Population, economy and family structure in Hertfordshire in 18 St Albans and its region

by Nigel Goose

The second of twelve volumes on
Population, economy and family structure in Hertfordshire in 1851

University of Hertfordshire Press

First published September 2000 in
Great Britain by
University of Hertfordshire Press
University of Hertfordshire
College Lane
Hatfield
Hertfordshire
AL10 9AB

ISBN 0-900458 83 6 paperback
ISBN 0-900458 84 4 casebound

Designed by Lisa Cordes

Page Layout by Margaret Smith

Printed by J W Arrowsmith Ltd

To Emily

My daughter

Population, economy and family structure in Hertfordshire in 1851

Contents

List of figures

Front cover
Based on W. Schmollinger's map of Hertfordshire from the 'Complete and Universal English Dictionary' by the Revd. James Barclay, revised by Henry W. Dewhurst and published by George Virtue in 1842. Reproduced courtesy of Hertford Museum.

PART 1

PART 2

Maps 3 to 12 were photographed by Peter Hoare. Maps 4 to 12 are reproduced courtesy of Hertfordshire Archives and Local Studies, Hertfordshire County Council, County Hall, Hertford.

List of tables

Acknowledgements

This book arises from a collaborative project launched in 1989, the Hertfordshire Historical Resources Project, which aims to computerise key historical documentation for the county of Hertfordshire, and which now falls under the umbrella of the University of Hertfordshire's Centre for Regional and Local History. It is the product of the combined work over several years of historians working at the University of Hertfordshire, local historians from both within and without the county and staff at the Hertfordshire County Record Office and Local Studies Library, which collectively now go under the title of Hertfordshire Archives and Local Studies (HALS).

Early work on transcription of the census data was conducted by Eveline Alty and Katherine Goad of the St Albans and Hertfordshire Architectural and Archaeological Society. The transcription and data entry for the Borough of St Albans for the present volume was partly the work of the author, but contributions were also made by Vera Baber. For the villages of Harpenden, Redbourn, Sandridge and Wheathampstead, thanks are also due to Marian Taylor and Michael Trenchard. The data entries have been checked by many hands, including Beverly Adams, R. Bunyan, Cliff Deamer, Lien Luu and Chris Pagan, and the final check was the work of Lucy Butters, research assistant to the project, from 1996–8.

At HALS Kate Thompson, former County Archivist, has taken an interest in the project since its inception in 1989, and all of her staff have invariably proved helpful, supportive and patient. In particular Sue Flood, Senior Archivist, has offered invaluable assistance to the project in a myriad of ways. Christine Shearman, former Local Studies Librarian, has been more than generous in making the census enumerators' returns freely available to our researchers, and has also contributed alongside Record Office staff to the often difficult process of co-ordinating the various contributors.

Within the University Paul Sawtell, my research assistant for three years between 1991 and 1994, saw the project take root and flourish. Subsequently Beverly Adams contributed to its administration, followed by Lucy Butters from 1996 to 1998, and more recently by Sheila Jennings and Margaret Smith. Khalid Khan provided valuable help on the computing front. Lisa Cordes provided both advice and assistance on design and layout, whilst the typescript was most efficiently laid out and converted into camera-ready form by Margaret Smith and John Stock.

Initial financial support for the project was provided by Royal Insurance Limited, Mitsubishi UK and Marks and Spencer plc., whilst the University of Hertfordshire has itself provided considerable financial assistance and continues to provide regular funding. Final preparation and publication of the present volume has been made possible by the award of a substantial British Academy personal research grant, which I am pleased to acknowledge.

PART ONE

Background and analysis

Chapter One

The Hertfordshire

Historical Resources Project

It was in 1989 that the Historical Studies Group at the University of Hertfordshire established the Hertfordshire Historical Resources Project, which is now subsumed within the Centre for Regional and Local History. The original intention was to establish a computerised collection of historical data, in either flatfile or relational databases as appropriate, to support these with related catalogues and bibliographies and then to use this resource base as a springboard for a range of activities. These activities were to include the development of courses in historical computing for undergraduates, the provision of short courses in historical computing, the supply to local schools of documentary teaching packs and machine-readable datasets for project work, the launch of a series of publications in Hertfordshire history and finally the establishment of a substantial database to which direct public access could be provided.[1]

This was undoubtedly an overly ambitious enterprise, and far from all these intended activities have actually materialised. No short courses in historical computing have run, whilst changes in staffing within the History Group have made it difficult to collaborate with the school sector in the manner originally planned. Amongst the historians at the University, what was originally envisaged as a group project has, as is so often the case, tended to become something of a one-man band, producing at times a somewhat frenetic and discordant performance rather than the smoothly orchestrated harmonies originally conceived. Without the successful bid made to the University for a Research Assistant in 1991, and further provision from the Faculty of Research Assistant support from 1996 to 1998, it is unlikely that the History Project would have prospered.

1　　A description of the initial thrust of the project can be found in *History and Computing,* Vol. 1, No. 2 (1989) pp. 170-1, and full contextualisation in N. Goose, "Participatory and Collaborative Research in English Regional and Local History", *Archives*, Vol. 23 (1997), pp. 1-13.

These caveats entered, however, prospered it has. Within the University a new course in History and Computing was first offered at Level Two in the academic year 1993/4 and again in 1994/5. This provided instruction and experience in the layout of academic articles using a state-of-the-art word processing package, demographic analysis of seventeenth century Hertfordshire parish registers employing Excel spreadsheets and exploitation of the Admissions and Discharges Register to the Hatfield Union Workhouse between the 1830s and 1860s held in a flatfile database called Reflex. Computer analysis of these datasets was supported by a series of lectures providing appropriate historical context, and discussions of methodological issues and ideas relating to the employment of these historical sources. All students were provided with workbooks to help ease their introduction to what was, for many, completely new ground.[2]

It would be an understatement to say that the course experienced teething troubles in its first year. Technical difficulties, underestimation of the problems the students would experience, overestimation of the competence of the tutor and inadequate provision of historical context all served to render this a difficult course for both students and staff. The results produced, however, were extremely encouraging, for the proficiency of many students in historical analysis came on in leaps and bounds through their employment of the computer as a tool to assist in that process. Our external examiner was impressed too, and in its second year the course ran remarkably smoothly, producing some impressive individual performances and the general approbation of the great majority of the students involved. A number of these subsequently put their new found skills to very good use in preparing computer-assisted undergraduate projects at Level Three, whilst others are laying plans for the employment of computer technology in postgraduate research.

In 1996/7 an element of historical computing was introduced into a Level One Group Project in Local History, where students were given the opportunity to analyse census data using Excel spreadsheets. Subsequently, in 1997/8, the Level Two History and Computing course was redeveloped by Lucy Butters, to focus also upon data from the 1851 census but employing the more sophisticated relational database management system Access. Again, historical context was provided by a series of lectures and discussion groups, whilst a substantial workbook led the students through a series of exercises to enable them to master the software.[3]

A more central thrust of the History Project has been the concerted attempt to establish, as quickly as possible, a series of substantial computer databases at the University. Indeed, without some progress in this direction it would have been difficult to run the undergraduate courses described above, although some of the data employed had been prepared previously. In particular the Cambridge Group for the History of Population and Social Structure kindly supplied copies of their parish register data for Hertfordshire, as well as the machine-readable material that they had collected for various parishes ofthe county on literacy as indicated by signatures.[4] The project's first research assistant, Paul Sawtell, focused his individual research upon the

2   These are available from the University: N. Goose, *Aldenham in the Seventeenth Century: an Introduction to Demographic Analysis Employing Excel Spreadsheets*, and N. Goose and P. Sawtell, *The Hatfield Union Workhouse c. 1830-1860 Employing Reflex Database*.

3   L. Butters, *Analysing the 1851 Census Using Access*.

4   The complete parish register aggregate data for the 404 parishes employed by the Cambridge Group is now available on CD ROM for just £6.50: R. Schofield, *Parish Register Aggregate Analyses: The Population History of England Database and Introductory Guide* (A *Local Population Studies* Supplement, Colchester, 1998). Orders should be sent to The Centre for Regional and Local History, University of Hertfordshire, Wall Hall, Watford Campus, Aldenham, Hertfordshire, WD2 8AT.

labouring poor in nineteenth century Hatfield, and hence he was personally responsible for inputting the data from the Admissions and Discharges Book for the Hatfield Union Workhouse as well as from the five decennial censuses for Hatfield between 1851 and 1891. Lucy Butters, research assistant from 1996 to 1998, worked particularly on the Baldock area, but has also been responsible for checking data for other parts of the county, including the St Albans region that is the subject matter of this book.

The key to the successful development of the History Project has, however, been collaboration: collaboration between professional historians working at the University, local and family historians and genealogists from both within and outside of the county working either as individuals or as part of teams provided by local history societies, and staff at both the Hertfordshire County Record Office and the Local Studies Library.[5] The University has played a key role in providing leadership, administration and co-ordination, to this end funding research assistant support for a total of five years. An Apple Macintosh was loaned to the County Record Office to facilitate the inputting of data by those who did not own their own computer or where documentation could not be copied but could only be examined in the Record Office itself. This has now been upgraded by HALS itself, and the 1851 census data for the Berkhamsted Superintendent Registrar's District can now be consulted there in machine-readable form. Extensive hardware and software has been provided at the University where a History Resource Room has been established and a body of expertise built up in the conversion of data between different formats and types of software. This, of course, allows volunteer data inputters to use their own hardware and software, leaving the University to worry about problems of compatibility and conversion. The Project has been publicised through a series of meetings and articles in local history journals and magazines, and a series of newsletters has been issued.[6]

The County Record Office and Local Studies Library have contributed in a number of ways. The Record Office found house room for our computer and has supervised its use, with its staff also playing a key role in establishing and maintaining links between the University and local history societies and groups. The Local Studies Library has provided free photocopies of the nineteenth century census enumerators' books, forgoing substantial charges that would have rendered it almost impossible for this aspect of the project to proceed, in return receiving bound surname indexes extracted from the census. Local Studies have also supported the Record Office in acting as a focal point for liaison between the University and local historians, and have provided the venue for a series of Project meetings.

The key players in this enterprise, however, have been the volunteer army of local historians upon whom all else depended, for without their concerted efforts rapid progress would have been impossible. More than seventy volunteer data inputters have been involved at one stage or another. Some contributions have been

---

5   Now merged to form Hertfordshire Archives and Local Studies (HALS).

6   N. Goose, "The University of Hertfordshire and Hertfordshire Local History", *Hertfordshire's Heritage*, No. 7 (July 1992), pp. 6-8; N. Goose, "Hatfield Historical Research Resources Project: Project 1851", *Hertfordshire People*, No. 46 (Summer 1992), pp. 9-11; N. Goose and P. Sawtell, "Computerising the Census: Towards a County Database for Hertfordshire 1851", *Computers in Genealogy*, Vol. 4, No. 8 (December 1992), pp. 342-6; N. Goose, "The Hertfordshire Historical Resources Project: Retrospect and Prospect", *Hertfordshire's Heritage*, No. 16 (October 1994), pp. 9-13; N. Goose, "Population, Economy and Family Structure", *Family Tree Magazine*, Vol. 12 No. 10 (August, 1996), pp. 21-2; N. Goose and L. Butters, "The Hertfordshire Historical Resources Project: a Progress Report", *Hertfordshire People*, No. 61 (June 1997), pp. 12-13.

modest, others substantial and one or two quite astonishing. They have worked from their own homes using their own equipment, commonly entering data in csv (comma separated value) format in various word processing packages though occasionally using spreadsheet or database software, or alternatively at the County Record Office using the facility made available for this purpose there. They have assisted with the photocopying of documentation at the Local Studies Library, and later proved invaluable as checkers of the work produced by fellow volunteers.

This collaborative venture was intended to produce mutual benefits. The University would gain a collection of machine-readable historical data to use as a basis for historical publications and undergraduate courses, the Record Office and Local Studies Library would gain a series of catalogues and indexes of key sets of historical documentation and local historians and genealogists would get access to a range of data in either machine-readable form or indexed hard copy which would be particularly useful for genealogical purposes. In all of these respects the History Project is proving to be a resounding success, and is serving as a profound stimulus to local historical research in the county. This is reflected in plans to launch a new local and regional historical journal and in the growing number of postgraduate research students registered at the University who are exploring aspects of local history. The first major publication to arise from the Project appeared in 1996 under the imprint of the University of Hertfordshire Press, analysing and reproducing the 1851 census for the Berkhamsted Superintendent Registrar's District of the county, and the present book is the second in a series that will eventually run to twelve volumes.[7] Volume 3, which will cover the Baldock area of the Hitchin Superintendent Registrar's District, is currently at an advanced stage of preparation.[8] The press is also to launch a new series of Studies in Regional and Local History, the first volume of which is due to appear shortly.[9]

Apart from the datasets either completed or in preparation mentioned above, collaborative work based at the County Record Office has produced a database of over 1,700 Hertfordshire pauper apprenticeships extant for the period 1599-1876. It is intended that in due course, once these have been thoroughly checked, they will be analysed, edited and published. Bastardy and Removal Orders are currently being added as a separate data set by the team working at the CRO . But without wishing to detract from these efforts, the largest project by far has been *Project 1851*, the drive to computerise all of the 167,298 individuals listed in the 1851 census enumerators' returns for Hertfordshire, upon which the Berkhamsted Region book and the current volume are based. Now that the basic task of inputting 1851 is complete, and it is safely stored in data banks of some 45 megabytes in both Access (PC) and Excel (Macintosh) software, many of our volunteers have shifted their attention to the 1891 census, the eventual completion of which will provide an invaluable point of comparison with 1851, an overview of economic, social and demographic change in Hertfordshire across the Victorian era as a whole. At the time of writing, approximately 40 per cent of the Hertfordshire 1891 census has been

---

7   N. Goose, *Population, Economy and Family Structure in Hertfordshire in 1851. Vol. 1 The Berkhamsted Region* (Hatfield, 1996).

8   Provisionally, N. Goose, L. Butters and R. Sharp, *Population, Economy and Family Structure in Hertfordshire in 1851. Vol. 3 The Baldock Region* (forthcoming).

9   C. Thornton (ed.), D.V. Stern, *A Hertfordshire Demesne of Westminster Abbey: Profits, Productivity and Weather* (University of Hertfordshire Press, due March 1999). Dr Margaret Shepherd, of Wolfson College, Cambridge, is currently re-writing her thesis on late nineteenth century Westmorland for publication as volume two of this series.

computerised. As one reviewer has put it, "present and future generations of Hertfordshire local historians and genealogists will have reason to be grateful to those who have undertaken this heroic task", for they have enabled the county's historians to "establish Hertfordshire as a pace-setter for others to follow".[10] Such plaudits amply testify to the benefits that collaborative work in regional, local and family history can produce.

---

10   W.A. Armstrong, review of Goose, *The Berkhamsted Region*, *Agricultural History Review*, Vol. 45 (1997), pp. 112-13.

Chapter Two

The making of the modern census

The genesis of the Census Enumerators' Returns of 1851

Enumerations of either national or local populations were not new to England in the nineteenth century, although many of those available to the historian before this time are only partial in their coverage in one sense or another. The Domesday Book was essentially a survey of landholding conducted for political and fiscal purposes.[1] Although it yields invaluable information on the extent of settlement in 1086, as well as a range of additional information of great interest to the economic and social historian, it is far from a complete head count of the population and needs careful adjustment before population totals can be derived for particular localities or for England as a whole.[2] The same is true of the Poll Taxes of the fourteenth century, the Exchequer lay subsidies of the early sixteenth century, the Hearth Taxes of the later seventeenth century, as well as the various ecclesiastical censuses that are extant for 1563, 1603 and 1676.[3] In each case substantial allowances need to be made for those missing from these lists, because they were female, because they were too young to be taxed, too young to be a communicant of the Church of England, because they were too poor to pay tax or because they successfully evaded taxation. Not surprisingly, these listings have been analysed in a variety of ways by different historians who in consequence have produced population estimates that are sometimes substantially at odds with each other.[4] In some cases their general reliability as a basis for the establishment of population totals has been questioned, as in a recent study of the 1563 'Bishops' Census' which employed Hertfordshire parish register data to test its validity and found it to seriously under-

---

1   It is published for Hertfordshire: J. Morris (ed.), *Domesday Book 12: Hertfordshire* (Chichester, 1976).

2   M.M. Postan, *The Medieval Economy and Society: an Economic History of Britain 1100-1500* (London, 1972), pp. 16-18, 27-8.

3   The figures from these and other similar extant sources for Hertfordshire have been usefully collected and published in L. Munby, *Hertfordshire Population Statistics 1563-1801* (Bedford, 1964).

4   See, for instance, Postan, *Medieval Economy and Society*, pp. 27-30; E.A. Wrigley and R.S. Schofield, *The Population History of England 1541-1871: a Reconstruction* (London, 1981), Appendix 5, pp. 563-72. Controversy has been particularly evident in an urban context: S.H. Rigby, "Urban Decline in the Later Middle Ages", *Urban History Yearbook 1979*, pp. 46-59; A. Dyer, "Growth and Decay in English Towns 1500-1700", *Urban History Yearbook 1979*, pp. 60-72; A. Dyer, *Decline and Growth in English Towns 1400-1640* (Basingstoke, 1991), esp. pp. 37-40, 64-74; N. Goose, "The Ecclesiastical Returns of 1563: a Cautionary Note", *Local Population Studies*, No. 34 (1985), pp. 46-7; A. Dyer, "The Bishops' Census of 1563: its Significance and Accuracy", *Local Population Studies*, No. 49 (1992), pp. 19-37; N. Goose, "Pre-industrial Urban Demography in England: What is to be Done?", *Urban History*, Vol. 21, Part 2 (1994), pp. 275-6.

enumerate the population of most parishes for which evidence survives.[5] Private estimates of the English population made by 'political arithmeticians' such as Gregory King and Charles Davenant towards the end of the seventeenth century are similarly open to interpretation.[6]

This is not to say that there are no reliable census-type sources available before the inception of the national census in 1801. In fact, a substantial number were compiled for a variety of reasons in particular localities, and have been the subject of considerable historical scrutiny since the Cambridge Group for the History of Population and Social Structure pioneered such work in the late 1960s.[7] Some contain immensely detailed information on the structure of the family and household, even rivalling that found in the nineteenth century censuses themselves, and have been subjected to detailed analysis.[8] Their survival is, however, sporadic and unpredictable: it is only after 1801 that the local historian can be guaranteed access to census type data relating to their area of interest.

What are the origins of the national census? The middle years of the eighteenth century witnessed considerable controversy between those who thought population had increased since the late seventeenth century and those who thought it had declined, a debate that was underpinned respectively by Whig champions of the rise of commerce on the one hand and an unholy alliance of agricultural conservatives and political radicals on the other. In its first stage, from 1755, the central protagonists were the Reverend William Brakenridge, Rector of St Michael Bassishaw, London, and the Reverend Richard Forster, Rector of Great Shefford in Berkshire, whose debate was conducted through the pages of the *Philosophical Transactions of the Royal Society*. But the controversy only truly entered centre stage with the intervention in 1771 of Dr Richard Price, whose pessimistic views were first attacked by Arthur Young in his *Political Arithmetic* (1774) and later by a battery of writers including William Eden, William Wales and perhaps most notably the Reverend John Howlett. So inadequate were contemporary population statistics and so open to interpretation were those that were available that, simultaneously around 1780, Richard Price could argue that the nation had lost nearly a quarter of its people in the past seventy years, whilst the likes of John Howlett could argue that numbers were steadily rising.[9]

From at least the mid-century there was also growing concern over the rising burden of poor relief. In simple cash terms poor relief expenditure rose over ten-fold during the eighteenth century, with a particularly rapid rate of growth evident in the second half of the century and a relative shift in the burden away from towns and industrial areas and towards the countryside. Allowing for price changes, this represented approximately a four-fold real increase, and a rise in expenditure as a proportion of national income from 0.8 per cent in 1696

5   N. Goose, "The Bishops' Census of 1563: a Re-examination of its Reliability", *Local Population Studies*, No. 56 (1996), pp. 43-53.

6   D.V. Glass, "Two Papers on Gregory King" in D.V. Glass and D.E.C. Eversley (eds.), *Population in History* (London, 1965), pp. 159-220; Wrigley and Schofield, *The Population History of England*, pp. 571-2.

7   P. Laslett, "Size and Structure of the Household in England Over Three Centuries", *Population Studies*, Vol. 23 (1969), pp. 199-223; P. Laslett and R. Wall (eds.), *Family and Household in Past Time* (Cambridge, 1972).

8   See, for example, N. Goose, "Household Size and Structure in Early Stuart Cambridge", *Social History*, Vol. 5, No. 3 (1980), pp. 347-85; D. Baker, *The Inhabitants of Cardington in 1782, Publications of the Bedfordshire Historical Record Society*, Vol. 52 (1973).

9   D.V. Glass, *Numbering the People. The Eighteenth Century Population Controversy and the Development of Census and Vital Statistics in Britain* (Farnborough, 1973), pp. 12-13, 24-6, 47-77. For a brief introduction, M. Nissel, *People Count. A History of the General Register Office* (London, 1987), pp. 48-9.

to around 2.0 per cent by the end of the century.[10] Into the controversy in 1798 entered Thomas Malthus, whose *Essay on the Principle of Population* argued, without any compelling empirical or historical foundation, that if left unchecked population would inevitably outgrow the means of subsistence, as it tends to increase in a geometrical ratio whilst food supply can only increase arithmetically.[11] Here, it seems, was the explanation for the apparently exponential increase in poor rates, an explanation that was immediately endorsed by the coincidence of war, harvest failure and high food prices at the turn of the century.[12] Malthus's essay may not in itself have been important in persuading parliament to agree to instigate the census, but it was a crystallisation of the growing tide of opinion that saw an expanding population as a potential threat rather than, following mercantilist thinking, as wholly advantageous.[13] It was against this background that the first Census Act was passed in 1800, and the prevailing economic difficulties and fears to which they gave rise doubtless eased its passage.[14] It was entitled "An Act for taking an Account of the Population of Great Britain, and the increase or diminution thereof", and as data was to be collected on baptisms, marriages and burials for the whole eighteenth century besides an immediate enumeration of the population, it seems clear that it was as much rooted in the controversies of the later eighteenth century as it was in the short term difficulties that accompanied the Napoleonic Wars.[15]

As the nineteenth century progressed the profound combination of political economy and the growing administrative sophistication of government produced an ever increasing spate of statistical surveys. J.F.C. Harrison has written of the 1830s and 1840s that "No previous age had been so much enquired into by select committees, royal commissions, statistical societies and local bodies... Documentation of the condition-of-England question was very thorough".[16] Census taking inevitably became intimately associated with this concern to reveal the true state of the nation. The influence of William Farr, superintendent of statistics at the General Register Office from 1838 until 1880 and one of the greatest medical statisticians of the century, produced a particular concern with the insight the census might provide into medical questions, especially as they related to population density, widely regarded as inversely proportional to general health.[17] Population density was, of course, associated with urbanisation, and the often overcrowded and insanitary conditions of urban life were in turn associated with moral as well as physical degeneracy.[18] By the mid-century, therefore, the intellectual framework that underpinned the census had broadened further, and this in turn resulted in the collection and recording of fuller and more precise information on a wide range of demographic, economic and social variables.

---

10   P. Slack, *The English Poor Law 1531-1782* (Basingstoke, 1990), pp. 30-34.

11   D.V. Glass (ed.), *Introduction to Malthus* (London, 1953).

12   Glass, *Numbering the People*, pp. 96-8.

13   Glass, *Numbering the People*, p. 90.

14   Nissel, *People Count*, p. 51.

15   E. Higgs, *Making Sense of the Census: the Manuscript Returns for England and Wales, 1801-1901* (London, 1989), p. 4. This book was re-issued in 1996 under the revised title *A Clearer Sense of the Census*, but as any changes are minimal all references here will be to the original publication.

16   J.F.C. Harrison, *The Early Victorians 1832-51* (St Albans, 1971), p. 80. See also M.J. Cullen, *The Statistical Movement in Early Victorian Britain: the Foundations of Empirical Social Research* (Hassocks, 1975).

17   Glass, *Numbering the People*, pp. 119-20, 130, 141-2; Higgs, *Making Sense of the Census*, pp. 15-16.

18   Cullen, *The Statistical Movement*, pp. 135-6.

The administrative machinery that supported the census was elaborated simultaneously. The 1801 Census Act had placed the burden of house-to-house enquiry squarely on the shoulders of the overseers of the poor, "other substantial householders" or, if needs be, "constables, tithingmen, headboroughs or other peace officers". The returns made by these officials required affirmation by local justices of the peace and endorsement by high constables before they were submitted to either town clerks or clerks of the peace for forwarding to the Home Office.[19] The task of census taking was, therefore, simply added to the burdens already borne by the system of parochial administration that had been established since Elizabethan times, although provision was made for payment of both fees and expenses.[20]

All this was to change in the 1830s. The inception of the Age of Reform brought not only electoral reform in the shape of the Reform Act of 1832, but a series of administrative changes that were to underpin radical re-organisation of the process of census taking. The Poor Law Amendment Act of 1834 established a new centralised administration controlled by a board of three commissioners who appointed, in turn, regional assistant commissioners. Parishes were now grouped together in 'unions', each union having just one large, central workhouse attached to it, and these Poor Law Unions were governed by Boards of Guardians elected by local ratepayers. These new administrative units, the 643 Unions, were soon adopted for the purpose of census taking. The Municipal Corporations Act of 1835 instituted borough councils elected by the ratepayers as the basis for local administration and these were to work through professional, salaried, officials, minimally a town clerk and a borough treasurer. The powers of the new councils extended to control over the police, the enactment of by-laws, management of municipal property and some aspects of local finance. This was an important landmark in the development of local government and, alongside the private legislation introduced since the eighteenth century and the numerous public Acts of the nineteenth, it underpinned the re-organisation of local government and its evolution from a largely amateur to a professional affair. In 1797 there were 15,884 public officials in Great Britain, most of whom were working in Customs and Excise or the Post Office, but by 1869 this number had grown to 108,000. This new army of local government officials was fundamental to the process of census enumeration.[21]

The final piece in the jigsaw was the introduction of compulsory civil registration of births, marriage and deaths by the Births and Deaths Registration Act of 1836, following which a registrar general was appointed with a central staff in the General Register Office, to which responsibility for the census was transferred in 1840. A hierarchical administrative structure was established with the largest units based on the Poor Law Unions, each with its own superintendent registrar. These were divided into sub-districts to which were appointed part-time registrars, and were then further divided into separate enumeration districts, for each of which a temporary enumerator was given responsibility at the appropriate juncture. These temporary enumerators were instituted via a new Census Act which formed the basis of the 1841 census. This Act also provided for the collection of a wider range of information and introduced the procedure of census taking on one night in the year rather than, as previously, over a more extended period of time. It was also in 1841 that household schedules, to be completed by the householders themselves, were introduced. Some of these changes were hurried through as census night approached and in many respects the 1841 census looks back to those

---

19   Higgs, *Making Sense of the Census*, pp. 5-6; Nissel, *People Count*, p. 52.
20   Nissel, *People Count*, p. 52.
21   Harrison, *The Early Victorians*, p. 108; H. Perkin, *The Origins of Modern English Society 1780-1880* (London, 1969), p. 123.

that preceded it rather than forward to those which followed. In particular, the population tables in the published reports followed the geography of traditional counties, and the hundreds, wapentakes, sokes, liberties and parishes within them, rather than the newly created administrative units. No special arrangements were made in 1841 for recording nightworkers, nor was the newly designed schedule for seamen put into use until 1851. Few detailed instructions were provided for the benefit of either enumerator or householder in 1841 and the manner in which lodgers and boarders were to be treated was left entirely unclear.[22]

The full transition to modern census taking was not made until 1851. In this census the new administrative structure and procedures elaborated from the 1830s were put into operation and remained in place through the nineteenth century. The 1851 census has a distinct advantage over previous ones in that relation to head of household was specified. This, together with the clearer instructions given to enumerators with regard to identification of households, means that it is the first census from which family and household structure can be established with confidence. Marital status was also specified from 1851 forwards, as were exact ages rather than the five year bands from 15 upwards employed in 1841. The 1851 census was the first to provide details of both county and town or parish of birth of each individual, whilst clearer instructions were provided for the recording of occupations, the work of members of the head's family and for recording details of farm size and agricultural labour force.[23] There is therefore a wealth of economic, social and demographic information contained in the 1851 census, whilst its consistent and highly structured format renders it ideally suited to treatment by database management systems. Furthermore, recent research has emphasised the accuracy of the census, particularly regarding birthplace statements, consistency of names and recording of ages, despite the relatively high propensity for birthplace disagreements between successive censuses in some London suburbs.[24] Occupational designations may sometimes be questionable, whilst the true position of those described as servants is somewhat problematic.[25] It is, however, easy to overdo scepticism.[26] Recent work comparing occupations in the Hertfordshire census enumerators books for 1851 with Kelly's Directory for the same year reveals a satisfying general congruence, whilst even in the case of women's work it is easy to overstate the difficulties posed by the census returns, for such employment was clearly *not* consistently omitted.[27]

Given their obvious historical value, it is surprising to find that so little use has been made of the census enumerators' returns, a bibliography prepared in 1989 by Dennis Mills and Carol Pearce identifying only 423 publications based substantially on the census enumerators' books (CEBs), only *two* of which relate to the

22   Higgs, *Making Sense of the Census*, pp. 8-10.

23   *Ibid*., pp. 71-2, 78-93.

24   P. Razzell, *Essays in English Population History* (London, 1994), pp. 100-1, 144, 148. See also D. Thomson, "Age Reporting by the Elderly and the Nineteenth-century Census", A. Perkyns, "Age Checkability and Accuracy in the Censuses of Six Kentish Parishes, 1851-1881", and A. Perkyns, "Birthplace Accuracy in the Censuses of Six Kentish Parishes, 1851-81", all reprinted in D. Mills and K. Schürer (eds.), *Local Communities in the Victorian Census Enumerators' Books* (Oxford, 1996), pp. 86-99, 115-34, 229-245.

25   E. Higgs, "The Tabulation of Occupations in the Nineteenth-Century Census, with Special Reference to Domestic Servants", *Local Population Studies*, No. 28 (1982), pp. 58-66.

26   A well balanced and constructive assessment, generally supportive of the validity of the census returns, is to be found in the editorial sections of D. Mills and K. Schürer (eds.), *Local Communities*.

27   C.A. Crompton, "Changes in Rural Service Occupations During the Nineteenth Century: an Evaluation of Two Sources for Hertfordshire, England", *Rural History*, Vol. 6 (1995), pp. 193-203; Goose, *The Berkhamsted Region*, pp. 34-40; For a more sceptical view, see C. Miller, "The Hidden Workforce: Female Field Workers in Gloucestershire, 1870-1901", *Southern History*, Vol. 6 (1984), pp. 139-61. See also below, Chapter 3, pp. 86-97.

county of Hertfordshire.[28] This global total is small indeed given the comprehensive geographical cover of the census and the fact that the pioneering work in this field by Armstrong and Anderson dates from the late 1960s,[29] whilst there is a particular dearth of studies which adopt a comparative perspective.[30] The work completed to date on Hertfordshire using this source is derisory. Mills and Pearce note a recent decline of interest in the census, occurring "at a time when computing facilities have become more widely available" and go on to suggest that "the real reason for lack of progress may lie in the census no longer being a fashionable new area in which to research, and in the lack of a sense of direction....".[31] In placing the 1851 census at the centre of the Hertfordshire Historical Resources Project the intention is to stimulate renewed interest in this invaluable source and to impart a sense of direction to Hertfordshire history.[32]

The Hertfordshire census of 1851: procedures and protocols

The database that was created to store the 1851 census for Hertfordshire was designed to be simple to use, compatible and comparable with other datasets and with census data from other dates. A flatfile format was employed, even though a copy is held on a relational database management system, and the fields basically followed the format of the columns in the CEBs, except that each entry was given its own record number, two fields were created for age and sex, and two to distinguish county of birth from town or parish. Completed datasets were then enriched by adding codings in four additional fields to aid occupational analysis: one giving a detailed identifier based on Booth's system of classification as modified by Armstrong,[33] another reflecting social status, a third classifying occupations by the raw material employed in each trade, and a fourth according to the type of product which resulted. These occupational classifications have been refined somewhat since the publication of the Berkhamsted Region volume, and now five different classifications are employed. The Booth, social status and raw material based classifications are retained, the latter being used here to enable comparison with the published Berkhamsted results, and also representing the best approximation to the approach adopted by the census authorities themselves.[34] The product-based comparison is now superseded by a more sensitive breakdown into the various occupational spheres as used in the work of Rubinstein, with further sub-divisions within those categories, whilst an additional classification by economic sector (agriculture, mining, manufacture, etc.) has been added. The data is therefore organised in a manner which will facilitate comparison with previous analyses where a range of different classificatory schemes are employed. Although the tabulations presented below use only the classification based upon raw

28　　D. Mills and C. Pearce, *People and Places in the Victorian Census*, Historical Geography Research Series No. 23 (November 1989). Work is currently underway on updating this bibliography, for publication as a *Local Population Studies* supplement.

29　　M. Anderson, *Family Structure in Nineteenth Century Lancashire* (Cambridge, 1971) and W.A. Armstrong, *Change and Stability in an English County Town: a Social Study of York 1801-51* (Cambridge, 1974). Both were refinements of PhD theses completed in the late 1960s.

30　　Mills and Schürer, *Local Communities*, p. 3. This is a failing that the present series has explicitly set out to address. See the review of *The Berkhamsted Region* by Schürer, *Local Population Studies*, No. 57 (1996), p. 77.

31　　Mills and Pearce, *People and Places*, p. 8.

32　　The contribution of the Hertfordshire census project has already been noticed by Mills and Schürer, who describe it as "an encouraging recent development": *Local Communities*, p. 3. The Hertfordshire Project, the work of the Cambridge Group on the censuses from 1891 to 1921 and the recent publication of the excellent Mills and Schürer edited volume all indicate something of a renaissance of interest in the census enumerators' returns.

33　　W.A. Armstrong, "The Use of Information About Occupation" in E.A. Wrigley (ed.), *Nineteenth Century Society: Essays in the Use of Quantitative Methods for the Study of Social Data* (Cambridge, 1972), pp. 191-310.

34　　Higgs, *Making Sense of the Census*, p. 79.

material, these various codings have permitted interrogation of the data from a range of perspectives to permit the detailed analysis of occupational structure that is provided in chapter three.[35]

Minimal standardisation has been employed. Surnames have not been standardised despite the insistence of some of the dedicated genealogists helping with the project that they should be. Ages of infants, recorded in weeks or months, were entered as "0" in the original database to facilitate numerical analysis, but the original entry restored for the final edition reproduced below. Corrections of the spelling of place names and occupational descriptions have been made, together with the adoption of a consistent approach to the use of capitals, abbreviations, hyphens and the like. In other words, the basic integrity of the data had been maintained *unless* the perpetuation of errors could only mislead and would convey no additional information of any historical value. Changes had to be made for the purposes of analysis, particularly household analysis, as when enumerators recorded step-sons or step-daughters as "son-in-law" and "daughter-in-law", an error that is often made plain by the very tender years and marital status of the individuals concerned. Unlike in the Berkhamsted volume, however, these have been changed back to their original form in the documentation reproduced below. Occasionally too, enumerators clearly made errors about the sex of those listed, or "widow" might be entered against an individual with a male forename. Wherever there can be *no doubt* that a simple error of nomenclature or transcription has occurred, the entry has been corrected. If it seems likely, although not certain, that an error had been made, the original entry is recorded followed by an interpretation in square brackets, with or without a query mark depending upon the confidence of the interpretation, a procedure also used for place names that were difficult to decipher. Place names that could be read but not located in the Place Names Society volumes or any other source are followed by a query in square brackets, whilst additional information not found in the original enumeration is also added in square brackets. These procedures stand very close to what is called a 'source orientated' approach to historical computing, although the most rigorous purist may yet not be satisfied. But we have adopted a pragmatic approach, guided by common sense, designed to protect the basic integrity of the census data whilst at the same time maximising its potential for use by both historians and genealogists, as well as facilitating the process of computer-assisted historical analysis.

The protocol established to ensure the integrity of the data was that each enumeration district, once computerised by a volunteer and then translated into standard format, would be checked by another volunteer for errors, omissions or typographical mistakes. Occupational codings were added by a research assistant using instructions drawn up by Project staff, and a third and final check was then made by a professional historian within the History Department. This threefold process has proved essential. It has proved essential because the standard of initial reading and inputting of the data has been highly variable. Second, it has proved essential to combat the irresistible temptation of those genealogists amongst our volunteers to excessively standardise. Third, experience has shown that even careful and experienced inputters make mistakes, checkers make mistakes too, and even the third line of defence has let through a few small errors, subsequently revealed during the process of data analysis. Finally, it was felt inappropriate to ask amateur historians to make historical judgements or expect them to be familiar with the literature concerning the reliability of the census in different respects or accepted interpretations that underpin its analysis. This

---

35   Full details of the classifications and of the protocol adopted in their construction are available on request from the Centre for Regional and Local History at the University of Hertfordshire, Wall Hall, Watford Campus, Aldenham, Hertfordshire, WD2 8AT.

expertise has to be brought by the professional historian who takes final responsibility for the decisions made. It goes without saying that the task of data collection and input, translation to standard format, checking, re-checking and administering all these activities has been enormous, involving many thousand man/woman hours of labour before the process of data analysis could even begin. Nevertheless, the end result is a series of datasets in which we can have a very high level of confidence indeed, obviating the need for users of this data to refer back to the original enumerations.[36]

Analytical procedures adopted have been informed by the work of the pioneer explorers of the census enumerators' returns, whilst Higgs' recent book has provided an invaluable short guide to possible pitfalls.[37] For the purposes of analysis and reproduction of the Hertfordshire census the basic units of Superintendent Registrars' Districts employed in 1851 have been adopted, for no other reason than their convenience as a collection of contiguous parishes and townships with a vague geographical coherence and of a suitable size to fill an individual volume. All enumerations districts have been included except those that clearly lay outside of the county of Hertfordshire. There are twelve Superintendent Registrars' Districts in the county and the St Albans District is the second to be analysed.

---

36   This is not, of course, true of some other group projects based upon the census, and family historians and genealogists will be aware of the shortcomings that have been identified in the 1881 transcription co-ordinated by the Mormon Church: see, for instance, G. Riggs, "1881 Index - Caution!", *Family Tree Magazine*, January 1996.

37   P.M. Tillott, "Sources of Inaccuracy in the 1851 and 1861 Censuses" and M. Anderson, "Standard Tabulation Procedures for the Census Enumerators' Books 1851-1891", both in Wrigley (ed.), *Nineteenth Century Society*, pp. 82-145; Higgs, *Making Sense of the Census, passim*. See also Mills and Schürer, *Local Communities, passim*.

Chapter Three

Population, economy and family structure in St Albans and its region in 1851

The St Albans Superintendent Registrar's District

If the Berkhamsted Superintendent Registrar's District forms the most westerly arm of Hertfordshire, the St Albans District is situated, as it were, on the shoulder, stretching lengthwise from the borders of Bedfordshire in the north to within a few miles of the Middlesex border to the south. The location within the county of the eight parishes that formed the district is shown in Figure 1. Its central feature is, of course, the City of St Albans, lying at its heart, which incorporates the whole of the parish of St Albans, and parts of St Peters, St Michaels and St Stephens. The parishes of Redbourn, Sandridge, Harpenden and Wheathampstead stretch out towards the north, and all but Harpenden are of ancient standing, identified as medieval vills in the Domesday survey of 1086.[1] Domesday includes St Albans as one of only five towns to be found in the entire county, and it was the only community within the District to possess an active market through from the early medieval period and into the sixteenth century.[2] By the mid-nineteenth century its regular Saturday market was reportedly "well frequented", and it could boast two annual fairs held in March and October.[3] Its importance as a thoroughfare was of long standing for the old Roman road, Watling Street, would deliver

---

1   T. Rook, *A History of Hertfordshire* (Chichester, 1984), pp. 34-5.

2   Rook, *History of Hertfordshire*, pp. 34, 40; A. Everitt, "The Marketing of Agricultural Produce" in J. Thirsk (ed.), *The Agrarian History of England and Wales Vol. IV 1500-1640* (Cambridge, 1967), pp. 473-4. The other four towns were Ashwell, Berkhamsted, Hertford and Stansted Abbotts.

3   *Kelly's Post Office Directory of Hertfordshire, 1855*, p. 230. The horse fair that had been held annually on 17th June was discontinued early in the nineteenth century: *VCH Herts*, Vol. 2, p. 482.

travellers from London in the south to its door, skirting the town after the foundation of St Albans Abbey towards the end of the eighth century, for onward progress to the Midlands and the north-west.[4] St Albans was, in fact, the first stage out of London, and the traffic generated by 1813 is graphically described by Solomon George Shaw, bookseller and stationer, who lived in Market Place:

> The mails and stage coaches which run through the town (supposing them to be pretty
> well loaded) have accommodation for upward of six hundred passengers daily; add to
> which the number of travellers who pass through by other conveyances and those on
> foot, it may reasonably be computed that not less than 1,000 persons pass through the
> town every day.[5]

By 1826 there were 72 coaches a day passing through the town, with steam carriages capable of carrying up to fifty people being run by the London and St Albans Steam Carriage Company.[6] In 1795 an Act of Parliament, passed in the face of opposition from local landowners and the Corporation of Hertford, had allowed for a collateral cut in the Grand Junction Canal to provide a connection with St Albans, although the canal was never completed, partly for financial reasons but possibly also because the additional duty of 2d per ton on goods carried on the canal built into the original Act rendered the project less attractive to the local trading community.[7] Perhaps as a consequence of its excellent road connections, St Albans also had to wait until 1858 for its first railway, some twenty years after the opening of the London and Birmingham Railway that ran through the Berkhamsted region to the west. On 5 May of that year a branch line from Watford was opened, on what had been known since 1846 as the London and North Western Railway, with a station at St Albans Abbey. The day was declared a general holiday, a public dinner held in the town hall, and the Corporation agreed that "a public subscription was to be raised to pay the cost of the same and to provide amusements for the humbler classes on so auspicious an occasion".[8] The Great Northern Railway opened a branch line between Hatfield and St Albans in 1865, whilst the Midland Railway opened the Bedford to London route via St Albans three years later.[9]

4   W. Page (ed.), *The Victoria County History of Hertfordshire*, 4 Vols. (London, 1908-14), Vol. 2, pp. 469-70.

5   Quoted in E. Toms, *The Story of St. Albans* (Luton, 1962), p. 138.

6   *Ibid.*, pp. 144-5.

7   H.C.F. Lansberry, "St Albans Canal", *Hertfordshire Past and Present*, No. 7 (1967), pp. 3-8.

8   A.E. Gibbs, *The Corporation Records of St Albans* (St Albans, 1890), p. 228. The Corporation had petitioned the House of Commons for
     powers to construct this branch line in 1847: *ibid.*, p. 212.

9   *VCH Herts*, Vol. 2, p. 470; Rook, *History of Hertfordshire*, pp. 94-7.

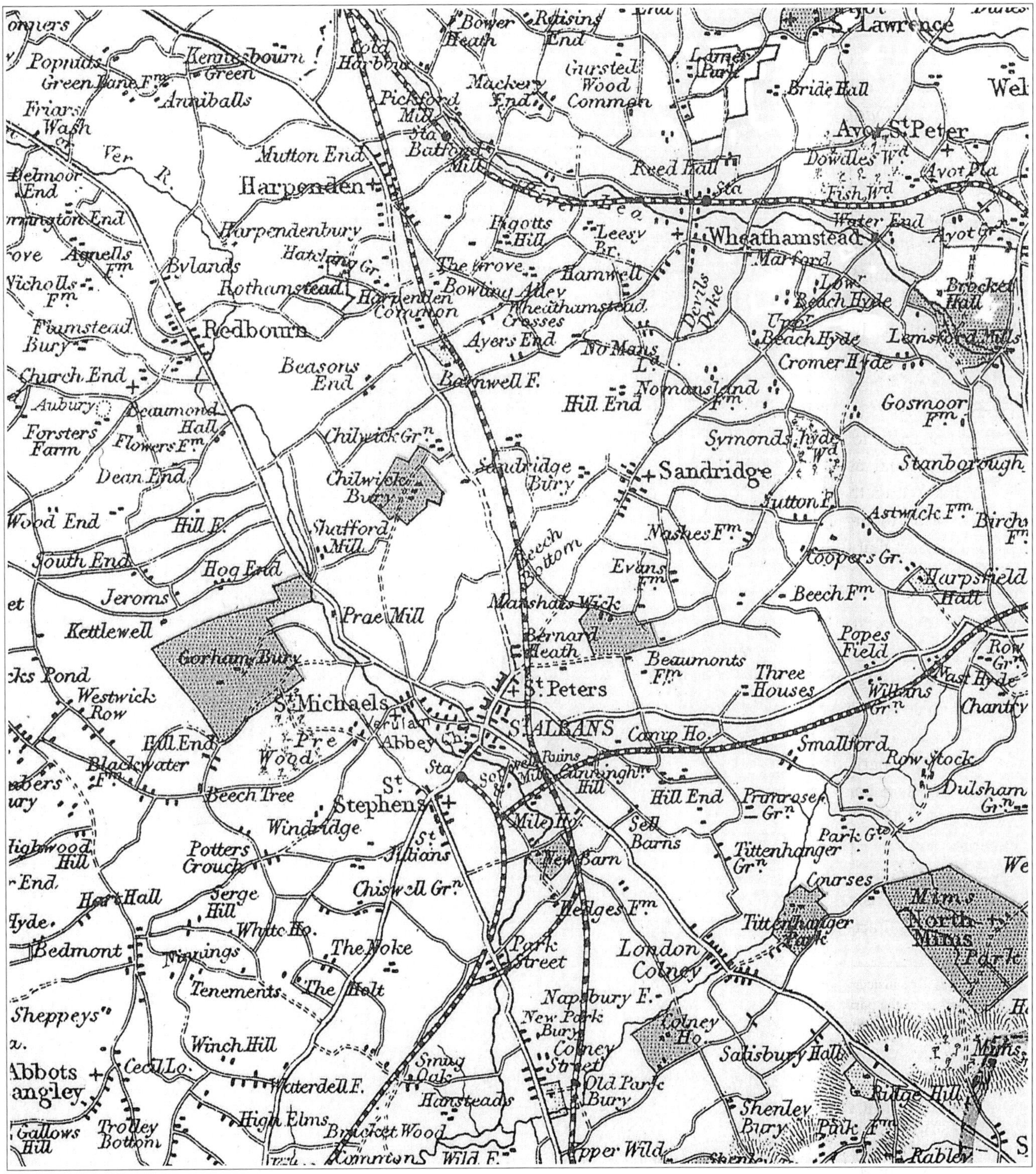

Figure 2 : Hertfordshire (1869) from Cussan's *History of Hertfordshire* Volume I (London 1870-3)

The organisation of the census enumerators' books into "Superintendent Registrar's Districts", "Registrar's Districts" and individual "Enumeration Districts" can pose severe problems for the historian wanting to identify appropriate and coherent units for analysis. For the St Albans district, the parishes to the north of the city pose no difficulty, for Wheathampstead, Harpenden, Redbourn and Sandridge are all clearly identified, the first three encompassed by three enumeration districts and Sandridge by two, with no apparent overlap between them. It is St Albans itself that poses the problem, for here the enumeration districts are identified partly by parish (St Albans, St Peters, St Michaels, St Stephens), partly by Ward (Middle, Holywell, Fishpool, Park and Windridge Wards), and partly by the names of hamlets (Sleapshyde, Smallford, Tyttenhanger), with numerous smaller sub-divisions mentioned along the way. This detail is, of course, very valuable to the local historian, particularly as individual streets are often identified in the city itself, whilst hamlets or villages such as Frogmore or Bricket Wood can also be located and isolated. The problem comes in deciding where the town starts and where it ends, for urban-rural contrasts are of obvious interest to the social and economic historian.[10] A particular problem is that there are different possibilities when it comes to the identification of urban boundaries, for either one could concentrate upon the area within the parliamentary borough boundaries (insofar as it is possible to identify them), or alternatively could include the much larger area incorporated within the Liberty of St Albans.[11] The strategy adopted here is to attempt to get the best of all possible worlds, by organising the data in such a way as to allow identification of the truly urban part of St Albans, that part that was essentially rural, and, by conflating the two, identifying separately the Liberty of St Albans.

Detailed examination of the occupational structure and topography of the various Enumeration Districts guided the divisions chosen. Hence the parish of St Albans itself is the only one that can be regarded as wholly urban.[12] St Michaels is easy to divide into its urban and rural components, for a separate Enumeration District is devoted to "all the houses in the parish and borough", with the rural component lying on the Childwick and Gorhambury side of the parish and stretching out towards Leverstock Green. The truly urban part of St Peters parish is also easy to identify as the relevant enumeration districts are headed "In the Borough of St Albans", whilst examination of street names and occupational composition provides confirmation.[13] The outlying parts of the parish are identified with the hamlets of Sleapshyde, Smallford, Tyttenhanger, Colney Heath and London Colney, collectively grouped for the purposes of analysis as "Out-hamlets" in the tables which follow. Tyttenhanger Green is included with this group, although this lay in the parish of St Stephens, as identified by the enumerator, whilst part of Smallford also appears to have extended into St Stephens. Parts of Colney Heath and Tyttenhanger also stretched into the parish of Ridge, whilst

---

10   This was not satisfactorily dealt with in the Berkhamsted volume, as the town of Tring itself was not separated out for the purposes of analysis from the parish as a whole, which included a large rural area: Goose, *The Berkhamsted Region*, pp. 23-5. This is currently being rectified with the assistance of Lyn Leader.

11   By no means the whole of St Albans Liberty is encompassed by the St Albans Superintendent Registrar's District, for at this date it was co-extensive with the Hundred of Cassio, and in 1841 it comprised 25 parishes and included a population in excess of 30,000: Gibbs, *Corporation Records of St Albans*, p. 215; W. Le Hardy (ed.), *Hertfordshire County Records. Calendar to the Sessions Books 1833-34* Vol. X (Hertford, 1957), p. xxvii; D. Dean *et al.*, *St Albans c. 1820. 'The Town'* (St Albans and Hertfordshire Architectural and Archaeological Society, 1982), p. 4.

12   Town maps for 1820 show that "all but a few square yards of the Abbey Parish [St Albans parish]" lay within the borough boundaries: Dean *et al.*, *St Albans c. 1820'*, p. 4.

13   Even those parishes or parts of parishes that clearly lay within the borough included some agricultural workers, however, particularly St Michaels.

roughly one-third of London Colney was situated in the parish of Shenley, these two parishes forming part of the Barnet Superintendent Registrar's District rather than that of St Albans. However, as the major portion of each of these hamlets fell within our district they are most appropriately considered here.[14] The parish of St Stephens was the only one to give greater pause for thought, for the borough does indeed extend into this parish. The first three households in enumeration district 6b of the St Albans Registrar's District are clearly identified as lying within the borough, but these have been included in the following analysis with the parish of St Stephens in order to maintain the integrity of the enumeration districts, rather than opting for excessive fine tuning of the data. Furthermore, as the *Victoria County History* noted at the turn of the present century, "The population is entirely agricultural",[15] whilst in 1893 Charles Ashdown described the parish in the following terms:

> It is strange that at such a short distance from the City should be found all the primitive
> concomitants which generally form the chief characteristics of village life; for here we
> see the Church (with its rectory) nestling in the trees, the almost deserted street, the village
> post-office, the inevitable inn occupying the customary position opposite the Church, the
> dwellings of rich and poor intermingled indiscriminately, whilst the scent of hay and kine
> is wafted on the air from the surrounding farmsteads.[16]

Such a description surely applies almost equally to the parish in 1851, with the caveat that at this date cottage industry was of considerable importance alongside agricultural employment. Standing immediately to the south of the town, St Stephens extends along Watling Street, incorporating the hamlets of Park Street, Frogmore,[17] Smug Oak and Bricket Wood. The portion that encompassed Tyttenhanger Green and part of Smallford is included with the Out-hamlets.

This strategy of distinguishing an urban and a rural part of St Albans has the added advantage that it is possible to compare and contrast the rural areas of the district as a whole (both within and without the Liberty of St Albans) with the town proper. The adopted divisions produce an area that had been identified as St Albans Urban, containing a population of 6,985. Although perhaps not precisely geographically coterminous with the borough, the population was almost identical, for the common boundaries of both the municipal and the parliamentary borough in 1851 included a population of exactly 7,000, suggesting that we have indeed achieved a close identification of the truly urban area within the Borough of St Albans.[18] In fact,

---

14　Tyttenhanger Green was in St Peters, and included 147 inhabitants in 1851, whilst Tyttenhanger in Ridge included just 45. The portion of Colney Heath in St Peters included 230 inhabitants compared to 35 in Ridge, whilst 321 people lived in London Colney, St Peters, in 1851 compared to 165 in London Colney, Shenley: Herts CRO, HO107/1701, E.D. 2, E.D. 3. The Hertfordshire place-names volume, confusingly, places Tyttenhanger under Ridge, whilst in a footnote stating that Tyttenhanger Green is in St Stephens, and also places London Colney under Shenley, whilst noting – correctly this time – that part lay in St Peters. Colney Heath is placed in St Peters, with no recognition of its extension into Ridge: J.E.B. Gover, A. Mawer and F.M. Stenton, *The Place-Names of Hertfordshire*, English Place-Name Society Vol. XV (repr. Nottingham, 1995, first publ. 1938), pp. 67, 85, 96.

15　*VCH Herts*, Vol. 2, p. 424.

16　C. H. Ashdown, *St. Albans, Historical and Picturesque* (London, 1893), p. 179.

17　Not to be confused with Frogmore, Kings Walden: Gover, Mawer and Stenton, *Place-Names of Hertfordshire*, p. 23.

18　*1851 Census Report. Population Tables I*, Parliamentary Papers 1852-3, Vol. LXXXV, p. ccvi.

the urban population identified in each of the three parishes coincides *exactly* with the number given for the borough in 1851 in Kelly's Directory of 1855.[19]

Of the 44 Registration Counties listed in the 1851 Census Report, Hertfordshire stood in 40th position in terms of the proportion urban, with just 24% of the total population living in its nine towns.[20] The existence of the two market towns of Great Berkhamsted and Tring within the Berkhamsted Superintendent Registrar's District rendered it notably urbanised compared with the county as a whole, with an urban population amounting to 53%, and the presence of the City of St Albans at the heart of the St Albans District produced a similar if less pronounced effect, with 40% of the population urban out of the total of 17,991 residents, if the occupants of the workhouse are included with the town.[21] St Albans was, in fact, the largest town in the county at this date, exceeding the population of the county's administrative capital, Hertford, by some 400, with the next nearest rivals, Bishop's Stortford, Hitchin and Ware, substantially smaller at around the 5,000 mark.[22] But if the City of St Albans dominated the district, in terms of population size and density, as the one parliamentary and municipal borough, as the centre of communications, as the oldest established market town and as the one truly urban economy, it would be a mistake to characterise the remainder of the district as a rural backwater. As we will see when we discuss the occupational structure of the region in more detail below, each of the rural parishes or parts of parishes had a significant if variable role to play in the straw plait industry, much like the rural population of the Berkhamsted region to the west.[23] Redbourn was a thriving community of 2,084 souls, and, being situated on Watling Street to the north-west of St Albans, could expect upwards of eighty coaches to pass through the town daily prior to the coming of the railway; in 1797 coaches bound for Birmingham, Liverpool and Carlisle all stopped here.[24] It could also boast three annual fairs at mid-century, held in early January, at Easter and at Whitsun.[25] Harpenden was a large village also approaching 2,000 inhabitants, with a substantial non-agricultural population, its own Literary Institute and a Chemical Laboratory, of which more below.[26] Sandridge, Wheathampstead and the Out-hamlets were the most agricultural of the areas under consideration, but again by no means exclusively. In particular, the involvement of all of these hamlets, villages and parishes in the plaiting of straw, producing a thriving cottage industry, tied them intimately to urban communities such as St Albans, for it was in the towns that straw hat industry itself was established, and to which individual plaiters and straw factors would come to sell both plait and straw.

---

19   *Kelly's Directory 1855*, p. 230.

20   *1851 Census Report. Population Tables I*, Parliamentary Papers 1852-3 Vol. LXXXV, pp. l, civ. The nine towns identified in the report are Bishops Stortford, Great Berkhamsted, Hemel Hempstead, Hertford, Hitchin, St Albans, Tring, Ware and Watford.

21   Goose, *The Berkhamsted Region*, p. 27. If the Workhouse is excluded, the urban proportion falls only marginally to 39%.

22   *1851 Census Report. Population Tables I*, Parliamentary Papers 1852-3 Vol. LXXXV, pp. cciv-ccvii.

23   Goose, *The Berkhamsted Region*, pp. 34-46.

24   *Kelly's Directory 1855*, p. 224; L.M. Munby, *The Hertfordshire Landscape* (London, 1977), p. 202. As early as 1777 it was described as "a great thoroughfare to London; it forms one street, and has four or five inns, where the wagons generally set up": A. Jones (ed.), *Hertfordshire 1731-1800 as Recorded in the Gentleman's Magazine* (Hertford, 1993), p. 38.

25   *Kelly's Directory 1855*, p. 224.

26   *Ibid.*, p. 203.

A profile of the population

Table 1 presents population totals, sex ratios, marital status and age structures for St Albans and its region, employing the subdivisions discussed above, together with sub-totals for the borough of St Albans (urban parishes), the Liberty of St Albans, and for all rural parishes, alongside comparative figures from the Berkhamsted region to the west and from an 'English Rural Norm' collected and calculated by Dr Dennis Mills and Joan Mills. The combined total of 17,991 individuals represents some 10.8% of the population of the county of Hertfordshire in 1851, with the borough of St Albans accounting for 40% of the total and the Liberty of St Albans for as much as 62%.

TABLE 1 : POPULATION, SEX RATIO, MARITAL STATUS AND AGE STRUCTURE

Place	No.	Population %		Marital Status %			Age Groups %					
		M	F	Unm	Mar	Wid	0-14	15-29	30-44	45-59	60-74	75+
St Albans Urban												
St Albans	3371	46.6	53.4	62.1	32.6	5.3	33.6	28.0	20.2	11.5	5.7	0.9
St Michaels (Urban)	1091	44.5	55.5	64.2	30.7	5.1	37.9	27.4	17.1	10.7	5.9	1.0
St Peters	2523	44.7	55.3	61.1	32.2	6.7	34.2	26.9	17.8	11.5	7.7	1.9
St Albans Rural												
St Michaels (Rural)	909	50.5	49.5	63.5	32.4	4.1	33.2	30.7	17.8	12.3	5.0	1.0
St Stephens	1553	49.6	50.4	61.0	33.3	5.7	36.8	27.0	15.5	12.4	6.9	1.4
Out-hamlets	1470	51.4	48.6	61.1	35.2	3.8	37.9	25.4	19.3	11.6	5.1	0.7
St Albans Workhouse	243	56.4	43.6	56.8	16.5	26.7	25.9	7.8	10.7	11.9	28.4	15.2
Harpenden	1979	47.8	52.2	60.1	33.9	5.9	35.7	25.4	19.4	11.9	6.2	1.4
Redbourn	2084	46.3	53.7	60.1	35.4	4.5	36.9	26.0	18.0	11.5	6.6	1.0
Sandridge	860	49.9	50.1	63.8	31.6	4.5	38.1	26.2	17.8	12.2	5.0	0.7
Wheathampstead	1908	49.5	50.5	60.9	34.7	4.4	40.5	23.0	18.9	10.3	6.2	1.1
Sub-Totals												
St Albans	11160	47.5	52.5	61.8	32.4	5.8	35.0	27.0	18.2	11.6	6.7	1.5
Urban Parishes	6985	45.6	54.4	62.1	32.2	5.8	34.5	27.5	18.9	11.4	6.4	1.3
Rural Parishes	10763	49.0	51.0	61.1	34.1	4.8	37.2	25.8	18.2	11.6	6.0	1.1
Total	17991	47.8	52.2	61.4	33.1	5.4	36.0	26.2	18.4	11.5	6.5	1.4
Berkhamsted Region	11578	47.4	52.6	61.4	32.9	5.7	36.8	27.1	17.9	11.2	5.8	1.2
Mills' Rural Norm	18490	51.1	48.9	59.8	35.0	5.2	36.6	25.4	17.2	11.8	6.9	1.7

N.B. marital status excludes 41 unstated, age groups exclude 12 unknown.

The first striking feature of this table is the remarkable similarity between the overall totals for the St Albans region and those for Berkhamsted, in terms of sex ratios, marital status and age structure, suggesting immediately that there may have been similar economic and social structures operating in both regions to underpin these demographic characteristics. The percentages for marital status are virtually identical, and thus show similar differences to Mills' Rural Norm, with a very slightly higher proportion widowed, a more markedly higher proportion unmarried and a lower percentage married. The percentages of widowed persons varies substantially between parishes, ranging from as low as 3.8% in the Out-hamlets to 6.7% in St Peters.

Looking at the sub-totals, in general there were more widowed persons in both the town and Liberty of St Albans than there were in the rural parishes taken together. The figure for the Liberty is, however, buoyed up by the inclusion of the workhouse, where 65 of the 243 inhabitants (39 men and 26 women) were widowed,

and if this is excluded the figure falls to 5.3%, very close indeed to Mills' Rural Norm. There is thus a tendency for the town to include a higher proportion of widows and widowers than did rural areas, both within and outside of this district, but the pattern is not clear cut between individual parishes. Low figures are indeed found in three of the four outlying villages, in the Out-hamlets and in rural St Michaels, but the figures for Harpenden and St Stephens both stand above average, whilst it is the influence of St Peters alone that produces the high urban figure, for the other two urban parishes stand very close to the mean.

Greater consistency is apparent when we turn to the sex ratio of the widowed population. Across the district as a whole, as in the Berkhamsted region, there were substantially more widows than widowers, the sex ratio (males per 100 females) standing at just 44.[27] This general picture is consistent across all parishes or parts of parishes except one: Sandridge, for no obvious reason, contained 22 widowers to just 17 widows. The urban-rural contrast is very clear cut indeed. The sex ratios in the urban parishes of St Albans, St Michaels and St Peters were as low as 29, 24 and 28 respectively, producing an average for the town of 28 (88 widowers to 313 widows). For the Liberty of St Albans the figure was 35, and for the rural parishes alone 59. These figures are the result of a combination of factors, the general excess of widows undoubtedly reflecting greater female longevity, as much a feature of the nineteenth century demographic regime as it is of today's, perhaps also allied to greater male opportunities for remarriage. But the urban-rural contrast must also reflect either important demographic, or social and economic, contrasts. It is possible, of course, that the discrepancy in life expectancy between men and women was greater in towns than in rural areas, although this remains to be established. A more plausible explanation is that urban communities provided greater opportunities for female independence than did rural areas, particularly in terms of employment opportunities, or that women of independent means were more likely to gravitate townwards to enjoy the culture and society that urban life could offer.[28] Indeed, this was a feature of towns recognised in the published census report for 1851, for whilst variation in the proportional numbers of widows was explained by various causes, including levels of marriage and remarriage and differential mortality rates, particular note was also made of "the accidental congregation in certain towns of women living on small annuities".[29]

A snapshot of the large female widowed population of St Peters might prove revealing. There were 131 widows living here in 1851, out of a total female population of 1,394, which, allowing for the four women whose status is not revealed, produces a proportion of 9.4%, or almost one in every ten.[30] Of these 89 (68%) headed their own household. Of the rest, the most common relationship was mother or mother-in-law to the head of household, accounting for a further 17, whilst seven were lodgers and seven were visitors. The remainder are made up of three daughters or daughters-in-law, three sisters and five servants. More revealing is the social status of these widows. As many as 23 (18%) fall into social classes A or B, which compares with only 11% of the female population of the parish as a whole.[31] Prominent here are annuitants, fundholders, proprietors of houses or women otherwise of independent means. But a look at the other end of the social scale is revealing too, for 28 of these 131 (21%) fall into the bottom class F, which compares with just 4% of the female population at large. Five of these are described as paupers, the remaining 23 are resident in almshouses, in Catharine Lane, in St Peters Almshouse, in Levingden Almshouse, and particularly in Marlborough

27   Goose, *The Berkhamsted Region*, p. 28. This calculation excludes the workhouse, the sex ratio rising to 48 if it is included.

28   This urban/rural contrast was also evident in pre-industrial England, and a similar range of factors have been suggested as the explanation: R. Wall, "Elderly Persons and Members of their Households in England and Wales from Preindustrial Times to the Present", in D. Kertzer and P. Laslett (eds.), *Aging in the Past: Demography, Society and Old Age* (London, 1995), pp. 87-90

29   *1851 Census Report. Population Tables II*, Parliamentary Papers 1852-3 Vol. LXXXVIII, Vol. 1, p. xl.

30   The figure for England and Wales as a whole was 7.2%, or one in every fourteen: *ibid*.

31   For classification by social status, see Appendix 1, p. 693.

Buildings, which housed as many as 15 and remains a familiar and imposing architectural feature of the City to this day, situated at the top of Hatfield Road, then known as Cock Lane.[32] Twenty widows (15%) fall into category C (dealers, clerical or skilled workers), 50 (38%) into D (semi-skilled) whilst a further 10 (8%) were unskilled workers in category E.

Comparing this with the situation in the four villages of Harpenden, Redbourn, Sandridge and Wheathampstead, which collectively contained 207 widows, the first difference is that here they formed a significantly lower proportion of the female population, at just 6% or one in seventeen. An almost identical proportion to that found in St Peters headed their households (67% compared to 68%), and mother, mother-in-law or step-mother, unsurprisingly, was again the most common relationship to the head of household amongst the rest. But there are two further notable differences. First, there were proportionally nearly twice as many widows employed as servants in the rural parishes than in St Peters, and, second, there were substantially fewer lodgers or visitors.

Turning to social class, it is perhaps surprising to find a similar proportion in categories A and B in the villages as in the town, at 16% (34 of 207), which compares with just 9.5% for the female population as a whole. Annuitants and fundholders were just slightly fewer in number in proportional terms in the villages, but as many as 11 widows were active farmers, a further four were retired farmers or retired farmers' widows, and six more were independent landed proprietors. The real contrast is found towards the bottom of the social scale, for only 14 of the 207 (8%) fall into category F, little more than one-third of the proportion found in St Peters, all being described as paupers. As for those who were employed, the great majority, 126 or 61% of all widows, fell into category D, largely semi-skilled workers, with slightly fewer in category C than in St Peters and substantially fewer in category E. The only other obvious difference between town and village with regard to widows was their age: almost half the rural widows were under 60, compared with little more than a third in the town. This discrepancy might weigh against the notion that higher urban male mortality was responsible for the size of the female widowed population in the town, for if this had been the case one might expect more, rather than fewer, younger urban widows.[33]

There is clearly considerable scope for further exploration of the similarities and contrasts in the female widowed population in the Victorian town and countryside, and indeed great opportunities to explore the position of the elderly more generally in Victorian society, for which the census provides an ideal point of departure.[34] For the St Albans district, however, we can conclude that towns were indeed able to support more widows than were rural areas, that they attracted more widows as temporary visitors but employed fewer as servants, and that urban widows tended to be older. Similar numbers in town and countryside were heads of household, however, and similar proportions belonged to the higher social groups, although unsurprisingly the source of their wealth and independence tended to differ. The real contrast lies in the ability of urban society to support a larger number of widows towards the bottom of the social scale, partly

32   Marlborough almshouses, then called The Buildings, were founded in 1736 by Sarah, Duchess of Marlborough, to provide accommodation for 36 poor inhabitants, 18 men and 18 women, who were each to receive £15 per year and an adequate allowance of coal. Robert Pemberton endowed an almshouse in 1627 in St Peters, for six aged widows, allowing £5 per annum to each: *Kelly's Directory 1855*, p. 230; F. B. Mason, *Gibb's Illustrated Handbook to St Albans* (St Albans, 1866), pp. 87-9; Anon. (by An Old Inhabitant), *A Guide to Hertfordshire* (Hertford, 1880), p. 328; *VCH Herts*, Vol. 2, p. 473.

33   To explore this further one would also need to consider the possibility of differential mortality by social class, particularly given the large number of low status widows in the town, and consider what was cause and what effect.

34   There is limited published work on the subject, but see P. Laslett, *A Fresh Map of Life. The Emergence of the Third Age* (London, 1989); Kertzer and Laslett (eds.), *Aging in the Past*.

through the opportunities provided for unskilled employment, but particularly through the mechanisms for social relief that lay outside of the confines of the poor law in the form of the almshouse.[35] Having ventured these conclusions, however, it must be appreciated that St Albans and its region may well be untypical, for we will shortly see that it offered employment opportunities for women, whether widowed or not, in both town and countryside, on a scale that has rarely been revealed in previous studies.

The proportion unmarried revealed in Table 1 is identical to that for the Berkhamsted region, and hence similarly lies slightly above Mills' Rural Norm, with the St Albans figure a little higher than the rural parishes, just as in the town of Great Berkhamsted compared to the region as a whole.[36] Similarly, the proportion married, as for the Berkhamsted region, stands below the Rural Norm, and particularly in the town. Examination of individual parishes generally reinforces this urban-rural contrast, although again Sandridge stands out as an exception to the rule, whilst the figures for St Michaels (rural) stand closer to those for the town than to the other rural parishes. The age structure of the population also suggests an urban-rural contrast, for the town included a smaller percentage in the 0-14 age group than the rural parishes both within and outside of the district, but contained a larger percentage aged 15-24. This was also a feature of the town of Great Berkhamsted, where just 34.2% of the population were aged 0-14, whilst the percentage aged 15-29 stood at 28.2, well above the rural average.[37] This may partly reflect differential fertility between town and countryside, either because urban marital fertility was lower or simply because a lower proportion of the population was married, a consideration we will return to when marriage levels are discussed below.[38] But it is no doubt also the product of patterns of migration, for the attraction to towns of adolescents and young, single adults, to take up positions in service or as apprentices, to simply take up a job or to marry, is a well-established feature of urban society through from the early modern to the modern periods.[39]

The most striking feature of Table 1, just as in the Berkhamsted region, is the sex ratio of the population. In the St Albans district there was once again a pronounced skew in favour of women, producing an excess of females very similar to that discovered for Berkhamsted, and standing in stark contrast to the situation in Mills' large rural sample which exhibits a bias towards males. Furthermore, whilst the imbalance was considerably more pronounced in the strictly urban parishes of St Albans, St Michaels (Urban) and St Peters, it was by no means a purely urban phenomenon, for the rural parishes as a group also included more females than males, and only St Michaels (rural) and the Out-hamlets stand out as exceptions, St Michaels only marginally so. Across the district as a whole, there was an excess of 843 females (excluding the workhouse), almost exactly 10% more females than males. Expressing the figures in terms of conventional sex ratios (males per 100 females) underlines the exceptional nature of this region. For whilst the national sex ratio (England and Wales) stood at 96 in 1851, and the figure for Hertfordshire as a whole at 99, in the St Albans district it was just 91, very similar to the Berkhamsted region figure of 90.[40] In the three urban parishes of St Albans, St Michaels (urban) and St Peters, the ratio stood as low as 87, 80 and 81 respectively, to produce a combined

35   This subject is explored further below, pp. 93-4.

36   Goose, *The Berkhamsted Region*, p. 27.

37   *Ibid*.

38   See pp. 42-50.

39   P. Clark and P. Slack (eds.), *Crisis and Order in English Towns 1500-1700* (London, 1972), pp. 17, 117-63; P. Clark and D. Souden (eds.), *Migration and Society in Early Modern England* (London, 1987), pp. 24, 77-106, 269-72; P. Corfield, *The Impact of English Towns 1700-1800* (Oxford, 1982), pp. 99-105; Anderson, *Family Structure in Nineteenth Century Lancashire*, pp. 39-40; Goose, *The Berkhamsted Region*, p. 58; and see below, pp. 138-41.

40   *1851 Census Report. Population Tables II*, Parliamentary Papers 1852-3 Vol. LXXXVIII, Vol. 1, p. 139; N.L. Tranter, *Population and Society 1750-1940: Contrasts in Population Growth* (London, 1985), p. 180; Goose, *The Berkhamsted Region*, p. 28.

urban figure of 84, even lower than those of 88 and 87 found respectively in Great Berkhamsted and the parish of Tring, suggesting that whilst even modest market towns tended to include more women than men, that advantage was even greater in the larger, economically more sophisticated, urban centres such as St Albans.[41] Again, however, it is clear that the rural parishes within this district were unusual, for whilst their combined sex ratio was identical to the national average it stood substantially below that normally found in rural populations. Furthermore, in some of the rural parishes the skew towards women was very pronounced indeed, the sex ratio standing at 92 in Harpenden, and rivalling the urban figure at just 86 in Redbourn.[42]

Just as in the Berkhamsted region, therefore, there are two features to be explained: an overall surplus of women across the St Albans District as a whole, and a more marked bias in the town itself compared with most, though not all, of the rural parishes. The general skew towards women is relatively easily explained, just as it was for Berkhamsted, by the ready availability of female employment in the area, which served both to attract them into the region from further to the north and east of the county and to discourage those born here from moving away. In the eastern half of the county the sex ratio was consistently higher, standing at 102 in the Ware Superintendent Registrar's District, at 104 in Hatfield, 105 in Royston and 106 in Hertford.[43] Indeed, contemporaries were themselves aware of this connection, for in 1866 it was noted that "The staple trade of the city is the manufacture of straw hats, in which women are principally employed, and which therefore accounts for the considerable numerical superiority of women over men in St Albans".[44] Nor was such insight confined to local residents, Dr H.J. Hunter, one of Her Majesty's Commissioners, writing in 1865 that "The Warwickshire beadwork has not yet filled the cots [cottages] with adult girls as has the straw plait further south".[45]

The combined effect of these two features, both retaining and attracting young women, is revealed by an examination of the sex ratio of the population by age group. For the age cohort 0-4, which will obviously be strongly influenced by the pattern of birth by sex, the sex ratio for the St Albans District as a whole stood at 97, and for the town proper at 94. The birth sex ratio for England and Wales in the 1840s and 1850s stood at 105, but as infant mortality tended to be higher amongst males than females, one would expect that this ratio would be lower for the age group 0-4 as a whole.[46] Indeed, the figure calculated for England from the 1821 census for those aged 0-4 is 101,[47] closer to, but still substantially higher than, the St Albans ratios. The low

41   Goose, *The Berkhamsted Region*, p. 28. The predominance of women in urban populations, particularly larger towns, is well established. In south-east England in 1801, the sex ratio in 931 rural parishes was 107, in 143 towns it stood at 97, and fell to 79 in 66 city parishes: M.J. Dobson, *Contours of Death and Disease in Early Modern England* (Cambridge, 1997), p. 180. In south Devon in 1851, women of all ages outnumbered men in the towns of Totnes, Buckfastleigh and Ashburton, particularly in the age range 10-30: D. Bryant, "Demographic Trends in South-Devon in the Mid-Nineteenth Century", in K.J. Gregory and W.L.D. Ravenhill (eds.), *Exeter Essays in Geography in Honour of Arthur Davies* (Exeter, 1971), p. 131.

42   The skew towards women in the urban sex ratio was evident from the start of the century, calculations for St Albans borough in 1801 and 1811 producing figures of 74 and 81 respectively. The rural areas of the district exhibited a sex ratio of 100 in 1801, but just 89 in 1811, by which date it stood as low as 80 in Harpenden. Calculations from census data given in R. Clutterbuck, *The History and Antiquities of the County of Hertford*, 3 Vols. (London, 1815-27), Vol. 1, pp. 3-4, 57, 277-8.

43   *1851 Census Report. Population Tables II*, Parliamentary Papers 1852-3 Vol. LXXXVIII, Vol. 1, p. 139.

44   Mason, *Gibb's Illustrated Handbook to St Albans*, p. 53.

45   *Medical Officer of the Privy Council, 7th Report*, Parliamentary Papers 1865 Vol. XXVI, p. 275, cited in M.J. Kingman, " 'Doing the Beads': By-employment for Women and Children in Rural Warwickshire", 1865-6, *Warwickshire History*, Vol. X (1996-7), pp. 82-6.

46   Wrigley and Schofield, *The Population History of England*, p. 128.

47   *Ibid.*, p. 591.

sex ratio for this age group in our district may have been the result of relatively high levels of both infant and early childhood mortality experienced here, levels that were most probably highest of all in the town of St Albans.[48] However, apart from the elderly, for whom the bias towards women has been discussed above, the largest skew in the sex ratio is to be found amongst teenagers and young adults. Across the district as a whole, the ratios for the age categories 15-19, 20-24, 25-29 and 30-34 were, respectively, 88, 88, 77 and 86, whilst for the town of St Albans they stood even lower, at 81, 75, 70 and 76.[49] As teenagers and young adults generally featured prominently amongst the migrant population of nineteenth century England, these figures clearly reflect the impact of sex specific migration, into the district as a whole but even more markedly into the town of St Albans itself.

The occupational structure of these parishes is presented in Table 2, and for the moment it is particularly female employment that concerns us. A more detailed examination of female employment will be conducted below,[50] but the figures in Table 2 show that it was at a high level. Of the total female population of all ages, 46.7% were recorded as in work, again a figure almost identical to the 46.5% revealed for the Berkhamsted region.[51] The association between female employment and a skewed sex ratio is quite clear, from the overall figures for employment as well as from a more detailed consideration of individual parishes. In rural St Michaels, St Stephens, the Out-hamlets, Sandridge and Wheathampstead, the proportion of females recorded as in employment ranged from 36.9% to 40.5%, relatively low figures, and in these same parishes the sex ratio tended to be high, ranging between 98 and 106.[52] Lower sex ratios tended to be associated with high levels of female employment. This is clearly the case in the three strictly urban parishes, most notably in St Michaels where a female employment rate of 50.3% was accompanied by the lowest sex ratio of all of the parishes at 80. But the two rural parishes with particularly high levels of female employment, Harpenden and Redbourn at 61.6% and 55.3% respectively, also exhibit low sex ratios at 92 and 86, considerably below the other rural parishes in our sample and very low indeed when compared with the norm in the other rural communities. The St Albans region thus clearly demonstrates an association between female employment opportunities and a skewed sex ratio, one that has more commonly been associated with larger towns and cities whose economy centred upon textile production, such as nineteenth century Dundee, where the imbalance in favour of women was particularly marked amongst the unmarried population aged 16 years and upwards.[53]

---

48   R. Woods and N. Shelton, *An Atlas of Victorian Mortality* (Liverpool, 1997), Maps 7a and 11a, pp. 49, 51, 66-7.

49   The age-specific figures for the town of St Albans mirror those found in Totnes, Ashburton and Buckfastleigh in south Devon, although in the rural area of this part of Devon there was a pronounced skew towards males in the age group 10-19, which is only occasionally found in parishes in our district, such as Sandridge, where there was a particularly strong demand for agricultural labour: Bryant, "Demographic Trends in South-Devon", p. 131.

50   See pp. 86-97.

51   Goose, *The Berkhamsted Region*, Table 2, p. 30.

52   The figures for female employment in Wheathampstead are, however, almost certainly understated: see below, p. 89.

53   D. Graham, "The Use of Published Census Burgh Ward Data for Local Population Studies: Dundee, 1901-1971", *Local Population Studies*, No. 58 (1997), p. 34. A similar skew towards women was evident in parts of Leicester in the third quarter of the 19th century, and has been explained in terms of the attraction of employment in the hosiery industry: S.M. Fletcher, "The Old Cricket Ground, Leicester: a Study of Two Contrasting Areas of Nineteenth-Century Development", unpubl. MA dissertation, University of Leciester, 1983, pp. 82-3, 86, 123.

TABLE 2 : OCCUPATIONAL STRUCTURE

St Albans

	All No.	All %	M No.	M %	F No.	F %
Agriculture	36	2.0	36	3.6	0	0.0
Textiles	491	26.6	181	18.1	310	36.6
Misc Manufs	22	1.2	21	2.1	1	0.1
Leather	71	3.8	59	5.9	12	1.4
Building	70	3.8	69	6.9	1	0.1
Metal	30	1.6	30	3.0	0	0.0
Wood	54	2.9	54	5.4	0	0.0
Food/Drink	158	8.6	140	14.0	18	2.1
Transport	27	1.5	27	2.7	0	0.0
Serv/Dom Serv	276	15.0	58	5.8	218	25.7
Publ Serv/Prof	93	5.0	75	7.5	18	2.1
Indep Means	52	2.8	11	1.1	41	4.8
Spec Ind (Straw)	265	14.4	50	5.0	215	25.4
Quarry/Mine	0	0.0	0	0.0	0	0.0
Retail/Distrib	46	2.5	38	3.8	8	0.9
Misc	155	8.4	149	14.9	6	0.7
Total	1846	100.0	998	100.0	848	100.0
Dependent/No Occ	1525	45.2	572	36.4	953	52.9

St Michaels (Urban)

	All No.	All %	M No.	M %	F No.	F %
Agriculture	77	12.2	77	23.7	0	0.0
Textiles	99	15.7	33	10.2	66	21.6
Misc Manufs	3	0.5	3	0.9	0	0.0
Leather	16	2.5	12	3.7	4	1.3
Building	17	2.7	17	5.2	0	0.0
Metal	5	0.8	5	1.5	0	0.0
Wood	12	1.9	12	3.7	0	0.0
Food/Drink	31	4.9	30	9.2	1	0.3
Transport	20	3.2	20	6.2	0	0.0
Serv/Dom Serv	89	14.1	27	8.3	62	20.3
Publ Serv/Prof	19	3.0	12	3.7	7	2.3
Indep Means	32	5.1	11	3.4	21	6.9
Spec Ind (Straw)	184	29.2	42	12.9	142	46.6
Quarry/Mine	5	0.8	5	1.5	0	0.0
Retail/Distrib	8	1.3	8	2.5	0	0.0
Misc	13	2.1	11	3.4	2	0.7
Total	630	100.0	325	100.0	305	100.0
Dependent/No Occ	461	42.3	160	33.0	301	49.7

St Peters

	All No.	All %	M No.	M %	F No.	F %
Agriculture	43	3.2	43	6.2	0	0.0
Textiles	331	25.0	106	15.3	225	35.7
Misc Manufs	7	0.5	7	1.0	0	0.0
Leather	42	3.2	35	5.0	7	1.1
Building	67	5.1	56	8.1	11	1.7
Metal	13	1.0	13	1.9	0	0.0
Wood	53	4.0	53	7.6	0	0.0
Food/Drink	69	5.2	65	9.4	4	0.6
Transport	27	2.0	26	3.7	1	0.2
Serv/Dom Serv	168	12.7	34	4.9	134	21.3
Publ Serv/Prof	62	4.7	40	5.8	22	3.5
Indep Means	53	4.0	10	1.4	43	6.8
Spec Ind (Straw)	208	15.7	28	4.0	180	28.6
Quarry/Mine	2	0.2	2	0.3	0	0.0
Retail/Distrib	21	1.6	18	2.6	3	0.5
Misc	159	12.0	159	22.9	0	0.0
Total	1325	100.0	695	100.0	630	100.0
Dependent/No Occ	1198	47.5	434	38.4	764	54.8

St Michaels (Rural)

	All No.	All %	M No.	M %	F No.	F %
Agriculture	206	41.8	204	62.8	2	1.2
Textiles	18	3.7	6	1.8	12	7.1
Misc Manufs	2	0.4	2	0.6	0	0.0
Leather	2	0.4	2	0.6	0	0.0
Building	0	0.0	0	0.0	0	0.0
Metal	1	0.2	1	0.3	0	0.0
Wood	16	3.2	16	4.9	0	0.0
Food/Drink	14	2.8	12	3.7	2	1.2
Transport	6	1.2	6	1.8	0	0.0
Serv/Dom Serv	108	21.9	41	12.6	67	39.9
Publ Serv/Prof	15	3.0	10	3.1	5	3.0
Indep Means	11	2.2	6	1.8	5	3.0
Spec Ind (Straw)	79	16.0	4	1.2	75	44.6
Quarry/Mine	0	0.0	0	0.0	0	0.0
Retail/Distrib	5	1.0	5	1.5	0	0.0
Misc	10	2.0	10	3.1	0	0.0
Total	493	100.0	325	100.0	168	100.0
Dependent/No Occ	416	45.8	134	29.2	282	62.7

St Stephens

	All No.	All %	M No.	M %	F No.	F %
Agriculture	399	46.8	398	73.7	1	0.3
Textiles	155	18.2	18	3.3	137	43.8
Misc Manufs	1	0.1	1	0.2	0	0.0
Leather	9	1.1	9	1.7	0	0.0
Building	8	0.9	8	1.5	0	0.0
Metal	10	1.2	10	1.9	0	0.0
Wood	22	2.6	22	4.1	0	0.0
Food/Drink	29	3.4	24	4.4	5	1.6
Transport	8	0.9	7	1.3	1	0.3
Serv/Dom Serv	91	10.7	20	3.7	71	22.7
Publ Serv/Prof	14	1.6	6	1.1	8	2.6
Indep Means	21	2.5	3	0.6	18	5.8
Spec Ind (Straw)	74	8.7	2	0.4	72	23.0
Quarry/Mine	0	0.0	0	0.0	0	0.0
Retail/Distrib	8	0.9	8	1.5	0	0.0
Misc	4	0.5	4	0.7	0	0.0
Total	853	100.0	540	100.0	313	100.0
Dependent/No Occ	700	45.1	230	29.9	470	60.0

Out-hamlets

	All No.	All %	M No.	M %	F No.	F %
Agriculture	350	43.8	346	67.7	4	1.4
Textiles	76	9.5	10	2.0	66	22.8
Misc Manufs	0	0.0	0	0.0	0	0.0
Leather	15	1.9	14	2.7	1	0.3
Building	17	2.1	17	3.3	0	0.0
Metal	5	0.6	5	1.0	0	0.0
Wood	13	1.6	13	2.5	0	0.0
Food/Drink	24	3.0	21	4.1	3	1.0
Transport	4	0.5	4	0.8	0	0.0
Serv/Dom Serv	95	11.9	37	7.2	58	20.1
Publ Serv/Prof	11	1.4	8	1.6	3	1.0
Indep Means	17	2.1	3	0.6	14	4.8
Spec Ind (Straw)	145	18.1	6	1.2	139	48.1
Quarry/Mine	0	0.0	0	0.0	0	0.0
Retail/Distrib	6	0.8	6	1.2	0	0.0
Misc	22	2.8	21	4.1	1	0.3
Total	800	100.0	511	100.0	289	100.0
Dependent/No Occ	670	45.6	245	32.4	425	59.5

Harpenden

	All No.	All %	M No.	M %	F No.	F %
Agriculture	391	30.6	388	60.4	3	0.5
Textiles	31	2.4	9	1.4	22	3.5
Misc Manufs	6	0.5	6	0.9	0	0.0
Leather	16	1.3	15	2.3	1	0.2
Building	17	1.3	17	2.6	0	0.0
Metal	10	0.8	10	1.6	0	0.0
Wood	25	2.0	25	3.9	0	0.0
Food/Drink	43	3.4	36	5.6	7	1.1
Transport	22	1.7	21	3.3	1	0.2
Serv/Dom Serv	125	9.8	34	5.3	91	14.3
Publ Serv/Prof	35	2.7	29	4.5	6	0.9
Indep Means	30	2.3	13	2.0	17	2.7
Spec Ind (Straw)	517	40.5	30	4.7	487	76.6
Quarry/Mine	0	0.0	0	0.0	0	0.0
Retail/Distrib	10	0.8	9	1.4	1	0.2
Misc	0	0.0	0	0.0	0	0.0
Total	1278	100.0	642	100.0	636	100.0
Dependent/No Occ	701	35.4	304	32.1	397	38.4

Redbourn

	All No.	All %	M No.	M %	F No.	F %
Agriculture	341	26.7	335	51.1	6	1.0
Textiles	51	4.0	13	2.0	38	6.1
Misc Manufs	5	0.4	5	0.8	0	0.0
Leather	19	1.5	19	2.9	0	0.0
Building	21	1.6	21	3.2	0	0.0
Metal	9	0.7	9	1.4	0	0.0
Wood	29	2.3	29	4.4	0	0.0
Food/Drink	46	3.6	41	6.3	5	0.8
Transport	10	0.8	10	1.5	0	0.0
Serv/Dom Serv	118	9.3	41	6.3	77	12.4
Publ Serv/Prof	16	1.3	8	1.2	8	1.3
Indep Means	20	1.6	6	0.9	14	2.3
Spec Ind (Straw)	528	41.4	58	8.8	470	75.9
Quarry/Mine	0	0.0	0	0.0	0	0.0
Retail/Distrib	14	1.1	13	2.0	1	0.2
Misc	48	3.8	48	7.3	0	0.0
Total	1275	100.0	656	100.0	619	100.0
Dependent/No Occ	809	38.8	309	32.0	500	44.7

Sandridge

	All No.	All %	M No.	M %	F No.	F %
Agriculture	204	45.5	202	69.7	2	1.3
Textiles	37	8.3	1	0.3	36	22.8
Misc Manufs	1	0.2	1	0.3	0	0.0
Leather	4	0.9	3	1.0	1	0.6
Building	9	2.0	9	3.1	0	0.0
Metal	6	1.3	6	2.1	0	0.0
Wood	9	2.0	9	3.1	0	0.0
Food/Drink	10	2.2	10	3.4	0	0.0
Transport	5	1.1	5	1.7	0	0.0
Serv/Dom Serv	73	16.3	25	8.6	48	30.4
Publ Serv/Prof	5	1.1	2	0.7	3	1.9
Indep Means	4	0.9	1	0.3	3	1.9
Spec Ind (Straw)	65	14.5	1	0.3	64	40.5
Quarry/Mine	1	0.2	1	0.3	0	0.0
Retail/Distrib	2	0.4	1	0.3	1	0.6
Misc	13	2.9	13	4.5	0	0.0
Total	448	100.0	290	100.0	158	100.0
Dependent/No Occ	412	47.9	139	32.4	273	63.3

	Wheathampstead						St Albans (Liberty)						Urban Parishes					
	All		M		F		All		M		F		All		M		F	
	No.	%	No.	%	No.	%	No.	%	No.	%	No.	%	No.	%	No.	%	No.	%
Agriculture	421	42.5	416	67.8	5	1.3	1111	18.7	1104	32.5	7	0.3	156	4.1	156	7.7	0	0.0
Textiles	14	1.4	4	0.7	10	2.7	1170	19.7	354	10.4	816	32.0	921	24.2	320	15.9	601	33.7
Misc Manufs	2	0.2	2	0.3	0	0.0	35	0.6	34	1.0	1	0.0	32	0.8	31	1.5	1	0.0
Leather	21	2.1	21	3.4	0	0.0	155	2.6	131	3.9	24	0.9	129	3.4	106	5.3	23	1.3
Building	12	1.2	12	2.0	0	0.0	179	3.0	167	4.9	12	0.5	154	4.1	142	7.0	12	0.7
Metal	13	1.3	13	2.1	0	0.0	64	1.1	64	1.9	0	0.0	48	1.3	48	2.4	0	0.0
Wood	34	3.4	34	5.5	0	0.0	170	2.9	170	5.0	0	0.0	119	3.1	119	5.9	0	0.0
Food/Drink	44	4.4	39	6.4	5	1.3	325	5.5	292	8.6	33	1.3	258	6.8	235	11.6	23	1.3
Transport	13	1.3	13	2.1	0	0.0	92	1.5	90	2.7	2	0.0	74	1.9	73	3.6	1	0.0
Serv/Dom Serv	76	7.7	21	3.4	55	14.6	827	13.9	217	6.4	610	23.9	533	14.0	119	5.9	414	23.2
Publ Serv/Prof	6	0.6	4	0.7	2	0.5	214	3.6	151	4.4	63	2.5	174	4.6	127	6.3	47	2.6
Indep Means	16	1.6	4	0.7	12	3.2	186	3.1	44	1.3	142	5.6	137	3.6	32	1.6	105	5.9
Spec Ind (Straw)	309	31.2	21	3.4	288	76.4	955	16.1	132	3.9	823	32.2	657	17.3	120	5.9	537	30.1
Quarry/Mine	0	0.0	0	0.0	0	0.0	7	0.1	7	0.2	0	0.0	7	0.2	7	0.3	0	0.0
Retail/Distrib	6	0.6	6	1.0	0	0.0	94	1.6	83	2.4	11	0.4	75	2.0	64	3.2	11	0.6
Misc	4	0.4	4	0.7	0	0.0	363	6.1	354	10.4	9	0.4	327	8.6	319	15.8	8	0.4
Total	991	100.0	614	100.0	377	100.0	5947	100.0	3394	100.0	2553	100.0	3801	100.0	2018	100.0	1783	100.0
Dependent/No Occ	917	48.1	331	35.0	586	60.9	4970	45.5	1775	34.3	3195	55.6	3184	45.6	1166	36.6	2018	53.1

	Rural Parishes						TOTAL					
	All		M		F		All		M		F	
	No.	%	No.	%	No.	%	No.	%	No.	%	No.	%
Agriculture	2312	37.7	2289	64.0	23	0.9	2468	24.8	2445	43.7	23	0.5
Textiles	382	6.2	61	1.7	321	12.5	1303	13.1	381	6.8	922	21.2
Misc Manufs	17	0.3	17	0.5	0	0.0	49	0.5	48	0.9	1	0.0
Leather	86	1.4	83	2.3	3	0.1	215	2.2	189	3.4	26	0.6
Building	84	1.4	84	2.3	0	0.0	238	2.4	226	4.0	12	0.3
Metal	54	0.9	54	1.5	0	0.0	102	1.0	102	1.8	0	0.0
Wood	148	2.4	148	4.1	0	0.0	267	2.7	267	4.8	0	0.0
Food/Drink	210	3.4	183	5.1	27	1.1	468	4.7	418	7.5	50	1.2
Transport	68	1.1	66	1.8	2	0.1	142	1.4	139	2.5	3	0.0
Serv/Dom Serv	686	11.2	219	6.1	467	18.2	1219	12.3	338	6.0	881	20.3
Publ Serv/Prof	102	1.7	67	1.9	35	1.4	276	2.8	194	3.5	82	1.9
Indep Means	119	1.9	36	1.0	83	3.2	256	2.6	68	1.2	188	4.3
Spec Ind (Straw)	1717	28.0	122	3.4	1595	62.3	2374	23.9	242	4.3	2132	49.1
Quarry/Mine	1	0.0	1	0.0	0	0.0	8	0.0	8	0.1	0	0.0
Retail/Distrib	51	0.8	48	1.3	3	0.1	126	1.3	112	2.0	14	0.3
Misc	101	1.6	100	2.8	1	0.0	428	4.3	419	7.5	9	0.2
Total	6138	100.0	3578	100.0	2560	100.0	9939	100.0	5596	100.0	4343	100.0
Dependent/No Occ	4625	43.0	1692	32.1	2933	53.4	7809	44.0	2858	33.8	4951	53.3

Just as in the Berkhamsted region, the bulk of this employment was created by the straw plait trade, as the figures in Table 2 reveal. In every parish a significant and often a substantial proportion of the female population were employed in the straw industry, most commonly simply as plaiters of straw. In the urban parishes of St Albans, however – and in this respect our district differs from the Berkhamsted region – straw plait was also worked up into straw hats, creating a symbiotic relationship between the more rural parishes which concentrated upon providing the raw material of straw plait, and the town which produced the finished article. The production of straw hats in turn created a demand for the trimmings of silk, lace or cotton that were increasingly fashionable towards the middle of the nineteenth century, giving an added boost to female employment under the heading of Textiles/clothing in Table 2. This may be one of the reasons why St Albans could also boast a significant silk weaving industry.[54] But an even more significant development was the growth of another related industry that can only have been inspired by the straw hat trade of the area, and this was the manufacture of the Brazilian hat, a hat woven from palm leaves mainly imported from Cuba. Brazilian hat-makers are also included under Textiles/clothing in Table 2, and their prominence largely

54   See below, p. 75.

explains the substantial number of females employed under this category in St Stephens, as well as boosting the figures in the town itself.

The range of female employment opportunities was, unsurprisingly, much greater in the borough of St Albans than it was in the more rural parishes of the district, even if the bulk of this employment was still to be found within the straw and textile sectors of the economy. This is a feature of English towns that has been traced back to at least the seventeenth century, and its impact upon the sex ratio of the population is well established,[55] whilst a recent study has revealed a similar situation in the towns and cities of seventeenth and eighteenth century France.[56] There were more openings, perhaps unsurprisingly, in the service sector in general and in domestic service in particular, but in St Albans the difference was one of degree rather than of kind, with 23% of total female employment in this sector in the town compared with 18% in rural areas. Furthermore, there were notable exceptions, with the parish of Sandridge exhibiting a figure of just over 30%, and rural St Michaels employing as many as 40% of its occupied female population in service and domestic service, the figure here boosted by the existence of substantial entourages at Childwick Hall, Prae House and most notably at Gorhambury, residence of the Earl and Countess of Verulam. Interestingly, these two parishes produced the two lowest overall proportions of females employed, as well as two of the three lowest figures for employment in straw and textiles combined, perhaps indicating a trade-off between female employment in industrial and in service industries.

In the Berkhamsted region marriage patterns were clearly affected by the imbalance between the sexes found there, and one would expect similar influences in the St Albans district. Table 3 presents the percentage of the population never married, by age and sex, for each parish, for the town of St Albans, for the Liberty, for the rural parishes and for the district as a whole. The fact that most first marriages took place within the age range 25-34 means that the percentages married in this age group are a good indicator of the propensity to marry, whilst the proportion remaining unmarried in the age group 45-54 will closely reflect the proportion who would never marry at all, particularly for women.[57]

The first obvious feature to emerge from Table 3 is the rarity of teenage marriage, with just 1% of the population marrying before the age of 20, a consistent feature of all parishes, and a situation that prevailed in the county as a whole at this date.[58] Across the district just one fifth of men married before their twenty-fifth birthday but almost 60% before the age of 30, figures which are slightly lower than those discovered for the Berkhamsted region.[59] Four men in every ten thus remained unmarried at the age of 30, almost a quarter at 35,

55   M. Anderson, "Marriage Patterns in Victorian Britain: an Analysis Based on a Registration District Data Sample for England and Wales 1861", *Journal of Family History*, Vol. 1 (1976), p. 61; Goose, *The Berkhamsted Region*, p. 28; P. Corfield, *The Impact of English Towns 1700-1800* (Oxford, 1982), p. 99; D. Souden, " 'East, West – Home's Best?' Regional Patterns in Migration in Early Modern England", in Clark and Souden (eds.), *Migration and Society*, pp. 292-332; D.J.M. Hooson, "The Straw Industry of the Chilterns in the Nineteenth Century", *East Midlands Geographer*, Vol. 4, pp. 342-50; Bryant, "Demographic Trends in South-Devon", pp. 131-2.

56   A. Fauve-Chamoux, "Servants in Pre-industrial Europe: Gender Differences", *Historical Social Research*, Vol. 23 (1998), pp. 112-29.

57   M. Anderson, "Marriage Patterns in Victorian Britain", p. 58; Wrigley and Schofield, *The Population History of England*, pp. 255-6, 436-7.

58   Of the 28,753 wives enumerated in Hertfordshire in 1851 just 3 were aged 16, 13 were 17, 42 were 18 and 112 were 19, hence those under 20 accounted for only 0.6% of the total: *1851 Census Report. Population Tables II*, Parliamentary Papers 1852-3 Vol. LXXXVIII, Vol. 1, p. 149.

59   Goose, *The Berkhamsted Region*, p. 32.

TABLE 3 : PERCENTAGE OF THE POPULATION NEVER MARRIED, BY AGE AND SEX

Age Group	St Albans M	F	All	St Michaels (Urb) M	F	All	St Peters M	F	All	St Michaels (Rur) M	F	All	St Stephens M	F	All
15-19	99	99	99	100	100	100	100	99	100	100	100	100	100	99	99
20-24	79	76	78	73	85	81	80	77	78	98	75	88	85	61	72
25-29	46	42	44	43	43	43	32	51	43	54	46	49	46	41	44
30-34	28	26	27	19	32	26	25	31	29	25	33	29	18	27	23
35-44	15	30	23	21	16	18	6	29	19	17	25	21	22	17	19
45-54	12	13	13	8	21	15	9	14	12	8	3	5	7	7	7
55-64	11	8	9	9	14	12	4	12	9	10	10	10	14	2	9
65+	9	16	14	25	3	10	9	12	11	0	0	0	0	4	2
25-34	36	35	35	33	38	36	29	41	37	40	41	40	35	35	35

Age Group	Out-hamlets M	F	All	Harpenden M	F	All	Redbourn M	F	All	Sandridge M	F	All	Wheathampstead M	F	All
15-19	100	99	99	100	99	99	99	98	99	100	98	99	100	98	99
20-24	88	62	76	76	72	74	79	70	74	80	72	76	65	62	64
25-29	41	26	34	42	44	43	28	38	34	32	37	35	39	41	40
30-34	29	20	25	20	28	25	21	17	19	17	41	28	15	16	16
35-44	10	11	11	18	15	16	6	15	11	16	18	17	12	10	11
45-54	9	7	8	17	11	14	8	15	12	8	28	18	11	11	11
55-64	10	2	6	7	7	7	11	3	7	6	14	9	4	12	8
65+	7	13	10	2	9	6	2	7	5	8	8	8	5	20	13
25-34	35	24	30	32	37	35	24	28	26	23	39	32	26	28	27

Age Group	St Albans (Lib) M	F	All	Urban Parishes M	F	All	Rural Parishes M	F	All	Total M	F	All
15-19	100	99	99	99	99	99	100	99	99	100	99	99
20-24	83	74	78	79	78	78	80	68	74	80	72	76
25-29	43	43	43	41	45	43	40	39	40	40	42	41
30-34	25	28	27	26	28	27	21	24	23	23	26	25
35-44	14	24	19	13	28	21	14	15	14	13	20	17
45-54	9	12	11	10	15	13	10	12	11	10	13	12
55-64	9	8	9	8	10	9	9	6	8	9	8	8
65+	7	11	9	10	13	12	3	9	6	5	11	9
25-34	35	36	35	34	37	36	31	32	32	32	35	33

and approximately 10% would never marry at all. More women married before their twenty-fifth birthday, 28%, but a similar proportion, roughly four in ten, remained single at 30. Fewer women married for the first time later in life, one in five remaining single through to their mid-forties, and approximately one in eight never marrying at all. Again these figures show similar tendencies to those found in the Berkhamsted region, but the differences in experience between the sexes are less pronounced: the marriage prospects of men were better than those of women in the St Albans district but not to the same degree as was found to the west. In St Albans the percentage never married in the age group 25-34 for men and women respectively was 32 and 35, compared with 28 and 35 in Berkhamsted, whilst those still unmarried in the age group 45-54 formed 10% and 13% respectively in St Albans, compared with 6% and 14% in Berkhamsted.[60] The corollary of this is that marriage patterns in this district conformed more closely to national averages than did those in Berkhamsted, the figure for men remaining unmarried at 25-34 being identical to that discovered for Britain in 1861, that for women

60   *Ibid.*, pp. 31-2.

standing four percentage points higher. Females still married relatively late here, therefore, but the prospects for men – after a slow start – were better. Furthermore, the proportions remaining unmarried at 45-54 also stood closer to national averages, for men just one percentage point down and for women just one percentage point up.[61]

Examination of the experiences of individual parishes as shown in Table 3 reveals significant variations within the district. Taking the age groups 25-34 and 45-54 as our key indicators, there was relatively little difference between the sexes in St Albans parish, St Stephens and Wheathampstead. The prospects for women to marry before the age of 35 were, however, significantly worse than for men in St Michaels (urban), St Peters, Harpenden, Redbourn and Sandridge, but significantly better than for men in the Out-hamlets. In terms of the proportion ever likely to marry at all, women fared substantially worse in St Michaels (urban), St Peters, Redbourn and Sandridge but were better placed in Harpenden and St Michaels (rural), with little evident difference in the Out-hamlets. In general these discrepancies conform fairly well with the imbalances in the sex ratios found in these parishes, confirming the expectation that the skewed sex ratio in this district would impact upon marriage patterns just as it had in the Berkhamsted region, as well as in the towns of eighteenth century France.[62] St Michaels (urban), St Peters and Redbourn exhibit the three lowest sex ratios, and here the prospects for women to marry early or at all were at their worst. In Harpenden the sex ratio was also low by rural standards, and here too a relatively high proportion of women remained unmarried in their mid-thirties. In the two areas with the highest sex ratios, the Out-hamlets and St Michaels (rural), female prospects to wed, either early or at all, were better than those for men.

Comparing the town with the rural parishes, there is a very clear contrast. There was relatively little difference in the eventual marriage prospects between the sexes overall in the rural areas, despite a clearly greater tendency for females to marry in their early twenties, whereas in the town the differentials in the age categories 25-34 and 45-54 reveal a more marked difference between the sexes which favoured male prospects in both the short and in the long term. In this respect, if again in more muted form, the St Albans data confirms the results found in the Berkhamsted region, and contradicts the hypothesis that early marriage, particularly for women, may have been more common in town than in countryside in the nineteenth century.[63] Of course there are exceptions to the rule. The urban parish of St Albans, with a sex ratio as low as 87, fails to indicate the expected discrepancies between the sexes in propensity to marry. Sandridge, on the other hand, does exhibit clear and very marked discrepancies despite its balanced overall sex ratio of 100. Such exceptions are not easily explained, although the very high proportion of women employed in the service and domestic service sector in Sandridge revealed in Table 2, standing at 30% compared with 18% in all rural parishes and 20% across the region as a whole, may have exerted an influence here. Forty-three female domestic servants worked in Sandridge in 1851, and 40 of these remained unmarried, with one married and two widowed. Most, however, were under the age of 25 (26 out of 40) with just seven in the age group 25-34, and a further seven above the age of 45. The incidence of domestic service is thus unlikely to explain the full extent of gender differences in marriage prospects in Sandridge, even if it did contribute. It is, of course, unrealistic to expect

61   Anderson, "Marriage Patterns in Victorian Britain", p. 59; Wrigley and Schofield, *The Population History of England*, Table 10.4, p. 437. Compare also Anderson, *Family Structure in Nineteenth Century Lancashire*, Table 35, p. 133.

62   Here Fauve-Chamoux notes that the prospects for female employment, especially in domestic service, created an "unbalanced matrimonial market": "Servants in pre-industrial Europe", p. 126.

63   Goose, *The Berkhamsted Region*, p. 32; Anderson, "Marriage Patterns in Victorian Britain", p. 60.

every individual parish fully to confirm our hypothesis. Nineteenth century marriage horizons, even if fairly circumscribed, were by no means limited to the parish of residence, and hence the general picture to emerge from the district as a whole and the clear urban/rural contrast is of greater note than individual exceptions in particular parishes.

What impact did the high levels of female employment in this district have upon marriage prospects? We have already noted that the high incidence of female domestic service in Sandridge may have at least contributed towards delayed marriage for women and the relatively high proportion that never married in this parish. St Michaels (rural) was another area to include a far greater than average proportion of employees in the service and domestic service sector, with as many as 40% of working females thus employed compared with the district total of 20%, and in this case exhibiting a high proportion for males too, at 13% compared with the district total of just 6%. Delayed marriage was quite clearly the result, and for both sexes, despite the fact that the sex ratio was well balanced here, standing at 102 males to every 100 females. Forty per cent of males remained unmarried in the age group 25-34, and 41% of females, compared with the district totals of 32% and 35% respectively, and the rural totals of 31% and 32%. Just a shade under half of the population remained unmarried through to their thirtieth birthday, after which the percentage fell rapidly, until by the age range 45-54 the proportions remaining single were particularly low. It is thus delayed marriage, rather than a tendency not to marry at all, that is revealed by these figures, and more detailed examination of domestic servants in rural St Michaels bears out these conclusions. Of the 24 males identified (including grooms, footmen and coachmen besides house servants) 19 remained single. Of the 61 female domestic servants, 55 were unmarried, with just three married and three widowed. Twenty four of these fell into the age range 25-34, eight were between 35 and 44, but there was only one above the age of 45. Taking all those of 'prime marriageable age' to lie within the age range 20-44, a realistic assumption in the light of the data in Table 3, there was a total of 166 women in this district, and of these as many as 45, or 27%, were unmarried domestic servants. Clearly, in the rural part of St Michaels parish a high incidence of domestic service and delayed marriage went hand in hand.

Whilst extreme levels of domestic service in individual parishes or parts of parishes clearly did impact upon age at marriage, particularly amongst women, its effect more generally is less easy to discern. In Harpenden, Redbourn and Wheathampstead the proportion of females in such employment was relatively low, at between 12 and 15% of the occupied female population, but whilst the proportion remaining unmarried in the age range 25-34 was indeed low in Redbourn and Wheathampstead, at 28% compared with 35% for the whole district, in Harpenden it stood above average, at 37%. Nor was the relatively high level of domestic service in the parish of St Albans reflected in any clear tendency to delay marriage compared with elsewhere, such as in St Peters where a lower incidence of domestic service is found side by side with a far more pronounced tendency for females to marry late. Despite these discrepancies, detailed analysis of particular parishes shows that domestic servants did indeed, as we would expect, tend to marry late. Thus whilst 41% of the female population aged 25-34 remained unmarried in St Peters, 100% (all 17) of the female domestic servants in this age group were yet to wed. In the parish of St Albans the situation was similar, with 35% of the female population aged 25-34 unmarried, compared with 91% (30 out of 33) of female servants.[64] Looking more widely at those of 'prime marriageable age' (20-44), 46% of the female population of St Peters remained unmarried, as did 44% in St Albans; but the figures for domestic servants in this age group stood at 94% and

---

64   This calculation excludes three servants of unspecified condition.

91% in the two parishes respectively.[65] The incidence of domestic service, therefore, may only have exerted an overriding impact upon age at marriage of women in areas where it was particularly prominent, but it undoubtedly exerted a contributory, if not a paramount, influence in other areas too. Given that domestic service tended to be a more common employment in town than in countryside, despite the exceptions found here in the wealthy suburban parts of the parish of St Michaels and in Sandridge, it clearly contributed towards the more marked tendency for marriage to be delayed in urban as compared with rural areas, for the population as a whole but for women in particular. Our regional analysis thus confirms the results produced by Anderson from the 1861 census nationally: high levels of female domestic service were "a crucial factor" reducing marriage proportions.[66]

Did other forms of employment exert any impact upon the timing and incidence of marriage? In terms of the seasonality of marriage it has been argued that the availability of female employment makes no difference at all, for Ann Kussmaul finds that the straw plaiting and lace-making areas remained "resolutely autumnal" in their marriage preferences, and are thus "indistinguishable from areas without that women's industrial work".[67] In the case of straw plait, the autumn months would most probably bring a fall-off in employment, even if the trade was far less seasonal than often assumed, whilst the alternative lure of harvest employment with the opportunities then available for high earnings, and subsequent gleaning, would also have passed.[68] It would therefore reinforce the expected autumnal preference in arable farming regions. Nevertheless, the fact that female employment in the lace trade and in spinning appears to have had no influence either does seem to indicate that male occupational priorities exerted the overriding influence, at least in agricultural areas. Towns, with their wider variety of occupations, were often least seasonal in their marriage patterns, although some small towns such as Banbury could resemble arable areas probably because they incorporated agricultural land within their boundaries and were also involved in supplying labour for the harvest in the surrounding fields beyond.[69] Hertfordshire, however, appears different from many other counties. Here the market towns of Baldock, Great Berkhamsted, Hemel Hempstead, Hitchin, Rickmansworth and Watford all exhibit the autumnal bias in marriage seasonality which is commonly associated with arable farming patterns, as does rural Harpenden from the St Albans region. No other county in Kussmaul's sample which includes such a substantial number of urban parishes exhibits such a pronounced tendency to depart from the expected norm. Furthermore, in nearby Huntingdonshire, Buckinghamshire, Bedfordshire and Oxfordshire, all of which provided substantial employment opportunities for women, six out of seven market towns similarly reveal an autumnal pattern.[70] It may well be, therefore, that whilst Kussmaul is correct to suggest that female employment opportunities had little impact upon marriage seasonality in rural areas, urban female employment opportunities in trades which themselves had a seasonal emphasis may have produced a departure from the expected non-seasonal marriage pattern to produce a bias towards the autumn months. At the very least, this is a hypothesis worth further exploration.

65   The calculation for St Albans excludes three servants and three other women of unspecified condition.
66   Anderson, "Marriage Patterns in Victorian Britain", pp. 66-7.
67   A. Kussmaul, *A General View of the Rural Economy of England, 1538-1840* (Cambridge, 1990), p. 17.
68   Goose, *The Berkhamsted Region*, pp. 36-7; Kussmaul, *General View*, pp. 13-17.
69   Kussmaul, *General View*, pp. 30, 55-6, 195.
70   From the data in Kussmaul, *General View*, Appendix, pp. 181-94.

With regard to the impact of female employment upon age at marriage, divergent views have been expressed. It was once argued by W. Ogle, on the basis of an analysis of the 1881 census and marriage registration data, that female employment opportunities encouraged early marriage, for "men might not unnaturally be more ready to marry girls or young women who were themselves earning money".[71] Contemporary opinion certainly does suggest that the accumulation of a modicum of savings was the common prerequisite to marriage, and that the woman would be expected to bring her share. Hence the Rev. J. Howlett wrote in 1795 that amongst farm servants "the young man [who] can scrape up £20 or £30 and finds a young woman possessed with nearly an equal sum" could then embark upon marriage, whilst another source from Hertfordshire in 1817 suggested that a normal precondition would be the accumulation of a combined sum of £40.[72] Contrary to Ogle, however, Snell and others have argued that the opportunity to accumulate savings amongst living-in farm servants, within the relatively secure confines of their steady employment, allied to the social restrictions that service inevitably also implied, resulted in delayed rather than early marriage, and a clear correlation has been identified between areas where farm service persisted and an enhanced tendency to marry later in mid-nineteenth century England. Where land was difficult to come by, employment insecure and wage levels lower, the labouring population lacked both the motive and the means to achieve such accumulation and hence to delay marriage.[73]

What impact did the availability of *industrial* employment for women have, in our region notably in the straw plait and hat trades? Proponents of the theory of 'proto-industrialisation' have argued, *inter alia,* that in areas of rural industry marriages tended to take place earlier, and a substantial body of empirical evidence has indeed been collected to support this argument, even if the possibility that there were alternative reasons for this phenomenon has not always been fully considered.[74] Nevertheless, if a falling age at marriage for women between the later seventeenth and earlier nineteenth centuries has been found consistently in *all* village reconstitutions completed to date, the declines appear to be above average in 'industrial' villages such as Shepshed in Leicestershire and Gedling in Nottinghamshire.[75] It is too early for hard and fast conclusions to be drawn, however. Only three of the 26 reconstitutions currently available relate to industrial villages, and although there was indeed a particularly steep fall in female age at marriage across the eighteenth century in these three, by the early nineteenth century the age at marriage was only slightly below that found elsewhere.[76] Moreover, the overwhelming emphasis in such analyses has been on the effect of rural industry, whilst the situation in towns – so difficult to reconstitute due to the mobility of their populations – has been largely ignored.[77] In attempting to explain such trends as have emerged we should also consider the potential impact of changing employment opportunities and wage levels over time, the impact of the poor law on both men

---

71 Quoted in Anderson, "Marriage Patterns in Victorian Britain", p. 66.

72 K.D.M. Snell, *Annals of the Labouring Poor. Social Change and Agrarian England 1660-1900* (Cambridge, 1985), pp. 212, 346.

73 *Ibid.*, pp. 212-13, 346-52.

74 H. Medick, "The Proto-Industrial Family Economy: the Structural Function of Household and Family During the Transition from Peasant Society to Industrial Capitalism", *Social History*, Vol. 3 (1976), pp. 291-315; D. Levine, *Family Formation in an Age of Nascent Capitalism* (New York, 1977); *idem, Reproducing Families* (Cambridge, 1987); L.A. Clarkson, *Proto-Industrialisation: the First Phase of Industrialisation?* (London, 1985).

75 E.A. Wrigley *et al., English Population History from Family Reconstitution 1580-1837* (Cambridge, 1997), pp. 134, 184-5, 549-50; D. Levine, "Industrialisation and the Proletarian Family in England", *Past and Present*, No. 107 (1985), p. 183.

76 Wrigley *et al., English Population History*, p. 191.

77 Clarkson, *Proto-Industrialisation*, pp. 53-4.

and women and the various social and cultural factors that might have affected the desire to marry. The diverse effects of this array of factors are likely to prove difficult to disentangle.[78]

TABLE 4 : FEMALE EMPLOYMENT AND AGE AT MARRIAGE

Place	Never Married 25-34 (%)	Sex Ratio	Female Employment (%)	Straw and Textiles (% of all females)	Domestic Service (% of all females)
St Albans Urban					
St Albans	35	87	47	29	9
St Michaels (Urban)	38	80	45	34	7
St Peters	41	81	50	29	7
St Albans Rural					
St Michaels (Rural)	41	102	37	19	14
St Stephens	34	98	40	27	6
Out-hamlets	24	106	41	29	6
Harpenden	37	92	62	49	7
Redbourn	28	86	55	45	5
Sandridge	39	100	37	23	10
Wheathampstead	28	98	39	31	4
Sub-Totals					
St Albans Liberty	36	90	44	29	8
Urban Parishes	37	84	47	30	8
Rural Parishes	32	96	47	35	7
Total	35	91	47	33	7

If the St Albans region in the mid-nineteenth century offers some coherence in terms of the substantial opportunities for female employment that it generally provided, it also offers the full gamut of complexity, with its urban and rural parishes, varying sex ratios, differing levels of domestic service, rural and urban industry and female wage levels that were doubtless past their peak. What the data shows, however, is a relatively high female age at marriage overall compared with the situation nationally, which – all other things being equal – would contradict the view that female employment opportunities and early marriage tended to go hand in hand. All other things were not equal, however, for the impact of domestic service and skewed sex ratios have already been laid bare. Close examination of the experience of individual parishes offers deeper insight, and this is provided in Table 4, where proportions of females remaining unmarried are juxtaposed with levels of female employment, employment in particular occupational sectors, and sex ratios. The impact of domestic service upon female age at marriage in the parish of Sandridge and the rural part of St Michaels, discussed above, is again evident. But the figures do not appear to indicate any clear association between female industrial employment and age at marriage. Redbourn and Harpenden both stand out as having particularly high proportions of their female populations employed in straw and textiles, at 45 and 49% respectively, but whilst in Redbourn only 28% of females aged 25-34 remained unmarried, in Harpenden the figure stood as high as 37%. Within the town, the parishes of St Albans and St Peters possessed identical proportions of females employed in these industries, at 29%, but quite different marriage patterns. The proportion so employed in the Out-hamlets also stood at 29%, but this area exhibited an extremely low figure for those remaining unmarried in their later twenties and early thirties, at just 24%, and in this case it is likely that a sex ratio that favoured men was a more potent influence. In St Michaels (rural) and Sandridge we find the lowest figures of all for percentages of females employed (37% in each) and for female industrial employment (19% and 23%

---

78   P. Sharpe, *Adapting to Capitalism. Working Women and the English Economy, 1700-1850* (Basingstoke, 1996), pp. 140-1.

respectively) and this corresponds with high figures for proportions remaining unmarried ages 25-34, but here a more potent influence was the high proportion of the female population employed in domestic service that we have already discussed.[79] Calculation of the correlation coefficient (Pearson's R) between proportion of females unmarried ages 25-34 and proportion employed in industrial occupations produces a figure of -0.29. Given that R would be 0 if the variables were totally unrelated and -1.0 would indicate a perfect inverse correlation, there is clearly just a very weak statistical association between female industrial employment and early female age at marriage.[80]

Clearly, there is a complex array of causes affecting the situation within particular parishes and these causes could easily offset one another to produce the results presented here. For example, St Michaels (rural) and Sandridge exhibit high proportions unmarried at ages 25-34 despite having a very balanced sex ratio, and this is the product of the high proportion of the female population employed in domestic service. If we look for a clear statistical association between sex ratio and female age at marriage across all the parishes or districts in our sample we will be disappointed, finding another fairly weak association at -0.34. However, is we remove these two unusual and atypical cases, the correlation coefficient rises to -0.74, indicating a fairly strong inverse correlation across the remaining parishes, and supporting the conclusions offered in the preceding discussion. To complete the statistical tests, a final correlation between domestic service and age at marriage was calculated, and this provided a fairly strong positive measure of 0.67, underlining the view that high levels of domestic service did indeed tend to lead to delayed marriage. All of this supports the conclusions drawn from the Berkhamsted region to the west: a weak association between female employment opportunities and early marriage, a strong association between domestic service and delayed marriage, and a generally strong connection between delayed marriage for women and a skewed sex ratio.[81] Our results also, once again, support the conclusions that have been drawn from analysis of the national census data for 1861.[82]

We must not forget, however, that the factors whose influence we are attempting to isolate statistically were often inter-related. Opportunities for female employment are clearly associated with a skewed sex ratio, here and elsewhere,[83] and an imbalance in favour of women clearly reduced female marriage opportunities to produce relatively high numbers remaining unmarried into their thirties. So even if female earnings in straw plait and the hat trade did indeed render early marriage more feasible, and perhaps also served to enhance women's eligibility in the eyes of potential husbands, the indirect and negative effect of these opportunities more than counteracted their positive impact upon age at marriage by producing an imbalance between the sexes, an imbalance that was further enhanced in the town of St Albans by the additional employment opportunities to be found there in service and domestic industries, and by the attraction it held for both wealthy and indigent widows. On the other hand, there does appear to be a trade-off between industrial employment and domestic service. In England and Wales in 1851 10% of the total female population was employed in domestic service,[84] whilst in the St Albans region the figure was only 7% overall, and fell as low

---

79   See above, p. 42.

80   For an approachable explanation of correlation coefficients and how to calculate them see R. Floud, *An Introduction to Quantitative Methods for Historians* (London, 1973), pp. 138-40.

81   Goose, *The Berkhamsted Region*, p. 34.

82   Anderson, "Marriage Patterns in Victorian Britain", pp. 61-9.

83   See above, pp. 37-8 and fn. 41.

84   E. Roberts, *Women's Work, 1840-1940* (Cambridge, 1988), Table 2.1, p. 19.

as 4-5% in some parishes. Where industrial employment opportunities were lower, most notably in St Michaels (rural) and Sandridge, a far higher proportion were employed as domestic servants. By discouraging young women from going into domestic service, an occupation that is very strongly associated indeed with delayed marriage, work for women in industrial employment may therefore have indirectly affected the overall age at marriage in a downward direction.

An urban economy

St Albans in the mid-nineteenth century was a small town. It could not be characterised otherwise when one appreciates the scale of England's larger towns and cities by this date, such as Sheffield with a population of 135,000, Manchester with almost 340,000 or Liverpool with nearly 400,000 inhabitants.[85] The relative scale is brought home even more sharply when one compares the population of St Albans with the mere growth achieved by these cities in the course of a decade, Manchester growing by 86,000 people between 1841 and 1851 and Liverpool by 96,000: with the population of St Albans standing at approximately 7,000, each of these towns effectively added the equivalent of a dozen or more St Albans to their mass within the compass of ten years.[86] In comparison with Greater London the town almost pales into insignificance, for by 1841 the capital had grown to over 2.2 million souls and was still expanding, reaching almost 2.7 million by mid-century and over 3.2 million ten years later.[87] Indeed, the dominance of the capital city of London, with its vast array of industrial activities, sophisticated financial centre, national and international commercial network and unsurpassed social and cultural facilities, must be largely responsible for the paucity of other large towns within its ambit, and notably in Hertfordshire itself.

One must not, however, get too carried away by the size and importance of England's great cities, for this is not all there was to the urban landscape, even at the height of the industrial revolution. 1851 is the date usually regarded as a benchmark when – following rapid urbanisation in the eighteenth and particularly the first half of the nineteenth centuries – over half of the population finally lived in urban areas. The precise figure is often debated, for the census authorities included in their definition of a town all communities of 2,000 or more people, as long as they fell into a single enumeration district and possessed a parish vestry, and it may well be that some of these were distinctly more rural than urban in character.[88] Furthermore, some towns included areas within their boundaries that can only be regarded as agricultural.[89] On the other hand, the census commissioners were also prepared to follow local wisdom, in this case the wisdom of the clerks to the county quarter sessions, and hence "several places containing more than 2,000 inhabitants [were] omitted, because in the opinion of those officers, they could not in strictness be so designated".[90] But such refinements to the statistics are really of little importance: by mid-century, either slightly more than half, half, or approaching half of the English population lived in urban rather than rural communities.[91]

85   G. Best, *Mid-Victorian Britain 1851-75* (revised edition, St Albans, 1973), p. 29.
86   *Ibid.*; F. Crouzet, *The Victorian Economy* (London, 1982), Table 23, p. 97.
87   Best, *Mid-Victorian Britain*, p. 25.
88   F.M.L. Thompson, "Town and City", in *idem*, (ed.), *The Cambridge Social History of Modern Britain 1750-1950. Volume 1: Regions and Communities* (Cambridge, 1990), p. 3.
89   A. Howkins, *Reshaping Rural England: a Social History 1850-1925* (London, 1991), pp. 7-8.
90   Quoted in P.J. Waller, *Town, City and Nation. England 1850-1914* (Oxford, 1983), p. 1.
91   Probably still the best discussion of the issue is C.M. Law, "The Growth of Urban Population in England and Wales, 1801-1911", *Transactions of the Institute of British Geographers*, Vol. 41 (1967), pp. 125-43.

Small towns formed a significant element of this expanding urban population. Even as late as 1901 there were 686 towns with fewer than 10,000 inhabitants, constituting 11.4% of the urban population of England and Wales, and hence P.J. Waller – echoing Alan Everitt's assertion of the importance of "the Banburys of England" for the early modern period – writes that "no urban historian can leave the Wallingfords of England out of account".[92] This is even more true for 1851. In that year 18.4% of the urban population, almost one-fifth, lived in towns with between 2,500 and 10,000 inhabitants, forming almost 10% of the total population of England and Wales.[93] Within Hertfordshire itself, where large towns were notable by their absence, towns such as St Albans stood at the peak of the urban hierarchy, such as it was, and dominated their local area in terms of both size and in terms of economic importance and complexity. So although Hertfordshire stood towards the bottom of the league table in terms of urbanisation at this date, its nine small towns accounted for as much ·s 24% of its population, and hence small town living assumes a proportionally greater significance here than it did in many other counties in England and Wales.[94]

At this date too we must recognise a high degree of integration between town and countryside, with these small towns providing markets and fairs for the sale of a wide variety of agricultural products as well as urban manufactures, providing a range of more specialised shops, professional services and entertainments, processing agricultural raw materials (often concentrating upon the quality end of the market in the case of industrial products) as well as participating in a regular two-way flow of labour, either permanent or temporary.[95] This economic interdependence, and more particularly the co-operation of town and countryside in industrial activity, was to wane during the course of the second half of the nineteenth century.[96] For the town of Hitchin a similar separation was noted at the end of the nineteenth century with regard to the marketing of agricultural produce. W.O. Times, clerk to the Urban District Council, wrote of how

> "town and village life were blended a century ago.... Hitchin seems to have been a centre
> of attraction, crowded at least every market day with all the farmers and their wives
> for miles around... [but] Now the rural residents of all classes go direct from the villages
> to the railway station and the town is only useful to them because it possesses that
> accommodation".[97]

But in 1851 this all lay in the future: as we see very clearly in the case of St Albans, a high degree of interdependence persisted in mid-century, between town and countryside and between agricultural and industrial activity, most notably in the form of the straw plait and straw hat trade.

---

92   Waller, *Town, City and Nation*, p. 6; A. Everitt, "The Banburys of England", *Urban History Yearbook 1974* (Leicester, 1974).
93   Waller, *Town, City and Nation*, p. 8.
94   See above, p. 33.
95   See, for example, P. Clark (ed.), *Small Towns in Early Modern Europe* (Cambridge, 1995), pp. 11-12; Waller, *Town, City and Nation*, pp. 193-4.
96   Waller, *Town, City and Nation*, p. 194.
97   Quoted in A.M. Foster, *Market Town. Hitchin in the Nineteenth Century* (Hitchin, 1987), p. 2.

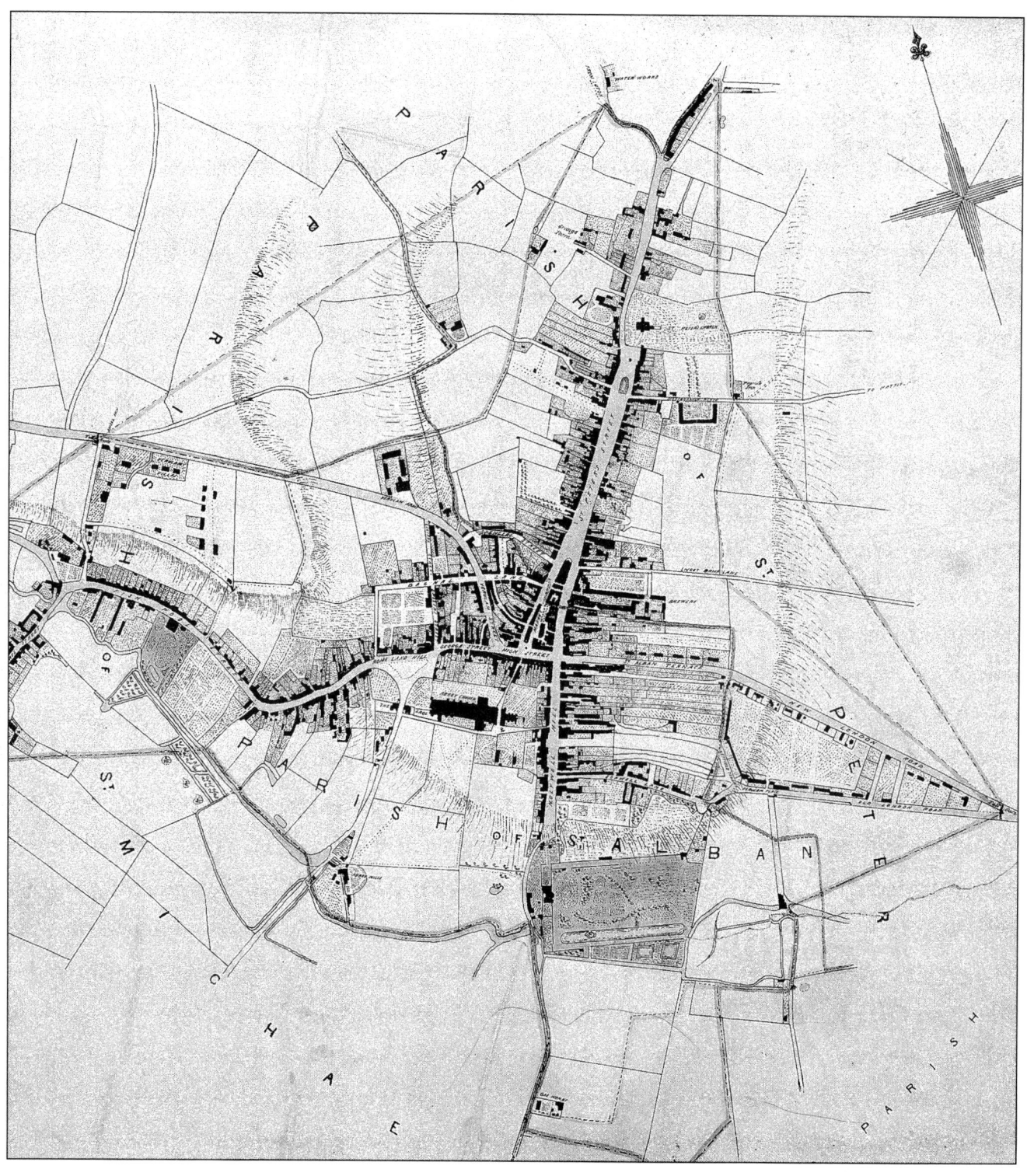

Map of the Borough of St Alban as determined by the commissioners appointed by The Honourable the Commons House of Parliament 1832 including all improvements to the 1st October 1835. Reproduced courtesy of the Museum of St Alban.

Figure 4 : THE TOWN CENTRE OF ST ALBANS

53

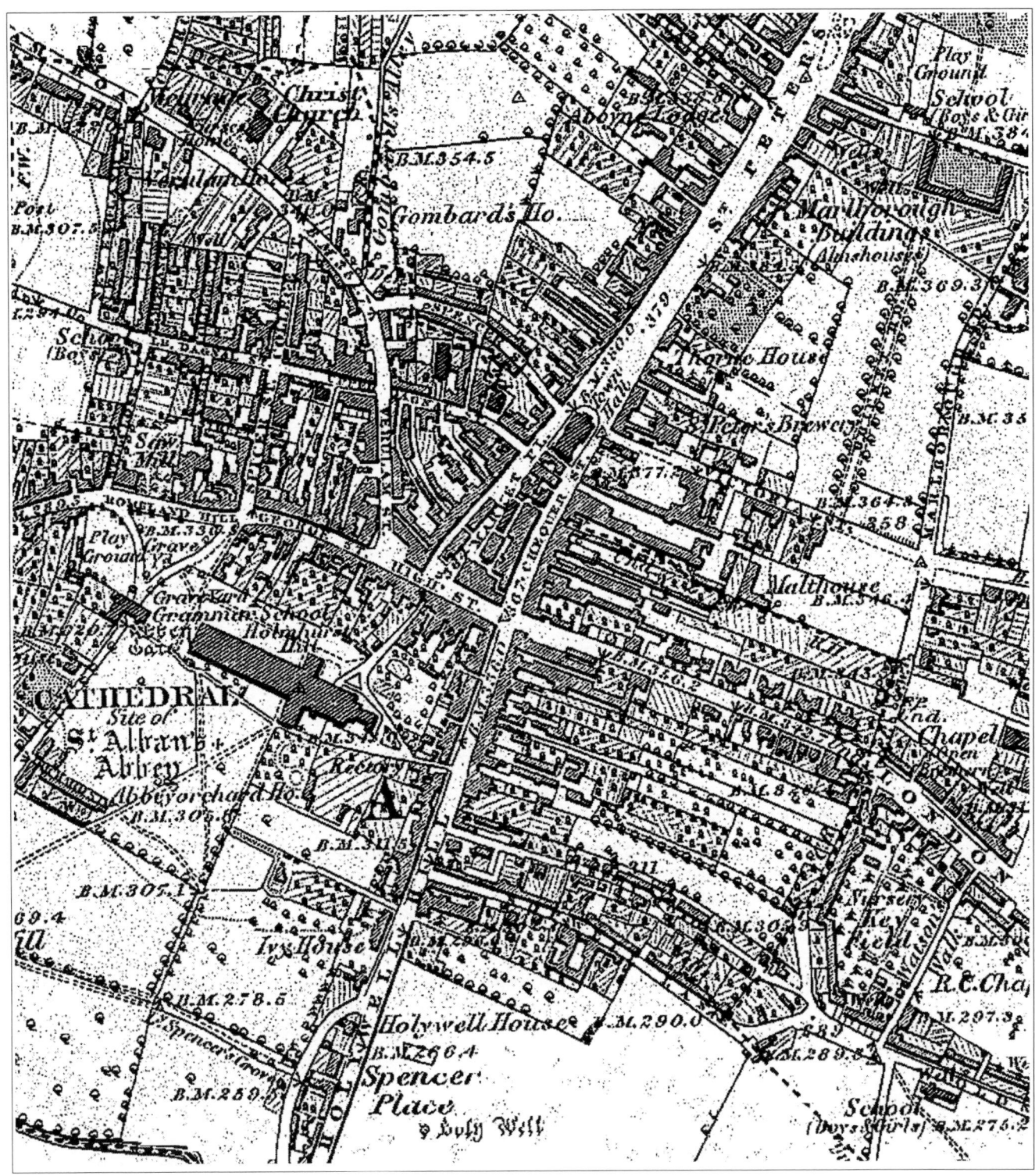

From the first edition of the 6 inch Ordinance Survey of Hertfordshire (1878), Sheet XXXIV

Approximate scale of reproduction: 1cm = 46m

Although the straw plait and straw bonnet trades were of crucial importance to St Albans in the mid-nineteenth century, this was far from all there was to the urban economy, for even a town of no more than 7,000 people displayed a wide diversity of economic activity. It was in the town, unsurprisingly, that were found the heaviest concentration of professional people and public servants. As the occupational breakdown given in Table 2 shows, 4.6% of the occupied population of the town was employed in the Public service/professional category, compared with just 1.7% in the rural parishes of the district.[98] In the mid-nineteenth century, of course, men predominated amongst the professional classes, and particularly in the town: 6.3% of the occupied male population of St Albans fell into this category, compared with just 1.9% in the rural parishes. In St Albans parish itself the figure was higher still, at 7.5%, whilst of the strictly rural parishes only Harpenden includes more than a handful of professional people.

TABLE 5 : PROFESSIONAL AND PUBLIC SERVICE OCCUPATIONS IN ST ALBANS 1851

	St Albans	St Michaels(Urban)	St Peters	Town	%
Government	19	4	1	24	13.8
Religion	10	3	8	21	12.1
Finance	3	0	1	4	2.3
Law	14	1	10	25	14.4
Policing	6	0	3	9	5.2
Medicine	11	4	14	29	16.7
Education	18	5	17	40	23.0
Building	0	0	1	1	0.6
Arts and Science	8	1	2	11	6.3
Miscellaneous	4	1	5	10	5.7
Total	93	19	62	174	100.0

A further breakdown of these professional and public service occupations for the town of St Albans is provided in Table 5, which reveals that they were mainly concentrated in the two parishes of St Albans and St Peters. Prominent amongst them were providers of educational, medical and religious services, catering respectively for mind, body and soul. Education alone provided employment for 40 inhabitants of the town in 1851, and – unusually for the professions – featured more women than men, 26 as against 14. The only school to be specifically mentioned by name is St Albans Grammar School, of which the 26 year-old bachelor, Herbert Williams BA, who originally hailed from Bath in Somerset, was "Second Master". Henry Turner, a 36 year-old bachelor living in Romeland and born at Deptford in Kent, is described as "Assistant Master in Grammar School" and presumably taught there too.[99] This was probably the establishment listed in the census in Fishpool Street run by Henry Hall, clergyman without cure, and his wife Elizabeth, with 29 resident pupils in 1851 aged 9 to 18, all boys, a cook and three domestic servants.[100] Others must have been employed at the National School, sponsored by the Church of England National Society for the Education of the Poor, which opened in 1848 in Spicer Street. The buildings, still standing today, had been erected at a cost of £390 17s 0d (£390.85p), and most of this sum was raised within the parish by subscription. No school records survive until 1869, but the submission to the National Society in 1846 indicates an expected roll call of 84 boys and 78

98 See Table 2, above, pp. 40–1.
99 Masters at the grammar school did not necessarily live in St Albans. Around 1860 there were 8 resident or visiting masters, amongst whom were the music master Mr Matthews of Bushey and the drawing master Mr Parry of Watford. This was a particularly prosperous period for the school: A.E. Gibbs, *Historical Records of St Albans* (St Albans, 1888), pp. 44-5.
100 Gibbs notes that the Rev. H. Hall was headmaster of the grammar school shortly after mid-century: *ibid.*, p. 44.

girls.[101] The nonconformist rival to the National Society, the British and Foreign Schools Society, already had its own school in Spencer Street when the National School was built, and Thomas McClane, a 25 year-old bachelor from Kirkudbright in Scotland, is described as "British Schoolmaster" in the census returns. The application for aid to the National Society also identifies a Blue Coat charity school operating in Fishpool Street, run by the Abbey vestry clerk, with a roll of 35 children, besides a substantial Sunday School and a number of dame schools.[102] The Blue Coat School is not specifically identified as such in the census, but in 1857 its finances were reported to be "in a very depressed state", and the Corporation directed the town clerk to write to the vicars of St Peters and St Michaels to ask them to make an annual collection for the school, which was ultimately to merge with the National School.[103] Another nonconformist school operated in Cross Street between 1836 and 1888, providing educational opportunities for 130 infants.[104] Additional educational provision was established by the Earl of Verulam in St Michaels parish in 1854.[105]

Again in St Albans parish Eliza Upton and her daughter, Sarah Amelia, were, respectively, Principal and Assistant of a "Ladies School", presumably a rather different enterprise from the charity schools described above, whilst Maria Upton, most probably Eliza's eldest daughter, is described as a "partner" in another "Establishment" in London Road.[106] Others clearly catering for the higher social echelons include two "Professors of Music", Mary E. Page and Francis M. Brown, who both lived in St Peters Street, and C.J.A. Marriette, "Professor of Languages", a 23 year-old spinster residing in Dagnall Lane, indicating once again that education could provide significant employment opportunities for women in mid-nineteenth century St Albans. Further examples suggesting small family run educational establishments are provided by Henry Hilliard and his wife, Charlotte, of Fishpool Street, and George Ivory and his sister, Jane, of Cock Lane (now Hatfield Road), all of whom are identified as schoolmasters or schoolmistresses. John Brooks, a bachelor of 30 years of age still living at home with his family, is identified as a "teacher of music and singing", and was assisted by his 22 year-old brother George.

Apart from formal schooling, the town possessed a Literary Society, established in 1823, holding lectures and debates on a variety of topics of public interest.[107] A Mechanics Institute was established in 1837, when it was conditionally granted accommodation in the town hall for a library, lecture room and a reading room, and St Albans Literary Institute was probably an offshoot of this.[108] Although the town's public library was not established until 1881, the Literary Institute had its own library of 500 books plus newspapers and periodicals, its reading room which was open every evening and a programme of winter lectures, explicitly designed to provide an educational and 'improving' alternative to the less cerebral entertainment to be found

---

101   A. Goodman, *The Story of The Abbey School. A Nineteenth Century National School,* Publication of *St Albans and Hertfordshire Architectural and Archaeological Society* (St Albans, 1991), pp. 1-5.

102   *Ibid.,* p. 3.

103   Gibbs, *Corporation Records of St Albans,* pp. 224-5; Goodman, *The Story of The Abbey School,* p. 3.

104   Corbett, *History of St Albans,* p. 93.

105   Anon., *A Guide to Hertfordshire,* p. 329.

106   These establishments, despite their titles, are unlikely to have been mere finishing schools, however, for Eliza Upton was married to the famous dissenting minister William Upton, pastor of Dagnall Lane Baptist Church, whose survey of nonconformity in Hertfordshire will be discussed below.

107   Toms, *Story of St Albans,* pp. 149-50.

108   Gibbs, *Corporation Records of St Albans,* p. 200.

in the town's numerous pubs and beer shops, of which more below.[109] For the very wealthy, of course, education was an even more private matter, and nine governesses are recorded in the census. Four of these lived with their fathers or husbands with no children present in the household, and must therefore have worked on a daily basis in the households of others, whilst two more, Louisa Webster and her sister Eliza who lived together in Verulam Road, are both explicitly described as "daily governess". Maria Hutchinson appears to have served as governess to her four younger sisters in the household of John Robert Hutchinson, for these are all described as "scholar at home". The other two lived in the household of their employer. Rebecca Callow was governess to the four children of Thomas Willshin of Kingsbury House, farmer of 600 acres, whose household also included three agricultural labourers and two domestic servants. Most exotic of all was one Madame Lavont, a 38 year-old spinster born in France, employed in the household of John Samuel Story, solicitor, in High Street, along with four servants, to instruct his three children and three grandchildren.

Medical practitioners are a more diverse group. Ten general practitioners, physicians or surgeons, with qualifications from Edinburgh, St Andrews and London, practised in the parishes of St Albans and St Peters, and were all male.[110] Most of the rest, 17 in number, were nurses, unsurprisingly all female. The balance is made up by a veterinary surgeon, James Sewell, a 65 year-old bachelor of Holywell Hill, and an "optician and farmer" *(sic)*, Samuel Dalton, 80 years of age, who thus had two good reasons to test the confidence of his patients.

The census for the town of St Albans includes 21 dispensers of religion, five of whom were engaged in church maintenance or administration, as sextons, vergers or "pew openers". Of the remaining 16, two served parishes outside of the town, Abbots Langley and Shipton Bellinger, leaving 14. Of these, eight were nonconformists, including two Wesleyans, three Independents, two "Dissenting" and one Primitive Methodist, indicating clearly the strength of nonconformity in the town in the mid-nineteenth century. Dagnall Street was a particularly important location for nonconformity, being home to the Old Presbyterian, Baptist and Wesleyan Chapels. A chapel that narrowly missed inclusion in the census was Bethel Baptist church, held by the Particular Baptists, which opened in Verulam Road in 1853, whilst the Plymouth Brethren began meeting in Lattimore Road twelve years later.[111]

It seems clear from the census, therefore, that St Albans could boast both a breadth and a depth of nonconformity, but far greater detail is provided by the national religious census that was also conducted in 1851, which in the case of Hertfordshire can be supplemented by the survey taken in 1847/8 by William Upton, pastor of the Dagnall Lane Baptist church since 1821 and secretary to the Hertfordshire Union of Baptists and Independents formed in 1810.[112] From the national ecclesiastical census the English Presbyterian

---

109   M.D. Ward, "Hertfordshire Fairs and the Fairs Act 1871", unpubl. MA dissertation, University of Hertfordshire 1997, p. 29; Toms, *Story of St Albans*, p. 158. By 1880 the Literary and Scientific Institution held about 1,000 books: Anon., *A Guide to Hertfordshire*, p. 331.

110   Nine are recorded in the 1822-3 trade directory, operating from seven discrete practices: Dean *et al.*, *St Albans c. 1820*, p. 7.

111   *VCH Herts*, Vol. 2, pp. 511-12.

112   Both are published in J. Burg (ed.), *Religion in Hertfordshire 1847-1851*, Hertfordshire Record Publications Vol. 11 (Linton, Cambridge, 1995). In the case of the national ecclesiastical census there is clearly some topographical confusion in the returns, for apart from the established parish churches of St Peters and St Michaels, all of the strictly urban religious establishments appear to be listed under the parish of "St Albans Abbey", which is equated with the borough itself: *Ibid.*, pp. 168-74.

chapel can now be dated back to 1694, whilst the Baptist chapel, large enough for a total of 550 sittings, was erected in 1720. The first Independent (or Congregationalist) chapel had been erected in Dagnall Lane in 1698,[113] but by the nineteenth century the Independents met on Spicer Street, in a chapel erected in 1811 to replace that previously situated in Sweet Briar Lane, with seating for a total of 568. The Wesleyan Methodist chapel was larger still, having been extended from a previous building in 1842, and with space for 700. According to the ecclesiastical census the Primitive Methodist chapel erected in Sopwell Lane in 1845 provided as many as 1,233 sittings, but Upton's estimate of accommodation for 200 is probably more accurate.[114] Still, these nonconformists congregations dwarfed the tiny Roman Catholic chapel on College Street which could house a mere 50.[115] Another tiny gathering was the Church of the Latter Day Saints which met from April 1850 onwards in what was once a part of the Crown Inn on Holywell Hill, with 42 free sittings and seven square yards of free space. And finally, with room for 300, a Temperance Chapel had been erected on Dagnall Lane in 1846, in a building appropriately shared with the St Albans Mutual Instruction Society. The average of the general congregation of this chapel, for morning, afternoon and evening respectively, is given as 36, 50 and 100, far smaller than attendances at the Wesleyan, Independent or Baptist congregations given in the census, or those at the parish churches. Upton, who does not give separate figures for different services but describes "attendance at its fullest", puts it at 50 out of a total of 3,075 churchgoers in the town plus a "very few" Roman Catholics, describing the character of the ministry as "teetotalism and little else".[116]

In 1797 Sir Frederic Eden had described religious adherence in the town in the following terms:

"The inhabitants are chiefly of the established Church; there is 1 Anabaptist chapel, and 1 Calvinist chapel, 1 Quaker's meeting-house, and a congregation of Independents; and once a week, a pious shoemaker quits his awl, and expounds the scriptures to an audience of old women; after which, he and his congregation attend divine service at the church."[117]

In 1815 an anonymous guide book concurred, arguing that "The whole body of Dissenters are inferior in numbers to those who favour the established religion in St Albans and any sect by itself is inconsiderable".[118] Fifty years later Eden's pious shoemaker was no doubt long gone, but Methodism had grown apace and now nonconformity had overhauled the established church in terms of appeal. Ignoring the Temperance and Roman Catholic chapels, the three parishes churches of St Albans, St Peters and St Michaels attracted a total congregation of 1,400 according to Upton, with the various nonconformist churches within the borough

113   G. Robinson, *Hertfordshire* (Chesham, 1978), p. 79.
114   *Ibid.*, p. 63.
115   In 1847 the Rev. William Mills, pastor of St Albans, launched an appeal for funding to erect a Catholic church, describing the existing Catholic chapel as "a room which will scarcely hold a hundred people": J. Corbett, *Celebration: the Story of a Parish. SS Alban and Stephen 1840-1900* (St Albans, 1990), p. 4.
116   Burg (ed.), *Religion in Hertfordshire*, p. 63.
117   F.M. Eden, *The State of the Poor: or an History of the Labouring Classes in England*, 3 Vols. (London, 1797), Vol. II, p. 271.
118   Quoted in A.R. Ruston, *Old Presbyterian Meeting House St Albans: the Story of a Building* (Oxhey, 1979), p. 15. This anonymous author also suggests that both the Baptist and Presbyterian congregations had once been large, but had declined as certain families had died out and others had changed their allegiance.

attracting 1,625.[119] Across the county as a whole he estimates that 41,430 attended Anglican places of worship, and 25,250 attended nonconformist chapels, figures that are remarkably similar to the 40,500 and 27,800 given in the national ecclesiastical census.[120] In St Albans, therefore, nonconformity loomed considerably larger than it did in Hertfordshire as a whole, whilst Roman Catholicism and Temperance remained distinctly minority interests.

Government servants, all of whom were male, also formed a significant group. The six national government officers were all tax officials, four Inland Revenue Officers, one Surveyor of Taxes and one Tax Collector. Local government officers, numbering a further eight, included the Mayor of St Albans, F.R. Silvester, a married man of 37 years of age living in London Road, originally from Colchester in Essex. Of the three identified as Aldermen, two were also stationers and the other a general practitioner and magistrate who, if he still practised medicine alongside his other responsibilities, should be added to the list of GPs described above. All but two of these national and local government officials lived in the parish of St Albans. Six more worked for the post office, including four described as "post boy", average age 54, whilst a further three were poor law officers of various kinds. Legal and police officers were only prominent in St Albans and St Peters, the former group dominated by solicitors and their clerks, the town boasting a dozen trained solicitors or attorneys. One, F.I. Osbaldeston of Holywell Hill, was also County Coroner, whilst two officials of St Albans County Court also feature in this category.[121] Six police and three prison officers of various ranks were present in the town to ensure that the Court was kept busy, police forces for the boroughs of Hertford and St Albans having been established in 1836.[122] The prison, formerly the Abbey Gatehouse, was manned by the Prison Governor and the Head Turnkey and their families, and contained 43 prisoners on census night, all but two of them men and all but seven described as labourers, but also including John Burnhill, a 57 year-old bachelor schoolmaster born in the parish of St Michaels. Finally, we should not ignore those categorised under "Arts and Science" in Table 5. Four printers operated in the town, including Richard Gibbs who was also a bookseller, and his son, also named Richard. Alfred Thomas Bayley of Verulam Street worked as a newspaper reporter. The town could also boast no fewer than five professional artists, two specified as portrait painters, one as a landscape artist and another as an "animal painter". The balance was made up by John Mauger, German by birth, musician, aged 32, who was lodging on Holywell Hill on census night, and two "tragedians", James Bradley and Edwin English, lodging together with their wives at the home of Charles Hewitt, butcher, in St Peters Street.

Professional people and public servants could of course be found in the suburban parishes of St Albans and its hinterland too, for these substantial villages were anything but rural backwaters. Schools and schoolmasters, lawyers, ministers, surgeons, bank clerks, police officers and the like can all be found, and particularly as we have noted in Harpenden, although it is impossible to tell whether they worked in their parish of residence or

---

119   St Albans 700, St Peters 500, St Michaels 200; Presbyterian 25 ("very indefinite and useless"), Baptist 600 (his own ministry, described as "full"), Independent 400, Wesleyan 500, Primitive Methodist ("energetic, but wild") 100: Burg (ed.), *Religion in Hertfordshire*, pp. 62-3.
120   *Ibid.*, pp. xxviii, 62-3.
121   St Albans was home of the County Court, as well as the Borough Petty Sessions and Liberty Petty Sessions, held every Friday and Saturday: Kelly's *Directory 1855*, p. 230.
122   Robinson, *Hertfordshire*, p. 102.

travelled into St Albans for that purpose.[123] But it was St Albans that possessed the critical mass in terms of size, the political and administrative responsibilities and infrastructure that only a true town could boast, the key position as a central place within a major transportation network, the ability to provide a wide range of goods and services, and the cultural manifestations that are an almost inevitable concomitant of all of this. The concentration and variety of these professional and public service occupations in the town, although by no means overwhelming numerically, are one crucial index of its very urbanity.

Another is the range of retail and distributive trades it could boast. This is an even smaller category in Table 2, accounting for just 2% of the occupied urban population, although this is more than double the proportion found in the rural areas. Nevertheless, the 75 individuals represented here help to define the distinctiveness of a truly urban community. The seven chemists with their three assistants, concentrated in the town centre in Market Place, Chequer Street, High Street, Holywell Hill and St Peters Street, provide a link with the medical men discussed above, and reflect the ability of the town to provide substantial medical services, not only to the urban residents themselves but also to the population of its hinterland.[124] The town's first dispensary opened in Verulam Street in the late 1840s, whilst a hospital and dispensary was erected on Holywell Hill in 1861, the £1,500 cost being met by public subscription.[125] Six coal dealers and one assistant also feature in this group, this time mainly situated further away from the town centre in locations such as Pound Field and Sopwell Lane. There were six booksellers and one bookseller's assistant, three of them in St Peters Street, catering for the educational and cultural needs of the community. The town's permanent shops provided employment for 11 "shopmen" or assistants, and many more will feature elsewhere in our occupational table attached to specific trades, whilst 13 individuals are described as general dealers. Itinerant traders – hawkers or travellers – were thirteen in number, ten of whom were lodgers. There was clearly a lodging house in Spicer Street, for five of these lived here at the same address, whilst another lodged at the Hare and Hounds on Old London Road. Fishpool Street, appropriately, housed two marine store dealers, and there were also a couple of rag merchants and tallow-chandlers. More specialised still, and epitomising the role of the town as a centre of consumption, was James Oakley of Spicer Street, furniture broker, and William Woodbridge of St Peters Street, china dealer. The town could also boast two specialist toyshops, one of which was run by two unmarried sisters, Jane and Harriett Giles, aged just 19 and 21, who still lived on High Street with their father, William, also employed in the retail trade as a draper's assistant. The other, a "fancy toyshop", was run by Elizabeth Coleman with the assistance of her 17 year-old niece, Ann Bletso. Elizabeth's husband, Vincent Coleman, was a dissenting minister, apparently prepared to indulge the distribution of vain fripperies rather than insisting upon a strict worldly asceticism, particularly where a profit was to be had: British Christianity, as Edward Miall wrote in *The Nonconformist* in 1849, was basically "Christianity developed by a middle class soil".[126]

The range of retail trades was far wider than this, however, for the organisation of our key occupational table by type of raw material – wood, textiles, metal and the like – will mean that many retailers appear under various other categories. Furthermore, for a number of crafts at this date the division between manufacture and

123   See below, pp. 80-1.

124   Only two "chemist and druggists" had been listed in the 1822-3 trade directory: Dean *et al.*, *St Albans c. 1820*, p. 7.

125   *Ibid.*; Anon, *A Guide to Hertfordshire*, p. 327. The hospital offered five beds, and the dispensary was open to out-patients three times a week.

126   A. Miall, *The Life of Edward Miall* (London, 1881), p. 151.

retail was less clear cut than it was subsequently to become: for example, many shoemakers were both manufacturers and retailers of the shoes they made. Such conflation of roles means that any classification will obscure as well as illuminate, and more detailed analysis is required if the true nature of the urban economy is to be revealed.

We can start with fuller consideration of the various occupations listed under "Food and Drink" in Table 2, again a category that employed a substantially higher proportion of the occupied population in town than in countryside, 6.8% compared with 3.4%, and which accounted for more than one in nine (11.6%) of the occupied male population as compared with one in twenty (5.1%) in the rural parishes of the district. Of the 258 individuals recorded as employed under this category in Table 2, 122 were dealers in foodstuffs of various kinds. Of these 32 are described as "grocer", who would commonly have bought in the wholesale market and have stocked a wide variety of foodstuffs, whilst 14 more were grocer's apprentices, assistants and the like. Of these 32, four conducted an additional sideline, and hence George Allen also dealt in china and glass, Edward Sutton was a tallow-chandler, Hannah Glasscock, widow, was a grocer and tea dealer and Thomas Young a grocer and baker. Additional to these were seven specified as greengrocers and two fruiterers, whilst two specialist tea dealers are also listed. Unfortunately the census provides no detailed indication of the range of foodstuffs sold in these various grocers' shops, and one is left to imagine the wide range of provision, both mundane and exotic, purveyed in these numerous establishments.

If we include victuallers, sixty-two more were dealers in drink, many of whom also provided accommodation.[127] Eight innkeepers are listed, two of whom were women: Martha Bryan, an unmarried woman of 40 years of age who ran the Fleur de Lys, and Mary Marks, a widow of 56, who ran an unspecified inn on Holywell Hill. Twenty-four are described as victuallers, licensed victuallers or eating-house keepers, one of whom, William Foreman of St Peters Street, was also a "coach proprietor". Two of these were widows, Elizabeth Aldridge, aged 45, who ran The Unicorn in Fishpool Street and Ann Dolling, a widow of 63 years of age who operated from Sopwell Lane with the help of her 35 year-old bachelor son Edward. Approximately half of these also provided accommodation, and hence the dividing line between innkeepers and victuallers was a thin one. Indeed, the proprietor of the St. Christopher Inn on Back Street, Neptune Smith, is described as a victualler by occupation, living here with his wife, Susannah, and William Griffin, a six year-old visitor. No lodgers were present at The Christopher on census night, despite the reputation that the inn apparently gained in the earlier nineteenth century as a favoured haunt for the unruly and disreputable, itinerants or Irish seasonal labourers.[128]

Additional to these innkeepers and victuallers there were 13 publicans, all male but one, which probably indicates 12 establishments as husband and wife are both listed in the case of James and Caroline Hawtree. Half of these provided accommodation too, usually for just two or three guests, but for as many as 12 in the case of James Varney of Chequer Street, whilst James Everett housed five lodgers in his establishment on Holywell Hill. Varney's guests give some indication of the transient element in the population of the town, for in the case of 10 of his 12 lodgers neither their names nor their occupations were known. A number of these inns, victualling houses and pubs have retained their identity to the present day, including The Portland Arms, The Rose and Crown in St Michaels, The Peahen Tap on London Road and The Black Lion in Fishpool Street, as well as the Fleur de Lys mentioned above. Others, The Cock and Flower Pot and The Unicorn in Fishpool

127   A slightly earlier version of this section is published as "Pubs, Inns and Beer Shops: the Retail Liquor Trade in St Albans in the mid-19th century", *Hertfordshire's Past*, Issue 43/4 (1998), pp. 55-60.
128   Ashdown, *St. Albans*, pp. 244-5.

Street, The Angel Inn on Verulam Road, The Dog and The Christopher Inn on Back Street, The Hare and Hounds in Old London Road, The Kings Head Inn on Market Street and The Woolpack Tap on London Road, have either ceased to trade or have since been renamed.

Seven more individuals kept "Beer Shops" or "Beer Houses", again including one husband and wife team, Joseph and Mary Ann Smith. Two women appear to have traded independently. Elizabeth Edwards, wife of James Edwards, labourer, ran a beer shop on London Road despite having three children under five years of age. Jane Howard is described as the head of her household, despite being listed as married, and managed her premises with as many as seven children aged between one year and twelve. James Hitcham, proprietor of The Hope Beer Shop in Dagnall, was also a seller of coal. Some of these beer shops were probably quite humble affairs, for not a single one of their households included a servant. On the other hand, the three in St Albans parish were more than mere beer shops, for two of them included lodgers, six and ten respectively, the other including three "visitors" on census night who may also have been temporary lodgers.

The Beer Act of 1830 had made it possible for any householder who paid towards the poor rate to become a licensed beer shop keeper, to sell beer for consumption on or off the premises, for a fee of just two guineas a year, although opening hours were much more restricted than those allowed for inns. By 1833 35,000 beer shops had sprung up in England and Wales, the number climbing steadily to approach 40,000 through the 1840s.[129] They were an easy target for contemporary moralisers and temperance reformers, even if many of the attacks upon them were often wholly unfair, and more than a little tinged with ignorance and class bias.[130] In evidence given to the Poor Law Commissioners in 1834, for example, John Carley Cook, Justice of the Peace of Nunsbury near Waltham Cross, Hertfordshire, complained that whilst prior to the Beer Act magistrates had striven to limit the number of public houses in Cheshunt to 20, in the four years since it was passed,

> beershops to the amount of 30 or more have been opened, many of which are supported
> entirely by the most infamous characters, who pass the day in gambling and forming
> plans for the purpose of poaching and hen-roost robbing... I may state without
> exaggeration... that the beershops have already increased, by their baneful influence,
> the poor rates from two and a half to five per cent in some parishes.[131]

In similar vein Thomas Lloyd, rector of Sacombe, Hertfordshire, linked the beer shops with criminal activity:

> I believe the new beershops to have produced more mischief, and demoralized the lower
> orders to an extent little known, except to those who have minutely watched their operation.
> I am borne out in this belief by every agricultural prisoner that has been committed to our
> prison for the last 12 months. The great evil arises from the beer being drunk on the
> premises.[132]

---

129   B. Harrison, *Drink and the Victorians* (2nd edition, Keele, 1994), pp. 79-80.
130   *Ibid.*, pp. 79-84.
131   *Report of the Royal Commission on the Poor Law 1834*, Appendix (C.), Parliamentary Papers, Vol. XXXVII, p. 416.
132   *Ibid.*, p. 417.

They clearly remained a cause for concern in St Albans into the late 1840s, where a number of Temperance Fetes were held,[133] this concern becoming married with another common target of the Temperance Movement, the fair, the commercial role of which had declined until, or so one reformer argued, they had become occasions "not for the transacting of business of any kind, but merely for what is called *pleasure*, alias *drinking...* gambling and fighting".[134] In response to the death of William White after a brawl in The Reformer public house in St Albans in October 1845, a deputation led by the Reverend Horatio Nelson Dudding, M.A., vicar of St Peters, called upon the Corporation to bring "the public-houses and beer-shops... under stricter supervision" and to limit the duration of the Michaelmas Fair, which, they argued, "gave rise to scenes of disorder and profligacy, that the Sabbath was violated, and that a deed of manslaughter was the direct consequence of the Fair".[135] The Town Council rejected this petition and defended the reputation of the fair, which continued until the pleasure fair was abolished by the Fairs Act of 1871. They did, however, order that in future shows and exhibitions should not be allowed to pack up on the Sabbath, and drew the attention of the borough Justices to the remarks of the deputation regarding public houses and beer shops.[136] The Temperance Fete itself, held in the summer, was taken over in 1853 by St Albans Literary Institute and renamed St Albans Grand Rural Fete.[137] From the economic point of view, what this episode clearly reveals is the role that inns, victualling houses, beer shops and the like played in servicing the needs of a wider clientele, not merely the urban residents but also those attracted to the town by the facilities and entertainments that it had to offer. The Fete, with its parade, dancing, sports, speeches, drinking booths and fireworks display, regularly attracted 3,000 people during the 1850s and 1860s, and hence brought a great deal of custom to the town.[138]

It is clear by reference to Kelly's trade directory that far from all of the inns, pubs and beer shops in the town can be identified by name from the census returns: in this respect the trade directory is a better source than is the census, although the census is far superior for the determination of overall occupational structure, and particularly for identification of more lowly occupational groups and categories.[139] In 1855 the directory, which encompasses the urban Liberty and not just the borough, included as many as 51 named inns or public houses, whilst from the census only 21 could be identified by name.[140] Three of those listed in the directory are distinguished from the rest. The Fleur de Lys in Market Place is described as "a commercial inn and posting house", and ran a regular service to London in the earlier nineteenth century.[141] The Peahen on High Street was also a coach office, assuming importance after the completion of the New London Road: in the earlier part of the nineteenth century most passenger coaches stopped there, and it was also used extensively by the wagoners carrying their merchandise through the town.[142] As late as 1893, despite the decline of the coaching

133   Ward, "Hertfordshire Fairs", p. 29

134   Quoted in Harrison, *Drink and the Victorians*, p. 318.

135   Gibbs, *Corporation Records of St Albans*, p. 208.

136   Gibbs, *Corporation Records of St Albans*, p. 208. In 1837 214 inhabitants had petitioned the Corporation for repeal of the bye-law prohibiting Sunday trading, which was opposed by a counter-petition with 164 signatories, on which occasion is was resolved not to alter the bye-law: *ibid.*, p. 200.

137   Ward, "Hertfordshire Fairs", pp. 28-9.

138   *Ibid.*, pp. 29-30.

139   For a comparison between the census returns and trade directories for rural Hertfordshire see C.A. Crompton, "Changes in Rural Service Occupations during the Nineteenth Century: an Evaluation of Two Sources for Hertfordshire, England", *Rural History*, Vol. 6 (1995), pp. 193-203.

140   *Kelly's Directory, 1855*, pp. 231-3.

141   Ashdown, *St. Albans*, p. 242.

142   *Ibid.*, p. 201.

trade with the advent of the railway, it could still be described as the "principal inn" of the town.[143] The Queen's Head in Chequer Street was also a commercial inn, and its proprietors, John Martin and Sons, were importers of foreign wines and spirits. The George on George Street is listed, with Henry Barrance as its proprietor, but somewhat surprisingly is given no special designation, despite the fact that – as the surviving courtyard testifies – it was a bustling place of call earlier in the nineteenth century, offering capacious stables and coach houses, accommodation and home brewed ale, with its own coach running daily to and from The Ram in Smithfield, London.[144]

Just four of these 51 named establishments were run by women, whilst seven of the proprietors conducted an additional, unrelated trade. In addition there were 35 "beer retailers", five of them female, and five pursuing an additional occupation.[145] Given that only 13 beer shops appear in the census for the Liberty of St Albans, it is possible that some of these had simply been differently described in the census. The directory lists no victuallers, and it is occasionally possible to link back to the census to find cases which merely represent a change of nomenclature, such as Mary Dell, a beer retailer in the directory but a public house keeper in the census, or John Hulks, beer retailer in the directory but a victualler in the census. One of these beer retailers is particularly interesting, due to the survival of the autobiography of Lucy Luck. At 13 years of age Lucy was sent by the parish relieving officer for Tring into service in St Albans with "Mr and Mrs H.", who kept a "shop and beer-house combined... they kept something of a general shop on one side of the doorway and a taproom on the other".[146] This would have been in 1851, just four years before the directory was compiled, at which date George Horsfield (Mr H?) ran a beer retailer's and chandler's shop on London Road.

All in all, therefore, the trade directory lists 86 establishments in the Liberty of St Albans providing alcoholic refreshments to the townsfolk and the various categories of visitor to the town. In the census returns, despite the problem in identifying specific establishments, there were 80 inns, victualling houses, pubs or beer shops within the same area, and thus the two sets of documents give overall numbers of much the same order of magnitude. If we take the figure of 86 from the directory as probably the more reliable of the two, this means that there was a pub, inn or beer shop for every 127 inhabitants (children included), or one for every 25 or so families, and the density within the borough proper would have been higher still.[147] A full list is provided in Appendix 2,[148] and it is notable just how many of them were situated upon the major thoroughfares through the town. In particular, the route from Watling Street, into Holywell Hill, and out of town via George Street and Fishpool Street towards Redbourn and thence to the Midlands is littered with inns, even though Verulam Road, opened in 1826, was by this time offering a more direct and spacious carriageway. Inns thus catered to the passenger trade, St Albans providing a convenient place for an overnight stop on the journey from London

---

143   *Ibid.*

144   *Ibid.*, pp. 257-8. For details on the architecture and history of St Albans inns and other historic buildings see J.T. Smith, *English Houses 1200-1800. The Hertfordshire Evidence* (London, 1992) and *idem, Hertforshire Houses. Selective Inventory* (London, 1993).

145   Details on multiple occupations in the directory are probably incomplete: Daniel Kentish, beer retailer, is listed as a "beer shop keeper and agricultural labourer" in the census; James Hitcham, beer retailer, is listed as a "beer and coal seller" in the census.

146   J. Burnett (ed.), *Useful Toil* (London, 1974), p. 71.

147   This compares with a figure for the number of persons per "on-license" in England and Wales as a whole in 1851 of 188: Harrison, *Drink and the Victorians*, Table 7, p. 304.

148   See below, pp. 695-6.

towards the Midlands and the north, as well as offering refreshment and accommodation to those conveying merchandise to and from the capital, whether by pack horse or wagon.[149]

Serving these various inns and beer shops and victualling houses were ten brewers, one of whom, Francis Searancke, doubled as a maltster and clearly operated on some scale as an employer of ten men.[150] Twelve "brewer's labourers" or "brewer's men" are also listed, and five additional maltsters. James Pain of Spencer Street catered for a more sober clientele as a ginger beer manufacturer. The town and its inns were also served by as many as 47 bakers, plus four journeyman bakers, two of whom lived in with their master Thomas McGeorge in Fishpool Street, whilst the other two headed their own households. Just two baker's apprentices are listed. There is little evidence of dual occupations amongst this group, although George Climance of Market Place also dealt in corn, and Thomas Moore of George Street was also a lodging house keeper, housing as many as eight lodgers on census night.[151] The town's bakers were served in their turn by five millers and one corn mill labourer, the Kingsbury Mill being run at this time by George Edwards and his brother, Frederick. Catering for the sweeter tooth were four specialist confectioners running three businesses, allowing for the family concern of Caleb Grimshaw and his 17 year-old son, Alfred. Meat was provided by 31 butchers, two journeyman butchers (one living-in, one living-out) and a butcher's boy, the 16 year-old Robert Hawes. John Pratt and his 28 year-old son Robert ran a business as "poulterers and carriers" in George Street, there were five fishmongers in the town and a solitary milkman. Again we find the occasional widow running her own business, such as Anne Furness, butcher, a 55 year-old widow who employed two men, Mary Bull, another butcher who worked with her bachelor son, William, and Susanna Davis, fishmonger, a 49 year-old widow living in the Market Place. Presumably they were continuing their late husbands' businesses, and their ability to do so might suggest that other women described in the census only as wives of butchers, fishmongers and the like may actually have been actively involved in these trades whilst their husbands still lived, a view that the published census report would appear to support for selected occupations at least.[152]

The sheer weight of numbers providing food, drink and accommodation in the town can only impress, although it might suggest that most of these businesses were small scale concerns, involving a duplication rather than a concentration of effort, still evident in the mid-nineteenth century just as it had been in pre-industrial England. However, it clearly also indicates that the town was a centre of consumption, not only for the urban residents themselves but also for numerous visitors, travellers and itinerant tradespeople, as well as for many of those living in the urban hinterland. Included amongst these, of course, would be the farming community who sold their produce in the town. Although some had apparently been deterred from using the St Albans market by the introduction of tolls on the new Redbourn road in 1826, by mid-century "the frequenters of the market" were petitioning the Corporation for an improvement to the market house, and in September 1857 the town's new Corn Exchange was completed, opened to general approval and celebrated with a public dinner "attended by

149   Ashdown, *St. Albans*, pp. 194-7, 276.
150   He is listed in the trade directory as a "brewer, maltster & spirit merchant": *Kelly's Directory, 1855*, p. 233.
151   Thomas Young, grocer and baker, has already been mentioned above.
152   The Census Report noted that "Widows often carry on the businesses of their deceased husbands, and are hence returned under occupations not commonly followed by women. The "Wives" of "Innkeepers", "Beershop-keepers", "Shoemakers", "Shopkeepers", "Butchers", "Farmers" are specifically returned in the Table, as they are generally engaged in the same business as their husbands." *1851 Census Report. Population Tables II*, Parliamentary Papers 1852-3 Vol. LXXXVIII, Vol. 1, p. 13, footnote.

the Lord Lieutenant and above 100 landowners, tenant farmers and inhabitants".[153] St Albans market was also, of course, important to the straw plait and hat trade, itself so crucial to the region's economy, which will be discussed more fully below.[154]

Consumption, of course, does not end with food and drink, and St Albans had far more to offer. Turning to clothing, there were 23 drapers in the town on census night, 19 of these in St Albans parish and the other four in St Peters. Three of these were described as "travelling drapers", James, Roger and Robert McAdam, all visiting James Harkness, tea dealer, and his family in College Street. Two more were also visitors, leaving 18 resident drapers. Only two women feature, Elizabeth and Charlotte Litchfield, unmarried sisters living in George Street. The size of these establishments is indicated in only two cases. James McCaw of St Peters Street employed four assistants, but larger by far was the operation of James Gibson. Gibson, a "draper and clothier" living in the High Street employed a total of 14 men, three of whom – a shopman and two apprentices – lived in with him, whilst his household also included two servants, described as a porter and a housekeeper. Eight draper's assistants, seven apprentices and two shopmen are also listed in the census, and others will no doubt have been included amongst the unspecified "shopmen" discussed above.[155] The service that such establishments provided to the wealthier residents of suburban premises, such as The Prae, is brought to life in Mary Carbery's reminiscences of a Victorian childhood, written between 1879 and 1885. Here she tells how her mother would only ever deign to set foot in one shop, Marshall and Snelgrove in London, "for at St Albans she sits in the carriage, and out run the shopmen with what she wants. If a helper in the shop gets out first, the owner rushes after him, snatches the tray of ribbons or buttons, jabs the young man with his elbow so that he nearly falls in the gutter, and apologizes to Mama for not having been on the spot first".[156] Securing the patronage of the local gentry was clearly well worth a little obsequious behaviour.

Many more either made, or made and sold, a variety of items of clothing. A total of 175 individuals worked with fabric cloth, including 38 tailors, two journeyman tailors and one apprentice. Three of these were also drapers, one also a hatter and – more unusually – Robert Potts of Dagnall Lane was a "tailor and newsagent". The clothing trades provided considerable opportunities for women, however, and the remaining 134 working in this sector were all female. There were as many as 88 dressmakers living in the town's three central parishes, plus one assistant dressmaker and six apprentices. Thirteen more are described as "needlewoman" or "needleworker", ten as seamstress or sempstress, whilst a further 14 were milliners (plus one apprentice), five of the latter also making dresses and one also making bonnets. The boot and shoe trade was also a considerable employer, accounting for a further 115 individuals, variously described as shoemaker, bootmaker, cordwainer, boot and shoemaker or shoebinder, and again including just a handful of identified apprentices. There was a clear sexual division of labour in the trade, for of the 22 women listed 21 were shoebinders, the most humble operation of a generally quite humble trade, with just one, Elizabeth Hisketh, a 73 year-old widow living on Holywell Hill, aspiring to the title of shoemaker.[157] Another indication of the status of the craft might be the large number of lodgers which feature amongst this group, fully 17 (15% of the

---

153   Gibbs, *Corporation Records of St Albans*, pp. 175-6, 219, 225.
154   See pp. 70-75.
155   See p. 59.
156   M. Carbery, *Happy World. The Story of a Victorian Childhood* (1st publ. London, 1941, repr. 1991), pp. 97-8.
157   Shoebinders sewed the uppers of shoes, most commonly in the home.

total) a far higher figure than the average for all occupations in the town as a whole.[158] Surprisingly, there was just one glover in the town, Charles Goldsmith of Spencer Street, but six staymakers – two of whom were the husband and wife team of Thomas and Mary Paul of High Street – catering to the vanity of the gentlewomen, and representing the vestiges of a trade that in the eighteenth century had been of greater importance as a source of female employment.[159] Discretion and privacy appears to have been of the essence here, for as Mary Carbery informs us "Most ladies, including Mama, have their stays made by a private person, living in her own house with a maid, and models of stays on dolls under a glass case".[160] The St Albans staymakers of 1851 would not have done at all: only one had a maidservant, and the rest lived, not alone, but alongside gunmakers, plasterers, labourers, plaitmakers and the like.

Food, clothing and shelter were the essential requisites of life, and trade and craftsmen in these sectors formed substantial elements of the occupational structure of towns through from the pre-industrial to the industrial era.[161] Food and clothing we have discussed, but the provision of shelter also features more prominently in town than in countryside in the St Albans district. The building trades accounted for 142 individuals, 7% of the occupied male population of the town compared with just 83 (2.3%) in the rural parishes. To these we should add the 67 carpenters included under "Wood" in Table 2, and perhaps also the 16 sawyers and one timber merchant who supplied the necessary raw material. Bricklayers and their labourers numbered 57, there were 27 painters or decorators, 10 general builders and the same number of plumbers. Seventeen stonemasons lived in St Albans, including two "stone and marble masons" and one "statuary and mason". Few of these businesses seem to have been very large, although William Bennett, builder and brickmaker, of St Peters Street stands out as an employer of 27 men: three carpenters, two bricklayers, fourteen labourers, six brickmakers and two "labs" (possibly "lads"). Two more builders, James Winterborn and James Webb, employed eight men each, the house decorator, Henry Smith, employed seven and John Kent, plumber, employed five. Not surprisingly, few females feature in the building trades in either town or country, but all twelve that do are to be found in the town. They were nearly all children, however, 11 of the 12 finding employment in just two families living side by side on Catherine Lane. William Slough, brickmaker, employed his six daughters, Emma, Susan, Amelia, Eliza, Marianne and Sarah, aged from 5 to 13, as well as two sons, Henry and James aged 4 and 7, all recorded under the occupational description "assists father", and conjuring visions of the squalor of the brickmaker's cottage described so graphically in *Bleak House*, which was, of course, also situated in St Albans.[162] Joseph Taylor, brickmaker, similarly called on the assistance of his five daughters aged from 9 to 19, Martha, Eliza, Susan, Sarah and Mary, as well as two sons, William and Henry, aged 8 and 16, with only the eldest daughter described as a brickmaker in her own right. The twelfth female employed in the building trade was Elizabeth Garland of College Place, described as an apprentice, presumably to her husband, John Garland, stonemason.

158   There was an inverse correlation between numbers of lodgers and social class: see below, pp. 169-70.

159   Eden, *The State of the Poor*, Vol. II, p. 271.

160   Carbery, *Happy World*, p. 98.

161   For discussion of urban occupational structures, implicitly or explicitly comparing pre-industrial with industrial England, see W.G. Hoskins, *Provincial England* (London, 1965), pp. 80, 88; J. Patten, *English Towns 1500-1700* (Folkestone, 1978), pp. 146-96; N. Goose, "English Pre-industrial Urban Economies", *Urban History Yearbook 1982* (Leicester, 1982), pp. 24-30.

162   Charles Dickens, *Bleak House* (Penguin edn., London, 1971 – first published 1853), pp. 130-2.

Three cabinet makers, a wood turner, a "carver and gilder" and a "chair bottomer" helped to fill the interior of St Albans homes, and we have already met our furniture broker and china and glass dealers above.[163] There were also four upholsterers plus one apprentice upholsterer operating from St Albans parish, which included the family business of Thomas Younger and his son, Henry, living in High Street with their apprentice, Frederick Howell. No doubt the numerous drapery wares available in the town were also put to good use adorning the homes as well as the bodies of its inhabitants. Five ironmongers, five whitesmiths, five tinplate workers, two tinmen and braziers and two braziers helped to supply these homes with a range of necessary domestic utensils. Less mundane domestic accoutrements were manufactured by William Brockley of Fishpool Street, barometer maker, whilst in the Marlborough Almshouses in St Peters lived Sarah Rowen "wife of a journeyman piano framemaker", whose husband was presumably away from the town on census night. Finally, to ensure the continued warmth of at least the wealthier inhabitants of the town in their grand houses, there were 12 chimney sweeps, all living in just two households in the parish of St Albans. John Warner and his 16 year-old son, George, operated from their home in Dagnall Lane, but far more interesting is the household headed by Sarah Perrin, a 40 year-old widow living in Spicer Street, described as "lodging house keeper and chimney sweep employing 8 sweeps". In fact, her household contained nine sweeps, including her son, James, her nephew, Charles Hyde, and seven servants. Dickensian visions of the brutal exploitation of tiny children are not borne out by the St Albans census, however, for the youngest of these was the nephew, Charles, aged 7, and the rest were between 15 and 24 years of age. On the other hand, the lowly status of the trade is suggested by a closer look at the lodging house that Sarah Perrin ran, which spread across three census schedules, and included a total of 21 "lodgers for the night". Thirteen of these were given the simple occupational designation "tramp", and additionally there were three tramp labourers, two tramp laundresses, and a tramp baker, silkweaver and needlewoman. They included four who shared the surname Eames, and ten members of the Collins family, whose exact inter-relationships are difficult to determine. The solitary inhabitant of the household in the very next schedule was George South, occupation beggar, suggesting that Spicer Street was not the most salubrious street in St Albans in the mid-nineteenth century.

Catering to the comfort and cleanliness of the wealthy and well off in the town was a veritable army of domestic servants. These and a range of other service trades are incorporated under "Service/domestic Service" in Table 2, and accounted for 14% of the occupied population of the town, and over 23% of all female occupations. A total of 345 indoor domestic servants of various descriptions were present in the town's three parishes on census night, 303 of them female and just 42 male. The great majority of the men, 38 of the 42, are described simply as servant, domestic servant or by a similar general title. Just one was a housekeeper, William Simons, a 52 year-old widower; another was a valet but not in the household where he was staying, being described as "lodger for the night"; a third, James Kelly, a 15 year-old servant to Joseph Cocking, innkeeper of Holywell Hill, is given the unflattering but graphic occupational designation "boots". The final manservant was John H. Playle, 39 years of age and a bachelor, who served as butler to Thomas F. Gape, landed proprietor, who lived with his three sisters, all fundholders, in Fishpool Street. Most of the women, 235 of them, were also described under a general title – domestic servant, housemaid, house servant and so forth – but there is more evidence of specialisation here. Thirty-one were housekeepers, three are described as "lady's maid" and another as a chamber maid. Twenty-two more were cooks, with just one kitchen maid. The complement is completed by ten nurses, specifically domestic servants as opposed to the independent nurses

---

163   See p. 59.

already considered above.[164] There are also some glimpses of the hierarchy of service, in the shape of the "under housemaid", "under nurse" and "house servant's assistant" who are listed, a topic we will return to when discussing the structure of households later in this chapter.[165]

Outdoor servants were far less numerous, and were universally male. Five of the 13 included here were footmen, catering to wealthy residents such as Henry Nicholson, rector of St Albans, Elizabeth Lydekker, fundholder, and Thomas Gape, landed proprietor. Another worked for Joseph Biddle of St Michaels, who lived with two brothers, two sisters, an aunt and a cousin, all annuitants, in a household that also included a cook and a housemaid. The fifth, Charles Blakemore, lived with his father John, John Blakemore being described as head of his household but occupied as a "servant" along with the rest of his family which included brother John, a groom. Two more grooms who were clearly servants are included, a coachman to Samuel Jones, optician and farmer employing three men who we have already met, and a single gardener, although other gardeners who did not live in will feature under other occupational categories. The balance is made up by a "postboy" and an errand boy.

The wealth of the middle and upper ranks of St Albans society also created employment in other service industries: in particular, the town overflowed with washerwomen and laundresses. In 1851 there were as many as 52 laundresses in the town, plus one – clearly more elevated – "laundry proprietress", Hannah Charles, a 74 year-old widow living in Fishpool Street with her servant, Mary Bidness. Additionally there were 10 washerwomen, including Mary Edwards, wife of James Edwards, gardener, in St Peters Street, who "takes in mangling". Scrubbing the floors rather than the clothes of the better off were 32 charwomen. Here were the menial jobs in the service sector of the economy of the town that helps to explain the skew in the sex ratio in favour of women that we have discussed above.[166] The age structure and marital condition of these women shows, however, that these trades were not attracting young immigrants, but helping generally more elderly women to make a living. Of the 95 laundresses, washerwomen and charwomen in the town, as many as 39, or 41%, were widows, whereas of all working women aged 15 or over widows formed just 14%. Indeed, these trades provided employment for almost one in five of all widows employed in the town. A further 41 (43%) were married, and hence took to washing and charring to supplement the family income. Just 15 (16%) were unmarried, and even amongst these only three were younger than 37, and only one in her teens. Looking at the age structure of this group as a whole, they were overwhelmingly middle aged or even elderly, 79% being in their forties, fifties and sixties, and more in excess of 70 years of age (eleven) than under 40 (nine). It was to these very trades that Lucy Luck, born at Tring in Hertfordshire, turned when the straw plait trade was dead, to support her children. As she writes in her autobiography, in the slack times "I have been out charring or washing, and I have looked after a gentleman's house a few times, and I have taken in needlework. This was before any of my children were old enough to work".[167]

---

164   See p. 56.
165   See below, pp. 164-5.
166   See pp. 37-42. Washing and charring were important sources of employment for women across the country, accounting for a total of 187,168 of the women employed according to the 1851 census report, only a little short of the 194,910 employed in cotton manufacture that receives so much attention, though well below the 715,704 employed in domestic service (general servant, housekeeper, cook or housemaid): calculated from *1851 Census Report. Population Tables II*, Parliamentary Papers 1852-3 Vol. LXXXVIII, Vol. 1, pp. ccxxvi-ccxxvii.
167   Burnett , *Useful Toil*, p. 77.

Whilst women washed and scrubbed, men dug and sowed: all 38 of the gardeners listed were men. Unlike in Tring and Great Berkhamsted, none of them are identified as horticulturists or market gardeners.[168] Nor did any possess any land worth mentioning in the census. It remains possible, of course, that some may have been growing fruit or vegetables on a small scale, but on this point the census returns are silent. If they were, their operations must have been very small scale: not a single one of these households included a servant, and there are only three instances of family involvement, two between father and son and one between the head of household and his nephew, all tending to suggest that the majority were probably domestic gardeners.

If men tidied the gardens of the better off in St Albans, they also tended to their hair, for all seven hairdressers listed, as in Tring, were men.[169] William and Joseph Mawbey, of Chequer Street and Verulam Street respectively, were both hairdressers; three more could be found on Holywell Hill, two of them – Stephen King and John Breech – lodging with James Everett, publican; whilst William Smith operated from St Peters Street and Ralph Lascelles from Waddington Row. Jewellery added the finishing touches to the coiffured classes, and they had two options. Simon Jones, interestingly, was born in Poland, and operated from Abbey Passage off High Street, whilst Joseph Wells, watchmaker and jeweller, was to be found in High Street itself, with his 16 year-old apprentice, Thomas Dell. Providing more useful decorations were five watchmakers (additional to Joseph Wells), the three in St Albans parish including the father and son business of John and John Thomas Crouch, the two in St Peters also forming one business, James Munns and his 31 year-old "servant", James Brodie.

There was another element of the economy of St Albans that would be a feature of any substantial town, reflecting its role as a central place within a network of trade and communications, and helping to give it its urban identity: this was the developed transport sector of its occupational structure, again occupying twice the proportion of males in the town as compared with the rural parishes. We have already discussed the numerous inns, victualling houses, pubs and beer shops from the viewpoint of provision of food and drink, but saw too that many of them also provided accommodation for visitors and itinerant traders. Lodging houses performed a similar function, and three were run by widows in St Albans and St Peters parishes, including the premises of Sarah Perrin with her 21 "tramp" lodgers introduced above.[170] William Sanders, labourer, and his wife, also of Spicer Street, entertained 12 lodgers, four of the five adults being described as "traveller" and the other as a hawker, perhaps again suggesting that the indigent knew where to gravitate to find cheap, temporary accommodation. Additionally, Thomas Moore of George Street was a "baker and lodging house keeper", housing eight guests on census night.

Providing transport and transport services proper were 73 men and boys and one woman, 21 of them — including the solitary female – oiling the wheels of internal communication and transport by running errands, whilst 10 carriers and two carmen took goods and passengers further afield. Others instrumental in facilitating longer distance travel were William Seymour, coach proprietor, operating from "Saracens" (Saracens Yard) in Holywell Hill, as well as two coachmen and one "coachman and gardener" to add to those who provided these services privately to their wealthy employers. Six coachmakers and four coach trimmers

168   Goose, *The Berkhamsted Region*, p. 53.
169   *Ibid.*, p. 54.
170   See p. 67.

plied their trade in the town, as did seven wheelwrights and a spring maker. Coaches, of course, imply horses and – again additional to those employed as domestic servants – there were 24 grooms, including Samuel and Henry Jones, both heads of their households, operating from Half Moon Yard, and Charles Nash and his four adult sons of Spencer Street in the parish of St Peters, besides 16 blacksmiths. Servicing the horses and carriages that arrived at the town's inns and victualling houses were six ostlers, whilst four more, described also as servants, are recorded elsewhere in our occupational table. Two toll-gate keepers collected the tolls payable on key roads, William Carter manning the Kingsbury Toll Gate and Winsler Wise that on London Road, which had been newly built in 1796 to cope with the weight of traffic.[171] Robert Lawes of Holywell Hill, driver of an omnibus, no doubt served either on the route which ran from Hatfield and Hertford to the Peahen inn, or on that running several times a day to the railway station at Watford, where William Gell, engine driver, was most probably employed.[172] Solomon George Shaw's suggestion, quoted above, that possibly 1,000 people passed through the town each day in the earlier nineteenth century, 600 of them by carriage, brings the activities of these various individuals to life.[173]

St Albans was thus a centre of trade, consumption, communications and culture, all of the immense variety of activities associated with these functions feeding off one another to produce a rich and diverse occupational structure clearly differentiated in so many ways from smaller towns and rural communities. But it was also a centre of industry. The importance of straw plait and the straw and Brazilian hat trades has already been introduced in our discussion of the skewed sex ratio that was a particular feature of the three urban parishes of the district, although also found in a less exaggerated form in other parishes with high levels of female employment.[174] Straw plait and straw hat-making was of regional rather than merely local importance, and to discuss it we must inevitably stray far beyond the urban boundaries. Nevertheless, despite its significance in rural areas – a subject to which we shall return – towns in the region such as Hemel Hempstead, Berkhamsted, Luton, Dunstable, Hitchin and St Albans played a crucial role as centres for marketing as well as, in some cases, for the manufacture of straw into hats. In St Albans in the mid-nineteenth century the straw hat trade, and the Brazilian hat trade to which it gave rise, were of central importance to the prosperity of the town.

In Hertfordshire in 1851 the straw plait and straw hat trade was thriving. Whilst some cottage industries were coming under pressure by the mid-nineteenth century in the face of mechanisation, straw plait continued to expand, producing a varied and high quality product that allowed it to compete successfully with foreign competition in the home market, and also to produce exports valued at approximately £43,000 per year in the mid-1850s.[175] It was not until the 1870s that cheaper imports, first from China and later from Japan, presented a serious threat, and signalled its long term decline.[176] The industry was heavily concentrated in Bedfordshire, Hertfordshire, Essex and the eastern part of Buckinghamshire, these counties including 84% of the 9,800 male and female plaiters recorded in the 1841 census for England and Wales.[177] It has been argued, however, that

---

171   Robinson, *Hertfordshire*, p. 93.

172   *Kelly's Directory, 1855*, p. 234.

173   See above, p. 29.

174   See above, pp. 37-42.

175   Hooson, "The Straw Industry", p. 345; G.E. Mingay (ed.), *The Agrarian History of England and Wales, Vol. VI 1750-1850* (Cambridge, 1989), pp. 858-9; A.J. Tansley, "On the Straw Plait Trade", *Journal of the Society of Arts*, Vol. IX, December 21 1860.

176   Hooson "The Straw Industry", pp. 346-7; C. Freeman, *Luton and the Hat Industry* (Luton, 1953), p. 13.

177   L.L. Grof, *Children of Straw. The Story of a Vanished Craft Industry in Bucks, Herts, Beds and Essex* (Buckingham, 1988), p. 28.

the Essex industry was highly localised, relied heavily upon markets outside the county such as Hitchin to buy and sell straw, and may have provided employment chiefly for children by the mid-nineteenth century.[178] Although this latter point is not borne out by the evidence of the 1851 census report, the main focus of the industry by this time was clearly the south and east Midlands where it was still expanding, whilst the Essex industry was in decline.[179]

TABLE 6 : STRAW PLAITERS IN FOUR ENGLISH COUNTIES 1841-1901

	1841	1851	1861	1871	1881	1891	1901
Bedfordshire	1,607	10,054	11,476	20,701	15,058	10,191	485
Buckinghamshire	1,181	2,922	2,976	3,412	1,654	515	173
Essex	431	3,058	2,444	2,839	922	37	0
Hertfordshire	4,415	8,753	8,598	12,089	7,543	3,133	681
Total	7,634	24,787	25,494	39,041	25,177	13,876	1,339

As only 8% of the total number of plaiters were male, the record of female employment provides an adequate reflection of its long term vitality, and these trends are shown in Table 6, which is reproduced from the important study of the straw industry by Laszlo Grof. The trade clearly expanded rapidly between 1841 and 1851, no doubt providing some relief from the years of depression which featured within a decade that was once described as "the hungry forties", even if it is now accepted that severe economic dislocation only characterised the years 1838-42 and 1847-8.[180] These difficulties find clear reflection in the Hertfordshire evidence in the form of rising admissions to the Hatfield Union Workhouse, in 1841-3 and again in 1847-8, with the admission of both males and the able-bodied dominating in these years in a manner not generally experienced in less distressed times, clearly indicating the spreading tide of unemployment.[181] The straw plait trade appears to have stagnated during the 1850s but, nevertheless, the 1861 census reveals 25,494 female straw plaiters, and as many as 44,228 including those who made up the plait into bonnets and hats.[182] The following decade saw renewed growth, after which quite rapid decline set in. By 1891 there was only one-quarter of the number of straw plaiters in Hertfordshire that there had been in the peak year of 1871, whilst in Essex and Buckinghamshire the trade had already virtually disappeared by this date. Bedfordshire hung on the strongest of the four counties but, like Hertfordshire, saw the virtual obliteration of the trade during the last decade of the century. By this time straw plaiters were paid a pittance and the industry had become clearly associated with poverty and low status.[183] Indeed, by 1881 it was "starving work" according to the few remaining straw plaiters found around Chelmsford in Essex.[184] By 1910, according to Mr Maberly Phillips writing of Hertfordshire in *The Connoisseur*, "only a few veterans of the art are left", and the rewards were

---

178 Sharpe, *Adapting to Capitalism*, pp. 56-63.

179 In Essex in 1851 there were 3,058 female straw plaiters, only 846 (28%) of whom were aged 14 years or under; 643 (21%) were aged 15-19, and 1,569 (51%) were twenty years of age or over. Calculated from *1851 Census Report. Population Tables II*, Parliamentary Papers 1852-3 Vol. LXXXVIII, Vol. 1, p. 273.

180 W.H. Chaloner, *The Hungry Forties: a Re-Examination* (London, 1957); F. Crouzet, *The Victorian Economy* (London, 1982), p. 54; E.P. Thompson, *The Making of the English Working Class* (Harmondsworth, 1969), p. 229.

181 Hertfordshire CRO, BG/HAT41.

182 *Children's Employment Commission: Second Report*, Parliamentary Papers 1864, Vol. XXII, p. xxxix.

183 Grof, *Children of Straw*, p. 103.

184 Quoted in Sharpe, *Adapting to Capitalism*, p. 62.

derisory.[185] By this time the hat trade imported nearly all of its straw, from Japan for quality and from China for price.[186]

In 1851, however, this all lay in the future, and the town of St Albans clearly relied heavily upon the straw plait and hat trade. Although the straw industry was less important as an employer of labour in the urban as opposed to the rural parts of the district, a feature as true of the urban Liberty as it is of the three purely urban parishes, it still accounted for 17.3% of all occupations in the town, and 16.1% in the Liberty. As elsewhere, most of these were female but in the town men were far more prominent than they were nationally. In 1841 and 1861 respectively, the census reveals that approximately 8% and 7% of straw plaiters nationally were male, the Hertfordshire figure for the latter year also standing at 7%.[187] These figures stand a little below the 10.2% in the St Albans District in 1851 and the 13.8% found in the Berkhamsted region to the west.[188] But in the three urban parishes of St Albans male participation stood much higher, at over 18%, with a particularly heavy concentration in St Michaels (urban) where men formed almost one quarter of the population occupied in the straw industry. It is clear that there was considerable variation between parishes, however, and no simple urban-rural divide either here or elsewhere in Hertfordshire. Notwithstanding the example of St Albans, the town of Berkhamsted exhibited a very low proportion of men in the trade, just 2.4%, whilst in other parishes in the region such as Tring (rural and urban) and Aldbury the figure reached 19%.

Whilst the straw industry accounted for over one in six of the occupied population of St Albans in 1851, and nearly one in three of all female occupations, the distinctive element of the urban industry was the existence of straw hat-making as well as straw plaiting. In 1860 the hat trade was described in a paper read to the Society of Arts as "the staple trade of that town", and this is amply borne out by the evidence of the census.[189] A detailed analysis of successive census returns conducted in 1871 by the Deputy Superintendent Registrar for Luton gives a total of 571 hat and bonnet makers in the St Albans registration district in 1851 and 870 in 1861, figures surpassed only by the Luton district itself where the totals stood at 2,907 and 4,866 for these two dates respectively.[190] It must be emphasised that precise classification of the various hatworkers is difficult, for hats could be made of felt as well as straw and also, notably in St Albans, of Brazilian grass. For the purposes of analysis here it has been assumed that all of those described by a generic title – "hat-maker", "bonnet maker", "bonnet sewer", "hat blocker" and the like – worked in straw; only those where Brazilian grass or an alternative raw material are specified are excluded from the Special Industry (Straw) category, and included instead under Textiles/clothing in Table 2. Those working with straw as a raw material rather than making hats out of prepared plait were in fact a distinct minority in the town, only some 129 (20%) of the 657 individuals employed in the industry. Eight of these were straw factors, dealers or merchants, emphasising the marketing role that the town performed. Even if it could not be numbered amongst the chief straw plait markets of the region, St Albans was undoubtedly of local importance, and the straw plaiters of Harpenden

185 *VCH Herts*, Vol. 4, p. 255.

186 *Ibid.*

187 *Children's Employment Commission: Second Report*, 1864, p. xxxix; calculations from *1861 Census Report, Population Tables II: Ages, Civil Condition, Occupations and Birth Places of the People*, Parliamentary Papers 1863, Vol. LIII (London, 1863), pp. 193, 196; Grof, *Children of Straw*, pp. 28-9.

188 Goose, *The Berkhamsted Region*, p. 36.

189 Tansley, "On the Straw Plait Trade", p. 73.

190 T.G. Austin, *The Straw Plaitting and Straw Hat and Bonnet Trade* (Luton, 1871), p. 11.

would walk the four miles into the town on Saturdays with their plait in time for the ringing of the market bell at 9 o' clock, whilst the straw plaiters of Hatfield, some six miles distant, also brought their plait to the town to sell at the weekly market.[191] Only one of these factors was a woman, Ann Edmonds of Sopwell Lane, the wife of William Edmonds, publican. If we exclude these straw factors from our calculation, the balance between the sexes in the plaiting of straw itself stands closer to the national figures than for the straw industry as whole, for just 11% of them were male.

Women were again predominant in the straw *hat* business, even if men were better represented at approaching 20% of the total, a figure which stands well above the 9% identified in the 1861 national census.[192] It is very difficult to differentiate between the various straw hat-makers, bonnet sewers, hatters or "fancy" hat-makers listed, but it is clear that this was no mere cottage industry, and in some instances was run on a very large scale indeed. Thomas Richardson of St Peters Street is listed as a "straw hat manufacturer and justice of the peace", and was thus clearly a man of some substance, his two sons, William, 28, and Henry, 18, remaining at home and "assisting in [the] manufactory", the household also including two servants. The census also provides other evidence that the trade was factory based. George Hailes of Verulam Road was foreman in a bonnet factory, whilst Maurice Britton of Dagnall Lane and James Bates, lodging in Verulam Street, were both "assistants" in a straw bonnet factory. But the most impressive evidence of the scale to which the business could aspire is provided by Thomas Harris of Chequer Street, described as "straw hat and canvas manufacturer employing 300 hands". His wife, Sarah, worked as "assistant in the manufactory", a daughter and step-daughter as straw hat-makers, and his household also included a seven year-old nephew and three month old infant, although surprisingly no servants. Judging by the small number of canvas weavers in the town, the great majority of Harris's employees were engaged in the straw hat trade, which would mean that his business must have dominated the industry. Like Luton and Dunstable, therefore, St Albans appears to have been able to boast a number of substantial hat-making factories, sewing, blocking, stiffening, pressing and trimming hats, operating alongside a large number of domestic outworkers who were either engaged in the early stages of manufacture before passing them on to the factories or in finishing the hats with trimmings of various descriptions.[193] The men's boater was a particular St Albans specialism, which it was said to supply to the world, whilst nearby Luton concentrated upon women's hats.[194] The straw and straw hat industry permeated the whole town, and straw hat-makers, blockers, trimmers and straw plaiters could be found in numbers in each of the three parishes and in most of its streets, but with a particular concentration in Fishpool Street which housed as many as 130 in 1851, the factory of Munt, Brown and Company being established here in the 1860s, the very last straw hats that St Albans produced being manufactured at numbers 9-11 Fishpool Street in 1937.[195]

---

191   The four chief markets were Luton, Dunstable, Hemel Hempstead and Hitchin. Nine more were held at St Albans, Chesham, Tring, Leighton Buzzard, Ivinghoe, Toddington, Ampthill, Shefford and Baldock: Tansley, "On the Straw Plait Trade", p. 72; Grey, *Cottage Life*, p. 87. It was the common procedure for individual plaiters from Hatfield to travel to St Albans to sell their plait, although "In some instances persons come round the country and buy the plait of the poor at their own cottages": *Report from the Select Committee of the House of Lords on the Poor Laws*, Parliamentary Papers, 1831 Vol. VIII, p. 279. In 1852 a dedicated Inspector was appointed to attend the plait markets, in 1867-8 making 269 visits to plait markets and districts, 817 calls at warehouses, travelling a total of 3,998 miles and detecting 2,538 cases of short measure of plait: Austin, *The Straw Plaitting and Straw Hat and Bonnet Trade*, pp. 20-1.

192   *Children's Employment Commission: Second Report*, 1864, p. xxxix.

193   W. Branch Johnson, *The Industrial Archaeology of Hertfordshire* (Newton Abbot, 1970), pp. 74-6.

194   Freeman, *Luton and the Hat Industry*, pp. 15-16; *VCH Herts*, Vol. 4, p. 255-6; E. Toms, *The New Book of St Albans* (Chesham, 1976), p. 97.

195   M. Fookes, *Made in St Albans* (St Albans, 1997), p. 12.

The St Albans hat industry did not end with straw hats, for by mid-century the Brazilian hat, made from split palm, which had been introduced into England at the end of the French Wars and manufactured in St Albans from about 1836, was also made in considerable quantities.[196] The Brazilian hat was made largely of raw material imported from Cuba and woven by hand, thus operating as a cottage rather than a factory industry.[197] Included in the Textile/clothing category of Table 2 for the town are some 475 additional individuals involved in one way or another in the making of hats. Of these 196 were employed as Brazilian hat-makers, blockers or pressers, and a further 14 as Brazilian grass splitters or openers, the great majority of them living in the parishes of St Albans and St Peters. The Brazilian hat industry thus employed almost two-fifths of the number employed making straw hats in 1851, but its success was relatively short-lived, for it succumbed to French competition from the 1870s leaving the town to concentrate on straw hats for men.[198]

Other hats were also made in St Albans in small quantities. Six "chip" hat-makers feature in the census, the chip hat being made out of woven splints of wood or woody fibres. All of them were young, unmarried women, five of the six sharing two households in Dagnall Lane. There was also a cloth cap maker, James Deamer, who lived in Christopher Yard, and a "waterproof hat-maker", Joseph Towersey of New England Place. But most of the rest of those included in this category and involved in hat-making were engaged in weaving or otherwise making trimmings for hats, and they number a further 260 individuals. They are variously described – as bonnet trimming maker, trimming weaver, hand loom weaver (trimming), trimming manufacturer, loom weaver, or simply as weaver – but there is little doubt that they were mainly concerned with the hat industry. The great majority, even of those specified as working on the loom, were women, and many of these were in their teenage years or occasionally younger, indicating that the work must have been at least relatively light. Hat trimmings woven on the loom could employ horsehair, cotton or silk, and could of course be applied to all hats, whether straw or Brazilian. If we take all of those involved in the hat trade – the straw plaiters, straw bonnet makers, trimming weavers, Brazilian hat-makers, as well as all the others described under a myriad of occupational titles – in total they number over 1,100, and constitute fully 30% of the town's occupied population in 1851, indicating a considerable level of specialisation by any standards.[199] Furthermore, when we turn to the town's hinterland, we will find a further concentration of Brazilian hat-makers in addition to the army of plaiters who helped to supply the town with the raw material for its straw hat trade.[200] Despite its role as a centre of consumption, of trade, of communication and culture, therefore, St Albans was also quite clearly an industrial town. Even if the industry in which it specialised was at this time only partly mechanised and partly centralised, and still rested squarely within the confines of the "advanced organic economy" rather than the "mineral-based energy economy" that was soon to take centre stage,[201] it made a real contribution to the multi-faceted process of industrialisation and modernisation, and was of profound importance to the economic vitality of its immediate hinterland and wider region.

---

196 Freeman, *Luton and the Hat Industry*, pp. 24-5; Fookes, *Made in St Albans*, pp. 15-16.
197 *VCH Herts*, Vol. 4, p. 254.
198 *Ibid.*; Fookes, *Made in St Albans*, p. 16.
199 Goose, "English Pre-industrial Urban Economies", pp. 28-9.
200 See below, p. 76-7.
201 For a fascinating reappraisal of the process of industrialisation and a fuller explanation of these terms see E.A. Wrigley, *Continuity, Chance and Change. The Character of the Industrial Revolution in England* (Cambridge, 1988).

Before we turn to the rural hinterland, however, there is one further facet of St Albans' industrial sector that cannot be ignored, and this is its silk industry. The Abbey Mill, a corn mill from the Middle Ages, was converted by John Woollam in 1804 to silk-throwing, and in this case both water and steam power were employed. In 1813 Solomon George Shaw estimated that there were 500 people, mostly children, employed in the town's silk mill and cotton mill, the latter giving its name to Cotton Mill Lane.[202] This may well have been an exaggeration, as contemporary estimates commonly were, but still by 1851 201 individuals are listed in the census as silk throwsters, spinners, winders, workers, labourers or simply "works at a silk mill", and hence the silk industry rivalled the Brazilian hat trade in terms of the number of hands it employed, even if it could not quite match the 300 silk workers operating at the same date in the parish of Tring to the west.[203] This was an industry where, in south-west Hertfordshire at least, there was no marked sexual division of labour. In St Albans there was a slight preponderance of males (56%) over females (44%), whilst in Tring we find the bias reversed, with 52% female and 48% male. Nor does there appear to be any distinction by sex according to the type of operation concerned, whether spinning, throwing, picking or sorting. This was in marked contrast to the situation nationally, for across the country silk factories employed roughly twice the number of females as males, and the unusual position here may well reflect the competing demand for female labour of the straw plait and hat trades.[204] Shaw was right, however, to emphasise the youth of the employees. Eighty-six of them (43%) were 14 years or younger, 18 of these below the age of 10. A further 38 (19%) were between 15 and 19, and only 77 (38%) were clearly adults, aged 20 and above.[205] The youngest was Eliza Taylor of Shrubbs Yard, aged just seven, and occupied as a silk throwster, whilst Ann Peacock and Betsey North, also throwsters, were eight. The remainder were aged nine or over, indicating that, unlike in the Essex industry where children were taken into the mills at the age of five or six, nine or ten was a more common age to start in St Albans.[206]

As for the cotton industry, little trace can be found, just one cotton spinner, the 52 year-old Charlotte Brothers and one cotton winder, 56 year-old Elizabeth Ratcliff, featuring in the record. The mill in Cotton Mill Lane had employed around 60 workers in 1840 but switched to Berlin tapestry wool in 1848.[207] It is quite possible, therefore, that some of the 68 individuals described simply as "weaver" were working here rather than, as assumed above, weaving trimmings for hats. Nor is there any trace of the mill dedicated to spinning candle-wick which had employed several children at the turn of the century.[208] There was, however, a small canvas factory in the town: we have already met Thomas Harris, "straw hat and canvas manufacturer employing 300 hands". In the three urban parishes, however, just six canvas weavers could be traced, plus Jeremiah Mayles, a married man of 34 years of age living on Old London Road, the foreman of a canvas factory, so the concern was clearly a small one. Finally, Phoebe Saddington and Rebecca Holland, aged 40 and 56 respectively, represent the ageing vestiges of the once important hand lace making industry, just as the mechanised silk mill points the way to the future.

---

202   Fookes, *Made in St Albans*, pp. 10-11, 21; Toms, *Story of St Albans*, p. 138.
203   Goose, *The Berkhamsted Region*, p. 38. Kelly's Directory for 1855 suggests that at that date St Albans silk mill employed 300 hands, but the census evidence indicates that this may have been a slight exaggeration: *Kelly's Directory, 1855*, p. 230.
204   B.R. Mitchell and P. Deane, *Abstract of British Historical Statistics* (Cambridge, 1962), p. 213.
205   The age and sex structure of the Essex silk industry was very different. Here there were half as many women again as men in 1841 (940 to 642), and only 37% were under the age of 20 compared to 62% in St Albans: Sharpe, *Adapting to Capitalism*, p. 41.
206   *Ibid.*, p. 47. Until 1830 Woollam's silk mill in St Albans provided employment for the parish children of nearby Hatfield: *VCH Herts*, Vol. 4, p. 221.
207   Ashdown, *St. Albans*, p. 192; Fookes, *Made in St Albans*, p. 21.
208   Eden, *The State of the Poor*, Vol. II, p. 271.

A rural hinterland

It is both easy and difficult to draw a distinction between a town and its rural hinterland. The easy part is to contrast the various parishes in terms of the proportions of the population engaged in the agricultural sector of the economy. In the three urban parishes just 4.1% of those who worked were so occupied; in the rural parishes together the figure stood at 37.7%. If we turn to male employment the contrast is even starker, with 7.7% of the urban population employed in agriculture, compared with an overwhelming 64.0% in the rural hinterland. The figures for the two most urban parishes of them all, St Albans and St Peters, are particularly low, at 3.6 and 6.2% respectively; the lowest rural figure is found in the parish of Redbourn, at 50.1%, with all of the other parishes exhibiting figures of between 61 and 74%, these figures generally standing higher than most of those for even the more rural parishes of the Berkhamsted region to the west.[209]

Nevertheless, if – perhaps by definition – agricultural activity and employment dominated the life of the town's rural hinterland, there are some complications to consider. First, exactly where does the town start and end? Reliance upon political and administrative boundaries, such as parliamentary borough or Liberty, is almost bound to prove unsatisfactory to some degree from the viewpoint of an economic and social analysis, for particular occupational or social categories did not necessarily confine themselves within such boundaries just to please latter-day historians who want, for the sake of clarity, to locate a particular trade or industry *in* a town. As we have seen, a small part of the parish of St Stephens did indeed fall within the town boundaries,[210] and hence we find that the town's gasworks, established in 1826, was situated here.[211] John B. Stammers, originally from London, "gas manufacturer", occupied a property called Holywell House at this time with his five young children and house servant, Emma Quilch.[212] The house in the next schedule is described simply as "gasworks", and was occupied by William Hardy from Belfast in Ireland, gasman, and his family. His household included a nine year-old "son-in-law", William Gibbs, who on account of his age must in fact have been his step-son. The next household again is headed by James Gibbs, labourer at the gasworks, suggesting a family tie by second marriage between the two men. Similarly, the Curate of St Peters Church, John Chippendale, lived along the Hatfield Road, and is thus included with the Out-hamlets, although his association was quite clearly with the town proper. Others may well have chosen to live on the fringes of the town, even though they participated fully in its economy by working there, but this is simply impossible to tell from the census. One wonders, for example, if George H. Saunders, solicitor's general clerk, of Westwick Row in St Michaels (rural) worked in his parish of residence, or whether he was employed by one of the solicitors in the town proper.

Even in those parts of the parish that clearly fell outside of the town boundaries we find occupations that were clearly associated with the urban economy, and not merely by feeding in raw materials. In particular, the Brazilian hat trade was extensively practised in the parish of St Stephens, just as it was in the borough itself, with as many as 137 Brazilian hat-makers living here, besides a handful of straw hat-makers. The same was true to a lesser extent of the Out-hamlets, where 49 Brazilian hat-makers could be found. The extent of the trade in these more outlying areas, of course, reflects the greater flexibility of a domestic industry compared with the factory production that characterised at least some aspects of straw hat production. If we were to

---

209   Goose, *The Berkhamsted Region*, Table 2, p. 30.

210   See above, p. 32.

211   Fookes, *Made in St Albans*, p. 22.

212   This was not, of course, the famous Holywell House built – or rebuilt – by the Duchess of Marlborough towards the end of the 17th century, for this had been pulled down in 1837 in order to restore Holywell Hill to its former straight course: see F. Harris, "Holywell House, St Albans: an Early Work by William Talman?", *Architectural History*, Vol. 28 (1985), pp. 32-6; *idem*, "Holywell House: a Gothic Villa at St Albans", *The British Library Journal*, Vol. 12 (1986), pp. 176-83; Ashdown, *St. Albans*, pp. 188-9.

add these in to the figures for the town proper discussed above, we virtually double the number of Brazilian hat-makers, this branch of the industry now increasing from two-fifths to four-fifths of the size of the straw hat trade in terms of numbers employed. Some slight restitution of the ascendancy of the straw hat trade is provided by the fact that straw hat-makers can be found in the suburbs too: 30 of them in the Out-hamlets, besides 18 more described simply as "hat-maker", and a handful of bonnet sewers and trimming weavers. In St Michaels (rural) there were a further 10 bonnet makers or sewers, three grass splitters or plaiters as well as six silk throwsters or winders, even if the 'urban' industry did not penetrate here to the same degree. There is a sense, therefore, in which the Liberty rather than the town forms a coherent economic entity, even if from the viewpoint of the dominance of agricultural employment there is a clear distinction to be drawn between the two.

There is a further complexity to this simple divide between town and hinterland to consider, over and above the difficulty that we inevitably have in drawing a clear line of demarcation in economic terms, for although both the urban Liberty and the surrounding villages were largely agricultural, there was far more to them than that. Indeed, we have touched upon this point in introducing the region above.[213] Redbourn was itself a major thoroughfare standing astride Watling Street and receiving as much through traffic as did St Albans itself, at least prior to the opening of the railway, and still hosting three fairs annually in 1855.[214] It could boast three nonconformist chapels, the Independent Chapel erected in Fish Street in 1806, the Mount Zion Primitive Baptist chapel erected in 1835 and the Wesleyan Methodist chapel built just two years later.[215] Wheathampstead, according to Kelly's Directory, was a place where "business to some considerable extent was formerly carried on, but of late years it has been gradually decreasing, and it now forms a place of little importance".[216] The village had, however, grown substantially during the first half of the nineteenth century, from a population of 1,043 in 1801 to 1,908, a factor of 1.83, which was only slightly below the national growth rate of 1.93, and above that achieved in the county as a whole, Hertfordshire's population expanding from 97,577 to 167,298, a factor of 1.71.[217] Growth in Wheathampstead was slower thereafter, but the village did not stagnate, and had added a further 500 to its numbers by 1901.[218] In mid-century it could boast two breweries, a range of other crafts apart from the straw plait trade, a National School built as early as 1815, an Independent Chapel erected in 1815, and a Methodist Chapel erected in 1839.[219] Its rail connection arrived only shortly after St Albans', in 1860.[220] Both Redbourn and Wheathampstead sustained friendly societies in the early nineteenth century, Redbourn in fact possessing three societies at the turn of the century, one more than could be found in St Albans itself.[221]

Sandridge was a less developed village, growing only marginally between 1821 and 1851 to achieve a population of 860, and contracting slightly thereafter until renewed growth set in during the last twenty years of the century. As such it contained no purpose-built nonconformist chapel, merely a "room in a dwelling house, licensed for religious worship", which was utilised according to the 1851 religious census by the "Baptist and Independent United" church, more generally known as the Hertfordshire Union which had been

---

213   See p. 33.
214   *Kelly's Directory, 1855*, p. 224.
215   Burg (ed.), *Religion in Hertfordshire*, pp. 167-8.
216   *Ibid.*, p. 249.
217   *VCH Herts*, Vol. 4, pp. 235-8; and calculations from Wrigley and Schofield, *Population History of England*, Table A3.1, p. 529.
218   *VCH Herts*, Vol. 4, pp. 235-8.
219   I. Freeman *et al.*, *Wheathampstead and Harpenden. Book V, The Old Order Changeth: The Places, The People, Their Work, Problems and Pleasures in the Nineteenth Century* (Harpenden, 1991), pp. 189, 196-206; Burg (ed.), *Religion in Hertfordshire*, pp. 165-6.
220   *Ibid.*, p. 207.
221   Eden, *The State of the Poor*, Vol. II, pp. 271, 275.

established in 1810.[222] Not surprisingly, as he had been secretary of the Union for over 20 years, William Upton adjudged this congregation to be "very useful" in his survey of 1847-8.[223] Sandridge had to wait until 1868 for substantial educational provision, in which year the Earl of Verulam provided grounds on which to erect schools for boys, girls and infants.[224]

Harpenden was in a rather different league to the small village of Sandridge. It expanded from a population of 1,112 in 1801, growing in each decade until 1831 when it approached 2,000, retaining its size in 1851 after a brief setback during the 1830s. Across the first half of the nineteenth century it had grown by a factor of 1.78, again above the county trend and not far short of that achieved nationally, and continued to grow steadily thereafter until again more rapid expansion occurred towards the end of the century.[225] The range of trades in Harpenden was wider than in the other villages in the hinterland, whilst in 1855 it could boast an Independent and a Wesleyan Methodist Chapel, the former erected in 1840 and the latter extended in 1839, a Literary Institute and a Chemical Laboratory.[226] A new British and Foreign School for boys and girls was built and opened in 1850, and in 1858 both an infant school and a new National School were opened, the latter requiring additional space just five years later to house its 70 pupils.[227] Horse racing was held on the large tract of unenclosed common from 1838 to 1914, twice a year by the 1870s, proving a popular attraction and providing considerable custom , not all of it welcome, for

> "Notwithstanding that these meetings are under the most unexceptionable patronage as regards the Stewards, yet for two days in the year all the London pickpockets, sharpers, and other blackguards who happen to be out of gaol, are permitted to make Harpenden their own, and to make travelling in a first class carriage of the Midland railway a danger to men, and an impossibility to ladies".[228]

Harpenden also achieved its rail connection in 1860.[229]

The census returns give a full indication of the range of activities found in the Liberty of St Albans and surrounding villages. Space prohibits the detailed analysis afforded above to the town itself, but each of these parishes exhibits the usual range of crafts and tradesmen found in towns and villages up and down the country. Here the word "men" is used advisedly, for – to an even greater extent than in the town of St Albans – it was indeed men who were overwhelmingly dominant in these occupations in the rural parishes, at least as

---

222   Burg (ed.), *Religion in Hertfordshire*, pp. ix, 168.

223   *Ibid.*, p. 66.

224   J.E. Cussans, *History of Hertfordshire* (London, 1879-81), Vol. III , Hundred of Cashio, p. 242.

225   *VCH Herts*, Vol. 4, pp. 235-8. The figure of 1980 given in the published census returns for 1851 is wrong: the correct population total is 1979.

226   *Kelly's Directory 1855*, p. 203; Freeman et al., *Wheathampstead and Harpenden*, pp. 193-206; Burg (ed.), *Religion in Hertfordshire*, p. 166.

227   Miss Vaughan, *Thirty-Three Years at Harpenden, being an Account Written by Miss Vaughan in 1893* (London, 1904), p. 10; *Kelly's Directory 1855*, p. 203; Cussans, *History of Hertfordshire*, Vol. III , The Hundred of Dacorum, p. 348.

228   Cussans, *History of Hertfordshire*, Vol. III, The Hundred of Dacorum, p. 350; E. Brandreth, *Harpenden* (Stroud, 1996), p. 9; Robinson, *Hertfordshire*, p. 103. For an introduction to early horse race meetings in the vicinity of St Albans see E. Edwards, *Friars Wash Point-to Point Races* (Flamstead, 1996).

229   Rook, *History of Hertfordshire*, p. 95.

far as is revealed by the evidence of the census.[230] If we combine all those men working in the textiles and clothing, miscellaneous manufactures, leather, building, metal, wood, food and drink, transport, quarrying and mining and retail and distribution categories of Table 2, hence excluding most of those engaged in the specialist straw and hat industry, then 744 or 21% of the occupied male population worked in these trades. There was variation from parish to parish, however. In the rural part of St Michaels only 15% of the occupied male population worked in these sectors, probably because proximity to the town rendered them less necessary or viable, but even here there was an array of bakers, beer sellers, carpenters (as many as eight of these), coalmen, drapers, general dealers, grocers, paperworkers, tinworkers, tailors and victuallers – if usually only one or two in each occupation. The Out-hamlets, probably for the same reason, also exhibit a slightly below average proportion engaged in these trades, at just over 17%. St Stephens stands close to the rural average at 20%, although here the figures are buoyed up by the number of male Brazilian hat-makers included within the textile and clothing category.

When we turn to the four villages in the rural hinterland, the percentages of men occupied in these crafts and trades is generally higher, reflecting their need for greater self-sufficiency given their distance from the town. In Harpenden, Redbourn and Wheathampstead the proportions were 23%, 24% and 23% respectively. Sandridge, no doubt because it was a substantially smaller village and situated only two as opposed to four and a half to five miles from the town, is the exception, with only 16% of its occupied male population in these crafts and trades. A cursory glance through the male occupations recorded in a substantial village like Wheathampstead gives a very different impression from that provided by rural St Michaels, an impression that the percentage differences that we have identified do not adequately convey. In Wheathampstead there were bakers, brewers, beer sellers, butchers and bricklayers, black, white and unspecified smiths, carriers, carpenters, coopers and coalmen, dealers, fishmongers, grocers and hawkers, innkeepers, papermakers, shoemakers, tailors and tea dealers. Here, however, there were more often than not at least two, frequently more, in each occupation, and several were small scale employers or keepers of apprentices. Occasionally, unusual dual occupations catch the eye, such as William Hunt blacksmith and grocer, George Gray shoemaker and publican or George Nash of the Red Lion Beer Shop, carpenter and beer shop keeper, although most individuals kept to just one trade. Harpenden and Redbourn present a very similar picture, one of a breadth and depth of craft and trade activities, clearly not on the same scale as in the town of St Albans, but nevertheless making a significant contribution to the economies of these villages, and reflecting the increased productivity and increased demand that was the essence of the process of industrialisation and modernisation.

Although the census provides only a snapshot at one point in time, one can see these village economies at mid-century as the culmination of a long term development that has recently been emphasised on a national scale. Between 1811 and 1851 the proportion of adult males employed in the agricultural sector fell from 39% to just 25%. As late as 1831, however, manufacturing, whether factory or domestic employment, constituted only 10% of the total – falling as low as 6% if Lancashire and the West Riding of Yorkshire are excluded – whereas retail and handicraft trades comprised 32% of the total. Examination of ten key occupations in the retail and service sectors across the first half of the nineteenth century shows clearly that it was these trades rather than

---

230   For a discussion of the tendency of the census to under-represent women's work, see E. Higgs, "Women, Occupations and Work in the Nineteenth Century Censuses", *History Workshop Journal* No. 23 (1987), pp. 59-80; B. Hill, "Women, Work and the Census: a Problem for Historians of Women", *History Workshop Journal*, No. 35 (1993), pp. 78-94.

the manufacturing sector that accounted for the bulk of additional male employment outside agriculture, underlining the perspective presented by Sir John Clapham over fifty years ago, and this was as much true of the more rural counties of England as it was of the rest of the country.[231] As Tony Wrigley concludes, "The steady, rapid growth of employment in [these] industries, all of which were engaged in providing goods and services to the local market, is in part a reflection of the boost to local demand arising from the prosperity produced by increasing efficiency in agriculture. In part, however, it may be regarded as an element in the process by which increasing productivity was achieved."[232] The evidence of the 1851 census for the St Albans district, like that for the Berkhamsted Superintendent Registrar's District to the west, provides a clear regional reflection of the culmination of this process by the mid-nineteenth century, emphasising the importance of retail and handicraft trades – particularly in small towns but to a lesser degree in the larger villages too – to the process of economic development that is so often unduly focused upon the industrial Midlands and the North.[233]

We have already seen that, apart from the more common crafts and trades, the parishes in the rural hinterland of St Albans could also include more specialist occupations, such as papermakers or tea dealers, or – in Redbourn – an "umbrella and parasol repairer", George Franklin of High Street. But by mid-century they often also included a range of professional men too, a reflection of the process of administrative and political modernisation that was now exerting its influence across the country. Their numbers varied considerably from parish to parish, as Table 2 reveals, with a considerably higher percentage of the occupied male population in the public service and professional category in Harpenden, and to a lesser extent in St Michaels (rural), than in the other parishes. Even parishes such as Sandridge, Redbourn and Wheathampstead included professional men, and even women, however. Apart from the omnipresent clergymen of the established church, such as Thomas Winbolt of Sandridge and Henry Hecker of Wheathampstead, curates in their respective parishes, dissenting ministers could be found in some rural areas, such as William Robinson, Independent Minister of the Fish Street Chapel in Redbourn, already mentioned above, indicating that if dissent was generally stronger in towns they certainly had no monopoly on it. Both Wheathampstead and Redbourn had their own police constables, Edward Beckwith and William Nicholls. In Sandridge, John F. Hutchinson of Bailiff's Cottage, Sandridgebury, served as collector of rates for the parish, in Redbourn William E. Otway served as assistant overseer and parish clerk, whilst again in Redbourn Samuel Farey was postmaster, doubling up as a glover. No schoolmasters were to be found in Sandridge, but there were two schoolmistresses, Sara Warbey aged 16 and Emma Mardling, 21, both described as "Teacher National School". In Wheathampstead there were two schoolmasters, besides a schoolmistress, whilst Redbourn could boast a schoolmaster and as many as six schoolmistresses (one at an infant school), who ranged in age between 19 and 74. Nurses and/or midwives were present in each parish, and in Redbourn a surgeon, Joseph B. Ayre, with L.A.C. qualifications from London.

---

231   E.A. Wrigley, "Men on the Land and Men in the Countryside: Employment in Agriculture in Early-Nineteenth Century England", in L. Bonfield, R. Smith and K. Wrightson (eds.), *The World We have Gained. Histories of Population and Social Structure* (Oxford, 1986), pp. 295-304; J.H. Clapham, *An Economic History of Modern Britain*, 3 vols. (Cambridge, 1926-38).

232   E.A. Wrigley, "Men on the Land and Men in the Countryside", p. 335.

233   Goose, *The Berkhamsted Region*, pp. 34, 54-5. The figures presented here, like those for the Berkhamsted region, relate to all male occupations rather than, as Wrigley's do, to men aged 20 or over, and thus – given the prominence of young men and boys in domestic service and the plaiting trade – are likely to understate the proportions found in the craft and retail sector.

In St Michaels (rural) and Harpenden professional people were more numerous still. Besides its clergymen, school teachers, nurses and postman, St Michaels was clearly an attractive location for those of a more elevated social standing. These included James Pennington, "one of her majesty's Yeomen ", and Henry Baillie, Member of Parliament, residing at Prae House with his family and 10 servants, taking pleasure on census night in a visit from George John, Marquis of Sligo, and his wife. This entourage is dwarfed, however, by that of the Earl of Verulam at Gorhambury. Besides his mother, the Dowager Countess of Verulam, his children, his brother, Robert Grimston, barrister at law, and two guests – Henry Unwin Addington, Under Secretary of State for Foreign Affairs and his wife – his household included no less than 29 servants of various descriptions, including the four travelling with his visitors.

Harpenden was a somewhat different matter, the relatively high proportion of professional people and public servants here reflecting a stronger middle or upper middle class presence. All six of the women who feature in this category in Harpenden were schoolteachers, one specifically at the British School, another at the "juvenile academy". In addition there were three schoolmasters, one specified as "master of the elementary school". There were also the usual clergymen, a Church of England curate and an Independent Minister, besides local officials such as the registrar of births and parish clerk, and a police officer, but the parish also possessed its own librarian, one Lewis Allen, and included three engaged in clerical work of one kind or another. The legal profession was represented by a solicitor, a lawyer and a barrister-at-law – the Attorney general of North Wales, John Wyatt. There were four surgeons (two not practising) as well as two surgeons and general practitioners. On census night a superannuated civil servant was visiting, as was Arthur G. Rumball, "superintendent of a private asylum for lunatics". Most particular to Harpenden, however, was the appearance in the census of a number of agricultural chemists, who deserve greater attention.

Far from being a rural backwater, Harpenden led the way for the rest of the nation in agricultural innovation, as the birthplace of the agro-chemical industry. The founding father was John Bennet Lawes, who inherited the Rothamsted estate in the parish of Harpenden in 1834, and immediately began his experiments, first with plants in pots and subsequently in the field. His key early discovery was the remarkable effect produced in turnip crops by dressing them with mineral phosphates that had been treated with sulphuric acid, and in 1842 he patented his process for the manufacture of superphosphate. By 1843 he was advertising his "Patent Manures" for sale:

> "J.B. LAWES PATENT MANURES, composed of Super Phosphate of Lime, Phosphate
> of Ammonia, Silicate of Potass, &c., are now for sale at his Factory, Deptford-creek,
> London, price 4s. 6d. per bushel. These substances can be had separately; the Super
> Phosphate of Lime alone is recommended for fixing the Ammonia of Dung-heaps,
> Cesspools, Gas Liquor, &c., Price 4s 6d. per bushel."

The renowned Rothamsted Experimental Station evolved from laboratories built on the estate during the 1840s and, underpinned by the Lawes Agricultural Trust established in 1889, still continues to this day. Systematic experiments were conducted, and carefully recorded, into the effect of the absence of manure, the use of farmyard manure and various chemical manures, both upon crops grown successively on the same land and on crops grown in various rotations. Lawes was also involved with J.T. Way in detailed monitoring of the

benefits to be had from the application of 'night soil' or sewage, concluding that the farmer might profitably give a halfpenny per ton for it, but no more than that, for the quantity required to produce any significant effect was substantial, and there was some contemporary suspicion that he may have deflated its worth due to his self-interest in the artificial fertilizer industry.[234] From 1847 experiments with farm animals also began, examining the effects of variations in diet on bodyweight, relative development of different parts of the animal and upon milk yield and composition. The unique feature of Rothamsted was, and is, the long unbroken continuity of the experiments conducted. Lawes' name is particularly associated with that of the chemist J. Henry Gilbert, with whom he enjoyed a long and fruitful partnership.[235]

Lawes himself, listed in the census as a "gentleman" and classified appropriately in our occupational table, lived on his estate at Rothamsted in 1851 with his wife, Caroline, his seven year-old son Charles Bennet, his six year-old daughter Caroline, and 13 servants covering the full range of duties, including one William Wade "vermin destroyer". Joseph H.J. Gilbert, "scientific and agricultural chemist" is also listed, living more humbly in The Village with his wife and just one general servant. But apart from Lawes and Gilbert, the prime movers behind the enterprise, there were four others engaged at Rothamsted at this date: Henry King, "laboratory man, agricultural chemical laboratory", William Simion, an assistant in the same laboratory, John Frederick Saunders, "engaged in connection with the science of agricultural chemistry" and George C. Churchill, "attorney and solicitor (not in practise) engaged in connection with the science of agricultural chemistry". It was these men who together led not merely the nation but the world in the development of an industry that has so profoundly affected agricultural practice ever since, and if for no other reason than this Harpenden has staked its claim to a place in history.

We will be exploring the agrarian structure of Harpenden and the rest of this region shortly, but before we do there is another industry, lying towards the other end of the technological spectrum from agricultural chemistry to consider – the straw plait trade – which, as we have seen, was thriving at mid-century. Here again we find a sense in which town and countryside, far from being separate entities, were inter-twined in a symbiotic relationship. For although a proportion of the straw plait used in the St Albans hat industry was produced in the town itself, the contribution of its hinterland was of far greater importance. Only some 120 or so straw plaiters could be traced in the town's three main parishes, for the great majority of those working in the straw industry here were engaged in the making up of hats. In the rural hinterland there was a total of 1,717 individuals working in straw, just 122 men (7%) but 1,595 women (93%), providing employment for 28% of the total occupied population, and for as much as 62% of the occupied female population. Here, however, the great majority were straw plaiters rather than hat or bonnet makers, 1,404 in all or 82% of the total.[236] Of these 94% were female, and just 6% male, almost identical figures to those for the straw industry as a whole.

---

234   N. Goddard, " 'A Mine of Wealth'? The Victorians and the Agricultural Value of Sewage", *Journal of Historical Geography*, Vol. 22 (1996), p. 277; J. Sheail, "Town Wastes, Agricultural Sustainability and Victorian Sewage", *Urban History*, Vol. 23 (1996), pp. 200-3.

235   W. Fream, "In Memoriam. Sir John Bennet Lawes, Bart.", *Journal of the Royal Agricultural Society*, 3rd series, Vol. 11 (1900), pp. 511-24; G.V. Dyke, *John Bennet Lawes: the Record of his Genius* (Taunton, 1991), pp. viii, 1-9. Lawes' experiments at Rothamsted are described in the contemporary account of J. Caird, *English Agriculture in 1850-51*, 2nd edition (London, 1968), pp. 459-64. For greater detail see Sir J.B. Lawes and Sir J.H. Gilbert, *The Rothamsted Experiments, being an Account of Some of the Results of the Agricultural Investigations Conducted at Rothamsted* (Edinburgh, 1895); Sir J.H. Gilbert, *Agricultural Investigations at Rothamsted, England, During a Period of Fifty Years* (Washington, 1895); A.D. Hall, *The Book of the Rothamsted Experiments* (London, 1905).

236   The figure of 1,404 includes two women described as "plaiter and bonnet sewer".

The industry was far from evenly spread between parishes. Those areas that we have designated 'rural' but which lay within the Liberty of St Albans generally depended less on the straw trade than did the outlying villages with the notable exception of Sandridge, which had more in common with the Liberty in this respect than with the villages, a feature we also discovered when examining crafts and trades generally.[237] Indeed, the proportion of the occupied population engaged in the straw industry in the Liberty as a whole is in fact slightly less than for the town proper. Furthermore, straw hat-making or bonnet sewing generally occupied a higher percentage of those employed in the straw industry in these rural parishes within the Liberty than in the villages, a little over one-third of the total, and we must also remember that there were significant concentrations of Brazilian hat-makers in St Stephens, the Out-hamlets and in Sandridge as well. That said, of the 298 individuals engaged in the straw trade in St Michaels (rural), St Stephens and the Out-hamlets, 190 were plaiters – some 70 more than the total in the three parishes within the borough – or nearly two-thirds of the total number of straw workers found here. In Sandridge, as many as 56 of the 65 straw workers were plaiters, 86% of the total, a figure very similar to that discovered in the other villages. As we move from town to countryside, therefore, the balance between hat-making and plaitmaking gradually changes, with those parishes lying closer to the town proper showing greater involvement in the hat industry – whether straw hat, Brazilian hat-making or a combination of the two – and those lying farther afield concentrating much more heavily upon servicing the town by providing raw materials in the form of plaited straw.

The concentrations of straw workers found in the three villages of Harpenden, Redbourn and Wheathampstead are quite remarkable, a total of 1,354 individuals, accounting for 41%, 41% and 31% of their total occupied populations respectively. These figures are not dissimilar, however, to those discovered in the Berkhamsted region. There, in rural parishes such as Aldbury, Frithsden, Puttenham and Wigginton, the proportion of the total occupied population engaged in the industry was also slightly over 40%, in Little Gaddesden and Northchurch it stood at just under 30%, in Tring (part urban, part rural) at exactly one-third, and only in the town of Great Berkhamsted itself did it fall as low as one-fifth.[238] The difference here, of course, is that there was no hat-making industry at all, only plaiting and associated occupations, and hence the region was engaged purely in the processing of straw to supply the hat-makers of towns lying outside of the region itself. In the villages within the St Albans district, there was at least some small involvement in the working up of straw plait into hats. Redbourn led the way with a total of 85 individuals described as straw bonnet maker or sewer, but even here this amounted to only 16% of those engaged in the straw industry, and only 7% of the total occupied population. Harpenden could boast just 38 straw hat-makers or sewers, only 7% of its straw workers and just 3% of its occupied population, whilst in Wheathampstead there were just 28, 9% of all those employed in the straw industry and again just 3% of its occupied population. More specialised hat workers were even rarer, just two hat blockers and a single hat presser featuring in the three parishes put together. On the other hand, there was a relatively large number of straw and straw plait factors, again re-emphasising the basic business of these villages, and demonstrating that towns had no monopoly of the marketing process. Altogether there were 17 straw factors, 11 straw plait factors, plus a husband and wife team described as "merchants (straw and fancy goods)" in the three villages, which compares with a total of only eight straw plait factors in the three urban parishes of the borough of St Albans, and only two more in the

237   See above, p. 79.
238   Goose, *The Berkhamsted Region*, p. 30.

remainder of the urban liberty.[239] Again Redbourn stands out, including 20 of these 30 dealers, followed by Harpenden and Wheathampstead together with five each. In Redbourn there were also two straw dyers, and in Harpenden two straw plait bleachers.

The division of labour between the sexes in both the urban and the rural straw industry has been touched upon above, where it was noted that there was generally a higher male participation in town than in countryside.[240] Only 122 men or boys were involved in the trade in all of the rural parishes within and outside of the Liberty, just over 7% of the total and only 3.4% of the total occupied male population. This is a rather different picture from that found in the Berkhamsted region, where some 14% of all straw workers were male, accounting for as much as 8% of recorded male occupations.[241] In the rural parishes of the St Albans district the more specialist occupations – hat blocking, ironing, dying, straw cutting and bleaching – were dominated by men, whilst of the 32 straw or straw plait dealers found in the rural parishes 22 were men and just 10 women. Of these 10 women five worked in partnership with their husbands, the partnership extending to husband and son in the case of Ann Abbott of Lamb Lane, Redbourn, and hence there were only five women independently dealing in straw or plait. Conversely, men were less heavily concentrated than women in the more menial aspects of the trade: only 78 were plaiters, or 64%, which compares with 83% of the women involved in the industry. Furthermore, these 78 male plaiters, again in contrast to the Berkhamsted region, were overwhelmingly boys or adolescents.[242] Forty-three were under 10, 27 were aged 10-19, and only eight were 20 years of age or over. If we take the cut-off point for maturity to be 15, then in the entire rural part of the district, incorporating seven parishes or parts of parishes and a total occupied male population of 3,577, there were only 10 adult male straw plaiters. The likes of Joey Russell of Harpenden, recalled as plaiting whilst driving his geese down to Cock Pond and continuing for hours whilst sat on the churchyard wall opposite the green, were very much the exception rather than the rule.[243]

Historians such as Pamela Horn have suggested that male involvement in straw plaiting was quite marginal, usually forming a secondary occupation to be taken up when demand was particularly brisk, although the national census reports as well as local studies do indicate a degree of full-time male involvement.[244] The report for 1861 reveals that 2,128 males gave straw plaiting as their main occupation, of which 1,561 were under 20 years of age, leaving just 567 who were clearly adult. By contrast there were 27,739 female plaiters, and hence men and boys accounted for just 7.1% of the total, although contemporary testimony suggests that there was more part-time or seasonal male involvement that the census fails to reveal.[245] The Berkhamsted region thus exhibited substantially greater than average male involvement, particularly of adult males, showing the need once again for regional variation to be taken into account. The rural part of the St Albans

239   The census, of course, gives no indication of the scale of individual businesses.
240   See above, p. 72-3.
241   Goose, *The Berkhamsted Region*, p. 36.
242   In Aldbury, Tring and Wigginton almost exactly one-third of male straw workers were fifteen years of age or over, 77 of the 227 listed: Goose, *The Berkhamsted Region*, p. 36.
243   Grey, *Cottage Life*, pp. 83-4.
244   P. Horn, *The Rural World 1780-1850* (London, 1980), p. 254. In Edlesborough in Buckinghamshire in 1851, 25 male householders (7.5% of the total) gave straw plaiting as their main occupation, even though the majority of male plaiters were aged 5-14: Grof, *Children of Straw*, p. 51.
245   P. Horn, *The Victorian Country Child* (new edn., Stroud, 1990), p. 122; Grey, *Cottage Life*, p. 68: D. Thorburn, "Gender, Work and Schooling in the Plaiting Villages", *The Local Historian*, Vol. 19 (1989), pp. 111-12.

district, by contrast, exhibits lower than average male involvement, just 5.5% of all plaiters recorded being male, and including a derisory number of adults amongst them. This accords well with the reminiscences of Harpenden in the 1860s of Edwin Grey, who wrote of male involvement in straw plaiting in the following terms:

> The cottage industry of straw plaiting played a very important part in the village life of these days. Very many of the women and girls were engaged in it: some of the men and the lads were also good at the work, doing it at odd times, or in the evenings after farm work, but this home industry was always looked upon really as women's work, and although there were men and also lads who were wonderfully good at it, yet their plait hardly ever came up to the standard of that made by the women... There were some men and lads who though not good at making any of the finer sorts would make the rough and coarser plait called "whole straw"... but this variety when all finished off and ready for sale realized but a few pence per score yards...[246]

Grey goes on to describe how the women would plait as they strolled through the commons and meadows, looping their plait around their arms to keep it clear of the ground. With a few exceptions, however, men plaited less publicly, for "men looked upon this work as appertaining to the women, so that although many men and youths did the plaiting at nights or odd times they preferred to do the work indoors or in the close vicinity of their homes."[247] Notwithstanding the limited participation of adult men, Grey's testimony only serves to underline the importance of the straw industry to villages such as Harpenden and others like them, an importance which is quite clear from the census returns, and one which had crucial implications for the family economy.

---

246   Grey, *Cottage Life*, pp. 68-9.
247   *Ibid.*, p. 83.

The family economy

The census returns for this part of Hertfordshire reveal very high levels of female employment indeed, but are these figures a true and accurate representation of female employment? We can first consider the possibility that the census returns actually *over*state the contribution of women to the labour force of this region. Many historians have suggested that the straw plait trade was seasonal, Hooson going so far as to identify a distinct straw 'season' running from January to May.[248] Lucy Luck in her autobiography refers to the "dull season", and reports "the straw-work is very bad, as a rule, from July up to about Christmas", whilst in contrast another contemporary commentator, A.J. Tansley, reports that "plait is made all year round, except during the interruption of harvest time".[249] Similarly Edwin Grey gives no indication of any clear seasonality in Harpenden, and actually describes women strolling in the lanes or plaiting in groups in the fields during the summer months, which would overlap with Lucy Luck's "dull season" and also extend well beyond the plaiting season identified by Hooson. Only on market days, "or at least for the better part of it", was there a general cessation of plaiting, whilst gleaning appears to have taken priority over plaiting for a short time, "though undoubtedly the stay-at-homes still kept on with their plait work".[250]

Such contradictory testimonies are difficult to harmonise, but the fact that a distinction was drawn between summer plait and winter plait would seem to indicate clearly that any seasonality was a question of degree rather than kind, even though earnings might well fluctuate between the seasons as spring and summer plait was double the price of that made in autumn and winter.[251] As Tansley explains, "winter plait is never so good as when it is done in spring and summer, away from the fire or in the open air, at the cottage door, or along the green lane."[252] Furthermore, the respondents to the Poor Law Commissioners for Hertfordshire in 1832-4, a slack period for the trade, also indicate the availability of work all year round. Hence from Redbourn it was stated that earnings could be had "throughout the year", whilst in Shenley straw plaiting was the only work available to women in winter, and at both Stevenage and Welwyn the employment of women and children in the trade during winter was also specifically noted.[253] Given the apparent paucity of agricultural employment for women and children in the winter months, where straw plaiting was available it must have been a veritable blessing. Clearly, at the very least the trade was far less seasonal than is sometimes suggested, and was undoubtedly much less seasonal than was agriculture.[254] Although the census was taken at the height of straw plaiting activity in late March, therefore, it seems reasonable to regard the figures it provides for female employment in the straw trade as a guide to, largely, full-time employment.

Whether or not other occupations, perhaps particularly female ones, were strictly full-time is difficult to determine. Were the numerous women recorded in the census returns as charwomen, laundresses or needlewomen regularly employed on a full-time basis, or did they operate as so many do today in a largely part-time capacity? It is at least possible that, by regarding such jobs on a par with full-time male occupations,

248   Hooson, "The Straw Industry of the Chilterns", p. 343.
249   Burnett (ed.), *Useful Toil*, p. 77; Tansley, "On the Straw Plait Trade", p. 71.
250   Grey, *Cottage Life*, pp. 70, 90, 118-19.
251   Freeman, *Luton and the Hat Industry*, p. 12; P. Horn, "Child Workers in the Pillow Lace and Straw Plait Trades of Victorian Buckinghamshire and Bedfordshire", *Historical Journal*, Vol. 4 (1974), p. 789.
252   Tansley, "On the Straw Plait Trade", p. 72.
253   *Poor Law Report*, Parliamentary Papers 1834, Vol. XXX, pp. 222, 224, 225, 227.
254   Grof, *Children of Straw*, p. 111; and see below, pp. 106-9.

we are in danger once again of overstating women's work. Unfortunately, the census gives no insight into the work patterns of particular occupations, but it is at least pertinent to ask such questions, given that so much emphasis is placed in the literature upon the *under*-recording of women's work.

The census clearly does understate women's work in some instances. It is clear, for instance, that much part-time and seasonal agricultural work undertaken by women is not captured in the census enumerators' returns, a subject we will return to when discussing agriculture below.[255] But it has also been suggested that under-recording of female employment may have gone far further than this. It has been argued that because the census returns were compiled by male enumerators and the schedules generally filled in by male household heads, "women tended to be defined as dependants, whatever their productive functions".[256] The Hertfordshire evidence examined to date shows that, as a generalisation, this statement is simply not true, for the occupational role of both single and married women is usually very accurately recorded. In south and west Hertfordshire the census reveals extremely high female participation rates, which would simply not have been apparent had women's work been so generally ignored by the enumerators. There are, however, two circumstances where under-recording of women's work may indeed have taken place. The first is when, on odd occasions, the enumerator clearly *did* subsume the wife under the husband's occupation, of which we have found a clear example in two Wheathampstead enumeration districts, and hence such faulty returns have simply to be excluded.[257] The second is in the case of a range of craft and, perhaps especially, retail trades, both in town and countryside. The fact that widows, on occasion, appear to have taken over their husbands' businesses after their deaths might well imply fuller involvement whilst they lived than the record appears to show. Enumerators were often unclear about what they were expected to do in the case of relatives, and – as in Great Berkhamsted – simply listed all wives and children as "carpenter's son", "brazier's daughter" and so forth, even in the case of very small infants who cannot possibly have been actively involved in their father's trade. Some did indeed clearly indicate husband and wife businesses, and we have identified a number of these above. Others gave them no occupational designation at all, even in the case of service occupations such as inns and pubs where it is highly likely that wives would have actively participated in the business.[258]

Rather than making blanket generalisations about the unreliability of the returns as a true reflection of women's work, therefore, we need to examine individual enumerations carefully, preferably on a regional basis, to look for internal and external consistency, and for clear evidence of under-representation of women and especially wives. For the great majority of enumerations that have been examined so far for south and west Hertfordshire, women's work appears to have been consistently and reliably recorded, notwithstanding the special case of seasonal agricultural employment. In the case of communities with large numbers of crafts and tradespeople, notably towns, we must simply accept that there is likely to be some understatement of female involvement, particularly in the middle ranks of society, where informal participation in family business has gone unrecognised. It may be, however, that there is also some overstatement of women's employment towards the lower end of the social scale, particularly in the town, and that the figures for this area of Hertfordshire,

255   See pp. 106-9.
256   Higgs, "Women, Occupations and Work", pp. 60-2.
257   See below, p. 89.
258   The published census report agrees, and hence specifically returns the wives of innkeepers, beer shop-keepers, shopkeepers, butchers, farmers and shoemakers as in employment: see fn. 152 above.

particularly in the rural parishes, may be buoyed up by the straw plait trade which was at its height when the census was taken.

One of the key discoveries to emerge from analysis of the 1851 census for the Berkhamsted region was the extremely high levels of female and child employment found there, which were largely the product of the existence of the thriving straw plait industry.[259] The importance of straw plaiting, bonnet making and Brazilian hat-making in the St Albans district exerted a similar effect, showing that these opportunities for women and children, far from being localised, extended over a considerable geographical area. The female occupational participation rate for England and Wales given in the 1871 census was 31%, and for Scotland 28%.[260] The Berkhamsted data, which like the data employed here also incorporated women and children of all ages, revealed an overall female occupational participation rate approaching 47%, compared with just under 65% for males, with the lowest female figure found in the town of Great Berkhamsted itself where it stood at 41%.[261] For the St Albans district as a whole the figures were virtually identical, female occupational participation also approaching 47%, whilst the figure for males was 66%.[262] Here, however, there was very little difference between town and countryside. A slightly higher proportion of men and boys were dependent in the town as compared with the surrounding rural parishes, but female participation was almost identical.

There appears, therefore, to be a notable difference between Great Berkhamsted and St Albans in terms of female employment prospects, but we need to explore further to establish this, in case there is a coincidental demographic explanation. We have seen that there was great similarity between the two regions in terms of overall sex ratios, and the marital status and age structures of their populations.[263] If we compare the town of Great Berkhamsted more closely with the three parishes of the borough of St Albans, the figures are again almost identical. There was a marginally greater skew towards women in St Albans than in Great Berkhamsted, which if anything might create greater competition between women for available employment, and hence favour female employment in Great Berkhamsted rather than in St Albans. But if we look at those categories of the population most likely to be dependent – the widowed, those aged under 15 and over 60 - the figures for the two towns are virtually the same.[264] The tabulations for both towns upon which these comparisons are based do, of course, incorporate both sexes, but a further breakdown by sex shows that the 'potentially dependent' female population was in fact larger in St Albans than in Great Berkhamsted. In the former town 31.8% of females were aged under 15, compared with 30.7% in the latter, whilst 8.8% were aged 60 and over compared with 7.3%. The higher female occupational participation rate in the town of St Albans as compared with Great Berkhamsted is thus not a reflection of any easily identifiable demographic divergence, but is a real reflection of the greater economic opportunities for women that the larger of the two towns had to offer.

Within the St Albans district there are substantial differences between parishes, and again a familiar pattern emerges of a general divergence between the rural parishes within the urban Liberty, and those within the

259   Goose, *The Berkhamsted Region*, pp. 37-43.
260   E. Roberts, *Women's Work, 1840-1940* (Cambridge, 1988), Table 1.2, p. 11.
261   Goose, *The Berkhamsted Region*, p. 37.
262   See Table 2, pp. 40-1.
263   Above, pp. 34, 37.
264   Goose, *The Berkhamsted Region*, Table 1, p. 27, and compare Table 1, p. 34, above.

borough and the outlying villages. The rural parishes within the Liberty, taken as a group, provided substantially fewer employment opportunities for women than did the other parishes, no doubt a reflection of the lesser importance of the straw plait and hat trade here and the absence of the countervailing opportunities that the town proper could provide. Here only 40% of the female population were occupied, a figure matched only by the village of Sandridge, which again reveals its close identity with suburban St Albans rather than with the three more substantial villages. On the face of it Wheathampstead, despite heavy involvement in the straw industry, also exhibits a relatively low proportion of occupied females, at 39%, but there is clearly a problem with the enumeration of married women's work in two of the village's three enumeration districts. In enumeration district 1a for Wheathampstead, 75% of married women are given an occupational designation, in 1b just 2% *(sic)*, the rest being recorded as wife to their husband's occupation ("agricultural labourer's wife", etc.), and in district 1c the proportion is just 4% with nothing at all entered for the vast majority of married women.[265] There is a similar, but less pronounced, problem with district 4b for Sandridge, which may mean that the prospects for women here were not quite as bleak as Table 2 suggests. In the case of Wheathampstead, however, the distortion is clear, the figures for female employment in Table 2 are severely suspect, and for this reason these particular enumeration districts have been excluded in the consideration of married women's work which is to follow.[266] In Harpenden the enumerations were conducted more reliably, producing the remarkable figures for the village shown in Table 2. Here the female occupational participation rate stood as high as 62%, almost approaching the figure for men in the parish and standing substantially above the female figure for every other parish, both within and without the borough of St Albans. The employment of adult (aged 15 or over) and married women, those unmarried and those widowed, is treated separately in Table 7.

For England and Wales as a whole just under 26% of all females aged 15 or over were in employment in 1851, whilst in the Berkhamsted region of south-west Hertfordshire the figure stood as high as 57%.[267] In the St Albans district, however, the proportion was higher still, at 63%, or 66% if the three suspect enumeration districts are excluded from the analysis. Figures of this order of magnitude have been discovered before for individual parishes, such as Great Horwood in Buckinghamshire,[268] or Cardington in Bedfordshire where 67% of females aged 15 or over were recorded as being in employment.[269] For Cardington, where lace-making provided the bulk of female employment, with straw plaiting playing a supporting role, it has been claimed that "The effect of cottage industry on the labour-force participation profiles of females was remarkable and perhaps even unique".[270] Far from Cardington being unique, however, figures in excess of 60% were quite commonly found in parishes in the St Albans region, as well as in other parts of south-west Hertfordshire.[271]

---

265 The two enumeration districts were examined closely for differences in terms of social structure that might account for this discrepancy, but proved to be very similar.

266 The fact that the percentages of unmarried women aged 20+ and widows employed in Wheathampstead compare favourably with other parishes underlines the view that married women's work was under-recorded here.

267 Best, *Mid-Victorian Britain*, p. 119; Goose, *The Berkhamsted Region*, pp. 37-8.

268 In Great Horwood 55% of the total female population were employed in 1871, mainly in lace-making, which would imply a very high level of employment for those aged 15 plus: P. Horn, "Victorian Villages from Census Returns", *The Local Historian*, Vol. 15 (1982), Table 2, p. 27.

269 Calculated from O. Saito, "Who Worked When? Lifetime Profiles of Labour-force Participation in Cardington and Corfe Castle in the Late-eighteenth and Mid-nineteenth Centuries", in Mills and Schürer (eds.), *Local Communities*, Table 16.2, p. 190.

270 *Ibid.*, p. 198. See also N.L. Tranter, "The Social Structure of a Bedfordshire parish in the Mid-nineteenth Century. The Cardington census Enumerators' Books, 1851", *International Review of Social History*, Vol. 18 (1973), pp. 90-106.

271 In Frithsden and Northchurch 65% and 61% of females aged 15 plus were employed, whilst the figure stood just a little lower at 59% in Little Gaddesden, Tring and Wigginton: Goose, *The Berkhamsted Region*, Table 4, p. 38.

Indeed, as a regional survey the Hertfordshire data is far more impressive, for no previous study has revealed such high female participation rates across such a wide geographical area, encompassing a total population of almost 18,000 individuals.

TABLE 7 : WORKING WOMEN

	Age 15 +			Married			Never Married Age 20 +			Widows		
	No.	Occ.	%	No.	Occ.	%	No.	Occ.	%	No.	Occ.	%
St Albans Urban												
St Albans	1225	747	61.0	549	183	33.3	349	307	88.0	137	108	78.8
St Michaels (Urban)	394	253	64.2	175	59	33.7	118	110	93.2	45	31	68.9
St Peters	972	546	56.2	415	125	30.1	278	226	81.3	131	80	61.1
St Albans Rural												
St Michaels (Rural)	299	148	49.5	145	36	24.8	77	65	84.4	25	17	68.0
St Stephens	487	275	56.5	260	88	33.8	101	87	86.1	55	38	69.1
Out-hamlets	437	238	54.5	260	106	40.8	74	55	74.3	36	28	77.8
Harpenden	674	555	82.3	335	248	74.0	162	146	90.1	77	68	88.3
Redbourn	727	504	69.3	373	213	57.1	156	124	79.5	66	49	74.2
Sandridge	269	142	52.8	135	23	17.0	77	68	88.3	17	11	64.7
Wheathampstead	584	287	49.1	332	75	22.6	116	102	87.9	47	36	76.6
Sub-Totals												
St Albans (Liberty)	3814	2207	57.9	1804	597	33.1	997	850	85.3	429	302	70.4
Urban Parishes	2591	1546	59.7	1139	367	32.2	745	643	86.3	313	219	70.0
Rural Parishes	3477	2149	61.8	1840	789	42.9	763	647	84.8	323	247	76.5
Total	6068	3695	60.9	2979	1156	38.8	1508	1290	85.5	636	466	73.3
Adjusted Figures*												
Rural Parishes	2929	1944	66.4	1526	774	50.7	653	554	84.8	279	218	78.1
Total	5520	3490	63.2	2665	1141	42.8	1398	1197	85.6	592	437	73.8

*Excludes districts 1b and 1c (Wheathampstead) and 4b (Sandridge)

The distinctiveness of the St Albans region is underlined if we turn to employment rates amongst married women. Female employment during the Industrial Revolution is so often associated with the opportunities provided in the rapidly expanding cotton textile trade of industrial Lancashire, or with the pottery industry of the Midland counties, notably Staffordshire. In the large cotton textile town of Preston in 1851 26% of all wives living with their husbands worked, whilst in the seven Lancashire registration districts studied by Margaret Hewitt, 30% of married women were employed in industrial occupations.[272] In the Staffordshire Potteries women made up one-third of the labour force in 1861, but here the age structure of the female labour force was relatively youthful, and only 14% of all married women worked in the pottery industry according to the most recent study, a figure that stands substantially below the more conventionally cited figure of approximately 30%.[273] Whatever the precise proportion in the Potteries, these figures for the advancing industrial regions of the country all fall short of the 35% of married women found in employment in the Berkhamsted region of Hertfordshire. [274] Once again, however, they fall even further short of the percentages discovered in the St Albans district, where the adjusted totals reveal that fully 43% of married women were

272 Anderson, *Family Structure in Nineteenth Century Lancashire*, pp. 71, 208 fn. 32.

273 M.W. Dupree, *Family Structure in the Staffordshire Potteries 1840-1880* (Oxford, 1995), pp. 147-8, 169-70. Cf. Harrison, *The Early Victorians*, p. 103.

274 Goose, *The Berkhamsted Region*, p. 37.

officially recorded to be in employment across the region as a whole. The importance of cottage industry to female employment is thus once again underlined, and in this respect the decline of such industries from the mid-nineteenth century forwards must have had serious implications for family incomes.[275] In the St Albans region, however, the remarkably high rates of employment of women in general, and of married women in particular, were the product of a combination of a thriving cottage industry in straw plait, opportunities both within and outside of the factories in the straw hat trade and, to a lesser extent, in silk production, in the domestic manufacture of Brazilian hats which developed upon the back of the straw hat trade, and in the openings provided in the economy of St Albans which - despite its relatively modest size – offered substantial employment in the more humble service and domestic service sectors, besides supporting a sizeable number of women of independent means.

There was considerable variation between parishes, both for adult women generally and for those who were married. Comparing town with countryside, the adjusted figures show slightly higher overall female employment rates in the rural areas, despite the fact that the rural areas within the Liberty exhibit a lower proportion (54.1%) than does the town. For married women, however, the position was rather different, with St Stephens and the Out-hamlets showing higher levels of female employment than the town as a whole, due to the existence of substantial participation in straw and Brazilian hat-making here. In St Michaels (rural), however, with its very heavy dependence upon domestic service as a source of employment for women, the proportion of married women working was, not surprisingly, distinctly low. It was the villages, however, that led the way, exhibiting levels of employment amongst married women substantially above the borough of St Albans itself. Sandridge again looks to be the exception, although it must be recalled that there is a question mark over the accuracy of the recording of married women's work here that might have prejudiced the results. In Wheathampstead there is no doubt that married women's employment was severely under-recorded: if we use the one clearly reliable enumeration district as a proxy for the village as a whole, then 75% of married women were in fact in work here, not the 23% shown in Table 7. This remarkable figure is equalled by the village of Harpenden, with 74% of married women in employment, whilst in Redbourn the figure of 57% stands substantially above the urban proportion and well above all of the parishes in the Berkhamsted region. Only in Cardington, where "about two-thirds" of married women worked, have figures approaching this level been reported before,[276] but this is just one parish, and it is the high level of employment of married women across the St Albans district as a whole, if in Harpenden and Wheathampstead in particular, that renders it so exceptional, at least in the current state of research.

Table 7 also gives information concerning those women aged 20 and over who remained single, as well as about widows. For unmarried women there is a quite consistent picture across the region, 86% overall in employment, with limited variation between parishes and no urban-rural divide. The figure for the Out-hamlets stood a little below the average, at 74%, but there are only 19 women involved here, and it is quite possible that this is an example of the under-recording of women's work in service industries discussed above, and in agriculture, to be discussed below.[277] Three of these unmarried women lived in pubs or victualling houses, and most probably served the family business. Five more were farmer's daughters, two of whom were

---

275   In some parishes the disappearance of cottage industries had already exerted an impact by 1851, in Corfe Castle in Devon, for instance: Saito, "Who Worked When?", p. 195. The longer term implications of the decline of trades such as hand lace-making, glove-making and – later in the century – of straw plait deserves further consideration.

276   Saito, "Who Worked When?", p. 195. A small sample for Colyton in Devon revealed an occupational participation rate amongst married women of 56%, with lace-making again an important source of employment: R. Wall, "Work, Welfare and Family", in Bonfield, Smith and Wrightson (eds.), *The World We Have Gained*, pp. 279-82.

277   See pp. 87, 106-9.

34 years old, and again it is at least likely that they worked on the farm in one capacity or another. Three more were visitors, and for this reason their occupation may have gone unrecorded. One was an elderly almswoman. The rest were young women still at home whose parents were presumably willing and able to support them. There was, therefore, probably nothing unusual about the Out-hamlets, but this more detailed look at this area does warn that the figures for the employment of unmarried women over 20 given in Table 7 should be regarded as *minima*.

To explore in detail the family circumstances of these apparently 'unemployed' women is a task too time-consuming to undertake here, but a glance at the parish of St Albans suggests that they were a diverse group. Some, such as Jessie Langridge the daughter of Edward Langridge, "justice and councillor and wine merchant", lived in households headed by professional men, and may thus have simply lived a life of leisure. Others (four in St Albans parish) were visitors, whose occupations may thus have gone unrecorded.[278] A couple lived in victualling/lodging houses, and may in fact have been employed there. A few lived with elderly relatives, such as Sarah Mates, 35, who lived with her father, a 67 year-old widower and Chelsea Pensioner, and these may therefore have in fact served as unpaid housekeepers, although in this respect they would be in the same position as numerous 'unemployed' wives. Hannah and Elizabeth Wiles, aged 43 and 32 respectively, are given no occupational designation, but they lived with their 79 year-old widowed mother, Hannah, who was a baker, and almost certainly would have been involved in the family business. A couple were themselves elderly, and retired or living on alms. The situation in the case of Alice, Ann and Emma Martin, aged 42, 39 and 36 respectively, is more difficult to fathom. They lived in Market Place with their younger, unmarried brother, Henry Gillam Martin – a chemist – but are all described in the census as "hatter's daughter". The position of others, those given no occupational designation at all or those described as "tailor's daughter", "carpenter's daughter" and so forth, is equally impossible to determine without further information.

In rural parishes such as Harpenden we meet a narrower range of ostensibly 'unoccupied' spinsters, although only 16 are represented here in this category. Of these seven lived in the household of a professional or landed father, and can thus be numbered amongst the leisured but no doubt cultivated classes. Six were farmer's daughters, two specified as such, two as "farmer's daughter at home" and two more with no designation at all. Elizabeth Rowe, 50, lived with her brother, a 71 year-old blacksmith, and may have served as housekeeper. Just two were daughters of trade or craftsmen. The balance in rural areas therefore, unsurprisingly, was somewhat different, although again one might speculate that at least some of these women worked in their family business, particularly on the farm. If this was indeed the case then it is even clearer that few adult women in the St Albans district in 1851, whether in town or countryside, were able to escape employment without resorting to marriage.

Those who did indeed marry but had outlived their partners also had to find a living, and Table 7 shows that almost three-quarters of widows across the district as a whole were officially recorded as in employment. With regard to the debate over whether widows relied mainly upon poor relief or upon employment, therefore, our region – exceptional though it is in terms of employment opportunities for women – clearly supports those who have emphasised the importance of work.[279] Again there is only a relatively small difference between the

---

278   Two of them are described as "visitor" in the 'relation to head of household' column and again as "visitor" under 'occupation'.

279   D. Thomson, "Workhouse to Nursing Home: Residential Care of the Elderly in Nineteenth Century England", *Ageing and Society*, Vol. 3 (1983), pp. 43-70; *idem*, "The Decline of Social Welfare: Falling State Support for the Elderly since Early Victorian Times", *Ageing and Society*, Vol. 4 (1984), pp. 451-82; E.H. Hunt. "Paupers and Pensioners: Past and Present", *Ageing and Society*, Vol. 9 (1990), pp. 407-30. Relative opportunities for employment in different communities would clearly affect the possibility of widows retaining

three urban parishes and the rest, but a greater difference between the borough and the four villages, where overall employment rates for widows were higher, although again Sandridge conforms more closely to the urban Liberty than to the other three parishes. We have already discussed the heavy concentration of widows amongst the lowlier service trades in the town of St Albans, charring, washing and laundering.[280] We have also considered the situation of the 131 widows in St Peters parish, 80 of whom were given occupational designations, and found above average proportions at the other end of the social scale, living as annuitants, fundholders or property owners, roughly one-quarter of the total. The remainder pursued a variety of trades though, as one might expect, with a heavy bias towards needlework, whether in dressmaking or in relation to the straw hat trade. Several worked as plaiters of straw or weavers of Brazilian hats, whilst as many as six of the 80 worked as nurses.

In the countryside, we have seen that in the four villages widows formed a smaller percentage of the total female population, that roughly twice as many proportionally were servants compared with urban St Peters, and there were fewer lodgers and visitors. Numbers towards the top of the social scale were similar due to the active involvement of many widows in farming, eleven in all, or as landed proprietors, whilst annuitants and fundholders could be found in these rural areas too, if in slightly smaller numbers. The most notable difference was the smaller numbers towards the bottom of the social scale, no doubt a reflection of the superior charitable endowments of the town compared with the countryside.[281] Unsurprisingly, most rural widows in this area worked as straw plaiters, 77 of the 164 employed, one dealt in plait and 10 more sewed bonnets. Charring, laundering and washing occupied 16 more, seven worked in the food and drink trades, and just six were needlewomen or dressmakers. The emphasis in terms of the employment of widows was thus again different, a reflection of the different thrust of the rural as compared with the urban economy, but both in town and in countryside a high percentage of widows worked for their living.

What of those widows who did not work? In the two urban parishes of St Albans and St Peters, 80 widows, 30% of the total, ostensibly fall into this category. Of these, 50 headed their own households. Most of these depended upon charity or parish relief, 33 being in receipt of alms or recorded as living in an almshouse, and four being described as paupers and thus presumably dependent upon outdoor poor relief. Twenty of the almswomen also have an occupation entered, usually in brackets, against their names, and it may well be that they were only partially dependent upon charity.[282] Six are described as "Almsperson (Annuitant)" which would clearly suggest that they had at least some alternative income. All four of those described as pauper lived with family, as did nine of the almswomen – most commonly unmarried daughters – and hence they also benefited from family earnings. Of the remaining 13 widowed household heads, eight lived with an array of children and/or grandchildren, whilst two lived with nephews and nieces. Thirty of the 80 did not head their household, and of these 20 were the mother or mother-in-law to the household head, and one was a sister. The balance was made up by three visitors, four lodgers – including the 91 year-old tramp, Elizabeth South, lodging for the night in Spicer Street – one prisoner in the gaol and one unknown. Widows in St Albans, therefore, made a variety of shifts to provide for their maintenance. Seventy per cent of them worked, and possibly a quarter of the remaining 80 worked at least part-time, although the census is unclear on this point.

economic independence, as it did in Nottinghamshire: S.O. Rose, "Widowhood and Poverty in Nineteenth-Century Nottinghamshire", in J. Henderson and R. Wall (eds.), *Poor Women and Children in the European Past* (London, 1994), pp. 281-3.

280   See above, pp. 36-7.

281   *Ibid.*

282   This view is supported by the fact that the Marlborough almshouses were intended for "elderly men and women in reduced circumstances, who have yet some small income of their own": Mason, *Gibb's Illustrated Handbook to St Albans*, pp. 88-9. It remains possible, however, that these entries indicate a previous occupation.

Fourteen per cent, roughly one in seven, were at least partially dependent upon charity, generally in the form of alms, but one-third of these also relied upon family support. Just 20 had joined the families of their offspring; one more lived with her sister.[283] If we add up all of those who relied at least partially on direct family support for their maintenance, we achieve a total of 34, showing that dependence upon charitable relief was therefore slightly more common for those widows without full-time employment than was dependence upon family.[284]

In the four villages, 43 of the 207 widows (21%) were ostensibly without employment, and just over half (22) headed their own households. Of these 10 were paupers, and hence a lower proportion depended upon charity than in the town, although here there was no private charity in the form of alms, just parish relief. Two of these paupers appear to have worked: 65 year-old Sarah Nash of Brewhouse Hill, Wheathampstead "Straw Plaiter (Pauper)", and Elizabeth Fensom, aged 59, of Lamb Lane, Redbourn, "Plaiter, 1s/6d per week from Redbourn parish". All but three lived with family, two more with lodgers and just one alone, and in this respect we again see a distinct difference between town and countryside, no doubt a product of the absence of accommodation in almshouses in the rural areas. Of the remaining 12 widowed heads, nine lived with family. One, 82 year-old Mary Pratt of Harpenden Lane, lived alone but is described as "supported by her children", another lived with a lodger and one more with a servant, also described as a pauper. Of the 21 who did not head their own household, 12 were mothers, step-mothers or mothers-in-law to the household head, five more lived with other relatives, and the balance is made up of three lodgers and a visitor. In the rural villages, therefore, a slightly higher proportion of all widows worked than in the town. A lower proportion, just 6%, depended upon charity, at least two of the ten concerned also worked and all but three also lived with family. A higher proportion had joined their family as a dependent, 17 out of 43 (40%) compared with 21 out of 80 (26%) in the town.[285] Adding up all of those who lived with family, as head of household or as a subordinate member, produces a total of 33, and thus the four villages again present a distinct contrast with the town of St Albans, for in the villages reliance upon the family amongst dependent widows was substantially more common than was resort to charitable relief.[286]

---

283   This would appear to contradict the conclusion reached from a detailed study of the parish of Colyton in Devon, from which it was concluded that "children, and particularly daughters, played a considerable part in caring for their elderly parents". The methodology employed in the Colyton study was, however, more sophisticated, involving employment of the extant family reconstitution data as well as the census returns: J. Robin, "Family Care of the Elderly in a Nineteenth-Century Devonshire Parish", *Ageing and Society*, Vol. 4 (1984), pp. 505-16.

284   Clearly we have only begun to explore the position of widows here, and have not been able to touch upon those receiving indoor workhouse relief or informal family assistance. There is great scope for more research into this subject.

285   This subject is returned to under the heading of household and family structure below, pp. 176-7.

286   Our conclusion for the rural parishes of the district, therefore, is more in line with the conclusion reached for Colyton, a rural parish of 2,500 people which incorporated a small market town: Robin, "Family Care of the Elderly". Rose's valuable study of two Nottinghamshire industrial villages remains rather vague over the relative importance of sources of support, concluding that widows relied upon "help from relatives, supplemented by parish relief and earnings", though the workhouse was very much a last resort: "Widows and Poverty in Nineteenth-Century Nottinghamshire", p. 287.

TABLE 8 : WORKING WOMEN BY AGE GROUP AND MARITAL STATUS

	Age 20-29						Age 30-39						Age 40-49					
	Married			Single			Married			Single			Married			Single		
	No.	Occ.	%	No.	Occ.	%	No.	Occ.	%	No.	Occ.	%	No.	Occ.	%	No.	Occ.	%
St Albans Urban																		
St Albans	128	52	40.6	206	186	90.3	162	52	32.1	81	63	77.8	126	43	34.1	30	28	93.3
St Michaels (Urban)	42	21	50.0	80	76	95.0	43	11	25.6	17	16	94.1	42	13	31.0	10	9	90.0
St Peters	83	28	33.7	157	137	87.3	120	39	32.5	59	44	74.6	105	35	33.3	28	21	75.0
St Albans Rural																		
St Michaels (Rural)	36	14	38.9	50	43	86.0	40	10	25	15	11	73.3	32	6	18.8	8	7	87.5
St Stephens	61	27	44.3	67	58	86.6	72	22	30.6	21	16	76.2	48	15	31.3	9	9	100.0
Out-hamlets	57	27	47.4	46	33	71.7	81	37	45.7	18	15	83.3	59	23	39.0	4	4	100.0
Harpenden	71	60	84.5	105	94	89.5	94	70	74.5	30	28	93.3	80	57	71.3	12	11	91.7
Redbourn	83	65	78.3	106	85	80.2	107	56	52.3	21	17	81.0	79	43	54.4	15	15	100.0
Sandridge	33	6	18.2	40	35	87.5	44	7	15.9	17	16	94.1	24	2	8.3	11	10	90.9
Wheathampstead	67	13	19.4	69	62	89.9	114	24	21.1	20	19	95.0	73	16	21.9	10	8	80.0
Sub-Totals																		
St Albans (Liberty)	407	169	41.5	606	533	88.0	518	171	33	211	165	78.2	412	135	32.8	89	78	87.6
Urban Parishes	253	101	39.9	443	399	90.1	325	102	31.4	157	123	78.3	273	91	33.3	68	58	85.3
Rural Parishes	408	212	52.0	483	410	84.9	552	226	40.9	142	122	85.9	395	162	41.0	69	64	92.8
Total	661	313	47.4	926	809	87.4	877	328	37.4	299	245	81.9	668	253	37.9	137	122	89.1
Adjusted Figures*																		
Rural Parishes	339	209	61.7	416	353	84.9	441	219	49.7	125	106	84.8	332	160	48.2	59	55	93.2
Total	592	310	52.4	859	752	87.5	766	321	41.9	282	229	81.2	605	251	41.5	127	113	89.0

*Excludes districts 1b and 1c (Wheathampstead) and 4b (Sandridge)

	Age 20-29						Age 30-39						Age 40-49					
Excluded districts	69	3	4.3	67	57	85.1	111	7	6.3	17	16	94.1	63	2	3.2	10	9	90.0

	Age 50-59						Age 60+					
	Married			Single			Married			Single		
	No.	Occ.	%	No.	Occ.	%	No.	Occ.	%	No.	Occ.	%
St Albans Urban												
St Albans	82	24	29.3	12	12	100.0	50	11	22.0	20	18	90.0
St Michaels (Urban)	27	9	33.3	7	6	85.7	21	5	23.8	4	3	75.0
St Peters	58	14	24.1	16	12	75.0	48	9	18.8	18	12	66.7
St Albans Rural												
St Michaels (Rural)	29	6	20.7	4	4	100.0	8	8	100.0	0	0	0.0
St Stephens	51	19	37.3	1	1	100.0	27	5	18.5	3	3	100.0
Out-hamlets	41	13	31.7	3	1	33.3	21	5	23.8	3	3	100.0
Harpenden	53	37	69.8	9	7	77.8	36	23	63.9	6	6	100.0
Redbourn	57	30	52.6	3	3	100.0	45	17	37.8	4	4	100.0
Sandridge	24	5	20.8	7	5	71.4	8	3	37.5	1	1	100.0
Wheathampstead	38	9	23.7	7	5	71.4	38	13	34.2	10	8	80.0
Sub-Totals												
St Albans (Liberty)	288	85	29.5	43	36	83.7	175	43	24.6	48	39	81.3
Urban Parishes	167	47	28.1	35	30	85.7	119	25	21.0	42	33	78.6
Rural Parishes	293	119	40.6	34	26	76.5	183	74	40.4	27	25	92.6
Total	460	166	36.1	69	56	81.2	302	99	32.8	69	58	84.1
Adjusted Figures*												
Rural Parishes	254	118	46.5	27	22	81.5	154	72	46.8	18	17	94.4
Total	421	165	39.2	62	52	83.9	273	97	35.5	60	50	83.3

*Excludes districts 1b and 1c (Wheathampstead) and 4b (Sandridge)

	Age 50-59						Age 60+					
Excluded districts	39	1	2.6	7	4	57.1	29	2	6.9	9	8	88.9

Returning to working women in general, Table 8 provides a breakdown by age group and marital status. The figures for single women amply confirm the position shown in Table 7, but show too that there was little or no respite for the high proportion of single women who had to work right through to the end of their lives. Across the region as a whole, 87.5% of single women in their twenties worked, as did 83.3% of single women aged 60

or over. There is, however, a degree of difference between town and countryside: more single women in their twenties worked in town than in country, 90% compared with 85%, whilst the position is reversed for the highest age category, the figures now standing at 79% and 94% respectively. Indeed, all but two single women aged 60 or over were in employment in the rural parishes. The discrepancy amongst young adults is no doubt the product of single women living at home on the farm but not officially recorded as in employment. The obverse difference amongst those aged 60 plus appears to be largely due to particularly low figures for the parish of St Peters, for St Albans parish exhibits a figure that approaches that found in the rural areas. Again the explanation lies in the availability of almshouse accommodation in St Albans, for four of the six apparently unoccupied in St Peters parish lived in the Marlborough Buildings. The numbers involved here are, of course, very small, but tend to support the conclusions drawn above regarding widows.

It was marriage that provided a way out of formal employment, if far less so in this region than in many other parts of the country, for employment levels amongst married women were, as we have seen, remarkably high. Nevertheless, if we compare married women with those who either remained single or had become widowed across the region as a whole, we find that 43% of the former worked compared with 82% of the latter, and thus married women had roughly double the chances of avoiding – or missing out on – paid employment. A feature held in common between town and countryside is the reduction in the proportion of married women in work in their thirties as compared with their twenties, a reduction of the order of 10 percentage points in each case, and which no doubt reflects the impact of the onset of child bearing and rearing. Child bearing *per se*, however, clearly did not persuade the majority of women to withdraw from employment, and in this respect we can contrast the situation in a region where cottage industry was predominant with those dominated by factory work, such as the Staffordshire Potteries.[287] Nor was there any further reduction in the proportion of married women working between their thirties and forties, in either town or countryside. So whilst it has been suggested that in cotton textile towns in both England and in France wives tended to withdraw from employment once their children were able to earn a wage,[288] the age profile of the working population of married women in the St Albans region would appear to indicate that no such mechanism operated here, again providing a contrast between factory work and cottage industry – a contrast that is also apparent from the age profile of the silk factory operatives in St Albans discussed above.[289]

Despite the similarities between town and country, there are interesting differences too. Firstly, employment was far more common for young married women in the rural parishes of the district, with some 62% in employment compared with 40% in the town.[290] Indeed, in Harpenden the figure rose as high as 85% – double the urban figure – and in Redbourn it stood at 78%. Here again we see the impact of the straw plait industry, providing ready employment for the wives of (largely) agricultural labourers whose earnings were modest at best. Secondly, whilst levels of employment decline in both town and countryside across the first two age cohorts, in the rural areas they then stabilise, to produce remarkably consistent proportions of married women

---

287 Dupree, *Family Structure in the Staffordshire Potteries*, pp. 169-70.

288 L.A. Tilly and J.W. Scott, *Women, Work and Family* (New York, 1978), p. 133. For a similar argument see, S. Horrell and J. Humphries, "Women's Labour Force Participation and the Transition to the Male Breadwinner Family, 1790-1865", *Economic History Review*, Vol. XLVIII (1995), p. 112.

289 See p. 75.

290 We must, of course, bear in mind the probability that some female urban employment, perhaps particularly amongst married women, may have gone unrecorded: see above, p. 87.

in employment through from those in their thirties to those aged 60 plus. The urban picture is, however, very different, for here married women tended to withdraw from employment once they reached their fifties, producing an enhanced urban-rural contrast for married women aged 50 and over. Thus whilst in the rural parishes 46% of married women aged 50 years or more worked, the urban figure was little more than half that, standing at just 25%. In the town, therefore, whilst fewer married women worked to begin with, a proportion of these took the opportunity to withdraw from employment as they advanced with age, a luxury that, in this region, was not available to their rural counterparts.

TABLE 9 : CHILD EMPLOYMENT BY AGE, SEX AND PARISH

| | Age 0-4 | | | | Age 5-9 | | | | Age 10-14 | | | |
| | M | | F | | M | | F | | M | | F | |
	No.	%	No.	%	No.	%	No.	%	No.	%	No.	%
St Albans Urban												
St Albans	1	0.6	2	1.0	13	6.2	22	12.0	71	41.5	77	41.6
St Michaels (Urban)	0	0.0	1	1.3	11	15.9	7	10.6	40	69.0	44	66.7
St Peters	1	0.7	1	0.7	22	13.5	10	6.9	38	29.9	74	53.2
St Albans Rural												
St Michaels (Rural)	0	0.0	0	0.0	2	4.4	3	5.1	20	45.5	17	40.5
St Stephens	0	0.0	0	0.0	5	5.3	5	5.2	50	60.2	33	37.1
Out-hamlets	0	0.0	1	0.9	10	11.5	14	14.9	44	56.4	36	47.4
Harpenden	2	1.6	3	2.4	12	9.2	20	17.2	52	54.7	58	50.0
Redbourn	0	0.0	0	0.0	23	18.7	40	29.4	67	55.8	75	62.0
Sandridge	0	0.0	0	0.0	0	0.0	3	4.9	38	70.4	14	31.1
Wheathampstead	0	0.0	1	0.7	14	9.6	29	24.2	64	54.2	60	56.1
Sub-Totals												
St Albans (Liberty)	2	0.3	5	0.7	63	9.4	61	9.5	263	46.9	281	47.1
Urban Parishes	2	0.5	4	0.9	46	10.4	39	9.9	149	41.9	195	50.0
Rural Parishes	2	0.3	5	0.7	66	9.7	114	16.7	335	56.6	293	49.2
Total	4	0.4	9	0.8	112	10.0	153	14.2	484	51.1	488	49.5

In the St Albans district, therefore, very substantial numbers of married women worked, even higher proportions than were found in the Berkhamsted region, hence contributing to the family wage economy or to family businesses. The economic structure of the region, again as in Berkhamsted, provided similar opportunities for children to supplement family budgets. Table 9 presents figures for the number and percentage of boys and girls employed in three age groups up to 14 years, together with percentages for the Berkhamsted region and available national data for ages 5-9 and 10-14. As in Berkhamsted, it is clear that very few children were employed below the age of five, just 13 in the entire district out of a total of 2,280. All but one worked in the straw plait or the hat industry, Henry Slough, age 4, of Catharine Lane in St Peters parish, one of eight children of William Slough, brickmaker, all recorded as assistants to their father. Harpenden had more than its share in this age group, all employed as straw plaiters, one as young as two years old and another two aged just three. Two more three year-olds worked in the parish of St Albans and in Sion Cottages in the Out-hamlets, a hat-maker and Brazilian hat-maker respectively. The Children's Employment Commissions of 1843 and 1864 had indeed found some children in plaiting schools as young as three years old, although concluding that most began work at four.[291]

---

291 *Children's Employment Commission: Second Report (Trades and Manufactures)*, Parliamentary Papers, 1843, Vol. XIII, p. 132; *Children's Employment Commission: Second Report*, 1864, p. xl; and see Tansley, "On the Straw Plait Trade", p. 71.

TABLE 10 : THE OCCUPATIONS OF CHILDREN BY AGE AND SEX

TOWN : St Albans, St Michaels (Urban), St Peters

	Age 0-4				Age 5-9				Age 10-14			
	M		F		M		F		M		F	
	No.	%	No.	%	No.	%	No.	%	No.	%	No.	%
No Occupation	350	87.9	369	87.2	164	37.1	138	34.9	92	25.8	82	21.0
Scholar	46	11.6	50	11.8	232	52.5	218	55.2	115	32.3	113	29.0
Straw Hat	1	0.3	2	0.5	12	2.7	8	2.0	36	10.1	92	23.6
Silk Industry	0	0.0	0	0.0	8	1.8	10	2.5	43	12.1	25	6.4
Brazilian Hat	0	0.0	2	0.5	10	2.3	9	2.3	22	6.2	31	7.9
Trimming Weaver	0	0.0	0	0.0	6	1.4	5	1.3	3	0.8	10	2.6
Domestic Service	0	0.0	0	0.0	1	0.2	1	0.3	4	1.1	18	4.6
Building Trades	1	0.3	0	0.0	2	0.5	4	1.0	5	1.4	6	1.5
Errand Boy	0	0.0	0	0.0	1	0.2	0	0.0	11	3.1	0	0.0
Straw Plaiter	0	0.0	0	0.0	2	0.5	2	0.5	0	0.0	6	1.5
Grass Opener	0	0.0	0	0.0	2	0.5	0	0.0	3	0.8	0	0.0
General Labourer	0	0.0	0	0.0	0	0.0	0	0.0	6	1.7	0	0.0
Dressmaker	0	0.0	0	0.0	0	0.0	0	0.0	0	0.0	6	1.5
Ag Lab/Shepherd	0	0.0	0	0.0	1	0.2	0	0.0	4	1.1	0	0.0
Food and Drink	0	0.0	0	0.0	0	0.0	0	0.0	4	1.1	0	0.0
Shoemaker	0	0.0	0	0.0	0	0.0	0	0.0	1	0.3	1	0.3
Other*	0	0.0	0	0.0	1	0.2	0	0.0	7	2.0	0	0.0
Total	398	100.0	423	100.0	442	100.0	395	100.0	356	100.0	390	100.0

* includes blacksmith, carman's assistant, chimney sweep, clerk, coal dealer's assistant, ostler, trainer, upholsterer's apprentice.

LIBERTY : St Michaels (Rural), Out-hamlets, St Stephens

	Age 0-4				Age 5-9				Age 10-14			
	M		F		M		F		M		F	
	No.	%	No.	%	No.	%	No.	%	No.	%	No.	%
No Occupation	254	92.4	256	95.5	81	35.7	100	40.2	36	17.6	43	20.8
Scholar	21	7.6	11	4.1	129	56.8	127	51.0	55	26.8	78	37.7
Ag Lab/Shepherd	0	0.0	0	0.0	5	2.2	0	0.0	90	43.9	0	0.0
Brazilian Hat	0	0.0	1	0.4	8	3.5	12	4.8	5	2.4	38	18.4
Straw Hat	0	0.0	0	0.0	1	0.4	4	1.6	1	0.5	23	11.1
Straw Plaiter	0	0.0	0	0.0	3	1.3	6	2.4	3	1.5	14	6.8
Domestic Service	0	0.0	0	0.0	0	0.0	0	0.0	8	3.9	6	2.9
Errand Boy	0	0.0	0	0.0	0	0.0	0	0.0	2	1.0	0	0.0
General Labourer	0	0.0	0	0.0	0	0.0	0	0.0	2	1.0	0	0.0
Other*	0	0.0	0	0.0	0	0.0	0	0.0	3	1.5	5	2.4
Total	275	100.0	268	100.0	227	100.0	249	100.0	205	100.0	207	100.0

* includes gamekeeper's helper, grass opener, grocer's son employed at home, laundress, needlewomen, nurse, shoemaker, silk winder.

VILLAGES : Harpenden, Redbourn, Sandridge, Wheathampstead

	Age 0-4				Age 5-9				Age 10-14			
	M		F		M		F		M		F	
	No.	%	No.	%	No.	%	No.	%	No.	%	No.	%
No Occupation	401	89.9	397	84.5	107	23.7	96	22.2	22	5.7	43	11.1
Scholar	43	9.6	69	14.7	295	65.4	245	56.6	144	37.2	139	35.7
Straw Plaiter(incl. cutter)	2	0.4	4	0.9	38	8.4	88	20.3	26	6.7	160	41.1
Ag Lab/Shepherd	0	0.0	0	0.0	11	2.4	1	0.2	155	40.1	0	0.0
Straw Hat	0	0.0	0	0.0	0	0.0	2	0.5	0	0.0	29	7.5
Domestic Service	0	0.0	0	0.0	0	0.0	0	0.0	7	1.8	8	2.1
Errand Boy	0	0.0	0	0.0	0	0.0	0	0.0	9	2.3	0	0.0
General Labourer	0	0.0	0	0.0	0	0.0	0	0.0	8	2.1	0	0.0
Brazilian Hat	0	0.0	0	0.0	0	0.0	1	0.2	0	0.0	6	1.5
Ostler/Groom	0	0.0	0	0.0	0	0.0	0	0.0	4	1.0	0	0.0
Food and Drink	0	0.0	0	0.0	0	0.0	0	0.0	4	1.0	0	0.0
Nurse	0	0.0	0	0.0	0	0.0	0	0.0	0	0.0	3	0.8
Wheelwright	0	0.0	0	0.0	0	0.0	0	0.0	2	0.5	0	0.0
Other*	0	0.0	0	0.0	0	0.0	0	0.0	6	1.6	1	0.3
Total	446	100.0	470	100.0	451	100.0	433	100.0	387	100.0	389	100.0

* includes apprentice carpenter, chimney sweep, apprentice dressmaker, hairdresser/glover's assistant, ropemaker, apprentice shoemaker, apprentice tailor.

Edwin Grey's reminiscences of Harpenden provide a similar indication: "The children, both boys and girls, learned to plait when very young; a friend of mine assured me that she had her first plaiting lesson when only three years old... at four years of age she had become so advanced in the art that she was able to earn 1s 6d per week by her plaiting".[292] If some started to earn at four, however, our figures indicate that very few indeed were recorded as gainfully employed at such a young age.

Whilst only 1-2% of girls and boys aged 5-9 in England and Wales were officially employed, the figures for the St Albans district were far higher: five times as high for boys and ten times as high for girls, at 10% and 14% respectively. The district as a whole could not challenge the very high overall proportions employed in this age group in the Berkhamsted region, where straw plaiting dominated child employment in every parish, but in the three plaiting parishes of Harpenden, Redbourn and Wheathampstead similar figures were indeed achieved. Redbourn stood out from all other parishes in providing the most substantial opportunities for children of both sexes, with almost one in five boys aged 5-9 in employment, and well over one in four girls. Table 10 indicates the type of employment available: in the villages straw plait dominated with agricultural labour playing a supporting role for boys, whilst in the rural part of the Liberty of St Albans, where child employment was lower overall, Brazilian hat weaving was the main source of employment with plaiting second. The town, with its more developed economy, offered a wider range of openings, although again the straw hat and Brazilian hat trades and the associated occupation of trimming weaver led the rankings, and relatively few were employed in other occupations in this age group. In the town slightly more boys were employed than girls, in the Liberty there was an almost equal balance, whilst in the villages nearly twice as many girls were employed as boys, again reflecting the predominant role played by women – even very young women – in the straw plaiting trade.

At ages 10-14 the St Albans figures again stand well above those for England and Wales, and now also challenge the numbers found in the Berkhamsted region. For boys 51% were employed in this age group, compared with 45% in the Berkhamsted region and just 37% in England and Wales. The figure for girls was very similar at 50%, a little below the Berkhamsted total of 56% but some two and a half times the 20% employed nationally. The county figures for this age group stood at 42% and 26% for boys and girls respectively, and are again comfortably exceeded in the St Albans district, but more particularly in the case of girls.[293] For both sexes, therefore, the region stands out as a substantial employer of children, providing work for considerable numbers of 5-9 year-olds where opportunities generally across the country were extremely limited, and substantially greater prospects for young teenagers, with girls enjoying an enormous advantage over their counterparts elsewhere. Whilst in many other regions of the country the problem by mid-century was the under-employment or unemployment of children, the scale of both domestic and factory based industry in the St Albans district create opportunities here which were quite exceptional.[294]

Just as for female employment, child labour in the Industrial Revolution has been commonly associated with factory work, and it has been the conditions of child labour in factories and mines that has attracted both contemporary and historical attention and debate. Most historians now accept that the Sadler Committee's

---

292   Grey, *Cottage Life*, pp. 70-1.
293   Cunningham, "The Employment and Unemployment of Children", Tables 3 and 4, pp. 144-5.
294   *Ibid.*, pp. 139-47. See also *idem, Children and Childhood in Western Society Since 1500* (Harlow, 1995), p. 83; P. Horn, *Children's Work and Welfare, 1780-1890* (Cambridge, 1994), p. 7 and *passim*.

report of 1835 was biased and partisan, but it formed the basis for contemporary condemnation of child labour and has fuelled the fury of many influential historians writing across the present century.[295] However, more recent assessments, even those concerned to condemn the increased intensity of child exploitation associated with factory work, have appreciated that through into the later nineteenth century "the most prevalent form of child labour was within the home or within the family economy".[296] Indeed, a recent estimate has concluded that as late as 1871 only 8.4% of children aged 10-14 were employed in factories and workshops, and that these formed less than one-third of the total employment of this age group.[297] Factory employment was heavily concentrated in the cotton textile industry of Lancashire, and in the woollen and worsted industries of the West Riding of Yorkshire, and this concentration rendered it highly visible, a potent symbol of the cutting edge of new technological processes that pointed the way to the future. Only the West Riding, however, with 52%, could match the proportion of the male population aged 10-14 in employment in the St Albans district in 1851, whilst at 44% the Lancashire figure stood substantially lower. Neither could approach the figure for female employment, both achieving roughly one-third as compared with the 50% found here.[298]

The cottage employment available to children in the St Albans and Berkhamsted districts of Hertfordshire was therefore the norm rather than the exception, although even here we can find both domestic *and* factory employment, the latter in the form of the silk industry where, as we have seen, 62% of silk workers were under the age of 20.[299] The silk industry was, in fact, the second largest employer of children in the town of St Albans after the straw hat trade, and was particularly important to the 10-14 age group, whilst straw hat-making was itself partly factory based. In terms of overall numbers silk was followed quite closely by the domestic industry of Brazilian hat-making, but it was also the leading employer of boys in the town. The town once again had a wider range of employment to offer 10-14 year-olds than did the rural parts of the district, despite the concentration in the key industries, although this range was appreciably wider for boys than for girls, reflecting employment patterns by sex for all ages.

Straw plait still dominated female employment at ages 10-14 in the villages, now supported by employment in the making of hats, and the only other female occupations found were in domestic service and nursing, with just one apprentice dressmaker in all four villages. Male employment in this age group, however, was now dominated by agricultural labour, a tendency that was also noted in the Berkhamsted region but one that is far more pronounced here.[300] Whilst in Berkhamsted the competing pull of straw plaiting left male agricultural employment at under half the 25% reported for Northamptonshire in 1851, in the villages of the St Albans district, and in the rural parts of the Liberty too, over 40% of this age group were agricultural workers. The rural parishes of the Liberty straddle the experience of town and country, hat-making still dominating female employment as in the town, but agricultural labour now by far the leading source of employment for boys.

295   J.L. and B. Hammond, *The Town Labourer* (London, 1932); E.P. Thompson, *The Making of the English Working Class* (Penguin edn., Harmondsworth, 1968), pp. 366-8; C. Nardinelli, *Child Labor and the Industrial Revolution* (Bloomington Indiana, 1990), pp. 1-8.
296   Thompson, *The Making of the English Working Class*, p. 367.
297   Nardinelli, *Child Labor and the Industrial Revolution*, p. 5.
298   M. Winstanley (ed.), *Working Children in Nineteenth-Century Lancashire* (Preston, 1995), Table 1.1, p. 8.
299   See above, p. 75.
300   Goose, *The Berkhamsted Region*, pp. 41-2.

What impact did the existence of these employment opportunities for 10-14 year-olds have on the family? Did it, as many contemporaries and some historians have suggested, lead to an early breakdown of family ties, a precocious independence and, as an almost inevitable concomitant, moral laxity? The question of the morality or otherwise of female straw plaiters and other domestic workers is not one that we can consider here, but those who have examined the issue appear to agree that, at the very least, contemporaries grossly exaggerated the problem.[301] With regard to suggestions that young plaiters sought early independence from their parents by leaving home to live as lodgers, we found very little evidence of this in the Berkhamsted region where plaiting was the overwhelming source of female employment.[302] Indeed, the evidence there tended to support the view of the contemporary agricultural writer Henry Evershed that, on the contrary, it "retains them at home", keeping families intact by allowing children to make a contribution to the family budget and providing an alternative to both agricultural labour and domestic service, which more commonly involved relatively early separation from parents.[303]

The St Albans district evidence is even more compelling on this point. Taking all of the female straw workers aged 10-14 in the seven rural parishes of the district, both within and without the Liberty, produces a total of 224, and of these just two (0.9%) were lodgers.[304] Sarah Warner, aged 12, lodged with Joshua Wheeler, agricultural labourer, and his wife Mary, on Marshalls Heath in Wheathampstead, all of them being native to the parish. Elizabeth Weedon, aged 11, lodged with John Pestill, agricultural labourer, and his wife Eleanor, herself a straw plaiter, on Turnpike Road in Harpenden, Elizabeth having been born in Wheathampstead. Two hundred of the 224 (over 89%) were the daughter or step-daughter of the head of household, seven were grandchildren, six nieces, three sisters and one a cousin, the balance being made up by four who were visiting on census night. In the age group 15-19 there were 273 straw workers, and of these just nine (3.3%) were described as lodgers.[305] Two hundred and twenty-three (nearly 82%) were the daughter or step-daughter of the household head, meaning that there was a slightly higher percentage of more distant relatives. In a population of 10,763, therefore, there were just 11 teenage female lodgers, workers in the straw industry, lodging in households to which they were unrelated. In the case of boys in this age range, of the 35 straw workers identified in the rural parishes, 34 were sons and one the nephew of the head of household. Far from providing an incentive for young men and women to leave home early, therefore, the straw industry would appear to have enabled families to remain intact.

The town of St Albans offers little more encouragement to the Victorian moralisers on this issue. There was a total of 1,351 individuals working in the straw, straw hat, Brazilian hat and other textile trades in the three urban parishes in 1851, and 163 of these were girls aged 10-14. Just three of these 163 were lodgers (1.8%), and two more were the children of lodgers and hence still with their parents. One hundred and thirty-nine (85%) were daughters or step-daughters of the household head, and apart from one visitor the rest were

301 L. Grof, *Children of Straw*, pp. 79-89; P. Horn, "The Buckinghamshire Straw Plait Trade in Victorian England", *Records of Buckinghamshire*, Vol. 19 (1971), pp. 49-52; C.A. and P. Horn, "The Social Structure of an 'Industrial' Community: Ivinghoe in Buckinghamshire in 1871", *Local Population Studies*, No. 31 (1983), pp. 12-13.

302 Goose, *The Berkhamsted Region*, pp. 44-5.

303 H. Evershed, "Agriculture of Hertfordshire", *Journal of the Royal Agricultural Society of England*, Vol. XXV (1864), p. 315. For a similar argument in relation to factory employment for children see Nardinelli, *Child Labor and the Industrial Revolution*, pp. 60-1.

304 This compares with almost 5% (7 out of 144) in the parish of Tring: Goose, *The Berkhamsted Region*, p. 45.

305 Again this is far lower than in Tring, where 10% of this age group were lodgers: *ibid*.

granddaughters, nieces and sisters. Of the 196 aged 15-19, a lower proportion (74%) were daughters or step-daughters than in the rural parishes, but still there were only 12 lodgers, just 6% of the total. Interestingly, six women in this age category headed their own households, all living in St Albans parish, four working in the hat trades and two in silk. Two of these were as young as 17, two 18 and two 19, suggesting that the opportunities available for female employment in the town, in a small number of cases at least, did create at least the possibility of early female independence. As in the rural parishes, the younger boys were particularly unadventurous, 104 of the 107 aged 10-14 being the son of the household head, and the remaining three were more distant relatives. At age 15-19 there were four unrelated male lodgers out of 76 (5%), one visitor and the remainder were related, although again there were slightly more distant relatives in this age category. Five headed their own households, four weavers and a straw factor, all in St Albans parish, again giving just minimal credibility to the argument that employment opportunities encouraged early independence. If more teenage boys and girls working in the straw and hat trades had left home in town than in countryside, therefore, it was a difference of degree rather than kind, and those who had ventured abroad were a small minority of the total.

With so many women and children working in the straw plaiting and hat trades of this region one would expect this to make a strong impact on family incomes, a far better measure of the standard of living than trends in individual wages. Indeed, it has been suggested that a general feature of the Industrial Revolution was increased labour force participation by women and children, which in turn was crucial to the achievement of surplus income above subsistence levels and hence to the increased home demand that was so vital to continued economic growth, the so-called "McKendrick effect".[306] Historians are not, however, universally convinced of the importance of the contribution that women and children could make to family budgets. A recent assessment by Sara Horrell and Jane Humphries, employing subsets from a sample of 1,781 detailed family budgets drawn from the years 1787 to 1865, concludes that "women's and children's contributions were relatively small at the end of the eighteenth century and remained so throughout the period", amounting overall to between 18% and 22 % of family incomes.[307] However, this is a judgement based upon a geographically and occupationally diverse sample, and they also conclude that "accounts of women's and children's contributions to family incomes must be conditional upon their occupational and regional identity".[308] The St Albans district, just like the Berkhamsted region to the west, stands out as possessing a very particular occupational and regional identity, and within such a region conclusions based upon aggregated figures from across the country simply do not apply. Here it is difficult to avoid the conclusion that the sheer weight of female and child employment must have made a significant contribution to many family budgets, and that it is most likely that the net result was an overall increase in domestic demand from working class families, which in turn provided a stimulus to regional and local economic development.[309]

306   N. McKendrick, "Home Demand and Economic Growth: a New View of the Role of Women and Children in the Industrial Revolution", in McKendrick (ed.), *Historical Perspectives in English Thought and Society in Honour of J.H. Plumb* (London, 1974). The trends in female and child employment are still the subject of debate: see, for instance, Snell, *Annals of the Labouring Poor*, pp. 49-66; M. Berg and P. Hudson, "Rehabilitating the Industrial Revolution", *Economic History Review*, Vol. XLV (1992), pp. 35-7.

307   Horrell and Humphries, "Women's Labour Force Participation", pp. 100-5. See also S. Horrell and J. Humphries, "'The Exploitation of Little Children': Child Labour and the Family Economy in the Industrial Revolution", *Explorations in Economic History*, Vol. 32 (1995), pp. 485-516.

308   Horrell and Humphries, "Women's Labour Force Participation", p. 105.

309   See also S. Horrell, "Home Demand and British Industrialisation", *Journal of Economic History*, Vol. 56 (1996), pp. 561-604. Here Horrell uses a smaller sample of family budgets, and finds little evidence for any marked escalation of working class demand for the

The earnings of women and children in the straw plait and hat trades were not, however, static over time. The golden age of plaiting was clearly during the Napoleonic Wars, when foreign plait was unobtainable and hence home produced plait was in great demand. It was in 1804 that Arthur Young reported earnings for female Hertfordshire plaiters of 21 shillings per week at Redbourn and Dunstable, 14-18 shillings at Berkhamsted and up to 5 shillings per day in St Albans, whilst for "a short time" some women earned 42 shillings per week. Children could earn 1s 6d to 2s 6d per week at age six, and a shilling a day at the age of seven, and by the age of 10 possibly 12 shillings per week or more.[310] Another reporter from early in the century revealed that at Hatfield "one woman had earned 22s in a week by plait".[311] These were extraordinary sums at a time when male agricultural labourers could command no more than 10-12 shillings per week, possibly only 8 shillings in cash.[312] They did not last, however, and rates of pay fell sharply at the end of the Napoleonic Wars and were never fully to recover. At Hatfield, Hertfordshire, in 1831 earnings had fallen to 8-10 shillings per week for women and 3-5 shillings for children, although these were still very significant sums compared with male agricultural wages of 9-12s, and calculations based upon the 1834 Poor Law Commission report suggest that in some parts of Buckinghamshire the earnings of wives and children could on occasion equal or even exceed that of male agricultural labourers.[313]

The trade was clearly subject to widely fluctuating fortunes over time, and the earnings quoted for Hertfordshire in the Poor Law Report of 1834 stand considerably below those for Hatfield just three years earlier. Hence in St Michaels parish in St Albans, the average earnings of women and children from straw plaiting across the year were put at just 2 shillings per week on average, and in St Peters at 1-2 shillings.[314] At Hemel Hempstead a wife's earnings from plaiting were put at 2s 6d per week, at Redbourn females in general earned 1s 6d to 3s 6d, whilst in Welwyn the earnings of "women and children" working at straw plait were put at 2 shillings or 2s 6d.[315] At Watford, where women and children were "chiefly employed in silk mills and straw-plait", they reportedly earned 2s 6d to 8 shillings in summer and 2 shillings to 6 shillings in winter. With harvest agricultural employment in addition, across the year a wife might earn 4 shillings per week, a child of fourteen 5 shillings, of eleven 2s 6d, of eight 2 shillings and of five 1 shilling.[316] Here, therefore, the earnings of family members could certainly rival those of an adult male, which were put at 10-14 shillings weekly.[317] More generally in 1832-4 our figures suggest that wages were low by previous standards, but this was due to a slump in trade, as the respondents to the Commission were well aware, and cannot be taken as typical. Hence from St Peters we are informed that the straw plait trade "is now very low", from Shenley "the families are large and young, and the straw plait very poor", from Welwyn "Straw-plaiting has generally superseded lace-making, but affords *at present* but a scanty subsistence" (my italics), whilst across the border at Amersham in Buckinghamshire lace-making and straw plaiting continued to be available to women and

---

products of the new, mechanised industries. She does, however, find significantly enhanced demand for the products of traditional trades in agricultural areas, such as those whose importance in a regional economic setting have been emphasised here.

310   A. Young, *General View of the Agriculture of the County of Hertfordshire* [1804] (repr. Plymouth, 1971), pp. 221-3. For those unfamiliar with what is now 'old money', one shilling equals five new pence, 6d equals 2.5 new pence.

311   *Report from the Select Committee of the House of Lords on the Poor Laws,* 1831, p. 277.

312   Young, *General View of the Agriculture of Hertfordshire,* pp. 217-20: Mingay (ed.), *Agrarian History,* Table IV.6, p. 1095.

313   *Report from the Select Committee of the House of Lords on the Poor Laws,* 1831, pp. 276, 279; Grof, *Children of Straw,* p. 91.

314   *Poor Law Report,* Parliamentary Papers 1834, Vol. XXX, p. 217.

315   *Ibid.,* pp. 219, 222, 227.

316   *Ibid.,* p. 226.

317   *Ibid.*

children, "both of which trades are very dull".[318] By 1843 it was reported that women needed to work a 12-14 hour day to earn 3 to 4 shillings a week, whilst children aged 8-13 could clear no more than 1s 6d per week once they had paid for their schooling.[319] This, however, was another untypical year, immediately following the removal of protective tariffs in 1842, and hence represented a particularly low point for earnings.[320] Indeed, the 1843 report itself noted that "the trade is so bad that many children are kept at home plaiting" to save the cost of attending plaiting schools, whilst "the earnings now of the plaiters were at least a third less than they were in former years".[321]

Figures cited in the 1860s for the Luton Union of just one shilling to 1s 6d per week also reflect a short-term slump in trade, and potential family earnings from plaiting at this date were put at 5 to 10 shillings, whilst other contemporary testimony suggests that children as young as 10-14 could clear 4-5 shillings per week after paying for their straw.[322] Tansley's assessment, made in 1860, is probably a reasonably reliable reflection of typical earnings. He reports earnings in straw plait for very young children of one shilling to 1s 6d, 2-3 shillings at ages eight or nine, 4-5 shillings on leaving the plaiting schools and possibly 7 shillings "after they become skilful". After deduction is made for the cost of the straws, "the earnings of a good plaiter will be from 5s to 7s 6d per week, in a good state of trade", and hence "a well ordered family will obtain as much or more than the husband who is at work on the neighbouring farm".[323] Grey too, in his reminiscences of Harpenden in the 1860s, agreed that labourers' wives "by straw plaiting would, if clever at the work, earn some weeks as much money or even more than the weekly wage of their husbands".[324] The 1867-8 Royal Commission Report similarly suggests that girls from sixteen years of age could earn 6 to 10 shillings per week when the plait trade was good.[325] These figures are far in excess of the 20% or so contribution suggested by Horrell and Humphries from their aggregated national figures, again emphasising the importance of a regional perspective and the distinctive nature of the region under consideration here. But there was also a hierarchy of both esteem and earnings within the straw plait and hat trades, for bonnet sewers would generally earn more than plaiters, a consideration of particular importance in St Albans where hat-making predominated over plaiting. Furthermore, those engaged directly in the manufactories earned more than those employed in "sale work", and the earnings of the so-called "room hands" were reportedly "superior to any similar class in the kingdom", ranging from 8-12 shillings per week for "medium" hands, to 16-20 shillings for "the best fancy hands", although these earnings too would fluctuate according to the state of trade as well as with the season.[326]

The evidence that opportunities in the straw plait and hat trades for women and children in the St Albans district must have made a substantial contribution to family incomes would appear to be compelling. The sheer weight of numbers employed, in the town mainly in hat-making, in the countryside predominantly in plaiting,

318 *Ibid.*, pp. 217, 224, 226; Vol. XXXVI, p. 11.

319 *Children's Employment Commission: Second Report*, 1843, p. 132.

320 Freeman, *Luton and the Hat Industry*, p. 12. This Children's Employment Commission report is probably the original source for Allen's figures of 3s 6d to 4s cited for the 1830s and 1840s: R.C. Allen, *Enclosure and the Yeoman* (Oxford, 1992), Figure 12-2, p. 256.

321 *Children's Employment Commission: Second Report*, 1843, p. 132.

322 Grof, *Children of Straw*, p. 93; Luton Museum Service, *The Straw Plait Pack*, no date or pagination.

323 Tansley, "On the Straw Plait Trade", pp. 73-4.

324 Grey, *Cottage Life*, p. 67.

325 *Report of the Royal Commission on the Employment of Children, Young Persons and Women in Agriculture*, Parliamentary Papers, 1867-8, Vol. XVII, p. 136.

326 Tansley, "On the Straw Plait Trade", pp. 72-3.

and the testimony of well-informed contemporaries, all point to this conclusion. There are, however, voices that dissent from this view, which suggest that males generally earned less in areas where female employment was available, that women and children lost out by being unable to participate in agricultural activities, and emphasise the seasonal nature of both plaiting and hat-making.[327] Clear evidence that male labourers earned substantially less in such areas has yet to be produced, however, and any reduction would need to be very substantial to offset earnings that could equal the male weekly wage.[328] Indeed, the view that there was such a trade-off is contradicted by comparison of occupational participation rates for children with adult agricultural wages for the period 1833-45, whilst Hunt's analysis of regional wage variations failed to show a general correspondence between low wages for men and employment opportunities for either women or children.[329] Agricultural earnings data available for the years 1824, 1837 and 1860 shows the Hertfordshire figure standing a little below the average for the 34 counties listed in each year, but when it is compared with the mean for 14 southern counties it stands a little above average in 1824, on the average for 1837, and just marginally below (by 8d) in 1860.[330] Nor is it clear that women would lose out on all aspects of agricultural work, for they reportedly left off plaiting in order to participate in the harvest, and either through choice or through the impact of technological changes their participation in agricultural work had anyway diminished substantially between the mid-eighteenth and mid-nineteenth centuries, at least across much of southern England.[331] The arguments regarding the degree of seasonality experienced in the plait trade have been considered above, and there is clear evidence that – despite fluctuations in intensity – the trade was practised on an ongoing basis.[332] And whilst it may be true that demand for straw hats peaked in summer, there is no reason to believe that there was only a very short summer season for hat production, even if the "fancy work" was concentrated in the summer months.[333] Indeed, the census enumerators were able to identify a veritable army of hat-makers at the end of March, and the fact that at least part of the industry was factory based by mid-century would also indicate that it was anything but a seasonal activity.

In the St Albans district, therefore, we can speak with confidence about a family economy, the region possessing a distinctive economic structure which produced a symbiotic relationship between town and country, extremely high levels of employment for women in general and married women in particular, and opportunities well in excess of national norms for children in both town and countryside. Here women and children made a substantial if ultimately unquantifiable contribution to family budgets, which in turn helped

327   P. Sharpe, "The Women's Harvest: Straw-Plaiting and the Representation of Labouring Women's Employment, c. 1793-1885", *Rural History*, Vol. 5 (1994), pp. 134-6.

328   Elsewhere Sharpe had argued that men's wages tended to be lower in parishes with female work of *any* type, so this is not an argument that applies simply to straw plaiting: Sharpe, *Adapting to Capitalism*, p. 59.

329   Nardinelli, *Child Labor and the Industrial Revolution*, Table 4.2 and pp. 82-5; E.H. Hunt, *Regional Wage Variations in Britain, 1850-1914* (Oxford, 1973), p. 126.

330   Calculated from F. Purdy, "On the Earnings of Agricultural Labourers in England and Wales, 1860", *Journal of the Royal Statistical Society*, Vol. 24 (1861), p. 342.

331   Tansley, "On the Straw Plait Trade", p. 71; Snell, *Annals of the Labouring Poor*, pp. 15-66; Roberts, *Women's Work, 1840-1940*, pp. 33-4; Goose, *The Berkhamsted Region*, pp. 39-40.

332   See p. 86.

333   Sharpe, "The Women's Harvest", p. 137. Sharpe's use of this reference, to Mr Harris's fancy straw weaving works, is potentially misleading, for although it was indeed reported that "This work is only carried for about two months in the year", it was also stated of the women who worked there that "the rest of the year they work at the straw plait": *Children's Employment Commission. Second Report*, 1843, p. A13.

to stimulate the local economy and hence to create the diversity of economic activity identified here in the thriving village communities, but above all in the town of St Albans itself.[334]

Agriculture

Despite the importance of the straw plait and hat-making trades to this region, and the diversity of economic activity found in St Albans and to a lesser degree in the substantial villages that surrounded it, agriculture remained of crucial importance. Straw, of course, was also itself a product of the land, and could prove to be a lucrative commodity, either for local consumption or for sale in the London market.[335] The census reveals that agriculture was the primary employer of all the occupational categories listed in Table 2, and clearly the dominant employer for men. It is also very likely that the census returns understate the size of the agricultural labour force. As noted above, the census was taken in late March, at the height of the straw plaiting season but at a relatively slack time for agriculture, and hence the substantial additional labour input of the harvest season will not be recorded.[336]

A range of factors may have resulted in understatement of agricultural employment in the printed census reports, including under-recording of women and of seasonal work, under-estimation of the contribution of family labour, recording of female farm servants as domestics, misplacement of agricultural workers into the category of general labourer and other residual factors. Together these might require a considerable upward revision of the orthodox figure for the number of agricultural workers in England and Wales in 1851, perhaps from 1.6 million to 2.1 million. This would raise the proportion of agricultural workers in the total labour force from 20 to 25%, and the percentage of the agricultural labour force who were women from 10 to 27%.[337] Such suggested revisions are, of course, only plausible orders of magnitude and are unlikely to relate consistently to every locality. But some of these criticisms of the printed census reports do apply equally to the occupational data for the St Albans district presented here, for female farm servants have been assigned to the 'domestic service' category unless there were indications to the contrary, whilst for the sake of consistency all women designated as 'farmer's wife' or 'farmer's daughter', as well as the youngest of the 'farmer's sons', were classified as unoccupied dependants. Our figures for agricultural employment must, therefore, be regarded as *minima*.

The census is particularly likely to under-record seasonal work undertaken by women in summer and autumn, such as harvesting and subsequent gleaning, and it was noted in 1861 by the principal of the statistical department of the London Poor Law Board that "Had the census of 1851 been taken two or three months later, the number of women and children employed in out-door labour would have been greater than...returned".[338] Indeed, it was suggested in 1860 by A.J. Tansley that the harvest was the one time of the year that the straw

---

334 For a similarly 'optimistic' interpretation of child employment during the industrial revolution which also emphasises rising family incomes see Nardinelli, *Child Labor and the Industrial Revolution, passim*. See also Horrell and Humphries, "'The Exploitation of Little Children'", pp. 502-12.

335 Evershed, "Agriculture of Hertfordshire", pp. 275, 314-15; Young, *General View of the Agriculture of Hertfordshire*, pp. 17, 92.

336 E. Higgs, "Occupational Censuses and the Agricultural Workforce in Victorian England and Wales", *Economic History Review*, Vol. 48 (1995), pp. 704-5.

337 Higgs, "Occupational Censuses", pp. 709-11.

338 Purdy, "On the Earnings of Agricultural Labourers in England and Wales", p. 331.

plait trade was interrupted.[339] Numerous other part-time and seasonal agricultural activities, such as weeding, stone-picking, dairying, hoeing, planting beans or pulling roots may generally also have gone unrecorded, even though examples can be found where such activities were occasionally listed.[340] Grey records that women (and children) were indeed involved in such activities in Harpenden in the 1860s, commenting upon gleaning in the following terms:

> "The gleaning season was made the most of by many of the cottage women, for the flour
> obtained as a result of this wheat gleaning was a great asset to the food supply of
> the household during the autumn and early winter. There were, of course, many women
> who, owing to home ties and duties, could not go out to glean, but the number who did
> so, together with the boys and girls, was quite considerable; I should think perhaps
> that this time of the year must have been somewhat slack as regards plaiting, for I
> cannot recollect seeing very much of it done during this period, though undoubtedly the
> stay-at-homes still kept on at their plait work."[341]

This echoes Mary Thompson's recollections of Lark Rise in Oxfordshire in the 1880s, where the "leazing" as it was known locally would last for two or three weeks, and in a good year would provide one or two bushels of flour, "or even more in large, industrious families", the sacks often being kept proudly on show on a chair in the living room for passers-by to step inside to inspect.[342] In Harpenden productivity was apparently higher still, with the range per family falling between two and six or even seven bushels, with one young woman alone able to achieve three bushels in one particularly good year.[343] If used prudently, such a supply could last a family well into the winter.[344]

The importance of gleaning to the family economy, long evident to contemporaries, has recently received recognition in the historical literature.[345] From nine parishes in southern England for which information is provided in the 1834 Poor Law Report it has been calculated that the average value of gleaning to a family stood at £2.64, which would represent as much as 6% of the annual income of high-earning labouring families and 9.5% of the income of those with low earnings.[346] With wheat prices standing at 55 shillings (£2.75) per quarter in the early 1870s, few Harpenden families would have earned as much as this, the average for a family perhaps amounting to about 30 shillings (£1.50).[347] It is possible that the introduction of reaping machinery in the area was already having an impact, for machine-cut fields left relatively little wheat to glean, although most farms in the area continued to cut corn by scythe at this date.[348] Some other reports do, however, also suggest lower sums, and hence at Hertingfordbury in 1834 the rector, Robert J. Eden, reported to the Poor

---

339   Tansley, "On the Straw Plait Trade", p. 71.
340   P. Horn, *Life and Labour in Rural England, 1760-1850* (London, 1987), pp. 75-7; Saito, "Who Worked When?", p. 189.
341   Grey, *Cottage Life*, pp. 118-19.
342   F. Thompson, *Lark Rise to Candleford* (Harmondsworth, 1973, 1st publ. 1939), pp. 28-9.
343   Grey, *Cottage Life*, pp. 124-5.
344   *Ibid.*, p. 126.
345   Eden, *The State of the Poor*, Vol. III, Appendix, p. cccxlii; P. King, "Customary Rights and Women's Earnings: the Importance of Gleaning to the Rural Labouring Poor, 1750-1850", *Economic History Review*, Vol. XLIV (1991), pp. 461-76.
346   *Ibid.*, pp. 463-4.
347   Wheat prices from Crouzet, *Victorian Economy*, Table 29, p. 167.
348   Grey, *Cottage Life*, pp. 63, 246-7; King, "Customary Rights and Women's Earnings", p. 473.

Law Commissioners that "In a fine harvest the gleaner on an average may get 20s (£1)", although it is unclear whether this figure applied to women only or to women and children in general.[349] A substantial survey of 338 Norfolk and Suffolk labouring families taken in 1837 also indicates a much lower figure, averaging just 21s 10d per family.[350] Such estimates do, at the very least, suggest that we should be cautious before accepting the evidence of the Poor Law Report at its face value, for the responses to the questionnaires were, after all, only the views of selected individuals, if usually fairly well-informed ones. Whatever the reason for the discrepancies between these various figures, there can be no doubt that the work of women and children in gleaning after harvest continued to make an important though perhaps variable contribution to family income, a contribution that is completely hidden from view in the census enumerators' books.

Many labouring families in Harpenden also kept a pig or two, and the task of tending to such animals naturally fell to the women of the household whilst the men were away working at the farm.[351] At Lark Rise, women and children also made an important contribution towards tending and feeding the labouring families' pigs.[352] Other agricultural activities in which women were involved at Harpenden included hay-baling, harvest work, mangold pulling, weeding, hoeing, stone-picking and acorn harvesting. It remains impossible to quantify from the evidence of such testimony but, whilst Grey appears to imply that plaiting was generally the most favoured female activity, still "there were always some women to be found working on the farm in certain seasons".[353]

Where quantification has been possible, female contributions to agricultural work have been discovered to be far from insignificant. Comparison between farm wage books and the 1871 census for five Gloucestershire parishes has revealed considerable under-enumeration of women who worked on the land for as much as one-third of the year, as well as discrepant treatment of female agricultural work between parishes, and it is possible that this was a feature of the 1851 returns as well as of later censuses.[354] Gloucestershire may well, however, have lacked the alternative employment opportunities that the St Albans district could provide, and there is certainly contemporary testimony that suggests that the many women may have preferred cottage industry to farm work for, as Arthur Young reported regarding plaiting in an oft-quoted phrase, "The farmers complain of it, as doing mischief, for it makes the poor saucy, and no servants can be procured, or any field-work done, where this manufacture establishes itself".[355] At Redbourn, the churchwarden George Lee Cane reported in 1834 that "The females generally work at straw-plaiting... throughout the year. They are not employed in harvest work".[356] Elsewhere in Hertfordshire the situation may also have been different from counties such as Gloucestershire, for the respondents to the Poor Law Commissioners in 1832-4 unanimously indicate that female agricultural employment was essentially casual or seasonal.[357] From Welwyn we hear that "The women in Hertfordshire seldom work at corn-harvest", although the same respondent estimates that

---

349   *Poor Law Report*, Parliamentary Papers 1834, Vol. XXX, p. 220.
350   J.P. Kay, "Earnings of Agricultural Labourers in Norfolk and Suffolk", *Journal of the Statistical Society of London*, Vol. 1, No. III (1838), p. 183.
351   Grey, *Cottage Life* , pp. 113-16.
352   Thompson, *Lark Rise to Candleford*, pp. 24-5.
353   *Ibid.*, pp. 92-3.
354   Miller, "The Hidden Workforce", pp. 137-61.
355   Young, *General View of the Agriculture of Hertfordshire*, p. 222; Horn, "Buckinghamshire Straw Plait Trade", p. 43.
356   *Poor Law Report*, Parliamentary Papers 1834, Vol. XXX, p. 222.
357   *Ibid.*, pp. 217-27.

they might earn 6s. to 7s. 6d. in summer, presumably in haymaking.[358] They were also able to find agricultural employment in the summer at Watford, although here their chief employment was in the silk mills and in straw plaiting, and also in Westmill, Shenley, Sacombe, St Margaret, Cheshunt, Hertford and Broxbourne. Again, however, this employment was generally marginal, and hence from Cheshunt we hear from John Earby Cook that the employment available to women and children was "None but casual; stone-picking, weeding and hay-making. They sometimes assist in reaping", whilst Thomas Rust of the same parish responded that there was "Little or none for women, except in hay and potato time, when they earn about 1s. per day".[359] The responses from Shenley are similarly instructive, from Thomas Newcombe, rector, "Hay-harvest, women, 1s. and beer; corn-harvest, little or nothing", and from J.M. Winter, J.P., "Harvest, scarce anything. Hay-harvest, women 15d. per day, and beer", whilst stone-picking, weeding and hay-making are again specified by William Heard, overseer and surveyor, of St Margaret near Ware.[360] The situation was similar at Woburn, Bedfordshire, some twenty-five years later, for here it was reported that whilst most women plaited straw, very few were employed in agriculture.[361]

Testimony from all quarters, therefore, indicates that by this time female agricultural employment in Hertfordshire was distinctly seasonal, and concentrated upon specific – generally unskilled – tasks. But if the respondents to the Poor Law Commissioners convey the impression that in consequence it was of little importance, we should not fall into the trap of accepting their judgement at face value. Quantification of potential earnings is extremely difficult, and it is clear that the estimates offered to the Commissioners were themselves only very rough and ready. Nevertheless, at Westmill it was indicated by both respondents that women might earn 48 shillings (£2.40) during the summer months in agriculture, in addition to what they might make by gleaning.[362] Robert Sworder, overseer of Westmill, estimated that a family of four (including boys aged 11 and 14) might earn about £50 8s (£50.40) in a year, and thus the wife's earnings amounted to 4.8% of annual income, in addition to her earnings from gleaning, estimated at £2 or a further 4.0%. The total contribution for a wife's agricultural employment, therefore, approached 9% of the annual earnings of the family, a sum that was far from insignificant in the budget of the average labouring family in the conditions prevailing in the second quarter of the nineteenth century. For Westmill we are told that "there is no average labourer who may not obtain employment nearly throughout the year", perhaps suggesting that constant employment was anything but guaranteed elsewhere, and raising the possibility that this parish may not be typical. Estimates from other Hertfordshire parishes, however, suggest a range of annual adult male earnings of £25-35, which places the Westmill figure of £30-32 at about average. Where wages were lower, possibly indicating a surplus of male labour, one might expect to find that female earning potential declined accordingly. But this is to speculate, and the best evidence we have to hand indicates that, although casual and seasonal, female agricultural employment could still make a significant contribution to family budgets.

Full-time, adult, male agricultural employment is without doubt recorded far better in the census than is the contribution of women and children, and the figures derived from the census enumerators' returns are probably a fairly accurate reflection of agricultural occupations. Our occupational table reveals that, even in

---

358   *Ibid.*, p. 226.
359   *Ibid.*, p. 219.
360   *Ibid.*, pp. 222, 224.
361   Purdy, "On the Earnings of Agricultural Labourers", p. 333.
362   *Poor Law Report*, Parliamentary Papers 1834, Vol. XXX, p. 227.

this relatively urbanised part of the county, one quarter of total employment overall was in the agricultural sector, and as much as 44% of male employment, both of these figures standing substantially above those found in the Berkhamsted region, and exceeding the national percentages that have been derived from the printed census reports.[363] In the rural parishes within and without the Liberty of St Albans, agricultural employment accounted for 38% of the total workforce and as much as 64% of male employment. Sandridge and Wheathampstead both exhibit high proportions, approaching 70%, whilst the two villages that possessed more developed non-agrarian economies – Harpenden and Redbourn – produce lower figures at 60% and 51% respectively. The percentages for the rural parishes within the Liberty of St Albans are also generally high, though tempered in St Michaels (rural) by the counteracting influence of the large number of male domestic servants found here, and reaching 74% in St Stephens which stretched out from the southern fringe of the town to incorporate Park Street, Smug Oak, Bricket Wood, Frogmore and Colney Street. Not only did these parishes incorporate substantial arable and pasture areas, but – as suggested above – they were in a better position than the more distant villages to rely upon the town of St Albans for the provision of a variety of goods and services, and hence the range of occupations found within their own borders was somewhat narrower.[364] In the town, unsurprisingly, agricultural activity was limited, accounting for only 4% of total employment and approaching 8% of male occupations. Roughly half of the urban male agricultural workers lived in St Michaels (urban), despite the relative paucity of agricultural land here, with just one farm of 600 acres owned by Thomas Willshin of Kingsbury House, employing 26 labourers. The remainder of the 74 agricultural workers living in this parish, mainly in Fishpool Street and Pound Field, must have been employed on neighbouring farms. But St Albans and St Peters too housed a clutch of farm labourers, some 27 in the former parish and 32 in the latter, again testifying to the inter-relationship between town and country.[365]

By this date the majority of agricultural labourers in Hertfordshire were hired rather than living in as farm servants, at least according to work published to date on this subject, the county exhibiting the lowest proportion of 'servants in husbandry' of all the counties in England.[366] These figures are, of course, based upon published census reports, and scrutiny of individual enumerators' returns seems to indicate that, although they are mostly reliable, some errors may have been made. For example, in St Michaels (rural), John Purrott of Maynes Farm is listed as a farmer without any acreage or number of labourers employed recorded, but there are six farm servants living in his household. A similar omission occurs in the case of Daniel Boulter of Old Park Bury in St Stephens, a farmer of 357 acres with no labourers listed although five lived in with him, and also in the case of Deborah Brinklow of Tyttenhanger Green. In Redbourn, Joseph Beaumont is described as farming 107 acres with one labourer but his household included three, designated as "agricultural labourer", "odd man" and "agricultural labourer, horsekeeper". Where farms were run by bailiffs or stewards, it is rare to find the number of acres or labourers employed recorded. In a number of cases, however, their households did include living-in labourers, such as William Croft of Wood End, Redbourn, whose

---

363   Goose, *The Berkhamsted Region*, p. 48; Higgs, "Occupational Censuses", pp. 709-11.

364   See above, p. 79.

365   For some comments on the 'rural' nature of some small towns and urban-rural inter-connections see Howkins, *Reshaping Rural England*, pp. 7-8 and Waller, *Town, City and Nation*, pp. 4-6.

366   A. Kussmaul, *Servants in Husbandry in Early Modern England* (Cambridge, 1981), p. 20. Snell's figures, which relate to males only and are more reliable in consequence, differ somewhat from those of Kussmaul, placing Hertfordshire towards, rather that at, the bottom in terms of the proportion of male agricultural labourers living in with their employers, at 7.9%: *Annals of the Labouring Poor*, Table 2.1, pp. 96-7.

household included a ploughman and an agricultural labourer, or in Wheathampstead Joseph Higgins, James Foster and Matthew Winch, with two, three and two living-in agricultural workers respectively. In Sandridge, James Hutchinson occupied the Sandridgebury Bailiff's Cottage, and housed five labourers, whilst in the previous schedule the household of James Kinder of Sandridgebury, magistrate and farmer of 700 acres employing 30 labourers – doubtless Hutchinson's employer – included none.

The returns for the Out-hamlets are particularly suspicious, for a number of entries occur here where young male servants living on farms are recorded either as "servant" under occupation as well as under relationship to head of household, or – more commonly – the occupation column is left blank, and it is probable that these were in fact farm servants. This is true of the farms of Henry Kerley, William George, George Longstaff and William Wise, amongst others, and the net effect is quite considerable. If all of the suspect cases are counted, then a total of 19 farm servants have been omitted, against a recorded total of just 27, and hence here the returns are clearly not to be trusted. Occasional examples of this practice can be found elsewhere, such as in the case of Sarah Norwood, widow, who ran Capt Hall Farm in Redbourn, employing 2 labourers, with a 31 year-old male servant living in but not identified as an agricultural labourer, whilst two other supposed male "servants" on Agnels Farm can be identified as agricultural workers only because, exceptionally, we are told that two of the eight labourers were employed indoors. In Redbourn, however, these are the only suspicious cases, and hence the returns can be regarded as at least generally reliable. In Sandridge the enumerator appears to have made a very clear distinction between farm and house servants, until the phrase "general servant" begins to appear towards the end of the enumeration, always against the names of male residents, which might indicate that the 11 individuals so described on the farms of Jonathan Cox, Robert Smith, William Holloway and Elizabeth Booth were both farm *and* household servants, and hence should be added to the 48 farm servants proper identified here.

Again the need to inspect individual enumerators' returns is highlighted, rather than relying upon blanket assessments of their general reliability or otherwise. For the St Albans region, farm servants appear to be reasonably well recorded, and distinguished from house servants, in all but the Out-hamlets and – to a lesser extent – in Sandridge, and hence in Table 11 which follows adjusted figures are presented for both of these districts. Although there are several examples in other parishes where no total number of labourers is given even though there are clearly some living in, with both farmers and with bailiffs, the exclusion of these cases will only affect the absolute numbers, and should not distort the percentages produced. The proportion of the total number of agricultural labourers living in as farm servants shown in Table 11, 23.4% overall, is surprisingly high, given that county by county calculations from the published 1851 census reports give a figure for the county of Hertfordshire of just 7.9%.[367] The percentages are fairly consistent between parishes, only Wheathampstead and the town of St Albans exhibiting notably lower proportions, but even here the figures remain double the county average. The situation could, however, vary considerably from one farm to the next. In Harpenden, for example, Robert Sibley of Annobles Farm employed 22 labourers, none of whom lived in at the farm, whilst of the 15 employed by Joseph Willmott at Cooters End, six did so. In St Michaels (rural) all six of Thomas Hollingshead's labourers at Kettlewell Farm lived in, whilst all other farms in this part of St Michaels parish included only between one and three live-in labourers, regardless of the size of the total labour force. In all, however, of the 149 farms suitable for analysis, 111 or fully 75% included at least

367   *Ibid.*

one living-in labourer. On the other hand, over 60% of farm servants were under the age of 20, and the majority of the remainder were in their twenties, indicative of the fact that farm service, like domestic service for many girls and young women, remained very predominantly a feature of a particular life-cycle stage.[368]

TABLE 11 : MALE LIVING-IN FARM SERVANTS

	No. Labourers	No. Living-in	% Living-in	No. Under 20*	% Under 20
St Albans (town)	34	6	17.6	3	50.0
St Michaels (rural)	119	33	27.7	23	69.7
St Stephens	198	46	23.2	30	65.2
Out-hamlets	181	47	26.0	25	53.2
Harpenden	177	38	21.5	18	47.4
Redbourn	126	35	27.8	24	68.6
Sandridge	255	59	23.1	34	57.6
Wheathampstead	167	28	16.8	20	71.4
Total	1257	292	23.2	177	60.6

* excludes the one labourer who lived in with Arthur Timperon, for whom no age is given.

On the face of it, therefore, our results for the St Albans district are difficult to square with those derived from the published census reports for the county. This is more apparent than real, however, for the two sets of figures are calculated in very different ways: the total number of labourers in Table 11 is derived from the statements of individual farmers of the numbers they employed, whilst the published figures use the total number designated as an agricultural labourer in the occupation column of the enumerators' books, in both cases relying upon examination of farmers' households to determine the proportion living in. If we re-work our data to conform with the method used in the published reports, the number of labourers found in the district increases from 1,257 to 2,160, and in consequence the proportion living-in falls considerably, from 23% down to 15.5%. Furthermore, differences between parishes are now considerably exaggerated, with only just over 9% living in in Wheathampstead and fully 37% in Sandridge. Indeed, Sandridge farmers can only have been importing farm labour from surrounding parishes, for they claim to have employed 255 labourers between them whilst only 173 lived within the bounds of the parish, and no doubt there were exchanges too between the parishes under discussion here and those bordering upon the St Albans district. These are, of course, imponderables, but if our data shows nothing else it clearly does suggest that any analysis based upon the individual parish is potentially entirely misleading. At the regional level the proportion of labourers who were living in is now reduced, but it still stands at double the level that has been calculated for the county from the published census reports.

Grey's reminiscences of Harpenden in the 1860s clearly testify to the continuation of living-in farm service in this parish.[369] Although the practice of yearly hiring was declining by this time, both lads and men would still present themselves at the annual hiring fairs held at St Albans or Luton, agreeing weekly wages, a lump sum of

368   Kussmaul's calculations from 265 eighteenth and early nineteenth century settlement examinations produce a median age of exit from farm service as low as 20, with just 20% remaining in service until they were 25 or over. This evidence is, however, inevitably biased towards the poor labourer, which may itself reflect low savings produced by an early exit from service. Kussmaul, *Servants in Husbandry*, p. 79.

369   Grey, *Cottage Life*, esp. pp. 57-62.

£2 at the end of the year's contract plus one shilling in binding money.[370] Although in some parts of the county farm servants still boarded with the farmer's family and ate at his table, the common practice in Harpenden was for the labourers to live in at the farm but to supply their own food. Whilst still young this was commonly brought or sent to them at the farm, either daily or if this was not possible then twice a week, and they would usually send their washing home to be done there. Older lads or young men were expected to buy their own provisions, which were cooked for them in the farm kitchen, usually twice a week, whilst nearly every farm provided a mess room where the labourers could prepare any extra food they wished.[371] Living in could, however, have a variety of meanings, as an unusual example from Wheathampstead shows. There, at Leasy Bridge Farm, Benjamin Welsh, agricultural labourer, headed the household, the enumerator's schedule including his wife, two sons, three daughters and two servants, Joseph Munt, shepherd and Henry George, horsekeeper. Where these two servants ate is not, of course, revealed, but where they slept appears to be, for whilst Welch's family occupied Leasy Bridge Farm, the address of Munt and George is recorded as "Leasy Bridge Cow Pen".[372]

The census enumerations thus show that between 15% and 23%, roughly one-sixth to one-quarter, of farm labourers still lived in in the St Albans district in 1851, and Grey's testimony indicates the continued prevalence of this practice in Harpenden at least. How can this be squared with the evidence of the published census reports, which appears to show little more than a vestige of farm service in Hertfordshire by the mid-nineteenth century? It is, of course, possible that this district was untypical of the county as a whole: the average number of labourers per farmer in the region was only half the county average, whilst across the country low proportions of farm-servant labour generally correlate with high labourer to farmer ratios.[373] This was not, however, a region of small farms but, as we shall see, quite the opposite, and farm service tended to survive longer in areas where many farms were small.[374] It is possible, on the other hand, that the published census reports under-count the numbers of living-in farm servants, but we will not be able to establish whether this is true or not until the individual census enumerators' books have been examined for the entire county. If this is indeed the case, the regional evidence presented here might indicate the need for a serious reconsideration of the chronology and the pace of the decline of service in husbandry, with all of the implications that this must have for our understanding of the nature of rural social relations in the mid-nineteenth century.[375]

---

370 Grey indicates that teenage boys would earn 3s. 6d. to 5s. per week, adult general farm hands 11s. to 13s weekly in summer and 9s. or even less in winter, whilst head ploughmen, cowmen or shepherds would earn 15s per week, although it was also possible to earn an extra 7-10s weekly at harvest time: *Cottage Life*, pp. 57, 59-62.

371 *Ibid.*, pp. 58-60.

372 For different forms of "living-in" and their implications for social relationships see A. Howkins, "Labour History and the Rural Poor", *Rural History*, Vol. 1 (1990), pp. 116-17.

373 Snell, *Annals of the Labouring Poor*, p. 95; and see below, pp. 123-4.

374 *Ibid.*

375 One thing that is clear is that it is not possible to rely upon the description given under occupation in the enumerations to determine the numbers of farm servants, and support for this conclusion comes from a region whose agricultural regime could not stand in more stark a contrast to that of Hertfordshire, the largely pastoral smallholdings of North Westmorland studied by Margaret Shepherd. In such regions, of course, farm service lingered far longer, but an examination of the 8,383-9,165 individuals listed in the censuses of 1841-81 reveals that, here too, far from all the living-in farm workers are identified as farm servants, and any analysis that relies simply on such a description rather than upon detailed examination of the census returns will seriously under-estimate the continued importance of living in: M.E. Shepherd, "North Westmorland 1841-1881: Aspects of its Historical Geography", unpubl. PhD thesis, Cambridge 1992, p. 298. Shepherd concludes that "the percentages quoted in Table 4.40 [for percentages living in] are

The considerable discrepancy between the two methods of calculating the proportion of farm servants must also give pause for thought. The published report does note that "Some uncertainty prevails as to whether farmers returned all their in-door farm servants" when reporting on the number they employed.[376] It is also clear, as we have seen, that in a few cases numbers were simply not given, and that they may be more generally missing for those described as landed proprietors and bailiffs.[377] The discrepancy between the two calculations is too large, however, to be wholly explained in this way. More likely, what we have here is, in effect, an index of the casualisation of farm labour that was a central feature of the agrarian development of southern England in the first half of the nineteenth century.[378] Furthermore, with the census being taken at the end of March it is likely that it catches the tail end of the winter dearth of employment that was also a feature of the primarily arable areas of the country.[379] By mid-century, therefore, rather than a simple dichotomy between living-in farm servants and outdoor agricultural labourers, there may have been another – possibly more important – divide within the agricultural labour force, between those who were in the regular employ of one or other of the farmers in the district and those who were not, but gained their livelihood on a more casual basis.[380]

Whilst bearing in mind the reservations expressed above about the representation of female agricultural employment, particularly part-time, in the census, our figures would seem to indicate that, just as we found in the Berkhamsted region, by this time *full*-time female agricultural employment was rare. Across the district as a whole only 23 of the 4,343 women with an occupational designation were engaged in agriculture, a mere 0.5%, an identical percentage to that found further to the west.[381] All of these were to be found in the rural parishes, where they formed just 1.0% of the occupied female population. Of these 23, as many as 17 were themselves farmers, 15 of them widows, farming acreages ranging from 11 to 419 and employing from one to 12 labourers. This leaves just six female agricultural employees. Judith Bates of Harpenden, Rebbecca Bigg of Wheathampstead , Charlotte Mansell of Colney Heath and Catherine Horton of London Colney are the only women described as agricultural labourers. The other two included here were Ann Bates of Redbourn, a "farmer's boy" *(sic)*, aged just eight and, in fact, the granddaughter of the head of household, and Charlotte

---

certainly under-estimates and that the living-in worker was far more important to agriculture in the area than even the 45.9% shown for 1881".

376   *1851 Census Report. Population Tables II*, Parliamentary Papers 1852-3, Vol. LXXXVIII, Vol. 1, p. lxxviii.

377   See above, pp. 110-11.

378   A. Armstrong, *Farmworkers: a Social and Economic History 1770-1980* (London, 1988), pp. 62-6. Casual labourers were not, of course, found only in the south, Marshall's interpretation of the 1831 census and extant account books for Lancashire leading him to conclude that this group was "very considerable in size" in this county: J.D. Marshall, "The Lancashire Rural Labourer in the Early Nineteenth Century", *Transactions of the Lancashire and Cheshire Antiquarian Society*, Vol. 71 (1961), pp. 92, 112.

379   Armstrong, *Farmworkers*, p. 64.

380   For similar reservations about the decline of farm service in Sussex see B. Short, "The Decline of Living-in Servants in the Transition to Capitalist Farming: a Critique of the Sussex Evidence", *Sussex Archaeological Collections*, Vol. 122 (1984), pp. 147-64; also M. Reed, "Indoor Farm Service in 19th-Century Sussex: Some Criticisms of a Critique" and B. Short, "A Rejoinder", *Sussex Archaeological Collections*, Vol. 123 (1985), pp. 225-41. For an alternative interpretation of the discrepancy between the different ways of counting agricultural labourers which blames failure by farmers to record indoor farm servants: J.A. Sheppard, "East Yorkshire's Agricultural Labour Force in the Mid-Nineteenth Century", *Agricultural History Review*, Vol. 9 (1961), pp. 43-54. This is not an explanation that could account for the size of the discrepancy in the St Albans district, whilst in some cases it is quite clear that farmers did indeed include living-in farm servants in their counts.

381   Goose, *The Berkhamsted Region*, Table 2, p. 30.

Saunders of St Michaels (rural), described as a "farmer's daughter employed at home".[382] The Select Committee of 1843 testified to the limited role that women were by then playing in agriculture, the preceding century having produced a substantial long term decline, and analysis of the published census reports provide further evidence. Although the returns for female living-in agricultural servants are unreliable, the percentage of outdoor labourers who were female by 1851 was tiny in many southern and south Midland counties. In nearby Bedfordshire and Buckinghamshire the figures stood at 0.2% and 0.6% respectively, whilst in Hertfordshire itself it only reached 1.4%.[383] With just four female outdoor agricultural labourers identified across the entire St Albans district, the region stood substantially below the county average.

In the light of this it is perhaps surprising to find Edwin Grey reporting that in Harpenden "There were also some of the young women and girls who hired themselves out, but I was never told what their agreements were, probably something after the same fashion as the boys and young men".[384] Perhaps the fact that Grey had no knowledge of "their agreements" is itself indicative of the rarity of this practice by the 1860s, whilst he had, as we have seen, a much clearer picture of part-time female involvement in agriculture.[385] It is possible, however, that some of the females listed as servants in farmers' households were engaged in more than domestic duties, but an examination of those listed for Harpenden is again unpromising. There were only 14 female servants on the 23 Harpenden farms, and of these 11 are described as "house servant", one as a housekeeper, one a nurse, and just one a "general servant".[386] What does seem to be clear is that by the mid-century there was considerable regional variation in the employment of women in agriculture. Thus whilst in the north and west of England the full-time employment of women remained common through into the third quarter of the century, "In the mainly arable areas of the south and east women tended to be more and more casual, brought into the productive process at particular times from the wives and daughters, widows and spinsters of the village based community, and paid by the piece for particular tasks".[387] We might add that the casualisation of female agricultural labour appears to have proceeded fastest and furthest in areas where substantial alternative employment was available, such as the Berkhamsted and St Albans regions of Hertfordshire. Indeed, the existence of industries such as straw plait and hat-making may have operated as both cause and effect, attracting women away from agricultural employment on the one hand, whilst declining opportunities for female agricultural employment stimulated their very growth on the other.[388] If women still played a supporting role in the agricultural regime, in a largely part-time or seasonal capacity, the main business of agriculture in this part of Hertfordshire by 1851 fell to the men, and the main business of Hertfordshire agriculture was the production of corn.

---

382   Additionally there were four "dairymaids", but all of these feature within the large entourages of domestic servants at Lamar Park in Wheathampstead, Rothamsted in Harpenden and Gorhambury and Childwick Hall in St Michaels, so they have appropriately been classified as domestic servants.

383   Snell, *Annals of the Labouring Poor*, pp. 21-2, 51-7, 95-6.

384   Grey, *Cottage Life*, p. 60.

385   See above, pp. 107.

386   In contrast to Higgs' view that "the exact status of female servants on the farm is especially difficult to determine", here at least the enumerators do appear to have attempted to distinguish clearly between female agricultural workers and domestic servants: Higgs, *Making Sense of the Census*, p. 87.

387   Howkins, *Re-shaping Rural England*, pp. 101-6.

388   M. Berg, *The Age of Manufactures 1700-1820* (London, 1985), p. 124.

The growing of corn dominated Hertfordshire agriculture, for as reported to the Board of Agriculture in 1795, "Hertfordshire is deemed the first corn county in the kingdom, for with the requisite advantages of climate, and of the various manures brought from London, to aid the production of the most valuable crops, nearly the whole of the soil is proper tillage land".[389] A few years later Arthur Young concurred. Arable cultivation was "the great object of the Hertfordshire husbandry. By far the greatest part of the county is under tillage, for which the county was singularly famous perhaps before the improvements in Norfolk began".[390] The proximity of London, allied to excellent connections by road, canal and subsequently rail, provided a vast and accessible market besides a valuable source of manure prior to the development of artificial fertilisers from the mid-nineteenth century, a development in which Hertfordshire, as we have seen, took the lead.[391] Sheep and cattle were not, of course, unknown in the county, but although they were fairly widely dispersed and valuable for their manure, Hertfordshire was not notable for its animal husbandry or dairying industry, and the trend in the first half of the nineteenth century was probably towards arable and away from pasture.[392] For Arthur Young, reporting to the Board of Agriculture in 1804, the subject of livestock was "as barren a one in Hertfordshire as any that can be named. It is merely an arable country; and the quantity of clover-hay carried to London is so great, and forms so profitable a husbandry, that livestock must be a very inferior object".[393] He does, however, note that at Gorhambury, at this date the estate of James Bucknall Grimston, Baron Verulam of Gorhambury, "the spotted polled breed" of cattle from Derbyshire were kept, as well as South Down sheep, whilst at Sandridgebury one Mr Clarke kept a flock of breeding Wiltshires.[394] Nevertheless, the returns for 1867 reveal that Hertfordshire stood bottom of the 40 counties of England and Wales in terms of the number of cattle per 100 acres of crops, whilst for sheep it stood in 32nd position.[395]

There clearly was at least some pasture farming taking place in the St Albans district in 1851. A total of 48 shepherds (including two shepherd boys) feature in the census, with at least a couple in each of the rural parishes and larger concentrations in St Michaels (rural), Redbourn and particularly in Wheathampstead, where 14 were to be found, three of them working together on Piggotts Hill Farm. A "sheep farm" at Wheathampstead consisting of 317 acres receives particular mention by the Reverend J. Clutterbuck in his agricultural notes on Hertfordshire relating to 1862-3, where a four-course crop rotation was managed with especial reference to sheep-stock, and in 1863 392 lambs, 356 sheep, 5 beasts, 50 calves and 198 pigs were fatted and sold from the farm.[396] Cowmen feature in far smaller numbers, just five in all, two of these again in

389   D. Walker, *General View of the County of Hertford Presented to the Board of Agriculture* (1795), quoted in *VCH Herts*, Vol. 2, p. 129.

390   Young, *General View of the Agriculture of Hertfordshire*, p. 55.

391   Evershed, "Agriculture of Hertfordshire", pp. 269, 283-4; J. Caird, *English Agriculture in 1850-51*, 2nd edition (London, 1968), pp. 459-64; N. Agar, "The Hertfordshire Farmer in the Age of the Industrial Revolution", in D. Jones-Baker (ed.), *Hertfordshire in History* (Hertfordshire Local History Council, 1991), pp. 252-3, 263; *VCH Herts*, Vol. 2, p. 129.

392   Agar, "The Hertfordshire Farmer", pp. 247-53; Mingay (ed.), *Agrarian History*, pp. 34, 49; Evershed, "Agriculture of Hertfordshire", pp. 270-2.

393   Young, *General View of the Agriculture of Hertfordshire*, p. 182. Evershed also noted that few sheep or stock of any kind were kept in the summer as the southern lands were generally unfit for permanent pasture and the clover was sold off as hay rather than used for feed: "Agriculture of Hertfordshire", p. 272.

394   Young, *General View of the Agriculture of Hertfordshire*, pp. 184-90; *VCH Herts*, Vol. 2, p. 396. The title Earl of Verulam was bestowed on James Walter Grimston in 1815.

395   Mingay (ed.), *Agrarian History*, Table III.10, pp. 1065-6. In terms of "stock units" (counting one ox or cow as equivalent to seven sheep) Hertfordshire, with 16.55 units per 100 acres of crops, stood 39th out of 40, just marginally ahead of Essex, with 16.12 units.

396   J. Clutterbuck, "Agricultural Notes on Hertfordshire", *Journal of the Royal Agricultural Society of England*, Vol. XXV (1864), pp. 308-10.

Wheathampstead. In Redbourn, apart from William Norwood, cowman on Redbournbury Farm, we find Bob Winchester working as a cow farrier, and, living separately, Joseph Winchester, a "cow's leech", who to judge from their ages were quite possibly father and son; despite the small number of cowmen, there was clearly enough work with cattle in the region to require specialist care. Three cattle drovers feature, in St Stephens, Sandridge and Harpenden, suggesting at least some participation in cattle trading, if more limited than was found in Tring to the west. However, in comparison with the total number of labourers declared by the farmers as employed on the various farms in the region, at least 1,257, and the 2,160 so designated under occupation, the numbers engaged in sheep and cattle farming are small, indicating clearly that pasture farming was very much a subsidiary activity. Indeed, a half century later, in 1905, the returns from the Board of Agriculture indicate that of a total acreage of 34,968 in the district, 23,560 acres were arable, 9,749 grass and 1,659 woodland.[397] The principal crop grown was undoubtedly wheat, supplemented by barley, oats, clover and roots, and by this date the Board was in no doubt that the soil of the region remained very well suited to grain production, both Harpenden and Wheathampstead producing "excellent wheat".[398]

The "common Hertfordshire course" of crop rotation, according to Young, was turnips, barley, clover, wheat and oats, and this was employed, with some slight variants, in and around St Albans, at Gorhambury and Wheathampstead, although on some of the heavier lands recourse was still had to a fallow year, a practice that in Hertfordshire he thought was confined to only the most difficult soils.[399] Almost fifty years later little had changed. In February 1851, a month or so before the census was taken, James Caird toured the county, similarly noting that the common system of cultivation involved five courses – turnips or fallow, barley, clover, wheat, oats – farms extending on average to 200 acres, with most farms of this size fattening sheep, pigs and cattle to supplement their arable husbandry and selling butter and straw as well.[400] This five course rotation, with swedes sometimes in place of turnips and occasionally interspersed with sainfoin, reportedly remained the most common practice in the southern half of the county in 1864.[401] Historians echo the view that five or six course rotations were usual in Hertfordshire, with fallow years not unknown despite the employment of root crops in place of fallow in areas where soils were sufficiently light.[402] Apart from corn, roots were the other chief crop in the rural parts of St Michaels in 1905, whilst in Sandridge farmers favoured wheat, barley, oats and clover, despite the fact that the soils of the two parishes – mixed clay, sand and gravel – were similar.[403]

Arthur Young, writing in 1804, noted that in Sandridge and around St Albans the soil was a deep, flinty loam on a chalk base, and "held to be very good land", whilst at Sandridgebury the sandy soil on the higher ground and the friable loams and clay and flint loams on the lower ground were also "excellent soil", and particularly good for turnips.[404] Turnips were also grown on the gravelly clay from Wheathampstead to St Albans, whilst similar soil from St Albans to Redbourn was "of an excellent quality, and superior to many

397   Calculated from the figures given in *VCH Herts*, Vol. 2, pp. 294, 365, 392, 412, 424, 432. No data is given for the parishes of St Albans or for St Michaels (urban).

398   *Ibid.*

399   Young, *General View of the Agriculture of Hertfordshire*, pp. 61, 69-71.

400   Caird, *English Agriculture in 1850-51*, pp. 455-6.

401   Evershed, "Agriculture of Hertfordshire", pp. 271-2.

402   Mingay (ed.), *Agrarian History*, pp. 281, 296.

403   *VCH Herts*, Vol. 2, pp. 392, 432.

404   Young, *General View of the Agriculture of Hertfordshire*, p. 5.

named". This was "a fine mellow turnip land, easily worked, and equal to the production of almost any crop".[405] William Cobbett too, writing sixteen years later, took note of the flint loams on chalk in the area, commenting that "wherever this is the soil, the wheat grows well". As he toured through the area in June 1822 he found "the crops, and especially that of the barley, are very fine and very forward".[406] Chalking of the land, at a rate of 40-50 bushels per acre, was as common here as it was elsewhere in the county, whilst wheat was generally top-dressed in the spring with soot and ashes, and at Sandridgebury with burnt bones, given the paucity of livestock and therefore dung in the county. Despite the opinion later to be expressed by John Bennett Lawes, Young regarded night soil as a most effective form of manure, and noted that "it is much used about St Albans", although animal dung was also employed in the area if available, often collected by the poor from the roads and sold to farmers at 2d per bushel.[407]

Wheat yields in Hertfordshire varied considerably between farms, ranging from just 15 bushels per acre in the poor open parish of Ashwell to 40 bushels per acre on the rich loams at Buntingford, with occasional examples in excess of that, and the figure for St Albans, Sandridge and Gorhambury standing midway at 24 or 25 bushels.[408] Sixty years later it was reported that on the lighter lands that predominated in the southern half of the county 28 bushels was considered an average crop.[409] From 17 examples in the county Young estimated the average barley crop at 32 bushels "and a small fraction" per acre, exactly the yield at St Albans and Sandridge, although inferior to the 40 bushels, sometimes 48 bushels, produced at Gorhambury, where oat yields were also well above average.[410] Other crops grown in the district on the farms visited by Young were beans and sainfoin, the latter very successfully at Sandridgebury. Particular note was also made of the oak woodlands of the Gorhambury estate, whilst in 1822 William Cobbett commented very favourably upon the fine oaks, ashes and beeches extending from Redbourn to Hemel Hempstead, and was characteristically pleased to find that "no villainous things of the *fir-tribe* offend the eye here".[411]

All of this, of course, pre-dates the revolutionary work to be commenced in the 1830s by John Bennett Lawes at Rothamsted.[412] But it is quite clear from contemporary observations that, long before this work was begun, Hertfordshire agriculture was well advanced, farmers of the 'improving' variety were numerous, and every effort was made through crop rotations and the use of various fertilisers to get the best out of the soil. The county had long been famous for its agriculture, even before the much vaunted improvements in Norfolk.[413] James Caird's figures for wheat yields in 1850-1 suggest that Hertfordshire's performance was respectable if by no means spectacular, but it is likely that the yields achieved in the St Albans district stood a little above the county average, particularly on well-managed estates such as that of the Earl of Verulam at Gorhambury.[414]

---

405   *Ibid.*, pp. 6, 10.
406   W. Cobbett, *Rural Rides*, 2 Vols. (Everyman edn., London, 1912), Vol. 1, p. 85.
407   *Ibid.*, pp. 82, 161-73.
408   *Ibid.*, pp. 87-8.
409   Evershed, "Agriculture of Hertfordshire", p. 275.
410   Young, *General View of the Agriculture of Hertfordshire*, pp. 95, 97.
411   *Ibid.*, pp. 98, 121, 146-7; Cobbett, *Rural Rides*, Vol. 1, p. 86.
412   See above, pp. 81-2.
413   Young, *General View of the Agriculture of Hertfordshire*, p. 55.
414   Caird, *English Agriculture in 1850-51*, p. 480.

In many parts of the county open field farming had long since disappeared, for Hertfordshire was one of the ten counties in England that was already largely enclosed as early as 1600.[415] The enclosure of land had proceeded piecemeal and usually by agreement, a process which continued through the sixteenth and seventeenth centuries, but one that had most impact in the south and west of the county rather than in the north and east, which shared a pattern of late enclosure with its neighbour, Cambridgeshire.[416] The arable land in open fields around St Albans was being enclosed during the seventeenth century, as were common lands in Harpenden in the late seventeenth and early eighteenth centuries, apparently without the controversy that erupted at Tring, Berkhamsted and Little Gaddesden to the west.[417] In the south of the county a very considerable proportion of the land was already enclosed by 1695, and it was largely waste land that was left to later parliamentary enclosure, although even then substantial areas remained unenclosed to survive as commons, in Harpenden and Wheathampstead in our region, as well as in Berkhamsted, Hemel Hempstead, Kings Langley and Royston.[418] Enclosure proceeded slowly in the early eighteenth century, more rapidly in the late eighteenth and early nineteenth centuries, although the proportion of arable land in the county enclosed by act of parliament prior to 1845 stood below 15 per cent, testifying to the impact of early enclosure by agreement.[419] Nevertheless, the steady further erosion of the common fields gradually changed the face of Hertfordshire agriculture, and facilitated agricultural innovation at an early stage.

For many contemporary agricultural writers, good farming practice not only required land to be held in discrete, enclosed plots, but it also generally required farms to be of a substantial size. Arthur Young was in little doubt on this score, writing that "It is the general opinion of the district, that the soil cannot be kept in that degree of fertility necessary to support the rental and other expenses of it, without bringing large quantities of manure from the capital: a business indifferently executed on very small farms. All the exertions of this kind, which claim any notice, are on large ones."[420] Furthermore, sheep folding, which was very prevalent in the county, simply could not be practised efficiently on small farms.[421] Writing in 1851 Caird noticed that in the broad region between Hitchin and Hemel Hempstead, which would incorporate much of the St Albans district, "Small farmers holding from 50 to 100 acres are not doing well. Some may manage just to keep going, but no more, whilst many of them must go out of the business".[422] William Ashby of High Street, Redbourn, a married man of 50 years with three young children, occupation "farmer out of business", may have been a case in point.

A few farmers supplemented their agricultural income with a by-employment, seven in total in our district, but far from all of these were smallholders, and most followed a trade quite closely tied to agriculture. Three were

415   R. Pope (ed.), *Atlas of British Social and Economic History Since c. 1700* (New York, 1989), p. 1. The other early enclosed counties were Cheshire, Cumberland, Durham, Essex, Kent, Lancashire, Suffolk, Surrey and Sussex.
416   Munby, *Hertfordshire Landscape*, pp. 164-6, 181-2.
417   *VCH Herts*, Vol. 4, pp. 221-2; G.H. Whybrow, *The History of Berkhamsted Common* (Letchworth, no date), pp. 37-52.
418   W.E. Tate, *A Handlist of English Enclosure Acts and Awards, part 16*, Hertfordshire (Lawes Agricultural Trust, Rothamsted, unpublished), p. 21, cited in L. Meredith, "Did Late Implementation Lessen the Effects of Enclosure on a Community? A Case Study of Aston, Hertfordshire", unpubl. undergraduate dissertation, University of Hertfordshire, 1995, p. 13; *VCH Herts*, Vol. 4, p. 222; Munby, *Hertfordshire Landscape*, p. 186.
419   Pope (ed.), *Atlas of British Social and Economic History*, Fig. 1.2, p. 4.
420   Young, *General View of the Agriculture of Hertfordshire*, pp. 25-6.
421   *Ibid.*, p. 26.
422   Caird, *English Agriculture in 1850-51*, pp. 455-6.

also millers, Jonathan Parsons of Shafford Mill in St Michaels (rural) who farmed 200 acres, Ernest Dixon in Redbourn, farmer of 150 acres who lived at the "Mill", and Edward Hawkins of Redbournbury Mill, a smallholder with just 27 acres. John House of Harpenden was a brewer and farmer of 120 acres, whilst in the same village Henry Oldaker was innkeeper at the Bull Inn and a smallholder of 50 acres. Busiest of all was Charles Dixon of Redbourn, "farmer, brewer and baker", whilst George Webb of Beaumont Hall in Redbourn was occupied as a maltster besides farming an extensive 530 acre holding and employing 23 labourers.

Young complained that farms in Hertfordshire were generally small, not one in the county exceeding 1,000 acres at the start of the nineteenth century.[423] His criterion was a demanding one, however, for across England and Wales as a whole in 1851 only 0.35% of farms were 1,000 acres or more in extent, a similar figure to the 0.33% in the south Midlands as a whole, although below the 1% in the eastern counties with which Young may have been particularly familiar.[424] By 1851 Caird put the average size at 200 acres.[425] The census enumerators' books allow us to examine farm sizes with more precision, but before we turn to the data presented in Table 12 some problems must be noted. The instructions given to the enumerators in 1851 were quite detailed, providing examples of how farmers were to be recorded, with their acreages and employees, and explicitly showing that landed proprietors were to be listed, also with the acreage of their estates and numbers employed.[426] In the St Albans district, however, these instructions were not faithfully followed. For those listed as landed proprietors, or designated by their title as "esquire", "gentleman" or the like, the acreages of their estates or the number of their employees are rarely given. This, of course, will mean that there are important omissions, particularly of the larger farms. One example of such a failure properly to record farm acreage is in the case of Arthur Timperon. Timperon resided at Childwick Hall in the parish of St Michaels (rural) with his mother, two sisters and an entourage of eleven servants. His occupational designation is simply "Esquire", with no indication of any farming activities at all. Amongst his household was one Elizabeth Cook, a "dairywoman", aged 40 and born in Twickenham, and it is this Elizabeth Cook who provides a link with an unusual entry in the Out-hamlets, for she is again listed here, and again as a servant, but as the first name in a new schedule. In the address column, the entry reads "New Barnes Farm. Farmer Arthur Timperon Esquire, 510 acres, 11 labourers one in and boys". In this instance, a fortunate link and a quirk in the procedure adopted by the St Peters' enumerator allowed his estate to be identified, but this was pure chance. If St Michaels parish had been examined in isolation, no clue would have been found at all regarding Timperon's agricultural activities.

In other instances the information is completely absent, and another important example is the Rothamsted Estate in Harpenden. Here, as we have seen, lived John Bennett Lawes with his wife, son, daughter and thirteen servants. But Lawes is described simply as a "gentleman", although, of course, we know that he was a highly active experimental farmer. His household included John Ransome, aged 28, a "farm bailiff", but again no further information is given. If we are to ascertain the size of the Rothamsted Estate, therefore, we would need to examine other documentation. In this case a report on the agriculture of Hertfordshire made in 1864

423   Young, *General View of the Agriculture of Hertfordshire*, p. 23.

424   Calculated from *1851 Census Report. Population Tables II*, Parliamentary Papers 1852-3, Vol. LXXXVIII, Vol. 1, Table 22, p. clxxv. The South Midland Division employed in the census report included Middlesex, Hertfordshire, Buckinghamshire, Oxfordshire, Northamptonshire, Bedfordshire and Cambridgeshire.

425   Caird, *English Agriculture in 1850-51*, p. 455.

426   Higgs, *Making Sense of the Census*, p. 86.

provides this information, revealing that about 56 acres were set aside for the purpose of experimentation alone, whilst the home farm consisted of 450 acres, including 94 acres of park, and from 1850-5 245 acres were kept under crops.[427] The Gorhambury estate of the Earl of Verulam is a similar example. Here the Earl, as head of the household, is given the occupational designation "Peer, Lord Lieutenant of Herts", and his household included his immediate family, his brother, distinguished visitors, and an army of servants, but the only indication of any agricultural activity is the presence of a single farm worker, John Pickett "cowman". No acreage is given, nor the number of agricultural labourers he employed, even though the advanced and productive farming practices at Gorhambury had caught the particular attention of Arthur Young.

It is not only in the case of such distinguished gentlemen that information on farm acreages is missing from the census enumerators' returns. Again in St Michaels (rural), and forming the very next schedule to the Earl of Verulam, is the household of John Purrott of Maynes Farm.[428] His household included two farm labourers, three ploughmen and a shepherd, but he is described simply as "farmer", with no further indication of the size of his farm or the total number of labourers he employed. In all there are eleven individuals described as farmer where no indication of acreage is given. Two of these were "partners", both brothers, to the head of household, two more were sons, and the acreage is given in the preceding entry, but this still leaves seven farmers, heads of their households, for whom no acreage is specified. Farm bailiffs pose a further problem. In just one instance, Frederick Faircloth of Fosters Farm, Redbourn, an acreage – in this case 140 acres – is specified, but for the remaining 19 bailiffs or stewards there is no indication of the size of the farm they managed. This is not, of course, a problem where they lived in at the farm they were running and the acreage is specified next to the head of household. Such is the case with James Batchelor, bailiff of Evan's Farm in Sandridge, who lived in with Elizabeth Booth, widow, farming 280 acres and employing 12 men. Nor is it a problem where the farm they managed can be found elsewhere in the census. Hence, in St Michaels (rural) we find James Glasscock, farm bailiff of St Stephens Farm, which can be traced in St Stephens parish in the ownership of Henry Cox, farmer of 100 acres employing 10 men. In other instances, the farm to which a bailiff was attached is unspecified, and we can only assume they worked for one or other of the farmers in the district, or possibly further afield. But occasionally they are described as bailiff to a farm that cannot be traced elsewhere in the census. Hence James Foster of Reed Hall Farm, Wheathampstead, is listed as bailiff to that farm, but no acreage is given, nor does the farm feature elsewhere in the listings for the village, and William Jordan of Nichols Farm, Redbourn, is a similar case. Once again, it would seem that there are some omissions from the census.

It is clear, therefore, that the returns exclude a – relatively small – number of farms, but may well exclude at least a few of the larger estates. On the other hand, such studies that have been conducted to date checking the acreages given in the census with other contemporary documentation do appear to indicate a fairly close correspondence.[429] It has also been suggested that, as only those describing themselves as farmers were obliged

---

427   Evershed, "Agriculture of Hertfordshire", pp. 285-91. In the interests of consistency, this information has not been added to that taken from the census presented in Table 12.

428   Maynes Farm was situated adjacent to Gorhambury, and still exists today.

429   S. Thomas, "The enumerators' returns as a source for a period picture of the parish of Llansantffraid, 1841-1851", *Ceredigion*, Vol. IV (1963), pp. 408-21; *Idem*, "The agricultural labour force in some south-west Carmarthenshire parishes in the mid-nineteenth century", *Welsh History Review*, Vol. III (1966-7), pp. 63-73. This is clearly a topic that deserves further investigation at the local and regional level. In the present state of knowledge, one can only speculate upon the extent to which the published national returns were affected by such factors.

to give details of land held, considerable numbers of smallholders may have been excluded from the census, and the agricultural returns made in 1875 tend to support this conclusion.[430] This would be true, of course, of all counties, although perhaps not equally, but as yet it is impossible to tell whether or not this means that the census is more accurate for some counties compared to others, at least before the very end of the nineteenth century.[431] It is with these considerations in mind, therefore, that we must approach the data presented in Table 12.

TABLE 12 : FARM SIZES (ACRES)

	Under 50	50-99	100-199	200-499	500+	Total	Total Acreage
St Albans (town)	0	0	0	1	1	2	815
St Michaels (rural)	2	2	5	9	0	18	3331
St Stephens	2	4	14	8	0	28	4832
Out-hamlets	4	5	12	6	3	30	5412
Harpenden	6	2	6	9	0	23	3755
Redbourn	3	4	10	4	1	22	3402
Sandridge	1	1	3	13	1	19	5419
Wheathampstead	3	6	6	5	0	20	3208
Total	21	24	56	55	6	162	30174
Percentage	13.0	14.8	34.6	34.0	3.7	100.0	
Berkhamsted Region(%)	14.6	13.4	37.8	32.9	1.2	99.9	
Great Britain (%)*	48.2	18.7	18.4	12.5	2.2	100.0	

* calculated from Mingay (ed.), *Agrarian History*, Table IV.2, p. 1072.

Despite the possible absence of a number of large farms, it is immediately apparent that Arthur Young gave a slightly misleading picture of Hertfordshire farms, at least in this area, by describing them as generally small.[432] In fact, just as in the Berkhamsted region, there was a far smaller percentage of very small farms, under 50 acres, in this district than was found nationally, only 13% compared with 48%. Nor was this compensated for by larger numbers between 50 and 100 acres, for here too the percentage was relatively low. By contrast, just over one-third of all farms stood between 100 and 199 acres, and a similar proportion between 200 and 499, compared with national figures of just 18 and 13% respectively. The figures for Great Britain, of course, include substantial regions of the country that were predominantly pastoral, James Caird having appreciated the fundamental division between a pastoral west and an arable east of England as early as 1851.[433] In pastoral areas Caird noted that farms tended to be smaller, and subsequent research has supported the view that farms of under 150 acres predominated in the north-west, north Midlands, Wales, the

---

430   M. Reed, "The Peasantry of Nineteenth-Century England: a Neglected Class?", *History Workshop Journal*, Issue 18 (1984), pp. 56-9. See also *idem*, "Nineteenth-Century Rural England. A Case for 'Peasant Studies'?", *Journal of Peasant Studies*, Vol. 14 (1986-7), pp. 78-99; A. Howkins, "Peasants, Servants and Labourers: The Marginal Workforce in British Agriculture, c.1870-1914", *Agricultural History Review*, Vol. 42 (1994), pp. 49-62: M. Winstanley, "Industrialisation and the Small Farm: Family and Household Economy in Nineteenth-Century Lancashire", *Past and Present*, No. 152 (1996), pp. 157-95.

431   The returns of 1895 confirm Hertfordshire as a county where a low proportion of the land was occupied by smallholders, whilst it stood in 4th place out of 43 counties for the proportion occupied by holdings of 100 acres or more: Winstanley, "Industrialisation and the Small Farm", Table 1, pp. 166-7.

432   See above, p. 120. Of course, the range of farm sizes could well have changed between 1804, when Young wrote, and 1851.

433   H.C. Prince, "The Changing Rural Landscape, 1750-1850", in Mingay (ed.), *Agrarian History*, pp. 73-6.

south-west and the Lincolnshire Fens.[434] Comparison between a corn growing county like Hertfordshire and a national average that incorporated both pastoral and arable areas may not, therefore, be entirely appropriate, but at least serves to underline the established orthodoxy concerning farm size and agricultural regime. Perhaps the point that Young was making was that the county was lacking in the largest holdings, those of over 500 acres, which as we have seen were more common in some other eastern and southern counties, and particularly in East Anglia.[435] Nevertheless, substantial, if not very large, farms dominated the region, again presenting a very similar pattern to that found in the Berkhamsted area. There were, however, more farms of 500 acres plus in the St Albans district than were found in Berkhamsted, six in all constituting 3.7% of the total, compared with 2.2% nationally and just 1.2% in the Berkhamsted region. If we take into account the omission of some estates that were probably amongst the largest in the district, this picture would be reinforced further.

The number of labourers employed is given for a total of 150 farms. We have already seen when discussing living in farm labourers that there are clearly some omissions in the census returns, most apparent when no labourers are recorded despite the fact that one or more clearly lived in at the farm.[436] Twelve farms record no employees even though they give the farm acreage. Eight of these 12 were farms of 20 acres or less, and hence were probably farmed solely with family labour. Another was 60 acres in extent, but the other three were 110, 180 and 357 acres respectively, and the two largest of these both included living in farm labourers. Possibly in the case of 20-25% of those farms which recorded no farm labour in this district, therefore, the entry is an error, and not a true reflection of the situation. If we assume that nine of our 162 farms actually employed no labour, then just 5.5% relied solely on family labour, which compares with a national figure for 1831 approaching one-half.[437] Of the 150 farms for which information is given on both acreage and number of labourers employed, 56 (37%) employed between one and five labourers, 56 between six and ten (37%), 21 between 11 and 15 (14%), seven between 16 and 20 (5%) and 10 employed 21 or more (7%), with two farms of 500 and 700 acres employing as many as 30 and one of 480 acres employing 32. These figures stand very close to those found in the Berkhamsted region of Hertfordshire, although here the largest concentration was a workforce of 20, again reflecting the greater prominence of large farms in the St Albans district.[438] The region thus emerges as a very substantial employer of agricultural labour, reflecting the greater labour demands (approximately double) of arable and mixed farming compared with pastoral, as well as the superior farm sizes found in predominantly arable regions.[439] On the national scale in 1851 the 306,767 farmers employed 1,460,896 labourers, a ratio of 4.8 per farm on average.[440] In the Berkhamsted region there were 89 farmers if all are included even where they specified no acreage or labour force, and 606 labourers, giving a ratio of 6.8. If the seven farms are excluded that mention no acreage or labour force the ratio rises further to 7.4.[441] In the St Albans district the figures were very similar, standing at 7.2:1 if all farmers are included, or 7.8:1 excluding those mentioning no acreage or labour force.

434   J.V. Beckett, "Land Ownership and Estate Management", in Mingay (ed.), *Agrarian History*, pp. 608-9.

435   *Ibid.*, pp. 607-9; *1851 Census Report. Population Tables II*, Parliamentary Papers 1852-3, Vol. LXXXVIII, Vol. 1, p. clxxv.

436   See above, pp. 110-11.

437   J.D. Chambers and G.E. Mingay, *The Agricultural Revolution 1750-1880* (London, 1966), p. 133.

438   Goose, *The Berkhamsted Region*, p. 52.

439   Chambers and Mingay, *The Agricultural Revolution*, pp. 133-4.

440   Calculated from Mingay (ed.), *Agrarian History*, Table IV.1, p. 1071.

441   Goose, *The Berkhamsted Region*, p. 52.

The returns made in connection with the Poor Law Commissioners' enquiries of 1832-4 and the report on the Employment of Women and Children in 1867 indicated that arable and mixed farming required one man for every 25 or 30 acres.[442] In the St Albans district overall the ratio stood at one man for every 24 acres, the figures for the sub-districts ranging from a low of 19-21 in Harpenden, Sandridge and Wheathampstead to 28-30 in St Michaels (rural) and the Out-hamlets. Again, as one would expect, there was a rough correspondence between individual farm sizes and labour force employed, although there were also many exceptions that are impossible to explain without further research. How was it, for instance, that Thomas Brown of Hill End could run a farm of 300 acres with just three agricultural labourers, even though his three sons were aged just 7, 9 and 13, and are described as "scholars", whilst Henry Cox of St Stephens needed as many as 10 to service his 100 acre farm? And how could Richard Brown of Lye Lane, St Stephens, manage 270 acres with just the help of four labourers and his one son, whilst at Chalk Dell farm in Sandridge, just 129 acres in extent, John Raggett required an many as 15?

If the ratio of 186 labourers to 34 farms (5.5:1) found in the village of Melbourn in Cambridgeshire represents "a guide to the extent of the proletarianisation of agriculture" in 1841, by 1851 this process had proceeded substantially further in the St Albans district, as indeed it had in the Berkhamsted region to the west.[443] Agricultural labourers in this area, however, or in Harpenden at least, were not necessarily wholly without access to land. Edwin Grey's reminiscences make much of the importance of pig-keeping to the agricultural labourers and their families, for even though the number of pig-keepers was declining somewhat in the third quarter of the century "even now there were quite a number".[444] Oral testimony to the same effect also survives for Wheathampstead.[445] The situation was again similar at Lark Rise in Oxfordshire a decade or so later, where "The family pig was everybody's pride and everybody's business", and an important source of bacon through the winter months or even longer.[446] Pigs were kept in cottagers' gardens in south Harpenden, nearer to or farther from the house depending upon the size of the plot, and here too they could assume considerable economic importance, "for it was the pig who was looked to for the rent money probably, and also to fill the pickle pot, the general custom at the time of killing being to sell one half of the carcase complete, and maybe the better joints of the other half, retaining the rest for home consumption...".[447] In turn the pig dung served as a dressing for the home garden or allotment. As Grey explains:

> "the housewife has, as a rule, plenty of fresh vegetables for her use, for besides the little
> vegetable gardens generally attached to most of the cottages, there was also the excellent
> Rothamsted Allotment Club, of which most of the married labourers in the South Harpenden
> district were members, holding allotments of ten or twenty poles area, the rent being at the
> rate of 3d. per pole per year."[448]

---

442 Chambers and Mingay, *The Agricultural Revolution*, p. 133.

443 D.R. Mills, "The Quality of Life in Melbourn, Cambridgeshire, in the Period 1800-50", *International Review of Social History*, Vol. 23 (1978), p. 397.

444 Grey, *Cottage Life*, p. 114.

445 M.A. Coburn, *George and Henry. Their Lives and Times in Victorian Wheathampstead* (Wheathampstead Local History Group, 1992), pp. 13-14.

446 Thompson, *Lark Rise to Candleford*, pp. 24-5.

447 Grey, *Cottage Life* , pp. 114-15.

448 *Ibid.*, p. 112.

John Bennett Lawes would allow his general hands to cease work at 2.00pm on Saturday afternoons, specifically to allow them to spend an hour or two working their allotments, and must thus clearly be included amongst those landowners who provided allotments for philanthropic reasons.[449] Such actions were noticed by contemporaries, for whilst expressing general concern about "the labourer's condition", Henry Evershed made particular reference to "the efforts made at Rothamsted and in other parts of the county to improve his lot and raise his social condition".[450] These holdings were quite small compared with the general situation across southern England as revealed in the 1834 Report of the Poor Law Commissioners, for twenty poles only amounted to one-eighth of an acre, whereas in 1834 one-quarter to half an acre was standard.[451] But despite the fact that this land was let in small parcels, the rent charged per acre was almost identical to that levied on allotments in the wider region some forty years before, despite the fact that rents generally had been buoyed up by the onset of agriculture's 'Golden Age' between the 1850s and 1870s.[452] There can be no doubt about the profitability of allotment cultivation, nor the nutritional benefit that must have derived from the ready availability of fresh vegetables, as Grey noted for Harpenden and Flora Thompson for Lark Rise.[453] Indeed, in 1861 it was suggested that it was "difficult, if not impossible" to compare agricultural earnings across the country because of the importance of the various perquisites that the labourer might enjoy – keeping a pig, rearing poultry for the market, growing potatoes in an allotment or cottage garden, cutting furze or turf for fuel, besides the value of gleaning and the other earnings of women and children.[454]

Grey does, of course, indicate that there were indeed hard times for these labouring families, generally in the winter when recourse might be had to free soup and warm clothing distributed by the wealthier ladies of the parish.[455] Mary Carbery's mother herself visited the poor with her daughter, whilst Mary's Grandma Wroughton of Woolley also attended the people of the parish, "with soup and rabbits and camphorated oil, and if poor, as most of them are, with flannel and calico from the Poor Persons' cupboard at Woolley".[456] Nevertheless, Grey also reported that in Harpenden "the youngsters, with very few exceptions, looked wonderfully sturdy and well, no doubt but that the various foods mentioned in their menus contained all the necessary 'vitamins' for body building".[457]

These cottage gardens apart, some evidence of commercial horticultural activity is also provided by the census. Two "nurserymen" are listed, John Watson of London Road in St Peters parish, and David Spriggins of St

449   Ibid., pp. 62-3; B. Moselle, "Allotments, Enclosure and Proletarianization in Early Nineteenth-century Southern England", Economic History Review, Vol. XLVIII (1995), pp. 484-5.

450   Evershed, "Agriculture of Hertfordshire", p. 302.

451   Moselle, "Allotments", p. 484.

452   Ibid., Table A1, p. 499; W.A. Armstrong, "The Countryside", in Thompson (ed.), Cambridge Social History of Britain 1750-1950, p. 113; R.A. Church, The Great Victorian Boom 1850-1873 (London 1975), pp. 28-30; Crouzet, Victorian Economy, pp. 159-66. Rents in general across England rose by an average of 16% between 1850 and 1873.

453   Moselle, "Allotments", pp. 489-93; Grey, Cottage Life, pp. 112-13; Thompson, Lark Rise to Candleford, pp. 27-8, 30. Recollections from Wheathampstead record that "all the vegetables were home grown, either in the garden or on land George rented": Coburn, George and Henry, p. 14. For pigs and gardens in Lancashire and Nottinghamshire, Marshall, "The Lancashire Rural Labourer", pp. 119-20, and idem, "Nottinghamshire Labourers in the Early Nineteenth Century", Transactions of the Thoroton Society of Nottinghamshire, Vol. 64 (1960), pp. 62-3.

454   Purdy, "On the Earnings of Agricultural Labourers", pp. 329-30.

455   Grey, Cottage Life, p. 111.

456   Carbery, Happy World, pp. 48, 71.

457   Grey, Cottage Life, p. 112.

Stephens Green, an employer of three men and three apprentices, two of whom, John Bracey and Charles Allen, lived in with him and his family. As in the Berkhamsted region, water cress was also grown here, in the River Colne, the Ver and adjacent brooks.[458] It was most notable at Redbourn, where William Payne, "cultivator of water cresses" lived at Water Cress Hall on the St Albans Road, whilst Thomas Slaughter, "labourer in water cress beds" lived in the village High Street. In the urban part of St Michaels parish Thomas Grace of Pound Field, who had himself been born in Redbourn, was a "water cress grower", but no water cress men appear in St Stephens, even though according to the Board of Agriculture cresses were being grown here some fifty years later.[459] This, however, was little more than a makeweight to an agricultural regime dominated by substantial farms producing wheat, barley and roots on a substantial scale, providing by far the most important source of employment for the male population of the district and, despite the importance of straw plait and hat-making, underpinning its wealth and economic vitality.

Migration

The analysis of patterns of migration from the census is rendered more difficult where a town exists which contains more than one parish, for although county of birth is very clear and straightforward in the enumerations, the place of birth recorded could be either a town, or a parish or a hamlet, or any other area that the householder chose to delimit. In the case of St Albans, we have also chosen to divide the parishes of St Peters and St Michaels into discrete urban and rural elements, and have hence imposed a further demarcation that would not necessarily have been recognised by those completing the census returns. Some did indeed recognise that they belonged to one of the Out-hamlets, and if they had been born there often stated as much. Others, however, clearly did not trouble themselves with such detail, and listed themselves as born in the parish of St Peters. Thus just 144 individuals living in the Out-hamlets in 1851 specified one or other of those hamlets as their birth-place, whilst as many as 569 entered the parish of St Peters, and it is inconceivable that this represents the number who had in fact been born in the town but had subsequently migrated to the Liberty.

It is even more difficult to segregate the urban and rural parts of St Michaels parish. But the problem does not end there, for many inhabitants clearly did not even distinguish between the three central parishes of the borough itself. Hence just 285 out of a total of 2,523 residents in St Peters parish in 1851 gave that parish as their place of birth, whilst as many as 1,039 entered St Albans, by which many of them can only have meant the town of St Albans rather than the parish. In contrast, 1,668 of the 3,371 inhabitants of St Albans parish gave St Albans as their place of birth, with just 13 listing St Michaels and 24 St Peters. It will not be possible, therefore, to analyse migration patterns according to proportions native and non-native on a parish by parish basis except for the four villages. The Liberty of St Albans can only be treated as a whole, and hence our figures for natives or migrants to the various parishes or parts of parishes within the Liberty refer to those native or migrant to the Liberty, and not to the parishes themselves. As this constitutes a large and populous geographical area, this is likely to minimise the amount of movement apparent in our data, for migration between birth and 1851 *within* the Liberty – even if it represented a significant rural to urban transition – will be obscured from view.

---

458   *VCH Herts*, Vol. 2, pp. 364-5, 424.
459   *Ibid.*, p. 424.

There are still few large scale studies of migration patterns for mid- or late nineteenth century England. Indeed, in a recent summary of those that are available for rural areas just four are highlighted, one of which is the Berkhamsted study that featured in Volume 1 of the present series.[460] The identification of place names in the census enumerators' books is an extremely time-consuming process when dealing with a large population, and one where unfamiliarity with particular places, on the part of both enumerator and researcher, can only serve to enhance the usual difficulties of poor handwriting and general legibility. Whilst serious efforts have been made, with the help of the various publications of the English Place-Name Society, to read and identify all the places of birth listed in the St Albans district, there are many that remain obscure, as indicated in the documentation which follows in Part Two. For the family historian or genealogist this may well be problematic if such obscurity affects the particular individual or family they are tracing. For the historian, however, interested in the larger picture created by the conflation of numerous individual cases, occasional omissions, or even errors where 'educated guesses' have been made, are unlikely to affect the overall trends revealed. Furthermore, county of birth is far easier to identify, as well as to analyse, and forms the basis of much of the discussion which follows. The central consideration will be the proportion of the population resident in their place of birth on census night, admittedly a limited window on patterns of migration but one that must suffice in view of the large sample under scrutiny, with the data further broken down by age, sex and social status.[461]

Ravenstein's "laws of migration", formulated in the later nineteenth century, have so often formed the starting point for discussion of migration that it might be appropriate to rehearse the key elements of them here.[462] Ravenstein felt that most migration was economically inspired, and hence the development of both industry and transport in the nineteenth century created a major flow from agricultural to industrial areas, with urban residents less likely to leave their birthplace. Most migrants moved over short distances, with variations according to levels of skill and by sex: males tended to move further, whilst more women migrated than men. Most migrants were young unmarried adults, and often migration proceeded by a series of steps to an ultimate destination. Heavy out-migration was often counter-balanced by a reverse inward flow. And finally, one of Ravenstein's hypotheses that has been seriously questioned, large towns grew more by migration than by natural increase.[463] Some of these "laws" can be put to the test in the discussion which follows, although others – particularly those which relate to out-migration and step-migration – cannot be fully tested from the data presented here.

---

460   Mills and Schürer (eds.), *Local Communities*, pp. 218-27.

461   Clearly, this will tell us nothing about any intermediate moves that might have taken place or reveal the timing of migration, although age specific figures will help in the latter respect. Additional insight would, of course, be provided by linking information between censuses, but this is an extremely time consuming process, particularly as registers of marriage and deaths must be consulted too, and it is therefore very difficult indeed to employ where a large, regional sample is involved. For some discussion of these issues, see C.G. Pooley and I.D. Whyte, "Introduction. Approaches to the Study of Migration and Social Change", in *idem* (eds.), *Migrants, Emigrants and Immigrants. A Social History of Migration* (London, 1991), pp. 1-15; and for an example of record linkage, K. Schürer, "The Role of the Family in the Process of Migration", in *ibid.*, pp. 106-42.

462   The following is based upon D.B. Grigg, "E.G. Ravenstein and the 'Laws of Migration'", *Journal of Historical Geography*, Vol. 3 (1977), pp. 41-54; see also Mills and Schürer (eds.), *Local Communities*, p. 219.

463   In fact for the urban registration districts of England and Wales, of 182% growth 1841-1911, 151% was due to natural increase and just 31% to migration: R. Woods, *The Population of Britain in the Nineteenth Century* (Cambridge, 1995), p. 23. Ravenstein did, however, refer to large towns, and the hypothesis thus deserves further testing.

TABLE 13 : MIGRATION – PROPORTION NATIVE*

	All		Male		Female	
	No.	%	No.	%	No.	%
St Albans Urban						
St Albans	1843	54.7	863	55.0	980	54.4
St Michaels (Urban)	670	61.4	303	62.5	367	60.6
St Peters	1421	56.3	679	60.1	742	53.2
St Albans Rural						
St Michaels (Rural)	401	44.1	195	42.5	206	45.8
St Stephens	1030	66.3	513	66.6	517	66.0
Out-hamlets	878	59.7	454	60.1	424	59.4
Harpenden	1127	56.9	529	55.9	598	57.9
Redbourn	1310	62.9	592	61.3	718	64.2
Sandridge	457	53.1	212	49.4	245	56.8
Wheathampstead	1232	64.6	604	63.9	628	65.2
Sub-Totals						
St Albans (Liberty)	6243	57.2	3007	58.2	3236	56.3
Urban Parishes	3934	56.3	1845	57.9	2089	55.0
Rural Parishes	6435	59.8	3099	58.8	3336	60.7
Total	10369	58.4	4944	58.5	5425	58.4
Berkhamsted Region		54.6		57.4		52.2
Mills' Rural Norm		55.3		58.8		51.7

* In relation to all of the St Albans parishes "native" means native to the Liberty of St Albans: see text for a fuller explanation.

An outline of the basic propensity to migrate and the patterns of migration found in the St Albans district in 1851 is shown in Tables 13 and 14. Table 13 shows that the proportion of the population who were still living in their place of birth varied from a low of 44% in St Michaels (rural) to a high of 66% in St Stephens, with both Redbourn and Wheathampstead also approaching the upper limit, with 63% and 65% native respectively. The figure for the St Albans district as a whole was a little over 58%. If, as Ravenstein posited, most migration followed emerging transportation networks and was most commonly in the direction of towns, this figure for the percentage still living in their place of birth might be regarded as surprisingly high, given the presence of the town of St Albans at the heart of the district. For the Berkhamsted region to the west just 53% remained in their parish of birth on census night in 1851, whilst Mills' Rural Norm, calculated from a widely dispersed sample of over 18,000 individuals living in essentially rural parishes, also gives a slightly lower figure of 55%. The St Albans figure is, however, almost identical to that discovered from a sample of 13,781 individuals in the Dart Valley in south Devon, where in the three small towns of Totnes, Ashburton and Buckfastleigh and in eight rural parishes 58% remained native to their place of birth. In Leicestershire, however, an impressive study of a population of over 34,000 people, incorporating the town of Loughborough, has revealed that as many as 61% remained resident in their birthplace, despite considerable variation from parish to parish that reflected the attractiveness of the new mining town of Coalville and the four mining villages amongst the sample.[464]

---

464   Bryant, "Demographic Trends in South-Devon", p. 125; other figures have been taken, or calculated, from Mills and Schürer (eds.), *Local Communities*, pp. 223-4. The original study for Leicestershire is C.T. Smith, "Population", in W.G. Hoskins and R.A. McKinley (eds.), *The Victoria County History of Leicester*, Vol. III (London, 1955), pp. 129-75.

The St Albans district figure is, therefore, very much in line with previous large scale studies of migration in either rural, or rural and *small* town, locations. Furthermore, the strictly urban parishes taken together do produce a slightly lower figure for the proportion that was native than do the rural parishes as a group, 56% as compared with 60%. There are, however, two methodological difficulties to consider, one of which has been introduced above.[465] As the manner in which the enumerations have been compiled means that it has only proved possible to detect migration into the strictly urban parishes from outside of the Liberty, any movement within it is hidden from view. There can be little question that a move from, say, Frogmore in St Stephens to the parish of St Albans would have constituted rural-urban migration, given the occupational structure of this part of the Liberty, and the same can be said for many other hamlets in St Stephens, the Out-hamlets or parts of St Michaels. A closer look at the St Albans enumeration shows that 58 individuals did indeed give St Stephens as their birthplace, whilst a further 24 recorded Park Street and 19 either Colney, Colney Heath or London Colney. All of this movement, as well as movement between the urban parishes themselves, is obscured in our tabulations. Nor do we know how many of those who simply recorded St Albans as their birthplace were referring to the parish of St Albans itself, the borough more generally, or the Liberty. The figures for the proportions native to those parishes or parts of parishes lying within the Liberty of St Albans, and perhaps particularly those for St Albans parish itself, must therefore be regarded very much as *maxima*, and can only understate – to a degree impossible to estimate – the amount of movement towards them.[466]

Related to the above consideration is a second methodological problem, which is one of comparing like with like. All other things being equal, the larger the area under consideration the smaller the amount of movement one will find. If the focus is upon a whole county, then as most migration was short distance the great majority of migration will occur within it, and the great majority of the inhabitants will be revealed as native. But the same consideration might also apply to smaller units of analysis, and an area as large as the Liberty of St Albans provides greater scope for internal migration, for economic reasons, to find more appropriate housing, or to establish a new household upon marriage, than does a small village such as Sandridge, where employment opportunities are likely to be more circumscribed, potential marriage partners fewer, and where a move of even a few yards could take an individual beyond the parish boundaries. In this context it is worth noting that a recent large scale study of migration across the period 1750-1930 found that over 38% of all moves took place *within* the same settlement.[467] Hence in south Devon in 1851 it was found that there was a clear relationship between the size of a parish and the apparent stability of its population.[468] This is an additional factor that might minimise apparent migration to larger, urban populations, and exaggerate the extent of rural movement. Apart from its effect on the St Albans figures, it may explain why the town of Loughborough in Leicestershire, with its population approaching 11,000, exhibited the relatively high proportion of 61% of its population native in 1851.[469]

---

465   See pp. 126-7.

466   The problems for urban-rural comparison have been similarly noted by Bryant for south-Devon, where it is argued that towns have a higher "movement absorbency": Bryant, "Demographic Trends in South-Devon", p. 132.

467   C.G. Pooley and J. Turnbull, "Changing Home and Workplace in Victorian London: the Life of Henry Jacques, Shirtmaker", *Urban History*, Vol. 24 (1997), p. 174.

468   Bryant, "Demographic Trends in South-Devon", p. 132.

469   Mills and Schürer (eds.), *Local Communities*, Table 18.2, p. 223.

Taking the above considerations into account, it would be safe to argue that the extent of migration into the town of St Albans was undoubtedly greater than the figures in Table 13 suggest, and that the discrepancy between town and countryside was considerably larger than that shown. This conclusion would thus support Ravenstein's hypothesis more fully, as well as the conclusion drawn from the Berkhamsted region, where it was easier to identify the small market town of Berkhamsted as a discrete entity, and to discover that the town's population contained a larger migrant population than did the more rural parts of the surrounding district.[470]

TABLE 14 : MIGRATION – COUNTY OF BIRTH (%)

	Herts			Beds/Bucks/M'sex			Other		
	All	M	F	All	M	F	All	M	F
St Albans Urban									
St Albans	72.4	70.6	74.0	13.1	12.5	13.5	14.5	16.8	12.5
St Michaels (Urban)	80.1	81.4	79.0	10.4	11.8	9.4	9.4	6.8	11.6
St Peters	74.4	76.8	72.4	11.7	11.4	11.9	14.0	11.8	15.7
St Albans Rural									
St Michaels (Rural)	76.5	78.4	74.4	11.2	10.5	12.0	12.3	11.1	13.6
St Stephens	86.0	88.1	83.9	7.4	6.6	8.2	6.6	5.3	7.9
Out-hamlets	82.4	83.7	81.1	7.7	7.9	7.4	9.9	8.3	11.5
Harpenden	81.1	80.7	81.5	10.8	11.2	10.5	8.1	8.1	8.0
Redbourn	85.7	86.0	85.3	9.7	9.4	10.0	4.6	4.6	4.6
Sandridge	87.4	86.9	87.9	6.5	7.2	5.8	6.0	5.8	6.3
Wheathampstead	90.7	90.9	90.6	6.8	7.2	6.4	2.5	1.9	3.0
Sub-Totals									
St Albans (Liberty)	77.2	78.2	76.4	10.8	10.5	11.1	12.0	11.3	12.5
Urban Parishes	74.3	74.5	74.2	12.1	12.0	12.3	13.5	13.5	13.5
Rural Parishes	84.7	85.3	84.1	8.7	8.6	8.7	6.6	6.1	7.2
Total	80.6	81.2	80.0	10.0	9.9	10.2	9.4	8.9	9.8
Berkhamsted Region	69.2			21.5			9.3		

Another of Ravenstein's hypotheses, the predominance of short range movement , has been amply supported by virtually all subsequent research on the subject, and is again borne out by the St Albans district data.[471] Only in the case of communities dominated by new and rapidly expanding industries, notably mining, has evidence been found, not only of above average rates of in-migration, but also of a preponderance of longer range movement, frequently from areas with a similar economic focus.[472] As Table 14 shows, almost 81% of the population of the St Albans district had been born in the county of Hertfordshire, a figure some 10 percentage points above that discovered for the Berkhamsted region.[473] Here, however, there is a clearer urban/rural contrast, though one of degree rather than of kind, with 74% of the urban population native to the county compared with 85% in the rural parishes of the district. Wheathampstead exhibits the highest figure of all with more than nine out of ten of its population having been born in Hertfordshire, whilst the lowest figures, at a little over seven in every ten, are for the two urban parishes of St Peters and St Albans. Clearly, the region as a

---

470   Goose, *The Berkhamsted Region*, Table 8, p. 57.
471   A. Redford, *Labour Migration in England, 1800-1850* (2nd edition Manchester 1964, first published 1926); C.G. Pooley and J. Turnbull, "Migration and Mobility in Britain from the Eighteenth to the Twentieth Centuries", *Local Population Studies*, No. 57 (1996), pp. 54-5, 65; Anderson, *Family Structure in Nineteenth Century Lancashire*, p. 37; Goose, *The Berkhamsted Region*, p. 56; Mills and Schürer (eds.), *Local Communities*, pp. 219-20.
472   Dupree, *Family Structure in the Staffordshire Potteries*, p. 91; Mills and Schürer (eds.) *Local Communities*, p. 223 (for Leicestershire).
473   Goose, *The Berkhamsted Region*, Table 8, p. 57.

whole, including the town itself, had far more in common with other small rural communities than it did with larger manufacturing centres, although it must be noted that the national sample from which this distinction is drawn focuses upon the adult population rather than the population as a whole, and will thus produce higher overall migration rates than a study such as the present one which incorporates the whole population.[474]

Over half of the individuals living in the St Albans district in 1851 were therefore resident, remembering the reservations expressed above about the urban parishes, in or adjacent to their parish of birth. Almost exactly two-thirds – to introduce a further breakdown which is not presented in Tables 13 or 14 – hailed from the St Albans Superintendent Registrar's District itself. Just one in five had been born outside Hertfordshire and, as Table 14 shows, half of these came from the neighbouring counties of Bedfordshire, Buckinghamshire and Middlesex (including London). Here again we can see an urban/rural contrast, with 12% of the population of the town coming from adjacent counties compared with under 9% in the rural parishes, with the Liberty as a whole occupying a mid-way position.[475] But there is more to this distinction than is apparent from Table 14. The great majority of migrants from Middlesex came from London, certainly from Greater London, and these make up a far larger element of the population of the town and Liberty of St Albans than they do of the population of the four villages. For the urban parishes a total of 849 individuals came from the three adjacent counties, but of these 419 (49%) came from Middlesex. There is no distinction in this respect between town and Liberty, 590 of the 1,179 migrants to the Liberty from these three adjacent parishes also coming from Middlesex, almost exactly 50%. The situation in the four villages was very different, for here only 191 out of 603 (32%) had lived in Middlesex, with the counties of Bedfordshire and Buckinghamshire a much more important source of recruitment. The situation in the Berkhamsted region was similar. Again focusing only upon recruits from these three adjacent counties, in the town of Great Berkhamsted itself 30% hailed from Middlesex, whilst in the rest of the region taken as a whole the figure stood as low as 16%. Clearly, therefore, the towns of south-west Hertfordshire, with their more developed industrial, professional and service sectors, exerted a stronger pull upon migrants from Middlesex in general but London in particular, than did the surrounding villages. Whilst it may be true, as Ravenstein suggested, that there was a considerable migratory flow from rural to urban areas, there was clearly also a small but by no means insignificant flow from town to town, even – as in this case – from the great capital city to the smaller towns within its orbit.[476]

At first sight it may be surprising to find that a higher proportion of migrants to the Berkhamsted region came from Bedfordshire, Buckinghamshire and Middlesex than is the case for the St Albans district, 22.5% compared with just 10% (see Table 14). This, however, is probably no more than an accident of geography. The Berkhamsted Superintendent Registrar's District forms a virtual peninsula of the county, reaching out to the west with Bedfordshire to the north and Buckinghamshire to the south. All the parishes that lie within it, therefore, sit upon one or other of the county borders, with Tring and Great Berkhamsted abutting both. Short range migration within this region would therefore more commonly involve a move across county boundaries. If distance of migration were to be calculated instead of crude county divisions, the discrepancy would most

474   R. Lawton, "Peopling the Past", *Institute of British Geographers Transactions*, Vol. 12 (1987), p. 265.

475   In south Devon a far lower proportion of the population as a whole, 6.4%, had been born outside the county, but there was again an urban-rural contrast, the figure for Totnes standing at 9.4%: Bryant, "Demographic Trends in South-Devon", pp. 133-4.

476   Pooley and Turnbull's recent study also emphasises the significance of movement down the urban hierarchy, and in fact challenges the view that migratory systems were dominated by movement to larger settlements in general and towns in particular: "Migration and Mobility in Britain", pp. 62-3.

probably disappear.[477] In terms of longer distance movement from counties other than those adjacent to south-west Hertfordshire, the figure for the St Albans district, at just over 9%, is virtually identical to that for Berkhamsted.[478] Although a relatively small percentage of the total population, this does, however, constitute a total of 1,660 individuals, almost as many as were attracted from the three neighbouring counties. Here again we find a clear urban/rural contrast, more than double the proportion travelling long distances settling in the three urban parishes as compared with the rural areas, 13.5% rather than 6.6%.

The Berkhamsted data indicated that, as Ravenstein predicted, females had a slightly higher propensity to migrate than males, 48% having been born outside of their parish of residence compared with 44%.[479] For the St Albans region as a whole, however, the figures are virtually identical for the two sexes. Indeed, in the rural parishes males proved marginally more mobile than females, a feature that is largely the product of the experience of the four villages where males were consistently more mobile, though most notably in Sandridge. The town of St Albans, however, does conform to Ravenstein's model, particularly the parish of St Peters, but the difference between the sexes for the borough as a whole is only three percentage points. We can, therefore, detect an urban-rural discrepancy that might have been predicted. The situation in the rural parishes, however, stands in marked contrast to that revealed in Mills' Rural Norm, for although an identical proportion of males were migrant, some 9% fewer females in the rural areas of the St Albans district had moved from their place of birth. The greater attraction of the town of St Albans for female migrants can readily be explained by the employment opportunities available there for women, in the straw and straw hat industry and in humbler service trades that were so prominent, charring, washing or general domestic service.[480] But it is also likely that similar factors were at play in the rural parishes, for the quite remarkable levels of female employment that were described above must surely have rendered out-migration for females less attractive or necessary, encouraging a higher proportion of the native population to remain in their parish of birth.[481] Sandridge is something of a conundrum in this respect, for there we have seen that female employment opportunities were substantially below those found in the other three villages.[482] However, it is largely the high level of male migration here that produces the substantial difference between the sexes, whilst the proportion of females who were native to the parish stood below that found in each of the other three villages.[483]

477　A common method of calculation is to employ concentric rings of different radiuses to measure distance moved. Mills' analysis of his rural sample usefully indicated those born within five miles and those born beyond five miles: Mills and Schürer (eds.), *Local Communities*, Table 18.3, p. 225. It is hoped to refine the present analysis to include distance moved at a future date.

478　Note that the figure of 9.3% given in Table 14 for the Berkhamsted region is substantially lower than that presented in Table 8 of *The Berkhamsted Region* (p. 57) simply because Middlesex has been transferred from "Other" and incorporated with Bedfordshire and Buckinghamshire.

479　Goose, *The Berkhamsted Region*, p. 57. Females were also more mobile than males in the Dengie and Hatfield areas of Essex: Schürer, "The Role of the Family in the Process of Migration", p. 112.

480　See above, pp. 88-97.

481　For a similar emphasis upon the *retention* of population by industrial villages, besides their ability to attract incomers, see D. Souden, "Movers and Stayers in Family Reconstitution Populations", *Local Population Studies*, No. 33 (1984), pp. 24-5. Unlike the argument offered here, Souden's interpretation is not gender specific, but Pooley and Turnbull offer a similar explanation of the very short distances over which females moved in nineteenth century textile communities: *Migration and Mobility in Britain*, pp. 172-6.

482　See above, p. 91.

483　Sandridge was the *only* parish where farmers claimed to employ more labourers than could be traced by occupation in the enumeration, and this need to attract labour may thus explain the high level of male mobility found here.

Turning to differences between individual parishes, it is clear that the area that we have designated as St Michaels (rural) had more in common with the urban parishes within the Liberty than it did with the other rural areas, in terms of the proportion native to the Liberty, the proportion from adjacent counties, and in terms of the relatively large number of longer distance migrants who settled there. It is likely that this was a product of its particular occupational and social structure.[484] In the case of the four villages, Harpenden and Wheathampstead stand out at either end of the spectrum. Harpenden exerted a greater pull upon the three adjacent counties than did the other three villages, although in this respect Redbourn sits not far behind. Interestingly, Redbourn received more migrants from Middlesex/London than did Harpenden, 72 as compared with 50, no doubt due to its location on Watling Street, the major thoroughfare from London to the Midlands and north-west. Harpenden, however, attracted a substantially higher proportion of long distance migrants (over 8%), although it is perhaps surprising to find the smaller village of Sandridge lying in second position in this respect. By contrast Wheathampstead included one of the highest proportions native of all of the parishes or sub-parishes, at 65%, and the highest of them all in terms of the proportion of its population born both within the St Albans district and within the county, at 75% and 91% respectively. Conversely, a mere 2.5% of Wheathampstead inhabitants hailed from counties situated further afield.

It is very tempting to draw conclusions about both perceptions and the reality of the opportunities that these communities had to offer from these figures. The centre of major settlement in the parish of Wheathampstead did indeed sit slightly further away from the county boundary than did the villages of Redbourn and Harpenden, and its border with Bedfordshire was a small one which might have helped to minimise movement across county boundaries, but these differences are ones of degree rather than kind, and should not in any case impact upon the figures for longer distance movement. It is a common assumption that the inclusion within a population of a higher proportion of migrants indicates growth and economic vitality.[485] But whilst this may appear to be no more than common sense, one might equally argue – as indeed we have for the female population of Harpenden, Redbourn and Wheathampstead – that the ability of a local community to *retain* the population born there might indicate the labour market opportunities that it had to offer, and if these opportunities were filled locally then in-migration from outside might well prove more difficult. Out-migration, therefore, needs consideration as well as in-migration.

It is generally very difficult indeed to analyse out-migration from the census enumerators' books, simply because emigrants from a particular parish could have gone anywhere within the British Isles, or even overseas, and no single researcher is likely to have the capacity to launch such a daunting search. This is, however, yet another respect in which genealogy and family history can fruitfully form an alliance with historical demography, exemplified by Pooley and Turnbull's analysis of the residential histories of 16,091 individuals born between 1750 and 1930 supplied to them by local researchers.[486] The employment of a regional approach also opens up new possibilities, particularly where the census data has been computerised,

---

484   See below, pp. 140-1.

485   For example, Mills and Schürer (eds.), *Local Communities*, pp. 223-5.

486   Pooley and Turnbull, "Migration and Mobility in Britain", *passim*. There are, of course, problems regarding the representativeness of such samples, which are inevitably biased towards men, the ever married and the middle classes. For a discussion of these issues see C. Pooley and J. Turnbull, *Migration and Mobility in England Since the 18th Century* (London, 1998), pp. 28-31, 38-50.

for as much movement took place over short distances it is possible to capture a high proportion of total movement by analysing migration between contiguous parishes.[487]

TABLE 15 : MIGRATION TO ST ALBANS FROM ITS HINTERLAND

	All			M			F		
	No.	%(1)	%(2)	No.	%(1)	%(2)	No.	%(1)	%(2)
St Albans Urban									
St Albans	174	5.2	2.5	73	4.6	2.2	101	5.6	2.8
St Michaels (Urban)	68	6.2	1.0	29	6.0	0.9	39	6.4	1.1
St Peters	170	6.7	2.5	73	6.5	2.2	97	7.0	2.7
St Albans Rural									
St Michaels (Rural)	75	8.3	1.1	51	11.1	1.6	24	5.3	0.7
St Stephens	33	2.1	0.5	19	2.5	0.6	14	1.8	0.4
Out-hamlets	70	4.8	1.0	34	4.5	1.0	36	5.0	1.0
Urban Parishes	412	5.9	6.0	175	5.5	5.3	237	6.2	6.7
Rural Parishes	178	4.5	2.6	104	5.2	3.2	74	3.8	2.1
St Albans (Liberty)	590	5.4	8.6	279	5.4	8.5	311	5.4	8.8

% (1) = percentage of the population of that parish in 1851
% (2) = percentage of the population of the four villages in 1851

Tables 15-17 present a closer look at migratory patterns within the St Albans district. The first of these focuses upon movement to the Liberty itself from the four villages in its hinterland. Taking the figures for the Liberty as a whole, 5.4% of its population in 1851 had been born in the four adjacent villages, the figure for men and women being identical. This constitutes only half the number who, as Table 14 showed, hailed from Bedfordshire, Buckinghamshire and Middlesex, and only 45% of those who came from further afield. Of course, the host population of these other areas was considerably larger, but given the proximity of these villages to St Albans, and the symbiotic economic relationship that existed between town and hinterland, this figure is surprisingly low. The strictly urban parishes drew a slightly higher proportion of their population from the villages compared with the rural parts of the Liberty, although St Michaels (rural) again stands out as the exception. In this respect women formed a higher proportion than did men, as would be expected. More men than women, however, migrated from the villages to the rural parishes, no doubt a reflection of the agricultural opportunities that these parishes had to offer in the form of farm labour. From the point of view of the villages themselves the picture looks a little different, for as the %(2) column of Table 15 shows 8.6% (over one in every twelve) of their inhabitants ended up living in the Liberty of St Albans in 1851.[488] The urban parishes of the Liberty now stand out far more clearly as the favoured destination for both sexes, with more than double the proportion settling here rather than in the rural areas, 6.0% compared with 2.6%. The overall figure for men and women is again very similar indeed, but the division between the sexes in terms of preferred destination is even clearer, with more than three times the proportion of the female population of the villages heading for the urban parishes as compared with the rural parts of the Liberty, at 6.7% and 2.1% respectively,

---

487   A very similar project, on an even broader canvas, is in progress at the University of Essex, employing the machine-readable 1881 census data collected by local and family historians on behalf of the Mormon Church and held at The Data Archive: see M. Woollard, "Creating a Machine-readable Version of the 1881 Census of England and Wales:, in C. Harvey and J. Press, *Databases in Historical Research* (London, 1996).

488   Comparison with the population of the four villages in 1851 itself is not strictly the correct procedure, for migration will have taken place over the preceding years and will hence relate to a different base population. However, the four villages as a group had grown only marginally between 1831 and 1851, from 6,495 to 6,831, so there should be little distortion: *VCH Herts*, Vol. 4, pp. 235-8. If the 1831 figure is preferred as a base population size, the percentage migrating to the Liberty rises from 8.6% to 9.1%.

whilst in the case of men the relative proportions were considerably closer, at 5.3% and 3.2%. The parish of St Stephens stands out as a particularly unattractive destination, but this might simply reflect its geographical position, stretching out from the southern end of the Liberty whilst each of the four villages lay to the north of the town.

TABLE 16 : MIGRATION TO THE FOUR VILLAGES FROM WITHIN THE ST ALBANS DISTRICT

Migrants From	Harpenden			Redbourn			Sandridge			Wheathampstead			Total		
	No.	%(1)	%(2)	No.	%(1)	%(2)	No.	%(1)	%(2)	No.	%(1)	%(2)	No.	%(1)	%(2)
Other 3 Villages															
All	185	9.3	3.8	95	4.6	2.0	93	10.8	1.6	160	8.4	3.3	533	7.8	7.8
M	90	9.5	3.8	44	4.6	1.9	51	11.9	1.8	78	8.3	3.3	263	8.0	8.0
F	95	9.2	3.8	51	4.6	2.1	42	9.7	1.3	82	8.5	3.2	270	7.6	7.6
Liberty of St Albans															
All	58	2.9	0.5	102	4.9	0.9	72	8.4	0.7	35	1.8	0.3	267	3.9	2.4
M	25	2.6	0.5	54	5.6	1.0	43	10.0	0.8	13	1.4	0.3	135	4.1	2.6
F	33	3.2	0.6	48	4.3	0.8	29	6.7	0.5	22	2.3	0.4	132	3.7	2.3
Total															
All	243	12.3	1.5	197	9.5	1.3	165	19.2	1.0	195	10.2	1.2	800	11.7	4.5
M	115	12.2	1.5	98	10.2	1.3	94	21.9	1.2	91	9.6	1.2	398	12.1	4.7
F	128	12.4	1.5	99	8.8	1.2	71	16.5	0.8	104	10.8	1.2	402	11.3	4.3

% (1) = percentage of the population of that parish in 1851
% (2) = percentage of the population of the parishes of origin in 1851

Table 16 examines migration to each of the four villages from the other three and from the Liberty of St Albans. The total figures (table header "%(2)") can be regarded as an index of internal movement within the St Albans Superintendent Registrar's District towards and between the four villages, and show that under 5% of the population made such a move during the course of their lives. From the perspective of the villages themselves (table header "%(1)"), almost 12% of their populations came from one of the other villages or from the Liberty of St Albans, which in this case, in contrast to St Albans itself, compares favourably with the proportion arriving from Bedfordshire, Buckinghamshire and Middlesex, and even more favourably with the proportion who had migrated from more distant counties (see Table 14). These movements, however, were dominated by migration between the villages rather than from the Liberty to the villages, exactly double the numbers coming from the former destinations compared with the latter. If we compare these totals with the figures for the reverse flow from hinterland to town presented in Table 15, then the primacy of rural-urban movement is clearly established. Just 267 individuals had migrated from the Liberty of St Albans to one of the four villages, constituting 3.9% of their population and representing just 2.4% of the population of the Liberty as it stood in 1851. By contrast 590 individuals from the four villages had made the move into the Liberty, to constitute 5.4% of its population and representing 8.6% of the villages' population in 1851. There were only marginal differences between the sexes, although in this case, as we have noted, it is impossible to distinguish between those leaving the urban and rural parishes that lay within the Liberty.

There are clear discrepancies between the experiences of the individual villages. Harpenden exerted the greatest pull of the four, although only by a fairly small margin, whilst Sandridge proved the least attractive. On the other hand, as the size of the population of Sandridge was substantially smaller than the other villages,

TABLE 17 : OUT-MIGRATION FROM THE FOUR VILLAGES

Destination	Harpenden All No.	%	M No.	%	F No.	%	Redbourn All No.	%	M No.	%	F No.	%	Sandridge All No.	%	M No.	%	F No.	%
St Albans Urban																		
St Albans	46	2.3	16	1.7	30	2.9	52	2.5	24	2.5	28	2.5	30	3.5	12	2.8	18	4.2
St Michaels (Urban)	14	0.7	7	0.7	7	0.7	29	1.4	15	1.6	14	1.3	19	2.2	7	1.6	12	2.8
St Peters	45	2.3	18	1.9	27	2.6	51	2.4	15	1.6	36	3.2	36	4.2	22	5.1	14	3.2
St Albans Rural																		
St Michaels (Rural)	16	0.8	9	1.0	7	0.7	21	1.0	14	1.5	7	0.6	19	2.2	18	4.2	1	0.2
St Stephens	11	0.6	9	1.0	2	0.2	5	0.2	3	0.3	2	0.2	9	1.0	5	1.2	4	0.9
Out-hamlets	14	0.7	9	1.0	5	0.5	4	0.2	3	0.3	1	0.1	37	4.3	16	3.7	21	4.9
Harpenden							33	1.6	17	1.8	16	1.4	15	1.7	6	1.4	9	2.1
Redbourn	62	3.1	29	3.1	33	3.2							6	0.7	3	0.7	3	0.7
Sandridge	13	0.7	9	1.0	4	0.4	6	0.3	4	0.4	2	0.2						
Wheathampstead	102	5.2	51	5.4	51	4.9	19	0.9	6	0.6	13	1.2	39	4.5	21	4.9	18	4.2
Sub-Totals																		
St Albans (Liberty)	146	7.4	68	7.2	78	7.6	162	7.8	74	7.7	88	7.9	150	17.4	80	18.6	70	16.2
Urban Parishes	105	5.3	41	4.3	64	6.2	132	6.3	54	5.6	78	7.0	85	9.9	41	9.6	44	10.2
Rural Parishes	218	11.0	116	12.3	102	9.9	88	4.2	47	4.9	41	3.7	125	14.5	69	16.1	56	13.0
Total	323	16.3	157	16.6	166	16.1	220	10.6	101	10.5	119	10.6	210	24.4	110	25.6	100	23.2

Destination	Wheathampstead All No.	%	M No.	%	F No.	%	Total All No.	%	M No.	%	F No.	%
St Albans Urban												
St Albans	46	2.4	21	2.2	25	2.6	174	2.5	73	2.2	101	2.8
St Michaels (Urban)	6	0.3	0	0.0	6	0.6	68	1.0	29	0.9	39	1.1
St Peters	38	2.0	18	1.9	20	2.1	170	2.5	73	2.2	97	2.7
St Albans Rural												
St Michaels (Rural)	19	1.0	10	1.1	9	0.9	75	1.1	51	1.6	24	0.7
St Stephens	8	0.4	2	0.2	6	0.6	33	0.5	19	0.6	14	0.4
Out-hamlets	15	0.8	6	0.6	9	0.9	70	1.0	34	1.0	36	1.0
Harpenden	137	7.2	67	7.1	70	7.3	185	2.7	90	2.7	95	2.7
Redbourn	27	1.4	12	1.3	15	1.6	95	1.4	44	1.3	51	1.4
Sandridge	74	3.9	38	4.0	36	3.7	93	1.4	51	1.6	42	1.2
Wheathampstead							160	2.3	78	2.4	82	2.3
Sub-Totals												
St Albans (Liberty)	132	6.9	57	6.0	75	7.8	590	8.6	279	8.5	311	8.8
Urban Parishes	90	4.7	39	4.1	51	5.3	412	6.0	175	5.3	237	6.7
Rural Parishes	280	14.7	135	14.3	145	15.1	711	10.4	367	11.2	344	9.7
Total	370	19.4	174	18.4	196	20.4	1123	16.4	542	16.5	581	16.4

here migrants from other parts of the district constituted almost one in five of its population (19.2%), compared with approximately one in ten in Redbourn and Wheathampstead (9.5% and 10.2%) and one in eight in Harpenden (12.3%). Harpenden and Wheathampstead proved particularly attractive to migrants from the other villages, Redbourn and Sandridge attracted larger proportions from the urban Liberty, and geographical proximity and dominant communication routes may well explain the latter result.[489] Wheathampstead proved particularly unattractive to the inhabitants of the Liberty of St Albans, recruiting just 35 migrants in total, 22 of these female, to make up just 1.8% of its total population and representing a mere 0.3% of the population of

489   Although the village of Sandridge stood approximately two miles from the town, the parish of Sandridge extended into Bernards Heath, and hence its border stood just a few hundred yards from the most populous parts of the parish of St Peters.

the urban Liberty. Slightly more migrants from the Liberty to Harpenden were also female, whilst Sandridge was more favoured by St Albans' men, and although the differences are relatively small they may again reflect the more considerable employment opportunities for women that Harpenden and Wheathampstead had to offer.[490]

The final analysis of local movement is presented in Table 17, which focuses upon out-migration from the four villages. Comparing the totals in this table with those in Table 16 shows clearly that the overall balance of movement within the district was away from the villages, for whilst they received a total of 800 immigrants 1,123 had left these parishes to settle elsewhere.[491] In all 16% of their combined populations made such a move, almost exactly one in six, and although the absolute number of women who moved exceeded the number of men by 39, there was no overall proportional difference between the sexes. These figures also shed further light on rural-urban movement, for although we have already established that substantially more people moved from the villages to the Liberty than moved from the Liberty to the villages, neither migration to the town of St Albans nor migration to the Liberty dominated these outward flows. Migration to the Liberty constituted little over half of the total outward movement from the villages, whilst the three urban parishes of St Albans accounted for little more than one-third. Despite the geographical proximity of the town of St Albans, therefore, and the very close economic ties that existed between town and countryside, almost two-thirds of the out-migration that the four villages experienced constituted a move to another rural area, and if it were possible to identify other moves to rural locations outside of the St Albans district there is no doubt that this proportion would be higher still. Furthermore, as we have already seen from Tables 15 and 16, the rural parts of the Liberty were the favoured destination for just 178 individuals, whilst the other villages attracted a total of 533. The town did, however, prove slightly more attractive to women than to men, again no doubt because of the economic opportunities that it had to offer, whilst the rural parts of the Liberty were more favoured by men, with the balance between the sexes for movement between the villages themselves almost exactly equal.

There are interesting differences between the four villages which allows us to return to the question of the light that migration data might throw on economic vitality.[492] Sandridge heads the list in terms of out-migration, with almost one in four of its population, as it stood in 1851, leaving to live elsewhere within the St Albans district, followed by Wheathampstead which lost almost one in five. The figure for Harpenden was slightly lower, at one in six almost identical with the average for the four villages as a whole, whilst Redbourn lost only one in ten. Any conclusions drawn from these figures can only be tentative, as they represent only a partial picture of the migratory tendencies of the inhabitants of these parishes. Nevertheless, when taken in conjunction with the data for proportions native, numbers of in-migrants from the Liberty and the numbers coming from adjacent or more distant counties discussed above, they would appear to confirm that Harpenden and Redbourn were both better able to retain their populations and were generally more attractive destinations for migrants locally and regionally, and – in the case of Harpenden – from further afield as well.

---

490   See above, p. 91.

491   This is not, of course, a measure of net migration, only of movement *within* the St Albans Superintendent Registrar's District. An alternative approach would be to examine proportions native, in-migration and out-migration from particular parishes to all contiguous parishes, as well as in-migration from other counties. The complete processing of the computerised Hertfordshire data will, of course, eventually allow such analysis.

492   See p. 133.

Migration patterns would therefore appear to support the view of Wheathampstead offered by the author of Kelly's Directory published in 1855, as well as the perspective upon Sandridge as compared with the other villages that has been presented here.[493]

The migratory flows from village to village underline the importance of geographical proximity and established transportation networks. Referring back to the outline map of Hertfordshire parishes in Figure 1, we can see that Harpenden inhabitants crossed the long borders into Redbourn and Wheathampstead in considerable numbers, but relatively few leaped the intervening parishes to reach Sandridge or the rural parts of the Liberty. Above average numbers left Redbourn for neighbouring St Michaels (urban and rural), whilst the border with Harpenden was again regularly crossed. Wheathampstead sent migrants back across the border to Harpenden, in greater numbers than travelled in the opposite direction. But considerable numbers also left Wheathampstead for Sandridge, a distinct contrast to the other villages, again crossing a long, common boundary. The importance of Watling Street is further underlined by the fact that Redbourn is the only one of the four villages to send more migrants to the three urban parishes than to the rural parts of the district, with a bias again fairly heavily weighted in favour of women. All of this serves to emphasise the closely circumscribed social and economic horizons of the population of these villages, for whilst the great majority in 1851 remained in their parish of birth the majority of those who *had* moved had simply crossed the nearest parish boundary, and can have ventured but a few miles at most. Movement into town did, however, usually represent a larger step, both physically and no doubt mentally too. The only parishes that were able to attract considerable numbers from other parishes within the district *without* sharing a common boundary were St Albans and St Peters, which adds a final dimension to our consideration of the significance of rural-urban migratory flows.

So far we have considered migration trends for the population as a whole, broken down only according to sex. Table 18 provides a further breakdown by age group. The overall age profile of migration is similar to that discovered for the Berkhamsted region, with an escalation into early adulthood followed by a levelling off, with just a slow upward drift in proportions migrant thereafter, to form a plateau from about the age of 50 onwards.[494] Here, however, the escalation in the teenage years was somewhat less pronounced, whilst the increase in proportions migrant between the later teens was of a similar order of magnitude, if from a lower base level. We have already seen that the population of this region was apparently somewhat less migratory overall than that in the Berkhamsted region, although there are geographical features that might render this more apparent than real, whilst the impossibility of ascertaining movement with the urban Liberty also makes strict comparison difficult. Nevertheless, the figures for migration by age, although subject to the same caveats, would tend to support this conclusion, and it is particularly noticeable once again that through the teenage years females were slightly less likely to be migrants than males. Thereafter, in the early twenties, the female figure surges ahead, and remains ahead through the second half of the twenties as well. As marriage was so rare for both sexes before the age of 20, the teenage figures undoubtedly reflect economically motivated moves into employment. In an area which was predominantly agricultural this would most commonly involve farm

---

493   *Kelly's Directory 1855*, p. 246; and see above, pp. 77-81.

494   This supports the results from the census linkage study of Dengie and Hatfield areas of Essex, where migration rose sharply for teenagers and young adults, to peak at about age 20, dropping steadily to age 50, after which it levelled off. In Essex, however, it was possible to detect a renewed increase amongst those aged 60 plus, which is not apparent from the St Albans figures: Schürer, "The Role of the Family in the Process of Migration", p. 115.

labour for boys, and we have seen that living-in farm labour was more important in this region than is often suggested for the county as a whole, whilst teenage boys feature very prominently amongst those living in.[495] For girls there would of course have been a considerable movement into domestic service, and it may well be that the competing pull of straw plaiting provides the explanation for levels of female migration in this age group that are lower than might be expected. Migration for those in their twenties, however, must undoubtedly have been influenced by marriage: indeed, it could be suggested that this would be likely to be the predominant motivation amongst this age group, and as women tended to marry slightly younger than men and might more regularly have been expected to move to their spouses' parish of residence rather than setting up home in their own parish, this would explain the divergence of migratory experiences between the two sexes amongst those in their early twenties.

TABLE 18 : MIGRATION BY AGE AND SEX (% MIGRANT)

Age Group	St Albans			St Michaels (U)			St Peters			St Michaels (R)			St Stephens			Out-hamlets			Harpenden		
	All	M	F	All	M	F	All	M	F	All	M	F	All	M	F	All	M	F	All	M	F
0-4	13	18	9	14	20	8	12	15	9	16	19	12	13	13	14	14	16	12	9	11	6
5-9	23	21	26	16	16	17	22	21	23	34	40	29	16	15	18	23	26	19	21	20	22
10-14	33	35	32	32	31	33	26	25	27	33	34	31	22	22	22	32	35	29	30	35	26
15-19	43	41	45	31	26	36	35	24	43	56	59	52	26	24	28	41	43	39	41	46	36
20-24	48	49	48	41	30	45	48	38	55	74	73	75	34	37	31	41	39	42	48	41	54
25-29	52	50	53	51	48	54	51	49	53	72	62	80	46	42	51	42	43	42	49	59	41
30-34	59	60	57	55	52	58	57	52	59	74	81	67	44	47	41	51	47	55	59	56	61
35-39	55	57	53	53	52	54	61	63	60	75	83	65	53	51	55	62	58	65	51	49	53
40-44	64	62	66	57	57	57	64	59	67	80	82	79	48	38	57	60	50	71	57	55	60
45-49	65	68	63	55	52	58	64	62	66	68	64	75	40	45	35	57	58	55	67	74	61
50-54	68	58	78	55	71	46	58	62	54	78	77	79	54	52	56	66	72	58	78	76	81
55-59	63	69	59	66	65	67	72	76	69	64	72	57	51	59	44	62	54	69	77	82	70
60-64	65	69	62	65	75	56	71	82	62	81	83	78	66	71	56	53	47	58	68	77	61
65+	74	74	73	56	67	52	71	68	73	73	71	75	52	43	60	62	52	74	65	64	65
Total	45	45	46	39	38	39	44	40	47	56	58	54	34	33	34	40	40	41	43	44	42

Age Group	Redbourn			Sandridge			Wheathamstead			St Albans Lib			Urban pars.			Rural pars.			Total		
	All	M	F	All	M	F	All	M	F	All	M	F	All	M	F	All	M	F	All	M	F
0-4	7	9	6	9	8	11	12	12	11	13	16	10	13	17	9	11	12	10	12	14	9
5-9	21	21	21	30	33	28	22	23	20	22	22	22	22	21	23	22	23	22	22	22	22
10-14	24	27	22	38	35	42	28	32	23	30	30	29	31	31	31	28	31	26	29	31	28
15-19	30	40	23	55	70	37	36	35	36	39	36	41	38	33	43	38	43	34	38	39	38
20-24	37	32	39	62	63	61	41	38	46	47	45	48	47	43	50	45	44	47	46	43	48
25-29	39	41	38	65	64	66	46	48	45	52	48	54	51	49	53	49	49	49	50	49	51
30-34	48	56	40	54	60	47	54	54	53	56	57	56	58	57	58	54	56	52	55	56	54
35-39	46	44	48	54	63	48	43	44	41	58	59	58	57	58	56	52	52	53	54	55	54
40-44	60	53	66	56	61	50	53	49	58	63	58	66	63	60	65	58	54	63	60	56	64
45-49	63	69	57	58	83	35	51	49	53	59	59	58	63	63	63	57	62	53	59	62	57
50-54	66	67	66	79	79	80	48	57	38	63	63	63	62	61	64	66	67	64	64	65	64
55-59	66	68	64	68	64	71	57	60	52	64	67	61	67	70	64	64	67	61	65	68	62
60-64	66	74	59	76	72	86	52	50	54	66	72	61	67	75	61	64	67	60	65	70	61
65+	68	63	72	46	58	33	42	41	42	66	62	69	70	70	70	58	55	62	63	60	66
Total	37	39	36	47	51	43	35	36	35	43	42	44	44	42	45	40	41	39	42	41	42

Ravenstein's view that most migration was economically motivated needs further examination, therefore. The proportions we have identified as moving in their teens represent a total of 1,242 individual migratory movements, whilst those in their twenties represent 1,404. Given the proportions that have been discovered

---

495   See above, pp. 111-14.

remaining unmarried into their early thirties,[496] a significant proportion of the 696 individuals who were migrant amongst those aged 30-34 must also have moved upon marriage, although one might expect movement for work-related reasons to assume increasing relative importance with age. On the other hand, we might realistically assume that the majority of the 756 individuals who moved in the age groups 0-9 did so to accompany their parents, whose movements with a young family are most likely to have been economically inspired. The analysis is admittedly crude, and cannot accommodate the diverse motivations of those in the higher age brackets, who could have migrated at any time since their birth and quite possibly on more than one occasion, but these results would nevertheless seem to suggest that – unless marriage itself is regarded as an economic motivation – migration for *social* reasons was at the very least a highly significant component of migration in this region in the mid-nineteenth century, and possibly represents a challenge to the ascendancy of economic motivation that Ravenstein suggested.[497]

There are interesting differences between the age profile of migrants in the urban as compared with the rural parishes. For males a major divergence appears in the age group 15-19, when a full 10% more rural males were migrant compared with their urban counterparts. This might partly reflect the initial take up of agricultural employment, but as a full 57% of rural males aged 10-14 were already employed,[498] must also indicate the mobility of labour in the agricultural sector amongst this age group.[499] For females there is also an urban-rural discrepancy in the same age group, but this time in the opposite direction, with some 9% more urban than rural females migrant. In the parish of St Albans itself the difference stood at 11%, with 45% of females aged 15-19 migrant compared with just 34% in the rural parishes as a group, and it is apparent that the difference between this urban parish and the rural ones was already emerging in the age group 10-14. Here again we see evidence of at least the relative stability of the female population in the rural parishes, a feature that appears to have been particularly marked in Redbourn, where only 23% of females aged 15-19 were migrant.[500] Conversely the figures indicate the attractiveness of the town for young females, and particularly as a source of employment in domestic service. In this regard it is notable that, despite the urban-rural disparity overall, the highest figures for migration amongst the age groups 15-24, and for both sexes, are found in St Michaels (rural) and Sandridge. Our occupational data showed that both of these areas were heavily agricultural, and hence offered substantial opportunities for male employment in agricultural labour, but both also provided considerable opportunities for males in the service/domestic service sector, in St Michaels amounting to more than double the average level for the region as a whole. The high female figure can also be explained by the very high levels of domestic service found in these parishes, the service/domestic service sector employing 30% and 40% of the occupied female population in Sandridge and St Michaels (rural) respectively. Here is our explanation for the

496 See above, pp. 42-4.
497 This emphasis is a little different to the conclusion of Pooley and Turnbull from their analysis of residential life histories, from which they argue that 47% of moves 1840-79 were work related but only 19% due to marriage, with 10% for housing reasons, 3% for family matters and a large residual of 15%for unspecified reasons ("other" or "crisis"). In one sense their analysis is less conjectural than that offered here, and they are able to consider a wider range of possible motives, but they also accept that "stated reasons for migration are probably the least reliable aspect of the dataset": Pooley and Turnbull, *Migration and Mobility in Britain*, pp. 71-2.
498 See above, Table 9, p. 97.
499 This corresponds with the age profile of rural migrants in early nineteenth century Lancashire: Marshall, "The Lancashire Rural Labourer", pp. 94, 114.
500 The rural parishes in our sample present a marked contrast with the situation in the agricultural areas of Dengie and Hatfield in Essex. In the St Albans district rural male migration took place earlier and was more pronounced than was female, whilst in Essex female migration was earlier and more marked than male: Schürer, "The Role of the Family in the Process of Migration", pp. 115-19.

divergence of experience between these and the other rural parishes that has been frequently noted in the foregoing discussion, and it is a divergence that does not disappear in the later age cohorts, possibly indicating that once a move was made into these parishes those individuals tended to remain there to feature as migrants to the parish throughout their lives.

Whilst in the urban parishes as a group a higher overall proportion of the population was migrant, a second quite marked discrepancy appears in the higher age ranges, and this is even more apparent if the exceptional instances of St Michaels (rural) and Sandridge are removed from the rural sample. Seventy per cent of those aged 65 or over in the urban parishes were migrant, the proportion being identical for the two sexes, whilst in the rural parishes the overall figure stood at just 58%, and for males and females respectively at 55% and 62%. The figures for the parish of St Albans are even higher, as is the figure for females of this age in St Peters. If we take the four villages on their own, the proportion for males was 57%, and for females 59%. This is an interesting divergence when seen in the light of the rather different experiences of widows in town and countryside that was identified above.[501] Furthermore, although the *proportions* migrant for the two sexes are similar in the urban parishes, as there was a marked imbalance in the sex ratio amongst this age group, in terms of *absolute* numbers substantially more women feature than men, 151 out of 215 compared with 81 of 115. To some extent, of course, this will represent the product of the cumulative effect of higher overall levels of in-migration to the urban parishes. It may, however, also have a wider social significance, as a consequence of the attractiveness of urban living to elderly people of independent means who, as we have seen, were more prominent in town than countryside, and also as a consequence of the greater availability of charitable support that the town could offer to those elderly people who were less financially fortunate.

Finally, it is clear from our age cohort analysis that the snapshot provided by the census will inevitably understate lifelong migratory experience. Indeed, it is possible that the census hides as much as it reveals, providing information only on current place of residence and place of birth, whilst intermediate moves are impossible to identify for all except those families whose children were born in diverse places. We must not, however, fall into the trap of believing that the frequency of movement exhibited by Lucy Luck and recorded in her autobiography was necessarily typical, for even a one-off move from Tring to London is likely to have been the exception rather than the rule.[502] She had, after all, started life in the unfortunate position of a parish pauper. On the other hand, analysis by age group does shed a slightly different light upon the migratory experience of the population compared with a simple count of the proportions migrant in 1851. For whilst the latter procedure indicates that only 42% of the population of the region as a whole had been born elsewhere (44% in the urban parishes and 40% in the rural areas), age cohort analysis shows that for those who achieved adulthood migration had been experienced by roughly half the population. For those who survived to what we might call middle age, the proportion who had migrated from their place of birth at some point in their lives was very close to two-thirds, and amongst the elderly population of the town the figure was even higher still, at 70% for both men and women.

---

501   See pp. 92-4.
502   Burnett (ed.), *Useful Toil*, pp. 67-77.

TABLE 19 : MIGRATION BY SOCIAL STATUS

| | | Number | | | Percentage | | | | | | | | | | | |
| | | | | | Native | | | Other Herts | | | Beds/Bucks/M'sex | | | Other | | |
	Status	All	M	F	All	M	F	All	M	F	All	M	F	All	M	F
St Albans	A	397	151	246	36.0	37.1	35.4	10.8	9.3	11.8	21.9	22.5	21.5	31.2	31.1	31.3
	B	691	356	335	38.2	40.4	35.8	17.2	15.7	18.8	20.3	19.4	21.2	24.3	24.4	24.2
	C	3656	1770	1886	58.4	57.9	58.8	17.0	16.6	17.3	12.7	12.6	12.8	12.0	12.9	11.1
	D	5035	2220	2815	59.7	61.5	58.4	23.6	24.3	23.1	7.9	7.5	8.2	8.8	6.8	10.3
	E	880	541	339	69.7	70.6	68.1	17.6	17.4	18.0	6.1	5.7	6.8	6.6	6.3	7.1
	F	215	103	112	31.2	23.3	38.4	28.8	36.9	21.4	13.5	12.6	14.3	26.5	27.2	25.9
	Z	43	28	15	30.2	35.7	20.0	7.0	3.6	13.3	16.3	21.4	6.7	46.5	39.3	60.0
	Total	10917	5169	5748	57.2	58.2	56.3	20.1	20.0	20.1	10.8	10.5	11.1	12.0	11.3	12.5
Urban parishes	A	304	111	193	36.8	36.9	36.8	11.8	10.8	12.4	17.4	17.1	17.6	33.9	35.1	33.2
	B	353	189	164	32.3	32.8	31.7	13.0	11.1	15.2	22.9	23.8	22.0	31.7	32.3	31.1
	C	2988	1447	1541	59.3	59.2	59.4	15.7	14.9	16.4	13.0	12.9	13.2	12.0	13.1	11.0
	D	2385	860	1525	57.0	62.1	54.1	22.1	19.2	23.7	10.4	10.3	10.4	10.5	8.4	11.7
	E	738	463	275	69.8	70.2	69.1	17.2	17.5	16.7	6.2	5.8	6.9	6.8	6.5	7.3
	F	186	92	94	28.0	20.7	35.1	27.4	34.8	20.2	14.5	14.1	14.9	30.1	30.4	29.8
	Z	31	22	9	29.0	31.8	22.2	9.7	4.5	22.2	16.1	18.2	11.1	45.2	45.5	44.4
	Total	6985	3184	3801	56.3	57.9	55.0	18.0	16.6	19.2	12.2	12.0	12.3	13.5	13.5	13.5
Rural parishes	A	248	105	143	35.5	35.2	35.7	16.1	14.3	17.5	27.8	28.6	27.3	20.6	21.9	19.6
	B	790	373	417	43.5	44.8	42.4	28.2	27.9	28.5	15.3	13.9	16.5	12.9	13.4	12.5
	C	1877	984	893	56.5	55.4	57.8	23.4	24.2	22.5	11.1	11.8	10.3	9.0	8.6	9.4
	D	7426	3570	3856	63.3	61.9	64.5	25.3	27.4	23.3	6.5	6.5	6.6	4.9	4.2	5.6
	E	331	205	126	61.6	62.0	61.1	23.0	23.4	22.2	10.0	8.8	11.9	4.2	3.9	4.8
	F	59	22	37	45.8	36.4	51.4	35.6	50.0	27.0	16.9	18.2	16.2	5.1	4.5	5.4
	Z	32	11	21	43.8	54.5	38.1	12.5	18.2	9.5	18.8	36.4	9.5	31.3	9.1	42.9
	Total	10763	5270	5493	59.8	58.8	60.7	24.9	26.5	23.4	8.7	8.6	8.7	6.6	6.1	7.2
4 Villages	A	155	65	90	36.8	33.8	38.9	21.3	20.0	22.2	22.6	23.1	22.2	19.4	23.1	16.7
	B	452	206	246	42.9	41.3	44.3	33.2	33.5	32.9	13.7	13.6	13.8	10.2	11.7	8.9
	C	1209	661	548	57.8	56.9	58.9	23.7	24.1	23.4	10.9	12.0	9.7	7.5	7.1	8.0
	D	4776	2210	2566	63.8	62.4	65.1	25.4	27.4	23.8	7.1	7.0	7.1	3.7	3.3	4.0
	E	189	127	62	56.1	55.1	58.1	25.4	27.6	21.0	13.2	11.0	17.7	3.2	3.1	3.2
	F	30	11	19	40.0	27.3	47.4	33.3	45.5	26.3	26.7	36.4	21.1	6.7	9.1	5.3
	Z	20	5	15	50.0	60.0	46.7	20.0	40.0	13.3	20.0	40.0	13.3	20.0	0.0	26.7
	Total	6831	3285	3546	60.4	59.0	61.7	25.6	27.0	24.2	8.8	9.0	8.7	5.2	5.0	5.4
Total	A	552	216	336	36.2	36.1	36.3	13.8	12.5	14.6	22.1	22.7	21.7	27.9	28.7	27.4
	B	1143	562	581	40.1	40.7	39.4	23.5	22.2	24.8	17.7	17.3	18.1	18.7	19.8	17.7
	C	4865	2431	2434	58.2	57.6	58.8	18.6	18.6	18.7	12.3	12.4	12.1	10.9	11.3	10.4
	D	9811	4430	5381	61.7	61.9	61.6	24.5	25.8	23.4	7.5	7.2	7.7	6.3	5.0	7.3
	E	1069	668	401	67.3	67.7	66.6	19.0	19.3	18.5	7.4	6.7	8.5	6.0	5.7	6.5
	F	245	114	131	32.2	23.7	39.7	29.4	37.7	22.1	15.1	14.9	15.3	24.1	25.4	22.9
	Z	63	33	30	36.5	39.4	33.3	11.1	9.1	13.3	17.5	24.2	10.0	38.1	33.3	43.3
	Total	17748	8454	9294	58.4	58.5	58.4	22.2	22.8	21.7	10.0	9.9	10.2	9.4	8.9	9.8

A final perspective upon movement into and within the St Albans district is provided in Table 19, which presents summary data for migration by social group. The most outstanding feature of this table is its remarkable symmetry, for very similar overall patterns are exhibited for each of the sub-groupings employed, as well as between the sexes in each category. For the population as a whole, as well as for each sub-grouping, the higher social groups – those in categories A and B – show a markedly higher propensity to migrate: little more than a third of those in category A were native to their parish of residence, and just 40% of those in

category B.[503] As we move down the social scale increasing proportions were living where they had been born, constituting two-thirds of the population by the time we reach category E, representing unskilled workers. The high figures for category D in both the rural parishes as a group and in the four villages reflects the particular immobility of the agricultural labourers that dominate this category, confirming the results for the Berkhamsted region and for rural Lancashire.[504] Only at the very bottom of the social scale is the trend reversed, and now we find a propensity to migrate that is very similar to those at the top of the social hierarchy.[505]

The picture is less clear for those born elsewhere in Hertfordshire, although again a relatively low proportion of those at the very top of the social scale had been born locally. For those who had travelled to the region from further afield, however, a symmetrical picture again re-emerges. The proportion born in Bedfordshire, Buckinghamshire and Middlesex was highest amongst social group A, and falls steadily as we descend the social scale down to and including group E, only to rise once again for groups F and Z. Over one-quarter of the very highest social group came from counties other than Hertfordshire, Bedfordshire, Buckinghamshire and Middlesex, and can thus be clearly categorised as long distance migrants. Again the proportions fall steadily, to less than one-fifth for social group B, one-tenth for group C, and to a low point of just one in sixteen for groups D and E, between which there was very little difference. In contrast, when we reach the bottom of the social scale the trend is again reversed, and the lowest social groups show a tendency for long distance migration of a very similar order of magnitude to those at the peak of the hierarchy.

Our data thus exhibits in very stark form a pattern that might have been predicted, and a pattern that emerged from a far more cursory consideration of migration by social class in the Berkhamsted region to the west.[506] Those with the greatest means at their disposal, with higher levels of education, with economic connections that would often extend well beyond their immediate region, and with the wider network of social contacts that were the inevitable concomitant of their elevated social standing – these showed the highest propensity to migrate in general, and to migrate over long distances in particular. A considerable gulf existed between such individuals and the rest of the population. Nevertheless, further down the social scale skilled workers were slightly more likely to migrate, particularly over long distances, than were semi-skilled workers, whilst the semi-skilled were in their turn slightly more likely to migrate than the unskilled, although at this level the difference in terms of long distance movement disappears. The indigent in nineteenth century society, however – and our figures exclude the exceptional category of those residing in St Albans workhouse in 1851 – were a particularly mobile section of the population, more frequently bereft of the social and economic ties that served to bind individuals to a particular place, in search of employment, in search of relief or in search of an opportunity to make their living through less socially acceptable means.

---

503   Previous research has shown that the higher socio-economic groups also tended to move longer distances: Pooley and Turnbull, *Migration and Mobility in Britain*, p. 13.

504   Goose, *The Berkhamsted Region*, p. 57; Marshall, "The Lancashire Rural Labourer", pp. 93-4, 114, 127.

505   Category Z, representing those of unknown social status, is constituted largely of lodgers and visitors of unknown occupation, and therefore ever likely to include a high proportion born elsewhere. On the other hand, the fact that their occupations were unknown, particularly in the case of lodgers, might indicate too that many of them formed part of a transient population of generally low social status.

506   Goose, *The Berkhamsted Region*, p. 57.

Despite the general symmetry of the data in Table 19, there are some noteworthy differences between town and countryside. Firstly, those included within category B in the town – largely professional people, reinforced by annuitants and smaller employers of labour – were considerably more mobile than their counterparts in the rural parishes, no doubt an indication of the greater attraction and opportunity that the town could offer these occupational groups. Indeed, in the urban parishes they were even a little more mobile than their social superiors in category A. Furthermore, a considerably higher proportion of both social group A and social group B who had migrated to the town came from beyond Hertfordshire, Bedfordshire, Buckinghamshire and Middlesex when compared with the rural parishes in general and the four villages in particular. Not only were they more often mobile, therefore, but they were more frequently prepared to travel long distances. Amongst those born in the adjacent counties, the connection with London/Middlesex featured very strongly for the higher social groups in both town and countryside, but again this connection was far stronger with the town, for of the 119 individuals in social groups A and B who had migrated from these three neighbouring counties to the parishes of St Albans and St Peters, as many as 75 hailed from Middlesex, the great majority of these from London itself.

Towards the middle of the social scale the urban and rural figures are, for the most part, quite similar. However, we can see that in the rural parishes generally, but particularly in the four villages, females in social class D were particularly immobile compared with the town, whilst the figures for the male population were very similar. From the urban viewpoint this can only reflect the higher levels of migration amongst the female domestic servants who feature in this category. From the rural perspective, we now have clearer evidence of a hypothesis introduced above: despite the prominence of relatively mobile female domestic servants in rural as well as urban areas, this social category was dominated in the countryside by female straw plaiters, whose relative immobility more than offset the impact of mobile domestic servants to produce the high overall proportions native amongst those in category D.[507] The proportions in the middle of the social scale coming from the neighbouring counties was similar, but again this hides the greater relative attraction that the town held for migrants from Middlesex/London, and in this respect the disparity between town and countryside increases as we move down through social categories C to D. Longer distance migrants formed a slightly higher proportion in town as compared with countryside, by a small margin for class C but more noticeably for class D, indicating that the greater pull that the town exerted upon the long distance migrant operated across all social categories and was not simply confined to those at the top of the social scale.

A final disparity to note appears at the bottom of the social hierarchy. Here the urban residents were considerably more migratory than those in the rural parishes, and were markedly more likely to have travelled longer distances. Indeed, the proportion arriving in the rural parishes from outside of the local region in category F was only marginally higher than that in category E. Furthermore, their number in the rural areas was considerably smaller than in the town, category F constituting only 0.5% of the total population, even though they were far from numerous in the borough of St Albans itself, where they formed just 2.7% of the population as a whole. The census would appear to indicate, therefore, that the problem posed by the pauper population in general and the indigent migrant population in particular, whilst of relatively modest proportions in both small town society and in rural villages in this part of Hertfordshire, was far more

---

507   This conforms closely to the situation in the rural parts of the Berkhamsted region, where straw plaiters formed a particularly immobile component of the population: Goose, *The Berkhamsted Region*, pp. 57-8.

apparent in town than it was in countryside. This reminds us once again of the lodging house in Spicer Street run by the chimney sweep Sarah Perrin, which on census night housed as many as 21 "lodgers for the night", all designated as "tramp", residing cheek by jowl with the Spicer Street Congregational Church and the Church of England National School, presenting a most incongruous social mix and a juxtaposition of social ethics that stood at the two extremities of mid-Victorian social values.[508]

Household size and structure

The final topic to be addressed is the structure of the household and family. The 1851 census is the first to allow full reconstruction of the family and household, for it is the first that specifies the relationship of each individual to the household head. The pioneering studies of Anderson and Armstrong led the way in such analyses, using a variety of records in harness with the census to establish key features of family structure in two very different mid-nineteenth century urban communities.[509] Surprisingly few historians have followed in their footsteps, however, despite the vast improvements in computational capabilities over the past twenty years, and there is a particular dearth for southern England.[510] Furthermore, most of the studies that have been undertaken have been much smaller in scale, focusing upon individual parishes or villages, or small collections of parishes, although the important recent work of Dupree on the Staffordshire Potteries represents a notable exception to this rule.[511] Other studies have presented the results of statistical analysis of various features of the family and household, but have made little or no attempt to explain the results produced.[512] In particular, what is needed is more comparative work, studies that can help reveal both the key similarities and the local and regional differences that undoubtedly exist beneath the bald averages that national samples produce, and studies that are placed within the more general social and economic context of the communities to which they relate.[513] This is often a complex process, for a number of variables could all interact in more or less subtle ways to influence various features of family and household formation. It is nevertheless a necessary procedure if we are to attempt to get behind the statistical tables that the census data can generate to write the history of communities, one that was attempted – hopefully with at least some success – in our study of the Berkhamsted region,[514] and one that will again be pursued here, this time with a clearer emphasis upon the differences that can be discovered between town and countryside.

A great deal of attention has been given to the various problems that the census enumerator's books present to the historian wishing to analyse family and household structure.[515] Whilst in the majority of cases a household was included within a discrete enumeration schedule, there are a number of instances where this clearly was not the case, with more than one head and their families sharing the same schedule number, or

508 See above, p. 67.

509 Anderson, *Family Structure in Nineteenth Century Lancashire*; Armstrong, *Stability and Change in an English County Town*.

510 D. Mills, M. Edgar and A. Hinde, "Southern Historians and their Exploitation of Victorian Censuses", *Southern History*, Vol. 18 (1996), p. 61.

511 Dupree, *Family Structure in the Staffordshire Potteries*. For some examples of small scale studies see Mills and Schürer, *Local Communities*, pp. 298-345; also Tranter, "The Social Structure of a Bedfordshire Parish".

512 For example, D. Constable, *Household Structure in Three English Market Towns, 1851-1871*, Geographical Papers, No. 55, University of Reading, 1977.

513 Mills and Schürer echo this view: *Local Communities*, pp. 280-1, 292.

514 Goose, *The Berkhamsted Region*, pp. 60-79.

515 Wrigley (ed.), *Nineteenth-Century Society*; Higgs, *A Clearer Sense*, pp. 68-77; Mills and Schürer (eds.), *Local Communities*, pp. 281-4.

where no head is listed at all in a separate schedule, or where there is confusion over the situation of lodgers as to whether or not they were members of the family with whom they appeared to live. On the latter issue, the instructions issued to the enumerators, whilst attempting to distinguish the position of lodgers who clearly lived with a family from those who should be regarded as having separate occupancy, only served to confuse, and it is quite apparent that the rules were interpreted in different ways by different individuals. It is particularly in towns, whether large or small, that such problems arise, for here we more commonly find the multiple occupancy of houses that is often the source of confusion.

It is important to keep these problems in perspective, however. Firstly, the great majority of households correspond to a schedule number and are clearly delineated, and the experience of analysing both the Berkhamsted and St Albans regions' census enumerations has indicated that, here at least, there are very few confusing instances indeed in the rural parishes. Secondly, it is possible to adopt standard procedures that will probably produce accurate identification of discrete households in the majority of cases where confusion is possible. Here, as in the Berkhamsted study, we have followed Anderson in ignoring schedule numbers, and deeming each new household to commence with every entry "head" in the column "relation to head of household".[516] Standard exceptions to this rule have been followed too, as in cases where a new schedule commences with an individual described as other than a head (most frequently "wife"), possibly indicating that the head of household was absent on census night. In such instances, where there can be no doubt that we are dealing with a new household and there can be no possible relationship to the previous schedule, these individuals are treated as equivalent to a household head. The situation of lodgers is more problematic, and particularly in St Albans itself, as they may well have been treated inconsistently by different enumerators. Each case has, therefore, to be treated on its merits, with recourse to the lines usually drawn to separate households by the enumerators, and to careful consideration of the interpretation of the rules that different enumerators appear to have followed. Some lodgers have, therefore, been assigned as lodgers to the previous schedule, others have been treated as occupants of separate households. In very few cases indeed was it impossible to decide how to proceed, and these were simply removed for the purposes of household analysis. Again, however, even for lodgers the majority of cases do not present difficulties, but can be dealt with by the standard procedures described above, or through common sense interpretation of particular entries.

There is also scope for confusion regarding the descriptions of the various members of a household and their relationship to the head. The most common error discovered to date in the Hertfordshire returns is the use of the term "in-law" for step children, but examination of the surnames and ages of those concerned makes their identification relatively easy.[517] Occasionally the relationship given is not that to the household head, but to another family member, and this too needs to be changed before analysis can proceed. "Housekeepers" were particularly problematic in Rochdale, where the great majority were clearly not servants but had a familial relationship to the household head, or were even heads themselves, but recent analysis of the National Sample from the 1851 census suggests that this may have been a particular feature of the region within which Rochdale was situated, and perhaps a product of the more common incidence of female employment outside of the

516   M. Anderson, "Standard Tabulation Procedures for the Census Enumerators' Books 1851-1891", in Wrigley (ed.), *Nineteenth-Century Society*, pp. 136-7.

517   This was standard (mis) usage in Victorian England, at least in the south: Mills, Edgar and Hinde, "Southern Historians and their Exploitation of the Victorian Censuses", p. 68.

home.[518] Certainly, although a degree of overlap between kinship and service relationships remains, the problem occurs at a markedly lower frequency at the national level.[519] In the St Albans region, of the 57 housekeepers listed in the occupational column of the enumerations, 23 were recorded as a servant in relation to the head of household, 34 were not. Daughter (9) and sister (8) were the most common relationships entered, there were seven heads and just three wives. Given these relatively small numbers, and the prominence of unmarried daughters and kin amongst these housekeepers, it does *not* appear that the term was regularly used to denote women in general who were engaged in domestic duties rather than participating in paid employment. Nor does the problem also occur for "housemaids" as it did in Rochdale, for 38 of the 39 thus described in the St Albans district by occupation are identified as servants in relation to the household head. Given that household analysis employs the "relationship to head of household" column to establish family composition, there should be no serious distortion, though we are reminded that one possible reason for kin to join a family unit, or for daughters to remain at home, might be to help in the domestic support of the household.

For the purposes of analysis, and to appropriately reflect their status within their households, living-in journeymen, apprentices, assistants and shopmen were classified as servants, as were two "articled pupils". They were, in any case, relatively few in number, with just 36 apprentices across the entire region despite its urban complexion, eight assistants, three shopmen and one living-in journeyman. "Boarders" and "inmates" have been regarded as lodgers whilst visitors have been treated separately, despite the occasional suspicion that the terms lodger and visitor may have been employed interchangeably by some enumerators. The "relationship to head of household" column is occasionally left blank by the enumerator, and these make up the small number included as "unknown" where an informed judgement as to their relationship proved impossible to make. "Other" includes three nurse children, a handful of servant's relatives who it did not seem appropriate to list as servants themselves, two "friends", one "partner" and one "companion". All major institutions have been excluded, notably the workhouse, the prison and the small hospital in Harpenden, as have all boarding schools, as well as the odd "pupil" found very occasionally in the homes of professional people. As for the analysis of household composition in the Berkhamsted region, it was decided also to remove lodging houses, hotels and inns, as by their very nature they are likely to include substantial numbers of servants not operating in a domestic capacity, as well as numerous temporary lodgers. Given the commonality between inns, hotels, victualling houses, pubs and beer shops, it was necessary to remove them all, and in the interests of consistency this was done whether or not they contained either servants or lodgers.[520] The net result is a sample size of 16,568 individuals, a little over 92% of the total population of the district, and between them forming 3,576 households.

Mean, median and modal household sizes for each parish, the various sub-districts and for the sample as whole are presented in Table 20, alongside the figures calculated for the Berkhamsted region. The consistency of the average size of the English household between the mid-sixteenth and early twentieth centuries, falling with the narrow range of 4.4 to 4.8 persons, is well known, the overall average calculated by Laslett standing

518 E. Higgs, "The Tabulation of Occupations in the Nineteenth Century Census, With Special Reference to Domestic Servants", *Local Population Studies*, No. 28 (1982), pp. 58-66; M. Anderson, "Mis-Specification of Servant Occupations in the 1851 Census: a Problem Revisited", *Local Population Studies*, No. 60 (1998), pp. 58-64.

519 *Ibid.*, p. 59.

520 This approach, therefore, has been followed even more rigorously than was the case for Berkhamsted.

at 4.47 and the figure for 1851 itself at 4.73.[521] Anderson's calculation for 1851, from the National Sample for Great Britain of 2,067 households, produces an almost identical mean of 4.75.[522] These are, of course, averages taken from large samples, and for individual parishes, or even groups of parishes, there was a wider range of mean household sizes. Hence for the twelve groups of communities included in Dennis Mills' English Rural Norm for 1851, the range lay between 4.09 and 6.07. In 1782 the average for the parish of Cardington in Bedfordshire stood as low as 3.88 whilst at the same date Aspley Guise in the same county exhibited a mean of 6.06, whilst just 70 years later the Cardington figure had risen to 5.11.[523] When we take larger areas, such as the 33 hundreds that constituted the county of Norfolk, the range again narrows, extending from 4.4 to 5.3 in 1811, whilst in the town of Norwich taken alone the figure stood as low as 3.85.[524] The more individual cases that are examined, however, the more it becomes clear that the range of averages lay within a fairly narrow band, generally between about four and six. Hence for Plumpton in Sussex the figure stood at between 5.3 and 5.7 in the successive censuses between 1841 and 1871, the three market towns of Horsham in Sussex and Salisbury and Swindon in Wiltshire exhibit a range between 4.3 and 5.4 in 1851, and the figure for Borden in north Kent stood at 4.9 for the same date.[525] In the three Cornish mining parishes of Camborne, Redruth and St Just in 1851 the range was from 5.2 to 5.5, whilst for the combined sample 20 years later it had fallen to 4.88 under the influence of economic depression.[526] In the city of York, expanding relatively slowly in the early nineteenth century on the basis of its traditional role as a supplier of a variety of trades and services to its region, the figure in 1851 was 4.7, whilst in Preston it stood somewhat higher at 5.4 due to the number of children remaining at home and the prominence of resident kin in this rapidly expanding textile manufacturing town.[527] The figure for the Potteries in both 1861 and 1881 stood at 5.0, a level very close to the national average, reflecting the combined influences of a relatively low age at marriage, slightly higher than average marital fertility and high death rates for infants, children and the adult population.[528]

---

521   P. Laslett, "Mean Household Size in England Since the Sixteenth Century", in Laslett and Wall (eds.), *Household and Family in Past Time*, pp. 133, 138.

522   M. Anderson, "Households, Families and Individuals: Some Preliminary Results from the National Sample from the 1851 Census of Great Britain", *Continuity and Change*, Vol. 3 (1988), Table 1, p. 425.

523   D. Baker, *The Inhabitants of Cardington in 1782. Bedfordshire Historical Records Society*, Vol. 52 (1973), pp. 31-3; Tranter, "The Social Structure of a Bedfordshire Parish", Table 3, p. 93.

524   T. Arkell and A. Whiteman, "Mean Household Size in Mid-Tudor England: Clackclose Hundred, Norfolk", *Local Population Studies*, No. 60 (1998), p. 30.

525   B. Short (ed.), *Scarpfoot Parish: Plumpton 1830-1880*, University of Sussex Centre for Continuing Education, Occasional Paper No. 16 (Brighton, 1981), p. 36; calculated from Constable, "Household Structure in Three English Market Towns", employing a 10% sample and relating to 'primary households' only; D. G. Jackson, *The Population of Borden in 1851. A Study of a North Kent Village Based on the 1851 Census Enumerators' Books* (private publication, Congleton, 1997), p. 13.

526   M. Brayshay, "Depopulation and Changing Household Structure in the Mining Communities of West Cornwall, 1851-1871", in Mills and Schürer (eds.), *Local Communities in the Victorian Census*, pp. 333, 335.

527   Armstrong, *Stability and Change in an English County Town*, pp. 28, 188, 195; Anderson, "Household Structure and the Industrial Revolution", pp. 215-35.

528   Calculated from Dupree, *Family Structure in the Staffordshire Potteries*, pp. 355-6. The 1861 figure is derived from a systematic 1 in 15 sample from the parliamentary borough of Stoke-on-Trent, although the figure for the number of households given in this methodological appendix (1,353) differs from that given earlier in the text on p. 100 (1,373). The sample for 1881 is 1 in 24, producing "approximately 6,000 individuals in 1,200 households". Dupree excluded visitors from her calculations but included quasi-institutions such as lodging houses. For marriage, fertility and death rates, see pp. 121-43. An independent study from the 1851 census of the townships of Hanley and Shelton which both lay within the parish and borough of Stoke on Trent (1 in 7 sample) produces an identical mean household size of 5.0: D.A. Gatley, *Hanley in 1851 Revisited: a Survey Based on the Census Returns* (Staffordshire University, 1996), p. 8.

TABLE 20 : MEAN, MEDIAN AND MODE HOUSEHOLD SIZES

	Number of Persons	Number of Households	Mean Household Size	Median Household Size	Mode Household Size
St Albans Urban					
St Albans	2960	695	4.26	4	3
St Michaels (Urban)	1040	216	4.81	4	6
St Peters	2384	561	4.25	4	2
St Albans Rural					
St Michaels (Rural)	866	159	5.45	5	6
St Stephens	1480	302	4.90	5	5
Out-hamlets	1365	278	4.91	5	5
Harpenden	1879	412	4.56	4	3
Redbourn	2004	436	4.60	4	3
Sandridge	831	153	5.43	5	5
Wheathampstead	1759	364	4.83	5	5
Sub-Totals					
St Albans (Liberty)	10095	2211	4.57	4	3
Urban Parishes	6384	1472	4.34	4	3
Rural Parishes	10184	2104	4.84	5	3
Total	16568	3576	4.63	4	3
Berkhamsted Region	11101	2300	4.83	4	3

In the light of these various figures the overall averages for the St Albans district are entirely unremarkable, as indeed they were for the Berkhamsted region to the west, the mean household size for the complete sample of 3,576 households standing just a little below the national average at 4.63. Again as in Berkhamsted, the range across the various parishes or parts of parishes was also quite narrow, in this case running from a low of 4.25 in St Peters to a high of 5.45 in the rural part of St Michaels. But whilst in the Berkhamsted region the more urban parishes showed a slight tendency to exhibit higher averages,[529] in St Albans the opposite is true, with the figure for the town proper standing at 4.34 compared with 4.84 for the rural parishes, and lower still for the two most wholly urban parishes of St Albans and St Peters at 4.26 and 4.25 respectively. This difference is also reflected in the fact that the median household size in the town stood at four, but at five in the rural parishes. In this regard the St Albans district conforms more closely to the situation nationally, for across England urban households tended to be smaller on average than rural ones in 1851, although the examples of towns such as Preston cited above show that there were exceptions to this rule as well as significant variations from town to town.[530] As in Berkhamsted, it is again surprising to find such a range in the modal household size, extending from just two in St Peters to six in both parts of St Michaels. But whilst this again helps explain the urban/rural contrast we have noted, just as in Berkhamsted the differences in the numbers of households within this range in each parish is generally very small, and they thus reflect fairly marginal rather than substantial discrepancies.

A more detailed breakdown of the number and proportion of households of different sizes and the number and proportion of the population they contained is presented in Tables 21 and 22. Looking at the smallest, solitary,

529   Goose, *The Berkhamsted Region*, pp. 61-2.
530   R. Wall, "The Household: Demographic and Economic Change in England 1650-1970", in R. Wall (ed.), *Family Forms in Historic Europe* (Cambridge, 1983), pp. 417, 510. Part of the difference between the more urban parts of the Berkhamsted region and the town of St Albans could, however, be due to the more rigorous exclusion of quasi-institutions such as lodging houses and inns in the present study, whilst the separation of town and countryside in the Berkhamsted analysis was incomplete, an anomaly that is currently being corrected, with the assistance of Lyn Leader, through a re-working of the Berkhamsted data for Tring.

households first, these figures indicate that one person households were far more common in the St Albans district than they were in Berkhamsted, accounting for as many as 6.49% of all households compared with just 3.65% in the region to the west. This figure also stands above the 5.7% discovered for 100 communities between 1574 and 1821, the 4.9% in the 1851 national sample, the 5.1% found in the city of York in 1851 and the 5.3% at Horsham in Sussex or 4.5% at Borden in Kent, and substantially above the 3% found in rural Lancashire, 2.5% in Hanley in the Potteries and the 1% in both industrial Preston and in Swindon in Wiltshire.[531] The discrepancy between the St Albans district figure and most others that have been reported to date is quite clearly due to the urban influence upon the overall figure, for one person households in the three parishes or parts of parishes that have been designated as urban amounted to as much as 10.26% of the total found there, and again the figures stand even higher for St Albans and St Peters at 11.80% and 10.70 respectively, proportions which are comparable to those revealed for England and Wales in the mid-*twentieth* century and more than double the norm for the mid-nineteenth.[532] By contrast, the proportion in the rural parishes of the district stood at just 3.85%, very similar to that for the Berkhamsted region as a whole and also comparable to rural Lancashire.

The discrepancy between town and countryside in this respect is thus a stark one, but also one that might have been predicted from our previous discussion of the social, demographic and occupational structure of the town. We have already seen that the town tended to contain higher proportions of widows and widowers, widows in particular, than did the rural parishes, and the discrepancy was particularly marked towards the bottom of the social scale, for parishes such as St Peters provided more substantial opportunities for independence in old age through the almshouse accommodation that was available there.[533] Furthermore, ostensibly unemployed urban widows were less likely than their rural counterparts to rely upon family members for support.[534] Of the 151 one person households in the urban parishes as many as 90 were headed by females, 43 of whom were widows, whilst in the rural parishes just 37 of the 81 one person households were headed by females, 19 of these being widows. But these figures also suggest that there must be more to the explanation, for the town also included 37 unmarried solitary women, constituting as much as one-quarter of all one person households, which compares with just 12 in the rural parishes where they constituted just 15% of all one person households, despite the considerably greater population of the latter area.[535] Clearly, there was substantially more opportunity for female independence in mid-nineteenth century St Albans, through employment as well as alms, than there was in the town's rural hinterland.[536] There were also far more unmarried men living alone in town than in countryside, 49 of the 61 male solitaries as compared with 22 out of 44, again no doubt

531   Laslett, "Mean Household Size in England", Table 4.6, p. 142; Anderson, "Households, Families and Individuals", pp. 424-5; Constable, *Household Structure*, pp. 28, 34, 46; Jackson, *The Population of Borden*, Table 5, p. 13; Anderson, "Household Structure and the Industrial Revolution", Table 7.1, p. 219; Gatley, *Hanley in 1851 Revisited*, Table 3.4, p. 8. It was exceeded slightly in Salisbury in Wiltshire, where 7.1% of households were solitaries: Constable, *ibid*. The figure for the Potteries in 1861 is not given by Dupree but stood below 5%, for only 5% of households consisted of either a head alone or a head with only unrelated persons: Dupree, *Family Structure in the Staffordshire Potteries*, Table 2.2, p. 103.

532   The figure for 1951 was 10.7% and for 1961 11.9%: Laslett, , "Mean Household Size in England", Table 4.6, p. 142.

533   See above, pp. 35-6.

534   See above, pp. 92-4.

535   In the town eight solitary females are described as married, two have no designation. In the rural parishes six are described as married. It is, of course, possible that their husbands were simply away from home on census night.

536   These features reflect in clearer terms the more tentative explanations offered for the relatively high proportion of solitary households found in Aldbury and Northchurch in the Berkhamsted region: Goose, The *Berkhamsted Region*, pp. 62-3.

TABLE 21 : NUMBER AND PERCENTAGE OF HOUSEHOLDS OF DIFFERENT SIZES

Household Size	St Albans No.	%	St Mich(Urban) No.	%	St Peters No.	%	St Mich (Rural) No.	%	St Stephens No.	%	Out-hamlets No.	%	Harpenden No.	%	Redbourn No.	%
1	82	11.80	9	4.17	60	10.70	8	5.03	13	4.30	9	3.24	23	5.58	16	3.67
2	109	15.68	32	14.81	98	17.47	13	8.18	42	13.91	34	12.23	63	15.29	72	16.51
3	120	17.27	31	14.35	95	16.93	25	15.72	43	14.24	44	15.83	78	18.93	78	17.89
4	104	14.96	37	17.13	87	15.51	26	16.35	41	13.58	42	15.11	67	16.26	77	17.66
5	81	11.65	21	9.72	66	11.76	20	12.58	47	15.56	48	17.27	51	12.38	56	12.84
6	70	10.07	38	17.59	53	9.45	27	16.98	37	12.25	33	11.87	52	12.62	54	12.39
7	53	7.63	21	9.72	37	6.60	10	6.29	34	11.26	32	11.51	32	7.77	26	5.96
8	34	4.89	12	5.56	29	5.17	10	6.29	23	7.62	19	6.83	17	4.13	24	5.50
9	25	3.60	8	3.70	19	3.39	8	5.03	14	4.64	7	2.52	13	3.16	20	4.59
10	8	1.15	3	1.39	10	1.78	4	2.52	6	1.99	5	1.80	5	1.21	7	1.61
11	3	0.43	2	0.93	2	0.36	4	2.52	1	0.33	2	0.72	4	0.97	3	0.69
12	2	0.29	1	0.46	3	0.53	0	0.00	0	0.00	1	0.36	5	1.21	2	0.46
13	3	0.43	0	0.00	1	0.18	1	0.63	0	0.00	1	0.36	1	0.24	0	0.00
14	0	0.00	1	0.46	1	0.18	0	0.00	1	0.33	1	0.36	0	0.00	0	0.00
15	1	0.14	0	0.00	0	0.00	1	0.63	0	0.00	0	0.00	1	0.24	1	0.23
16-20	0	0.00	0	0.00	0	0.00	1	0.63	0	0.00	0	0.00	0	0.00	0	0.00
21-25	0	0.00	0	0.00	0	0.00	0	0.00	0	0.00	0	0.00	0	0.00	0	0.00
26-30	0	0.00	0	0.00	0	0.00	0	0.00	0	0.00	0	0.00	0	0.00	0	0.00
31-35	0	0.00	0	0.00	0	0.00	0	0.00	0	0.00	0	0.00	0	0.00	0	0.00
36-40	0	0.00	0	0.00	0	0.00	1	0.63	0	0.00	0	0.00	0	0.00	0	0.00
Total	695	99.99	216	99.99	561	100.01	159	100.01	302	100.01	278	100.01	412	99.99	436	100.00

Household Size	Sandridge No.	%	Wheath'pstead No.	%	St Albans (Liberty) No.	%	Urban Parishes No.	%	Rural Parishes No.	%	Total No.	%	Berkhamsted Region No.	%
1	0	0.00	12	3.30	181	8.19	151	10.26	81	3.85	232	6.49	84	3.65
2	15	9.80	56	15.38	328	14.83	239	16.24	295	14.02	534	14.93	304	13.22
3	24	15.69	50	13.74	358	16.19	246	16.71	342	16.25	588	16.44	385	16.74
4	21	13.73	57	15.66	337	15.24	228	15.49	331	15.73	559	15.63	378	16.43
5	26	16.99	59	16.21	283	12.80	168	11.41	307	14.59	475	13.28	370	16.09
6	20	13.07	46	12.64	258	11.67	161	10.94	269	12.79	430	12.02	263	11.43
7	21	13.73	35	9.62	187	8.46	111	7.54	190	9.03	301	8.42	206	8.96
8	11	7.19	25	6.87	127	5.74	75	5.10	129	6.13	204	5.70	127	5.52
9	5	3.27	11	3.02	81	3.66	52	3.53	78	3.71	130	3.64	96	4.17
10	4	2.61	7	1.92	36	1.63	21	1.43	38	1.81	59	1.65	40	1.74
11	3	1.96	4	1.10	14	0.63	7	0.48	21	1.00	28	0.78	23	1.00
12	0	0.00	0	0.00	7	0.32	6	0.41	8	0.38	14	0.39	9	0.39
13	2	1.31	1	0.27	6	0.27	4	0.27	6	0.29	10	0.28	9	0.39
14	0	0.00	0	0.00	4	0.18	2	0.14	2	0.10	4	0.11	1	0.04
15	0	0.00	1	0.27	2	0.09	1	0.07	2	0.10	3	0.08	0	0.00
16-20	1	0.65	0	0.00	1	0.05	0	0.00	4	0.19	4	0.11	3	0.13
21-25	0	0.00	0	0.00	0	0.00	0	0.00	0	0.00	0	0.00	1	0.04
26-30	0	0.00	0	0.00	0	0.00	0	0.00	0	0.00	0	0.00	1	0.04
31-35	0	0.00	0	0.00	0	0.00	0	0.00	0	0.00	0	0.00	0	0.00
36-40	0	0.00	0	0.00	1	0.05	0	0.00	1	0.05	1	0.03	0	0.00
Total	153	100.00	364	100.00	2211	100.00	1472	100.02	2104	100.02	3576	99.98	2300	99.98

TABLE 22 : NUMBER AND PERCENTAGE OF PEOPLE IN HOUSEHOLDS OF DIFFERENT SIZES

Household Size	St Albans No.	%	St Mich (Urban) No.	%	St Peters No.	%	St Mich (Rural) No.	%	St Stephens No.	%	Out-hamlets No.	%	Harpenden No.	%	Redbourn No.	%
1	82	2.77	9	0.87	60	2.52	8	0.92	13	0.88	9	0.66	23	1.22	16	0.80
2	218	7.36	64	6.15	196	8.22	26	3.00	84	5.68	68	4.98	126	6.71	144	7.19
3	360	12.16	93	8.94	285	11.95	75	8.66	129	8.72	132	9.67	234	12.45	234	11.68
4	416	14.05	148	14.23	348	14.60	104	12.01	164	11.08	168	12.31	268	14.26	308	15.37
5	405	13.68	105	10.10	330	13.84	100	11.55	235	15.88	240	17.58	255	13.57	280	13.97
6	420	14.19	228	21.92	318	13.34	162	18.71	222	15.00	198	14.51	312	16.60	324	16.17
7	371	12.53	147	14.13	259	10.86	70	8.08	238	16.08	224	16.41	224	11.92	182	9.08
8	272	9.19	96	9.23	232	9.73	80	9.24	184	12.43	152	11.14	136	7.24	192	9.58
9	225	7.60	72	6.92	171	7.17	72	8.31	126	8.51	63	4.62	117	6.23	180	8.98
10	80	2.70	30	2.88	100	4.19	40	4.62	60	4.05	50	3.66	50	2.66	70	3.49
11	33	1.11	22	2.12	22	0.92	44	5.08	11	0.74	22	1.61	44	2.34	33	1.65
12	24	0.81	12	1.15	36	1.51	0	0.00	0	0.00	12	0.88	60	3.19	24	1.20
13	39	1.32	0	0.00	13	0.55	13	1.50	0	0.00	13	0.95	13	0.69	0	0.00
14	0	0.00	14	1.35	14	0.59	0	0.00	14	0.95	14	1.03	0	0.00	0	0.00
15	15	0.51	0	0.00	0	0.00	15	1.73	0	0.00	0	0.00	0	0.00	0	0.00
16-20	0	0.00	0	0.00	0	0.00	20	2.31	0	0.00	0	0.00	17	0.90	17	0.85
21-25	0	0.00	0	0.00	0	0.00	0	0.00	0	0.00	0	0.00	0	0.00	0	0.00
26-30	0	0.00	0	0.00	0	0.00	0	0.00	0	0.00	0	0.00	0	0.00	0	0.00
31-35	0	0.00	0	0.00	0	0.00	0	0.00	0	0.00	0	0.00	0	0.00	0	0.00
36-40	0	0.00	0	0.00	0	0.00	37	4.27	0	0.00	0	0.00	0	0.00	0	0.00
Total	2960	99.98	1040	99.99	2384	99.99	866	99.99	1480	100.00	1365	100.01	1879	99.98	2004	100.01

Household Size	Sandridge No.	%	Wheath'pstead No.	%	St Albans (Liberty) No.	%	Urban Parishes No.	%	Rural Parishes No.	%	Total No.	%	Berkhamsted Region No.	%
1	0	0.00	12	0.68	181	1.79	151	2.37	81	0.80	232	1.40	84	0.76
2	30	3.61	112	6.37	656	6.50	478	7.49	590	5.79	1068	6.45	608	5.48
3	72	8.66	150	8.53	1074	10.64	738	11.56	1026	10.07	1764	10.65	1155	10.40
4	84	10.11	228	12.96	1348	13.35	912	14.29	1324	13.00	2236	13.50	1512	13.62
5	130	15.64	295	16.77	1415	14.02	840	13.16	1535	15.07	2375	14.33	1850	16.67
6	120	14.44	276	15.69	1548	15.33	966	15.13	1614	15.85	2580	15.57	1578	14.21
7	147	17.69	245	13.93	1309	12.97	777	12.17	1330	13.06	2107	12.72	1442	12.99
8	88	10.59	200	11.37	1016	10.06	600	9.40	1032	10.13	1632	9.85	1016	9.15
9	45	5.42	99	5.63	729	7.22	468	7.33	702	6.89	1170	7.06	864	7.78
10	40	4.81	70	3.98	360	3.57	210	3.29	380	3.73	590	3.56	400	3.60
11	33	3.97	44	2.50	154	1.53	77	1.21	231	2.27	308	1.86	253	2.28
12	0	0.00	0	0.00	84	0.83	72	1.13	96	0.94	168	1.01	108	0.97
13	26	3.13	13	0.74	78	0.77	52	0.81	78	0.77	130	0.78	117	1.05
14	0	0.00	0	0.00	56	0.55	28	0.44	28	0.27	56	0.34	14	0.13
15	0	0.00	15	0.85	30	0.30	15	0.23	30	0.29	45	0.27	0	0.00
16-20	16	1.93	0	0.00	20	0.20	0	0.00	70	0.69	70	0.42	52	0.47
21-25	0	0.00	0	0.00	0	0.00	0	0.00	0	0.00	0	0.00	21	0.19
26-30	0	0.00	0	0.00	0	0.00	0	0.00	0	0.00	0	0.00	27	0.24
31-35	0	0.00	0	0.00	0	0.00	0	0.00	0	0.00	0	0.00	0	0.00
36-40	0	0.00	0	0.00	37	0.37	0	0.00	37	0.36	37	0.22	0	0.00
Total	831	100.00	1759	100.00	10095	100.00	6384	100.01	10184	99.98	16568	99.99	11101	99.99

reflecting more diverse occupational opportunities, and perhaps also a greater transience amongst one element of the population at least. In the town, male solitaries were far younger on average than were females who lived alone, just 11% being aged 60 or over compared with 53% of the women, whilst in the rural parishes there was little difference between the sexes in this respect. In the rural areas as many as 20 widowers were found living alone, compared with a mere four in the whole of the town, which helps explain the relative age differences between the two. Finally, before we leave the subject of one person households, we should simply note that whilst they constituted quite substantial proportions of all households, when we consider these individuals as a proportion of the total population the percentages are far smaller, standing at just 2.37% for the town, 0.8% for the rural parishes, and 1.4% overall.

The majority of the population, just as in the Berkhamsted region and indeed across the country, lived in nuclear families of moderate size. Small households, comprising just one or two members, constituted only 21% of the total, which compares with 17% in the Berkhamsted region, 20% in 100 communities 1564-1821, 21% in the 1851 national sample, 20% in York, 11% in Preston, 12% in Hanley in the Potteries and 15% in a Lancashire rural sample. The urban/rural contrast found for solitary households is only very slightly enhanced by the consideration of all containing one or two members, for there was only a marginally higher proportion of two person households in town than in countryside. Nevertheless, with 27% of its households in the 'small' category, the town of St Albans presents a considerable contrast to the large industrial towns in both Staffordshire and Lancashire for which we have evidence, even if the region as a whole mirrors the national average almost exactly, with 21% of households containing 8% of individuals.[537] Most households were of moderate size, those containing 3-6 members accounting for 57% of all households in the district as a whole, with relatively little difference between town (55%) and countryside (59%). These figures are again of the same order of magnitude as the 61% in the Berkhamsted region, 59% in 100 communities 1564-1821, 61% in York, 59% in Preston, 59% in Swindon in Wiltshire, and 54% in Salisbury in Wiltshire, Borden in north Kent and Horsham in Surrey.[538] In studies to date the range for the proportion of households that might be regarded as moderately sized tended to fall between half and two-thirds, with Plumpton in Sussex (50%) and Anderson's Lancashire rural sample (51%) falling at the lower end of the range and Hanley in the Potteries at the upper end (65%), and hence the St Albans district sat squarely in the middle.[539] Comparison with the 1851 national sample is only possible in terms of households with 3-5 members, but here our district conforms exactly to the national average, with an identical 45% in this category, and even less difference between town (44%) and countryside (47%).[540] The proportion of *individuals* found in these households tended to be slightly lower, however, as Table 22 reveals. The category we have defined as of moderate size, with 3-6 members, accounted for 54% of the population of the St Albans district, with identical figures for town and

537   The market towns of Horsham in Sussex, with 25% and Salisbury in Wiltshire with 28% in this category are more comparable with the St Albans figure, though the fact Swindon in Wiltshire included only 10% shows that this was not invariably a feature of towns of this stature: Constable, *Household Structure in Three English Market Towns*, pp. 28, 34, 46.

538   Goose, *The Berkhamsted Region*, p. 63; calculations from Laslett, "Mean Household Size in England", Table 4.6, p. 142; Anderson, "Household Structure and the Industrial Revolution", Table 7.1, p. 219; Constable, *Household Structure in Three English Market Towns*, pp. 28, 34, 46; Jackson, *The Population of Borden in 1851*, Table 5, p. 13.

539   Short (ed.), *Scarpfoot Parish*, Table 12, p. 37; Anderson, "Household Structure and the Industrial Revolution", Table 7.1, p. 219; Gatley, *Hanley in 1851 Revisited*, Table 3.4, p. 8.

540   National sample figure calculated from Anderson, "Households, Families and Individuals", pp. 424-5.

countryside.[541] And if we compare Tables 21 and 22 more closely, we find that whilst the most common household size was one of three members, followed by four, two, five and six in that order, the highest number of individuals actually lived in households with six members, followed by five, four, seven and three. This takes us close to what Anderson has described as "mean experienced household size", or household size weighted by the number of persons in each household, which he calculates at 6.2 for the 1851 national sample.[542]

Larger households, with 7-9 members, accounted for 18% of the total (16% in the urban and 19% in the rural parishes), which again conforms closely to the Berkhamsted figure of 19%, the 100 community sample of 17%, the Potteries figure of 19% as well as to that for a city of comparable stature to St Albans, Salisbury in Wiltshire, with 16%.[543] The range for households of this size could be quite wide, however, with Horsham (11%) and York (14%) towards the bottom and Preston and Plumpton (23%) and Borden, Swindon and the Lancashire rural sample (26%) at the upper end.[544] Generally between one in four and one in seven of all households fell into this category, and within our sample of parishes St Stephens and Sandridge approached the top of this range with 24% of households, and Harpenden stood at the lower end with just 15%. Very large households, with 10 or more members, accounted for 3.4% of the total for the district, 2.8% in the town of St Albans and 3.9% in the rural parishes collectively. Again this is a very similar figure to Salisbury (3%), Berkhamsted, the Potteries and Borden (4%), 100 communities 1564-1821 and York (5%), whilst those for Preston and the Lancashire rural sample stood a little higher at 8% and 9% respectively.[545] The range of household sizes was, however, considerable, and in the St Albans district included one as large as 37, that of the Earl of Verulam at Gorhambury on the rural side of the parish of St Michaels, whilst seven more included over 15 members, all but one situated in rural parishes. In the town it is not surprising to find that the professional classes and more elevated retailers feature strongly amongst those heading very large households, although more humble urban workers are represented too, including five labourers, two shoemakers, a silk throwster and two bricklayers, one of whom was a mere journeyman. In the rural parishes, again it is no surprise to find that farmers were particularly prominent, but as many as 24 agricultural labourers (including two shepherds) headed households with 10 or more members out of a rural total of just 82 (29%), whilst another was headed by Sarah Baines, a widow of 50 years of age, plaiter, who lived in Harpenden with her four children, three grandchildren and two lodgers.

---

541   Viewed in this way the proportion of the population living in moderately sized households could fall below half, as in the example of Borden in Kent where only 46% of the population resided in households with 3-6 members: calculated from Jackson, *The Population of Borden in 1851*, Table 5, p. 13.

542   Anderson, "Households, Families and Individuals", p. 424 and fn. 11.

543   Goose, *The Berkhamsted Region*, p. 66; calculations from Laslett, "Mean Household Size in England", Table 4.6, p. 142; p. 219; Gatley, *Hanley in 1851 Revisited*, Table 3.4; p. 8; Constable, *Household Structure in Three English Market Towns*, p. 34.

544   Constable, *Household Structure in Three English Market Towns*, pp. 28, 46; Short (ed.), *Scarpfoot Parish*, Table 12, p. 37; Anderson, "Household Structure and the Industrial Revolution", Table 7.1, p. 219.

545   Constable, *Household Structure in Three English Market Towns*, p. 34; Goose, *The Berkhamsted Region*, p. 66; calculations from Laslett, "Mean Household Size in England", Table 4.6, p. 142; Gatley, *Hanley in 1851 Revisited*, Table 3.4; Jackson, *The Population of Borden in 1851*, Table 5, p. 13; Anderson, "Household Structure and the Industrial Revolution", Table 7.1, p. 219. The figures also stood a little higher for Swindon (6%), Plumpton (9%) and Horsham (11%), but the sample sizes in each case are small, with a total of only 85, 70 and 57 households respectively, and just a handful of households in this category in each case.

If most households in Victorian England were of relatively modest size, therefore, a considerable minority were large, by present day standards at least, and the range of sizes was considerable. In the St Albans district as a whole, a total of 758 households included seven or more members, 21% or just over one in every five, rising to 23%, approaching one in every four, in the rural parishes. Given that, by definition, these households contained more individuals than did the smaller ones, the proportion of people who experienced life in these large establishments was greater still. Those at the very top of the range were sufficiently few in number to account for quite a limited proportion of all inhabitants, and hence just 8% of the population lived in households containing 10 or more residents, 7% in the town and 9% in the rural parishes. If we focus upon those households that we have defined as large, however, those with seven or more residents, the picture looks very different indeed. Across the St Albans district as a whole as much as 38% of the population lived in such households in 1851, 36% in the town of St Albans and 39% in the rural parishes collectively, the overall figure standing very close indeed to the 39% discovered for the Berkhamsted region to the west.[546] Comparison with the 1851 national sample and the average for 100 communities 1574-1821 is only possible in terms of the proportion of individuals living in households with *six* or more members, both of these producing a figure of 55%, which compares very closely with the 54% in the St Albans district and the 53% in Berkhamsted.[547] If we extend our definition of 'large' households to those with six or more members, therefore, they incorporated over half of the total population. When expressed in this way it becomes clearer that living in large family groups, whether the members of those groups be immediate or distant relatives or unrelated servants, although by no means the universal experience, was far more common in Victorian England than it was to become by the mid to late twentieth century, when the proportion of larger households had dwindled.[548]

The composition of the family and household is explored further in Table 23 through a consideration of the influence of social class.[549] The figures for the district as a whole show a positive association between socio-economic status and mean household size through from categories A to D, and this is confirmed by the very low figure for the unemployed and indigent population represented in category F. In this respect our results exactly match those discovered for the Berkhamsted region, with the exception of category A.[550] In Berkhamsted the figure for category A stood slightly below that for B and C, probably largely due to the influence of the large number of proprietors of houses included here, not all of whom were necessarily of considerable means.[551] In St Albans, however, their impact is less noticeable, and although we will shortly see that those of independent means, which includes the annuitants in category B, did indeed exhibit a below average mean household size, this was more than counterbalanced by the large households of other occupational groups towards the top of

546 Goose, *The Berkhamsted Region*, p. 66.
547 Anderson, "Households, Families and Individuals", p. 424; calculated from Goose, *The Berkhamsted Region*, Table 12, p. 65.
548 In England and Wales in 1966 mean household size stood at just 3.0, only 6% of the population lived in households with six or more members and just 2% in households with seven or more; by 1981 mean household size was just 2.7, and now just 4% of households contained six or more members: Anderson, "Household Structure and the Industrial Revolution", Table 7.1, p. 219; idem, "Households, Families and Individuals", p. 424. See also idem, "What is New About the Modern Family?", in M. Drake (ed.), *Time, Family and Community. Perspectives on Family and Community History* (Oxford, 1994), pp. 67-90.
549 For an explanation of the social groupings see Appendix 1, p. 693.
550 Goose, *The Berkhamsted Region*, pp. 66-7.
551 Mills, Edgar and Hinde agree, noting that " 'independent' sometimes implied little more than independence from poor relief, and 'annuitants' often existed on very meagre annuities", whilst " 'proprietor of houses' could imply only a couple of tumbledown cottages": "Southern Historians and their Exploitation of the Victorian Censuses", p. 70. On the other hand, we will see shortly that if the keeping of servants is any guide to social status, then as an occupational category those of independent means are appropriately regarded as of relatively high social standing overall (pp. 172-3, below).

the social scale, at least when we consider the district as a whole. In Berkhamsted we found that combining social categories A and B produced a mean household size of 5.42, which stood very close to the 5.31 discovered for a comparable social range in the city of York, and in similar fashion this exercise for the St Albans district produces a figure of 5.36.[552]

TABLE 23 : MEAN HOUSEHOLD SIZE BY SOCIO-ECONOMIC GROUP

				Social Group				Total
	A	B	C	D	E	F	Z	
St Albans Urban								
St Albans	4.83	3.33	4.47	3.95	4.42	2.13	7.00	4.26
St Michaels (Urban)	7.89	3.67	5.15	4.64	5.50	3.45	0.00	4.81
St Peters	4.62	4.04	4.60	4.07	4.87	2.00	0.00	4.25
St Albans Rural								
St Michaels (Rural)	16.00	5.36	5.15	4.92	4.38	3.50	0.00	5.45
St Stephens	6.36	5.71	4.98	4.78	4.00	3.20	0.00	4.90
Out-hamlets	6.86	5.71	4.67	4.86	4.00	2.50	3.00	4.91
Harpenden	5.38	4.84	4.39	4.53	2.00	2.67	0.00	4.56
Redbourn	5.58	5.86	4.84	4.37	4.52	2.75	4.00	4.60
Sandridge	9.20	7.00	6.20	4.76	4.50	5.67	0.00	5.43
Wheathampstead	7.00	5.14	4.71	4.76	5.20	2.00	0.00	4.83
Sub-Totals								
St Albans (Liberty)	5.97	4.64	4.62	4.55	4.61	2.39	5.00	4.57
Urban Parishes	5.05	3.61	4.57	4.20	4.71	2.23	7.00	4.34
Rural Parishes	7.34	5.51	4.82	4.67	4.31	3.23	3.50	4.84
Total	6.12	4.95	4.66	4.56	4.60	2.50	4.67	4.63
No. Households	163	294	1036	1702	267	111	3	3576
Berkhamsted Region	4.87	5.64	4.98	4.72	4.90	3.74	n/a	4.83

Note: the scheme of socio-economic classification is presented in Appendix 1 below, p. 693.

It is when we reach category E, representing unskilled workers, that our results deviate from a simple association between household size and social class. At this level in the social scale, the mean household size rises again to stand slightly above that for category D. Indeed, the differences between those represented in all three categories C, D and E are small, and certainly cannot be taken to indicate any *clear cut* distinction in mean household size between the skilled and lower clerical, semi-skilled and unskilled occupational groups. What is clear, however, is that at the lower (but not lowest) levels in the socio-economic hierarchy the positive relationship between status and household size breaks down, representing a departure from the pre-industrial norm identified by Laslett and found also in selected pre-industrial urban studies, hence confirming the results discovered for the Berkhamsted region to the west.[553] Furthermore, despite the fact that some studies of other communities in 1851 have claimed to have found a generally positive association between social class and mean household size, the results for both Cardington and York are, in fact, in line with those discovered here, with the lower socio-occupational categories exhibiting larger households than the social groups immediately

552   *Ibid.*, p. 66; Armstrong, *Stability and Change in an English County Town*, Table 7.13, p. 189.
553   Laslett. "Mean Household Size in England", Table 4.15, p. 154; Goose, "Household Size and Structure", pp. 365-70; *idem, The Berkhamsted Region*, p. 67.

above them.[554] By the mid-nineteenth century, therefore, the simple and consistent positive association between social status and mean household size found in English pre-industrial communities had been superseded by a more complex, less tidy, reality.

Table 23 reveals some interesting differences between town and countryside, as well as some irregularities between individual parishes. For the rural parishes the positive association between social group and mean household size that had prevailed in pre-industrial England again reasserts itself, with a distinct gradient from category A to C, a more gentle decline through C to E, and a distinct drop once again at the very bottom of the hierarchy. The decline through categories A to C is confirmed for every rural parish in the sample, but the continued, if more gentle, downward trend from the middle to the bottom of the scale is less regularly realised. Hence in the Out-hamlets, Harpenden and Wheathampstead, the mean for category D stands slightly above rather than below that for category C, whilst for Redbourn and Wheathampstead the mean for category E stands above that for category D, quite noticeably in the latter case. In Wheathampstead, however, only five households are represented in category E, there is only one in this group in Harpenden, and just three in category F in Sandridge, and it may therefore be wise to ignore these results. The Redbourn result, however, is based upon 23 households in category E, and should not be due to chance distortion. Furthermore, if we extract the four villages from the rural parishes as a group, the mean household sizes for categories D and E respectively stood at 4.58 and 4.54, and hence the distinction at this level in the social scale is purely the product of the influence of those rural parishes which lay within the Liberty of St Albans, where the households of those classed as semi-skilled were significantly larger than those of the unskilled.

In the town of St Albans the picture was different again, and the association between social class and household size even less clear. Households in category A were, at a mean of 5.05, larger than the average of 4.34, but the difference is far less pronounced than that found in the rural parishes, and there is even less of a distinction in the two most clearly urban parishes of St Albans and St Peters. Across the town and consistently in all three parishes the mean household size for social group B was small, producing an overall average of 3.61, falling to just 3.33 in the parish of St Albans. This is primarily the result of the influence upon the figures of the large number of annuitants living in the town who are included in social group B, 30 in number out of a total of 88 in this category, and exhibiting a mean household size of just 2.83.[555] Only four of these annuitants were married, 13 were unmarried and 13 were widows, their average age was 58.4 years, with 19 aged 60 and over and only seven less than 50 years of age. With this demographic profile, it is not surprising that their households were generally small. Towards the middle of the social scale, we find that the households of the skilled and lower clerical workers in category C were noticeably larger than those of the semi-skilled in category D, and consistently so across all three parishes. In contrast to the rural parishes as a group, however, and particularly in contrast to the situation in the rural parishes within the Liberty of St Albans, the position is reversed when we reach category E, for in the town as a whole and in each of the three individual parishes the households headed by the unskilled were larger than those headed by the semi-skilled. Furthermore, in two of the three parishes mean household size for category E was larger than that for category C and equal to it in the remaining parish of St Albans. For category F, household size was again very small. Hence in the town it is only at the two extremes of the social scale that a positive association between household size and social class is apparent, although even here this was only consistently and significantly

---

554   Armstrong, "A Note on the Household Structure", Table 6.3, p. 207: Armstrong does note that "the class V results for York appear to be out of line"; Tranter, "The Social Structure of a Bedfordshire Parish", p. 93.

555   The mean household size of annuitants in the Berkhamsted region was also low: Goose, *The Berkhamsted Region*, p. 66.

apparent at the very bottom of the social scale, and whilst skilled households tended to be larger than those of the semi-skilled, those headed by unskilled workers were on average larger still.

A more detailed analysis of the composition of the household is provided in Table 24, which includes comparative data taken from the 1851 national sample.[556] During the course of the eighteenth and early nineteenth centuries the structure of English households appears to have changed in three key respects. First, there was a slight rise in the number of children they contained, of the order of 17%, already apparent by the second half of the eighteenth century but sustained to 1851. Second, the proportion of living-in servants decreased substantially, from almost 14% in the period 1650-1749 to about 7% in rural areas and 3% in towns by 1851. Third, the proportion of resident kin grew, from 3.6% in 1650-1749 to 6.1% and 7.1% in urban and rural areas respectively in 1851, involving an approximate doubling of the mean number of kin per household across the period.[557] All of these developments are reflected in the data presented in Table 24, which shows that the St Albans district, again like the Berkhamsted region, conformed very closely indeed to the national picture. For the district as a whole the mean number of heads and spouses, children and servants per household are all virtually identical to the national sample figures, differing by a mere 0.01 in each case. There were just slightly more kin in St Albans, 0.33 compared with 0.30, but again this is a small difference amounting to just three individuals for every 100 households.

TABLE 24 : HOUSEHOLD COMPOSITION – MEAN NUMBER OF PERSONS PER HOUSEHOLD

Relationship to Head	Total	St Albans District Urban	Rural	Berkhamsted Region	1851 National Sample	1851 Urban Sample	1851 Rural Sample
Head + Spouse	1.70	1.63	1.75	1.72	1.69	1.64	1.71
Children	2.08	1.92	2.19	2.20	2.07	1.91	2.10
Kin	0.33	0.33	0.33	0.38	0.30	0.27	0.33
Servants	0.31	0.24	0.36	0.26	0.30	0.14	0.33
Subtotal	4.42	4.12	4.63	4.56	4.36	3.96	4.47
Lodgers/Visitors	0.20	0.21	0.20	0.26	0.40	0.50	0.24
Other/Unknown	0.01	0.01	0.01	0.01	n/a	n/a	n/a
Total	4.63	4.34	4.84	4.83	4.75	4.46	4.71
No. of Households	3576	1472	2104	2300	2067	1961	2467

Notes: Children included step-children; servants include apprentices, living-in journeymen, shopmen etc

The only category to show a marked discrepancy is that for lodgers and visitors, for the St Albans figure is only half that found nationally. This may partly, however, be a product of the rigorous exclusion from the St Albans analysis of inns, lodging houses and similar businesses, where numerous strictly temporary lodgers are likely to have been housed and clearly would not usually form part of either the family or household of the

---

556   1851 national sample from a one-fortieth sub-sample of a one-fiftieth sample of the 1851 census by Anderson, "Households, Families and Individuals", Table 1, p. 425; 1851 urban and rural samples from a one-sixteenth sub-sample of a one-fiftieth sample from the 1851 census again provided by Anderson, analysed by Wall and published in "The Household: Demographic and Economic Change in England", Table 16.2, p. 497. Although billed as "national", "urban" and "rural" 1851 samples, it must be emphasised that they are not identical, and the urban and rural sub-samples combined do not equal the national sample, hence conflation of the urban and rural sub-samples produces a mean household size of 4.60, well below the 4.75 calculated from the national sample.

557   Wall, "The Household: Demographic and Economic Change in England", Tables 16.2 and 16.3, pp. 497-8.

relevant head.[558] From the sample used for household analysis for the St Albans district, 16,568 individuals in 3,576 households, a total of 433 lodgers and 296 visitors were identified. Using the complete enumeration, all 17,991 individuals and hence including lodgers staying in inns, lodging houses and similar establishments, the figure for lodgers rises to 672 and for visitors to 324, producing a total of 996 as compared with 729.[559] The exclusion of these premises cannot, therefore, account for more than a proportion of the discrepancy between St Albans and the national figure, approximately one-third of the difference, and if all households had been included in the St Albans sample the mean number of lodgers and visitors per household would have risen to about 0.26, still well below the national sample mean of 0.40. The urban/rural difference in the number of lodgers and visitors apparent from the national sample itself seems to provide the explanation. The rural figure of 0.24 stands only slightly above the St Albans district totals, and if the St Albans rural sample had included inns, lodging houses and the like it would have been identical to this. The figure from the national urban sample, however, far exceeds the St Albans totals, and even if inns and the like had been included for the town of St Albans itself, the local urban figure would rise only to a mean of 0.29. It can only be, therefore, that the higher national figure reflects the inclusion of a sample from larger towns, where average numbers of lodgers and visitors must have stood substantially above those found in Hertfordshire small town and rural society.

There were, therefore, a similar number of lodgers in domestic households in town and countryside in the St Albans district in 1851, although the town of St Albans attracted more temporary residents as lodgers and visitors to inns, pubs, victualling and lodging houses, amounting in total to some 67 per 1,000 population compared with 49 per 1,000 in the rural parishes collectively.[560] But there are also other urban/rural contrasts apparent from Table 24. Fewer spouses were to be found in town than in countryside, a reflection of the higher proportion of widows and widowers found here that we have already identified, and a feature which is also apparent in the urban and rural sub-samples from the national data.[561] More children were to be found in the rural compared with the urban parishes, again as revealed in the national figures, although the St Albans rural average stands a little above that found nationally, suggesting the possibility that the opportunities for child labour here were exerting an impact, as may also have been the case for the Berkhamsted region.[562] The proportions of kin are identical in the town and the surrounding rural parishes, with the local rural figure again mirroring that found nationally whilst the urban totals stood significantly higher, a reversal of the situation with regard to lodgers and visitors, suggesting that there may perhaps have been a trade-off between the two. And finally, servants were present in similar numbers to those found nationally, but were considerably more prominent in the town of St Albans than in the national urban sample.[563] These figures would appear to indicate that small towns such as St Albans included proportionally more servants than did larger urban concentrations, even though they remained fewer in number here than in the surrounding rural areas due to the inclusion in the rural figures of living-in farm servants.

---

558   There is no indication that such establishments are excluded from the national sample: Anderson, ""Households, Families and Individuals", pp. 422-4.

559   Only the workhouse, prison and school boarders are excluded from this calculation.

560   Calculation based on all lodgers, boarders, visitors etc., and excluding only the workhouse.

561   See above, p. 35.

562   Goose, The Berkhamsted Region, pp. 70-1.

563   The national urban sample figure is, however, suspiciously low, and a rough calculation indicates that conflation of the 1851 urban and rural samples produces a combined total substantially below that calculated from the national sample, at approximately 0.25 per household compared to 0.30: calculated from Wall, "The Household: Demographic and Economic Change in England", Tables 16.2 and 16.3, pp. 497-8.

A finer breakdown is provided in Tables 25a and 25b where the components of the household are analysed by parish. The effect of the presence of substantially larger numbers of widows and widowers in the three urban parishes is immediately apparent in the figures for wives, with particularly low mean numbers per household in St Peters and St Albans as we would expect. Expressed as a percentage of the population the figures are also low for each of the urban parishes, but the lowest figure in Table 25b is now from Sandridge, reflecting the effect upon these percentages of the larger numbers of other categories of household member. Of the four villages Harpenden included a higher than average proportion of widows and widowers in its population and this is again reflected in Table 25a, whilst the two highest figures for wives are found in St Michaels (rural) and the Out-hamlets which included fewer widows than any of the other parishes or parts of parishes in the sample.[564] Both of these also exhibited relatively low proportions of their population aged 60 or above, at 6.0% and 5.8% respectively, compared with 7.9% for the district as a whole and 8.6% in Mills' rural norm.

TABLE 25a : COMPONENTS OF THE HOUSEHOLD BY PARISH – MEAN NUMBER OF PERSONS PER HOUSEHOLD

	Head	Wife	Children	Kin	Servant	Lodger	Visitor	Other/ Unknown	SubTotal*	MHS	Pop.	No. Househ'ds
St Albans Urban												
St Albans	1.00	0.63	1.83	0.34	0.27	0.09	0.10	0.01	4.06	4.26	2960	695
St Michaels (Urban)	1.00	0.69	2.42	0.32	0.24	0.10	0.04	0.01	4.67	4.81	1040	216
St Peters	1.00	0.62	1.83	0.33	0.20	0.19	0.06	0.01	3.98	4.25	2384	561
St Albans Rural												
St Michaels (Rural)	1.00	0.78	2.37	0.29	0.82	0.06	0.01	0.01	5.26	5.45	866	159
St Stephens	1.00	0.75	2.28	0.39	0.32	0.10	0.02	0.02	4.74	4.90	1480	302
Out-hamlets	1.00	0.82	2.31	0.21	0.31	0.12	0.01	0.01	4.65	4.91	1365	276
Harpenden	1.00	0.70	2.00	0.33	0.33	0.12	0.00	0.00	4.35	4.56	1879	412
Redbourn	1.00	0.74	2.12	0.31	0.25	0.08	0.01	0.01	4.42	4.60	2004	436
Sandridge	1.00	0.77	2.34	0.39	0.69	0.11	0.01	0.01	5.19	5.43	831	153
Wheathampstead	1.00	0.76	2.16	0.39	0.26	0.19	0.00	0.00	4.60	4.83	1759	364
Sub-Totals												
St Albans (Liberty)	1.00	0.68	2.05	0.32	0.30	0.12	0.09	0.01	4.35	4.57	10095	2211
Urban Parishes	1.00	0.63	1.92	0.33	0.24	0.13	0.08	0.01	4.12	4.34	6384	4172
Rural Parishes	1.00	0.75	2.19	0.33	0.36	0.12	0.08	0.01	4.63	4.84	10184	2104
Total	1.00	0.70	2.08	0.33	0.31	0.12	0.08	0.01	4.42	4.63	16568	3576
Berkhamsted Region	1.00	0.72	2.20	0.38	0.26	0.18	0.07	0.01	4.56	4.83	11101	2300
1851 Rural Sample	1.00	0.71	2.10	0.33	0.33	0.24	n/a	n/a	4.47	4.71	11630	2467
1851 Urban Sample	1.00	0.64	1.91	0.27	0.14	0.50	n/a	n/a	3.96	4.46	8734	1961
1851 National Sample	1.00	0.69	2.07	0.30	0.30	0.40	n/a	n/a	4.36	4.75	9828	2067

* Excludes lodgers, visitors other/unknown

Where the Sub-Total and MHS do not equal the sum of the household components this is due to the effect of rounding decimal places.

The figures for children show substantial variation from parish to parish, from a low of just 1.83 in the two most urban parishes of St Albans and St Peters to 2.42 in the urban portion of the parish of St Michaels, the variations from area to area being faithfully reflected in the percentages given in Table 25b, if often in more muted form. These variations are not easily explained. The town clearly did exhibit a range of demographic features that might have produced low mean numbers of children per household: higher proportions widowed, slightly higher proportions unmarried and a distinct tendency for marriage to take place later than it did in the rural parishes, particularly for women.[565] The urban portion of St Michaels, however, shared all of these

564   See above, Table 1, p. 34.
565   See above, Tables 1 and 3, pp 34, 43.

features with St Albans and St Peters but still included the highest proportion of children. On the other hand, all of the rural parishes apart from Harpenden do show relatively high figures for children, and this one exception may have been due to the fact that there were more widows here than in all the other rural parishes, as well as a relatively high proportion of females still unmarried in the age group 25-34, at 37% compared with 32% in the rural parishes collectively.[566]

TABLE 25b : COMPONENTS OF THE HOUSEHOLD BY PARISH – PERCENTAGES

	Head	Wife	Children	Kin	Servant	Lodger	Visitor	Other	Unknown	Total	Pop.	No. H'Holds
St Albans Urban												
St Albans	23.5	14.7	42.9	8.0	6.3	2.1	2.3	0.0	0.2	100.0	2960	695
St Michaels (Urban)	20.8	14.3	50.2	6.7	5.0	2.0	0.8	0.2	0.0	100.0	1040	216
St Peters	23.5	14.6	43.1	7.7	4.7	4.5	1.8	0.1	0.0	100.0	2384	561
St Albans Rural												
St Michaels (Rural)	18.4	14.3	43.5	5.3	15.1	1.0	2.2	0.0	0.1	99.9	866	159
St Stephens	20.4	15.2	46.5	8.0	6.6	2.0	1.0	0.3	0.0	100.0	1480	302
Out-hamlets	20.4	16.8	47.0	4.2	6.4	2.5	2.6	0.0	0.2	100.1	1365	278
Harpenden	21.9	15.3	43.7	7.1	7.3	2.7	1.8	0.1	0.1	100.0	1879	412
Redbourn	21.8	16.2	46.2	6.7	5.3	1.7	1.9	0.2	0.0	100.0	2004	436
Sandridge	18.4	14.2	43.1	7.1	12.8	2.0	2.3	0.1	0.0	100.0	831	153
Wheathampstead	20.7	15.8	45.2	8.1	5.3	3.9	1.0	0.0	0.0	100.0	1759	364
Sub-Totals												
St Albans (Liberty)	21.9	15.0	44.8	7.0	6.6	2.6	1.9	0.1	0.1	100.0	10095	2211
Urban Parishes	23.1	14.6	44.2	7.7	5.5	3.0	1.8	0.1	0.1	100.1	6384	1472
Rural Parishes	20.7	15.6	45.2	6.8	7.5	2.4	1.7	0.1	0.0	100.0	10184	2104
Total	21.6	15.2	44.8	7.1	6.7	2.6	1.8	0.1	0.1	100.0	16568	3576
Berkhamsted Region	20.7	15.0	45.6	8.0	5.3	3.8	1.5	0.1	0.1	100.1	11101	2300
1851 Rural Sample	21.2	15.2	44.4	7.1	7.1	5.0	n/a	n/a	n/a	100.0	11630	2467
1851 Urban Sample	22.4	14.3	42.8	6.1	3.1	11.2	n/a	n/a	n/a	99.9	8734	1961

When the relatively high proportion of children found in the population of the Berkhamsted region was considered, it was suggested that this may have been due to the considerable employment opportunities available there for children, and this appeared to be borne out by the correspondence between those parishes with the highest proportions of children, and those with the greatest opportunities for employment in the straw industry both in general and for children in particular.[567] This argument is supported by the experiences of Preston, Cardington and York in the mid-nineteenth century, for the first two of these offered substantial opportunities for child employment and included relatively high proportions of children amongst their populations (49% and 53% respectively), whilst the latter offered far more limited prospects and included a much lower proportion (37%).[568] It has already been suggested that the relatively high figure for mean number of children per household for the rural parishes as a whole in the St Albans district revealed in Table 24 might be similarly explained. The situation in the St Albans district is more complex than Berkhamsted, however, for here straw and Brazilian hat-making was an important presence in the town and Liberty in addition to the straw plaiting that was to be found in both town and countryside, though particularly in the latter. The occupational figures for St Michaels (urban) do, however, suggest that the correspondence may hold here too,

---

566   *Ibid.*

567   Goose, *The Berkhamsted Region*, pp. 70-1.

568   Anderson, "Household Structure and the Industrial Revolution", Table 7.10, p. 232; Tranter, "The Social Structure of a Bedfordshire Parish", pp. 91, 94, 106; Cunningham, "The Employment and Unemployment of Children", p. 136.

for the straw industry was more significant in St Michaels than it was in the other two urban parishes, whilst child employment levels were also substantially higher, particularly for the age group 10-14.[569] Whereas the demographic structure of the parish was more likely to produce the low proportions of children found elsewhere in the town, therefore, this appears to have been more than offset by its economic structure which pulled in the opposite direction.

In the rural parishes, however, there is no clear cut correspondence between employment opportunities for children and mean numbers per household on a parish-by-parish basis.[570] The four parishes or areas with the highest mean number were St Michaels (rural), Sandridge, the Out-hamlets and St Stephens, but of these only the Out-hamlets appear to have provided above average employment opportunities for children, and here only marginally so, whilst in St Stephens and Sandridge, where hat-making rather than plaiting employed relatively large numbers of women, employment opportunities for children, particularly girls, were comparatively poor.[571] In Redbourn and Wheathampstead where the employment of children, girls aged 5-14 in particular, stood at very high levels indeed, the mean number of children per household, although above the two very low urban figures, was not particularly high.

TABLE 26 : SONS AND DAUGHTERS IN HOUSEHOLDS – BY PARISH

	No. Sons*	No. Daus*	Sex ratio	Sons per H'hold	Daus per H'hold	Difference (daus – sons)	Total No. Children	No. H'Holds
St Albans Urban								
St Albans	586	684	86	0.84	0.98	0.14	1270	695
St Michaels (Urban)	243	279	87	1.13	1.29	0.17	522	216
St Peters	486	542	90	0.87	0.97	0.10	1028	561
St Albans Rural								
St Michaels (Rural)	184	193	95	1.16	1.21	0.06	377	159
St Stephens	338	350	97	1.12	1.16	0.04	688	302
Out-hamlets	332	310	107	1.19	1.12	-0.08	642	278
Harpenden	386	436	89	0.94	1.06	0.12	822	412
Redbourn	413	512	81	0.95	1.17	0.23	925	436
Sandridge	167	191	87	1.09	1.25	0.16	358	153
Wheathampstead	373	422	88	1.02	1.16	0.13	795	364
Sub-Totals								
St Albans (Liberty)	2169	2358	92	0.98	1.07	0.09	4527	2211
Urban Parishes	1315	1505	87	0.89	1.02	0.13	2820	1472
Rural Parishes	2193	2414	91	1.04	1.15	0.11	4607	2104
4 Villages	1339	1561	86	0.98	1.14	0.16	2900	1365
Total	3508	3919	90	0.98	1.10	0.11	7427	3576

* Sons and daus include step-children

569   See above, Tables 2 and 9, pp. 40-1, 97.
570   The relevant figures here are those for boys aged 5-9, and for girls aged 5-14, for most boys aged 10-14 were employed in agriculture, commonly living in as farm servants rather than remaining at home.
571   In Sandridge and St Stephens respectively just 33% and 37% of girls aged 10-14 were employed, compared with an overall figure for the district of 50%: above, Table 9, p. 97.

Table 26 provides additional insight by comparing children in households by sex. Those parishes with relatively high mean numbers of children per household – St Michaels (urban), St Michaels (rural), Sandridge, the Out-hamlets and St Stephens – all exhibit above average numbers of *sons* per household. They also included above average numbers of daughters per household, but are less distinctive in this respect in comparison with the figures for parishes such as Redbourn and Wheathampstead. This suggests two possibilities. Either families in these parishes tended, out of choice or necessity, to retain their sons at home for longer, or there were general demographic variables in operation to produce these high figures entirely unrelated to sex-specific occupational opportunities, such as the age and marital structure of the population already considered. When we look, however, at the differentials between mean numbers of sons and daughters and the sex ratios that resulted, we have a measure of the tendency to retain children at home that is unrelated to any general demographic feature of the population, and one that may well be influenced by relative employment prospects. Employment of girls aged 10-14 was at its highest in St Michaels (urban), Redbourn and Wheathampstead, and these three all show relatively large differences in favour of daughters compared with sons remaining at home. Sandridge yet again stands out as an exception, as it has in so many previous analyses, whilst the parish of St Albans shares the relatively greater tendency for urban households to favour daughters.

There was clearly a range of variables that could produce the differences in mean numbers of children between parishes that we have discovered, and the inter-relationship between them must have been complex. In seeking to discover whether or not employment opportunities had a bearing, we need to remember that employment for children – particularly girls – went hand in hand with employment for women in general. As we have already found an association between female employment opportunities, a skewed sex ratio and a tendency to marry later, these opportunities may thus have pulled in two directions at once, tending towards a reduction in family size via later marriage but also towards an enhancement of family size by encouraging the retention of female children at home rather than putting them out to service at the earliest possible age.[572] Furthermore, in seeking such associations on a parish-by-parish basis we may be being too demanding of our data, for the smaller the unit of analysis the higher the possibility of chance variation.[573] Perhaps we should close this discussion by reminding ourselves that whilst the age and marital structure of the two most urban parishes clearly depressed the mean number of children per household here, the rural parishes as a group exhibit mean numbers of children very similar to those found in the Berkhamsted region, and substantially above those found in the 1851 national sample or, indeed, in the 1851 rural sample.[574]

The figures for kin in Tables 25a and 25b fall within a fairly narrow range though again show variation from parish to parish, from a low of 0.21 per household in the Out-hamlets (4.2% of the population) to a high of 0.39 in St Stephens, Sandridge and Wheathampstead (respectively 8.0, 7.1 and 8.1% of the population). There is no clear relationship between numbers of kin and numbers of children, for whereas in the Out-hamlets and St Michaels (rural) low figures for kin stand alongside high figures for children, high figures for kin in St Stephens and Sandridge are found side by side with figures for children that are well above the regional

---

572   There may also have been an impact upon marital fertility, but to make such a claim would be too speculative before further research has been conducted.

573   It may be more than a coincidence that the one parish that seems invariably to prove exceptional – Sandridge – was the smallest of the lot.

574   Further comparison with other areas within the county where fewer female employment opportunities were available and with other areas both locally and nationally, when this becomes possible, will prove instructive.

average, and also above the rural average. Furthermore, the mean numbers are very similar in each of the three urban parishes, despite the considerable discrepancy between St Michaels (urban) and the other two parishes in terms of the proportions of children. The relatively large numbers of resident kin found in the mid-nineteenth century, amply confirmed by these figures, is of course one of the distinctive features of the household structure of the period, and for this reason the composition of these kin will be considered in more detail below.[575]

TABLE 27 : DISTRIBUTION OF SERVANTS IN HOUSEHOLDS – BY PARISH

	0		1		2		3		4		5		6+		No.	1+
	No.	%	No.	%	No.	%	No.	%	No.	%	No.	%	No.	%	H'holds	%
St Albans Urban																
St Albans	571	82.2	89	12.8	18	2.6	10	1.4	4	0.6	3	0.4	0	0.0	695	17.8
St Michaels (Urban)	192	88.9	13	6.0	4	1.9	3	1.4	2	0.9	0	0.0	2	0.9	216	11.1
St Peters	493	87.9	44	7.8	12	2.1	7	1.2	3	0.5	2	0.4	0	0.0	561	12.1
St Albans Rural																
St Michaels (Rural)	128	80.5	6	3.8	7	4.4	6	3.8	6	3.8	0	0.0	6	3.8	159	19.5
St Stephens	259	85.8	17	5.6	9	3.0	9	3.0	5	1.7	2	0.7	1	0.3	302	14.2
Out-hamlets	244	87.8	9	3.2	9	3.2	7	2.5	6	2.2	3	1.1	0	0.0	278	12.2
Harpenden	356	86.4	23	5.6	17	4.1	6	1.5	1	0.2	4	1.0	5	1.2	412	13.6
Redbourn	388	89.0	21	4.8	12	2.8	4	0.9	8	1.8	2	0.5	1	0.2	436	11.0
Sandridge	125	81.7	5	3.3	3	2.0	3	2.0	7	4.6	5	3.3	5	3.3	153	18.3
Wheathampstead	324	89.0	20	5.5	10	2.7	4	1.1	2	0.5	1	0.3	3	0.8	364	11.0
Sub-Totals																
St Albans (Liberty)	1887	85.3	178	8.1	59	2.7	42	1.9	26	1.2	10	0.5	9	0.4	2211	14.7
Urban Parishes	1256	85.3	146	9.9	34	2.3	20	1.4	9	0.6	5	0.3	2	0.1	1472	14.7
Rural Parishes	1824	86.7	101	4.8	67	3.2	39	1.9	35	1.7	17	0.8	21	1.0	2104	13.3
4 Villages	1193	87.4	69	5.1	42	3.1	17	1.2	18	1.3	12	0.9	14	1.0	1365	12.6
Total	3080	86.1	247	6.9	101	2.8	59	1.6	44	1.2	22	0.6	23	0.6	3576	13.9

There was greater variation in the mean number of servants per household by parish, and consequently also in the proportion of the population they formed, from a low of 4.7% in St Peters to a high of 15.1% in St Michaels (rural). Two parishes stand out from the rest, St Michaels (rural) and Sandridge, with mean numbers of servants per household as high as 0.82 and 0.69 respectively, compared with the average for the district as a whole of just 0.31. Partly this reflects the presence of a relatively small number of households that were very large indeed, as the additional information in Table 27 reveals, for in St Michaels (rural) there were six households with six or more servants and five in Sandridge, constituting 3.8 and 3.3% of all households respectively, whilst for the district as a whole only 0.6% of households contained such large servant groups. In St Michaels this reflected the presence of a number of residences of some distinction, for Arthur Timperon Esquire of Childwick Hall kept 11 servants, as did Henry Baillie, Member of Parliament, at Prae House, whilst the entourage of the Earl of Verulam, Lord Lieutenant of Hertfordshire, at Gorhambury ran to as many as 25. In Sandridge it was the presence of a number of large farms that was responsible, for all of those who employed six or more servants here were farmers of between 248 and 700 acres, and none employed more than seven in total. The high figures shown in Tables 25a and 25b for these two parishes are not, however, solely the product of these small numbers of very large servant groups, for in Table 27 both also exhibit figures for the proportion of households containing at least one servant that are considerably above average, and hence also relatively low figures for the proportion of households without any servants at all. As the keeping of servants was, as we shall see, strongly related to social class, this would thus indicate that these two parishes

---

575   See pp. 174-80.

included more than their share of wealthier residents, the propensity to keep servants possibly providing a more sensitive indicator of social standing than the crude socio-economic groupings that have been employed in our various tabulations both above and below. Given this, we may have found a further, and crucial, explanation as to why these two parishes both exhibit such high mean household sizes: their respective social structures produced larger numbers of servants, hence adding to the effect of the relatively low proportions widowed and high mean number of children per household.

In the remaining parishes the mean numbers of servants per household and percentages they formed of the total population lay within a fairly narrow band, with the slight advantage in favour of the rural parishes that we have already noted, produced by the inclusion of some farm servants in these figures. The additional information in Table 27 shows that across the district one household in every seven included at least one resident servant, although now there is a slight advantage in favour of the town and Liberty as compared with the rural parishes as a group, whilst the figure for the four villages drops to one in every eight. These figures compare with one in six found in the market town of Great Berkhamsted and stand markedly above the one in ten in industrial Preston but slightly below the one in five in York.[576] Within the town the parish of St Albans stands out above the rest, approaching the higher proportion with servants found in York, and reflecting the more elevated overall social and economic profile of the heart of the town. Even here, however, it was rare for a household to include more than one servant, and only 35 out of a total of 695 (5%) did so, and similarly low proportions are also found in the other two urban parishes. Again the rural parishes include more households with groups of two or more servants, although even here this was only a feature of 9% of the total, with St Michaels (rural) and Sandridge, with 16% and 15% respectively, again standing out from the rest.

Lodgers and visitors formed the smallest component of the household, usually by a substantial margin, in every parish except the Out-hamlets where they exceeded the proportions and mean numbers of kin. From Table 25b we can now see that they formed a slightly higher proportion of the population of the town of St Albans than they did in rural areas, although even here the figures stand well below those found in the market towns of Great Berkhamsted and Tring, to which only the one parish of St Peters presents a challenge.[577] The variation within the town of St Albans, with St Peters including proportionally twice as many lodgers as the other two parishes, is mirrored in the rural areas where Wheathampstead also exhibits a particularly high proportion. If we combine the figures for lodgers and visitors, then the range in the rural parishes lies between 3.0 and 5.1% of the population, representing a mean per household of from 0.15 to 0.25, now with the Out-hamlets showing the highest proportion rather than Wheathampstead. It is tempting to suggest that a trade-off was operating between kin and lodgers in the rural parishes within the urban Liberty, for the Out-hamlets exhibit the highest figure for lodgers and visitors and the lowest of all the parishes for kin by a significant margin, whilst St Stephens shares the highest mean number of kin but the lowest figure of all for lodgers and visitors. No such clear cut association holds for the urban parishes, however, whilst amongst the four villages the two parishes with relatively high numbers of kin, Sandridge and Wheathampstead, also include above average proportions and mean numbers of lodgers and visitors per household.

---

576   Goose, *The Berkhamsted Region*, p. 71; Anderson, "Household Structure and the Industrial Revolution", Table 7.3, p. 220.

577   In Great Berkhamsted lodgers formed 4.9% of the population and visitors 1.7%, in Tring 5.5% and 1.5%: Goose, *The Berkhamsted Region*, Table 15, p. 70.

TABLE 28 : HOUSEHOLDS WITH LODGERS, VISITORS AND KIN

	1+ Lodger		1+ Visitor		Lodger and/or Visitor		Lodger plus Visitor		1+ Kin		Lodger plus Kin		Visitor plus Kin		Lodger and/or Visitor plus Kin		H'hs.
	No.	%	No.	%	No.	%	No.	%	No.	%	No.	%	No.	%	No.	%	
St Albans Urban																	
St Albans	41	5.9	44	6.3	80	11.5	5	0.7	148	21.3	13	1.9	9	1.3	21	3.0	695
St Michaels (Urban)	20	9.3	4	1.9	23	10.6	1	0.5	48	22.2	3	1.4	1	0.5	4	1.9	216
St Peters	57	10.2	33	5.9	89	15.9	1	0.2	118	21.0	10	1.8	9	1.6	19	3.4	561
St Albans Rural																	
St Michaels (Rural)	8	5.0	10	6.3	18	11.3	0	0.0	32	20.1	0	0.0	3	1.9	3	1.9	159
St Stephens	22	7.3	12	4.0	34	11.3	0	0.0	71	23.5	6	2.0	3	1.0	9	3.0	302
Out-hamlets	25	9.0	27	9.7	50	18.0	2	0.7	35	12.6	1	0.4	2	0.7	3	1.1	278
Harpenden	34	8.3	30	7.3	61	14.8	3	0.7	91	22.1	13	3.2	6	1.5	18	4.4	412
Redbourn	27	6.2	34	7.8	58	13.3	3	0.7	80	18.3	5	1.1	5	1.1	10	2.3	436
Sandridge	9	5.9	16	10.5	24	15.7	1	0.7	34	22.2	3	2.0	3	2.0	5	3.3	153
Wheathampstead	40	11.0	13	3.6	51	14.0	2	0.5	88	24.2	2	0.5	2	0.5	3	0.8	364
Sub-Totals																	
St Albans (Liberty)	173	7.8	130	5.9	294	13.3	9	0.4	452	20.4	33	1.5	27	1.2	59	2.7	2211
Urban Parishes	118	8.0	81	5.5	192	13.0	7	0.5	314	21.3	26	1.8	19	1.3	44	3.0	1472
Rural Parishes	165	7.8	142	6.7	296	14.1	11	0.5	431	20.5	30	1.4	24	1.1	51	2.4	2104
4 Villages	110	8.1	93	6.8	194	14.2	9	0.7	293	21.5	23	1.7	16	1.2	36	2.6	1365
Total	283	7.9	223	6.2	488	13.6	18	0.5	745	20.8	56	1.6	43	1.2	95	2.7	3576

Table 28 presents details of the proportions of households in the various parishes that included lodgers, visitors and lodgers and/or visitors alongside kin. Across the district one household in every 13 or 7.9% included one or more lodgers, and once again there was only a marginal difference between the urban and rural parishes in favour of the town. This figure stands well below the 12% calculated from the 1851 national sample, where lodgers formed 5% of the total population compared with just 2.6% here, and even further below the figures of 21% and 23% discovered in the two large towns of York and Preston respectively.[578] The figure for Hanley in the Potteries in 1851 stood mid-way, at 15%.[579] As one would expect, larger towns and expanding industrial areas tended to include more lodgers than did rural areas and small towns, and hence the figure for the village of Borden in Kent was similar to that for the St Albans district, standing at just 9%.[580] But the number of lodgers could vary across time as well as space, and hence in Plumpton in Sussex the proportion rose from 9% in 1851 and 1861 to 19% in 1871, as living-in farm servants were transformed into independent wage labourers, often lodging in the households of their social equals.[581] Again, both local and temporal variations deserve further investigation, and there were distinct differences between parishes within the St Albans district itself in 1851. St Peters and Wheathampstead again head the rankings, as they did for mean numbers of lodgers per household, although now St Michaels (urban) and the Out-hamlets stand close behind. Sandridge now joins St Michaels (rural) at the bottom of the rural order, whilst in the parish of St Albans only 5.9% of households included a lodger compared with 9.9% for the other two urban parishes combined.

---

578   Anderson, "Households, Families and Individuals", p. 428; *idem*, "Household Structure and the Industrial Revolution", Table 7.3, p. 220. We must again remember that inns, lodging houses and similar establishments have all been excluded from the St Albans data, unlike the national sample, and hence the latter must be expected to show significantly higher figures.

579   Gatley, *Hanley in 1851 Revisited*, Table 3.5, p. 9. In the larger 1861 Potteries sample analysed by Dupree lodgers formed 6% of the population compared to 12% in Preston: Dupree, *Family Structure in the Staffordshire Potteries*, p. 108.

580   Jackson, *The Population of Borden in 1851*, Table 7, p. 14.

581   Short (ed.), *Scarpfoot Parish*, pp. 37-8.

The differences in the ranking of parishes for proportions of households with lodgers compared with mean numbers per household are the product of the greater tendency for lodgers to be found in groups of two or more in some parishes than in others. Of the 283 households across the district which housed one or more lodgers, 187 (66%) included just one, and hence 96 (34%) included two or more. In St Peters, however, whilst 29 households included one lodger, as many as 28 (49%) included two or more, and four of these included three, three included four, and four included five. Thus whilst in the town as a whole the percentage of single lodgers was almost identical to the whole district at 64%, the experience of St Peters parish was very different. Again this experience is mirrored in the rural parishes by Wheathampstead, where 20 households included just one lodger but 20 more, exactly 50%, included two or more, although this time only two included four or over. The district as a whole shows a considerable difference in this respect from the results of the national sample, from which it has been calculated that only 28% of all lodgers lived in groups of one compared with 43% here, whilst the figures for St Peters and Wheathampstead, at 27% and 29% respectively, are more comparable, and again underline the considerable variation that could be found between parishes.[582]

Visitors were to be found in a higher proportion of rural than urban households, 6.7% compared with 5.9%, again this discrepancy with the mean numbers and percentages shown in Tables 25a and 25b arising due to the greater tendency for individual urban households to include more than one visitor, particularly a feature of the parishes of St Albans and St Peters. The overall figure for the district, at 6.2% or one household in every 16, stands at only half the figure calculated from the national sample, and of these only 23% were to be found in groups of two or more compared with 56% nationally.[583] Variation between parishes was even wider than for lodgers, the figures ranging from just 1.9% in St Michaels (urban) to 9.7% in the Out-hamlets and 10.5% in Sandridge. Relatively few households included both a lodger and a visitor on census night, a mere 18 or 0.5% of all households, with identical urban and rural totals.[584] When we consider the two categories together, the variations between parishes become less marked, all lying within the range 10.6% to 18.0%.

Across the district as a whole 20.8% of all households included at least one relative apart from members of the nuclear family, with very little difference at all between town and countryside. This figure stands remarkably close to those discovered for the larger towns of Oldham, Preston and York, where the proportions stood at 21%, 23% and 22% respectively, although slightly above the figure of 18% found both in the Potteries and the 1851 national sample, or the 15% calculated for selected sub-districts from the census of 1861.[585] More substantial variations can be found around these figures, however, at both the regional and the local level, for in a Lancashire rural sample for 1851 27% of households included kin, whilst in the village of Borden in Kent the figure was as low as 13%, and again such variations deserve further exploration.[586]

582   Anderson, "Households, Families and Individuals", p. 428.
583   *Ibid*, p. 429. The figure for Borden in Kent stood at 6.5%: Jackson, *The Population of Borden in 1851*, Table 7, p. 14.
584   It may be that there was some confusion in the minds of enumerators concerning the distinction between the two, a possibility that can only have been enhanced by the lack of guidance in the instructions provided to them *Ibid.*, p. 428.
585   J. Foster, *Class Struggle and the Industrial Revolution: Early Industrial Capitalism in Three English Towns* (London, 1974), p. 99; Armstrong, *Stability and Change in an English County Town*, p. 185; Anderson, "Household Structure and the Industrial Revolution", Table 7.3, p. 220; *idem*, "Households, Families and Individuals", p. 425; Dupree, *Family Structure in the Staffordshire Potteries*, pp. 102-3.
586   Anderson, "Household Structure and the Industrial Revolution", Table 7.3, p. 220; calculated from Jackson, *The Population of Borden in 1851*, Table 9, p. 15.

Table 28 also provides details on households which contained lodgers or visitors as well as kin, and at first sight appears to indicate a high degree of exclusivity between these three categories of household member. Only 1.6% of all households included both a lodger *and* kin, whilst just 1.2% included both a visitor and kin. If lodgers and visitors are combined then either one and/or the other were found in 13.6% of all households but only 2.7% also included one or more kin. But whilst these figures for households including lodgers and/or visitors as well as kin seem low, they are in fact only marginally lower for each category – lodgers, visitors and lodgers and visitors combined – than a random distribution would have produced. This also holds true for most individual parishes, but there are exceptions. We have already seen that the Out-hamlets show particularly high figures for lodgers and visitors and low figures for kin, and Table 28 confirms that the proportion of households containing both was particularly low, under half what would be expected given a random distribution.[587] The only other parish to produce such as result was Wheathampstead, where the number of households including either a lodger and/or a visitor and one or more kin was only one-quarter of what a random distribution would have produced. As these two parishes included two of the three highest figures for proportions of households with lodgers, whilst the Out-hamlets exhibit the highest figure of all for households with lodgers or visitors, it might be suggested that where lodgers were to be found in substantially above average numbers there may indeed have been a trade-off with resident kin. This was not, however, invariably the case, and nor does such a trade-off appear to have operated in the urban parish of St Peters. Generally, the urban parishes show slightly higher figures than would be expected from a random distribution for lodgers and/or visitors and kin, whilst the rural parishes show somewhat lower figures. Again there is an exception, however, for in Harpenden the figure stands some 50% above the expected level.

TABLE 29a : COMPONENTS OF THE HOUSEHOLD BY SOCIAL GROUP – MEAN NUMBER OF PERSONS PER HOUSEHOLD

Social Group	Head	Wife	Children	Kin	Servant	Lodger	Visitor	Other/ Unknown	Sub- Total*	MHS	Pop.	No. H'Holds
A	1.00	0.49	1.53	0.52	2.33	0.04	0.18	0.02	5.87	6.12	997	163
B	1.00	0.50	1.48	0.37	1.39	0.06	0.14	0.01	4.74	4.95	1454	294
C	1.00	0.76	2.10	0.33	0.26	0.12	0.08	0.01	4.45	4.66	4830	1036
D	1.00	0.75	2.28	0.30	0.03	0.13	0.07	0.01	4.36	4.56	7767	1702
E	1.00	0.78	2.26	0.30	0.00	0.18	0.07	0.00	4.34	4.60	1228	267
F	1.00	0.24	0.61	0.47	0.06	0.07	0.05	0.00	2.39	2.50	278	111
Z	1.00	0.33	2.67	0.00	0.00	0.00	0.67	0.00	4.00	4.67	14	3
Total	1.00	0.70	2.08	0.33	0.31	0.12	0.08	0.01	4.42	4.63	16568	3576

* Excludes lodgers, visitors, other/unknown

Where the Sub-total and MHS does not equal the sum of the houshold components this is due to the effect of rounding decimal places.

The components of the household are broken down further in Tables 29a, 29b, 30a and 30b which present analyses by social class and by occupational group. Heads were found together with spouses in three-quarters of households in the middle to lower social range, categories C to E, but both above and below this the picture was very different indeed, with half of all households in categories A and B comprising a lone head, and as many as three-quarters in category F – paupers, the unemployed, prisoners and vagrants. As far as children are concerned there is a generally *inverse* correspondence between numbers of children and social class, with the exception of the indigent at the bottom of the social scale. This is again identical to the results discovered for the Berkhamsted region, and hence again contradicts the previous research that has identified a positive

---

587   We must note, however, that the numbers concerned here are very low indeed.

correlation.[588] In this respect categories A and B are difficult to distinguish, whilst the same is true to an even greater extent of categories D and E, the semi-skilled and unskilled, and hence the position with regard to children mirrors the results found for mean household size.

TABLE 29b : COMPONENTS OF THE HOUSEHOLD BY SOCIAL GROUP – PERCENTAGES

Social Group	Head	Wife	Children	Kin	Servant	Lodger	Visitor	Other/ Unknown	Total	Pop.	No. H'Holds
A	16.3	8.0	25.1	8.5	38.0	0.6	3.0	0.4	99.9	997	163
B	20.2	10.0	30.0	7.5	28.1	1.2	2.8	0.2	100.0	1454	294
C	21.4	16.3	45.0	7.0	5.7	2.6	1.8	0.2	100.0	4830	1036
D	21.9	16.3	50.0	6.6	0.6	2.9	1.5	0.1	99.9	7767	1702
E	21.7	16.9	49.2	6.5	0.0	4.0	1.5	0.1	99.9	1228	267
F	39.9	9.7	24.5	18.7	2.5	2.9	1.8	0.0	100.0	278	111
Z	21.4	7.1	57.1	0.0	0.0	0.0	14.3	0.0	99.9	14	3
Total	21.6	15.2	44.8	7.1	6.7	2.6	1.8	0.2	100.0	16568	3576

The higher mean household size of those at the top of the social scale was thus achieved despite the fact that their average nuclear family group was substantially smaller than the average for all classes, standing at just 3.02 compared with 3.78. Their advantage in terms of mean household size was mainly due to the presence of servants in larger numbers, 2.33 per household compared with an average of 0.31, servants forming as much as 38% of the population of households in category A compared with 6.7% across the social range. The relatively high mean household size of those in social category B was similarly achieved, for here the nuclear family size stood even lower at 2.98, with servants averaging 1.39 per household and forming 28.1% of the population of their households. In the case of servants, apart from the appearance of a handful at the very bottom of the social scale, some of whom resided with their employers in almshouses, there was a very strong positive association with social class, as would be expected. They were quite rare below the level of category C, comprising skilled craftsmen, dealers and clerks, and altogether absent from the households of the unskilled.

The presence of servants in substantial numbers was not, however, the only reason why households were larger towards the top of the social scale, for – again with the indigent in category F standing out as the exception – there was also a positive correspondence between social class and numbers of resident kin, with the figure for category A in particular, at 0.52 per household, standing well above the overall mean of 0.33. In terms of percentages of the population they formed, there is a steady downward trend from categories A to E, although again the figures for groups D and E are almost indistinguishable. Visitors appear in households across the social scale, but once again there is a positive correlation with social class, and they were to be found in considerably greater numbers in categories A and B than in the other groups, whilst this time the numbers in categories D and E – the semi-skilled and unskilled – are identical. Interestingly, and perhaps suggesting that the enumerators did indeed distinguish lodgers from visitors, the correlation between social class and mean numbers and percentages of lodgers is inverse, again until we reach the indigent in category F, many of whom, living in almshouses, would not have been able to accommodate lodgers even had they so wished. In this regard there is a noticeable difference between social groups D and E, with respective means per household of 0.13 and 0.18 and percentages of their populations of 2.9 and 4.0, and it is this factor that is largely responsible for the marginally higher mean household size of the lower of these two social groups. The

588 Armstrong, *Stability and Change in an English County Town*, pp. 178-9; Tranter, "The Social Structure of a Bedfordshire Parish", p. 94.

prominence of lodgers in the households of the unskilled is not highlighted in the summary results from the 1851 national sample, which emphasises their concentration in the homes of the urban self-employed and semi-skilled.[589] For the St Albans district, however, it now appears clear that as we approach the lower rungs of the social ladder households, whilst accommodating more children, found room for slightly higher numbers of lodgers, but for slightly lower numbers of kin.

One of the advantages of analysing household composition for the total population of a region of this size is that it makes it possible to consider particular social or occupational categories without reducing the numbers of households below the level of viability.[590] Hence in Tables 30a and 30b our 3,576 households are divided into the 17 occupational categories previously employed, whilst separate breakdowns are provided for farmers, agricultural labourers and straw workers, and for virtually all occupational categories the numbers are large enough to be regarded as meaningful. The figures show wide variation in numbers of spouses present.

TABLE 30a : COMPONENTS OF THE HOUSEHOLD BY OCCUPATIONAL GROUP – MEAN NUMBER OF PERSONS PER HOUSEHOLD

	Head	Wife	Children	Kin	Servant	Lodger	Visitor	Other/ Unknown	Sub-Total*	MHS	Pop.	No. H'Holds
Agriculture	1.00	0.88	2.41	0.27	0.37	0.13	0.06	0.01	4.93	5.13	6519	1272
Textiles	1.00	0.45	1.65	0.41	0.25	0.18	0.08	0.03	3.76	4.06	824	203
Misc Manufs	1.00	0.86	1.83	0.26	0.23	0.06	0.26	0.00	4.17	4.49	157	35
Leather	1.00	0.82	2.33	0.37	0.11	0.18	0.04	0.00	4.62	4.83	551	114
Building	1.00	0.91	2.65	0.29	0.07	0.08	0.06	0.01	4.92	5.08	726	143
Metal	1.00	0.91	2.46	0.28	0.13	0.12	0.10	0.01	4.79	5.03	337	67
Wood	1.00	0.89	2.30	0.26	0.03	0.10	0.01	0.00	4.49	4.59	812	177
Food/Drink	1.00	0.78	2.11	0.34	0.42	0.07	0.09	0.00	4.66	4.83	1121	232
Transport	1.00	0.85	1.94	0.19	0.06	0.05	0.19	0.00	4.05	4.29	266	62
Serv/Dom Serv	1.00	0.50	2.00	0.37	0.06	0.10	0.04	0.00	3.94	4.07	769	189
Publ Serv/Prof	1.00	0.65	1.73	0.27	0.92	0.06	0.12	0.01	4.57	4.76	752	158
Indep Means	1.00	0.18	0.64	0.52	1.42	0.11	0.18	0.01	3.77	4.06	572	141
Spec Ind (Straw)	1.00	0.24	1.87	0.50	0.08	0.20	0.17	0.00	3.68	4.05	1045	258
Quarry/Mine	1.00	1.00	4.25	0.25	0.00	0.00	0.00	0.00	6.50	6.50	26	4
Retail/Distrib	1.00	0.76	1.85	0.19	0.31	0.11	0.16	0.00	4.11	4.37	328	75
Misc	1.00	0.89	2.29	0.27	0.00	0.16	0.07	0.00	4.45	4.68	1063	227
Dep/No Occ	1.00	0.24	1.10	0.51	0.16	0.10	0.10	0.00	3.00	3.20	700	219
Total	1.00	0.70	2.08	0.33	0.31	0.12	0.08	0.01	4.42	4.63	16568	3576
Farmers	1.00	0.64	2.01	0.44	2.56	0.04	0.16	0.02	6.65	6.88	1115	162
Agric. Labourers	1.00	0.91	2.48	0.24	0.01	0.14	0.04	0.01	4.65	4.84	5181	1070
Straw Workers	1.00	0.11	1.80	0.54	0.00	0.22	0.15	0.00	3.45	3.83	815	213

* Excludes lodgers, visitors, other/unknown

Where the Sub-total and MHS does not equal the sum of the houshold components this is due to the effect of rounding decimal places.

In most cases this reflects the prominence of widows in particular occupational groups, notably straw workers, those of independent means and with no identified occupation, where the figures for wives stand as low as 0.11, 0.18 and 0.24 respectively, whilst the same is true but to a lesser degree in the service and domestic service trades and in textiles, which included many hat workers. Less predictable are the relatively low figures for farmers and public service and professional occupations, at 64 and 65% respectively. This can in

589 Anderson, "Households, Families and Individuals", p. 428.

590 Anderson felt that for the 1851 national sub-sample of 2,067 households, the "numbers are too small to use this sub-sample for a definitive analysis of the occupational correlates of household composition": ibid., p. 427.

large measure be attributed to their marriage patterns, particularly for the professional category. In all there were 1,058 households in which the head lacked a spouse, and in 333 or 31% of these this was because the head remained unmarried. Of the 56 professional lone heads, however, 30 or 54% remained unmarried, and for farmers the figure stood at 26 out of 59 cases, or 44%. For both groups, therefore, but particularly the first of these, marriage was either delayed or never entered into at all. For the public service/professional category, the proportion of heads who were widows or widowers stood slightly below the average for the whole population, whilst their average age at 46 years was identical to the overall mean. Farmer household heads were, however, on average two years older than heads as a whole, but more pertinently they also included a substantially higher proportion of widowers amongst their number, 8.6% compared with the overall figure of 4.6%. In the case of farmers, therefore, the prominence of widowers as heads of household is a further reason for the relatively large proportion discovered without a spouse. For the other occupational categories differences are much smaller, but craftsmen in the wood, metal, miscellaneous manufacturing and building trades, as well as agricultural labourers, stand well above average for the proportion with a spouse present, although again this is largely due to the fact that males were overwhelmingly dominant in these occupations, whereas in some other trades, notably food and drink, at least some females were household heads, if in relatively small numbers.

TABLE 30b : COMPONENTS OF THE HOUSEHOLD BY OCCUPATIONAL GROUP – PERCENTAGES

	Head	Wife	Children	Kin	Servant	Lodger	Visitor	Other/ Unknown	Total	Pop.	No. H'Holds
Agriculture	19.5	17.2	47.0	5.3	7.3	2.4	1.2	0.2	100.1	6519	1272
Textiles	24.6	11.2	40.7	10.2	6.1	4.5	1.9	0.8	100.0	824	203
Misc Manufs	22.3	19.1	40.8	5.7	5.1	1.3	5.7	0.0	100.0	157	35
Leather	20.7	16.9	48.3	7.6	2.2	3.6	0.7	0.0	100.0	551	114
Building	19.7	17.9	52.2	5.8	1.4	1.7	1.1	0.3	100.1	726	143
Metal	19.9	18.1	49.0	5.6	2.7	2.4	2.1	0.3	100.1	337	67
Wood	21.8	19.5	50.1	5.7	0.7	2.1	0.1	0.0	100.0	812	177
Food/Drink	20.7	16.2	43.7	7.0	8.7	1.5	2.0	0.1	99.9	1121	232
Transport	23.3	19.9	45.1	4.5	1.5	1.1	4.5	0.0	99.9	266	62
Serv/Dom Serv	24.6	12.4	49.2	9.1	1.6	2.3	0.9	0.0	100.1	769	189
Publ Serv/Prof	21.0	13.6	36.4	5.6	19.4	1.2	2.5	0.3	100.0	752	158
Indep Means	24.7	4.5	15.7	12.9	35.0	2.6	4.4	0.2	100.0	572	141
Spec Ind (Straw)	24.7	5.9	46.1	12.2	1.9	4.9	4.1	0.1	99.9	1045	258
Quarry/Mine	15.4	15.4	65.4	3.8	0.0	0.0	0.0	0.0	100.0	26	4
Retail/Distrib	22.9	17.4	42.4	4.3	7.0	2.4	3.7	0.0	100.1	328	75
Misc	21.4	19.0	48.9	5.7	0.1	3.4	1.4	0.1	100.0	1063	227
Dep/No Occ	31.3	7.4	34.3	15.9	5.1	3.0	3.0	0.0	100.0	700	219
Total	21.6	15.2	44.8	7.1	6.7	2.6	1.8	0.2	100.0	16568	3576
Farmers	14.5	9.3	29.2	6.5	37.1	0.6	2.3	0.4		1115	162
Agric. Labourers	20.7	18.9	51.2	5.0	0.3	2.8	0.9	0.2		5181	1070
Straw Workers	26.1	2.9	47.0	14.1	0.0	5.6	4.0	0.1		815	213

Turning to children, the high proportion of elderly and widowed amongst those of independent means and dependents with no stated occupation finds clear reflection in the low numbers of children in their households, at a mean of just 0.64 and 1.10 respectively, but there is a difference between the two categories. Both groups were relatively elderly with an average age for dependents of 63 and for independents of 58, compared with an overall average for household heads of 46. Both included high proportions of widows and widowers, at 52% and 41% respectively compared with just 16% for the whole sample. But whilst just 7% of the dependent

category were not, and never had been, married, a figure below the overall average of 9%, for those of independent means the proportion was as high as 35%, and it is the avoidance of marriage (or failure to marry) by such a high proportion of those of independent means that largely explains the very low mean numbers of children found in their households. Again we find at least relatively low figures for other occupations where women – and particularly widows – were prominent as household heads, notably the straw and textile trades, a feature that was also apparent in the Berkhamsted region.[591] No doubt this reflects the impact of an early end to child-bearing and perhaps also the poverty that could result from the absence of an adult male wage earner, a view that receives some support from the fact that not a single servant was to be found in any of the 213 households headed by straw workers. Other relatively low figures are found for the public service and professional sector, and for the retail and distribution trades, the former figure again reflecting the unusual marriage patterns of this group discussed above. As for the retail and distribution trades, there is nothing obvious in their demographic profile that marks them out from the population as a whole, but it is at least possible that the relative mobility of many within this category may have impacted adversely upon their levels of fertility, and a similar argument might also explain the below average performance in this respect of those in the transport sector. In general, larger mean numbers of children are more commonly found in occupational groups with high proportions of heads and wives, as one might expect, as in the building trades, wood, leather, metal and miscellaneous categories in particular. Agricultural labourers stand high in the rankings, and – again underlining the inverse correlation of social class and numbers of resident children – exhibit a substantially higher mean number per household than do farmers. For farmers, the mean number is below the overall average, hence once again confirming the Berkhamsted region results but in an even more exaggerated form.[592] Again, however, there was a considerable discrepancy between the marital conditions of these two groups, for we have already discovered that a relatively high proportion of farmers were either unmarried or were widowers.[593] Unmarried or widowed farmers formed 34% of household heads, whilst the comparable figure for agricultural labourers was just 7%.[594] If we focus only upon those in each occupational group who were married, then the 107 married farmers' households included an average of 2.40 children, whilst the 991 married agricultural labourers' households included an average of 2.59, a much reduced disparity but one which favours labourers nevertheless.

When we turn to servants the distinction between farmers and agricultural labourers could hardly be more stark, with farmers at the top of the rankings by a considerable margin at 2.56 per household and labourers virtually at the bottom, their mean of 0.01% reflecting the presence of just 16 servants in all, and being undercut only by straw workers and the small quarrying and mining group where servants were completely unknown. Indeed, farmers' households included more servants, either domestic or farm servants, than they did children of the head, forming fully 37.1% of the population of their households, and this is a feature that needs to be borne firmly in mind in the context of arguments concerning the decline of farm service and growing social distance between the classes in the countryside in the first half of the nineteenth century.[595] Those of independent means stand next in the rankings for numbers of servants employed, with a mean per household of 1.42, indicating

591   Goose, *The Berkhamsted Region*, pp. 69, 73.
592   *Ibid.*, Table 16, p. 73.
593   Above, p. 171.
594   18% of farmer household heads were widows or widowers, 5% of agricultural labourers, 16% for the whole sample; 16% of farmer household heads were unmarried, 2% of agricultural labourers, 9% for the whole sample.
595   For example Snell, *Annals of the Labouring Poor*, p. 101.

that if some in this category were annuitants of fairly modest means, as an occupational group they are appropriately classified as of high social standing. The other category to stand out, as one might expect, is the professional and public service group, with 0.92 servants per household. As both of these groups included high percentages of heads without a spouse and relatively low numbers of children, servants formed substantial proportions of the population of their households, 19.4% for professional and as much as 35.0% for those of independent means. The only other category to stand above the average was food and drink, and this despite the exclusion of innkeepers, beerhouse keepers and the like from this sample. Sixty-four of the 232 households in this category included one or more servants, 27.6% compared with 13.9% in all households across the district, with butchers, bakers and grocers the most prominent employers of servants, and a few millers and brewers accounting for most of the rest. Low figures are found in a number of the craft industries – building, metal, wood and leather in particular – in all of which we found numbers of children to be substantially above average, suggesting that there may have been a trade-off operating here. Low numbers were also found in the transport and service/domestic service sectors, a reflection of the generally low social standing of many of the occupations which fall into these categories. With a mean per household of 0.16 servants, those with no occupation exhibit higher figures than might have been expected, but this category includes a number of retired trade and craftsmen living off accumulated wealth as well as dependent paupers and almspeople, and only seven of the 29 households which included a servant fall into the latter categories.

The highest mean numbers of lodgers were found in households headed by straw workers, with 0.22 per household compared with the overall average of 0.12, followed by the textile/clothing trades and leather crafts jointly in second place with 0.18. We have already seen that the straw plait and textiles/clothing categories included considerable numbers of households headed by women, and as a consequence of the absence of spouses and an early end to child-bearing there were also fewer children present. Their nuclear family groups were thus very small, creating more space for lodgers, whilst the low economic status of their occupations and the absence of a wage-earning partner must have rendered their financial position precarious, placing a premium upon the additional income a lodger would bring. As we will shortly see, these occupational groups also included relatively large numbers of kin in their households, subverting the more general positive association between numbers of kin and social class identified above. No similar explanation applies to the leather trades, for here spouses and children were both present in above average numbers as, by a smaller margin, were kin. But if the presence of servants is indeed a reliable predictor of social status, and the positive association between social status and numbers of visitors also holds good, then the low figures for each of these categories for this occupational group indicates their relative poverty, known to have been frequently a feature of the boot and shoe trade. Again, therefore, economic necessity might explain their somewhat heavier reliance upon lodgers, despite the substantial presence of children, to produce a mean household size that was above the overall average. Agricultural labourers housed a slightly above average number of lodgers, but they were particularly rare in the households of farmers and those in the professions and public service, again underlining the inverse correlation with social standing. Low numbers were, however, also found in the transport and food and drink categories, and whilst in the case of the latter the mean numbers of servants in their households might indicate an above average status, there is no obvious explanation for the transport sector. Here every category of household member except wives and visitors stands below average to produce a relatively low mean household size, the high number of visitors no doubt the product of the wider geographical horizons their occupations produced. Visitors were also prominent in certain high status occupational groups,

such as the professions, the retail trades and farming, but again straw workers housed high numbers, and again this contradicts the more general positive association we have identified between visitors and social class.

The distribution of kin by occupation is particularly interesting. High mean figures occur in the households of straw workers (0.54), those of independent means (0.52), those with no occupation (0.51), farmers (0.44) and textile workers (0.41). All of these occupations, as we have seen, exhibit high proportions of lone heads, either because they were widowed or had never married, and their households included below average numbers of children.[596] Farmers stand closest to the average of this group in terms of numbers of children and spouses present, and in this case their relative wealth as well as the opportunities they provided for employment must also have been important factors in creating openings for kin in their households. The motivation in the case of the other four occupational groups may have been more varied, over and above the fact that their small nuclear family sizes, ranging from just 1.82 to 3.10 compared with the average of 3.78, clearly left more space for additional occupants. In the case of those of independent means and those without an occupation, their high average age and marital condition might indicate that they welcomed kin into their homes for companionship or support. We have seen that those we have classified as dependents were 63 years old on average, and 52% of them were widowed; of the 59 who housed kin, however, their average age was 67, and 68% of them were widowed. For those of independent means, the situation was somewhat different. Their average age was 58 whilst 41% were widowed, but the average age of those housing kin was also 58, whilst only 30% of these (12 out of 40) were widowed. In this case it was those who had remained unmarried who accounted for the majority of households with kin, 24 out of 40, 14 of these in the town of St Albans and a further three in the urban Liberty.

The age, sex and marital profile of those in the textiles/clothing and straw trades might also provide an insight into the high proportions with kin here. Both groups of heads were younger than average, at 39 and 44 years respectively, but straw workers included a very high proportion of widowed persons amongst their number, 49% compared with the average of 16%, all but one of them female. They also, however, included a high proportion unmarried, at 23% compared with the average for all household heads of just 9%, and 48 of the 50 represented here were female. In the textile and clothing trades, only 19% were widowed, but here an even higher proportion were unmarried, 30% of the total, with women again predominant with 42 representatives whilst this time men feature in greater numbers with 19.[597] These figures clearly indicate that both of these occupational categories created opportunities for female independence, as unmarried households heads and also in widowhood in the case of the straw industry. But it was also these same households that either created opportunities for, or relied upon, kin. Across the whole sample of households we have seen that 21% included one or more kin, whilst of those households with a married head the figure stood at 17%. For married straw workers the figure was 16% and for married textile and clothing workers 18%, almost exactly the same as the average figure for the district. Amongst *un*married straw workers, however, the figure was 42%, and for widowed straw workers 31%, with the respective totals for the textile and clothing trades standing at 34% and 33%.

---

596   In Corfe Castle, Dorset, high concentrations of relatives were found in households where the household head was without children of his/her own: Wall, "Characteristics of European Family and Household Systems", p. 62.

597   The occupations predominantly represented here were dressmaking and various aspects of Brazilian hat-making.

With regard to the other occupational categories any differences are far smaller, the range for mean numbers of kin per household falling between 0.19 and 0.37, with the retail/distributive trades and the transport sector at the bottom of this range and leather workers and the service and domestic service trades at the top. In the latter case the relatively high proportion of widows heading households again exerted an impact, for 33% of household heads in this group were widowed, and 30% of these included one or more kin. For other occupations, there is no clear or obvious patterns to explain the relatively small differences that existed.

TABLE 31 : CATEGORIES OF KIN

	Liberty		Urban Parishes		Rural Parishes		4 Villages		Total	
	No.	%	No.	%	No.	%	No.	%	No.	%
AUNT	5	0.7	5	1.0	4	0.6	4	0.9	9	0.8
BROTHER	41	5.8	28	5.7	31	4.5	18	3.8	59	5.0
BROTHER IN LAW	13	1.8	8	1.6	18	2.6	13	2.8	26	2.2
COUSIN	10	1.4	7	1.4	6	0.9	3	0.6	13	1.1
DAU IN LAW	18	2.5	11	2.2	21	3.1	14	3.0	32	2.7
FATHER	5	0.7	2	0.4	9	1.3	6	1.3	11	0.9
FATHER IN LAW	12	1.7	6	1.2	17	2.5	11	2.3	23	2.0
GRANDAU	113	15.9	71	14.5	137	19.9	95	20.3	208	17.7
GRANDSON	106	15.0	72	14.7	124	18.0	90	19.2	196	16.6
GT GRANDAU	5	0.7	3	0.6	2	0.3	0	0.0	5	0.4
GT GRANDSON	4	0.6	1	0.2	3	0.4	0	0.0	4	0.3
GT NEPHEW	5	0.7	5	1.0	1	0.1	1	0.2	6	0.5
GT NIECE	1	0.1	0	0.0	5	0.7	4	0.9	5	0.4
MOTHER	33	4.7	22	4.5	27	3.9	16	3.4	49	4.2
MOTHER IN LAW	25	3.5	16	3.3	18	2.6	9	1.9	34	2.9
NEPHEW	67	9.4	47	9.6	46	6.7	26	5.5	93	7.9
NIECE	69	9.7	55	11.2	68	9.9	54	11.5	123	10.4
RELATIVE	2	0.3	0	0.0	2	0.3	0	0.0	2	0.2
SISTER	127	17.9	103	21.0	76	11.0	52	11.1	179	15.2
SISTER IN LAW	33	4.7	23	4.7	31	4.5	21	4.5	54	4.6
SON IN LAW	16	2.3	4	0.8	42	6.1	30	6.4	46	3.9
STEP MOTHER	0	0.0	0	0.0	2	0.3	2	0.4	2	0.2
STEP SISTER	1	0.1	1	0.2	0	0.0	0	0.0	1	0.1
Total	711	100.0	490	100.0	690	100.0	469	100.0	1180	100.0
Identified Total*	709	100.0	490	100.0	688	100.0	469	100.0	1178	100.0
M	269	38.5	173	35.8	291	42.7	195	41.8	464	39.8
F	430	61.5	310	64.2	391	57.3	271	58.2	701	60.2
M+F (known)**	699	100.0	483	100.0	682	100.0	466	100.0	1165	100.0
Parents (in law)	75	10.6	46	9.4	73	10.6	44	9.4	119	10.1
M	17	2.4	8	1.6	26	3.8	17	3.6	34	2.9
F	58	8.2	38	7.8	47	6.8	27	5.8	85	7.2
Siblings (in law)	215	30.3	163	33.3	156	22.7	104	22.2	319	27.1
M	54	7.6	36	7.3	49	7.1	31	6.6	85	7.2
F	161	22.7	127	25.9	107	15.6	73	15.6	234	19.9
Son/dau in law	34	4.8	15	3.1	63	9.2	44	9.4	78	6.6
Grandchildren	219	30.9	143	29.2	261	37.9	185	39.4	404	34.3
Niece/nephew	136	19.2	102	20.8	114	16.6	80	17.1	216	18.3

*   excludes "relative",   ** excludes "relative" and "cousin"

Before we leave our consideration of kin, however, we should note that those found in the St Albans district bore similar relationships to the families they joined as they did in the national sample. Table 31 provides a complete breakdown of kin by relation to the head of household, with sub-totals for the Liberty of St Albans, the urban parishes, the rural parishes and the four villages. The wide range of kin types is immediately evident, and in this respect our region supports the conclusions drawn by Wall for Corfe Castle in Dorset, which reveals a wider range of kin than in selected communities elsewhere in Europe where complex households were more common. [598] Grandchildren were the most common category of kin across the district as a whole, accounting for 34.3% of the total. They are prominent in each sub-category too, but there is a clear urban/rural divide. In the rural parishes they account for 37.9% of all kin, the figure rising to 39.4% for the four villages alone, whereas in the town of St Albans they account for only 29.2%. The proportion of resident kin who were grandchildren derived from the 1851 national sample was 36.9% with girls in a very slight majority, very similar to our overall figures but with the total standing substantially above that for the town where the sexes were also virtually equal in number.[599] Siblings or siblings-in-law were the next largest category, accounting for 27.1% of the whole sample, again very similar to the 24.1% derived from the national sample, whilst the proportion of these who were siblings rather than in-laws, at 75%, was also similar to the national figure of 79%.[600] In the town, however, they form the largest category of kin, at 33.3% exceeding the proportion who were grandchildren, the figure falling to 22.2% in the four villages.[601] But there is another substantial deviation from the national pattern too, for in the St Albans district 73% of siblings or siblings-in-law were female compared with just 59% nationally, the figure rising to 78% in the town, a distinctive feature that no doubt again reflects the considerable female employment opportunities available. The next largest group were nieces and nephews, at 18.3% again of a similar order to the 16.8% found nationally,[602] the town on this occasion showing a much smaller lead over the rural parishes, with nieces outnumbering nephews by more than two to one in the four villages whilst the urban sex ratio was much closer. Again it is possible that the exceptional opportunities for the employment of girls as young as 5-9 in the villages of Harpenden, Redbourn and Wheathampstead was exerting an impact here.[603]

Those relatives whose presence would reflect a vertical extension of the household – parents, parents-in-law and sons and daughters-in-law – were found in far fewer numbers, as they were nationally. Only 10.1% of resident kin were parents or parents-in-law, compared with the national sample figure of 11.1%: here there were exactly 2.5 females for every male, nationally women outnumbered men by "almost two to one".[604] In the

598   R. Wall, "Characteristics of European Family and Household Systems", *Historical Social Research*, Vol. 23 (1998), p. 62. Wall's conclusion is worth quoting at greater length: "In England one can see the household functioning as a welfare agency, taking in a wide variety of persons who would find it difficult to live on their own, whereas in the other two populations the kin group was much less diverse and primarily associated with the process of the transfer of the headship of the household".

599   Anderson, "Households, Families and Individuals", p. 426.

600   *Ibid.*

601   The situation in the town of St Albans mirrors that found in Hanley in the Potteries, where siblings or siblings-in-law also formed a higher proportion of resident kin than did grandchildren, 28.3% compared to 25.0%: calculated from Gatley, *Hanley in 1851 Revisited*, Table 3.7, p. 10. In rural Borden grandchildren outnumbered siblings, but the numbers involved are very small: Jackson, *The Population of Borden in 1851*, Tables 11 and 12, pp. 15-16.

602   *Ibid.*

603   See above, Table 9, p. 97.

604   *Ibid.* The decisive factor here, of course, was greater female longevity: across the district as a whole widows outnumbered widowers by a ratio of 2.9:1. Sandridge is again an oddity, being the only parish where widowers outnumbered widows, and including only 1 solitary parent/in-law amongst the 59 resident kin here (1.7%), a single father-in-law.

town, however, the advantage in favour of women was again far greater, standing as high as 4.8 to 1.[605] Sons and daughters-in-law were present in even fewer numbers, accounting for just 6.6% of resident kin overall, again close to the national figure of 7.7%, although the St Albans district figure favours males by a substantial margin whilst the national figure shows women "in a slight majority".[606] Again, however, our region reveals a clear urban/rural divide, for the proportions reach as high as 9.2% and 9.4% respectively for the rural parishes and four villages, and fall as low as 3.1% in the town; in the former sons-in-law outnumber daughters by a ratio of 2:1, whilst in the town 11 daughters-in-law were found alongside just four sons, producing a ratio of 2.75:1 in favour of females. These figures again suggest that whilst the district as a whole reflects the national experience in terms of approximate proportions of different categories of resident kin, there are differences in the sex ratios and substantial intra-regional variations that can only reflect local economic and social differences, particularly between town and countryside.

There is, of course, one final conclusion that arises from this analysis of the different categories of kin, and this is the now well rehearsed fact that, even in the mid-nineteenth century when families shared their homes with non-nuclear relatives to a greater extent than they had before or were to do afterwards, households that were vertically extended were relatively rare. In cases where households were extended upwards to incorporate parents, the great majority of parents or parents-in-law were to be found singly, in 105 households in total, 90 of which were headed by a married couple, 11 by an unmarried head and four by a widowed head. In only seven households were two parents/parents-in-law present, in five cases with a married head, in one with a widowed head and in one with a head who had remained single.[607] Six of these seven cases, including all five where the head was married, were found in rural rather than urban parishes. In all just 112 households out of 3,576 were vertically extended upwards, just 3.1%, and the proportion in which a married couple shared with a married parent was tiny, at 0.1%.

Extension downwards was no more common, although definition is problematic here. To deal first with the clear cases of downward extension, there were 43 households where a married head shared with a married son or daughter and his or her spouse, and hence sharing by two lineally related couples was far more common down a generation than up, accounting for 1.2% of all households. Thirty-two of these were found in the rural parishes and just 11 in the town, and hence in proportional terms they were twice as common in the rural areas, accounting for 1.5% of all households compared with 0.75% in the three urban parishes. A further thirty-two households headed by a widow or widower included a married son or daughter and their partners, twenty-seven in the rural parishes and just five in the town. Combining these two categories of household head gives a total of 75, 2.1% of all households. Fifty-nine were in the rural parishes, 2.8% of the number of households here, and 16 for the town, or 1.1% of households. There was just a single instance where a married head shared with more than one child and his/her partner, and this was Joseph Constable, gardener, of Harpenden, whose household included his wife Ann, two married daughters and son-in-laws, and also four grandchildren aged from three months to eleven years. Lone in-laws were very rare, featuring in just seven

605   The ratio between widows and widowers in general was also high in the town, standing at 3.6:1.

606   Anderson, "Households, Families and Individuals", p. 426.

607   The proportion of households headed by married and single heads respectively which housed either one or two parents/parents-in-law was identical, at 3.6% (3.5% for one parent); for widowed heads it was lower at 0.9%, no doubt due to their higher average age.

households in all, three with married heads and four with widowed heads, three occurring in the town and four in the rural parishes.

If we extend our analysis to include ever-married children, there were 25 more households that included widowed sons and daughters, ten sons and fifteen daughters.[608] Seven of the ten widowed sons had children with them, and either eleven or twelve of the fifteen daughters,[609] and no doubt the need for child care played its part in the return to the parental home. They were virtually equally divided between households where the head was married and where the head was him/herself widowed, which means that proportionally they were far more common in the households of widowed heads.[610] In relation to total numbers of households, they were again almost twice as common in the rural parishes as they were in the town. A further 35 households included sons or daughters who are described as married but have no partner present, nine sons and 26 daughters, 20 living with a married head of household and 15 with a widow or widower. There are a number of possible explanations for this. First, the enumerators may have made errors, but the internal evidence from surnames and presence of children suggests that this cannot have been common, nor would it explain the disparity between the sexes. Second, respective partners may simply have been absent on census night, but this is something we have no way of knowing. It would, however, probably explain the fact that there were substantially more lone married daughters than sons, and might also explain their greater prominence in the town where 15 of the 26 daughters lived. If this were indeed the main explanation, we would need to substantially increase our estimates of the number of married couples living with either one or two parents.[611] A third possibility is that these, or some of these, represent cases where couples had, for one reason or another, separated, but again this can only be speculation.[612]

There is therefore some uncertainty with regard to the exact extent of vertical extension of households in the district, but whatever interpretation is placed upon the ambiguous cases in total they remain proportionally quite small. In the 1851 national sample just 6% of households contained two lineally related ever-married persons. Adding up all of those lineally related downwards that we have just considered produces a total for the St Albans region as a whole of 142 households, or 4% of the total. Adding the 112 that were related upwards gives a grand total of 254, or 7.1% of the total, just slightly above the national figure. There was virtually no urban/rural difference in terms of upward extension, but downward extension was – as we have seen – far more common in rural areas than it was in the town, accounting for 4.8% of total households compared with 2.9%. Overall 87 urban households were vertically extended through lineally related ever-married persons, 5.9% of the total, as were 167 rural households, or 7.9% of the total. In the national sample, just 22 out of 2,067 households (1.1%) included a married head living with a married parent or a married child. In our sample the proportion is just slightly higher. If only co-resident married couples are included the total is

608 It is probably appropriate that they are treated separately, for it is likely that the majority of these had initially set up a distinct household with their partners only to return to the parental home upon widowhood.
609 One case is unclear, as the widow has the same surname (Smith) as a married son and daughter-in-law who are also present, and hence the grandchildren could belong to either.
610 2,669 households had a married head, 571 a widowed head.
611 If this were the sole explanation, then the number of couples living with a married head would rise to 63 (1.8%), and with a widowed head to 47 (1.3%), the combined total of 110 amounting to 3.1% of all households, rather than the 2.1% calculated previously.
612 The Deputy Superintendent Registrar for Luton explained the imbalance between the number of husbands and wives as a product of "the *desertion* or temporary absence of the husband at the taking of the Census" (my italics): Austin, *The Straw Plaitting, Straw Hat and Bonnet Trade*, p. 27.

48 (43 children, five parents), or 1.3%, but if lone married children are included too the total rises to 83, or 2.3%. For the town the proportions stand at 0.7% and 1.8% respectively, for the rural parishes at 1.8% and 2.7%.

Scattered amongst these various extended households are examples that exhibit considerable complexity. Thus in Harpenden we find Henry Smith, a 66 year-old agricultural labourer and his wife, Phoebe, straw plaiter, living with a widowed daughter, a married son and his wife, five unmarried sons, two grandchildren, and entertaining a six year-old visitor on census night, to produce a household of thirteen members, eleven of whom were employed either in agricultural labour or straw plait. In the Out-hamlets Deborah Brinklow, a widow of 63 years, was a farmer at Tyttenhanger Green. She shared her house with her son, William, farm bailiff, his wife, Ann, and their four children, as well as her unmarried son, Alfred, her nephew, Frederick Watkins, a female servant and three male servants, all farm labourers. Another example of a widowed head, this time a humble straw plaiter, sharing with a range of kin is Hannah Toms of St Stephens, aged 44, whose household included her married son, William, his wife and daughter, an unmarried daughter, her unmarried sister, Elizabeth Hall, and a child of three years, Emma Hall, described – possibly misleadingly – as the granddaughter of the head. In Wheathampstead we find William Ramsdon, an unmarried agricultural labourer of 48 years, with his widowed mother, an unmarried sister aged just 13 and a married sister (with no partner present) and her two children, his nephew and niece. In the same parish James Beck and his wife, Sarah, lived with two young daughters, two slightly older step-daughters, his widowed mother-in-law and his unmarried brother-in-law, and again as many as seven out of this household of eight were gainfully employed in agriculture or straw plait. In Redbourn we find another example from the upper end of the social scale in the household headed by Martha Vere Brown, a widow of 75 years, "Lady. Landed proprietor and Fundholder". She lived with her married son, Charles, and his wife, four grandchildren who shared their surname, two additional grandchildren with the surname Hampson, besides eight servants, ranging from a housekeeper to a "gardening man". As an example from the town of St Albans Elizabeth Ratcliff of Catherine Lane, widow and cotton winder, shared with two unmarried sons, a son who was a widower, two grandchildren (presumably his children), a lodger, as well as her unmarried brother. And finally, a particularly interesting example from Redbourn appears to openly admit illegitimacy, twice in the same household. Ann Green was the *un*married head, a 43 year-old straw plaiter living in Lamb Lane, who shared with her father, Joseph, widower, and her brother, Francis, but also with two daughters aged 13 and 6, an *un*married lodger, Martha Lay, aged 25, and one Henry Lay, aged 2 years, her son.

Further examples of similarly complex households could easily be produced, but they catch the eye not because they feature frequently but because they are unusual, accounting for a very small proportion of the 3,576 households in the sample for the district as a whole. It would therefore be appropriate to end our discussion with a reminder of just how ordinary the majority of households were. In all 2,106 households, or 59% of the total, included only the head, a head and spouse, or a head and/or spouse plus children – the simple nuclear family group. Households which contained only related persons, without any servants, lodgers or visitors, numbered 2,645, 74% of the total. Whilst 745 households included relatives other than children (21%), only 458, 13% of the total, included both children and more distant kin, and only 95 households (2.7%) included both kin and a lodger and/or a visitor. Thus although examples of quite complex households can indeed be found, and whilst the proportions including unrelated persons in the form of lodgers or servants or relatives

from beyond the immediate family group were considerably larger in the mid-nineteenth century than they were to become by the mid-twentieth century, the majority of households remained of modest size, were simple in construction, focused heavily upon the nuclear family group, and were generally restricted to just two generations.

In many respects the composition of the household and family in the St Albans district was similar to that which has emerged from the national 1851 sample. It was not, however, identical, nor was it uniform in all of its features throughout the district. We have found, for example, that our region included a higher proportion of people living on their own than emerged from the national sample, and – particularly in the town of St Albans – a high proportion of generally small households compared with other larger urban centres. Fewer lodgers lived in St Albans than in towns across the country, but its population included a higher proportion of kin, whilst there were also more servants here than in the national urban sample. Across the district children formed a slightly larger component of the population than was more generally the case, as they had in the Berkhamsted region to the west, and this was particularly true of the rural parishes of the district. Discrepancies between the sexes in the retention of children at home appear to indicate that this was influenced by the relative opportunities for the early employment of female children, although the relationship between employment prospects and the numbers of children on a parish-by-parish basis was not straightforward, and the skewed sex ratio that these very same opportunities produced may simultaneously have pulled in the opposite direction through its impact upon the age at marriage and hence fertility.

In other respects the national data as yet provides no point of comparison, for we still await breakdowns by social class and occupational group.[613] The St Albans district results do, however, fundamentally conflict with the orthodox view that has emerged from other local studies, to show that there was *no* simple positive correlation between household size and social class except at the very top and the very bottom of the social scale, and that the households headed by unskilled workers were often larger on average that those of their immediate social superiors. In the town, the association between social class and mean household size was even less clear than it was in the rural parishes. Mean numbers of children were inversely related to social class except at the very bottom of the social scale, although there was no difference in this respect between semi- and unskilled workers. A very important influence here was the age and marital condition of the household heads of the respective groups, with the figures being strongly influenced by high proportions of households headed by widows, the associated prominence of women heading households in particular social and occupational groups, and by the high proportions headed by those who had never married. The positive association between social class and servants, as found in previous studies, was entirely expected, but there was also a positive association with both kin and visitors, although particular occupational groups where women were prominent as household heads stand out as notable exceptions. For lodgers the association was inverse, this result emphasising the need for those towards the bottom of the social scale to supplement their incomes by letting accommodation, and in some cases lodgers may have substituted for kin. Occupational categories with particularly high proportions of households headed by women, straw plait and textiles/clothing, housed high mean numbers of lodgers as well as high mean numbers of kin, whilst straw plaiters' households also included above average number of visitors.[614]

---

613   This was underway in 1988: Anderson, "Households, Families and Individuals", p. 427.
614   As noted above, these conclusions do not hold for category F at the very foot of the social scale.

The analysis of kin proved particularly interesting, although it is again only possible to draw comparisons with the national sample results in general rather than social or occupational terms. In the St Albans district occupations which included substantial proportions of heads without a spouse, found both high and low in the social hierarchy, included relatively large numbers of kin, and again both the age and marital status of the head played a crucial part in this, though in different ways for different occupations.[615] The distribution of the various categories of kin showed a clear urban/rural divide, whilst their sex ratio differed markedly from that found in the national sample, particularly in the town. Again the opportunities across the district for the employment of women and children in the hat-making and straw plaiting industries was clearly exerting an influence, whilst the town also presented other openings for women that were to be found in towns more generally. Although lineally related co-resident couples were only slightly more prominent here than they were nationally, again a distinct urban/rural contrast has emerged with far higher proportions discovered in the rural areas, underlining the fact that these parishes attracted larger numbers of young, female kin, whilst older women showed a greater tendency to favour the town.

Within the context of the general parameters which shaped the family and household in mid-nineteenth century England there was thus scope for considerable variation. The St Albans district, whilst conforming in many ways to the overall profile of the English household in this period, was in all of the above respects different to a greater or lesser degree, and these differences were themselves the product of the particular and inter-related demographic, economic and social profile of the region. There were also a number of respects in which the town of St Albans presented a contrast with the rural parishes both within and outside of the Liberty, and often a more stark contrast with the four villages when considered separately. Variety, however, went further than this, and in terms of variables such as the proportions and mean numbers of servants, lodgers and kin per household, some parishes exhibited figures that were double or even treble those found in others. Clearly, we must not lose sight of the broad picture, whether it be established at the national or the regional level, nor forget that the parish was an administrative unit, often relatively small, and one which by no means bound the customs and horizons of the inhabitants within it. Nevertheless, local differences cannot be ignored, for although not always easily susceptible to explanation they can often be related to other equally local social and economic features, in consequence helping us to understand the processes involved in household and family formation. The foregoing discussion will, we hope, shed some light on those processes, through our consideration of the local and regional, the urban and rural, within a broader comparative context, whilst the full variety and complexity of individual households can be traced in the documentation that follows in Part 2.

---

615   Consideration of the composition of households by age of the household head might prove to be a fruitful path for further research.

PART TWO

The census enumerators' returns

The main procedures and protocols for the collection, organisation and presentation of the census documentation have been described in Chapter Two above. The approach has been to maintain the basic integrity of the original data unless the reproduction of errors would mislead or convey no useful information, and hence corrections have been made to spellings and to place names, though not to surnames which have in all cases been transcribed as written.

The layout of the documentation follows the census enumerators' books, except that age and sex are entered in separate columns, as are county and town or parish of birth. The disability column of the census enumerators' books, which contains only very sparse and scant information, has been merged with the occupational information column in the data which follows. All subsidiary information, largely relating to houses unoccupied or being built, has been included where it occurs.

Each individual in every parish has been given a separate identifying record number. This allows more precise referencing than would the use of either the census schedule number or the folio numbers that can be found in the original documentation. The Name Index reference employs the first letter of the relevant parish (A for St Albans, P for St Peter etc.) and the individual record number. Sandridge is SA to distinguish it from St Stephens, MU and MR are St Michael Urban and St Michael Rural, whilst the Workhouse is WKH to distinguish it from Wheathampstead. A full key is provided at the start of the index.

Each enumeration district within each parish commences with the name of the Registrar's District, enumeration district number and Public Record Office reference.

This is followed by the description of the district as given in the enumeration book. All further descriptive details presented by the enumerators interspersed amongst the census data itself has been entered wherever it occurs. The headers contained in the original enueration books vary considerably in the extent of the detail that they provide, but where they convey additional information this too has been entered as a sub-heading. Where these headers merely repeat information given elsewhere, such as under address, or where they give information that is confusing or contradictory, they have been omitted.

The appearance of information in square brackets indicates additional information provided by the author, either to aid identification or to suggest possible corrections. Confident amendments are simply enclosed in square brackets, whilst less confident suggestions include a query mark. Query marks alone in square brackets indicate difficulties in reading or identifying place names where no clear ideas could be offered. In these cases readers must have recourse to the original returns and decide for themselves.

The maps included at the start of each chapter have been reproduced from the first edition 25 inch ordinance survey maps of 1878, some 27 years after the census date. These maps include the most populous parts of each parish, and as much of the more outlying areas as could be included within the page size available.

Chapter Four

The parish of Wheathampstead

Registrar's District: Harpenden   Enumeration District 1a   Ref. HO107/1713 folios 1-10

All that part of the parish of Wheathampstead which lies to the east of the road from St Albans to Kimpton; including the east side of the village, East Lane, the houses adjoining the Place Farm, part of Gustard Wood, Lamar, Reed Hall, Marford, to the King William public house, "No Mans Land".

The Village of Wheathampstead

No	Surname	Forename	House	Address	Relation	Condition	Age	Sex	Occupation	County	Birthplace
1	ADAMS	William	1	High Street	Head	Mar	46	M	Cordwainer Master	Leics	[Unknown]
2	ADAMS	Elizabeth	1		Wife	Mar	40	F		Herts	Wheathampstead
3	GATWOOD	William	1		Appr	Unm	14	M	Cordwainers Appr	Herts	Wheathampstead
4	REN	William	2	High Street	Head	Mar	30	M	Agric Lab	Herts	Hatfield
5	REN	Eliza	2		Wife	Mar	28	F	Straw Plaiter	Herts	Wheathampstead
6	REN	Isabella	2		Dau		6	F	Scholar	Herts	Wheathampstead
7	REN	George	2		Son		5	M	Scholar	Herts	Wheathampstead
8	REN	Betsy	2		Dau		1	F		Herts	Wheathampstead
9	GATHARD	Thomas	2		Father-in-law	Mar	68	M	Agric Lab	Herts	Wheathampstead
10	GATHARD	Hannah	2		Mother-in-law	Mar	60	F	Washerwoman	Herts	Wheathampstead
11	DUNHAM	James	3	High Street	Head	Mar	62	M	Bricklayer & Beer Seller	Herts	Wheathampstead
12	DUNHAM	Rebecca	3		Wife	Mar	61	F	Beer Seller	Herts	Wheathampstead
13	EDMUNDS	John	3		Lodger	Unm	45	M	Agric Lab	Herts	Wheathampstead
14	BROWNSELL	William	3		Lodger	Unm	45	M	Agric Lab	Herts	Sandridge
15	TWIDLE	William	3		Lodger	Unm	34	M	Agric Lab	Herts	Wheathampstead
16	OLNEY	William	3		Lodger	Unm	41	M	Agric Lab	Herts	Harpenden
17	THRALE	William	4	High Street	Head	Unm	23	M	Baker Master	Beds	Luton
18	LATTIMORE	William	5	High Street	Head	Widower	68	M	Retired Mealman	Middx	London
19	LATTIMORE	William Higby	5		Son	Mar	33	M	Brewer & Maltster	Herts	Wheathampstead
20	LATTIMORE	Ann	5		Dau-in-law	Mar	33	F		Herts	Digswell
21	LATTIMORE	William H	5		Grandson		7	M	Scholar	Herts	Wheathampstead
22	LATTIMORE	Charles F	5		Grandson		5	M	Scholar	Herts	Wheathampstead
23	LATTIMORE	Sophia	5		Grandson		2	F		Herts	Wheathampstead
24	SEABROOK	Mary	5		Serv	Widow	53	F	House Servant	Herts	Wheathampstead
25	SMITH	Eliza	5		Serv	Unm	17	F	House Servant	Herts	Wheathampstead

Figure 5 : WHEATHAMPSTEAD

From the first edition of the 6 inch Ordinance Survey of Hertfordshire (1878), Sheet XXVII and XXVIII

Approximate scale of reproduction: 1cm = 193m

WHEATHAMPSTEAD

No.	Surname	Forename		Address	Relation	Status	Age	Sex	Occupation	County	Birthplace
26	SIBLEY	Sarah	6	High Street	Head	Widow	35	F	Independent Landed Property	Herts	Kimpton
27	YOUNG	Mary	6		Visitor	Mar	30	F	Independent Annuitant	Herts	Sandridge
28	IVORY	Ann E	6		Niece	Unm	6	F	Scholar at Home	Herts	Kimpton
29	DORRINGTON	Sarah	6		Boarder	Unm	25	F	Governess	Herts	Digswell
30	DICKINSON	Mary	6		Serv	Unm	30	F	House Servant	Herts	Park Street
31	JENNINGS	Benjamin	7	High Street	Head	Mar	44	M	Plumber Glazier etc Master, employing 2 Plumbers	Middx	London
32	JENNINGS	Ann	7		Wife	Mar	49	F	Wife	Herts	Royston
33	JENNINGS	Sarah A	7		Dau	Unm	14	F		Herts	Welwyn
34	JENNINGS	Frederick	7		Son	Unm	12	M	Scholar	Herts	Welwyn
35	JENNINGS	Martha	7		Dau	Unm	6	F	Scholar	Herts	Wheathampstead
36	THRALE	Thomas	8	High Street (The Boot)	Head	Mar	25	M	Baker & Beer Seller	Beds	Luton
37	THRALE	Sarah	8		Dau		2	F		Herts	Wheathampstead
38	THRALE	Thomas R	8		Son		1m	M		Herts	Wheathampstead
39	THRALE	Eliza	8		Wife	Mar	24	F		Herts	Wheathampstead
40	PEACOCK	James	8		Relative	Unm	26	M	Agric Lab	Herts	Wheathampstead
41	ODELL	Henry	8		Lodger	Unm	22	M	Fishmonger	Herts	Wheathampstead
42	MCCULLOCH	John	9	High Street	Head	Mar	34	M	Baker Master	Scotland	[Unknown]
43	MCCULLOCH	Mary Ann	9		Wife	Mar	30	F	Plait Dealer	Herts	Wheathampstead
44	MCCULLOCH	Mary A	9		Dau		6	F	Scholar	Herts	Whitwell
45	MCCULLOCH	William	9		Son		2	M		Herts	Wheathampstead
46	LINES	Eliza	9		Visitor	Unm	16	F	Plaiter	Herts	Wheathampstead
47	LIGHTFOOT	John	10	High Street	Head	Mar	32	M	Maltster Journeyman	Herts	Unknown
48	LIGHFOOT	Ann	10		Wife	Mar	35	F	Plaiter	Herts	Unknown
49	LIGHTFOOT	Charles	10		Son	Unm	11	M	Scholar	Herts	Unknown
50	LIGHTFOOT	Susan	10		Dau		4	F	Scholar	Herts	Unknown
51	LIGHTFOOT	Jesse	10		Son		11m	M		Herts	Wheathampstead
52	BROWNSELL	Matilda	11	High Street	Head	Unm	35	F	Straw Plaiter	Herts	Wheathampstead
53	BROWNSELL	John	11		Son	Unm	13	M	Agric Lab	Herts	Wheathampstead
54	BROWNSELL	Emma	11		Dau	Unm	13	F	Plaiter	Herts	Wheathampstead
55	CATLEY	Naomi	12	High Street	Head	Unm	29	F	Plaiter	Herts	Wheathampstead
56	CATLEY	Emma	12		Dau	Unm	7	F	Plaiter	Herts	Wheathampstead
57	SMITH	John	13	High Street	Head	Mar	67	M	Agric Lab	Herts	Sandridge
58	SMITH	Susanna	13		Wife	Mar	62	F	Plaiter	Herts	Harpenden
59	SMITH	Maria	13		Dau	Unm	20	F	Plaiter	Herts	Harpenden
60	BRAY	Robert	14	High Street The Bell Inn	Head	Mar	46	M	Cooper & Victualler	Herts	Wheathampstead
61	BRAY	Sarah	14		Wife	Mar	46	F		Herts	Wheathampstead
62	BRAY	George	14		Son	Unm	12	M	Scholar	Herts	Wheathampstead
63	BEASLEY	Samuel	14		Lodger	Unm	50	M	Cooper (Journeyman)	Herts	Wheathampstead
64	GLADMAN	Maria	15	High Street	Head	Unm	79	F	Annuitant	Herts	Wheathampstead
65	PALMER	Martha	15		Serv	Unm	19	F	House Servant	Herts	Wheathampstead
66	HAWKINS	Robert	16	High Street	Head	Mar	39	M	Butcher	Herts	Wheathampstead
67	HAWKINS	Elizabeth	16		Wife	Mar	39	F	Plaiter	Herts	Peters Green
68	HAWKINS	Harriet	16		Dau		7	F	Plaiter	Herts	Peters Green
69	HAWKINS	Amos	16		Son		7	M	Plaiter	Herts	Peters Green

	SURNAME	FORENAME	SCHEDULE NUMBER	ADDRESS	RELATIONSHIP	STATUS	AGE	SEX	OCCUPATION	COUNTY OF BIRTH	PLACE OF BIRTH
70	BLOW	William	17	High Street	Head	Mar	30	M	Groom	Lincs	[Unknown]
71	BLOW	Ann	17		Wife	Mar	28	F	Straw Plaiter	Herts	Wheathampstead
72	BLOW	Robert	17		Son		7	M	Scholar	Herts	Wheathampstead
73	BLOW	Emma	17		Dau		6	F	Scholar	Herts	Wheathampstead
74	BLOW	Harriet	17		Dau		3	F		Herts	Wheathampstead
75	BLOW	Ann	17		Dau		3m	F		Herts	Wheathampstead
76	NASH	George	18	High Street	Head	Unm	48	M	Grocer & Draper	Herts	Wheathampstead
77	NASH	Sarah	18		Sister	Unm	50	F	Grocer & Draper Partner with Brother	Herts	Wheathampstead
78	GRUNDON	Ann E	18		Niece	Unm	16	F	Drapers Assistant	Herts	Hitchin
79	WELSH	Sarah	18		Serv	Unm	15	F	House Servant	Herts	Wheathampstead
80	HARRIS	William	19	High Street (White Hart)	Head	Widower	46	M	Journeyman Miller & Beer Seller	Herts	Welwyn
81	HARRIS	Jemima	19		Dau	Unm	19	F	House Keeper	Herts	Welwyn
82	HARRIS	William	19		Son	Unm	14	M	Scholar	Herts	Wheathampstead
83	HARRIS	C	19		Son		12	M	Scholar	Herts	Wheathampstead
84	HARRIS	Mary	19		Dau		10	F	Scholar	Herts	Wheathampstead
85	DICKINSON	Robert	20	High Street	Head	Mar	42	M	Wheelwright Master	Herts	Abbots Langley
86	DICKINSON	Elizabeth	20		Wife	Mar	38	F		Herts	Wheathampstead
87	DICKINSON	Emily	20		Dau		10	F	Scholar	Herts	Wheathampstead
88	DICKINSON	Elizabeth	20		Dau		7	F	Scholar	Herts	Wheathampstead
89	DICKINSON	Henry	20		Son		2	M		Herts	Wheathampstead
90	PEARMAN	George	21	High Street	Head	Mar	27	M	Carrier	Herts	Wheathampstead
91	PEARMAN	Hannah	21		Wife	Mar	26	F		Herts	Wheathampstead
92	PEARMAN	Jane	21		Dau		5	F	Scholar	Herts	Wheathampstead
93	PEARMAN	Mary Ann	21		Dau		2	F		Herts	Wheathampstead
94	HOOPER	Joanna	22	The Bull Inn	Head	Widow	67	F	Innkeeper	Cornwall	Truro
95	HOOPER	Eliza	22		Dau	Unm	38	F	Governess	Cornwall	Penzance
96	HOOPER	Frances	22		Dau	Unm	33	F	Governess	Staffs	Ingestre
97	HOOPER	Jane	22		Dau	Unm	31	F	Dress Maker	Herts	Hatfield
98	HOOPER	Ann E	22		Dau	Unm	25	F	Governess	Herts	Wheathampstead
99	MATTHEWS	Charles	22		Lodger	Unm	21	M	Groom	Surrey	Bagshot
100	ARNOLD	Albert	22		Serv	Unm	38	M	Servant	Herts	Wheathampstead
101	WELLS	John	22		Serv	Mar	56	M	Servant	Northants	Peterborough
102	CHAPMAN	Louisa	23	High Street	Head	Mar	38	F	Straw Plaiter	Herts	Wheathampstead
103	JACKSON	Eliza	23		Dau	Unm	15	F	Straw Plaiter	Herts	Wheathampstead
104	CHAPMAN	Charles	23		Son		9	M	Straw Plaiter	Herts	Wheathampstead
105	CHAPMAN	Maria	23		Dau		4	F	Scholar	Herts	Wheathampstead
106	CHAPMAN	William	23		Son		2	M		Herts	Wheathampstead
107	ODLE	Harriet	23		Visitor	Unm	21	F	Bonnet Sewer	Herts	Wheathampstead
108	ARNOLD	Ruth	23		Visitor	Unm	22	F	Bonnet Sewer	Herts	Wheathampstead
109	ARNOLD	Joseph	24	High Street	Head	Unm	54	M	Agric Lab	Herts	Wheathampstead
110	TAYLOR	Charles	24		Lodger	Unm	42	M	Agric Lab	Herts	Wheathampstead
111	PEARCE	William	24		Lodger	Unm	29	M	Agric Lab	Herts	Wheathampstead
112	COLEMAN	Thomas	25	Bull Yard	Head	Mar	36	M	Wheelwright-Journeyman	Beds	Unknown
113	COLEMAN	Dinah	25		Wife	Mar	30	F	Straw Plaiter	Herts	Wheathampstead

114	COLEMAN	William	25		Son		6	M	Scholar	Herts	Wheathampstead
115	COLEMAN	Arthur	25		Son		18 m	M		Herts	Wheathampstead
116	ARNOLD	James	26	Bull Yard	Head	Mar	46	M	Agric Lab	Herts	Wheathampstead
117	ARNOLD	Ann	26		Wife	Mar	40	F	Straw Plaiter	Herts	Wheathampstead
118	ARNOLD	Sarah	26		Dau	Unm	15	F	Straw Plaiter	Herts	Wheathampstead
119	ARNOLD	William	26		Son		9	M	Scholar	Herts	Wheathampstead
120	ARNOLD	Emily	26		Dau		7	F	Scholar	Herts	Wheathampstead
121	ARNOLD	Jane	26		Dau		3	F	Scholar	Herts	Wheathampstead
122	PALMER	Elizabeth	27	Bull Yard	Head	Widow	60	F	Washerwoman	Herts	Wheathampstead
123	PALMER	John	27		Son	Unm	28	M	Agric Lab	Herts	Wheathampstead
124	HULKS	Joseph	28	Bull Yard	Head	Mar	42	M	Agric Lab	Herts	Wheathampstead
125	HULKS	Eliza	28		Wife	Mar	36	F	Straw Plaiter	Essex	Unknown
126	HULKS	Thomas	28		Son	Unm	17	M	Agric Lab	Herts	Wheathampstead
127	HULKS	Joseph	28		Son		9	M	Agric Lab	Herts	Wheathampstead
128	HULKS	Sarah	28		Dau		7	F	Scholar	Herts	Wheathampstead
129	HULKS	Susan	28		Dau		5	F	Scholar	Herts	Wheathampstead
130	HULKS	Lydia	28		Dau		2	F		Herts	Wheathampstead
131	EAST	Susan	29	East Lane	Head	Widow	42	F	Straw Plaiter	Herts	Wheathampstead
132	EAST	George	29		Son	Unm	27	M	Agric Lab	Herts	Wheathampstead
133	EAST	Mary	29		Dau	Unm	23	F	Straw Plaiter	Herts	Wheathampstead
134	EAST	William	29		Son	Unm	21	M	Agric Lab	Herts	Wheathampstead
135	EAST	Eliza	29		Dau	Unm	18	F	Straw Plaiter	Herts	Wheathampstead
136	EAST	Charles	29		Son	Unm	13	M	Agric Lab	Herts	Wheathampstead
137	EAST	Ann	29		Grandau		4	F		Herts	Wheathampstead
138	EAST	Thomas	29		Grandson		2 m	M		Herts	Wheathampstead

Two houses uninhabited

139	CROFT	William	30	East Lane	Head	Mar	66	M	Agric Lab	Herts	Wheathampstead
140	CROFT	Ann	30		Wife	Mar	64	F	Straw Plaiter	Herts	Wheathampstead
141	CROFT	Harriet	30		Dau	Unm	28	F	Straw Plaiter	Herts	Wheathampstead
142	TOMLIN	Frederic	30		Son-in-law	Mar	24	M	Journeyman Baker	Herts	Wheathampstead
143	TOMLIN	Eliza	30		Dau	Mar	26	F	Straw Plaiter	Herts	Wheathampstead
144	TOMLIN	Henry	30		Grandson		1	M		Herts	Wheathampstead
145	DAWES	George	31	East Lane	Head	Mar	35	M	Agric Lab	Herts	Wheathampstead
146	DAWES	Sarah	31		Wife	Mar	32	F	Straw Plaiter	Herts	Wheathampstead
147	DAWES	William	31		Son	Unm	15	M	Agric Lab	Herts	Wheathampstead
148	DAWES	Mary	31		Dau		10	F	Straw Plaiter	Herts	Wheathampstead
149	DAWES	Charles	31		Son		7	M	Straw Plaiter	Herts	Wheathampstead
150	DAWES	George	31		Son		5	M		Herts	Wheathampstead
151	DAWES	Thomas	31		Son		2	M		Herts	Wheathampstead
152	WOODWARDS	Mary	32	East Lane	Head	Widow	70	F	Straw Plaiter	Herts	Wheathampstead
153	WOODWARDS	Sarah	32		Dau	Unm	27	F	Straw Plaiter	Herts	Wheathampstead
154	WOODWARDS	Harriet	32		Grandau		3	F		Herts	Wheathampstead
155	BLAND	James	33	East Lane	Head	Mar	60	M	Agric Lab	Herts	Wheathampstead
156	BLAND	Sarah	33		Wife	Mar	41	F	Straw Plaiter	Herts	Wheathampstead

	SURNAME	FORENAME	SCHEDULE NUMBER	ADDRESS	RELATIONSHIP	STATUS	AGE	SEX	OCCUPATION	COUNTY OF BIRTH	PLACE OF BIRTH
157	MONDIN	Henry	34	East Lane	Head	Mar	39	M	Agric Lab	Herts	Wheathampstead
158	MONDIN	Eliza	34		Wife	Mar	35	F	Straw Plaiter	Herts	Wheathampstead
159	MONDIN	Rebecca	34		Dau	Unm	13	F	Straw Plaiter	Herts	Wheathampstead
160	MONDIN	Emma	34		Dau		9	F	Straw Plaiter	Herts	Wheathampstead
161	MONDIN	George	34		Son		4	M		Herts	Wheathampstead
162	WEBB	Thomas	35	East Lane	Head	Mar	64	M	Agric Lab	Herts	Wheathampstead
163	WEBB	Elizabeth	35		Wife	Mar	62	F	Straw Plaiter	Herts	Wheathampstead
164	WEBB	Alice	35		Dau	Unm	27	F	Straw Plaiter	Herts	Wheathampstead
165	WEBB	Hannah	35		Dau	Unm	22	F	Straw Plaiter	Herts	Wheathampstead
166	WEBB	William	35		Grandson		6	M	Straw Plaiter	Herts	Wheathampstead
167	BECK	James	36	East Lane	Head	Mar	37	M	Agric Lab	Herts	Wheathampstead
168	BECK	Sarah	36		Wife	Mar	32	F	Straw Plaiter	Herts	Wheathampstead
169	BECK	Mary	36		Dau		6	F	Straw Plaiter	Herts	Wheathampstead
170	BECK	Lucy	36		Dau		1	F		Herts	Wheathampstead
171	GRISSEL	Emma	36		Dau-in-law	Unm	14	F	Straw Plaiter	Herts	Wheathampstead
172	GRISSEL	Eliza	36		Dau-in-law		12	F	Straw Plaiter	Herts	Wheathampstead
173	GRISSEL	Rebecca	36		Mother-in-law	Widow	62	F	Straw Plaiter	Herts	Wheathampstead
174	GRISSEL	William	36		Brother-in-law	Unm	27	M	Agric Lab	Herts	Wheathampstead
175	NASH	James	37	East Lane	Head	Mar	60	M	Agric Lab	Herts	Wheathampstead
176	NASH	Mary	37		Wife	Mar	54	F	Straw Plaiter	Herts	Wheathampstead
177	NASH	Eliza	37		Dau	Unm	17	F	Straw Plaiter	Herts	Wheathampstead
178	NASH	Sarah	37		Dau	Unm	15	F	Straw Plaiter	Herts	Wheathampstead
179	MORRIS	William	38	East Lane	Head	Mar	49	M	Agric Lab	Herts	Wheathampstead
180	MORRIS	Sarah	38		Wife	Mar	47	F	Straw Plaiter	Herts	Wheathampstead
181	MORRIS	Emma	38		Dau	Unm	15	F	Straw Plaiter	Herts	Wheathampstead
182	MORRIS	John	38		Son		11	M	Scholar	Herts	Wheathampstead
183	MORRIS	Sarah	38		Dau		9	F	Scholar	Herts	Wheathampstead
184	SMITH	Mary	38		Mother-in-law	Widow	71	F	Straw Plaiter	Beds	Unknown
185	GRAY	William	39	East Lane	Head	Mar	34	M	Sawyer	Herts	Wheathampstead
186	GRAY	Hannah	39		Wife	Mar	34	F	Straw Plaiter	Herts	Wheathampstead
187	GRAY	Mary	39		Dau	Unm	13	F	Straw Plaiter	Herts	Wheathampstead
188	GRAY	George	39		Son		11	M	Errand Boy	Herts	Wheathampstead
189	GRAY	Hallah-beenah	39		Dau		8	F	Straw Plaiter	Herts	Wheathampstead
190	GRAY	Fanny E	39		Dau		3	F		Herts	Wheathampstead
191	GRAY	Lizzy	39		Dau		1	F		Herts	Wheathampstead
192	MALES	Joseph	40	East Lane	Head	Mar	21	M	Maltman	Herts	Codicote
193	MALES	Ann	40		Wife	Mar	23	F	Straw Plaiter	Herts	Wheathampstead
194	MALES	Mary Ann	40		Dau		1	F		Herts	Wheathampstead
195	SEABROOK	Michael	40		Brother-in-law	Unm	14	M	Farmers labr	Herts	Wheathampstead
196	SEABROOK	George	40		Visitor	Mar	24	M	Tea Dealer	Herts	Wheathampstead
197	SEABROOK	Sarah	40		Visitors Wife	Mar	26	F		Herts	Datchworth
198	SEABROOK	Mary Anne	40		Visitors Dau		1	F		Herts	Watton
199	DAY	James	41	East Lane	Head	Mar	35	M	Agric Lab	Herts	Wheathampstead

200	DAY	Elizabeth	41		Wife	Mar	28	F	Straw Plaiter	Herts	Wheathampstead
201	DAY	Thomas	41		Son		5	M	Straw Plaiter	Herts	Wheathampstead
202	DAY	William	41		Son		2	M		Herts	Wheathampstead
203	FREEMAN	William	41		Lodger	Widower	55	M	Agric Lab	Herts	Wheathampstead
204	FREEMAN	David	41		Visitor	Unm	15	M	Blacksmiths Appr	Herts	Wheathampstead
205	DAY	Alfred	41		Lodger	Unm	13	M	Agric Lab	Herts	Wheathampstead
206	FREEMAN	Francis	42	East Lane	Head	Mar	51	M	Agric Lab	Herts	Kimpton
207	FREEMAN	Sarah	42		Wife	Mar	52	F	Straw Plaiter	Beds	Bedford
208	READ	James	43	East Lane	Head	Widower	77	M	Agric Lab	Herts	Wheathampstead
209	HONOUR	Joseph	44	East Lane	Head	Widower	62	M	Agric Lab	Herts	Kings Langley
210	HONOUR	Dorcas	44		Sister	Unm	60	F	Brothers Housekeeper	Herts	Kings Langley
211	ARNOLD	George	45	High Street	Head	Mar	38	M	Carpenter Master	Middx	Chelsea
212	ARNOLD	Mary	45		Wife	Mar	34	F		Herts	Wheathampstead
213	ARNOLD	Julia M	45		Dau		6	F	Scholar	Herts	Wheathampstead
214	ARNOLD	Harriet	45		Dau		2	F		Herts	Wheathampstead
215	MERKINS	William	46	High Street	Head	Mar	39	M	Agric Lab	Herts	Wheathampstead
216	MERKINS	Martha	46		Wife	Mar	41	F	Straw Plaiter	Herts	Wheathampstead
217	MERKINS	George	46		Son	Unm	11	M	Agric Lab	Herts	Wheathampstead
218	MERKINS	Sarah	46		Dau		8	F	Plaiter	Herts	Wheathampstead
219	MERKINS	William	46		Son		5	M	Scholar	Herts	Wheathampstead
220	MERKINS	James	46		Son		2	M		Herts	Wheathampstead
221	ADDINGTON	Emma	46		Niece		4	F	Scholar	Herts	Wheathampstead
222	EDMUNDS	Elizabeth	47	High Street	Head	Widow	68	F	Straw Plaiter	Herts	Wheathampstead
223	EDMUNDS	Charlotte	47		Dau	Unm	28	F	Straw Plaiter	Herts	Wheathampstead
224	EDMUNDS	Eliza	47		Dau	Unm	22	F	Straw Plaiter	Herts	Wheathampstead
225	EDMUNDS	George	47		Grandson		1	M		Herts	Wheathampstead
226	HUTCHINGS	William	48	High Street	Head	Mar	79	M	Agric Lab	Herts	Wheathampstead
227	HUTCHINGS	Mary	48		Wife	Mar	70	F	Straw Plaiter	Herts	Wheathampstead
228	HUTCHINGS	Joseph	48		Son	Unm	35	M	Agric Lab	Herts	Wheathampstead
229	ROE	George	49	High Street	Head	Mar	30	M	Agric Lab	Herts	Wheathampstead
230	ROE	Mary	49		Wife	Mar	28	F	Straw Plaiter	Herts	Wheathampstead
231	ROE	Sarah	49		Dau		6	F	Scholar	Herts	Wheathampstead
232	ROE	Rhoda	49		Dau		4	F	Scholar	Herts	Wheathampstead
233	HIGGINS	Joseph	50	High Street	Head	Mar	51	M	Farming Bailiff	Herts	Flamstead
234	HIGGINS	Phoebe	50		Wife	Mar	44	F		Herts	Wheathampstead
235	ODELL	George	50		Serv	Unm	21	M	Ploughman	Herts	Wheathampstead
236	HONNOR	Thomas	50		Serv	Unm	19	M	Horsekeeper	Herts	Wheathampstead
237	ABBOTT	Henry	51	High Street	Head	Mar	26	M	Cowman	Herts	Redbourn
238	ABBOTT	Mary Ann	51		Wife	Mar	27	F		Bucks	Winslow
239	SMITH	George	51		Lodger	Mar	22	M	Groom	Herts	Harpenden
240	STEVENS	Joseph	51		Lodger	Unm	20	M	Ploughman	Herts	Wheathampstead
241	MILLARD	William	51		Lodger	Unm	15	M	Shepherd	Herts	Wheathampstead
242	ABBOTT	Jane	51		Dau		4	F		Herts	Wheathampstead
243	ABBOTT	Elizabeth A	51		Dau		1	F		Herts	Wheathampstead

	SURNAME	FORENAME	SCHEDULE NUMBER	ADDRESS	RELATIONSHIP	STATUS	AGE	SEX	OCCUPATION	COUNTY OF BIRTH	PLACE OF BIRTH
244	ARNOLD	James	52	High Street	Head	Mar	83	M	Miller Journeyman	Herts	Wheathampstead
245	ARNOLD	Sarah	52		Wife	Mar	70	F	Straw Plaiter	Herts	Wheathampstead
246	SPRIGS	Mary	52		Dau	Mar	27	F	Straw Plaiter	Herts	Wheathampstead
247	SPRIGS	John	52		Son-in-law	Mar	24	M	Gardener	Herts	Wheathampstead
248	HECKER	Henry Tousle	53	High Street	Head	Mar	44	M	M.A. Curate of Wheathamstead	Herts	Hornsey
249	HECKER	Emma C. T.	53		Dau		8	F	Scholar at Home	Kent	Sevenoaks
250	HECKER	Charles H. T.	53		Son		6	M	Scholar at Home	Herts	Wheathampstead
251	HECKER	Frances L. T.	53		Dau		3	F		Herts	Wheathampstead
252	HECKER	Margaret E. T.	53		Dau		1	F		Herts	Wheathampstead
253	FOXLEY	Caroline	53		Serv	Unm	25	F	House Servant	Herts	Welwyn
254	PURSSELL	Mahalah	53		Serv	Unm	19	F	House Servant	Herts	Shenley
255	YOUNG	Rebecca	53		Serv	Unm	18	F	House Servant	Herts	Codicote
256	LATTIMORE	Charles Higby	54	High Street (The Place Farm)	Head	Unm	42	M	Farmer of 273 acres employing 26 labourers (20 men and 6 boys)	Herts	Wheathampstead
257	LATTIMORE	Anne	54		Sister	Unm	46	F	No occupation	Herts	Wheathampstead
258	LATTIMORE	Mary	54		Sister	Unm	44	F	No occupation	Herts	Wheathampstead
259	DIXON	Mary	54		Serv	Unm	50	F	Household Servant	Herts	Wheathampstead
260	CRISP	Harriet	55	Wheathampstead Hill	Head	Unm	18	F	Surgeons Daughter	Middx	Harrow
261	CRISP	Fanny	55		Sister	Unm	17	F	Surgeons Daughter	Middx	Harrow
262	CRISP	Marianne	55		Sister	Unm	16	F	Surgeons Daughter	Middx	London
263	CRISP	Clara L	55		Sister	Unm	12	F	Surgeons Daughter	Bucks	Chalfont
264	CRISP	George C A	55		Brother		9	M	Surgeons Son	Bucks	Chalfont
265	MARDALL	Harriet	56	Wheathampstead Hill	Head	Widow	49	F		Herts	Sandridge
266	MARDALL	James	56		Son	Unm	28	M	Farmer of 150 acres employing 6 men & 2 boys	Herts	Wheathampstead
267	FRANKLIN	Eliza	56		Serv	Unm	15	F	House Servant	Herts	Wheathampstead
268	WOODARDS	George	57	Wheathampstead Hill	Head	Widower	60	M	Agric Lab	Herts	Wheathampstead
269	WOODARDS	Emma	57		Dau	Unm	10	F	Straw Plaiter	Herts	Wheathampstead
270	NASH	John	57		Son-in-law	Mar	30	M	Miller Journeyman	Herts	Wheathampstead
271	NASH	Rebecca	57		Dau	Mar	25	F	Straw Plaiter	Herts	Wheathampstead
272	FITZJOHN	Edward	58	Wheathampstead Hill	Head	Mar	41	M	Agric Lab	Herts	Wheathampstead
273	FITZJOHN	Mary	58		Wife	Mar	39	F	Straw Plaiter	Herts	Wheathampstead
274	FITZJOHN	Eliza	58		Dau	Unm	13	F	Straw Plaiter	Herts	Wheathampstead
275	FITZJOHN	Mary	58		Dau		11	F	Straw Plaiter	Herts	Wheathampstead
276	FITZJOHN	Frank	58		Son		6	M	Scholar	Herts	Wheathampstead
277	WYNTER	George Jacob	59	Wheathampstead Hill	Head	Widower	69	M	Annuitant	Bucks	Tilgram
278	WYNTER	Hephzibah	59		Dau	Unm	35	F	Governess	Beds	Evershot
279	WYNTER	Jane	59		Dau	Unm	30	F	Governess	Beds	Evershot
280	FLOYD	Sarah	59		Serv	Unm	17	F	House Servant	Herts	Wheathampstead
281	BYLES	James E	59		Boarder		9	M	Scholar	London	London
282	SAMS	Joseph H	59		Boarder		7	M	Scholar	London	London
283	CHENNELS	Amelia	60	Wheathampstead Hill	Head	Widow	50	F	Farmer of 80 acres employing 4	Herts	Tewin
284	CHENNELS	George	60		Son	Unm	28	M	Farmers Son	Herts	Wheathampstead

| 285 | CHENNELS | John | 60 | | Son | Unm | 20 | M | Farmers Son | Herts | Wheathampstead |
| 286 | MUMFORD | John | 60 | | Lodger | Unm | 40 | M | Butcher Master | Herts | Hertford |

End of the east side of the Village of Wheathampstead

287	BOZIER	John	61	Gustard Wood	Head	Mar	40	M	Gardener	Herts	St Albans
288	BOZIER	Ann	61		Wife	Mar	41	F	Straw Plaiter	Herts	St Albans
289	BOZIER	William	61		Son	Unm	12	M	Straw Plaiter	Herts	St Albans
290	BOZIER	Mary	61		Dau		13	F	Straw Plaiter	Herts	St Albans
291	BOZIER	Henry	61		Son		9	M	Straw Plaiter	Herts	St Albans
292	BOZIER	Ann	61		Dau		7	F	Scholar	Herts	Wheathampstead
293	BOZIER	Eliza	61		Dau		2	F		Herts	Wheathampstead
294	BOZIER	Sarah	61		Dau		3 m	F		Herts	Wheathampstead
295	GROOM	James	62	Gustard Wood	Head	Mar	35	M	Agric Lab	Herts	Wheathampstead
296	GROOM	Susanna	62		Wife	Mar	37	F	Straw Plaiter	Beds	[Unknown]
297	GROOM	William	62		Son		5	M	Scholar	Herts	Wheathampstead
298	GROOM	James	62		Son		3	M		Herts	Wheathampstead
299	PARSONS	George	62		Father-in-law	Widower	56	M	Agric Lab	Herts	Bendish Kings Walden [St Pauls Walden?]
300	FRENCH	William	63	Gustard Wood	Head	Mar	29	M	Agric Lab	Herts	Wheathampstead
301	FRENCH	Hannah	63		Wife	Mar	28	F	Straw Plaiter	Herts	Kimpton
302	BROTHERS	Abraham	64	Royal Exchange	Head	Mar	57	M	Boot & Shoemaker & Beer Seller	Beds	Holwell
303	BROTHERS	Elizabeth	64		Wife	Mar	50	F		Herts	Wheathampstead
304	BROTHERS	Sarah	64		Dau	Unm	18	F	Plaiter	Herts	Wheathampstead
305	BROTHERS	Diana	64		Dau	Unm	15	F	Plaiter	Herts	Wheathampstead
306	BROTHERS	Abraham	64		Son		11	M	Plaiter	Herts	Wheathampstead
307	BROTHERS	John	64		Son		8	M	Scholar	Herts	Wheathampstead
308	WRIGHT	Robert	65	Gustard Wood	Head	Mar	42	M	Agric Lab	Herts	Wheathampstead
309	WRIGHT	Ann	65		Wife	Mar	51	F	Plaiter	Herts	Wheathampstead
310	REED	Benjamin	65		Lodger	Mar	26	M	Shepherd	Herts	Wheathampstead
311	REED	Martha	65		Lodger	Mar	23	F	Plaiter	Herts	Wheathampstead
312	REED	David	65		Lodger		2	M		Herts	Wheathampstead
313	KINGHAM	James	66	Gustard Wood	Head	Widower	64	M	Agric Lab	Herts	Wheathampstead
314	KINGHAM	Mary Ann	66		Dau	Unm	32	F	Plaiter	Herts	Wheathampstead
315	BARTON	Sarah	66		Lodger		5	F		Herts	Wheathampstead
316	NORRIS	John	67	Gustard Wood	Head	Mar	51	M	Sawyer	Herts	Wheathampstead
317	NORRIS	Caroline	67		Wife	Mar	42	F	Straw Plaiter	Herts	Sandridge
318	GROOM	Thomas	68	Gustard Wood	Head	Mar	64	M	Agric Lab	Herts	Wheathampstead
319	GROOM	Ann	68		Wife	Mar	65	F	Straw Plaiter	Herts	Wheathampstead
320	GROOM	Thomas	68		Son	Mar	30	M	Straw Plaiter	Herts	Wheathampstead
321	GROOM	Ann	68		Dau-in-law	Mar	30	F	Straw Plaiter	Herts	Wheathampstead
322	GROOM	Charles	68		Grandson		9	M	Straw Plaiter	Herts	Wheathampstead
323	GROOM	William	68		Grandson		7	M	Scholar	Herts	Wheathampstead
324	GROOM	Arthur	68		Grandson		5	M	Scholar	Herts	Wheathampstead
325	GROOM	George	68		Grandson		2	M		Herts	Wheathampstead
326	PARSONS	Edward	69	Gustard Wood	Head	Mar	33	M	Agric Lab	Herts	Wheathampstead

	SURNAME	FORENAME	SCHEDULE NUMBER	ADDRESS	RELATIONSHIP	STATUS	AGE	SEX	OCCUPATION	COUNTY OF BIRTH	PLACE OF BIRTH
327	PARSONS	Mary	69		Wife	Mar	26	F	Straw Plaiter	Herts	Wheathampstead
328	PARSONS	Henry	69		Son		2	M		Herts	Wheathampstead
329	BYGRAVE	John	70	Gustard Wood	Head	Mar	72	M	Journeyman Smith	Herts	Red Hill
330	BYGRAVE	Sarah	70		Wife	Mar	75	F	Plaiter	Herts	Redbourn
331	BYGRAVE	Martha	70		Dau	Unm	26	F	Plaiter	Herts	Ayot St Lawrence
332	HOLLINSWORTH	Joseph	71	Gustard Wood	Head	Mar	40	M	Agric Lab	Herts	Wheathampstead
333	HOLLINSWORTH	Jemima	71		Wife	Mar	48	F	Plaiter	Herts	Wheathampstead
334	HOLLINSWORTH	George	71		Son	Unm	20	M	Agric Lab	Herts	Wheathampstead
335	CLARK	George	72	Gustard Wood	Head	Mar	39	M	Agric Lab	Herts	Sandridge
336	CLARK	Sarah	72		Wife	Mar	37	F	Straw Plaiter	Herts	Wheathampstead
337	CLARK	William	72		Son	Unm	12	M	Agric Lab	Herts	Wheathampstead
338	CLARK	Sarah	72		Dau		8	F	Straw Plaiter	Herts	Wheathampstead
339	CLARK	Jane	72		Dau		5	F	Straw Plaiter	Herts	Wheathampstead
340	CLARK	Charles	72		Son		2	M		Herts	Wheathampstead
341	ELLIS	Ann	73	Gustard Wood	Head	Mar	30	F	Servants Wife	Herts	Northchurch
342	CLARK	George	74	Gustard Wood	Head	Mar	69	M	Agric Lab	Herts	Sandridge
343	CLARK	Esther	74		Wife	Mar	62	F	Plaiter	Herts	Sandridge
344	CLARK	Mary	74		Dau	Unm	25	F	Bonnet Sewer	Herts	Wheathampstead
345	CLARK	Maria	74		Grandau		4	F		Herts	Wheathampstead
346	GEORGE	George	75	Gustard Wood	Head	Mar	68	M	Carpenter Journeyman	Herts	Wheathampstead
347	GEORGE	Maria	75		Wife	Mar	56	F	Straw Plaiter	Bucks	Taplow
348	GEORGE	Daniel	75		Son	Unm	32	M	Agric Lab	Herts	Wheathampstead
349	GEORGE	Mary Ann	75		Dau	Unm	30	F	Plaiter	Herts	Wheathampstead
350	GEORGE	James	75		Son	Unm	26	M	Servant	Herts	Wheathampstead
351	BRITTON	Harriet	75		Niece	Unm	20	F	Plaiter	Herts	St Albans
352	ADAMS	Daniel	76	Gustard Wood	Head	Mar	21	M	Carter (employing 1 man)	Herts	Wheathampstead
353	ADAMS	Ruth	76		Wife	Mar	22	F	Carters Wife	Herts	Wheathampstead
354	ADAMS	Elizabeth	76		Dau		2	F	Carters Daur	Herts	Wheathampstead
355	ADAMS	Harriet	76		Dau		9 m	F	Carters Daur	Herts	Wheathampstead
356	ADAMS	Abel	76		Brother	Unm	16	M	Labourer (Carters)	Herts	Wheathampstead
357	KILBY	William	77	Gustard Wood	Head	Mar	28	M	Carpenter Master	Herts	Wheathampstead
358	KILBY	Jane	77		Wife	Mar	30	F		Herts	Wheathampstead
359	KILBY	Charles John	77		Son		3	M		Herts	Wheathampstead
360	KILBY	John Charles	77		Son		3	M		Herts	Wheathampstead
361	CHALKLEY	Louisa	77		Serv	Unm	16	F	House Servant	Herts	St Pauls Walden
362	EDMONDS	Elizabeth	78	Gustard Wood	Head	Widow	69	F	Straw Plaiter	Herts	Wheathampstead
363	EDMONDS	Jane	78		Dau	Unm	26	F	Straw Plaiter	Herts	Wheathampstead
364	MILLARD	Daniel	79	Gustard Wood	Head	Mar	42	M	Agric Lab	Herts	Wheathampstead
365	MILLARD	Frances	79		Wife	Mar	43	F	Straw Plaiter	Herts	Wheathampstead
366	MILLARD	Frances S	79		Dau	Unm	13	F	Straw Plaiter	Herts	Wheathampstead
367	MILLARD	Elizabeth	79		Dau	Unm	12	F	Straw Plaiter	Herts	Wheathampstead
368	MILLARD	John D	79		Son		11	M	Straw Plaiter	Herts	Wheathampstead
369	MILLARD	Rhoda	79		Dau		8	F	Scholar	Herts	Wheathampstead
370	MILLARD	Emma	79		Dau		6	F	Scholar	Herts	Wheathampstead

371	MILLARD	Jane	79		Dau		4	F	Scholar	Herts	Wheathampstead
372	ROFE	Samuel	80	Gustard Wood	Head	Mar	39	M	Agric Lab	Herts	Wheathampstead
373	ROFE	Anna	80		Wife	Mar	49	F	Straw Plaiter	Herts	Wheathampstead
374	ROFE	Mary Ann	80		Dau	Unm	11	F	Straw Plaiter	Herts	Wheathampstead
375	ROFE	Catherine	80		Dau		9	F	Straw Plaiter	Herts	Wheathampstead
376	ROFE	John	80		Son		7	M	Scholar	Herts	Wheathampstead
377	ROFE	Emanuel	80		Son		2	M		Herts	Wheathampstead
378	BUTCHER	Mary	80		Lodger	Unm	24	F	Plaiter	Herts	Unknown
379	BUTCHER	Rebecca	80		Lodgers Dau		under 1 m	F		Herts	Wheathampstead
380	WOOD	Joseph	81	Gustard Wood	Head	Mar	51	M	Agric Lab	Herts	Wheathampstead
381	WOOD	Mary	81		Wife	Mar	64	F	Straw Plaiter	Cambs	[Unknown]
382	PECKS	William	82	Gustard Wood	Head	Mar	48	M	Carpenter Journeyman	Herts	Wheathampstead
383	PECKS	Ann	82		Wife	Mar	49	F	Straw Plaiter	Herts	Wheathampstead
384	PECKS	Livinia	82		Dau	Unm	16	F	Straw Plaiter	Herts	Wheathampstead
385	PECKS	James	82		Son	Unm	22	M	Agric Lab	Herts	Wheathampstead
386	PECKS	Eve	82		Dau		9	F	Plaiter	Herts	Wheathampstead
387	PECKS	Lot	82		Son		6	M		Herts	Wheathampstead
388	CARTER	William	83	Gustard Wood	Head	Widower	74	M	Carpenter Journeyman	Herts	Wheathampstead
389	CARTER	William	84	Gustard Wood	Head	Mar	42	M	Agric Lab	Herts	Wheathampstead
390	CARTER	Caroline	84		Wife	Mar	35	F	Straw Plaiter	Herts	Kimpton
391	CARTER	Amelia	84		Dau		9	F	Straw Plaiter	Herts	Wheathampstead
392	CARTER	Ann M	84		Dau		6	F	Straw Plaiter	Herts	Wheathampstead
393	CARTER	Moses	84		Son		1	M		Herts	Wheathampstead
394	SHAMBROOK	Daniel	85	Gustard Wood	Head	Mar	46	M	Agric Lab	Herts	Wheathampstead
395	SHAMBROOK	Mary	85		Wife	Mar	40	F	Straw Plaiter	Herts	Codicote
396	SHAMBROOK	Elizabeth	85		Dau	Unm	20	F	Straw Plaiter	Herts	Codicote
397	SHAMBROOK	Caroline	85		Dau	Unm	13	F	Straw Plaiter	Herts	Wheathampstead
398	SHAMBROOK	Eliza	85		Dau	Unm	10	F	Scholar	Herts	Wheathampstead
399	SHAMBROOK	Joshua	85		Son		7	M	Scholar	Herts	Wheathampstead
400	SHAMBROOK	Hester	85		Dau		4	F	Scholar	Herts	Wheathampstead
401	SHAMBROOK	Martha	85		Dau		1	F		Herts	Wheathampstead
402	CRAWLEY	Mary	86	Gustard Wood	Head	Unm	21	F	Straw Plaiter	Herts	Wheathampstead
403	CRAWLEY	Emily	86		Dau		1	F		Herts	Wheathampstead
404	SIBLEY	Esther	87	Gustard Wood	Head	Mar	63	F	Farmer of 80 acres employing 4 men	Durham	Sunderland
405	SIBLEY	Charles	87		Son	Unm	26	M	Farmers Son	Herts	Wheathampstead
406	KILBY	Emily	87		Visitor		5	F		Herts	Wheathampstead
407	SIBLEY	John	88	Gustard Wood (Cross Keys)	Head	Mar	43	M	Shoemaker & Victualler	Herts	Wheathampstead
408	SIBLEY	Mary	88		Wife	Mar	39	F		Herts	Wheathampstead
409	TURNER	Thomas	88		Nephew	Unm	22	M	Shoemaker Journeyman	Herts	Wheathampstead
410	LATCHFORD	Thomas	88		Appr	Unm	17	M	Shoemaker Appr	Herts	Wheathampstead
411	THRALE	Norman	88		Nephew	Unm	19	M	Miller Journeyman	Beds	Luton
412	WINCH	Samuel	88		Lodger	Unm	24	M	Shoemaker Journeyman	Herts	Stevenage
413	ATTWOOD	Amos	88		Lodger	Unm	28	M	Agric Lab	Herts	Kimpton
414	HEDGES	Thomas	89	Gustard Wood	Head	Mar	67	M	Agric Lab	Herts	Wheathampstead

	SURNAME	FORENAME	SCHEDULE NUMBER	ADDRESS	RELATIONSHIP	STATUS	AGE	SEX	OCCUPATION	COUNTY OF BIRTH	PLACE OF BIRTH
415	HEDGES	Martha	89		Wife	Mar	55	F	Charwoman	Herts	Wheathampstead
416	WICKS	William	89		Lodger	Mar	25	M	Agric Lab	Herts	Wheathampstead
417	WICKS	Eliza	89		Lodgers Wife	Mar	22	F	Straw Plaiter	Herts	Wheathampstead
418	WICKS	Ellen	89		Lodgers Dau		2	F		Herts	Wheathampstead
419	IZZARD	William	90	Gustard Wood	Head	Mar	39	M	Agric Lab	Beds	Unknown
420	IZZARD	Sarah	90		Wife	Mar	32	F	Straw Plaiter	Herts	Wheathampstead
421	IZZARD	Lydia	90		Dau	Unm	15	F	Straw Plaiter	Herts	Wheathampstead
422	IZZARD	James	90		Son	Unm	13	M	Agric Lab	Herts	Wheathampstead
423	IZZARD	Samuel	90		Son		8	M	Scholar	Herts	Wheathampstead
424	IZZARD	William	90		Son		6	M	Scholar	Herts	Wheathampstead
425	IZZARD	Robert	90		Son		2	M		Herts	Wheathampstead
426	BOON	William	91	Gustard Wood	Head	Mar	34	M	Agric Lab	Herts	Wheathampstead
427	BOON	Hannah	91		Wife	Mar	45	F	Straw Plaiter	Herts	Wheathampstead
428	WHEELER	Mary	91		Visitor	Unm	39	F	Straw Plaiter	Herts	Wheathampstead
429	GARRARD	Charles B. D.	92	Lamar Park	Head	Mar	45	M	Landed Proprietor	Middx	Mill Hill
430	GARRARD	Honora D.	92		Wife	Mar	37	F	Landed Proprietor	Bucks	Great Brickhill
431	LINFORD	Maria	92		Serv	Widow	33	F	Housekeeper	Kent	Tonbridge
432	GEARING	Caroline	92		Serv	Unm	31	F	Ladys Maid	Suffolk	Stone
433	HILL	Sophia	92		Serv	Unm	27	F	Laundry Maid	Dorset	Branscombe
434	RAMSAY	Eliza	92		Serv	Unm	41	F	House Maid	Herts	Hertford
435	ROBERTS	Sarah	92		Serv	Unm	24	F	Kitchen Maid	Beds	Risley
436	CRANE	Sarah	92		Serv	Unm	23	F	House Maid	Bucks	Bletchley
437	MEACHAM	Priscilla	92		Serv	Unm	31	F	Dairy Maid	Bucks	Great Brickhill
438	ELLIS	John	92		Serv	Mar	31	M	Butler	Oxon	Shipton
439	SIBLEY	Charles	92		Serv	Mar	58	M	Coachman	Herts	Wheathampstead
440	SIBLEY	Samuel	92		Serv	Mar	30	M	Groom	Herts	Wheathampstead
441	WILLIAMS	James	92		Serv	Unm	22	M	Footman	Somerset	Uphill
442	BUCKLE	Thomas	92		Serv	Unm	26	M	Helper	Herts	Kimpton
443	BOZIER	Sarah	92		Serv	Widow	63	F	Washerwoman	Herts	Stapleford
444	FOSTER	James	93	Reed Hall Farm	Head	Mar	56	M	Bailiff to a Farmer	Herts	Lilley
445	FOSTER	Frances	93		Wife	Mar	56	F		Cambs	Burwell
446	FOSTER	Esther	93		Dau	Unm	22	F	Bonnet Sewer	Herts	Lilley
447	FOSTER	Sarah	93		Dau	Unm	18	F	Straw Plaiter	Herts	Lilley
448	ROLPH	John	93		Serv	Unm	31	M	Agric Lab	Herts	Kimpton
449	PEARSE	James	93		Serv	Unm	16	M	Agric Lab	Herts	Wheathampstead
450	DARBON	William	93		Serv	Unm	14	M	Agric Lab	Herts	Wheathampstead

The end of the east side of Gustard Wood

	SURNAME	FORENAME	SCHEDULE NUMBER	ADDRESS	RELATIONSHIP	STATUS	AGE	SEX	OCCUPATION	COUNTY OF BIRTH	PLACE OF BIRTH
451	THREADER	Joseph	94	Marford	Head	Mar	36	M	Agric Lab	Herts	Wheathampstead
452	THREADER	Harriet	94		Wife	Mar	32	F	Straw Plaiter	Herts	Hatfield
453	THREADER	William	94		Son	Unm	11	M	Straw Plaiter	Herts	Sandridge
454	THREADER	Hannah	94		Dau		6	F	Straw Plaiter	Herts	Wheathampstead
455	THREADER	Emma	94		Dau		3	F		Herts	Wheathampstead
456	THREADER	William	94		Son		1	M		Herts	Wheathampstead
457	MARDELL	William	95	Marford	Head	Mar	48	M	Agric Lab	Herts	Hitchin

458	MARDELL	Charlotte	95		Wife	Mar	46	F	Plaiter	Herts	Sandridge
459	MARDELL	James	95		Grandson		8	M	Scholar	Herts	Wheathampstead
460	TRUSTRUM	William	96	Marford	Head	Mar	30	M	School Master	Herts	Royston
461	TRUSTRAM	Eliza	96		Wife	Mar	36	F		Cambs	Gamlingay
462	TRUSTRAM	Emma E. M.	96		Dau		4	F	Scholar	Herts	Wheathampstead
463	TRUSTRAM	Lucy A.	96		Dau		2	F		Herts	Wheathampstead
464	SCOREY	Joseph	96		Boarder		11	M	Scholar	Middx	Marylebone
465	STRATTON	Samuel T.	96		Boarder		11	M	Scholar	Middx	Paddington
466	STRATTON	George Harry	96		Boarder		8	M	Scholar	Middx	Paddington
467	COX	Charles F	96		Boarder		14	M	Scholar	Middx	Paddington
468	SAMS	William	96		Boarder		12	M	Scholar	Herts	Hatfield
469	WOODHAM	William	96		Boarder		12	M	Scholar	Beds	Barton
470	RUMSLEY	Thomas	96		Boarder		10	M	Scholar	Middx	Marylebone
471	STEVENS	Charles J	96		Boarder	Unm	16	M	Scholar	Middx	Paddington
472	STEVENS	Henry	96		Boarder	Unm	13	M	Scholar	Middx	Paddington
473	SAVILL	Enoch	96		Boarder		12	M	Scholar	Beds	Luton
474	GARRAS	Julias	96		Boarder		6	M	Scholar	Herts	Hatfield
475	GRAY	Phoebe	96		Serv	Unm	16	F	House Servant	Herts	Wheathampstead
476	WOODWARDS	George	97	Marford	Head	Mar	39	M	Agric Lab	Herts	Wheathampstead
477	WOODWARDS	Caroline	97		Wife	Mar	38	F	Straw Plaiter	Herts	Wheathampstead
478	WOODWARDS	William	97		Son	Unm	17	M	Farmers Boy	Herts	Wheathampstead
479	WOODWARDS	James	97		Son	Unm	13	M	Farmers Boy	Herts	Wheathampstead
480	WOODWARDS	Charlotte	97		Dau		11	F	Straw Plaiter	Herts	Wheathampstead
481	WOODWARDS	Ann	97		Dau		7	F	Straw Plaiter	Herts	Wheathampstead
482	WOODWARDS	Alfred	97		Son		9	M	Straw Plaiter	Herts	Wheathampstead
483	WOODWARDS	John	97		Son		6	M	Straw Plaiter	Herts	Wheathampstead
484	WOODWARDS	Ellen	97		Dau		4	F		Herts	Wheathampstead
485	WOODWARDS	George	97		Son		2	M		Herts	Wheathampstead
486	WOODWARDS	Emma	97		Dau		2m	F		Herts	Wheathampstead
487	FLOYD	Elizabeth	98	Marford	Head	Widow	45	F	Straw Plaiter	Herts	Wheathampstead
488	FLOYD	Caroline	98		Dau	Unm	19	F	Straw Plaiter	Herts	Wheathampstead
489	FLOYD	Phillis	98		Dau	Unm	15	F	Straw Plaiter	Herts	Wheathampstead
490	FLOYD	George	99	Marford	Head	Mar	44	M	Brewers Lab	Herts	Wheathampstead
491	FLOYD	Mary	99		Wife	Mar	45	F	Straw Plaiter	Herts	Wheathampstead
492	FLOYD	Mary	99		Dau	Unm	11	F	Straw Plaiter	Herts	Wheathampstead
493	FLOYD	James	99		Son		8	M	Scholar	Herts	Wheathampstead
494	FLOYD	Ruth	99		Dau		4	F	Scholar	Herts	Wheathampstead
495	GRAY	Samuel	100	Marford (Melbourne Arms)	Head	Mar	42	M	Sawyer & Keeper of Beer Shop	Herts	Wheathampstead
496	GRAY	Mary Ann	100		Wife	Mar	36	F		Herts	Wheathampstead
497	GRAY	James	100		Son	Unm	13	M	Agric Lab	Herts	Wheathampstead
498	GRAY	Jesse	100		Son		10	M	Scholar	Herts	Wheathampstead
499	GRAY	Martha	100		Dau		8	F	Scholar	Herts	Wheathampstead
500	GRAY	Henry	100		Son		6	M		Herts	Wheathampstead
501	GRAY	Mary	100		Dau		2	F		Herts	Wheathampstead

	SURNAME	FORENAME	SCHEDULE NUMBER	ADDRESS	RELATIONSHIP	STATUS	AGE	SEX	OCCUPATION	COUNTY OF BIRTH	PLACE OF BIRTH
502	CLARK	George	100		Nephew		7	M	Scholar	Herts	Welwyn
503	GRAY	James	101	Marford	Head	Mar	58	M	Sawyer	Herts	Wheathampstead
504	GRAY	Elizabeth	101		Wife	Mar	57	F	Sawyers Wife	Herts	Colney Heath
505	GRAY	Samuel	101		Son	Unm	20	M	Sawyer	Herts	Hatfield
506	GRAY	Mercy	101		Dau	Unm	11	F	Scholar	Herts	Wheathampstead
507	GRAY	John	101		Grandson		3	M	Butchers Son	Herts	Wheathampstead
508	BRUTON	George	101		Son-in-law	Mar	23	M	Sawyer	Herts	Wheathampstead
509	BRUTON	Jane	101		Dau	Mar	24	F	Sawyers Wife	Herts	Hatfield
510	FRANKLIN	Henry	102	Marford	Head	Mar	41	M	Agric Lab	Herts	Sandridge
511	FRANKLIN	Jane	102		Wife	Mar	50	F	Plaiter	Herts	Wheathampstead
512	FRANKLIN	Jane	102		Dau	Unm	14	F	Plaiter	Herts	Wheathampstead
513	FRANKLIN	Mary	102		Dau	Unm	12	F	Scholar (partially deaf)	Herts	Wheathampstead
514	FRANKLIN	Henry	102		Son		10	M	Scholar	Herts	Wheathampstead
515	FRANKLIN	Charles	102		Son		8	M	Scholar	Herts	Wheathampstead
516	DAY	James	103	Marford	Head	Mar	35	M	Agric Lab	Herts	Wheathampstead
517	DAY	Maria	103		Wife	Mar	38	F	Plaiter (Deaf)	Herts	Wheathampstead
518	DAY	Mary	103		Dau	Unm	14	F	Plaiter	Herts	Wheathampstead
519	DAY	William	103		Son	Unm	7	M	Scholar	Herts	Wheathampstead
520	DAY	Sophia	103		Dau		6	F		Herts	Wheathampstead
521	DAY	John	103		Son		4	M		Herts	Wheathampstead
522	DAY	Charles	103		Son		1	M		Herts	Wheathampstead

The end of the Hamlet of Marford in the parish of Wheathampstead

	SURNAME	FORENAME	SCHEDULE NUMBER	ADDRESS	RELATIONSHIP	STATUS	AGE	SEX	OCCUPATION	COUNTY OF BIRTH	PLACE OF BIRTH
523	HUMPHREY	James	104	Wheathampstead Hill	Head	Mar	54	M	Agric Lab	Herts	Wheathampstead
524	HUMPHREY	Jane	104		Wife	Mar	54	F	Straw Plaiter	Herts	Wheathampstead
525	HUMPHREY	George	104		Son	Unm	12	M	Farmers Boy	Herts	Wheathampstead
526	HUMPHREY	Charles	104		Son		10	M	Farmers Boy	Herts	Wheathampstead
527	LEWIN	Mary	104		Sister-in-law	Unm	56	F	Straw Plaiter	Herts	Wheathampstead
528	PEACOCK	William	105	Wheathampstead Hill	Head	Mar	56	M	Agric Lab	Herts	Wheathampstead
529	PEACOCK	Mary	105		Wife	Mar	46	F	Plaiter	Herts	Sandridge
530	WARNER	Edward	106	Wheathampstead Hill	Head	Mar	57	M	Agric Lab	Herts	Wheathampstead
531	WARNER	Mary	106		Wife	Mar	58	F	Plaiter	Herts	Wheathampstead
532	WARNER	Betsy	106		Dau	Unm	21	F	Plaiter	Herts	Wheathampstead
533	WARNER	David	106		Son	Unm	18	M	Agric Lab	Herts	Wheathampstead
534	WARNER	Harriet	106		Dau		7	F	Plaiter	Herts	Wheathampstead
535	ARNOLD	James	107	Wheathampstead Hill	Head	Mar	64	M	Cordwainer	Herts	Kings Walden
536	ARNOLD	Ann	107		Wife	Mar	81	F		Middx	Unknown
537	FARNELL	Charles	108	The King William, Wheathampstead Hill	Head	Mar	51	M	Plumber & Victualler	Beds	Ampthill
538	FARNELL	Jane	108		Wife	Mar	50	F		Beds	Luton
539	CRANE	George	108		Lodger	Unm	18	M	Groom	Herts	Barnet
540	SOLLOWAY	Samuel	108		Lodger	Unm	19	M	Groom	Herts	Baldock
541	NIGHTGALE	John	108		Lodger	Unm	18	M	Horse Trainer	Herts	Brickwall

The end of the District 1a in the parish of Wheathampstead in the County of Hertford.

Registrar's District: Harpenden   Enumeration District 1b   Ref. HO107/1713 folios 11-41

All that part of the parish of Wheathampstead which lies to the west of the road leading from St Albans to Kimpton and to the north of the road leading from Wheathampstead to Luton, including part of Gustard Wood, Hog Island, Turners Hall Farm, Raisins, Bower Heath, the Hill, Great and Little Cutts, Marshalls Heath and thence to Wheathampstead

542	BARNES	James	1	Larner Lane	Head	Mar	57	M	Retired Glazier	London	London City
543	BARNES	Mary	1		Wife	Mar	61	F	Retired Glaziers Wife	Suffolk	Glemham
544	ENGLAND	Hannah	1		Serv	Unm	18	F	House Servant	Herts	Sandridge
545	NASH	Robert	2	Larner Lane	Head	Mar	74	M	Timber Merchant	Herts	Wheathampstead
546	NASH	Sarah	2		Wife	Mar	68	F	Timber Merchants Wife	Herts	Wheathampstead
547	BROWN	George	3	Village	Head	Mar	50	M	Builder	Herts	Wheathampstead
548	BROWN	Mary	3		Wife	Mar	42	F	Builders Wife	Cornwall	Penzance
549	BROWN	Sarah	3		Dau	Unm	22	F	Builders Daughter	Herts	Wheathampstead
550	BROWN	Henry	3		Son	Unm	19	M	Builder	Herts	Wheathampstead
551	BROWN	Emily	3		Dau	Unm	18	F	Builders Daughter	Herts	Wheathampstead
552	BROWN	Fanny	3		Dau	Unm	15	F	Builders Daughter	Herts	Wheathampstead
553	BROWN	Julia	3		Dau	Unm	13	F	Builders Daughter	Herts	Wheathampstead
554	BROWN	Emily	3		Grandau	Unm	3	F	Builders Grand Daughter	London	Borough
555	SIMONS	George	4	Village	Head	Mar	30	M	Butcher	Herts	Harpenden
556	SIMONS	Eliza	4		Wife	Mar	33	F	Butchers Wife	Herts	St Stephens
557	SIMONS	Mary	4		Dau		5	F	Butchers Daughter	Herts	Wheathampstead
558	SIMONS	Emma	4		Dau		2	F	Butchers Daur	Herts	Wheathampstead
559	SIMONS	Robert	4		Son		1	M	Butchers Son	Herts	Wheathampstead
560	SIMONS	Harriett	4		Dau		1	F	Butchers Daur	Herts	Wheathampstead
561	NEAL	Richard	4		Nephew		11	M	Butchers Boy	Herts	Watford
562	CRAFT	Elizabeth	4		Serv		17	F	House Servant	Herts	St Stephens
563	HALSEY	Joseph	5	Village	Head	Widower	50	M	Cordwainer	Herts	Sandridge
564	HALSEY	Joseph	5		Son	Unm	31	M	Labourer	Herts	Wheathampstead
565	HALSEY	Sarah	5		Dau	Unm	28	F	Hat Maker	Herts	Wheathampstead
566	HALSEY	William	5		Son	Unm	22	M	Labourer	Herts	Wheathampstead
567	HALSEY	John	5		Son	Unm	18	M	Labourer	Herts	Wheathampstead
568	HALSEY	Susan	5		Dau	Unm	16	F	Hat Maker	Herts	Wheathampstead
569	HALSEY	Mercy	5		Dau	Unm	13	F	Hat Maker	Herts	Wheathampstead
570	HALSEY	Charles B	5		Grandson		8	M		Herts	Wheathampstead
571	HALSEY	George B	5		Grandson		5	M		Herts	Wheathampstead
572	HALSEY	Elizabeth B	5		Grandau		1	F		Herts	Wheathampstead
573	ARCHER	William	6	Gustard Wood	Head	Mar	44	M	Shepherd	Herts	Wheathampstead
574	ARCHER	Mary	6		Wife	Mar	43	F	Shepherds Wife	Herts	Wheathampstead
575	ARCHER	George	6		Son	Unm	16	M	Agric Lab	Herts	Wheathampstead
576	ARCHER	Sarah	6		Dau		13	F	Scholar	Herts	Wheathampstead
577	ARCHER	Elizabeth	6		Dau		10	F	Scholar	Herts	Wheathampstead
578	RUSSEL	Francis	7	Gustard Wood	Head	Mar	26	M	Agric Lab	Herts	Kings Walden
579	RUSSEL	Lucy	7		Wife	Mar	26	F	Agric Labs Wife	Herts	Redbourn
580	RUSSEL	Sarah J	7		Dau		4	F	Agric Labs Daughter	Herts	Wheathampstead

	SURNAME	FORENAME	SCHEDULE NUMBER	ADDRESS	RELATIONSHIP	STATUS	AGE	SEX	OCCUPATION	COUNTY OF BIRTH	PLACE OF BIRTH
581	RUSSEL	Ann M	7		Dau		2	F	Agric Labs Daughter	Herts	Wheathampstead
582	WILSON	Edward	7		Serv	Unm	17	M	Agric Lab	Herts	Hitchin
583	KILBY	John	8	Gustard Wood	Head	Mar	54	M	Carpenter (Master) employing 5 men & 2 labs	Herts	Wheathampstead
584	KILBY	Mary Ann	8		Wife	Mar	55	F	Carpenters Wife	Herts	Sandridge
585	KILBY	Sarah	8		Dau	Unm	19	F	Carpenters Daur	Herts	Wheathampstead
586	KILBY	Alfred	8		Son		13	M	Scholar	Herts	Wheathampstead
587	WRIGHT	Sarah	9	Gustard Wood	Head	Unm	47	F	Straw Plaiter	Herts	Kimpton
588	GILBERT	William	9		Lodger	Mar	38	M	Tailor	Herts	St Albans
589	GILBERT	Louisa	9		Wife	Mar	37	F	Tailors Wife	Herts	Kimpton
590	GILBERT	William	9		Son		6	M	Tailors Son	Herts	Wheathampstead
591	GILBERT	Henry	9		Son		4	M	Tailors Son	Herts	Wheathampstead
592	GILBERT	Emily	9		Dau		3	F	Tailors Daur	Herts	Wheathampstead
593	LINES	William	10	Gustard Wood	Head	Mar	32	M	Blacksmith	Herts	Wheathampstead
594	LINES	Ann	10		Wife	Mar	35	F	Blacksmiths Wife	Herts	Wheathampstead
595	LINES	Harriet	10		Dau		8	F	Blacksmiths Daur	Herts	Wheathampstead
596	LINES	Alfred	10		Son		5	M	Blacksmiths Son	Herts	Wheathampstead
597	LINES	George	10		Son		2	M	Blacksmiths Son	Herts	Wheathampstead
598	LINES	Ann	10		Dau		11 m	F	Blacksmiths Daur	Herts	Wheathampstead
599	MUNT	William	10		Appr	Unm	20	M	Shop Apprentice	Herts	Wheathampstead
600	PLUMB	Sarah	10		Serv	Unm	15	F	House Servant	Herts	Woolmer Green
601	ARCHER	George	11	Gustard Wood	Head	Mar	41	M	Agric Lab	Herts	Wheathampstead
602	ARCHER	Ann	11		Wife	Mar	35	F	Agric Labs Wife	Herts	Wheathampstead
603	ARCHER	Mary Ann	11		Dau	Unm	15	F	Straw Plaiter	Herts	Wheathampstead
604	ARCHER	Maria	11		Dau		12	F	Straw Plaiter	Herts	Wheathampstead
605	ARCHER	Esther	11		Dau		7	F	Straw Plaiter	Herts	Wheathampstead
606	ARCHER	Sarah	11		Dau		5	F	Scholar	Herts	Wheathampstead
607	ARCHER	Jane	11		Dau		3	F		Herts	Wheathampstead
608	ARCHER	Elizabeth	11		Dau		1	F		Herts	Wheathampstead
609	EPHGRAVE	Thomas	12	Gustard Wood Hearns Farm	Head	Mar	65	M	Farmer of 140 acres employing 7 men & 2 boys	Herts	Wheathampstead
610	EPHGRAVE	Elizabeth	12		Wife	Mar	60	F	Farmers Wife	Herts	Wheathampstead
611	EPHGRAVE	Frederick	12		Son	Unm	24	M	Farmers Son	Herts	Wheathampstead
612	EPHGRAVE	Ann E	12		Grandau		8	F	Scholar	London	Southwark
613	EPHGRAVE	Thomas	12		Grandson		6	M	Scholar	London	Ludgate Hill
614	PEARCE	Charles	12		Serv	Unm	18	M	Agric Lab	Herts	Offley
615	EDMONDS	George	12		Serv	Unm	16	M	Agric Lab	Herts	Wheathampstead
616	RAFT	Joseph	13	Gustard Wood	Head	Mar	42	M	Agric Lab	Herts	Kimpton
617	RAFT	Hannah	13		Wife	Mar	34	F	Agric Labs Wife	Herts	Wheathampstead
618	RAFT	Edith	13		Dau		9	F	Straw Plaiter	Herts	Wheathampstead
619	RAFT	Amos	13		Son		4	M	Scholar	Herts	Wheathampstead
620	SAUNDERS	John	14	Gustard Wood	Head	Mar	38	M	Agric Lab	Herts	Ippollitts
621	SAUNDERS	Sarah	14		Wife	Mar	41	F	Agric Labs Wife	Herts	Offley
622	SAUNDERS	Alfred	14		Son		14	M	Farm Labourer	Herts	Wheathampstead
623	SAUNDERS	Abraham	14		Son		12	M	Farm Labourer	Herts	Wheathampstead

624	SAUNDERS	George	14		Son		10	M	Farm Labourer	Herts	Wheathampstead
625	SAUNDERS	Mary	14		Dau		8	F	Scholar	Herts	Wheathampstead
626	SAUNDERS	Mark	14		Son		6	M	Scholar	Herts	Wheathampstead
627	SAUNDERS	Emily	14		Dau		4	F	Scholar	Herts	Wheathampstead
628	SAUNDERS	Henry	14		Son		1	M		Herts	Wheathampstead
629	WILSHIRE	William	15	Gustard Wood	Head	Mar	42	M	Cow Man	Herts	St Pauls Walden
630	WILSHIRE	Frances	15		Wife	Mar	47	F	Cowmans Wife	Beds	[Unknown]
631	DAY	William	16	Gustard Wood	Head	Mar	50	M	Agric Lab	Herts	Hitchin
632	DAY	Esther	16		Wife	Mar	44	F	Agric Labs Wife	Herts	Preston
633	DAY	Rebecca	16		Dau	Unm	17	F	Straw Plaiter	Herts	Kimpton
634	DAY	Mille	16		Dau		12	F	Scholar	Herts	Kimpton
635	DAY	Samuel	16		Son		10	M	Scholar	Herts	Wheathampstead
636	GIBBS	Thomas	17	Gustard Wood	Head	Mar	30	M	Agric Lab	Herts	Wheathampstead
637	GIBBS	Susan	17		Wife	Mar	28	F	Agric Labs Wife	Herts	Wheathampstead
638	GIBBS	William	17		Son		9	M	Scholar	Herts	Wheathampstead
639	GIBBS	Lydia	17		Dau		2	F		Herts	Wheathampstead
640	WOOD	Thomas	18	Gustard Wood	Head	Mar	48	M	Agric Lab	Herts	Wheathampstead
641	WOOD	Susan	18		Wife	Mar	38	F	Agric Labs Wife	Herts	Wheathampstead
642	WOOD	Jessey	18		Son	Unm	14	M	Agric Lab	Herts	Wheathampstead
643	WOOD	Ellen	18		Dau		11	F	Straw Plaiter	Herts	Wheathampstead
644	WOOD	Prentice	18		Son		9	M	Scholar	Herts	Wheathampstead
645	WOOD	Frederick	18		Son		6	M	Scholar	Herts	Wheathampstead
646	WOOD	Louisa	18		Dau		4	F		Herts	Wheathampstead
647	WOOD	Caroline	18		Dau		2	F		Herts	Wheathampstead
648	WOOD	Arthur	18		Son		2m	M		Herts	Wheathampstead
649	FIELD	James	19	Gustard Wood	Head	Mar	53	M	Agric Lab	Herts	Wheathampstead
650	FIELD	Mary	19		Wife	Mar	48	F	Agric Labs Wife	Herts	Wheathampstead
651	FIELD	Sarah	19		Dau	Unm	19	F	Straw Plaiter	Herts	Wheathampstead
652	FIELD	James	19		Son		14	M	Agric Lab	Herts	Wheathampstead
653	FIELD	Mary Ann	19		Dau		9	F	Scholar	Herts	Wheathampstead
654	FIELD	Charlotte	19		Dau		7	F	Scholar	Herts	Wheathampstead
655	BANGS	John	20	Gustard Wood	Head	Widower	23	M	Agric Lab	Herts	Kimpton
656	BANGS	Henry	20		Son		1	M		Herts	Wheathampstead
657	FIELD	Eliza	20		Lodger	Unm	26	F	Straw Plaiter	Herts	Ayot St Lawrence
658	FIELD	Ann	20		Lodger	Unm	17	F	Straw Plaiter	Herts	Wheathampstead
659	SMITH	William	21	Gustard Wood	Head	Mar	56	M	Agric Lab	Herts	St Pauls Walden
660	SMITH	Sarah	21		Wife	Mar	61	F	Agric Labs Wife	Herts	Wheathampstead
661	SMITH	Charlotte	21		Dau	Unm	25	F	Dress Maker	Herts	Wheathampstead
662	VAUGHAN	James	22	Gustard Wood	Head	Mar	37	M	Agric Lab	Herts	Kimpton
663	VAUGHAN	Sarah	22		Wife	Mar	36	F	Agric Labs Wife	Herts	Kimpton
664	VAUGHAN	Ann	22		Dau	Unm	15	F	Straw Plaiter	Herts	Kimpton
665	VAUGHAN	Daniel	22		Son		6	M	Scholar	Herts	Wheathampstead
666	VAUGHAN	Arthur	22		Son		4	M		Herts	Wheathampstead
667	VAUGHAN	Emma	22		Dau		3	F		Herts	Wheathampstead
668	VAUGHAN	Harriett	22		Dau		5m	F		Herts	Wheathampstead

	SURNAME	FORENAME	SCHEDULE NUMBER	ADDRESS	RELATIONSHIP	STATUS	AGE	SEX	OCCUPATION	COUNTY OF BIRTH	PLACE OF BIRTH
669	SLOUGH	Frederick	23	Gustard Wood	Head	Mar	21	M	Agric Lab	Herts	Wheathampstead
670	SLOUGH	Ann	23		Wife	Mar	27	F	Agric Labs Wife	Herts	Wheathampstead
671	DAUBIN	William	24	Gustard Wood	Head	Mar	56	M	Agric Lab	Beds	Lilley
672	DAUBIN	Susan	24		Wife	Mar	50	F	Agric Labs Wife	Herts	Wheathampstead
673	DAUBIN	Jane	24		Dau	Unm	16	F	Straw Plaiter	Herts	Wheathampstead
674	DAUBIN	Mary	24		Dau		11	F	Scholar	Herts	Wheathampstead
675	DAUBIN	Thomas	24		Son		7	M	Scholar	Herts	Wheathampstead
676	EPHGRAVE	Charles	25	Gustard Wood	Head	Mar	37	M	Carpenter	Herts	Wheathampstead
677	EPHGRAVE	Sarah	25		Wife	Mar	34	F	Carpenters Wife	Herts	Wheathampstead
678	EPHGRAVE	Arthur	25		Son		11	M	Farmers Boy	Herts	Wheathampstead
679	EPHGRAVE	Walter	25		Son		10	M	Scholar	Herts	Wheathampstead
680	EPHGRAVE	Alfred	25		Son		8	M	Scholar	Herts	Wheathampstead
681	EPHGRAVE	Harriet	25		Dau		7	F	Scholar	Herts	Wheathampstead
682	EPHGRAVE	Henry	25		Son		5	M	Scholar	Herts	Wheathampstead
683	EPHGRAVE	George	25		Son		3	M		Herts	Wheathampstead
684	EPHGRAVE	Julia	25		Dau		2	F		Herts	Wheathampstead
685	EPHGRAVE	Emily	25		Dau		7m	F		Herts	Wheathampstead
686	EDMONS	John	26	Gustard Wood	Head	Mar	39	M	Agric Lab	Herts	Wheathampstead
687	EDMONS	Elizabeth	26		Wife	Mar	39	F	Agric Labs Wife	Herts	Wheathampstead
688	EDMONS	Sarah	26		Dau		12	F	Scholar	Herts	Wheathampstead
689	EDMONS	Elizabeth	26		Dau		9	F	Scholar	Herts	Wheathampstead
690	EDMONS	Walter	26		Son		6	M	Scholar	Herts	Wheathampstead
691	EDMONS	Arther	26		Son		3	M		Herts	Wheathampstead
692	EDMONS	Harriet	26		Dau		6m	F		Herts	Wheathampstead
693	DOLLIMORE	Henry	27	Gustard Wood	Head	Mar	27	M	Agric Lab	Herts	Codicote
694	DOLLIMORE	Ann	27		Wife	Mar	21	F	Agric Labs Wife	Herts	Kimpton
695	DOLLIMORE	George	27		Son		3m	M		Herts	Wheathampstead
696	WHEELER	Isaac	28	Gustard Wood	Head	Mar	36	M	Agric Lab	Herts	Harpenden
697	WHEELER	Emma	28		Wife	Mar	38	F	Agric Labs Wife	Herts	Wheathampstead
698	WHEELER	Elizabeth	28		Dau	Unm	17	F	Straw Plaiter	Herts	St Albans
699	WHEELER	Joseph	28		Son		9	M	Scholar	Herts	Wheathampstead
700	WHEELER	Eliza	28		Dau		7	F	Straw Plaiter	Herts	Wheathampstead
701	WHEELER	Ann	28		Dau		4	F	Straw Plaiter	Herts	Wheathampstead
702	WHEELER	Sarah	28		Dau		1	F		Herts	Wheathampstead
703	TEMPEL	Joseph	29	Gustard Wood	Head	Mar	35	M	Agric Lab	Herts	Bedmond [Abbots Langley]
704	TEMPEL	Susan	29		Wife	Mar	37	F	Agric Labs Wife	Herts	Wheathampstead
705	TEMPEL	David	29		Son		7	M		Herts	Wheathampstead
706	TEMPEL	William	29		Son		5	M		Herts	Wheathampstead
707	TEMPEL	Mary	29		Dau		2	F		Herts	Wheathampstead
708	DEAMER	Phebe	30	Gustard Wood	Head	Widow	70	F	Straw Plaiter	Herts	Kimpton
709	DEAMER	George	30		Son	Unm	36	M	Agric Lab	Herts	Kimpton
710	THOMPSON	John	31	Gustard Wood	Head	Mar	60	M	Agric Lab	Herts	Lilley
711	THOMPSON	Hannah	31		Wife	Mar	60	F	Agric Labs Wife	Herts	Codicote
712	THOMPSON	John	31		Son	Unm	20	M	Agric Lab	Herts	Codicote

713	THOMPSON	Charles	32	Gustard Wood	Head	Mar	24	M	Agric Lab	Herts	Codicote
714	THOMPSON	Mary	32		Wife	Mar	21	F	Agric Labs Wife	Herts	Kimpton
715	THOMPSON	George	32		Son		1	M		Herts	Wheathampstead
716	SMITH	James	33	Gustard Wood	Head	Mar	23	M	Agric Lab	Herts	Wheathampstead
717	SMITH	Harriett	33		Wife	Mar	21	F	Agric Labs Wife	Herts	Kimpton
718	JEEVES	William	34	Gustard Wood	Head	Mar	42	M	Agric Lab	Middx	London
719	JEEVES	Sophia	34		Wife	Mar	40	F	Agric Labs Wife	Herts	Kimpton
720	JEEVES	Ann	34		Dau		13	F	Straw Plaiter	Herts	Kimpton
721	JEEVES	Emma	34		Dau		10	F	Straw Plaiter	Herts	Kimpton
722	JEEVES	Eliza	34		Dau		8	F		Herts	Kimpton
723	JEEVES	Louis	34		Son		5	M		Herts	Wheathampstead
724	JEEVES	Susannah	34		Dau		9m	F		Herts	Wheathampstead
725	ALLEN	John	35	Gustard Wood	Head	Mar	32	M	Agric Lab	Beds	Barton
726	ALLEN	Sophia	35		Wife	Mar	28	F	Agric Labs Wife	Herts	Kimpton
727	ALLEN	Ann	35		Dau		7	F	Straw Plaiter	Herts	Kimpton
728	ALLEN	Sarah	35		Dau		3	F		Herts	Wheathampstead
729	ALLEN	Henry	35		Son		8m	M		Herts	Wheathampstead
730	DAWS	James	35		Lodger	Unm	70	M	Agric Lab	Herts	Kimpton
731	SIBLEY	Edward	36	Gustard Wood	Head	Mar	52	M	Grocer	Herts	Wheathampstead
732	SIBLEY	Maria	36		Wife	Mar	42	F	Grocers Wife	Herts	Kimpton
733	SIBLEY	Henry	36		Son	Unm	16	M	Baker	Herts	Wheathampstead
734	SIBLEY	John	36		Son		11	M	Scholar	Herts	Wheathampstead
735	BOON	John	37	Gustard Wood	Head	Mar	27	M	Agric Lab	Herts	Wheathampstead
736	BOON	Ellen	37		Wife	Mar	51	F	Agric Labs Wife	Herts	Redbourn
737	MATHEWS	James	37		Son-in-law	Mar	22	M	Agric Lab	Herts	Kimpton
738	MATHEWS	Eliza	37		Dau-in-law	Mar	20	F	Agric Labs Wife	Herts	Kimpton
739	WHEELER	Thomas	37		Son-in-law	Unm	17	M	Agric Lab	Herts	Wheathampstead
740	WHEELER	Henry	37		Son-in-law		15	M	Agric Lab	Herts	Wheathampstead
741	WHEELER	John	37		Son-in-law		6	M	Son at home	Herts	Wheathampstead
742	SLOUGH	William	38	Gustard Wood	Head	Mar	53	M	Agric Lab	Herts	Wheathampstead
743	SLOUGH	Matilda	38		Wife	Mar	37	F	Agric Labs Wife	Herts	Wheathampstead
744	SLOUGH	Mary	38		Dau	Unm	18	F	Straw Plaiter	Herts	Wheathampstead
745	SLOUGH	Edmund	38		Son		11	M		Herts	Wheathampstead
746	SLOUGH	John	38		Son		6	M		Herts	Wheathampstead
747	SLOUGH	Arthur	38		Son		2	M		Herts	Wheathampstead
748	CATLIN	George	39	Gustard Wood	Head	Unm	37	M	Agric Lab	Herts	Wheathampstead
749	STUDMAN	Susan	39		Lodger	Unm	47	F	Straw Plaiter	Herts	Wheathampstead
750	SWALLOW	Ann	39		Lodger		8	F	Straw Plaiter	Herts	Wheathampstead
751	BOSHER	James	40	Gustard Wood	Head	Mar	33	M	Gardener	Herts	Wheathampstead
752	BOSHER	Emma	40		Wife	Mar	22	F	Gardeners Wife	Herts	Wheathampstead
753	BOSHER	Julia	40		Dau		6m	F		Herts	Wheathampstead
754	NORTH	William	41	Gustard Wood	Head	Mar	58	M	Agric Lab	Herts	Wheathampstead
755	NORTH	Sarah	41		Wife	Mar	40	F	Agric Labs Wife	Herts	Codicote
756	NORTH	James	41		Son	Unm	22	M	Agric Lab	Herts	Kimpton
757	NORTH	Daniel	41		Son	Unm	17	M	Agric Lab	Herts	Kimpton

	SURNAME	FORENAME	SCHEDULE NUMBER	ADDRESS	RELATIONSHIP	STATUS	AGE	SEX	OCCUPATION	COUNTY OF BIRTH	PLACE OF BIRTH
758	NORTH	Louisa	41		Dau		16	F	Straw Plaiter	Herts	Kimpton
759	NORTH	Selina	41		Dau		14	F	Scholar	Herts	Kimpton
760	NORTH	Samuel	41		Son		10	M	Scholar	Herts	Wheathampstead
761	NORTH	Alfred	41		Son		8	M	Scholar	Herts	Wheathampstead
762	CARTER	George	42	Gustard Wood	Head	Mar	37	M	Agric Lab	Herts	Wheathampstead
763	CARTER	Mary	42		Wife	Mar	36	F	Agric Labs Wife	Herts	Sandridge
764	CARTER	Caroline	42		Dau		12	F	Straw Plaiter	Herts	Wheathampstead
765	CARTER	Sarah	42		Dau		9	F	Straw Plaiter	Herts	Wheathampstead
766	CARTER	Mercy	42		Dau		4	F		Herts	Wheathampstead
767	CARTER	William	42		Son		1	M		Herts	Wheathampstead
768	WRIGHT	George	43	Gustard Wood	Head	Mar	32	M	Agric Lab	Herts	Wheathampstead
769	WRIGHT	Sarah	43		Wife	Mar	34	F	Agric Labs Wife	Herts	Wheathampstead
770	WRIGHT	Frederick	43		Son		8	M	Scholar	Herts	Wheathampstead
771	WRIGHT	Daniel	43		Son		5	M		Herts	Wheathampstead
772	WRIGHT	James	43		Son		1	M		Herts	Wheathampstead
773	PEW	George	44	Gustard Wood	Head	Mar	40	M	Retired Carpenter. Owner of Houses	Herts	East Barnet
774	PEW	Catharine	44		Wife	Mar	30	F	Retired Carpenters Wife	Herts	Hatfield
775	PEW	James	44		Son		16	M		Herts	Wheathampstead
776	PEW	Mary	44		Dau		14	F		Herts	Wheathampstead
777	PEW	Harriett	44		Dau		4	F		Herts	Wheathampstead
778	PEW	Henry	44		Son		3	M		Herts	Wheathampstead
779	PEW	John	44		Son		1	M		Herts	Wheathampstead
780	BOZIER	Ann	45	Gustard Wood	Head	Unm	29	F	Straw Plaiter	Herts	Wheathampstead
781	BOZIER	Thomas	45		Brother	Unm	20	M	Agric Lab	Herts	Wheathampstead
782	SIBLEY	Thomas	46	Gustard Wood	Head	Mar	34	M	Baker	Herts	Wheathampstead
783	SIBLEY	Matilda	46		Wife	Mar	36	F	formerly Needle Woman	Bucks	Gt Brickhill
784	SIBLEY	Edwin S	46		Son		7	M	Scholar	Herts	Wheathampstead
785	SIBLEY	George F	46		Son		2	M		Herts	Wheathampstead
786	LEE	James	47	Gustard Wood	Head	Mar	34	M	Agric Lab	Herts	St Pauls Walden
787	LEE	Eliza	47		Wife	Mar	34	F	Agric Labs Wife	Herts	Hitchin
788	WOOD	Abraham	47		Son-in-law	Unm	13	M	Agric Lab	Herts	Codicote
789	WOOD	Emma	47		Dau-in-law		11	F	Straw Plaiter	Herts	Kimpton
790	LEE	James	47		Son		4	M		Herts	Whitwell
791	LEE	Stephen	47		Son		1	M		Herts	Whitwell
792	PARSONS	Thomas	48	Gustard Wood	Head	Mar	75	M	Agric Lab	Herts	Wheathampstead
793	PARSONS	Elizabeth	48		Wife	Mar	74	F	Agric Labs Wife	Herts	Wheathampstead
794	ARCHER	Thomas	49	Gustard Wood	Head	Mar	34	M	Agric Lab	Herts	Wheathampstead
795	ARCHER	Elizabeth	49		Wife	Mar	30	F	Agric Labs Wife	Herts	Kimpton
796	ARCHER	Thomas	49		Son		10	M	Farm Boy	Herts	Wheathampstead
797	ARCHER	Susannah	49		Dau		7	F	Scholar	Herts	Wheathampstead
798	EDMONDS	James	50	Gustard Wood	Head	Mar	43	M	Agric Lab	Herts	Wheathampstead
799	EDMONDS	Mary	50		Wife	Mar	46	F	Agric Labs Wife	Herts	Wheathampstead
800	EDMONDS	Hannah	50		Dau		11	F	Straw Plaiter	Herts	Wheathampstead
801	EDMONDS	Sarah	50		Dau		9	F	Straw Plaiter	Herts	Wheathampstead

No.	Surname	Forename		Place	Relation	Status	Age	Sex	Occupation	County	Birthplace
802	EDMONDS	Elizabeth	50		Dau		7	F		Herts	Wheathampstead
803	EDMONDS	Eliza	50		Dau		4	F		Herts	Wheathampstead
804	FISHER	Joseph	50		Lodger	Mar	21	M	Agric Lab	Herts	Wheathampstead
805	FISHER	Ann	50		Lodgers Wife	Mar	22	F	Agric Labs Wife	Herts	Stevenage
806	SIBLEY	Eliza	51	Gustard Wood	Head	Unm	25	F	Baker	Herts	Wheathampstead
807	PEW	Sarah	51		Visitor	Unm	20	F	Dress Maker	Herts	Wheathampstead
808	NORRIS	Mary	52	Gustard Wood	Head	Widow	67	F	Retired Farmer	Oxon	Benson
809	NORRIS	James	52		Son	Unm	28	M	Gardener	Herts	Wheathampstead
810	HENLY	Thomas	53	Gustard Wood	Head	Mar	35	M	Agric Lab	Herts	Wheathampstead
811	HENLY	Sarah	53		Wife	Mar	34	F	Agric Labs Wife	Herts	Kimpton
812	HENLY	Louisa	53		Dau		8	F	Straw Plaiter	Herts	Harpenden
813	HENLY	William	53		Son		5	M		Herts	Harpenden
814	HENLY	George	53		Son		3	M		Herts	Harpenden
815	HENLY	Emma	53		Dau		6m	F		Herts	Wheathampstead
816	POLLARD	Thomas	53		Lodger	Unm	45	M	Agric Lab	Herts	Kimpton
817	POLLARD	William	53		Lodger	Unm	14	M	Agric Lab	Herts	Kimpton
818	HOWARD	Charles E	54	Gustard Wood	Head	Mar	28	M	Beer Seller	Beds	Lilley
819	HOWARD	Jane Ann	54		Wife	Mar	23	F	Beer Sellers Wife	London	Marylebone
820	HOWARD	William	54		Son		4	M	Scholar	Middx	Willesden
821	HOWARD	Jane	54		Dau		2	F		Middx	Willesden
822	HOWARD	Harriet	54		Dau		7wks	F		Herts	Wheathampstead
823	BOON	Henry	55	Gustard Wood	Head	Mar	72	M	Agric Lab	Herts	Wheathampstead
824	BOON	Elizabeth	55		Wife	Mar	63	F	Agric Labs Wife	Beds	Southwold
825	BOON	Henry	55		Son	Unm	20	M	Agric Lab	Herts	Wheathampstead
826	WEBB	Maria	55		Lodger	Unm	26	F	Straw Plaiter	Herts	Redbourn
827	SEARS	Dinah	56	Gustard Wood	Head	Mar	30	F	Straw Plaiter	Herts	Wheathampstead
828	BOON	Emma	56		Dau		11	F	Straw Plaiter	Herts	Wheathampstead
829	BOON	Susan	56		Lodger	Unm	22	F	Straw Plaiter	Herts	Wheathampstead
830	BOON	Harriet	56		Dau		2	F		Herts	Wheathampstead
831	BURTON	William	57	Gustard Wood	Head	Mar	51	M	Agric Lab	Herts	Kimpton
832	BURTON	Hannah	57		Wife	Mar	44	F	Agric Labs Wife	Herts	Kimpton
833	BURTON	Emma	57		Dau	Unm	22	F	Straw Plaiter	Herts	Kimpton
834	BURTON	Joseph	57		Son	Unm	19	M	Agric Lab	Herts	Kimpton
835	BURTON	Sophia	57		Dau	Unm	14	F	Straw Plaiter	Herts	Kimpton
836	BURTON	Charles	57		Son		12	M	Agric Lab	Herts	Kimpton
837	BURTON	William	57		Son		10	M		Herts	Kimpton
838	BURTON	Sarah	57		Dau		7	F	Straw Plaiter	Herts	Wheathampstead
839	BURTON	Maria	57		Dau		2	F		Herts	Wheathampstead
840	WOODWARD	James	58	Gustard Wood	Head	Mar	47	M	Wheelwright	Herts	Kings Langley
841	WOODWARD	Charlotte	58		Wife	Mar	46	F	Wheelwrights Wife	Herts	Hatfield
842	WOODWARD	George	58		Son	Unm	15	M		Middx	Whetstone
843	WOODWARD	Mary A	58		Dau	Unm	13	F		Middx	Enfield
844	WOODWARD	Elizabeth	58		Dau		5	F		Herts	Wheathampstead
845	BROWN	John	59	Gustard Wood	Head	Mar	21	M	Agric Lab	Herts	Wheathampstead

	SURNAME	FORENAME	SCHEDULE NUMBER	ADDRESS	RELATIONSHIP	STATUS	AGE	SEX	OCCUPATION	COUNTY OF BIRTH	PLACE OF BIRTH
846	BROWN	Amelia	59		Wife	Mar	24	F	Agric Labs Wife	Herts	Kimpton
847	BROWN	Louisa	59		Dau		1	F		Herts	Wheathampstead
848	COALMAN	William	60	Gustard Wood	Head	Mar	45	M	Shoemaker	[Sussex]	Brighton
849	COALMAN	Charlotte	60		Wife	Mar	44	F	Shoemakers Wife	Beds	Evershaw
850	COALMAN	William	60		Son	Unm	23	M	Agric Lab	Beds	Evershaw
851	COALMAN	Sarah A	60		Dau	Unm	16	F	Straw Plaiter	Beds	Evershaw
852	COALMAN	Louisa	60		Dau		14	F	Straw Plaiter	Beds	Evershaw
853	COALMAN	Thomas	60		Son		10	M	Scholar	Beds	Evershaw
854	COALMAN	Henry	60		Son		6	M		Beds	Evershaw
855	COALMAN	Elizabeth	60		Dau		1	F		Bucks	Mentmore
856	ARCHER	William	61	Hog Island	Head	Mar	72	M	Carpenter	Herts	Wheathampstead
857	ARCHER	Jane	61		Wife	Mar	69	F	Carpenters Wife	Herts	Wheathampstead
858	ARCHER	James	61		Son	Mar	27	M	Agric Lab	Herts	Wheathampstead
859	ARCHER	Hannah	61		Dau-in-law	Mar	27	F	Agric Labs Wife	Herts	Kimpton
860	ARCHER	Ann	61		Grandau		4	F		Herts	Wheathampstead
861	ARCHER	Joseph	61		Grandson		1	M		Herts	Wheathampstead
862	BLAIN	Thomas	62	Turners Hall Farm	Head	Mar	40	M	Farmer of 186 acres employing 8 labourers	Herts	Wheathampstead
863	BLAIN	Elizabeth	62		Wife	Mar	41	F	Farmers Wife	Herts	Sandridge
864	BLAIN	Eleanor	62		Dau	Unm	20	F	Farmers Daur	Herts	Wheathampstead
865	BLAIN	William	62		Son	Unm	19	M	Farmers Son	Herts	Sandridge
866	BLAIN	George	62		Son	Unm	16	M	Farmers Son	Herts	Sandridge
867	BLAIN	Charles	62		Son		6	M	Farmers Son	Herts	Wheathampstead
868	WEATHERLEY	Ellen	62		Visitor	Unm	15	F	Servant	Herts	St Peters
869	BRADBURY	Thomas	62		Serv	Unm	20	M	Agric Lab	Herts	Redbourn
870	PIERCE	Joseph	62		Serv	Unm	22	M	Agric Lab	Herts	Wheathampstead
871	FENSOM	James	62		Serv	Unm	16	M	Agric Lab	Herts	Wheathampstead
872	BOON	George	62		Serv	Unm	14	M	Agric Lab	Herts	Wheathampstead
873	BANGS	Job	63	Raisins Farm	Head	Mar	29	M	Agric Lab	Herts	Kimpton
874	BANGS	Mary	63		Wife	Mar	24	F	Agric Labs Wife	Herts	Wheathampstead
875	BANGS	William	63		Son		5	M		Herts	Wheathampstead
876	BANGS	Eliza	63		Dau		3	F		Herts	Wheathampstead
877	BANGS	John	63		Son		1	M		Herts	Wheathampstead
878	BANGS	Maria	63		Lodger	Unm	21	F	Straw Plaiter	Herts	Kimpton
879	BANGS	William	63		Lodgers Son		2	M		Herts	Hitchin
880	BANGS	David	63		Lodger	Unm	19	M	Agric Lab	Herts	Kimpton
881	SEABROOK	George	64	Dane Farm	Head	Mar	43	M	Farmer of 88 acres employing 1 man & 2 boys	Herts	Wheathampstead
882	SEABROOK	Mary	64		Wife	Mar	42	F	Farmers Wife	Herts	Wheathampstead
883	SEABROOK	George	64		Son	Unm	22	M	Farmers Son	Herts	Wheathampstead
884	SEABROOK	Elizabeth	64		Dau	Unm	18	F	Farmers Daur	Herts	Wheathampstead
885	SEABROOK	Mary A	64		Dau	Unm	16	F	Farmers Daur	Herts	Wheathampstead
886	SEABROOK	Mille	64		Dau	Unm	14	F	Farmers Daur	Herts	Wheathampstead
887	SEABROOK	Emma	64		Dau		11	F	Farmers Daur	Herts	Wheathampstead
888	SEABROOK	William	64		Son		8	M	Farmers Son	Herts	Wheathampstead

889	SEABROOK	Harriet	64		Dau		5	F	Farmers Daur	Herts	Wheathampstead
890	SEABROOK	John	64		Son		3	M	Farmers Son	Herts	Wheathampstead
891	SEABROOK	Elizabeth	64		Mother	Widow	77	F	Late Farmers Wife	Herts	Wheathampstead
892	SWALLOW	George	64		Serv	Unm	19	M	Agric Lab	Herts	Wheathampstead
893	SWALLOW	Thomas	64		Serv	Unm	16	M	Agric Lab	Herts	Wheathampstead
894	ILOTT	Elizabeth	65	Hill Farm	Head	Widow	63	F	Farmer of 114 acres employing 6 men	Merion	Towan
895	ILOTT	William	65		Son	Unm	30	M	Farmers Son	Herts	Codicote
896	BANGS	Henry	65		Serv	Unm	24	M	Agric Lab	Herts	Kimpton
897	SIBLEY	Aaron	66	Little Cutts Cottage	Head	Mar	24	M	Game Keeper	Herts	Harpenden
898	SIBLEY	Mary	66		Wife	Mar	25	F	Game Keepers Wife	Herts	Kimpton
899	SIBLEY	James	66		Son		5	M		Herts	Harpenden
900	SIBLEY	George	66		Son		3	M		Herts	Wheathampstead
901	SIBLEY	William	66		Son		1	M		Herts	Wheathampstead
902	BIGG	Thomas	67	Little Cutts Cottage	Head	Mar	27	M	Agric Lab	Herts	Kimpton
903	BIGG	Mary	67		Wife	Mar	30	F	Agric Labs Wife	Herts	Harpenden
904	BIGG	James	67		Son		4	M		Herts	Wheathampstead
905	BIGG	George	67		Son		2	M		Herts	Wheathampstead
906	SIBLEY	William	67		Lodger	Unm	21	M	Agric Lab	Herts	Harpenden
907	BIGG	William	68	Little Cutts Cottage	Head	Mar	31	M	Agric Lab	Herts	Cloth Hall
908	BIGG	Rebecca	68		Wife	Mar	29	F	Agric Lab	Bucks	Tring
909	BIGG	Henry	68		Son		6	M		Herts	Peters Green
910	BIGG	Jane	68		Dau		4	F		Herts	Peters Green
911	BIGG	Hannah	68		Dau		1	F		Herts	Peters Green
912	SWAIN	Elizabeth	69	Bower Heath	Head	Widow	71	F	Charwoman	Norfolk	[Unknown]
913	REED	Edward	69		Son-in-law	Mar	48	M	Agric Lab	Herts	Wheathampstead
914	REED	Susannah	69		Dau	Mar	45	F	Agric Labs Wife	Norfolk	[Unknown]
915	REED	John	69		Grandson		10	M	Scholar	Herts	Wheathampstead
916	REED	George	69		Grandson		4	M		Herts	Wheathampstead
917	BENTLEY	James	70	Bower Heath	Head	Mar	45	M	Game keeper	Herts	Ayot St Lawrence
918	BENTLEY	Harriett	70		Wife	Mar	49	F	Game Keepers Wife	Worcs	Castle Motons
919	BENTLEY	Marian	70		Dau		9	F	Scholar	Herts	Wheathampstead
920	BENTLEY	James	70		Son		6	M	Scholar	Herts	Wheathampstead
921	BENTLEY	Helen	70		Dau		5	F	Scholar	Herts	Wheathampstead
922	SMITH	Anne	70		Aunt	Unm	76	F		Hereford	Whitburn
923	ILOTT	Edmund	71	Bower Heath Farm	Head	Mar	33	M	Farmer of 72 acres employing 6 men	Herts	Codicote
924	ILOTT	Mary Ann	71		Wife	Mar	34	F	Farmers Wife	Herts	Aston
925	ILOTT	Edmund Henry	71		Son		8	M	Scholar	Herts	Wheathampstead
926	ILOTT	Georgiana M. F	71		Dau		4	F		Herts	Wheathampstead
927	ILOTT	Ellen L	71		Dau		2	F		Herts	Wheathampstead
928	ILOTT	Oswald R	71		Son		6 m	M		Herts	Wheathampstead
929	FIELD	Ann	72	Bower Heath Lodge	Head	Widow	45	F	Needle Woman	Northants	Oakley
930	FIELD	Eliza	72		Dau		11	F	Scholar	Herts	Wheathampstead
931	FIELD	James	72		Son		7	M	Scholar	Herts	Wheathampstead
932	FIELD	Jane	72		Dau		4	F	Scholar	Herts	Wheathampstead

	SURNAME	FORENAME	SCHEDULE NUMBER	ADDRESS	RELATIONSHIP	STATUS	AGE	SEX	OCCUPATION	COUNTY OF BIRTH	PLACE OF BIRTH
933	LINES	William	73	Bower Heath	Head	Mar	56	M	Smith	Beds	Luton
934	LINES	Charlotte	73		Wife	Mar	47	F	Smiths Wife	Herts	Kings Walden
935	LINES	Henry	73		Son	Unm	28	M	Smith	Herts	Wheathampstead
936	LINES	John	73		Son	Unm	20	M	Smith	Herts	Wheathampstead
937	LINES	Ann	73		Dau	Unm	18	F	Bonnet Sewer	Herts	Wheathampstead
938	LINES	William	73		Son	Unm	16	M	Apprentice to Cordwainer	Herts	Wheathampstead
939	LINES	Clementina	73		Dau		14	F	Scholar	Herts	Wheathampstead
940	LINES	Edward	73		Son		12	M	Scholar	Herts	Wheathampstead
941	LINES	Albert	73		Son		11	M	Scholar	Herts	Wheathampstead
942	LINES	Elizabeth	73		Dau		9	F	Scholar	Herts	Wheathampstead
943	LINES	Mary	73		Dau		7	F	Scholar	Herts	Wheathampstead
944	COWIE	Andrew	74	Cutts Farm	Head	Mar	43	M	Coachman	Scotland	Aberdeen
945	COWIE	Ellen	74		Wife	Mar	38	F	Coachmans Wife	Ireland	Limerick
946	COWIE	Ann	74		Dau		10	F	Scholar	Herts	Cutts Farm
947	COWIE	Andrew	74		Son		8	M	Scholar	Herts	Cutts Farm
948	COWIE	Isabella	74		Dau		4	F		Herts	Cutts Farm
949	COWIE	Ellen	74		Dau		4m	F		Herts	Cutts Farm
950	THRUSSELL	James	75	Great Cutts	Head	Mar	37	M	Shepherd	Herts	Purton
951	THRUSSELL	Eliza	75		Wife	Mar	38	F	Shepherds Wife	Beds	Luton
952	THURSSELL	Joseph	75		Son		13	M	Shepherd Boy	Beds	Luton
953	THURSSELL	Mary Ann	75		Dau		9	F	Scholar	Beds	Luton
954	THURSSELL	Elizabeth	75		Dau		7	F	Scholar	Herts	Wheathampstead
955	THURSSELL	George	75		Son		6	M	Scholar	Herts	Wheathampstead
956	THURSSELL	Edward	75		Son		4	M	Scholar	Herts	Wheathampstead
957	THURSSELL	Ellen	75		Dau		1	F		Herts	Wheathampstead
958	FIELD	John	76	Great Cutts	Head	Mar	23	M	Woodman	Herts	Ayot St Peter
959	FIELD	Elizabeth	76		Wife	Mar	29	F	Woodmans Wife	Suffolk	Thelnetham
960	FIELD	Walter	76		Son		2	M		Herts	Wheathampstead
961	FIELD	Harriett	76		Dau		3m	F		Herts	Wheathampstead
962	PRENTICE	William	77	Cold Arbour	Head	Mar	47	M	Agric Lab	Herts	Wheathampstead
963	PRENTICE	Elizabeth	77		Wife	Mar	45	F	Agric Labs Wife	Beds	Luton
964	ATTWOOD	Joseph	78	Cold Arbour	Head	Mar	50	M	Agric Lab	Herts	Wheathampstead
965	ATTWOOD	Charlotte	78		Wife	Mar	51	F	Agric Labs Wife	Herts	Harpenden
966	ATTWOOD	Eliza	78		Dau	Unm	20	F	Straw Plaiter	Herts	Wheathampstead
967	ATTWOOD	Harriet	78		Dau	Unm	18	F	Straw Plaiter	Herts	Wheathampstead
968	ATTWOOD	George	78		Son		11	M	Scholar	Herts	Wheathampstead
969	COOK	John	79	Cold Arbour	Head	Mar	44	M	Agric Lab	Beds	Luton
970	COOK	Elizabeth	79		Wife	Mar	45	F	Agric Labs Wife	Herts	Redbourn
971	COOK	Joseph	79		Son		15	M	Agric Lab	Herts	Wheathampstead
972	COOK	Charles	79		Son		13	M	Agric Lab	Herts	Wheathampstead
973	COOK	Emma	79		Dau		11	F	Scholar	Herts	Wheathampstead
974	COOK	Hannah	79		Dau		7	F	Scholar	Herts	Wheathampstead
975	FAULDER	Thomas	80	Cold Arbour	Head	Mar	67	M	Agric Lab	Herts	Wheathampstead
976	FAULDER	Elizabeth	80		Wife	Mar	64	F	Agric Labs Wife	Beds	Luton
977	WARREN	George	80		Grandson	Unm	15	M	Agric Lab	Herts	Wheathampstead

978	HUNT	William	81	Cold Arbour	Head	Mar	65	M	Agric Lab	Herts	Wheathampstead
979	HUNT	Mary	81		Wife	Mar	63	F	Agric Labs Wife	Herts	Wheathampstead
980	WESTON	Charles	81		Grandson		13	M		Herts	Harpenden
981	WESTON	Ellen	81		Grandau		8	F		Herts	Harpenden
982	NORMAN	Joseph	82	Cold Arbour	Head	Mar	46	M	Agric Lab	Herts	Digswell
983	NORMAN	Mary	82		Wife	Mar	45	F	Agric Labs Wife	Herts	Wheathampstead
984	WRIGHT	Samuel	83		Head	Mar	45	M	Gardener	Herts	Kimpton
985	WRIGHT	Susan	83		Wife	Mar	48	F	Gardeners Wife	Herts	Wheathampstead
986	WRIGHT	Charles	83		Son	Unm	21	M	Agric Lab	Herts	Wheathampstead
987	WRIGHT	Mary	83		Dau	Unm	18	F	Straw Plaiter	Herts	Wheathampstead
988	WRIGHT	Emily	83		Dau		12	F	Straw Plaiter	Herts	Wheathampstead
989	LEWIN	William	84	Cold Arbour	Head	Mar	49	M	Agric Lab	Herts	Wheathampstead
990	LEWIN	Eliza	84		Wife	Mar	34	F	Agric Labs Wife	Herts	Harpenden
991	LEWIN	William	84		Son		14	M	Agric Lab	Herts	Wheathampstead
992	LEWIN	Charles	84		Son		12	M	Scholar	Herts	Wheathampstead
993	LEWIN	George	84		Son		10	M	Scholar	Herts	Wheathampstead
994	LEWIN	Thomas	84		Son		8	M	Scholar	Herts	Wheathampstead
995	LEWIN	Lucy	84		Dau		6	F		Herts	Wheathampstead
996	LEWIN	John	84		Son		4	M		Herts	Wheathampstead
997	LEWIN	Samuel	84		Son		2	M		Herts	Wheathampstead
998	LEWIN	Joseph	84		Son		3m	M		Herts	Wheathampstead
999	BRUTON	John	85	Cold Arbour	Head	Mar	52	M	Agric Lab	Herts	Wheathampstead
1000	BRUTON	Rebecca	85		Wife	Mar	51	F	Agric Labs Wife	Herts	Wheathampstead
1001	BRUTON	John	85		Son	Unm	24	M	Agric Lab	Herts	Wheathampstead
1002	BRUTON	William	85		Son	Unm	21	M	Agric Lab	Herts	Wheathampstead
1003	BRUTON	Frederick	85		Son	Unm	17	M	Agric Lab	Herts	Wheathampstead
1004	BRUTON	Sarah	85		Dau	Unm	16	F	Straw Plaiter	Herts	Wheathampstead
1005	WHEELER	Elizabeth	85		Visitor	Unm	19	F		Herts	Wheathampstead
1006	BROWN	Thomas	86	Cold Arbour	Head	Mar	27	M	Agric Lab	Beds	Luton
1007	BROWN	Elizabeth	86		Wife	Mar	27	F	Agric Labs Wife	Herts	Harpenden
1008	BROWN	Eliza H	86		Dau		1	F		Herts	Wheathampstead
1009	PARROTT	Thomas	87	Pickford Mills	Head	Mar	35	M	Beer Seller	Herts	Harpenden
1010	PARROTT	Hannah	87		Wife	Mar	33	F	Beer Sellers Wife	Herts	Wheathampstead
1011	PARROTT	Maria	87		Dau		10	F	Scholar	Herts	Harpenden
1012	PARROTT	Sarah	87		Dau		5	F	Scholar	Herts	Harpenden
1013	LAY	Hannah	87		Lodger	Unm	30	F	Bonnet Maker	Beds	Luton
1014	ROBERTS	Henry	88	Pickford Mills	Head	Mar	53	M	Paper Maker	Norfolk	[Tab..?]
1015	ROBERTS	Mercy	88		Wife	Mar	53	F	Paper Makers Wife	Herts	Preston
1016	WILLSON	James	89	Pickford Mills	Head	Mar	27	M	Agric Lab	Herts	Wheathampstead
1017	WILLSON	Susan	89		Wife	Mar	29	F	Agric Labs Wife	Herts	Hatfield
1018	WILLSON	James	89		Son		9	M		Herts	Hatfield
1019	WILLSON	Elizabeth	89		Dau		4	F		Herts	Hatfield
1020	WILLSON	Mary	89		Dau		6m	F		Herts	Wheathampstead
1021	DAY	Thomas	90	Pickford Mills	Head	Mar	37	M	Agric Lab	Herts	Harpenden
1022	DAY	Mary	90		Wife	Mar	38	F	Agric Labs Wife	Herts	Harpenden

	SURNAME	FORENAME	SCHEDULE NUMBER	ADDRESS	RELATIONSHIP	STATUS	AGE	SEX	OCCUPATION	COUNTY OF BIRTH	PLACE OF BIRTH
1023	DAY	Hannah	90		Dau		11	F	Straw Plaiter	Herts	Harpenden
1024	DAY	George	90		Son		9	M	Straw Plaiter	Herts	Harpenden
1025	DAY	James	90		Son		6	M	Scholar	Herts	Harpenden
1026	ATTWOOD	Charles	91	Pickford Mills	Head	Mar	29	M	Agric Lab	Herts	Wheathampstead
1027	ATTWOOD	Sarah	91		Wife	Mar	33	F	Agric Labs Wife	Bucks	Warden
1028	ATTWOOD	Alfred	91		Son		8	M	Scholar	Herts	Harpenden
1029	ATTWOOD	Ann	91		Dau		5	F		Herts	Harpenden
1030	ATTWOOD	Mary	91		Dau		2	F		Herts	Harpenden
1031	SHADBOLT	Richard	92	Pickford Mills	Head	Mar	26	M	Agric Lab	Herts	Kimpton
1032	SHADBOLT	Ann	92		Wife	Mar	24	F	Agric Labs Wife	Bucks	Wingrove
1033	SHADBOLT	George	92		Son		3	M		Herts	Harpenden
1034	SHADBOLT	Sarah	92		Dau		1	F		Herts	Wheathampstead
1035	HILSDON	George	93	Pickford Mills	Head	Mar	40	M	Agric Lab	Herts	Wheathampstead
1036	HILSDON	Joanna	93		Wife	Mar	42	F	Agric Labs Wife	Ireland	Cork
1037	SYGROVE	John	94	Pickford Mills	Head	Mar	31	M	Agric Lab	Herts	Wheathampstead
1038	SYGROVE	Hannah	94		Wife	Mar	32	F	Agric Labs Wife	Herts	Preston
1039	SYGROVE	Ellen	94		Dau		7	F	Scholar	Herts	Harpenden
1040	SYGROVE	George	94		Son		5	M		Herts	Harpenden
1041	SYGROVE	Joseph	94		Son		3	M		Herts	Harpenden
1042	SYGROVE	Rachel	94		Dau		1	F		Herts	Harpenden
1043	NEWSON	Richard	95	Batford Mills	Head	Mar	44	M	Agric Lab	Beds	Luton
1044	NEWSON	Mary	95		Wife	Mar	46	F	Agric Labs Wife	Herts	Wheathampstead
1045	NEWSON	George	95		Son	Unm	19	M	Agric Lab	Herts	Wheathampstead
1046	NEWSON	Hannah	95		Dau		12	F	Straw Plaiter	Herts	Wheathampstead
1047	NEWSON	Mary	95		Dau		9	F	Straw Plaiter	Herts	Wheathampstead
1048	NEWSON	Sarah	95		Dau		4	F		Herts	Wheathampstead
1049	WEBB	Hannah	95		Niece	Unm	16	F	Straw Plaiter	Herts	Wheathampstead
1050	HENLY	Mary	96	Batford Mills	Head	Widow	45	F	Straw Plaiter	Beds	Luton
1051	BINGHAM	Thomas	96		Lodger	Mar	24	M	Smith	Beds	Caddington
1052	BINGHAM	Sarah	96		Dau	Mar	26	F	Smiths Wife	Herts	Wheathampstead
1053	BINGHAM	Isabella	96		Grandau		6m	F		Herts	Wheathampstead
1054	HENLY	Sophia	96		Dau	Unm	24	F	Straw Plaiter	Herts	Wheathampstead
1055	HENLY	Martha	96		Dau	Unm	21	F	Straw Plaiter	Herts	Wheathampstead
1056	HENLY	Sarah	96		Niece		9	F	Straw Plaiter	Herts	Wheathampstead
1057	PARROTT	James	97	Batford Mills	Head	Mar	30	M	Dealer	Herts	Harpenden
1058	PARROTT	Elizabeth	97		Wife	Mar	36	F	Dealers Wife	Herts	Wheathampstead
1059	PARROTT	Frederick	97		Son		11	M	Scholar	Herts	Harpenden
1060	PARROTT	James A	97		Son		10	M	Scholar	Herts	Harpenden
1061	HUCKLESBY	James	97		Father-in-law	Widower	64	M	Agric Lab	Herts	Harpenden
1062	NEALE	George	98	Batford Mills Road The Gibraltar	Head	Mar	45	M	Publican	Herts	Wheathampstead
1063	NEALE	Elizabeth	98		Wife	Mar	40	F	Publicans Wife	Herts	Wheathampstead
1064	NEALE	Emma	98		Dau	Unm	15	F	Bonnet Sewer	Herts	Wheathampstead
1065	NEALE	Ann	98		Dau	Unm	15	F	Straw Plaiter	Herts	Wheathampstead
1066	NEALE	Mathew	98		Son		10	M	Scholar	Herts	Wheathampstead

1067	NEALE	William	98		Son		10	M	Scholar	Herts	Wheathampstead
1068	NEALE	Sarah	98		Dau		5	F	Scholar	Herts	Wheathampstead
1069	NEALE	Eliza	98		Dau		3	F		Herts	Wheathampstead
1070	NEALE	Elizabeth	98		Dau		2	F		Herts	Wheathampstead
1071	NEALE	George	98		Son		6m	M		Herts	Wheathampstead
1072	MADDOCK	Charles	98		Lodger	Unm	20	M	Agric Lab	Herts	Wheathampstead
1073	WEBSTER	James	98		Lodger	Unm	20	M	Agric Lab	Herts	Wheathampstead
1074	FISHER	John	99	Batford Mills	Head	Mar	56	M	Shepherd	Herts	Harpenden
1075	FISHER	Maria	99		Wife	Mar	37	F	Shepherds Wife	Herts	Harpenden
1076	FISHER	Emma	99		Dau	Unm	14	F	Straw Plaiter	Herts	Harpenden
1077	FISHER	Harriott	99		Dau		10	F	Straw Plaiter	Herts	Harpenden
1078	FISHER	Ellen	99		Dau		5	F		Herts	Harpenden
1079	DUNHAM	Francis	100	Cherry Trees	Head	Mar	30	M	Bricklayer	Herts	Wheathampstead
1080	DUNHAM	Hannah	100		Wife	Mar	31	F	Bricklayers Wife	Herts	Wheathampstead
1081	DUNHAM	Ann Maria	100		Dau		1	F		Herts	Wheathampstead
1082	BURGOINE	George	101	Cherry Trees	Head	Mar	39	M	Agric Lab	Herts	Wheathampstead
1083	BURGOINE	Esther	101		Wife	Mar	35	F	Agric Labs Wife	Herts	Harpenden
1084	BURGOINE	John	101		Son		9	M	Scholar	Herts	Harpenden
1085	BURGOINE	Mary	101		Dau		6	F		Herts	Wheathampstead
1086	BURGOINE	Peter	101		Son		4	M		Herts	Wheathampstead
1087	BURGOINE	Stephen	101		Son		1	M		Herts	Wheathampstead
1088	GIDDENS	Eliza	101		Sister-in-law	Unm	18	F	Straw Plaiter	Herts	Harpenden
1089	BRACEY	John	102	Cherry Trees	Head	Mar	50	M	Agric Lab	Herts	Broad Water
1090	BRACEY	Mary	102		Wife	Mar	51	F	Agric Labs Wife	Herts	Kimpton
1091	BRACEY	Harriett	102		Dau	Unm	28	F	Dress Maker	Herts	Wheathampstead
1092	BRACEY	Frederick	102		Son	Unm	21	M	Carpenter	Herts	Wheathampstead
1093	BRACEY	George	102		Son		11	M	Agric Lab	Herts	Wheathampstead
1094	ATTWOOD	Sarah	102		Lodger		6	F	Scholar	Middx	Paddington
1095	HAWES	John	103	Cherry Trees	Head	Mar	52	M	Agric Lab	Beds	Dunstable
1096	HAWES	Mary	103		Wife	Mar	53	F	Agric Labs Wife	Herts	Wheathampstead
1097	BURGOINE	William	104	Cherry Trees	Head	Mar	34	M	Agric Lab	Herts	Wheathampstead
1098	BURGOINE	Ann	104		Wife	Mar	36	F	Agric Labs Wife	Herts	Aldenham
1099	BURGOINE	Emily	104		Dau		10	F	Scholar	Herts	Wheathampstead
1100	BURGOINE	Alfred	104		Son		8	M	Scholar	Herts	Wheathampstead
1101	BURGOINE	Eliza	104		Dau		6	F	Scholar	Herts	Wheathampstead
1102	BURGOINE	Mary	104		Dau		4	F		Herts	Wheathampstead
1103	MUNT	Mathew	105	Cherry Trees	Head	Mar	46	M	Agric Lab	Herts	Caddington
1104	MUNT	Rebecca	105		Wife	Mar	42	F	Agric Labs Wife	Beds	Kensworth
1105	MUNT	Sarah A	105		Dau		14	F	Bonnet Sewer	Herts	Wheathampstead
1106	MUNT	Mary	105		Dau		12	F	Straw Plaiter	Herts	Wheathampstead
1107	MUNT	ELiza	105		Dau		10	F	Straw Plaiter	Herts	Wheathampstead
1108	MUNT	Elizabeth	105		Dau		8	F	Scholar	Herts	Wheathampstead
1109	MUNT	Alfred	105		Son		4	M		Herts	Wheathampstead
1110	MUNT	George	105		Son		1	M		Herts	Wheathampstead
1111	WRIGHT	William	106	Marshalls Heath	Head	Mar	59	M	Agric Lab	Herts	Kimpton

	SURNAME	FORENAME	SCHEDULE NUMBER	ADDRESS	RELATIONSHIP	STATUS	AGE	SEX	OCCUPATION	COUNTY OF BIRTH	PLACE OF BIRTH
1112	WRIGHT	Sophia	106		Wife	Mar	52	F	Agric Labs Wife	Herts	Flamstead
1113	WRIGHT	Charles	106		Son	Unm	22	M	Agric Lab	Herts	Wheathampstead
1114	WRIGHT	David	106		Son	Unm	19	M	Agric Lab	Herts	Wheathampstead
1115	WRIGHT	George	106		Son		9	M		Herts	Wheathampstead

Three houses uninhabited

	SURNAME	FORENAME	SCHEDULE NUMBER	ADDRESS	RELATIONSHIP	STATUS	AGE	SEX	OCCUPATION	COUNTY OF BIRTH	PLACE OF BIRTH
1116	FENSOM	John	107	Marshalls Heath	Head	Mar	23	M	Agric Lab	Herts	Wheathampstead
1117	FENSON	Emily	107		Wife	Mar	20	F	Agric Labs Wife	Herts	Wheathampstead
1118	FENSOM	Ann M	107		Dau		5m	F		Herts	Wheathampstead
1119	PECKS	Eliza	107		Sister-in-law		11	F	Straw Plaiter	Herts	Wheathampstead
1120	WOOD	David	108	Marshalls Heath	Head	Mar	55	M	Agric Lab	Herts	Studham
1121	WOOD	Martha	108		Wife	Mar	49	F	Agric Labs Wife	Oxon	Hook Norton
1122	WOOD	James	108		Father	Widower	86	M	Agric Lab	Herts	Harridge [?]
1123	HARRIS	William	109	Marshalls Heath	Head	Mar	40	M	Agric Lab	Herts	Mangrove
1124	HARRIS	Sarah	109		Wife	Mar	30	F	Agric Labs Wife	Herts	Wheathampstead
1125	HARRIS	John	109		Son		10	M	Agric Lab	London	St Lukes
1126	HARRIS	Thomas	109		Son		7	M		London	St Lukes
1127	HARRIS	Charlotte	109		Dau		1	F		Herts	Wheathampstead
1128	WHEELER	Joshua	110	Marshalls Heath	Head	Mar	37	M	Agric Lab	Herts	Wheathampstead
1129	WHEELER	Mary A	110		Wife	Mar	27	F	Agric Labs Wife	Herts	Wheathampstead
1130	WARNER	Sarah	110		Lodger	Unm	12	F	Straw Plaiter	Herts	Wheathampstead
1131	SALES	Sarah	110		Lodger	Unm	20	F	Straw Plaiter	Herts	Wheathampstead
1132	BROWN	James	111	Marshalls Heath	Head	Mar	32	M	Agric Lab	Herts	Harpenden
1133	BROWN	Ann	111		Wife	Mar	30	F	Agric Labs Wife	Herts	Harpenden
1134	BROWN	Charles	111		Son		12	M	Straw Plaiter	Herts	Harpenden
1135	BROWN	Sophia	111		Dau		8	F	Straw Plaiter	Herts	Harpenden
1136	BROWN	William	111		Son		6	M		Herts	Harpenden
1137	BROWN	James	111		Son		2	M		Herts	Harpenden
1138	FENSOM	James	112	Marshalls Heath	Head	Mar	50	M	Agric Lab	Herts	Kimpton
1139	FENSOM	Maria	112		Wife	Mar	52	F	Agric Labs Wife	Herts	Wheathampstead
1140	NORRIS	Charlotte	112		Dau	Widow	29	F	Straw Plaiter	Herts	Kimpton
1141	NORRIS	William	112		Grandson		9m	M		Herts	Harpenden
1142	LAWRENCE	Thomas	112		Son-in-law	Mar	22	M	Agric Lab	Herts	Harpenden
1143	LAWRENCE	Ann	112		Wife	Mar	20	F	Agric Labs Wife	Herts	Wheathampstead
1144	LAURENCE	Mary	112		Grandau		1	F		Herts	Wheathampstead
1145	FENSOM	Eliza	112		Dau		13	F	Straw Plaiter	Herts	Wheathampstead
1146	ROLFE	Mathew	113	Mackery End	Head	Mar	33	M	Agric Lab	Herts	Kimpton
1147	ROLFE	Charlotte	113		Wife	Mar	25	F	Agric Labs Wife	Herts	Redbourn
1148	ROLFE	Mathew	113		Son		5	M	Scholar	Herts	Redbourn
1149	ROLFE	George	113		Son		4	M		Herts	Redbourn
1150	ROLFE	Elizabeth	113		Dau		1	F		Herts	Redbourn
1151	WILLMOTT	Elizabeth	114	Mackery End Farm	Head	Widow	46	F	Farmer of 300 acres employing 12 labourers	Herts	Frogmore Kings Walden
1152	WILLMOTT	Elizabeth	114		Dau	Unm	20	F	Farmers Daughter	Herts	Bendish
1153	WILLMOTT	Mary	114		Dau	Unm	18	F	Farmers Daughter	Herts	Frogmore
1154	WILLMOTT	Charlotte	114		Dau	Unm	16	F	Farmers Daughter	Herts	Frogmore

1155	WILLMOTT	Samuel	114		Son	Unm	13	M	Farmers Son	Herts	Kimpton
1156	WILLMOTT	Edward	114		Son		11	M	Farmers Son	Herts	Kimpton
1157	WILLMOTT	Anne	114		Dau		8	F	Scholar	Herts	Kimpton
1158	SWAIN	Thomas	114		Serv	Unm	31	M	Shepherd	Herts	Kimpton
1159	CARRINGTON	Thomas	114		Serv	Unm	23	M	Agric Lab	Herts	Abbots Langley
1160	ROLFE	Thomas	114		Serv	Unm	18	M	Agric Lab	Herts	St Pauls Walden
1161	NORTH	Charles	114		Serv		13	M	Agric Lab	Herts	Kings Walden
1162	WILLMOTT	Charles	115	Holly Bush Hall	Head	Mar	22	M	Farmer of 12 acres employing 1 man	Herts	Kings Walden
1163	WILLMOTT	Emma	115		Wife	Mar	30	F	Farmers Wife	Herts	Hatfield

Two houses uninhabited

1164	WELCH	Mary	116	Holly Bush Hall	Head	Widow	65	F	Charwoman	Herts	Wheathampstead
1165	COLLINS	Francis	116		Son	Mar	26	M	Agric Lab	Herts	Wheathampstead
1166	COLLINS	Ann	116		Wife	Mar	31	F	Agric Labs Wife	Herts	Kimpton
1167	COLLINS	William	116		Grandson		3	M		Herts	Wheathampstead
1168	COLLINS	George	116		Grandson		0	M		Herts	Wheathampstead
1169	WELCH	Edward	116		Son of the widow	Unm	19	M	Agric Lab	Herts	Wheathampstead
1170	WILSHIRE	Susan	117	Luton Road	Head	Widow	79	F	Late Farmers Wife Retired	Herts	Ayot St Lawrence
1171	ANSELL	Charlotte	117		Lodger	Widow	57	F		Herts	Codicote
1172	LAURENCE	Thomas	118	Luton Road	Head	Mar	21	M	Agric Lab	Herts	Wheathampstead
1173	LAURENCE	Elizabeth	118		Wife	Mar	22	F	Agric Labs Wife	Herts	Harpenden
1174	WEBB	James	119	Luton Road	Head	Mar	36	M	Agric Lab	Ireland	[Unknown]
1175	WEBB	Maria	119		Wife	Mar	36	F	Agric Labs Wife	Herts	Wheathampstead
1176	DELLAR	William	120	Luton Road	Head	Mar	49	M	Shoemaker & Beerseller	Cambs	Melbourn
1177	DELLAR	Louisa	120		Wife	Mar	42	F	Shoemakers Wife	Herts	Harpenden
1178	LATCHFORD	James	121	Luton Road	Head	Mar	37	M	Agric Lab	Herts	Wheathampstead
1179	LATCHFORD	Sarah	121		Wife	Mar	26	F	Agric Labs Wife	Herts	Harpenden
1180	ROBERTS	Sarah	122	Luton Road	Head	Mar	23	F	Carpenters Wife	Herts	Shenley
1181	ROBERTS	[?]	122		Son		under 1 m	M		Herts	Wheathampstead
1182	DUNHAM	Hannah	122		Serv	Widow	57	F	Monthly Nurse	Herts	Wheathampstead
1183	HAWKINS	James	123	Village	Head	Mar	38	M	Agric Lab	Herts	Preston
1184	HAWKINS	Ann	123		Wife	Mar	35	F	Agric Labs Wife	Herts	Wheathampstead
1185	HAWKINS	George	123		Son		9	M	Scholar	Herts	Wheathampstead
1186	HAWKINS	Harriett	123		Dau		6	F	Scholar	Herts	Wheathampstead
1187	HAWKINS	William	123		Son		3	M		Herts	Wheathampstead
1188	EAST	Eliza	123		Lodger	Unm	19	F	Straw Plaiter	Herts	Wheathampstead
1189	ROW	Edward	124	Village	Head	Mar	61	M	Agric Lab	Herts	Wheathampstead
1190	ROW	Hannah	124		Wife	Mar	61	F	Agric Labs Wife	Herts	Wheathampstead
1191	ROW	Edward	124		Son	Unm	23	M	Agric Lab	Herts	Wheathampstead
1192	ROW	Charles	124		Son	Unm	21	M	Shepherd	Herts	Wheathampstead
1193	HALSEY	James	124		Lodger	Unm	20	M	Agric Lab	Herts	Wheathampstead
1194	WINCH	Daniel	125	Village	Head	Mar	34	M	Agric Lab	Herts	Stevenage
1195	WINCH	Charlott	125		Wife	Mar	31	F	Agric Labs Wife	Herts	Wheathampstead
1196	WINCH	Caroline	125		Dau		9	F	Scholar	Herts	Wheathampstead

	SURNAME	FORENAME	SCHEDULE NUMBER	ADDRESS	RELATIONSHIP	STATUS	AGE	SEX	OCCUPATION	COUNTY OF BIRTH	PLACE OF BIRTH
1197	WINCH	Mary Ann	125		Dau		4	F	Scholar	Herts	Wheathampstead
1198	WINCH	Fanny	125		Dau		2	F		Herts	Wheathampstead
1199	LINES	John	126	Village	Head	Mar	43	M	Agric Lab	Herts	Wheathampstead
1200	LINES	Sarah	126		Wife	Mar	31	F	Agric Labs Wife	Herts	Wheathampstead
1201	LINES	Joseph	126		Son		11	M		Herts	Wheathampstead
1202	LINES	Mary Ann	126		Dau		9	F	Scholar	Herts	Wheathampstead
1203	LINES	Jessey	126		Son		6	M	Scholar	Herts	Wheathampstead
1204	LINES	John	126		Son		3	M		Herts	Wheathampstead
1205	LINES	George	126		Son		6m	M		Herts	Wheathampstead
1206	DAY	Joseph	127	Village	Head	Mar	36	M	Agric Lab	Herts	Wheathampstead
1207	DAY	Charlotte	127		Wife	Mar	36	F	Agric Labs Wife	Herts	Wheathampstead
1208	DAY	Ann	127		Dau		5	F	Scholar	Herts	Wheathampstead
1209	DAY	John	127		Son		8m	M		Herts	Wheathampstead
1210	DAY	Sarah	127		Mother	Widow	64	F		Herts	Bushey
1211	ADDINGTON	Sarah	127		Niece		9	F	Hat Maker	Herts	Wheathampstead

One house uninhabited

The end of the Enumeration District 1b of the parish of Wheathampstead

Registrar's District: Harpenden   Enumeration District 1c   Ref. HO107/1713 folios 42-64

All that part of the parish of Wheathampstead which lies to the west of the road leading from St Albans to Kimpton and to the south of the road leading from Wheathampstead to Luton, including No Mans Land, Hamwell, Ayres end, Pipers, part of Harpenden Common, Pickford and Batford Mills, thence to Wheathampstead, Bury Green and farms within the said boundary

	SURNAME	FORENAME	SCHEDULE NUMBER	ADDRESS	RELATIONSHIP	STATUS	AGE	SEX	OCCUPATION	COUNTY OF BIRTH	PLACE OF BIRTH
1212	SMITH	James	1	No Mans Land Common	Head	Mar	52	M	Agricultural Labourer	Herts	St Pauls Walden
1213	SMITH	Elizabeth	1		Wife	Mar	56	F		Herts	Hatfield
1214	DAWES	Richard	1		Son-in-law	Mar	29	M	Agric Lab	Herts	Codicote
1215	DAWES	Ann	1		Dau	Mar	26	F		Herts	Hatfield
1216	SMITH	Dan	1		Grandson		7	M		Herts	Wheathampstead
1217	ARCHER	Thomas	2	No Mans Land Common	Head	Mar	61	M	Agric Lab	Herts	Wheathampstead
1218	ARCHER	Sarah	2		Wife	Mar	61	F		Herts	Wheathampstead
1219	ARCHER	James	3	No Mans Land Common	Head	Mar	31	M	Agric Lab	Herts	Wheathampstead
1220	ARCHER	Hannah	3		Wife	Mar	30	F		Herts	Sandridge
1221	ARCHER	Emily	3		Dau		3	F		Herts	Wheathampstead
1222	DAWES	David	3		Lodger	Unm	26	M	Agric Lab	Herts	Codicote
1223	ADDINGTON	James	4	No Mans Land Common	Head	Widower	44	M	Agric Lab	Herts	Sandridge
1224	RANCE	Thomas	5	No Mans Land Common	Head	Mar	44	M	Agric Lab	Herts	Stevenage
1225	RANCE	Maria	5		Wife	Mar	33	F	Agric Labs Wife	Herts	Harpenden
1226	RANCE	Thomas	5		Son		12	M	Agric Lab	Herts	Harpenden
1227	IVORY	Ann	5		Step-dau		9	F	At Home	Herts	Harpenden
1228	IVORY	Eliza	5		Step-dau		6	F	At Home	Herts	Wheathampstead
1229	FIELD	Sarah	6	No Mans Land Common	Head	Mar	45	F	Straw Plaiter	Herts	Harpenden
1230	FIELD	Mary Anne	6		Dau	Unm	21	F	Straw Plaiter	Herts	Wheathampstead
1231	FIELD	Harriett	6		Dau	Unm	19	F	Straw Plaiter	Herts	Wheathampstead
1232	FIELD	Emma	6		Dau		15	F	Straw Plaiter	Herts	Wheathampstead

1233	FIELD	Sarah	6		Dau		12	F	Straw Plaiter	Herts	Wheathampstead
1234	FIELD	James	6		Son		10	M	Straw Plaiter	Herts	Wheathampstead
1235	FIELD	Joseph	6		Son		7	M	At Home	Herts	Wheathampstead
1236	WEBB	John	7	No Mans Land Common	Head	Widower	45	M	Agric Lab	Herts	Wheathampstead
1237	WEBB	Mary	7		Dau	Unm	20	F	Straw Plaiter	Herts	Wheathampstead
1238	WEBB	Sarah	7		Dau		14	F	Straw Hat Maker	Herts	Wheathampstead
1239	WEBB	John	7		Son		12	M	Agric Lab	Herts	Wheathampstead
1240	ODELL	George	8	No Mans Land Common	Head	Mar	27	M	Bricklayer (Journeyman)	Herts	Wheathampstead
1241	ODELL	Mary	8		Wife	Mar	27	F		Herts	Wheathampstead
1242	ODELL	Thirza M	8		Dau		3	F	At Home	Herts	Wheathampstead
1243	ODELL	Ellen	8		Dau		6 m	F		Herts	Wheathampstead
1244	RAGGETT	John	9	No Mans Land Common	Head	Mar	31	M	Farmer of 22 acres employing 1 boy	Beds	Studham
1245	RAGGETT	Sarah	9		Wife	Mar	32	F		Herts	St Peters
1246	RAGGETT	Sarah M	9		Dau		8	F	At Home	Herts	Wheathampstead
1247	RAGGETT	Jane	9		Dau		3	F		Herts	Wheathampstead
1248	RAGGETT	John J	9		Son		7	M		Herts	Wheathampstead
1249	ROBERTS	Richard	10	No Mans Land Common	Head	Mar	30	M	Agric Lab	Herts	North Mimms
1250	ROBERTS	Ann	10		Wife	Mar	30	F		Herts	Wheathampstead
1251	ROBERTS	William	10		Son		7	M	At Home	Herts	Wheathampstead
1252	ROBERTS	Thomas	10		Son		4	M	At Home	Herts	Wheathampstead
1253	SMITH	William	11	No Mans Land Common	Head	Mar	52	M	Agric Lab	Herts	North Mimms
1254	SMITH	Elizabeth	11		Wife	Mar	50	F		Herts	Wheathampstead
1255	SMITH	William	11		Son	Unm	24	M	Agric Lab	Herts	Wheathampstead
1256	SMITH	Sarah	11		Dau	Unm	22	F	Bonnet Sewer	Herts	Wheathampstead
1257	SMITH	John	11		Son	Unm	19	M	Agric Lab	Herts	Wheathampstead
1258	SMITH	Elizabeth	11		Dau		15	F	Straw Hat Maker	Herts	Wheathampstead
1259	SMITH	Eliza	11		Dau		13	F	Straw Hat Maker	Herts	Wheathampstead
1260	SMITH	Mercy	11		Dau		11	F	Straw Hat Maker	Herts	Wheathampstead
1261	LATCHFORD	Thomas	12	No Mans Land Common	Head	Mar	39	M	Agric Lab	Herts	Wheathampstead
1262	LATCHFORD	Ann	12		Wife	Mar	29	F		Herts	Sandridge
1263	RAMSDON	John	13	No Mans Land Common	Head	Mar	42	M	Agric Lab & Beer Shop Keeper	Herts	Wheathampstead
1264	RAMSDON	Martha	13		Wife	Mar	32	F		Herts	Redbourn
1265	RAMSDON	John	13		Son		11	M	Agric Lab	Herts	Wheathampstead
1266	RAMSDON	William	13		Son		4	M	At Home	Herts	Wheathampstead
1267	RAMSDON	Isaac	13		Son		2	M	At Home	Herts	Wheathampstead
1268	MILLARD	William	14	No Mans Land Common	Head	Mar	53	M	Agric Lab	Herts	Wheathampstead
1269	MILLARD	Maria	14		Wife	Mar	51	F		Herts	Wheathampstead
1270	MILLARD	David	14		Son		15	M	Agric Lab	Herts	Wheathampstead
1271	MILLARD	Daniel	14		Son		10	M	At Home	Herts	Wheathampstead
1272	ANSELL	Charles	15	No Mans Land Common	Head	Mar	38	M	Agric Lab	Herts	Wheathampstead
1273	ANSELL	Mary	15		Wife	Mar	33	F		Herts	Hatfield
1274	ANSELL	Ann	15		Mother	Widow	73	F	Straw Plaiter	Herts	Wheathampstead
1275	VYSE	George	16	No Mans Land Common	Head	Mar	28	M	Coal Carrier (late a Groom)	Herts	Boxmoor
1276	VYSE	Sarah	16		Wife	Mar	29	F		Beds	Totternhoe

	SURNAME	FORENAME	SCHEDULE NUMBER	ADDRESS	RELATIONSHIP	STATUS	AGE	SEX	OCCUPATION	COUNTY OF BIRTH	PLACE OF BIRTH
1277	VYSE	George W.	16		Son		4	M	At Home	Herts	Hemel Hempstead
1278	CHAPMAN	Richard	17	No Mans Land Common	Head	Mar	35	M	Agric Lab	Herts	Wheathampstead
1279	CHAPMAN	Ann	17		Wife	Mar	38	F		Herts	Wheathampstead
1280	CHAPMAN	William	17		Son		14	M	Agric Lab	Herts	Wheathampstead
1281	CHAPMAN	Emma	17		Dau		8	F	Scholar	Herts	Wheathampstead
1282	CHAPMAN	Samuel	17		Son		4	M	At Home	Herts	Wheathampstead
1283	CHAPMAN	Ann	17		Dau		1	F	At Home	Herts	Wheathampstead
1284	CHAPMAN	Lucy	17		Mother	Widow	73	F	Straw Plaiter (Pauper)	Beds	Barton
1285	KING	William	18	Amwell	Head	Mar	31	M	Agric Lab	Herts	Wheathampstead
1286	KING	Mary	18		Wife	Mar	29	F		Herts	Wheathampstead
1287	KING	William	18		Son		4	M	At Home	Herts	Wheathampstead
1288	KING	James	18		Son		3	M	At Home	Herts	Wheathampstead
1289	FRENCH	William	19	Amwell	Head	Unm	33	M	Agric Lab	Herts	Kimpton
1290	FRENCH	Sarah	19		Mother	Widow	53	F	Straw Plaiter	Herts	Kimpton
1291	DAY	Thomas	20	Amwell	Head	Mar	62	M	Agric Lab	Herts	Offley
1292	DAY	Elizabeth	20		Wife	Mar	72	F		Herts	Offley
1293	LAWRANCE	Eliza	20		Lodger	Unm	20	F	Straw Hat Maker	Herts	Sandridge
1294	LAWRANCE	George	21	Amwell	Head	Mar	60	M	Agric Lab	Herts	Welwyn
1295	LAWRANCE	Jane	21		Wife	Mar	53	F		Herts	Wheathampstead
1296	LAWRANCE	Henry	21		Son	Unm	25	M	Agric Lab	Herts	Wheathampstead
1297	LAWRANCE	Fanny	21		Dau	Unm	18	F	Straw Plaiter	Herts	Wheathampstead
1298	RAMSDON	William	22	Amwell	Head	Unm	48	M	Agric Lab	Herts	Wheathampstead
1299	RAMSDON	Ann	22		Mother	Widow	73	F	Straw Plaiter Pauper	Herts	Wheathampstead
1300	RAMSDON	Elizabeth	22		Sister		13	F	Scholar	Herts	Wheathampstead
1301	CREW	Mary	22		Sister	Mar	32	F	Straw Plaiter	Herts	Wheathampstead
1302	CREW	Mary Ann	22		Niece		8	F		Herts	Northaw
1303	CREW	William	22		Nephew		1	M	At Home	Herts	Wheathampstead
1304	STREDDER	John	23	Amwell	Head	Mar	71	M	Carpenter & Beershop keeper	Herts	Wheathampstead
1305	STREDDER	Hannah	23		Wife	Mar	71	F		Beds	Luton
1306	STREDDER	Charlotte	23		Dau	Unm	35	F	Straw Plaiter	Herts	Wheathampstead
1307	STREDDER	Sarah	23		Dau	Unm	25	F	Straw Plaiter	Herts	Wheathampstead
1308	FLETCHER	John	24	Amwell	Head	Mar	34	M	Blacksmith (Journeyman)	Unknown	
1309	FLETCHER	Eliza	24		Wife	Mar	26	F		Herts	Wheathampstead
1310	FLETCHER	Mary Ann	24		Dau		2	F	At Home	Herts	Wheathampstead
1311	FLETCHER	Eliza	24		Dau		5m	F	At Home	Herts	Wheathampstead
1312	SPRING	Isaac	25	Amwell	Head	Mar	46	M	Agric Lab	Herts	Offley
1313	SPRING	Caroline	25		Wife	Mar	41	F		Herts	Wheathampstead
1314	BURGOYNE	Thomas	26	Amwell	Head	Widower	69	M	Agric Lab	Herts	Sandridge
1315	JOINER	Joseph	26		Son-in-law	Mar	32	M	Agric Lab	Herts	Sandridge
1316	JOINER	Joyce	26		Dau	Mar	38	F		Herts	Wheathampstead
1317	BROWNSELL	David	27	Amwell	Head	Mar	40	M	Agric Lab	Herts	Sandridge
1318	BROWNSELL	Jane	27		Wife	Mar	35	F		Herts	Sandridge
1319	BROWNSELL	George	27		Son		7	M	Scholar	Herts	Wheathampstead
1320	HALE	Thomas	28	Amwell	Head	Mar	32	M	Agric Lab	Herts	Flamstead

1321	HALE	Eliza	28		Wife	Mar	37	F		Beds	Luton
1322	HALE	Frederick	28		Son		11	M	Scholar	Herts	Wheathampstead
1323	HALE	Eliza	28		Dau		8	F	At Home	Herts	Wheathampstead
1324	HALE	Harriet	28		Dau		6	F	At Home	Herts	Wheathampstead
1325	HALE	Sarah	28		Dau		3	F	At Home	Herts	Wheathampstead
1326	HALE	William	28		Son		1	M	At Home	Herts	Wheathampstead
1327	FREEMAN	Joseph	29	Amwell	Head	Mar	71	M	Farmer of 20 acres employing 1 boy	Herts	Hempstead [Hemel]
1328	FREEMAN	Elizabeth	29		Wife	Mar	76	F		Beds	Shortnall
1329	FITZGERALD	Henry	29		Serv		11	M	Farmers boy	Middx	Kentish Town
1330	YOUNG	Charles	30	Amwell	Head	Mar	55	M	Agric Lab	Herts	Wheathampstead
1331	YOUNG	Sarah	30		Wife	Mar	56	F		Herts	Wheathampstead
1332	PUTT	Sarah	31	Amwell	Head	Widow	90	F	Retired Milliner	Herts	Wheathampstead
1333	DAY	Mary	31		Serv	Unm	69	F	Straw Plaiter Pauper	Herts	Wheathampstead
1334	FARR	George	32	Bull Farm	Head	Mar	54	M	Farmer of 80 acres employing 2 labourers	Herts	Kimpton
1335	FARR	Sophia	32		Wife	Mar	51	F		Herts	St Albans
1336	FARR	Sophia	32		Dau		12	F	At home	Herts	North Mimms
1337	FARR	Frederick E.	32		Son		10	M	At Home	Herts	North Mimms
1338	FARR	Charles	32		Son		8	M	At Home	Herts	North Mimms
1339	HIRST	Eliza	32		Sister-in-law	Unm	59	F	Assistant in Family	Herts	St Albans
1340	MUNT	William	33	Ayres End	Head	Mar	40	M	Agric Lab	Herts	Harpenden
1341	MUNT	Eliza	33		Wife	Mar	30	F		Herts	Harpenden
1342	MUNT	Emily	33		Dau		10	F	Scholar	Herts	Wheathampstead
1343	MUNT	Eliza	33		Dau		13	F	Scholar	Herts	Wheathampstead
1344	MUNT	Alfred	33		Son		3	M	At Home	Herts	Wheathampstead
1345	MUNT	Mary Ann	33		Dau		1	F	At Home	Herts	Wheathampstead
1346	BAILEY	William	34	Ayres End	Head	Mar	58	M	Agric Lab	Beds	Houghton
1347	BAILEY	Mary	34		Wife	Mar	49	F		Beds	Totternhoe
1348	BAILEY	Elizabeth	34		Dau	Unm	20	F	Dress Maker	Herts	Wheathampstead
1349	BAILEY	Charles	34		Son		9	M	Agric Lab	Herts	Wheathampstead
1350	BAILEY	Harriet	34		Dau		5	F	At Home	Herts	Wheathampstead
1351	SLOUGH	William	35	Ayres End	Head	Mar	47	M	Agric Lab	Herts	Wheathampstead
1352	SLOUGH	Mary	35		Wife	Mar	52	F		Beds	Caddington
1353	SLOUGH	Susan	35		Dau	Unm	23	F	Bonnet Sewer	Herts	Wheathampstead
1354	SLOUGH	Ellen	35		Dau	Unm	18	F	Bonnet Sewer	Herts	Wheathampstead
1355	SLOUGH	Mary	35		Dau		15	F	Scholar	Herts	Wheathampstead
1356	SLOUGH	Eliza	35		Dau		12	F	Scholar	Herts	Wheathampstead
1357	GAWER	Thomas	36	Ayres End Farm	Head	Mar	32	M	Baker	Bucks	Wing
1358	GAWER	Georgiana	36		Wife	Mar	33	F		Herts	Sandridge
1359	GAWER	Ellen	36		Dau		6	F	At Home	Herts	Harpenden
1360	GAWER	Frederick	36		Son		5	M	At Home	Herts	Harpenden
1361	GAWER	Ann	36		Dau		2	F	At Home	Herts	Harpenden
1362	GAWER	George	36		Son		6m	M	At Home	Herts	Harpenden
1363	DICKENSON	Henry	36		Brother-in-law	Unm	37	M	Farmers Son	Herts	Sandridge
1364	GODFREY	Thomas	36		Serv	Widower	58	M	Agric Lab Shepherd	Herts	St Peters

	SURNAME	FORENAME	SCHEDULE NUMBER	ADDRESS	RELATIONSHIP	STATUS	AGE	SEX	OCCUPATION	COUNTY OF BIRTH	PLACE OF BIRTH
1365	SCRIVENER	George	37	Harpenden Common	Head	Mar	50	M	Agric Lab	Beds	Sundon
1366	SCRIVENER	Sarah	37		Wife	Mar	48	F		Herts	Harpenden
1367	SCRIVENER	Rose	37		Dau	Unm	19	F	Straw Plaiter	Herts	Harpenden
1368	SCRIVENER	Susan	37		Dau	Unm	17	F	Straw Plaiter	Herts	Harpenden
1369	SCRIVENER	Emma	37		Dau		14	F	Straw Plaiter	Herts	Harpenden
1370	SCRIVENER	William	37		Son		12	M	Agric Lab	Herts	Harpenden
1371	SCRIVENER	Charles	37		Son		10	M	Scholar	Herts	Harpenden
1372	SCRIVENER	Maria	37		Dau		8	F	Scholar	Herts	Harpenden
1373	SCRIVENER	Eliza	37		Grandau		5m	F		Herts	Wheathampstead
1374	SCRIVENER	Infant	37		Grandau		2wks	F		Herts	Wheathampstead
1375	GRAY	William	38	Harpenden Common	Head	Mar	23	M	Agric Lab	Herts	Wheathampstead
1376	GRAY	Maria	38		Wife	Mar	26	F		Herts	Harpenden
1377	JARVIS	David	39	Harpenden Common	Head	Mar	51	M	Agric Lab	Herts	Lilley
1378	JARVIS	Ann	39		Wife	Mar	49	F		Herts	Wheathampstead
1379	RUSSEL	Emily	39		Niece		15	F	Straw Plaiter	Herts	Wheathampstead
1380	RUSSEL	Louisa	39		Niece		13	F	Straw Plaiter	Herts	Harpenden
1381	HUNT	William	40	Harpenden Common	Head	Mar	32	M	Blacksmith & Grocer	Herts	Harpenden
1382	HUNT	Eliza	40		Wife	Mar	32	F		Herts	Wheathampstead
1383	HUNT	Edward	40		Son		6	M	At Home	Herts	Wheathampstead
1384	HUNT	Fanny	40		Dau		3	F	At Home	Herts	Wheathampstead
1385	HUNT	Sarah	40		Dau		1	F		Herts	Wheathampstead
1386	SAUNDERS	George	41	Harpenden Common	Head	Mar	25	M	Agric Lab	Herts	Harpenden
1387	SAUNDERS	Sarah	41		Wife	Mar	34	F		Herts	Bovingdon
1388	BELCHER	Elizabeth	42	Harpenden Common	Head	Widow	36	F	Straw Plaiter	Herts	Wheathampstead
1389	BELCHER	Mary Ann	42		Dau		15	F	Straw Plaiter	Herts	Wheathampstead
1390	WALKER	Emma	42		Visitor		8	F		Herts	Wheathampstead
1391	WALKER	Mary Ann	42		Visitor		6	F		Herts	Wheathampstead
1392	GRAY	George	43	Harpenden Common	Head	Mar	60	M	Shoemaker & Publican	Herts	Wheathampstead
1393	GRAY	Phoebe	43		Wife	Mar	56	F		Herts	Wheathampstead
1394	GRAY	George	43		Son	Mar	31	M	Shoemaker	Herts	Wheathampstead
1395	GRAY	Ann	43		Dau-in-law	Mar	31	F		Herts	Harpenden
1396	GRAY	George	43		Grandson		6	M	At Home	Herts	Wheathampstead
1397	GRAY	Ann	43		Grandau		4	F	At Home	Herts	Wheathampstead
1398	GRAY	Alice	43		Grandau		10 m	F		Herts	Wheathampstead
1399	SLATER	Sarah	43		Grandau		12	F	At Home	Herts	Wheathampstead
1400	WEBB	George	44	Harpenden Common	Head	Mar	40	M	Agric Lab	Herts	Wheathampstead
1401	WEBB	Sarah	44		Wife	Mar	40	F		Herts	Ippollitts
1402	WEBB	Mary	44		Dau	Unm	18	F	Straw Plaiter	Herts	Wheathampstead
1403	WEBB	Sarah	44		Dau		15	F	Scholar	Herts	Wheathampstead
1404	WEBB	Hannah	44		Dau		12	F	Scholar	Herts	Wheathampstead
1405	WEBB	Phoebe	44		Dau		9	F	Scholar	Herts	Wheathampstead
1406	WEBB	Edith	44		Dau		4	F	At Home	Herts	Wheathampstead
1407	AUSTIN	William	45	Harpenden Common	Head	Mar	54	M	Straw Plait Dealer	Herts	Redbourn
1408	AUSTIN	Ann	45		Wife	Mar	54	F		Herts	Redbourn

1409	SEARS	Thomas	46	Harpenden Common	Head	Mar	39	M	Farmer of 50 acres employing I labourer	Herts	Wheathampstead
1410	SEARS	Jane	46		Wife	Mar	39	F		Herts	Wheathampstead
1411	SEARS	Anne	46		Mother	Unm	66	F	Housekeeper	Herts	Wheathampstead
1412	SEARS	William	46		Son	Unm	16	M	Farmers Son	Herts	Harpenden
1413	SEARS	Anne	46		Dau		14	F	At Home	Herts	Harpenden
1414	SEARS	Thomas	46		Son		10	M		Herts	Harpenden
1415	SEARS	Charles	46		Son		8	M	At Home	Herts	Harpenden
1416	SEARS	John	46		Son		5	M	At Home	Herts	Wheathampstead
1417	SEARS	Jane	46		Dau		3	F	At Home	Herts	Wheathampstead
1418	SEARS	Harriet	46		Dau		7m	F	At Home	Herts	Wheathampstead
1419	COTTON	John	47	St Albans Road	Head	Widower	60	M	Publican	Herts	Kings Walden
1420	PARKINS	William	47		Serv		14	M	Ostler	Herts	Hemel Hempstead
1421	RICHARDSON	John	47		Lodger	Widower	67	M	Pensioner (Royal Marines)	Herts	St Albans
1422	WINCH	Matthew	48	Harpenden Common	Head	Mar	60	M	Farm Bailiff	Herts	Hitchin
1423	WINCH	Elizabeth	48		Wife	Mar	44	F		Herts	Harpenden
1424	BENT	John	48		Serv	Unm	28	M	Agric Lab	Herts	Harpenden
1425	CLARIDGE	James	48		Serv	Unm	17	M	Agric Lab	Herts	Wheathampstead
1426	SYGROVE	John	49	Harpenden Common	Head	Mar	65	M	Agric Lab	Herts	Wheathampstead
1427	SYGROVE	Fanny	49		Wife	Mar	63	F		Herts	St Albans
1428	GIBBONS	George	49		Son-in-law	Mar	22	M	Agric Lab	Herts	Harpenden
1429	GIBBONS	Elizabeth	49		Dau	Mar	23	F		Herts	Wheathampstead
1430	GIBBONS	Rebecca	49		Grandau		2	F		Herts	Wheathampstead
1431	GIBBONS	William	49		Grandson		9m	M		Herts	Wheathampstead
1432	GRAY	Edward	50	Harpenden Common	Head	Mar	77	M	Agric Lab	Herts	Wheathampstead
1433	GRAY	Susannah	50		Wife	Mar	62	F		Herts	Wheathampstead
1434	GRAY	George	50		Son	Unm	22	M	Hat Blocker	Herts	Wheathampstead
1435	WESTON	Joseph	51	Harpenden Common	Head	Mar	44	M	Agric Lab	Herts	Wheathampstead
1436	WESTON	Martha	51		Wife	Mar	42	F		Herts	Kings Walden
1437	WESTON	Charles	51		Son		12	M	Agric Lab	Herts	Wheathampstead
1438	WESTON	Ann	51		Dau		9	F	Scholar	Herts	Wheathampstead
1439	WESTON	Alfred	51		Son		7	M	At Home	Herts	Wheathampstead
1440	WESTON	William	51		Son		4	M	At Home	Herts	Wheathampstead
1441	WESTON	Thomas	51		Son		1	M	at Home	Herts	Wheathampstead
1442	BRACEY	Caleb	52	Harpenden Common	Head	Mar	29	M	Agric Lab	Herts	Harpenden
1443	BRACEY	Helen	52		Wife	Mar	28	F		Herts	Wheathampstead
1444	BRACEY	Fanny	52		Dau		6	F	At Home	Herts	Wheathampstead
1445	BRACEY	George	52		Son		5	M	At Home	Herts	Wheathampstead
1446	BRACEY	Charles	52		Son		1	M		Herts	Wheathampstead
1447	GRAY	Ellen	52		Visitor	Unm	17	F	Bonnet Sewer	Herts	Wheathampstead
1448	MIAS	Esther	53	Harpenden Common	Head	Widow	38	F	Straw Plaiter	Herts	Wheathampstead
1449	MIAS	William	53		Son	Unm	19	M	Agric Lab	Herts	St Albans
1450	MIAS	Elizabeth	53		Dau	Unm	17	F	Straw Plaiter	Herts	Wheathampstead
1451	MIAS	John	53		Son		15	M	Agric Lab	Herts	Wheathampstead
1452	MIAS	James	53		Son		13	M	Agric Lab	Herts	St Albans

	SURNAME	FORENAME	SCHEDULE NUMBER	ADDRESS	RELATIONSHIP	STATUS	AGE	SEX	OCCUPATION	COUNTY OF BIRTH	PLACE OF BIRTH
1453	SYGROVE	James	53		Father	Widower	73	M	Agric Lab	Herts	Wheathampstead
1454	WESTON	John	54	Harpenden Common	Head	Mar	69	M	Agric Lab	Herts	Wheathampstead
1455	WESTON	Sophia	54		Wife	Mar	67	F		Herts	Redbourn
1456	WESTON	Eliza	54		Grandau		4	F		Herts	Harpenden
1457	LARGE	William	55	Cross Orchard	Head	Mar	22	M		Herts	Redbourn
1458	LARGE	Hannah	55		Wife	Mar	21	F		Herts	Redbourn
1459	HOWELL	James	56	Cross Orchard	Head	Mar	75	M	Agric Lab	Herts	Colney
1460	HOWELL	Sarah	56		Wife	Mar	55	F		Herts	Barnet
1461	HOWELL	William	56		Son	Unm	23	M	Agric Lab	Herts	St Peters
1462	HOWELL	Henry	56		Son	Unm	17	M	Hawker	Herts	St Albans
1463	DICKENSON	George	57	Cross Farm	Head	Mar	64	M	Farmer of 312 acres employing 9 labourers	Herts	Abbots Langley
1464	DICKENSON	Elizabeth	57		Wife	Mar	68	F		Herts	Redbourn
1465	DICKENSON	Rebecca	57		Dau	Unm	25	F	At Home	Herts	Sandridge
1466	DICKENSON	John	57		Son	Unm	24	M	At Home	Herts	Sandridge
1467	DICKENSON	Ann	57		Grandau	Unm	15	F	At Home	Herts	Sandridge
1468	ATKINS	Phoebe	57		Serv	Unm	18	F	House Servant	Herts	Abbots Langley
1469	BAILEY	George	57		Serv		12	M	Agric Lab	Herts	Wheathampstead
1470	DUNHAM	Alfred	57		Grandson		10	M	At Home	Herts	Harpenden
1471	BAILEY	James	57		Serv		9	M	Agric Lab	Herts	Wheathampstead
1472	HOUSE	Thomas	58	Grove Farm	Head	Unm	27	M	Farmer of 480 acres employing 32 labourers	Herts	Wheathampstead
1473	HOUSE	Sarah	58		Sister	Unm	30	F	At Home	Herts	Wheathampstead
1474	KIDMAN	Harriet	58		Cousin	Unm	22	F		Herts	Offley
1475	SMITH	Mary A	58		Serv	Unm	26	F	House Servant	Herts	Gaddesden
1476	SMITH	Hannah	58		Serv	Unm	19	F	House Servant	Herts	Harpenden
1477	KINGHAM	George	58		Serv	Unm	26	M	Ploughman	Herts	Wheathampstead
1478	ALLEN	James	58		Serv	Unm	17	M	Horsekeeper	Beds	Luton
1479	HUMPHREY	William	58		Serv	Unm	16	M	Horsekeeper	Herts	Flamstead
1480	GOTHARD	John	59	Pipers Lane	Head	Mar	44	M	Agric Lab	Herts	Kimpton
1481	GOTHARD	Eliza	59		Wife	Mar	34	F		Herts	Kimpton
1482	GOTHARD	Selina	59		Dau		12	F	Servant	Herts	Wheathampstead
1483	GOTHARD	George	59		Son		9	M	Scholar	Herts	Wheathampstead
1484	CLARIDGE	Joshua	60	Pipers Lane	Head	Mar	43	M	Agric Lab	Herts	Cockernhoe
1485	CLARIDGE	Lydia	60		Wife	Mar	43	F		Herts	Wheathampstead
1486	CLARIDGE	William	60		Son		14	M	Agric Lab	Herts	Wheathampstead
1487	CLARIDGE	Sophia	60		Dau		9	F	Scholar	Herts	Wheathampstead
1488	CLARIDGE	Thomas	60		Son		6	M	Scholar	Herts	Wheathampstead
1489	CLARIDGE	Joseph	60		Son		2	M	At Home	Herts	Wheathampstead
1490	DAY	George	61	Pipers Lane	Head	Widower	64	M	Agric Lab	Herts	Offley
1491	PARKINS	John	62	Pipers Lane	Head	Mar	55	M	Agric Lab	Herts	Wheathampstead
1492	PARKINS	Eliza	62		Wife	Mar	49	F		Beds	Leagrave
1493	PARKINS	Charles	62		Grandson		11	M	Scholar	Herts	Wheathampstead
1494	BARTON	Edward	62		Son-in-law	Widower	25	M	Agric Lab	Unknown	

One house uninhabited

1495	LATCHFORD	John	63	Down Green	Head	Mar	44	M	Agric Lab	Herts	Wheathampstead

1496	LATCHFORD	Sarah	63		Wife	Mar	42	F		Herts	Wheathampstead
1497	LATCHFORD	Thomas	63		Son		9	M	Agric Lab	Herts	Wheathampstead
1498	LATCHFORD	Ann	63		Dau		7	F	Scholar	Herts	Wheathampstead
1499	LATCHFORD	Lizzie	63		Dau		2	F	At Home	Herts	Wheathampstead
1500	CHAPMAN	James	63		Lodger		16	M	Agric Lab	Herts	Wheathampstead
1501	LATCHFORD	William	64	Down Green	Head	Widower	47	M		Herts	Wheathampstead
1502	WEBSTER	Joseph	64		Son-in-law	Mar	25	M	Agric Lab	Unknown	
1503	WEBSTER	Elizabeth	64		Dau	Mar	29	F		Herts	Wheathampstead
1504	WEBSTER	Charlotte E	64		Grandau		2 m	F		Herts	Wheathampstead
1505	CHAPMAN	John	65	Down Green	Head	Mar	44	M	Straw Factor	Herts	Hatfield
1506	CHAPMAN	Hannah	65		Wife	Mar	47	F		Herts	Wheathampstead
1507	CHAPMAN	Alice E	65		Dau	Unm	16	F	Straw Plaiter	Herts	Wheathampstead
1508	WEBB	William	65		Father-in-law	Widower	87	M	Agric Lab (Pauper)	Beds	Luton
1509	WELCH	Benjamin	66	Leasy Bridge Farm	Head	Mar	36	M	Agric Lab	Herts	Wheathampstead
1510	WELCH	Mary	66		Wife	Mar	44	F		Northants	Boddington
1511	WELCH	Emma	66		Dau		12	F	Straw Plaiter	Herts	Wheathampstead
1512	WELCH	Benjamin	66		Son		10	M	Agric Lab	Herts	Wheathampstead
1513	WELCH	William	66		Son		7	M	Scholar	Herts	Wheathampstead
1514	WELCH	Mary	66		Dau		5	F	At Home	Herts	Wheathampstead
1515	WELCH	Helen	66		Dau		2	F	At Home	Herts	Wheathampstead
1516	MUNT	Joseph	66		Serv	Unm	18	M	Shepherd	Herts	Sandridge
1517	GEORGE	Henry	66		Serv	Unm	18	M	Horsekeeper	Herts	Wheathampstead
1518	STEBBINGS	Thomas	67	Leasy Bridge	Head	Mar	58	M	Agric Lab	Herts	Ippollitts
1519	STEBBINGS	Jane	67		Wife	Mar	48	F		Herts	St Pauls Walden
1520	STEBBINGS	Emma	67		Dau		12	F	Straw Plaiter	Herts	Wheathampstead
1521	BALES	Elizabeth	68	Piggots Hill Farm	Head	Widow	65	F	Annuitant	Herts	Harpenden
1522	WARNER	Ann	68		Serv	Unm	30	F	House Servant	Herts	Wheathampstead
1523	SMITH	John	68		Serv	Unm	23	M	Agric Lab	Herts	Wheathampstead
1524	SLOUGH	Alfred	68		Serv	Unm	17	M	Agric Lab	Herts	Wheathampstead
1525	DAWES	James	68		Serv	Unm	17	M	Agric Lab	Herts	Kimpton
1526	GRAY	Thomas	68		Serv	Unm	16	M	Agric Lab	Herts	Wheathampstead
1527	GRAY	Charles	68		Serv		14	M	Agric Lab	Herts	Wheathampstead
1528	WOOD	Frederick	68		Serv	Unm	17	M	Shepherd	Herts	Whitwell
1529	WOOD	William	68		Serv	Mar	40	M	Shepherd	Herts	Wheathampstead
1530	CREW	Benjamin	68		Serv		14	M	Shepherd	Herts	St Pauls Walden
1531	WEEDON	Philip	69	Paper Mill	Head	Mar	29	M	Paper Maker	Bucks	High Wycombe
1532	WEEDON	Elizabeth	69		Wife	Mar	25	F		Herts	Wheathampstead
1533	WEEDON	Joseph	69		Son		5	M	At Home	Herts	Wheathampstead
1534	WEEDON	Edwin	69		Son		2	M	At Home	Herts	Wheathampstead
1535	HAPPY	William	70	Nr Pickford Mill	Head	Mar	49	M	Whitesmith	Middx	Bethnal Green
1536	HAPPY	Mary	70		Wife	Mar	43	F		Herts	Harpenden
1537	HAPPY	Emma	70		Dau	Unm	15	F	At Home	Herts	Harpenden
1538	LINFORD	Alfred	70		Lodger	Mar	22	M	Tailor	Bucks	Amersham
1539	LINFORD	Mary A	70		Lodgers Wife	Mar	18	F		Middx	Spitalfields

	SURNAME	FORENAME	SCHEDULE NUMBER	ADDRESS	RELATIONSHIP	STATUS	AGE	SEX	OCCUPATION	COUNTY OF BIRTH	PLACE OF BIRTH
1540	DYMOCK	David	71	Nr Pickford Mill	Head	Mar	23	M	Agric Lab	Herts	Wheathampstead
1541	DYMOCK	Mary	71		Wife	Mar	26	F		Herts	Harpenden
1542	DYMOCK	Infant	71		Son		1 m	M		Herts	Wheathampstead
1543	HARRIS	Thomas	72	Nr Pickford Mill	Head	Mar	37	M	Horsekeeper	Northants	Wittlebury
1544	HARRIS	Elizabeth	72		Wife	Mar	33	F		Middx	South Mimms
1545	HARRIS	Mary A	72		Dau		10	F	At Home	Middx	Hadley
1546	HARRIS	George	72		Son		7	M	At Home	Middx	Hadley
1547	HARRIS	Joseph	72		Son		5	M	At Home	Middx	Hadley
1548	HARRIS	William	72		Son		3	M	At Home	Middx	Hadley
1549	DIVERS	William	73	Batford Mill	Head	Unm	30	M	Farmer of 160 acres employing 7 men	Herts	Tewin
1550	DIVERS	Henry	73		Brother	Unm	27	M	Miller employing 1 Lab	Herts	Tewin
1551	DIVERS	Mary A	73		Sister	Unm	25	F	At Home	Herts	Hertford
1552	DIVERS	Eliza	73		Sister	Unm	23	F	At Home	Herts	Hertford
1553	ARNOLD	Matthew	74	Batford Mills	Head	Mar	52	M	Agric Lab	Herts	Harpenden
1554	ARNOLD	Ann	74		Wife	Mar	47	F		Herts	Hatfield
1555	ARNOLD	Matthew	74		Son		16	M	Agric Lab	Herts	Wheathampstead
1556	ARNOLD	Ann	74		Dau		15	F	Straw Plaiter	Herts	Wheathampstead
1557	ARNOLD	James	74		Son		11	M	Agric Lab	Herts	Wheathampstead
1558	ARNOLD	William	74		Son		9	M	At Home	Herts	Wheathampstead
1559	ARNOLD	George	74		Son		7	M	At Home	Herts	Wheathampstead
1560	DYMOCK	Thomas	75	Batford Mills	Head	Mar	57	M	Agric Lab	Herts	Wheathampstead
1561	DYMOCK	Susan	75		Wife	Mar	57	F		Herts	Watton
1562	DYMOCK	John	75		Grandson		12	M	Agric Lab	Herts	Wheathampstead
1563	NORTH	Thomas	76	Batford Mills	Head	Mar	48	M	Agric Lab	Herts	Wheathampstead
1564	NORTH	Elizabeth	76		Wife	Mar	47	F		Herts	Wheathampstead
1565	NORTH	Hannah	76		Dau	Unm	18	F	Straw Plaiter	Herts	Wheathampstead
1566	NORTH	Mary	76		Dau		11	F	Straw Plaiter	Herts	Wheathampstead
1567	NORTH	Alfred	76		Son		6	M	At Home	Herts	Wheathampstead
1568	GRIGG	William A	77	Causewell Farm	Head	Mar	36	M	Farmer of 150 acres employing 7 labourers	Berks	Newbury
1569	GRIGG	Ellen	77		Wife	Mar	33	F		Wilts	Ramsbury
1570	SWAIN	Emma	77		Serv	Unm	19	F	House Servant	Herts	Colney
1571	BURGIN	Joseph	77		Serv		15	M	Agric Lab	Herts	Wheathampstead
1572	WOODWARD	Charles	77		Serv		14	M	Agric Lab	Herts	Wheathampstead
1573	WILTSHIRE	Joseph	77		Visitor	Unm	41	M	Brewer	Herts	Sandridge
1574	GROOM	Charles	78	The Folly	Head	Mar	29	M	Agric Lab	Herts	Wheathampstead
1575	GROOM	Anne	78		Wife	Mar	30	F		Herts	Ayot St Lawrence
1576	GROOM	Susan	78		Dau		9	F	At Home	Herts	Wheathampstead
1577	GROOM	John	78		Son		4	M	At Home	Herts	Wheathampstead
1578	GROOM	Elizabeth	78		Dau		1	F		Herts	Wheathampstead
1579	CRAWLEY	William	78		Lodger	Unm	38	M	Agric Lab	Herts	Wheathampstead
1580	ROBERTS	Mark	78		Lodger	Mar	24	M	Sawyer	Herts	Wheathampstead
1581	NORRIS	Joseph	79	The Folly	Head	Mar	36	M	Sawyer	Herts	Wheathampstead
1582	NORRIS	Sarah	79		Wife	Mar	31	F		Herts	Wheathampstead
1583	NORRIS	Ann M	79		Dau		9	F	At Home	Herts	Wheathampstead

1584	NORRIS	John	79		Son		7	M	At Home	Herts	Wheathampstead
1585	NORRIS	Joseph	79		Son		4	M	At Home	Herts	Wheathampstead
1586	NORRIS	Hannah	79		Dau		4m	F		Herts	Wheathampstead
1587	FENSOME	Elizabeth	79		Sister-in-law	Unm	28	F	Straw Plaiter	Herts	Wheathampstead
1588	PEARCE	Thomas	80	Wheathampstead Hill	Head	Mar	71	M	Agric Lab	Herts	Harpenden
1589	PEARCE	Mary	80		Wife	Mar	65	F	Laundress	Herts	Wheathampstead
1590	PEARCE	Sarah	80		Dau	Unm	33	F	Straw Plaiter	Herts	Wheathampstead
1591	BLOW	Robert	80		Grandson		7	M		Herts	Wheathampstead
1592	THOMSON	William	81	Wheathampstead Hill	Head	Mar	40	M	Straw Factor	Herts	Codicote
1593	THOMSON	Hannah	81		Wife	Mar	37	F		Herts	Wheathampstead
1594	THOMSON	Eliza	81		Dau	Unm	18	F	Straw Plaiter	Herts	Wheathampstead
1595	THOMSON	Susan	81		Dau		15	F	Straw Plaiter	Herts	Wheathampstead
1596	THOMSON	James	81		Son		13	M	Scholar	Herts	Wheathampstead
1597	THOMSON	Mary	81		Dau		10	F	Scholar	Herts	Wheathampstead
1598	THOMSON	Charles	81		Son		7	M	Scholar	Herts	Wheathampstead
1599	THOMSON	Sophia	81		Dau		5	F	Scholar	Herts	Wheathampstead
1600	THOMSON	Henry	81		Son		5m	M		Herts	Wheathampstead
1601	HILLS	John	82	Wheathampstead Hill	Head	Mar	35	M	Brewers Labourer	Herts	Ware
1602	HILLS	Jane	82		Wife	Mar	30	F		Herts	Datchworth
1603	HILLS	Ann	82		Dau		11	F	Scholar	Herts	Hertford
1604	HILLS	Albert	82		Son		9	M	Scholar	Herts	Hertford
1605	HILLS	Louisa	82		Dau		7	F	Scholar	Herts	Hertford
1606	HILLS	Fanny	82		Dau		4	F		Middx	Islington
1607	HILLS	Harriet	82		Dau		1	F		Herts	Wheathampstead
1608	GROOM	James	83	Wheathampstead Hill	Head	Mar	26	M	Agric Lab	Herts	Hitchin
1609	GROOM	Susan	83		Wife	Mar	25	F		Herts	Wheathampstead
1610	GROOM	Reuben	83		[Son]		7m	M		Herts	Wheathampstead
1611	JOINER	John	84	Wheathampstead Hill	Head	Mar	36	M	Agric Lab	Herts	Preston
1612	JOINER	Sarah	84		Wife	Mar	37	F		Herts	Preston
1613	JOINER	Jane	84		Dau	Unm	16	F	Straw Plaiter	Herts	Preston
1614	JOINER	Frederick	84		Son		8	M	Scholar	Herts	Preston
1615	JOINER	Matilda	84		Dau		6	F	At Home	Herts	Preston
1616	JOINER	Edmund	84		Son		3	M	At Home	Herts	Gaddesden
1617	JOINER	Henry	84		Son		5m	M	At Home	Herts	Wheathampstead
1618	HANDLEY	John	85	Wheathampstead Hill	Head	Mar	32	M	Agric Lab	Herts	Kings Walden
1619	HANDLEY	Sarah	85		Wife	Mar	35	F		Herts	Wheathampstead
1620	DICKENSON	Eli	86	Wheathampstead Hill	Head	Mar	36	M	Sawyer	Herts	Wheathampstead
1621	DICKENSON	Phoebe	86		Wife	Mar	36	F		Herts	Wheathampstead
1622	DICKENSON	George	86		Son		16	M	Agric Lab	Herts	Wheathampstead
1623	DICKENSON	Sarah	86		Dau		12	F	Scholar	Herts	Wheathampstead
1624	DICKENSON	Reuben	86		Son		3	M	At Home	Herts	Wheathampstead
1625	DICKENSON	Anne	86		Dau		5m	F	At Home	Herts	Wheathampstead
1626	BRACEY	Daniel	87	Wheathampstead Hill	Head	Mar	36	M	Bricklayers Labr	Herts	Sandridge
1627	BRACEY	Mary A	87		Wife	Mar	36	F		Herts	Wheathampstead
1628	BRACEY	John	87		Son-in-law		15	M	Agric Lab	Herts	Wheathampstead

	SURNAME	FORENAME	SCHEDULE NUMBER	ADDRESS	RELATIONSHIP	STATUS	AGE	SEX	OCCUPATION	COUNTY OF BIRTH	PLACE OF BIRTH
1629	BRACEY	Francis	87		Son		12	M	Agric Lab	Herts	Wheathampstead
1630	BRACEY	Edith	87		Dau		7	F	At Home	Herts	Wheathampstead
1631	BRACEY	Maria	87		Dau		5	F	At Home	Herts	Wheathampstead
1632	BRACEY	Anne	87		Dau		3	F	At Home	Herts	Wheathampstead
1633	BRACEY	Thomas	87		Son		2	M	At Home	Herts	Wheathampstead
1634	BRACEY	Infant	87		Son		1wk	M	At Home	Herts	Wheathampstead
1635	GRAY	Charles	88	Wheathampstead Hill	Head	Mar	32	M	Brewers Labr & Beer shopkeeper	Herts	Gosmore
1636	GRAY	Ann	88		Wife	Mar	29	F		Herts	Preston
1637	GRAY	Thomas	88		Son		9	M	Scholar	Herts	Gosmore
1638	GRAY	Charles	88		Son		6	M	Scholar	Herts	Wheathampstead
1639	GRAY	Frederick	88		Son		4	M	At Home	Herts	Wheathampstead
1640	GRAY	Edward	88		Son		2	M	At Home	Herts	Wheathampstead
1641	GRAY	Mary A	88		Dau		2m	F		Herts	Wheathampstead
1642	JOINER	Emma	88		Niece		10	F		Herts	Preston
1643	KEMP	John	88		Lodger	Unm	16	M	Shepherd	Herts	North Mimms
1644	NASH	William	89	Wheathampstead Hill	Head	Widower	60	M	Carpenter	Herts	Wheathampstead
1645	NASH	Sarah	89		Dau	Unm	26	F	Straw Plaiter	Herts	Wheathampstead
1646	NASH	Charlotte	89		Dau	Unm	23	F	Straw Plaiter	Herts	Wheathampstead
1647	NASH	Harriet	89		Dau	Unm	14	F	Straw Plaiter	Herts	Wheathampstead
1648	ODELL	John	89		Lodger	Widower	62	M	Agric Lab (Deaf)	Beds	Stopsley
1649	MUNT	Thomas	90	Wheathampstead Hill	Head	Mar	39	M	Agric Lab	Herts	Wheathampstead
1650	MUNT	Maria	90		Wife	Mar	35	F		Herts	Wheathampstead
1651	MUNT	Charles	90		Son		16	M	Agric Lab	Herts	Wheathampstead
1652	MUNT	George	90		Son		14	M	Agric Lab	Herts	Wheathampstead
1653	MUNT	Harriet	90		Dau		11	F	At Home	Herts	Wheathampstead
1654	MUNT	Amos	90		Son		8	M	At Home	Herts	Wheathampstead
1655	MUNT	Alfred	90		Son		6	M	Scholar	Herts	Wheathampstead
1656	MUNT	Thomas	90		Son		4	M	At Home	Herts	Wheathampstead
1657	MUNT	Anne	90		Dau		1	F	At Home	Herts	Wheathampstead
1658	BURGOYNE	John	91	Wheathampstead Hill	Head	Mar	42	M	Agric Lab	Herts	Wheathampstead
1659	BURGOYNE	Mary	91		Wife	Mar	33	F		Herts	Wheathampstead
1660	BURGOYNE	Joyce	91		Dau		15	F	Straw Plaiter	Herts	Wheathampstead
1661	BURGOYNE	Lucy	91		Dau		13	F	Straw Plaiter	Herts	Wheathampstead
1662	BURGOYNE	Edith	91		Dau		11	F		Herts	Wheathampstead
1663	PARKINS	Alfred	91		Son-in-law		9	M	Scholar	Herts	Wheathampstead
1664	BURGOYNE	Henry	91		Son		2	M		Herts	Wheathampstead
1665	BURGOYNE	Infant	91		Son		1wk	M		Herts	Wheathampstead
1666	PARKINS	Eliza	91		Lodger	Mar	50	F	Nurse	Herts	Wheathampstead
1667	PARKINS	Thomas	92	Wheathampstead Hill	Head	Mar	30	M	Agric Lab	Herts	Wheathampstead
1668	PARKINS	Mary	92		Wife	Mar	29	F		Bucks	Wadsden
1669	PARKINS	Eliza	92		Dau		3	F		Herts	Wheathampstead
1670	PARKINS	Ann	92		Dau		1	F		Herts	Wheathampstead
1671	BURGESS	Charles	93	The Swan Inn	Head	Mar	37	M	Innkeeper	Herts	Tewin
1672	BURGESS	Maria	93		Wife	Mar	33	F		Herts	St Margarets [Stanstead St Margarets]

1673	HEWSON	Alfred W	93		Son-in-law		7	M	Scholar	Herts	Wheathampstead
1674	HEWSON	Laura	93		Dau-in-law		6	F	Scholar	Herts	Wheathampstead
1675	HEWSON	Edward	93		Son-in-law		2	M		Herts	Wheathampstead
1676	BURGESS	Frederick	93		Son		2m	M		Herts	Wheathampstead
1677	BASS	Ellen	93		Serv	Unm	20	F	Domestic Servant	Herts	Wheathampstead
1678	DAY	John	93		Serv	Unm	20	M	Horsekeeper	Herts	Kimpton
1679	REID	John	93		Lodger	Unm	60	M	Agric Lab (Pensioner)	Herts	Wheathampstead
1680	ODELL	William	93		Lodger	Unm	20	M	Agric Lab	Herts	Wheathampstead
1681	SAUNDERS	William	93		Lodger	Unm	29	M	Shoemaker	Herts	St Albans
1682	MESSER	John	94	Wheathampstead Village	Head	Mar	50	M	Blacksmith employing 2 men	Herts	Wheathampstead
1683	MESSER	Mary	94		Wife	Mar	44	F		Herts	Wheathampstead
1684	MESSER	James	94		Son	Unm	20	M	Blacksmith	Herts	Wheathampstead
1685	MESSER	Thomas	94		Son	Unm	18	M	Servt to a Baker	Herts	Wheathampstead
1686	MESSER	Ebenezer	94		Son	Unm	14	M	Errand boy	Herts	Wheathampstead
1687	MESSER	William	94		Son		12	M	Scholar	Herts	Wheathampstead
1688	MESSER	Alfred	94		Son		7	M	Scholar	Herts	Wheathampstead
1689	MESSER	Mary	94		Dau		2	F		Herts	Wheathampstead
1690	MESSER	John	94		Nephew		13	M	Scholar	Herts	Wheathampstead
1691	WILSHER	John	95	Wheathampstead Village	Head	Mar	40	M	Carpenter	Herts	Sandridge
1692	WILSHER	Sarah	95		Wife	Mar	35	F		Herts	Wheathampstead
1693	WILSHER	William	95		Son	Unm	16	M	Appr Grocer	Herts	Wheathampstead
1694	WILSHER	Sarah	95		Dau	Unm	14	F	Appr Bonnet Sewer	Herts	Wheathampstead
1695	WILSHER	Thomas	95		Son		11	M	Scholar	Herts	Wheathampstead
1696	WILSHER	John	95		Son		8	M	Scholar	Herts	Wheathampstead

Two houses uninhabited

1697	FOSTER	Mary	96	Wheathampstead Village	Head	Widow	54	F	School Mistress	Herts	Wheathampstead
1698	REED	Eliza	96		Lodger	Unm	28	F	Straw Plaiter	Herts	Wheathampstead
1699	CHENNELLS	Ann	97	Wheathampstead Street	Head	Unm	86	F	Annuitant	Herts	Wheathampstead
1700	CHENNELLS	Esther	97		Sister	Unm	77	F	Annuitant	Herts	Wheathampstead
1701	NASH	John	98	Wheathampstead Street	Head	Mar	26	M	Grocers Assistant	Herts	Wheathampstead
1702	NASH	Sarah S	98		Wife	Mar	19	F		Herts	Hitchin
1703	NASH	Thomas	98		Son		1	M		Herts	Wheathampstead
1704	MERKINS	Mary	98		Serv	Unm	13	F	House Servant	Herts	Wheathampstead
1705	POULTER	John	99	Workhouse Yard	Head	Widower	35	M	Agric Lab	Herts	Wheathampstead
1706	POULTER	Caroline	99		Dau		6	F	At Home	Herts	Wheathampstead
1707	POULTER	Lucy	99		Dau		5	F		Herts	Wheathampstead
1708	POULTER	James	99		Father	Mar	71	M	Tailor	Herts	Ickleford
1709	POULTER	Jane	99		Mother	Mar	73	F		Herts	Wheathampstead
1710	STREDDER	William	100	Workhouse Yard	Head	Widower	54	M	Agric Lab	Herts	Harpenden
1711	MORGAN	William	101	Workhouse Yard	Head	Mar	53	M	Agric Lab	Herts	Preston
1712	MORGAN	Margaret	101		Wife	Mar	49	F		Herts	Wheathampstead
1713	PIXLEY	William	101		Lodger	Widower	42	M	Agric Lab	Herts	Wheathampstead
1714	PIXLEY	Sarah	101		Lodgers Dau		12	F	Scholar	Herts	Wheathampstead
1715	PIXLEY	William	101		Lodgers Son		11	M	Scholar	Herts	Wheathampstead

	SURNAME	FORENAME	SCHEDULE NUMBER	ADDRESS	RELATIONSHIP	STATUS	AGE	SEX	OCCUPATION	COUNTY OF BIRTH	PLACE OF BIRTH
1716	PIXLEY	George	101		Lodgers Son		8	M	Scholar	Herts	Wheathampstead
1717	SMITH	Henry	102	Workhouse Yard	Head	Mar	48	M	Agric Lab	Herts	St Pauls Walden
1718	SMITH	Sarah	102		Wife	Mar	49	F		Herts	St Pauls Walden
1719	SMITH	Mary	102		Dau	Unm	18	F	Straw Plaiter	Herts	St Pauls Walden
1720	SMITH	George	102		Son	Unm	15	M	Agric Lab	Herts	Wheathampstead
1721	SMITH	Charlotte	102		Lodger		2	F		Herts	Kings Walden
1722	JOHNSON	James	103	Workhouse Yard	Head	Unm	37	M	Boot & Shoemaker employing 2 workers	Middx	Clerkenwell
1723	SEABROOK	Thomas	103		Appr	Unm	16	M	Appr to Boot & Shoemaker	Herts	Wheathampstead
1724	LEE	Edmund	103		Lodger	Unm	27	M	Journeyman Shoemaker	Herts	Ayot St Peter
1725	PEARMAN	Thomas	104	Workhouse Yard	Head	Mar	59	M	Agric Lab	Herts	Yardley
1726	PEARMAN	Sarah	104		Wife	Mar	52	F		Herts	Wheathampstead
1727	MOWBRAY	Elizabeth	105	Workhouse Yard	Head	Unm	46	F	Dress Maker	Herts	St Albans
1728	EDMONDS	Mary	106	Workhouse Yard	Head	Unm	77	F	Annuitant	Middx	St Pancras
1729	SMITH	Louisa	107	Wheathampstead Street	Head	Mar	34	F	Bonnet Sewer	Herts	St Albans
1730	LINES	Mary A	107		Sister		14	F	Bonnet Sewer	Herts	St Albans
1731	PAUL	Sophia	107		Lodger	Unm	23	F	Dress Maker	Herts	Sandridge
1732	JAMES	John E	107		Lodger	Unm	17	M	Schoolmaster	Middx	Brompton
1733	ARNOLD	James	108	Wheathampstead Street	Head	Mar	40	M	Boot & Shoemaker	Herts	Kings Walden
1734	ARNOLD	Elizabeth	108		Wife	Mar	46	F		Herts	Wheathampstead
1735	RUDD	William	109	Wheathampstead Street	Head	Widower	42	M	Beer Shop keeper	Herts	Sandridge
1736	RUDD	Ann	109		Dau	Unm	19	F	Straw Plaiter	Herts	Kimpton
1737	RUDD	Daniel	109		Son	Unm	17	M	At Home	Herts	Wheathampstead
1738	RUDD	Joseph	109		Son		7	M	Scholar	Herts	Wheathampstead
1739	RUDD	Philip	109		Son		5	M	Scholar	Herts	Wheathampstead
1740	TONG	Mary	110	Wheathampstead Street	Head	Widow	50	F	Tailors Widow	Herts	Wheathampstead
1741	TONG	Mary A	110		Dau	Unm	21	F	Dress Maker	Herts	Wheathampstead
1742	TONG	Thomas	110		Son	Unm	18	M	Tailor	Herts	Wheathampstead
1743	TONG	William	110		Grandson		4m	M		Herts	Wheathampstead
1744	BRAY	Ann	111	Wheathampstead Street	Head	Unm	45	F	Straw Plaiter	Herts	Wheathampstead
1745	BRAY	Sarah	111		Dau		9	F	Straw Plaiter	Herts	Wheathampstead
1746	BRAY	Alfred	111		Son		5	M		Herts	Wheathampstead
1747	ARNOLD	Sarah	112	Wheathampstead Street	Head	Widow	67	F	Straw Plaiter	Herts	Wheathampstead
1748	ARNOLD	Oliver	112		Son	Unm	37	M	Sawyer	Middx	Chelsea
1749	ARNOLD	Mary A	112		Dau	Unm	28	F	Straw Plaiter	Herts	Wheathampstead
1750	ARNOLD	Susan E	112		Grandau		11	F	Scholar	Herts	St Albans
1751	ARNOLD	John	112		Grandson		9	M	Scholar	Herts	Wheathampstead
1752	ARNOLD	Julia	112		Grandau		3	F	Scholar	Herts	Wheathampstead
1753	BURTON	Edward	113	Wheathampstead Mill	Head	Mar	41	M	Miller & Farmer of 40 acres employing 3 labourers	Herts	Wheathampstead
1754	BURTON	Eliza	113		Wife	Mar	33	F		Herts	St Albans
1755	BURTON	Harriet	113		Dau		12	F	Scholar	Herts	Wheathampstead
1756	BURTON	Sarah A	113		Dau		10	F	Scholar	Herts	Wheathampstead
1757	BURTON	Edward	113		Father	Widower	73	M	Retired Farmer	Herts	Kimpton
1758	ADAMS	William	114	Near the Mill	Head	Mar	49	M	Hay Binder	Herts	Wheathampstead

1759	ADAMS	Anne	114		Wife	Mar	52	F		Herts	Wheathampstead
1760	ADAMS	Albert	114		Son		13	M	Agric Lab	Herts	Wheathampstead
1761	HOLLINGS-WORTH	Thomas	115	Near the Mill	Head	Mar	65	M	Agric Lab	Herts	Wheathampstead
1762	HOLLINGS-WORTH	Harriet	115		Wife	Mar	66	F		Herts	Wheathampstead
1763	BAR	Mahala	115		Lodger	Widow	32	F	Straw Plaiter	Herts	Wheathampstead
1764	BAR	Arthur	115		Lodgers Son		9	M	Scholar	Herts	Wheathampstead
1765	EDMONDS	William	116	Near the Mill	Head	Mar	40	M	Agric Lab	Herts	Wheathampstead
1766	EDMONDS	Mary A	116		Wife	Mar	40	F		Herts	Wheathampstead
1767	EDMONDS	Alfred	116		Son		10	M	Scholar	Herts	Wheathampstead
1768	BATCHELOR	Thomas	117	Near the Mill	Head	Mar	29	M	Baker employs 2 Men	Herts	Wheathampstead
1769	BATCHELOR	Sally	117		Wife	Mar	27	F		Herts	Studham
1770	EZZARD	George N	117		Serv	Unm	18	M	Baker	Herts	Hitchin
1771	SMITH	George	117		Serv	Unm	23	M	Baker	Herts	Hemel Hempstead
1772	DELLAR	William	118	Near the Red Lion	Head	Unm	21	M	Shoemaker	Herts	Anstey
1773	GREGORY	Elizabeth	119	Near the Red Lion	Head	Unm	58	F	Retired Grocer	Herts	Harpenden
1774	DICKENSON	Mary A	119		Serv		13	F	House Servant	Herts	Wheathampstead
1775	NASH	George	120	The Red Lion Beer Shop	Head	Mar	65	M	Carpenter & Beer Shopkeeper	Herts	Wheathampstead
1776	NASH	Maria	120		Wife	Mar	62	F		Herts	Wheathampstead
1777	NASH	Amelia	120		Dau	Unm	26	F	Straw Plaiter	Herts	Wheathampstead
1778	NASH	Francis	120		Son	Unm	22	M	Bricklayers Labr	Herts	Wheathampstead
1779	NASH	Charles	120		Grandson		6	M	Scholar	Herts	Wheathampstead
1780	HALSEY	Elizabeth	121	Near the Red Lion	Head	Mar	23	F	Sawyers Wife	Herts	Abbots Langley
1781	HALSEY	Sarah	121		Dau		3	F		Herts	Redbourn
1782	FISHER	James	122	Near the Red Lion	Head	Widower	40	M	Agric Lab	Herts	Wheathampstead
1783	FISHER	Emma	122		Dau		12	F	Straw Plaiter	Herts	Wheathampstead
1784	FISHER	Ann	122		Dau		10	F	Scholar	Herts	Wheathampstead
1785	FITZJOHN	Hester	122		Lodger	Unm	35	F	Straw Plaiter	Herts	Wheathampstead
1786	FITZJOHN	Thomas	122		Lodger		8	M	Scholar	Herts	Harpenden
1787	NASH	David	123	Near the Red Lion	Head	Mar	34	M	Carpenter	Herts	Wheathampstead
1788	NASH	Maria	123		Wife	Mar	34	F		Herts	Wheathampstead
1789	NASH	Hannah	123		Dau		10	F	Scholar	Herts	Wheathampstead
1790	NASH	George	123		Son		8	M	At Home	Herts	Wheathampstead
1791	NASH	John	123		Son		5	M		Herts	Hatfield
1792	NASH	Jabez	123		Son		1	M		Herts	Hatfield
1793	ELLINGHAM	John	124	Bury Green	Head	Widower	60	M	Late Gardener	Beds	Totternhoe
1794	ELLINGHAM	Mary	124		Dau	Unm	26	F	Bonnet Sewer	Herts	Wheathampstead
1795	CLARK	William	125	Bury Green	Head	Mar	33	M	Carrier & Farmer	Herts	Ayot St Peter
1796	CLARK	Mary	125		Wife	Mar	32	F		Herts	Wheathampstead
1797	CLARK	Catherine	125		Dau		8	F	Scholar	Herts	Wheathampstead
1798	CLARK	George	125		Son		6	M	At Home	Herts	Wheathampstead
1799	CLARK	Thomas	125		Son		4	M	At Home	Herts	Wheathampstead
1800	CLARK	Mary A	125		Dau		3	F		Herts	Wheathampstead
1801	CLARK	William	125		Son		1	M		Herts	Wheathampstead

	SURNAME	FORENAME	SCHEDULE NUMBER	ADDRESS	RELATIONSHIP	STATUS	AGE	SEX	OCCUPATION	COUNTY OF BIRTH	PLACE OF BIRTH
1802	GROOM	William	125		Serv	[Unm]	17	M	Servant	Middx	[Unknown]
1803	WOOD	Emma	125		Serv		13	F	House Servt	Herts	Wheathampstead
1804	GROOM	Arthur	125		Lodger		13	M	Groom & Gardener	Middx	[Unknown]
1805	DUNHAM	Francis	126	Bury Green	Head	Mar	56	M	Bricklayer	Herts	Wheathampstead
1806	DUNHAM	Maria	126		Wife	Mar	56	F		Herts	Wheathampstead
1807	DUNHAM	Matilda	126		Dau	Unm	34	F	Bonnet Sewer	Herts	Wheathampstead
1808	DUNHAM	Thomas	126		Son	Unm	21	M	Bricklayer	Herts	Wheathampstead
1809	DUNHAM	Mary A	127	Bury Green	Head	Unm	46	F	Beer Shop keeper	Herts	Wheathampstead
1810	DUNHAM	Eliza	127		Niece		3	F		Beds	New Mill End
1811	SMITH	William	127		Lodger	Mar	38	M	Bricklayer	Herts	Bishops Stortford
1812	EVANS	George	127		Lodger	Unm	30	M	Agric Lab	Herts	Hatfield
1813	PEACOCK	Mary	128	The Rectory	Head	Unm	68	F	Housekeeper	Herts	St Albans
1814	WEBB	Joseph	128		Serv	Unm	50	M	Gardener & Pensioner (Army)	Herts	Wheathampstead

One house uninhabited

	SURNAME	FORENAME	SCHEDULE NUMBER	ADDRESS	RELATIONSHIP	STATUS	AGE	SEX	OCCUPATION	COUNTY OF BIRTH	PLACE OF BIRTH
1815	BARKER	James	129	Bury Green	Head	Mar	54	M	Agric Lab	Herts	Hitchin
1816	BARKER	Dinah	129		Wife	Mar	56	F		Herts	Wheathampstead
1817	BARKER	Matilda	129		Dau		12	F	Scholar	Herts	Wheathampstead
1818	BARKER	Sophia	129		Dau		9	F	Scholar	Herts	Wheathampstead
1819	FREEMAN	Mary A	129		Grandau		3	F		Herts	Wheathampstead
1820	FREEMAN	James	130	Bury Green	Head	Mar	32	M	Agric Lab	Beds	[Unknown]
1821	FREEMAN	Mary	130		Wife	Mar	30	F		Herts	Wheathampstead
1822	FREEMAN	James	130		Son		1	M		Herts	Wheathampstead
1823	BARKER	James	130		Brother-in-law		17	M	Agric Lab	Herts	Wheathampstead
1824	BARKER	John	130		Brother-in-law		13	M	Agric Lab	Herts	Wheathampstead
1825	LINES	Charles	131	Bury Green	Head	Mar	46	M	Coal Carter & dealer	Herts	Wheathampstead
1826	LINES	Mary	131		Wife	Mar	42	F		Herts	Walkern
1827	LINES	George	131		Son	Unm	19	M	Coal Carter	Herts	Wheathampstead
1828	LINES	Charles	131		Son		13	M	Scholar	Herts	Wheathampstead
1829	LINES	Kitty	131		Dau		11	F	Straw Plaiter	Herts	Wheathampstead
1830	LINES	John	131		Son		8	M	Scholar	Herts	Wheathampstead
1831	LINES	Ann	131		Dau		4	F	At Home	Herts	Wheathampstead
1832	LINES	James	131		Son		2	M		Herts	Wheathampstead
1833	LATTIMORE	Thomas	132	Bury Green	Head	Mar	76	M	Proprietor of Houses	Herts	Wheathampstead
1834	LATTIMORE	Hannah	132		Wife	Mar	66	F		Herts	Wheathampstead
1835	DICKENSON	Charles	132		Grandson		14	M	Wheelwright	Herts	Wheathampstead
1836	GRIMSDALE	George	133	Bury Green	Head	Mar	30	M	Gardener	Herts	Wheathampstead
1837	GRIMSDALE	Ann	133		Wife	Mar	40	F		Herts	Wheathampstead
1838	GRIMSDALE	Elizabeth	133		Dau		7	F	At Home	Beds	[Unknown]
1839	GRIMSDALE	Arthur	133		Son		5	M	At Home	Beds	[Unknown]
1840	DOVER	James	134	Bury Farm	Head	Mar	41	M	Farmer of 439 acres employing 20 labourers	Bucks	North Marston
1841	DOVER	Elizabeth	134		Wife	Mar	41	F		Oxon	Cropredy
1842	OLNEY	David	134		Serv	Unm	37	M	Agric Lab	Herts	Harpenden
1843	NASH	Joseph	134		Serv	Unm	20	M	Agric Lab	Herts	Wheathampstead

1844	WESTON	George	134		Serv	Unm	19	M	Agric Lab	Herts	Harpenden
1845	EDMUNDS	William	134		Serv	Unm	17	M	Agric Lab	Herts	Wheathampstead
1846	LATCHFORD	James	134		Serv	Unm	13	M	Agric Lab	Herts	Wheathampstead
1847	LATCHFORD	William	134		Serv		12	M	Agric Lab	Herts	Wheathampstead
1848	GREY	James	134		Serv	Unm	15	M	Agric Lab	Herts	Wheathampstead
1849	DYMOCK	John	135	Bury Green	Head	Unm	60	M	Agric Lab	Herts	Wheathampstead
1850	DYMOCK	Mary	135		Sister	Unm	59	F	Straw plaiter	Herts	Wheathampstead
1851	GALER	William	136	Bury Green	Head	Widower	73	M	Gardener	Herts	St Pauls Walden
1852	GALER	Sarah	136		Dau	Unm	45	F	Laundress	Herts	St Albans
1853	NEWSON	Mary A	136		Niece	Unm	43	F	Straw Plaiter	Middx	[Unknown]
1854	ROBARDS	Halsey	137	Bury Green	Head	Unm	66	M	Shoemaker	Herts	Wheathampstead
1855	NASH	Henry	138	Bury Green	Head	Mar	32	M	Journeyman Smith	Herts	Wheathampstead
1856	NASH	Elizabeth	138		Wife	Mar	32	F		Herts	Wheathampstead
1857	NASH	Ann	138		Dau		5	F	Scholar	Herts	Wheathampstead
1858	NASH	Elizabeth	138		Dau		2	F	At Home	Herts	Wheathampstead
1859	NASH	Sarah	138		Dau		2m	F		Herts	Wheathampstead
1860	ANDERSON	John	139	Bury Green	Head	Mar	40	M	Brewers Labr	Herts	Wheathampstead
1861	ANDERSON	Ann	139		Wife	Mar	37	F		Herts	Colney Heath
1862	ANDERSON	Arthur	139		Son		10	M	Scholar	Herts	Wheathampstead
1863	ANDERSON	Charles	139		Son		5	M	At Home	Herts	Wheathampstead
1864	ANDERSON	Richard	139		Father	Widower	76	M	Agric Lab (Pauper)	Herts	St Michaels
1865	BECKWITH	Edward	140	Brewhouse Hill	Head	Mar	25	M	Police Constable	Herts	Waltham Cross [Cheshunt]
1866	BECKWITH	Harriet	140		Wife	Mar	29	F		Essex	Epping
1867	BECKWITH	George	140		Son		5	M	Scholar	Herts	Watford
1868	BECKWITH	William	140		Son		3	M	At Home	Herts	Hoddesdon
1869	BECKWITH	James	140		Son		1	M		Herts	Wheathampstead
1870	FOSTER	Henry	140		Brother-in-law	Mar	33	M	Railway Porter	Essex	Epping
1871	CHENNELLS	William	141	Brewhouse Hill	Head	Mar	23	M	Farmers Son	Herts	Wheathampstead
1872	CHENNELLS	Mary	141		Wife	Mar	31	F		Herts	Wheathampstead

One house building

1873	PARROTT	Ann	142	Brewhouse Hill	Head	Unm	70	F	Gentlewoman Annuitant	Middx	[Unknown]
1874	WHITE	Maria	142		Sister	Widow	62	F	Gentlewoman Annuitant	Herts	Welwyn
1875	PARROTT	Phoebe	142		Sister	Unm	56	F	Gentlewoman Annuitant	Herts	Welwyn
1876	GREY	Ann	142		Serv	Unm	28	F	Cook	Herts	Hatfield
1877	BRIGHT	Jane	142		Serv		12	F	Parlour Maid	Middx	[Unknown]
1878	MERRISON	Alexina	143	Brewhouse Hill	Head	Widow	38	F	Gentlewoman Annuitant	Middx	Westminster
1879	SEABROOK	Matthew	144	Brewhouse Hill	Head	Mar	29	M	Agric Lab	Herts	Hemel Hempstead
1880	SEABROOK	Sarah	144		Wife	Mar	34	F		Herts	Wheathampstead
1881	SEABROOK	Infant	144		Dau		1m	F		Herts	Wheathampstead

One house uninhabited

1882	ISAACS	John	145	Brewhouse Hill	Head	Mar	60	M	Agric Lab	Middx	St Georges in East
1883	ISAACS	Mary	145		Wife	Mar	61	F		Herts	Stevenage

	SURNAME	FORENAME	SCHEDULE NUMBER	ADDRESS	RELATIONSHIP	STATUS	AGE	SEX	OCCUPATION	COUNTY OF BIRTH	PLACE OF BIRTH
1884	NASH	James	146	Brewhouse Hill	Head	Mar	38	M	Sawyer	Herts	Wheathampstead
1885	NASH	Mary	146		Wife	Mar	25	F		Herts	Harpenden
1886	NASH	William J	146		Son		11 m	M		Herts	Wheathampstead
1887	MORRICE	Philip	147	Brewhouse Hill	Head	Mar	45	M	Agric Lab Pensioner (Army)	Herts	Sandridge
1888	MORRICE	Eliza	147		Wife	Mar	30	F		Herts	Wheathampstead
1889	MORRICE	Sarah	147		Dau		1	F		Herts	Wheathampstead
1890	PARKINS	Eliza	147		Step-dau		8	F	At Home	Herts	Wheathampstead
1891	PARKINS	Emma	147		Sister-in-law	Unm	25	F	Straw Plaiter	Herts	Wheathampstead
1892	PARKINS	Sarah	147		Sister-in-law		11	F	At Home	Herts	Wheathampstead
1893	PEARMAN	Maria	148	Brewhouse Hill	Head	Widow	58	F	Straw plaiter	Herts	Wheathampstead
1894	PEARMAN	Alfred	148		Grandson		7	M	At Home	Herts	Wheathampstead
1895	LINES	Ketturah	149	Brewhouse Hill	Head	Widow	65	F	Straw Plait dealer	Herts	Wheathampstead
1896	MCCULLOCH	John	149		Grandson		5	M	At Home	Herts	Wheathampstead
1897	LINES	Mary A	149		Niece	Widow	43	F	Bonnet Sewer	Herts	Wheathampstead
1898	FRENCH	George	150	Brewhouse Hill	Head	Mar	45	M	Carpenter	Herts	Kimpton
1899	FRENCH	Eliza	150		Wife	Mar	40	F		Beds	Luton
1900	FRENCH	Emma	150		Dau	Unm	20	F	Straw Plaiter	Beds	Luton
1901	FRENCH	Charles	150		Son		11	M	Scholar	Herts	Wheathampstead
1902	FRENCH	James	150		Son		8	M	Scholar	Herts	Wheathampstead
1903	NASH	Sarah	151	Brewhouse Hill	Head	Widow	65	F	Straw Plaiter (Pauper)	Herts	Wheathampstead
1904	DAY	Elizabeth	151		Dau	Unm	37	F	Straw Plaiter	Herts	Wheathampstead
1905	ROLFE	James	152	Brewhouse Hill	Head	Mar	33	M	Agric Lab	Herts	Wheathampstead
1906	ROLFE	Ann	152		Wife	Mar	28	F		Herts	Wheathampstead
1907	ROLFE	George	152		Son		6 m	M		Herts	Wheathampstead
1908	BAILEY	Mary	152		Sister-in-law	Unm	17	F	Bonnet Sewer	Herts	Wheathampstead

End of District 1c in the parish of Wheathampstead

Chapter Five

The parish of Harpenden

Registrar's District: Harpenden   Enumeration District 2a   Ref. HO107/1713 folios 65-91

All that part of the parish of Harpenden which lies to the south of the road called Stakers Lane, and of a line drawn from the western end of such lane to the gate on Harpenden Common leading to Rothamsted, and from such gate in a westward direction, leaving Rothamsted, Harpenden Bury and Bylands to the south thereof, into the Holyhead Road, including the Bowling Alley, Harpenden Common, Hatchin Green and the farms within such boundary.

1	GREEN	William	1	The Village	Head	Mar	47	M	Gardener and Groom	Bucks	[?]
2	GREEN	Eliza	1		Wife	Mar	46	F	Plaiter	Berks	Tilehurst
3	GREEN	Mary	1		Dau	Unm	24	F	Plaiter	Beds	Leighton Buzzard

Two uninhabited

4	GILBERT5	Joseph H.J.	2	The Village	Head	Mar	33	M	Scientific & Agricultual Chemist	Yorks	Hull
5	GILBERT	Eliza Forbes	2		Wife	Mar	31	F		Berks	Reading
6	STEGGALL	Ann Elizabeth	2		Serv	Unm	23	F	General Servant	Essex	Barking
7	GROOM	George	3	The Village	Head	Mar	64	M	Agric Lab	Beds	Dunstable, Houghton
8	GROOM	Mary	3		Dau	Widow	21	F		Northants	Northampton
9	HARDY	John	4	The Village	Head	Unm	54	M	Chelsea Pensioner	Herts	Harpenden
10	HARDY	James	4		Brother	Unm	52	M	Agric Lab	Herts	Harpenden
11	HARDY	Ann	4		Sister	Unm	49	F	Plaiter	Herts	Harpenden
12	GIDDENS	Sarah	5	The Village	Head	Widow	67	F	Plaiter	Herts	Kimpton
13	LUCK	Francis	5		Son-in-law	Mar	24	M	Agric Lab	Herts	Harpenden
14	LUCK	Amy	5		Dau	Mar	25	F	Plaiter	Herts	Kimpton
15	LUCK	Emma	5		Grandau		1	F		Herts	Harpenden
16	ARCHER	Susan	6	The Village	Head	Unm	45	F	Plaiter	Herts	Harpenden
17	READ	Eliza	6		Niece	Unm	19	F	Plaiter	Herts	Harpenden
18	SMITH	Henry	7	The Village	Head	Mar	66	M	Agric Lab	Beds	Sundon
19	SMITH	Phoebe	7		Wife	Mar	64	F	Plaiter	Herts	North Mimms
20	SMITH	Elizabeth	7		Dau	Widow	29	F	Plaiter	Herts	Harpenden
21	SMITH	William	7		Son	Unm	27	M	Agric Lab	Herts	Harpenden
22	SMITH	George	7		Son	Mar	23	M	Agric Lab	Herts	Harpenden
23	SMITH	James	7		Son	Unm	18	M	Agric Lab	Herts	Harpenden
24	SMITH	Thomas	7		Son	Unm	15	M	Agric Lab	Herts	Harpenden

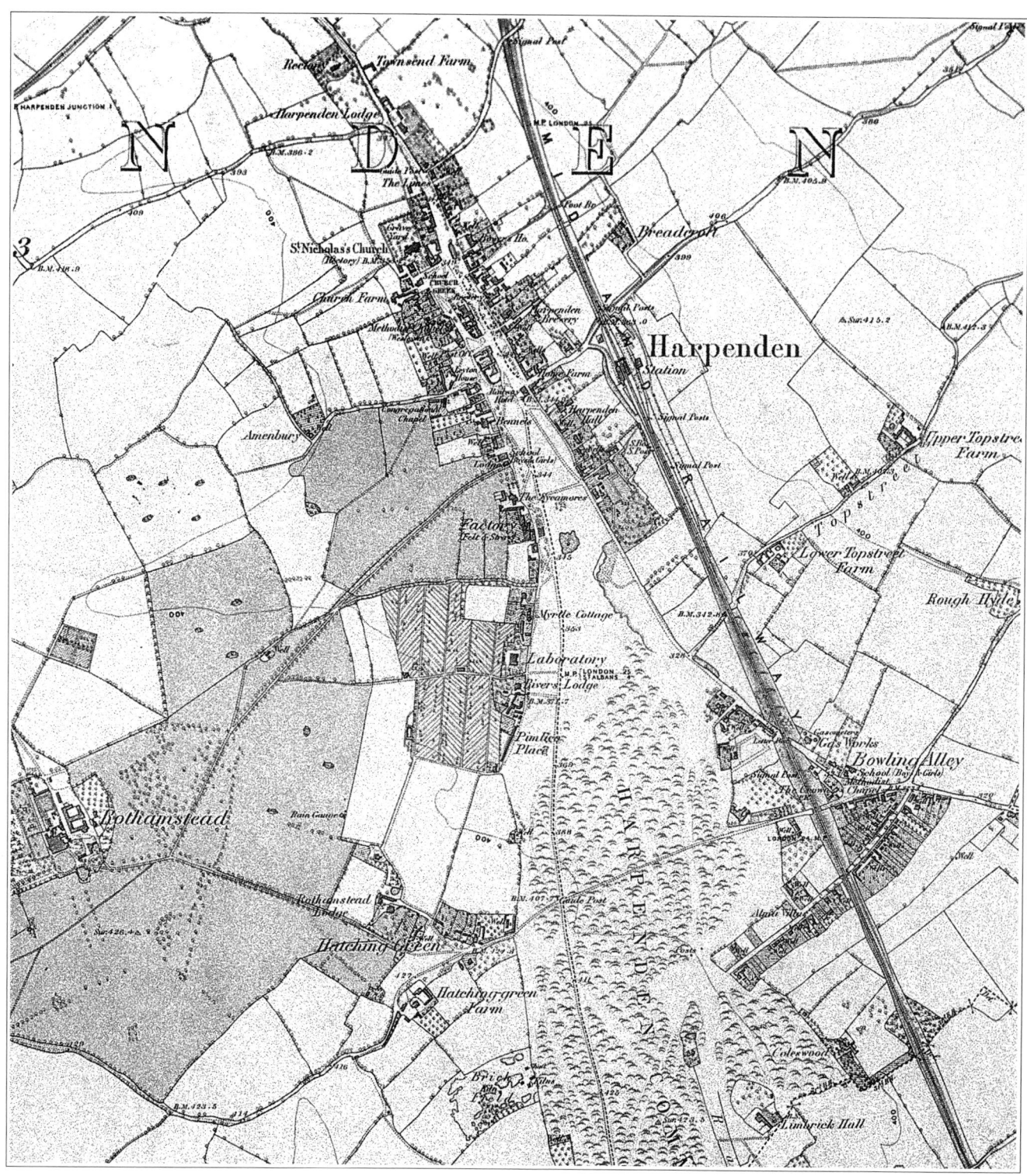

From the first edition of the 6 inch Ordinance Survey of Hertfordshire (1878), Sheet XXVII

Approximate scale of reproduction: 1cm = 123m

25	SMITH	George	7		Son	Unm	17	M	Agric Lab	Herts	Harpenden
26	SMITH	Charles	7		Son		14	M	Agric Lab	Herts	Harpenden
27	SMITH	Mary Ann	7		Dau-in-law	Mar	23	F	Plaiter	Beds	Hevington [Everton?]
28	SMITH	Thomas	7		Grandson		3	M		Herts	Harpenden
29	SMITH	Jane	7		Grandau	2m	F			Herts	Harpenden
30	WESTON	George	7		Visitor		6	M	Plaiter	Herts	Harpenden
31	RUMBALL	James R.	8	The Village	Head	Mar	54	M	Surgeon practising R. C. of Surg. London	Berks	Abingdon
32	RUMBALL	Rebecca	8		Wife	Mar	52	F		Kent	Dartford
33	RUMBALL	George	8		Son	Unm	20	M		London	
34	RUMBALL	Selina	8		Dau	Unm	23	F		London	
35	RUMBALL	James	8		Son	Unm	22	M	Bankers Clerk	London	
36	RUMBALL	Frederick	8		Son	Unm	18	M		London	
37	ROYER	Sarah	8		Sister-in-law	Widow	42	F	Lady (Annuitant)	Kent	Dartford
38	M.	I	8		Patient	Unm	40	M	Surgeon not practising	Unknown	
39	T.	P.	8		Patient	Unm	34	M	Gent	Unknown	
40	C.	W.	8		Patient	Unm	67	M	Gent	Unknown	
41	P.	H.	8		Patient	Unm	35	M	Formerly Stock Brokers Clerk	Herts	St Albans
42	D.	M.	8		Patient	Unm	87	F	Lady	Hants	Hurst [Hursley]
43	C.	A	8		Patient	Unm	55	F	Lady	Unknown	
44	LONG	Harriet	8		Serv	Unm	26	F	Ladys Maid	Herts	St Albans
45	ARNOLD	Susan	8		Serv	Unm	28	F	Cook	Herts	Wheathampstead
46	ADDINGTON	Ann	8		Serv	Unm	20	F	House Maid	Herts	Bedmond [Abbots Langley]
47	PURSELL	John	8		Serv	Unm	20	M	House Servant	Herts	St Peters, St Albans
48	GARDNER	George	9	The Village	Head	Mar	31	M	Plumber	Beds	Luton
49	GARDNER	Mary	9		Wife	Mar	36	F		Beds	Breachwood Green
50	GARDNER	Ellen	9		Dau		10	F	Scholar	Herts	Harpenden
51	GARDNER	Emma	9		Dau		8	F	Scholar	Herts	Harpenden
52	GARDNER	Thomas	9		Son		6	M	Scholar	Herts	Harpenden
53	GARDNER	William	9		Son		5	M	Scholar	Herts	Harpenden
54	GARDNER	Mary Ann	9		Dau		3	F	Scholar	Herts	Harpenden
55	GARDNER	Eliza	9		Dau		1	F		Herts	Harpenden
56	MORRICE	Charles	9		Apprentice	Unm	17	M	Plumbers Apprentice	Beds	Dunstable
57	HANSCOMBE	John	10	The Village	Head	Mar	51	M	Agric Lab	Herts	Exton [?]
58	HANSCOMBE	Ann Caroline	10		Wife	Mar	34	F	Dress Maker	London	Oxford Street
59	HANSCOMBE	William M.	10		Son		10	M	Scholar	Herts	Harpenden
60	RADWELL	Joseph	11	The Village	Head	Mar	60	M	Carpenter	Herts	Harpenden
61	RADWELL	Martha	11		Wife	Mar	50	F	Bonnet Sewer	Herts	St Pauls Walden
62	BINT	George	12	The Village	Head	Mar	39	M	Agric Lab	Herts	Harpenden
63	BINT	Sarah	12		Wife	Mar	40	F	Plaiter	Herts	Harpenden
64	BINT	Elizabeth	12		Dau		8	F	Scholar	Herts	St Albans
65	BINT	Mary Ann	12		Dau		5	F	Scholar	Herts	Harpenden
66	ALLEN	John	13	The Village	Head	Mar	57	M	Agric Lab	Beds	Luton
67	ALLEN	Sarah	13		Wife	Mar	57	F	Plaiter	Herts	Harpenden

	SURNAME	FORENAME	SCHEDULE NUMBER	ADDRESS	RELATIONSHIP	STATUS	AGE	SEX	OCCUPATION	COUNTY OF BIRTH	PLACE OF BIRTH
68	ALLEN	Ann	13		Dau	Unm	27	F	Plaiter	Herts	Harpenden
69	ALLEN	Louisa	13		Dau	Unm	19	F	Plaiter	Herts	Harpenden
70	ALLEN	John	13		Son	Unm	35	M	Agric Lab	Herts	Harpenden
71	ALLEN	William	13		Son	Unm	23	M	Agric Lab	Herts	Harpenden
72	READ	James	14	The Village	Head	Mar	51	M	Agric Lab	Beds	Maulden
73	READ	Eliza	14		Wife	Mar	47	F	Plaiter	Herts	Harpenden
74	NOTT	Daniel	15	The Village	Head	Mar	40	M	Drayman	Beds	Sundon
75	NOTT	Hannah	15		Wife	Mar	42	F	Plaiter	Herts	Harpenden
76	NOTT	Mary Ann	15		Dau		14	F		Herts	Harpenden
77	NOTT	George	15		Son		13	M	Scholar	Herts	Harpenden
78	POULTON	William	16	The Village	Head	Mar	29	M	Carpenter	Beds	Clipson [Clipstone]
79	POULTON	Elisabeth	16		Wife	Mar	36	F	Plaiter	Herts	Harpenden
80	BIGG	William	17	Stakers Lane	Head	Mar	29	M	Wheelwright	Herts	Flamstead
81	BIGG	Ellen	17		Wife	Mar	30	F	Plaiter	Herts	Harpenden
82	BIGG	Lucia	17		Dau		2	F		Herts	Harpenden
83	WHITEHOUSE	Job	18	Stakers Lane	Head	Mar	46	M	Schoolmaster	Herts	Hertford
84	WHITEHOUSE	Martha	18		Wife	Mar	50	F	Plaiter	Hants	Basingstoke
85	WHITEHOUSE	Levi	18		Son		14	M	Plaiter	Herts	Harpenden
86	WHITEHOUSE	Ann	18		Dau		11	F	Plaiter	Herts	Harpenden
87	SIMMONS	David	19	Stakers Lane	Head	Mar	35	M	Agric Lab	Herts	Harpenden
88	SIMMONS	Sarah	19		Wife	Mar	36	F	Plaiter	Herts	Wheathampstead
89	SIMMONS	Emma	19		Dau		8	F	Plaiter	Herts	Harpenden
90	SIMMONS	Mary	19		Dau		6	F	Plaiter	Herts	Harpenden
91	HOOK	Abena	19		Visitor		5	F		Herts	Hemel Hempstead
92	BREWER	Thomas	20	Stakers Lane	Head	Mar	32	M	Carter	Herts	Harpenden
93	BREWER	Faith	20		Wife	Mar	26	F	Plaiter	Herts	Harpenden
94	HALE	William	21	The Village Stakers Lane	Head	Mar	34	M	Grocer	Hants	[Unknown]
95	HALE	Eliza	21		Wife	Mar	34	F		Herts	Harpenden
96	TOMPKINS	Thomas	22	The Village Stakers Lane	Head	Mar	56	M	Gardener	Bucks	Chesham
97	TOMPKINS	Sarah	22		Wife	Mar	56	F	Plaiter	Herts	Hemel Hempstead
98	NICHOLLS	Milly	23	The Village Stakers Lane	Head	Widow	38	F	Plaiter and Bonnet Sewer	Herts	Harpenden
99	NICHOLLS	Maria	23		Dau		17	F	Plaiter and Bonnet Sewer	Herts	Harpenden
100	NICHOLLS	Frederick	23		Son		13	M	Scholar	Herts	Harpenden
101	CRANE	Elizabeth	24	The Village Stakers Lane	Head	Unm	56	F	Plaiter	Herts	Harpenden
102	LINES	Elizabeth	24		Visitor		9	F		Herts	Harpenden
103	PROCTOR	Ellen	25	The Village Stakers Lane	Head	Widow	67	F	Plaiter	Herts	Harpenden
104	HARRIS	Elizabeth	25		Visitor	Unm	43	F	Plaiter	Herts	St Albans
105	IVORY	Thomas	26	The Village Stakers Lane	Head	Mar	36	M	Agric Lab	Herts	Harpenden
106	IVORY	Martha	26		Wife	Mar	31	F	Plaiter	Herts	Hitchin
107	SEARS	John	27	The Village Stakers Lane	Head	Mar	27	M	Agric Lab	Herts	Harpenden
108	SEARS	Mary	27		Wife	Mar	26	F	Plaiter	Herts	Harpenden
109	SEARS	Frederic	27		Son		4	M		Herts	Harpenden
110	SEARS	Mary Ann	27		Dau		2	F		Herts	Harpenden

111	SEARS	Charles	27		Son		4 m	M		Herts	Harpenden
112	MUNT	Mary	28	The Village Stakers Lane	Head	Widow	43	F	Plaiter	Herts	Harpenden
113	IVORY	Emma	28		Visitor		11	F	Plaiter	Herts	Harpenden
114	ALLEN	Maria	29	The Village Stakers Lane	Head	Widow	43	F	Plaiter	Herts	Wheathampstead
115	ALLEN	Matilda	29		Dau	Unm	20	F	Plaiter	Herts	Offley
116	ALLEN	Mary	29		Dau	Unm	17	F	Plaiter	Beds	Luton
117	ALLEN	Thomas	29		Son	Unm	12	M	Scholar	Beds	Luton
118	ALLEN	William	29		Son	Unm	10	M	Scholar	Beds	Luton
119	LEE	John	30	The Village Stakers Lane	Head	Widower	38	M	Groom	Herts	Flamstead
120	LEE	George	30		Son		16	M	Helper	Herts	Flamstead
121	LEE	John	30		Son		11	M		Herts	Flamstead
122	LEE	Thomas	30		Son		9	M		Herts	Flamstead
123	TOWNSEND	Elizabeth	30		Visitor	Unm	40	F	Plaiter	Herts	Caddington
124	MANEN	James	31	The Village Stakers Lane	Head	Widower	34	M	Agric Lab	Herts	Harpenden
125	MANEN	William	31		Son		9	M	Scholar	Herts	Harpenden
126	SEABROOK	George	32	The Village Stakers Lane	Head	Mar	28	M	Storehouseman Brewery	Herts	Harpenden
127	SEABROOK	Elizabeth	32		Wife	Mar	28	F		Warks	Warwick
128	SEABROOK	Jane	32		Dau		3	F		Herts	Harpenden
129	SEABROOK	Lousia	32		Dau		1	F		Herts	Harpenden
130	OGGLESBY	Robert	33	The Village Stakers Lane	Head	Mar	41	M	General Dealer	Herts	Wheathampstead
131	OGGLESBY	Ann	33		Wife	Mar	45	F		Lincs	Louth
132	ADAMS	John	34	The Village Stakers Lane	Head	Mar	44	M	Agric Lab	Herts	Wheathampstead
133	ADAMS	Sarah	34		Wife	Mar	42	F	Plaiter	Herts	Wheathampstead
134	ADAMS	Emma	34		Dau	Unm	16	F	Plaiter	Herts	Wheathampstead
135	WILSHIRE	Thomas	35	The Village Stakers Lane	Head	Mar	44	M	Agric Lab	Herts	Bendith [St Pauls Walden]
136	WILSHIRE	Phoebe	35		Wife	Mar	45	F	Plaiter	Herts	Lilley
137	HILLIARD	James	36	The Village Stakers Lane	Head	Mar	39	M	Agric Lab	Herts	Offley
138	HILLIARD	Fanny	36		Wife	Mar	52	F	Plaiter	Herts	Kimpton
139	BANGS	Hariet	36		Dau-in-law		17	F	Plaiter	Herts	Kimpton
140	BANGS	Amy	36		Dau-in-law		14	F	Plaiter	Herts	Kimpton
141	BANGS	Sophia	36		Dau-in-law		9	F	Plaiter	Herts	Kimpton
142	BANGS	Susanna	36		Dau-in-law		4	F		Herts	Kimpton
143	DOGGETT	Joseph	37	The Village Stakers Lane	Head	Mar	53	M	Bricklayer	Herts	St Albans
144	DOGGETT	Susan	37		Wife	Mar	53	F		Herts	St Stephens
145	DOGGETT	David	37		Son	Unm	19	M	Bricklayer	Herts	Wheathampstead
146	DOGGETT	William	37		Grandson		9 m	M		Herts	Harpenden
147	FIELD	John	38	The Village Stakers Lane	Head	Mar	34	M	Miller	Beds	Clophill
148	FIELD	Jemmia	38		Wife	Mar	34	F		Herts	Hitchin
149	FIELD	William	38		Son		8	M		Herts	Hitchin
150	FIELD	John	38		Son		7	M		Herts	Hertford
151	FIELD	Elizabeth	38		Dau		5	F		Middx	Enfield
152	FIELD	Thomas	38		Son		4	M		Herts	Harpenden
153	FIELD	Samuel	38		Son		1	M		Herts	Harpenden
154	DAVIES	William	39	The Village Stakers Lane	Head	Mar	27	M	Agric Lab	Herts	Holwell

	SURNAME	FORENAME	SCHEDULE NUMBER	ADDRESS	RELATIONSHIP	STATUS	AGE	SEX	OCCUPATION	COUNTY OF BIRTH	PLACE OF BIRTH
155	DAVIES	Sarah	39		Wife	Mar	30	F		Herts	Harpenden
156	DAVIES	Sarah	39		Dau		5	F		Herts	Harpenden
157	DAVIES	William	39		Son		4	M		Herts	Harpenden
158	DAVIES	Elisabeth	39		Dau		2	F		Herts	Harpenden
159	BREWER	Samuel	40	The Marquis	Head	Mar	35	M	Publican	Herts	Harpenden
160	BREWER	Elizabeth	40		Wife	Mar	31	F		Beds	Silsoe
161	DAVIES	George	41	Upper Top Street	Head	Unm	23	M	Farmer of 196 acres employing 7 labourers	Herts	Hexton
162	GREY	Mary	41		Aunt	Widow	56	F		Herts	Ickleford
163	SMITH	Frederick	41		Serv		14	M	Agric Lab	Herts	Harpenden
164	LUCK	James	41		Serv	[blank]	16	M	Agric Lab	Herts	Harpenden
165	FITZJOHN	John	42	Upper Top Street	Head	Mar	31	M	Agric Lab	Herts	Harpenden
166	FITZJOHN	Eliza	42		Wife	Mar	27	F	Plaiter	Herts	Wheathampstead
167	FITZJOHN	George	42		Son		5	M	Scholar	Herts	Wheathampstead
168	FITZJOHN	Eliza	42		Dau		3	F	Scholar	Herts	Wheathampstead
169	FITZJOHN	Charles	42		Son		11 m	M		Herts	Harpenden
170	WARNER	Mary	43	Upper Top Street	Head	Widow	46	F	Plaiter	Herts	Wheathampstead
171	WARNER	Susan	43		Dau	Unm	16	F	Plaiter	Herts	Harpenden
172	HORNET	William	43		Son	Unm	21	M	Agric Lab	Herts	Wheathampstead
173	HORNET	Maria	43		Dau	Unm	18	F	Plaiter	Herts	Wheathampstead
174	INNANCE	William	43		Lodger	Mar	41	M	Carpenter	Herts	Harpenden
175	DAVIES	William	44	Lower Top Street	Head	Mar	51	M	Farmer of 97 acres employing 8 labourers	Herts	Harpenden
176	DAVIES	Mary	44		Wife	Mar	52	F		Herts	Hexton
177	DAVIES	Mary	44		Dau	Unm	24	F		Herts	Holwell
178	DAVIES	Sarah	44		Dau	Unm	15	F		Herts	Harpenden
179	DAVIES	Charles Thomas	44		Son		10	M	Scholar	Herts	Harpenden
180	BARKER	Hannah	44		Serv	[blank]	55	F	House Servant	Herts	Harpenden
181	DAY	George	44		Serv		13	M	Farm Servant	Herts	Harpenden
182	ELLS	Sarah	45	Rough Hyde	Head	Widow	46	F	Farmer of 108 acres employing 5 labourers	Herts	Redbourn
183	ELLS	Charles	45		Son	Unm	23	M		Herts	Harpenden
184	ELLS	Elizabeth	45		Dau	Unm	20	F		Herts	Harpenden
185	ASHBY	Charles	45		Brother	Unm	38	M		Herts	Redbourn
186	PEARCE	John	45		Serv	Unm	17	M	Farm Servant	Herts	Harpenden
187	LUCK	Caleb	45		Serv		13	M	Farm Servant	Herts	Harpenden
188	WESTON	Thomas	46	The Common Bowling Alley	Head	Mar	41	M	Agric Lab	Herts	Wheathampstead
189	WESTON	Sarah	46		Wife	Mar	37	F	Plaiter	Herts	Wheathampstead
190	WESTON	Thomas	46		Son		7	M	Scholar	Herts	Harpenden
191	WESTON	William	46		Son		4	M	Scholar	Herts	Harpenden
192	SEABROOK	William	47	The Common Bowling Alley	Head	Mar	50	M	Beer House Keeper	Herts	Hemel Hempstead
193	SEABROOK	Frances	47		Wife	Mar	40	F		Herts	Wheathampstead
194	SEABROOK	Ann	47		Dau	Unm	14	F	Plaiter	Herts	Harpenden
195	SEABROOK	Frederic	47		Son		12	M	Scholar	Herts	Harpenden
196	SEABROOK	James	47		Son		10	M	Scholar	Herts	Harpenden
197	SEABROOK	Eliza	47		Dau		7	F		Herts	Harpenden
198	SEABROOK	William	47		Son		5	M		Herts	Harpenden

199	SEABROOK	Francis	47		Son		3	M		Herts	Harpenden
200	SEABROOK	John	47		Son		4m	M		Herts	Harpenden
201	TURDLE	Richard	48	The Common Bowling Alley	Head	Mar	58	M	Agric Lab	Norfolk	Hillington
202	TURDLE	Sophia	48		Wife	Mar	52	F	Plaiter	Herts	Wheathampstead
203	TURDLE	George	48		Son		12	M	Agric Lab	Herts	Wheathampstead
204	TURDLE	Edward	48		Son	Mar	30	M	Agric Lab	Herts	Wheathampstead
205	TURDLE	Mary	48		Dau-in-law	Mar	21	F	Plaiter	Herts	Wheathampstead
206	TURDLE	Sarah	48		Grandau		1	F		Herts	Wheathampstead
207	GIDDENS	James	49	The Common Bowling Alley	Head	Mar	40	M	Shepherd	Herts	Harpenden
208	GIDDENS	Mary	49		Wife	Mar	45	F	Plaiter	Herts	Harpenden
209	GIDDENS	Sophia	49		Dau	Unm	16	F	Plaiter	Herts	Harpenden
210	GIDDENS	Ellen	49		Dau		4	F	Scholar	Herts	Harpenden
211	OGGELSBY	William	49		Lodger	Widower	66	M	Agric Lab	Herts	Harpenden
212	FREEMAN	Francis	50	The Common Bowling Alley	Head	Mar	25	M	Agric Lab	Herts	Harpenden
213	FREEMAN	Hannah	50		Wife	Mar	25	F	Plaiter	Herts	Harpenden
214	SYGROVE	Eliza	50		Sister	Unm	16	F	Plaiter	Herts	Harpenden
215	SLOUGH	William	51	The Common Bowling Alley	Head	Mar	80	M	Agric Lab	Beds	Caddington
216	SLOUGH	Jane	51		Wife	Mar	75	F	Plaiter	Herts	Wheathampstead
217	SLOUGH	George	51		Son	Unm	35	M	Agric Lab	Herts	Wheathampstead
218	GREY	Edward	51		Son-in-law	Mar	27	M	Agric Lab	Herts	Wheathampstead
219	GREY	Mary Ann	51		Dau	Mar	27	F	Plaiter	Herts	Wheathampstead
220	BURGESS	Thomas	52	The Common Bowling Alley	Head	Mar	32	M	Carpenter	Herts	Harpenden
221	BURGESS	Hannah	52		Wife	Mar	36	F	Plaiter	Herts	Harpenden
222	BURGESS	Joseph	52		Brother	Unm	18	M	Agric Lab	Herts	Harpenden
223	GIDDENS	William	53	The Common Bowling Alley	Head	Mar	38	M	Agric Lab	Herts	Harpenden
224	GIDDENS	Eliza	53		Wife	Mar	34	F	Plaiter	Herts	Harpenden
225	GIDDENS	Alfred	53		Son		7	M	Scholar	Herts	Harpenden
226	GIDDENS	John	53		Son		5	M	Scholar	Herts	Harpenden
227	GIDDENS	Betsey	53		Dau		2	F		Herts	Harpenden
228	GIDDENS	Eliza	53		Dau		8m	F		Herts	Harpenden
229	LUCK	Sarah	54	The Common Bowling Alley	Head	Widow	45	F	Beer Seller	Herts	Harpenden
230	LUCK	William	54		Son	Unm	20	M	Coal Dealer	Herts	Harpenden
231	LUCK	Sophia	54		Dau	Unm	16	F	Plaiter	Herts	Harpenden
232	LUCK	Charles	54		Son		8	M	Scholar	Herts	Harpenden
233	LUCK	Frederic	54		Son		6	M	Scholar	Herts	Harpenden
234	WESTON	George	54		Lodger	Unm	29	M	Agric Lab	Herts	Wheathampstead
235	BARKER	James	55	The Common Bowling Alley	Head	Mar	34	M	Agric Lab	Unknown	
236	BARKER	Maria	55		Wife	Mar	30	F	Plaiter	Herts	Harpenden
237	BARKER	Emily	55		Dau		9	F		Herts	Wheathampstead
238	BARKER	Mary Ann	55		Dau		7	F		Herts	Harpenden
239	BARKER	Eliza	55		Dau		6	F		Herts	Harpenden
240	BARKER	William	55		Son		1	M		Herts	Harpenden
241	WESTON	William	56	The Common Bowling Alley	Head	Mar	25	M	Agric Lab	Herts	Wheathampstead
242	WESTON	Mary Ann	56		Wife	Mar	20	F	Plaiter	Herts	Harpenden
243	WESTON	Fanny	56		Dau		1	F		Herts	Harpenden

	SURNAME	FORENAME	SCHEDULE NUMBER	ADDRESS	RELATIONSHIP	STATUS	AGE	SEX	OCCUPATION	COUNTY OF BIRTH	PLACE OF BIRTH
244	ENGLISH	George	57	The Common Bowling Alley	Head	Mar	36	M	Agric Lab	Herts	Hitchin
245	ENGLISH	Charlotte	57		Wife	Mar	36	F	Plaiter	Beds	Luton
246	ENGLISH	Sarah	57		Dau		14	F	Plaiter	Herts	Harpenden
247	ENGLISH	Mary	57		Dau		12	F	Plaiter	Herts	Harpenden
248	ENGLISH	George	57		Son		10	M	Plaiter	Herts	Harpenden
249	ENGLISH	Ann	57		Dau		8	F	Plaiter	Herts	Harpenden
250	ENGLISH	Martha	57		Dau		6	F	Plaiter	Herts	Harpenden
251	ENGLISH	Amos	57		Son		5	M		Herts	Harpenden
252	ENGLISH	Charlotte	57		Dau		3	F		Herts	Harpenden
253	ENGLISH	Fanny	57		Dau		4m	F		Herts	Harpenden
254	DUNKLEY	Robert	58	The Common Bowling Alley	Head	Mar	76	M	Smith B.	Northants	Northampton
255	DUNKLEY	Martha	58		Wife	Mar	70	F		Herts	Harpenden
256	DUNKLEY	Emily	58		Dau	Unm	19	F	Plaiter	Herts	Harpenden
257	REED	Charles	59	The Common Bowling Alley	Head	Mar	28	M	Agric Lab	Herts	Harpenden
258	REED	Mary Ann	59		Wife	Mar	25	F	Plaiter	Herts	Harpenden
259	REED	Mary Ann	59		Dau		4	F	Scholar	Herts	Harpenden
260	REED	Jane	59		Dau		1	F		Herts	Harpenden
261	STEED	George	60	The Common Bowling Alley	Head	Mar	45	M	Agric Lab	Herts	Whitwell
262	STEED	Mary	60		Wife	Mar	47	F	Plaiter	Herts	Gaddesden
263	STEED	Elizabeth	60		Dau		7	F		Herts	Wheathampstead
264	NORTH	William	61	The Common Bowling Alley	Head	Mar	26	M	Agric Lab	Herts	Kimpton
265	NORTH	Matilda	61		Wife	Mar	23	F	Plaiter	Herts	Wheathampstead
266	NORTH	Thomas	61		Son		1	M		Herts	Harpenden
267	LUCK	Nat	62	The Common Bowling Alley	Head	Mar	43	M	Agric Lab	Herts	Harpenden
268	LUCK	Mary	62		Wife	Mar	43	F	Plaiter	Herts	Harpenden
269	LUCK	Sarah	62		Dau	Unm	18	F	Plaiter	Herts	Harpenden
270	LUCK	Ann	62		Dau	Unm	15	F	Plaiter	Herts	Harpenden
271	LUCK	Maria	62		Dau		9	F	Plaiter	Herts	Harpenden
272	LUCK	David	62		Son		6	M		Herts	Harpenden
273	LUCK	Sophia	62		Dau		2	F		Herts	Harpenden
274	REED	James	63	The Common Bowling Alley	Head	Mar	32	M	Agric Lab	Herts	Harpenden
275	REED	Zelpha	63		Wife	Mar	27	F	Plaiter	Herts	Flamstead
276	REED	William	63		Son		3	M		Herts	Harpenden
277	REED	George	63		Son		5	M		Herts	Flamstead
278	LUCK	Charlotte	64	The Common Bowling Alley	Head	Widow	53	F	Plaiter	Unknown	
279	LUCK	George	64		Son	Unm	30	M	Agric Lab	Herts	Harpenden
280	LUCK	Ann	64		Dau		15	F	Plaiter	Herts	Wheathampstead
281	PECK	Thomas	65	The Common Bowling Alley	Head	Unm	21	M	Baker	Herts	Harpenden
282	PECK	George	65		Brother		12	M	Baker	Herts	Harpenden
283	DEACON	David	65		Lodger	Unm	45	M	Tailor	Unknown	
284	WINGRAVE	George	66	The Common Bowling Alley	Head	Mar	25	M	Agric Lab	Herts	Kimpton
285	WINGRAVE	Ann	66		Wife	Mar	25	F	Plaiter	Herts	Harpenden
286	WINGRAVE	Alfred	66		Son		3	M		Herts	Harpenden
287	WESTON	Charles	67	The Common Bowling Alley	Head	Mar	27	M	Agric Lab	Herts	Wheathampstead

288	WESTON	Sarah	67		Wife	Mar	25	F	Plaiter	Herts	Harpenden
289	WESTON	Ann	67		Dau		4 m	F		Herts	Harpenden
290	GODMAN	Charles	68	The Common Bowling Alley	Head	Mar	42	M	Agric Lab	Herts	Aldenham
291	GODMAN	Mary	68		Wife	Mar	46	F	Plaiter	Herts	Harpenden
292	GODMAN	George	68		Son	Unm	15	M	Agric Lab	Herts	Harpenden
293	GODMAN	Emma	68		Dau		11	F	Plaiter	Herts	Harpenden
294	GODMAN	Eliza	68		Dau		8	F	Plaiter	Herts	Harpenden
295	COLLINS	William	69	The Common Bowling Alley	Head	Mar	47	M	Agric Lab	Herts	Wheathampstead
296	COLLINS	Elizabeth	69		Wife	Mar	42	F	Plaiter	Herts	Harpenden
297	COLLINS	Charles	69		Son	Unm	16	M	Agric Lab	Herts	Harpenden
298	COLLINS	Elizabeth	69		Dau		9	F		Herts	Wheathampstead
299	COLLINS	John	69		Son		6	M		Herts	Wheathampstead
300	COLLINS	Frederic	69		Son		3	M		Herts	Harpenden
301	BENNETT	Mary	70	The Common Bowling Alley	Head	Widow	48	F	Plaiter	Beds	Sundon
302	BENNETT	Susan	70		Dau	Unm	22	F	Plaiter	Herts	Harpenden
303	BENNETT	Ann	70		Dau		12	F	Plaiter	Herts	Harpenden
304	BENNETT	Edward	70		Son		7	M	Scholar	Herts	Harpenden
305	BAINES	Susan	71	The Common Bowling Alley	Head	Widow	50	F	Plaiter	Herts	Hemel Hempstead
306	BAINES	Thomas	71		Son	Unm	28	M	Agric Lab	Herts	Redbourn
307	BAINES	Eliza	71		Dau	Unm	23	F	Plaiter	Herts	Wheathampstead
308	BAINES	George	71		Grandson		4	M	Scholar	Herts	Redbourn
309	BAINES	Sarah	71		Grandau		1	F		Herts	Harpenden
310	BAINES	Emma	71		Dau	Unm	21	F	Plaiter	Herts	Wheathampstead
311	BAINES	Ann	71		Grandau		2	F		Herts	Harpenden
312	BAINES	Fanny	71		Dau		13	F	Plaiter	Herts	Wheathampstead
313	WALKER	Sarah	71		Lodger	Unm	21	F	Plaiter	Herts	Redbourn
314	HUTCHINGS	George	71		Lodger	Unm	28	M	Agric Lab	Herts	Wheathampstead
315	REED	Thomas	72	The Common Bowling Alley	Head	Mar	57	M	Agric Lab	Herts	Harpenden
316	REED	Elizabeth	72		Wife	Mar	54	F	Plaiter	Unknown	
317	REED	Mathew	72		Son		13	M	Agric Lab	Herts	Harpenden
318	GREY	Thomas	73	The Common Bowling Alley	Head	Mar	53	M	Agric Lab	Herts	Lilley
319	GREY	Sarah	73		Wife	Mar	50	F	Plaiter	Herts	Harpenden
320	GREY	John	73		Son	Unm	26	M	Agric Lab	Herts	Harpenden
321	GREY	Samuel	73		Son	Unm	18	M	Agric Lab	Herts	Harpenden
322	GREY	Phillis	73		Dau		13	F	Plaiter	Herts	Harpenden
323	GREY	Eliza	73		Dau		9	F	Plaiter	Herts	Harpenden
324	GREY	Frederic	73		Son		5	M		Herts	Harpenden
325	PESTELL	Ann	73		Lodger	Unm	28	F	Plaiter	Herts	Harpenden
326	PESTELL	William	73		Lodgers Son		5	M		Herts	Harpenden
327	COX	Susan	74	The Common Bowling Alley	Head	Mar	41	F	Plaiter	Herts	Sandridge
328	COX	Elizabeth	74		Dau		13	F	Plaiter	Herts	Kensworth
329	COX	Susan	74		Dau		10	F	Scholar	Herts	Kensworth
330	COX	Thomas	74		Son		6	M	Scholar	Herts	Kensworth
331	COX	Henry	74		Son		1wk	M		Herts	Harpenden

	SURNAME	FORENAME	SCHEDULE NUMBER	ADDRESS	RELATIONSHIP	STATUS	AGE	SEX	OCCUPATION	COUNTY OF BIRTH	PLACE OF BIRTH
332	COX	Charlotte	74		Dau		2	F		Herts	Hoddesdon
333	BRACKLEY	Lucy	74		Visitor	Unm	19	F	Plaiter	Unknown	
334	STREATON	Joseph	75	The Common Bowling Alley	Head	Widower	62	M	Plaiter	Herts	Harpenden
335	STREATON	Richard	75		Son	Unm	25	M	Plaiter	Herts	Harpenden
336	BLOWS	Louisa	75		Niece	Unm	20	F	Plaiter	Unknown	
337	BRACEY	Issac	76	The Common Bowling Alley	Head	Mar	25	M	Agric Lab	Herts	Harpenden
338	BRACEY	Martha	76		Wife	Mar	23	F	Plaiter	Beds	Luton
339	BRACEY	Joseph	76		Son		5	M	Scholar	Herts	Harpenden
340	BRACEY	William	76		Son		3	M	Scholar	Herts	Harpenden
341	BRACEY	Sarah Ann	76		Dau		1	F		Herts	Harpenden
342	CROFT	Martha	76		Visitor	Widow	61	F	Plaiter	Beds	Luton
343	MORLEY	Samuel	77		Head	Mar	47	M	Tile Maker	Beds	Luton
344	MORLEY	Ann	77	The Common Bowling Alley	Wife	Mar	46	F	Plaiter	Herts	Little Wymondley
345	MORLEY	Sophia	77		Dau	Unm	22	F	Plaiter	Herts	Hitchin
346	MORLEY	John	77		Son	Unm	17	M	Butcher	Herts	Hitchin
347	MORLEY	Thomas	77		Son		14	M	Agric Lab	Herts	Hitchin
348	MORLEY	Rebecca	77		Dau		6	F	Scholar	Herts	Hitchin
349	MORLEY	William	77		Son		3	M		Herts	Harpenden
350	FREEMAN	Sarah	78	The Common Bowling Alley	Head	Unm	24	F	Plaiter	Herts	Harpenden
351	FREEMAN	Susan	78	The Common Bowling Alley	Sister	Unm	20	F	Plaiter	Herts	Harpenden
352	FREEMAN	James	78		Brother	Unm	11	M	Agric Lab	Herts	Harpenden
353	INNARD	Sarah	79	The Common Bowling Alley	Head	Widow	75	F	Proprietor of Houses	Herts	Harpenden
354	DICKINSON	Lucy	79		Dau	Mar	34	F	Dress Maker	Herts	Harpenden
355	INNARD	Sarah	79		Grandau	Unm	17	F	Dress Maker	Herts	Harpenden
356	BRINDELL	Thomas	80	The Common Bowling Alley	Head	Mar	29	M	Straw Plaits Bleacher	Beds	Luton
357	RINDELL	Mary	80		Wife	Mar	29	F	Plaiter	Herts	Harpenden
358	BRINDELL	George	80		Son		4	M		Herts	Harpenden
359	STROUD	Thomas	81	The Common Bowling Alley	Head	Mar	30	M	Brewers Lab	Wilts	Ramsbury
360	STROUD	Ann	81		Wife	Mar	22	F		Herts	St Albans
361	PATMORE	Charlotte	82	The Common Bowling Alley	Head	Widow	48	F	Farmer of 11 acres employing 2 labourers	Herts	Harpenden
362	PATMORE	Joseph	82		Son	Unm	25	M	Agric Lab	Herts	Harpenden
363	PATMORE	Maria	82		Dau	Unm	22	F	Plaiter	Herts	Harpenden
364	PATMORE	Emma	82		Dau	Unm	20	F	Plaiter	Herts	Harpenden
365	PATMORE	George	82		Son		16	M	Agric Lab	Herts	Harpenden
366	BURGESS	Thomas	83	The Common Bowling Alley	Head	Mar	38	M	Beer Seller	Herts	Kimpton
367	BURGESS	Elizabeth	83		Wife	Mar	34	F	Plaiter	Herts	Hitchin
368	WALLER	William	83		Lodger	Mar	32	M	Groom	Beds	Barton
369	WALLER	Charlotte	83		Lodgers Wife	Mar	37	F	Dress Maker	Suffolk	Levington
370	WARREN	William	84	The Common Bowling Alley	Head	Mar	74	M	Superannuated	Herts	Wheathampstead
371	WARREN	Martha	84		Wife	Mar	72	F	Plaiter	Herts	St Michaels
372	WARREN	Eliza	84		Dau	Unm	33	F	Plaiter	Herts	Wheathampstead
373	WALKER	James	84		Lodger	Widower	77	M	Superannuated Independent	Herts	Hitchin
374	JOHNSON	George Tiny [?]	85	The Common Bowling Alley	Head	Mar	56	M	Minister of the Independent Chapel	Middx	Clerkenwell
375	JOHNSON	Eliza	85		Wife	Mar	51	F		Middx	St Lukes

376	JOHNSON	Eliza Jemima	85		Dau	Unm	30	F	Governess	Hants	Christchurch
377	JOHNSON	Martha	85		Dau		12	F	Scholar	Essex	Horden on the Hill
378	ANDREW	William	86	The Common Bowling Alley	Head	Mar	41	M	Shoemaker (Journeyman)	Herts	Harpenden
379	ANDREW	Priscilla	86		Wife	Mar	43	F	Plaiter	Herts	Harpenden
380	ANDREW	Emma	86		Dau		12	F	Scholar	Herts	Harpenden
381	ANDREW	Jabez	86		Son		4	M		Herts	Harpenden
382	LAURENCE	George	87	The Common Bowling Alley	Head	Widower	44	M	Agric Lab	Beds	Stopsley
383	LAURENCE	Sophia	87		Dau	Unm	18	F	Plaiter	Herts	Harpenden
384	BRACEY	Sarah	88	The Common Bowling Alley	Head	Widow	60	F	Needle Woman	Bucks	Buckingham
385	BRACEY	Caroline	88		Dau	Unm	22	F	Plaiter	Herts	Harpenden
386	BRACEY	Hannah	88		Dau	Unm	20	F	Plaiter	Herts	Harpenden
387	BRACEY	Mary	88		Dau	Unm	18	F	Plaiter	Herts	Harpenden
388	BORDERS	John	88		Lodger	Unm	22	M	Agric Lab	Herts	Harpenden
389	BRACEY	Hannah	88		Grandau		2	F		Herts	Harpenden
390	NEALE	Thomas	89	The Common Bowling Alley	Head	Mar	54	M	Agric Lab	Herts	Wheathampstead
391	NEALE	Ann	89		Wife	Mar	46	F	Plaiter	Herts	Hatfield
392	NEALE	Elizabeth	89		Dau		8	F	Scholar	Herts	Harpenden
393	WALKER	William	90	The Common Bowling Alley	Head	Mar	49	M	Merchant in Straw Plait	Herts	Sandridge
394	WALKER	Emily	90		Wife	Mar	45	F		Middx	London
395	WALKER	Eliza	90		Dau	Unm	24	F	Straw Bonnet Manufacturer	Herts	Kimpton
396	WALKER	Lucy	90		Dau	Unm	23	F		Herts	Wheathampstead
397	WALKER	Ellen	90		Dau	Unm	19	F		Herts	Wheathampstead
398	WALKER	Alfred	90		Son	Unm	18	M		Herts	Wheathampstead
399	WALKER	Fanny	90		Dau	Unm	16	F		Herts	Wheathampstead
400	WELLS	Sophia	90		Serv	Unm	16	F	House Servant	Middx	Primrose Hill [London]
401	LANGLEY	George	90		Serv	Unm	14	M	House Servant	Beds	Dunstable
402	GIDDENS	William	91	The Common Bowling Alley	Head	Mar	71	M	Agric Lab	Herts	Harpenden
403	GIDDENS	Sarah	91		Wife	Mar	64	F	Plaiter	Herts	Harpenden
404	GIDDENS	Eliza	91		Grandau		8	F		Herts	Harpenden
405	FREEMAN	Frederic	92	The Common Bowling Alley	Head	Mar	23	M	Agric Lab	Herts	Harpenden
406	FREEMAN	Jane	92		Wife	Mar	31	F	Plaiter	Herts	Wheathampstead
407	FREEMAN	George	92		Son		7	M		Herts	Harpenden
408	FREEMAN	Thomas	92		Son		9m	M		Herts	Harpenden
409	MESSER	John	93	The Common Bowling Alley	Head	Mar	28	M	Smith	Herts	Wheathampstead
410	MESSER	Eliza	93		Wife	Mar	24	F		Herts	Hatfield
411	MESSER	Zachariah	93		Son		2	M		Herts	Harpenden
412	MESSER	Enos	93		Son		1	M		Herts	Harpenden
413	PIGGOTT	Thomas	94	The Common	Head	Mar	34	M	Agric Lab	Herts	Harpenden
414	PIGGOTT	Sarah	94		Wife	Mar	26	F	Plaiter	Herts	Hitchin
415	PIGGOTT	George	94		Son		6	M		Herts	Harpenden
416	PIGGOTT	William	94		Son		5	M		Herts	Harpenden
417	PIGGOTT	Rebecca	94		Dau		3	F		Herts	Harpenden
418	PIGGOTT	Matilda	94		Dau		8m	F		Herts	Harpenden
419	SLOUGH	Timothy	95	The Common Limbrick Farm	Head	Mar	38	M	Agric Lab	Herts	Wheathampstead

	SURNAME	FORENAME	SCHEDULE NUMBER	ADDRESS	RELATIONSHIP	STATUS	AGE	SEX	OCCUPATION	COUNTY OF BIRTH	PLACE OF BIRTH
420	SLOUGH	Mary Ann	95		Wife	Mar	34	F	Plaiter	Herts	Wheathampstead
421	WARNER	Mary Ann	95		Visitor	Unm	14	F		Herts	Wheathampstead
422	CROULON	Thomas	95		Serv	Unm	18	M	Agric Lab	Herts	Wheathampstead
423	DELEON	Charles	95		Serv		13	M	Agric Lab	Herts	Redbourn
424	LODGE	John	96	The Common St Albans Road	Head	Mar	55	M	Agric Lab	Herts	Welwyn
425	LODGE	Elizabeth	96		Wife	Mar	43	F	Plaiter	Herts	Wheathampstead
426	LODGE	Mary	96		Dau		13	F	Plaiter	Herts	Wheathampstead
427	LODGE	Martha	96		Dau		11	F		Herts	Wheathampstead
428	LODGE	James	96		Son		7	M		Herts	Wheathampstead
429	EWER	James	97	The Common St Albans Road	Head	Mar	59	M	Agric Lab	Herts	Hatfield
430	EWER	Hannah	97		Wife	Mar	52	F	Plaiter	Herts	Hemel Hempstead
431	EWER	Joseph	97		Son	Unm	24	M	Agric Lab	Herts	Colney Heath
432	EWER	James	97		Son	Unm	20	M	Agric Lab	Herts	St Albans
433	EWER	Ann	97		Dau	Unm	18	F	Plaiter	Herts	St Albans
434	EWER	Esther	97		Dau		13	F	Plaiter	Herts	St Albans

Two uninhabited houses

	SURNAME	FORENAME	SCHEDULE NUMBER	ADDRESS	RELATIONSHIP	STATUS	AGE	SEX	OCCUPATION	COUNTY OF BIRTH	PLACE OF BIRTH
435	ROWE	James	98	The Common St Albans Road	Head	Mar	71	M	Blacksmith	Herts	St Albans
436	ROWE	Elizabeth	98		Sister	Unm	50	F		Herts	Harpenden
437	SEABROOK	Eliza	98		Visitor	Unm	29	F	Plaiter	Herts	Redbourn
438	SEABROOK	Selina Alice	98		Visitors Dau		1	F		Herts	Harpenden
439	RUTHERFORD	Peter	99	The Common	Head	Mar	60	M	Annuitant	Scotland	[Unknown]
440	RUTHERFORD	Sarah	99		Wife	Mar	60	F		Herts	Harpenden
441	PEARCE	Sophia	99		Serv	Unm	21	F	House Servant	Herts	Harpenden
442	SEABROOK	Micheal	100	The Common	Head	Mar	40	M	Agric Lab	Herts	Redbourn
443	SEABROOK	Hannah	100		Wife	Mar	41	F	Plaiter	Herts	Harpenden
444	SEABROOK	Emma	100		Dau	Unm	16	F	Plaiter	Herts	Harpenden
445	SEABROOK	Maria	100		Dau		14	F	Plaiter	Herts	Harpenden
446	SEABROOK	Charles	100		Son		12	M	Agric Lab	Herts	Harpenden
447	SEABROOK	Eliza	100		Dau		9	F	Plaiter	Herts	Harpenden
448	SEABROOK	Jane	100		Dau		7	F	Plaiter	Herts	Harpenden
449	SEABROOK	Robert	100		Son		5	M		Herts	Harpenden
450	BROWN	Daniel	101	The Common	Head	Mar	46	M	Brick Maker	Herts	Hitchin
451	BROWN	Phoebe	101		Wife	Mar	45	F	Plaiter	Herts	Hitchin
452	BROWN	Maria	101		Dau	Unm	24	F	Plaiter	Herts	Hitchin
453	BROWN	Thomas	101		Son	Unm	20	M	Agric Lab	Herts	Hitchin
454	BROWN	Elizabeth	101		Dau	Unm	18	F	Plaiter	Herts	Hitchin
455	BROWN	James	101		Son		10	M	Agric Lab	Herts	Hitchin
456	BROWN	Anne	101		Dau		7	F		Herts	Harpenden
457	BROWN	Eliza	101		Dau		4	F		Herts	Harpenden
458	ABBOTT	George	101		Son-in-law	Mar	25	M	Agric Lab	Herts	Harpenden
459	SYGROVE	Edward	102	Hatchen Green	Head	Mar	35	M	Agric Lab	Herts	Wheathampstead
460	SYGROVE	Catherine	102		Wife	Mar	33	F	Plaiter	Herts	Redbourn
461	SYGROVE	Mary	102		Dau		9	F		Herts	Harpenden

462	SYGROVE	Elizabeth	102		Dau		6	F		Herts	Harpenden
463	SYGROVE	Ellen	102		Dau		4	F		Herts	Harpenden
464	SYGROVE	Fanny	102		Dau		1	F		Herts	Harpenden
465	COX	Azer [?]	103	Hatchen Green	Head	Mar	54	M	Agric Lab	Unknown	
466	COX	Hannah	103		Wife	Mar	54	F	Plaiter	Herts	Redbourn
467	TRENCH	James	103		Son-in-law	Unm	22	M	Agric Lab	Herts	Redbourn
468	HAYDON	William	104	Hatchen Green	Head	Mar	54	M	Agric Lab	Beds	Luton
469	HAYDON	Susannah	104		Wife	Mar	42	F	Plaiter	Herts	Hemel Hempstead
470	HAYDON	Eliza	104		Dau	Unm	17	F	Plaiter	Herts	Wheathampstead
471	HAYDON	Isaac	104		Brother	Unm	45	M	Agric Lab	Herts	Harpenden
472	BURCHMORE	George	105	Hatchen Green	Head	Mar	40	M	Farmer of 130 acres employing 5 labourers	Herts	Flamstead
473	BURCHMORE	Hannah	105		Wife	Mar	45	F		Herts	Harpenden
474	BURCHMORE	Elizabeth Hannah	105		Dau		4	F		Herts	Harpenden
475	SHAMBROOK	Mary	105		Serv	Unm	18	F	House Servant	Herts	Wheathampstead
476	HOWARD	William	105		Serv	Unm	20	M	Agric Lab	Herts	Wheathampstead
477	WHEELER	Thomas	105		Serv	Unm	16	M	Agric Lab	Herts	Redbourn
478	PEACOCK	John	106	Hatchen Green	Head	Mar	59	M	Gardener	Herts	Harpenden
479	PEACOCK	Elizabeth	106		Wife	Mar	58	F	Plaiter	Herts	Harpenden
480	PEACOCK	Jeremiah	106		Son	Unm	34	M	Gardener	Herts	Harpenden
481	PEACOCK	Elizabeth	106		Dau	Unm	20	F	Plaiter	Herts	Harpenden
482	WRIGHT	Mary	107	Hatchen Green	Head	Widow	71	F	Seamster	Herts	Harpenden
483	WRIGHT	William	107		Son	Unm	36	M	Wheelwright	Herts	Harpenden
484	STRATFORD	John Paxton	107		Son-in-law	Widower	39	M	Carpenter	Herts	Harpenden
485	STRATFORD	George	107		Grandson	Unm	16	M	Carpenter	Herts	Harpenden
486	STRATFORD	Ann Maria	107		Grandau		14	F	Bonnet Sewer	Herts	Harpenden
487	STRATFORD	Elisa Mary	107		Grandau		13	F	Scholar	Herts	Harpenden
488	ANGLE	Charles	108	Hatchen Green	Head	Mar	36	M	Agric Lab	Beds	Luton
489	ANGLE	Mary	108		Wife	Mar	35	F	Plaiter	Herts	Harpenden
490	ANGLE	Hannah	108		Dau		15	F	Plaiter	Herts	Harpenden
491	ANGLE	Eliza	108		Dau		12	F	Plaiter	Herts	Harpenden
492	ANGLE	Henry	108		Son		10	M	Scholar	Herts	Harpenden
493	ANGLE	Charlotte	108		Dau		7	F	Scholar	Herts	Harpenden
494	ANGLE	George	108		Son		5	M		Herts	Harpenden
495	IVORY	Charles	108		Lodger	Unm	22	M	Agric Lab	Herts	Harpenden
496	HULL	James	109	Hatchen Green	Head	Mar	34	M	Agric Lab	Herts	Harpenden
497	HULL	Jane	109		Wife	Mar	30	F	Plaiter	Herts	Bovingdon
498	HULL	George	109		Son		8	M	Scholar	Herts	St Michaels
499	HULL	David	109		Son		6	M		Herts	Wheathampstead
500	HULL	James	109		Son		4	M		Herts	Wheathampstead
501	HULL	Daniel	109		Son		1	M		Herts	Wheathampstead
502	PIGGOTT	Joseph	110	Hatchen Green	Head	Mar	56	M	Agric Lab	Beds	Leagrave
503	PIGGOTT	William	110		Son	Unm	20	M	Agric Lab	Herts	Harpenden
504	PIGGOTT	Frederic	110		Son		12	M	Agric Lab	Herts	Harpenden
505	LUNUN	Alice	111	Hatchen Green	Head	Widow	63	F	Plaiter	Herts	Harpenden

	SURNAME	FORENAME	SCHEDULE NUMBER	ADDRESS	RELATIONSHIP	STATUS	AGE	SEX	OCCUPATION	COUNTY OF BIRTH	PLACE OF BIRTH
506	LUNUN	Joseph	111		Son	Unm	24	M	Agric Lab	Herts	Harpenden
507	PIGGOTT	Susan	111		Visitor	Unm	25	F	Plaiter	Herts	Harpenden
508	ROAL	Thomas	112	Hatchen Green	Head	Mar	54	M	Agric Lab	Herts	Flamstead
509	ROAL	Mary	112		Wife	Mar	42	F	Plaiter	Beds	Luton
510	ROAL	Fanny	112		Dau		1	F		Herts	Harpenden
511	MATHIAS	Lewis	113	Hatchen Green	Head	Mar	38	M	Justice of the Peace	Somerset	Wells
512	MATHIAS	Emily Catherine	113		Wife	Mar	30	F		Herts	Harpenden
513	MATHIAS	Caroline	113		Dau		3	F		Wales	Lamphey
514	MATHIAS	Charles	113		Son		1	M		Wales	Lamphey
515	MATHIAS	Lewis	113		Son		2m	M		Herts	Harpenden
516	WARD	Henry Charles	113		Nephew		5	M		Warks	Stratford
517	MCGIBBON	Margaret	113		Serv	Unm	30	F	Cook	Scotland	[Unknown]
518	RICHARDS	Ann	113		Serv	Unm	27	F	Nurse	Wales	Jeffreston
519	PHILLIPS	Martha	113		Serv	Unm	20	F	Nurse	Wales	Carew
520	FISHER	Elizabeth	113		Serv	Widow	59	F	Monthly Nurse	Herts	Tewin
521	MATHEWS	John	113		Serv	Unm	15	M	Groom	Wales	Lamphey
522	WESTON	Ralph	114	Hatchen Green	Head	Mar	38	M	Agric Lab	Herts	Harpenden
523	WESTON	Mary Ann	114		Wife	Mar	34	F	Plaiter	Herts	Harpenden
524	WESTON	William	114		Son		11	M	Scholar	Herts	Harpenden
525	WESTON	Sarah	114		Dau		8	F	Scholar	Herts	Harpenden
526	DEAMER	Reuben	115	Hatchen Green	Head	Mar	37	M	Agric Lab	Herts	Harpenden
527	DEAMER	Ann	115		Wife	Mar	35	F	Plaiter	Beds	Luton
528	DEAMER	George	115		Son		9	M	Scholar	Herts	Harpenden
529	DEAMER	Ann	115		Dau		6	F	Scholar	Herts	Harpenden
530	DEAMER	David	115		Son		4	M		Herts	Harpenden
531	DEAMER	William	115		Son		1	M		Herts	Harpenden
532	FARR	Edward	116	Hatchen Green	Head	Mar	52	M	Agric Lab	Herts	St Pauls Walden
533	FARR	Jane	116		Wife	Mar	45	F		Leics	Whatton
534	FARR	Jane	116		Dau		12	F	Scholar	Leics	Whatton
535	FARR	Mary	116		Dau		10	F	Scholar	Herts	Redbourn
536	FARR	Sarah	116		Dau		8	F	Scholar	Herts	Redbourn
537	MATTHEWS	George	117	Hatchen Green	Head	Mar	31	M	Agric Lab	Herts	Harpenden
538	MATTHEWS	Maria	117		Wife	Mar	27	F	Plaiter	Herts	Harpenden
539	MATTHEWS	Francis	117		Son		9m	M		Herts	Harpenden
540	SEARS	William	118	Hatchen Green	Head	Mar	37	M	Agric Lab	Herts	St Stephens
541	SEARS	Eliza	118		Wife	Mar	36	F	Dress Maker	Beds	Luton
542	PIGGOTT	Henry	119	Hatchen Green	Head	Mar	64	M	Agric Lab	Beds	Leagrave
543	PIGGOTT	Sarah	119		Wife	Mar	60	F	Plaiter	Beds	Luton
544	PIGGOTT	Emma	119		Dau	Unm	26	F	Plaiter	Herts	Harpenden
545	PIGGOTT	George	119		Son		6	M	Scholar	Herts	Harpenden
546	HARPER	George William	120	Hatchen Green	Head	Mar	42	M	Agric Lab	Herts	Ayot St Peter
547	HARPER	Mary	120		Wife	Mar	41	F	Plaiter	Herts	Harpenden
548	HARPER	Sarah	120		Dau		14	F	Plaiter	Herts	Harpenden
549	HARPER	Mary Ann	120		Dau		11	F	Plaiter	Herts	Harpenden

550	HARPER	Charlotte	120		Dau		7	F		Herts	Harpenden
551	HARPER	Jane Elizabeth	120		Dau		1	F		Herts	Harpenden
552	LEWIS	Samuel	121	Hatchen Green	Head	Mar	49	M	Agric Lab	Herts	Harpenden
553	LEWIS	Faith	121		Wife	Mar	47	F		Herts	Hitchin
554	LEWIS	Sarah	121		Mother	Widow	80	F		Herts	Harpenden
555	PEARCE	John	122	Hatchen Green	Head	Mar	50	M	Agric Lab	Herts	Pirton
556	PEARCE	Hannah	122		Wife	Mar	45	F	Plaiter	Beds	Luton
557	PEARCE	William	122		Son	Unm	22	M	Agric Lab	Herts	Harpenden
558	PEARCE	Elizabeth	122		Dau		12	F	Plaiter	Herts	Harpenden
559	PEARCE	Abram	122		Son		10	M	Agric Lab	Herts	Harpenden
560	PEARCE	Frederick	122		Son		8	M	Scholar	Herts	Harpenden
561	PEARCE	Eliza	122		Dau		6	F		Herts	Harpenden
562	PEARCE	James	122		Son		4	M		Herts	Harpenden
563	THRUSSELL	James	123	Hatchen Green	Head	Mar	38	M	Agric Lab	Herts	Harpenden
564	THRUSSELL	Jane	123		Wife	Mar	35	F	Plaiter	Herts	Harpenden
565	THRUSSELL	George	123		Son		8	M	Scholar	Herts	Harpenden
566	THRUSSELL	Mary Ann	123		Dau		5	F		Herts	Harpenden
567	THRUSSELL	Sarah	123		Dau		2	F		Herts	Harpenden
568	SCRIVENER	Ann Elizabeth	123		Visitor		14	F	Plaiter	Herts	Harpenden
569	IVORY	James	124	Hatchen Green	Head	Mar	37	M	Agric Lab	Herts	Harpenden
570	IVORY	Elizabeth	124		Wife	Mar	35	F	Plaiter	Herts	Harpenden
571	IVORY	Eliza	124		Dau		15	F	Plaiter	Herts	Harpenden
572	IVORY	Ann	124		Dau		14	F	Plaiter	Herts	Harpenden
573	IVORY	Alfred	124		Son		11	M		Herts	Harpenden
574	IVORY	James	124		Son		7	M		Herts	Harpenden
575	IVORY	Emily	124		Dau		5	F		Herts	Harpenden
576	IVORY	Thomas	124		Son		2	M		Herts	Harpenden
577	THORN	William	124		Lodger	Widower	28	M	Agric Lab	Herts	Harpenden
578	IVORY	Mary A.	124		Dau		13	F	Plaiter	Herts	Harpenden
579	IVORY	Sarah	124		Dau		10	F	Plaiter	Herts	Harpenden
580	MATHEWS	Joseph	125	Hatchen Green	Head	Mar	41	M	General Dealer	Herts	Harpenden
581	MATHEWS	Ann	125		Wife	Mar	41	F		Herts	Bendish
582	GINGER	Daniel	125		Son-in-law	Unm	18	M	Agric Lab	Herts	Bushey
583	MATHEWS	Emma	125		Dau	Unm	14	F		Herts	Harpenden
584	MATHEWS	Eliza	125		Dau		11	F	Scholar	Herts	Harpenden
585	MATHEWS	Maria	125		Dau		9	F	Scholar	Herts	Harpenden
586	MATHEWS	Rose	125		Dau		7	F	Scholar	Herts	Harpenden
587	MATHEWS	Catherine	125		Dau		6	F	Scholar	Herts	Harpenden
588	MATHEWS	Georgiana	125		Dau		4	F	Scholar	Herts	Harpenden
589	MATHEWS	Susan	125		Dau		1	F		Herts	Harpenden
590	MATHEWS	Mary	125		Mother	Widow	66	F		Herts	St Albans
591	DUGGEON	Robert	125		Visitor	Unm	25	M	Agric Lab	Scotland	Latton [?]
592	WARREN	John	126	Hatchen Green	Head	Mar	57	M	Agric Lab	Beds	Luton
593	WARREN	Lydia	126		Wife	Mar	52	F	Plaiter	Beds	Hockliffe

	SURNAME	FORENAME	SCHEDULE NUMBER	ADDRESS	RELATIONSHIP	STATUS	AGE	SEX	OCCUPATION	COUNTY OF BIRTH	PLACE OF BIRTH
594	PLACEAM	James	126		Son-in-law	Unm	24	M	Agric Lab	Herts	Harpenden
595	PLACEAM	Sarah	126		Dau-in-law	Unm	19	F	Plaiter	Herts	Harpenden
596	PLACEAM	Eliza	126		Dau-in-law		14	F	Plaiter	Herts	Harpenden
597	PLACEAM	Mary Ann	126		Dau-in-law		16	F	Plaiter	Herts	Harpenden
598	HUMPHREY	Charles	127	The Common	Head	Mar	59	M	Agric Lab	Herts	Wheathampstead
599	HUMPHREY	Mary	127		Wife	Mar	63	F	Plaiter	Herts	Harpenden
600	HUMPHREY	Anne	127		Grandau		2	F		Herts	Harpenden
601	SYGROVE	William	128	Pimlico	Head	Mar	36	M	Agric Lab	Herts	Wheathampstead
602	SYGROVE	Sarah	128		Wife	Mar	36	F	Plaiter	Herts	Harpenden
603	SYGROVE	John	128		Son	Unm	15	M	Agric Lab	Herts	Harpenden
604	SYGROVE	Thomas	128		Son		10	M	Scholar	Herts	Harpenden
605	SYGROVE	William	128		Son		7	M	Scholar	Herts	Harpenden
606	SYGROVE	Robert	128		Son		5	M	Scholar	Herts	Harpenden
607	SYGROVE	Dinah	128		Dau		2	F		Herts	Harpenden
608	HANSCOMBE	Emma	128		Lodger	Unm	20	F	Plaiter	Herts	Harpenden
609	HINE	James	129	Pimlico	Head	Widower	58	M	Agric Lab	Unknown	
610	HINE	Sarah	129		Dau	Unm	16	F	Plaiter	Herts	Harpenden
611	HINE	Mary	129		Dau		14	F	Plaiter	Herts	Harpenden
612	HINE	Ann	129		Dau		8	F	Plaiter	Herts	Harpenden
613	WHEELER	William	130	Pimlico	Head	Mar	40	M	Agric Lab	Herts	Harpenden
614	WHEELER	Martha	130		Wife	Mar	41	F	Plaiter	Beds	Luton
615	WHEELER	Mary	130		Dau	Unm	19	F	Plaiter	Herts	Harpenden
616	WHEELER	Samuel	130		Son		16	M	Agric Lab	Herts	Wheathampstead
617	WHEELER	Joseph	130		Son		14	M	Agric Lab	Herts	Wheathampstead
618	WHEELER	John	130		Son		11	M	Agric Lab	Herts	Harpenden
619	WHEELER	George	130		Son		9	M	Plaiter	Herts	Harpenden
620	WHEELER	Charles	130		Son		7	M	Plaiter	Herts	Harpenden
621	WHEELER	Ellen	130		Dau		4	F	Scholar	Herts	Harpenden
622	WHEELER	Joshua	130		Son		2	M		Herts	Harpenden
623	WHEELER	Mary	130		Dau		2m	F		Herts	Harpenden
624	IVORY	Ann	131	Pimlico	Head	Widow	60	F	Plaiter	Herts	Harpenden
625	IVORY	Sarah	131		Dau	Unm	28	F	Plaiter	Herts	Harpenden
626	IVORY	Susan	131		Dau	Unm	26	F	Plaiter	Herts	Harpenden
627	IVORY	Francis	131		Son		4	M		Herts	Harpenden
628	IVORY	George	131		Son	Unm	19	M	Agric Lab	Herts	Harpenden
629	LUCK	Eliza	131		Lodger	Unm	19	F	Plaiter	Herts	Harpenden
630	LUCK	Thomas	132	Pimlico	Head	Mar	50	M	Agric Lab	Herts	Harpenden
631	LUCK	Alice?	132		Wife	Mar	46	F	Plaiter	Herts	Harpenden
632	LUCK	Elizabeth	132		Dau	Unm	22	F	Plaiter	Herts	Harpenden
633	LUCK	William	132		Son	Unm	18	M		Herts	Harpenden
634	LUCK	Millia	132		Dau		13	F	Plaiter	Herts	Harpenden
635	LUCK	Charles	132		Son		8	M	Scholar	Herts	Harpenden
636	LUCK	Ann	132		Grandau		1	F		Herts	Harpenden
637	BORDERS	William	133	Pimlico	Head	Widower	58	M	Agric Lab	Herts	Harpenden
638	SMITH	Eliza	133		Dau	Widow	35	F	Plaiter	Herts	Harpenden

639	BORDERS	Isaac	133		Son	Unm	19	M		Herts	Harpenden
640	SMITH	Ellen	133		Grandau		12	F		Herts	Harpenden
641	SMITH	Keziah	133		Grandau		9	F		Herts	Harpenden
642	SMITH	Isabella	133		Grandau		2m	F		Herts	Harpenden
643	PARK	James	134	Pimlico	Head	Mar	44	M	Bricklayer	Beds	Shillington
644	PARK	Mary	134		Wife	Mar	43	F	Plaiter	Beds	Dunstable
645	PARK	Mary Ann	134		Dau	Unm	18	F	Plaiter	Herts	Harpenden
646	PARK	Louisa	134		Dau		16	F	Plaiter	Herts	Harpenden
647	PARK	Alfred	134		Son		9	M	Scholar	Herts	Harpenden
648	PARK	William	134		Son		6	M	Scholar	Herts	Harpenden
649	PARK	Frederick	134		Son		3	M	Scholar	Herts	Harpenden
650	PARK	Albert	134		Son		2wks	M		Herts	Harpenden
651	SOUTH	William	135	Pimlico	Head	Mar	37	M	Agric Lab	Herts	Wheathampstead
652	SOUTH	Charlotte	135		Wife	Mar	34	F	Plaiter	Herts	Harpenden
653	SOUTH	Eliza	135		Dau		9	F		Herts	Harpenden
654	SOUTH	Charles	135		Son		6	M		Herts	Harpenden
655	ROBERTS	William	136	Pimlico	Head	Mar	32	M	General Dealer	Herts	Harpenden
656	ROBERTS	Sarah	136		Wife	Mar	28	F	Plaiter	Herts	Harpenden
657	ROBERTS	Emma	136		Dau		6	F		Herts	Harpenden
658	ROBERTS	Mary	136		Dau		5	F		Herts	Harpenden
659	ROBERTS	Ivory	136		Dau		3	F		Herts	Harpenden
660	PLACEAM	Charlotte	137	Pimlico	Head	Widow	48	F	Plaiter	Herts	Whitwell
661	ROW	John	137		Lodger	Mar	36	M	Agric Lab	Herts	Caddington
662	ROW	Lucy	137		Lodgers Wife	Mar	26	F	Plaiter	Herts	Harpenden
663	ROW	Emma	137		Lodgers Dau		2	F		Herts	Harpenden
664	PLACEAM	William	137		Son	Unm	21	M	Agric Lab	Herts	Harpenden
665	SHEPPARD	William	138	Pimlico	Head	Mar	58	M	Agric Lab	Beds	Woburn
666	SHEPPARD	Sarah	138		Wife	Mar	53	F	Plaiter	Herts	Redbourn
667	PARKINS	Maria	138		Lodger	Widow	67	F	Plaiter	Herts	Harpenden
668	BURGESS	Ann	139	Pimlico	Head	Mar	32	F	Shepherds Wife	Herts	Harpenden
669	BURGESS	Alfred	139		Son		3	M		Herts	Harpenden
670	BURGESS	Edward	139		Son		1	M		Herts	Harpenden
671	BATES	Alfred	139	Pimlico	Visitor		9	M		Herts	Harpenden
672	PLUMER	Thomas	140	Pimlico	Head	Widower	43	M	Agric Lab	Herts	Harpenden
673	PLUMER	Charles	140		Son	Unm	18	M	Agric Lab	Herts	Harpenden
674	PLUMER	John	140		Son		10	M	Scholar	Herts	Harpenden
675	PLUMER	Alfred	140		Son		7	M	Scholar	Herts	Harpenden
676	HAWKINS	Anne	140		Lodger	Unm	29	F	Plaiter	Herts	Kings Walden
677	HAWKINS	Agnas	140		Lodgers Dau		6	F	Scholar	Herts	Harpenden
678	HAWKINS	Oscar	140		Lodgers Son		3	M		Herts	Harpenden
679	HAWKINS	Eliza	140		Lodgers Sister	Unm	27	F	Plaiter	Herts	Harpenden
680	HAWKINS	William	140		Lodgers Brother	Unm	23	M	Agric Lab	Herts	Harpenden
681	HEALAND	William	141	Pimlico	Head	Mar	36	M	Agric Lab	Herts	Harpenden

	SURNAME	FORENAME	SCHEDULE NUMBER	ADDRESS	RELATIONSHIP	STATUS	AGE	SEX	OCCUPATION	COUNTY OF BIRTH	PLACE OF BIRTH
682	HEALAND	Diana	141		Wife	Mar	29	F	Plaiter	Herts	Harpenden
683	HEALAND	Mary Ann	141		Dau		9	F	Scholar	Herts	Harpenden
684	HEALAND	Eliza	141		Dau		6	F	Scholar	Herts	Harpenden
685	HEALAND	Ann	141		Dau		1	F		Herts	Harpenden
686	BATES	James	142	Pimlico	Head	Mar	58	M	Agric Lab	Beds	Eaton Bray
687	BATES	Judith	142		Wife	Mar	53	F	Agric Lab	Herts	Harpenden
688	BATES	Frederick	142		Son	Unm	23	M	Dealer in Coals	Herts	Harpenden
689	KING	Henry	143	Pimlico	Head	Mar	40	M	Laboratory Man, Agricultural Chemical Laboratory	Oxon	Oxford
690	KING	Susan	143		Wife	Mar	32	F		Herts	St Albans
691	KING	Henry	143		Son		7	M		Herts	St Albans
692	KING	Robert	143		Son		6	M		Herts	Harpenden
693	KING	John	143		Son		1	M		Herts	Harpenden
694	KING	Alfred	143		Son		1	M		Herts	Harpenden
695	ROBINSON	Ann	144	Pimlico	Head	Widow	53	F	Grocer	Herts	Harpenden
696	ROBINSON	Rosa	144		Grandau		5	F		Herts	Harpenden
697	HANSCOMBE	William	144		Lodger	Unm	57	M	Retired Farmer	Herts	Hexton
698	TWIDLE	Sophia	144		Serv	Unm	17	F	House Servant	Herts	Wheathampstead
699	SIMION [?]	William	144		Head	Unm	19	M	Assistant, Agricultural Chemical Laboratory	Middx	London
700	SEARS	Thomas	145	The Common	Head	Mar	60	M	Agric Lab	Herts	Harpenden
701	SEARS	Ann	145		Wife	Mar	54	F	Plaiter	Herts	Harpenden
702	SEARS	William	145		Son	Unm	32	M	Agric Lab	Herts	Harpenden
703	SEARS	Mary Ann	145		Dau	Unm	22	F	Plaiter	Herts	Harpenden
704	SEARS	Frederick	145		Son	Unm	20	M	Agric Lab	Herts	Harpenden
705	SEARS	Ann	145		Grandau		7	F		Herts	Harpenden
706	GREY	Thomas	146	The Common	Head	Mar	83	M	Agric Lab	Herts	Wheathampstead
707	GREY	Ann	146		Wife	Mar	74	F		Beds	Langford
708	GREY	George	146		Son	Unm	48	M	Agric Lab	Herts	Wheathampstead
709	GREY	Mary	146		Dau	Unm	35	F	Plaiter	Herts	Wheathampstead

Two uninhabited houses

	SURNAME	FORENAME	SCHEDULE NUMBER	ADDRESS	RELATIONSHIP	STATUS	AGE	SEX	OCCUPATION	COUNTY OF BIRTH	PLACE OF BIRTH
710	ROW	Thomas	147	The Common	Head	Mar	42	M	Agric Lab	Beds	Luton
711	ROW	Mary	147		Wife	Mar	42	F	Plaiter	Herts	Harpenden
712	ROW	Elisabeth	147		Dau		13	F	Plaiter	Herts	Harpenden
713	ROW	Eliza	147		Dau		9	F		Herts	Harpenden
714	ROW	James	147		Brother	Unm	34	M	Agric Lab	Beds	Luton
715	SLOUGH	John	148	The Common	Head	Mar	25	M	Agric Lab	Herts	Wheathampstead
716	SLOUGH	Sarah	148		Wife	Mar	22	F	Plaiter	Herts	Wheathampstead
717	SLOUGH	Emma	148		Sister		11	F	Plaiter	Herts	Wheathampstead
718	LITTLE	George	149	The Common	Head	Mar	40	M	Baker	Herts	Redbourn
719	LITTLE	Ann	149		Wife	Mar	31	F		Beds	Flitton
720	LITTLE	Mary	149		Dau		14	F		Herts	St Albans
721	LITTLE	William	149		Son		11	M		Herts	St Albans
722	ABBISS	Mary Ann	149		Visitor	Unm	18	F	Plaiter	Beds	Luton
723	DEAMER	Elizabeth	150	The Common	Head	Widow	68	F	Plaiter	Herts	Harpenden

724	DEAMER	Aron	150		Son	Unm	27	M	Plaiter	Herts	Harpenden
725	DEAMER	Abigal	150		Dau	Unm	24	F	Plaiter	Herts	Harpenden
726	DEAMER	Eliza	150		Grandau		3	F		Herts	Harpenden
727	DEAMER	Emma	150		Grandau		1	F		Herts	Harpenden
728	FREEMAN	Richard	151	The Common	Head	Mar	38	M	Gardener	Herts	Harpenden
729	FREEMAN	Sarah	151		Wife	Mar	42	F	Plaiter	Herts	Wheathampstead
730	FREEMAN	Maria	151		Dau		15	F	Plaiter	Herts	Harpenden
731	FREEMAN	William	151		Son		12	M		Herts	Wheathampstead
732	FREEMAN	Sarah	151		Dau		10	F		Herts	Harpenden
733	FREEMAN	John	151		Son		9	M	Scholar	Herts	Harpenden
734	FREEMAN	Joseph	151		Son		7	M	Scholar	Herts	Harpenden
735	FREEMAN	James	151		Son		3	M		Herts	Harpenden
736	FREEMAN	Emma	151		Dau		7m	F		Herts	Harpenden
737	BAILEY	George	152	The Common	Head	Unm	42	M	Leather Seller	Middx	Long Acre [London]
738	HOAR	Ann	152		Serv	Widow	48	F	Housekeeper	Herts	Harpenden
739	HAYDON	Samuel	153	Chapel Row	Head	Unm	43	M	Agric Lab	Herts	Harpenden
740	DEAMER	John	154	Chapel Row	Head	Mar	30	M	Servant	Herts	Harpenden
741	DEAMER	Sarah	154		Wife	Mar	40	F	Plaiter	Herts	Wheathampstead
742	SEABROOK	William	155	Chapel Row	Head	Mar	38	M	Agric Lab	Herts	Harpenden
743	SEABROOK	Mary	155		Wife	Mar	37	F	Plaiter	Herts	Harpenden
744	SEABROOK	Elizabeth	155		Dau		11	F	Plaiter	Herts	Harpenden
745	SEABROOK	John	155		Son		9	M	Plaiter	Herts	Harpenden
746	SEABROOK	Mary Ann	155		Dau		6	F	Plaiter	Herts	Harpenden
747	SEABROOK	Margaret	155		Dau		2	F		Herts	Harpenden
748	SEYMORE	Thomas	156	Chapel Row	Head	Mar	31	M	Agric Lab	Herts	Baldock
749	SEYMORE	Hannah	156		Wife	Mar	29	F	Plaiter	Herts	Harpenden
750	SEYMORE	Emily	156		Dau		1	F		Herts	Harpenden
751	BOSWORTH	Henry	157	Chapel Row	Head	Mar	30	M	Agric Lab	Unknown	
752	BOSWORTH	Eliza	157		Wife	Mar	27	F	Plaiter	Herts	Tewin
753	BOSWORTH	Sarah	157		Dau		2m	F		Herts	Harpenden
754	FELLS	William	158	Chapel Row	Head	Mar	32	M	Agric Lab	Herts	Harpenden
755	FELLS	Catherine	158		Wife	Mar	31	F	Plaiter	Herts	Hitchin
756	FELLS	George	158		Son		9	M	Scholar	Herts	Harpenden
757	FELLS	John	158		Son		6	M	Scholar	Herts	Harpenden
758	FELLS	Maria	158		Dau		4	F		Herts	Harpenden
759	FELLS	Matilda	158		Dau		4m	F		Herts	Harpenden
760	STREATON	John	159	Chapel Row	Head	Mar	61	M	Agric Lab	Herts	Harpenden
761	STREATON	Elizabeth	159		Wife	Mar	51	F	Plaiter	Herts	Hitchin
762	STREATON	William	159		Son	Unm	21	M	Agric Lab	Herts	Harpenden
763	STREATON	Emma	159		Dau	Unm	19	F	Plaiter	Herts	Harpenden
764	STREATON	Harriet	159		Dau		14	F	Plaiter	Herts	Harpenden
765	STREATON	Elizabeth	159		Dau		12	F	Plaiter	Herts	Harpenden
766	STREATON	George	159		Son		10	M		Herts	Harpenden
767	FENDELL	James	160	Chapel Row	Head	Mar	65	M	Agric Lab	Unknown	

	SURNAME	FORENAME	SCHEDULE NUMBER	ADDRESS	RELATIONSHIP	STATUS	AGE	SEX	OCCUPATION	COUNTY OF BIRTH	PLACE OF BIRTH
768	FENDELL	Ann	160		Wife	Mar	68	F	Plaiter	Herts	Harpenden
769	FENDELL	James	160		Grandson	Unm	17	M	Agric Lab	Herts	St Albans
770	GIDDENS	Joseph	161	Chapel Row	Head	Mar	34	M	Agric Lab	Herts	Harpenden
771	GIDDENS	Lucia	161		Wife	Mar	29	F	Plaiter	Herts	Harpenden
772	GIDDENS	Rosa	161		Dau		5	F		Herts	Harpenden
773	GIDDENS	Alfred	161		Son		3	M		Herts	Harpenden
774	GIDDENS	Emma	161		Dau		5m	F		Herts	Harpenden
775	FELLS	John	162	Chapel Row	Head	Mar	26	M	Agric Lab	Herts	Harpenden
776	FELLS	Emma	162		Wife	Mar	19	F	Plaiter	Herts	Sandridge
777	COX	Jesse	163	Chapel Row	Head	Mar	47	M	Agric Lab	Unknown	
778	COX	Ann	163		Wife	Mar	48	F	Plaiter	Herts	Abbots Langley
779	COX	Eliza	163		Dau	Unm	24	F	Plaiter	Herts	St Albans
780	COX	George	163		Son	Unm	18	M	Agric Lab	Herts	St Albans
781	COX	Emma	163		Dau		16	F	Plaiter	Herts	St Albans
782	COX	David	163		Son		13	M		Herts	St Albans
783	COX	Mary Ann	163		Dau		9	F		Herts	St Albans
784	FISHER	William	164	Chapel Row	Head	Mar	32	M	Agric Lab	Unknown	
785	FISHER	Sarah	164		Wife	Mar	29	F	Plaiter	Herts	Harpenden
786	FISHER	Eliza	164		Dau		1	F		Herts	Harpenden
787	LOVITT	Thomas	165	Chapel Row	Head	Mar	43	M	Agric Lab	Herts	Flamstead
788	LOVITT	Ann	165		Wife	Mar	41	F		Herts	Harpenden
789	LOVITT	Thomas	165		Son	Unm	19	M	Agric Lab	Herts	Harpenden
790	LOVITT	William	165		Son	Unm	17	M	Agric Lab	Herts	Harpenden
791	LOVITT	George	165		Son		13	M	Agric Lab	Herts	Harpenden
792	LOVITT	Frederick	165		Son		10	M	Scholar	Herts	Harpenden
793	LOVITT	Betsey	165		Dau		8	F	Scholar	Herts	Harpenden
794	LOVITT	Arteezer [?]	165		Son		6	M	Scholar	Herts	Harpenden
795	LOVITT	Albert	165		Son		2	M		Herts	Harpenden
796	LOVITT	Jaber	165		Son		2	M		Herts	Harpenden
797	SMITH	George	166	Chapel Row	Head	Mar	29	M	Agric Lab	Herts	Harpenden
798	SMITH	Mary Ann	166		Wife	Mar	36	F	Plaiter	Herts	Harpenden
799	SMITH	Eliza	166		Dau		10	F		Herts	Harpenden
800	SMITH	Henry	166		Son		1	M		Herts	Harpenden
801	FELLS	Mary	167	Chapel Row	Head	Mar	64	F	Plaiter	Unknown	
802	LOWEN	William	167		Lodger	Mar	26	M	Agric Lab	Herts	Weston
803	LOWEN	Eliza	167		Lodgers Wife	Mar	25	F	Plaiter	Herts	Harpenden
804	LOWEN	Mary	167		Grandau		4	F		Herts	Harpenden
805	LOWEN	John	167		Grandson		1	M		Herts	Harpenden
806	ADEY	Goodson	168	Chapel Row	Head	Mar	55	M	Solicitor	Herts	St Albans
807	ADEY	Priscilla	168		Wife	Mar	58	F		Herts	Harpenden
808	PALMER	Ann	168		Serv	Unm	30	F	House Servant	Herts	Wheathampstead
809	GIDDENS	William	169	Rothamstead Lane	Head	Mar	40	M	Gardener	Herts	Wheathampstead
810	GIDDENS	Mary	169		Wife	Mar	41	F		Essex	Newport
811	GIDDENS	Emily	169		Dau		6	F		Herts	Bovingdon

812	GIDDENS	William	169		Son		2 m	M		Herts	Harpenden
813	HOW	William	170	Hammonds End	Head	Unm	45	M	Farmer of 335 acres employing 12 labourers	Herts	St Albans
814	WINCHESTER	Lydia	170		Serv	Unm	40	F	House Servant	Herts	Redbourn
815	PARROT	Eliza	170		Serv	Unm	18	F	House Servant	Herts	Essenden
816	UCKLESBY	George	170		Serv	Unm	21	M	Farm Servant	Herts	Harpenden
817	COOK	James	170		Serv	Unm	21	M	Farm Servant	Beds	Luton
818	SHEPHARD	James	170		Serv	Unm	15	M	Farm Servant	Herts	Redbourn
819	FARR	Thomas	171	Schute Farm	Head	Mar	38	M	Farmer of 220 acres employing 10 labourers	Herts	Hatfield
820	FARR	Sarah	171		Wife	Mar	36	F		Herts	Hatfield
821	FARR	Robert	171		Son		8	M	Scholar	Herts	Harpenden
822	FARR	Sarah	171		Dau		6	F	Scholar	Herts	Harpenden
823	FARR	George	171		Son		5	M		Herts	Harpenden
824	FARR	Thomas	171		Son		4	M		Herts	Harpenden
825	FARR	William	171		Son		2	M		Herts	Harpenden
826	FARR	Maria	171		Dau		1	F		Herts	Harpenden
827	WRIGHT	Jane	171		Serv	Unm	26	F	House Servant	Herts	Harpenden
828	PRATT	Elizabeth	171		Serv	Unm	13	F	Nurse	Herts	Harpenden
829	MADDERS	Joseph	171		Serv	Unm	40	M	Farm Lab	Herts	Harpenden
830	BROWN	Mathew	171		Serv	Unm	26	M	Farm Lab	Herts	Harpenden
831	HAWKINS	John	172	Myelands	Head	Widower	66	M	J.P. Landed Proprietor	Herts	Harpenden
832	HAWKINS	Maria Augusta	172		Dau	Unm	26	F		Herts	Harpenden
833	HAWKINS	Emma Sarah	172		Dau	Unm	22	F		Herts	Harpenden
834	MANSEL	Mary	172		Serv	Unm	40	F		Herts	Harpenden
835	HAWKINS	Frances Ann	172		Dau	Unm	24	F		Herts	Harpenden
836	PUDDEPHAT	Sarah	172		Serv	Unm	22	F	Housemaid	Herts	Abbots Langley
837	ARBER	Mary Ann	172		Serv	Unm	30	F	Cook	Herts	Flamstead
838	HILL	Margaret	172		Serv	Unm	23	F	Kitchen Maid	Herts	Flamstead
839	AYNSWORTH	Joseph	172		Serv	Unm	40	M	House Servant	Herts	Abbots Langley
840	HALSEY	George	172		Serv	Unm	18	M	Farm Servant	Herts	Abbots Langley
841	MATTREHEAD [?]	Joseph	172		Serv	Unm	14	M	Farm Servant	Herts	Abbots Langley
842	MANNS	Francis	172		Visitor	Unm	56	M	Superannuated Civil Servant (Navy)	Berks	Barkham
843	BATES	John	173	Bury Farm	Head	Unm	30	M	Farmer of 470 acres employing 20 labourers	Herts	Harpenden
844	HUGHES	Elizabeth	173		Serv	Unm	40	F	House Servant	Herts	Harpenden
845	HOOTON	William	173		Serv	Unm	22	M	Farm Servant	Herts	Harpenden
846	LOVETT	John	173		Serv	Unm	28	M	Shepherd	Herts	Harpenden
847	SMITH	James	173		Serv	Unm	26	M	Farm Servant	Herts	Harpenden
848	PAUDDER	George	173		Serv	Unm	27	M	Farm Servant	Herts	Harpenden
849	PUDDIT	John	173		Serv	Unm	21	M	Farm Servant	Herts	Harpenden
850	EDWARDS	George	173		Serv	Unm	24	M	Farm Servant	Herts	Harpenden
851	LAWES	John Bennett	174	Rothamstead	Head	Mar	36	M	Gentleman	Herts	Harpenden
852	LAWES	Caroline	174		Wife	Mar	28	F		Norfolk	Narford
853	LAWES	Charles Bennett	174		Son		7	M		Devon	Teignmouth
854	LAWES	Caroline	174		Dau		6	F		Middx	Hampstead

	SURNAME	FORENAME	SCHEDULE NUMBER	ADDRESS	RELATIONSHIP	STATUS	AGE	SEX	OCCUPATION	COUNTY OF BIRTH	PLACE OF BIRTH
855	REVILL	Elizabeth	174		Serv	Unm	76	F	House Keeper	Devon	Holbeton
856	SHARPE	Ann	174		Serv	Unm	36	F	Ladys Maid	Norfolk	Nodlple [?]
857	CARR	Margaret	174		Serv	Unm	22	F	Nurse	Middx	Chelsea
858	WARFF	Ann	174		Serv	Unm	24	F	Laundry Maid	Norfolk	Narborough
859	BAKER	Ann	174		Serv	Unm	25	F	House Maid	Warks	Warburton
860	PATMORE	Mary	174		Serv	Unm	25	F	Cook	Herts	Harpenden
861	SEABROOK	Alice	174		Serv	Unm	19	F	Kitchen Maid	Herts	Wheathampstead
862	RANSOME	John	174		Serv	Unm	28	M	Farm Bailiff	Norfolk	Necton
863	COTTERITH	John	174		Serv	Unm	28	M	Footman	Warks	Barton
864	DOLLING	William	174		Serv	Unm	25	M	Groom	Herts	Redbourn
865	BROOKS	Elizabeth	174		Serv	Widow	55	F	Dairy Maid	Herts	St Albans
866	WADE	William	174		Serv	Unm	36	M	Vermin Destroyer	Herts	Harpenden
867	SYGROVE	William	174		Serv	Unm	15	M	Farm Servant	Herts	Harpenden

The end of the Enumerator's District No. 2a

Registrar's District: Harpenden   Enumeration District 2b   Ref. HO107/1713 folios 92-107

All that part of the parish of Harpenden that lies to the north of the road called Stakers Lane, and east of the Turnpike Road leading from St Albans to Luton, including Cold Harbour, Back Lane, Breadcroft, the east side of the village, and the farms within the said boundary.

	SURNAME	FORENAME	SCHEDULE NUMBER	ADDRESS	RELATIONSHIP	STATUS	AGE	SEX	OCCUPATION	COUNTY OF BIRTH	PLACE OF BIRTH
868	SMART	Francis	1	Cold Harbour	Head	Mar	60	M	Agric Lab	Beds	Caddington
869	SMART	Sarah	1		Wife	Mar	54	F	Straw Plaiter	Herts	Wheathampstead
870	SMART	Matilda	1		Dau	Unm	20	F	Straw Plaiter	Herts	Harpenden
871	SMART	Ann	1		Dau	Unm	16	F	Straw Plaiter	Herts	Harpenden
872	SMART	Josiah	1		Son	Unm	14	M	Agric Lab	Herts	Harpenden
873	SMART	Emma	1		Dau		11	F	Straw Plaiter	Herts	Harpenden
874	SMART	Frederick	1		Grandson		2	M		Herts	Harpenden
875	HULL	William	2	Cold Harbour	Head	Mar	39	M	Agric Lab	Herts	Harpenden
876	HULL	Mary	2		Wife	Mar	36	F	Straw Plaiter	Herts	Harpenden
877	HULL	William	2		Son	Unm	15	M	Agric Lab	Herts	Harpenden
878	HULL	George	2		Son		6	M	Scholar	Herts	Harpenden
879	HULL	Thomas	2		Son		3	M		Herts	Harpenden
880	ATTWOOD	William	3	Cold Harbour	Head	Mar	24	M	Agric Lab	Herts	Harpenden
881	ATTWOOD	Lydia	3		Wife	Mar	26	F	Straw Plaiter	Herts	Kimpton
882	ATTWOOD	Sarah	3		Dau		3	F	Scholar	Herts	Harpenden
883	WESTON	Thomas	4	Cold Harbour	Head	Widower	37	M	Agric Lab	Herts	Harpenden
884	WESTON	Eliza	4		Sister	Unm	39	F	Straw Plaiter	Herts	Harpenden
885	WESTON	Rose	4		Dau		11	F	Straw Plaiter	Herts	Harpenden
886	WESTON	Henry	4		Son		7	M	Scholar	Herts	Harpenden
887	WESTON	Charles	4		Nephew		9	M	Scholar	Herts	Harpenden
888	WESTON	George	4		Nephew		2	M		Herts	Harpenden
889	MEAD	William	5	Cold Harbour	Head	Mar	58	M	Agric Lab	Herts	Wheathampstead
890	MEAD	Mary	5		Wife	Mar	57	F	Straw Plaiter	Beds	Luton
891	MEAD	Eliza	5		Dau	Unm	34	F	Straw Plaiter	Herts	Wheathampstead
892	MEAD	William	5		Grandson		3	M	Straw Plaiter	Herts	Harpenden
893	SIBLEY	James	6	Cold Harbour	Head	Widower	75	M	Agric Lab	Herts	Harpenden

894	SIBLEY	George	7	Cold Harbour	Head	Mar	50	M	Agric Lab	Herts	Harpenden
895	SIBLEY	Ann	7		Wife	Mar	49	F	Straw Plaiter	Herts	Harpenden
896	SIBLEY	James	7		Son	Unm	18	M	Agric Lab	Herts	Harpenden
897	SIBLEY	Julia	7		Dau	Unm	15	F	Straw Plaiter	Herts	Harpenden
898	SIBLEY	George	7		Son		13	M	Agric Lab	Herts	Harpenden
899	SIBLEY	Charles	7		Son		9	M	Agric Lab	Herts	Harpenden
900	SIBLEY	Agnes	7		Niece		7	F	Scholar	Middx	Finchley
901	ARNOLD	George	8	Cold Harbour	Head	Mar	43	M	Agric Lab	Beds	Luton
902	ARNOLD	Sarah	8		Wife	Mar	55	F	School Mistress	Herts	Harpenden
903	ARNOLD	Mary Ann	8		Dau	Unm	19	F	Straw Plaiter	Herts	Harpenden
904	ARNOLD	George	8		Son	Unm	17	M	Agric Lab	Herts	Harpenden
905	ARNOLD	Martha	8		Dau		13	F	Straw Plaiter	Herts	Harpenden
906	ARNOLD	Thomas	8		Son		11	M	Scholar	Herts	Harpenden
907	DAY	Thomas	9	Cold Harbour	Head	Widower	67	M	Agric Lab	Herts	Harpenden
908	DAY	Hannah	9		Dau	Unm	29	F	Straw Plaiter	Herts	Harpenden
909	DAY	John	9		Son	Mar	24	M	Commercial Labourer Ag	Herts	Harpenden
910	DAY	Amos	9		Son	Unm	18	M	Agric Lab	Herts	Harpenden
911	ATTWOOD	William	10	Cold Harbour	Head	Mar	42	M	Agric Lab & Beershop Keeper	Herts	Wheathampstead
912	ATTWOOD	Elizabeth	10		Wife	Mar	39	F	Straw Plaiter	Herts	Harpenden
913	ATTWOOD	Amos	10		Son	Unm	18	M	Agric Lab	Herts	Harpenden
914	ATTWOOD	George	10		Son	Unm	14	M	Agric Lab	Herts	Harpenden
915	HAWKINS	Fanny	10		Niece	Unm	14	F	Straw Plaiter	Herts	Harpenden
916	HUNT	William	11	Cold Harbour	Head	Mar	44	M	Shoemaker	Herts	Harpenden
917	HUNT	Sophia	11		Wife	Mar	42	F	Straw Plaiter	Herts	Harpenden
918	HUNT	William	11		Son	Unm	19	M	Agric Lab	Herts	Harpenden
919	HUNT	Aradora	11		Dau	Unm	17	F	Straw Plaiter	Herts	Harpenden
920	HUNT	Jane	11		Dau	Unm	13	F	Scholar	Herts	Harpenden
921	HUNT	Rosa	11		Dau		10	F	Scholar	Herts	Harpenden
922	HUNT	Ann	11		Dau		7	F	Scholar	Herts	Harpenden
923	HUNT	Harriet	11		Dau		4	F		Herts	Harpenden
924	FINDELL	Charles	12	Cold Harbour	Head	Mar	33	M	Brick Maker	Herts	Harpenden
925	FINDELL	Sarah	12		Wife	Mar	29	F	Straw Plaiter	Beds	Luton
926	FINDELL	William	12		Son		4	M	Scholar	Herts	Hatfield
927	FINDELL	Alfred	12		Son		1	M		Herts	Hemel Hempstead
928	WESTON	Abraham	13	Cold Harbour	Head	Mar	30	M	Agric Lab	Herts	Harpenden
929	WESTON	Hannah	13		Wife	Mar	23	F	Straw Plaiter	Herts	Harpenden
930	WESTON	Sarah	13		Dau		2	F	Scholar	Herts	Harpenden
931	WESTON	Hannah	13		Dau		7 m	F		Herts	Harpenden
932	WESTON	Joshua	14	Cold Harbour	Head	Mar	32	M	Agric Lab	Herts	Harpenden
933	WESTON	Eliza	14		Wife	Mar	32	F	Straw Plaiter	Herts	Harpenden
934	WESTON	Frederick	14		Son		11	M	Scholar	Herts	Harpenden
935	WESTON	Sophia	14		Dau		9	F	Scholar	Herts	Harpenden
936	WESTON	Emma	14		Dau		7	F	Scholar	Herts	Harpenden
937	WESTON	Louisa	14		Dau		5	F	Scholar	Herts	Harpenden

	SURNAME	FORENAME	SCHEDULE NUMBER	ADDRESS	RELATIONSHIP	STATUS	AGE	SEX	OCCUPATION	COUNTY OF BIRTH	PLACE OF BIRTH
938	WESTON	Thomas	14		Son		3	M		Herts	Harpenden
939	WESTON	Mary Ann	14		Dau		1	F		Herts	Harpenden
940	ELLINGHAM	Thomas	15	Back Lane	Head	Mar	26	M	Agric Lab	Herts	Kimpton
941	ELLINGHAM	Maria	15		Wife	Mar	27	F	Straw Plaiter	Herts	Harpenden
942	ELLINGHAM	Edmond	15		Son		1	M		Herts	Harpenden
943	SMART	Emma	15		Sister		10	F	Scholar	Herts	Harpenden
944	MADDOX	John	16	Back Lane	Head	Mar	70	M	Agric Lab	Beds	Barton [in the] Clay
945	MADDOX	Hannah	16		Wife	Mar	41	F	Straw Plaiter	Herts	Wheathampstead
946	MADDOX	Daniel	16		Son	Unm	17	M	Agric Lab	Herts	Wheathampstead
947	MOLES	William	17	Back Lane	Head	Mar	49	M	Agric Lab	Herts	Stevenage
948	MOLES	Mary	17		Wife	Mar	45	F	Straw Plaiter	Herts	Sandridge
949	MOLES	William	17		Son	Unm	20	M	Agric Lab	Herts	Datchworth
950	MOLES	Aaron	17		Son		10	M	Straw Plaiter	Herts	Kimpton
951	PARSONS	James	18	Back Lane	Head	Mar	40	M	Agric Lab	Herts	Harpenden
952	PARSONS	Elizabeth	18		Wife	Mar	21	F	Straw Plaiter	Herts	Harpenden
953	HUMPHREY	George	19	Back Lane	Head	Mar	35	M	Agric Lab	Herts	Harpenden
954	HUMPHREY	Esther	19		Wife	Mar	28	F	Straw Plaiter	Herts	Harpenden
955	HUMPHREY	William	19		Son		3	M		Herts	Harpenden
956	HUMPHREY	Georgiana	19		Dau		1	F		Herts	Harpenden

End of Cold Harbour and Back Lane

	SURNAME	FORENAME	SCHEDULE NUMBER	ADDRESS	RELATIONSHIP	STATUS	AGE	SEX	OCCUPATION	COUNTY OF BIRTH	PLACE OF BIRTH
957	HOAR	John	20	Broad Croft	Head	Mar	24	M	Straw Hat Maker	Herts	Harpenden
958	HOAR	Mary Ann	20		Wife	Mar	22	F	Bonnet Sewer	Beds	Luton
959	ABBOTT	William	21	Broad Croft	Head	Mar	36	M	Agric Lab	Herts	Harpenden
960	ABBOTT	Bryomer	21		Wife	Mar	33	F	Straw Plaiter	Herts	Redbourn
961	ABBOTT	Meheler R.	21		Dau		14	F	Scholar	Herts	Harpenden
962	ABBOTT	William	21		Son		6	M	Scholar	Herts	Harpenden
963	ABBOTT	Jane	21		Dau		3	F		Herts	Harpenden
964	ABBOTT	Amos	21		Son		1	M		Herts	Harpenden
965	PESTLE	William	22	Broad Croft	Head	Mar	42	M	Agric Lab	Herts	Harpenden
966	PESTLE	Mary	22		Wife	Mar	40	F	Straw Plaiter	Herts	Harpenden
967	PESTLE	Elizabeth	22		Dau	Unm	20	F	Bonnet Sewer	Herts	Harpenden
968	PESTLE	William	22		Son		14	M	Straw Plaiter	Herts	Harpenden
969	PESTLE	Ann	22		Dau		10	F	Scholar	Herts	Harpenden
970	PESTLE	Eliza	22		Dau		7	F	Scholar	Herts	Harpenden
971	PESTLE	Mary Ann	22		Dau		4	F	Scholar	Herts	Harpenden
972	PESTLE	Fanny	22		Dau		2	F		Herts	Harpenden
973	HALE	Martha	23	Broad Croft	Head	Widow	62	F	Straw Plaiter	Beds	Luton
974	HALE	Emma	23		Dau	Unm	21	F	Straw Plaiter	Herts	Harpenden
975	HALE	Thomas	23		Son	Unm	18	M	Apprentice to Tailor	Herts	Harpenden
976	SWALLOW	Thomas	24	Broad Croft	Head	Mar	39	M	Agric Lab	Herts	Harpenden
977	SWALLOW	Ann	24		Wife	Mar	46	F	Straw Plaiter	Beds	Eaton Bray
978	SWALLOW	Emma	24		Dau	Unm	15	F	Straw Plaiter	Herts	Harpenden
979	SWALLOW	Enock	24		Son		8	M	Scholar	Herts	Harpenden
980	SWALLOW	Ann	24		Dau		3	F		Herts	Harpenden

981	WEEDON	James	25	Broad Croft	Head	Mar	34	M	Paper Maker	[Beds]	Woburn
982	WEEDON	Mary Ann	25		Wife	Mar	43	F	Straw Plaiter	Herts	Harpenden
983	WEEDON	Mary Ann	25		Dau		10	F	Scholar	Herts	Harpenden
984	WEEDON	Joshua	25		Son		8	M	Scholar	Herts	Harpenden
985	WEEDON	Caroline	25		Dau		7	F	Scholar	Herts	Harpenden
986	WEEDON	William	25		Son		6	M	Scholar	Herts	Harpenden
987	WEEDON	Benjaman	25		Son		2	M		Herts	Harpenden
988	PALMER	James	26	Broad Croft	Head	Mar	40	M	Agric Lab	Herts	Flampstead
989	PALMER	Lydia	26		Wife	Mar	36	F	Straw Plaiter	Herts	Flampstead
990	ABBOTT	Rosa	26		Step-dau		9	F	Scholar	Herts	Harpenden
991	ABBOTT	Ann	26		Step-dau		7	F	Scholar	Herts	Harpenden
992	ABBOTT	Lydia	26		Step-mother	Widow	74	F	Straw Plaiter	Herts	Kings Walden
993	SWALLOW	William	27	Broad Croft	Head	Mar	40	M	Agric Lab	Herts	Wheathampstead
994	SWALLOW	Susan	27		Wife	Mar	30	F	Straw Plaiter	Herts	Wheathampstead
995	SWALLOW	Mary	27		Dau	Unm	18	F	Straw Plaiter	Herts	Wheathampstead
996	DEAN	Richard	28	Broad Croft	Head	Mar	42	M	Malt Maker	Herts	Harpenden
997	DEAN	Mary	28		Wife	Mar	34	F	Straw Plaiter	Herts	Kimpton
998	DEAN	Sarah	28		Dau		8	F	Scholar	Herts	Harpenden
999	DEAN	Asahel	28		Son		5	M	Scholar	Herts	Harpenden
1000	DEAN	Elizabeth	28		Dau		2	F		Herts	Harpenden
1001	DEAN	Emma	28		Niece	Unm	19	F	Straw Plaiter	Herts	Harpenden
1002	HULL	William	28		Lodger	Unm	39	M	Agric Lab	Herts	Harpenden
1003	WARREN	William	29	Broad Croft	Head	Mar	37	M	Agric Lab	Herts	Harpenden
1004	WARREN	Sarah	29		Wife	Mar	36	F	Straw Plaiter	Herts	Harpenden
1005	WARREN	Thomas	29		Son		14	M	Agric Lab	Herts	Wheathampstead
1006	WARREN	William	29		Son		11	M	Agric Lab	Herts	Wheathampstead
1007	WARREN	Mary Ann	29		Dau		9	F	Scholar	Herts	Wheathampstead
1008	WELSH	William	29		Step-son		11	M	Agric Lab	Herts	Harpenden
1009	WELSH	George	29		Step-son		9	M	Scholar	Herts	Harpenden
1010	ANDREW	Elizabeth	30	Broad Croft	Head	Widow	63	F	Straw Plaiter	Herts	Harpenden
1011	ANDREW	Ann	30		Dau	Unm	23	F	Bonnet Sewer	Herts	Harpenden
1012	ANDREW	Eliza	30		Dau	Unm	20	F	Straw Plaiter	Herts	Harpenden
1013	HANSCOMBE	Mary	30		Lodger	Unm	23	F	Straw Plaiter	Herts	Harpenden
1014	HANSCOMBE	Elizabeth	30		Lodger	Unm	18	F	Straw Plaiter	Herts	Harpenden
1015	JONES	Fanny	30		Visitor		4	F	Scholar	Herts	Harpenden
1016	SWALLOW	William	31	Broad Croft	Head	Mar	42	M	Agric Lab	Herts	Harpenden
1017	SWALLOW	Elizabeth	31		Wife	Mar	41	F	Straw Plaiter	Herts	Redbourn
1018	SWALLOW	William	31		Son	Unm	19	M	Agric Lab	Herts	Harpenden
1019	SWALLOW	Emily	31		Dau	Unm	16	F	Straw Plaiter	Herts	Harpenden
1020	SWALLOW	Matilda	31		Dau	Unm	13	F	Straw Plaiter	Herts	Harpenden
1021	SWALLOW	Maria	31		Dau		11	F	Scholar	Herts	Harpenden
1022	SWALLOW	Lydia	31		Dau		8	F	Scholar	Herts	Harpenden
1023	SWALLOW	Ann	31		Dau		6	F	Scholar	Herts	Harpenden
1024	SWALLOW	George	31		Son		3	M	Scholar	Herts	Harpenden

	SURNAME	FORENAME	SCHEDULE NUMBER	ADDRESS	RELATIONSHIP	STATUS	AGE	SEX	OCCUPATION	COUNTY OF BIRTH	PLACE OF BIRTH
1025	BELCHER	James	32	Stakers Lane	Head	Mar	53	M	Agric Lab	Bucks	[Unknown]
1026	BELCHER	Elizabeth	32		Dau	Unm	31	F	Straw Plaiter	Herts	Harpenden
1027	BELCHER	Eliza	32		Dau	Unm	19	F	Straw Plaiter	Herts	Harpenden
1028	BELCHER	Emily	32		Dau		11	F	Scholar	Herts	Harpenden
1029	LINES	James	33		Head	Mar	36	M	Agric Lab	Herts	Wheathampstead
1030	LINES	Sarah	33		Wife	Mar	29	F	Straw Plaiter	Herts	Harpenden
1031	LINES	James	33		Son		7	M	Scholar	Herts	Harpenden
1032	GREEN	William	34	Stakers Lane	Head	Mar	54	M	Agric Lab	Herts	Flampstead
1033	GREEN	Fanny	34		Wife	Mar	67	F	Straw Plaiter	Herts	Flampstead
1034	HOPKINS	John	34		Lodger	Mar	51	M	Agric Lab	Herts	Flampstead
1035	HOPKINS	Sarah	34		Lodger	Mar	57	F	Straw Plaiter	Herts	Flampstead
1036	FITZJOHN	Ann	35	Stakers Lane	Head	Widow	73	F	Straw Plaiter	Herts	Harpenden
1037	FITZJOHN	Mary	35		Dau	Unm	38	F	Straw Plaiter	Herts	Harpenden
1038	PATERNOSTER	Martha	36	Stakers Lane	Head	Widow	61	F	Laundress	Middx	Hampstead
1039	LOVETT	Sarah	37	Stakers Lane	Head	Widow	58	F	Straw Plaiter	Herts	Redbourn
1040	DEAN	Diana	37		Visitor	Unm	17	F	Straw Plaiter	Herts	Harpenden
1041	NOTT	William	38	Stakers Lane	Head	Mar	38	M	Brewers Labourer	Beds	Sundon
1042	NOTT	Hannah	38		Wife	Mar	35	F	Straw Plaiter	Beds	Leagrave
1043	NOTT	Susanna	38		Dau		9	F	Scholar	Beds	Leagrave
1044	NOTT	Ann	38		Dau		6	F	Scholar	Beds	Leagrave
1045	NOTT	Daniel	38		Son		2	M		Beds	Leagrave
1046	MAWLEY	Susanna	38		Mother	Widow	70	F	Straw Plaiter	Beds	Luton
1047	SHARMAN	Jane	39	Stakers Lane	Head	Widow	40	F	Straw Plaiter	Oxon	Chadlington
1048	SHARMAN	James	39		Son	Unm	16	M	Agric Lab	Sussex	Newick
1049	SHARMAN	William	39		Son	Unm	14	M	Agric Lab	Sussex	Newick
1050	SHARMAN	Maria	39		Dau		13	F	Straw Plaiter	Sussex	Newick
1051	BENT	Samuel	39		Lodger	Unm	23	M	Agric Lab	Herts	Harpenden
1052	SIMMONDS	Fanny	39		Lodger	Unm	20	F	Straw Plaiter	Herts	Harpenden
1053	SIMMONDS	Frederick	39		Lodger		6m	M		Herts	Harpenden
1054	HUMPHREY	William	40	Stakers Lane	Head	Widower	71	M	Agric Lab	Bucks	Mentmore
1055	HUMPHREY	William	40		Son	Unm	40	M	Bricklayers Labourer	Herts	Harpenden
1056	BRACKLEY	Elizabeth	40		Dau	Widow	43	F	Straw Plaiter	Herts	Harpenden
1057	BRACKLEY	Joshua	40		Grandson	Unm	16	M	Agric Lab	Herts	Harpenden
1058	REED	Eliza	40		Boarder		11	F	Scholar	Herts	Harpenden
1059	WILLMOTT	Henry	41	Village	Head	Mar	44	M	Farmer of 180 acres employing 10 labourers	Herts	Kings Walden
1060	WILLMOTT	Lousia	41		Wife	Mar	43	F	Farmers Wife	Herts	Kings Walden
1061	WILLMOTT	Joseph	41		Son	Unm	20	M	Farmers Son	Herts	Kings Walden
1062	WILLMOTT	Henry	41		Son	Unm	19	M	Farmers Son	Herts	Sandridge
1063	WILLMOTT	Elizabeth	41		Dau	Unm	14	F	Farmers Dau	Herts	Sandridge
1064	WILLMOTT	William B.	41		Son		13	M	Scholar	Herts	Sandridge
1065	WILLMOTT	Lousia	41		Dau		11	F	Scholar	Herts	Sandridge
1066	WILLMOTT	Samuel	41		Son		9	M	Scholar	Herts	Sandridge
1067	WILLMOTT	Frederick	41		Son		6	M	Scholar	Herts	Harpenden
1068	WILLMOTT	Sarah	41		Dau		4	F	Scholar	Herts	Harpenden

1069	WILLMOTT	Jane	41		Dau		7 m	F		Herts	Harpenden
1070	CREW	Henry	41		Nephew		13	M	Agric Lab	Herts	Kimpton
1071	OSBORN	William	42	Village	Head	Mar	44	M	Victualler	Beds	Dunstable
1072	OSBORN	Sarah	42		Wife	Mar	50	F	Victuallers Wife	Herts	Harpenden
1073	FISHER	John	42		Lodger	Mar	32	M	Painter	Norfolk	Wymondham
1074	NOBB	John	42		Lodger	Widower	40	M	Watch Jobber	Essex	Brightlingsea
1075	JENNINGS	Joseph	43	Village	Head	Mar	43	M	Agric Lab	Herts	Harpenden
1076	JENNINGS	Ann	43		Wife	Mar	38	F	Straw Plaiter	Herts	Harpenden
1077	JENNINGS	Joseph	43		Son	Unm	17	M	Agric Lab	Herts	Harpenden
1078	JENNINGS	Elizabeth	43		Dau	Unm	15	F	Straw Plaiter	Herts	Harpenden
1079	JENNINGS	Charles	43		Son		13	M	Agric Lab	Herts	Harpenden
1080	JENNINGS	Henry	43		Son		11	M	Agric Lab	Herts	Harpenden
1081	JENNINGS	Edward	43		Son		8	M	Scholar	Herts	Harpenden
1082	JENNINGS	Sarah	43		Dau		5	F	Scholar	Herts	Harpenden
1083	JENNINGS	Frederick	43		Son		2	M		Herts	Harpenden
1084	SMITH	Sarah	44	Village	Head	Mar	46	F	Shop Keeper	Herts	Harpenden
1085	THOMPSON	James	45	Village	Head	Mar	82	M	Agric Lab	Beds	[Studham?]
1086	THOMPSON	Sarah	45		Wife	Mar	77	F	Straw Plaiter	Herts	Wheathampstead
1087	GULSTON	Sarah	45		Lodger	Mar	26	F	Millers Wife	Herts	Harpenden
1088	BAKER	Jacob	45		Lodger	Unm	22	M	Groom	Yorks	Sutton [?]
1089	LANGHAM	William	45		Lodger	Unm	16	M	Groom	Middx	London
1090	RAMSDEN	Francis	46	Village	Head	Mar	34	M	Brewers Labourer	Herts	Wheathampstead
1091	RAMSDEN	Elizabeth	46		Wife	Mar	33	F	Straw Plaiter	Herts	Harpenden
1092	RAMSDEN	Edward	46		Son		11	M	Scholar	Herts	Harpenden
1093	RAMSDEN	Charles	46		Son		6	M	Scholar	Herts	Harpenden
1094	RAMSDEN	Alfred	46		Son		4	M		Herts	Harpenden
1095	RAMSDEN	Emily	46		Dau		2	F		Herts	Harpenden
1096	RAMSDEN	Lizzy	46		Dau		6 m	F		Herts	Harpenden
1097	NOTT	William	47	Village	Head	Mar	54	M	Farmer of 135 acres employing 4 labourers & Grocer	Beds	Chalgrave
1098	NOTT	Susan	47		Wife	Mar	53	F	Farmers Wife	Herts	Harpenden
1099	NOTT	Mary	47		Dau	Unm	24	F	Farmers Dau	Herts	Harpenden
1100	NOTT	Charles	47		Son	Unm	23	M	Farmers Son	Herts	Harpenden
1101	NOTT	George	47		Son	Unm	22	M	Farmers Son	Herts	Harpenden
1102	NOTT	Ellen	47		Dau	Unm	19	F	Farmers Dau	Herts	Harpenden
1103	NOTT	Jane	47		Dau		13	F	Farmers Dau	Herts	Harpenden
1104	CHALKLEY	Thomas	48	Village	Head	Mar	51	M	Malt Maker	Herts	Gosmore
1105	CHALKLEY	Elizabeth	48		Wife	Mar	51	F	Straw Plaiter	[Surrey]	Bermondsey
1106	CHALKLEY	James	48		Son		11	M	Agric Lab & Shepherd	Herts	Sandridge
1107	CHALKLEY	Charles	48		Son		8	M	Scholar	Herts	Wheathampstead
1108	CURTIS	James	49	Village	Head	Mar	41	M	Brewer & Maltster	Hants	Alton
1109	CURTIS	Catherine	49		Wife	Mar	41	F	Brewer & Maltsters Wife	Herts	St Albans
1110	MORRIS	Mary Jane	49		Niece	Unm	16	F	Scholar at home	Beds	Ampthill
1111	CHATER	Esther	49		Serv	Unm	52	F	House Servant	Beds	Ampthill
1112	TURNER	Mary	49		Serv	Unm	45	F	House Servant	Hants	Ropley

	SURNAME	FORENAME	SCHEDULE NUMBER	ADDRESS	RELATIONSHIP	STATUS	AGE	SEX	OCCUPATION	COUNTY OF BIRTH	PLACE OF BIRTH
1113	REID	Ellen	49		Serv	Unm	20	F	House Servant	Hants	Alton
1114	CHILD	William	50	Village	Head	Mar	42	M	Tailormaster employing one man	Herts	Harpenden
1115	CHILD	Mary	50		Wife	Mar	46	F	Straw Plaiter	Herts	Harpenden
1116	CHILD	Harry	50		Son	Unm	15	M	Errand Boy	Herts	Harpenden
1117	HAWKINS	Sarah	51	Village	Head	Widow	72	F	Straw Plaiter	Bucks	Causgrove [Cosgrove, Northants?]
1118	HAWKINS	William	51		Son	Widower	52	M	Sawyer	Herts	Harpenden
1119	HAWKINS	James	51		Son	Unm	37	M	Sawyer	Herts	Harpenden
1120	HAWKINS	William	51		Grandson		10	M	Scholar	Herts	Harpenden
1121	HAWKINS	Alfred	51		Grandson		5	M	Scholar	Herts	Harpenden
1122	HOUSE	John	52	Village	Head	Unm	33	M	Brewer & Farmer of 120 acres employing 10 labourers	Herts	Wheathampstead
1123	ROWED	Elizabeth	52		Companion &Sister	Unm	32	F	House Keeper	Herts	Flampstead
1124	MCGERY	Mary Ann	52		Serv	Unm	19	F	House Servant	Scotland	[Unknown]
1125	FARNELL	John	53	Village	Head	Widower	55	M	Butcher	Beds	Ampthill
1126	FARNELL	Frederick	53		Son	Unm	29	M	Butcher	Herts	Harpenden
1127	PARBERG	Judith	53		Serv	Unm	53	F	House Servant	Northants	Towcester
1128	PHILLPOTT	Sarah	54	Village	Head	Widow	68	F	Landed Proprietor	Beds	Luton
1129	PHILLPOTT	Elizabeth	54		Dau	Unm	31	F	Straw Plaiter	Herts	Wheathampstead
1130	HUSON	Elizabeth	55	Village	Head	Widow	74	F	House Work	Herts	St Michaels
1131	HUSON	Thomas	55		Son	Unm	44	M	Shoemaker	Herts	Harpenden
1132	HUSON	George	55		Son	Unm	37	M	Shoemaker	Herts	Harpenden
1133	HUSON	Mary Ann	55		Dau	Unm	34	F	Shoe Binder	Herts	Harpenden
1134	FREMAN	Elizabeth	56	Village	Head	Widow	46	F	Landed Proprietor	Herts	Harpenden
1135	ROBINSON	Elizabeth	57	Village	Head	Unm	28	F	Straw Bonnet Maker	Herts	Harpenden
1136	ROBINSON	Mary	57		Sister	Unm	15	F	Apprentice	Herts	Harpenden
1137	BUTTERWORTH	Robert	58	Village	Head	Unm	26	M	Gentleman	Middx	St Dunstans
1138	BROWN	Charles	59	Village	Head	Mar	30	M	Grocer	Bucks	Little Marlow
1139	BROWN	Charlotte	59		Wife	Mar	30	F	Grocers Wife	Bucks	Great Marlow
1140	COCKS	Mary	59		Step-mother	Widow	60	F	Retired Shoemaker	Berks	Boxford
1141	DARBON	John	60	Vinegar Lane	Head	Mar	67	M	Agric Lab	Herts	Offley
1142	DARBON	Sarah	60		Wife	Mar	60	F	Straw Plaiter	Herts	Sandridge
1143	DEAMER	John	61	Vinegar Lane	Head	Mar	36	M	Agric Lab	Herts	Harpenden
1144	DEAMER	Mary	61		Wife	Mar	41	F	Straw Plaiter	Herts	Harpenden
1145	DEAMER	Frederick	61		Son		4	M	Scholar	Herts	Harpenden
1146	DEAMER	Emma	61		Dau		2	F		Herts	Harpenden
1147	DEAMER	Sophia	61		Dau		2m	F		Herts	Harpenden

One house uninhabited

	SURNAME	FORENAME	SCHEDULE NUMBER	ADDRESS	RELATIONSHIP	STATUS	AGE	SEX	OCCUPATION	COUNTY OF BIRTH	PLACE OF BIRTH
1148	LINES	Elizabeth	62	Village	Head	Widow	60	F	Laundress	Northants	Pitsford
1149	PAYNE	Sarah	63	Village	Head	Unm	65	F	Laundress	Northants	Maidwell
1150	ARCHER	Ann	64	Cross Keys	Head	Widow	49	F	Victualler	Herts	Sandon
1151	HANSCOMBE	Charles	64		Serv	Unm	14	M	Errand Boy	Herts	Harpenden
1152	EDWARDS	James	64		Lodger	Widower	38	M	Coachman	Herts	St Albans

1153	SIMONS	William	65	Village	Head	Mar	70	M	Surgeon	Beds	Ridgmont
1154	SIMONS	Rebecca	65		Wife	Mar	65	F	Surgeons Wife	Herts	St Albans
1155	SIMONS	Ann	65		Dau	Unm	25	F	Surgeons Dau	Herts	Harpenden
1156	CORTERTON	Elizabeth	65		Serv	Unm	15	F	Domestic Servant	Lincs	Holbeach
1157	FIELD	James	66	Village	Head	Mar	53	M	Merchant (Straw & Fancy Goods)	London	Cripplegate
1158	FIELD	Eliza	66		Wife	Mar	58	F	Merchant (Straw & Fancy Goods)	Middx	Piccadilly
1159	NEWTON	James F.	66		Grandson		7	M	Scholar	Middx	St John Hackney
1160	DAVAY	John	66		Serv	Unm	30	M	Groom and Gardener	Devon	[Unknown]
1161	HOPKIN	Sarah	66		Serv	Unm	25	F	Servant	Oxon	Hook Norton
1162	GEEVE [?]	William	67	Village	Head	Mar	43	M	Wheelwright	Herts	Hitchin
1163	GEEVE [?]	Sarah	67		Wife	Mar	50	F	Wheelwrights Wife	Essex	Brentwood
1164	BROWN	Joseph	67		Step-son	Unm	17	M	Wheelwright	Herts	Kings Walden
1165	BROWN	James	67		Step-son	Unm	15	M	Scholar	Beds	Luton
1166	PATERNOSTER [?]	John	67		Apprentice	Unm	20	M	Apprentice Wheelwright	Middx	Hampstead
1167	CHILD	Elizabeth	68	Village	Head	Unm	36	F	Milliner and Dressmaker	Wilts	Brocksfield [?]
1168	RODWELL	Mary	68		Aunt	Unm	66	F	Straw Plait Sewer	Herts	Harpenden
1169	HAYWARD	Betsy	68		Boarder	Unm	30	F	British School Mistress	Surrey	Wandsworth Road [London]
1170	CHASE	Frederick	69	Village	Head	Widower	40	M	Harness Maker employing 1 man	Herts	Harpenden
1171	CHASE	Sarah	69		Dau		11	F	Scholar	Herts	Harpenden
1172	CHASE	Frederick J.	69		Son		9	M	Scholar	Herts	Harpenden
1173	CHASE	Amelia	69		Dau		7	F	Scholar	Herts	Harpenden
1174	CHASE	Emily	69		Dau		5	F	Scholar	Herts	Harpenden
1175	CHASE	Caroline	69		Sister	Unm	27	F	Dress Maker	Herts	Harpenden
1176	GAITTERIDGE	Mary	69		Serv	Unm	20	F	House Servant	Beds	Whipsnade
1177	ELLS	Elizabeth	70	Village	Head	Widow	71	F	Proprietor of House and Land	Herts	Caddington
1178	CRAWLEY	Mary	70		Serv	Unm	25	F	Domestic Servant	Herts	Harpenden
1179	BROSIER [?]	Luke	71	Village	Head	Mar	37	M	Agric Lab	Beds	Barton [in the] Clay
1180	BROSIER [?]	Eliza	71		Wife	Mar	35	F	Straw Plaiter	Herts	Kimpton
1181	BROSIER [?]	Ann	71		Dau		6	F	Scholar	Herts	Harpenden
1182	BROSIER [?]	Thomas	71		Son		4	M		Herts	Harpenden
1183	VALLANCE	William	72	Village	Head	Mar	66	M	Stationer and Ironmonger	Middx	London
1184	VALLANCE	Elizabeth	72		Wife	Mar	68	F		Beds	Dunton
1185	VALLANCE	Martha	72		Dau	Unm	34	F		Herts	Wheathampstead
1186	ROLT	Thomas	73	Village	Head	Mar	30	M	Agric Lab	Herts	Flampstead
1187	ROLT	Sarah	73		Wife	Mar	31	F	Straw Plaiter	Herts	Harpenden
1188	ROLT	William	73		Son		4	M	Scholar	Herts	Harpenden
1189	ROLT	George	73		Son		7 m	M		Herts	Harpenden
1190	HOLLAND	James	73		Father-in-law	Widower	55	M	Agric Lab	Beds	Totternhoe
1191	LINES	Henry	74	Village	Head	Mar	36	M	Blacksmith	Herts	Great Gaddesdon
1192	LINES	Sophia	74		Wife	Mar	46	F	Blacksmiths Wife	Herts	Harpenden
1193	LINES	Ann Jane	74		Dau		12	F	Scholar	Herts	Harpenden
1194	LINES	Sarah Ann	74		Dau		10	F	Scholar	Herts	Harpenden

	SURNAME	FORENAME	SCHEDULE NUMBER	ADDRESS	RELATIONSHIP	STATUS	AGE	SEX	OCCUPATION	COUNTY OF BIRTH	PLACE OF BIRTH
1195	LINES	Henry	74		Son		6	M	Scholar	Herts	Harpenden
1196	LINES	John	74		Son		2	M	At home	Herts	Harpenden
1197	BOOKER	Mary Ann	74		Visitor	Mar	38	F	Gardeners Wife	Herts	Harpenden
1198	LINES	Sarah	74		Visitor	Unm	28	F	Servant	Herts	Great Gaddesdon
1199	HAWKINS	George	75	Village	Head	Mar	59	M	Carpenter (Journeyman)	Herts	Harpenden
1200	HAWKINS	Susanna	75		Wife	Mar	60	M	Carpenters Wife	Suffolk	Bury St Edmunds
1201	HAWKINS	Martha	75		Dau	Unm	33	F	Straw Plaiter	Herts	Harpenden
1202	HAWKINS	Mary	75		Dau	Unm	18	F	Bonnet Sewer	Herts	Harpenden
1203	HAWKINS	Ann	75		Grandau		5	F	Scholar	Herts	Harpenden

One house uninhabited

	SURNAME	FORENAME	SCHEDULE NUMBER	ADDRESS	RELATIONSHIP	STATUS	AGE	SEX	OCCUPATION	COUNTY OF BIRTH	PLACE OF BIRTH
1204	TIDY	Harriet	76	Village	Head	Mar	40	F	Livery Servants Wife	Herts	Hoddesdon
1205	TIDY	James	76		Son		8	M	Scholar	Middx	Stepney
1206	TIDY	Elizabeth	76		Mother	Widow	75	F	Laundress	Middx	St Giles
1207	HOLLAND	William	77	Village	Head	Mar	35	M	Agric Lab	Herts	Harpenden
1208	CLAY	Josiah	77		Nephew		10	M	Scholar	Herts	Harpenden
1209	HOLLAND	Eliza	77		Wife	Mar	32	F	Straw Plaiter	Herts	Harpenden
1210	ALLEN	Lewis	78	Village	Head	Mar	56	M	Librarian	Middx	St James, Westminster
1211	ALLEN	Mary	78		Wife	Mar	39	F		Middx	St Margaret, Westminster
1212	ALLEN	William	78		Son		16	M	Scholar (at home)	Middx	St John, Westminster
1213	ALLEN	Lousia S.	78		Dau		12	F	Scholar (at home)	Middx	St John, Westminster
1214	ALLEN	Elvia Maria	78		Dau		7	F	Scholar (at home)	Beds	Bedford St Mary
1215	STOOKS	Thomas	79	Village	Head	Mar	39	M	Tailor	Unknown	
1216	STOOKS	Maria	79		Wife	Mar	34	F	Straw Plaiter	Herts	Harpenden
1217	STOOKS	Alfred	79		Son	Unm	9	M	Scholar	Herts	Harpenden
1218	ATTWOOD	James	79		Father-in-law	Widower	70	M	Bricklayer	Herts	Harpenden
1219	SPENCER	Leigh	80	Village	Head	Unm	34	M	Curate of Harpenden	Middx	London
1220	STEVENSTON	Mary	80		Serv	Unm	22	F	House Servant	Beds	Carlton
1221	EYLES	John	81	Village	Head	Mar	42	M	Tailor employing 1 man	Herts	Harpenden
1222	EYLES	Ann	81		Wife	Mar	39	F		Middx	Hadley
1223	EYLES	Edward	81		Son		10	M	Scholar	Herts	Harpenden
1224	EYLES	Henry	81		Son		8	M	Scholar	Herts	Harpenden
1225	EYLES	Julia	81		Dau		7	F	Scholar	Herts	Harpenden
1226	EYLES	Fanny	81		Dau		6	F	Scholar	Herts	Harpenden
1227	EYLES	Ida	81		Dau		4	F	Scholar	Herts	Harpenden
1228	EYLES	Amy	81		Dau		2	F	Scholar	Herts	Harpenden
1229	EYLES	Frederick	81		Son		1	M		Herts	Harpenden
1230	WEBB	John	81		Apprentice	Unm	19	M	Apprentice Tailor	Herts	Harpenden
1231	DAY	Emma	81		Serv	Unm	19	F	House Servant	Herts	Hitchin
1232	PRENTICE	John	82	Village	Head	Mar	37	M	Agric Lab	Herts	Harpenden
1233	PRENTICE	Mary A.	82		Wife	Mar	41	F	Straw Plaiter	Herts	Kimpton
1234	PRENTICE	William	82		Son		9	M	Scholar	Herts	Harpenden
1235	PRENTICE	George	82		Son		6	M	Scholar	Herts	Harpenden
1236	PRENTICE	James	82		Son		5 m	M		Herts	Harpenden

1237	GREGORY	Charlotte	82		Step-dau		10	F	Scholar	Herts	Harpenden
1238	GREGORY	George	82		Step-son		9	M	Scholar	Herts	Harpenden
1239	GREGORY	William	82		Step-son		6	M	Scholar	Herts	Harpenden
1240	GREGORY	James	83	Village	Head	Mar	73	M	Agric Lab	Herts	Hexton
1241	GREGORY	Charlotte	83		Wife	Mar	73	F	Straw Plaiter	Herts	Northall
1242	DUNKLEY	Elizabeth	84	Village	Head	Widow	74	F	Straw Plaiter	Herts	Harpenden
1243	LUCK	Elizabeth	84		Dau	Mar	38	F	Straw Plaiter	Herts	Harpenden
1244	CREW	Vincent	84		Son-in-law	Mar	39	M	Agric Lab	Herts	Kimpton
1245	CREW	Sarah	84		Dau	Mar	36	F	Straw Plaiter	Herts	Harpenden
1246	CREW	Vincent	84		Grandson		9	M	Scholar	Herts	Harpenden
1247	CREW	William	84		Grandson		7	M	Scholar	Herts	Harpenden
1248	CREW	Emily	84		Grandau		4	F		Herts	Harpenden
1249	CREW	Gary [?]	84		Grandson		1 m	M		Herts	Harpenden
1250	ROBINSON	John	85	Village	Head	Mar	62	M	Master Carpenter employing 1 man	Middx	[Unknown]
1251	ROBINSON	Jane	85		Wife	Mar	55	F	Master Carpenters Wife	Scotland	Edinburgh
1252	ROBINSON	Thomas	85		Son	Unm	22	M	Carpenter	Herts	Harpenden
1253	PARSONS	Jonathan	86	Village	Head	Widower	50	M	Agric Lab	Beds	Luton
1254	PARSONS	Harriet	86		Dau	Unm	21	F	Straw Plaiter	Herts	Harpenden
1255	PARSONS	Henry A.	86		Grandson		3	M	Scholar	Herts	Harpenden
1256	ALLEN	Charlotte	86		Visitor	Unm	21	F	Straw Plaiter	Herts	Harpenden
1257	TRUSTRAM	John	87	Sun Lane	Head	Mar	44	M	Agric Lab	Herts	Harpenden
1258	TRUSTRAM	Martha	87		Wife	Mar	43	F	Straw Plaiter	Herts	Wheathampstead
1259	TRUSTRAM	Martha	87		Dau	Unm	15	F	Straw Plaiter	Herts	Wheathampstead
1260	TRUSTRAM	Lucy	87		Dau		12	F	Scholar	Herts	Wheathampstead
1261	TRUSTRAM	John	87		Son		11	M	Scholar	Herts	Wheathampstead
1262	TRUSTRAM	Thomas	87		Son		8	M	Scholar	Herts	Wheathampstead
1263	SIMONS	Mary	88	Starveget Hall	Head	Unm	63	F	Annuitant	Beds	Ampthill
1264	SINFAIL	Robert	89	Starveget Hall	Head	Mar	70	M	Agric Lab	Herts	Offley
1265	SINFAIL	Elizabeth	89		Wife	Mar	67	F	Straw Plaiter	Herts	Thundridge
1266	ELMER	Richard	90	Starveget Hall	Head	Widower	59	M	Farmer of 25 acres employing 2 men	Beds	Westoning
1267	ELMER	Ann	90		Dau	Unm	33	F	Farmers Daughter	Beds	Silsoe
1268	SLATER	Thomas	91	Lodge Row	Head	Mar	34	M	Gardener	Beds	Elstow
1269	SLATER	Mary	91		Wife	Mar	31	F	Gardeners Wife	Beds	Elstow
1270	SLATER	Emma	91		Dau		10	F	Scholar	Beds	Bedford
1271	SLATER	Elizabeth	91		Dau		8	F	Scholar	Beds	Bedford
1272	SLATER	William	91		Son		6	M	Scholar	Beds	Bedford
1273	SLATER	Charles	91		Son		5	M	Scholar	Herts	Harpenden
1274	SLATER	Louisa	91		Dau		11 m	F		Herts	Harpenden

One house uninhabited

1275	REEVES	James	92	Lodge Row	Head	Mar	27	M	Agric Lab	Herts	Harpenden
1276	REEVES	Eliza	92		Wife	Mar	27	F	Straw Plaiter	Herts	Harpenden
1277	REEVES	Alfred	92		Son		9	M	Scholar	Herts	Harpenden
1278	REEVES	William	92		Son		7	M	Scholar	Herts	Harpenden

	SURNAME	FORENAME	SCHEDULE NUMBER	ADDRESS	RELATIONSHIP	STATUS	AGE	SEX	OCCUPATION	COUNTY OF BIRTH	PLACE OF BIRTH
1279	REEVES	Charles	92		Son		5	M	Scholar	Herts	Harpenden
1280	REEVES	Julia	92		Dau		2	F		Herts	Harpenden
1281	REEVES	James	92		Son		4 m	M		Herts	Harpenden
1282	BENT	William	93	Lodge Row	Head	Mar	76	M	Agric Lab	Herts	Wheathampstead
1283	BENT	Mary	93		Wife	Mar	59	F	Straw Plaiter	Herts	Harpenden
1284	SHEFFIELD	Harriet	94	Lodge Row	Head	Mar	39	M	Straw Plaiter	Herts	Harpenden
1285	SHEFFIELD	Emma	94		Dau	Unm	16	F	Straw Plaiter	Bucks	Ivinghoe
1286	SHEFFIELD	Maria	94		Dau		11	F	Straw Plaiter	Herts	Harpenden
1287	SHEFFIELD	William	94		Son		9	M	Straw Plaiter	Herts	Harpenden
1288	SHEFFIELD	Eliza	94		Dau		6	F	Straw Plaiter	Herts	Harpenden
1289	SHEFFIELD	Mary	94		Dau		3	F		Herts	Harpenden
1290	SHEFFIELD	Ellen	94		Dau		1	F		Herts	Harpenden
1291	ATTWOOD	Frank	95	Lodge Row	Head	Widower	71	M	Carpenter	Herts	Harpenden
1292	MAITLAND	Isabella R.	96	The Lodge	Head	Unm	58	F	Fund Holder	Essex	Leyton, Whipps Cross
1293	RUTTY	Stephen H.	96		Visitor	Mar	76	M	Annuitant	Wilts	Siond [?]
1294	RUTTY	Sarah	96		Serv	Mar	74	F	House Keeper	Bucks	Moulsoe
1295	FUGE	Jane	96		Serv	Widow	40	F	Cook	Derby	Denby Town
1296	SIMPSON	Charlotte	96		Serv	Unm	23	F	Housemaid	Kent	Strood
1297	PEDY	James	96		Serv	Mar	43	M	Man Servant	Hants	Petersfield
1298	COX	Thomas	96		Serv	Mar	40	M	Coachman	Norfolk	North Walsham
1299	WILLMOTT	Joseph	97	Cooters End	Head	Widower	40	M	Farmer of 300 acres employing 15 Lab.	Herts	Kings Walden
1300	WILLMOTT	Mary	97		Dau	Unm	14	F	Farmers Daughter	Herts	Kings Walden
1301	WILLMOTT	Sarah	97		Dau		10	F	Farmers Daughter	Herts	Kings Walden
1302	ARCHER	William	97		Serv	Unm	20	M	Agric Lab	Herts	St Albans
1303	MARTIN	Abraham	97		Serv	Unm	60	M	Agric Lab	Surrey	Chertsey
1304	LAWRENCE	Samuel	97		Serv	Unm	18	M	Agric Lab	Herts	Kings Walden
1305	WALLER	George	97		Serv	Unm	16	M	Agric Lab	Beds	Toddington
1306	THRUSELL	Charles	97		Serv	Unm	16	M	Agric Lab	Herts	St Pauls Walden
1307	PROCTER	William	97		Serv	Unm	17	M	Agric Lab	Beds	Luton

End of the District No. 2b in the parish of Harpenden

Registrar's District: Harpenden

Enumeration District 2c

Ref. HO 107/1713 folios 108-28

All that part of the parish of Harpenden that lies to the west of the Turnpike road leading from St Albans to Luton, and north of the road called Stakers Lane, and of the line drawn from the western end of such lane to the gate on Harpenden Common leading to Rothamsted, and from thence in a western direction into the Holyhead Road, including the western side of the village, Kingsbourne Green, and the farms within such boundary.

	SURNAME	FORENAME	SCHEDULE NUMBER	ADDRESS	RELATIONSHIP	STATUS	AGE	SEX	OCCUPATION	COUNTY OF BIRTH	PLACE OF BIRTH
1308	JAMES	Thomas	1	Turnpike Road	Head	Unm	51	M	Toll Collector	Shrop	Hopton Castle
1309	PATMORE	John	2	The Red Lion	Head	Mar	49	M	Licensed Victualler	Herts	Wheathampstead
1310	PATMORE	Amelia	2		Wife	Mar	49	F		Herts	Harpenden
1311	LINES	Joseph	2		Lodger	Widower	65	M	Blacksmith Journeyman	Herts	Wheathampstead
1312	BUTCHER	Thomas	2		Lodger	Mar	63	M	Harness Maker	Beds	Eversholt
1313	BRAGGE	Benjamin	2		Lodger	Unm	40	M	Harness Maker	Sussex	[Unknown]
1314	BOULTON	Charles	3	Turnpike Road	Head	Mar	28	M	Tinman & Brazier	Herts	St Michaels
1315	BOULTON	Louisa	3		Wife	Mar	31	F	Dress Maker	Herts	St Michaels
1316	PATMORE	Elizabeth	4	Turnpike Road	Head	Widow	76	F	Annuitant	Herts	Sandridge

1317	FREEMAN	Sarah	4		Dau	Mar	35	F	Needlewoman	Herts	Wheathampstead
1318	GOODRIDGE	William	5	Turnpike Road	Head	Mar	57	M	Out of business (no stated occ.)	Northants	Hartwell
1319	GOODRIDGE	Elizabeth	5		Wife	Mar	61	F		Northants	West Haddon
1320	GOODRIDGE	Mary	5		Dau	Unm	22	F	Grocer & Dress Maker	Bucks	Stony Stratford
1321	MARVIN	William	6	Turnpike Road	Head	Mar	77	M	Farmer of 2 acres employing 1 man	Herts	Wheathampstead
1322	MARVIN	Hannah	6		Wife	Mar	78	F		Herts	All Saints, Hertford
1323	MARVIN	William	6		Son	Widower	49	M	Waggoner	Herts	Wheathampstead
1324	MISSENDEN	John	7	Turnpike Road	Head	Mar	54	M	Baker, Master employing 1 man	Herts	St Albans
1325	MISSENDEN	Sarah	7		Wife	Mar	49	F	Assistant in Bakehouse	Beds	Luton
1326	MISSENDEN	Sarah	7		Dau	Unm	19	F	Bonnet Sewer	Herts	Harpenden
1327	MISSENDEN	Eliza	7		Dau		12	F	Scholar	Herts	Harpenden
1328	ELMES	George	7		Visitor		11	M	Scholar	Herts	Hertford
1329	ROBINS	Walter	7		Journeyman	Unm	21	M	Journeyman Baker	Herts	Watton
1330	TRUSTRAM	Joseph W	8	The Cock Inn	Head	Mar	37	M	Carpenter	Herts	Harpenden
1331	TRUSTRAM	Sophia	8		Wife	Mar	37	F		Herts	Sandridge
1332	TRUSTRAM	Mary Ann	8		Dau		9	F	Scholar	Herts	Harpenden
1333	TRUSTRAM	Sophia	8		Dau		2	F	Scholar	Herts	Harpenden
1334	TRUSTRAM	Walter	8		Son		1	M		Herts	Harpenden
1335	TRUSTRAM	Lucy	8		Mother	Widow	70	F	Supported by her Family	Suffolk	Ipswich
1336	TRUSTRAM	William	8		Nephew	Unm	20	M	Apprentice	Herts	Harpenden
1337	RUDD	Samuel	8		Serv		10	M	Errand Boy	Herts	Wheathampstead
1338	SMALLBROOK	John	9	Turnpike Road	Head	Mar	55	M	Gardener	Oxon	Bletchingdon
1339	SMALLBROOK	Charlotte	9		Wife	Mar	53	F	School Mistress	Beds	Woburn
1340	EAMEY [?]	James	10	Turnpike Road	Head	Mar	77	M	Annuitant	Herts	Whipsnade
1341	EAMEY [?]	Rebecca	10		Wife	Mar	75	F		Beds	Dunstable
1342	JOHNSON	Mary Mercer?	11	Turnpike Road	Head	Unm	24	F	Juvenile Academy	Essex	Stanford Rivers
1343	TOMALIN	Matthew	12	Turnpike Road	Head	Mar	42	M	Dealer	Middx	London
1344	TOMALIN	Frances	12		Wife	Mar	41	F	Plaiter	Herts	Harpenden
1345	TOMALIN	Joseph	12		Son	Unm	11	M	Plaiter	Herts	Harpenden
1346	TOMALIN	Frances E	12		Dau	Unm	10	F	Plaiter	Herts	Harpenden
1347	TOMALIN	Maria	12		Dau	Unm	5	F	Plaiter	Herts	Harpenden
1348	TOMALIN	Frederick	12		Son		3	M		Herts	Harpenden
1349	HUGHES	Charles	13	Turnpike Road	Head	Mar	53	M	Agric Lab	London	
1350	HUGHES	Phoebe	13		Wife	Mar	49	F	Plaiter	Beds	Luton
1351	HUGHES	Frederick	13		Son	Unm	19	M	Agric Lab	Herts	Harpenden
1352	HUGHES	Elizabeth	13		Dau	Unm	15	F	Plaiter	Herts	Harpenden
1353	HUGHES	Charles	13		Son		12	M	Servant	Herts	Harpenden
1354	HUGHES	John	13		Son		10	M	Scholar	Herts	Harpenden
1355	HUGHES	Eliza	13		Grandau		2	F	Scholar	Herts	Harpenden
1356	GREAVES	James	14	Turnpike Road	Head	Unm	49	M	Paper Maker	Bucks	Chesham
1357	MITCHELL	Eliza	14		Serv	Unm	26	F	House Keeper	Herts	Harpenden
1358	ROLT	Elizabeth	15	Turnpike Road	Head	Unm	32	F	Plaiter	Herts	St Michaels
1359	RUSSELL	George	15		Brother-in-law	Mar	20	M	Agric Lab	Herts	Harpenden

	SURNAME	FORENAME	SCHEDULE NUMBER	ADDRESS	RELATIONSHIP	STATUS	AGE	SEX	OCCUPATION	COUNTY OF BIRTH	PLACE OF BIRTH
1360	RUSSELL	Ellen	15		Sister	Mar	21	F	Plaiter	Herts	Harpenden
1361	ROLT	Sarah	15		Sister		13	F	Plaiter	Herts	Harpenden
1362	ROLT	Thomas	15		Nephew		4	M	Plaiter	Herts	St Albans Union
1363	HARDY	George	16	Turnpike Road	Head	Mar	47	M	Agric Lab	Herts	Harpenden
1364	HARDY	Elizabeth	16		Wife	Mar	45	F	Plaiter	Beds	Luton
1365	HARDY	Mary	16		Dau	Unm	19	F	Plaiter	Herts	Harpenden
1366	HARDY	James	16		Son	Unm	16	M	Agric Lab	Herts	Harpenden
1367	HARDY	Maria	16		Dau		14	F	Plaiter	Herts	Harpenden
1368	HARDY	William	16		Son		12	M	Butchers Boy	Herts	Harpenden
1369	HARDY	Eliza	16		Dau		9	F	Plaiter	Herts	Harpenden
1370	HARDY	Jane	16		Dau		7	F	Plaiter	Herts	Harpenden
1371	HARDY	Henry	16		Son		4	M	At home	Herts	Harpenden
1372	HAWKINS	John	17	Turnpike Road	Head	Mar	23	M	Cattle Drover	Herts	Harpenden
1373	HAWKINS	Martha	17		Wife	Mar	23	F	Plaiter	Herts	Caddington
1374	HAWKINS	George	17		Son		3	M		Herts	Harpenden
1375	HAWKINS	Sarah	17		Dau		1	F		Herts	Harpenden
1376	WHITEHOUSE	Josiah	18	Turnpike Road	Head	Mar	23	M	Tailor	Herts	Harpenden
1377	WHITEHOUSE	Mary Ann	18		Wife	Mar	24	F	Plaiter	Herts	Harpenden
	One house uninhabited		19								
1378	HAWKINS	George	20	Turnpike Road	Head	Mar	41	M	Lawyer	Herts	Harpenden
1379	HAWKINS	Susanah	20		Wife	Mar	39	F	Plaiter	Herts	Harpenden
1380	HAWKINS	Frederick	20		Son		13	M	Scholar	Herts	Harpenden
1381	HAWKINS	Emily	20		Dau		9	F	Scholar	Herts	Harpenden
1382	DURLEY	William	21	Turnpike Road	Head	Mar	50	M	Traveller	Bucks	Hardwick
1383	DURLEY	Sophia	21		Wife	Mar	30	F	Plaiter	Herts	Harpenden
1384	WHITEHOUSE	Thomas	22	Turnpike Road	Head	Mar	62	M	School Master	Staffs	[Unknown]
1385	WHITEHOUSE	Elizabeth	22		Wife	Mar	54	F	School Mistress	Herts	Harpenden
1386	DELLOR	William	23	Turnpike Road	Head	Mar	62	M	Agric Lab	Herts	Offley
1387	DELLOR	Ann	23		Wife	Mar	56	F	Charwoman	Herts	Hitchin
1388	DELLOR	David	23		Son		14	M	Agric Lab	Herts	Harpenden
1389	DELLOR	William	23		Son		11	M	Agric Lab	Herts	Harpenden
1390	RUSSELL	Joseph	23		Lodger	Unm	48	M	Plaiter	Herts	Harpenden
1391	BREWER	William	24	Turnpike Road	Head	Mar	62	M	Agric Lab	Beds	Toddington
1392	BREWER	Hannah	24		Wife	Mar	57	F	Plaiter	Herts	Watford
1393	SWAIN	Elizabeth	24		Lodger	Widow	55	F	Plaiter	Herts	Hexton
1394	BREWER	William	24		Son	Unm	20	M	Agric Lab	Herts	Harpenden
1395	SMITH	Joseph	25	Turnpike Road	Head	Mar	56	M	Agric Lab	Herts	Offley
1396	SMITH	Harriett	25		Wife	Mar	55	F	Plaiter	Herts	Flamstead
1397	SMITH	Josiah	25		Son		9	M	Plaiter	Herts	Harpenden
1398	PARKINS	James	25		Son-in-law	Mar	23	M	Agric Lab	Herts	Wheathampstead
1399	PARKINS	Martha	25		Dau	Mar	22	F	Plaiter	Herts	Flamstead
1400	SIMMONS	Charles	25		Lodger	Unm	21	M	Agric Lab	Herts	Harpenden
1401	TAYLOR	George	26	Turnpike Road	Head	Mar	23	M	Blacksmith/Journeyman	Herts	Ickleford
1403	TAYLOR	Emma	26		Dau		1	F		Herts	Harpenden

1402	TAYLOR	Sarah	26		Wife	Mar	24	F	Plaiter	Herts	Harpenden
1404	SAUNDERS	William	27	Turnpike Road	Head	Mar	53	M	Agric Lab	Beds	Houghton Regis
1405	SAUNDERS	Sarah	27		Wife	Mar	53	F	Plaiter	Beds	Houghton Regis
1406	SAUNDERS	Sarah	27		Dau		15	F	Plaiter	Herts	Harpenden
1407	SAUNDERS	Matilda	27		Dau		13	F	Plaiter	Herts	Harpenden
1408	SAUNDERS	Frederick	27		Son		9	M	Plaiter	Herts	Harpenden
1409	WELLS	Thomas	27		Son-in-law	Widower	26	M	Agric Lab	Herts	Flamstead
1410	WELLS	Ann	27		Grandau		6	F	Plaiter	Herts	Harpenden
1411	WELLS	George	27		Grandson		4	M	At home	Herts	Harpenden
1412	SWAIN	Emma	27		Lodger	Unm	17	F	Plaiter	Herts	Harpenden
1413	LEEDHAM	Henry J.	28	Turnpike Road	Head	Mar	40	M	Rope Maker	Herts	Harpenden
1414	LEEDHAM	Maria	28		Wife	Mar	38	F		Herts	Harpenden
1415	LEEDHAM	William H.	28		Son		13	M	Rope Maker	Herts	Harpenden
1416	LEEDHAM	Eliza	28		Dau		10	F	Bonnet Sewer	Herts	Harpenden
1417	STARKINGS	Joseph	29	Turnpike Road	Head	Mar	81	M	Watch Maker	Herts	Harpenden
1418	STARKINGS	Mary	29		Wife	Mar	82	F	Plaiter	Herts	Harpenden
1419	FREEMAN	Sarah	30	Turnpike Road	Head	Widow	75	F	Annuitant	Herts	Harpenden
1420	COE	Ann	30		Inmate	Widow	73	F	Annuitant	Herts	Wheathampstead
1421	SMITH	Maria	30		Grandau	Unm	23	F	House Servant	Herts	Wheathampstead
1422	DILLEY	Mary	31	Turnpike Road	Head	Widow	63	F	Plaiter	Herts	Harpenden
1423	DILLEY	Elizabeth	31		Dau	Unm	29	F	Plaiter	Herts	Harpenden
1424	DILLEY	Mary Ann	31		Grandau		8	F	Plaiter	Herts	Harpenden
1425	MITCHELL	Charles	32	Turnpike Road	Head	Unm	28	M	Agric Lab	Herts	Harpenden
1426	FAULKNER	Maria	32		Sister	Widow	23	F	Plaiter	Herts	Harpenden
1427	FAULKNER	Eliza	32		Niece		2	F	Plaiter	Herts	Harpenden
1428	VAUGHAN	Mary Ann	32		Lodger	Unm	29	F	Plaiter	Herts	Wheathampstead
1429	VAUGHAN	Eliza	32		Lodger		5	F	Plaiter	Herts	Wheathampstead
1430	BORDERS	Amos	33	Turnpike Road	Head	Unm	22	M	Agric Lab	Herts	Harpenden
1431	MITCHELL	Ann	33		H'keeper	Unm	20	F	Plaiter	Herts	Harpenden
1432	MITCHELL	Charles	33		H'keepers Son		1	M		Herts	Harpenden
1433	SLOW	Edward	34	Turnpike Road	Head	Mar	43	M	Agric Lab	Herts	Wheathampstead
1434	SLOW	Abi	34		Wife	Mar	38	F	Plaiter	Oxon	Churchill
1435	SLOW	Emma	34		Dau		6	F	Scholar	Herts	Harpenden
1436	SLOW	Edmund	34		Son		2	M		Herts	Harpenden
1437	SPACKMAN	Frederic R.	35	Turnpike Road	Head	Mar	31	M	MB Lond: MRCSE. LSA.Gen:Pract:Surgeon	Leics	Lutterworth
1438	SPACKMAN	Caroline H.	35		Wife	Mar	34	F		Leics	Lutterworth
1439	SPACKMAN	Harriet M.	35		Dau		4	F	Scholar at home	Herts	Harpenden
1440	SPACKMAN	Frederic H.	35		Son		3	M	Scholar at home	Herts	Harpenden
1441	SPACKMAN	Johnson W.	35		Son		10 m	M		Herts	Harpenden
1442	SAWBRIDGE	Jane	35		Serv	Unm	25	F	House Maid	Northants	[Unknown]
1443	BAILEY	Eliza	35		Serv	Unm	27	F	Cook	Bucks	Cuddington
1444	DUNKLEY	John	35		Serv	Unm	20	M	Groom	Herts	Harpenden
1445	BRASH	Helen	36	Turnpike Road	Head	Mar	31	F	Tea Dealer	Scotland	[Unknown]
1446	BRASH	David H	36		Son		6	M	Scholar	Scotland	[Unknown]

	SURNAME	FORENAME	SCHEDULE NUMBER	ADDRESS	RELATIONSHIP	STATUS	AGE	SEX	OCCUPATION	COUNTY OF BIRTH	PLACE OF BIRTH
1447	BRASH	Thomas	36		Son		5	M	Scholar	Scotland	[Unknown]
1448	BRASH	Helen	36		Dau		3	F	Scholar	Yorks	Hull
1449	BRASH	Johan M.	36		Dau		1	F		Herts	Harpenden
1450	COOPER	Albucia	37	Turnpike Road	Head	Unm	21	M	Master of Elementary School	Cumb	Garrigill
1451	ASHBY	Harriott	38	Turnpike Road	Head	Mar	57	F	Proprietor of Houses	Beds	Shefford
1452	TRUSTRAM	Mary Ann	38		Niece	Unm	18	F	Plaiter	Herts	Harpenden
1453	SIMPSON	Henry	39	Turnpike Road	Head	Mar	30	M	Brewers Clerk	Hants	Wield
1454	SIMPSON	Sarah	39		Wife	Mar	28	F		Bucks	Newport Pagnell
1455	WILSON	Mary Ann	40	Turnpike Road	Head	Unm	40	F	Annuitant	Herts	Harpenden
1456	SIMONS	Maria	41	Turnpike Road	Head	Widow	48	F	Retired Baker	Herts	St Albans
1457	SIMONS	Maria E.	41		Dau	Unm	18	F	Dress Maker	Herts	Harpenden
1458	SAUNDERS	John Frederick	42	Turnpike Road	Head	Unm	18	M	Engaged in connection with the Science of Agricultural Chemistry	Surrey	Cobourg, Old Kent Rd [?]
1459	CONSTABLE	Joseph	43	Turnpike Road	Head	Mar	58	M	Gardener	Herts	Harpenden
1460	CONSTABLE	Ann	43		Wife	Mar	64	F	Plaiter	Herts	Harpenden
1461	YOUNG	Thomas	43		Son-in-law	Mar	40	M	(Dom.) Servant	Herts	Wheathampstead
1462	YOUNG	Mary Ann	43		Dau	Mar	37	F	Plaiter	Herts	Harpenden
1463	HAWKINS	Henry	43		Son-in-law	Mar	33	M	Sawyer	Herts	Harpenden
1464	HAWKINS	Sophia	43		Dau	Mar	32	F	Bonnet Sewer	Herts	St Michaels
1465	HAWKINS	Susan	43		Grandau		11	F	Bonnet Sewer	Herts	Harpenden
1466	HAWKINS	Alfred	43		Grandson		5	M	Scholar	Herts	Harpenden
1467	HAWKINS	Jane	43		Grandau		1	F		Herts	Harpenden
1468	HAWKINS	Joseph	43		Grandson		3m	M		Herts	Harpenden
1469	ATTWOOD	Mary	44	Turnpike Road	Head	Unm	67	F	Bonnet Sewer	Herts	Harpenden
1470	SAUNDERS	John	45	Turnpike Road	Head	Mar	35	M	Dealer	Herts	Baldock
1471	SAUNDERS	Henrietta	45		Wife	Mar	27	F		Herts	Abbots Langley
1472	SAUNDERS	Mary	45		Dau		2	F		Herts	Harpenden
1473	SAUNDERS	Louisa	45		Dau		10m	F		Herts	Harpenden
1474	DICKENSON	Henry	45		Nephew		5	M	Scholar	Herts	St Albans
1475	ARCHER	George	46	Turnpike Road	Head	Mar	66	M	Cordwainer	Herts	Harpenden
1476	ARCHER	Sarah	46		Wife	Mar	65	F	Bonnet Sewer	Herts	Ridge
1477	ARCHER	Thomas	46		Son	Unm	36	M	Cordwainer	Herts	Harpenden
1478	WORRALL	Joseph	47	Turnpike Road	Head	Mar	45	M	Dealer in Straw	Bucks	Chesham
1479	WORRALL	Georgiana	47		Wife	Mar	47	F		Herts	Wheathampstead
1480	IRONS	Thomas	48	Turnpike Road	Head	Widower	72	M	Carpenter	Herts	Harpenden
1481	OGGLESBY	Thomas	49	Turnpike Road	Head	Mar	72	M	Carpenter	Herts	Harpenden
1482	OGGLESBY	Hannah	49		Wife	Mar	70	F		Herts	Weston
1483	OGGLESBY	Thomas	49		Son	Widower	45	M	Carpenter	Herts	Harpenden
1484	PESTILL	John	50	Turnpike Road	Head	Mar	72	M	Agric Lab	Herts	Harpenden
1485	PESTILL	Eleanor	50		Wife	Mar	66	F	Plaiter	Herts	Norton
1486	WEEDON	Elizabeth	50		Lodger		11	F	Plaiter	Herts	Wheathampstead
1487	MESSENGER	Daniel	51	Turnpike Road	Head	Mar	39	M	Agric Lab	Beds	Houghton Regis
1488	MESSENGER	Hannah	51		Wife	Mar	39	F	Plaiter	Beds	Houghton Regis
1489	MESSENGER	James	51		Son	Unm	18	M	Agric Lab	Herts	Harpenden

1490	MESSENGER	Jane	51		Dau		13	F	Plaiter	Herts	Harpenden
1491	MESSENGER	Emma	51		Dau		11	F	Plaiter	Herts	Harpenden
1492	MESSENGER	Sarah	51		Dau		7	F	Plaiter	Herts	Harpenden
1493	MESSENGER	George	51		Son		5	M	Plaiter	Herts	Harpenden
1494	MESSENGER	William	51		Son		2	M		Herts	Harpenden
1495	MESSENGER	Mary Ann	51		Dau		7 m	F		Herts	Harpenden
1496	BOYS	Phillip	52	Turnpike Road	Head	Widower	60	M	Miller	London	
1497	BOYS	Jabez	52		Son	Unm	23	M	Bonnet Ironer	Herts	Harpenden
1498	BOYS	Maria	52		Dau	Unm	30	F	Bonnet Sewer	Herts	Harpenden
1499	GILBERT	Thomas	53	Turnpike Road	Head	Mar	49	M	Tailor	Middx	London
1500	GILBERT	Frances	53		Wife	Mar	47	F		Herts	Harpenden
1501	TEWIN	Joseph	54	Turnpike Road	Head	Mar	31	M	Grocer & Druggist, 2 men	Herts	St Albans
1502	TEWIN	Sarah	54		Wife	Mar	27	F		London	
1503	TEWIN	Francis	54		Son		7	M		Herts	Harpenden
1504	WINTERBONE	Jonas	54		Serv	Unm	34	M	Assistant Druggist	London	
1505	HARRIS?	Elizabeth	54		Serv	Unm	19	F	House Servant	Surrey	Southwark
1506	TEWIN	William	55	Turnpike Road	Head	Mar	63	M	Retired Grocer	Herts	St Albans
1507	TEWIN	Elizabeth	55		Wife	Mar	70	F		Herts	Watford
1508	TRUSSELL [?]	Ann	55		Serv	Widow	38	F	House Servant	Herts	Hatfield
1509	WESTON	Joseph	56	Turnpike Road	Head	Mar	40	M	House Servant	Herts	Harpenden
1510	WESTON	Elizabeth	56		Wife	Mar	41	F	Laundress	Oxon	Drayton
1511	WESTON	Sarah	56		Dau	Unm	17	F	Bonnet Sewer	Warks	Leamington
1512	WESTON	Edward	56		Son		14	M	Scholar	Warks	Leamington
1513	WESTON	Joseph	56		Son		9	M	Scholar	Herts	Harpenden
1514	ROBINSON	William	57	The Marten Cat	Head	Mar	33	M	Beer House Keeper & Hair Dresser	Middx	Clerkenwell
1515	BOFF	Mary	57		H'keeper	Unm	38	F		Herts	Harpenden
1516	RADWELL	Catherine	58	Turnpike Road	Head	Widow	65	F	Bonnet Sewer	Herts	St Michaels
1517	HULL	John	58		Son-in-law	Mar	46	M	Agric Lab	Beds	Luton
1518	HULL	Caroline	58		Dau	Mar	45	F	Bonnet Sewer	Middx	London
1519	HULL	Sarah	58		Grandau		15	F	Bonnet Sewer	Herts	Harpenden
1520	HULL	Catherine	58		Grandau		12	F	Scholar	Herts	Harpenden
1521	HULL	Joseph	58		Grandson		8	M	Scholar	Herts	Harpenden
1522	HULL	Elizabeth	58		Grandau		3	F		Herts	Harpenden
1523	BUNYAN	James	59	Turnpike Road	Head	Mar	20	M	Agric Lab	Herts	Harpenden
1524	BUNYAN	Ann	59		Wife	Mar	30	F	Plaiter	Herts	Harpenden
1525	BUNYAN	Eliza	59		Dau		7 m	F		Herts	Harpenden
1526	CRAWLEY	Richard	60	Turnpike Road	Head	Mar	28	M	Agric Lab	Herts	Flamstead
1527	CRAWLEY	Susanah	60		Wife	Mar	26	F	Plaiter	Herts	Harpenden
1528	CRAWLEY	John	60		Son		5	M	Plaiter	Herts	Harpenden
1529	CRAWLEY	Mary Ann	60		Dau		1	F		Herts	Harpenden
1530	JENNINGS	Charlotte	60		Mother-in-law	Mar	48	F	Plaiter	Herts	Abbots Langley
1531	JENNINGS	Sarah	60		Sister-in-law	Unm	19	F	Bonnet Sewer	Herts	Harpenden
1532	BUNYAN	Thomas	61	Turnpike Road	Head	Mar	47	M	Agric Lab	Herts	Kimpton
1533	BUNYAN	Maria	61		Wife	Mar	50	F	Plaiter	Norfolk	Martin

SURNAME	FORENAME	SCHEDULE NUMBER	ADDRESS	RELATIONSHIP	STATUS	AGE	SEX	OCCUPATION	COUNTY OF BIRTH	PLACE OF BIRTH
1534	BUNYAN	Mary	61		Dau	Unm	22	F	Bonnet Sewer	Herts	Harpenden
1535	WALKER	William	62	Turnpike Road	Head	Mar	22	M	Straw Bonnet Manufacturer	Herts	Wheathampstead
1536	WALKER	Ellen	62		Wife	Mar	22	F		Surrey	Walworth
1537	HOUGHTON	Joseph	62		Brother-in-law	Unm	28	M	Straw Bonnet Manufacturer	Surrey	Southwark
1538	LINES	Hannah	62		Serv	Unm	14	F	House Servant	Herts	Harpenden
1539	WARD	Jessie	63	Odd Fellows Arms	Head	Mar	52	M	Beer House Keeper	Herts	Harpenden
1540	WARD	Sarah	63		Wife	Mar	48	F		Herts	Redbourn
1541	WARD	Eliza	63		Dau	Unm	16	F	Plaiter	Herts	Harpenden
1542	GROVER	William	64	Turnpike Road	Head	Mar	37	M	Brewers Labourer	Herts	Sarratt
1543	GROVER	Maria	64		Wife	Mar	27	F	Plaiter	Herts	St Albans
1544	GROVER	Eliza	64		Dau		8	F	Scholar	Herts	St Albans
1545	GROVER	Caroline	64		Dau		2	F		Herts	Harpenden
1546	GROVER	George	64		Son		3m	M		Herts	Harpenden
1547	NASH	Sarah	64		Visitor	[blank]	38	F	Plaiter	Herts	St Albans
1548	FARR	John	65	Turnpike Road	Head	Mar	36	M	Agric Lab	Herts	Harpenden
1549	FARR	Emma	65		Wife	Mar	30	F	Trimming Weaver	Herts	Harpenden
1550	FARR	George	65		Son		9	M	Scholar	Herts	Harpenden
1551	FARR	Harriett	65		Dau		6	F	Scholar	Herts	Harpenden
1552	HASTINGS	Richard	66	Turnpike Road	Head	Mar	48	M	MRCS London SAC London G.Practioner	Ireland	[Unknown]
1553	BROWN	Sarah	66		Serv	Unm	28	F		Herts	St Albans
1554	BROWN	Elizabeth	66		Serv	Unm	37	F		Herts	St Albans
1555	FREEMAN	Elizabeth	67	Turnpike Road	Head	Widow	72	F	Laundress	Herts	Harpenden
1556	NICHOLLS	Emily	67		Grandau		9	F	Scholar	Middx	London
1557	FREEMAN	Ann	68	Turnpike Road	Head	Widow	45	F	Plaiter	Herts	Harpenden
1558	FREEMAN	Louisa	68		Niece		15	F	Bonnet Sewer	Surrey	Brixton
1559	DIMMOCK [?]	Sarah	69	Turnpike Road	Head	Unm	43	F	Plaiter	Herts	Harpenden
1560	DIMMOCK [?]	Sarah	69		Mother	Widow	72	F	Plaiter	Herts	Harpenden
1561	JOHNSON	Charlotte	70	Turnpike Road	Head	Widow	80	F	Relief from parish	Herts	Offley
1562	JOHNSON	Rhoda	70		Dau	Unm	30	F	Plaiter	Herts	Harpenden
1563	JOHNSON	Rebecca	70		Grandau	Unm	20	F	Plaiter	Middx	St Pancras
1564	WINCH	Elizabeth	71	Turnpike Road	Head	Widow	37	F	Plaiter	Herts	Harpenden
1565	WINCH	Mary Ann	71		Sister-in-law	Unm	16	F	Plaiter	Herts	Harpenden
1566	MARIN	Ann	71		Niece		11	F		Herts	Harpenden
1567	BIGGS	John	72	Turnpike Road	Head	Mar	46	M	Agric Lab	Herts	Harpenden
1568	BIGGS	Elizabeth	72		Wife	Mar	38	F	Laundress	Beds	Sewell
1569	RADWELL	Emma	72		Dau-in-law		13	F	Scholar	Herts	Harpenden
1570	RADWELL	Mary	72		Dau-in-law		11	F	Scholar	Herts	Harpenden
1571	RADWELL	Caroline	72		Dau-in-law		9	F	Scholar	Herts	Harpenden
1572	BIGGS	Maria	72		Dau		13	F	Scholar	Herts	Harpenden
1573	BIGGS	George	72		Son		5m	M		Herts	Harpenden
1574	GIBBONS	William	73	Turnpike Road	Head	Mar	66	M	Agric Lab	Beds	Toddington
1575	GIBBONS	Sarah	73		Wife	Mar	60	F	Bonnet Sewer	Beds	Sewell
1576	GIBBONS	John	73		Grandson		6	M	Scholar	Herts	Harpenden
1577	HINSON	William	74	Turnpike Road	Head	Mar	58	M	Shoemaker	Northants	Northampton

1578	HINSON	Priscilla	74		Wife	Mar	47	F		Herts	Harpenden
1579	BUNYAN	James	75	Turnpike Road	Head	Mar	45	M	Agric Lab (Shepherd)	Herts	Kimpton
1580	BUNYAN	Martha	75		Wife	Mar	46	F	Plait Dealer	Herts	Harpenden
1581	BUNYAN	Ann	75		Dau	Unm	19	F	Bonnet Sewer	Herts	Harpenden
1582	BUNYAN	Mary	75		Dau		10	F	Scholar	Herts	Harpenden
1583	JENNINGS	Martha	75		Mother-in-law	Widow	88	F	Plaiter	Herts	Harpenden
1584	BUNYAN	Amelia	75		Sister	Unm	37	F	Plaiter	Herts	Harpenden
1585	JENNINGS	James	75		Nephew	Unm	15	M	Bonnet Blocker	Herts	Harpenden
1586	THOMPSON	William	76	Turnpike Road	Head	Mar	60	M	Brewers Labourer	Beds	Caddington
1587	THOMPSON	Alice	76		Wife	Mar	61	F		Bucks	Wing
1588	HULL	James	77	Turnpike Road	Head	Widower	74	M	Hay Binder	Herts	Much Wymondley
1589	SYGROVE	George	78	Turnpike Road	Head	Mar	25	M	Agric Lab	Herts	Wheathampstead
1590	SYGROVE	Elizabeth	78		Wife	Mar	37	F	Plaiter	Herts	Harpenden
1591	SYGROVE	Charles	78		Son		3	M		Herts	Harpenden
1592	SYGROVE	James	78		Son		1	M		Herts	Harpenden
1593	DAY	Shadrach	78		Son-in-law		11	M	Agric Lab	Herts	Harpenden
1594	BEAN	Sophia	79	Turnpike Road	Head	Widow	62	F	Plaiter	Herts	Harpenden
1595	DUNHAM	Daniel	79		Son-in-law	Mar	28	M	Cordwainer	Herts	Wheathampstead
1596	DUNHAM	Eliza	79		Dau	Mar	28	F	Bonnet Sewer	Herts	Harpenden
1597	WARDE	Marianne	80	Turnpike Road	Head	Mar	37	F	Annuitant	Herts	Harpenden
1598	WARDE	Ada Lloyd	80		Dau		12	F	Scholar at Home	Warks	Stratford on Avon
1599	WARDE	Charlotte L	80		Dau		9	F	Scholar at home	Warks	Stratford on Avon
1600	WARDE	Emily L	80		Dau		7	F	Scholar at home	Warks	Stratford on Avon
1601	LAWES	Marianne	80		Visitor	Widow	59	F	Fund Holder	Herts	St Michaels
1602	MATTHIAS	Emily	80		Visitor		5	F		Wales	Lamphey
1603	DIETERICH	Mary	80		Governess	Unm	38	F	Governess	Middx	St James
1604	MILLER	Harriott	80		Serv	Unm	50	F	Ladys Maid	Middx	St Brides
1605	LAKIN	Mary	80		Serv	Unm	52	F	Cook	Staffs	Alrewas
1606	REEDMAN	Mary Anne	80		Serv	Unm	38	F	Housemaid	Middx	Kingsland [London]
1607	MACDOUGALL	Elizabeth	80		Serv	Unm	22	F	Kitchen Maid	Scotland	[Unknown]
1608	ABBOTT	Jane	80		Serv	Unm	19	F	Parlour Maid	Herts	Harpenden
1609	GIFKINS	George	81	Turnpike Road	Head	Mar	47	M	Registrar of Births & Parish Clerk	Herts	Great Berkhamsted
1610	GIFKINS	Fanny L.	81		Wife	Mar	27	F		Middx	Stanmore
1611	GIFKINS	Caroline L.	81		Dau	Unm	25	F	Dress Maker	Herts	Wheathampstead
1612	GIFKINS	Henry G.	81		Son	Unm	17	M	Brewers Clerk	Herts	Wheathampstead
1613	GIFKINS	Fanny M.	81		Dau		15	F	Scholar at Home	Herts	Wheathampstead
1614	GIFKINS	Laura S.B.	81		Dau		4	F	Scholar at Home	Herts	Harpenden
1615	GIFKINS	Percy R.R.	81		Son		2	M		Herts	Harpenden
1616	REID	Emelie M.R.	81		Boarder		7	F	Scholar	Middx	Chelsea
1617	RUMBALL	Arthur G.	81		Visitor	Unm	24	M	Superintendent of Private Asylum for Lunatics	Herts	Barnet
1618	OLDAKER	Henry	82	The Bull Inn	Head	Mar	56	M	Innkeeper & Farmer, 50 acres, 2 labourers	Gloucs	Beckley [Beckford?, Beckley, Oxon?]
1619	OLDAKER	Georgiana	82		Wife	Mar	52	F		London	

	SURNAME	FORENAME	SCHEDULE NUMBER	ADDRESS	RELATIONSHIP	STATUS	AGE	SEX	OCCUPATION	COUNTY OF BIRTH	PLACE OF BIRTH
1620	OLDAKER	Thomas	82		Son	Unm	28	M	Farmers Son at Home	Herts	Rickmansworth
1621	OLDAKER	Emma	82		Dau	Unm	26	F	Farmers Daughter at Home	Herts	Rickmansworth
1622	OLDAKER	Mary	82		Dau	Unm	22	F	Farmers Daughter at Home	Herts	Rickmansworth
1623	OLDAKER	Charles	82		Son	Unm	16	M	Farmers Son at Home	Herts	Harpenden
1624	OLDAKER	William	82		Son		10	M	Scholar	Herts	Harpenden
1625	OLDAKER	Rosa	82		Dau		7	F	Scholar	Herts	Harpenden
1626	KING	William	82		Lodger	Unm	29	M	Horse Trainer	Yorks	Sandbeck
1627	POINTER	Mary	82		Serv	Unm	24	F	House Servant	Bucks	Brill
1628	DEAN	James	82		Lodger	Widower	46	M	Groom	Herts	Harpenden
1629	WYATT	John	83	Turnpike Road	Head	Widower	86	M	Barrister of law & Attorney General of North Wales	London	St Anns, Westminster
1630	WYATT	Susan N.	83		Dau	Unm	50	F		Beds	Silsoe
1631	WYATT	Abbina S.N.	83		Dau	Unm	47	F		Beds	Maulden
1632	HIBBERT	Leonard	83		Serv	Unm	25	M	General Servant	Herts	Kings Langley
1633	PARSONS	Clara	83		Serv	Unm	19	F	House Maid	Herts	Harpenden
1634	MACKEY	Hannah	83		Serv	Widow	75	F	Cook	Herts	Harpenden
1635	FELLS	George	84	Turnpike Road	Head	Mar	30	M	Bricklayers Lab	Herts	Harpenden
1636	FELLS	Susan	84		Wife	Mar	27	F	Plaiter	Herts	Harpenden
1637	FELLS	George	84		Son		3	M		Herts	Harpenden
1638	FELLS	Eliza	84		Dau		1	F		Herts	Harpenden
1639	BATES	Matthew	85	Turnpike Road	Head	Widower	55	M	Agric Lab	Beds	Eaton Bray
1640	BATES	James	85		Son	Unm	16	M	Groom	London	
1641	BATES	Thomas	85		Son		11	M	Groom	London	
1642	HALES	Ann	85		H'keeper	Mar	32	F	Plaiter	Herts	Redbourn
1643	HEATH	George	86	Turnpike Road	Head	Mar	66	M	Butcher	Herts	Harpenden
1644	HEATH	Penelope	86		Wife	Mar	54	F	Plaiter	Northants	Brington
1645	HEATH	Abigail	86		Dau	Unm	26	F	Plaiter	Herts	Harpenden
1646	HEATH	William	86		Son		12	M	Scholar	Herts	Harpenden
1647	HEATH	Charles	86		Grandson		1	M		Herts	Harpenden
1648	ROBINSON	Mary Ann	86		Visitor	Mar	36	F	Bonnet Sewer	Herts	Markyate
1649	ARCHER	William	87	Turnpike Road	Head	Mar	42	M	Shoemaker	Herts	Harpenden
1650	ARCHER	Sarah	87		Wife	Mar	41	F	Plaiter	Herts	Harpenden
1651	ARCHER	Thomas	87		Son	Unm	13	M	Groom	Beds	Luton
1652	ARCHER	William	87		Son		10	M	Scholar	Herts	Harpenden
1653	ARCHER	George	87		Son		6	M	Scholar	Herts	Harpenden
1654	ARCHER	Sarah	87		Dau		2	F	Scholar	Herts	Harpenden
1655	ATTWOOD	Ann	88	Turnpike Road	Head	Widow	63	F	Laundress	Herts	Harpenden
1656	LOVETT	Mary Ann	88		Grandau		14	F	Scholar	Herts	Harpenden
1657	SMITH	William	89	Turnpike Road	Head	Mar	25	M	Agric Lab	Herts	Harpenden
1658	SMITH	Hannah	89		Wife	Mar	29	F	Plaiter	Herts	Harpenden
1659	SMITH	Emma	89		Dau		12	F	Plaiter	Herts	Harpenden
1660	WESTON	Emma	89		Niece		2	F		Herts	Harpenden
1661	ATTWOOD	Frank	90	Turnpike Road	Head	Mar	32	M	Agric Lab	Herts	Harpenden
1662	ATTWOOD	Eliza	90		Wife	Mar	33	F	Plaiter	Herts	St Albans

1663	ATTWOOD	Ann	90		Dau		13	F	Scholar	Herts	St Albans
1664	ATTWOOD	Eliza	90		Dau		7	F	Scholar	Herts	Harpenden
1665	ATTWOOD	Rose	90		Dau		4	F	Scholar	Herts	Harpenden
1666	ATTWOOD	Thomas	90		Son		1	M		Herts	Harpenden
1667	WELLS	William	91	Turnpike Road	Head	Mar	51	M	Builder	Herts	Ayot St Peter
1668	WELLS	Mary	91		Wife	Mar	52	F		Cambs	Sutton
1669	WELLS	Sarah Ann	91		Dau	Unm	24	F	Dress Maker	Herts	Harpenden
1670	WELLS	Susan	91		Dau	Unm	20	F	Dress Maker	Herts	Harpenden
1671	WELLS	Elizabeth	91		Dau	Unm	17	F	At Home	Herts	Harpenden
1672	WELLS	Thomas J.	91		Son		8	M	Scholar	Herts	Harpenden
1673	WELLS	James	92	Turnpike Road	Head	Mar	45	M	Bricklayer	Herts	Ayot St Peter
1674	WELLS	Mary Ann	92		Wife	Mar	55	F	Needlewoman	Herts	Hertingfordbury
1675	WELLS	John	92		Son	Unm	20	M	Bricklayer	Herts	Ayot St Peter
1676	MARTIN	Joseph	93	Turnpike Road	Head	Mar	36	M	Bricklayer	Suffolk	Unknown
1677	MARTIN	Sarah	93		Wife	Mar	50	F		Herts	Ickleford
1678	HAWKINS	Agnes	93		Grandau		12	F	Scholar	Herts	Harpenden
1679	MARDLING	Mary Ann	93		Visitor	Unm	27	F	Plaiter	Herts	Sandridge
1680	HULL	John	93		Lodger	Mar	45	M	Shepherd	Herts	Harpenden
1681	CHURCHILL	George C.	94	Turnpike Road	Head	Unm	28	M	Attorney & Solicitor (not in Practice) engaged in connection with the Science of Agricultural Chemistry	Notts	Nottingham
1682	ELMER	James	95	The George	Head	Mar	30	M	Publican	Beds	Silsoe
1683	ELMER	Sarah	95		Wife	Mar	34	F		Herts	Kimpton
1684	MOSS	Fanny	95		Mother-in-law	Widow	69	F	Bonnet Sewer	Beds	Luton
1685	CLARIDGE	George	95		Lodger	Unm	34	M	Groom	Warks	Kenilworth
1686	MORLEY	James	95		Lodger	Unm	22	M	Groom	Herts	Harpenden
1687	KINGSTON	Francis	96	Turnpike Road	Head	Mar	64	M	Surgeon	Herts	Harpenden
1688	BRACEY	Sarah	96		Serv	Unm	31	F	Housekeeper	Herts	Kimpton
1689	BRACEY	Emma	96		Serv	Unm	17	F	Housemaid	Herts	Wheathampstead
1690	BATCHELOR	Richard	97	Turnpike Road	Head	Unm	45	M	Baker	Herts	Flamstead
1691	IRONS	Sarah	97		H'keeper	Unm	45	F		Herts	Harpenden
1692	CONSTABLE	Charles	98	Turnpike Road	Head	Mar	35	M	Agric Lab	Herts	Harpenden
1693	CONSTABLE	Mary	98		Wife	Mar	36	F	Plaiter	Herts	Harpenden
1694	CONSTABLE	William	98		Son	Unm	16	M	Agric Lab	Herts	Harpenden
1695	CONSTABLE	Charles	98		Son		12	M	Scholar	Herts	Harpenden
1696	SEABROOK	Thomas	99	Turnpike Road	Head	Mar	36	M	Brewers Labourer	Herts	Redbourn
1697	SEABROOK	Hannah	99		Wife	Mar	35	F	Plaiter	Herts	Harpenden
1698	SEABROOK	Emma	99		Dau		13	F		Herts	Harpenden
1699	SEABROOK	Caroline	99		Dau		11	F	Plaiter	Herts	Harpenden
1700	SEABROOK	George	99		Son		9	M	Scholar	Herts	Harpenden
1701	SEABROOK	Charles	99		Son		11 m	M		Herts	Harpenden
1702	STRATTON	William	100	Turnpike Road	Head	Mar	70	M	Agric Lab	Herts	Sandridge
1703	STRATTON	Susan	100		Wife	Mar	58	F	Plaiter	Herts	Harpenden
1704	STRATTON	Lucy	100		Dau	Unm	24	F	Plaiter	Herts	Harpenden

	SURNAME	FORENAME	SCHEDULE NUMBER	ADDRESS	RELATIONSHIP	STATUS	AGE	SEX	OCCUPATION	COUNTY OF BIRTH	PLACE OF BIRTH
1705	STRATTON	Ann	100		Dau	Unm	23	F	Plaiter	Herts	Harpenden
1706	STRATTON	George	100		Grandson		3	M	Scholar	Herts	Harpenden
1707	IRONS	William	101	Turnpike Road	Head	Mar	41	M	Carpenter, employing 4 men	Herts	Harpenden
1708	IRONS	Eliza	101		Wife	Mar	40	F		Herts	St Albans
1709	IRONS	Thomas	101		Son	Unm	17	M	Carpenter employed at home	Herts	Harpenden
1710	IRONS	Frederick	101		Son		15	M	Bakers Errand Boy	Herts	Harpenden
1711	IRONS	Elizabeth	101		Dau		12	F	Scholar	Herts	Harpenden
1712	IRONS	Sarah	101		Dau		11	F	Scholar	Herts	Harpenden
1713	IRONS	John	101		Son		9	M	Scholar	Herts	Harpenden
1714	IRONS	Ann	101		Dau		5	F	Scholar	Herts	Harpenden
1715	SWAIN	John	102	Turnpike Road	Head	Mar	33	M	Blacksmith, employing 2 men	Herts	Harpenden
1716	SWAIN	Emma	102		Wife	Mar	31	F		Herts	Totteridge
1717	SWAIN	Thomas	102		Son		10	M	Scholar	Herts	Totteridge
1718	SWAIN	John	102		Son		6	M	Scholar	Herts	Harpenden
1719	SWAIN	Mary	102		Dau		4	F	Scholar	Herts	Harpenden
1720	SWAIN	Richard	102		Son		2	M		Herts	Harpenden
1721	FREEMAN	Charles	102		Apprentice	Unm	19	M	Blacksmiths Apprentice	Herts	Harpenden
1722	SHANNON	James	102		Serv	Unm	16	M	Lab B. [Blacksmith]	Sussex	Newick
1723	PHILLPOTT	David	103	Turnpike Road	Head	Mar	29	M	Butcher	Herts	Wheathampstead
1724	PHILLPOTT	Eliza	103		Wife	Mar	30	F		Herts	Kimpton
1725	PHILLPOTT	David	103		Son		4	M	Scholar	Herts	Harpenden
1726	PHILLPOTT	Selina	103		Dau		11 m	F		Herts	Harpenden
1727	TOWNSEND	Edmund	104	Turnpike Road	Head	Mar	36	M	Police Officer	Essex	Thaxted
1728	TOWNSEND	Sarah	104		Wife	Mar	40	F		Herts	Standon
1729	TOWNSEND	Thomas	104		Son		12	M	Scholar	Herts	Bishops Stortford
1730	TOWNSEND	Walter	104		Son		8	M	Scholar	Herts	Little Amwell
1731	TOWNSEND	Constantine	104		Son		3	M		Herts	Datchworth
1732	TOWNSEND	Charles	104		Son		2	M		Herts	Little Munden
1733	TOWNSEND	Edward	104		Son		6	M	Scholar	Herts	Hertford
1734	ARCHER	Edward	105	Turnpike Road	Head	Mar	27	M	Cordwainer	Herts	Harpenden
1735	ARCHER	Hannah	105		Wife	Mar	26	F		Herts	Harpenden
1736	ARCHER	Rose	105		Dau		5	F	Scholar	Herts	Harpenden
1737	ARCHER	John	105		Son		4	M	Scholar	Herts	Harpenden
1738	ARCHER	Emma	105		Dau		1	F		Herts	Harpenden
1739	ARCHER	Ellen	105		Dau		3 m	F		Herts	Harpenden
1740	ELLS	John	105		Father-in-law	Widower	62	M	Butcher	Beds	Luton
1741	ARCHER	John	106	Turnpike Road	Head	Mar	39	M	Cordwainer	Herts	Harpenden
1742	ARCHER	Sarah	106		Wife	Mar	37	F	Dress Maker	Herts	Wheathampstead
1743	ARCHER	Elizabeth	106		Dau	Unm	15	F	Dress Maker	Herts	Harpenden
1744	ARCHER	Emily	106		Dau		14	F	Scholar	Herts	Harpenden
1745	ARCHER	Jane	106		Dau		12	F	Scholar	Herts	Harpenden
1746	ARCHER	Ann	106		Dau		9	F	Scholar	Herts	Harpenden
1747	ARCHER	Frederick	106		Son		5	M	Scholar	Herts	Harpenden
1748	ARCHER	Jessie	106		Son		2	M		Herts	Harpenden

1749	SIMONS	Thomas	107	Turnpike Road	Head	Mar	24	M	Baker & Corn Dealer	Herts	Harpenden
1750	SIMONS	Ann	107		Wife	Mar	24	F		Herts	Lilley
1751	KINGHAM	Matthew	107		Apprentice	Unm	18	M	Baker/Apprentice	Herts	Redbourn
1752	READ	Thomas	107		Serv	Unm	17	M	Baker Labourer	Herts	Harpenden
1753	KEIL [KERL]	William	108	Turnpike Road	Head	Mar	45	M	Annuitant	Middx	St Olave Wood St
1754	KEIL [KERL]	Anne R.	108		Wife	Mar	42	F		Middx	St Martin in Field
1755	KEIL [KERL]	Anne	108		Dau		3	F		Middx	St James, Westminster
1756	WILLIAMS	Ann	108		Serv	Unm	20	F	House Servant	Bucks	Princes Risborough
1757	KINGSTON	Jane	109	Turnpike Road	Head	Mar	66	F	Annuitant	Middx	London
1758	SHARPE	Lucy	109		Serv	Widow	40	F	House Servant	Herts	Caddington
1759	DAVIS	Thomas	110	New Farm	Head	Unm	42	M	Farmer of 231 acres employing 8 men and 2 boys	Herts	Harpenden
1760	DAVIS	James	110		Brother	Unm	40	M	Partnership with Brother [Farmer]	Herts	Harpenden
1761	DAVIS	John	110		Brother	Unm	50	M	Annuitant	Herts	Harpenden
1762	LINES	Sarah	110		Niece	Unm	24	F	House Keeper	Herts	Bovingdon
1763	MUNDAY	William	110		Serv	Unm	21	M	Agric Lab	Herts	Harpenden
1764	ENGLISH	William	110		Serv	Unm	16	M	Agric Lab	Herts	Harpenden
1765	FRENCH	William	110		Serv	Unm	14	M	Agric Lab	Herts	Redbourn
1766	WALLER	William	111	Faulkners End	Head	Mar	68	M	Agric Lab	Beds	Streatley
1767	WALLER	Sarah	111		Wife	Mar	66	F	Plaiter	Herts	Harpenden

One house uninhabited

1768	GOODYEAR	James	112	Nr. the Holyhead Road	Head	Mar	23	M	Agric Lab	Herts	Caddington
1769	GOODYEAR	Sarah	112		Wife	Mar	27	F	Plaiter	Lincs	Helpstone [Helpston, Northants?]
1770	GOODYEAR	Eliza	112		Dau		1	F		Herts	Harpenden
1771	FENSOM	William	113	Nr. the Holyhead Road	Head	Mar	50	M	Agric Lab	Herts	Caddington
1772	FENSOM	Ann	113		Wife	Mar	49	F	Plaiter	Beds	Luton
1773	FENSOM	Maria	113		Dau		16	F	Plaiter	Herts	Harpenden
1774	FENSOM	David	113		Son		14	M	Agric Lab	Herts	Harpenden
1775	FENSOM	Samuel	113		Son		12	M	Agric Lab	Herts	Harpenden
1776	MORRICE	Mary	114	Turnpike Gate Holyhead Road	Head	Widow	42	F	Toll Collector	Northants	Daventry
1777	MORRICE	Jane	114		Dau	Unm	16	F	Dress Maker	Beds	Caddington
1778	MORRICE	Arthur	114		Son		13	M	Scholar	Herts	Kensworth
1779	MORRICE	Joseph	114		Son		11	M	Scholar	Herts	Harpenden
1780	MORRICE	Alexander	114		Son		8	M	Scholar	Herts	Harpenden
1781	BANDY	Dinah	114		Visitor	Unm	26	F	Plaiter	Herts	Flamstead
1782	BUNN	Henry	115	Poplars Farm	Head	Mar	65	M	Farmer of 40 acres employing 2 labourers	Herts	Harpenden
1783	BUNN	Sarah	115		Wife	Mar	56	F		Beds	Luton
1784	FENSOM	Edward	115		Serv		16	M	Agric Lab	Unknown	
1785	PAPWORTH	Stephen	115		Serv	Mar	29	M	Agric Lab	Herts	Flamstead
1786	PARISH	Solomon	116	Near Poplars Farm	Head	Mar	45	M	Agric Lab	Staffs	[Unknown]
1787	PARISH	Sarah	116		Wife	Mar	55	F	Lace Maker	[Herts]	Wigginton
1788	FARR	Robert	117	Near Poplars Farm	Head	Mar	37	M	Agric Lab	Herts	Harpenden

	SURNAME	FORENAME	SCHEDULE NUMBER	ADDRESS	RELATIONSHIP	STATUS	AGE	SEX	OCCUPATION	COUNTY OF BIRTH	PLACE OF BIRTH
1789	FARR	Mary	117		Wife	Mar	39	F	Plaiter	Herts	Flamstead
1790	FARR	William	117		Son		11	M	Agric Lab	Beds	Luton
1791	FARR	Joseph	117		Son		8	M	Agric Lab	Beds	Luton
1792	FARR	Mary	117		Dau		7m	F		Herts	Harpenden
1793	JANES	George	118	Turners Hall Farm	Head	Mar	59	M	Farmer of 254 acres employing 12 labourers	Bucks	Hughenden
1794	JANES	Sarah	118		Wife	Mar	56	F		Herts	Watford
1795	JANES	William	118		Son	Unm	22	M	Farmers Son/ at Home	Herts	Abbots Langley
1796	JANES	Augusta	118		Dau	Unm	14	F	Farmers Daughter/ at Home	Herts	Watford
1797	PHILPOTT	Charlotte	118		Serv	Unm	21	F	General Servant	Herts	Abbots Langley
1798	STARKEY	George	118		Serv	Unm	21	M	Agric Lab	Herts	Redbourn
1799	DAVIS	Samuel	118		Serv	Unm	17	M	Agric Lab	Beds	Offley
1800	SIBLEY	Robert	119	Annobles Farm	Head	Mar	39	M	Farmer of 360 acres employing 22 men & boys	Herts	Wheathampstead
1801	SIBLEY	Susanna	119		Wife	Mar	37	F		Herts	Flamstead
1802	SIBLEY	Elizabeth	119		Dau		8	F	Scholar at Home	Herts	Harpenden
1803	SIBLEY	Maria	119		Dau		5	F	Scholar at Home	Herts	Harpenden
1804	SIBLEY	Emma	119		Dau		3	F	Scholar at Home	Herts	Harpenden
1805	SIBLEY	Susan	119		Dau		1	F	Scholar at Home	Herts	Harpenden
1806	TIPPING	Fanny	119		Visitor	Unm	17	F	Governess	Herts	Hemel Hempstead
1807	FOLLY	Elizabeth	119		Serv	Unm	26	F	House Servant	Berks	Cookham
1808	FRENCH	Elizabeth	119		Serv	Unm	18	F	House Servant	Herts	Wheathampstead
1809	MANNING	Grace	119		[blank]	Widow	65	F	Charwoman	Beds	Meppershall
1810	WARREN	William	120	Near Annobles Farm	Head	Mar	60	M	Agric Lab	Beds	Luton
1811	WARREN	Mary	120		Wife	Mar	60	F	Plaiter	Herts	Ippollitts
1812	DELLOR	James	120		Serv	Unm	17	M	Agric Lab	Herts	Harpenden
1813	GOODYEAR	Robert	120		Serv	Unm	15	M	Agric Lab	Herts	Harpenden
1814	LOITERTON	John	121	Near Annobles Farm	Head	Mar	41	M	Agric Lab	Lincs	Holbeach
1815	LOITERTON	Elizabeth	121		Wife	Mar	42	F	Plaiter	Lincs	Gedney
1816	LOITERTON	John	121		Son		13	M	Agric Lab	Lincs	Holbeach
1817	LOITERTON	Sarah Ann	121		Dau		11	F	Plaiter	Lincs	Holbeach
1818	HOBBS	John	122	Near Annobles Farm	Head	Mar	23	M	Agric Lab	Herts	Flamstead
1819	HOBBS	Phoebe	122		Wife	Mar	24	F	Plaiter	Herts	Wheathampstead
1820	HOBBS	Jonas	122		Son		2	M		Herts	Wheathampstead
1821	HOBBS	John	122		Son		8m	M		Herts	Harpenden
1822	WRIGHT	Emily	122		Visitor		14	F	Plaiter	Herts	Wheathampstead
1823	REDHEAD	Matthew	123	Kingsbourne Green	Head	Mar	51	M	Farmer of 270 acres employing 8 labourers	Lincs	St Edmunds [?]
1824	REDHEAD	Sarah	123		Wife	Mar	52	F		Lincs	Holbeach
1825	HUCKBODY	Elizabeth	123		Serv	Unm	19	F	House Servant	Lincs	Pinchback
1826	ABRAHAMS	George	123		Serv	Unm	15	M	Agric Lab	Unknown	
1827	HOW	John	124	Kingsbourne Green	Head	Unm	25	M	Farmer of 200 acres employing 10 labourers	Herts	Aldbury
1828	GREEN	Elizabeth	124		Serv	Unm	39	F	House Keeper	Bucks	Wendover
1829	WILLMOTT	John	124		Serv	Unm	45	M	Agric Lab	Herts	Redbourn
1830	WOOD	Frederick	124		Serv	Unm	18	M	Agric Lab	Herts	Willian
1831	PRATT	John	124		Serv	Unm	17	M	Agric Lab	Herts	Gravely

1832	HOWELL	Charles	124		Serv	Unm	24	M	Agric Lab	Herts	London Colney
1833	SAPWELL	William	125	Kingsbourne Green	Head	Mar	48	M	Agric Lab	Beds	Dunstable
1834	SAPWELL	Ellen	125		Wife	Mar	47	F	Plaiter	Herts	Flamstead
1835	SAPWELL	Ann	125		Dau	Unm	15	F	Plaiter	Herts	Harpenden
1836	SAPWELL	James	125		Son		10	M	Agric Lab	Herts	Harpenden
1837	CLARK	John	126	Kingsbourne Green	Head	Mar	38	M	Farmer of 10 acres	Sussex	Lewes
1838	CLARK	Mary Ann	126		Wife	Mar	37	F		Sussex	Lewes
1839	CLARK	Edward	126		Son		10	M	Scholar	Sussex	Brighton
1840	CLARK	Mary Ann	126		Dau		6	F		Sussex	East Grinstead
1841	CLARK	Alfred	126		Son		4	M		Sussex	East Grinstead
1842	BARTRAM	Kitty	126		Serv	Unm	16	F	House Servant	Herts	Redbourn
1843	BASSILL	Samuel	127	Kingsbourne Green	Head	Mar	35	M	Agric Lab	Herts	Flamstead
1844	BASSILL	Maria	127		Wife	Mar	33	F	Plaiter	Herts	Harpenden
1845	BASSILL	William	127		Son		10	M	Scholar	Herts	Harpenden
1846	BASSILL	Robert	127		Son		8	M	Scholar	Herts	Harpenden
1847	BASSILL	Ann	127		Dau		6	F	Scholar	Herts	Harpenden
1848	BASSILL	Emily	127		Dau		4	F	Scholar	Herts	Harpenden
1849	BASSILL	Ellen	127		Dau		2	F	Scholar	Herts	Harpenden
1850	HUNT	Richard	128	Kingsbourne Green	Head	Mar	54	M	Agric Lab	Beds	Luton
1851	HUNT	Alice	128		Wife	Mar	55	F	Plaiter	Herts	Harpenden
1852	HUNT	Thomas	128		Son	Unm	22	M	Agric Lab	Herts	Harpenden
1853	CRAWLEY	Thomas	129	Kingsbourne Green	Head	Mar	60	M	Agric Lab	Herts	Ippollitts
1854	CRAWLEY	Mary	129		Wife	Mar	62	F	Plaiter	Norfolk	Larthing [Larling]
1855	CRAWLEY	James	129		Son	Unm	36	M	Agric Lab	Herts	Caddington
1856	GRAY	George	129		Son-in-law	Mar	23	M	Agric Lab	Herts	Harpenden
1857	GRAY	Eliza	129		Dau	Mar	22	F	Plaiter	Herts	Harpenden
1858	MARRIN [?]	Eliza	130	Kingsbourne Green	Head	Unm	30	F	Plaiter	Herts	Harpenden
1859	MARRIN [?]	William	130		Son		8	M	Scholar	Herts	Harpenden
1860	HALE	John	131	Kingsbourne Green	Head	Mar	28	M	Agric Lab	Herts	Flamstead
1861	HALE	Helen	131		Wife	Mar	23	F	Plaiter	Herts	Harpenden
1862	HALE	William	131		Son		2	M		Herts	Harpenden
1863	HALE	Eliza	131		Dau		1 m	F		Herts	Harpenden
1864	DAVIS	George	132	Kingsbourne Green	Head	Mar	39	M	Proprietor of Houses	Herts	Harpenden
1865	DAVIS	Ann	132		Wife	Mar	45	F		Beds	Luton
1866	COLLINGS	Henry	133	Gibraltar Gate	Head	Unm	39	M	Toll Collector	Bucks	Aylesbury
1867	SIMPKINS	James	134	Kingsbourne Green - Kennel	Head	Mar	42	M	Huntsman	Herts	Kimpton
1868	SIMPKINS	Mary	134		Wife	Mar	50	F		Sussex	Firle
1869	SIMPKINS	Mary	134		Dau	Unm	16	F	Bonnet Sewer	Herts	Harpenden
1870	SIMPKINS	Sarah	134		Dau		14	F		Herts	Harpenden
1871	MITCHELL	John	134		Nephew	Unm	20	M	Agric Lab	Herts	St Stephens
1872	HASTINGS	Thomas	134		Serv	Unm	18	M	Groom	Herts	Barnet
1873	WILSON	Daniel	134		Serv	Unm	35	M	Groom	Herts	Preston
1874	MUNNS	Alfred	135	Kingsbourne Green - Kennel	Head	Unm	24	M	Whipper In to Hounds	Herts	Little Berkhamsted
1875	DOLLIMORE	Joseph	135		Lodger	Unm	24	M	Groom	Herts	Redbourn

	SURNAME	FORENAME	SCHEDULE NUMBER	ADDRESS	RELATIONSHIP	STATUS	AGE	SEX	OCCUPATION	COUNTY OF BIRTH	PLACE OF BIRTH
1876	SCRIVENOR	Reuben	136	Kingsbourne Green	Head	Mar	32	M	Whipper In to Hounds	Oxon	Yardley [Ardley]
1877	SCRIVENOR	Sarah	136		Wife	Mar	25	F	Plaiter	Herts	Harpenden
1878	SCRIVENOR	Catherine	136		Dau		8	F	Scholar	Herts	Harpenden
1879	SCRIVENOR	Henry B.	136		Son		5	M	Scholar	Herts	Harpenden
1880	SCRIVENOR	John	136		Son		2	M		Herts	Harpenden
1881	SCRIVENOR	Sarah	136		Dau		4m	F		Herts	Harpenden
1882	BONFIELD	John	137	Kingsbourne Green	Head	Widower	70	M	Agric Lab	Unknown	
1883	BONFIELD	Sarah	137		Dau	Unm	27	F	Plaiter	Herts	Harpenden
1884	HUNT	William	138	Kingsbourne Green	Head	Mar	28	M	Agric Lab	Herts	Harpenden
1885	HUNT	Maria	138		Wife	Mar	27	F	Plaiter	Beds	Luton
1886	HUNT	Frances	138		Dau		3	F	Plaiter	Herts	Harpenden
1887	HOLT	James	139	Kingsbourne Green	Head	Unm	26	M	Agric Lab	Herts	Watton
1888	HUNT	Richard	140	Kingsbourne Green	Head	Mar	28	M	Agric Lab	Herts	Harpenden
1889	HUNT	Mary	140		Wife	Mar	27	F	Plaiter	Herts	Harpenden
1890	HUNT	Jane	140		Dau		6	F	Scholar	Herts	Harpenden
1891	HUNT	Mary Ann	140		Dau		4	F	Scholar	Herts	Harpenden
1892	HUNT	Sarah	140		Dau		1	F		Herts	Harpenden
1893	BUNN	Thomas	141	Kingsbourne Green	Head	Mar	31	M	Agric Lab	Herts	Wheathampstead
1894	BUNN	Mary Ann	141		Wife	Mar	28	F	Plaiter	Beds	Luton
1895	BUNN	Thomas	141		Son		5	M	Scholar	Herts	Harpenden
1896	BUNN	Henry	141		Son		4	M	Scholar	Herts	Harpenden
1897	BUNN	Maria	141		Dau		1	F		Herts	Harpenden
1898	BUNN	Benjamin	141		Son		1m	M		Herts	Harpenden
1899	GOODYEAR	Robert	142	Kingsbourne Green	Head	Mar	48	M	Agric Lab	Herts	Caddington
1900	GOODYEAR	Elizabeth	142		Wife	Mar	48	F	Plaiter	Herts	Redbourn
1901	GOODYEAR	Charlotte	142		Dau	Unm	18	F	Plaiter	Herts	Harpenden
1902	GOODYEAR	Elizabeth	142		Dau		11	F	Plaiter	Herts	Harpenden
1903	GOODYEAR	Edward	142		Son		9	M	Agric Lab	Herts	Harpenden
1904	GOODYEAR	Emma	142		Dau		7	F	Scholar	Herts	Harpenden
1905	GOODYEAR	Joseph	142		Son		5	M	Scholar	Herts	Harpenden
1906	FENSOM	William	143	Kingsbourne Green	Head	Mar	28	M	Agric Lab	Beds	Luton
1907	FENSOM	Ann	143		Wife	Mar	23	F	Plaiter	Beds	Luton
1908	FENSOM	Jim	143		Son		4	M		Beds	Luton
1909	FENSOM	William	143		Son		3	M		Herts	Harpenden
1910	FENSOM	George	143		Son		1	M		Herts	Harpenden
1911	ADAMS	William	145	Kingsbourne Green	Head	Mar	24	M	Bricklayer	Herts	Harpenden
1912	ADAMS	Sarah	145		Wife	Mar	30	F	Plaiter	Bucks	Wingrave
1913	ADAMS	Mary	145		Dau		11	F	Plaiter	Herts	Hemel Hempstead
1914	ADAMS	Joseph	145		Son		1	M		Herts	Harpenden
1915	READ	Joshua	146	Kingsbourne Green	Head	Mar	27	M	Groom	Herts	Harpenden
1916	READ	Hannah	146		Wife	Mar	28	F	Plaiter	Herts	Harpenden
1917	READ	William	146		Son		5	M	Scholar	Herts	Harpenden
1918	READ	Sarah	146		Dau		3	F	Scholar	Herts	Harpenden
1919	DEAMER	Frederick	147	Kingsbourne Green	Head	Mar	33	M	Agric Lab	Herts	Harpenden

1920	DEAMER	Elizabeth	147		Wife	Mar	28	F	Plaiter	Herts	Harpenden
1921	DEAMER	Elizabeth	147		Dau		9	F	Scholar	Herts	Harpenden
1922	DEAMER	Frederick	147		Son		7	M	Scholar	Herts	Harpenden
1923	DEAMER	Charles	147		Son		4	M		Herts	Harpenden
1924	DEAMER	John	147		Son		2	M		Herts	Harpenden
1925	FARR	Francis	148	Kingsbourne Green	Head	Mar	40	M	Beer House Keeper	Herts	Harpenden
1926	FARR	Hannah	148		Wife	Mar	41	F		Herts	Harpenden
1927	FARR	George	148		Son		14	M	Scholar	Herts	Harpenden
1928	FARR	Emma	148		Dau		12	F	Scholar	Herts	Harpenden
1929	FARR	Ann	148		Dau		8	F	Scholar	Herts	Harpenden
1930	FARR	Thomas	148		Son		5	M	Scholar	Herts	Harpenden
1931	BROOKS	William	148		Lodger	Unm	22	M	Agric Lab	Unknown	
1932	BASSILL	George	149	The Fox	Head	Mar	68	M	Beer House Keeper	Herts	Redbourn
1933	BASSILL	Mary	149		Wife	Mar	64	F		Herts	Stevenage
1934	BASSILL	Mary	149		Dau	Unm	27	F	Dress Maker	Herts	Harpenden
1935	JACKSON	Sarah	149		Dau	Mar	21	F	Bonnet Sewer	Herts	Harpenden
1936	JACKSON	William	149		Grandson		5 m	M		Wales	Newport
1937	BASSILL	Ellen	149		Grandau		4	F	Plaiter	Herts	Great Gaddesdon
1938	FARR	George	150	Kingsbourne Green	Head	Mar	22	M	Agric Lab	Herts	Harpenden
1939	FARR	Ann	150		Wife	Mar	21	F	Plaiter	Herts	St Michaels
1940	FARR	Alfred	150		Son		5 m	M		Herts	Harpenden
1941	WOOD	Susannah	151	Kingsbourne Green	Head	Widow	42	F	School Mistress	Beds	Luton
1942	WOOD	Maria	151		Dau		10	F	Scholar	Beds	Caddington
1943	WOOD	John	151		Son		9	M	Scholar	Beds	Caddington
1944	WOOD	Thomas	151		Son		7	M	Scholar	Herts	Harpenden
1945	LUCK	Jacob	152	Kingsbourne Green	Head	Mar	45	M	Agric Lab	Herts	Harpenden
1946	LUCK	Rose	152		Wife	Mar	44	F	Plaiter	Herts	Harpenden
1947	CHAMBERS	John	153	Kingsbourne Green	Head	Mar	35	M	Agric Lab	Herts	Kimpton
1948	CHAMBERS	Sarah	153		Wife	Mar	39	F	Plaiter	Beds	Luton
1949	CHAMBERS	Emma	153		Dau		13	F	Plaiter	Beds	Luton
1950	CHAMBERS	George	153		Son		8 m	M		Herts	Harpenden
1951	BASSILL	Edward	154	Kingsbourne Green	Head	Mar	40	M	Agric Lab	Herts	Flamstead
1952	BASSILL	Sophia	154		Wife	Mar	33	F	Plaiter	Herts	Harpenden
1953	BASSILL	Frederick	154		Son		13	M	Scholar	Herts	Harpenden
1954	BASSILL	Mary	154		Dau		10	F	Scholar	Herts	Harpenden
1955	BASSILL	William	154		Son		7	M	Scholar	Herts	Harpenden
1956	BASSILL	Maria	154		Dau		5	F	Scholar	Herts	Harpenden
1957	BASSILL	Sophia	154		Dau		3	F	Scholar	Herts	Harpenden
1958	BASSILL	George	154		Son		8 m	M		Herts	Harpenden
1959	IVORY	Joseph	155	The Old Bell	Head	Mar	47	M	Agric Lab	Herts	Harpenden
1960	IVORY	Harriett	155		Wife	Mar	44	F	Plaiter	Beds	Luton
1961	IVORY	Emily	155		Dau	Unm	19	F	Plaiter	Herts	Harpenden
1962	IVORY	Harriett	155		Dau	Unm	16	F	Plaiter	Herts	Harpenden
1963	IVORY	Mary	155		Dau		14	F	Plaiter	Herts	Harpenden
1964	IVORY	James	155		Son		10	M	Agric Lab	Herts	Harpenden

	SURNAME	FORENAME	SCHEDULE NUMBER	ADDRESS	RELATIONSHIP	STATUS	AGE	SEX	OCCUPATION	COUNTY OF BIRTH	PLACE OF BIRTH
1965	TOMALIN	Matthew	156	The Old Bell	Head	Mar	68	M	Farmer/ 11 acres	Herts	Harpenden
1966	TOMALIN	Ann	156		Wife	Mar	60	F		Herts	Harpenden
1967	TOMALIN	William	156		Grandson		9	M	Scholar	Herts	Harpenden
1968	LEWIS	Joseph	156		Lodger	Unm	44	M	Agric Lab	Herts	Harpenden
1969	FENSOM	Joseph	156		Lodger	Unm	57	M	Tailor	Herts	Harpenden
1970	HOW	John	156		Lodger	Widower	77	M	Agric Lab	Herts	Harpenden
1971	TOMALIN	Thomas	156		Brother	Unm	53	M	Agric Lab & Hostler	Herts	Harpenden
1972	PRESTON	Isaac	156		Lodger	Unm	26	M	Agric Lab	Leics	Great Weston
1973	TRUSTRAM	William	157	Moreton End Farm	Head	Unm	44	M	Agric Lab left in charge of premises	Herts	Harpenden
1974	BIGGS	Daniel	158	Lewins Green	Head	Mar	57	M	Agric Lab	Herts	Markyate St.
1975	BIGGS	Sarah	158		Wife	Mar	53	F	Plaiter	Herts	Flamstead
1976	BIGGS	Eliza	158		Dau	Unm	22	F	Bonnet Sewer	Herts	Harpenden
1977	BIGGS	Sarah	158		Dau	Unm	17	F	Bonnet Sewer	Herts	Harpenden
1978	BIGGS	Mary	158		Dau		12	F	Bonnet Sewer	Herts	Harpenden
1979	ATTWOOD	Emily	158		Lodger	Unm	26	F	Bonnet Sewer	Herts	Harpenden

End of Enumeration District No. 2c in the parish of Harpenden.

Chapter Six

The parish of Redbourn

Registrar's District: Harpenden   Enumeration District 3a   Ref. HO 107/1713 folios 129-52

All that part of the parish of Redbourn which lies to the north east of the London and Holyhead Road, and of the districts between the roads called Fish Street and Lamb Lane, leading therefrom towards Hempstead, including the village, Bisney End, Redbourn Bury etc. towards Shafford Mill.

1	SEABROOK	George	1	Beeson End Farm	Head	Mar	66	M	Farmer of 150 acres employing 5 labourers (1 in, 4 out)	Herts	Wheathampstead
2	SEABROOK	Hannah	1		Wife	Mar	52	F	Farmers Wife	Herts	Harpenden
3	SEABROOK	Mary Ann	1		Dau	Unm	22	F	Straw Bonnet Sewer	Herts	Redbourn
4	SEABROOK	John	1		Son	Unm	18	M	Farmers Son	Herts	Redbourn
5	SEABROOK	Sarah	1		Dau	Unm	14	F	Plaiter	Herts	Redbourn
6	SEABROOK	Harriett	1		Dau	Unm	12	F	Scholar	Herts	Redbourn
7	SEABROOK	Emma M.	1		Dau	Unm	8	F	Scholar	Herts	Redbourn
8	COLEMAN	Charles	1		Serv	Unm	17	M	Farm Lab	Beds	Luton
9	DICKINSON	Henry	2	Beeson End Farm	Head	Mar	42	M	Farmer of 143 acres employing 6 labourers (3 in, 3 out)	Herts	Aldenham
10	DICKINSON	Elizabeth	2		Wife	Mar	33	F	Farmers Wife	Herts	Redbourn
11	DICKINSON	Sarah	2		Mother	Widow	83	F	Retired Farmers Widow	Herts	Aldenham
12	BURGOINE	Joyce	2		Serv	Unm	15	F	House Servant	Herts	Wheathampstead
13	STREADER	William	2		Serv	Unm	19	M	Farm Labourer	Herts	Flamstead
14	LUNNON	Charles	2		Serv	Unm	17	M	Farm Labourer	Herts	Harpenden
15	POCOCK	George	3	Redbournbury Farm	Head	Mar	50	M	Farmer of 322 acres employing 12 labourers (3 in, 9 out)	Herts	St Stephens
16	POCOCK	Charlotte	3		Wife	Mar	44	F	Farmers Wife	Herts	St Stephens
17	CLARK	Edward	3		Inmate	Unm	21	M	Independent	Middx	Hackney
18	CLARK	Susan	3		Serv	Unm	19	F	House Servant	Oxon	Garsington
19	NORWOOD	William	3		Serv	Unm	34	M	Cow Man	Herts	St Stephens
20	FITZJOHN	George	3		Serv	Unm	17	M	Farm Servant	Herts	St Michaels
21	HILL	Matthew	3		Serv		14	M	Farm Servant	Herts	St Peters
22	HAWKINS	Edward	4	Redbournbury Mill	Head	Mar	33	M	Miller & Farmer 27 acres, 3 labourers	Herts	Redbourn
23	HAWKINS	Mary H.	4		Wife	Mar	23	F		Herts	Aldenham
24	HAWKINS	Edward	4		Son		3	M		Herts	Redbourn

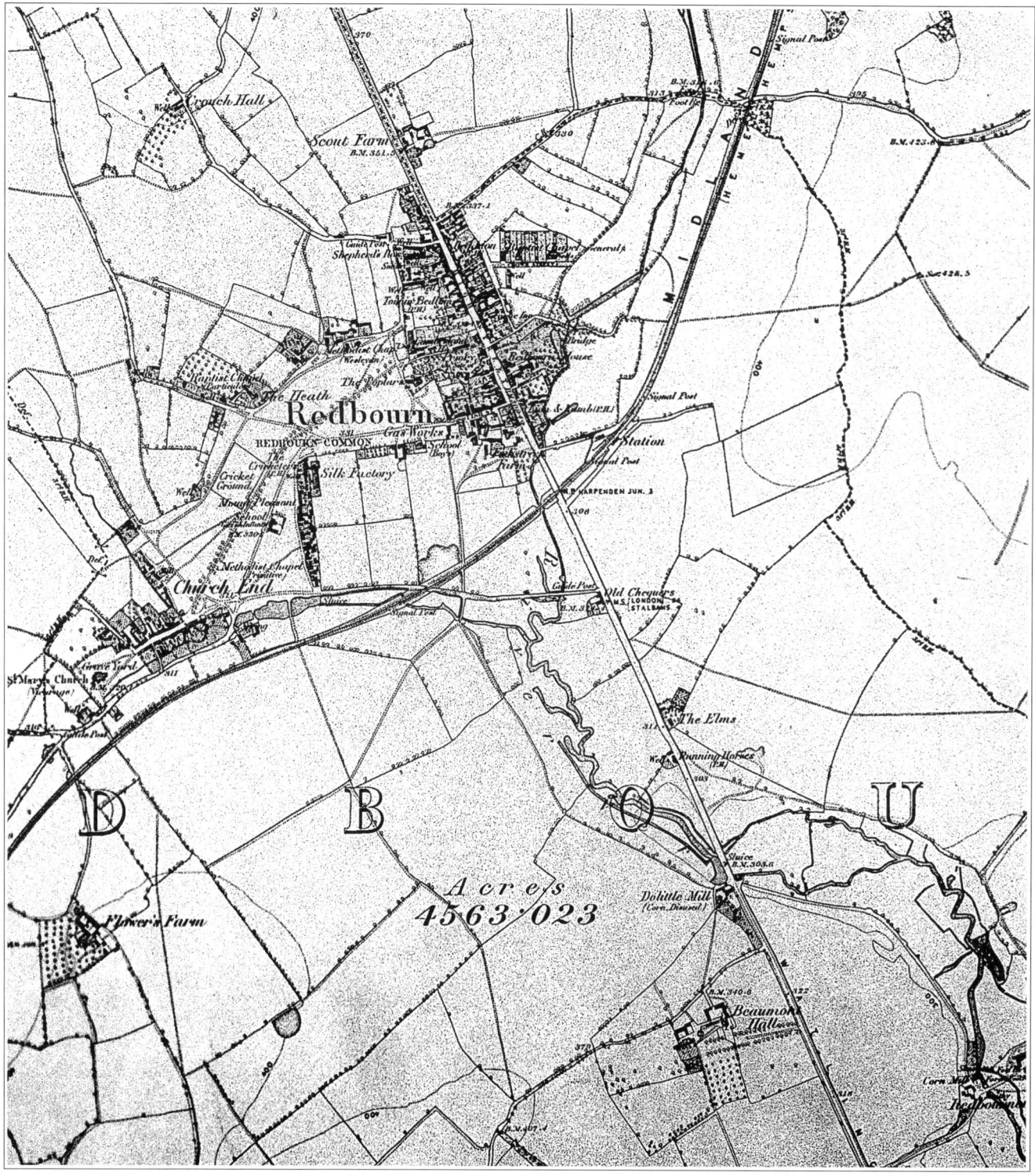

From the first edition of the 6 inch Ordinance Survey of Hertfordshire (1878), Sheet XXVII

Approximate scale of reproduction: 1cm = 119m

No.	Surname	Forename	Sch.	Address	Relation	Cond.	Age	Sex	Occupation	County	Birthplace
25	HAWKINS	Helen	4		Dau		1	F		Herts	Redbourn
26	TURNER	Henry	4		Apprentice	Unm	17	M	Millers App	Herts	Wheathampstead
27	TURNER	Esther	4		Serv	Unm	15	F	House Servant	Herts	Wheathampstead
28	DEAMER	George	5	Redbournbury Lane	Head	Mar	40	M	Farm Lab	Herts	St Pauls Walden
29	DEAMER	Ann	5		Wife	Mar	30	F	Plaiter	Herts	St Peters
30	DEAMER	Charles	5		Son	Unm	13	M	Farm Servant	Herts	St Peters
31	DEAMER	George	5		Son		5	M		Herts	St Peters
32	DEAMER	David	5		Son		3	M		Herts	St Peters
33	HOWARD	Jane	5		Mother-in-law	Widow	80	F		Herts	St Stephens
34	HOWARD	Hannah	5		Sister-in-law	Unm	40	F		Herts	St Peters
35	HILL	Joseph	6	Redbournbury Lane	Head	Mar	55	M	Farm Lab	Herts	St Stephens
36	HILL	Dinah	6		Wife	Mar	52	F		Herts	St Peters
37	HILL	William	6		Son	Mar	31	M	Farm Lab	Herts	St Michaels
38	HILL	Elizabeth	6		Dau	Unm	23	F	Grass Hat Maker	Herts	St Peters
39	TURNER	Thomas	7	St Albans Road Cottage	Head	Mar	53	M	Miller	Herts	Hitchin
40	TURNER	Esther	7		Wife	Mar	52	F		Herts	Wheathampstead
41	TURNER	Mary	7		Dau	Unm	11	F	Scholar	Herts	Wheathampstead
42	SEABROOK	William	8	Punch Bowl, St Albans Road	Head	Mar	37	M	Victualler	Herts	Redbourn
43	SEABROOK	Elizabeth	8		Wife	Mar	37	F		Herts	Redbourn
44	SEABROOK	Ann	8		Dau	Unm	13	F	Plaiter	Herts	Redbourn
45	SEABROOK	William	8		Son		9	M	Scholar	Herts	Redbourn
46	SEABROOK	John	8		Son		7	M	Scholar	Herts	Redbourn
47	SEABROOK	Walter	8		Son			M		Herts	Redbourn
48	SEABROOK	Joseph	8		Son		3	M		Herts	Redbourn
49	SEABROOK	Charlotte	8		Dau		1	F		Herts	Redbourn
50	DOLLIMORE	Thomas	8		Lodger	Unm	23	M	Labourer	Herts	Redbourn
51	PAYNE	William	9	Water Cress Hall, St Albans Road	Head	Mar	35	M	Cultivator of Water Cresses	Herts	Rickmansworth
52	PAYNE	Harriet	9		Wife	Mar	35	F		Herts	Rickmansworth
53	PAYNE	William	9		Son	Unm	11	M	Scholar	Herts	Redbourn
54	PAYNE	Charles	9		Son	Unm	9	M	Scholar	Herts	Redbourn
55	PAYNE	Eliza	9		Dau	Unm	8	F	Scholar	Herts	Redbourn
56	PAYNE	Mary Ann	9		Dau	Unm	7	F	Scholar	Herts	Redbourn
57	PAYNE	Harriett	9		Dau	Unm	5	F	Scholar	Herts	Redbourn
58	SLAUGHTER	John	9		Father-in-law	Mar	60	M	Labourer	Herts	Rickmansworth
59	SLAUGHTER	Sarah	9		Mother-in-law	Mar	56	F	Plaiter	Herts	Rickmansworth
60	GIBBS	George	9		Serv	Unm	47	M	Lab	Herts	Rickmansworth
61	SLAUGHTER	George	9		Serv	Unm	22	M	Lab	Herts	Rickmansworth
62	PUGH	Thomas	10	Elm Cottage, St Albans Road	Head	Mar	70	M	Clergyman Est. Church not having cure of souls	Middx	London
63	PUGH	Mary Basil	10		Wife	Mar	55	F		Herts	Redbourn
64	PUGH	Isabella	10		Dau	Unm	27	F		Herts	Redbourn
65	PUGH	Emily	10		Dau	Unm	25	F		Herts	Redbourn
66	PUGH	Charlotte A	10		Dau	Unm	19	F		Herts	Redbourn
67	BETT	Mary	10		Serv	Unm	20	F	Servant	Bucks	Ludgershall

	SURNAME	FORENAME	SCHEDULE NUMBER	ADDRESS	RELATIONSHIP	STATUS	AGE	SEX	OCCUPATION	COUNTY OF BIRTH	PLACE OF BIRTH
68	HOW	Joseph	10		Serv	Unm	17	M	Groom	Herts	St Stephens
69	ASHBY	Thomas	11	High Street	Head	Mar	36	M	Farmers Bailiff	Herts	Redbourn
70	ASHBY	Maria A.	11		Wife	Mar	35	F		Kent	Farnborough
71	ASHBY	John S.	11		Son	Unm	9	M	Scholar	Herts	Redbourn
72	ASHBY	Sarah A.	11		Dau		8	F	Scholar	Herts	Redbourn
73	ASHBY	Maria E.	11		Dau		6	F	Scholar	Herts	Redbourn
74	ASHBY	Samuel	11		Son		4	M	Scholar	Herts	Redbourn
75	ASHBY	Joseph	11		Son		2	M		Herts	Redbourn
76	ASHBY	Mary	11		Dau		1	F		Herts	Redbourn
77	DIXEY	Hannah	12	High Street	Head	Widow	61	F	Laundress	Herts	Redbourn
78	DIXEY	Ellen	12		Dau	Unm	18	F	Dress Maker	Herts	Redbourn
79	DIXEY	Phoebe	12		Dau	Unm	17	F	Straw Bonnet Maker	Herts	Redbourn
80	GREEN	George	12		Lodger	Unm	22	M	Journeyman Fellmonger	Herts	Watford
81	NEWNHAM	William	12		Lodger	Unm	19	M	Journeyman Fellmonger	Herts	Watford
82	BISNEY	Joseph	13	High Street	Head	Mar	35	M	Journeyman Carpenter	Herts	Redbourn
83	BISNEY	Sarah	13		Wife	Mar	36	F	Plaiter	Herts	Redbourn
84	BISNEY	Henry	13		Son	Unm	12	M	Farm Lab	Herts	Redbourn
85	BISNEY	Mary Ann	13		Dau		10	F	Scholar	Herts	Redbourn
86	BISNEY	Elizabeth	13		Dau		2	F		Herts	Redbourn
87	COLE	William	14	High Street	Head	Mar	31	M	Journeyman Wheelwright	Herts	Redbourn
88	COLE	Celia	14		Wife	Mar	30	F	Plaiter	Herts	Redbourn
89	COLE	Sarah A.	14		Dau	Unm	3	F		Herts	Redbourn
90	COLE	Robert W.	14		Son		1	M		Herts	Redbourn
91	COLE	William G.	14		Son		3m	M		Herts	Redbourn
92	FAREY	James	15	High Street	Head	Widower	52	M	Labourer	Herts	Redbourn
93	FAREY	George	15		Son	Unm	34	M	Labourer	Herts	Redbourn
94	FAREY	Fanny	15		Dau	Unm	21	F	Straw Bonnet Sewer	Herts	Redbourn
95	HARRADINE	Charlotte	16	High Street	Head	Widow	63	F	Bonnet Manufacturer	Herts	Redbourn
96	HARRADINE	Katherine	16		Dau	Unm	29	F	Bonnet Manufacturer	Herts	Redbourn
97	ASLIN	Frederick	16		Visitor	Unm	25	M	Farm Bailiff	Herts	Redbourn
98	HALL	George	17	High Street	Head	Mar	52	M	Hostler	Herts	London Colney
99	HALL	Ruth	17		Wife	Mar	51	F		Middx	Chelsea [London]
100	HALL	Betsey	17		Dau	Unm	20	F	Straw Bonnet Maker	Herts	Redbourn
101	READING	Ellen	17		Niece	Widow	30	F	Straw Bonnet Maker	Herts	Redbourn
102	DOLLING	Ernest	17		Nephew	Unm	22	M	Groom out of place	Herts	Redbourn
103	DOLLING	Edwin	17		Nephew	Unm	19	M	Groom out of place	Herts	Redbourn
104	DOLLING	Mary Ann	17		Niece	Unm	16	F	Straw Bonnet Maker	Herts	Redbourn
105	READING	Ernest	17		Nephew		5	M	Scholar	Herts	Redbourn
106	READING	Henry	17		Nephew		4	M	Scholar	Herts	Redbourn
107	AYRE	Joseph B.	18	High Street	Head	Mar	34	M	L.A.C. London Surgeon	Norfolk	Lynn Regis [Kings Lynn]
108	AYRE	Catherine	18		Wife	Mar	24	F		Devon	Totnes
109	ROLAND	Alice	18		Serv	Unm	20	F	Servant	Bucks	Marsworth
110	PEACOCK	Thomas	19	High Street	Head	Mar	74	M	Toll Collector	Herts	Redbourn
111	PEACOCK	Mary	19		Wife	Mar	73	F	Deaf	Herts	Redbourn

112	FAREY	Samuel	20	High Street	Head	Mar	66	M	Postmaster & Glover	Herts	Redbourn
113	FAREY	Ann	20		Wife	Mar	65	F		Middx	St Andrews, Holborn
114	HERRON	George	21	High Street	Head	Mar	30	M	Fellmonger employing 5 Men	Kent	Rochester
115	HERRON	William	21		Son		8	M	Scholar	Kent	Maidstone
116	HERRON	George	21		Son		6	M	Scholar	Kent	Maidstone
117	ABBOTT	Thomas	22	Saracens Head, High Street	Head	Mar	27	M	Straw Factor & Victualler	Herts	Redbourn
118	ABBOTT	Ann	22		Wife	Mar	24	F		Bucks	Clifton
119	ABBOTT	William	22		Son		8 m	M		Herts	Redbourn
120	JACKSON	William	22		Visitor	Unm	56	M	Labourer	Herts	Redbourn
121	WHEATLEY	William	22		Visitor	Unm	50	M	Labourer	Herts	St Albans
122	SIMMONS	George	23	High Street	Head	Mar	45	M	Labourer	Oxon	Sheepluck
123	SIMMONS	Mary	23		Wife	Mar	46	F		Northants	Badby
124	SIMMONS	Charles	23		Son		11	M	Farm Labourer	Bucks	Chalfont St Giles
125	SIMMONS	George	23		Son		10	M	Scholar	Bucks	Chalfont St Giles
126	SIMMONS	William	23		Son		7	M	Scholar	Middx	Hayes
127	SIMMONS	Sarah	23		Dau		5	F	Scholar	Middx	Hayes
128	SKILLMAN	Thomas	24	High Street	Head	Mar	26	M	Butcher	Herts	Redbourn
129	SKILLMAN	Susanna	24		Wife	Mar	33	F		Herts	Hoddesden
130	SKILLMAN	Thomas H.	24		Son		1	M		Herts	Redbourn
131	BURCHMORE	Charlotte	25	High Street	Head	Unm	45	F	Independent	Herts	Flamstead
132	BURCHMORE	Ann	25		Sister	Unm	42	F	Independent	Herts	Flamstead
133	BURCHMORE	Mary Ann	25		Sister	Unm	37	F	Independent	Herts	Flamstead
134	WINCHESTER	Letitia	25		Serv	Unm	17	F	House Servant	Herts	Redbourn
135	PITKIN	Sarah	26	High Street	Head	Widow	47	F	Grocer	Herts	Ayot St Lawrence
136	PITKIN	Sarah A.	26		Dau	Unm	16	F		Herts	Redbourn
137	PLOWMAN	Rachael	26		Serv	Unm	28	F	Servant	Herts	Redbourn
138	MOSS	Anna M.	27	High Street, Redbourn House	Serv	Widow	44	F	Servant, in charge of Lady Glamis Mansion	Herts	Hitchin
139	THOROGOOD	Rebecca	27		Serv	Mar	51	F	Servant, in charge of Lady Glamis Mansion	Herts	Willian

One house uninhabited

140	AUSTIN	Alice	28	High Street	Head	Widow	71	F	Pauper-Household Duties	Beds	Toddington
141	HILL	Elizabeth	28		Lodger	Widow	72	F	Pauper-no employment	Herts	Redbourn
142	FORD	Charles	29	High Street	Head	Mar	31	M	Journeyman Plumber	Kent	Deptford
143	FORD	Elizabeth	29		Wife	Mar	31	F		Herts	Hemel Hempstead
144	FORD	Thomas	29		Son		7	M	Scholar	Herts	Hemel Hempstead
145	FORD	Charles	29		Son		6	M	Scholar	Herts	Hemel Hempstead
146	FORD	Elizabeth	29		Dau		5	F	Scholar	Kent	Eltham
147	FORD	Alice	29		Dau		2	F		Kent	Deptford
148	FORD	Richard	29		Son		6 m	M		Herts	Redbourn
149	WADE	William S.	30	High Street	Head	Mar	50	M	Vicar of Redbourn	Middx	Mary le Bone [St Marylebone]
150	WADE	Mary A.M.	30		Dau	Unm	6	F	Scholar at Home	Herts	St Albans
151	WADE	Ellen E.	30		Dau	Unm	3	F		Herts	Redbourn
152	WADE	Arthur G.S.	30		Son	Unm	1	M		Herts	Redbourn

	SURNAME	FORENAME	SCHEDULE NUMBER	ADDRESS	RELATIONSHIP	STATUS	AGE	SEX	OCCUPATION	COUNTY OF BIRTH	PLACE OF BIRTH
153	CARRINGTON	Amos	30		Serv	Unm	17	M	Page	Herts	Great Gaddesden
154	KEMPSTER	Sarah	30		Serv	Unm	21	F	Cook	Bucks	Chesham
155	FENSOM	Mary A.	30		Serv	Unm	24	F	Housemaid	Herts	St Albans
156	LINES	Georgiana	30		Serv	Unm	30	F	Nurse	Herts	Great Gaddesden
157	CHIPPERFIELD	Mary	30		Serv	Unm	20	F	Under Nurse	Herts	Redbourn
158	DIXON	Charles	31	High Street	Head	Mar	43	M	Farmer, Brewer & Baker	Herts	Redbourn
159	DIXON	Hannah	31		Wife	Mar	44	F		London	Parish Unknown
160	DIXON	Hannah	31		Dau	Unm	10	F	Scholar	Herts	Redbourn
161	DIXON	Emma	31		Dau		7	F	Scholar	Herts	Redbourn
162	DIXON	William	31		Son		6	M	Scholar	Herts	Redbourn
163	DIXON	Anne	31		Dau		3	F	Scholar	Herts	Redbourn
164	WRANGLE	Mary A.	31		Niece	Unm	21	F	Visitor	London	Parish Unknown
165	CURRELL	Eliza	31		Serv	Unm	23	F	Servant	Herts	Redbourn
166	ADAMS	Daniel	31		Serv	Unm	15	M	Bakers Boy	Herts	Markyate Street
167	BOWDLER	Joseph	32	High Street	Head	Mar	32	M	Journeyman Tailor	Shrop	Shrewsbury
168	BOWDLER	Sarah	32		Wife	Mar	31	F		Herts	Redbourn
169	BOWDLER	Mary Ann	32		Dau		7	F	Scholar	Herts	Redbourn
170	BOWDLER	Thomas	32		Son		5	M	Scholar	Herts	Redbourn
171	BOWDLER	Fanny	32		Dau		3	F		Herts	Redbourn
172	BOWDLER	Elizabeth	32		Dau		3m	F		Herts	Redbourn
173	WOODS	Thomas	32		Father-in-law	Widower	59	M	Tailor	Beds	Ashful Bridge [?]
174	WOODS	Elizabeth	32		Sister-in-law	Unm	23	F	Straw Manufacturer	Herts	Redbourn
175	CURTIS	Leah	32		Visitor	Unm	17	F	Straw Manufacturer	Northants	Unknown
176	NEAL	John	33	High Street	Head	Widower	56	M	Carpenter & Joiner	Herts	Wheathampstead
177	NEAL	Susannah	33		Dau	Unm	26	F	Fathers Housekeeper	Herts	Redbourn
178	NEAL	Emma	33		Dau		11	F	Scholar	Herts	Redbourn
179	NEAL	Joseph	33		Son		9	M	Scholar	Herts	Redbourn
180	NEAL	Charles	33		Son		7	M	Scholar	Herts	Redbourn
181	NEAL	Caroline	33		Grandau		5	F	Scholar	Herts	Redbourn
182	HINDS	Henry	34	High Street, The George	Head	Mar	61	M	Watch Finisher	Bucks	Olney
183	HINDS	Elizabeth	34		Wife	Mar	65	F		Beds	Bedford
184	WATCHAM	Sarah Ann	35	High Street	Head	Mar	28	F	Journeyman Carpenters Wife	Lincs	Grantham
185	OLNEY	Martha	36	High Street	Head	Widow	72	F	Butchers Widow	Herts	Redbourn
186	OLNEY	Elizabeth	36		Dau	Unm	32	F	Dressmaker	Herts	Redbourn

One house uninhabited

	SURNAME	FORENAME	SCHEDULE NUMBER	ADDRESS	RELATIONSHIP	STATUS	AGE	SEX	OCCUPATION	COUNTY OF BIRTH	PLACE OF BIRTH
187	PRATT	Edmund	37	High Street	Head	Mar	27	M	Tailor	Herts	Redbourn
188	PRATT	Ann	37		Wife	Mar	31	F	Bonnet Manufacturer	Bucks	Fleet Marston
189	PRATT	Jane	37		Dau		4	F		Herts	Redbourn
190	PRATT	Arthur	37		Son		3m	M		Herts	Redbourn
191	RICHARDSON	Sarah	37		Visitor	Unm	19	F	Bonnet Manufacturer	Bucks	Fleet Marston
192	LORD	William	38	White Horse, High Street	Head	Mar	32	M	Wheelwright & Victualler	Herts	Redbourn
193	LORD	Ann	38		Wife	Mar	31	F		Herts	Redbourn
194	LORD	William	38		Son	Unm	8	M	Scholar	Herts	Redbourn

195	LORD	Frederick	38		Son		6	M	Scholar	Herts	Redbourn
196	LORD	Thomas	38		Son		4	M	Scholar	Herts	Redbourn
197	BULL	Charlotte	39	High Street	Head	Widow	56	F		Herts	Redbourn
198	BULL	Charlotte	39		Dau	Unm	19	F	Servant	Herts	Redbourn
199	BULL	John	39		Son	Unm	17	M	Gardener	Herts	Redbourn
200	ROBERTS	John	40	High Street	Head	Mar	34	M	Baker	Surrey	Chertsey
201	ROBERTS	Caroline	40		Wife	Mar	29	F	Dressmaker	Herts	Redbourn
202	HARRIS	Elizabeth	40		Apprentice	Unm	14	F	Apprentice to Dressmaker	Herts	Park Street [St Stephens]
203	EAMES	John	41	High Street	Head	Mar	51	M	Labourer	Herts	Redbourn
204	EAMES	Sarah	41		Wife	Mar	51	F	Plaiter	Herts	Redbourn
205	EAMES	Mary A.	41		Grandau		9	F	Plaiter	Herts	Redbourn
206	HUDSON	Frederick	41		Lodger	Mar	51	M	Brewer	Surrey	Bermondsey
207	BROWN	John	42	High Street	Head	Mar	60	M	Labourer	Beds	Luton
208	BROWN	Jane	42		Wife	Mar	45	F	Plaiter	Herts	Redbourn
209	GREEN	Charlotte	42		Sister-in-law	Unm	30	F	Trimming Weaver	Herts	Redbourn
210	GREEN	Eliza	42		Dau-in-law	Unm	22	F	Servant	Herts	Redbourn
211	BROWN	William	42		Son		8	M	Farmers Boy	Herts	Redbourn
212	BROWN	Charlotte	42		Dau		7	F	Plaiter	Herts	Redbourn
213	BROWN	Emma	42		Dau		5	F	Plaiter	Herts	Redbourn
214	BROWN	George	42		Son		2	M		Herts	Redbourn
215	SEABROOK	Mary	43	High Street	Head	Widow	43	F	Plaiter	Herts	Redbourn
216	SEABROOK	Alice	43		Dau	Unm	15	F	Plaiter	Herts	Redbourn
217	SEABROOK	Thomas	43		Son		11	M	Plaiter	Herts	Redbourn
218	SEABROOK	Joseph	43		Son		9	M	Plaiter	Herts	Redbourn
219	CLARK	William	44	High Street	Head	Mar	71	M	Cordwainer	Herts	Redbourn
220	CLARK	Elizabeth	44		Wife	Mar	71	F	Plaiter	Beds	Caddington
221	ALLEN	John C.	45	High Street	Head	Mar	45	M	Labourer	Herts	Gaddesden
222	ALLEN	Eliza	45		Wife	Mar	39	F	Plaiter	Herts	Little Wymondley
223	ALLEN	Lydia	45		Dau	Unm	17	F	Plaiter	Herts	Redbourn
224	ALLEN	Ann	45		Dau		11	F	Scholar	Herts	Redbourn
225	ALLEN	William	45		Son		11	M	Scholar	Herts	Redbourn
226	CHERRY	Jabez	46	High Street	Head	Mar	45	M	Draper & Tailor, 3 Men & 3 App.	Herts	St Albans
227	CHERRY	Sarah	46		Wife	Mar	40	F		Herts	Redbourn
228	CHERRY	Samuel	46		Son	Unm	12	M	Scholar	Herts	Redbourn
229	CHERRY	Luke	46		Son	Unm	10	M	Scholar	Herts	Redbourn
230	CHERRY	Sarah	46		Dau	Unm	6	F	Scholar	Herts	Redbourn
231	AUNSCOMBE	Allen	46		Assistant	Unm	26	M	Drapers Assistant	Middx	Hampton
232	GUTTERIDGE	George	46		Apprentice	Unm	15	M	Drapers Apprentice	Herts	Markyate Street
233	BURGOYNE	Jane	46		Serv	Unm	38	F	Domestic Servant	Herts	Redbourn
234	MESSENGER	Henry	47	High Street	Head	Mar	56	M	Agric Lab	Herts	Studham
235	MESSENGER	Mary	47		Wife	Mar	51	F	Plaiter	Herts	Redbourn
236	MESSENGER	Hannah	47		Dau	Unm	28	F	Plaiter	Herts	Redbourn
237	MESSENGER	Emma	47		Dau	Unm	19	F	Plaiter	Herts	Redbourn
238	MESSENGER	Sarah	47		Dau	Unm	17	F	Plaiter	Herts	Redbourn

	SURNAME	FORENAME	SCHEDULE NUMBER	ADDRESS	RELATIONSHIP	STATUS	AGE	SEX	OCCUPATION	COUNTY OF BIRTH	PLACE OF BIRTH
239	MESSENGER	Thomas	47		Son	Unm	15	M	Farm Lab	Herts	Redbourn
240	THOROGOOD	John	48	High Street	Head	Mar	38	M	Carpenter	Herts	Redbourn
241	THOROGOOD	Sarah	48		Wife	Mar	42	F		Herts	Harnstead
242	THOROGOOD	Martha	48		Dau	Unm	16	F	Bonnet Sewer	Herts	Redbourn
243	THOROGOOD	Emma	48		Dau		11	F	Scholar	Herts	Redbourn
244	JONES	Ann	49	High Street	Head	Widow	34	F	Bonnet Sewer	Herts	Redbourn
245	JONES	Ellen	49		Dau	Unm	4	F	Scholar	Herts	Redbourn
246	JONES	William C.	49		Son		1	M		Herts	Redbourn
247	SMITH	Charlotte	49		Sister	Unm	20	F	Bonnet Sewer	Herts	Redbourn
248	PRATT	William	50	High Street	Head	Mar	26	M	Bricklayers Lab	Herts	Redbourn
249	PRATT	Ann	50		Wife	Mar	25	F	Plaiter	Herts	Flamstead
250	PRATT	Ann	50		Dau		5	F	Scholar	Herts	Redbourn
251	PRATT	Emily E.	50		Dau		2	F	Scholar	Herts	Redbourn
252	PEDDER	John	51	The Crown	Head	Mar	51	M	Harness Maker & Victualler	Herts	Redbourn
253	PEDDER	Ann	51		Wife	Mar	50	F	Plaiter	Herts	Harpenden
254	PEDDER	Alexander	51		Son	Unm	18	M	Poulterer	Herts	Redbourn
255	PEDDER	Harriet	51		Dau	Unm	15	F	Bonnet Sewer	Herts	Redbourn
256	PEDDER	Albina	51		Dau		11	F	Scholar	Herts	Redbourn
257	PEDDER	Albert	51		Son		9	M	Scholar	Herts	Redbourn
258	TYLER	Michael	51		Lodger	Unm	28	M	Labourer (Woodman)	Herts	St Pauls Walden
259	SAUNDERS	Edward	51		Lodger	Unm	32	M	Labourer (Woodman)	Herts	St Pauls Walden
260	SHADBOLT	George	51		Lodger	Unm	25	M	Labourer (Woodman)	Herts	St Pauls Walden
261	SEARLE	James	51		Lodger	Unm	20	M	Coach Painter	Oxon	Banbury
262	LUNN	Robert	52	High Street	Head	Mar	21	M	Fellmonger	London	Parish Unknown
263	LUNN	Elizabeth	52		Wife	Mar	22	F		Berks	Reading
264	LUNN	Robert	52		Son		1	M		Berks	Reading
265	BAIL	Eliza	53	High Street	Head	Unm	26	F	Straw Bonnet Sewer	Herts	Redbourn
266	MARTIN	Elizabeth H.	53		Visitor	Unm	16	F	Straw Bonnet Sewer	Bucks	Aylesbury
267	CLARK	John	54	High Street	Head	Mar	62	M	Shoemaker	Herts	Redbourn
268	CLARK	Charlotte	54		Wife	Mar	60	F	Straw Bonnet Sewer	Herts	Redbourn
269	SKILLMAN	John	55	High Street	Head	Mar	61	M	Master Tailor	Herts	Kings Langley
270	SKILLMAN	Mary	55		Wife	Mar	62	F		Herts	Redbourn
271	SKILLMAN	Mary Ann	55		Dau	Unm	32	F	Dressmaker	Herts	Redbourn
272	SKILLMAN	Eliza	55		Dau	Unm	27	F	Dressmaker	Herts	Redbourn
273	SKILLMAN	Daniel	55		Son	Unm	22	M	Tailor	Herts	Redbourn
274	SKILLMAN	Henry C.	55		Son	Unm	18	M	Butcher (App)	Herts	Redbourn
275	ABBOTT	John	56	High Street	Head	Mar	36	M	Agric Lab	Herts	Redbourn
276	ABBOTT	Sarah	56		Wife	Mar	39	F	Charwoman	London	Parish Unknown
277	ABBOTT	Charles	56		Son	Unm	12	M	Plaiter	Herts	Redbourn
278	ABBOTT	Eliza	56		Dau		11	F	Plaiter	Herts	Redbourn
279	ABBOTT	Emma	56		Dau		9	F	Plaiter	Herts	Redbourn
280	ABBOTT	Charlotte	56		Dau		7	F	Plaiter	Herts	Redbourn
281	ABBOTT	Henry	56		Son		5	M	Plaiter	Herts	Redbourn
282	ABBOTT	George	56		Son		3	M		Herts	Redbourn

No.	Surname	Name		Address	Relation	Cond.	Age	Sex	Occupation	County	Birthplace
283	ABBOTT	Daniel	56		Son		8 m	M		Herts	Redbourn
284	OSBORN	Elizabeth	57	High Street	Head	Unm	73	F	Laundress	Herts	Redbourn
285	OSBORN	Barbara	57		Sister	Unm	71	F	Laundress	Herts	Redbourn
286	MAY	Walter	58	Red Lion	Head	Mar	38	M	Victualler & Horse Trainer	Norfolk	Havenham [Hevingham]
287	MAY	Ann	58		Wife	Mar	39	F		Glos	Duresh [Dursley ?]
288	MAY	William	58		Son		12	M	Scholar	Middx	Chelsea
289	MAY	Edith	58		Dau		9	F	Scholar	Surrey	Epsom
290	JENKINS	Hector	58		Inmate	Unm	24	M	Dealer	Essex	Cranham
291	STEABBENS	Emma	58		Inmate		11	F	Scholar	Middx	St Pancras
292	PETIT	James	58		Serv	Unm	18	M	Groom	Beds	Dunstable
293	ASHBY	William	59	High Street	Head	Mar	50	M	Farmer out of Business	Herts	Redbourn
294	ASHBY	Sarah	59		Wife	Mar	42	F		Herts	Gaddesden
295	ASHBY	Sarah	59		Dau	Unm	12	F	Straw Bonnet Maker	Herts	Redbourn
296	ASHBY	Daniel	59		Son		7	M	Scholar	Herts	Redbourn
297	ASHBY	Mary Ann	59		Dau		3 m	F		Herts	Redbourn
298	HULKS	Alfred	60	High Street	Head	Mar	36	M	Plumber, Glazier & Painter	Herts	Abbey Parish [St Albans]
299	HULKS	Mary	60		Wife	Mar	32	F		Herts	Abbey Parish [St Albans]
300	HULKS	Alfred	60		Son		11	M	Scholar	Herts	Abbey Parish [St Albans]
301	HULKS	Joshua	60		Son		9	M	Scholar	Herts	Abbey Parish [St Albans]
302	HULKS	Henry	60		Son		7	M	Scholar	Herts	Abbey Parish [St Albans]
303	HULKS	Charles	60		Son		3	M		Herts	Redbourn
304	HULKS	Frederick	60		Son		1	M		Herts	Redbourn
305	CHEESEMAN	Joseph	61	High Street	Head	Mar	58	M	Blacksmith employing 4 Men	Middx	Cripplegate
306	CHEESEMAN	Elizabeth	61		Wife	Mar	49	F	Domestic Duties	Dorset	Shaftesbury
307	SIBLEY	Sarah	61		Dau	Mar	30	F	Domestic Duties	Herts	Redbourn
308	SIBLEY	William	61		Son-in-law	Mar	39	M	Blacksmith Journeyman	Herts	St Michaels
309	SIBLEY	Eliza	61		Grandau		5	F	Scholar	Herts	Redbourn
310	SIBLEY	Eleanor	61		Grandau		3	F	At Home	Herts	Redbourn
311	SIBLEY	Joseph	61		Grandson		2	M	At Home	Herts	Redbourn
312	HORN	Robert	62	High Street	Head	Mar	68	M	Chelsea Pensioner	Herts	Redbourn
313	HORN	Susan	62		Wife	Mar	48	F	Sempstress	Ireland	Kings, County Philipstown
314	HORN	Ann E.	62		Dau	Unm	17	F	Straw Bonnet Maker	Herts	Redbourn
315	WHITEHOUSE	William	63	High Street	Head	Mar	52	M	Schoolmaster	Staffs	Wolverhampton
316	WHITEHOUSE	Jane	63		Wife	Mar	54	F	Schoolmistress	Herts	South Mimms
317	WHITEHOUSE	Sophia	63		Dau	Unm	20	F	Bonnet Sewer	Herts	Markyate Street
318	FRANKLIN	Sarah	64	High Street	Head	Widow	64	F	Midwife	Essex	Livlingham [?]
319	FRANKLIN	George	64		Son	Unm	22	M	Umbrella & Parasol Repairer	Herts	Redbourn
320	MARSHALL	Henry	64		Lodger	Unm	20	M	Barber	Herts	Redbourn
321	KEENE	John	65	High Street	Head	Mar	47	M	Jobber	Beds	Dunstable
322	KEENE	Sarah	65		Wife	Mar	44	F		Bucks	Aylesbury
323	KEENE	William	65		Son	Unm	19	M	Boot & Shoe Mender	Herts	Kensworth
324	KEENE	Jane	65		Dau	Unm	12	F	Bonnet Sewer	Herts	Redbourn

	SURNAME	FORENAME	SCHEDULE NUMBER	ADDRESS	RELATIONSHIP	STATUS	AGE	SEX	OCCUPATION	COUNTY OF BIRTH	PLACE OF BIRTH
325	KEENE	Joseph	65		Son		10	M	Errand Boy	Herts	Redbourn

One house uninhabited

326	GREEN	Jonathan	66	High Street	Head	Mar	25	M	Baker	Herts	Flamstead
327	GREEN	Mary	66		Wife	Mar	26	F	Bonnet Sewer	Herts	Redbourn
328	GREEN	Thomas	66		Son	Unm	3	M		Herts	Redbourn
329	GREEN	Marian	66		Dau		4m	F		Herts	Redbourn
330	ASHBY	John	67	High Street	Head	Mar	38	M	Grocer	Herts	Redbourn
331	ASHBY	Sarah	67		Wife	Mar	40	F		Herts	Park Street [St Stephens]
332	ASHBY	Sarah	67		Dau	Unm	16	F	Straw Bonnet Sewer	Herts	Park Street [St Stephens]
333	ASHBY	John T.	67		Son	Unm	14	M	Grocer	Bucks	Beaconsfield
334	ASHBY	Daniel	67		Son	Unm	12	M	Scholar	Herts	Redbourn
335	ASHBY	Ann	67		Dau	Unm	11	F	Scholar	Herts	Redbourn
336	ASHBY	Georgiana	67		Dau		8	F	Scholar	Herts	Redbourn
337	ASHBY	Catherine	67		Dau		7	F	Scholar	Herts	Redbourn
338	ASHBY	Elizabeth	67		Dau		4	F	Scholar	Herts	Redbourn
339	GREEN	Elizabeth	67		Visitor	Widow	39	F	Dressmaker	Herts	Tring

Uninhabited — 68 — *Miss Hoar no return. Slept out [struck through]*

340	ANSELL	John J.	69	High Street	Head	Mar	44	M	Groom	Herts	North Mimms
341	ANSELL	Ann	69		Wife	Mar	40	F	Domestic Duties	Herts	Redbourn
342	PARROTT	John	70	High Street	Head	Mar	37	M	Journeyman Blacksmith	Herts	Wheathampstead
343	PARROTT	Frances	70		Wife	Mar	36	F	Plaiter	Herts	Preston
344	PARROTT	John	70		Son	Unm	12	M	Farmers Lab	Herts	Hatfield
345	PARROTT	Lucy	70		Dau	Unm	8	F	Scholar	Herts	Wheathampstead
346	PARROTT	George	70		Son	Unm	5	M		Herts	Hatfield
347	PARROTT	William	70		Son		3m	M		Herts	Redbourn
348	HOOTON	Thomas	71	High Street	Head	Mar	59	M	Labourer	Herts	Redbourn
349	HOOTON	Martha	71		Wife	Mar	58	F		Beds	Luton
350	BARNES	Simon	72	High Street	Head	Mar	27	M	Jobbing Lab	Herts	Flamstead
351	BARNES	Emma	72		Wife	Mar	22	F	Hat Maker	Herts	St Albans
352	BARNES	Emily	72		Dau		1	F		Herts	Redbourn
353	BARNES	William	72		Son		6m	M		Herts	Redbourn
354	STEABBENS	Joseph	73	High Street	Head	Mar	44	M	Butcher	Herts	St Albans
355	STEABBENS	Susannah	73		Wife	Mar	39	F		Norfolk	Beeston
356	STEABBENS	Joseph	73		Son	Unm	14	M	Scholar	Middx	St Pancras
357	STEABBENS	William	73		Son	Unm	12	M	Scholar	Middx	St Pancras
358	STEABBENS	Arthur	73		Son	Unm	9	M	Scholar	Middx	St Pancras
359	STEABBENS	Zephah	73		Dau	Unm	7	F	Scholar	Middx	St Pancras
360	STEABBENS	George	73		Son	Unm	5	M		Middx	St Pancras
361	STEABBENS	Walter	73		Son	Unm	4	M		Middx	St Pancras
362	BROWN	Elizabeth	73		Sister-in-law	Unm	28	F	Straw Bonnet Maker	Norfolk	Fransham
363	HARRIS	Charlotte	74	High Street	Head	Widow	64	F	Lady (Houses, Land & Fund Holder)	Herts	Redbourn
364	SIMMONS	Mary Ann	74		Serv	Unm	15	F	Household Servant	London	Parish UnKnown
365	SMITH	Michael	74		Head	Mar	74	M	Confectioner	Beds	St Pauls, Bedford

366	SMITH	Sarah	74		Wife	Mar	72	F		Herts	Hatfield
367	HULKS	Hannah	74		Visitor	Unm	49	F	Annuitant	Herts	Aldenham
368	BURTON	Jeremiah	74		Visitor	Unm	60	M	Annuitant	Norfolk	Sporle
369	HUTCHINS	John	75	High Street	Head	Mar	49	M	Lab & Beer Shop Keeper	Beds	Caddington
370	HUTCHINS	Phebe	75		Wife	Mar	51	F		Herts	Redbourn
371	ROBERTS	Angelina	75		Visitor	Unm	6	F		Middx	South Mimms
372	BURGESS	William	76	High Street	Head	Mar	26	M	Farmers Lab	Herts	Redbourn
373	BURGESS	Ann	76		Wife	Mar	26	F	Plaiter	Herts	Redbourn
374	BARNES	Thomas	77	High Street	Head	Mar	46	M	Baker, 1 man	Herts	Redbourn
375	BARNES	Ann	77		Wife	Mar	36	F		Herts	Redbourn
376	BARNES	Amy	77		Niece	Unm	20	F	Milliner	Herts	Redbourn
377	BARNES	Eliza	77		Niece	Unm	18	F		Herts	Redbourn
378	THOROGOOD	Thomas	77		Nephew	Unm	19	M	Journeyman Baker	Herts	Redbourn
379	THOROGOOD	Thomas	78	High Street	Head	Mar	34	M	Carpenter employing 2 men	Herts	Redbourn
380	THOROGOOD	Mary Ann	78		Wife	Mar	32	F		Herts	Redbourn
381	THOROGOOD	Betsey	78		Dau	Unm	14	F	Plaiter	Herts	Redbourn
382	THOROGOOD	Tryphena	78		Dau		7	F	Deaf & Dumb	Herts	Redbourn
383	THOROGOOD	Mary Ann	78		Dau		4	F	Deaf & Dumb	Herts	Redbourn
384	THOROGOOD	Sarah	78		Dau		2	F		Herts	Redbourn
385	THOROGOOD	Rosa	78		Dau		4m	F		Herts	Redbourn
386	GREEN	Elizabeth	79	High Street	Head	Widow	60	F	Plaiter	Herts	Crouchfield [Hemel Hempstead]
387	GREEN	Elizabeth	79		Dau	Unm	19	F	Bonnet Sewer	Herts	Redbourn
388	SILSBY	Charles	80	High Street	Head	Mar	41	M	Plait Dealer	Herts	Watford
389	SILSBY	Mary	80		Wife	Mar	31	F	Bonnet Sewer	Northants	Piddington
390	SILSBY	Charles	80		Son	Unm	13	M	Scholar	Herts	St Albans
391	SILSBY	William	80		Son	Unm	10	M	Scholar	Herts	St Albans
392	MITCHELL	Elizabeth	80		Niece	Unm	12	F	Appr to Straw Bonnet Maker	Bucks	Newport Pagnell
393	DIXON	Charles (Jnr)	81	High Street (White Hart Inn)	Head	Unm	16	M	Innkeeper	Herts	Redbourn
394	DIXON	Eliza	81		Sister	Unm	13	F	Scholar	Herts	Redbourn
395	NASH	Maria	81		Serv	Unm	20	F	Domestic Servant	Herts	Wheathampstead
396	ADAMS	William	81		Serv	Unm	14	M	Errand Boy	Herts	Markyate Street
397	GARRATT	John	82	High Street (Ton of Bedlam)	Head	Mar	34	M	Victualler	Bucks	Hudnall
398	GARRATT	Eliza	82		Wife	Mar	42	F		Herts	Little Gaddesden
399	GARRATT	Ann	82		Dau		10	F	Scholar	Herts	Little Gaddesden
400	REED	Charles	83	High Street	Head	Mar	43	M	Chelsea Pensioner	Herts	St Albans
401	REED	Eliza	83		Wife	Mar	27	F	Bonnet Sewer	Herts	Redbourn
402	REED	Adelaide	83		Dau	Unm	15	F	Bonnet Sewer	Ireland	[Unknown]
403	REED	Charles	83		Son	Unm	11	M	Scholar	Ireland	[Unknown]
404	REED	Caroline	83		Dau		10	F	Scholar	Berks	Windsor
405	FIGG	Leah	84	High Street	Head	Mar	44	F	Grocer	Bucks	Ivinghoe
406	FIGG	Sarah	84		Dau	Unm	17	F	Bonnet Sewer	Bucks	Cheddington
407	FIGG	Rebecca	84		Dau	Unm	15	F	Bonnet Sewer	Bucks	Cheddington
408	FIGG	James	84		Son		12	M	Tailor (App.)	Bucks	Cheddington

	SURNAME	FORENAME	SCHEDULE NUMBER	ADDRESS	RELATIONSHIP	STATUS	AGE	SEX	OCCUPATION	COUNTY OF BIRTH	PLACE OF BIRTH
409	FIGG	Davill	84		Son		9	M	Scholar	Bucks	Cheddington
410	FIGG	Mary	84		Dau		6	F	Scholar	Herts	Redbourn
411	CHURCH	John	85	High Street	Head	Mar	32	M	Butcher, 1 man	Beds	Potton
412	CHURCH	Hannah	85		Wife	Mar	25	F		Beds	Roxton
413	CHURCH	Anne	85		Dau		4	F	Scholar	Herts	Redbourn
414	NEAL	Mary Ann	85		Serv	Unm	20	F	Servant	Herts	Wheathampstead
415	MARTIN	William	86	High Street	Head	Mar	39	M	Cordwainer	Oxon	Thame
416	MARTIN	Ann	86		Wife	Mar	44	F	Housekeeper	Bucks	Aylesbury
417	MARTIN	John H.	86		Son	Unm	18	M	Cordwainer	Bucks	Aylesbury
418	MARTIN	Ann	86		Dau	Unm	14	F	Bonnet Sewer	Bucks	Aylesbury
419	MARTIN	Emma	86		Dau	Unm	12	F	Bonnet Sewer	Herts	Hemel Hempstead
420	MARTIN	Sarah	86		Dau	Unm	10	F	Bonnet Sewer	Herts	Hemel Hempstead
421	MARTIN	Thomas	86		Son	Unm	8	M	Scholar	Herts	Hemel Hempstead
422	McDONALD	James	86		Apprentice	Unm	16	M	Apprentice to Cordwainer	Middx	London
423	SEABROOK	John	86		Apprentice	Unm	17	M	Apprentice to Cordwainer	Herts	Redbourn
424	BURGOYNE	Sarah	87	High Street	Head	Widow	67	F	Plaiter	Herts	Sandridge
425	BURGOYNE	George	87		Son	Unm	33	M	Baker	Herts	Redbourn
426	PRATT	Betsey	87		Dau	Mar	30	F	Bonnet Sewer	Herts	Redbourn
427	PRATT	Henry	87		Son-in-law	Mar	28	M	Bricklayer	Herts	Redbourn
428	PRATT	Bob	87		Grandson		2	M		Herts	Redbourn
429	LARGE	James (Jnr)	88	High Street	Head	Mar	26	M	Agric Lab	Herts	Redbourn
430	LARGE	Ellen	88		Wife	Mar	26	F	Plaiter of Straw	Herts	Redbourn
431	LARGE	Amos	88		Son		2m	M		Herts	Redbourn
432	LARGE	James (Snr)	89	High Street	Head	Mar	66	M	Agric Lab	Beds	Luton
433	LARGE	Sarah	89		Wife	Mar	55	F	Bonnet Sewer	Beds	Luton
434	LARGE	Ann	89		Dau	Unm	17	F	Bonnet Sewer	Herts	Redbourn
435	LARGE	Emma	89		Dau	Unm	14	F	Bonnet Sewer	Herts	Redbourn
436	LARGE	John	89		Son	Unm	12	M	Labourer	Herts	Redbourn
437	LARGE	Matthew	89		Son	Unm	10	M	Labourer	Herts	Redbourn
438	DIXON	Mary B.	90	High Street	Head	Widow	66	F	Retired Millers Widow	Dorset	Shaftesbury
439	DIXON	Kitty	90		Dau	Unm	32	F	Governess	Herts	Redbourn
440	DIXON	Tryphena	90		Dau	Unm	30	F	Dressmaker	Herts	Redbourn
441	DIXON	Mary	90		Grandau		7	F	Visitor	N'thumb	Newcastle-upon-Tyne
442	HARRISON	James	91	High Street	Head	Unm	46	M	Chemist & Druggist	Suffolk	Timworth
443	INNOUS	Susannah	91		Visitor	Unm	31	F		Essex	Stratford
444	INNOUS	Ann	91		Visitors Dau	Unm	13	F		Essex	Stratford
445	HOWIE	Robert	92	High Street	Head	Mar	51	M	Agent	Ireland	Banff, County Grange
446	HOWIE	Rose F.	92		Wife	Mar	41	F		Herts	Redbourn
447	HOWIE	Sarah E.	92		Dau		9m	F		Herts	Redbourn
448	GIFKINS	Caroline	92		Serv	Unm	15	F	Servant	Herts	St Michaels
449	OSBORN	Richard	93	High Street	Head	Widower	74	M	Annuitant	Cornwall	Kilkhampton
450	GILBERT	William	94	High Street	Head	Mar	36	M	Plait Dealer	Herts	St Michaels
451	GILBERT	Ann E.	94		Wife	Mar	35	F	Dressmaker	Middx	Poplar

452	BROWN	Martha Vere	95	High Street	Head	Widow	75	F	Lady. Landed proprietor & Fundholder	Staffs	Handsworth
453	BROWN	Charles F.	95		Son	Mar	44	M	Com. Royal Navy (Half Pay), Land Holder	Herts	St Albans
454	BROWN	Elizabeth A.	95		Dau-in-law	Mar	28	F	Lady	Herts	Harpenden
455	BROWN	Elizabeth M.	95		Grandau	Unm	8	F	Scholar at Home	Herts	St Michaels
456	BROWN	Mary F.	95		Grandau	Unm	6	F	Scholar at Home	Herts	Redbourn
457	BROWN	Jane E.	95		Grandau	Unm	3	F	Scholar at Home	Herts	Redbourn
458	BROWN	John W.	95		Grandson	Unm	2	M	Scholar at Home	Herts	Redbourn
459	HAMPSON	Jane	95		Grandau	Unm	24	F	Lady, Fundholder	Middx	London
460	HAMPSON	William S.	95		Grandson	Unm	20	M	Student, Christchurch Oxford	Middx	London
461	BROTHERS	Mary	95		Serv	Unm	50	F	Housekeeper	Unknown	[Unknown]
462	TAYLOR	Susanna	95		Serv	Unm	39	F	House Servant	Herts	Great Gaddesden
463	AUSTIN	Ann	95		Serv	Unm	23	F	Cook	Lincs	Thurlby
464	TOMS	John	95		Serv	Unm	20	M	Man Servant	Herts	Hemel Hempstead
465	MAYNE	Harriett	95		Serv	Mar	34	F	Nurse	Herts	St Albans
466	MANNING	Temperance	95		Serv	Unm	19	F	House Servant	Herts	Redbourn
467	WOODBINE	Sarah	95		Serv	Mar	70	F	Monthly Nurse	Middx	London
468	SHIRLY	John	95		Serv	Mar	57	M	Gardening Man	Herts	Redbourn
469	JENNINGS	Joshua	96	High Street	Head	Widower	60	M	Dealer	Yorks	Harewood
470	JENNINGS	Julia	96		Dau	Unm	18	F		Herts	Harpenden
471	OSBORN	Jane	97	High Street	Head	Unm	50	F	Independent. House & Funds	Middx	St James, Westminster
472	OSBORN	Frances	97		Sister	Unm	45	F	Independent. House & Funds	Middx	St James, Westminster
473	SAUNDERS	Jane M.	97		Niece		6	F	Scholar at Home	Herts	Flamstead
474	PRATT	Matthew	98	High Street	Head	Mar	29	M	Bricklayer	Herts	Redbourn
475	BURGOYNE	William	99	High Street	Head	Unm	44	M	Bricklayers Lab	Herts	Redbourn
476	TROT	Martha	99		Lodger	Unm	43	F	Charwoman	Herts	Hemel Hempstead
477	SLAUGHTER	Thomas	100	High Street	Head	Mar	30	M	Labourer in Water Cress Beds	Herts	Rickmansworth
478	SLAUGHTER	Lucy	100		Wife	Mar	25	F	Plaiter	Herts	St Albans
479	SLAUGHTER	Henry	100		Son		4	M		Herts	Redbourn
480	SLAUGHTER	William	100		Son		2	M		Herts	Redbourn
481	SLAUGHTER	Walter	100		Son		7 m	M		Herts	Redbourn
482	STONE	John	101	High Street	Head	Mar	34	M	Baker employing 1 man	Herts	Redbourn
483	STONE	Mary Ann	101		Wife	Mar	33	F		Herts	Studham
484	STONE	Thomas	101		Son	Unm	8	M	Scholar	Herts	Studham
485	STONE	Sarah	101		Dau	Unm	6	F	Scholar	Herts	Redbourn
486	STONE	Emily	101		Dau	Unm	3	F		Herts	Redbourn
487	STONE	Harriett	101		Dau	Unm	9 m	F		Herts	Redbourn
488	WELLS	Eliza	101		Serv	Unm	16	F	House Serv	Herts	Redbourn
489	HALSEY	George	101		Serv	Unm	23	M	Journeyman Baker	Herts	Redbourn
490	ADAMS	Daniel	102	High Street	Head	Mar	41	M	Journeyman Baker	Herts	Redbourn
491	ADAMS	Sarah	102		Wife	Mar	40	F		Herts	Flamstead
492	ADAMS	Thomas	102		Son		10	M	Scholar	Herts	Markyate Street
493	ADAMS	Arthur	102		Son		9	M	Scholar	Herts	Markyate Street

	SURNAME	FORENAME	SCHEDULE NUMBER	ADDRESS	RELATIONSHIP	STATUS	AGE	SEX	OCCUPATION	COUNTY OF BIRTH	PLACE OF BIRTH
494	ADAMS	Alfred	102		Son		6	M	Scholar	Herts	Markyate Street
495	ADAMS	Frederick	102		Son		3	M		Herts	Markyate Street
496	ADAMS	Walter	102		Son		4m	M		Herts	Redbourn
497	EAMES	Samuel	103	High Street	Head	Mar	30	M	Hairdresser & Glover	Herts	Redbourn
498	EAMES	Mary	103		Wife	Mar	28	F		Devon	Devonport
499	EAMES	Ellen J.	103		Dau		6m	F		Herts	Redbourn
500	LONGHURST	George	103		Brother-in-law	Unm	14	M	Assistant [Hairdresser & Glover]	Devon	Devonport
501	HALL	Thomas	104	High Street	Head	Mar	45	M	Shopkeeper	Herts	Kensworth
502	HALL	Mary	104		Wife	Mar	43	F	Plaiter	[Beds]	Caddington
503	HALL	William	104		Son	Unm	12	M	Servant	Herts	Hemel Hempstead
504	HALL	Elizabeth	104		Dau	Unm	10	F	Plaiter	Herts	Hemel Hempstead
505	HALL	Matilda	104		Dau		10m	F		Herts	Redbourn
506	RUMBALL	William	105	High Street	Head	Mar	21	M	Cordwainer	Herts	Harpenden
507	RUMBALL	Martha	105		Wife	Mar	23	F	Bonnet Sewer	Bucks	Shalstone
508	VICKERS	Mary Ann	105		Cousin	Unm	14	F	Bonnet Sewer	Northants	Sulgrave

One house uninhabited

	SURNAME	FORENAME	SCHEDULE NUMBER	ADDRESS	RELATIONSHIP	STATUS	AGE	SEX	OCCUPATION	COUNTY OF BIRTH	PLACE OF BIRTH
509	THOROGOOD	John	106	Harpenden Lane	Head	Mar	70	M	Retired Carpenter (Houses)	Beds	Luton
510	THOROGOOD	Martha	106		Wife	Mar	65	F		Oxon	Chesterton
511	THOROGOOD	Ann	106		Dau	Unm	36	F	Plaiter	Herts	Redbourn
512	THOROGOOD	James	106		Son	Unm	21	M	Journeyman Carpenter	Herts	Redbourn
513	THOROGOOD	Mary	106		Grandau		15	F	Bonnet Sewer	Herts	Redbourn
514	MESSEDER	John	107	Harpenden Lane	Head	Mar	60	M	Straw Dealer	Herts	Kensworth
515	MESSEDER	Rebecca	107		Wife	Mar	57	F		Herts	Hemel Hempstead
516	LACEY	Jabez	108	Harpenden Lane	Head	Mar	28	M	Chair Turner	Bucks	Princes Risborough
517	LACEY	Caroline	108		Wife	Mar	27	F		Herts	Kensworth
518	LACEY	Ruth	108		Dau		4	F	Scholar	Herts	Kensworth
519	LACEY	James	108		Son		1	M		Herts	Markyate Street
520	BENT	Charles	109	Harpenden Lane	Head	Mar	33	M	Agric Lab	Herts	Harpenden
521	BENT	Phebe	109		Wife	Mar	32	F	Bonnet Sewer	Herts	Harpenden
522	SHEPPARD	George	110	Harpenden Lane	Head	Mar	31	M	Agric Lab	Herts	Redbourn
523	SHEPPARD	Sophia	110		Wife	Mar	32	F	Bonnet Sewer	Herts	Harpenden
524	DUNCKLEY	William	111	Harpenden Lane	Head	Mar	40	M	Painter	Herts	Flamstead
525	DUNCKLEY	Hannah	111		Wife	Mar	35	F		Middx	Uxbridge
526	DUNCKLEY	Emma E.	111		Dau		7	F	Scholar	Herts	Redbourn
527	DUNCKLEY	Sarah Ann	111		Dau		5	F		Herts	Redbourn
528	DUNCKLEY	Dennis	111		Son		2	M		Herts	Redbourn
529	DUNCKLEY	Dorcas	111		Dau		2	F		Herts	Redbourn
530	HOW	Joseph	112	Harpenden Lane	Head	Mar	43	M	Agric Lab	Herts	Flamstead
531	HOW	Susannah	112		Wife	Mar	51	F	Straw Plaiter	Herts	Harpenden
532	CLAYTON	William	113	Harpenden Lane	Head	Widower	67	M	Coal Merchants Labourer	Herts	Flamstead
533	BENNETT	William	114	Harpenden Lane	Head	Mar	45	M	Shepherd	Herts	Essendon
534	BENNETT	Phebe	114		Wife	Mar	41	F	Plaiter	Herts	Ashwell

535	BENNETT	George	114		Son	Unm	19	M	Shepherd	Herts	Wheathampstead
536	BENNETT	Eliza	114		Dau	Unm	17	F	Plaiter	Herts	Hatfield
537	BENNETT	James	114		Son		10	M	Scholar	Herts	Wheathampstead
538	PENNY	William	115	Harpenden Lane	Head	Mar	68	M	Agric Lab	Herts	Redbourn
539	PENNY	Mary	115		Wife	Mar	71	F		Herts	Barnet
540	LUCK	Joseph	116	Harpenden Lane	Head	Mar	42	M	Agric Lab	Herts	Harpenden
541	LUCK	Sarah	116		Wife	Mar	37	F	Plaiter	Herts	Flamstead
542	LUCK	Louisa	116		Dau	Unm	15	F	Bonnet Sewer	Herts	Redbourn
543	LUCK	Thomas	116		Son	Unm	12	M	Straw Cutter	Herts	Redbourn
544	HYDE	William	117	Harpenden Lane	Head	Mar	25	M	Agric Lab	Herts	Weston
545	HYDE	Hannah	117		Wife	Mar	26	F	Plaiter	Herts	Redbourn
546	PRATT	Mary	118	Harpenden Lane	Head	Widow	82	F	Supported by her children	Herts	Redbourn
547	GREEN	Mary	119	Harpenden Lane	Head	Unm	46	F	Plaiter	Herts	Redbourn
548	GREEN	Charlotte	120	Harpenden Lane	Head	Widow	57	F	Laundress	Somerset	Newton
549	GREEN	Edward C.	120		Son	Unm	20	M	Painter & Glazier (App)	Herts	Redbourn
550	PRATT	Joseph	121	Fish Street	Head	Mar	50	M	Bricklayer	Herts	Redbourn
551	PRATT	Ann	121		Wife	Mar	52	F	Plaiter	Herts	Harpenden
552	PRATT	Joseph	121		Son	Unm	20	M	Bricklayers Lab	Herts	Redbourn
553	PRATT	James	121		Son	Unm	18	M	Bricklayers Lab	Herts	Redbourn
554	PRATT	Ann	121		Dau	Unm	15	F	Bonnet Sewer	Herts	Redbourn
555	PRATT	John	121		Son		11	M	Scholar	Herts	Redbourn
556	SLOW	Mary	122	Fish Street	Head	Widow	56	F	Plaiter	Herts	Hemel Hempstead
557	DOLLING	George	123	Fish Street	Head	Mar	50	M	Groom	Herts	Redbourn
558	DOLLING	Lucy	123		Wife	Mar	25	F	Needlewoman	Hants	Odiham
559	DOLLING	Harriett	123		Dau		4	F		Herts	Redbourn
560	MAY	John	123		Visitor	Unm	16	M	Groom	Suffolk	Newmarket
561	BAYLEY	Charlotte	124	Fish Street	Head	Mar	51	F	Grooms Wife	Herts	Redbourn
562	BAYLEY	Charlotte	124		Dau	Unm	16	F	Bonnet Sewer	Herts	Redbourn
563	BAYLEY	Mary Ann	124		Dau	Unm	9	F	Scholar	Herts	Redbourn
564	TWINDELLS	Jessie	124		Visitor	Unm	8	F	Scholar	London	Aldersgate Street
565	TWINDELLS	Maria	124		Visitor	Unm	7	F	Scholar	London	Aldersgate Street
566	TWINDELLS	Charles	124		Visitor		5	M	Scholar	London	Aldersgate Street
567	LOVETT	Esther	125	Fish Street	Head	Widow	79	F	Plaiter	Herts	Wheathampstead
568	LOWE	Ellen	125		Visitor	Unm	17	F	Grass Hat Maker	Herts	Redbourn
569	SMITH	Daniel (Snr)	126	Fish Street	Head	Mar	68	M	Labourer	Herts	St Peters, St Albans
570	SMITH	Mary	126		Wife	Mar	58	F		Herts	Redbourn
571	SMITH	Susannah	126		Dau	Unm	22	F	Plaiter	Herts	Redbourn
572	SMITH	John	126		Son	Unm	19	M	Blacksmiths Lab	Herts	Redbourn
573	SMITH	James	126		Son	Unm	17	M	Agric Lab	Herts	Redbourn
574	JACKSON	Hannah	126		Inmate	Unm	19	F	Bonnet Sewer	Herts	Redbourn
575	KITCHENER	Frederick	127	Fish Street	Head	Mar	33	M	Labourer	Beds	Luton
576	KITCHENER	Pamelia	127		Wife	Mar	43	F		Herts	Redbourn
577	KITCHENER	William	127		Son	Unm	10	M	Scholar	Herts	St Albans
578	KITCHENER	Kezia A.	127		Dau	Unm	8	F		Herts	Redbourn

	SURNAME	FORENAME	SCHEDULE NUMBER	ADDRESS	RELATIONSHIP	STATUS	AGE	SEX	OCCUPATION	COUNTY OF BIRTH	PLACE OF BIRTH
579	KITCHENER	James	127		Son		6	M		Herts	Redbourn
580	DAVIS	Richard	128	Fish Street	Head	Widower	42	M	Agric Lab	Herts	Flamstead
581	DAVIS	Caroline	128		Dau	Unm	19	F	Plaiter	Herts	Redbourn
582	DAVIS	Eliza	128		Dau	Unm	18	F	Plaiter	Herts	Redbourn
583	DAVIS	William	128		Son	Unm	14	M	Agric Lab	Herts	Redbourn
584	DAVIS	Mary Ann	128		Dau	Unm	9	F	Plaiter	Herts	Redbourn
585	PROCTOR	Louisa	128		Lodger	Unm	19	F	Plaiter	Herts	Hemel Hempstead
586	GEEVES	James	129	Fish Street	Head	Mar	61	M	Carrier	Herts	Redbourn
587	GEEVES	Frances	129		Wife	Mar	60	F		Herts	St Albans
588	ROBINSON	William	130	Fish Street	Head	Unm	44	M	Independent Minister of Fish St. Chapel	Lincs	Grantham
589	ASHBY	Thomas (Snr)	131	Fish Street	Head	Mar	61	M	Ret. Butcher. Funds, Houses & Land	Herts	Redbourn
590	ASHBY	Sarah	131		Wife	Mar	54	F		Beds	Caddington
591	ASHBY	Mary D.	131		Dau	Unm	21	F	Schoolmistress in Fathers House	Herts	Redbourn
592	ASHBY	Frances	131		Dau	Unm	19	F	Schoolmistress in Fathers House	Herts	Redbourn
593	ASHBY	Catherine	131		Dau	Unm	16	F	Scholar	Herts	Redbourn
594	CLARK	Jane	131		Boarder		4	F	Scholar	Middx	St Andrews, Holborn
595	GEEVES	Henry	132	Fish Street	Head	Mar	41	M	Poulterer	Herts	Redbourn
596	GEEVES	Alice	132		Wife	Mar	42	F		Herts	Redbourn
597	GEEVES	Sarah	132		Dau	Unm	20	F	Bonnet Sewer	Herts	Redbourn
598	GEEVES	Frances	132		Dau	Unm	15	F	Bonnet Sewer	Herts	Redbourn
599	GEEVES	Rose	132		Dau	Unm	13	F	Scholar	Herts	Redbourn
600	GEEVES	Alfred	132		Son	Unm	10	M	Scholar	Herts	Redbourn
601	GEEVES	Walter	132		Son	Unm	8	M	Scholar	Herts	Redbourn
602	GEEVES	William	132		Son	Unm	6	M	Scholar	Herts	Redbourn
603	GEEVES	James	132		Son	Unm	4	M	Scholar	Herts	Redbourn
604	GEEVES	Agnes	132		Dau	Unm	9 m	F		Herts	Redbourn
605	PHILPOTT	Ann	133	Fish Street	Head	Widow	58	F		Herts	Redbourn
606	PHILPOTT	Jesse	133		Son	Mar	30	M	Jobbing Labourer	Herts	Redbourn
607	PHILPOTT	Hannah	133		Dau-in-law	Mar	30	F	Plaiter	Herts	Redbourn
608	PHILPOTT	John	133		Grandson		6	M		Herts	Redbourn
609	BARNES	George	133		Lodger	Unm	33	M	Footman out of place	Herts	Redbourn
610	STEPHENS	Abraham	134	Fish Street	Head	Mar	54	M	Jobbing Lab	Beds	Luton
611	STEPHENS	Ann	134		Wife	Mar	50	F		Beds	Sundon
612	BALDWIN	John	135	Fish Street	Head	Mar	29	M	Jobbing Lab (Generally with Butcher)	Herts	Redbourn
613	BALDWIN	Elizabeth	135		Wife	Mar	30	F	Straw Bonnet Maker	Beds	Luton
614	BALDWIN	Elizabeth	135		Dau	Unm	6	F		Herts	Redbourn
615	BALDWIN	Frances	135		Dau		3	F		Herts	Redbourn
616	BALDWIN	William	135		Son		5 m	M		Herts	Redbourn
617	BARNES	Hannah	136	Fish Street	Head	Widow	47	F	Straw Bonnet Maker	Herts	Redbourn
618	BARNES	Elizabeth	136		Dau	Unm	16	F	Dressmaker	Herts	Redbourn
619	BARNES	Mary Ann	136		Dau	Unm	15	F	Straw Plait Maker	Herts	Redbourn
620	LOVELL	Ann	137	Fish Street	Head	Mar	33	F	Straw Plait Maker	Herts	Redbourn
621	LOVELL	William	137		Son		3	M	Scholar	Herts	Redbourn

622	LOVELL	Ann E.	137		Dau		1	F		Herts	Redbourn
623	BARNES	Sarah	137		Niece	Unm	13	F	Straw Plait Maker	Herts	Redbourn
624	BINGHAM	Elizabeth	138	Fish Street	Head	Widow	77	F	Straw Plait Maker	Herts	Redbourn
625	BINGHAM	Hannah	138		Dau	Unm	47	F	Straw Plait Maker	Herts	Redbourn
626	BINGHAM	Eliza	138		Dau	Unm	39	F	Straw Plait Maker	Herts	Redbourn
627	HALSEY	Ann	138		Grandau	Unm	17	F	Straw Plait Maker	Herts	Redbourn
628	HALSEY	Emma	138		Grandau	Unm	14	F	Straw Plait Maker	Herts	Redbourn
629	HALSEY	Eliza	138		Grandau		8	F	Scholar	Herts	Redbourn
630	COLE	William (Snr)	139	Fish Street	Head	Mar	76	M	Wheelwright	Herts	Redbourn
631	COLE	Elizabeth	139		Wife	Mar	65	F		Herts	Redbourn
632	COLE	Jane	139		Dau	Unm	23	F	Straw Bonnet Sewer	Herts	Redbourn
633	SHIRLEY	Elizabeth	140	Fish Street	Head	Mar	49	F	Domestic Duties	Herts	Redbourn
634	SHIRLEY	Mary	140		Dau	Unm	24	F	Straw Plait Maker	Herts	Redbourn
635	SHIRLEY	Josephus	140		Son	Unm	16	M	Servant (no employ)	Herts	Redbourn
636	SHIRLEY	Henry	140		Son	Unm	9	M	Scholar	Herts	Redbourn
637	SHIRLEY	Edwin	140		Grandson		2	M		Herts	Redbourn
638	BISNEY	Francis	141	Fish Street	Head	Mar	74	M	Chelsea Pensioner	Herts	Flamstead
639	BISNEY	Mary	141		Wife	Mar	66	F	Plait Dealer & Chandler	Herts	St Stephens
640	BISNEY	William	141		Grandson	Unm	14	M	Wheelwright (App)	Herts	Redbourn
641	HARRIS	James	141		Visitor	Unm	50	M	Agric Lab	Herts	St Stephens
642	MARSHALL	Elizabeth	142	Redbourn Common	Head	Widow	48	F	Plaiter	Herts	Sandridge
643	MARSHALL	William	142		Son	Unm	17	M	Hawkers Servant	Herts	Redbourn
644	MARSHALL	Emma	142		Dau	Unm	11	F	Plaiter	Herts	Redbourn
645	MARSHALL	Stephen	142		Son	Unm	8	M	Farm Serv	Herts	Redbourn
646	MARSHALL	Sarah	142		Dau	Unm	5	F	Plaiter	Herts	Redbourn
647	ARNOLD	James	143	Redbourn Common	Head	Mar	38	M	Farm Lab	Herts	Harpenden
648	ARNOLD	Elizabeth	143		Wife	Mar	33	F	Infant Schoolmistress	Herts	Redbourn
649	COLES	Joseph	144	Redbourn Common	Head	Mar	40	M	Wheelwright employing 1 man	Herts	Redbourn
650	COLES	Rose	144		Wife	Mar	37	F	Plaiter	Herts	Redbourn
651	COLES	Ann	144		Dau	Unm	12	F	Scholar	Herts	Redbourn
652	COLES	Sarah	144		Dau		9	F	Scholar	Herts	Redbourn
653	SLYTHE	Sarah	145	Redbourn Common	Head	Unm	74	F	Schoolmistress	Essex	Halsted
654	GRIMSHEAD (Esq.)	Thomas	146	Redbourn Common	Head	Unm	47	M	Gent; Fundholder	Surrey	Epsom
655	GRIMSHEAD	Frances	146		Sister	Unm	42	F	Lady (Mortgagee etc.)	Surrey	Epsom
656	MANNING	Susan	146		Serv	Widow	87	F	Cook	London	Parish Unknown
657	FAIRCLOTH	Sophia	146		Serv	Unm	22	F	Housemaid	Herts	Hatfield

Two houses uninhabited

658	PROCTOR	William	147	Lamb Lane, Bricklayers Arms	Head	Mar	34	M	Victualler & Hawker	Herts	Hemel Hempstead
659	PROCTOR	Eliza	147		Wife	Mar	29	F		Herts	Flamstead
660	PROCTOR	George	147		Son		4	M	Scholar	Herts	Redbourn
661	PROCTOR	John	147		Son		2	M		Herts	Redbourn
662	PROCTOR	William	147		Son		5m	M		Herts	Redbourn
663	GREEN	Thomas	147		Lodger	Unm	39	M	Labourer	Herts	Redbourn

	SURNAME	FORENAME	SCHEDULE NUMBER	ADDRESS	RELATIONSHIP	STATUS	AGE	SEX	OCCUPATION	COUNTY OF BIRTH	PLACE OF BIRTH
664	CLARK	George	148	Lamb Lane	Head	Mar	35	M	Agric Lab	Beds	Luton
665	CLARK	Eliza	148		Wife	Mar	35	F	Plaiter	Herts	Redbourn
666	CLARK	William	148		Son		10	M	Straw Cutter	Herts	Redbourn
667	CLARK	Eliza	148		Dau		6	F	Scholar	Herts	Redbourn
668	POULTER	John	149	Lamb Lane	Head	Mar	31	M	Agric Lab	Herts	St Pauls Walden
669	POULTER	Sarah	149		Wife	Mar	30	F	Plaiter	Herts	Redbourn
670	POULTER	Alice	149		Dau		9	F	Plaiter	Herts	Redbourn
671	POULTER	William	149		Son		7	M		Herts	Redbourn
672	POULTER	Sarah	149		Dau		4	F		Herts	Redbourn
673	CHALKLEY	George	150	Lamb Lane	Head	Mar	23	M	Agric Lab	Herts	Redbourn
674	CHALKLEY	Eliza	150		Wife	Mar	19	F	Plaiter	Herts	Redbourn
675	CHALKLEY	Emma	150		Dau		under 1 m	F		Herts	Redbourn
676	CHRISTMAS	John	151	Lamb Lane	Head	Mar	50	M	Journeyman Blacksmith	Herts	Bennington
677	CHRISTMAS	Mary Ann	151		Wife	Mar	47	F	Plaiter	Herts	Redbourn
678	CHRISTMAS	Sarah	151		Dau	Unm	18	F	Plaiter	Herts	Redbourn
679	CHRISTMAS	Mary	151		Dau	Unm	15	F	Plaiter	Herts	Redbourn
680	CHRISTMAS	Owen W.	151		Son	Unm	11	M	Scholar	Herts	Redbourn
681	CHRISTMAS	Elizabeth	151		Dau		6	F	Scholar	Herts	Redbourn
682	CHRISTMAS	Emma	151		Dau		5	F	Scholar	Herts	Redbourn
683	BALDWIN	Thomas	152	Lamb Lane	Head	Mar	58	M	Agric Lab	Herts	Redbourn
684	BALDWIN	Fanny	152		Wife	Mar	56	F	Laundress	Middx	South Mimms
685	BALDWIN	Thomas	152		Son	Unm	26	M	Bricklayers Lab	Herts	Redbourn
686	BALDWIN	Eliza	152		Dau	Unm	16	F	Grass Hat Maker	Herts	Redbourn
687	BALDWIN	George	152		Son		12	M	Farm Lab	Herts	Redbourn
688	FRANKLIN	Alfred	153	Lamb Lane	Head	Mar	25	M	Straw Cutter	Herts	Redbourn
689	FRANKLIN	Mary	153		Wife	Mar	23	F	Bonnet Sewer	Herts	Redbourn
690	FRANKLIN	George	153		Son		3	M		Herts	Redbourn
691	FRANKLIN	Mary A.	153		Dau		1	F		Herts	Redbourn
692	MARSHALL	John	154	Lamb Lane	Head	Mar	25	M	Agric Lab	Herts	Redbourn
693	MARSHALL	Ann	154		Wife	Mar	28	F	Plaiter	Herts	Redbourn
694	GREEN	Elizabeth	155	Lamb Lane	Head	Mar	42	F	Farmers Wife	Herts	Redbourn
695	CURRELL	Elizabeth	155		Serv	Widow	59	F	Servant	Beds	Tilsworth
696	THOROGOOD	Henry	156	Lamb Lane	Head	Mar	23	M	Journeyman Carpenter	Herts	Redbourn
697	THOROGOOD	Emma	156		Wife	Mar	22	F	Bonnet Sewer	Herts	Redbourn
698	WOODSTOCK	Charles	157	Lamb Lane	Head	Mar	56	M	Master Blacksmith	Bucks	Chesham
699	WOODSTOCK	Sarah	157		Wife	Mar	62	F		Herts	Redbourn
700	DOLLING	Elizabeth S.	157		Grandau		6	F	Scholar	Middx	St Marylebone
701	ASLIN	Benjamin	158	Lamb Lane	Head	Mar	38	M	Agric Lab	Herts	Redbourn
702	ASLIN	Eliza	158		Wife	Mar	32	F	Plaiter	Herts	Studham
703	ASLIN	Charlotte E	158		Dau		10	F	Scholar	Herts	Redbourn
704	ASLIN	John	158		Son		4	M		Herts	Redbourn
705	ASLIN	Samuel	158		Son		2	M		Herts	Redbourn
706	ASLIN	Walter	158		Son		7 m	M		Herts	Redbourn
707	FENSOM	Elizabeth	159	Lamb Lane	Head	Widow	59	F	Plaiter 1/6d per week from Redbourn parish	Herts	St Pauls Walden

708	FENSOM	Ann	159		Dau	Unm	37	F	Plaiter	Herts	Redbourn
709	GROVER	Ann	159		Inmate	Unm	51	F	Formerly Chandler, parochial relief 1s per week Redbourn	Herts	Redbourn
710	POULTER	William	160	Lamb Lane	Head	Mar	33	M	Agric Lab	Herts	St Pauls Walden
711	POULTER	Mary	160		Wife	Mar	30	F	Plaiter	Herts	Redbourn
712	THOROGOOD	Charles	161	Lamb Lane	Head	Mar	26	M	Journeyman Carpenter	Herts	Redbourn
713	THOROGOOD	Sarah	161		Wife	Mar	27	F	Dressmaker	Herts	Wheathampstead
714	THOROGOOD	William	161		Son		1	M		Herts	Redbourn
715	BONNIC	Samuel	162	Lamb Lane	Head	Mar	48	M	Agric Lab	Herts	Harpenden
716	BONNIC	Martha	162		Wife	Mar	42	F	Plaiter	Herts	Redbourn
717	BONNIC	Samuel	162		Son	Unm	22	M	Labourer	Herts	Harpenden
718	BONNIC	James	162		Son	Unm	16	M	Labourer	Herts	Harpenden
719	BONNIC	Thomas	162		Son	Unm	14	M	Labourer	Herts	Harpenden
720	BONNIC	Mary	162		Dau	Unm	12	F	Scholar	Herts	Harpenden
721	BONNIC	George	162		Son	Unm	7	M	Scholar	Herts	Redbourn
722	BONNIC	Charles	162		Son	Unm	5	M	Scholar	Herts	Redbourn
723	BONNIC	Ann	162		Dau	Unm	2	F	Scholar	Herts	Redbourn
724	POWELL	Samuel	163	Lamb Lane	Head	Mar	51	M	Dealer	Northants	Towcester
725	POWELL	Eliza	163		Wife	Mar	38	F		Herts	Redbourn
726	POWELL	Eliza	163		Dau		12	F	Bonnet Sewer	Herts	Redbourn
727	POWELL	Emma	163		Dau		10	F	Plaiter	Herts	Redbourn
728	POWELL	Rebecca	163		Dau		9	F	Plaiter	Herts	Redbourn
729	POWELL	Henrietta	163		Dau		7	F	Plaiter	Herts	Redbourn
730	POWELL	John Thomas	163		Son		3	M		Herts	Redbourn
731	POWELL	Infant	163		Son		under 1 m	M		Herts	Redbourn
732	WHOOTON	Sarah	163		Serv	Widow	47	F	Monthly Nurse	Beds	Barton
733	WHOOTON	Charlotte	164	Lamb Lane	Head	Unm	24	F	Plaiter	Herts	Redbourn
734	WHOOTON	Sarah	164		Dau		2	F		Herts	Redbourn
735	WHOOTON	Joshua	164		Brother	Unm	18	M	Agric Lab	Herts	Redbourn
736	BLAIRD	John	165	Lamb Lane	Head	Mar	44	M	Agric Lab	Middx	Whetstone
737	BLAIRD	Mary	165		Wife	Mar	48	F	Charwoman	Herts	Berkhamsted
738	BLAIRD	Charles	165		Son	Unm	20	M	Agric Lab	Herts	Redbourn
739	BLAIRD	Elizabeth	165		Dau	Unm	18	F	Plaiter	Herts	Redbourn
740	MARE	Thomas	165		Brother-in-law	Unm	44	M	Parish Allowance (Idiot)	Herts	Redbourn
741	GREGG	Edmond	165		Nursechild		5	M		Herts	Redbourn
742	ABBOTT	Daniel	166	Lamb Lane	Head	Mar	53	M	Straw Dealer	Herts	Redbourn
743	ABBOTT	Ann	166		Wife	Mar	56	F	Straw Dealer	Herts	Redbourn
744	ABBOTT	Daniel	166		Son	Unm	17	M	Straw Dealer	Herts	Redbourn
745	ABBOTT	Ann	166		Dau	Unm	13	F	Bonnet Sewer	Herts	Redbourn
746	PETIT	James	167	Lamb Lane	Head	Mar	52	M	Jobbing Lab	Herts	Redbourn
747	PETIT	Susanna	167		Wife	Mar	54	F	Plaiter	Herts	Redbourn
748	PETIT	Elizabeth	167		Dau	Unm	16	F	Bonnet Sewer	Herts	Redbourn
749	HALSEY	Richard	168	Lamb Lane	Head	Mar	35	M	Lab	Herts	Redbourn
750	HALSEY	Matilda	168		Wife	Mar	29	F	Plaiter	Herts	Chipperfield [Kings Langley]

	SURNAME	FORENAME	SCHEDULE NUMBER	ADDRESS	RELATIONSHIP	STATUS	AGE	SEX	OCCUPATION	COUNTY OF BIRTH	PLACE OF BIRTH
751	HALSEY	Sarah	168		Dau	Unm	11	F	Plaiter	Herts	Redbourn
752	HALSEY	Eliza	168		Dau		2	F		Herts	Redbourn
753	CURD	Clara	168		Sister-in-law	Unm	18	F	Hand Loom Weaver	Herts	Redbourn
754	CURD	Ann	168		Sister-in-law	Unm	16	F	Bonnet Sewer	Herts	Redbourn
755	KING	John	169	Lamb Lane	Head	Mar	72	M	Agric Lab	London	Parish Unknown
756	KING	Ann	169		Wife	Mar	60	F		Herts	Flamstead
757	KING	Joseph	169		Son	Unm	34	M	Agric Lab	Herts	Flamstead
758	KING	Hannah	169		Dau	Unm	28	F	Plaiter	Herts	Harpenden
759	HILL	Josiah	169		Lodger	Unm	21	M	Agric Lab	Herts	Hemel Hempstead
760	COSTIN	Henry	170	Lamb Lane	Head	Mar	33	M	Plaiter	Berks	Slough
761	COSTIN	Ann	170		Wife	Mar	29	F	Plaiter	Beds	Leighton
762	COSTIN	Julia	170		Dau		3	F		Herts	Redbourn
763	GREEN	Joseph	171	Lamb Lane	Head	Mar	47	M	Agric Lab	Herts	Flamstead
764	GREEN	Alice	171		Wife	Mar	47	F	Plaiter	Beds	Whipsnade
765	GREEN	Mary	171		Dau	Unm	20	F	Plaiter	Herts	Flamstead
766	BURTON	Mary A.	171		Visitor		2	F		Herts	Redbourn
767	CHIPPERFIELD	Mary	172	Lamb Lane	Head	Widow	58	F	Laundress	Kent	Chalk
768	CHIPPERFIELD	Charles	172		Son	Unm	15	M	Scholar	Herts	Redbourn
769	SHARP	William	173	Lamb Lane	Head	Mar	68	M	Agric Lab	Herts	Kensworth
770	SHARP	Ann	173		Wife	Mar	60	F	Plaiter	Bucks	Marsworth
771	SHARP	Elizabeth	173		Dau	Unm	24	F		Herts	Flamstead
772	WEATHERHEAD	John	174	Lamb Lane	Head	Mar	39	M	Master Shoemaker	Herts	Flamstead
773	WEATHERHEAD	Harriett	174		Wife	Mar	37	F	Plaiter	Beds	Luton
774	WEATHERHEAD	Mary Ann	174		Dau	Unm	18	F	Plaiter	Herts	Redbourn
775	WEATHERHEAD	Eliza	174		Dau	Unm	10	F	Plaiter	Herts	Redbourn
776	WEATHERHEAD	Betsy	174		Dau		8	F	Scholar	Herts	Redbourn
777	WEATHERHEAD	John	174		Son		5	M	Scholar	Herts	Redbourn
778	WEATHERHEAD	Sophia	174		Dau		7m	F		Herts	Redbourn
779	ABRAHAMS	William	175	Lamb Lane	Head	Mar	22	M	Agric Lab	Beds	Dunstable
780	ABRAHAMS	Caroline	175		Wife	Mar	25	F	Plaiter	Herts	Flamstead
781	COOK	James	176	Lamb Lane	Head	Mar	48	M	Straw Dyer	Herts	Flamstead
782	COOK	Elizabeth	176		Wife	Mar	48	F	Plaiter	Herts	Flamstead
783	COOK	Mary	176		Dau	Unm	19	F	Bonnet Sewer	Herts	Flamstead
784	THOROGOOD	George	177	Lamb Lane	Head	Mar	45	M	Master Carpenter	Herts	Redbourn
785	THOROGOOD	Mary	177		Wife	Mar	44	F	Bonnet Sewer	Herts	Redbourn
786	THOROGOOD	John	177		Son	Unm	17	M	Carpenter	Herts	Redbourn
787	THOROGOOD	James	177		Son	Unm	15	M	Scholar	Herts	Redbourn
788	THOROGOOD	Adeliza	177		Dau		13	F	Scholar	Herts	Redbourn
789	THOROGOOD	William	177		Son		11	M	Scholar	Herts	Redbourn
790	THOROGOOD	Tryphena	177		Dau		7	F	Scholar	Herts	Redbourn
791	THOROGOOD	Emily	177		Dau		2	F		Herts	Redbourn
792	GREEN	Ann	178	Lamb Lane	Head	Unm	43	F	Plaiter	Herts	Redbourn
793	GREEN	Joseph	178		Father	Widower	75	M	Agric Lab	Herts	Redbourn
794	GREEN	Francis	178		Brother	Unm	27	M	Agric Lab	Herts	Redbourn

No.	Surname	Name	#	Place	Relation	Status	Age	Sex	Occupation	County	Birthplace
795	GREEN	Martha	178		Dau		13	F	Plaiter	Herts	Redbourn
796	GREEN	Jane	178		Dau		6	F	Plaiter	Herts	Redbourn
797	LAY	Martha	178		Inmate	Unm	25	F	Plaiter	Herts	Redbourn
798	LAY	Henry	178		Inmate		2	M		Herts	St Michaels

Three houses building

The end of the District 3a Redbourn parish, Hertfordshire

Registrar's District: Harpenden Enumeration District 3b Ref. HO 107/1713 folios 153-77

All that part of the parish of Redbourn which lies to the north west of the London and Holyhead Road and of the road called Lamb Lane near the Red Lion public house leading to Hempstead, including part of Redbourn Common, Church End, Revel End, Holsemere End, Agnels, North Place and farms within the said boundary.

No.	Surname	Name	#	Place	Relation	Status	Age	Sex	Occupation	County	Birthplace
799	PRATT	Edward	1	North Place	Head	Widower	53	M	Builder (5 men)	Herts	Redbourn
800	MAY	Mary	1		Dau	Mar	24	F	Housekeeper	Herts	Redbourn
801	MAY	Julia	1		Grandau		5	F	Scholar	Herts	Redbourn
802	MAY	Henry	1		Grandson		3	M	Scholar	Surrey	Mickleham
803	MAY	Edward	1		Grandson		11 m	M		Herts	Redbourn
804	ELMES	Elizabeth	1		Visitor	Widow	51	F	Dressmaker	Herts	St Albans
805	GEEVES	Elizabeth	1		Niece	Unm	16	F	Plaiter	Herts	Redbourn
806	OTWAY	William E.	2	North Place	Head	Mar	56	M	Assistant Overseer & Parish Clerk	Herts	Tewin
807	OTWAY	Ann	2		Wife	Mar	36	F	Domestic Duties	Middx	St Clement Danes - Westminster
808	OTWAY	Mary E.	2		Dau	Unm	14	F	Scholar	Herts	Welwyn
809	OTWAY	William A.	2		Son		12	M	Scholar	Herts	Welwyn
810	OTWAY	Sarah A.	2		Dau		9	F	Scholar	Herts	Welwyn
811	OTWAY	Thomas J.G.	2		Son		5	M	Scholar	Herts	Redbourn
812	OTWAY	Fanny M.M.	2		Dau		2	F		Herts	Redbourn
813	OTWAY	Ada F.	2		Dau		under 4 m	F		Herts	Redbourn
814	PRATT	John	3	North Place	Head	Mar	46	M	Builder (4 men)	Herts	Redbourn
815	PRATT	Caroline	3		Wife	Mar	31	F		Herts	Redbourn
816	PRATT	John F.	3		Son		11	M	Scholar	Herts	Redbourn
817	PRATT	Caroline	3		Dau		9	F	Scholar	Herts	Redbourn
818	PRATT	Samuel	3		Son		7	M	Scholar	Herts	Redbourn
819	PRATT	David	3		Son		4	M	Scholar	Herts	Redbourn
820	PRATT	Mary	3		Dau		2	F		Herts	Redbourn
821	PRATT	Martha	3		Dau		1	F		Herts	Redbourn
822	RUSH	William	3		Visitor	Mar	48	M	Tin Plate Worker	Beds	Bedford
823	AUBURN	Sarah	3		Serv	Unm	18	F	Domestic Servant	Herts	St Albans
824	HANSCOMBE	Ann	4	North Place	Head	Unm	56	F	From dividends, Independent	Herts	Hexton
825	HANSCOMBE	Jane	4		Sister	Unm	46	F	From dividends, Independent	Herts	Harpenden
826	HARBOROUGH	Micael	5	North Place	Head	Mar	28	M	Servant Groom	Herts	Redbourn
827	HARBOROUGH	Caroline	5		Wife	Mar	30	F		Herts	Gaddesden
828	HARBOROUGH	Charlotte	5		Dau	Unm	7	F	Scholar	Herts	Gaddesden
829	HARBOROUGH	Henry	5		Son	Unm	4	M	Scholar	Herts	Redbourn
830	HARBOROUGH	Elizabeth	5		Dau	Unm	1	F		Herts	Redbourn

	SURNAME	FORENAME	SCHEDULE NUMBER	ADDRESS	RELATIONSHIP	STATUS	AGE	SEX	OCCUPATION	COUNTY OF BIRTH	PLACE OF BIRTH
831	HARBOROUGH	Emma	5		Dau		3m	F		Herts	Redbourn
832	STONE	Eliza	6	North Place	Head	Mar	48	F	Bonnet Sewer	Middx	Whetstone
833	STONE	Catherine	6		Dau	Unm	16	F	Bonnet Sewer	Herts	Redbourn
834	STONE	Louisa	6		Dau	Unm	7	F	Scholar	Herts	Redbourn
835	KING	Thomas	7	North Place	Head	Mar	55	M	Journeyman, Blacksmith	Herts	Hertford
836	KING	Ann	7		Wife	Mar	63	F	Bonnet Sewer	Herts	Hitchin
837	EAMES	Mary	8	North Place	Head	Mar	58	F	Straw Plaiter	Herts	Redbourn
838	EAMES	Eliza	8		Dau	Unm	24	F	Straw Bonnet Sewer	Herts	Redbourn
839	EAMES	Elizabeth	8		Dau	Unm	20	F	Straw Bonnet Sewer	Herts	Redbourn
840	EAMES	Ann	8		Dau	Unm	18	F	Straw Bonnet Sewer	Herts	Redbourn
841	SMITH	John	9	North Place	Head	Mar	60	M	Agric Lab	Herts	Redbourn
842	SMITH	Sarah	9		Wife	Mar	55	F		Herts	Redbourn
843	SMITH	Mary Ann	9		Dau	Unm	30	F	Straw Bonnet Maker	Herts	Redbourn
844	SMITH	Eliza	9		Dau	Unm	25	F	Straw Bonnet Maker	Herts	Redbourn
845	MOORCROFT	John	10	North Place	Head	Mar	65	M	Poulterer	Beds	Leighton
846	MOORCROFT	Caroline [?]	10		Wife	Mar	44	F	Dressmaker	Herts	St Albans
847	MOORCROFT	Charles	10		Son	Unm	20	M	Dealer	Herts	Redbourn
848	MOORCROFT	Ebenezer	10		Son	Unm	17	M	Servant	Herts	Redbourn
849	MOORCROFT	Emily	10		Dau	Unm	13	F	Brazilian Hat Maker	Herts	Redbourn
850	MOORCROFT	William	10		Son		9	M	Scholar	Herts	Redbourn
851	MOORCROFT	Elizabeth	10		Dau		7	F	Scholar	Herts	Redbourn
852	MOORCROFT	Maria	10		Dau		5	F	Scholar	Herts	Redbourn
853	SANDERS	James	11	High Street	Head	Mar	39	M	Coal Dealer (1 Man)	Middx	Whetstone
854	SANDERS	Mary	11		Wife	Mar	36	F		Herts	Hemel Hempstead
855	SANDERS	Walter	11		Son		9	M	Scholar	Herts	Redbourn
856	SANDERS	Julia	11		Dau		5	F		Herts	Redbourn
857	STONE	Emma	11		Niece	Unm	18	F	Sewer	Herts	Redbourn
858	MILLER	Thomas	12	High Street	Head	Mar	40	M	Gardener	Wilts	Horningsham
859	MILLER	Martha	12		Wife	Mar	40	F		Wilts	Horningsham
860	MILLER	Herbert	12		Son	Unm	12	M	Scholar	Somerset	Camerton
861	MILLER	Harry	12		Son	Unm	10	M	Scholar	Somerset	Camerton
862	MILLER	Adolphus	12		Son		8	M	Scholar	Herts	Redbourn
863	MILLER	Jesse	12		Son		6	M	Scholar	Herts	Redbourn
864	MILLER	Augusta	12		Dau		4	F	Scholar	Herts	Redbourn
865	MILLER	Walter	12		Son		2	M		Herts	Redbourn
866	MILLER	Thomas	12		Son		3m	M		Herts	Redbourn
867	NICHOLLS	William	13	High Street	Head	Mar	32	M	Police Constable	Herts	Bayford
868	NICHOLLS	Elizabeth	13		Wife	Mar	40	F		Wilts	Chiseldon
869	NICHOLLS	Ann	13		Dau	Unm	14	F	Straw Plait Worker	Middx	Hornsey
870	NICHOLLS	Ruth	13		Dau	Unm	12	F	Straw Plait Worker	Herts	Widford
871	NICHOLLS	Elizabeth A.	13		Dau		9	F	Scholar	Surrey	Camberwell
872	NICHOLLS	Harriett	13		Dau		7	F	Scholar	Herts	Widford
873	NICHOLLS	William	13		Son		4	M	Scholar	Herts	Amwell
874	NICHOLLS	James S.	13		Son		under 5m	M		Herts	Redbourn

875	SMITH	Daniel	14	High Street	Head	Mar	42	M	Blacksmith & Grocer	Herts	Redbourn
876	SMITH	Sarah	14		Wife	Mar	49	F	Grocer	Herts	Redbourn
877	SANDERS	Henry	14		Son-in-law	Unm	18	M	Tailors Apprentice	Middx	Holborn
878	THOROGOOD	Joseph	15	High Street	Head	Mar	32	M	Journeyman Carpenter	Herts	Redbourn
879	THOROGOOD	Elizabeth	15		Wife	Mar	31	F	Sewer	Herts	Redbourn
880	THOROGOOD	Eliza	15		Dau	Unm	10	F	Scholar	Herts	Redbourn
881	THOROGOOD	Walter	15		Son		9	M	Scholar	Herts	Redbourn
882	JOHNSON	William	16	High Street	Head	Mar	29	M	Cordwainer	Herts	Redbourn
883	JOHNSON	Mary	16		Wife	Mar	34	F		Herts	Redbourn
884	JOHNSON	Elizabeth	16		Dau		5	F		Herts	Redbourn
885	JOHNSON	William	16		Son		2	M		Herts	Redbourn
886	JOHNSON	John	16		Son		1	M		Herts	Redbourn
887	PRATT	Thomas	17	High Street	Head	Mar	37	M	Journeyman, Bricklayer	Herts	Redbourn
888	PRATT	Sarah A.	17		Wife	Mar	38	F	Laundress	Herts	Hemel Hempstead
889	PRATT	Emily	17		Dau	Unm	6	F	Scholar	Herts	Redbourn
890	PRATT	Harriett	17		Dau		4	F	Scholar	Herts	Redbourn
891	PRATT	James	18	High Street (The Princes Head)	Head	Mar	40	M	Victualler	Herts	Redbourn
892	PRATT	Mary	18		Wife	Mar	38	F		Herts	Harpenden
893	PRATT	George	18		Son	Unm	14	M	Carpenters App.	Herts	Redbourn
894	HALSEY	Richard Snr	19	Lamb Lane	Head	Widower	81	M	Coal Dealer	Herts	Redbourn
895	COLLIER	Thomas	19		Lodger	Widower	59	M	Agric Lab	Herts	Harpenden
896	SAUNDERS	Alfred W.	20	Crouch Hall	Head	Mar	34	M	Farmer of 12 acres employing 1 man	Herts	Redbourn
897	SAUNDERS	Anne	20		Wife	Mar	40	F		[London]	St James, Westminster
898	SAUNDERS	Thomas D.	20		Son		5	M		Herts	Flamstead
899	SELLS	William	21	Blackhorse	Head	Mar	25	M	Victualler	Beds	Luton
900	SELLS	Eliza	21		Wife	Mar	21	F		Herts	Redbourn
901	SELLS	Charles	21		Son		7m	M		Herts	Redbourn
902	BRITMAN	William	21		Lodger	Mar	34	M	Agric Lab	Unknown	Unknown
903	ARBOROUGH	John	22	Cottage near Blackhorse	Head	Mar	55	M	Agric Lab	Beds	Luton
904	ARBOROUGH	Mary	22		Wife	Mar	53	F		Herts	Flamstead
905	ARBOROUGH	Emma	22		Dau	Unm	17	F	Sewer	Herts	Redbourn
906	ARBOROUGH	Jane	22		Dau	Unm	13	F	Sewer	Herts	Redbourn
907	GOODRICH	Thomas	23	Cottage near Blackhorse	Head	Mar	42	M	Shepherd	Herts	St Albans
908	GOODRICH	Susan	23		Wife	Mar	37	F		Herts	Hemel Hempstead
909	GOODRICH	Harriett	23		Dau	Unm	16	F	Sewer	Herts	Redbourn
910	GOODRICH	Emma	23		Dau	Unm	12	F	Sewer	Herts	Redbourn
911	PROCTOR	Fanny	23		Niece		4	F		London	London, Parish Not Known
912	SEABROOK	Susannah	24	Norrington End Farm	Head	Widow	62	F	Farming 101 acres, 1 man in doors	Herts	Redbourn
913	SEABROOK	George	24		Son	Unm	37	M	Farmers Son	Herts	Redbourn
914	SEABROOK	John	24		Son	Unm	33	M	Farmers Son	Herts	Redbourn
915	SEABROOK	Ann	24		Dau	Unm	27	F	Farmers Daur	Herts	Redbourn
916	SEABROOK	Eliza	24		Dau	Unm	25	F	Farmers Daur	Herts	Redbourn
917	SEABROOK	Alice	24		Dau	Unm	22	F	Farmers Daur	Herts	Redbourn

	SURNAME	FORENAME	SCHEDULE NUMBER	ADDRESS	RELATIONSHIP	STATUS	AGE	SEX	OCCUPATION	COUNTY OF BIRTH	PLACE OF BIRTH
918	SEABROOK	Emma M.	24		Dau	Unm	18	F	Farmers Daur	Herts	Redbourn
919	PALMER	Thomas	24		Serv	Unm	18	M	Hired Servant	Herts	Flamstead
920	SAUNDERS	George T.	25	Agnels Farm	Head	Mar	30	M	Farmer of 250 acres employing 8 labourers, 2 in doors	Herts	Redbourn
921	SAUNDERS	Fanny	25		Wife	Mar	25	F	Farmers Wife	Herts	Hemel Hempstead
922	SAUNDERS	Jane F.	25		Dau	Unm	3	F		Herts	Redbourn
923	SAUNDERS	Amy M.	25		Dau	Unm	2	F		Herts	Redbourn
924	SAUNDERS	Emily	25		Dau	Unm	1	F		Herts	Redbourn
925	MILLER	Ann	25		Serv	Unm	19	F	Household Servant	Bucks	Hardwicke
926	FRANKLIN	Sarah	25		Serv		14	F	Nursemaid	Herts	Hemel Hempstead
927	BELCHER	Thomas	25		Serv	Unm	18	M	Serv	Herts	Harpenden
928	HOBBS	Thomas	25		Serv	Unm	19	M	Serv	Herts	Flamstead

Two cottages uninhabited

	SURNAME	FORENAME	SCHEDULE NUMBER	ADDRESS	RELATIONSHIP	STATUS	AGE	SEX	OCCUPATION	COUNTY OF BIRTH	PLACE OF BIRTH
929	JORDAN	William	26	Nichols Farm	Head	Mar	60	M	Bailiff	Beds	Meppershall
930	JORDAN	Ruth	26		Wife	Mar	70	F		Herts	Offley
931	LAWRENCE	Hannah	26		Serv	Unm	20	F	Maid of all work	Herts	Kings Walden
932	BIGG	Thomas	26		Serv	Unm	25	M	Agric Lab	Herts	Harpenden
933	MASON	William	26		Serv	Unm	18	M	Agric Lab	Herts	Childwick [St Michaels]
934	DEACON	Matthew	26		Serv	Unm	18	M	Agric Lab	Herts	Redbourn
935	EMERTON	John	27	Holtsmere End	Head	Mar	35	M	Agric Lab	Beds	Luton
936	EMERTON	Harriett	27		Wife	Mar	35	F		Beds	Barton
937	SYGRAVE	Emma	27		Niece	Unm	8	F		Herts	Harpenden
938	FALLDER	William	28	Holtsmere End	Head	Mar	33	M	Agric Lab	Beds	Barton
939	FALLDER	Hannah	28		Wife	Mar	29	F	Plaiter	Herts	Redbourn
940	FALLDER	Emma	28		Dau	Unm	7	F	Plaiter	Herts	Redbourn
941	FALLDER	Hannah	28		Dau	Unm	2	F		Herts	Redbourn
942	SHERWOOD	Ann	29	Revel End Farm	Head	Widow	31	F	Farmer of 200 acres employing 5 labourers	Herts	Kings Langley
943	SHERWOOD	John	29		Son	Unm	4	M		London	[London] Newgate Street
944	GRAVESTOCK	Daniel	29		Serv	Unm	17	M	Agric Lab	Herts	Redbourn
945	BANGS	Eliza	29		Serv	Unm	29	F	House Servant	Herts	Kimpton
946	FENN	John	29		Serv	Unm	35	M	Farm Bailiff	Herts	Redbourn
947	ELWOOD	Edward	29		Serv	Unm	25	M	Agric Lab	Herts	St Stephens
948	HODSDEN	Samuel	30	Revel End Cottage	Head	Mar	50	M	Agric Lab	Herts	Park Street [St Stephens]
949	HODSDEN	Susan	30		Wife	Mar	48	F		Bucks	Whelpley Hill [?]
950	SEABROOK	William	31	Revel End Cottage	Head	Mar	26	M	Agric Lab	Herts	Redbourn
951	SEABROOK	Charlotte	31		Wife	Mar	21	F	Plaiter	Herts	Redbourn
952	SEABROOK	Charles	31		Son		4m	M		Herts	Redbourn
953	BOGGIS	George	32	Revel End Cottage	Head	Mar	29	M	Gardener	Suffolk	Clare
954	BOGGIS	Mary	32		Wife	Mar	29	F	Formerly Milliner	London	[London] Bloomsbury
955	BOGGIS	Mary Ann	32		Dau		3	F		Middx	Bow
956	BOGGIS	George	32		Son		1	M		Herts	Redbourn
957	FENN	Mary Ann	33	Revel End Farm	Head	Widow	56	F	Farmers Widow 175 acres 5 labourers	Herts	Redbourn

958	FENN	Elizabeth	33		Dau	Unm	30	F	Farmers Daur	Herts	Redbourn
959	FENN	Emma S.	33		Dau	Unm	24	F	Farmers Daur	Herts	Redbourn
960	FENN	Alfred J.	33		Son	Unm	21	M	Farmers Son	Herts	Redbourn
961	FENN	Jane	33		Dau	Unm	15	F	Farmers Daur	Herts	Redbourn
962	FENN	Catherine	33		Dau	Unm	13	F	Scholar	Herts	Redbourn
963	FENN	Louisa	33		Dau	Unm	10	F	Scholar	Herts	Redbourn
964	PENNY	James	33		Serv	Unm	19	M	Farm Servant	Herts	Redbourn
965	DOLLIMORE	Charles	33		Serv	Unm	15	M	Farm Servant	Herts	Redbourn
966	SEABROOK	George	34	Revel End Lodge	Head	Mar	54	M	Agric Lab	Herts	Hemel Hempstead
967	SEABROOK	Mary	34		Wife	Mar	48	F	Plaiter	Herts	Redbourn
968	SEABROOK	Thomas	34		Son	Unm	23	M	Agric Lab	Herts	Redbourn
969	SEABROOK	Ann	34		Dau	Unm	19	F	Plaiter	Herts	Redbourn
970	SEABROOK	Ellen	34		Dau	Unm	14	F	Plaiter	Herts	Redbourn
971	FAIRCLOTH	Frederick	35	Fosters Farm	Head	Mar	46	M	Bailiff of 140 acres 8 Lab	Herts	North Mimms
972	FAIRCLOTH	Susan	35		Wife	Mar	45	F		Herts	Wheathampstead
973	FAIRCLOTH	Susan	35		Dau	Unm	19	F		Herts	Hatfield
974	FAIRCLOTH	Eliza	35		Dau	Unm	16	F		Herts	Hatfield
975	FAIRCLOTH	Mary Ann	35		Dau		7	F		Herts	Harpenden
976	FAIRCLOTH	Emma	35		Grandau		9 m	F		Herts	Redbourn
977	NORTH	William	35		Serv	Unm	19	M	Shepherd	Herts	St Albans
978	SEABROOK	William	35		Serv	Unm	18	M	Horse Keeper	Herts	St Albans
979	TAYLOR	William	36	Camps Meadow	Head	Mar	28	M	Agric Lab	Herts	Redbourn
980	TAYLOR	Jane	36		Wife	Mar	26	F	Plaiter	Herts	London Colney
981	TAYLOR	Ann	36		Dau		5	F	Plaiter	Herts	Redbourn
982	TAYLOR	Emma	36		Dau		4	F		Herts	Redbourn
983	TAYLOR	Jane	36		Dau		0	F		Herts	Redbourn
984	ABBOTT	William	37	Camps Meadow	Head	Mar	56	M	Agric Lab	Herts	Redbourn
985	ABBOTT	Ann	37		Wife	Mar	54	F	Monthly Nurse	Herts	Hemel Hempstead
986	ALLEN	John	38	Camps Meadow	Head	Mar	45	M	Agric Lab	Herts	Redbourn
987	ALLEN	Eliza	38		Wife	Mar	41	F	Plaiter	Herts	Harpenden
988	WARREN	Charles	38		Lodger	Unm	19	M	Agric Lab	Herts	Harpenden
989	LIBERTY	Henry	38		Visitor	Unm	8	M	Plaiter	Herts	Redbourn
990	LIBERTY	William	39	Camps Meadow	Head	Widower	65	M	Agric Lab	Herts	Kensworth
991	LIBERTY	Eliza	39		Dau	Unm	23	F	Plaiter	Herts	Kensworth
992	SEABROOK	James	40	Camps Meadow Church End	Head	Mar	45	M	Agric Lab & Beer Shop Keeper	Herts	Harpenden
993	SEABROOK	Ann	40		Wife	Mar	42	F		Herts	Harpenden
994	SEABROOK	George	40		Son	Unm	17	M	Shepherd	Herts	Harpenden
995	WHITEHEAD	William	41	Church End	Head	Mar	21	M	Agric Lab	Herts	Redbourn
996	WHITEHEAD	Mary	41		Wife	Mar	18	F	Plaiter	Herts	Redbourn
997	PLOWMAN	Joseph	42	Church End	Head	Mar	58	M	Agric Lab	Beds	Lilley
998	PLOWMAN	Esther	42		Wife	Mar	57	F	Domestic Duties	Beds	Lilley
999	PLOWMAN	David	42		Son	Unm	28	M	Imbecile mind from fits	Herts	Redbourn
1000	PLOWMAN	Emma	42		Dau	Unm	25	F	Cook out of Place	Herts	Redbourn
1001	PLOWMAN	Harriett	42		Dau	Unm	18	F	Plaiter	Herts	Redbourn

	SURNAME	FORENAME	SCHEDULE NUMBER	ADDRESS	RELATIONSHIP	STATUS	AGE	SEX	OCCUPATION	COUNTY OF BIRTH	PLACE OF BIRTH
1002	PLOWMAN	Eliza	42		Dau	Unm	13	F	Plaiter	Herts	Redbourn
1003	WHEELER	George	43	Church End	Head	Mar	43	M	Agric Lab	Herts	Redbourn
1004	WHEELER	Esther	43		Wife	Mar	41	F	Straw Plaiter	Herts	Redbourn
1005	WHEELER	Eliza	43		Dau	Unm	16	F	Straw Plaiter	Herts	Redbourn
1006	WHEELER	John	43		Son	Unm	7	M	Scholar	Herts	Redbourn
1007	WHEELER	George	43		Son	Unm	3	M		Herts	Redbourn
1008	WHEELER	Hannah	43		Dau		6m	F		Herts	Redbourn
1009	HARDWICK	James	44	Church End	Head	Mar	46	M	Agric Lab	Beds	Upper Graveness [Gravenhurst]
1010	HARDWICK	Mary Ann	44		Wife	Mar	40	F	Domestic Duties	Herts	Redbourn
1011	HARDWICK	William	44		Son	Unm	13	M	Farm Serv	Herts	Redbourn
1012	HARDWICK	Joseph	44		Son	Unm	11	M	Farm Serv	Herts	Redbourn
1013	HARDWICK	Sarah	44		Dau	Unm	9	F	Scholar	Herts	Redbourn
1014	HARDWICK	Susan	44		Dau	Unm	5	F	Scholar	Herts	Redbourn
1015	HARDWICK	Mary Ann	44		Dau	Unm	2	F		Herts	Redbourn
1016	PALMER	John	45	Church End	Head	Unm	73	M	Retired Servant & Fundholder	Herts	Flamstead
1017	LUNNON	William	46		Head	Mar	38	M	Agric Lab	Herts	Harpenden
1018	LUNNON	Ann	46		Wife	Mar	34	F	Domestic Duties at Home	Herts	Redbourn
1019	LUNNON	Ann	46		Dau	Unm	13	F	Plaiter	Herts	Redbourn
1020	LUNNON	Joseph	46		Son	Unm	11	M	Scholar	Herts	Redbourn
1021	LUNNON	George	46		Son	Unm	9	M	Scholar	Herts	Redbourn
1022	LUNNON	Esther	46		Dau	Unm	8	F	Scholar	Herts	Redbourn
1023	LUNNON	Edwin	46		Son	Unm	2	M		Herts	Redbourn
1024	ABBOTT	John	47	Church End	Head	Mar	30	M	Baker	Herts	Flamstead
1025	ABBOTT	Ann	47		Wife	Mar	23	F		Herts	Harpenden

One house uninhabited

	SURNAME	FORENAME	SCHEDULE NUMBER	ADDRESS	RELATIONSHIP	STATUS	AGE	SEX	OCCUPATION	COUNTY OF BIRTH	PLACE OF BIRTH
1026	WHITELOCK	Joseph	48	Church End	Head	Mar	47	M	Agric Lab	Herts	Redbourn
1027	WHITELOCK	Sarah	48		Wife	Mar	46	F	Charwoman	Beds	Luton
1028	WHITELOCK	Daniel	48		Son	Unm	12	M	Scholar	Herts	Redbourn
1029	WHITELOCK	Sarah	48		Dau	Unm	8	F	Scholar	Herts	Redbourn
1030	FIELD	John	48		Son-in-law	Mar	30	M	Agric Lab	Herts	Hatfield
1031	FIELD	Martha	48		Dau	Mar	24	F	Plaiter	Herts	Redbourn
1032	FIELD	Joseph	48		Grandson		2	M		Herts	Redbourn
1033	FIELD	John	48		Grandson		1	M		Herts	Redbourn
1034	KIMPTON	John	49	Church End	Head	Mar	29	M	Agric Lab	Herts	Baldock
1035	KIMPTON	Caroline	49		Wife	Mar	31	F	Plaiter	Herts	Redbourn
1036	KIMPTON	Sarah	49		Dau		6	F		Herts	Redbourn
1037	KIMPTON	Thomas	49		Son		3	M		Herts	Redbourn
1038	KIMPTON	William	49		Son		4m	M		Herts	Redbourn
1039	ABBOTT	Sarah	49		Visitor	Unm	14	F	Plaiter	Herts	Redbourn
1040	HALL	John	50	Church End	Head	Mar	34	M	Agric Lab	Herts	Flamstead
1041	HALL	Charlotte	50		Wife	Mar	28	F	Plaiter	Herts	Harpenden
1042	HALL	Mary	50		Dau	Unm	8	F	Idiot child	Herts	Redbourn
1043	HALL	Abraham	50		Son		6m	M		Herts	Redbourn
1044	POLLARD	Charity	51	Church End	Head	Mar	49	F	Plaiter	Herts	Redbourn

1045	POLLARD	Alice	51		Dau	Unm	22	F	Plaiter	Herts	Redbourn
1046	POLLARD	Henry	51		Son	Unm	15	M	Agric Lab	Herts	Redbourn
1047	POLLARD	Josiah	51		Son	Unm	11	M	Plaiter	Herts	Redbourn
1048	HALSEY	Maria	52	Church End	Head	Widow	45	F	Plaiter	Herts	St Pauls Walden
1049	HALSEY	George	52		Son	Mar	22	M	Sawyer	Herts	Redbourn
1050	HALSEY	Sarah	52		Dau	Unm	20	F	Plaiter	Herts	Redbourn
1051	HALSEY	Henry	52		Son	Unm	18	M	Agric Lab	Herts	Redbourn
1052	HALSEY	Josiah	52		Son	Unm	15	M	Agric Lab	Herts	Redbourn
1053	HALSEY	Mary	52		Dau	Unm	13	F	Plaiter	Herts	Redbourn
1054	HALSEY	Emily	52		Dau	Unm	10	F	Plaiter	Herts	Redbourn
1055	HALSEY	Eliza	52		Dau		7	F	Plaiter	Herts	Redbourn
1056	POLLARD	James	53	Church End	Head	Mar	56	M	Carrier	Herts	Hatfield
1057	POLLARD	Ann	53		Wife	Mar	54	F	Plait Dealer	Herts	Redbourn
1058	POLLARD	John	53		Son	Mar	28	M	Fishmonger	Herts	Redbourn
1059	POLLARD	Samuel	53		Son	Unm	17	M	Plaiter	Herts	Redbourn
1060	POLLARD	Thomas	53		Son		10	M	Plaiter	Herts	Redbourn
1061	POLLARD	William	53		Son		8	M	Plaiter	Herts	Redbourn
1062	POLLARD	Caroline	53		Dau-in-law	Mar	21	F	Plaiter	Herts	Harpenden
1063	POLLARD	Henry	53		Grandson		4	M		Herts	Redbourn
1064	POLLARD	Thomas	53		Grandson		1	M		Herts	Redbourn
1065	FALLDER	John	54	Church End	Head	Mar	42	M	Agric Lab	Herts	Harpenden
1066	FALLDER	Sophia	54		Wife	Mar	36	F		Herts	Redbourn
1067	FALLDER	Elizabeth	54		Dau	Unm	16	F	Plaiter	Herts	Redbourn
1068	FALLDER	William	54		Son	Unm	14	M	Labourer	Herts	Redbourn
1069	FALLDER	George	54		Son		10	M	Plaiter	Herts	Redbourn
1070	FALLDER	Charles	54		Son		8	M	Plaiter	Herts	Redbourn
1071	FALLDER	Thomas	54		Son		6	M	Plaiter	Herts	Redbourn
1072	FALLDER	Mary Ann	54		Dau		4	F		Herts	Redbourn
1073	FALLDER	Rose	54		Dau		2	F		Herts	Redbourn
1074	ATTWOOD	William	55	Church End	Head	Widower	59	M	Gardener	Herts	Flamstead
1075	ATTWOOD	Joseph	55		Son	Unm	20	M	Labourer	Herts	Redbourn
1076	READING	William	56	Church End	Head	Mar	48	M	Agric Lab	Herts	Redbourn
1077	READING	Ann	56		Wife	Mar	40	F	Plaiter	Herts	Redbourn
1078	STRATFORD	John	57	Church End	Head	Mar	81	M	Relief from Parish 2/6d per week	Herts	Harpenden
1079	STRATFORD	Sarah	57		Wife	Mar	73	F	Plaiter	Herts	Harpenden
1080	STRATFORD	William	57		Son	Widower	30	M	Agric Lab	Herts	Harpenden
1081	STRATFORD	William	57		Grandson		2	M		Herts	Redbourn
1082	ARBORN	Joseph	58	Church End	Head	Mar	32	M	Agric Lab	Herts	Harpenden
1083	ARBORN	Sarah	58		Wife	Mar	32	F	Plaiter	Beds	Luton
1084	ARBORN	Eliza	58		Dau	Unm	12	F	Plaiter	Herts	Redbourn
1085	ARBORN	Hannah	58		Dau		8	F	Plaiter	Herts	Redbourn
1086	ARBORN	Emma	58		Dau		4	F		Herts	Redbourn
1087	ARBORN	Theresa	58		Dau		under 2 m	F		Herts	Redbourn
1088	SAGE	Thomas	59	Church End	Head	Mar	39	M	Agric Lab	Herts	Redbourn

	SURNAME	FORENAME	SCHEDULE NUMBER	ADDRESS	RELATIONSHIP	STATUS	AGE	SEX	OCCUPATION	COUNTY OF BIRTH	PLACE OF BIRTH
1089	SAGE	Elizabeth	59		Wife	Mar	39	F	Plaiter	Herts	Kensworth
1090	SAGE	Ann	59		Dau	Unm	16	F	Plaiter	Herts	Redbourn
1091	SAGE	Charlotte	59		Dau		11	F	Plaiter	Herts	Redbourn
1092	SAGE	George	59		Son		8	M	Plaiter	Herts	Redbourn
1093	SAGE	William	59		Son		5	M	Plaiter	Herts	Redbourn
1094	QUICK	James	60	Church End	Head	Mar	25	M	Agric Lab	Herts	Redbourn
1095	QUICK	Emma	60		Wife	Mar	25	F	Plaiter	Herts	Redbourn
1096	QUICK	George	60		Son	Unm	3	M		Herts	Redbourn
1097	QUICK	William	60		Son		1	M		Herts	Redbourn
1098	HELBORN	George	61	Church End	Head	Mar	45	M	Agric Lab	Herts	St Albans
1099	HELBORN	Sarah	61		Wife	Mar	42	F	Plaiter	Herts	Harpenden
1100	HELBORN	George	61		Son	Unm	20	M	Agric Lab	Herts	Redbourn
1101	HELBORN	Elizabeth	61		Dau	Unm	18	F	Plaiter	Herts	Redbourn
1102	HELBORN	Sarah	61		Dau	Unm	15	F	Plaiter	Herts	Redbourn
1103	HELBORN	Mary	61		Dau	Unm	12	F	Plaiter	Herts	Redbourn
1104	HELBORN	Eliza	61		Dau		10	F	Plaiter	Herts	Redbourn
1105	HELBORN	James	61		Son		8	M	Farm Serv	Herts	Redbourn
1106	HELBORN	William	61		Son		5	M		Herts	Redbourn
1107	HELBORN	Joseph	61		Son		2	M		Herts	Redbourn
1108	ABRAMS	Joseph	62	Church End	Head	Mar	50	M	Agric Lab	Bucks	Mentmore
1109	ABRAMS	Mary	62		Wife	Mar	45	F	Plaiter	Herts	Berkhamsted
1110	ABRAMS	Mary	62		Dau	Unm	24	F	Plaiter	Herts	Redbourn
1111	ABRAMS	Sarah	62		Dau	Unm	18	F	Plaiter	Herts	Redbourn
1112	ABRAMS	Ann	62		Dau	Unm	13	F	Plaiter	Herts	Redbourn
1113	ABRAMS	Eliza	62		Dau	Unm	11	F	Plaiter	Herts	Redbourn
1114	HOWARD	Ellen	63	Church End	Head	Widow	68	F	Plaiter	Herts	Redbourn
1115	HOWARD	Emma	63		Dau	Unm	27	F	Plaiter	Herts	Redbourn
1116	BUNNAGE	William	64	Church End	Head	Mar	35	M	Agric Lab	Herts	Harpenden
1117	BUNNAGE	Mary	64		Wife	Mar	35	F	Plaiter	Herts	Redbourn
1118	TRAVELLEN	Sarah	64		Visitor	[Unm]	9	F	Plaiter	Herts	Bovingdon
1119	TRAVELLEN	Mary	64		Visitor	[Widow?]	65	F	Plaiter	Herts	Harpenden
1120	WINCHESTER	Joseph	65	Church End	Head	Mar	43	M	Cows Leech (see Vet Surgeon)	Herts	Redbourn
1121	WINCHESTER	Lydia	65		Wife	Mar	39	F	Domestic Duties	Herts	Redbourn
1122	WINCHESTER	Mary	65		Dau	Unm	18	F	Sewer	Herts	Redbourn
1123	WINCHESTER	Joseph	65		Son		9	M	Scholar	Herts	Redbourn
1124	WINCHESTER	William	65		Son		5	M	Scholar	Herts	Redbourn
1125	WINCHESTER	Charles	65		Son		2	M		Herts	Redbourn
1126	ASLIN	Avery	66	Church End	Head	Mar	37	M	Straw Factor	Herts	Redbourn
1127	ASLIN	Mary	66		Wife	Mar	38	F	Straw Factor	Beds	Luton
1128	SMITH	Jeremiah	66		Visitor	Widower	76	M	Straw Cutter	Beds	Chorl End [?]
1129	READING	Thomas	67	Church End	Head	Mar	50	M	Agric Lab	Herts	Redbourn
1130	READING	Sarah	67		Wife	Mar	48	F	Plaiter	Herts	Redbourn
1131	READING	Ann	67		Dau	Unm	27	F	Plaiter	Herts	Redbourn
1132	READING	Rebecca	67		Dau	Unm	25	F	Plaiter	Herts	Redbourn

1133	READING	Thomas	67		Son	Unm	16	M	Agric Lab	Herts	Redbourn
1134	READING	William	67		Son	Unm	14	M	Agric Lab	Herts	Redbourn
1135	READING	Betsey	67		Dau	Unm	12	F	Plaiter	Herts	Redbourn
1136	READING	George	67		Son	Unm	10	M	Plaiter	Herts	Redbourn
1137	READING	Albert	67		Son	Unm	8	M	Plaiter	Herts	Redbourn
1138	READING	Jane	67		Grandau		1 m	F		Herts	Redbourn
1139	ABBOTT	Charles	68	Church End	Head	Mar	50	M	Straw Factor	Herts	Redbourn
1140	ABBOTT	Hannah	68		Wife	Mar	49	F	Plaiter	Herts	Redbourn
1141	ABBOTT	Mary Ann	68		Dau	Unm	24	F	Plaiter	Herts	Redbourn
1142	ABBOTT	Ann	68		Dau	Unm	16	F	Plaiter	Herts	Redbourn
1143	ABBOTT	Hannah	68		Dau	Unm	8	F	Plaiter	Herts	Redbourn
1144	KINGHAM	George	69	Church End	Head	Mar	50	M	Lab at Mill	Beds	Barton
1145	KINGHAM	Rachael	69		Wife	Mar	47	F	Plaiter	Herts	Redbourn
1146	KINGHAM	Caroline	69		Dau	Unm	15	F	Plaiter	Herts	Redbourn
1147	KINGHAM	Edward	69		Son	Unm	10	M	Agric Lab	Herts	Redbourn
1148	KINGHAM	Hannah	69		Dau		8	F	Plaiter	Herts	Redbourn
1149	KINGHAM	Susan	69		Dau		5	F	Plaiter	Herts	Redbourn
1150	TAYLOR	William	70	Church End	Head	Mar	32	M	Agric Lab	Herts	Redbourn
1151	TAYLOR	Eliza	70		Wife	Mar	25	F	Plaiter	Bucks	Ringshall
1152	TAYLOR	David	70		Son		2	M		Herts	Redbourn
1153	TAYLOR	Walter J.	70		Son		under 1 m	M		Herts	Redbourn
1154	WALTERTON	Maria	70		Visitor	Unm	21	F	Lace Maker	Bucks	Ringshall
1155	THOROGOOD	Thomas	71	Church End	Head	Mar	28	M	Agric Lab	Herts	Redbourn
1156	THOROGOOD	Jane	71		Wife	Mar	29	F	Plaiter	Herts	Redbourn
1157	THOROGOOD	George	71		Son		3	M		Herts	Redbourn
1158	SEARS	Rebecca	71		Niece		3 m	F		Herts	Redbourn
1159	TAYLOR	Benjamin	72	Church End	Head	Mar	32	M	Agric Lab	Herts	Redbourn
1160	TAYLOR	Ann	72		Wife	Mar	32	F	Plaiter	Beds	Luton
1161	IMPEY	Mary Ann	72		Niece	Unm	12	F	Plaiter	Herts	Redbourn
1162	IMPEY	Emma	72		Niece		7	F	Plaiter	London	[London] Parish Not Known
1163	HEDGES	James	73	Church End	Head	Mar	35	M	Agric Lab	Herts	Flamstead
1164	HEDGES	Mary Ann	73		Wife	Mar	40	F	Plaiter	Herts	Harpenden
1165	STRATFORD	Mary	73		Niece	Unm	4	F		Herts	Redbourn
1166	BRICK	John	74	Church End	Head	Mar	50	M	Agric Lab	Beds	Luton
1167	BRICK	Elizabeth	74		Wife	Mar	50	F	Plaiter	Herts	Redbourn
1168	HODSDEN	William	74		Visitor	Unm	22	M	Agric Lab	Herts	Redbourn
1169	MALIN	John	75	Church End	Head	Mar	47	M	Gardener	Herts	Redbourn
1170	MALIN	Elizabeth	75		Wife	Mar	42	F	Plaiter	Herts	Redbourn
1171	MALIN	Ann	75		Dau	Unm	14	F	Sewer of Bonnets	Herts	Redbourn
1172	MALIN	Thomas	75		Son		11	M	Scholar	Herts	Redbourn
1173	MALIN	David	75		Son		9	M	Scholar	Herts	Redbourn
1174	MALIN	Sarah	75		Dau		6	F	Plaiter	Herts	Redbourn
1175	MALIN	Daniel	75		Son		4	M		Herts	Redbourn
1176	MALIN	Emma	75		Dau		1	F		Herts	Redbourn

	SURNAME	FORENAME	SCHEDULE NUMBER	ADDRESS	RELATIONSHIP	STATUS	AGE	SEX	OCCUPATION	COUNTY OF BIRTH	PLACE OF BIRTH
1177	POCOCK	Mary	76	Church End (Vicarage)	Head	Widow	47	F	Bonnet Sewer	Bucks	Aylesbury
1178	POCOCK	Sarah R.	76		Dau	Unm	28	F	Bonnet Sewer	Herts	Redbourn
1179	POCOCK	Mary	76		Dau	Unm	24	F	Bonnet Sewer	Herts	Redbourn

Two cottages uninhabited

	SURNAME	FORENAME	SCHEDULE NUMBER	ADDRESS	RELATIONSHIP	STATUS	AGE	SEX	OCCUPATION	COUNTY OF BIRTH	PLACE OF BIRTH
1180	HEBBES	David	77	Church End	Head	Mar	48	M	Carpenter	Herts	Redbourn
1181	HEBBES	Charlotte	77		Wife	Mar	48	F	Plaiter	Herts	Redbourn
1182	PRATT	Nancy	77		Dau	Mar	27	F	Plaiter	Herts	Redbourn
1183	PRATT	Elizabeth	77		Grandau		2	F		Herts	Redbourn
1184	PRATT	Clement	77		Grandson		2m	M		Herts	Redbourn
1185	MOODY	Henry	78	Church End	Head	Widower	37	M	Agric Lab	Herts	Redbourn
1186	MOODY	George	78		Son		12	M	Agric Lab	Herts	Redbourn
1187	MOODY	Sarah	78		Dau		9	F	Plaiter	Herts	Redbourn
1188	MOODY	Amy	78		Dau		7	F	Plaiter	Herts	Redbourn
1189	MOODY	Henry	78		Son		2	M		Herts	Redbourn
1190	SWAINSON	William	78		Brother-in-law	Mar	27	M	Agric Lab	Herts	Kings Walden
1191	SWAINSON	Mary	78		Sister-in-law	Mar	22	F	Plaiter	Herts	Redbourn
1192	SWAINSON	Elizabeth	78		Niece		1	F		Herts	Redbourn
1193	MOODY	Moses	79	Church End	Head	Mar	40	M	Straw Cutter	Herts	Redbourn
1194	MOODY	Elizabeth	79		Wife	Mar	40	F	Plaiter	Beds	Luton
1195	MOODY	Sarah	79		Niece	Unm	9	F	Plaiter	Herts	Redbourn
1196	HALSEY	Thomas	80	Church End	Head	Mar	60	M	Sawyer	Herts	Redbourn
1197	HALSEY	Mary	80		Wife	Mar	48	F	Plaiter	Herts	Redbourn
1198	HALSEY	Nancy	80		Dau	Unm	27	F	Plaiter	Herts	Redbourn
1199	HALSEY	James	80		Son	Unm	20	M	Sawyer	Herts	Redbourn
1200	HALSEY	Charlotte	80		Dau	Unm	16	F	Plaiter	Herts	Redbourn
1201	HALSEY	Edmund	80		Son	Unm	13	M	Plaiter	Herts	Redbourn
1202	HALSEY	Phebe	80		Dau		11	F	Plaiter	Herts	Redbourn
1203	HALSEY	Walter	80		Son		9	M	Plaiter	Herts	Redbourn
1204	HALSEY	David	80		Son		5	M	Plaiter	Herts	Redbourn
1205	ALLCOCK	Daniel	81	Church End	Head	Mar	44	M	Bricklayers Lab	Herts	Redbourn
1206	ALLCOCK	Charlotte	81		Wife	Mar	38	F	Plaiter	Herts	Redbourn
1207	PENNY	Henry	81		Son-in-law	Unm	18	M	Agric Lab	Herts	Redbourn
1208	SKINNER	Joseph	82	Church End	Head	Mar	24	M	Farm Servant	Herts	Redbourn
1209	SKINNER	Mary	82		Wife	Mar	24	F	Plaiter	Herts	Redbourn
1210	SKINNER	Emma	82		Dau		3	F		Herts	Redbourn
1211	HOOTON	Elizabeth	83	Church End	Head	Widow	55	F	Plaiter	Herts	Redbourn
1212	HOOTON	Jesse	83		Son	Unm	30	M	Plaiter	Herts	Redbourn
1213	HOOTON	Daniel	83		Son	Unm	21	M	Agric Lab	Herts	Redbourn
1214	HOOTON	Sarah	83		Dau	Unm	19	F	Plaiter	Herts	Redbourn
1215	HOOTON	Isaac	83		Son		14	M	Labourer	Herts	Redbourn
1216	HOOTON	Benjamin W.	83		Grandson		4	M		London	[London]
1217	TENNANT	Joseph	84	Church End	Head	Mar	34	M	Agric Lab	Beds	Luton
1218	TENNANT	Charity	84		Wife	Mar	34	F		Herts	Redbourn
1219	TENNANT	Eliza	84		Dau	Unm	12	F	Plaiter	Herts	Redbourn

1220	TENNANT	Betsey	84		Dau		10	F	Plaiter	Herts	Redbourn
1221	TENNANT	William	84		Son		7	M	Plaiter	Herts	Redbourn
1222	TENNANT	Ann	84		Dau		5	F	Plaiter	Herts	Redbourn
1223	TENNANT	Sarah	84		Dau		2	F		Herts	Redbourn
1224	TENNANT	Fanny	84		Dau		5 m	F		Herts	Redbourn
1225	HOPCROFT	John	85	Church End (Holly Bush)	Head	Mar	43	M	Victualler	Herts	Little Gaddesden
1226	HOPCROFT	Mary	85		Wife	Mar	49	F		Herts	Little Gaddesden
1227	HOPCROFT	George	85		Son	Unm	22	M	Butcher	Bucks	Ivinghoe
1228	HOPCROFT	Margaret	85		Dau	Unm	18	F	Dressmaker	Bucks	Ivinghoe
1229	SUMS	Hannah	85		Visitor	Unm	37	F		Bucks	Ivinghoe
1230	GRACE	Matthew	86	Church End	Head	Mar	40	M	Cordwainer	Herts	Redbourn
1231	GRACE	Esther	86		Wife	Mar	40	F	Cordwainers Wife	Herts	Redbourn
1232	GRACE	Charlotte	86		Dau	Unm	19	F	Straw Plaiter	Herts	Redbourn
1233	GRACE	Thomas	86		Son	Unm	16	M	Labourer	Herts	Redbourn
1234	GRACE	Alice	86		Dau	Unm	14	F	Straw Plaiter	Herts	Redbourn
1235	GRACE	Sarah	86		Dau	Unm	12	F	Plaiter	Herts	Abbotts Langley
1236	GRACE	Matthew	86		Son	Unm	9	M	Plaiter	Herts	St Michaels
1237	GRACE	Walter	86		Son		6	M		Herts	Redbourn
1238	HEDGES	William	87	Church End	Head	Mar	29	M	Agric Lab	Herts	Flamstead
1239	HEDGES	Hannah	87		Wife	Mar	25	F	Plaiter	Herts	Redbourn
1240	HEDGES	William	87		Son		4	M		Herts	Redbourn
1241	HEDGES	Hannah	87		Dau		3	F		Herts	Redbourn
1242	HEDGES	Henry	87		Son		3 m	M		Herts	Redbourn
1243	GROOM	William	88	Church End	Head	Mar	31	M	Labourer	Herts	Bendish
1244	GROOM	Elizabeth	88		Wife	Mar	29	F	Plaiter	Herts	Redbourn
1245	GROOM	Mary Ann	88		Dau		2	F		Herts	Redbourn
1246	GROOM	James	88		Son		1	M		Herts	Redbourn
1247	GRAY	Thomas	89	Church End	Head	Unm	58	M	Tailor	Herts	Redbourn
1248	GRAY	John	89		Brother	Unm	56	M	Tailor	Herts	Redbourn
1249	GRAY	Sarah	89		Sister	Unm	40	F	Cripple	Herts	Redbourn
1250	SKINNER	Alice	90	Church End	Head	Widow	65	F	Plaiter	Beds	Leagrave
1251	SKINNER	Mary	90		Dau	Unm	19	F	Plaiter	Herts	Redbourn
1252	PENNY	John	90		Lodger	Unm	25	M	Agric Lab	Herts	Redbourn
1253	SMITH	Edward	91	Church End	Head	Mar	67	M	Labourer	Beds	Eaton Bray
1254	SMITH	Esther	91		Wife	Mar	66	F	Needlework	Northants	Daventry
1255	GREENHILL	Thomas	91		Nephew	Unm	31	M	Agric Lab	Herts	Redbourn
1256	AXTELL	William	91		Grandson		13	M	Labourer	Herts	Redbourn
1257	WHEELER	James	92	Church End	Head	Mar	42	M	Agric Lab	Herts	Wheathampstead
1258	WHEELER	Elizabeth	92		Wife	Mar	41	F	Plaiter	Herts	Flamstead
1259	WHEELER	Mary	92		Dau	Unm	12	F	Plaiter	Herts	Flamstead
1260	WHEELER	Eliza	92		Dau		10	F	Plaiter	Herts	Flamstead
1261	WHEELER	Sarah	92		Dau		7	F	Plaiter	Herts	Flamstead
1262	WHEELER	James	92		Son		5	M		Herts	Flamstead
1263	WHEELER	Emma	92		Dau		4	F		Herts	Flamstead
1264	WHEELER	Martha	92		Dau		2	F		Herts	Flamstead

	SURNAME	FORENAME	SCHEDULE NUMBER	ADDRESS	RELATIONSHIP	STATUS	AGE	SEX	OCCUPATION	COUNTY OF BIRTH	PLACE OF BIRTH
1265	SUMMERS	William	93	Church End	Head	Mar	71	M	Agric Lab	Herts	Stevenage
1266	SUMMERS	Ruth	93		Wife	Mar	63	F	Chandlers Shop	Herts	Kings Walden
1267	STRATFORD	John	94	Church End	Head	Mar	66	M	Grocer	Herts	Redbourn
1268	STRATFORD	Mary	94		Wife	Mar	63	F	Domestic Duties	Herts	Harpenden
1269	STRATFORD	Sarah	94		Dau	Unm	40	F		Herts	Redbourn
1270	STRATFORD	Alfred	94		Son	Unm	25	M	Fathers Assistant [Grocer]	Herts	Redbourn
1271	GREGORY	William	95	Church End	Head	Mar	31	M	Straw Factor	Herts	Flamstead
1272	GREGORY	Emma	95		Wife	Mar	26	F	Plaiter	Herts	Redbourn
1273	GREGORY	George	95		Son		1	M		Herts	Redbourn
1274	IMPEY	William	96	Church End	Head	Mar	59	M	Chelsea Pensioner (Blind)	Middx	St Pancras
1275	IMPEY	Ann	96		Wife	Mar	62	F	Pensioners Wife, Plaiter	Herts	St Albans
1276	DOLLIMORE	James	97	Frogmore	Head	Mar	60	M	Shoemaker	Herts	Harpenden
1277	DOLLIMORE	Maria	97		Wife	Mar	61	F		Herts	Wheathampstead
1278	BIGG	Daniel	97		Son-in-law	Mar	25	M	Agric Lab	Herts	Harpenden
1279	BIGG	Hannah	97		Dau	Mar	21	F	Plaiter	Herts	Redbourn
1280	DRAPER	Elizabeth	97		Visitor		10	F	Scholar	Herts	St Michaels
1281	COCKLE	Abel	98	Common	Head	Mar	25	M	Straw Cutter	Herts	Redbourn
1282	COCKLE	Mary	98		Wife	Mar	24	F	Plaiter	Herts	Redbourn
1283	COCKLE	David	98		Son		2	M		Herts	Redbourn
1284	COCKLE	Emma	98		Dau		7m	F		Herts	Redbourn
1285	HUTCHINS	William	99	Common	Head	Mar	25	M	Straw Factor	Beds	Tebworth
1286	HUTCHINS	Charlotte	99		Wife	Mar	23	F	Plaiter	Herts	Redbourn
1287	HUTCHINS	Thomas	99		Son		2	M		Herts	Redbourn
1288	SCRIVENER	William	100	Common	Head	Mar	57	M	Coal Dealer	Herts	Flamstead
1289	SCRIVENER	Sophia	100		Wife	Mar	57	F		Herts	Berkhamsted
1290	SCRIVENER	Jonathan	100		Son	Unm	22	M	Agric Lab	Herts	Redbourn
1291	HOW	Henry	101	Common	Head	Mar	43	M	Agric Lab	Herts	Studham
1292	HOW	Charlotte	101		Wife	Mar	50	F	Plaiter	Herts	Redbourn
1293	JACKSON	Hannah	101		Visitor	Unm	9	F	Plaiter	Herts	Redbourn
1294	SEARS	Joseph	102	Common	Head	Widower	35	M	Agric Lab	Herts	Redbourn
1295	SEARS	George	102		Son		9	M	Scholar	Herts	Redbourn
1296	SEARS	William	102		Son		7	M	Scholar	Herts	Redbourn
1297	SEARS	Elizabeth	102		Dau		3	F		Herts	Redbourn
1298	LITTLE	James	103	Common	Head	Widower	66	M	Agric Lab	Herts	Wheathampstead
1299	LITTLE	Jane	103		Dau	Unm	42	F	Plaiter	Herts	Redbourn
1300	NORRIS	William	104	Common	Head	Mar	29	M	Jobbing Labourer	Herts	Redbourn
1301	NORRIS	Elizabeth	104		Wife	Mar	27	F	Plaiter	Herts	Redbourn
1302	NORRIS	Lizzy	104		Dau		1	F		Herts	Redbourn
1303	TIBBS	George	105	Common	Head	Mar	31	M	Lab	Surrey	Croydon
1304	TIBBS	Eliza	105		Wife	Mar	30	F	Plaiter	Herts	Redbourn
1305	TIBBS	James	105		Son		10	M	Plaiter	Herts	Redbourn
1306	TIBBS	George	105		Son		8	M	Plaiter	Herts	Redbourn
1307	TIBBS	Eliza	105		Dau		5	F	Plaiter	Herts	Redbourn
1308	TIBBS	Ann	105		Dau		2	F		Herts	Redbourn

1309	JOHNSON	John	106	Common	Head	Mar	31	M	Cordwainer	Herts	Redbourn
1310	JOHNSON	Sarah	106		Wife	Mar	32	F	At Home	Herts	Redbourn
1311	JOHNSON	William	106		Son		5	M	Scholar	Herts	Redbourn
1312	JOHNSON	Mary A.	106		Dau		3	F	Scholar	Herts	Redbourn
1313	JOHNSON	Thomas	106		Son		2	M	At Home	Herts	Redbourn
1314	JOHNSON	John	106		Son		1	M	At Home	Herts	Redbourn
1315	HEDGES	George	106		Son-in-law		10	M	At Home	Herts	Redbourn
1316	HALSEY	James	107	Common	Head	Widower	50	M	Lab	Herts	Redbourn
1317	HALSEY	Emanuel	107		Son	Unm	24	M	Lab	Herts	Redbourn
1318	HALSEY	Thomas	107		Son		17	M	Lab	Herts	Redbourn
1319	SMART	Jonas	108	Common	Head	Mar	59	M	Chimney Sweep	Herts	Hertford
1320	SMART	Esther	108		Wife	Mar	58	F		Herts	Hunsdon
1321	SMART	William	108		Son	Unm	22	M	Sweep	Herts	Redbourn
1322	SMART	George	108		Son	Unm	20	M	Sweep	Herts	Redbourn
1323	SMART	Susan	108		Dau	Unm	18	F	Plaiter	Herts	Redbourn
1324	SMART	Esther	108		Dau	Unm	16	F	Plaiter	Herts	Redbourn
1325	SMART	Maria	108		Dau	Unm	15	F	Plaiter	Herts	Redbourn
1326	SMART	Charles	108		Son	Unm	13	M	Sweep	Herts	Redbourn
1327	BATES	Henry	108		Serv	Unm	15	M	Sweep	Beds	Luton
1328	HEDGES	Thomas	109	Common	Head	Mar	55	M	Agric Lab	Bucks	Pitstone
1329	HEDGES	Charlotte	109		Wife	Mar	54	F	Plaiter	Herts	Great Gaddesden
1330	HEDGES	Charlotte	109		Dau	Unm	18	F	Plaiter	Herts	Flamstead
1331	HEDGES	Emma	109		Dau	Unm	15	F	Plaiter	Herts	Flamstead
1332	BARR	Joseph	110	Common	Head	Mar	35	M	Agric Lab	Herts	Redbourn
1333	BARR	Sarah	110		Wife	Mar	35	F	Plaiter	Herts	Redbourn
1334	BARR	Ann	110		Dau	Unm	13	F	Plaiter	Herts	Redbourn
1335	BARR	Harriett	110		Dau		9	F	Plaiter	Herts	Redbourn
1336	BARR	George	110		Son		6	M	Plaiter	Herts	Redbourn
1337	BARR	Mary	110		Dau		3	F		Herts	Redbourn
1338	AUSTIN	Henry	111	Common	Head	Mar	23	M	Lab	Herts	Redbourn
1339	AUSTIN	Sarah	111		Wife	Mar	23	F	Plaiter	Herts	Redbourn
1340	FALLDER	David	112	Common	Head	Mar	26	M	Agric Lab	Herts	Harpenden
1341	FALLDER	Ann	112		Wife	Mar	23	F	Plaiter	Herts	Redbourn
1342	FALLDER	George	112		Son		2	M		Herts	Redbourn
1343	WHITEHEAD	William	113	Common	Head	Mar	44	M	Agric Lab	Herts	St Albans
1344	WHITEHEAD	Hannah	113		Wife	Mar	33	F	Plaiter	Herts	Redbourn
1345	WHITEHEAD	Betsy	113		Dau	Unm	10	F	Plaiter	Herts	Redbourn
1346	WHITEHEAD	Ann	113		Dau		8	F	Plaiter	Herts	Redbourn
1347	WHITEHEAD	Selina	113		Dau		6	F	Plaiter	Herts	Redbourn
1348	WHITEHEAD	Joseph	113		Son		5	M	Plaiter	Herts	Redbourn
1349	WHITEHEAD	William	113		Son		2	M		Herts	Redbourn
1350	MALIN	William	114	Common	Head	Mar	27	M	Agric Lab	Bucks	Dagnall
1351	MALIN	Eliza	114		Wife	Mar	21	F	Plaiter	Herts	Gaddesden Row
1352	MALIN	Joseph	114		Son		6m	M		Herts	Redbourn
1353	BARTRAM	Samuel	115	Common	Head	Mar	70	M	Agric Lab	Herts	Berkhamsted

	SURNAME	FORENAME	SCHEDULE NUMBER	ADDRESS	RELATIONSHIP	STATUS	AGE	SEX	OCCUPATION	COUNTY OF BIRTH	PLACE OF BIRTH
1354	BARTRAM	Elizabeth	115		Wife	Mar	60	F		Herts	Redbourn
1355	BARTRAM	Betsy	115		Dau	Unm	21	F	Plaiter	Herts	Redbourn
1356	BARTRAM	Rose	115		Dau	Unm	19	F	Plaiter	Herts	Redbourn
1357	BARTRAM	Catherine	115		Dau	Unm	10	F	Plaiter	Herts	Redbourn
1358	BARTRAM	Charlotte	115		Grandau		1	F		Herts	Redbourn
1359	LEA	John	116	Common	Head	Mar	57	M	Agric Lab	Herts	Redbourn
1360	LEA	Mary (Snr)	116		Wife	Mar	54	F	Plaiter	Herts	Redbourn
1361	LEA	Mary	116		Dau	Unm	20	F	Plaiter	Herts	Redbourn
1362	LEA	Hannah	116		Dau	Unm	18	F	Plaiter	Herts	Redbourn
1363	LEA	James	116		Son	Unm	13	M	Farm Boy	Herts	Redbourn
1364	SQUIRES	Daniel	117	Common	Head	Mar	53	M	Agric Lab	Beds	Luton
1365	SQUIRES	Sophia	117		Wife	Mar	53	F	Plaiter	Herts	Redbourn
1366	SQUIRES	William	117		Son	Unm	12	M	Farm Servant	Herts	Redbourn
1367	SQUIRES	Daniel	117		Son	Unm	10	M	Farm Servant	Herts	Redbourn
1368	SQUIRES	Hannah	117		Dau	Unm	16	F	Plaiter	Herts	Redbourn
1369	DOGGETT	Daniel	118	Common	Head	Mar	23	M	Agric Lab	Herts	Redbourn
1370	DOGGETT	Lydia	118		Wife	Mar	26	F	Plaiter	Herts	Redbourn
1371	SIMPSON	Thomas	118		Lodger	Unm	46	M	Agric Lab	Herts	Redbourn
1372	HULL	John	119	Common	Head	Mar	45	M	Shepherd	Herts	Harpenden
1373	HULL	Ann	119		Wife	Mar	45	F	Plaiter	Herts	Colney
1374	HULL	Betsy	119		Dau	Unm	26	F	Plaiter	Herts	Redbourn
1375	HULL	Adelaide	119		Dau	Unm	20	F	Plaiter	Herts	Redbourn
1376	HULL	Eliza	119		Dau	Unm	14	F	Plaiter	Herts	Redbourn
1377	WESTROPE	James	120	Common	Head	Mar	74	M	Retired Miller	Beds	Stotfold
1378	WESTROPE	Elizabeth	120		Wife	Mar	72	F		Beds	Houghton Regis
1379	SMITH	James	121	Common	Head	Mar	82	M		Beds	Luton
1380	SMITH	Judith	121		Wife	Mar	72	F	Almspeople, Formerly Agric Labs	Herts	Flamstead
1381	DUNCKLEY	Joseph	122	Common	Head	Mar	44	M	Well Digger	Herts	Flamstead
1382	DUNCKLEY	Elizabeth	122		Wife	Mar	43	F	Plaiter	Herts	Flamstead
1383	DUNCKLEY	William	122		Son	Unm	9	M	Farmers Boy	Herts	Flamstead
1384	DUNCKLEY	John	122		Son	Unm	5	M		Herts	Flamstead
1385	SMITH	James	123	Common	Head	Mar	38	M	Agric Lab	Herts	Redbourn
1386	SMITH	Susan	123		Wife	Mar	38	F	Charwoman	Herts	Redbourn
1387	SMITH	Betsey	123		Dau		12	F	Plaiter	Herts	Redbourn
1388	SMITH	Susan	123		Dau		9	F	Plaiter	Herts	Redbourn
1389	SMITH	Silas	123		Son		6	M		Herts	Redbourn
1390	SMITH	Henry	123		Son		4	M		Herts	Redbourn
1391	SMITH	James	123		Son		1	M		Herts	Redbourn
1392	HUCKLESBY	George	124	Common	Head	Mar	22	M	Agric Lab	Herts	Redbourn
1393	HUCKLESBY	Eliza	124		Wife	Mar	21	F	Plaiter	Herts	Redbourn
1394	HUCKLESBY	William	124		Son		0	M		Herts	Redbourn
1395	LAY	James	125	Common	Head	Mar	35	M	Agric Lab	Herts	Flamstead
1396	LAY	Susan	125		Wife	Mar	35	F	Plaiter	Herts	Redbourn
1397	LAY	William	125		Son	Unm	11	M	Scholar	Herts	Redbourn

1398	LAY	Jane	125		Dau	Unm	7	F	Scholar	Herts	Redbourn
1399	WHITEHEAD	Joseph	126	Common	Head	Mar	52	M	Agric Lab	Herts	Childwick [St Michaels]
1400	WHITEHEAD	Ann	126		Wife	Mar	41	F	Plaiter	Herts	Boxmoor [Hemel]

One uninhabited

1401	GILBERT	Joseph	127	Common	Head	Mar	61	M	Plait Dealer	Herts	St Michaels
1402	GILBERT	Mary	127		Wife	Mar	58	F	Plait Dealer	Herts	St Michaels
1403	GILBERT	Sarah	127		Dau	Unm	22	F	At Home	Herts	St Michaels

One house uninhabited

1404	CHALKLY	William	128	Common	Head	Mar	48	M	Agric Lab	Herts	Redbourn
1405	CHALKLY	Mary	128		Wife	Mar	45	F	Plaiter	Herts	Flamstead
1406	CHALKLY	James	128		Son	Unm	21	M	Agric Lab	Herts	Redbourn
1407	CHALKLY	Ann	128		Dau		12	F	Plaiter	Herts	Redbourn
1408	CHALKLY	David	128		Son		7	M	At Home	Herts	Redbourn
1409	CHALKLY	Mary	128		Mother	Widow	72	F		Beds	Leighton
1410	HILL	Isaac	129	Common	Head	Mar	37	M	Labourer	Herts	Redbourn
1411	HILL	Mary	129		Wife	Mar	33	F	Plaiter	Herts	Redbourn
1412	HILL	Louisa	129		Dau		11	F	Plaiter	Herts	Redbourn
1413	HILL	Samuel	129		Son		7	M	Scholar	Herts	Redbourn
1414	HILL	Mary Ann	129		Dau		3	F		Herts	Redbourn
1415	HILL	William	129		Son		7m	M		Herts	Redbourn
1416	THORN	Thomas	130	Common	Head	Mar	40	M	Agric Lab	Herts	Redbourn
1417	THORN	Sarah	130		Wife	Mar	30	F	Plaiter	Herts	Redbourn
1418	THORN	Thomas	130		Nephew	Unm	10	M	Farmers Boy	Herts	Redbourn
1419	THORN	Eliza	130		Niece	Unm	12	F	Plaiter	Herts	Redbourn
1420	ALLEN	Mary	130		Mother-in-law	Widow	74	F		Beds	Dunstable
1421	ARNOLD	William	131	Common	Head	Mar	35	M	Lab	Herts	Redbourn
1422	ARNOLD	Patty	131		Wife	Mar	36	F	Plaiter	Herts	Redbourn
1423	ARNOLD	John	131		Son	Unm	11	M	Farmers Boy	Herts	Redbourn
1424	ARNOLD	Ann	131		Dau		8	F	Plaiter	Herts	Redbourn
1425	ARNOLD	William	131		Son		5	M	Plaiter	Herts	Redbourn
1426	ARNOLD	Mary	131		Dau		3	F		Herts	Redbourn
1427	ROWE	Thomas	131		Inmate	Mar	64	M	Lab	Herts	Harpenden
1428	ROWE	Mary	131		Inmate	Mar	74	F		Herts	Redbourn
1429	HUCKLESBY	James	132	Common	Head	Mar	53	M	Agric Lab	Beds	Leagrave
1430	HUCKLESBY	Dinah	132		Wife	Mar	56	F	Plaiter	Herts	Hitchin
1431	HUCKLESBY	John	132		Son	Unm	18	M	Agric Lab	Herts	Redbourn
1432	HUCKLESBY	William	132		Son	Unm	15	M	Agric Lab	Herts	Redbourn
1433	DEAYTON	David	133	Common	Head	Mar	45	M	Agric Lab	Herts	Hemel Hempstead
1434	DEAYTON	Ann	133		Wife	Mar	55	F	Charwoman	Herts	Hitchin
1435	DEAYTON	Louisa	133		Dau	Unm	20	F	Plaiter	Herts	Redbourn
1436	DEAYTON	Edward	133		Grandson		3	M		Herts	Gaddesden
1437	SMITH	Joseph	134	Common	Head	Widower	57	M	Brewer	Herts	Great Gaddesden
1438	SMITH	Eliza	134		Dau	Unm	20	F	Plaiter	Herts	Redbourn

	SURNAME	FORENAME	SCHEDULE NUMBER	ADDRESS	RELATIONSHIP	STATUS	AGE	SEX	OCCUPATION	COUNTY OF BIRTH	PLACE OF BIRTH
1439	QUICK	Fanny	134		Visitor	Unm	18	F	Plaiter	Herts	Redbourn
1440	PEACOCK	Emanuel	135	Common	Head	Mar	55	M	Journeyman Carpenter	Herts	Redbourn
1441	PEACOCK	Dinah	135		Wife	Mar	49	F	Plaiter	Herts	Redbourn
1442	PEACOCK	Emanuel	135		Son	Unm	22	M	Lab	Herts	Redbourn
1443	PEACOCK	Ruth	135		Dau	Unm	16	F	Plaiter	Herts	Redbourn
1444	QUICK	Thomas	136	Common	Head	Mar	52	M	Game Keeper	Beds	Luton
1445	QUICK	Fanny	136		Wife	Mar	54	F	Plaiter	Beds	Luton
1446	QUICK	Thomas	136		Son	Unm	20	M	Labourer	Herts	Redbourn
1447	QUICK	Amy	136		Dau		15	F	Plaiter	Herts	Redbourn
1448	QUICK	Harriett	136		Dau		12	F	Plaiter	Herts	Redbourn
1449	MANNING	Patience	137	Tassel Hall Lane	Head	Unm	21	F	Dressmaker	Herts	Redbourn
1450	MANNING	Jabez	137		Brother		12	M	Scholar	Herts	Redbourn
1451	PITKIN	Jane	137		Visitor	Unm	18	F		Herts	Redbourn
1452	BRADBURY	William	138	Tassel Hall Lane	Head	Mar	36	M	Agric Lab	Beds	Milton
1453	BRADBURY	Mary Ann	138		Wife	Mar	30	F	Plaiter	Herts	Harpenden
1454	BRADBURY	Daniel	138		Son	Unm	10	M	Scholar	Herts	Redbourn
1455	BRADBURY	William	138		Son		2	M		Herts	Redbourn
1456	SPRIGGS	John	138		Father-in-law	Mar	70	M	Agric Lab	Herts	Redbourn
1457	SPRIGGS	Ann	138		Mother-in-law	Mar	75	F	Washerwoman	Herts	Redbourn
1458	DOLLIMORE	George	139	Tassel Hall Lane	Head	Mar	70	M	Agric Lab	Herts	Redbourn
1459	DOLLIMORE	Phoebe	139		Wife	Mar	70	F	Plaiter	Herts	Redbourn
1460	AXTELL	James	140	Tassel Hall Lane	Head	Mar	42	M	Agric Lab	Herts	Redbourn
1461	AXTELL	Mary	140		Wife	Mar	44	F	Plaiter	Herts	Redbourn
1462	AXTELL	Daniel	140		Son	Unm	12	M	Lab	Herts	Redbourn
1463	SMITH	Robert	141	Tassel Hall Lane	Head	Mar	32	M	Agric Lab	Herts	Redbourn
1464	SMITH	Ann	141		Wife	Mar	25	F	Plaiter	Herts	Redbourn
1465	SMITH	Sarah	141		Dau	Unm	2	F		Herts	Redbourn
1466	SMITH	Mary A.	141		Dau	Unm	1	F		Herts	Redbourn
1467	ABBOTT	Sarah	142	Tassel Hall Lane	Head	Widow	82	F	Straw Factors Widow	Herts	Redbourn
1468	ABBOTT	Thomas	142		Son	Unm	55	M	Straw Factor	Herts	Redbourn
1469	SMITH	Sarah	143	Tassel Hall Lane	Head	Mar	28	F	Plaiter	Herts	Flamstead
1470	SMITH	Selina	143		Dau		9	F	Scholar	Middx	London
1471	SMITH	Alexander	143		Son		6	M	Scholar	Herts	Redbourn
1472	READING	Daniel	144	Tassel Hall Lane	Head	Mar	37	M	Agric Lab	Herts	Redbourn
1473	READING	Caroline	144		Wife	Mar	36	F	Plaiter	Herts	Redbourn
1474	READING	Emily	144		Dau	Unm	13	F	Plaiter	Herts	Redbourn
1475	READING	Alfred	144		Son	Unm	10	M	Scholar	Herts	Redbourn
1476	READING	Caroline	144		Dau	Unm	6	F	Scholar	Herts	Redbourn
1477	READING	Rose	144		Dau	Unm	2	F		Herts	Redbourn
1478	FALLDER	Thomas	145	Tassel Hall Lane	Head	Mar	30	M	Agric Lab	Herts	Redbourn
1479	FALLDER	Rose	145		Wife	Mar	28	F	Plaiter	Herts	Redbourn
1480	FALLDER	William	145		Son	Unm	2	M		Herts	Redbourn
1481	BELCHER	William	146	Tassel Hall Lane	Head	Mar	40	M	Agric Lab	Herts	Redbourn
1482	BELCHER	Mary	146		Wife	Mar	38	F	Plaiter	Herts	Redbourn

1483	BELCHER	Sarah	146		Dau	Unm	10	F	Plaiter	Herts	Redbourn
1484	BELCHER	John	146		Son	Unm	7	M	Scholar	Herts	Redbourn
1485	BELCHER	Hannah	146		Dau	Unm	2	F		Herts	Redbourn
1486	SEABROOK	Sarah	147	Tassel Hall Lane	Head	Widow	53	F	Plaiter	Herts	Hatfield
1487	SEABROOK	Mary Ann	147		Dau	Unm	22	F	Bonnet Sewer	Herts	Harpenden
1488	SEABROOK	Eliza	147		Dau	Unm	20	F	Bonnet Sewer	Herts	Harpenden
1489	SEABROOK	Maria	147		Dau	Unm	11	F	Plaiter	Herts	Redbourn
1490	LILEY	Joseph	148	The Heath	Head	Mar	65	M	Retired Inn Keeper	Hants	Blackwater
1491	LILEY	Frances	148		Wife	Mar	52	F		Herts	Hatfield
1492	LILEY	Frances	148		Dau	Unm	27	F	Governess	Beds	Hockliffe
1493	LILEY	Catherine	148		Dau	Unm	25	F		Herts	Redbourn
1494	LILEY	Ann	148		Dau	Unm	23	F		Herts	Redbourn
1495	LILEY	Harriett M.	148		Dau	Unm	20	F	Dressmaker	Herts	Redbourn
1496	STEPHENS	Mary	148		Niece	Unm	9	F	Pupil	Herts	Redbourn
1497	SEABROOK	William	148		Serv	Unm	14	M	Servant	Herts	Redbourn
1498	BURGESS	Mary	149	Snatchup	Head	Widow	56	F	Plaiter	Herts	Redbourn
1499	BURGESS	Elizabeth	149		Dau	Unm	21	F	Plaiter	Herts	Redbourn
1500	BURGESS	Hannah	149		Dau	Unm	13	F	Plaiter	Herts	Redbourn
1501	AXTELL	Francis	150	Snatchup	Head	Mar	62	M	Agric Lab	Herts	Flamstead
1502	AXTELL	Sarah	150		Wife	Mar	68	F	Plaiter	Herts	Redbourn
1503	AXTELL	Joseph	150		Son	Unm	25	M	Agric Lab	Herts	Redbourn
1504	BATES	Sarah	150		Dau	Widow	34	F	Plaiter	Herts	Redbourn
1505	BATES	William	150		Grandson	Unm	10	M	Farmers Boy	Herts	Redbourn
1506	BATES	Ann	150		Grandau		8	F	Farmers Boy	Herts	Redbourn
1507	WELLS	Mary	151	Snatchup	Head	Widow	65	F	Plaiter	Herts	Redbourn
1508	WELLS	William	151		Son	Unm	33	M	Agric Lab	Herts	Redbourn
1509	WELLS	Jess	151		Son	Unm	25	M	Agric Lab	Herts	Redbourn
1510	WELLS	Joseph	151		Son	Unm	22	M	Agric Lab	Herts	Redbourn
1511	STARKINS	James	152	Snatchup	Head	Mar	66	M	Agric Lab	Herts	Harpenden
1512	STARKINS	Esther	152		Wife	Mar	62	F		Herts	St Albans
1513	STARKINS	Thomas	152		Son	Unm	18	M	Agric Lab	Herts	Redbourn
1514	BIGG	James	153	Snatchup	Head	Mar	46	M	Agric Lab	Herts	Harpenden
1515	BIGG	Mary	153		Wife	Mar	39	F	Plaiter	Herts	Redbourn
1516	BIGG	James	153		Son	Unm	17	M	Agric Lab	Herts	Redbourn
1517	BIGG	Emma	153		Dau	Unm	15	F	Plaiter	Herts	Redbourn
1518	BIGG	George	153		Son	Unm	12	M	Agric Lab	Herts	Redbourn
1519	BIGG	Daniel	153		Son		10	M	Agric Lab	Herts	Redbourn
1520	BIGG	Mary Ann	153		Dau		4	F		Herts	Redbourn
1521	BIGG	Louisa	153		Dau		1	F		Herts	Redbourn
1522	BARR	George	154	Snatchup	Head	Mar	66	M	Agric Lab	Herts	Redbourn
1523	BARR	Mary	154		Wife	Mar	66	F		Herts	Hemel Hempstead
1524	BARR	George	154		Son	Unm	33	M	Agric Lab	Herts	Redbourn
1525	WHEELER	Sarah	155	Snatchup	Head	Widow	60	F	Charwoman	Middx	Shenley
1526	NASH	Thomas	155		Son-in-law	Mar	27	M	Agric Lab	Herts	Kings Walden

	SURNAME	FORENAME	SCHEDULE NUMBER	ADDRESS	RELATIONSHIP	STATUS	AGE	SEX	OCCUPATION	COUNTY OF BIRTH	PLACE OF BIRTH
1527	NASH	Ann	155		Dau	Mar	24	F	Plaiter	Herts	Redbourn
1528	WHEELER	Elenor	155		Dau	Unm	19	F	Plaiter	Herts	Redbourn
1529	ABBOTT	James	156	Snatchup	Head	Mar	40	M	Agric Lab	Herts	Redbourn
1530	ABBOTT	Georgiana	156		Wife	Mar	39	F	Plaiter	Herts	St Albans
1531	GRAVESTOCK	James	157	Snatchup	Head	Mar	54	M	Agric Lab	Middx	Finchley
1532	GRAVESTOCK	Elizabeth	157		Wife	Mar	44	F	Plaiter	Beds	Dunstable
1533	GRAVESTOCK	Sarah	157		Dau	Unm	20	F	Plaiter	Herts	Redbourn
1534	GRAVESTOCK	Emma	157		Dau	Unm	14	F	Plaiter	Herts	Redbourn
1535	GRAVESTOCK	George	157		Son	Unm	11	M	Agric Lab	Herts	Redbourn
1536	GRAVESTOCK	Ann	157		Dau		9	F	Plaiter	Herts	Redbourn
1537	GRAVESTOCK	William	157		Son		7	M	Scholar	Herts	Redbourn
1538	MONTAGUE	John	158	Snatchup	Head	Mar	59	M	Agric Lab	Herts	Kensworth
1539	MONTAGUE	Kezia	158		Wife	Mar	56	F		Beds	Luton
1540	MONTAGUE	John	158		Son	Unm	24	M	Agric Lab	Herts	Redbourn
1541	MONTAGUE	Emily	158		Dau	Unm	19	F	Plaiter	Herts	Redbourn
1542	MONTAGUE	Daniel	158		Son	Unm	15	M	Agric Lab	Herts	Redbourn
1543	SMITH	David	159	Snatchup	Head	Mar	38	M	Agric Lab	Herts	Great Gaddesden
1544	SMITH	Phillis	159		Wife	Mar	38	F	Plaiter	Herts	Redbourn
1545	SMITH	Susan	159		Dau	Unm	17	F	Plaiter	Herts	Redbourn
1546	SMITH	Ann	159		Dau	Unm	16	F	Plaiter	Herts	Flamstead
1547	SMITH	Mary Ann	159		Dau	Unm	15	F	Plaiter	Herts	Redbourn
1548	SMITH	William	159		Son	Unm	13	M	Agric Lab	Herts	Redbourn
1549	HARRIS	Thomas	159		Son-in-law	Unm	12	M	Agric Lab	Herts	Redbourn
1550	SMITH	John	159		Son	Unm	10	M	Agric Lab	Herts	Redbourn
1551	SMITH	Joseph	159		Son		3	M		Herts	Redbourn
1552	SMITH	Jane	159		Dau		2	F		Herts	Redbourn
1553	SMITH	Alice	159		Dau		3m	F		Herts	Redbourn
1554	PENNY	Dorcas	160	Snatchup	Head	Widow	57	F	Plaiter	Herts	Redbourn
1555	PENNY	William	160		Son	Unm	26	M	Agric Lab	Herts	Redbourn
1556	PENNY	Sarah	160		Dau	Unm	24	F	Plaiter	Herts	Redbourn
1557	PENNY	Charlotte	160		Dau	Unm	18	F	Plaiter	Herts	Redbourn
1558	PENNY	George	160		Son	Unm	20	M	Agric Lab	Herts	Redbourn
1559	PENNY	Thomas	160		Son	Unm	11	M	Agric Lab	Herts	Redbourn
1560	PENNY	John	160		Son	Unm	6	M		Herts	Redbourn
1561	HUNT	William	161	Snatchup	Head	Mar	34	M	Bricklayers Lab (Beer Shop)	Oxon	Tadmarton
1562	HUNT	Elizabeth	161		Wife	Mar	30	F	Plaiter	Herts	Flamstead
1563	BRADBURY	Daniel	161		Son-in-law	Unm	12	M	Agric Lab	Herts	Lilley
1564	JARMIN	Benjamin	162	Snatchup	Head	Mar	49	M	Straw Factor	Herts	Great Gaddesden
1565	JARMIN	Ann	162		Wife	Mar	43	F	Straw Factors Wife	Herts	Redbourn
1566	JARMIN	Charles	162		Son	Unm	20	M	Straw Cutter	Herts	Redbourn
1567	JARMIN	Ann	162		Dau	Unm	16	F	Plaiter at Home	Herts	Redbourn
1568	JARMIN	Joseph	162		Son	Unm	12	M	Straw Cutter	Herts	Redbourn
1569	JARMIN	Edward	162		Son	Unm	10	M	Straw Cutter	Herts	Redbourn
1570	JARMIN	Catherine	162		Dau	Unm	9	F	Plaiter at Home	Herts	Redbourn
1571	JARMIN	George	162		Son	Unm	7	M	Plaiter at Home	Herts	Redbourn

1572	JARMIN	Thomas	162		Son	Unm	5	M		Herts	Redbourn
1573	JARMIN	Elizabeth	162		Dau	Unm	4	F		Herts	Redbourn
1574	JARMIN	Sarah	162		Dau	Unm	2	F		Herts	Redbourn
1575	JARMIN	David	162		Son	Unm	1	M		Herts	Redbourn
1576	REED	Stephen	163	Snatchup	Head	Mar	20	M	Shoebinder	Middx	St Lukes
1577	REED	Sarah	163		Wife	Mar	24	F	Bonnet Sewer	Herts	Redbourn
1578	REED	Charlotte E	163		Dau		8 m	F		Herts	Redbourn
1579	REED	Emily	163		Sister	Unm	15	F	Bonnet Sewer	Middx	St Lukes
1580	WELLS	David	164	Snatchup	Head	Mar	38	M	Agric Lab	Herts	Gaddesden
1581	WELLS	Jane	164		Wife	Mar	42	F	Needlewoman	Herts	Flamstead
1582	WELLS	Charles	164		Son		12	M	Errand Boy	Herts	Flamstead
1583	ASHBY	William	164		Son-in-law	Unm	21	M	Builder	Herts	Flamstead
1584	BURN	Joseph	165	Snatchup	Head	Mar	40	M	Coal Dealer	Herts	Redbourn
1585	BURN	[?]	165		Wife	Mar	30	F		Herts	Harpenden
1586	BURN	Joseph	165		Son	Unm	15	M	Agric Lab	Herts	Redbourn
1587	BURN	Benjamin	165		Son		10	M	Agric Lab	Herts	Redbourn
1588	BURN	Kitty	165		Dau		6	F	Scholar	Herts	Redbourn
1589	STRATTON	Mary Ann	166	Snatchup	Head	Widow	33	F	Plaiter	Herts	Redbourn
1590	STRATTON	Ann	166		Dau	Unm	8	F	Plaiter	Herts	Redbourn
1591	STRATTON	Hannah	166		Dau	Unm	3	F		Herts	Redbourn
1592	SMITH	Emma	166		Niece	Unm	15	F	Plaiter	Herts	Redbourn
1593	COOPER	Thomas	167	Snatchup	Head	Mar	37	M	Agric Lab	Herts	Redbourn
1594	COOPER	Susan	167		Wife	Mar	26	F	Plaiter	Bucks	Weedon
1595	COOPER	Eliza	167		Dau	Unm	8	F	Plaiter	Herts	Redbourn
1596	COOPER	William	167		Son		3	M		Herts	Redbourn
1597	COOPER	Thomas	167		Son		1 m	M		Herts	Redbourn
1598	BENT	Mary	168	Snatchup	Head	Widow	59	F	Plaiter	Herts	Redbourn
1599	BENT	Ann	168		Dau	Unm	24	F	Plaiter at Home	Herts	Redbourn
1600	BENT	Sarah	168		Grandau		12	F	Plaiter at Home	Herts	Redbourn
1601	BENT	Mary	168		Grandau		11	F	Plaiter at Home	Herts	Redbourn
1602	BENT	Susannah	168		Grandau		8	F	Plaiter at Home	Herts	Redbourn
1603	FOURTH	Mary	169	Snatchup	Head	Unm	70	F	Schoolmistress	Herts	Redbourn
1604	ANDREWS	Laura	169		Cousin		5	F	Scholar	Middx	[London] Kings Cross
1605	BRADBURY	James	170	Snatchup	Head	Mar	32	M	Agric Lab	Beds	Woburn
1606	BRADBURY	Mary	170		Wife	Mar	26	F	Plaiter	Herts	Kimpton
1607	BRADBURY	George	170		Son		4	M		Herts	Hatfield
1608	BRADBURY	Elizabeth	170		Mother	Widow	66	F	Plaiter	Beds	Woburn
1609	BARNES	Thomas	171	Snatchup	Head	Widower	74	M	Carrier	Herts	Redbourn
1610	SMITH	Esther	171		Niece	Unm	45	F	Nurse	Herts	Redbourn
1611	THOROGOOD	George	171		Grandson	Unm	21	M	Carrier	Herts	Redbourn

The end of the District 3b, parish of Redbourn Herts.

Registrar's District: Harpenden   **Enumeration District 3c**   **Ref. HO 107/1713 folios 178-93**

All that part of the parish of Redbourn that lies between the London and Holyhead Road and on the south west side of the road called Fish Street leading therefrom to Hempstead, including the south west side of Fish Street, that part of Redbourn Common known as the Dirt Houses, thence to Wood End, Cherry Trees, South End, Butlers and farms within the said boundary.

	SURNAME	FORENAME	SCHED	ADDRESS	RELATIONSHIP	STATUS	AGE	SEX	OCCUPATION	COUNTY	PLACE OF BIRTH
1612	HESTER	James	1	High Street	Head	Mar	37	M	Agric Lab	Herts	St Albans
1613	HESTER	Ann	1		Wife	Mar	43	F		Herts	Redbourn
1614	HESTER	James	1		Son	Unm	11	M	Scholar	Herts	Redbourn
1615	HESTER	George	1		Son	Unm	6	M	Scholar	Herts	Redbourn
1616	CARPENTER	Eliza	2	High Street	Head	Unm	30	F	Straw Plaiter	Herts	Redbourn
1617	BURRETT	William	3	High Street	Head	Mar	60	M	Agric Lab	Middx	Shoreditch
1618	BURRETT	Elizabeth	3		Wife	Mar	56	F		Devon	Exeter
1619	BURRETT	Keziah	3		Dau	Unm	29	F		Herts	Redbourn
1620	BURRETT	Daniel	3		Son	Unm	17	M	At Home	Herts	Redbourn
1621	HUDSON	Elizabeth	3		Grandau		9	F	Scholar	Herts	Redbourn
1622	SCRIVENER	John	3		Lodger	Unm	27	M	Agric Lab	Herts	Redbourn
1623	SMITH	John	4	High Street	Head	Mar	32	M	Lath Render	Herts	Harpenden
1624	SMITH	Alice	4		Wife	Mar	29	F		Herts	Redbourn
1625	SEABROOK	Mary Ann	4		Visitor		6	F		Herts	St Michaels, St Albans
1626	THOROGOOD	James	5	High Street	Head	Mar	55	M	Agric Lab	Herts	St Pauls Walden
1627	THOROGOOD	Mary	5		Dau	Unm	22	F	Straw Plaiter	Herts	Willian
1628	THOROGOOD	Maria	5		Dau	Unm	20	F	Straw Plaiter	Herts	Willian
1629	THOROGOOD	Eliza	5		Dau		7	F	Scholar	Herts	Redbourn
1630	TONSEY	Sarah	6	High Street	Head	Widow	50	F	Grocer	Herts	St Stephens, St Albans
1631	COLE	Mary Ann	6		Dau	Mar	22	F	Bonnet Sewer	Bucks	Aylesbury
1632	AMERY	Robert	7	High Street (Lion & Lamb)	Head	Mar	50	M	Victualler	Somerset	Taunton
1633	AMERY	Elizabeth	7		Wife	Mar	50	F		Middx	London
1634	STYLES	Hannah	7		Visitor	Mar	45	F	Unknown	Middx	London
1635	GREEN	Sarah	7		Serv	Unm	20	F	Servant	Herts	Redbourn
1636	FELLOWS	James	8	Fish Street	Head	Mar	58	M	Agric Lab	Herts	Hemel Hempstead
1637	FELLOWS	Elizabeth	8		Wife	Mar	57	F		Herts	Hemel Hempstead
1638	FELLOWS	Jane	8		Dau	Unm	19	F	Straw Plaiter	Herts	Redbourn
1639	FELLOWS	James	9	Fish Street	Head	Mar	28	M	Agric Lab	Herts	Redbourn
1640	FELLOWS	Emma	9		Wife	Mar	27	F		Herts	Abbotts Langley
1641	FELLOWS	Caroline	9		Dau		5	F	Scholar	Herts	Abbotts Langley
1642	FELLOWS	William	9		Son		1m	M		Herts	Redbourn
1643	SEAR	Ann	10	Fish Street	Head	Widow	66	F	Pauper	Herts	Wheathampstead
1644	WOODWARD	John	11	Fish Street	Head	Mar	42	M	Agric Lab	Herts	Sandridge
1645	WOODWARD	Susan	11		Wife	Mar	40	F		Herts	Sandridge
1646	WOODWARD	Charles	11		Son		12	M	Scholar	Herts	Wheathampstead
1647	WOODWARD	Louisa	11		Dau		10	F	Scholar	Herts	Wheathampstead
1648	WOODWARD	William	11		Son		6	M	Scholar	Herts	Redbourn
1649	WOODWARD	Ann	11		Dau		2	F		Herts	Redbourn
1650	CHAMBERS	William	12	Fish Street	Head	Mar	34	M	Agric Lab	Unknown	

1651	CHAMBERS	Hannah	12		Wife	Mar	33	F		Herts	Redbourn
1652	CHAMBERS	Ann	12		Lodger	Unm	26	F	Straw Plaiter	Herts	St Pauls Walden
1653	STARKINS	Eliza	12		Visitor		12	F	Scholar	Herts	Redbourn
1654	WELLS	William	13	Fish Street	Head	Mar	48	M	Agric Lab	Herts	St Stephens, St Albans
1655	WELLS	Catherine	13		Wife	Mar	45	F		Kent	Ramsgate
1656	WELLS	Mary A.	13		Dau	Unm	21	F	Straw Plaiter	Herts	Redbourn
1657	WELLS	Elizabeth	13		Dau	Unm	18	F	Straw Plaiter	Herts	Redbourn
1658	WELLS	Maria	13		Dau		11	F	Bonnet Sewer	Herts	Redbourn
1659	WELLS	William	13		Son		9	M	Scholar	Herts	Redbourn
1660	WELLS	Sarah Starkins	13		Grandau		4m	F		Herts	Redbourn
1661	DOLLING	James	14	Fish Street	Head	Mar	42	M	Agric Lab	Herts	Hemel Hempstead
1662	DOLLING	Abigail	14		Wife	Mar	35	F		Herts	Flamstead
1663	DOLLING	Emma	14		Dau		11	F	Scholar	Herts	Redbourn
1664	DOLLING	Ann	14		Dau		1	F		Herts	Redbourn
1665	STARKINS	Joseph	15	Fish Street	Head	Mar	35	M	Agric Lab	Herts	Redbourn
1666	STARKINS	Eliza	15		Wife	Mar	33	F		Herts	Redbourn
1667	STARKINS	Mary	15		Dau		10	F	At Home	Herts	Redbourn
1668	STARKINS	Fanny	15		Dau		3	F		Herts	Redbourn
1669	STARKINS	Emma	15		Dau		1	F		Herts	Redbourn
1670	READING	Richard	16	Fish Street	Head	Mar	44	M	Carpenter	Herts	Redbourn
1671	READING	Elizabeth	16		Wife	Mar	44	F	Seamstress	Cambs	Wisbech
1672	READING	Mary Ann	16		Dau	Unm	14	F	Straw Bonnet Sewer	Herts	Redbourn
1673	READING	Eliza	16		Dau		11	F	Straw Plaiter	Herts	Redbourn
1674	READING	William	16		Son		6	M	Scholar	Herts	Redbourn
1675	READING	Elizabeth	16		Dau		2	F		Herts	Redbourn
1676	AUSTIN	John	17	Fish Street	Head	Mar	25	M	Agric Lab	Herts	Redbourn
1677	AUSTIN	Hannah	17		Wife	Mar	26	F	Straw Plaiter	Herts	Redbourn
1678	AUSTIN	George	17		Son		4	M	Scholar	Herts	Redbourn
1679	AUSTIN	Samuel	17		Son		1	M		Herts	Redbourn
1680	CAMBERS	Jane	18	Fish Street	H'keeper	Unm	42	F	Housekeeper	Middx	Hampton
1681	BURRETT	Maria	18		Serv	Unm	25	F	Servant	Herts	Redbourn
1682	PARTRIDGE	Peter	18		Serv	Unm	14	M	Farm Servant	Herts	Redbourn
1683	DOLLIMORE	William	18		Serv	Unm	18	M	Farm Servant	Herts	Redbourn
1684	BROWN	John	18		Serv	Unm	14	M	Farm Servant	Herts	Redbourn
1685	WEBB	John	19	Redbourn Common	Head	Widower	61	M	Farmer of 16 acres employing 1 labourer	Sussex	Hastings
1686	WEBB	George	19		Son	Unm	23	M	At Home	Herts	Markyate Street
1687	GEARY	Ellen	19		Serv	Unm	17	F	House Servant	Bucks	Hanslope
1688	SMITH	William	20	Dirt House Row	Head	Mar	28	M	Agric Lab	Herts	Redbourn
1689	SMITH	Mary	20		Wife	Mar	25	F	Straw Plaiter	Herts	Redbourn
1690	SMITH	James	21	Dirt House Row	Head	Mar	59	M	Lath Render	Herts	Hemel Hempstead
1691	SMITH	Ann	21		Wife	Mar	57	F		Hunts	Abbotsley
1692	SMITH	Jane	21		Dau	Unm	19	F	Bonnet Sewer	Herts	Redbourn
1693	SMITH	Elizabeth	21		Dau	Unm	17	F	Straw Plaiter	Herts	Redbourn

	SURNAME	FORENAME	SCHEDULE NUMBER	ADDRESS	RELATIONSHIP	STATUS	AGE	SEX	OCCUPATION	COUNTY OF BIRTH	PLACE OF BIRTH
1694	MARKHAM	Thomas	22	Dirt House Row	Head	Mar	32	M	Agric Lab	Herts	Kimpton
1695	MARKHAM	Sarah	22		Wife	Mar	34	F	Straw Plaiter	Herts	Harpenden
1696	WEBB	William	23	Dirt House Row	Head	Widower	64	M	Agric Lab	Beds	Luton
1697	WEBB	Joseph	23		Son	Mar	23	M	Agric Lab	Herts	Redbourn
1698	WEBB	Susannah	23		Dau-in-law	Mar	22	F	Straw Plaiter	Herts	Redbourn
1699	WEBB	Alice	23		Grandau		10 m	F		Herts	Redbourn
1700	WILSON	Godfrey	24	Dirt House Row	Head	Mar	48	M	Agric Lab	Herts	Great Gaddesden
1701	WILSON	Dorcas	24		Wife	Mar	59	F	Straw Plaiter	Herts	Redbourn
1702	WILSON	Eli	24		Son		5	M	Scholar	Herts	Hemel Hempstead
1703	CLARK	James	25	Dirt House Row	Head	Widower	74	M	Agric Lab	Herts	Kimpton
1704	CLARK	James	25		Son	Mar	55	M	Agric Lab	Herts	Redbourn
1705	CLARK	Ann	25		Dau-in-law	Mar	60	F	Straw Plaiter	Herts	Redbourn
1706	LONDON	Daniel	26	Dirt House Row	Head	Mar	26	M	Agric Lab	Herts	Redbourn
1707	LONDON	Sarah	26		Wife	Mar	25	F	Straw Plaiter	Herts	Redbourn
1708	LONDON	George	26		Son		1	M		Herts	Redbourn
1709	COOPER	George	27	Dirt House Row	Head	Mar	30	M	Agric Lab	Herts	Redbourn
1710	COOPER	Rebecca	27		Wife	Mar	29	F		Herts	Redbourn
1711	ABBOTT	John	27		Lodger	Unm	20	M	Agric Lab	Herts	Redbourn
1712	ABBOTT	Charles	27		Lodger		10	M		Herts	Redbourn
1713	THOROGOOD	Ann	28	Dirt House Row	Head	Mar	28	F	Straw Plaiter	Herts	Redbourn
1714	THOROGOOD	Mary A.	28		Dau		5	F		Herts	Redbourn
1715	THOROGOOD	Charles	28		Son		4	M		Herts	Redbourn
1716	THOROGOOD	Alfred	28		Son		3 m	M		Herts	Redbourn
1717	BATES	Sarah	28		Lodger	Unm	33	F	Straw Plaiter	Herts	Redbourn
1718	HALE	William	29	Dirt House Row	Head	Mar	29	M	Agric Lab	Herts	Flamstead
1719	HALE	Hannah	29		Wife	Mar	24	F	Straw Plaiter	Herts	Redbourn
1720	HALE	Eliza	29		Dau		7	F	Scholar	Herts	Redbourn
1721	HALE	Mary	29		Dau		3	F		Herts	Redbourn
1722	HALE	Hannah	29		Dau		5 m	F		Herts	Redbourn
1723	LONDON	Edward	30	Dirt House Row	Head	Mar	64	M	Agric Lab	Herts	Hemel Hempstead
1724	LONDON	Susan	30		Wife	Mar	60	F	Straw Plaiter	Herts	Redbourn

One house uninhabited

	SURNAME	FORENAME	SCHEDULE NUMBER	ADDRESS	RELATIONSHIP	STATUS	AGE	SEX	OCCUPATION	COUNTY OF BIRTH	PLACE OF BIRTH
1725	POULTER	Peter	31	Dirt House Row	Head	Mar	43	M	Agric Lab	Beds	Bendich [Bendish, Herts?]
1726	POULTER	Mary	31		Wife	Mar	36	F		Herts	Redbourn
1727	POULTER	Ann	31		Sister	Unm	26	F	At Home	Herts	Redbourn
1728	POULTER	Emma	31		Dau	Unm	16	F	Scholar	Herts	Redbourn
1729	POULTER	Eliza	31		Dau		11	F	Scholar	Herts	Redbourn
1730	PLYMOUTH	James	32	Dirt House Row	Head	Mar	36	M	Agric Lab	Herts	Redbourn
1731	PLYMOUTH	Harriett	32		Wife	Mar	39	F	Straw Bonnet Sewer	Herts	Redbourn
1732	PLYMOUTH	George	32		Son		10	M	Scholar	Herts	Redbourn
1733	PLYMOUTH	Eliza	32		Dau		8	F	At Home	Herts	Redbourn
1734	PLYMOUTH	Henry	32		Son		6	M	Scholar	Herts	Redbourn
1735	PLYMOUTH	Ann	32		Dau		1	F		Herts	Redbourn

1736	SMITH	Thomas	33	Dirt House Row	Head	Mar	36	M	Straw Dyer	Herts	Redbourn
1737	SMITH	Eliza	33		Wife	Mar	34	F		Herts	Redbourn
1738	SMITH	Sarah	33		Dau		13	F	Bonnet Sewer	Herts	Redbourn
1739	SMITH	Eliza	33		Dau		12	F	Scholar	Herts	Redbourn
1740	SMITH	Daniel	33		Son		9	M	Scholar	Herts	Redbourn
1741	SMITH	Selina	33		Dau		7	F	Scholar	Herts	Redbourn
1742	SMITH	Hannah	33		Dau		4	F		Herts	Redbourn
1743	SMITH	Joseph	33		Son		3	M		Herts	Redbourn
1744	SMITH	Mary	33		Dau		2	F		Herts	Redbourn
1745	HEBBS	William	34	Dirt House Row	Head	Mar	30	M	Agric Lab	Herts	Redbourn
1746	HEBBS	Sarah	34		Wife	Mar	26	F	Straw Plaiter	Middx	London
1747	HEBBS	John	34		Son		9	M	Scholar	Herts	Redbourn
1748	HEBBS	Mary	34		Dau		6	F	Scholar	Herts	Redbourn
1749	HEBBS	Ann	34		Dau		4	F		Herts	Redbourn
1750	HEBBS	Alfred	34		Son		1	M		Herts	Redbourn
1751	WOODSTOCK	Sherach	35	Dirt House Row	Head	Mar	35	M	Agric Lab	Herts	Redbourn
1752	WOODSTOCK	Hannah	35		Wife	Mar	35	F		Herts	Redbourn
1753	WOODSTOCK	George	35		Son	Unm	15	M	Straw Factor	Herts	Redbourn
1754	WOODSTOCK	William	35		Son	Unm	13	M	Scholar	Herts	Redbourn
1755	WOODSTOCK	Abenego	35		Son		10	M	Scholar	Herts	Redbourn
1756	WOODSTOCK	Joreal (?)	35		Son		8	M	Scholar	Herts	Redbourn
1757	WOODSTOCK	Rose	35		Dau		6	F	Scholar	Herts	Redbourn
1758	WOODSTOCK	Emma	35		Dau		4	F		Herts	Redbourn
1759	WELLS	Richard	36	Dirt House Row	Head	Mar	66	M	Bricklayer	Herts	Redbourn
1760	WELLS	Elizabeth	36		Wife	Mar	54	F	Straw Plaiter	Herts	Hemel Hempstead
1761	WELLS	Ephraim	36		Son	Unm	22	M	Bricklayer	Herts	Redbourn
1762	WELLS	Ann	36		Dau	Unm	20	F	Straw Plaiter	Herts	Redbourn
1763	WELLS	Henry	36		Son		14	M	Straw Plaiter	Herts	Redbourn
1764	WELLS	Edmund	36		Son		12	M	Straw Plaiter	Herts	Redbourn
1765	PLYMOUTH	Robert	37	Dirt House Row	Head	Mar	74	M	Agric Lab	Herts	Pirton [Hitchin]
1766	PLYMOUTH	Emma	37		Wife	Mar	60	F	Straw Plaiter	Beds	Shillington
1767	AUSTIN	Joseph	38	Dirt House Row	Head	Mar	66	M	Agric Lab	Herts	Redbourn
1768	AUSTIN	Mary	38		Wife	Mar	62	F		Herts	Redbourn
1769	AUSTIN	Elizabeth	38		Dau	Unm	22	F	Straw Plaiter	Herts	Redbourn
1770	LIBERTY	Emily	38		Niece		15	F	Straw Plaiter	Herts	Redbourn
1771	LIBERTY	Selina	38		Niece		5	F	Scholar	Herts	Redbourn
1772	HALSEY	Jane	38		Lodger	Unm	19	F	Straw Plaiter	Herts	Redbourn
1773	LEE	Hannah	39	Dirt House Row	Head	Unm	36	F	Straw Plaiter	Herts	Redbourn
1774	SMITH	Thomas	39		Lodger	Unm	22	M	Agric Lab	Herts	Redbourn
1775	HALL	Henry	39		Lodger	Unm	30	M	Agric Lab	Herts	Abbotts Langley
1776	LEE	Samuel	40	Dirt House Row	Head	Mar	39	M	Agric Lab	Herts	Redbourn
1777	LEE	Esther	40		Wife	Mar	36	F	Straw Plaiter	Beds	Caddington
1778	LEE	Charles	40		Son	Unm	16	M	Agric Lab	Herts	Redbourn
1779	LEE	Henry	40		Son		12	M	Agric Lab	Herts	St Michaels, St Albans

	SURNAME	FORENAME	SCHEDULE NUMBER	ADDRESS	RELATIONSHIP	STATUS	AGE	SEX	OCCUPATION	COUNTY OF BIRTH	PLACE OF BIRTH
1780	LEE	Eliza	40		Dau		9	F	Scholar	Herts	Redbourn
1781	LEE	Mary A.	40		Dau		6	F	Scholar	Herts	Redbourn
1782	CASTLE	Frances	41	Dirt House Row	Head	Mar	58	F	Straw Plaiter	Herts	St Stephens, St Albans
1783	LEE	Edward	42	Dirt House Row	Head	Unm	30	M	Agric Lab	Herts	Redbourn
1784	HALSEY	Elizabeth	42		Serv	Unm	30	F	Servant	Herts	Redbourn
1785	HALSEY	Thomas	42		Servants Son		10	M	Scholar	Herts	Redbourn
1786	HALSEY	John	42		Servants Son		7	M	Scholar	Herts	Redbourn
1787	HALSEY	Edward	42		Servants Son		5	M	Scholar	Herts	Redbourn
1788	HALSEY	Amy	42		Servants Dau		1	F	Scholar	Herts	Redbourn
1789	WALDOCK	Thomas	43	Dirt House Row	Head	Widower	48	M	Agric Lab	Beds	Luton
1790	WALDOCK	Emily	43		Dau	Unm	19	F	Straw Plaiter	Herts	Redbourn
1791	WALDOCK	Henry	43		Son		11	M	Agric Lab	Herts	Redbourn
1792	WALDOCK	Maria	43		Dau		4	F	Scholar	Herts	Redbourn
1793	HEBBES	John	44	Dirt House Row	Head	Mar	40	M	Agric Lab	Herts	Redbourn
1794	HEBBES	Jane	44		Wife	Mar	39	F		Herts	Watford
1795	HEBBES	John C.	44		Son	Unm	19	M	Agric Lab	Herts	Redbourn
1796	HEBBES	Susannah	44		Dau	Unm	15	F	Straw Plaiter	Herts	Redbourn
1797	HEBBES	Sarah A.	44		Dau		12	F	Straw Plaiter	Herts	Redbourn
1798	HEBBES	Louisa	44		Dau		8	F	Straw Plaiter	Herts	Redbourn
1799	HEBBES	Goodinspire	44		Son		6	M	Straw Plaiter	Herts	Redbourn
1800	HEBBES	Walter	44		Son		4	M		Herts	Redbourn
1801	HEBBES	Eliza	44		Dau		1	F		Herts	Redbourn
1802	HEBBES	Charles	45	Dirt House Row	Head	Mar	47	M	Straw Factor	Herts	Redbourn
1803	HEBBES	Sarah	45		Wife	Mar	50	F	Straw Plaiter	Herts	Redbourn
1804	HEBBES	Joseph	46	Dirt House Row	Head	Mar	72	M	Lure Maker	Herts	Redbourn
1805	HEBBES	Mary Ann	46		Wife	Mar	70	F		Bucks	Nettleden [Hillesden?]
1806	TAYLOR	Thomas	47	Dirt House Row	Head	Mar	59	M	Agric Lab	Herts	Redbourn
1807	TAYLOR	Sarah	47		Wife	Mar	59	F		Herts	Wheathampstead
1808	WALDOCK	George	47		Grandson		7	M	Scholar	Herts	Redbourn
1809	WALDOCK	James	48	Dirt House Row	Head	Mar	30	M	Agric Lab	Beds	Luton
1810	WALDOCK	Judith	48		Wife	Mar	32	F	Straw Plaiter	Herts	Redbourn
1811	WALDOCK	Eliza	48		Dau		5	F	Scholar	Herts	Redbourn
1812	WALDOCK	James	48		Son		8	M	Scholar	Herts	Redbourn
1813	WALDOCK	William	48		Son		2	M		Herts	Redbourn
1814	WALDOCK	Benjamin	48		Son		6m	M		Herts	Redbourn
1815	TAYLOR	Thomas	48		Lodger	Unm	19	M	Agric Lab	Herts	Redbourn
1816	TAYLOR	Mary	49	Dirt House Row	Head	Widow	81	F	Straw Plaiter	Herts	Hemel Hempstead
1817	LIBERTY	John	50	Dirt House Row	Head	Unm	21	M	Agric Lab	Herts	Kensworth
1818	CROSS	John	50		Lodger	Unm	27	M	Agric Lab	Herts	Royston
1819	ASLIN	Thomas	51	Dirt House Row	Head	Mar	39	M	Agric Lab	Herts	Redbourn
1820	ASLIN	Susan	51		Wife	Mar	35	F		Herts	Hemel Hempstead
1821	ASLIN	William	51		Son		13	M	Scholar	Herts	Redbourn

1822	ASLIN	Robert	51		Son		5	M		Herts	Redbourn
1823	DOLLIMORE	James	52	Dirt House Row	Head	Mar	31	M	Agric Lab	Herts	Wheathampstead
1824	DOLLIMORE	Mary	52		Wife	Mar	25	F	Straw Plaiter	Herts	Redbourn
1825	HUCKELL	Thomas	52		Step-son		9	M	Scholar	Herts	Redbourn
1826	ASLIN	William	53	Dirt House Row	Head	Mar	50	M	Agric Lab	Herts	Redbourn
1827	ASLIN	Mary	53		Wife	Mar	49	F		Herts	Redbourn
1828	ASLIN	Rose	53		Dau	Unm	19	F	Straw Plaiter	Herts	Redbourn
1829	ASLIN	Avery	53		Son		10	M	Scholar	Herts	Redbourn
1830	ASLIN	Susan	53		Dau		7	F	Scholar	Herts	Redbourn
1831	AUSTIN	Thomas	54	Dirt House Row	Head	Mar	30	M	Agric Lab	Herts	Redbourn
1832	AUSTIN	Eliza	54		Wife	Mar	28	F	Straw Plaiter	Herts	Redbourn
1833	COCKLE	Maria	54		Step-dau		9	F	Scholar	Herts	Redbourn
1834	AUSTIN	Rose	54		Dau		3	F	Scholar	Herts	Redbourn
1835	AUSTIN	Charles	54		Son		1	M		Herts	Redbourn
1836	HALSEY	John	55	Dirt House Row	Head	Mar	40	M	Carpenter	Herts	Redbourn
1837	HALSEY	Rose	55		Wife	Mar	27	F	Straw Plaiter	Herts	Redbourn
1838	HALSEY	Jane	55		Dau	Unm	19	F	Straw Plaiter	Herts	Redbourn
1839	HALSEY	Louisa	55		Dau		3	F		Herts	Redbourn
1840	ROBBINS	William	56	Dirt House Row	Head	Mar	66	M	Carpenter	Beds	Tebworth
1841	ROBBINS	Mary	56		Wife	Mar	66	F		Herts	St Peters, St Albans
1842	BAIL	Richard	57	Dirt House Row	Head	Mar	66	M	Agric Lab	Herts	Redbourn
1843	BAIL	Catherine	57		Wife	Mar	61	F	Charwoman	Herts	St Albans
1844	HAWKINS	James	58	Bottom of Common	Head	Mar	42	M	Agric Lab	Herts	Caddington
1845	HAWKINS	Eliza	58		Wife	Mar	37	F		Herts	Redbourn
1846	HAWKINS	Mary	58		Dau	Unm	18	F	Straw Plaiter	Herts	Redbourn
1847	HAWKINS	George	58		Son	Unm	16	M	Agric Lab	Herts	Redbourn
1848	HAWKINS	Elizabeth	58		Dau		14	F	Straw Plaiter	Herts	Redbourn
1849	HAWKINS	Susannah	58		Dau		12	F	Scholar	Herts	Redbourn
1850	HAWKINS	James	58		Son		10	M	Scholar	Herts	Redbourn
1851	HAWKINS	Benjamin	58		Son		6	M	Scholar	Herts	Redbourn
1852	HAWKINS	Eliza	58		Dau		3	F		Herts	Redbourn
1853	HAWKINS	Amos	58		Son		1wk	M		Herts	Redbourn
1854	COLEMAN	Susannah	59	Bottom of Common	Head	Widow	75	F	Pauper	Beds	Cranfield
1855	COLEMAN	Mary	59		Dau	Unm	47	F	Straw Plaiter	Herts	Redbourn
1856	COLEMAN	Sarah	59		Dau	Unm	45	F	Charwoman	Herts	Redbourn
1857	SKINNER	John	60	Bottom of Common	Head	Mar	37	M	Agric Lab	Herts	Redbourn
1858	SKINNER	Kezia	60		Wife	Mar	49	F	Straw Plaiter	Herts	Harpenden
1859	WINCHESTER	Bob	61	Common House	Head	Widower	73	M	Cow Farrier	Bucks	Chenies
1860	WINCHESTER	Susan	61		Dau	Unm	23	F	Straw Plaiter	Herts	Redbourn
1861	DOLLIMORE	George	62	Old House Lane	Head	Mar	37	M	Agric Lab	Herts	Redbourn
1862	DOLLIMORE	Eliza	62		Wife	Mar	36	F	Straw Plaiter	Herts	Redbourn
1863	DOLLIMORE	Eliza	62		Dau		11	F	Scholar	Herts	Redbourn
1864	DOLLIMORE	Charles	62		Son		6	M	Scholar	Herts	Redbourn
1865	DOLLIMORE	Alfred	62		Son		4	M		Herts	Redbourn

	SURNAME	FORENAME	SCHEDULE NUMBER	ADDRESS	RELATIONSHIP	STATUS	AGE	SEX	OCCUPATION	COUNTY OF BIRTH	PLACE OF BIRTH
1866	DOLLIMORE	Charlotte	62		Dau		11 m	F		Herts	Redbourn
1867	DOLLIMORE	Joseph	62		Son		11 m	M		Herts	Redbourn
1868	WHEATLY	Charles	63	Old House Lane	Head	Mar	37	M	Agric Lab	Herts	St Albans
1869	WHEATLY	Eliza	63		Wife	Mar	37	F		Herts	Redbourn
1870	WHEATLY	Harriett	63		Dau		11	F	Scholar	Herts	Redbourn
1871	WHEATLY	Emma	63		Dau		9	F	Scholar	Herts	Redbourn
1872	WHEATLY	Mary	63		Dau		6	F	Scholar	Herts	Redbourn
1873	WHEATLY	George	63		Son		4	M		Herts	Redbourn
1874	WHEATLY	Daniel	63		Son		2	M		Herts	Redbourn
1875	WELLS	John	64	Hog End	Head	Mar	65	M	Agric Lab	Bucks	Whicombe [Wycombe]
1876	WELLS	Elizabeth	64		Wife	Mar	59	F		Herts	St Albans
1877	WHEATLY	David	64		Visitor		11	M	Scholar	Herts	Redbourn
1878	SKINNER	William	65	Hog End	Head	Mar	26	M	Agric Lab	Herts	Redbourn
1879	SKINNER	Ann	65		Wife	Mar	24	F	Straw Plaiter	Herts	Redbourn
1880	SKINNER	Ann M.	65		Dau		10	F		Herts	Redbourn
1881	AUBERN	John	66	Butlers	Head	Mar	39	M	Agric Lab	Herts	Sandridge
1882	AUBERN	Ann	66		Wife	Mar	41	F	Straw Plaiter	Bucks	Oving
1883	AUBERN	Emma	66		Dau		11	F	Scholar	Herts	St Albans
1884	AUBERN	George	66		Son		8	M	Scholar	Herts	St Albans
1885	AUBERN	Eliza	66		Dau		4	F		Herts	Redbourn
1886	CLARK	Isaac	66		Serv	Unm	20	M	Servant	Unknown	
1887	HILL	Samuel	66		Serv	Unm	15	M	Servant	Herts	St Stephens, St Albans
1888	SMITH	Frederick	66	Butlers	Head	Mar	50	M	Retired Farmer	Herts	St Stephens, St Albans
1889	SMITH	Elizabeth	66		Wife	Mar	40	F		Herts	Flamstead
1890	SMITH	Dorcas	66		Dau	Unm	22	F	At Home	Herts	Great Gaddesden
1891	SMITH	Caroline	66		Dau	Unm	20	F	At Home	Herts	Great Gaddesden
1892	SMITH	Henry	66		Son	Unm	14	M	At Home	Herts	Great Gaddesden
1893	JAMES	George	66		Visitor	Unm	24	M	Blind Maker	Middx	London
1894	READ	Edmund	67	Jerrams	Head	Mar	30	M	Gamekeeper	Middx	St Georges, London
1895	READ	Susannah	67		Wife	Mar	31	F	Straw Plaiter	Herts	St Michaels, St Albans
1896	READ	John H.	67		Son		9	M	Scholar	Herts	St Albans
1897	READ	Edmund	67		Son		3	M		Herts	Redbourn
1898	READ	William	67		Son		1	M		Herts	Redbourn
1899	DAY	John	68	New Jerrams	Head	Mar	37	M	Agric Lab	Herts	St Pauls Walden
1900	DAY	Susan	68		Wife	Mar	35	F		Herts	Watford
1901	DAY	Elizabeth	68		Dau		11	F	Scholar	Herts	Redbourn
1902	DAY	George	68		Son		10	M	Scholar	Herts	Redbourn
1903	DAY	Thomas	68		Son		9	M	Scholar	Herts	Redbourn
1904	ASLIN	Thomas	69	South End Farm	Head	Widower	65	M	Farmer of 179 acres employing 10 labourers	Herts	Redbourn
1905	ASLIN	Thomas	69		Son	Mar	42	M	At Home	Herts	Redbourn
1906	ASLIN	Mary	69		Dau	Unm	21	F	At Home	Herts	Redbourn
1907	ASLIN	Charles	69		Son	Unm	18	M	At Home	Herts	Redbourn
1908	ASLIN	Edmund	69		Son	Unm	14	M	At Home	Herts	Redbourn

1909	ASLIN	William	69		Serv	Unm	13	M	Farm Servant	Herts	Redbourn
1910	ASLIN	Maria	70	South End	Head	Mar	30	F	Domestic	Kent	Seven Oaks
1911	ASLIN	Emily	70		Dau		10	F	At Home	Herts	Redbourn
1912	ASLIN	Ann	70		Dau		8	F	At Home	Herts	Redbourn
1913	ASLIN	George	70		Son		5	M		Herts	Redbourn
1914	FREEMAN	Mary	71	South End	Head	Widow	86	F	Pauper	Bucks	Chesham
1915	WEST	Eliza	71		Dau	Widow	35	F	Charwoman	Herts	Redbourn
1916	WEST	Keturah	71		Grandau	Unm	13	F	Straw Plaiter	Herts	Redbourn
1917	WEST	William	71		Grandson		8	M	Scholar	Herts	Redbourn
1918	STRATTON	George	72	Small Beer Hall	Head	Mar	22	M	Agric Lab	Herts	Redbourn
1919	STRATTON	Elizabeth	72		Wife	Mar	22	F	Straw Plaiter	Herts	Abbotts Langley
1920	STRATTON	Thomas	73	Small Beer Hall	Head	Mar	63	M	Agric Lab	Herts	Wheathampstead
1921	STRATTON	Mary	73		Wife	Mar	56	F	Straw Plaiter	Herts	Redbourn
1922	STRATTON	Elizabeth	73		Dau	Unm	23	F	Idiot	Herts	Redbourn
1923	STRATTON	Eliza	73		Dau	Unm	17	F	Straw Plaiter	Herts	Redbourn
1924	ORCHARD	John	74	Hill Farm	Head	Mar	56	M	Farmer of 73 acres employing 3 labourers	Herts	St Michaels, St Albans
1925	ORCHARD	Sarah	74		Wife	Mar	50	F		Herts	St Michaels, St Albans
1926	ORCHARD	Mary A.	74		Dau		12	F	Scholar	Herts	Redbourn
1927	ORCHARD	Rosanna	74		Dau		10	F	Scholar	Herts	Redbourn
1928	DAY	William	74		Serv	Unm	14	M	Farm Servant	Herts	St Michaels, St Albans
1929	CROFT	Henry	75	Running Horses	Head	Mar	71	M	Victualler	Herts	St Pauls Walden
1930	CROFT	Mary	75		Wife	Mar	70	F		Herts	Harpenden
1931	CROFT	Susan	75		Dau	Unm	20	F	Bonnet Sewer	Herts	Hatfield
1932	WILSON	Thomas	76	St Albans Road	Head	Mar	66	M	Agric Lab	Herts	Kensworth
1933	WILSON	Mary	76		Wife	Mar	63	F		Middx	London
1934	COCKLE	William	77	St Albans Road	Head	Mar	63	M	Agric Lab	Herts	Redbourn
1935	COCKLE	Hannah	77		Wife	Mar	66	F		Herts	St Albans
1936	PARTRIDGE	Keziah	78	Chequers	Head	Widow	44	F	Victualler	[Leics]	Wilson
1937	PARTRIDGE	William	78		Son	Unm	19	M	At Home	Herts	Redbourn
1938	PARTRIDGE	Sarah	78		Dau	Unm	15	F	At Home	Herts	Redbourn
1939	PARTRIDGE	Elizabeth	78		Dau		12	F	Scholar	Herts	Redbourn
1940	FIELD	Robert	78		Lodger	Unm	35	M	Agric Lab	Unknown	
1941	DIXON	Ernest	79	Mill	Head	Mar	41	M	Farmer & Miller. 150 acres employing 8 labourers	Herts	Redbourn
1942	DIXON	Harriett	79		Wife	Mar	35	F		Herts	Redbourn
1943	DIXON	Isabel	79		Dau		12	F	Scholar	Herts	Redbourn
1944	DIXON	Julia	79		Dau		10	F	Scholar	Herts	Redbourn
1945	DIXON	Ernest	79		Son		7	M	Scholar	Herts	Redbourn
1946	DIXON	Walter	79		Son		5	M	Scholar	Herts	Redbourn
1947	DIXON	James	79		Son		3	M		Herts	Redbourn
1948	DIXON	Albert	79		Son		10	M		Herts	Redbourn
1949	SAUNDERS	Rose	79		Visitor	Unm	16	F	Milliner	Herts	Redbourn
1950	MARTIN	Sarah	79		Serv	Unm	19	F	House Servant	Herts	London Colney
1951	SIMONS	Jane	79		Serv	Unm	14	F	House Servant	Middx	London

	SURNAME	FORENAME	SCHEDULE NUMBER	ADDRESS	RELATIONSHIP	STATUS	AGE	SEX	OCCUPATION	COUNTY OF BIRTH	PLACE OF BIRTH
1952	DOLLIMORE	Robert	79		Serv	Unm	20	M	Farm Servant	Herts	Redbourn
1953	DRAPER	James	80	Mill Bank	Head	Mar	27	M	Agric Lab	Herts	Lovedale [?]
1954	DRAPER	Sarah	80		Wife	Mar	22	F		Herts	Redbourn
1955	PAYNE	Joseph	81	Mill Bank	Head	Mar	28	M	Agric Lab	Herts	Caddington
1956	PAYNE	Ann	81		Wife	Mar	28	F		Berks	Wallgrave [Wargrave]
1957	PAYNE	Emma	81		Dau		9 m	F		Herts	Redbourn
1958	MOODY	George	82	Mill Bank	Head	Mar	39	M	Agric Lab	Herts	Redbourn
1959	MOODY	Harriett	82		Wife	Mar	36	F		Herts	Redbourn
1960	MOODY	Henry	82		Son		6	M	Scholar	Herts	Redbourn
1961	MOODY	Edward	82		Son		5	M		Herts	Redbourn
1962	MOODY	John	82		Son		2	M		Herts	Redbourn
1963	MOODY	William	82		Son		4 m	M		Herts	Redbourn
1964	FULLER	Henry	83	Mill Bank	Head	Mar	48	M	Agric Lab	Berks	Walgrave [Wargrave]
1965	FULLER	Rebecca	83		Wife	Mar	43	F		Berks	Walgrave [Wargrave]
1966	FULLER	Emma	83		Dau	Unm	19	F	At Home	Herts	Redbourn
1967	FULLER	William	83		Son		13	M	Agric Lab	Herts	Redbourn
1968	WEBB	George	84	Beaumont Hall	Head	Mar	45	M	Farmer & Malster, 530 acres employing 23 labourers	Middx	Clerkenwell
1969	WEBB	Ruth	84		Wife	Mar	44	F		Berks	Streatley
1970	WEBB	Caroline	84		Dau		10	F	Scholar	Herts	Redbourn
1971	WEBB	George	84		Son		8	M	Scholar	Herts	Redbourn
1972	FULLER	Ann	84		Serv	Unm	21	F	Cook	Herts	Redbourn
1973	READ	Ann	84		Serv	Unm	20	F	Housemaid	Herts	Redbourn
1974	HANDLEY	John	84		Serv	Unm	20	M	Groom	Herts	Essendon
1975	PAYNE	Samuel	84		Serv	Unm	23	M	Ploughman	Beds	Caddington
1976	HOBBS	Matthew	84		Serv	Unm	24	M	Ploughman	Beds	Luton
1977	HICKS	Ellen	84		Visitor	Unm	23	F	Merchants Daughter	Berks	Sonning
1978	TAYLOR	John	85	Beaumont Hall	Head	Mar	35	M	Agric Lab	Hants	Woodinitt [?] [?Woodmancott?]
1979	TAYLOR	Ann	85		Wife	Mar	32	F	Straw Plaiter	Herts	Bushey
1980	COTTERALL	Elizabeth	85		Step-dau	Unm	14	F	At Home	Herts	Bushey
1981	TAYLOR	William	85		Son		10	M	Scholar	Herts	Bushey
1982	TAYLOR	Ann	85		Dau		4	F		Beds	Luton
1983	TAYLOR	Eliza	85		Dau		1	F		Herts	Redbourn
1984	DOLLIMORE	Sarah	86	Dane End	Head	Widow	47	F	Straw Plaiter	Herts	Redbourn
1985	DOLLIMORE	George	86		Son		11	M	Scholar	Herts	Redbourn
1986	WRIGHT	Daniel	86		Lodger	Unm	16	M	Deaf & Dumb	Herts	Redbourn
1987	WRIGHT	James	86		Lodger		11	M	Deaf & Dumb	Herts	Redbourn
1988	WRIGHT	Emily	86		Lodger		7	F	Deaf & Dumb	Herts	Redbourn
1989	DOLLIMORE	Joseph	87	Dane End	Head	Mar	30	M	Agric Lab	Herts	Redbourn
1990	DOLLIMORE	Caroline	87		Wife	Mar	31	F	Straw Plaiter	Bucks	Wendover
1991	DOLLIMORE	Sarah J.	87		Dau		12	F	Scholar	Bucks	Wendover
1992	DOLLIMORE	Emmily	87		Dau		8	F	Scholar	Herts	Redbourn
1993	DOLLIMORE	Abel	87		Son		5	M	Scholar	Herts	Redbourn
1994	DOLLIMORE	Elizabeth	87		Dau		3	F		Herts	Redbourn

1995	BURCHMORE	William	88	Dane End Farm	Head	Mar	59	M	Farmer of 134 acres employing 5 labourers	Herts	Flamstead
1996	BURCHMORE	Sarah	88		Wife	Mar	59	F		Herts	Flamstead
1997	KINGSTON	Elizabeth	88		Step-dau	Unm	26	F		Herts	Harpenden
1998	BURRIDGE	Susan	88		Serv	Unm	19	F	Servant	Herts	Markyate Street
1999	CHALKLEY	Joseph	88		Serv	Unm	18	M	Farm Servant	Herts	Wheathampstead
2000	DOLLIMORE	William	88		Serv	Unm	18	M	Farm Servant	Herts	Redbourn
2001	VINCENT	William	88		Serv	Mar	25	M	Farm Servant	Herts	Kimpton
2002	BISHOP	John	89	Bottom House Farm	Head	Mar	50	M	Farmer of 94 acres employing 2 labourers	Herts	Unknown
2003	BISHOP	Elizabeth	89		Wife	Mar	32	F		Yorks	Sheffield
2004	BISHOP	John	89		Son		15	M	At Home	Herts	St Stephens, St Albans
2005	BISHOP	Edward	89		Son		11	M	Scholar	Herts	St Stephens, St Albans
2006	BISHOP	Emily	89		Dau		5	F		Herts	St Stephens, St Albans
2007	WEEDON	Mary	89		Serv	Unm	17	F	Servant	Cambs	Cambridge
2008	SEABROOK	John	90	Bakers Farm	Head	Mar	68	M	Farmer of 80 acres employing 2 labourers	Herts	Redbourn
2009	SEABROOK	Frances	90		Wife	Mar	66	F		Herts	Wheathampstead
2010	JACKSON	William	90		Serv	Unm	16	M	Servant	Herts	Redbourn
2011	SEABROOK	Eliza	90		Visitor	Unm	11	F	Scholar	Herts	Redbourn

One house uninhabited

2012	HOW	Mary	91	Beech Hyde	Head	Widow	70	F	Farmer of 166 acres employing 7 labourers	Middx	London
2013	HOW	Margaret	91		Dau	Unm	42	F	At Home	Herts	St Albans
2014	HOW	Mary	91		Dau	Unm	36	F	At Home	Herts	Redbourn
2015	HOW	John	91		Son	Unm	34	M	At Home	Herts	Redbourn
2016	HOW	Jane	91		Dau	Unm	28	F	At Home	Herts	Redbourn
2017	HUTCHINS	Ann	91		Serv	Unm	20	F	House Servant	Herts	St Albans
2018	TURNER	Jane	91		Serv	Unm	19	F	House Servant	Herts	St Albans
2019	PRESTON	Henry	91		Serv	Unm	19	M	Groom	Herts	Hemel Hempstead
2020	FREEMAN	Thomas	91		Serv	Unm	16	M	Horsekeeper	Herts	St Albans
2021	GEORGE	Benjamin	92	Cherry Trees	Head	Mar	43	M	Farmer of 319 acres employing 8 labourers	Herts	Redbourn
2022	GEORGE	Jane	92		Wife	Mar	36	F		Herts	Redbourn
2023	GEORGE	John	92		Son	Unm	17	M	Shepherd	Herts	Kensworth
2024	GEORGE	James	92		Son		15	M	Herdsman	Herts	Redbourn
2025	JACKSON	Mary	92		Visitor	Unm	21	F		Bucks	Unknown
2026	JEFFERY	Samuel	92		Serv	Unm	27	M	Agric Lab	Herts	Unknown
2027	COCKLE	George	92		Serv	Unm	19	M	Agric Lab	Herts	Redbourn
2028	SANDERS	Susan	92		Serv	Unm	23	F	Domestic Servant	Bucks	Unknown
2029	TAYLOR	Thomas	93	Cherry Trees	Head	Mar	51	M	Agric Lab	Herts	St Peters
2030	TAYLOR	Ann	93		Wife	Mar	47	F		Herts	Hemel Hempstead
2031	GURNEY	George	93		Serv	Unm	17	M	Shepherd	Beds	Whipsnade
2032	HEWITT	Thomas	93		Serv	Unm	16	M	Horsekeeper	Herts	St Stephens, St Albans
2033	CROFT	William	94	Wood End	Head	Mar	41	M	Farm Bailiff	Herts	Sandridge
2034	CROFT	Mary	94		Wife	Mar	36	F		Herts	St Michaels, St Albans
2035	CROFT	Henry	94		Son		11	M		Herts	Redbourn

	SURNAME	FORENAME	SCHEDULE NUMBER	ADDRESS	RELATIONSHIP	STATUS	AGE	SEX	OCCUPATION	COUNTY OF BIRTH	PLACE OF BIRTH
2036	CROFT	Matilda	94		Dau		9	F	Scholar	Herts	Redbourn
2037	CROFT	George	94		Son		6	M	Scholar	Herts	Redbourn
2038	CROFT	Susan	94		Dau		4	F		Herts	Redbourn
2039	CROFT	Louisa	94		Dau		1	F		Herts	Redbourn
2040	CROFT	Sarah	94		Dau	Unm	22	F	Straw Plaiter	Herts	Hemel Hempstead
2041	CROFT	Mary Ann	94		Grandau		1	F		Herts	Redbourn
2042	IMPEY [?]	Henry	94		Serv	Unm	21	M	Ploughman, Agric Lab	Herts	Redbourn
2043	SAUNDERS	William	94		Serv	Unm	17	M	Agric Lab	Herts	Great Gaddesden
2044	BOWRA [?]	William	95	Wood End	Head	Mar	65	M	Gamekeeper	Kent	Seven Oaks
2045	BOWRA [?]	Mary	95		Wife	Mar	67	F		Kent	Brasted
2046	BOWRA [?]	Sarah	95		Dau	Unm	28	F	Bonnet Sewer	Herts	St Michaels, St Albans
2047	SMITH	George	96	Cross Lanes	Head	Mar	36	M	Agric Lab	Herts	Redbourn
2048	SMITH	Mary	96		Wife	Mar	31	F		Herts	Redbourn
2049	SMITH	Joseph	96		Son		11	M	Scholar	Herts	Redbourn
2050	SMITH	Esther	96		Dau		8	F	Scholar	Herts	Redbourn
2051	SMITH	Edward	96		Son		5	M	Scholar	Herts	Redbourn
2052	SMITH	James	96		Son		3	M		Herts	Redbourn
2053	SMITH	Mary	96		Dau		1	F		Herts	Redbourn
2054	SMITH	Thomas	97	Cross Lanes	Head	Mar	41	M	Agric Lab	Herts	Caddington
2055	SMITH	Sarah	97		Wife	Mar	36	F		Herts	Kensworth
2056	SMITH	Mary	97		Dau	Unm	16	F	Straw Plaiter	Herts	Redbourn
2057	SMITH	Rebecca	97		Dau		15	F	Scholar	Herts	Redbourn
2058	SMITH	Abraham	97		Son		11	M	Scholar	Herts	Redbourn
2059	SMITH	Louisa	97		Dau		8	F	Scholar	Herts	Redbourn
2060	SMITH	Ann	97		Dau		6	F	Scholar	Herts	Redbourn
2061	SMITH	Sarah	97		Dau		7m	F		Herts	Redbourn
2062	BEAUMONT	Joseph	98	Flowers Farm	Head	Mar	31	M	Farmer of 107 acres employing 1 labourer	Herts	Redbourn
2063	BEAUMONT	Hannah	98		Wife	Mar	33	F		Middx	Hillingdon
2064	COLLINS	Mary	98		Sister-in-law	Widow	36	F	Retired Butcher	Middx	Hillingdon
2065	COLLINS	Edward	98		Nephew		7	M	Scholar	Herts	Hemel Hempstead
2066	COLLINS	Caroline	98		Niece		6	F		Herts	Hemel Hempstead
2067	RICHARDSON	Ann	98		Serv	Unm	19	F	Servant	Beds	Clophill
2068	ABRAMS	William	98		Serv	Unm	20	M	Agric Lab	Herts	Redbourn
2069	SQUIRES	John	98		Serv	Unm	19	M	Agric Lab, Oddman.	Herts	Redbourn
2070	LIBERTY	William	98		Serv	Unm	14	M	Agric Lab, Horsekeeper	Herts	Redbourn
2071	NORWOOD	Sarah	99	Capt Hall Farm	Head	Widow	81	F	Farmer of 61 acres employing 2 labourers	Herts	Chipperfield [Kings Langley]
2072	NORWOOD	Jane	99		Dau	Unm	61	F	Blind	Herts	St Stephens, St Albans
2073	NORWOOD	George	99		Son	Unm	55	M	Agric Lab	Herts	Watford
2074	NORWOOD	Ann	99		Dau	Unm	52	F		Herts	Redbourn
2075	STEPHENS	William	99		Serv	Unm	31	M	Servant	Herts	Abbotts Langley
2076	GADSBURY	Mary	100	Church Gate	Head	Widow	76	F	Pauper	Herts	Flamstead
2077	SMITH	William	100		Lodger	Unm	58	M	Agric Lab	Bucks	Ivinghoe
2078	SEABROOK	Sarah	100		Visitor		13	F	Scholar	Herts	Harpenden

2079	LEE	Thomas	101	Church Gate	Head	Mar	45	M	Agric Lab	Herts	Redbourn
2080	LEE	Elizabeth	101		Wife	Mar	54	F	Straw Plaiter	Herts	Preston
2081	DOLLIMORE	Edward	101		Grandson		3	M		Herts	Redbourn
2082	LEE	William	101		Son	Mar	19	M	Agric Lab	Herts	Redbourn
2083	LEE	Elizabeth	101		Dau-in-law	Mar	23	F	Lace Maker	Oxon	Kingston
2084	LEE	Emma	101		Grandau		1	F		Herts	Redbourn

End of the 3c District, parish of Redbourn

Chapter Seven

The parish of Sandridge

Registrar's District: Harpenden   Enumeration District 4a   Ref. HO 107/1713 folios 194-209

All that part of the parish of Sandridge which lies to the east of the road from Hardems Marsh through Sandridge to Wheathampstead, including Church End, Marford, Bride Hall, Water End, Coleman Green and farms within the said boundary.

Village of Sandridge

1	KERRISON	Levi	1	House Lane	Head	Mar	38	M	Builder employing 4 men	Norfolk	East Marling
2	KERRISON	Mary	1		Wife	Mar	34	F	Shopkeeper	Herts	Sandridge
3	KERRISON	Louisa	1		Dau	Unm	10	F	Scholar	Herts	Sandridge
4	KERRISON	Emma J	1		Dau	Unm	8	F	Scholar	Herts	Sandridge
5	KERRISON	Solomon	1		Son	Unm	6	M	Scholar	Herts	Sandridge
6	KERRISON	James	1		Son	Unm	6	M	Scholar	Herts	Sandridge
7	KERRISON	Mark	1		Son	Unm	3	M	Scholar	Herts	Sandridge
8	KERRISON	Horatio	1		Son	Unm	1	M		Herts	Sandridge
9	PAUL	Jesse	1		Visitor	Unm	17	M	Tailor (Journeyman)	Herts	Sandridge
10	WARBEY	James	2	House Lane	Head	Mar	48	M	Blacksmith (Journeyman)	Herts	Tewin
11	WARBEY	Kitty	2		Wife	Mar	45	F	Domestic Duties	Herts	Sandridge
12	WARBEY	William	2		Son	Unm	21	M	Blacksmith (Journeyman)	Herts	Sandridge
13	WARBEY	Ann	2		Dau	Unm	18	F	Straw Plaiter	Herts	Sandridge
14	WARBEY	Benjamin	2		Son	Unm	14	M	Agric Lab	Herts	Sandridge
15	WARBEY	Sarah	2		Dau	Unm	16	F	Teacher National School	Herts	Sandridge
16	WARBEY	George	2		Son	Unm	12	M	Scholar	Herts	Sandridge
17	WARBEY	Eliza	2		Dau	Unm	10	F	Scholar	Herts	Sandridge
18	WARBEY	John	2		Son	Unm	6	M	Scholar	Herts	Sandridge
19	WARBEY	Charles	2		Son	Unm	4	M	Scholar	Herts	Sandridge
20	FILLER	William	3	Village Street	Head	Mar	36	M	Groom	Herts	Hatfield
21	FILLER	Rebecca	3		Wife	Mar	39	F		Herts	Sandridge
22	FILLER	Ann M	3		Dau	Unm	7	F	Scholar	Herts	Sandridge
23	FILLER	Emma	3		Dau	Unm	5	F	Scholar	Herts	Sandridge
24	FILLER	Jesse M	3		Son		2	M	Scholar	Herts	Sandridge
25	FILLER	Elizabeth	3		Dau		2 m	F		Herts	Sandridge

Figure 8 : SANDRIDGE

331

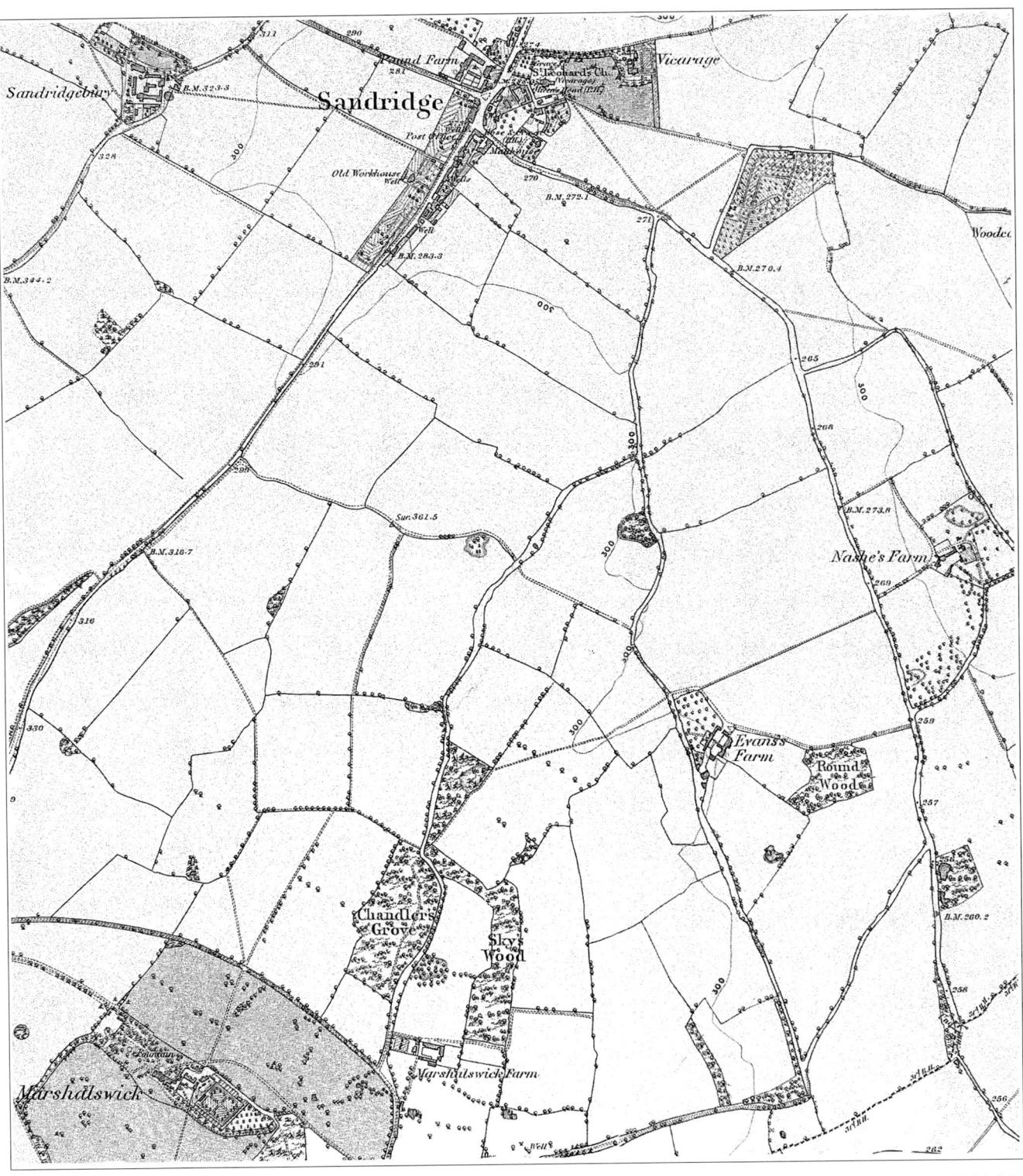

From the first edition of the 6 inch Ordinance Survey of Hertfordshire (1878), Sheet XXXIV AND XXXV

Approximate scale of reproduction: 1cm = 112m

	SURNAME	FORENAME	SCHEDULE NUMBER	ADDRESS	RELATIONSHIP	STATUS	AGE	SEX	OCCUPATION	COUNTY OF BIRTH	PLACE OF BIRTH
26	FRANKLING	Martha	3		Sister-in-law	Unm	24	F	Straw plaiter	Herts	Sandridge
27	MARDLING	John	4	Village Street	Head	Mar	56	M	Agric Lab	Herts	Sandridge
28	MARDLING	Dinah	4		Wife	Mar	55	F	Agric Lab Wife (Blind)	Herts	Redbourn
29	MARDLING	Rebecca	4		Dau	Unm	26	F	Brazilian Hat Maker	Herts	Sandridge
30	MARDLING	Emma	4		Dau	Unm	21	F	Teacher National School	Herts	Sandridge
31	HEDGES	Joseph	5	Village Street	Head	Mar	61	M	Agric Lab	Herts	Wheathampstead
32	HEDGES	Ann	5		Wife	Mar	59	F	Domestic	Herts	Tewin
33	HEDGES	Maria	5		Dau	Unm	27	F	Straw plaiter	Herts	Wheathampstead
34	HEDGES	Eliza	5		Dau	Unm	22	F	Brazilian Hat Maker	Herts	Wheathampstead
35	PAUL	William	6	Village Street	Head	Mar	30	M	Carpenter employing 4 Labourers	Herts	Sandridge
36	PAUL	Mary	6		Wife	Mar	31	F		Herts	St Peters
37	PAUL	William	6		Son		6	M	Scholar	Herts	Sandridge
38	PAUL	Peter	6		Son		1	M	Scholar	Herts	Sandridge
39	PAUL	Caroline	6		Dau		3	F	Scholar	Herts	Sandridge
40	HEDGES	John	6		Apprentice	Unm	18	M	Carpenter (App)	Herts	St Peters
41	PARSONS	James	7	Village Street	Head	Mar	61	M	Carrier	Herts	Sandridge
42	PARSONS	Elizabeth	7		Wife	Mar	58	F	Domestic	Herts	Sandridge
43	PARSONS	Susan	7		Dau	Unm	27	F	Trimming Weaver	Herts	Sandridge
44	ALDRIDGE	Isabel	7		Visitor	Unm	19	F	Brazilian Hat Maker	Herts	Sandridge
45	GAYTON	Samuel	8	Village Street	Head	Mar	50	M	Agric Lab	Bucks	Brick Hill
46	GAYTON	Ann	8		Wife	Mar	46	F	Charwoman	Herts	Sandridge
47	GAYTON	Sarah	8		Dau	Unm	16	F	House Servant	Herts	Sandridge
48	GAYTON	William	8		Son	Unm	13	M	Agric Lab	Herts	Sandridge
49	GAYTON	Ann	8		Dau	Unm	10	F	Scholar	Herts	Sandridge
50	GAYTON	Emma	8		Dau		3	F	Scholar	Herts	Sandridge
51	LATTIMORE	Joshua	9	Village Street	Head	Mar	44	M	Timber Merchant employing 10 men	Herts	Sandridge
52	LATTIMORE	Mary	9		Wife	Mar	47	F		Wilts	Highworth
53	GEGG	Ann	9		Aunt	Widow	84	F	Retired Hat Manufacturer	Wilts	Highworth
54	DAVIS	John	9		Serv	Unm	18	M	General Servant	Herts	Gustard Wood
55	POLLARD	Joseph	9		Serv	Unm	14	M	General Servant	Beds	Luton
56	IMPEY	John	10	Village Street	Head	Mar	58	M	Agric Lab	Herts	St Albans
57	IMPEY	Sarah	10		Wife	Mar	35	F	Charwoman	Herts	Shephall
58	IMPEY	Joshua	10		Son	Unm	11	M	Errand Boy	Herts	St Albans
59	IMPEY	Thomas	10		Son	Unm	6	M	Scholar	Herts	St Albans
60	IMPEY	Joseph	10		Son		4	M	Scholar	Herts	Sandridge
61	SMITH	Thomas	10		Brother-in-law	Widower	28	M	Agric Lab	Herts	Wheathampstead
62	SMITH	Roda	10		Niece	Unm	4	F	Scholar	Herts	St Albans
63	TRUSSELL	William	11	Church End	Head	Mar	63	M	Agric Lab	Herts	Hitchin
64	TRUSSELL	Sarah	11		Wife	Mar	56	F	Charwoman	Herts	St Albans
65	TRUSSELL	Eliza	11		Dau	Unm	15	F	Brazilian Hat Maker	Herts	Sandridge
66	TRUSSELL	James	11		Son	Unm	12	M	Agric Lab	Herts	Sandridge
67	BARFORD	William	12	Church End	Head	Widower	64	M	Agric Lab	Herts	Sandridge
68	BARFORD	George	12		Son	Mar	32	M	Agric Lab	Herts	Sandridge

69	BARFORD	Sophia	12		Dau-in-law	Mar	35	F		Herts	St Albans
70	MATTHEWS	John	12		Step-son	Unm	11	M	Agric Lab	Herts	Sandridge
71	TAYLOR	Thomas	13	Church End	Head	Mar	29	M	Agric Lab	Herts	St Albans
72	TAYLOR	Anna	13		Wife	Mar	29	F		Herts	Colney Heath
73	TAYLOR	Sarah	13		Dau	Unm	4	F	Scholar	Herts	Sandridge
74	TAYLOR	William	13		Son	Unm	1	M		Herts	Sandridge
75	FARR	John	14	Church End	Head	Mar	64	M	Agric Lab	Herts	Kings Walden
76	FARR	Elizabeth	14		Wife	Mar	62	F		Herts	Sandridge
77	HARDY	Rebecca	14		Sister-in-law	Unm	47	F	Straw plaiter	Herts	Sandridge
78	IRONS	John	15	Church End (Queens Head Inn)	Head	Mar	45	M	Victualler	Herts	St Albans
79	IRONS	Elizabeth	15		Wife	Mar	43	F		Herts	Harpenden
80	IRONS	Susan	15		Dau	Unm	4	F	Scholar	Herts	Sandridge
81	IRONS	Ellen	15		Dau		1	F		Herts	Sandridge
82	CROFT	Rosa	15		Niece		7	F	Scholar	Herts	Hatfield
83	HARDY	James	15		Visitor	Unm	53	M	Pensioner Chelsea	Herts	Sandridge
84	GEORGE	John	15		Visitor	Unm	34	M	Farm Servant	Herts	Sandridge
85	PARSONS	John	15		Visitor	Unm	33	M	Bricklayer (Journeyman)	Hants	Winchester
86	WINBOLT	Thomas Hy	16	Church End Vicarage	Head	Mar	53	M	Curate of Sandridge	Middx	Edmonton
87	WINBOLT	Mary S	16		Wife	Mar	37	F		Ireland	[Unknown]
88	WINBOLT	Ann E	16		Dau	Unm	5	F	Scholar	Middx	Hadley
89	WINBOLT	Henry H	16		Son		12	M	Scholar	Middx	Hadley
90	WINBOLT	John S	16		Son		10	M	Scholar	Middx	Hadley
91	WINBOLT	Sophia S	16		Visitor	Unm	40	F	Annuitant	Middx	Edmonton
92	TRACHAD	Fred S	16		[blank]	Unm	16	M	Scholar	France	[Unknown]
93	STEER	Charles B	16		[blank]	Unm	15	M	Scholar	E. Indies	[Unknown]
94	ROBERTSON	John J E	16		[blank]	Unm	14	M	Scholar	E. Indies	[Unknown]
95	STEER	Edmund D	16		[blank]	Unm	13	M	Scholar	E. Indies	[Unknown]
96	BALL	Francis	16		Serv	Unm	34	F	House Servant	Middx	Enfield
97	SALMON	Elizabeth	16		Serv	Unm	27	F	House Servant	Gloucs	Hanham
98	WRIGHT	Ann	16		Serv	Unm	17	F	House Servant	Herts	St Stephens
99	LAWRENCE	John	17	Church End	Head	Mar	50	M	Agric Lab	Herts	Kimpton
100	LAWRENCE	Charlotte	17		Wife	Mar	44	F		Herts	Sandridge
101	LAWRENCE	Charlotte	17		Dau	Unm	16	F	Brazilian Hat Maker	Herts	Sandridge
102	LAWRENCE	Ann	17		Dau	Unm	12	F	Brazilian Hat Maker	Herts	Sandridge
103	LAWRENCE	Charles	17		Son	Unm	10	M	Farm Servant	Herts	Sandridge
104	LAWRENCE	Lizzy	17		Dau	Unm	8	F	Scholar	Herts	Sandridge
105	LAWRENCE	Fanny	17		Dau		6	F	Scholar	Herts	Sandridge
106	LAWRENCE	James	17		Son		4	M	Scholar	Herts	Sandridge
107	MARDLING	Joseph	18	Church End	Head	Mar	25	M	Agric Lab	Herts	Stevenage
108	MARDLING	Ann	18		Wife	Mar	27	F		Herts	Colney Heath
109	LOVETT	Betsey	18		Visitor	Unm	16	F	Brazilian Hat Maker	Herts	Sandridge
110	MARDLING	James	18		Son		2	M		Herts	St Albans
111	MARDLING	Ann	18		Dau		8m	F		Herts	St Albans
112	LAWRENCE	Henry	19	Church End	Head	Widower	44	M	Baker	Herts	Sandridge
113	LAWRENCE	Walter	19		Son		11	M	Scholar	Herts	Sandridge

	SURNAME	FORENAME	SCHEDULE NUMBER	ADDRESS	RELATIONSHIP	STATUS	AGE	SEX	OCCUPATION	COUNTY OF BIRTH	PLACE OF BIRTH
114	LAWRENCE	Susan	19		Sister	Unm	48	F	Straw plaiter	Herts	Sandridge
115	LAWRENCE	Sarah	19		Sister	Unm	42	F	Straw plaiter	Herts	Sandridge
116	LAWRENCE	Rose	19		Niece		7	F	Scholar	Herts	Sandridge
117	HANDLEY	John	20	Church End	Head	Mar	60	M	Agric Lab	Herts	Hitchin
118	HANDLEY	Susan	20		Wife	Mar	57	F		Herts	Offley
119	HANDLEY	Sarah	20		Dau	Unm	16	F	Brazilian Hat Maker	Herts	Sandridge
120	HANDLEY	Richard	21	Church End	Head	Mar	33	M	Farm Servant	Herts	Kings Walden
121	HANDLEY	Susan	21		Wife	Mar	31	F		Herts	Sandridge
122	HANDLEY	Charles	21		Son	Unm	8	M	Scholar	Herts	St Albans
123	HANDLEY	George	21		Son		4	M	Scholar	Herts	Sandridge
124	HANDLEY	Jesse	21		Son		2	M		Herts	Sandridge
125	MATTHEWS	John	22	Church End	Head	Mar	22	M	Agric Lab	Herts	Kimpton
126	MATTHEWS	Sarah	22		Wife	Mar	22	F		Herts	Sandridge
127	MATTHEWS	Emma	22		Dau		1	F		Herts	Sandridge
128	PAYNE	Elizabeth	23	Church End	Head	Widow	57	F	Straw plaiter	Herts	Northchurch
129	PAYNE	Ann	23		Dau	Unm	26	F	Straw plaiter	Herts	Sandridge
130	JEEVES	Jesse	24	Church End	Head	Mar	26	M	Chalk drawer	Beds	Leighton [Buzzard]
131	JEEVES	Ann	24		Wife	Mar	20	F		Herts	Wheathampstead
132	MARDLING	Thomas	25		Head	Widower	85	M	(Pauper) Agric Lab	Beds	Shillington
133	MARDLING	William	25		Son	Widower	59	M	Pauper (Agric Lab)	Herts	Sandridge
134	MARDLING	John	25		Grandson	Unm	28	M	Bricklayers Labourer	Herts	Sandridge
135	LAWRENCE	John	26	Church End	Head	Mar	40	M	Agric Lab	Herts	Colney Heath
136	LAWRENCE	Eliza	26		Wife	Mar	35	F		Herts	Hatfield
137	LAWRENCE	James	26		Son	Unm	15	M	Agric Lab	Herts	Sandridge
138	LAWRENCE	William	26		Son	Unm	13	M	Agric Lab	Herts	Sandridge
139	LAWRENCE	Sarah	26		Dau		11	F	Brazilian Hat Maker	Herts	Sandridge
140	LAWRENCE	George	26		Son		8	M	Scholar	Herts	Sandridge
141	LAWRENCE	Alfred	26		Son		3	M	Scholar	Herts	Sandridge
142	HARTLEY	Frederick	27	Church End	Head	Mar	31	M	Agric Lab	Herts	St Albans
143	HARTLEY	Sarah	27		Wife	Mar	31	F		Herts	Colney Heath
144	HARTLEY	Anna	27		Dau		6	F	Scholar	Herts	Sandridge
145	HARTLEY	Thomas	27		Son		4	M	Scholar	Herts	Sandridge
146	HARTLEY	Sarah	27		Dau		1	F		Herts	Sandridge
147	DENNISS	William	28	Church End	Head	Mar	30	M	Lath Render	Herts	Sandridge
148	DENNISS	Elizabeth	28		Wife	Mar	32	F		Herts	Sandridge
149	DENNISS	William	28		Son		1	M		Herts	Sandridge
150	DENNISS	Frank	28		Son		2m	M		Herts	Sandridge
151	BARFORD	William	29	Church End	Head	Mar	37	M	Gardener	Herts	Sandridge
152	BARFORD	Eliza	29		Wife	Mar	35	F		Herts	Sandridge
153	BARFORD	Charles	29		Son		11	M	Agric Lab	Herts	Sandridge
154	BARFORD	Jane	29		Dau		9	F	Scholar	Herts	Sandridge
155	BARFORD	Rosa	29		Dau		7	F	Scholar	Herts	Sandridge
156	BARFORD	Alfred	29		Son		5	M	Scholar	Herts	Sandridge
157	BARFORD	Eliza	29		Dau		2	F		Herts	Sandridge
158	BARFORD	Emily	29		Dau		2m	F		Herts	Sandridge

159	GATHARD	Hannah	30	Church End	Head	Unm	45	F	Straw plaiter	Herts	Sandridge
160	ARCHER	Elizabeth	30		Visitor	Unm	13	F	Brazilian Hat Maker	Herts	Sandridge
161	ARCHER	William	31	Church End	Head	Mar	44	M	Agric Lab & Sexton	Herts	Sandridge
162	ARCHER	Sarah	31		Wife	Mar	42	F	Labourers Wife	Herts	Sandridge
163	ARCHER	James	31		Son		11	M	Agric Lab	Herts	Sandridge
164	ARCHER	Emma	31		Dau		9	F	Scholar	Herts	Sandridge
165	ARCHER	Sarah	31		Dau		7	F	Scholar	Herts	Sandridge
166	ARCHER	Edward	31		Son		3	M	Scholar	Herts	Sandridge
167	ARCHER	George	31		Son		1	M		Herts	Sandridge
168		Infant	31		Son		7days	M		Herts	Sandridge
169	BIGG	Percival	32	Church End	Head	Mar	36	M	Agric Lab	Herts	Studham Com
170	BIGG	Emma	32		Wife	Mar	32	F		Herts	Childwick [St Michaels]
171	BIGG	Henry	32		Son		10	M	Agric Lab	Herts	Sandridge
172	BIGG	Kitty	32		Dau		12	F	Scholar	Herts	Sandridge
173	BIGG	Ann	32		Dau		6	F	Scholar	Herts	Sandridge
174	BIGG	William	32		Son		2	M		Herts	Sandridge
175	LARMAN	Matthew	33	Church End	Head	Widower	72	M	Retired Gardener	Herts	Hare Street, Hertford
176	PAUL	James	33		Nephew	Mar	26	M	Bricklayer (Journeyman)	Herts	Sandridge
177	PAUL	Ruth	33		Nephews Wife	Mar	24	F		Beds	Toddington
178	PAUL	Fredk J	33		Nephews Son		8m	M		Herts	Sandridge

End of the Village of Sandridge

179	WATSON	William	34	Pudding Green	Head	Mar	52	M	Gardener employing 2 Men	Herts	St Peters
180	WATSON	Frances	34		Wife	Mar	54	F		Herts	Shenley
181	WATSON	Susan	34		Sister	Unm	50	F	Idiot	Herts	St Peters
182	KENNCIS	James	35	Flint Lodge	Head	Mar	63	M	Agric Lab	Herts	Colney Heath
183	KENNCIS	Mary	35		Wife	Mar	61	F		Herts	North Mimms
184	KENNCIS	William	35		Son	Unm	21	M	Agric Lab	Herts	Colney Heath
185	KENNCIS	Joseph	35		Son	Unm	19	M	Agric Lab	Herts	Sleapshyde [St Peters]
186	BRACEY	Susan	36	Flint Lodge	Head	Widow	60	F	Straw plaiter	Herts	St Albans
187	BRACEY	Kesiah	36		Dau	Unm	30	F	Straw plaiter	Herts	Sandridge
188	BRACEY	Emily	36		Dau	Unm	23	F	Straw plaiter	Herts	Sandridge
189	BRACEY	Jane	36		Grandau		10	F	Scholar	Herts	Sandridge
190	BRACEY	Charles	36		Grandson		4	M		Herts	Sandridge
191	YOUNG	George	37	Woodcock Hill (Nashs Farm)	Head	Mar	47	M	Farmer of 290 acres employing 14 labourers	Herts	Harpenden
192	YOUNG	Mary	37		Wife	Mar	45	F	Farmers Wife	Herts	Sandridge
193	SIMPKINS	Eliza	37		Serv	Unm	30	F	House Servant	Herts	Sandridge
194	THUSSELL	William	37		Serv	Unm	18	M	Ploughman	Herts	Sandridge
195	DEAN	Joseph	37		Serv	Unm	17	M	Horse Keeper	Herts	Hemel Hempstead
196	STANLEY	William	38	Woodcock Hill (Hooks)	Head	Mar	36	M	Agric Lab	Herts	Baldock
197	STANLEY	Sarah	38		Wife	Mar	29	F	Agric Lab Wife	Herts	Sandridge
198	STANLEY	John	38		Son		8	M	Scholar	Herts	Sandridge
199	STANLEY	Emma	38		Dau		5	F		Herts	Sandridge

	SURNAME	FORENAME	SCHEDULE NUMBER	ADDRESS	RELATIONSHIP	STATUS	AGE	SEX	OCCUPATION	COUNTY OF BIRTH	PLACE OF BIRTH
200	STANLEY	Sarah	38		Dau		2	F		Herts	Sandridge
201	STANLEY	George	38		Son		6m	M		Herts	Sandridge
202	HUCKLE	Thomas	38		Visitor	Mar	60	M	(Agric Lab) Pauper	Herts	Wheathampstead
203	BRACEY	Isaac	39	Woodcock Hill (Hooks)	Head	Mar	38	M	Agric Lab	Herts	Sandridge
204	BRACEY	Anna	39		Wife	Mar	40	F		Herts	Sandridge
205	BRACEY	Ann	39		Dau	Unm	17	F	Brazilian Hat Maker	Herts	Sandridge
206	SIMPKINS	James	40	Woodcock Hill (Upper Caps)	Head	Mar	57	M	Agric Lab	Herts	North Mimms
207	SIMPKINS	Harriet	40		Dau	Unm	30	F	Straw plaiter	Herts	Sandridge
208	SIMPKINS	Joseph	40		Son	Unm	21	M	Agric Lab	Herts	Sandridge
209	SIMPKINS	Thomas	40		Son		12	M	Agric Lab	Herts	Sandridge
210	SIMPKINS	Samuel	40		Son		10	M	Agric Lab	Herts	Sandridge
211	WOODWARD	Charles	41	Woodcock Hill (Upper Caps)	Head	Mar	31	M	Agric Lab	Herts	Wheathampstead
212	WOODWARD	Elizabeth	41		Wife	Mar	27	F		Beds	Ampthill
213	WOODWARD	James	41		Son	Unm	1	M		Herts	Sandridge
214	WOODWARD	Mary Ann	41		Dau		7	F	Scholar	Herts	Wheathampstead
215	WOOLMER	William	42	Woodcock Hill (Lower Caps)	Head	Mar	36	M	Agric Lab	Herts	Sandridge
216	WOOLMER	Elizabeth	42		Wife	Mar	35	F		Herts	Sandridge
217	WOOLMER	Sophia	42		Dau		10	F	Scholar	Herts	Sandridge
218	WOOLMER	Thomas	42		Son		8	M	Scholar	Herts	Sandridge
219	WOOLMER	James	42		Son		8	M	Scholar	Herts	Sandridge
220	WOOLMER	Walter	42		Son		2	M		Herts	Sandridge
221	LITTLE	William	42		Father-in-law	Widower	63	M	Road Mending	Herts	Redbourn
222	GEORGE	Mary Ann	43	Woodcock Hill (Fairfolds Farm)	Head	Unm	30	F	Farmers sister inhab. house belonging to her brother (200 acres, 7 labourers)	Herts	Sandridge
223	GEORGE	Eliza	43		Sister	Unm	25	F		Herts	Sandridge
224	PAYNE	Thomas	43		Serv	Mar	38	M	Agric Lab	Herts	St Peters
225	PAYNE	Mary	43		Serv Wife	Mar	39	F	House Servant	Bucks	Little Kimble
226	PAYNE	Mary	43		Serv Dau		11	F		Herts	St Peters
227	SMART	Joseph	43		Serv	Unm	18	M	Agric Lab	Herts	Sandridge
228	RANCE	George	43		Serv	Unm	17	M	Agric Lab	Herts	Wheathampstead

One house uninhabited

	SURNAME	FORENAME	SCHEDULE NUMBER	ADDRESS	RELATIONSHIP	STATUS	AGE	SEX	OCCUPATION	COUNTY OF BIRTH	PLACE OF BIRTH
229	DENNISS	Thomas	44	Woodcock Hill	Head	Mar	57	M	Late Lathrender	Herts	Hertford
230	DENNISS	Susan	44		Wife	Mar	58	F		Herts	North Mimms
231	DENNISS	Mary	44		Dau	Unm	18	F	Straw plaiter	Herts	Sandridge
232	GATHARD	William	45	Woodcock Hill	Head	Mar	52	M	Agric Lab	Herts	Sandridge
233	GATHARD	Elizabeth	45		Wife	Mar	43	F		Herts	Sandridge
234	GATHARD	Charles	45		Son	Unm	19	M	Agric Lab	Herts	Sandridge
235	GATHARD	William	45		Son		13	M	Agric Lab	Herts	Sandridge
236	GATHARD	Mary Ann	45		Dau		10	F	Straw plaiter	Herts	Sandridge
237	GATHARD	Thomas	45		Son		7	M	Scholar	Herts	Sandridge
238	GATHARD	Emily	45		Dau		3	F		Herts	Sandridge
239	COOK	William	45		Step-son	Unm	24	M	Agric Lab	Herts	Sandridge
240	SMITH	Charles	46	Woodcock Hill	Head	Mar	30	M	Agric Lab	Herts	Sandridge
241	SMITH	Sarah	46		Wife	Mar	25	F		Beds	Caldecote

242	SMITH	Sarah	46		Dau		under 1 m	F		Herts	Sandridge
243	COOK	Ann	46		Niece	Unm	19	F	Straw plaiter	Herts	Wheathampstead
244	COX	Thomas	47	Tower Hill Hammonds Farm	Head	Mar	56	M	Farmer of 360 acres employing 16 labourers	Herts	Hatfield
245	COX	Mary Anne	47		Wife	Mar	46	F		Herts	Hatfield
246	COX	Henry	47		Son	Unm	24	M	Farmers Son	Herts	Hatfield
247	COX	Sarah	47		Dau		14	F		Herts	Sandridge
248	COX	Elizabeth	47		Dau		10	F		Herts	Sandridge
249	GATHARD	Hannah	47		Serv	Unm	24	F	House Servant	Herts	Sandridge
250	LOWE	David	47		Serv	Unm	17	M	Agric Lab	Herts	Wheathampstead
251	SIMPKINS	William	47		Serv	Unm	15	M	Agric Lab	Herts	Sandridge
252	HANDLEY	Charles	47		Serv	Unm	14	M	Farm Servant	Herts	Little Ayott
253	SMART	Samuel	48	Tower Hill (Holly Bush)	Head	Mar	40	M	Agric Lab	Herts	Hatfield
254	SMART	Hannah	48		Wife	Mar	36	F		Herts	Sandridge
255	SMART	Sophia	48		Dau	Unm	10	F	Scholar	Herts	St Albans
256	SIMPKINS	Lucy	48		Visitor	Mar	50	F	Midwife	Herts	Hunton Bridge
257	OAKLY	William	49	Tower Hill (Holly Bush)	Head	Mar	40	M	Agric Lab	Herts	Stevenage
258	OAKLY	Sarah	49		Wife	Mar	40	F		Herts	Hatfield
259	OAKLY	Elizabeth	49		Dau	Unm	13	F	Scholar	Herts	Hatfield
260	OAKLY	Mary	49		Dau		12	F	Scholar	Herts	Hatfield
261	OAKLY	Emma	49		Dau		9	F	Scholar	Herts	Sandridge
262	OAKLY	Henry	49		Son		7	M	Scholar	Herts	Sandridge
263	OAKLY	James	49		Son		5	M	Scholar	Herts	Sandridge
264	ENGLAND	James	50	Tower Hill	Head	Mar	47	M	Agric lab	Herts	St Stephens
265	ENGLAND	Grace	50		Wife	Mar	48	F	Labourers Wife	Bucks	Taplow
266	ENGLAND	Maria	50		Dau		12	F		Herts	Sandridge
267	ENGLAND	Charlotte	50		Dau		10	F		Herts	Sandridge
268	ENGLAND	Jabez	50		Son		8	M	Scholar	Herts	Sandridge
269	ENGLAND	George	50		Son		5	M	Scholar	Herts	Sandridge
270	ENGLAND	Emily	50		Dau		4	F		Herts	Sandridge
271	BEASNEY	Charlotte	51	Tower Hill	Head	Unm	44	F	Annuitant	Herts	Hatfield
272	SIMSON	Charlotte	51		Serv	Widow	47	F	House Servt	Herts	Sandridge
273	WOOLLATT	George Sidn	52	Beech Hyde	Head	Mar	43	M	Farmer of 248 acres employing 13 labourers	Herts	Sandridge
274	WOOLLATT	Harriet	52		Wife	Mar	42	F		Herts	Redbourn
275	WOOLLATT	Harriet	52		Dau		9	F	Scholar	Herts	Sandridge
276	WOOLLATT	George	52		Son		7	M	Scholar	Herts	Sandridge
277	WOOLLATT	Katherine	52		Dau		2	F		Herts	Sandridge
278	MAY	Susan	52		Serv	Unm	21	F	House Servant	Essex	Moultling
279	WOOLLATT	Joseph	52		Serv	Unm	35	M	Agric Lab	Herts	Watton
280	WITHMORE	William	52		Serv	Widower	30	M	Agric Lab	Herts	Sandridge
281	PARKINS	John	52		Serv	Unm	21	M	Agric Lab	Herts	Wheathampstead
282	SLOW	James	52		Serv	Unm	17	M	Agric Lab	Herts	Wheathampstead
283	ADDINGTON	Charles	52		Serv	Unm	16	M	Agric Lab	Herts	Wheathampstead

One house uninhabited

	SURNAME	FORENAME	SCHEDULE NUMBER	ADDRESS	RELATIONSHIP	STATUS	AGE	SEX	OCCUPATION	COUNTY OF BIRTH	PLACE OF BIRTH
284	MILES	William	53	Beech Hyde	Head	Mar	23	M	Agric Lab	Beds	Statfore [Stratford?, Stotfold?]
285	MILES	Ruth	53		Wife	Mar	32	F		Herts	Sandridge
286	MILES	Lizzy	53		Dau		10	F	Straw plaiter	Herts	Wheathampstead
287	MILES	Anna	53		Dau		9	F	Straw plaiter	Herts	Wheathampstead
288	MILES	Ann	53		Dau		2	F		Herts	Wheathampstead
289	MILES	James	53		Son		3m	M		Herts	Sandridge
290	MUNT	Richard	54	Coleman Green	Head	Mar	51	M	Agric Lab	Herts	Sandridge
291	MUNT	Maria	54		Wife	Mar	52	F	Straw plaiter	Herts	Hatfield
292	MUNT	Aaron	54		Son	Unm	11	M	Straw plaiter	Herts	Sandridge
293	PIGGOTT	Henry	55	Coleman Green	Head	Mar	61	M	Agric Lab	Beds	Luton
294	PIGGOTT	Sarah	55		Wife	Mar	61	F	Straw plaiter	Beds	Luton
295	PIGGOTT	Hannah	55		Dau	Unm	35	F	Brazilian Hat Maker	Herts	Sandridge
296	PIGGOTT	James	55		Son	Unm	24	M	Agric Lab	Herts	Sandridge
297	SEALES	Elizabeth	55		Grandau	Unm	14	F	Brazilian Hat Maker	Herts	Hatfield
298	SEALES	Sarah	55		Grandau	Unm	5	F	Brazilian Hat Maker	Herts	Hatfield
299	PEARMAN	Alfred	56	Coleman Green	Head	Mar	22	M	Agric Lab	Herts	Wheathampstead
300	PEARMAN	Emma	56		Wife	Mar	23	F	Brazilian Hat Maker	Herts	Sandridge
301	PEARMAN	Sarah	56		Dau		3	F		Herts	Sandridge
302	PEARMAN	Elizabeth	56		Dau		6m	F		Herts	Sandridge
303	WALLER	George	56		Visitor	Unm	24	M	Farm Labourer	Unknown	
304	SOUTHAM	John	57	Coleman Green	Head	Mar	48	M	Blacksmith employing 1 man	Herts	Rickmansworth
305	SOUTHAM	Susanna	57		Wife	Mar	47	F		Herts	Sandridge
306	SOUTHAM	Lydia	57		Dau	Unm	22	F	Bonnet Sewer	Herts	Sandridge
307	SOUTHAM	Charles	57		Son	Unm	18	M	Blacksmith (Journeyman)	Herts	Sandridge
308	SOUTHAM	Sophia	57		Dau	Unm	16	F	Bonnet Sewer	Herts	Sandridge
309	SOUTHAM	Alfred	57		Son		13	M	Agric Lab	Herts	Sandridge
310	SOUTHAM	John	57		Son		11	M	Agric Lab	Herts	Sandridge
311	SOUTHAM	Thomas	57		Son		9	M	Scholar	Herts	Sandridge
312	SOUTHAM	George	57		Son		5	M	Scholar	Herts	Sandridge
313	MATTHEWS	Daniel	58	Coleman Green	Head	Mar	27	M	Agric Lab	Herts	Kimpton
314	MATTHEWS	Mary	58		Wife	Mar	25	F	Brazilian Hat Maker	Herts	Hatfield
315	WALLER	Charles	59	Coleman Green	Head	Mar	54	M	Agric Lab	Unknown	
316	WALLER	Hannah	59		Wife	Mar	51	F	Straw plaiter	Unknown	
317	WALLER	Charles	59		Son	Unm	22	M	Agric Lab	Herts	Welwyn
318	WALLER	Sarah	59		Dau	Unm	16	F	Brazilian Hat Maker	Herts	Welwyn
319	WALLER	Daniel	59		Son		12	M	Farm Labourer	Herts	Welwyn
320	WALLER	James	59		Son		8	M	Scholar	Herts	Welwyn
321	FISHER	Rebecca	60	Coleman Green	Head	Widow	63	F	Straw plaiter	Herts	Hertingfordbury
322	FISHER	Joseph	60		Son	Unm	17	M	Agric Lab	Herts	Sandridge
323	FISHER	Sarah	60		Dau	Unm	15	F	Straw plaiter	Herts	Sandridge
324	COLEMAN	Sarah	60		Visitor	Unm	71	F	Straw plaiter	Herts	Sandridge
325	GEORGE	Edward	61	Samwells Farm	Head	Mar	35	M	Owner of 179 acres Farmer of 383 acres, inclusive, employing 13 labourers	Herts	Sandridge

#	Surname	Forename		Address	Relation	Status	Age	Sex	Occupation	County	Birthplace
326	GEORGE	Mary A	61		Wife	Mar	36	F		London	St Lukes
327	GEORGE	Mary A	61		Dau		2	F		Herts	Sandridge
328	GEORGE	Anne E	61		Dau		1	F		Herts	Sandridge
329	BYLES	George	61		Nephew		7	M		Herts	Hemel Hempstead
330	WILLIAMS	Anne S	61		Sister-in-law	Unm	32	F	N.K.	London	St Lukes
331	HANNAL	Mary A	61		Serv	Unm	21	F	House Servant	Herts	Aldenham
332	HONNER	Elizabeth	61		Serv	Unm	15	F	House Servant	Herts	Wheathampstead
333	MUNT	Jonathan	61		Serv	Unm	22	M	Agric Lab	Herts	Hatfield
334	SMITH	James	61		Serv	Unm	16	M	Agric Lab	Herts	Wheathampstead
335	STEPHENS	Jesse	61		Serv	Unm	13	M	Agric Lab	Herts	Wheathampstead
336	RAGGETT	John	62	Chalk Dell Farm	Head	Widower	68	M	Farmer of 129 acres employing 15 labourers	Herts	Redbourn
337	TOOLEY	Richard	62		Serv	Widower	50	M	Agric Lab	Herts	Wheathampstead
338	RANCE	William	62		Serv	Unm	20	M	Agric Lab	Herts	Stevenage
339	IVORY	George	62		Serv	Unm	12	M	Agric Lab	Herts	Harpenden
340	WHITT	Mary	62		Serv	Unm	48	F	House Servant	Herts	Hitchin
341	WRIGHT	George	63	Wacketts Farm	Head	Mar	28	M	Farmer of 58 acres employing 2 labourers	Herts	Sandridge
342	WRIGHT	Emma	63		Wife	Mar	26	F		Herts	Ippollitts
343	WRIGHT	Elizabeth	63		Dau		4	F		Herts	Sandridge
344	WRIGHT	Rosa	63		Dau		2	F		Herts	Sandridge
345	WRIGHT	Edwin G	63		Son		3m	M		Herts	Sandridge
346	LEE	Mary Ann	63		Serv	Unm	17	F	House Servant	Herts	Welwyn
347	SHARPE	William	64	Water End	Head	Mar	31	M	Agric Lab	Herts	Ayot St Peters
348	SHARPE	Betsy	64		Wife	Mar	23	F	Straw plaiter	Herts	Bendon
349	SHARPE	Louisa	64		Dau		11m	F		Herts	Bendon
350	FLOYD	Thomas	65	Water End	Head	Mar	63	M	Agric Lab	Herts	Wheathampstead
351	FLOYD	Mary	65		Wife	Mar	66	F	Straw plaiter	Herts	Harpenden
352	MINNARD	William	66	Water End Sparrow Hall	Head	Mar	49	M	Agric Lab	Wilts	Ramsbury
353	MINNARD	Sarah	66		Wife	Mar	46	F		Wilts	Ramsbury
354	MINNARD	William	66		Son		13	M	Agric Lab	Wilts	Wanborough
355	MINNARD	Mary A	66		Dau		10	F	Scholar	Wilts	Ramsbury
356	MINNARD	Martha	66		Dau		5	F	Scholar	Wilts	Wanborough
357	SMITH	Dolphin	67	Water End	Head	Mar	45	M	Farmer of 480 acres employing 22 labourers	Wilts	Ramsbury
358	SMITH	Maria	67		Wife	Mar	39	F	Farmers Wife	Wilts	Frecksfield
359	SMITH	Ellen	67		Dau		10	F	Scholar	Wilts	Ramsbury
360	SMITH	John H	67		Son		8	M	Scholar	Wilts	Ramsbury
361	SMITH	Agnes	67		Dau		4	F	At Home	Herts	Sandridge
362	SMITH	William A	67		Son		2	M	At Home	Herts	Sandridge
363	SMITH	Elizabeth	67		Dau		11m	F	At Home	Herts	Sandridge
364	WOODWARDS	Anna	67		Serv	Unm	17	F	House Servant	Herts	Wheathampstead
365	RUMNEY	Jane	67		Serv	Unm	16	F	House Servant	Herts	Hatfield
366	JONES	Thomas	67		Serv	Widower	58	M	Agric Lab	Wilts	Mildenhall
367	HONNOR	James	67		Serv	Unm	18	M	Agric Lab	Herts	Wheathampstead
368	WARBEE	Mark	67		Serv	Unm	16	M	Agric Lab	Herts	Wheathampstead
369	WOODWARD	Henry	67		Serv	Unm	13	M	Agric Lab	Herts	Wheathampstead

	SURNAME	FORENAME	SCHEDULE NUMBER	ADDRESS	RELATIONSHIP	STATUS	AGE	SEX	OCCUPATION	COUNTY OF BIRTH	PLACE OF BIRTH
370	DORRINGTON	Charles	68	Bride Hall	Head	Unm	28	M	Farmer of 374 acres employing 16 labourers	Herts	Stapleford
371	DORRINGTON	Ellenor	68		Sister	Unm	32	F	Farmers Sister	Herts	Stapleford
372	HAYES	Emma	68		Serv	Unm	16	F	House Servant	Herts	Bengeo
373	JARVIS	Steven	68		Serv	Unm	17	M	Farm Servant	Herts	Kimpton
374	DARLOW	James	68		Serv	Unm	24	M	Farm Servant	Herts	Wheathampstead
375	PAYNE	Charles	68		Serv	Unm	17	M	Farm Servant	Herts	Sandridge
376	KINGHAM	William	68		Serv	Unm	17	M	Farm Servant	Herts	Wheathampstead
377	EAST	William	69	Marford Cottage	Head	Mar	58	M	Farmer of 7 acres employing 1 labourer	Herts	Wheathampstead
378	EAST	Jane	69		Wife	Mar	60	F	Farmers Wife	Herts	Stevenage
379	EAST	William	69		Son	Unm	31	M	Farmers Son	Herts	Sandridge
380	EAST	Sarah	69		Dau	Unm	21	F	Farmers Daughter	Herts	Wheathampstead
381	EAST	Matthew	69		Son	Unm	14	M	Farmers Son	Herts	Wheathampstead
382	CURELL	George	69		Visitor	Unm	61	M	Agric Lab	Herts	Wheathampstead
383	WOODWARD	George	69		Visitor	Unm	22	M	Agric Lab	Herts	Wheathampstead
384	FREEMAN	Fredk	69		Visitor	Unm	19	M	Agric Lab	Herts	Wheathampstead
385	PEARMAN	John	70	Beech Hyde Lower	Head	Unm	44	M	Farmer of 170 Acres employing 7 labourers	Herts	Sandridge
386	PEARMAN	Jane	70		Sister	Unm	55	F	House Keeper	Herts	Sandridge
387	PEARMAN	Sarah	70		Sister	Unm	53	F	House Servant	Herts	Sandridge
388	PEARMAN	Mary Ann	70		Sister	Unm	51	F	House Servant	Herts	Sandridge
389	PEARMAN	Joseph	70		Nephew	Unm	20	M	Farm Servant	Herts	St Stephens
390	GIDDINS	George	70		Serv	Unm	17	M	Farm Servant	Herts	Harpenden
391	THRALE	Ralph	71	No Mans Land	Head	Widower	72	M	Farmer of 220 acres employing 10 labourers	Herts	Sandridge
392	THRALE	Ralph Norman	71		Son	Unm	47	M	Farmers Son	Herts	Sandridge
393	THRALE	William	71		Son	Unm	45	M	Farmers Son	Herts	Sandridge
394	PLUMMER	Sophia	71		Serv	Unm	48	F	House Servant	Herts	Sandridge
395	HANSCOMBE	Fanny	71		Serv	Unm	14	F	House Servant	Herts	Sandridge
396	MUNT	George	71		Serv	Unm	20	M	Farm Servant	Herts	Sandridge
397	ARCHER	John	71		Serv	Unm	14	M	Agric Lab	Herts	Sandridge
398	MUNT	Charles	71		Serv	Unm	17	M	Agric Lab	Herts	Sandridge
399	PIKE	William	72	No Mans Land	Head	Mar	31	M	Agric Lab	Berks	Froxfell
400	PIKE	Caroline	72		Wife	Mar	28	F	Straw Plaiter	Wilts	Ramsbury
401	STEVENS	Joseph	73	No Mans Land	Head	Mar	51	M	Farm Labourer	Herts	Wheathampstead
402	STEVENS	Hannah	73		Wife	Mar	50	F	Straw Plaiter	Herts	Wheathampstead
403	STEVENS	Hannah	73		Dau	Unm	23	F	Servant	Herts	Wheathampstead
404	STEVENS	Mary	73		Dau	Unm	18	F	Straw Plaiter	Herts	Wheathampstead
405	STEVENS	Susan	73		Dau	Unm	11	F	Straw Plaiter	Herts	Wheathampstead

End of District 4a, Sandridge parish

Registrar's District: Harpenden   Enumeration District 4b   Ref. HO 107/1713 folios 210-27

All that part of the parish of Sandridge which lies to the west of the road from Hardens Marsh through Sandridge to Wheathampstead, including part of the village, Marshalls Wick, Bernards Heath, Sleep Side [Sleapshyde], the Bury, Hill End and thence to the village.

406	BOOTH	Elizabeth	1	Evans Farm	Head	Widow	50	F	Farming 280 acres employing 12 men	Herts	Sandridge

407	BATCHELOR	James	1		Bailiff	Unm	44	M	Farmers Bailiff	Herts	Flamstead
408	RENTE... [?]	Jane	1		Serv	Unm	16	F	House Servant	Cambs	Chapel Shudy
409	COOTE	John	1		Serv	Unm	16	M	General Servant	Herts	Park St., St Stephens
410	SWAIN	James	1		Serv	Unm	14	M	General Servant	Herts	Sleapshyde, St Peters
411	HOLLOWAY	William	2	Marshalls Wick Farm	Head	Mar	32	M	Farmer of 229 acres employing 8 men	Herts	Aldenham
412	HOLLOWAY	Mary	2		Wife	Mar	37	F	Farmers Wife	Sussex	Ditchling
413	HOLLOWAY	Sarah A	2		Dau	Unm	8	F	Farmers Daur at home Scholar	Herts	Aldenham
414	HOLLOWAY	Mary H	2		Dau	Unm	7	F	Farmers Daur at home Scholar	Herts	Aldenham
415	HOLLOWAY	Elizabeth	2		Dau	Unm	6	F	Farmers Daur at home, Scholar	Herts	Aldenham
416	DEACON	Charlotte	2		Serv	Unm	24	F	House Servt	Herts	Leavesden Woodside
417	PITKIN	Fredrick	2		Serv	Unm	19	M	General Servant	Herts	Colney Street [St Stephens]
418	ALDRIDGE	Henry	2		Serv	Unm	14	M	General Servant	Herts	Sandridge
419	ARCHER	Willm	2		Serv	Unm	18	M	Farm Labourer	Herts	Sandridge
420	SPARY	David	3	Marshalls Wick	Head	Mar	43	M	Gardener for G.B. Martin, Park/Garden/Woods 100 acres 5 men	Herts [Essex]	Brentwood
421	SPARY	Mary	3		Wife	Mar	39	F	Gardeners Wife	Herts	Sandridge
422	SPARY	Rosana	3		Dau	Unm	10	F	At Home	Herts	Sandridge
423	SPARY	Arthar	3		Son	Unm	7	M	At Home	Herts	Sandridge
424	SEWEERL	A	3		Serv	Unm	29	F	House Servant	Sussex	Petworth
425	BROADWAY	A	3		Serv	Unm	26	F	House Servant	Middx	Elingdon [Hillingdon]
426	SMITH	Robert	4	Bernards Heath	Head	Mar	64	M	Farmer of 460 acres employing 23	Herts	St Albans
427	SMITH	Elizabeth	4		Wife	Mar	65	F	Farmers Wife	Herts	Flamstead
428	SMITH	Susan	4		Dau	Unm	28	F	Farmers daur	Herts	Sandridge
429	SMITH	Edmund	4		Son	Unm	25	M	Farmers Son	Herts	Sandridge
430	SMITH	Ellen	4		Dau	Unm	22	F	Farmers Daur	Herts	Sandridge
431	COOK	Ann	4		Serv	Unm	20	F	House Servant	Bucks	Long Crendon
432	HARDY	George	4		Serv	Unm	41	M	General Servant	Herts	Sandridge
433	GOSS	Peter	4		Serv	Unm	28	M	General Servant	Herts	Gt. Berkhamsted
434	BUSH	William	4		Serv	Unm	21	M	General Servant	Herts	Sandridge
435	CHAPMAN	John	4		Serv	Unm	16	M	General Servant	Herts	Smallford St Peters
436	BRADSHAW	John	5	Bernards Heath	Head	Mar	56	M	Gentleman	Herts	St Albans, St Michaels
437	BRADSHAW	Sarah Manfield	5		Wife	Mar	59	F	Gentlemans Wife	Herts	St Peters
438	EDWARDS	Maria	5		Serv	Unm	16	F	House Servant	Herts	St Albans
439	ROBERTS	Anna	6	Bernards Heath	Head	Unm	35	F	Fund Holder	Sussex	Hurstpierpoint
440	GRIFFITHS	Frederick W	6		Visitor	Widower	45	M	Solicitor retired from practice	Middx	Islington
441	GRIFFITHS	Ernest H	6		Nephew	Unm	7	M	Scholar at Home	Middx	Islington
442	BARRETT	Hannah	6		Serv	Unm	62	F	Housekeeper	Sussex	Ditchling
443	WOODGATE	Caroline	6		Serv	Unm	23	F	Cook	Sussex	Fulmer
444	GREEN	William	7	Bernards Heath	Head	Mar	60	M	Labourer	Herts	Sandridge
445	GREEN	Mary	7		Wife	Mar	50	F	Labourers Wife	Beds	[E...?]
446	GREEN	William	7		Son	Unm	20	M	Labourer	Herts	Bernards Heath [St Albans]

	SURNAME	FORENAME	SCHEDULE NUMBER	ADDRESS	RELATIONSHIP	STATUS	AGE	SEX	OCCUPATION	COUNTY OF BIRTH	PLACE OF BIRTH
447	SMITH	Mary	7		Visitor	Mar	35	F	Straw Bonnet Sewer	Beds	Dunstable
	Unoccupied.		8	*Greens Farm – Family not at home on the 30th*							
448	HEDGES	Elizabeth	9	Greens Farm	Head	Widow	27	F	Straw Hat Worker	Herts	Sandridge
449	HEDGES	James	9		Son		5	M		Herts	Sandridge
450	HEDGES	Charles	9		Son		3	M		Herts	Sandridge
451	HART	Mathew	10	Greens Farm	Head	Mar	35	M	Labourer	Herts	Harpenden
452	HART	Eliza	10		Wife	Mar	28	F	Labourers Wife	Herts	Sandridge
453	HART	James	10		Son		10	M	Labourer	Herts	St Michaels
454	HART	John	10		Son		8	M	Scholar	Herts	St Michaels
455	HART	Ellen	10		Dau		5	F	Scholar	Herts	St Michaels
456	HART	William	10		Son		2	M		Herts	Sandridge
457	DICKINSON	George	11	Cheap Side Farm	Head	Mar	39	M	Farmer of 228 acres employing 10 labourers	Herts	Sandridge
458	DICKINSON	Susannah	11		Wife	Mar	35	F	Farmers Wife	Herts	Wheathampstead
459	DICKINSON	Richard	11		Son		13	M	Farmers Son	Herts	Sandridge
460	DICKINSON	Ellen	11		Dau		11	F	Scholar	Herts	Sandridge
461	DICKINSON	Rosa	11		Dau		8	F	Scholar	Herts	Sandridge
462	DICKINSON	Emma	11		Dau		6	F	Scholar	Herts	Sandridge
463	RUSSEL	James	11		[blank]	Widower	51	M	Farm Labourer	Beds	Luton
464	REED	William	11		Serv	Unm	18	M	Farm Labourer	Beds	Chalton
465	GATHERD	Joseph	11		Serv	Unm	16	M	Farm Labourer	Herts	Sandridge
466	BLAIN	James	11		Drover	Mar	33	M	Drover	Herts	Wheathampstead
467	BANGBOURN	George	12	Beech Bottom	Head	Mar	24	M	Game Keeper	Herts	St Michaels
468	BANGBOURN	Emma	12		Wife	Mar	32	F	Game Keepers Wife	Herts	St Michaels
469	BANGBOURN	Harriotte	12		Dau		5	F		Herts	St Michaels
470	BANGBOURN	Joseph	12		Son		2	M		Herts	Flamstead
471	KINDER	John	13	Sandridge Bury	Head	Unm	67	M	Magistrate, Farmer, 700 acres employing 30 labourers	Herts	St Albans
472	KINDER	Thomas	13		Nephew	Mar	35	M		Herts	St Albans
473	KINDER	Caroline	13		Niece	Mar	36	F		Herts	Long Milford
474	KINDER	Anna Maria	13		Dau of		9	F	Scholar at home	Herts	Sandridge Bury
475	KINDER	Emma	13		Dau of		7	F	Scholar at home	Herts	Sandridge Bury
476	KINDER	Fanny E	13		Dau of		5	F	Scholar at home	Herts	Sandridge Bury
477	KINDER	Caroline A	13		Dau of		1	F		Herts	Sandridge Bury
478	BOUTELL	Mary E L	13		Visitor		9	F	Scholar at home	Herts	Sandridge Bury
479	KINDER	Anna Maria	13		Visitor	Widow	65	F		London	
480	ANDERSSON	Laura M	13		Governess	Unm	25	F	Governess	London	
481	BEBER	Ann	13		Serv	Unm	32	F	Cook	[Unknown]	Newford [?]
482	HOPPER	Hannah	13		Serv	Unm	28	F	House Maid	Kent	[Unknown]
483	WESTON	Eliza	13		Serv	Unm	21	F	Nurse Maid	[Unknown]	Downham Market
484	ARCHER	Emely	13		Serv	Unm	16	F	Kitchen Maid	Herts	Sandridge
485	MAUNDER	Maria	13		Serv	Unm	20	F	Ladies Maid	Devon	[Unknown]
486	GIBBS	Thomas	13		Serv	Mar	42	M	Man Servant	Herts	St Albans
487	HUTCHINSON	James	14	Sandridge Bury, Bailiffs Cottage	Head	Mar	53	M	Farming Bailiff	Scotland	[Unknown]
488	HUTCHINSON	Sophy	14		Wife	Mar	27	F	Bailiffs Wife	Herts	St Albans

489	HUTCHINSON	John F	14		Son	Unm	18	M	Collector of Rates for Sandridge	Herts	St Albans
490	HUTCHINSON	Ann	14		Dau		3	F	Scholar	Herts	Sandridge
491	HUTCHINSON	James M	14		Son		2	M	Scholar	Herts	Sandridge
492	HUTCHINSON	Isabella	14		Dau		8 m	F	Infant	Herts	Sandridge
493	BRACEY	Susan	14		Serv	Unm	15	F	House Servant	Herts	Sandridge
494	CRANE	William	14		Serv	Unm	21	M	Hired Agric Lab	Herts	Sandridge
495	BROWN	James	14		Serv	Unm	18	M	Hired Agric Lab	Herts	St Albans
496	BUNCE	Charles	14		Serv	Unm	22	M	Hired Agric Lab	Herts	Sandridge
497	LAWRENCE	George	14		Serv	Unm	15	M	Hired Agric Lab	Herts	Sandridge
498	WELSH	David	14		Serv	Unm	33	M	Shepherd	Herts	Kimpton
499	SEABROOK	David	14		Serv	Unm	15	M	Errand Boy	Herts	St Albans
500	COX	Jonathan	15	Hill End Farm	Head	Mar	29	M	Farmer of 372 acres employing 20 labourers	Herts	Hatfield
501	COX	Mary Ann	15		Wife	Mar	25	F	Farmers Wife	Herts	Lilley
502	COX	Henry	15		Son		2	M	Farmers Son	Herts	Sandridge
503	COX	Jonathan	15		Son		1	M	Farmers Son	Herts	Sandridge
504	JAMES	Fanny	15		Serv	Unm	20	F	House Servant	Herts	Norton
505	MINALL	Ann	15		Serv	Unm	17	F	Nurse Maid	Wilts	Memsbury
506	PAIN	William	15		Labourer	Mar	51	M	Agric Lab	Herts	Little Wymondley
507	PAIN	William	15		Labourer	Unm	20	M	Agric Lab	Herts	Sandridge
508	WELCH	George	15		Serv	Unm	16	M	General Servant	Herts	Hitchin
509	WOOD	Joseph	15		Serv	Unm	16	M	General Servant	Herts	Whitwell
510	ARNOLD	John	15		Serv	Unm	16	M	General Servant	Herts	Whitwell
511	PAYNE	Mary	16	Sandridge	Head	Mar	39	F	Labourers Wife	Herts	[Unknown]
512	PAYNE	Zilpha	16		Dau	Unm	16	F	Straw Hat Worker	Herts	Whitwell
513	PAYNE	Sarah	16		Dau	Unm	13	F	Straw Hat Worker	Herts	Hatfield
514	PAYNE	Eliza	16		Dau		8	F	Straw Hat Worker	Herts	Sandridge
515	PAYNE	James	16		Son		5	M	Scholar	Herts	Sandridge
516	PAYNE	Ann	16		Dau		3	F		Herts	Sandridge
One unoccupied			17	Mrs Hooper – not sleeping in her house on the 30th							
517	SHARP	Thomas	18	Sandridge	Head	Mar	33	M	Farm Labourer	Herts	Sandridge
518	SHARP	Elizabeth	18		Wife	Mar	42	F	Labourers Wife	Northants	Stony Stratford
519	SHARP	Sarah	18		Dau		10	F	Scholar	Herts	Sandridge
520	SHARP	Thomas	18		Son		6	M	Scholar	Herts	Sandridge
521	SHARP	James	19	Sandridge	Head	Mar	70	M	Labourer on Road	Herts	Hitchin
522	SHARP	Sarah	19		Wife	Mar	70	F	Labourers Wife	Herts	Sandridge
523	SHARP	Mary	19		Dau	Unm	39	F	Straw Plaiter	Herts	Sandridge
524	SMITH	James	20	Sandridge	Head	Mar	40	M	Farm Labourer	Herts	St Albans
525	SMITH	Dinah	20		Wife	Mar	37	F	Labourers Wife	Herts	Sandridge
526	SMITH	Ann	20		Dau		11	F	Straw hat worker	Herts	Sandridge
527	SMITH	George	20		Son		9	M	Scholar	Herts	Sandridge
528	SMITH	Emma	20		Dau		8	F		Herts	Sandridge
529	SMITH	Hannah	20		Dau		6	F		Herts	Sandridge
530	SMITH	Ellen	20		Dau		1 m	F	Infant	Herts	Sandridge
531	ARCHER	Thomas	21	Sandridge	Head	Mar	37	M	Agric Lab	Herts	Sandridge

	SURNAME	FORENAME	SCHEDULE NUMBER	ADDRESS	RELATIONSHIP	STATUS	AGE	SEX	OCCUPATION	COUNTY OF BIRTH	PLACE OF BIRTH
532	ARCHER	Ann	21		Wife	Mar	35	F	Labourers Wife	Herts	Sandridge
533	ARCHER	William	21		Son		8	M	Scholar	Herts	Sandridge
534	ARCHER	Rebecca	21		Dau		5	F	Scholar	Herts	Sandridge
535	ARCHER	Alfred	21		Son		2	M		Herts	Sandridge
536	ARCHER	Ann	21		Dau		4 m	F	Infant	Herts	Sandridge
537	ADDINGTON	William	22	Sandridge	Head	Mar	29	M	Agric Lab	Herts	Sandridge
538	ADDINGTON	Hannah	22		Wife	Mar	26	F	Labourers Wife	Herts	St Peters
539	ADDINGTON	Lizzey	22		Dau		3	F	Scholar	Herts	Sandridge
540	ADDINGTON	Sarah	22		Dau		10 m	F	Infant	Herts	Sandridge
541	PEARMAN	Elizabeth	23	Sandridge	Head	Widow	56	F	Laundress	Herts	Ware
542	ARCHER	Jane	23		Visitor		11	F		Herts	Sandridge
543	SMITH	Thomas	24	Sandridge	Head	Mar	31	M	Farmer of 435 acres employing 16 labourers	Herts	Sandridge
544	SMITH	Elizabeth	24		Wife	Mar	28	F	Farmers Wife	Herts	Flamstead
545	PARROTT	Susan	24		Serv	Unm	50	F	House Servant	Beds	Mettanesthitt [?]
546	DOLERMORE	Frank	24		Serv	Unm	22	M	Agric Lab	Herts	Wheathampstead
547	HIGGARD	Joseph	24		Serv	Unm	16	M	Agric Lab	Herts	Kings Walden
548	HAMMETT	Henry	24		Serv	Unm	13	M	Agric Lab	Herts	Kimpton
549	HILL	Joseph	24		Serv	Unm	25	M	Agric Lab	Herts	Sandridge
550	WILLS	John	25	Sandridge	Head	Mar	66	M	Labourer	Beds	Dunstable
551	WILLS	Susan	25		Wife	Mar	54	F	Labourers Wife	Herts	Ippollitts
552	WILLS	Sarah	25		Dau	Unm	34	F	Straw Plaiter	Herts	Sandridge
553	WILLS	Elizabeth	25		Dau	Unm	30	F	Straw Plaiter	Herts	Sandridge
554	WILLS	Rose	25		Dau	Unm	18	F	Straw Plaiter	Herts	Sandridge
555	WILLS	Charles	25		Son		11	M	Scholar	Herts	Sandridge
556	ALDRIDGE	James	26	Sandridge	Head	Mar	45	M	Agric Lab	Essex	Little End
557	ALDRIDGE	Mary	26		Wife	Mar	34	F	Labourers Wife	Herts	Sandridge
558	ALDRIDGE	Charles	26		Son		11	M	Scholar	Herts	Sandridge
559	ALDRIDGE	Ann	26		Dau		9	F	Scholar	Herts	Sandridge
560	ALDRIDGE	Susan	26		Dau		6	F	Scholar	Herts	Sandridge
561	ALDRIDGE	William	26		Son		2	M		Herts	Sandridge
562	ALDRIDGE	Edward	26		Son		1 m	M		Herts	Sandridge
563	PARSONS	Jonathan	27	Sandridge	Head	Widower	83	M	Baker employing 2 men	Herts	Sandridge
564	PARSONS	Susanah	27		Dau	Unm	56	F	Bakers Daughter	Herts	Sandridge
565	SMITH	Mary A	27		Grandau	Unm	13	F	Visitor	Herts	Hadley
566	LITTLE	Sophy	27		Serv		15	F	House Servant	Herts	Hatfield
567	PARSONS	Charles	27		Serv	Mar	59	M	Baker (Journeyman)	Herts	Sandridge
568	FENSOM	Mark	27		Serv	Unm	16	M	Baker (Journeyman)	Herts	St Stephens

One house building

	SURNAME	FORENAME	SCHEDULE NUMBER	ADDRESS	RELATIONSHIP	STATUS	AGE	SEX	OCCUPATION	COUNTY OF BIRTH	PLACE OF BIRTH
569	MALES	William	28	Sandridge	Head	Mar	28	M	Agric Lab	Herts	Codicote
570	MALES	Rebecca	28		Wife	Mar	26	F	Labourers Wife	Herts	Wheathampstead
571	MALES	James	28		Son		5	M	Scholar	Herts	Sandridge
572	MALES	John	28		Son		3	M	Scholar	Herts	Hatfield
573	MALES	George	28		Son		6 m	M		Herts	Kimpton
574	FRANKLIN	John	29	Sandridge	Head	Mar	30	M	Agric Lab	Herts	Sandridge

575	FRANKLIN	Elizabeth	29		Wife	Mar	25	F	Labourers Wife	Herts	Wheathampstead
576	FRANKLIN	Sophia	29		Dau		5	F	Labourers Daur	Herts	Wheathampstead
577	FRANKLIN	Charles	29		Son		3	M	Labourers Son	Herts	Sandridge
578	FRANKLIN	Luke	29		Son		1	M	Labourers Son	Herts	Sandridge
579	RUDD	Elizabeth	30	Sandridge	Head	Mar	67	F	Straw Plaiter	Herts	Sandridge
580	RUDD	Mary	30		Dau	Unm	45	F	Straw Plaiter	Herts	Sandridge
581	COX	Edwin	30		Grandson		5	M	Visitor	Beds	Kingsworth
582	SAYER	Robert	31	Sandridge	Head	Mar	30	M	Bricklayer	Norfolk	Harling
583	SAYER	Sarah	31		Wife	Mar	30	F	Bricklayers Wife	Herts	Sandridge
584	SAYER	Mary	31		Dau		7	F	Scholar	Herts	Sandridge
585	SAYER	Charles	31		Son		5	M		Herts	Sandridge
586	SAYER	Samuel	31		Son		3	M		Herts	Sandridge
587	SAYER	Charlotte	31		Dau		1	F	Infant	Herts	Sandridge
588	PAUL	Charles	31		Brother-in-law	Unm	21	M	Carpenter	Herts	Sandridge
589	EDMONDS	William	31		Lodger	Unm	43	M	Labourer	Herts	Wheathampstead
590	RANDALL	Joseph	32	Sandridge	Head	Unm	26	M	Shoemaker	Herts	Beech Farm [St Peters]
591	RANDALL	Elizabeth	32		Sister	Unm	20	F	Straw Bonnet sewer	Herts	Beech Farm [St Peters]
592	LINES	John	33	Sandridge	Head	Mar	43	M	Maltster	Herts	Sandridge
593	LINES	Ann	33		Wife	Mar	41	F	Maltsters Wife	Herts	Wheathampstead
594	LINES	Eliza	33		Dau	Unm	22	F	Maltsters Daughter	Herts	Wheathampstead
595	LINES	John	33		Son	Unm	16	M	General Labourer	Herts	Wheathampstead
596	LINES	Sophia	33		Dau	Unm	13	F	Straw Plaiter	Herts	Wheathampstead
597	LINES	Elizabeth	33		Dau	Unm	11	F	Scholar	Herts	Wheathampstead
598	LINES	Charles	33		Son		7	M	Scholar	Herts	Sandridge
599	EVANS	Charles	34	Sandridge (Rose & Crown Inn)	Head	Mar	30	M	Victualler	Herts	Wheathampstead
600	EVANS	Sarah	34		Wife	Mar	29	F	Victuallers Wife	Beds	Luton
601	EVANS	Henry	34		Son		2	M	Victuallers Son	Herts	Sandridge
602	HIGGINS	Sarah	34		Serv	Unm	13	F	Nurse Maid	Herts	Sandridge
603	HIGGINS	John	34		Lodger	Widower	55	M	Labourer	Beds	Luton
604	PETER	Henry	34		Visitor	Unm	27	M	Training Groom	Herts	Watford
605	MORGAN	Henry	34		Lodger	Widower	45	M	Labourer	Beds	Luton
606	EDWARDS	Frederick	35	Sandridge	Head	Mar	30	M	Trainer of Horses	Suffolk	New Market
607	EDWARDS	Jocelene	35		Wife	Mar	23	F	Trainers Wife	Belgium	Brussels
608	EDWARDS	James	35		Son		5	M	Scholar	Surrey	Epsom
609	EDWARDS	Ellen	35		Dau		1	F	Infant	Surrey	Epsom
610	JOHNSON	Robert	35		Serv	Unm	21	M	Groom	Yorks	York
611	BEVERLEY	William	35		Serv	Unm	23	M	Groom	Cambs	Cambridge
612	BACON	George	35		Serv	Unm	16	M	Groom	Norfolk	Bunham
613	BARKER	Emma	35		Serv	Unm	20	F	House Servant	Herts	Wheathampstead
614	EPHGRAVE	John	36	Sandridge	Head	Mar	38	M	Blacksmith employing 2 men	Herts	Watton
615	EPHGRAVE	Eliza	36		Wife	Mar	38	F	Smiths Wife. Dressmaker	Herts	Wheathampstead
616	EPHGRAVE	Walter	36		Son	Unm	15	M	Blacksmith	Herts	Sandridge
617	EPHGRAVE	Sarah	36		Dau		13	F	Scholar	Herts	Sandridge

	SURNAME	FORENAME	SCHEDULE NUMBER	ADDRESS	RELATIONSHIP	STATUS	AGE	SEX	OCCUPATION	COUNTY OF BIRTH	PLACE OF BIRTH
618	EPHGRAVE	George	36		Son		10	M	Scholar	Herts	Sandridge
619	EPHGRAVE	Mary	36		Dau		8	F	Scholar	Herts	Sandridge
620	EPHGRAVE	Eliza	36		Dau		5	F	Scholar	Herts	Sandridge
621	EPHGRAVE	Edward	36		Son		2	M	Infant	Herts	Sandridge
622	WEBB	Sarah	37	Sandridge	Head	Widow	73	F	Pauper	Herts	Sandridge
623	WEBB	James	37		Son	Unm	35	M	Agric Lab	Herts	Sandridge
624	WEBB	John	37		Son	Mar	30	M	Agric Lab	Herts	Sandridge
625	WEBB	Sarah	37		Sons wife	Mar	35	F	Labourers Wife	Herts	Wheathampstead
626	WEBB	William	37		Grandson		2	M	Infant	Herts	Sandridge
627	WEBB	Joseph	37		Grandson		7wks	M	Infant	Herts	Sandridge
628	HALE	Daniel	38	Sandridge	Head	Mar	63	M	Agric Lab	Beds	Sundon
629	HALE	Mary	38		Wife	Mar	59	F	Labrs Wife	Herts	Great Harden
630	AMES	Mary	38		Lodger	Unm	34	F	Straw Plaiter	Beds	Sundon
631	BURGIN	William	39		Head	Mar	29	M	Gardener	Herts	Redbourn
632	BURGIN	Eliza	39		Wife	Mar	28	F	Gardeners Wife	Herts	Welwyn
633	SIMPSON	James	40	Sandridge	Head	Mar	42	M	Agric Lab	Herts	Wheathampstead
634	SIMPSON	Susan	40		Wife	Mar	45	F	Agric Labs Wife	Herts	Sandridge
635	SIMPSON	George	40		Son		5	M	Scholar	Herts	Sandridge
636	CRANE	Thomas	41	Sandridge	Head	Mar	43	M	Agric Lab	Herts	Codicote
637	CRANE	Sophia	41		Wife	Mar	39	F	Labr Wife	Herts	Sandridge
638	ALLEN	William	41		Lodger	Mar	24	M	Malters Man	Herts	North Mimms
639	ALLEN	Mahalla	41		Lodgers Wife	Mar	19	F	Malters Wife	Herts	Codicote
640	ALLEN	Mary	41		Lodgers Dau		9m	F	Infant	Herts	Sandridge
641	FRANKLIN	Joshua	41		Lodger	Unm	18	M	Agric Lab	Herts	St Michaels
642	KING	George	42	Sandridge	Head	Mar	48	M	Agric Lab	Herts	Wheathampstead
643	KING	Sophia	42		Wife	Mar	53	F		Herts	St Peters
644	KING	Eliza	42		Dau	Unm	19	F	Brazilian Hat worker	Herts	Sandridge
645	KING	Hannah	42		Dau	Unm	17	F	Brazilian Hat worker	Herts	Sandridge
646	KING	Ephraim	42		Son	Unm	16	M	Agric Lab	Herts	Sandridge
647	KING	George	42		Son	Unm	13	M	Agric Lab	Herts	Sandridge
648	KING	Ann	42		Dau		10	F	Scholar	Herts	Sandridge
649	BARKER	Thomas	43	Sandridge	Head	Mar	51	M	Agric Lab	Herts	Wheathampstead
650	BARKER	Sophia	43		Wife	Mar	53	F	Labrs Wife	Herts	Harpenden
651	BARKER	Mary	43		Dau	Unm	27	F	Straw Plaiter	Herts	St Peters
652	BARKER	Jane	43		Dau	Unm	24	F	Straw Plaiter	Herts	St Peters
653	BARKER	Eliza	43		Dau	Unm	19	F	Straw Plaiter	Herts	Sandridge
654	ALLEN	George	43		Lodger	Unm	19	M	Shoemakers Apprentice	Herts	Harpenden
655	RENOLDS	Levi	44	Sandridge	Head	Mar	25	M	Agric Lab	Herts	Hatfield
656	RENOLDS	Sarah	44		Wife	Mar	28	F	Agric Labr Wife	Herts	Flamstead
657	RENOLDS	Emmely	44		Dau		3	F	Labr daughter	Herts	Sandridge
658	RENOLDS	John	44		Son		9m	M	Labr Son	Herts	Sandridge
659	FRANKLIN	William	45	Sandridge	Head	Mar	26	M	Labourer	Herts	Sandridge
660	FRANKLIN	Harriotte	45		Wife	Mar	26	F	Labourers Wife	Herts	Sandridge
661	PLUMMER	Sarah	46	Sandridge	Head	Widow	75	F	Straw Plaiter	Herts	Sandridge

662	PLUMMER	Lucy	46		Dau	Unm	43	F	Blind	Herts	Sandridge
663	PLUMMER	Sarah	46		Dau	Unm	41	F	Straw Plaiter	Herts	Sandridge
664	PLUMMER	Thomas	46		Son	Unm	31	M	Agric Lab	Herts	Sandridge
665	PLUMMER	Jane	46		Grandau	Unm	15	F	Straw Plaiter	Herts	Sandridge
666	SHARP	John	47	Sandridge	Head	Mar	54	M	Beer House Keeper	Beds	Kingsworth
667	SHARP	Hannah	47		Wife	Mar	44	F	Straw Plaiter	Herts	Sandridge
668	SHARP	Susan	47		Dau	Unm	15	F	Straw Plaiter	Herts	Sandridge
669	SHARP	Hannah	47		Dau	Unm	13	F	Straw Plaiter	Herts	Sandridge
670	SHARP	Thomas	47		Son		10	M	Scholar	Herts	Sandridge
671	SHARP	Sarah	47		Dau		7	F	Scholar	Herts	Sandridge
672	SHARP	Charles	47		Son		4	M	Scholar	Herts	Sandridge
673	SHARP	Alfred	47		Grandau		1	M	Infant	Herts	Sandridge
674	ARCHER	Thomas	47		Lodger	Unm	21	M	Agric Lab	Herts	Sandridge
675	WRIGHT	James	47		Lodger	Unm	23	M	Agric Lab	Ireland	North
676	HILL	William	48	Sandridge	Head	Mar	50	M	Agric Lab	Herts	St Pauls Walden
677	HILL	Mary	48		Wife	Mar	50	F	Agric Labrs Wife	Herts	St Pauls Walden
678	HILL	Harriotte	48		Dau	Unm	21	F	Brazilian Hatter	Herts	St Pauls Walden
679	HILL	Emma	48		Dau	Unm	17	F	Brazilian Hatter	Herts	Sandridge
680	HILL	Lizzy	48		Dau	Unm	15	F	Brazilian Hatter	Herts	Sandridge
681	HILL	Sarah	48		Dau	Unm	11	F	Brazilian Hatter	Herts	Sandridge
682	FRANKLIN	Thomas	49	Sandridge	Head	Mar	57	M	Agric Lab	Herts	Sandridge
683	FRANKLIN	Sarah	49		Wife	Mar	58	F	Labourers Wife	Northants	Stony Stratford
684	BRAIZER	Thomas	50	Sandridge	Head	Mar	37	M	Agric Lab	Herts	Hitchin
685	BRAIZER	Eliza	50		Wife	Mar	36	F	Labr Wife	Herts	Sandridge
686	BRAIZER	William	50		Son	Unm	14	M	Agric Lab	Herts	Sandridge
687	BRAIZER	George	50		Son		12	M	Agric Lab	Herts	Sandridge
688	BRAIZER	Eliza	50		Dau		10	F	Scholar	Herts	Sandridge
689	BRAIZER	James	50		Son		6	M	Scholar	Herts	Sandridge
690	BRAIZER	John	50		Son		2	M		Herts	Sandridge
691	HADAWAY	Henry	51	Sandridge	Head	Mar	25	M	Sawyer	Bucks	Princes Risborough
692	HADAWAY	Eliza	51		Wife	Mar	29	F	Sawyers Wife	Beds	Studham
693	MANNING	William	51		Lodger	Unm	19	M	Labourer	Herts	Harpenden
694	CROFT	William	52	Sandridge	Head	Mar	25	M	Shoemaker	Herts	Hatfield
695	CROFT	Elizabeth	52		Wife	Mar	32	F	Boot Binder	Herts	Bayfordbury
696	CROFT	Harriotte	52		Dau		1	F	Infant	Herts	Sandridge
697	GEORGE	Edward	52		Nephew		10	M	Errand Boy	Herts	Little Berkhamsted
698	BREWER	George	53	Sandridge	Head	Mar	46	M	Agric Lab	Beds	Toddington
699	BREWER	Ann	53		Wife	Mar	48	F	Labourers Wife	Beds	Toddington
700	BREWER	George	53		Son	Unm	13	M	Agric Lab	Beds	Toddington
701	BREWER	Alfred	53		Son		11	M	Scholar	Beds	Toddington
702	BREWER	Sarah	53		Dau		9	F	Scholar	Herts	Sandridge
703	BREWER	Ann	53		Dau		3	F		Herts	Sandridge
704	ROLF	Thomas	54	Sandridge	Head	Mar	34	M	Agric Lab	Herts	Kimpton
705	ROLF	Rebecca	54		Wife	Mar	48	F	Labourers Wife	Herts	Sandridge

	SURNAME	FORENAME	SCHEDULE NUMBER	ADDRESS	RELATIONSHIP	STATUS	AGE	SEX	OCCUPATION	COUNTY OF BIRTH	PLACE OF BIRTH
706	ROLF	John	54		Son		7	M	Scholar	Herts	Sandridge
707	EVANS	George	55	Sandridge	Head	Mar	32	M	Carpenter	Herts	Wheathampstead
708	EVANS	Mary Ann	55		Wife	Mar	30	F	Carpenters Wife	Herts	Sandridge
709	EVANS	Charles	55		Son		9	M	Scholar	Herts	Sandridge
710	EVANS	George	55		Son		6	M	Scholar	Herts	St Michaels
711	EVANS	Susan	55		Dau		3	F		Herts	Sandridge

One house uninhabited

	SURNAME	FORENAME	SCHEDULE NUMBER	ADDRESS	RELATIONSHIP	STATUS	AGE	SEX	OCCUPATION	COUNTY OF BIRTH	PLACE OF BIRTH
712	HADAWAY	Lakey	56	Sandridge	Head	Mar	34	M	Sawyer	Bucks	Princes Risborough
713	HADAWAY	Patience	56		Wife	Mar	34	F	Sawyers Wife	Bucks	Buckland Common
714	HADAWAY	Jane	56		Dau		10	F	Scholar	Bucks	Buckland Common
715	HADAWAY	Ann	56		Dau		7	F	Scholar	Bucks	Buckland Common
716	HADAWAY	William	56		Son		5	M	Scholar	Bucks	Buckland Common
717	HADAWAY	Lizzy	56		Dau		3	F	Scholar	Herts	Sandridge
718	HADAWAY	Edward	56		Son		2	M	Infant	Herts	Sandridge
719	HADAWAY	James	56		Son		5 m	M	Infant	Herts	Sandridge
720	HODDINGTON	Thomas	57	Sandridge	Head	Mar	52	M	Agric Lab	Herts	Sandridge
721	HODDINGTON	Sarah	57		Wife	Mar	54	F	Agric Labr Wife	Herts	St Pauls Walden
722	DIMMOCK	David	58	Sandridge	Head	Mar	33	M	Labourer	Herts	St Stephens
723	DIMMOCK	Mary	58		Wife	Mar	27	F	Labr Wife	Herts	Sandridge
724	DIMMOCK	George	58		Son		11	M	Scholar	Herts	Sandridge
725	DIMMOCK	Alfred	58		Son		9	M	Scholar	Herts	Sandridge
726	DIMMOCK	William	58		Son		7	M	Scholar	Herts	Sandridge
727	DIMMOCK	Emma	58		Dau		1	F		Herts	Sandridge
728	ADAMS	Susana	58		Step-dau		5	F	Scholar	Herts	Sandridge
729	SLATER	Sarah	59	Sandridge	Head	Unm	53	F	Straw Plaiter	Herts	Sandridge
730	SLATER	Sophia	59		Sister	Unm	32	F	Straw Plaiter	Herts	Sandridge
731	SHARP	Daniel	59		Lodger	Mar	32	M	Game Keeper	Herts	Caddington [?]
732	SHARP	Elizabeth	59		Lodgers Wife	Mar	32	F	Keepers Wife	Herts	Sandridge
733	SHARP	Alfred	59		Lodgers Son		11	M	Scholar	Herts	Sandridge
734	SHARP	Sarah	59		Lodgers Dau		8	F	Scholar	Herts	St Peters
735	SHARP	Joseph	59		Lodgers Son		1	M	Infant	Herts	Sandridge
736	SLATER	Joseph	60	Sandridge	Head	Mar	29	M	Bricklayer	Herts	Sandridge
737	SLATER	Susan	60		Wife	Mar	29	F	Bricklayers Wife	Herts	Sandridge
738	HUGHES	James	61	Sandridge	Head	Mar	45	M	Agric Lab	Herts	Redbourn
739	HUGHES	Sophia	61		Wife	Mar	36	F	Labr Wife	Herts	Sandridge
740	HUGHES	Fanny	61		Dau		16	F	Brazilian Hatter	Herts	Sandridge
741	HUGHES	Henry	61		Son		13	M	Agric Lab	Herts	Sandridge
742	HUGHES	Alfred	61		Son		11	M	Scholar	Herts	Sandridge
743	HUGHES	Eliza	61		Dau		9	F	Scholar	Herts	Sandridge
744	HUGHES	Elizabeth	61		Dau		6	F	Scholar	Herts	Sandridge
745	HUGHES	Susan	61		Dau		3	F	Scholar	Herts	Sandridge
746	HUGHES	James	61		Son		1	M	Infant	Herts	Sandridge

SANDRIDGE

	Surname	Name		Place	Relation	Status	Age	Sex	Occupation	County	Birthplace
747	DICKENSON	Thomas	61		Lodger	Widower	85	M	Labourer	Beds	Dunstable
748	HALSEY	William	62	Sandridge	Head	Widower	64	M	Agric Lab	Herts	Sandridge
749	TRUSSELL	Joshua	62		Lodger	Mar	22	M	Agric Lab	Herts	Sandridge
750	TRUSSELL	Susan	62		Lodgers Wife	Mar	23	F	Labr Wife	Herts	Sandridge
751	HALSEY	Fanny	62		Grandau		2	F	Scholar	Herts	Sandridge
752	HALSEY	Samuel	62		Visitor	Unm	20	M	Bricklayer	Essex	Ilford
753	ANDREWS	James	63	Sandridge	Head	Mar	32	M	Agric Lab	Beds	Harford
754	ANDREWS	Maria	63		Wife	Mar	31	F	Labr Wife	Herts	Sandridge
755	ANDREWS	Mary	63		Dau		8	F	Scholar	Herts	Sandridge
756	ANDREWS	William	63		Son		7	M	Scholar	Herts	Sandridge
757	ANDREWS	Sarah	63		Dau		4	F	Scholar	Herts	Sandridge
758	ANDREWS	George	63		Son		3	M	Scholar	Herts	Sandridge
759	ANDREWS	Elizabeth	63		Dau		1	F	Infant	Herts	Sandridge
760	SWALEY	Sarah	64	Sandridge	Head	Widow	70	F	(Pauper) late husband an Agric Lab	Herts	Sandridge
761	SWALEY	John	64		Son	Unm	28	M	Agric Lab	Herts	Sandridge
762	LATCHFORD	Joseph	64		Son-in-law	Mar	34	M	Agric Lab	Herts	Wheathampstead
763	LATCHFORD	Mary	64		Dau	Mar	35	F	Labr Wife	Herts	Sandridge
764	LATCHFORD	Sarah	64		Grandau		9	F	Scholar	Herts	Sandridge
765	LATCHFORD	Mary	64		Grandau		7	F	Scholar	Herts	Sandridge
766	LATCHFORD	William	64		Grandson		5	M	Scholar	Herts	Sandridge
767	LATCHFORD	Susan	64		Grandau		6 m	F	Infant	Herts	Sandridge
768	LATTIMORE	John	65	Sandridge	Head	Widower	68	M	Timber Merchant employing 10 men	Herts	Sandridge
769	LATTIMORE	Joseph	65		Brother	Unm	64	M	Retired Timber Merchant	Herts	Sandridge
770	WILLIS	Eliza	65		Dau	Widow	45	F	Housekeeper	Herts	Sandridge
771	WILLIS	John	65		Grandson		9	M	Scholar	Beds	Woburn
772	WILLIS	Thomas	65		Grandson		7	M	Scholar	Beds	Woburn

One house uninhabited

	Surname	Name		Place	Relation	Status	Age	Sex	Occupation	County	Birthplace
773	ADAMS	William	66	Sandridge	Head	Mar	63	M	Agric Lab	Herts	Harpenden
774	ADAMS	Susan	66		Wife	Mar	59	F	Labr Wife	Herts	Sandridge
775	ADAMS	Thomas	66		Son	Unm	33	M	Agric Lab	Herts	Sandridge
776	ADAMS	Ann	66		Dau	Unm	25	F	Straw Plaiter	Herts	Sandridge
777	ADAMS	Elizabeth	66		Dau	Unm	15	F	Straw Plaiter	Herts	Sandridge
778	NORMAN	Joseph	67	Sandridge	Head	Mar	23	M	Sawyer	Herts	Tewin
779	NORMAN	Eliza	67		Wife	Mar	23	F	Straw Plaiter	Herts	Sandridge
780	NORMAN	William	67		Son		2	M	Infant	Herts	Sandridge
781	NORMAN	Michal	68	Sandridge	Head	Mar	54	M	Agric Lab	Herts	Welwyn
782	NORMAN	Hannah	68		Wife	Mar	52	F	Labr Wife	Herts	Tewin
783	NORMAN	Elizabeth	68		Dau	Unm	20	F	Straw Plaiter	Herts	Tewin
784	NORMAN	Esther	68		Dau		11	F	Scholar	Herts	Wheathampstead
785	NORMAN	Hannah	68		Grandau		1	F	Infant	Herts	Sandridge
786	SLATER	Elizabeth	69	Sandridge	Head	Widow	33	F	Straw Plaiter	Herts	Wheathampstead
787	SLATER	Ann	69		Dau		10	F	Scholar	Herts	Wheathampstead
788	SLATER	Sophia	69		Dau		7	F	Scholar	Herts	Wheathampstead

	SURNAME	FORENAME	SCHEDULE NUMBER	ADDRESS	RELATIONSHIP	STATUS	AGE	SEX	OCCUPATION	COUNTY OF BIRTH	PLACE OF BIRTH
789	SLATER	Susana	69		Dau		5	F	Scholar	Herts	Wheathampstead
790	GRAY	Sarah	69		Visitor	Unm	26	F	Straw Plaiter	Herts	Wheathampstead
791	CHARLES	William	70	Sandridge	Head	Mar	31	M	Gardener	Herts	Sandridge
792	CHARLES	Hanna	70		Wife	Mar	28	F	Gardeners Wife	Herts	Sandridge
793	CHARLES	Alfred	70		Son		7	M	Scholar	Herts	St Peters
794	CHARLES	Jane	70		Dau		4	F	Scholar	Herts	St Peters
795	CHARLES	Albert	70		Son		1	M	Infant	Herts	Harpenden
796	MORRICE	Henry	71	Sandridge	Head	Mar	55	M	Agric Lab	Herts	St Peters
797	MORRICE	Sarah	71		Wife	Mar	53	F	Agric Labr Wife	Herts	Wheathampstead
798	MORRICE	Elizabeth	71		Dau	Unm	20	F	Brazilian Hatter	Herts	Sandridge
799	GURNEY	William	72	Sandridge	Head	Mar	47	M	Agric Lab	Herts	Sandridge
800	GURNEY	Eliza	72		Wife	Mar	44	F	Labr Wife	Herts	Abbey, St Albans
801	GURNEY	Hannah	72		Lodger	Widow	70	F	Pauper (formerly Plaiter)	Herts	Sandridge
802	FAULDER	Rhoda	73	Sandridge	Head	Widow	49	F	Dress Maker	Herts	Harpenden
803	FAULDER	Maria	73		Dau	Unm	16	F	Brazilian Hatter	Herts	Sandridge
804	FAULDER	Henry	73		Son		11	M	Scholar	Herts	Sandridge
805	FAULDER	Sarah	73		Dau		9	F	Scholar	Herts	Sandridge
806	FAULDER	Jane	73		Dau		7	F	Scholar	Herts	Sandridge
807	WEBB	Henry	74	Sandridge	Head	Mar	70	M	Agric Lab	Herts	Sandridge
808	WEBB	Hannah	74		Wife	Mar	65	F	Labr Wife	Herts	Sandridge
809	WEBB	Maria	74		Dau	Unm	35	F	Brazilian Hatter	Herts	Sandridge
810	WEBB	Eliza	74		Dau	Unm	33	F	Brazilian Hatter	Herts	Sandridge
811	WEBB	Elizabeth	74		Dau	Unm	23	F	Brazilian Hatter	Herts	Sandridge
812	WEBB	Mary	74		Grandau		7	F	Scholar	Herts	Sandridge
813	WEBB	Emma	74		Grandau		6	F	Scholar	Herts	Sandridge
814	WEATHERLEY	Jeremiah	75	Sandridge	Head	Widower	59	M	Agric Lab	Herts	Sandridge
815	WEATHERLEY	Elizabeth	75		Dau	Unm	24	F	Brazilian Hatter	Herts	Sandridge
816	WEATHERLEY	Eliza	75		Dau	Unm	19	F	Brazilian Hatter	Herts	Sandridge
817	MESSENGER	James	76	Sandridge	Head	Mar	49	M	Agric Lab	Herts	Harpenden
818	MESSENGER	Mary	76		Wife	Mar	42	F	Labr Wife	Herts	Sandridge
819	MESSENGER	John	76		Son	Unm	20	M	Agric Lab	Herts	Sandridge
820	MESSENGER	James	76		Son	Unm	14	M	Agric Lab	Herts	Sandridge
821	MESSENGER	Henry	76		Son		12	M	Agric Lab	Herts	Sandridge
822	MESSENGER	Thomas	76		Son		9	M	Scholar	Herts	Sandridge
823	LAWRENCE	Charles	77	Sandridge	Head	Mar	30	M	Wheelwright	Herts	Barnet
824	LAWRENCE	Maria	77		Wife	Mar	23	F	Dress Maker	Herts	Wheathampstead
825	LAWRENCE	Charles	77		Son		8	M	Scholar	Herts	North Mimms
826	LAWRENCE	George	77		Son		1	M	Infant	Herts	Sandridge
827	HORNET	William	78	Sandridge	Head	Mar	33	M	Agric Lab	Herts	Preston
828	HORNET	Hannah	78		Wife	Mar	33	F	Labr Wife	Herts	Wheathampstead
829	HORNET	Letticia	78		Dau		10	F	Scholar	Herts	Wheathampstead
830	HORNET	Amos	78		Son		8	M	Scholar	Herts	Wheathampstead
831	HORNET	Mary	78		Dau		6	F	Scholar	Herts	Sandridge
832	HORNET	Dinah	78		Dau		4	F	Scholar	Herts	Sandridge

833	HORNET	Alice	78		Dau		1	F	Infant	Herts	Sandridge
834	SIMMONS	John	79	Sandridge	Head	Mar	50	M	Agric Lab	Bucks	Ivinghoe
835	SIMMONS	Ann	79		Wife	Mar	52	F	Labr Wife	Herts	Hemel Hemps·ead
836	SIMMONS	John	79		Son	Unm	17	M	Agric Lab	Herts	St Peters
837	ALLEN	John	80	Sandridge	Head	Mar	39	M	Shepherd	Herts	St Peters
838	ALLEN	Charlotte	80		Wife	Mar	33	F	Shepherds Wife	Herts	St Stephens
839	ALLEN	Louisa	80		Dau		10	F	Scholar	Herts	Hemel Hempstead
840	ALLEN	Isabella	80		Dau		7	F·	Scholar	Herts	Hemel Hempstead
841	ALLEN	Allice	80		Dau		1	F	Infant	Herts	Sandridge

One house uninhabited

842	DOLLIMORE	Charles	81	Sandridge	Head	Mar	40	M	Agric Lab	Herts	Wheathampstead
843	DOLLIMORE	Susan	81		Wife	Mar	44	F	Labr Wife	Herts	Baldock
844	DOLLIMORE	Emma	81		Dau		1	F	Infant	Herts	Sandridge
845	WELSH	John	82	Sandridge	Head	Mar	26	M	Agric Lab	Herts	Flamstead
846	WELSH	Sarah	82		Wife	Mar	23	F	Labr Wife	Herts	Sandridge
847	WELSH	George	82		Son		4	M		Herts	Sandridge
848	WELSH	Sarah	82		Dau		8 m	F	Infant	Herts	Sandridge
849	BREAD	William	83	Sandridge	Head	Mar	45	M	Agric Lab	Herts	Abbey [St Albans]
850	BREAD	Mary	83		Sister	Widow	36	F		Herts	Sandridge
851	CHARLES	George	84	Sandridge	Head	Mar	37	M	Agric Lab	Middx	Marylebone
852	CHARLES	Elizabeth	84		Wife	Mar	34	F	Labr Wife	Herts	Hatfield
853	CHARLES	Fanny	84		Dau		11	F	Scholar	Herts	Hatfield
854	CHARLES	Jesse	84		Son		8	M	Cripple	Herts	Hatfield
855	CHARLES	Sarah	84		Dau		5	F		Herts	Sandridge
856	CHARLES	Walter	84		Son		3	M		Herts	Sandridge
857	CHARLES	Alfred	84		Son		1	M		Herts	Sandridge
858	JONES	William	85	Sandridge	Head	Widower	76	M	Corn Salesman	Herts	Sandridge
859	SAUNDERS	Sophia	85		Dau	Mar	39	F	Dress Maker	Herts	Sandridge
860	SAUNDERS	William	85		Grandson		12	M	Scholar	Herts	Sandridge

The end of the District 4b in the parish of Sandridge.

Chapter Eight

The parish of St Peters in the borough of St Albans

Registrar's District: St Albans   Enumeration District 1a   Ref. HO 107/1713 folios 228-58

The part west of the road from the Market Place to Luton, including part of St Peters Street, Spencer Street, Adelaide Street, Waddingtons Yard and Catherine Lane.

1	HADNUTT	Jemima	1	Market Place	Head	Unm	62	F	Annuitant	Herts	Aldenham
2	MERRIOTT	Mary	1		Sister	Widow	74	F	Annuitant	Herts	Aldenham
3	RUSSELL	William Alexander	2	St Peters Street	Head	Mar	36	M	Surgeon M.R.C.S.E.	Cambs	Wisbech
4	RUSSELL	Jane	2		Wife	Mar	34	F		Middx	Shoreditch
5	RUSSELL	Alexander Thomas	2		Son		4	M		Herts	St Albans
6	RUSSELL	Harry Goodman B.	2		Son		1	M		Herts	St Albans
7	BEAGGOOD	Sophia	2		Mother-in-law	Widow	65	F		Middx	Holbom
8	WELCH	Catherine	2		Nurse	Widow	65	F	Nurse	[Herts]	Hitchin
9	HALE	Ann	2		Serv	Unm	37	F	Cook	Herts	Datchworth
10	EMMETT	Maryanne	2		Serv	Unm	19	F	Housemaid	Bucks	Olney
11	SIMPSON	William Balcombe	3	St Peters Street	Head	Mar	36	M	Solicitor	Sussex	Brighton
12	SIMPSON	Elizabeth	3		Wife	Mar	31	F		Sussex	Cuckfield
13	SIMPSON	Albert Leppard	3		Son		14	M		Sussex	Brighton
14	BURTON	Emily	3		Serv	[Unm]	16	F	General Servant	Herts	Haileybury [Great Amwell]
15	EAMES	George	4	St Peters Street	Head	Mar	57	M	Innkeeper	Somerset	[Unknown]
16	EAMES	Elizabeth	4		Wife	Mar	60	F		Herts	St Albans
17	EAMES	George	4		Son	Unm	18	M		Herts	St Albans
18	LINNELL	Richard	4		Lodger	Unm	32	M	Traveller	Shrop	[Unknown]
19	EGAN	William	4		Lodger	Mar	55	M	Traveller	Ireland	Dublin
20	LANE	James William	5	St Peters Street	Head	Unm	23	M	Grocer employing 3 youths	Kent	Chatham
21	LANE	Mary Elizabeth	5		Sister	Unm	26	F		Kent	Gillingham
22	HULL	George	5		Assistant	Unm	20	M	Grocers Assistant	Herts	St Albans
23	LANE	George	5		Assistant	Unm	18	M	Grocers Apprentice	Kent	Rochester
24	LOVETT	John	5		Serv	Unm	16	M	Grocers Servant	Herts	Harpenden
25	CHILDS	Henry	6	St Peters Street	Head	Mar	59	M	Baker	Herts	Shenley

ST PETERS353

26	CHILDS	Francoise	6		Wife	Mar	55	F	Bakers Wife	Switz	[Unknown]
27	CHILDS	Frances	6		Dau	Unm	18	F	Bakers Daughter	Herts	Redbourn
28	HEWITT	Charles	7	St Peters Street	Head	Mar	25	M	Butcher	Herts	St Albans
29	HEWITT	Mary	7		Wife	Mar	23	F	Butchers Wife	Middx	Kentish Town
30	BRADLEY	James	7		Lodger	Mar	30	M	Tragedian	Leics	Leicester
31	ENGLISH	Edwin	7		Lodger	Mar	25	M	Tragedian	London	City
32	ENGLISH	Caroline	7		Lodgers Wife	Mar	26	F	Tragedians Wife	Notts	Kingston Upon Soar
33	BRADLEY	Hannah	7		Lodgers Wife	Mar	29	F	Tragedians Wife	Staffs	[Unknown]
34	ENGLISH	Maryanne	7		Lodgers Dau		2	F		Middx	Chelsea
35	MACBETH	William	8	St Peters Street	Head	Mar	25	M	Foundry Ironmonger	Herts	St Albans
36	MACBETH	Elizabeth	8		Wife	Mar	25	F		Herts	St Albans
37	MACBETH	Elizabeth	8		Dau		10 m	F		Herts	St Albans
38	HAGGER	Louisa	9	St Peters Street	Head	Mar	25	F	Wife	Herts	Kimpton
39	HAGGER	Alfred	9		Son		2	M		Herts	St Albans
40	HAGGER	Henry	9		Lodger		2 m	M		Herts	St Albans
41	COWING	John James	10	St Peters Street	Head	Unm	23	M	Bookseller employing 1 person	Herts	Barnet
42	ARNOLD	Robert	10		Visitor	Unm	20	M	Unemployed	Herts	St Albans
43	DAY	Amelia	10		Serv	Unm	32	F	House Servant	Herts	Totteridge
44	SMITH	William	11	St Peters Street	Head	Mar	39	M	Hair Dresser	Herts	Watford
45	SMITH	Mary Ann	11		Wife	Mar	37	F		Herts	Watford
46	SMITH	Hannah Rebecca	11		Dau		8	F		Herts	St Albans
47	SMITH	William James Arthur	11		Son		6	M		Herts	St Albans
48	SMITH	Joseph	11		Son		3	M		Herts	St Albans
49	WALFORD	Hannah	11		Lodger	Mar	28	F		Essex	Witham
50	BUTLER	Mary Ann	11		[blank]		6	F		Middx	Marylebone
51	JOYNER	Daniel	11		Lodger	Mar	21	M		Herts	Welwyn
52	JOYNER	Mary Elizabeth	11		[Lodgers Wife]	Mar	22	F		Essex	Colchester
53	WOODBRIDGE	William	12	St Peters Street	Head	Mar	36	M	China Dealer	Herts	Amersham
54	WOODBRIDGE	Ann	12		Wife	Mar	38	F	China Dealers Wife	Herts	Coleshill [Northaw]
55	WOODBRIDGE	Ruth	12		Dau		14	F	Scholar	Herts	Coleshill [Northaw]
56	HILL	William	13	St Peters Street	Head	Mar	55	M	Victualler	Hunts	Diddington
57	HILL	Mary	13		Wife	Mar	45	F	Victuallers Wife	Herts	Baldock
58	HILL	Thomas	13		Son		14	M	Scholar	Herts	St Albans
59	HILL	Arthur James	13		Son		13	M	Errand Boy	Herts	St Albans
60	HILL	William	13		Son		11	M		Herts	St Albans
61	HILL	Frederick	13		Son		8	M		Herts	St Albans
62	HILL	George	13		Son		6	M		Herts	St Albans
63	HILL	Horace Hade	13		Son		3	M		Herts	St Albans
64	DIX	James William	14	St Peters Street	Head	Unm	25	M	Painter	Middx	Edmonton
65	PAGE	Philip Inglis	15	St Peters Street	Head	Mar	35	M	Land Surveyor & Auctioneer	Herts	Redbourn
66	PAGE	Anne	15		Wife	Mar	28	F		Herts	Barnet

	SURNAME	FORENAME	SCHEDULE NUMBER	ADDRESS	RELATIONSHIP	STATUS	AGE	SEX	OCCUPATION	COUNTY OF BIRTH	PLACE OF BIRTH
67	PAGE	Philip Henry	15		Son		5	M		Herts	St Albans
68	PAGE	Annie Emily	15		Dau		3	F		Herts	St Albans
69	PAGE	Edward Burnett	15		Son		2	M		Herts	St Albans
70	PAGE	Thomas Jowland	15		Son		2 m	M		Herts	St Albans
71	ILGOOD	George J.	15		Pupil	[Unm]	17	M	Articled Pupil	Middx	Marylebone
72	MCDERMOTT	Reginald	15		Pupil	[Unm]	16	M	Articled Pupil	Yorks	Leeds
73	GOODE	Maria	15		Serv	[Unm]	22	F	Cook	Oxon	Lewknor
74	FINCHES	Priscilla	15		Serv	[Unm]	22	F	Nurse	Herts	Tring
75	FINCHES	Elizabeth	15		Serv	[Unm]	18	F	Under Housemaid	Herts	Tring
76	AMSDEN	Benjamin	16	St Peters Street	Head	Mar	30	M	Straw Hat Manufacturer	Herts	Tring
77	AMSDEN	Frances	16		Wife	Mar	38	F		Herts	St Albans
78	AMSDEN	Harriet F.	16		Dau		4	F		Herts	St Albans
79	AMSDEN	Mary A.	16		Dau		2	F		Herts	St Albans
80	WELLS	Eliza	16		Serv	Unm	20	F	General Servant	Herts	Sandridge
81	CRAWLEY	Eliza	16		Serv	Unm	20	F	General Servant	Herts	St Albans
82	LEWIS	Olivia	17	St Peters Street	Head	Widow	30	F		Kent	Sittingbourne
83	LEWIS	Olivia Ann	17		Dau		5	F		Herts	St Albans
84	LEWIS	Augusta Mary	17		Dau		1	F		Herts	St Albans
85	PARKINS	Hannah	17		Serv	Unm	32	F	House Servant	Herts	Harpenden
86	SMITH	Henry	18	St Peters Street	Head	Mar	59	M	House Decorator employing 7 men	Middx	Paddington
87	SMITH	Lydia	18		Wife	Mar	48	F		Middx	Clerkenwell

One house uninhabited

	SURNAME	FORENAME	SCHEDULE NUMBER	ADDRESS	RELATIONSHIP	STATUS	AGE	SEX	OCCUPATION	COUNTY OF BIRTH	PLACE OF BIRTH
88	THOMPSON	William	19	St Peters Street	Head	Mar	52	M	Bootmaker	Herts	St Albans
89	THOMPSON	Elizabeth	19		Wife	Mar	47	F		Herts	St Albans
90	THOMPSON	Ellen Woollatt	19		Dau		15	F		Herts	St Albans
91	THOMPSON	Joseph Sturgo	19		Son		13	M		Herts	St Albans
92	THOMPSON	Samuel	19		Son		9	M		Herts	St Albans
93	THOMPSON	William	19		Son		7	M		Herts	St Albans
94	THOMPSON	Catherin Beaumont	19		Dau		3	F		Herts	St Albans
95	REDRUP	James	19		Appr	Unm	17	M	Bootmakers Apprentice	Herts	St Albans
96	WHITE	Henry	20	St Peters Street	Head	Mar	28	M	Mason	Somerset	Bath
97	WHITE	Elizabeth	20		Wife	Mar	23	F	Formerly Dressmaker	Norfolk	Norwich
98	WHITE	Ann Eliza	20		Dau		9 m	F		Herts	St Albans
99	BROACH	George	21	St Peters Street	Head	Unm	33	M	Draper	Scotland	Dumfries
100	RICHARDS	Joseph	22	St Peters Street	Head	Mar	65	M	Saddler	Warks	Warwick
101	RICHARDS	Hannah	22		Wife	Mar	61	F	Bonnet Sewer	Herts	Shenley
102	RICHARDS	Fitzgerald	22		Son	Unm	23	M	Grocer	Herts	St Albans
103	PEASE	Harriet	22		Lodger	Unm	18	F	Bonnet Sewer	Norfolk	Scoulton
104	GILBERT	Ann	22		Serv	Unm	20	F	House Servant	Herts	St Albans
105	WHEELDON	Mary	23	St Peters Street	Inmate	Unm	72	F	Annuitant	Herts	St Albans
106	FOTHERGILL	Elizabeth	24	St Peters Street	Head	Mar	49	F	Fundholder	[Devon]	Tiverton
107	BATHURST	Sophia	24		Visitor	Unm	22	F	Fundholder	Kent	Strood

108	FOTHERGILL	Lydia	24		Visitor	Unm	18	F		Cumb	St Bees
109	THICK	Caroline	24		Serv	Unm	27	F	Servant of all work	Herts	East Barnet
110	EDWARDS	Elizabeth	25	St Peters Street	Head	Unm	48	F	Dressmaker	Herts	St Albans
111	EDWARDS	Thomas	25		Nephew		10	M	Scholar	Herts	St Albans
112	BEASBY	Ann	25		Cousin	Unm	39	F	Dressmaker	Herts	Stevenage
113	COOK	Emily	25		Appr	Unm	18	F	[Apprentice] Dressmaker	Middx	London
114	MORGAN	Elizabeth	25		Appr		14	F	[Apprentice] Dressmaker	Herts	Sandridge
115	PEPPERCORN	John	26	St Peters Street	Head	Widower	60	M	Retired Farmer	Beds	Little Staughton
116	PEPPERCORN	Sarah	26		Sister	Unm	54	F		Beds	Little Staughton
117	PEPPERCORN	Elizabeth	26		Sister	Unm	46	F		Hunts	Great Paxton
118	MCCAW	James	27	St Peters Street	Head	Unm	33	M	Draper employing 4 assistants	Scotland	[Unknown]
119	ARMSTRONG	Mary	27		Visitor	Widow	54	F	Annuitant	Scotland	[Unknown]
120	ARMSTRONG	Ann	27		Serv	Unm	30	F	House Servant	Scotland	[Unknown]
121	ARMSTRONG	Agnes	27		Niece		15	F	Scholar	Scotland	[Unknown]
122	STUBBS	Phineas	27		Serv	Unm	23	M	Drapers Assistant	Scotland	[Unknown]
123	BOYES	John	27		Serv	Unm	21	M	Drapers Assistant	Scotland	[Unknown]
124	KERR	George	27		Serv	Unm	22	M	Drapers Assistant	Scotland	[Unknown]
125	ARMSTRONG	Andrew	27		Serv	Unm	18	M	Drapers Assistant	Scotland	[Unknown]
126	BRADSHAW	John	28	St Peters Street	Head	Mar	79	M	Retired Builder	Herts	St Albans
127	BRADSHAW	Elizabeth	28		Wife	Mar	65	F		Leics	Little Dalby
128	BRADSHAW	Emma	28		Dau	Unm	28	F	Dressmaker	Herts	St Albans
129	BRADSHAW	Elvina	28		Dau	Unm	26	F	Dressmaker	Herts	St Albans
130	PAYNE	James	29	St Peters Street	Head	Mar	59	M	Cordwainer	Herts	St Albans
131	PAYNE	Ann Maria	29		Wife	Mar	59	F	Cordwainers Wife	Herts	Park Street [St Stephens]
132	JOHNSON	John	29		Nephew	Unm	29	M	Cordwainer	Warks	Birmingham
133	PETERS	Pamela	29		Lodger	Unm	17	F	Bonnet Sewer	England	[Unknown]
134	BUCKLER	Elizabeth	30	St Peters Street	Head	Unm	65	F	House Servant	Northants	Northampton
135	DEAYTON	James	31	St Peters Street	Head	Mar	31	M	Licensed Victualler	Herts	St Albans
136	DEAYTON	Ann	31		Wife	Mar	35	F		Beds	Toddington
137	DEAYTON	George James	31		Son		5	M	At Home	Herts	St Albans
138	DEAYTON	Clarissa	31		Dau		2	F		Herts	St Albans
139	DEAYTON	Laura Ann	31		Dau		1	F		Herts	St Albans
140	CURBY	Jane	31		Lodger	Unm	18	F	Servant	[Beds]	Bidden [Biddenham]
141	HICKMAN	William	31		Serv	Widower	60	M	Servant Gardener	Bucks	Buckingham
142	CHILDS	Jesse	32	St Peters Street	Head	Mar	41	M	Wheelwright	Herts	Elstree
143	CHILDS	Eliza	32		Wife	Mar	40	F	Wheelwrights Wife	Herts	Elstree
144	CHILDS	Jesse	32		Son	Unm	18	M	Wheelwright	Herts	St Stephens
145	CHILDS	Mary Ann	32		Dau	Unm	16	F	Bonnet Sewer	Middx	Finchley
146	CHILDS	David	32		Son	Unm	12	M		Herts	St Albans
147	CHILDS	William	32		Son		10	M		Herts	St Albans
148	CHILDS	Susan	32		Dau		8	F		Herts	St Albans
149	CHILDS	Walter	32		Son		3	M		Herts	St Albans
150	CHILDS	Emma	32		Dau		1	F		Herts	St Albans

	SURNAME	FORENAME	SCHEDULE NUMBER	ADDRESS	RELATIONSHIP	STATUS	AGE	SEX	OCCUPATION	COUNTY OF BIRTH	PLACE OF BIRTH
151	FOREMAN	William	33	St Peters Street	Head	Mar	49	M	Victualler & Coach Proprietor	Essex	Saffron Walden
152	FOREMAN	Mary Ann	33		Wife	Mar	42	F		Middx	Clerkenwell
153	FOREMAN	Elizabeth	33		Dau	Unm	19	F		Middx	Clerkenwell
154	FOREMAN	Mary Ann	33		Dau		4	F		Herts	St Albans
155	FOREMAN	James	33		Son		2	M		Herts	St Albans
156	FOREMAN	Ellen	33		Dau		1	F		Herts	St Albans
157	FALKNALL	Ann	33		Serv	[Unm]	18	F	House Servant	Herts	St Albans
158	CLARKE	Robert	34	St Peters Street	Head	Mar	53	M	General Practitioner	N'thumb	Newcastle
159	CLARKE	Lydia	34		Wife	Mar	40	F		Herts	Wheathampstead
160	CLARKE	James	34		Son	Unm	15	M		Herts	Wheathampstead
161	CLARKE	Mary Ann	34		Dau	Unm	13	F		Herts	Wheathampstead
162	CLARKE	Lydia	34		Dau		10	F		Herts	St Albans
163	CLARKE	William	34		Son		7	M		Herts	St Albans
164	CLARKE	Margaret	34		Dau		6	F		Herts	St Albans
165	CLARKE	Maria	34		Dau		5	F		Herts	St Albans
166	CLARKE	Eira [?]	34		Dau		3	F		Herts	St Albans
167	EDMONDS	John	35	St Peters Street	Head	Mar	52	M	Grocer	Bucks	Aylesbury
168	EDMONDS	Mary	35		Wife	Mar	52	F	Grocers Wife	Beds	Stotford
169	BENNETT	John	35		Serv	Unm	17	M	Shopman	Herts	St Albans
170	WRIGHT	Elizabeth	35		Serv	Unm	22	F	House Servant	Herts	Bayford
171	SMITH	Sarah	36	St Peters Street	Head	Widow	50	F	Straw Bonnet Maker	Herts	Sandridge
172	LUFF	George	37	St Peters Street	[Head]	Unm	34	M	Boot Maker	Herts	St Albans
173	LUFF	James	37		[blank]	Unm	33	M	Boot Maker	Herts	St Albans
174	TEWKESBURY	William	38	St Peters Street	Lodger	Unm	50	M		Dorset	Weymouth
175	BENNETT	William	39	St Peters Street	Head	Mar	48	M	Builder & Brickmaker employing 27 men: viz 3 Carpenters 2 Bricklayers 14 labourers 6 brickmakers and 2 labs	Middx	Hackney
176	BENNETT	Martha	39		Wife	Mar	37	F		Herts	St Albans
177	BENNETT	Mary Ann	39		Dau		14	F	Scholar	Herts	St Albans
178	BENNETT	Eleanor M.	39		Dau		7	F		Herts	St Albans
179	BENNETT	Harriet L.	39		Dau		5	F		Herts	St Albans
180	BENNETT	Alice H.	39		Dau		3	F		Herts	St Albans
181	BENNETT	Henry C.	39		Son		1	M		Herts	St Albans
182	BATES	Hannah	39		Serv	Unm	18	F	House Servant	Middx	Paddington
183	PEPPERCORN	James (Jnr)	40	St Peters Street	Head	Mar	24	M	Butcher	Herts	St Albans
184	PEPPERCORN	Mary Ann	40		Wife	Mar	24	F	Butchers Wife	Essex	Barking
185	FISHER	Martha	40		Serv	Unm	15	F	House Servant	Essex	Barking
186	PEPPERCORN	James (Snr)	41	St Peters Street	Head	Mar	59	M	Butcher, employing 2 men	Beds	Little Staughton
187	PEPPERCORN	Elizabeth	41		Wife	Mar	60	F	Butchers Wife	Herts	St Albans
188	PEPPERCORN	Benjamin	41		Son	Unm	26	M	Chemist	Herts	St Albans
189	PEPPERCORN	Sarah	41		Dau	Unm	19	F	Butchers Daughter	Herts	St Albans
190	PEPPERCORN	Hannah	41		Dau	Unm	17	F	Butchers Daughter	Herts	St Albans
191	KNOWLES	Sarah	41		Serv	Unm	17	F	House Servant	Herts	Park Street [St Stephens]

192	NIGHTINGALE	James Parkinson	42	St Peters Street	Head	Mar	31	M	Grocer	Herts	Hatfield
193	NIGHTINGALE	Caroline Augusta	42		Wife	Mar	34	F	Grocers Wife	Surrey	Woking
194	NIGHTINGALE	Emma	42		Dau		8	F		Herts	St Albans
195	NIGHTINGALE	Caroline Prudence	42		Dau		6	F		Herts	St Albans
196	NIGHTINGALE	James Reading	42		Son		4	M		Herts	St Albans
197	NIGHTINGALE	Walter John	42		Son		2	M		Herts	St Albans
198	NIGHTINGALE	Horace Parkinson	42		Son		6 m	M		Herts	St Albans
199	BIRD	Mary	42		Serv	Unm	23	F	House Servant	Surrey	Woking
200	BOWEN	William Mogg	43	St Peters Street	Head	Widower	83	M	D.D. Vicar of Shipton Bellinger, Magistrate	Somerset	Taunton
201	BOWEN	Aubrey William Spencer	43		Son	Mar	37	M	Gentleman	Herts	St Albans
202	BOWEN	Elizabeth Ann	43		Dau-in-law	Mar	32	F		Herts	Bovingdon
203	BOWEN	Sarah Harriot Elizabeth	43		Grandau		7	F		Herts	Bovingdon
204	BOWEN	Henry Francis	43		Grandson		6	M		Herts	Bovingdon
205	BOWEN	Aubrey William Percy	43		Grandson		1	M		Herts	St Albans
206	BLUNT	Charlotte	43		Serv	Unm	25	F	House Servant	Herts	Cheshunt
207	KILBY	James	43		Serv	Unm	21	M	House Servant	Middx	Wembley [?]
208	STEVENS	Mary	44	St Peters Street	Head	Widow	63	F	Annuitant	Bucks	Missenden
209	STEVENS	Mary	44		Dau	Unm	27	F	Dressmaker	Bucks	Wycombe
210	STEVENS	James	44		Grandson		9	M	Scholar	Bucks	Wycombe
211	FARR	Elisha Davis	45	St Peters Street	Head	Mar	35	M	Plumber & Engineer to Waterworks	Herts	Baldock
212	FARR	Emma	45		Wife	Mar	45	F	Dressmaker	Herts	St Albans
213	AGUTTER	Emma	45		Sister-in-law	Unm	20	F	Dressmaker	Herts	St Albans
214	AGUTTER	Sarah	45		Sister-in-law		13	F	Scholar	Herts	St Albans
215	WINCH	Sarah	46	St Peters Street	Head	Widow	60	F	Annuitant	Herts	St Albans
216	SWAIN	Elizabeth	46		Serv		13	F	General Servant	Herts	St Albans
217	LUNON	John	47	St Peters Street	Head	Mar	57	M	Farm Servant	Herts	Hemel Hempstead
218	LUNON	Elizabeth	47		Wife	Mar	45	F		Herts	Redbourn
219	LUNON	Susan	47		Dau	Unm	22	F		Herts	Redbourn
220	LUNON	Edward	47		Son	Unm	20	M	Labourer	Herts	Hemel Hempstead
221	LUNON	Sarah	47		Dau	Unm	17	F		Herts	Hemel Hempstead
222	LUNON	Hannah	47		Dau	Unm	15	F	Works at Silk Mill	Herts	Hemel Hempstead
223	LUNON	Maryanne	47		Dau		13	F	Works at Silk Mill	Herts	Hemel Hempstead
224	LUNON	William	47		Son		10	M	Works at Silk Mill	Herts	Redbourn
225	LUNON	Shalet	47		Dau		5	F		Herts	Redbourn
226	LUNON	George	47		Son		2	M		Herts	Redbourn
227	LUNON	Infant	47		Grandson		1 m	M		Herts	St Albans
228	HILTON	William	47		Visitor	Unm	17	M	Weaver	Herts	St Albans
229	FIELD	William	48	St Peters Street	Head	Mar	73	M	Carpenter	Lincs	Grantham
230	WOODLAND	William	48		Lodger	Unm	26	M	Carpenter	Herts	St Albans

	SURNAME	FORENAME	SCHEDULE NUMBER	ADDRESS	RELATIONSHIP	STATUS	AGE	SEX	OCCUPATION	COUNTY OF BIRTH	PLACE OF BIRTH
231	KINGHORN	Frederick	48		Lodger		8	M		London	Marylebone
232	NORRISS	William	49	St Peters Street	Head	Mar	46	M	Butcher, employing 2 servants	Herts	Park Street [St Stephens]
233	NORRISS	Elizabeth	49		Wife	Mar	43	F	Butchers Wife	Herts	Harpenden
234	LITCHFIELD	Harriot	49		Dau	Mar	23	F	Butchers Daughter	Herts	Harpenden
235	LITCHFIELD	William	49		Son		1 m	M		Herts	St Albans
236	WILLIS	John	49		Serv	Unm	22	M	Servant	Herts	St Albans
237	KING	Eliza	49		Serv		14	F	House Servant	Herts	St Albans
238	ARNOLD	George Farr	50	St Peters Street	Head	Mar	41	M	Joiner and Builder	Beds	Apsley
239	ARNOLD	Susannah	50		Wife	Mar	39	F		Beds	Apsley
240	YOUNG	Thomas	51	St Peters Street	Head	Mar	43	M	Grocer and Baker	Herts	St Albans
241	YOUNG	Mary	51		Wife	Mar	35	F	Grocer and Bakers Wife	Herts	Welwyn
242	YOUNG	Susannah	51		Dau	Unm	15	F	At Home	Herts	St Albans
243	YOUNG	Charlotte	51		Dau		13	F	At Home	Herts	St Albans
244	YOUNG	Henry	51		Son		11	M	Scholar	Herts	St Albans
245	YOUNG	Frances	51		Dau		9	F	Scholar	Herts	St Albans
246	YOUNG	Maria	51		Dau		7	F	Scholar	Herts	St Albans
247	YOUNG	Thomas	51		Son		5	M	Scholar	Herts	St Albans
248	YOUNG	George	51		Son		2	M	Scholar	Herts	St Albans
249	TITMASS	William	52	St Peters Street	Head	Mar	32	M	Hat Presser	Herts	Wheathampstead
250	TITMASS	Jane	52		Wife	Mar	27	F		Herts	St Albans
251	TITMASS	William	52		Son		5	M		Herts	St Albans
252	TITMASS	Harriet	52		Dau		4	F		Herts	St Albans
253	LOGGAN	Joseph	53	St Peters Street	Head	Mar	52	M	Painter	Herts	St Albans
254	LOGGAN	Mary	53		Wife	Mar	50	F		Herts	St Albans
255	YOUNG	Thomas	54	St Peters Street	Head	Widower	71	M	Baker	Herts	St Albans
256	YOUNG	Daniel	54		Son	Unm	37	M	Baker	Herts	St Albans
257	WILLIS	Joseph	54		Serv	Mar	55	M	Baker	Herts	St Albans
258	WOODHOUSE	Frances	55	St Peters Street	Head	Widow	73	F	Proprietor of Houses	Essex	Witham
259	BOYS	Edward	55		Lodger	Unm	52	M	Solicitor	Herts	Kings Langley
260	SIMMONDS	Mary Ann	55		Lodger	Unm	30	F	Fundholder	Kent	Canterbury
261	ADAMS	Emma	55		Serv	Unm	18	F	House Servant	Herts	Wheathampstead
262	COX	Daniel Harford	56	St Peters Street	Head	Mar	29	M	Tax Collector	Middx	Shoreditch
263	COX	Hannah	56		Wife	Mar	30	F	Domestically Employed	Beds	Luton
264	COX	John	56		Son		6	M	Scholar	Herts	Harpenden
265	COX	Henry	56		Son		4	M	Scholar	Herts	Harpenden
266	COX	Emma	56		Dau		1	F	At Home	Herts	St Albans
267	CANNON	Emily	56		Visitor	Unm	40	F	Annuitant	Herts	Welwyn
268	BIGNELL	Hannah	56		Serv	Unm	16	F	Servant of all Work	Herts	Leesdon [Leavesden]
269	READING	James	57	St Peters Street	Head	Unm	21	M	Independent Minister	Bucks	Aylesbury
270	HULKS	John Francis	58	St Peters Street	Head	Mar	43	M	Victualler	Herts	St Albans
271	HULKS	Mary	58		Wife	Mar	40	F	Victuallers Wife	Essex	Longford
272	HULKS	John Joseph	58		Son		12	M		Herts	St Albans
273	JOHNSON	Mary Ann	59	St Peters Street	Head	Unm	40	F	Dressmaker	Herts	Harpenden

274	JOHNSON	Caroline	59		Sister	Unm	35	F	Dressmaker	Herts	Harpenden
275	HENMAN	Mary Ann	59		Niece	Unm	24	F	Milliner	Herts	Harpenden
276	CARTER	Jane	59		Friend	Unm	34	F	Straw Business	Warks	Coventry

Three houses uninhabited

277	RUMBALL	John Homer	60	St Peters Street	Head	Mar	57	M	Land Agent Surveyor & Auctioneer	Surrey	Croydon
278	RUMBALL	Eliza Ann	60		Wife	Mar	56	F		Herts	St Albans
279	RUMBALL	George Horace	60		Son	Unm	28	M	Assistant to Father [Surveyor & Architect]	Herts	St Albans
280	RUMBALL	Sampson John	60		Son	Unm	24	M	Assistant to Father [Surveyor & Architect]	Herts	St Albans
281	RUMBALL	Charles	60		Son	Unm	21	M	Collegian at Oxford	Herts	St Albans
282	RUMBALL	Aubrey	60		Son		14	M		Herts	St Albans
283	RUMBALL	Rosa Mary	60		Dau		11	F		Herts	St Albans
284	APPLEBY	Elizabeth	60		Visitor	Unm	66	F		Middx	St Georges East
285	RUMBALL	Henry John	60		Nephew	Unm	30	M	Clerk to his Uncle	Herts	St Albans
286	HODGSON	Ann	60		Serv	Unm	29	F	General Servant	Herts	Redbourn
287	DUDDING	Horatio Nelson	61	St Peters Street	Head	Mar	42	M	Vicar of St Peters (St Albans) Oxford MA	Middx	Marylebone
288	DUDDING	Margaretta	61		Wife	Mar	33	F		Surrey	Guildford
289	DUDDING	Eleanor Georgianna	61		Dau		12	F		Suffolk	Little Stonham
290	DUDDING	Mary	61		Dau		7	F		Herts	St Albans
291	DUDDING	Margaretta	61		Dau		6	F		Herts	St Albans
292	DUDDING	Edward Ban	61		Son		3	M		Herts	St Albans
293	DUDDING	Horatio Nelson	61		Son		1	M		Herts	St Albans
294	DUDDING	Mary	61		Mother	Widow	74	F		Lincs	Lincoln
295	WALFORD	John Francis	61		Pupil	Unm	19	M	Pupil	Notts	Nottingham
296	PEARCE	Charles Henry	61		Pupil	Unm	18	M	Pupil	Middx	Hampstead
297	HOLFORD	George	61		Pupil	Unm	18	M	Pupil	Middx	Hampstead
298	MULLER	Julia	61		Serv	Unm	20	F	Ladys Maid	Switz	Geneva
299	CLARKE	Harriet	61		Serv	Unm	26	F	Cook	Somerset	Oldford [Ford?]
300	PROPER	Eliza	61		Serv	Unm	21	F	Housemaid	Somerset	Oldford [Ford?]
301	CLARKE	Jenny	61		Serv	Unm	23	F	Housemaid	Worcs [Surrey?]	Malden
302	LORD	Ann	62	St Peters Street	Head	Widow	75	F	Levingden Alms House	Herts	Redbourn
303	LINNEY	Rosannah	63	St Peters Street	Head	Widow	77	F	Labourers Daughter	Herts	St Albans
304	EDMONDS	Sarah	63		Visitor	Mar	60	F	Gardeners Wife	Herts	St Albans
305	NORWOOD	Harriet	64	St Peters Street	Head	Widow	74	F	Servant	Herts	Watford
306	DUNTON	Martha	65	St Peters Street	Head	Widow	75	F	Levingden Alms House	Bucks	Aylesbury
307	ROBERTS	Mary	65		Serv	Unm	61	F	General Servant	Herts	St Albans
308	FINDELL	Elizabeth	66	St Peters Street	Head	Widow	85	F	St Peters Almshouse	Herts	St Albans
309	HULL	Elizabeth	66		Serv	Unm	17	F	General Servant	Herts	St Albans
310	BOOBYER	William	67	St Peters Street	Head	Mar	35	M	Bookseller	Middx	Kensington
311	BOOBYER	Emily Carpenter	67		Wife	Mar	39	F	Booksellers Wife	Middx	Kensington
312	BOOBYER	Mary Ann Ruth	67		Dau	Unm	16	F	Booksellers Daughter	Middx	Kensington
313	BOOBYER	Adam Edwin	67		Son		12	M	Scholar	Middx	Kensington

	SURNAME	FORENAME	SCHEDULE NUMBER	ADDRESS	RELATIONSHIP	STATUS	AGE	SEX	OCCUPATION	COUNTY OF BIRTH	PLACE OF BIRTH
314	BOOBYER	Emma Diana Jane	67		Dau		8	F	Scholar	Middx	Kensington
315	BOOBYER	James Clarke	67		Son		6	M	Scholar	Middx	Kensington
316	BOOBYER	Sarah Priscilla	67		Dau		3	F		Herts	St Albans
317	BOOBYER	Henry Richard	67		Son		1	M		Herts	St Albans
318	HUNT	Ann	67		Mother-in-law	Widow	69	F	Formerly Grocer	Warks	Honington
319	MORETON	Anne	67		Serv		15	F	House Servant	Herts	St Stephens
320	LYDEKKER	Elizabeth	68	St Peters Street	Head	Widow	73	F	Fundholder	Essex	Boxwell [Boxted?]
321	LYDEKKER	Cornelia	68		Dau	Unm	41	F		Herts	St Albans
322	NORWOOD	Elizabeth	68		Serv	Unm	57	F	Cook	Herts	Batford [Wheath'pstead]
323	PERCY	Anne B.	68		Serv	Unm	27	F	Housemaid	Herts	Ware
324	CLARKE	Samuel	68		Serv	Unm	22	M	Footman	Beds	Luton
325	BERNER	George Manfield	69	St Peters Street	Head	Unm	66	M	Gentleman	Herts	St Peters
326	BERNER	Benjamin Manfield	69		Brother	Mar	66	M	Gentleman	Herts	St Peters
327	BERNER	Charlotte	69		Sister-in-law	Mar	61	F		Bucks	Chesham
328	NICHOLLS	Elizabeth	69		Serv	Widow	65	F	General Servant	Bucks	Stoke
329	HARDING	James	70	Spencer Street	Head	Mar	66	M	Basket Maker	Bucks	Chesham
330	HARDING	Mary Ann	70		Wife	Mar	67	F		Herts	St Albans
331	BIRCH	Susanna	70		Sister-in-law	Unm	55	F	Deaf & Dumb	Herts	St Albans
332	MAUNDER	Vincent	70		Grandson		9	M	Scholar	Herts	St Peters
333	JAQUES	Peter	71	Spencer Street	Head	Widower	61	M	Police Constable	Herts	St Albans
334	JAQUES	Charles	71		Son	Unm	29	M	Carpenter	Herts	St Albans
335	JAQUES	Susannah	71		Dau	Unm	27	F	Hat Maker	Herts	St Albans
336	JAQUES	Rosetta Jane	71		Dau	Unm	18	F	Hat Maker	Herts	St Albans
337	ADAMS	Sarah	72	Spencer Street	Head	Mar	31	F		Herts	St Albans
338	ADAMS	George	72		Son		9	M		Herts	St Albans
339	ADAMS	John	72		Son		7	M		Herts	St Albans
340	ADAMS	Sarah	72		Dau		3	F		Herts	St Albans
341	ADAMS	James	72		Son		6m	M		Herts	St Albans
342	GREENHILL	Sarah	73	Spencer Street	Head	Unm	20	F	Straw Hat Maker	Middx	London
343	JONES	Mary Ann	74	Spencer Street	Head	Widow	44	F	Seamstress	Herts	Norton
344	PURRIER	John	75	Spencer Street	Head	Unm	61	M	Tailor	Beds	Ampthill
345	PARSONS	Henry	75		Lodger	Unm	20	M	Labourer	Herts	St Albans
346	EAGLE	Eliza	76	Spencer Street	Head	Unm	30	F	Bonnet Sewer	Herts	Hatfield
347	EAGLE	Ann	76		Dau		4	F		Herts	St Albans
348	WALLER	James	77	Spencer Street	Head	Mar	45	M	Servant	Suffolk	Ipswich
349	WALLER	Frederick	77		Son		14	M	Servant	Herts	St Albans
350	WALLER	Henry	77		Son		10	M	At Home	Herts	St Albans
351	WALLER	James	77		Son		5	M	At Home	Herts	St Albans
352	GILLIGAN	Mary	78	Spencer Street	Head	Mar	38	F	Annuitant	Worcs	Dudley
353	GILLIGAN	Rebecca	78		Dau		6	F	Scholar	Ireland	Cork
354	GILLIGAN	David	78		Son		4	M	Scholar	Ireland	Mullingar
355	PECK	Susannah	79	Spencer Street	Head	Widow	48	F	Grocer	Herts	Stevenage

356	PECK	Eliza	79		Sister	Unm	39	F	Dressmaker	Herts	Hertingfordbury
357	DANESON	George	80	Spencer Street	Head	Widower	64	M	Ropemaker	Beds	Luton
358	DANESON	George	80		Grandson		8	M		Middx	London
359	CUSTANCE	Jenny	80		Serv	[Unm]	22	F	General Servant	Herts	St Albans
360	CREW	Caleb	81	Spencer Street	Head	Mar	48	M	Sawyer	Herts	Kimpton
361	CREW	Mary	81		Wife	Mar	41	F	Dressmaker	Herts	St Albans
362	CREW	William	81		Son		13	M	Scholar	Herts	St Albans
363	CREW	Mary	81		Dau		11	F	Scholar	Herts	St Albans
364	CREW	Susannah	81		Dau		9	F	Scholar	Herts	St Albans
365	CREW	Frederick	81		Son		7	M	Scholar	Herts	St Albans
366	CREW	Louisa	81		Dau		4	F	Scholar	Herts	St Albans
367	WILSON	Susannah	81		Sister-in-law	Unm	43	F	Dressmaker	Herts	St Albans
368	CHAPPLE YOUNG	Samuel	82	Spencer Street	Head	Mar	40	M	Baker	Herts	St Albans
369	CHAPPLE YOUNG	Frances	82		Wife	Mar	48	F	Hat Maker	S. Wales	Haverfordwest
370	LEAR	Thomas	83	Spencer Street	Head	Mar	43	M	Labourer	Wilts	Devizes
371	LEAR	Hannah	83		Wife	Mar	50	F		Herts	Potters Crouch [St Michaels]
372	LEAR	Thomas	83		Son		11	M	At Home	Herts	St Stephens
373	LEAR	Jane	83		Dau	[Unm]	20	F	Bonnet Sewer	Herts	St Albans
374	SMITH	Elizabeth	84	Spencer Street	Head	[blank]	27	F	Silk Sorter	Herts	Hatfield
375	MATTHEWS	Robert	85	Spencer Street	Head	Widower	41	M	Boot Maker	Suffolk	Ipswich
376	MATTHEWS	George	85		Son	Unm	20	M	Closer	Middx	London
377	HIGDEN	Joseph	85		Lodger	Mar	22	M	Wood Turner	Herts	St Albans
378	HIGDEN	Elizabeth	85		Lodgers Wife	Mar	25	F	Wood Turners Wife	Herts	St Albans
379	HIGDEN	Thomas	85		Lodgers Son		2	M		Middx	London
380	HIGDEN	Emma	85		Lodgers Dau		1	F		Herts	St Albans
381	NASH	Charles	86	Spencer Street	Head	Mar	53	M	Groom	Herts	Bennington
382	NASH	Jane	86		Wife	Mar	55	F	Grooms Wife	Cambs	Swaffham
383	NASH	Ann	86		Dau [in-law]	Mar	30	F	Grooms Daughter	Cambs [Suffolk]	Newmarket
384	NASH	Henry	86		Son	Mar	28	M	Grooms Son	Cambs [Suffolk]	Newmarket
385	NASH	Charles	86		Son	Unm	26	M	Grooms Son	Cambs [Suffolk]	Newmarket
386	NASH	Elizabeth	86		Dau	Unm	24	F	Grooms Daughter	Cambs [Suffolk]	Newmarket
387	NASH	George	86		Son	Unm	22	M	Grooms Son	Herts	St Albans
388	NASH	Jane	86		Dau	Unm	20	F	Grooms Daughter	Herts	St Albans
389	NASH	Francis	86		Son	Unm	18	M	Grooms Son	Herts	St Albans
390	LANE	John	87	Spencer Street	Head	Mar	54	M	Journeyman Carpenter	Herts	Studham
391	LANE	Maria	87		Wife	Mar	43	F	Carpenters Wife	Herts	Colney
392	LANE	Henry Thomas	87		Son	Unm	18	M	Carpenters Son	Herts	St Albans
393	LANE	Mary Ann	87		Dau	Unm	16	F	Hat Maker	Herts	St Albans
394	LANE	John	87		Son		14	M	Carpenters Son	Herts	St Albans
395	MENLOVE	John	88	Spencer Street	Head	Mar	39	M	Gardener	Middx	London
396	MENLOVE	Mary	88		Wife	Mar	40	F		Herts	Beech Wood Green [Flamstead]
397	MENLOVE	John	88		Son		11	M	Works at Silk Mill	Herts	St Albans

	SURNAME	FORENAME	SCHEDULE NUMBER	ADDRESS	RELATIONSHIP	STATUS	AGE	SEX	OCCUPATION	COUNTY OF BIRTH	PLACE OF BIRTH
398	MENLOVE	Joseph	88		Son		10	M	Scholar	Herts	St Albans
399	MENLOVE	James	88		Son		7	M	Scholar	Herts	St Albans
400	MENLOVE	Mary Ann	88		Dau		5	F	At Home	Herts	St Albans
401	MENLOVE	Susan	88		Dau		1	F	At Home	Herts	St Albans
402	GOODWIN	William	89	Spencer Street	Head	Mar	37	M	Gardener	Cheshire	Astbury
403	GOODWIN	Catherine	89		Wife	Mar	42	F	Gardeners Wife	Shrop	Andlann [?]
404	GOODWIN	William	89		Son		13	M	Scholar	Herts	St Albans
405	CLARKE	Hester	90	Spencer Street	Head	Widow	60	F	Independent	Herts	Redbourn
406	GRAHAM	Sarah	90		Lodger	Unm	40	F	Bonnet Sewer	Beds	Dunstable
407	PELLANT	James	91	Spencer Street	Head	Mar	28	M	Groom	London	Cripplegate
408	PELLANT	Anne	91		Wife	Mar	31	F	Wife	Northants	Harlestone
409	PELLANT	Anne	91		Dau		7 m	F		Herts	St Albans
410	MICHELL	Frederick	92	Spencer Street	Head	Widower	33	M	Carpenter	Herts	Gaddesden
411	JENNINGS	Emma	92		Niece		7	F		Herts	St Albans
412	HART	Emma	92		H'keeper	Widow	55	F	Housekeeper	Herts	Hatfield
413	WADDINGTON	Joseph	93	Spencer Street	Head	Mar	52	M	Straw Bonnet Manufacturer	Leics	Melbourne
414	WADDINGTON	Sarah	93		Wife	Mar	49	F		Leics	Leicester
415	WADDINGTON	Louisa	93		Dau	Unm	19	F		Leics	Leicester
416	WADDINGTON	Henry Lee	93		Son		12	M	Scholar	Herts	St Albans
417	HILL	Mary Ann	93		Serv	Unm	21	F	House Servant	Herts	Sleapshyde [St Peters]
418	GOODRIDGE	Ann	94	Spencer Street	Head	Widow	70	F	School Mistress	Bucks	Stony Stratford
419	SHENSTONE	Mary	94		Sister	Unm	73	F	Assistant	Bucks	Stony Stratford
420	DODD	Julia A.	94		Grandau		9	F		Bucks	Stony Stratford
421	POLLARD	Robert	95	Spencer Street	Head	Mar	25	M	Bookseller	Suffolk	Ipswich
422	POLLARD	Sarah	95		Wife	Mar	25	F	Booksellers Wife	Suffolk	Pettaugh
423	POLLARD	Walter	95		Son		3	M		Herts	St Albans
424	POLLARD	Robert	95		Son		1 wk	M		Herts	St Albans
425	MEXEY [?]	Ann	95		Visitor	Unm	28	F	Shoe Binder	Norfolk	Haydon [?]
426	WYATT	Philis	95		Visitor	Widow	55	F	Nurse	Herts	Harpenden
427	BARRETT	William	96	Spencer Street	Head	Widower	69	M	Bricklayer	Beds	Luton
428	EGAN	Hannah Maria	96		Dau	Mar	42	F	Straw Bonnet Maker	Beds	Luton
429	BARRETT	Frederick	96		Grandson	Unm	22	M	Painter	Beds	Luton
430	BARRETT	Emma	96		Grandau	Unm	17	F	Straw Bonnet Maker	Warks	Birmingham
431	TOMPSON	Ann	96		Serv	Unm	14	F	House Servant	Kent	Woolwich
432	IVES	Ann	97	Spencer Street	Head	Mar	62	F	Proprietor of Houses	Bucks	Olney
433	WEBB	Charles	98	Spencer Street	Head	Mar	25	M	Plasterer	Herts	St Albans
434	WEBB	Emma Clayton	98		Wife	Mar	24	F		Herts	St Albans
435	WEBB	Maryanne Elizabeth	98		Dau		9 m	F		Herts	St Albans
436	BEAGLEY	Joseph	99	Spencer Street	Head	Mar	35	M	Journeyman Bricklayer	Middx	Hammersmith
437	BEAGLEY	Mary	99		Wife	Mar	34	F		Middx	Hammersmith
438	BEAGLEY	George	99		Son		5	M		Middx	Hammersmith
439	BEAGLEY	James	99		Son		3	M		Middx	Hammersmith
440	BEAGLEY	Thomas	99		Son		1	M		Middx	Hammersmith

No.	Surname	First Name	House	Street	Relationship	Status	Age	Sex	Occupation	County	Birthplace
441	WEBB	William	100	Spencer Street	Head	Mar	50	M	Labourer	Herts	Potters Crouch [St Michaels]
442	WEBB	Hannah	100		Wife	Mar	53	F		Herts	St Michaels
443	WEBB	Jane Cole	100		Grandau		13	F		Herts	St Peters
444	HAYLLER	William	100		Lodger	Mar	38	M	Carpenter	Sussex	Syddisham [Sidlesham?]
445	HAYLLER	Lucy	100		Lodgers Wife	Mar	36	F		Surrey	Bletchingley [?]
446	HAYLLER	Sarah	100		Lodgers Dau		8	F	Scholar	Middx	Westminster
447	HAYLLER	Elizabeth	100		Lodgers Dau		7	F	Scholar	Middx	Westminster
448	HAYLLER	Mary Ann	100		Lodgers Dau		5	F	Scholar	Middx	Westminster
449	WATERS	Eliza	101	Spencer Street	Head	Widow	35	F	Straw Bonnet Maker	Herts	St Albans
450	WATERS	Thomas	101		Son		7	M		Herts	St Albans
451	WATERS	Edward	101		Son		4	M		Herts	St Albans
452	IVORY	Jonathan	101		Lodger	Mar	60	M	Gardener	Herts	Great Gaddesden
453	FOWELL	Ann	101		Visitor	Unm	30	F	Straw Bonnet Maker	Herts	St Albans
454	BROWN	Sarah	102	Spencer Street	Head	Widow	50	F	Laundress	Herts	Sandridge
455	BROWN	Maria	102		Dau	Unm	24	F	Dressmaker	Herts	Childwick Green [St Michaels]
456	BROWN	Harriet	102		Dau	Unm	15	F	Servant	Herts	St Albans
457	BROWN	Emma	102		Dau		11	F	Scholar	Herts	St Albans
458	HEWITT	Emma	103	Spencer Street	Head	Unm	31	F	Hat Sewer	Herts	St Albans
459	CHALKLEY	William	103		Brother-in-law	Mar	27	M	Stone Mason	Middx	Kentish Town
460	CHALKLEY	Eleanor	103		Sister	Mar	28	F		Herts	St Albans
461	MACKINTOSH	Emma	103		Niece		7	F	Scholar	Kent	Dartford
462	GOLDSMITH	Charles	104	Spencer Street	Head	Mar	51	M	Glover	Herts	Welwyn
463	GOLDSMITH	Jane	104		Wife	Mar	38	F	Dressmaker	Herts	St Albans
464	GOLDSMITH	Anne	104		Dau	Unm	15	F	Hat Maker	Herts	St Albans
465	GOLDSMITH	Eliza	104		Dau		14	F	Hat Maker	Herts	St Albans
466	GOLDSMITH	Emma	104		Dau		11	F	Hat Maker	Herts	St Albans
467	GOLDSMITH	Charles	104		Son		7	M	Scholar	Herts	St Albans
468	GOLDSMITH	Ellen	104		Dau		1	F	At Home	Herts	St Albans
469	ANSELL	George	105	Spencer Street	Head	Mar	40	M	Boot Maker	Herts	Bell Bar [North Mimms]
470	ANSELL	Amelia	105		Wife	Mar	40	F		Northants	Old Stratford
471	BRUNT	William	106		Head	Mar	51	M	Currier & Leather Seller	Middx	Enfield
472	BRUNT	Frances	106		Wife	Mar	57	F		Berks	Pangham [Pangbourn]
473	HUTSON	David	107	Spencer Street	Head	Mar	57	M	Assistant Clerk in St Albans County Court	Cambs	Haddenham
474	HUTSON	Ruth	107		Wife	Mar	49	F		Herts	St Albans
475	HUTSON	William Philip	107		Son	Unm	20	M	No Business	Herts	St Albans
476	MCBELLAR	Peter	108	Spencer Street	Head	Mar	37	M	Draper	Scotland	Argyleshire
477	MCBELLAR	Elizabeth	108		Wife	Mar	28	F		Scotland	Renfrewshire
478	EWING	William	108		Appr	Unm	18	M	Drapers Apprentice	Scotland	Renfrewshire
479	WILKINS	Frederick	109	Spencer Street	Head	Mar	34	M	Coach Maker	Herts	St Albans
480	WILKINS	Mary	109		Wife	Mar	30	F		Herts	St Albans
481	WILKINS	Louisa A.	109		Dau		10	F	Scholar	Herts	St Albans
482	WILKINS	Frederick John	109		Son		8	M	Scholar	Herts	St Albans

	SURNAME	FORENAME	SCHEDULE NUMBER	ADDRESS	RELATIONSHIP	STATUS	AGE	SEX	OCCUPATION	COUNTY OF BIRTH	PLACE OF BIRTH
483	WILKINS	Harriet I.	109		Dau		5	F	Scholar	Herts	St Albans
484	WILKINS	Mary Martha	109		Dau		3	F	At Home	Herts	St Albans
485	WILKINS	Catherine Clarissa	109		Dau		1	F	At Home	Herts	St Albans
486	RICHARDSON	John	110	Spencer Street	Head	Mar	52	M	Carpenter	Beds	Toddington
487	RICHARDSON	Ann	110		Wife	Mar	52	F	Straw Plaiter	Herts	Caddington
488	PAIN	James	111	Spencer Street	Head	Mar	31	M	Ginger Beer Manufacturer	Herts	St Albans
489	PAIN	Margaret	111		Wife	Mar	31	F	Straw Plait Worker	Herts	Hemel Hempstead
490	PAIN	Ann	111		Dau		8	F	Scholar	Herts	Hemel Hempstead
491	PAIN	Margaret	111		Dau		7	F	Scholar	Herts	Hemel Hempstead
492	PAIN	Edward	111		Son		6	M	Scholar	Herts	Hemel Hempstead
493	PAIN	Emma	111		Dau		4	F	Scholar	Herts	Hemel Hempstead
494	WILDBORE	James	112	Spencer Street	Head	Mar	45	M	Carrier	Herts	St Albans
495	WILDBORE	Sarah	112		Wife	Mar	31	F		Herts	Watford
496	WILDBORE	William	112		Brother	Unm	50	M	Tallow Chandler	Herts	St Albans
497	WILDBORE	Thomas	112		Son	Unm	18	M		Herts	St Albans
498	WILDBORE	George	112		Son		15	M		Herts	St Albans
499	CROFT	James	113	Spencer Street	Head	Mar	37	M	Letter Carrier	Herts	Wheathampstead
500	CROFT	Susan	113		Wife	Mar	38	F	Needlewoman	Herts	Wheathampstead
501	CROFT	Maryanne	113		Dau		11	F	Scholar	Herts	Wheathampstead
502	CROFT	Emily	113		Dau		9	F	Scholar	Herts	Wheathampstead
503	CROFT	Lucy	113		Dau		7	F	Scholar	Herts	Wheathampstead
504	COOK	Thomas	114	Spencer Street	Head	Mar	35	M	Wheelwright	Herts	Kimpton
505	COOK	Catherine	114		Wife	Mar	45	F	Domestic Duties	Middx	London
506	COOK	Catherine	114		Dau		12	F	Home	Herts	St Albans
507	COOK	Robert	114		Son		8	M	School	Herts	St Albans
508	COOK	Emma	114		Dau		5	F	School	Herts	St Albans
509	COOK	John	114		Son		3	M	Home	Herts	St Albans
510	COOK	Thomas	114		Son		1	M	Home	Herts	St Albans
511	PAIN	William	115	Spencer Street	Head	Mar	25	M	Journeyman Baker	Herts	Abbots Langley
512	PAIN	Eleanor	115		Wife	Mar	30	F	Dressmaker	Herts	St Albans
513	PIDGEON	Stephen	116	Spencer Street	Head	Mar	31	M	Police Constable	Yorks	Wakefield
514	PIDGEON	Ann Cashbourne	116		Wife	Mar	29	F	Police Constables Wife	Cambs	Soham
515	PIDGEON	Frederick William	116		Son		9 m	M		Herts	Hoddesden
516	MUNNS	James	117	Spencer Street	Head	Mar	66	M	Watchmaker	Herts	Hitchin
517	MUNNS	Elizabeth	117		Wife	Mar	65	F		Norfolk	Weasenham
518	MUNNS	Maria	117		Dau	Unm	37	F		Herts	Hertford
519	BRODIE	James	117		Serv	Unm	21	M	Watchmaker	Herts	Hertford
520	ALLWAY	Elizabeth	118	Spencer Street	Head	Unm	60	F	Straw Plait Manufacturer	Herts	St Albans
521	BAKER	Sophia	118		Visitor	Widow	48	F		Ireland	[Unknown]
522	GREY	Sophia	118		Visitor	Widow	64	F		Ireland	[Unknown]
523	BENSON	Terence	119	Spencer Street	Head	Unm	54	M	General Practitioner, L.I.A.	Ireland	[Unknown]

524	HUTCHINSON	John Robert	120	Spencer Street	Head	Mar	47	M	General Practitioner, member of the Royal College of Surgeons	Surrey	Southwark
525	HUTCHINSON	Mary	120		Wife	Mar	46	F		Suffolk	Bromeswell
526	HUTCHINSON	Maria	120		Dau	Unm	20	F	Governess	Middx	Harrow
527	HUTCHINSON	Elizabeth H.	120		Dau		14	F	Scholar at Home	Bucks	Beaconsfield
528	HUTCHINSON	Emily	120		Dau		13	F	Scholar at Home	Bucks	Beaconsfield
529	HUTCHINSON	Amelia	120		Dau		11	F	Scholar at Home	Bucks	Beaconsfield
530	HUTCHINSON	Margaret Janet	120		Dau		7	F	Scholar at Home	Bucks	Beaconsfield
531	CLARKE	Edmund	121	Waddington Row	Head	Mar	25	M	Butcher	Herts	Abbots Langley
532	CLARKE	Elizabeth	121		Wife	Mar	23	F		Herts	Abbots Langley
533	CLARKE	Sydney	121		Nephew		3m	M		Herts	Abbots Langley
534	POINTON	Thomas	122	Waddington Row	Head	Unm	21	M	Labourer	Herts	St Albans
535	ASHWELL	William	123	Waddington Row	Head	Mar	47	M	Labourer	Herts	St Albans
536	ASHWELL	Georgianna	123		Wife	Mar	37	F		Herts	St Albans
537	ASHWELL	Thomas	123		Son	Unm	21	M	Labourer	Herts	St Albans
538	ASHWELL	William	123		Son	Unm	30	M	Labourer	Herts	St Albans
539	NICHOLLS	Isaac	124	Waddington Row	Head	Mar	30	M	Blacksmith	Herts	St Albans
540	NICHOLLS	Elizabeth	124		Wife	Mar	28	F	Hand Loom Weaver	Herts	St Albans
541	CRAWLEY	Daniel	125	Waddington Row	Head	Mar	38	M	Labourer	Herts	Kings Walden
542	CRAWLEY	Ann	125		Wife	Mar	30	F		Herts	Kings Walden
543	CRAWLEY	Richard	125		Son		9	M	Scholar	Herts	Sandridge
544	CRAWLEY	Sarah	125		Dau		2	F		Herts	St Albans
545	CRAWLEY	Mary Ann	125		Dau		4m	F		Herts	St Albans
546	BARBER	James	126	Waddington Row	Head	Mar	31	M	Labourer	Herts	St Albans
547	BARBER	Maria	126		Wife	Mar	29	F		Herts	St Albans
548	BARBER	Joseph	126		Son		4	M		Herts	St Albans
549	SMITH	Mary Ann	127	Waddington Row	Head	Widow	60	F	Lodging House Keeper	Herts	Harpenden
550	CHAPMAN	Henry	127		Lodger	Widower	52	M	Cordwainer	Beds	Maulden
551	SUTTON	Andrew	127		Lodger	Unm	25	M	Cordwainer	Middx	Edmonton
552	BARBER	Sarah	127		Lodger	Mar	48	F		Herts	St Albans
553	WEAVER	Louisa Ann	127		Lodger	Unm	24	F	Straw Weaver	Hunts	Brampton
554	MAJOR	John	128	Waddington Row	Head	Mar	33	M	Bricklayer	Herts	St Albans
555	MAJOR	Mary Ann	128		Wife	Mar	31	F		Herts	St Albans
556	MAJOR	Emily	128		Dau		9	F		Herts	St Albans
557	MAJOR	Thomas	128		Son		7	M		Herts	St Albans
558	MAJOR	George	128		Son		4	M		Herts	St Albans
559	MAJOR	Selina	128		Dau		2	F		Herts	St Albans
560	MAJOR	Harriet Ann	128		Dau		3m	F		Herts	St Albans
561	WESTFIELD	John	129	Waddington Row	Head	Mar	29	M	Journeyman Millwright	Bucks	Princes Risborough
562	WESTFIELD	Betsey	129		Wife	Mar	31	F	Bonnet Sewer	Beds	Leighton Buzzard
563	WESTFIELD	Mary Ann	129		Dau		4	F		Herts	St Albans
564	WESTFIELD	Elizabeth Sarah	129		Dau		4m	F		Herts	St Albans
565	HULL	William	130	Waddington Row	Head	Mar	50	M	Labourer	Herts	St Albans
566	HULL	Sarah	130		Wife	Mar	48	F		Herts	St Albans

	SURNAME	FORENAME	SCHEDULE NUMBER	ADDRESS	RELATIONSHIP	STATUS	AGE	SEX	OCCUPATION	COUNTY OF BIRTH	PLACE OF BIRTH
567	HULL	Thomas	130		Son	Unm	25	M	Weaver	Herts	St Albans
568	HULL	Eliza	130		Dau	Unm	20	F	Silkworker	Herts	St Albans
569	HULL	Mary	130		Dau	Unm	16	F	Hat Maker	Herts	St Albans
570	COCKLE	James	131	Waddington Row	Head	Mar	40	M	Labourer	Herts	St Albans
571	COCKLE	Sarah	131		Wife	Mar	36	F		Herts	Tring
572	COCKLE	Emily	131		Dau		5	F		Herts	St Albans
573	LASCELLES	Ralph	132	Waddington Row	Head	Mar	34	M	Hair Dresser	Lincs	Skellingthorpe
574	LASCELLES	Precious	132		Wife	Mar	38	F		Lincs	Bourne
575	LASCELLES	Eliza Angelina	132		Dau		4	F		Lincs	Bourne
576	FLINT	Judith	133	Waddington Row	Head	Widow	64	F	Plait Worker	Herts	St Albans
577	FLINT	Robert	133		Son	Unm	24	M	Tailor	Herts	St Albans
578	FLINT	Sarah	133		Dau	Unm	20	F	Bonnet Sewer	Herts	St Albans
579	PEW	Catherine	133		Visitor	Widow	85	F		Middx	Enfield
580	WHITE	Elizabeth	134	Waddington Row	Head	Widow	33	F	Charring	Herts	St Albans
581	WHITE	Eliza	134		Dau		14	F	Hat Maker	Herts	St Albans
582	WHITE	Alfred	134		Son		11	M	Silk Worker	Herts	St Albans
583	WHITE	Sarah	134		Dau		10	F	Silk Worker	Herts	St Albans
584	WHITE	Emily	134		Dau		8	F	School	Herts	St Albans
585	WHITE	Ann	134		Dau		5	F	School	Herts	St Albans
586	WHITE	Harriet	134		Dau		3	F	School	Herts	St Albans
587	WHITE	James	134		Son		6	M	School	Herts	St Albans
588	TRIPLETTS	Maria	134		Lodger	[blank]	57	F	Silk Worker	Herts	St Albans
589	PURCELL	Jane	134		Lodger	[Unm]	17	F	Hat Maker	Herts	St Albans
590	MATTHEWS	Elizabeth	135	Waddington Row	Head	Widow	58	F	Dealer	Ireland	Dublin
591	HAYS	John	135		Lodger	Mar	42	M	Shoemaker	Ireland	Bandon
592	HAYS	Ellen	135		Lodgers Wife	Mar	40	F	Shoe Binder	Ireland	Bandon
593	HAYS	Margaret	135		Serv		12	F		Middx	London
594	BIRCH	Charles	136	Waddington Row	Head	Mar	37	M	Basket Maker	Herts	St Albans
595	BIRCH	Eliza	136		Wife	Mar	35	F		Herts	Weston
596	BIRCH	Elizabeth Mary	136		Dau		8	F		Herts	St Albans
597	BIRCH	Eliza	136		Dau		6	F		Herts	St Albans
598	SMITH	Edward	137	Adelaide Street	Head	Mar	28	M	Baker	Herts	Mimms
599	SMITH	Marianne	137		Wife	Mar	28	F		Herts	Redbourn
600	SMITH	James	137		Son		11	M		Herts	St Albans
601	WHEATLEY	Joseph	138	Adelaide Street	Head	Mar	28	M	Wheelwright	Herts	Childwick [St Michaels]
602	WHEATLEY	Elizabeth	138		Wife	Mar	31	F		Herts	St Albans
603	WHEATLEY	Neathan	138		Son		6	M		Herts	Childwick [St Michaels]
604	WHEATLEY	John	138		Son		4	M		Herts	St Albans
605	WHEATLEY	Henry	138		Son		1	M		Herts	St Albans
606	POLLARD	John	139	Adelaide Street	Lodger	Mar	68	M	Labourer	Herts	Kimpton
607	PAYNE	Hannah	140	Adelaide Street	Head	Widow	46	F	Laundress	Herts	Kings Walden
608	PAYNE	Alfred	140		Son	Unm	17	M	Shoemaker	Herts	St Albans
609	PAYNE	Henry	140		Son		7	M	Scholar	Herts	St Albans

610	PAYNE	James	140		Son		4	M		Herts	St Albans
611	COTTON	Sarah	141	Adelaide Street	Head	Unm	76	F	Proprietor of Houses	Middx	Stoke Newington
612	JARVIS	Elizabeth	141		Serv	Unm	36	F	Servant	Somerset	Wedmore
613	HAGGAR	James	141		Serv	Unm	55	M	Servant	Herts	Welwyn
614	WHITBREAD	Henry	142	Adelaide Street	Head	Widower	66	M	Farmer	Beds	Silsoe
615	WHITBREAD	Elizabeth	142		Dau	Unm	32	F		Beds	Ampthill
616	WARREN	George	143	Adelaide Street	Head	Mar	46	M	Miller	Herts	Redbourn
617	WARREN	Maria	143		Wife	Mar	48	F		Beds	Luton
618	WARREN	Alfred	143		Son		16	M	Errand Boy	Herts	Park Street [St Stephens]
619	WARREN	Ann	143		Dau		14	F	Scholar	Herts	Park Street [St Stephens]
620	WARREN	Naomi	143		Dau		12	F	Scholar	Herts	St Albans
621	WARREN	Henrietta	143		Dau		8	F	Scholar	Herts	St Albans
622	WARREN	Selina	143		Dau		4	F	Scholar	Herts	St Albans
623	DENCH	William	144	Adelaide Street	Head	Mar	36	M	Painter & Glazier	Cambs	Ely
624	DENCH	Mary	144		Wife	Mar	34	F		Surrey	Bermondsey
625	GRAY	Sarah	145	Adelaide Street	Head	Unm	30	F	Dressmaker	Herts	Harpenden
626	GLADMAN	James	146	Adelaide Street	Head	Mar	50	M	Bricklayers Labourer	Herts	St Albans
627	GLADMAN	Elizabeth	146		Wife	Mar	50	F	Laundress	Herts	Shenley
628	BEAN	William	147	Adelaide Street	Head	Mar	39	M	Sawyer	Herts	St Albans
629	BEAN	Elizabeth	147		Wife	Mar	39	F	Dressmaker	Herts	Northaw
630	BEAN	Mary Jane	147		Dau		13	F	Bonnet Sewer	Herts	St Albans
631	BEAN	Sarah	147		Dau		8	F	Scholar	Herts	St Albans
632	CREW	Thomas	148	Adelaide Street	Head	Mar	57	M	Cordwainer	Herts	Kimpton
633	CREW	Sophia	148		Wife	Mar	54	F		Cambs	Comberton
634	CREW	Charles	148		Son	Unm	20	M	Gardener	Herts	St Albans
635	LOOKER	Louisa	148		Niece		7	F	Scholar	Herts	St Albans
636	LINES	Emma	149	Adelaide Street	Lodger	Unm	24	F	Bonnet Maker	Northants	Northampton
637	DUDLEY	John	150	Adelaide Street	Head	Mar	56	M	Straw Factor	Beds	Eggington
638	DUDLEY	Martha	150		Wife	Mar	44	F		Beds	Eggington
639	DUDLEY	Pheobe	150		Grandau	Unm	15	F	Weaver	Beds	Eggington
640	OSMAN	Thomas	151	Adelaide Street	Head	Mar	28	M	Labourer	Herts	St Peters
641	OSMAN	Rebecca	151		Wife	Mar	27	F		Herts	Bedmond [Abbots Langley]
642	OSMAN	John	151		Son		2	M		Herts	St Peters
643	LAWRENCE	James	152	Adelaide Street	Head	Mar	29	M	Cordwainer	Herts	St Albans
644	LAWRENCE	Sarah	152		Wife	Mar	32	F		Herts	St Albans
645	LAWRENCE	George	152		Son		9	M		Herts	St Albans
646	LAWRENCE	Ann	152		Dau		8	F		Herts	St Albans
647	LAWRENCE	Maria	152		Dau		6	F		Herts	St Albans
648	DOWNES	James	152		Lodger	Unm	22	M	Cordwainer	Herts	St Albans
649	SHRUBB	Samuel J.	153	Adelaide Street	Head	Unm	20	M	Rope Maker	Herts	St Albans
650	SHRUBB	Martha	153		Mother	Widow	51	F	Nurse	Northants	Cold Ashby
651	HAMMONDS	Martha	153		Cousin	Unm	27	F	Milliner & Dressmaker	Northants	Ravensthorpe
652	TOWNSEND	James	154	Adelaide Street	Lodger	Unm	22	M	Schoolmaster	London	Whitechapel

	SURNAME	FORENAME	SCHEDULE NUMBER	ADDRESS	RELATIONSHIP	STATUS	AGE	SEX	OCCUPATION	COUNTY OF BIRTH	PLACE OF BIRTH
653	JAURER [?]	John	155	Adelaide Street	Head	Mar	61	M	Labourer	Herts	Preston
654	JAURER [?]	Deborah	155		Wife	Mar	63	F		Herts	Ippollitts
655	CHALK	Ann	155		Grandau	Unm	16	F		Herts	[Unknown]
656	JAURER [?]	Charles	155		Son	Mar	22	M	Labourer	Herts	Sandridge
657	CONSTABLE	William	156	Adelaide Street	Head	Mar	34	M	Green Grocer	Herts	St Albans
658	CONSTABLE	Jane	156		Wife	Mar	30	F		Herts	St Albans
659	HARDING	William	157	Adelaide Street	Head	Mar	24	M	Basket Maker	Herts	St Albans
660	HARDING	Susan	157		Wife	Mar	21	F		Warks	[Unknown]
661	BUTCHER	Charles	158	Adelaide Street	Head	Mar	28	M	Labourer	Herts	St Albans
662	BUTCHER	Amey	158		Wife	Mar	23	F		Herts	St Albans
663	BUTCHER	George	158		Son		3	M		Herts	St Albans
664	BUTCHER	James	158		Son		1	M		Herts	St Albans
665	EAMES	Robert	159	Adelaide Street	Head	Mar	41	M	Labourer	Herts	St Peters
666	EAMES	Elizabeth	159		Wife	Mar	40	F	Weaver of Straw	Herts	St Peters
667	EAMES	Alfred	159		Son	Unm	18	M	Weaver of Straw	Herts	St Peters
668	EAMES	Thomas	159		Son		13	M	Hat Maker	Herts	St Peters
669	EAMES	Eliza	159		Dau		12	F	Hat Maker	Herts	St Peters
670	EAMES	James	159		Son		8	M	Hat Maker	Herts	St Peters
671	EAMES	Sarah	159		Dau		6	F	Scholar	Herts	St Peters
672	EAMES	Joseph	159		Son		4	M	Scholar at Home	Herts	St Peters
673	EAMES	Ann	159		Dau		1m	F		Herts	St Peters
674	BIGGS	Thomas	160	Adelaide Street	Head	Mar	41	M	Bricklayers Labourer	Herts	Sandridge
675	BIGGS	Dinah	160		Wife	Mar	37	F	Hat Maker	Bucks	Chesham
676	STONE	William	160		Brother-in-law	Mar	40	M	Labourer	Bucks	Chesham
677	STONE	Sarah	160		Sister-in-law	Mar	41	F		Bucks	Amersham
678	STONE	Sophia	160		Niece		5m	F		Bucks	Chesham
679	LENT	George	161	Adelaide Street	Head	Mar	40	M	Tin Plate Worker	Yorks	Rotherham
680	LENT	Eliza	161		Wife	Mar	36	F	Straw Bonnet Maker	Beds	Luton
681	LENT	Elizabeth	161		Dau		13	F	Straw Bonnet Maker	Beds	Luton
682	LENT	Jane	161		Dau		10	F	Scholar	Beds	Luton
683	RICHARDSON	George	162	Adelaide Street	Head	Mar	35	M	Carpenter	Herts	St Albans
684	RICHARDSON	Elizabeth	162		Wife	Mar	37	F		Herts	Puckeridge
685	CONNELLY	Thomas	162		Son		14	M	Carpenters Son	Herts	Stapleford
686	RICHARDSON	Maryann	162		Dau		6	F		Herts	St Albans
687	RICHARDSON	Emma	162		Dau		3	F		Herts	St Albans
688	RICHARDSON	Ellen Elizabeth	162		Dau		1	F		Herts	St Albans
689	GENTLE	Samuel	163	Adelaide Street	Head	Mar	43	M	Brewer	Herts	Kimpton
690	GENTLE	Mary Ann	163		Wife	Mar	40	F		Herts	Sandridge
691	GENTLE	James	163		Son		14	M		Herts	Sandridge
692	GENTLE	Amelia	163		Dau		12	F		Herts	St Albans
693	GENTLE	Daniel	163		Son		10	M		Herts	St Albans
694	GENTLE	Samuel	163		Son		8	M		Herts	St Albans
695	GENTLE	Charles	163		Son		6	M		Herts	St Albans
696	GENTLE	David	163		Son		4	M		Herts	St Albans

697	GENTLE	Philip	163		Son		1 m	M		Herts	St Albans
698	ADDINGTON	Eliza	164	Adelaide Street	Head	Unm	19	F	Bonnet Sewer	Herts	St Albans
699	LAWRENCE	Jonathan	165	Adelaide Street	Head	Mar	51	M	Collar & Harness Maker	Herts	St Albans
700	LAWRENCE	Ann	165		Wife	Mar	50	F		Herts	St Albans
701	SOTCHER	Mary Ann	165		Dau	Mar	26	F		Herts	St Albans
702	LAWRENCE	William Henry	165		Son	Unm	20	M	Printer	Herts	St Albans
703	LAWRENCE	Sarah	165		Dau		14	F		Herts	St Albans
704	LAWRENCE	Joseph	165		Son		14	M		Herts	St Albans
705	CLAY	Sarah	166	Adelaide Street	Head	Widow	52	F	Schoolmistress	Herts	St Albans
706	CLAY	Martha	166		Dau	Unm	22	F	Bonnet Sewer	Herts	St Albans
707	CLAY	Joseph	166		Son	Unm	18	M	Servant	Herts	St Albans
708	DOGGETT	Ellen	166		Visitor	Unm	24	F	Bonnet Sewer	Middx	Uxbridge
709	TOWERS	John	167	Adelaide Street	Head	Mar	45	M	Cordwainer	Berks	Reading
710	TOWERS	Susan	167		Wife	Mar	46	F		Herts	Sandridge
711	TOWERS	William	167		Son	[Unm]	21	M	Carpenter	Herts	St Albans
712	TOWERS	Rupert	167		Son	[Unm]	20	M	Grocer	Herts	Sandridge
713	TOWERS	Isabella	167		Dau		15	F	Hat Coverer	Herts	Sandridge
714	BEESON	John	168	Adelaide Street	Head	Mar	34	M	Tinman & Brazier	Herts	St Albans
715	BEESON	Elizabeth	168		Wife	Mar	32	F	Bonnet Sewer	Herts	St Albans
716	LICHFIELD	William	169	Adelaide Street	Lodger	Unm	22	M	Tinman & Brazier	Herts	Flamstead
717	COLEMAN	Amelia	170	Adelaide Street	Head	Widow	70	F	Housekeeper	Herts	Cheshunt
718	YOUNG	Ann	170		Dau	Mar	48	F	Needlewoman	Middx	South Mimms
719	BLAKEMORE	Elizabeth	170		Grandau	Unm	14	F	Hat Maker	Herts	St Albans
720	WILSHIRE	William	171	Adelaide Street	Head	Mar	36	M	Carpenter	Herts	Hitchin
721	WILSHIRE	Sarah	171		Wife	Mar	38	F		Herts	Hitchin
722	WILSHIRE	Sarah Emily	171		Dau		8	F	Scholar	Herts	St Peters
723	BAYLEY	Mary Catherine	172	Adelaide Street	Head	Widow	45	F	Bonnet Maker	Herts	St Albans
724	BAYLEY	Catherine	172		Dau	Unm	22	F	Bonnet Maker	Herts	St Albans
725	BAYLEY	Thomas	172		Son	Unm	18	M	Green Grocer	Herts	St Albans
726	BIRCH	Mary	172		Mother	Widow	68	F		Middx	Highgate
727	GOSBEE	James	173	Adelaide Street	Head	Mar	37	M	Carpenter	Herts	Harpenden
728	GOSBEE	Mary	173		Wife	Mar	35	F		Herts	St Albans
729	GOSBEE	John	173		Son		13	M	Scholar	Herts	St Albans
730	GOSBEE	Sarah	173		Dau		11	F	Scholar	Herts	St Albans
731	GOSBEE	Ann	173		Dau		9	F	Scholar	Herts	St Albans
732	SMITH	Hannah	174	Adelaide Street	Head	Widow	51	F	Housekeeper	Oxon	[Unknown]
733	SMITH	Eliza	174		Dau	Unm	19	F	Weaver	Herts	St Albans
734	SMITH	Frederick	174		Son	Unm	16	M		Herts	St Albans
735	FREEMAN	George	175	Adelaide Street	Head	Mar	36	M	Labourer	Beds	Dunstable
736	FREEMAN	Elizabeth	175		Wife	Mar	32	F		Herts	Gaddesden
737	BARKER	Charlotte	175		Sister	Unm	20	F	Bonnet Sewer	Bucks	Buckingham
738	FITZGERALD	Emily Mary	176	Adelaide Street	Head	Widow	29	F	Dressmaker	Herts	Kings Langley
739	FITZGERALD	George Isaac	176		Son		9	M	Scholar	Herts	St Albans

	SURNAME	FORENAME	SCHEDULE NUMBER	ADDRESS	RELATIONSHIP	STATUS	AGE	SEX	OCCUPATION	COUNTY OF BIRTH	PLACE OF BIRTH
740	WINTER	Catherine	176		Sister	Unm	36	F	Milliner & Dressmaker	Herts	Abbots Langley
741	EAMES	Mathew	177	Adelaide Street	Head	Widower	27	M	Carpenter	Herts	Newgate [Hatfield]
742	EAMES	Ann	177		Mother	Widow	73	F		Herts	St Albans
743	EAMES	Ephraim	177		Son		3	M		Herts	St Albans
744	GEORGE	Mary	177		Visitor	[Unm]	18	F	Plait Worker	Herts	St Albans
745	JEFFREYS	Henry	178	Middle Row	Head	Unm	44	M	Fishmonger	Herts	St Albans
746	BALL	William	178		Brother	Mar	40	M	Fishmonger	Herts	St Albans
747	BALL	Sarah	178		Sister-in-law	Mar	42	F		Herts	St Albans
748	BALL	Harriet	178		Dau		13	F		Herts	St Albans
749	SMITH	Samuel T.	179	Middle Row	Head	Mar	47	M	Butcher	Herts	St Albans
750	SMITH	Louisa	179		Wife	Mar	37	F		Herts	Redbourn
751	SMITH	Louisa	179		Dau	Unm	17	F		Herts	St Albans
752	SMITH	Eliza	179		Dau		15	F		Herts	St Albans
753	SMITH	Edward	179		Son		13	M		Herts	St Albans
754	SMITH	Emily	179		Dau		9	F		Herts	St Albans
755	SMITH	Henry	179		Son		7	M		Herts	St Albans
756	SMITH	Sarah	179		Dau		3	F		Herts	St Albans
757	WHITE	Samuel	179		Serv	Unm	17	M	Journeyman Butcher	Herts	Redbourn
758	SAGE	Eliza	179		Serv	Unm	20	F	House Servant	Herts [Staffs]	Penkridge
759	SAMS	Joseph	180	Middle Row	Head	Mar	50	M	Victualler	Herts	St Albans
760	SAMS	Ann	180		Wife	Mar	51	F	Victuallers Wife	N'thumb	[Unknown]
761	SAMS	Joseph	180		Son	Unm	19	M		Herts	St Albans
762	SAMS	Margaret	180		Dau	Unm	10	F		Herts	St Albans
763	SAMS	Sarah	180		Serv	Unm	25	F	House Servant	Herts	St Albans
764	GRUBB	George	180		Visitor	Mar	40	M	Annuitant	Herts	St Albans
765	ARNOLD	David	181	Middle Row	Head	Mar	56	M	Town Hall Keeper	Herts	Ayot St Lawrence
766	ARNOLD	Mary Ann	181		Wife	Mar	46	F	Domestic Duties	Hants [Northants?]	Gretton
767	ARNOLD	Mary Ann	181		Dau	Unm	17	F	Dressmaker	Herts	St Albans
768	ARNOLD	Charlotte	181		Dau	Unm	15	F	Household Duties	Herts	St Albans
769	ARNOLD	James	181		Son		12	M	Scholar	Herts	St Albans
770	ARNOLD	David	181		Son		9	M	Scholar	Herts	St Albans
771	ARNOLD	Esther	181		Dau		7	F	Scholar	Herts	St Albans
772	ARNOLD	Francis Joseph	181		Son		3	M	Scholar	Herts	St Albans
773	CANDLE	Thomas	182	Catherine Lane	Head	Mar	68	M	Labourer	Herts	St Albans
774	CANDLE	Elizabeth	182		Wife	Mar	66	F		Herts	St Albans
775	CANDLE	Joseph	183	Catherine Lane	Head	Mar	60	M	Labourer	Herts	St Albans
776	CANDLE	Elizabeth	183		Wife	Mar	48	F		Herts	St Albans
777	CANDLE	Frederick	183		Son	Unm	18	M	Labourer	Herts	St Albans
778	CANDLE	Ann	183		Dau	Unm	11	F		Herts	St Albans
779	DENTON	Jemima	184	Catherine Lane	Head	Unm	27	F	Silkworker	Herts	St Albans
780	BAIL	Ann	185	Catherine Lane	Head	Widow	60	F	Charwoman	Herts	St Albans
781	BAIL	Ann	185		Dau	Unm	19	F	Brazilian Hat Maker	Herts	St Albans
782	HEALEY	Charles	186	Catherine Lane	Head	Mar	25	M	Silk Throwster	Herts	St Albans
783	HEALEY	Sarah	186		Wife	Mar	29	F	Needle Worker	Herts	Essenden

ST PETERS

371

784	HEALEY	Eliza	186		Dau		3	F		Herts	St Albans
785	HEALEY	James	186		Son		6	M		Herts	St Albans
786	HEALEY	Charles	186		Son		1	M		Herts	St Albans
787	GROOM	Elizabeth	187	Catherine Lane	Head	Widow	74	F	Inmate of Alms House	Herts	Caddington
788	BRANDON	Mary	188	Catherine Lane	Head	Widow	80	F	Inmate of Alms House	Herts	St Albans
789	RATCLIFFE	Elizabeth	189	Catherine Lane	Head	Widow	56	F	Charwoman	Herts	St Albans
790	RATCLIFFE	Benjamin	189		Son	Widower	32	M	Labourer	Herts	St Albans
791	RATCLIFFE	John	189		Grandson		5	M	At Home	Herts	St Albans
792	RATCLIFFE	James	189		Grandson		4	M	At Home	Herts	St Albans
793	TURNER	Sarah	190	Catherine Lane	Head	Widow	67	F	Nurse	Herts	Redbourn
794	GOLSBY	Elizabeth	190		Lodger	Unm	38	F	Weaver	Herts	St Albans
795	HOULSTON	Louisa	190		Lodger	Widow	67	F	Nurse	Middx	Hadley [?]
796	SEABROOK	Charlotte	190		Lodger	Widow	70	F	Straw Plaiter	Herts	Redbourn
797	DAWS	James	190		Lodger	Widower	86	M	Sawyer	Herts	St Pauls Walden
798	AUSTEN	William	190		Lodger	Unm	21	M	Labourer	Herts	Redbourn
799	LOUGHTON	Sarah	191	Catherine Lane	Head	Widow	56	F	Laundress	Beds	Luton
800	LOUGHTON	James	191		Son	Unm	22	M	Farm Labourer	Herts	St Albans
801	LOUGHTON	Sarah	191		Dau		12	F	Scholar	Herts	St Albans
802	RATCLIFF	Elizabeth	192	Catherine Lane	Head	Widow	56	F	Cotton Winder	Herts	St Albans
803	RATCLIFF	John	192		Son	Unm	28	M	Labourer	Herts	St Albans
804	RATCLIFF	Frederick	192		Son	Unm	23	M	Labourer	Herts	St Albans
805	RATCLIFF	Benjamin	192		Son	Widower	32	M	Labourer	Herts	St Albans
806	RATCLIFF	John	192		Grandson		5	M	At Home	Herts	St Albans
807	RATCLIFF	James	192		Grandson		4	M	At Home	Herts	St Albans
808	WALLER	Henry	192		Lodger	[blank]	24	M	Labourer	Herts	St Albans
809	JEFFS	James	192		Brother	Unm	47	M	Labourer	Herts	St Albans
810	AVIS	Mary	193	Catherine Lane	Head	Widow	64	F	Inmate of Alms House	Herts	St Albans
811	NORTH	Ann	194	Catherine Lane	Head	Widow	77	F	Inmate of Alms House	Herts	St Albans
812	RATCLIFF	William	195	Catherine Lane	Head	Mar	39	M	Carrier	Herts	St Albans
813	RATCLIFF	Fanney	195		Wife	Mar	37	F	Weaver	Herts	St Albans
814	RATCLIFF	Sarah	195		Dau	Unm	19	F	Weaver	Herts	St Albans
815	RATCLIFF	William	195		Son		9	M	At Home	Herts	St Albans
816	RANDALL	William	196	Catherine Lane	Head	Mar	42	M	Cordwainer	Herts	Newnham
817	RANDALL	Elizabeth	196		Wife	Mar	32	F		Herts	St Albans
818	RANDALL	George	196		Son		12	M	Scholar	Herts	St Albans
819	RANDALL	Robert	196		Son		10	M	Scholar	Herts	St Albans
820	RANDALL	Eliza	196		Dau		8	F	Scholar	Herts	St Albans
821	RANDALL	Alice	196		Dau		5	F	Scholar	Herts	St Albans
822	RANDALL	Arthur	196		Son		2	M	At Home	Herts	St Albans
823	DAWES	William	197	Catherine Lane	Head	Mar	50	M	Labourer	Herts	St Pauls Walden
824	DAWES	Ann	197		Wife	Mar	55	F	Laundress	Staffs	[Unknown]
825	HILLIARD	William	198	Catherine Lane	Head	Mar	39	M	Butcher	Herts	St Albans
826	HILLIARD	Sarah	198		Wife	Mar	30	F	Butchers Wife	Herts	St Albans
827	HILLIARD	Alfred	198		Son		13	M	Scholar	Herts	St Albans

	SURNAME	FORENAME	SCHEDULE NUMBER	ADDRESS	RELATIONSHIP	STATUS	AGE	SEX	OCCUPATION	COUNTY OF BIRTH	PLACE OF BIRTH
828	HILLIARD	John	198		Son		11	M	Scholar	Herts	St Albans
829	HILLIARD	George	198		Son		9	M	Scholar	Herts	St Albans
830	HILLIARD	Henry	198		Son		1	M	At Home	Herts	St Albans
831	UNDERWOOD	James	199	Cross Street	Head	Mar	36	M	Coachman	Kent	Woolwich
832	UNDERWOOD	Emma	199		Wife	Mar	34	F		Essex	West Ham
833	UNDERWOOD	Emily	199		Dau		6	F		Herts	St Albans
834	UNDERWOOD	Regia	199		Dau		4	F		Herts	St Albans
835	UNDERWOOD	James	199		Son		2	M		Herts	St Albans
836	UNDERWOOD	Sarah	199		Dau		3m	F		Herts	St Albans
837	SMITH	Elizabeth	200	Cross Street	Head	Widow	32	F	Dressmaker	Kent	Ashford
838	SMITH	Jane	200		Dau		8	F	Scholar	Herts	Hitchin
839	SMITH	Mary Anne	200		Dau		6	F	Scholar	Herts	Stevenage
840	SMITH	Walter	200		Son		3	M		Herts	St Albans
841	SMITH	Mary Anne	200		Sister	Unm	28	F	Bonnet Maker	Herts	St Albans
842	MOOR	Mary	200		Visitor	Unm	17	F	House Servant	Herts	St Albans
843	RUSSELL	Sarah	200		Visitor	Unm	16	F	Bonnet Sewer	Herts	Harpenden
844	ROBERTS	Emma	201	Cross Street	Head	Unm	18	F	Stay Maker	Middx	St Olaves
845	LAWRENCE	Ethel	202	Cross Street	Head	Widow	62	F	Straw Plait Maker	Herts	St Albans
846	LAWRENCE	Ann	202		Dau	Mar	24	F	Grass Hat Maker	Herts	St Albans
847	EPPGRAVE	David	202		Lodger	Unm	35	M	Shoemaker	Herts	Sandridge
848	SLOUGH	Charles	202		Lodger	Unm	20	M	Tailor	Herts	Wheathampstead
849	LITTLE	Henry	203	Cross Street	Head	Mar	58	M	Labourer	Bucks	Marlow
850	LITTLE	Caroline	203		Wife	Mar	56	F	Charwoman	Herts	St Albans
851	LITTLE	Eliza	203		Dau	Unm	25	F	Hat Maker	Herts	St Albans
852	LITTLE	Rosanna	203		Grandau		6	F	Scholar	Herts	St Albans
853	GOSEBY [?]	Mary	204	Cross Street	Head	Unm	49	F	Needlewoman	Herts	St Albans
854	DICKINS	Jonathan	205	Cross Street	Head	Mar	41	M	Carpenter	Northants	Wellingborough
855	DICKINS	Ann	205		Wife	Mar	29	F	Bonnet Sewer	Beds	Toddington
856	DICKINS	Jane	205		Dau		12	F	Brazilian Hat Maker	Herts	St Albans
857	DICKINS	Mary Ann	205		Dau		10	F	Brazilian Hat Maker	Herts	St Albans
858	SWAIN	Rose	206	Cross Street	Head	Widow	57	F	Plain Needleworker	Herts	Braughing
859	SWAIN	Susannah	206		Dau	Unm	22	F	Dressmaker	Herts	St Albans
860	TURNER	Thomas	207	Cross Street	Head	Widower	45	M	Carpenter	Herts	Weston
861	TURNER	Ellen Elizabeth	207		Dau	Unm	9	F	Scholar	Herts	St Peters
862	SEYMOUR	John	208	Cross Street	Head	Mar	25	M	Carpenter	Middx	Highgate
863	SEYMOUR	Emma	208		Wife	Mar	23	F		Herts	St Albans
864	HARTWELL	John	209	Cross Street	Head	Mar	67	M	Carpenter	Herts	Bedmond [Abbots Langley]
865	HARTWELL	Sarah	209		Wife	Mar	66	F		Herts	St Albans
866	SAVAGE	George	210	Cross Street	Head	Mar	27	M	Bricklayer	Beds	Hockliffe
867	SAVAGE	Mary	210		Wife	Mar	27	F		Herts	St Albans
868	SAVAGE	James	210		Son		7	M	Scholar	Herts	St Albans
869	RUSH	Hannah	211	Cross Street	Head	Unm	28	F	Trimming Maker	Herts	St Albans
870	RUSH	Frederick	211		Son		4	M		Herts	St Albans
871	SLOUGH	Maria	211		Lodger	Unm	26	F	Trimming Maker	Herts	St Albans

872	SIBLEY	James	212	Cross Street	Head	Mar	35	M	Gardener	Herts	Colney
873	SIBLEY	Mary	212		Wife	Mar	38	F	Gardeners Wife	Herts	St Albans
874	SIBLEY	Sarah	212		Dau		9	F		Herts	St Albans
875	SIBLEY	Henry	212		Son		2	M		Herts	St Albans
876	SIBLEY	Emma	212		Dau		2 m	F		Herts	St Albans
877	SAVAGE	Daniel	213	Cross Street	Head	Mar	52	M	Bricklayer, employing 2 men	Beds	Cranfield
878	SAVAGE	Ann	213		Wife	Mar	51	F		Beds	Toddington
879	SAVAGE	Mary	213		Dau	Unm	20	F	Bonnet Sewer	Herts	St Albans
880	SAVAGE	John	213		Son	Unm	18	M	Bricklayer	Herts	St Albans
881	SAVAGE	William	213		Son		15	M	Scholar	Herts	St Albans
882	SAVAGE	Harriet	213		Dau		13	F	Dressmaker	Herts	St Albans
883	LAWRENCE	David	214	Cross Street	Head	Mar	40	M	Boot Maker	Herts	St Albans
884	LAWRENCE	Hannah	214		Wife	Mar	37	F	Domestic	Herts	St Albans
885	LAWRENCE	William	214		Son		11	M		Herts	St Albans
886	LAWRENCE	Thomas	214		Son		9	M	Scholar	Herts	St Albans
887	LAWRENCE	Sarah	214		Dau		8	F	Scholar	Herts	St Albans
888	LAWRENCE	David	214		Son		6	M	Scholar	Herts	St Albans
889	LAWRENCE	Aaron	214		Son		4	M	Scholar	Herts	St Albans
890	LAWRENCE	Walter	214		Son		2	M		Herts	St Albans
891	BIGGS	William	215	Cross Street	Head	Mar	38	M	Bricklayer	Herts	Sandridge
892	BIGGS	Mary	215		Wife	Mar	38	F		Warks	Coventry
893	BIGGS	Sarah Ann	215		Dau	Unm	17	F		Herts	St Albans
894	BIGGS	Henry	215		Son		15	M	Bricklayers Son	Herts	St Albans
895	BIGGS	Sidney James	215		Son		10	M	Scholar	Herts	St Albans
896	BIGGS	Emily	215		Dau		3	F		Herts	St Albans
897	HYDE	Sarah	215		Visitor	Widow	60	F	Bonnet Sewer	Herts	Wheathampstead
898	JONES	Samuel	216	Dalton House	Head	Unm	80	M	Optician & Farmer employing 3 men	Middx	St Andrews, Holborn
899	BARKER	Richard	216		Serv	Mar	46	M	Coachman	Middx	Hammersmith
900	MANN	Elizabeth	216		Serv	Widow	65	F	Housekeeper	Middx	Westminster
901	DYMMOCK	Sarah	216		Serv	Unm	40	F	Cook	Herts	Colney
902	WOODLAND	James	217	Catherine Lane	Head	Mar	48	M	Carpenter	Herts	St Albans
903	WOODLAND	Sarah	217		Wife	Mar	49	F		Herts	St Albans
904	WOODLAND	Mary	217		Dau	Unm	23	F	Bonnet Sewer	Herts	St Albans
905	WOODLAND	James	217		Son	Unm	21	M	Labourer	Herts	St Albans
906	WOODLAND	Robert	217		Son	Unm	19	M	Silk Worker	Herts	St Albans
907	WOODLAND	John	217		Son	[Unm]	17	M	Errand Boy	Herts	St Albans
908	WOODLAND	Joseph	217		Son		15	M	Errand Boy	Herts	St Albans
909	WOODLAND	Sarah	217		Dau		13	F	Scholar	Herts	St Albans
910	WOODLAND	Thomas	217		Son		11	M	Scholar	Herts	St Albans
911	GOODGAME	Thomas	218	Catherine Lane	Head	Widower	60	M	Beer Shop Keeper	Bucks	Denham
912	HESTER	Ann	218		Dau	Widow	33	F	Bonnet Sewer	Herts	Park Street [St Stephens]
913	HESTER	Thomas	218		Grandson		13	M	Scholar	Herts	St Albans
914	GOODGAME	Sabina	218		Grandau		15	F	Dressmaker	Middx	Islington
915	KING	William	219	Catherine Lane	Head	Mar	56	M	Labourer	Herts	St Albans

	SURNAME	FORENAME	SCHEDULE NUMBER	ADDRESS	RELATIONSHIP	STATUS	AGE	SEX	OCCUPATION	COUNTY OF BIRTH	PLACE OF BIRTH
916	KING	Maria	219		Wife	Mar	53	F		Herts	St Albans
917	KING	Thomas	219		Son		12	M	At Home	Herts	St Albans
918	NORTH	William	220	Catherine Lane	Head	Mar	37	M	Bricklayers Labourer	Herts	St Albans
919	NORTH	Sarah	220		Wife	Mar	34	F		Herts	St Albans
920	NORTH	Edmund	220		Son	Unm	14	M	Scholar	Herts	St Albans
921	NORTH	Rose	220		Dau		7	F	Scholar	Herts	St Albans
922	NORTH	William	220		Son		3	M	At Home	Herts	St Albans
923	HUMPHREYS	Francis	221	Catherine Lane	Head	Mar	62	M	Painter	Herts	St Albans
924	HUMPHREYS	Charlotte	221		Wife	Mar	55	F		Middx	London
925	HUMPHREYS	Frederick	221		Son		8	M		Herts	St Albans
926	HUMPHREYS	Charlotte	221		Dau		6	F		Herts	St Albans
927	MOORE	Henry	221		Son-in-law	Unm	16	M	Weaver	Herts	St Albans
928	LITTLE	Henry	222	Catherine Lane	Head	Mar	32	M	Labourer	Herts	St Albans
929	LITTLE	Sarah	222		Wife	Mar	25	F	Labourers Wife	Herts	Wheathampstead
930	LITTLE	Sarah Anne	222		Dau		4	F		Herts	St Albans
931	JONES	John	223	Catherine Lane	Lodger	Unm	25	M	Carver & Gilder	Lancs	Liverpool
932	STAMFORD	Edward	224	Catherine Lane	Lodger	Unm	21	M	House Painter	Middx	Edmonton
933	RICHARDSON	William	225	Catherine Lane	Head	Mar	49	M	Bricklayer	Northants	Hartwell
934	RICHARDSON	Ann	225		Wife	Mar	58	F	Hat Maker	Beds	Cranfield
935	RICHARDSON	William	225		Grandson		8	M	Scholar	Herts	St Peters
936	BURRIDGE	Mary	226	Catherine Lane	Head	Widow	57	F	Nurse	Herts	St Albans
937	BURRIDGE	Harriet	226		Dau	Unm	27	F	Bonnet Sewer	Herts	St Albans
938	BURRIDGE	Esther	226		Dau	Unm	24	F	Bonnet Sewer	Herts	St Albans
939	BURRIDGE	Sydney Edward Perkins	226		Grandson		5	M	Scholar	Herts	St Albans
940	BURRIDGE	Mary Anne Elizabeth	226		Grandau		2	F	Scholar	Herts	St Albans
941	HAUGHTEN	Pheobe	227	Catherine Lane	Head	Widow	69	F	Pauper	Herts	Hitchin
942	BASSEL	Ann	228	Catherine Lane	Head	Widow	66	F	Pauper	Bucks	Stoke
943	MORETON	Emma	228		Grandau	Unm	25	F	Weaver	Herts	St Peters
944	SLOUGH	William	229	Catherine Lane	Head	Mar	46	M	Brickmaker	Herts	Wheathampstead
945	SLOUGH	Louisa	229		Wife	Mar	46	F	Brickmakers Wife	Middx	[Unknown]
946	SLOUGH	Sarah	229		Dau		13	F	Assists Father [Brickmaker]	Herts	St Albans
947	SLOUGH	Marianne	229		Dau		11	F	Assists Father [Brickmaker]	Herts	St Albans
948	SLOUGH	Eliza	229		Dau		10	F	Assists Father [Brickmaker]	Herts	St Albans
949	SLOUGH	Amelia	229		Dau		9	F	Assists Father [Brickmaker]	Herts	St Albans
950	SLOUGH	Susan	229		Dau		8	F	Assists Father [Brickmaker]	Herts	St Albans
951	SLOUGH	James	229		Son		7	M	Assists Father [Brickmaker]	Herts	St Albans
952	SLOUGH	Emma	229		Dau		5	F	Assists Father [Brickmaker]	Herts	St Albans
953	SLOUGH	Henry	229		Son		4	M	Assists Father [Brickmaker]	Herts	St Albans
954	TAYLOR	Joseph	230	Catherine Lane	Head	Mar	39	M	Brickmaker	Herts	St Albans
955	TAYLOR	Eliza	230		Wife	Mar	38	F	Brickmakers Wife	Herts	St Albans
956	TAYLOR	Mary	230		Dau	[Unm]	19	F	Brickmaker	Herts	St Albans

957	TAYLOR	Henry	230		Son	[Unm]	16	M	Assists Father [Brickmaker]	Herts	St Albans
958	TAYLOR	Sarah	230		Dau		14	F	Assists Father [Brickmaker]	Herts	St Albans
959	TAYLOR	Susan	230		Dau		12	F	Assists Father [Brickmaker]	Herts	St Albans
960	TAYLOR	Eliza	230		Dau		10	F	Assists Father [Brickmaker]	Herts	St Albans
961	TAYLOR	Martha	230		Dau		9	F	Assists Father [Brickmaker]	Herts	St Albans
962	TAYLOR	William	230		Son		8	M	Assists Father [Brickmaker]	Herts	St Albans
963	CRAWLEY	Joseph	231	Catherine Lane	Head	Mar	51	M	Labourer	Herts	St Albans
964	CRAWLEY	Elizabeth	231		Wife	Mar	51	F		Herts	St Albans
965	CRAWLEY	Mary	231		Dau	Unm	19	F	Bonnet Sewer	Herts	St Albans
966	CRAWLEY	Joseph	231		Son		15	M	Errand Boy	Herts	St Albans
967	CRAWLEY	Marian	231		Dau		14	F	At School	Herts	St Albans
968	CRAWLEY	Martha	231		Dau		8	F	At School	Herts	St Albans
969	BIBBY	Ann	232	Catherine Lane	Head	Unm	24	F	Hat Maker	Herts	St Albans
970	BIBBY	Sarah	232		Sister	Unm	22	F	Hat Maker	Herts	St Albans
971	BIBBY	Mary Ann	232		Sister	Unm	13	F	Hat Maker	Herts	St Albans
972	LITTEL	George	232		Nephew		4	M	Scholar	Herts	St Albans
973	EBBORN	William	233	Catherine Lane	Head	Mar	42	M	Labourer	Herts	St Albans
974	EBBORN	Fanny	233		Wife	Mar	49	F		Herts	St Albans
975	EBBORN	George	233		Son	Unm	26	M	Labourer	Herts	St Albans
976	EBBORN	Charles	233		Son	Unm	15	M		Herts	St Albans
977	EBBORN	William	233		Son		11	M		Herts	St Albans
978	EBBORN	Alfred	233		Son		7	M		Herts	St Albans
979	EBBORN	Joseph	233		Son		4	M		Herts	St Albans
980	CONSTABLE	James	234	Catherine Lane	Head	Mar	29	M	Labourer, Alms Relief	Herts	St Albans
981	CONSTABLE	Ann	234		Wife	Mar	28	F		Herts	St Albans
982	HILL	Mary	235	Catherine Lane	Head	Widow	75	F	Straw Plaiter, Alms Relief	Herts	Redbourn
983	HILL	Hannah	235		Dau	Unm	46	F	Straw Plaiter, Alms Relief	Herts	Redbourn
984	HILL	Sarah	235		Dau	Unm	44	F	Straw Plaiter, Alms Relief	Herts	Redbourn
985	ELTHRIDGE	Samuel	236	Catherine Lane	Head	Mar	27	M	Silk Throwster	Herts	St Albans
986	ELTHRIDGE	Susan	236		Wife	Mar	29	F	Hat Maker	Beds	Ampthill
987	HULL	Thomas	237	Catherine Lane	Head	Mar	37	M	Labourer	Herts	St Albans
988	HULL	Susan	237		Wife	Mar	35	F		Herts	Hitchin
989	HULL	Emma	237		Dau		14	F	Hat Maker	Herts	St Albans
990	HULL	Ann	237		Dau		10	F	Hat Maker	Herts	St Albans
991	HULL	Isabella	237		Dau		8	F	Scholar	Herts	St Albans
992	HULL	Helen	237		Dau		4	F	Scholar	Herts	St Albans
993	HULL	William	237		Son		2	M		Herts	St Albans
994	HONNER	Ann	238	Catherine Lane	Head	Mar	80	F	Alms Relief, Charwoman	Herts	St Albans
995	HONNER	Martha	238		Dau	Unm	47	F	Charwoman	Herts	St Albans
996	HONNER	Eliza	238		Dau	Unm	38	F	Weaver	Herts	St Albans
997	HONNER	Jane	238		Dau	Unm	21	F	Weaver	Herts	St Albans
998	HONNER	Hannah	238		Niece	Unm	15	F	Weaver	Herts	St Albans

	SURNAME	FORENAME	SCHEDULE NUMBER	ADDRESS	RELATIONSHIP	STATUS	AGE	SEX	OCCUPATION	COUNTY OF BIRTH	PLACE OF BIRTH
999	HONNER	Ann	238		Niece		13	F	Hat Maker	Herts	St Albans
1000	WHEELER	Thomas	239	Catherine Lane	Head	Mar	56	M	Labourer	Herts	St Albans
1001	WHEELER	Sarah	239		Wife	Mar	56	F		Herts	Kimpton
1002	WHEELER	Ann	239		Dau	Unm	17	F		Herts	St Albans
1003	FURNESS	William	239		Visitor	Unm	68	M	Labourer	Beds	Hockliffe
1004	BERNER	Benjamin Manfield	240	Catherine Lane	Head	Mar	33	M	Annuitant	Herts	Abbots Langley
1005	BERNER	Sophia	240		Wife	Mar	44	F	Annuitant	Beds	Wilden
1006	WOODWARD	George	241	Catherine Lane	Head	Mar	55	M	Carpenter	Herts	Bushey
1007	WOODWARD	Elizabeth	241		Wife	Mar	59	F		Herts	Therfield
1008	WOODWARD	George	241		Son	Unm	29	M	Carpenter	Herts	St Stephens
1009	WOODWARD	Emma	241		Dau	Unm	25	F	Domestic Duties	Herts	St Albans
1010	WOODWARD	Sarah	241		Dau	Unm	23	F	Domestic Duties	Herts	St Albans
1011	WOODWARD	Elizabeth	241		Dau	Unm	15	F	Domestic Duties	Herts	St Albans
1012	BEAN	John	242	Catherine Lane	Head	Mar	70	M	Sawyer	Herts	St Albans
1013	BEAN	Mary	242		Wife	Mar	70	F		Herts	St Albans
1014	BEAN	Ann	242		Dau	Unm	40	F	Bonnet Sewer	Herts	St Albans
1015	BEAN	Elizabeth	242		Dau	Unm	35	F	Bonnet Sewer	Herts	St Albans
1016	BEAN	Jane	242		Dau	Unm	30	F	Bonnet Sewer	Herts	St Albans
1017	HULL	Thomas	243	Catherine Lane	Head	Mar	31	M	Gardener	Herts	St Albans
1018	HULL	Susan	243		Wife	Mar	31	F		Herts	St Albans
1019	HULL	Eliza	243		Dau		6	F	Scholar	Herts	St Albans
1020	HULL	Susan	243		Dau		4	F		Herts	St Albans
1021	HULL	Thomas James	243		Son		2	M		Herts	St Albans
1022	HULL	Infant	243		Son		1 m	M		Herts	St Albans
1023	LOWE	George	244	Catherine Lane	Head	Mar	42	M	Labourer	Herts	St Albans
1024	LOWE	Susan	244		Wife	Mar	37	F		Herts	St Albans
1025	LOWE	Eliza	244		Dau	Unm	18	F	Bonnet Sewer	Herts	St Albans
1026	LOWE	William	244		Son		15	M	Errand Boy	Herts	St Albans
1027	LOWE	Amos	244		Son		9	M	Scholar	Herts	St Albans
1028	LOWE	Robert	244		Son		6	M	Scholar	Herts	St Albans
1029	LOWE	Caroline	244		Dau		3	F		Herts	St Albans
1030	GOLDSBY	Charles	245	Catherine Lane	Head	Mar	30	M	Labourer	Herts	St Albans
1031	GOLDSBY	Maria	245		Wife	Mar	29	F		Herts	St Albans
1032	GOLDSBY	Charles	245		Son		10	M		Herts	St Albans
1033	GOLDSBY	Adelaide [?]	245		Dau		9	F		Herts	St Albans
1034	GOLDSBY	Isabella	245		Dau		5	F		Herts	St Albans
1035	GOLDSBY	Susannah	245		Dau		2	F		Herts	St Albans
1036	GOLDSBY	Joseph	245		Son		2 m	M		Herts	St Albans
1037	WARNER	Thomas	245		Father-in-law	Widower	68	M	Labourer	Herts	Stevenage
1038	POWELL	William	246	Catherine Lane	Head	Mar	37	M	Labourer	Herts	St Albans
1039	POWELL	Rebecca	246		Wife	Mar	38	F		Herts	St Albans
1040	POWELL	Thomas	246		Son		9	M	Scholar	Herts	St Albans
1041	POWELL	Mary	246		Dau		6	F	Scholar	Herts	St Albans
1042	POWELL	James	246		Son		4	M	Scholar	Herts	St Albans

1043	POWELL	William	246		Son		2	M		Herts	St Albans
1044	MANN	Emma	247	Catherine Lane	Head	Widow	33	F	Bonnet Sewer	Middx	London
1045	MANN	William	247		Son		12	M	Scholar	Middx	London
1046	MANN	Sarah	247		Dau		10	F	Scholar	Herts	St Albans
1047	MANN	Abel	247		Son		8	M	Scholar	Herts	St Albans
1048	MANN	Eliza	247		Dau		5	F	Scholar	Herts	St Albans
1049	MANN	Joseph	247		Son		3	M		Herts	St Albans

Registrar's District: St Albans   Enumeration District 1b   Ref. HO 107/1713 folios 259-79

The part east of the road from Luton to the Market Place, and north east of the road from St Albans to Barnet, including part of St Peters Street, Snatchup Alley, Cock Lane and Marlborough Buildings.

1050	DIXON	Sophia	1	St Peter Street, Bell Yard	Head	Widow	63	F	Pauper Late Laundress	Herts	Hemel Hempstead
1051	LINES	Elizabeth	1		Dau	Widow	38	F	Bonnet Sewer	Herts	St Albans
1052	DIXON	Mary	1		Dau	Unm	35	F	Hatmaker	Herts	St Albans
1053	LINES	John	1		Grandson	Unm	19	M	Silkwinder	Herts	St Albans
1054	LINES	Eliza	1		Grandau	Unm	13	F	Hatmaker	Herts	St Albans
1055	SEARS	Ann	2	St Peter Street, Bell Yard	Head	Widow	71	F	Laundress	Herts	St Albans
1056	OAKLEY	James	3	St Peter Street, Bell Yard	Head	Mar	40	M	Ostler	Beds	Eversholt
1057	OAKLEY	Susan	3		Wife	Mar	40	F	Straw Trimming Weaver	Beds	Maulden
1058	HANSELL	Edward	4	St Peters Street	Head	Mar	47	M	Innkeeper	Unknown	
1059	HANSELL	Elizabeth	4		Wife	Mar	35	F		Wilts [Bucks?]	Iver
1060	HANSELL	Charles	4		Son	Unm	7	M	Scholar At Home	Middx	London
1061	HANSELL	Frederick	4		Son	Unm	4	M	Scholar At Home	Middx	London
1062	HANSELL	Thomas	4		Son	Unm	2	M		Herts	St Albans
1063	SMITH	Mary	4		Serv	Unm	22	F	Servant	Herts	St Stephens
1064	SWAIN	William	4		Serv	Unm	20	M	Servant	Herts	Harpenden
1065	DEBENHAM	Alfred E	5	St Peters Street	Head	Mar	32	M	Brewer	Suffolk	Ickworth Thorpe
1066	DEBENHAM	Mary A	5		Wife	Mar	30	F		Norfolk	Thetford
1067	DEBENHAM	James	5		Son		7	M		Norfolk	Thetford
1068	DANIELS	Amelia	5		Serv	Unm	22	F	Servant	Surrey	Lambeth
1069	GAYLER	Ellen	5		Serv	Unm	19	F	Servant	Herts	Ayot St Peter
1070	NEWPORT	William B	6	St Peters Street	Head	Mar	24	M	Solicitors Managing Clerk	Berks	Hurst
1071	NEWPORT	Maria	6		Wife	Mar	23	F		Middx	St Georges
1072	HOWARD	James	7	St Peters Street	Head	Mar	50	M	Brewers Man	Herts	Sandridge
1073	HOWARD	Elizabeth	7		Wife	Mar	45	F	Does Wash	Herts	Bennington
1074	HOWARD	John	7		Son		11	M	Scholar At Home	Herts	St Albans
1075	HOWARD	Lydia	7		Dau		9	F	Scholar At Home	Herts	St Albans
1076	HOWARD	Jesse	7		Son		7	M	Scholar At Home	Herts	St Albans
1077	HOWARD	Esther	7		Dau		5	F	Scholar At Home	Herts	St Albans
1078	HEARN	Charles	8	St Peters Street	Head	Unm	40	M	Agric Lab	Herts	Sandridge
1079	HARVEY	William	9	St Peters Street	Head	Mar	28	M	Brewers Cooper & Store House Man	Unknown	
1080	HARVEY	Harriet	9		Wife	Mar	27	F		Norfolk	Thetford

	SURNAME	FORENAME	SCHEDULE NUMBER	ADDRESS	RELATIONSHIP	STATUS	AGE	SEX	OCCUPATION	COUNTY OF BIRTH	PLACE OF BIRTH
1081	HARVEY	Joseph W	9		Son		3	M		Herts	St Albans
1082	HARVEY	Mary A	9		Dau		10m	F		Herts	St Albans
1083	CARR	William	10	St Peters Street	Head	Mar	71	M	Superann Excise Officer	Beds	Biggleswade
1084	CARR	Elizabeth	10		Wife	Mar	40	F		Bucks	Stony Stratford
1085	CARR	Amelia	10		Dau	Unm	20	F	Straw Hat Worker	Bucks	Stony Stratford
1086	CARR	William	10		Son	Unm	17	M		Bucks	Olney
1087	CARR	Sophia	10		Dau	Unm	14	F		Herts	Baldock
1088	CARR	John	10		Son		10	M		Herts	Baldock
1089	CARR	Joseph	10		Son		9	M		Herts	St Albans
1090	CARR	Frederick	10		Son		6	M		Herts	St Albans
1091	CARR	Edwin	10		Son		4	M		Herts	St Albans
1092	CARR	Mary Ann	10		Dau		2	F		Herts	St Albans
1093	MILLS	Ann	11	St Peters Street	Head	Unm	52	F	Schoolmistress	Herts	St Albans
1094	MILLS	Susan	11		Sister	Unm	39	F	Schoolmistress	Herts	St Albans
1095	AYRES	Charlotte	11		Teacher	Unm	18	F	Teacher	Middx	Camden Town
1096	TOMLIN	Mary	11		Scholar		14	F		Herts	Whitwell
1097	MASON	Elizabeth	11		Scholar		13	F		Herts	St Albans
1098	MASON	Emily	11		Scholar		12	F		Herts	St Albans
1099	DALTON	Jane	11		Scholar		11	F		Unknown	
1100	DALTON	Mary	11		Scholar		7	F		Unknown	
1101	HALES	Eliza	11		Serv	Unm	27	F	Serv	Herts	Colney
1102	WOODS	Maria A	12	St Peters Street	Head	Unm	23	F	Milliner	Norfolk	Ayleholm [Aylsham ?]
1103	PEACOCK	Annie	12		Partner	Unm	27	F	Dressmaker	Herts	St Albans
1104	PAYNE	Emma B	12		Visitor	Unm	22	F	Assistant Dressmaker	Herts	Watford
1105	HOWIE	Rosetta	12		Visitor	Unm	17	F	Apprentice [Dressmaker]	Herts	St Albans
1106	PARSONS	Henry	13	St Peters Street	Head	Mar	43	M	Common Brewer	Herts	St Albans
1107	PARSONS	Sarah	13		Wife	Mar	39	F		Beds	Toddington
1108	PARSONS	Edwin	13		Son	Unm	16	M	Common Brewer	Herts	St Albans
1109	PARSONS	Francis	13		Son	Unm	8	M	Scholar	Herts	St Albans
1110	WRAY	Elizabeth	13		Serv	Unm	30	F		Herts	Tewin
1111	SHELLEY	Mary	13		Serv	Unm	20	F		Staffs	Croxton
1112	SMITH	William	14	St Peters Street	Head	Mar	44	M	Carpenter employing 3	Middx	St Andrews
1113	SMITH	Mary A	14		Wife	Mar	43	F		Herts	St Albans
1114	SMITH	William	14		Son	Unm	17	M	Butcher	Herts	St Albans
1115	SMITH	Rosannah	14		Dau	Unm	16	F		Herts	St Albans
1116	SMITH	James T	14		Son		12	M	Scholar At Home	Herts	St Albans
1117	SMITH	Mary L	14		Dau		10	F	Scholar At Home	Herts	St Albans
1118	SMITH	Lucy	14		Dau		8	F	Scholar At Home	Herts	St Albans
1119	SMITH	Emma	14		Dau		6	F	Scholar At Home	Herts	St Albans
1120	SMITH	Elizabeth R	14		Dau		4	F	Scholar At Home	Herts	St Albans
1121	SMITH	Maria	14		Dau		2	F		Herts	St Albans
1122	LOWE	Richard G	15	St Peters Street	Head	Unm	49	M	Solicitor	Herts	St Albans
1123	SEARANCKE	Mary E	15		Sister	Widow	55	F	Proprietor & Fundholder	Herts	St Albans
1124	LOWE	Ann	15		Mother	Widow	82	F		Herts	St Albans

1125	HARRIS	Elizabeth	16	St Peters Street	Head	Unm	54	F	Fundholder	Herts	St Albans
1126	HARRIS	Sarah	16		[blank]	Unm	52	F	Independent	Herts	St Albans
1127	APTED [?]	Emma	16		Visitor	Unm	16	F	Independent	Middx	Isleworth
1128	KENT	Charlotte	17	St Peters Street	Head	Unm	34	F	Schoolmistress	Herts	Redbourn
1129	RIDLEY	Susannah	17		Partner	Unm	28	F	Schoolmistress	Kent	Dover
1130	RIDLEY	Sarah	17		Visitor	Unm	36	F		Kent	Dover
1131	EDMONDS	Amelia	17		Scholar	Unm	14	F		Gloucs	Gloucester
1132	PALMER	Maria	17		Serv	Unm	17	F	Housemaid	Herts	St Albans
1133	EDMONDS	Anne	17		Scholar	Unm	8	F		Somerset	Bath
1134	SPEEDY	Harriet	17		Scholar	Unm	9	F		Middx	London
1135	POTTER	Elizabeth	17		Scholar		8	F		Surrey	Clapham
1136	POTTER	Mary	17		Scholar		6	F		Surrey	Clapham
1137	KENT	Herbert	17		Scholar		7	M		Middx	Dalston
1138	KENT	Arthur	17		Scholar		6	M		Middx	Dalston
1139	KENT	Henry	17		Scholar		6	M		Middx	Islington
1140	KENT	George A	17		Scholar		4	M		Herts	Cheshunt
1141	HUGGETT	Henry	17		Scholar		7	M		Middx	London
1142	JOHNSON	Ann	17		Serv	Unm	19	F	Cook	Middx	London
1143	PAGE	Mary E	18	St Peters Street	Head	Unm	40	F	Professor Of Music	Herts	St Albans
1144	HOWARD	Thomas	19	St Peters Street	Head	Mar	38	M	Bricklayers Journeyman	Herts	St Albans
1145	HOWARD	Mary Ann	19		Wife	Mar	41	F		Herts	South Mimms
1146	HOWARD	Sarah	19		Mother	Widow	67	F		Herts	St Albans
1147	HOWARD	Joseph	19		Son		13	M		Herts	St Albans
1148	HOWARD	Elisabeth	19		Dau		11	F		Herts	St Albans
1149	HOWARD	Sarah	19		Dau		8	F		Herts	St Albans
1150	MAWE	George	19		Nephew		2	M		Herts	St Albans
1151	VASS	James	20	St Peters Street	Head	Mar	46	M	Builder	Middx	London
1152	VASS	Maria	20		Wife	Mar	61	F		Herts	Ayot St Peter
1153	BAYFORD	Mary	21	St Peters Street	Head	Widow	44	F		Herts	Harpenden
1154	FREEMAN	Charles F	21		Nephew	[Unm]	17	M		Herts	Harpenden
1155	JORDAN	Elizabeth	21		Serv	[blank]	63	F	Servant	Herts	Watford
1156	BACON	Elizabeth	22	St Peters Street	Head	Widow	75	F	Fundholder	Beds	Biggleswade
1157	FREEMAN	Phillis	22		Serv	Unm	57	F	Serv	Herts	Watford
1158	FAIRTHORNE	Thomas	23	St Peters Street	Head	Mar	67	M	Solicitor	Wilts	Swindon
1159	FAIRTHORNE	Sarah W	23		Wife	Mar	57	F		London	Cripplegate
1160	WELLS	Ann	23		Serv	Unm	23	F	Serv	Herts	Sandridge
1161	MCKENZIE	John D	24	St Peters Street	Head	Mar	49	M	Banker	Middx	London
1162	MCKENZIE	Hannah	24		Wife	Mar	43	F		Wilts	Marlborough
1163	MCKENZIE	Alice M	24		Dau		10	F		Middx	Brompton
1164	MCKENZIE	Douglas	24		Son		9	M		Middx	Brompton
1165	MCKENZIE	Ellen S	24		Dau		7	F		Suffolk	Ipswich
1166	MCKENZIE	Jessie M	24		Dau		6	F		Suffolk	Ipswich
1167	MCKENZIE	Kenneth	24		Son		4	M		Hunts	St Neots
1168	MCKENZIE	Edith M	24		Dau		2	F		Hunts	St Neots
1169	MCKENZIE	Harry W	24		Son		4m	M		Herts	St Albans

	SURNAME	FORENAME	SCHEDULE NUMBER	ADDRESS	RELATIONSHIP	STATUS	AGE	SEX	OCCUPATION	COUNTY OF BIRTH	PLACE OF BIRTH
1170	LAWRENCE	Martha	24		Serv	Unm	43	F	Serv	Sussex	Winchelsea
1171	PAGE	Emma	24		Serv	Unm	21	F	Serv	Norfolk	Ormesby
1172	CLARKE	Susan	24		Serv	Unm	14	F	Serv	Herts	St Albans
1173	EVANS	William H	25	St Peters Street	Head	Mar	39	M	Medical General Practitioner. M.R.C.S. London	Cambs	Ely
1174	EVANS	Eliza A	25		Wife	Mar	31	F		Cambs	Ely
1175	EVANS	Bertha E	25		Dau		4	F		Cambs	Ely
1176	EVANS	William E	25		Son		9m	M		Herts	St Albans
1177	BERRY	Mary A	25		Serv	Unm	21	F	Housemaid	Hants	Alton
1178	WELLS	Sarah A	25		Serv	Unm	20	F	Nursemaid	Unknown	
1179	EACOTT	Mary A	25		Serv	Unm	28	F	Cook	Wilts	Marlborough
1180	HARDWICK	George	25		Serv	Unm	16	M	Groom	Herts	Flamstead
1181	MARCON	Catherine	26	St Peters Street	Head	Unm	40	F	Fundholder	Norfolk	Swaffham
1182	TURNER	Elizabeth	26		Serv	Unm	65	F		Herts	St Albans
1183	SEARS	Thomas	27	St Peters Street	Head	Mar	45	M	Gardener	Herts	St Albans
1184	SEARS	Priscilla	27		Wife	Mar	44	F		Herts	St Albans
1185	SEARS	John	27		Son	Unm	17	M		Herts	St Albans
1186	SEARS	Ann	27		Dau	Unm	14	F	Scholar	Herts	St Albans
1187	SEARS	Thomas	27		Son		10	M	Scholar	Herts	St Albans
1188	SEARS	William	27		Son		5	M	Scholar	Herts	St Albans
1189	HILL	Daniel	28	St Peters Street	Head	Mar	61	M	Tailor Employs 1 Apprentice	Surrey	Mitcham
1190	HILL	Eliza	28		Wife	Mar	49	F		Bucks	Marlow
1191	ELLINGWORTH	Sarah J	28		Step-dau		25	F		Rutland	Okeham [Oakham]
1192	HILL	Emmelina	28		Dau		13	F		Bucks	Marlow
1193	HILL	Angenina	28		Dau		12	F		Herts	St Albans
1194	HILL	Albert A	28		Son		8	M		Herts	St Albans
1195	HILL	Clara A.	28		Dau		5	F		Herts	St Albans
1196	SILSBY	James T	28		Appr		15	M	Apprentice [to Tailor]	Herts	St Albans
1197	BROWN	Francis M	29	St Peters Street	Head	Mar	37	M	Professor Of Music	Herts	St Albans
1198	BROWN	Hannah I	29		Wife	Mar	37	F		Middx	St Giles
1199	BROWN	Francis	29		Son		15	M	Scholar At Home	Herts	St Albans
1200	BROWN	John F	29		Son		12	M	Scholar At Home	Herts	St Albans
1201	BROWN	Frederick D	29		Son		10	M	Scholar At Home	Herts	St Albans
1202	BROWN	George M	29		Son		9	M	Scholar At Home	Herts	St Albans
1203	BROWN	Edwin P	29		Son		2	M		[Unknown]	
1204	SMITH	Sarah	30	St Peters Street	Head	Widow	60	F	Washerwoman	Herts	St Albans
1205	DOUGLAS	Joseph	31	St Peters Street	Head	Mar	63	M	Superintendant of Boro' Police	Bucks	Shenley
1206	DOUGLAS	Mary F	31		Wife	Mar	44	F		Beds	Holcot
1207	DOUGLAS	Elizabeth M	31		Dau	Unm	16	F		Herts	St Albans
1208	WOOD	Charles	32	St Peters Street	Head	Mar	39	M	Schoolmaster	[Unknown]	
1209	WOOD	Anna M	32		Wife	Mar	45	F		[Unknown]	
1210	WOOD	Charles	32		Son	Unm	14	M	Scholar at home	[Unknown]	
1211	WOOD	Edward	32		Son	Unm	12	M	Scholar at home	[Unknown]	
1212	WOOD	Matilda	32		Sister	Unm	29	F		Surrey	Camberwell

1213	SEALE	Archibald A	32		Brother-in-law	Mar	57	M	Army Pension, service at St Helena	[Unknown]	
1214	DENT	Dinah	32		Serv	Unm	44	F	Servant	Herts	St Albans
1215	FULLER	Henry	32		Assistant	Unm	20	M	School Assistant	Sussex	Lewes
1216	TOWNSEND	Charles	32		Scholar	Unm	13	M	Scholar	Herts	Hatfield
1217	REEVES	Thomas	32		Scholar	Unm	9	M	Scholar	Herts	St Albans
1218	ODELL	Christopher	32		Scholar	Unm	10	M	Scholar	Middx	London
1219	ODELL	Thomas	32		Scholar	Unm	8	M	Scholar	Middx	London
1220	BRIDGES	Thomas	32		Scholar	Unm	14	M	Scholar	U.S.A.	
1221	GREENWOOD	John	32		Scholar	Unm	14	M	Scholar	Oxon	Easington
1222	GREENWOOD	Thomas	32		Scholar	Unm	12	M	Scholar	Middx	Kensington
1223	BOOME	Henry	32		Scholar	Unm	10	M	Scholar	Herts	Colney
1224	WESTON	James	32		Scholar	Unm	11	M	Scholar	Middx	Fulham
1225	WESTON	Spencer	32		Scholar	Unm	9	M	Scholar	Middx	Fulham
1226	CHASE	Horace	32		Scholar	Unm	12	M	Scholar	Beds	Luton
1227	CHASE	Sydney	32		Scholar	Unm	8	M	Scholar	Beds	Luton
1228	GREEN	Albert	32		Scholar	Unm	14	M	Scholar	Middx	Regents Park
1229	GREEN	Henry	32		Scholar	Unm	10	M	Scholar	Sussex	Brighton
1230	BLEWITT	Charles	32		Scholar	Unm	14	M	Scholar	N'thumb	Newcastle
1231	RUMBALL	Stanley	32		Scholar	Unm	14	M	Scholar	Herts	St Albans
1232	RUMBALL	Stewart	32		Scholar	Unm	10	M	Scholar	Herts	St Albans
1233	ATKINS	Sarah	33	St Peters Street	Head	Unm	76	F	Fundholder	London	City
1234	WELLS	Dorcas	33		Serv	Unm	24	F	Housemaid	Herts	Redbourn
1235	LOVETT	Hannah	33		Serv	Unm	45	F	Cook	Herts	Leverstock Green
1236	CANNON	William	34	St Peters Street	Head	Unm	36	M	Gent Fundholder	Herts	St Peters
1237	CANNON	Harriet	34		Sister	Unm	34	F	Fundholder	Herts	St Peters
1238	CANNON	Maria	34		Sister	Unm	28	F	Fundholder	Herts	St Peters
1239	GEORGE	Sarah	34		Serv	Unm	25	F		Essex	Margaretting
1240	RICHARDSON	Thomas	35	St Peters Street	Head	Mar	61	M	Straw Hat Manufacturer, Justice of Peace	Kent	Minster
1241	RICHARDSON	Ann	35		Wife	Mar	47	F	Wife	Kent	Faversham
1242	RICHARDSON	Hester	35		Dau	Unm	33	F		Kent	Sittingbourne
1243	RICHARDSON	William	35		Son	Unm	28	M	Assistant To Head Of Family	Kent	Sittingbourne
1244	RICHARDSON	Eliza	35		Dau	Unm	22	F		Kent	Sittingbourne
1245	RICHARDSON	Granville	35		Son	Unm	21	M	Draper	Kent	Sittingbourne
1246	RICHARDSON	Henry	35		Son	Unm	18	M	Assist To Head	Herts	St Albans
1247	RUSHTON	Mary	35		Serv	Unm	24	F	House Servant	Northants	Northampton
1248	FOWLER	Catherine	35		Serv	Unm	15	F	House Servant	Herts	Shenley
1249	NICHOLLS	Mary	36	St Peters Street	Head	Unm	52	F	Proprietor Of Houses & Fundholder	Herts	St Albans
1250	SIMPSON	Nancy W	36		Niece	Mar	24	F		Middx	London
1251	SIMPSON	Alfred W	36		Gt. Nephew		4	M		Hants	Southampton
1252	SIMPSON	John A	36		Gt. Nephew		7	M		Hants	Southampton
1253	KEEL	Thomas	37	St Peters Street	Head	Mar	53	M	Bricklayer	Herts	St Albans
1254	KEEL	Ann	37		Wife	Mar	60	F		Herts	St Albans
1255	KEEL	Jane	37		Dau	Unm	19	F		Herts	St Albans

	SURNAME	FORENAME	SCHEDULE NUMBER	ADDRESS	RELATIONSHIP	STATUS	AGE	SEX	OCCUPATION	COUNTY OF BIRTH	PLACE OF BIRTH
1256	HOLLOWAY	George	37		Lodger	Unm	19	M	Labourer	Herts	St Albans
1257	HARBURN	Benjamin	37		Lodger	Unm	18	M	Labourer	Herts	St Albans
1258	POWELL	Samuel	37		Lodger	Unm	18	M	Labourer	Herts	St Albans
1259	CARRIDGE	Samuel	38	St Peters Street	Head	Mar	57	M	Licenced Victualler	Suffolk	East Soham
1260	CARRIDGE	Elizabeth	38		Wife	Mar	60	F	Wife	Suffolk	Thorndon
1261	WEBB	Sarah	38		Niece	Unm	5	F	Scholar	Herts	St Albans
1262	STANBRIDGE	William	38		Serv	Unm	30	M	Ostler	Herts	Hertford
1263	CUTTS	Ann	38		Serv	Unm	19	F	House Serv	Herts	Welwyn
1264	GREENE	George	38		Lodger	Unm	24	M	Coach Painter	Herts	Hertford
1265	WORBY [HORBY]	George	38		Lodger	Widower	61	M	Labourer	Herts	St Albans
1266	BROWN	John	38		Lodger	Mar	67	M	Labourer	Herts	Hoddesdon
1267	BRADSHAW	George	38		Lodger	Mar	25	M	Bookseller	Middx	Hanwell
1268	DOWDLE	George	39	St Peters Street	Head	Mar	26	M	Labourer	Surrey	Walworth
1269	DOWDLE	Hannah	39		Wife	Mar	27	F	Wife	Herts	St Stephens
1270	DOWDLE	James	39		Son	Unm	6	M		Herts	St Albans
1271	DOWDLE	Harriet	39		Dau	Unm	2	F		Herts	St Albans
1272	DOWDLE	Thomas	39		Son		5m	M		Herts	St Albans
1273	DOWDLE	Dinah	39		Mother	Widow	56	F	Straw Plaiter	Herts	Redbourn
1274	DOWDLE	Dinah	39		Sister	Unm	24	F	Straw Trimming Weaver	Middx	Westminster
1275	WARRELL	Ann	39		Visitor	Unm	15	F	Straw Hat Maker	Herts	St Stephens
1276	WHITE	Elizabeth	40	St Peters Street	Head	Mar	30	F	Straw Trimming Weaver	Unknown	
1277	WHITE	George	40		Son	Unm	5	M	Scholar	Unknown	
1278	WHITE	Sarah	40	St Peters Street	Head	Mar	41	F	Straw Trimming Weaver	Herts	Harpenden
1279	WHITE	Alfred	40		Son	Unm	17	M	Horseclipper	Herts	Harpenden
1280	WHITE	Ellen	40		Dau	Unm	15	F	Bonnet Maker	Herts	Harpenden
1281	WHITE	Julia	40		Dau	Unm	12	F	Hatmaker	Herts	Harpenden
1282	WHITE	Arthur	40		Son	Unm	5	M		Herts	St Albans
1283	WHITE	Charles	40		Son	Unm	2	M		Herts	St Albans
1284	HULL	Henry	41	St Peters Street	Head	Mar	35	M	Labourer	Herts	St Peters
1285	HULL	Sarah	41		Wife	Mar	35	F	Handloom Weaver	Herts [Middx]	Stanmore
1286	HULL	George	41		Son	Unm	14	M	Silkweaver	Herts	St Peters
1287	HULL	William	41		Son	Unm	13	M	Silkweaver	Herts	St Peters
1288	HULL	Thomas	41		Son	Unm	9	M	Silkweaver	Herts	St Peters
1289	GARNER	Henry	41		Head	Mar	45	M	Army Chelsea Pensioner	Notts	Nottingham
1290	GARNER	Mary	41		Wife	Mar	37	F	Wife	Herts	St Albans
1291	CATLIN	Ann	41		Niece	Unm	7	F		Herts	St Albans
1292	EDWARDS	James	42	St Peters Street	Head	Mar	59	M	Gardener	Herts	St Albans
1293	EDWARDS	Mary	42		Wife	Mar	59	F	Takes In Mangling	[Hereford]	Stoke Prior
1294	EDWARDS	Mary A	42		Grandau		10	F	Scholar	Ireland	Newcastle Longford
1295	EDWARDS	Robert	42		Grandson		5	M	Scholar	Ireland	Londonderry
1296	CORDELL	Charles	43	St Peters Street	Head	Mar	27	M	Labourer	Herts	St Albans
1297	CORDELL	Elizabeth	43		Wife	Mar	30	F		Herts	Hatfield
1298	CORDELL	Ann	43		Dau	Unm	8	F	Scholar	Herts	St Albans

1299	DENTON	Frederick	44	St Peters Street	Head	Mar	44	M	Agric Lab	Herts	St Peters
1300	DENTON	Mary	44		Wife	Mar	52	F		Herts	St Peters
1301	DENTON	George	44		Son	Unm	20	M	Silk Winder	Herts	St Peters
1302	DENTON	Jane	44		Dau	Unm	17	F	Straw Hat Maker	Herts	St Peters
1303	DENTON	Emma	44		Dau	Unm	13	F	Straw Hat Maker	Herts	St Peters
1304	DENTON	William	44		Son		3	M		Herts	St Peters
1305	LITTLE	William	45	St Peters Street	Head	Mar	39	M	Labourer	Herts	Redbourn
1306	LITTLE	Sarah	45		Wife	Mar	38	F	Straw Plaiter	Herts	St Stephens
1307	LITTLE	Thomas	45		Son		11	M	Scholar	Herts	St Peters
1308	LITTLE	Elizabeth	45		Dau		10	F	Scholar	Herts	St Peters
1309	LITTLE	Martha	45		Dau		8	F	Scholar	Herts	St Peters
1310	LITTLE	Charles	45		Son		2	M		Herts	St Peters
1311	PURCELL	Harriet	46	St Peters Street	Head	Widow	42	F	Laundress	Cornwall	Falmouth
1312	PURCELL	Harriet	46		[Dau]	Unm	18	F	Straw Hat Maker	Middx	London
1313	PURCELL	Eliza	46		[Dau]		15	F	Straw Hat Maker	Middx	London
1314	PURCELL	Emily	46		[Dau]		12	F	Straw Hat Maker	Middx	London
1315	CRAWLEY	William	47	St Peters Street	Head	Mar	67	M	Agric Lab	Herts	Wheathampstead
1316	CRAWLEY	Elizabeth	47		Wife	Mar	54	F		Herts	St Peters
1317	CRAWLEY	Barnewell	47		Son	Unm	20	M	Agric Lab	Herts	St Stephens
1318	CRAWLEY	Caroline	47		Dau	Unm	16	F	Hat Maker	Herts	St Stephens
1319	CRAWLEY	Rosetta	47		Dau	Unm	11	F	Silk Winder	Herts	St Stephens
1320	HEDGES	Thomas	48	Cock Lane	Head	Mar	47	M	Labourer In Brickyard	Herts	Sandridge
1321	HEDGES	Sarah	48		Wife	Mar	44	F		Herts	St Albans
1322	HEDGES	Henry	48		Son	Unm	22	M	Lab In Brickyard	Herts	St Albans
1323	HEDGES	James	48		Son	Unm	18	M	Brazil Grass Splitter	Herts	St Albans
1324	HEDGES	Emma	48		Dau	Unm	20	F	Silk Winder	Herts	St Albans
1325	HEDGES	Joseph	48		Son	Unm	15	M	Brazil Grass Splitter	Herts	St Albans
1326	HEDGES	Ellen	48		Dau	Unm	12	F	Silk Winder	Herts	St Albans
1327	CARTER	Richard	49	Marlborough Buildings	Head	Mar	74	M	Almsperson (tailor)	Herts	St Albans
1328	CARTER	Elizabeth	49		Wife	Mar	73	F		Dorset	Dalwood
1329	ENGLISH	Thomas B	50	Marlborough Buildings	Head	Widower	65	M	Almsperson (Commercial Trav)	Worcs	Feckenham
1330	WAGSTAFF	Mary	51	Marlborough Buildings	Head	Widow	73	F	Almsperson (servant)	Berks	Reading
1331	MATTHEWS	Amelia J	52	Marlborough Buildings	Head	Unm	69	F	Almsperson (dressmaker)	Northants	Brington
1332	COCKINGTON	John	53	Marlborough Buildings	Head	Mar	74	M	Almsperson (Prop of Houses)	Herts	St Albans
1333	COCKINGTON	Susan	53		Wife	Mar	73	F		Unknown	
1334	STRINGER	James	54	Marlborough Buildings	Head	Unm	67	M	Almsperson (Butler)	Sussex	Steyning
1335	DEIGHTON	Ann	54		Serv	Widow	45	F	Housekeeper	Surrey	Rotherhithe
1336	WILLIAMS	Catherine	55	Marlborough Buildings	Head	Widow	77	F	Almsperson (Widow Of Saddler)	Beds	Elstow
1337	SPICER	Anne	56	Marlborough Buildings	Head	Widow	75	F	Almsperson (Nurse)	Herts	Hatfield
1338	SPICER	Frederick	56		Son	Unm	35	M		Herts	St Albans
1339	HALE	Maria	56		Visitor	Unm	34	F		Herts	St Albans
1340	REEVES	Emmanuel	57	Marlborough Buildings	Head	Mar	65	M	Almsperson (Coach proprietor)	Bucks	Quainton
1341	REEVES	Elizabeth	57		Wife	Mar	67	F		Essex	Witham

	SURNAME	FORENAME	SCHEDULE NUMBER	ADDRESS	RELATIONSHIP	STATUS	AGE	SEX	OCCUPATION	COUNTY OF BIRTH	PLACE OF BIRTH
1342	RICHARDSON	Eliza	57		Dau	Mar	38	F	Housekeeper	Herts	Rickmansworth
1343	HORNS	Eliza	57		Serv	Unm	39	F	House Serv	Herts	St Albans
1344	GALER	John	58	Marlborough Buildings	Head	Mar	77	M	Almsperson (Grocer)	Herts	St Pauls Walden
1345	GALER	Charlotte	58		Wife	Mar	68	F		Herts	St Albans
1346	WHITE	Mary	59		Head	Widow	65	F	Almsperson (Annuitant)	Northants	Walgrave
1347	WHITE	Elizabeth	59		Dau	Unm	44	F	Fundholder	Northants	Pytchley
1348	KELLON	Ann	60	Marlborough Buildings	Head	Widow	82	F	Almsperson (Annuitant)	Herts	Watford
1349	GROOM	Sarah	60		Niece	Unm	26	F		Middx	Laleham
1350	BEESTON	Francis	61	Marlborough Buildings	Head	Widower	69	M	Almsperson (Cook)	Derby	Bakewell
1351	ROWEN	Sarah	61		Dau	Mar	28	F	Wife Of Journeyman Piano Frame Maker Scholar	Middx	Chelsea
1352	ROWEN	William E	61		Grandson	Unm	7	M		Middx	London
1353	ROWEN	John B	61		Grandson	Unm	4	M		Middx	London
1354	ROWEN	Albert H	61		Grandson		7m	M		Middx	London
1355	THORNE	James	62	Marlborough Buildings	Head	Mar	69	M	Almsperson (Butler)	Bucks	Aylesbury
1356	THORNE	Elizabeth	62		Wife	Mar	57	F		Herts	St Albans
1357	COOK	Henry	62		Visitor		13	M		Surrey	Kingston
1358	COOK	James	62		Visitor		8	M		Surrey	Kingston
1359	WEBSTER	Sarah	63	Marlborough Buildings	Head	Widow	73	F	Almsperson/Pension Widow [of] Surgeon Royal Navy	Hunts	Kimbolton
1360	WEBSTER	Fanny	63		Dau	Unm	40	F		Hunts	Kimbolton
1361	MARSTON	Ann	64	Marlborough Buildings	Head	Widow	67	F	Almsperson Widow [of] Farmer	N'thumb [?]	Burickton [Buckton?]

Uninhabited

	SURNAME	FORENAME	SCHEDULE NUMBER	ADDRESS	RELATIONSHIP	STATUS	AGE	SEX	OCCUPATION	COUNTY OF BIRTH	PLACE OF BIRTH
1362	TANNER	William	65	Marlborough Buildings	Head	Mar	73	M	Almsperson (Annuitant)	Berks	Midgham
1363	TANNER	Elizabeth	65		Wife	Mar	71	F	Annuitant	Oxon	Standlake
1364	TANNER	Jane	65		Dau	Unm	27	F	Dressmaker	Surrey	Southwark
1365	SANDISON	Sarah	66	Marlborough Buildings	Head	Widow	69	F	Almsperson (Nurse)	Oxon	Goring
1366	EAGLESFIELD	Abigail	67	Marlborough Buildings	Head	Widow	81	F	Almsperson Housekeeper	Northants	Flore [?] [Floore]
1367	DEAYTON	William	68	Marlborough Buildings	Head	Widower	72	M	Almsperson (Mess. P. Office)	Herts	St Albans
1368	DEAYTON	Emma	68		Dau	Unm	33	F		Herts	St Albans
1369	MITCHELL	George	69	Marlborough Buildings	Head	Mar	63	M	Almsperson (Annuitant)	Dorset	Pulham
1370	MITCHELL	Elizabeth	69		Wife	Mar	65	F	Dressmaker	Berks	Ashampstead
1371	MITCHELL	William	69		Son	Unm	26	M	Tailor (Journeymn)	Herts	St Albans
1372	FOWLER	Elizabeth	70	Marlborough Buildings	Head	Widow	74	F	Almsperson (Annuitant)	Derby	Melbourne
1373	HIGGINS	Elizabeth	70		Sister	Unm	24	F	Grocers Dau	Middx	Kensington
1374	GOLDSMITH	Jane	71	Marlborough Buildings	Head	Widow	80	F	Almsperson Widow of Capt. in Royal Lancashire Voluntary[?]	Scotland	Edinburgh
1375	WARD	Samuel	72	Marlborough Buildings	Head	Widower	73	M	Almsperson Tailor	Warks	Tiddington
1376	PHILPOT	Sarah	72		Serv	Unm	16	F	House Serv	Herts	Bedmond [Abbots Langley]
1377	BOLTON	Joseph	73	Marlborough Buildings	Head	Widower	73	M	Almsperson (Coalmerchant)	U.S.A.	
1378	MARTIN	Lucy A	73		Grandau	Unm	18	F	Housekeeper	Kent	[Unknown]
1379	WEBSTER	Sophia	74	Marlborough Buildings	Head	Widow	66	F	Almsperson (Annuitant)	Herts	Bramfield

1380	BENNET	Harriet	74		Grandau	Unm	12	F		Middx	St Pancras
1381	FREEMAN	Elizabeth	75	Marlborough Buildings	Head	Widow	95	F	Almsperson (Milliner)	Herts	Buntingford
1382	FREEMAN	Maria	75		Dau	Unm	53	F	Milliner	Herts	St Albans
1383	TAYLOR	Amelia	76	Marlborough Buildings	Wife	Mar	43	F	Almsperson	Wales	Montgomery
1384	RAWLEY	Samuel	77	Marlborough Buildings	Head	Mar	77	M	Almsperson Cordwainer	Herts	St Albans
1385	RAWLEY	Elizabeth	77		Wife	Mar	66	F	None	Lincs	Spalding
1386	BASTON	Sarah	78	Marlborough Buildings	Head	Unm	79	F	Almsperson (Annuitant)	Cheshire	Knutsford
1387	BASTON	Mary	78		Sister	Unm	70	F	Annuitant	Cheshire	Knutsford
1388	WATSON	Susannah	79	Marlborough Buildings	Head	Unm	78	F	Almsperson (Annuitant)	Scotland	Meigle [?]
1389	FRANCIS	Robert	80	Marlborough Buildings	Head	Mar	80	M	Almsperson (Annuitant)	Lincs	Uffington
1390	FRANCIS	Sarah	80		Wife	Mar	80	F		Middx	St Anns Lewisham
1391	BATTEN	Luke	81	Marlborough Buildings	Head	Widower	76	M	Almsperson (annitt)	Herts	St Albans
1392	MORFITT	Elizabeth	81		[Step-]Sister	Unm	73	F		Yorks	Cawood
1393	ROSS	Elizabeth	82	Marlborough Buildings	Head	Widow	77	F	Almsperson (Annuitant)	Herts	Abbots Langley
1394	JENKINSON	Mary	83	Marlborough Buildings	Head	Widow	63	F	Almsperson (Annuitant)	Yorks	Tadcaster
1395	IVORY	George	84	Cock Lane	Head	Unm	30	M	Schoolmaster	Berks	Reading
1396	IVORY	Jane	84		Sister	Unm	27	F	Schoolmistress	Berks	Reading
1397	IVORY	Jane	84		Mother	Widow	65	F		Berks	Newbury
1398	BRADSHAW	Martha	84		Scholar		5	F		Herts	Hatfield
1399	EVANS	John	85	Cock Lane	Head	Mar	27	M	Journeyman, Bricklayer	Herts	St Albans
1400	EVANS	Harriet	85		Wife	Mar	23	F	Straw Plaiter	Herts	Ayot St Peter
1401	LAWRENCE	Priscilla	86	Cock Lane	Head	Widow	50	F	Brazil Grass Hat Maker	Herts	St Albans
1402	LAWRENCE	Reuben	86		Son		10	M	Scholar	Herts	St Albans
1403	EMILY	Joseph	86		Nephew	Unm	35	M	Labourer	Herts	St Albans
1404	EMILY	Sarah	86		Sister	Widow	62	F	Errand Woman	Herts	St Albans
1405	SLOUGH	Rebecca	87	Cock Lane	Head	Widow	56	F	Brazil Grass Worker	Herts	Welwyn
1406	SLOUGH	Frederick	87		Son	Unm	25	M	Labourer	Herts	St Peters
1407	SLOUGH	Henry	87		Son	Unm	23	M	Labourer	Herts	St Peters
1408	SLOUGH	Susan	87		Dau	Unm	21	F	Straw Hat Maker	Herts	St Peters
1409	SLOUGH	Charles	87		Son	Unm	17	M	Labourer	Herts	St Albans
1410	SLOUGH	Emma	87		Dau	Unm	15	F	Straw Hat Maker	Herts	St Albans
1411	STANLEY	Mary	88	Cock Lane	Head	Widow	58	F	Straw Plaiter	Herts	Wheathampstead
1412	STANLEY	Emma	88		Dau	Unm	18	F	Straw Plaiter	Herts	St Peters
1413	STANLEY	Hannah	88		Dau	Unm	14	F	Straw Plaiter	Herts	St Peters
1414	GEORGE	William	88		Head	Unm	20	M	Brewery Man	Herts	St Albans
1415	HORWOOD	Henry	89	Cock Lane	Head	Widower	52	M	Fishmonger	Bucks	Buckland
1416	BOWATER	Susannah	89		Head	Widow	81	F	Farmers Daughter	Northants	Weslay Lodge
1417	SANDERS	James	90	Cock Lane	Head	Mar	50	M	Brewers Man	Herts	St Albans
1418	SANDERS	Charlotte	90		Wife	Mar	51	F	Washerwoman	Beds	Luton
1419	SANDERS	Elizabeth	90		Dau	Unm	19	F	Silkwinder	Herts	St Peters
1420	SANDERS	Sarah	90		Dau	Unm	17	F	Silkwinder	Herts	St Peters
1421	SANDERS	Thomas	90		Son		12	M	Silkwinder	Herts	St Peters

	SURNAME	FORENAME	SCHEDULE NUMBER	ADDRESS	RELATIONSHIP	STATUS	AGE	SEX	OCCUPATION	COUNTY OF BIRTH	PLACE OF BIRTH
1422	SANDERS	William	90		Son		10	M	Silkwinder	Herts	St Peters
1423	ROBERSON	Henry	90		Visitor	Unm	20	M	Silkwinder		[Unknown]
1424	ELLINGHAM	Thomas	91	Cock Lane	Head	Unm	21	M	Straw Trimming Weaver	Herts	St Albans
1425	ELLINGHAM	Sarah	91		Dau	Unm	23	F	Straw Trimming Weaver	Herts	St Albans
1426	FENSON	William	92	Cock Lane	Head	Mar	34	M	Brewers Man	Herts	Kimpton
1427	FENSON	Harriet	92		Wife	Mar	27	F	Wife	Herts	Kimpton
1428	FENSON	Emily	92		Dau		1	F		Herts	Kimpton
1429	SLOUGH	Isaac	93	Cock Lane	Head	Mar	49	M	Works Brickmaker	Herts	Harpenden
1430	SLOUGH	Ann	93		Wife	Mar	48	F	Straw Hat Maker		[Unknown]
1431	SLOUGH	Mary	93		Dau	Unm	24	F	Straw Hat Maker	Herts	St Albans
1432	SLOUGH	Joseph	93		Son	Unm	22	M	Labourer	Herts	St Albans
1433	SLOUGH	Julia	93		Dau	Unm	20	F	Straw Hat Maker	Herts	Redbourn
1434	SLOUGH	Rebecca	93		Dau	Unm	18	F	Straw Hat Maker	Herts	Redbourn
1435	SLOUGH	George	93		Son	Unm	10	M	Straw Hat Maker	Herts	St Peters
1436	SLOUGH	Jesse	93		Son		6	M		Herts	St Peters
1437	PARKINS	John	94	Cock Lane	Head	Mar	44	M	Sawyer	Herts	St Albans
1438	PARKINS	Sarah	94		Wife	Mar	42	F	Bonnet Sewer	Herts	St Albans
1439	PARKINS	Joseph	94		Son		12	M	Errand Boy	Herts	St Albans
1440	PARKINS	Mary A	94		Dau		10	F	Brazilian Hat Maker	Herts	St Albans
1441	PARKINS	Alfred	94		Son		7	M	Scholar	Herts	St Albans
1442	PARKINS	Edward	94		Son		6	M	Scholar	Herts	St Albans
1443	PARKINS	Elizabeth	94		Dau		3	F		Herts	St Albans
1444	BEAN	Mary	94		Mother-in-law	Widow	69	F	Late Bonnet Sewer	Herts	St Albans
1445	HUNT	Susan	95	Cock Lane	Head	Unm	23	F	Dressmaker	Herts	Harpenden
1446	BALDWIN	Hannah	95		Visitor	Unm	20	F	Trimming Weaver	Herts	St Michaels
1447	BALDWIN	Georgiana	95		Visitors Dau		7m	F		Herts	St Albans
1448	HULKS	Eliza	96	St Peters Street	Head	Unm	19	F	Grocer	Herts	St Albans
1449	HULKS	Ruth	96		Sister	Unm	17	F		Herts	St Albans
1450	HULKS	Charlotte	96		Sister	Unm	13	F	Scholar	Herts	St Albans
1451	MAIN	Mary	96	St Peters Street	Head	Widow	68	F	Needle Woman	Herts	St Albans
1452	MAIN	Emma	96		Dau	Unm	32	F	Bonnet Maker	Herts	St Albans
1453	WALKER	Samuel	97	St Peters Street	Head	Mar	52	M	Coach Trimmer	Staffs	Lichfield
1454	WALKER	Ann	97		Wife	Mar	53	F		Herts	St Albans
1455	SEARS	John	97	St Peters Street	[Head]	Mar	60	M	Gardener	Bucks	Ivinghoe
1456	SWIFT	George	98	St Peters Street	Head	Mar	38	M	Tailor	Yorks	Doncaster
1457	SWIFT	Maria	98		Wife	Mar	36	F		Herts	St Albans
1458	ARCHER	Charles	98		Nephew		9	M	Scholar	Herts	St Albans
1459	PAGE	William	99	St Peters Street	Head	Mar	38	M	Blacksmith employs 2 men	Herts	Datchworth
1460	PAGE	Mary	99		Wife	Mar	38	F		Beds	Toddington
1461	DOWNING	Elizabeth	99		Step-dau	Unm	14	F	Dressmakers Apprentice	Herts	St Albans
1462	DOWNING	Sarah A	99		Step-dau	Unm	12	F	Apprentice Bonnet Sewer	Herts	St Albans
1463	PAGE	George W	99		Son		5	M		Herts	St Albans
1464	PAGE	William	99		Son		2	M		Herts	St Albans

1465	PAGE	Emily	99		Dau		7m	F		Herts	St Albans
1466	CURRELL	Thomas	100	St Peters Street	Head	Widower	32	M	Labourer	Herts	Gustardwood [Wheathampstead]
1467	AUSTIN	Joseph	101	St Peters Street	Head	Mar	69	M	Blacksmith	Herts	St Albans
1468	AUSTIN	Eliza	101		Wife	Mar	68	F		Middx [Herts]	Totteridge
1469	HARCOURT	Thomas	102	St Peters Street	Head	Widower	69	M	Miller & Engineer employs 2 men	Worcs	Abberley [?]
1470	WHARTON	Ann	102		Niece	Unm	44	F	Housekeeper	Hereford	Kingsland
1471	HALE	William	103	St Peters Street	Head	Mar	48	M	Proprietor Of Houses	Herts	St Albans
1472	HALE	Mary A	103		Wife	Mar	42	F		London	
1473	PARKINS	George	104	St Peters Street	Head	Mar	27	M	Boot & Shoemaker	Herts	Wheathampstead
1474	PARKINS	Martha	104		Wife	Mar	26	F		Herts	St Albans
1475	PARKINS	Ann	104		Dau	Unm	2	F		Herts	St Albans
1476	PARKINS	Frederick	104		Son	Unm	1	M		Herts	St Albans
1477	BURGOINE	Lucy	104		Visitor	Unm	14	F	Straw Hat Maker	Herts	Wheathampstead
1478	FOWLER	Joseph	105	Church Green	Head	Mar	35	M	Journeyman Bricklayer	Herts	St Albans
1479	FOWLER	Amelia	105		Wife	Mar	28	F		Herts	St Albans
1480	FOWLER	Ellen	105		Dau		9	F		Herts	St Albans
1481	FOWLER	Charles	105		Son		7	M		Herts	St Albans
1482	FOWLER	Elizabeth	105		Dau		6	F		Herts	St Albans
1483	FOWLER	Emma	105		Dau		4	F		Herts	St Albans
1484	FOWLER	Amelia	105		Dau		2	F		Herts	St Albans
1485	FOWLER	Sarah	105		Dau		1	F		Herts	St Albans
1486	BRACEY	James	105		Lodger	[blank]	22	M	Labourer	Herts	St Albans
1487	PULMAN	Joseph	105		Lodger	[blank]	50	M	Gardener	Herts	St Albans
1488	EVANS	Elizabeth	106	Church Green	Head	Mar	63	F	Laundress	Middx	Tottenham
1489	EVANS	Eliza	106		Dau	Unm	18	F	Laundress	Herts	St Peters
1490	EVANS	Anne	106		Dau	Unm	12	F		Herts	St Peters
1491	GEORGE	William	106	Church Green	Head	Unm	19	M	Bricklayers Labourer	Herts	Kimpton
1492	HONER [?]	James H	106	Church Green	Head	Unm	22	M	Agric Lab	Herts	St Peters
1493	MUNNINGS	Hannah	107	Church Green	Head	Widow	63	F	Laundress	Herts	St Peters
1494	WHITE	Thomas	108	Church Green	Head	Mar	39	M	Labourer	Herts	St Albans
1495	WHITE	Eliza	108		Wife	Mar	42	F		Herts	Wheathampstead
1496	PAYNE	John	109	Church Green	Head	Mar	50	M	Sexton	Herts	St Albans
1497	PAYNE	Dinah	109		Wife	Mar	51	F		Warks	Warwick
1498	PAYNE	William	109		Son	Unm	29	M	Labourer	Herts	St Albans
1499	PAYNE	Eliza	109		Dau	Unm	20	F	Bonnet Sewer	Herts	St Albans
1500	PAYNE	Charles	109		Grandson		9	M	Scholar	Herts	St Albans
1501	PAYNE	Abel	109		Grandson		4	M		Herts	St Albans
1502	COE	Philip	110	Church Green	Head	Mar	46	M	Gardener	Norfolk	Dereham
1503	COE	Sarah	110		Wife	Mar	44	F	Pew Opener	Herts	St Albans
1504	COE	Louisa	110		Dau	Unm	16	F	Pew Opener	Herts	St Albans
1505	AGGELTON	Mary	110		Lodger	Unm	56	F	Nurse	Herts	St Albans
1506	RUFFETT [RUSSELL?]	Thomas	111	Church Green	Head	Mar	44	M	Coal Dealer	Beds	Woburn
1507	RUFFETT [RUSSELL?]	Margaret	111		Wife	Mar	42	F	Laundress	Unknown	

	SURNAME	FORENAME	SCHEDULE NUMBER	ADDRESS	RELATIONSHIP	STATUS	AGE	SEX	OCCUPATION	COUNTY OF BIRTH	PLACE OF BIRTH
1508	RUFFETT [RUSSELL?]	John	111		Son	Unm	20	M	Grocers Shopman	Herts	St Peters
1509	RUFFETT [RUSSELL?]	George	111		Son	Unm	17	M	Carman	Herts	St Peters
1510	HENSLOW	John Prentis	112	Bowgate	Head	Mar	80	M	Retired Solicitor & Merchant	Hants	Portsea
1511	HENSLOW	Frances	112		Wife	Mar	76	F	Wife	Kent	Rochester
1512	HENSLOW	Ann F	112		Dau	Unm	51	F		Kent	Rochester
1513	HENSLOW	Charlotte	112		Dau	Unm	44	F		Kent	Rochester
1514	HENSLOW	Eleanor	112		Dau	Unm	42	F		Kent	Rochester
1515	HENSLOW	Louisa	112		Dau	Unm	39	F		Kent	Rochester
1516	WIMBUSH	Elizabeth	112		Serv	Unm	40	F		Herts	Berkhamsted
1517	CHAPMAN	Ann	112		Serv	Unm	33	F		Herts	Hertford
1518	SCHOOLING	Martha	112		Serv	Unm	25	F		Herts	Little Hadham
1519	BRABANT	Richard W	113	Bowgate	Head	Mar	61	M	Attorney not Practising	London	
1520	BRABANT	Ann	113		Wife	Mar	60	F		Herts	St Stephens
1521	BRABANT	Emma	113		Dau	Unm	31	F	Portrait Painter	Middx	London
1522	BRABANT	Jane	113		Dau	Unm	30	F	Governess	Herts	St Albans
1523	BRABANT	Henry	113		Son	Unm	27	M	Solicitors General Clerk	Herts	St Albans
1524	BRABANT	Mary	113		Sister	Unm	75	F	Fundholder	Middx	London
1525	SAYER	Ann	113		Niece	Unm	50	F	Fundholder	Herts	St Albans
1526	WALKLATE	Rebecca	113		Serv	Unm	23	F	General Servant	Herts	St Albans
1527	BROWN	William C	114	Bowgate	Head	Unm	42	M	Farmer of 215 acres employing 8 men	Herts	St Albans
1528	BROWN	Thomas H	114		Brother	Unm	34	M	Partner	Herts	St Albans
1529	MUCKLE	Eliza	114		Serv	Unm	36	F	General Servant	Herts	St Stephens
1530	EAMES	Jeffrey	114		Serv	Widower	55	M	Farm Servant	Beds	Houghton Regis
1531	ANDERSON	John	114		Serv	Unm	22	M	Farm Servant	Herts	St Peters
1532	HAWKINS	William	114		Serv	Unm	15	M	Farm Servant	Herts	St Stephens
1533	PACKMAN	William	115		Head	Widower	59	M	Proprietor of Houses	Herts	Northaw
1534	RISELY [?]	Susannah I	115		Niece	Unm	25	F	Proprietor of Houses	Essex	Plaistow
1535	SMITH	Philadelpha	115		Visitor	Mar	46	F	Servant	Herts	St Peters
1536	NICHOLLS	Isaac	116	Snatchup Alley	Head	Mar	57	M	Town Blacksmith & Beerseller	Herts	Sandridge
1537	NICHOLLS	Maria	116		Wife	Mar	48	F		Middx	London
1538	PALMER	Aubrey	116		Step-son		13	M	Town Blacksmith	Herts	St Albans
1539	TURLEY	Emma	116		Guest	Mar	25	F	Wife of a Painter	Middx	London
1540	TURLEY	Alfred	116		Guest	Unm	1	M	Son of Painter	Middx	London
1541	BAMFIELD	James	117	Snatchup Alley	Head	Mar	43	M	Labourer	Essex	Unknown
1542	BAMFIELD	Anne	117		Wife	Mar	42	F	Hat Worker	Herts	Kings Walden
1543	BAMFIELD	Betsy	117		Dau	Unm	12	F	Hat Worker	Herts	St Albans
1544	BAMFIELD	George	117		Son	Unm	7	M	Scholar	Herts	St Albans
1545	BAMFIELD	Emma	117		Dau	Unm	4	F		Herts	St Albans
1546	BAMFIELD	Frederick	117		Son	Unm	2	M		Herts	St Albans

Uninhabited

	SURNAME	FORENAME	SCHEDULE NUMBER	ADDRESS	RELATIONSHIP	STATUS	AGE	SEX	OCCUPATION	COUNTY OF BIRTH	PLACE OF BIRTH
1547	CRAWLEY	George	118	Snatchup Alley	Head	Mar	44	M	Labourer	Herts	St Albans
1548	CRAWLEY	Ann	118		Wife	Mar	40	F		Beds	Barton in [the] Clay
1549	CRAWLEY	George	118		Son	Unm	22	M	Labourer	Herts	St Albans

1550	CRAWLEY	William	118		Son	Unm	18	M	Straw Weaver	Herts	St Peters
1551	CAWDLE	William	118	Snatchup Alley	Head	Mar	31	M	Bricklayers Labourer	Herts	St Albans
1552	CAWDLE	Ann	118		Wife	Mar	26	F	Plaiter Of Straw	Herts	St Albans
1553	CAWDLE	Mary A	118		Dau	Unm	1	F		Herts	St Albans
1554	CAWDLE	William	118		Son	Unm	3	M		Herts	St Albans
1555	RADLETT	Thomas	118		Visitor	Unm	1	M		Herts	St Albans
1556	WARNER	Daniel	119	Snatchup Alley	Head	Mar	55	M	Labourer	Herts	Bennington
1557	WARNER	Charlotte	119		Wife	Mar	44	F	Plaiter	Herts	Wheathampstead
1558	WARNER	Maria	119		Dau	Unm	18	F	Straw Hat Worker	Herts	Hatfield
1559	WARNER	Dinah	119		Dau	Unm	13	F	Silkwinder	Herts	Wheathampstead
1560	WARNER	Emma	119		Dau	Unm	12	F	Straw Hat Worker	Herts	Wheathampstead
1561	WARNER	Elizabeth	119		Dau	Unm	9	F	Silkwinder	Herts	Wheathampstead
1562	WARNER	Thomas	119		Son	Unm	7	M	Scholar	Herts	Sandridge
1563	WARNER	Daniel	119		Son	Unm	3	M		Herts	Sandridge
1564	HEDGES	William	120	Snatchup Alley	Head	Mar	45	M	Hawker Of Small Wares	Herts	Sandridge
1565	HEDGES	Eliza	120		Wife	Mar	40	F	Plaiter	Herts	St Albans
1566	HEDGES	James	120		Son		14	M	Silkwinder	Herts	St Albans
1567	HEDGES	Eliza	120		Dau		4	F		Herts	St Albans
1568	KILBY	John	121	Snatchup Alley	Head	Mar	50	M	Publican	Herts	Smallford
1569	KILBY	Mary	121		Wife	Mar	46	F		Herts	Hexton
1570	KILBY	George	121		Son		12	M		Herts	St Albans
1571	KILBY	William	121		Son		10	M	Scholar	Herts	St Albans
1572	KILBY	Samuel	121		Son		8	M		Herts	St Albans
1573	DAWS	Thomas	121		Lodger		45	M	Agric Lab	Herts	Kings Walden
1574	CARTER	James	121		Lodger		19	M	Labourer	Herts	St Albans
1575	DOGGETT	Frederick	122	Snatchup Alley	Head	Mar	26	M	Journeyman, Bricklayer	Herts	St Albans
1576	DOGGETT	Elizabeth	122		Wife	Mar	31	F	Strawplaiter	Herts	Great Gaddesden
1577	DOGGETT	Edwin	122		Son		6	M	Scholar	Herts	Harpenden
1578	DOGGETT	Emily	122		Dau		3	F		Herts	St Michaels
1579	DOGGETT	Elizabeth	122		Dau		3m	F		Herts	St Albans
1580	HARCOURT	William	123	Snatchup Alley	Head	Mar	79	M	Agric Lab	Beds	Luton
1581	HARCOURT	Mary	123		Wife	Mar	79	F		Herts	St Albans
1582	MUNT	John	124	Snatchup Alley	Head	Mar	52	M	Labourer	Herts	St Albans
1583	MUNT	Rhoda	124		Wife	Mar	41	F		Beds	Bedford
1584	MUNT	William	124		Son	Unm	19	M	Labourer	Herts	St Albans
1585	MUNT	Frederick	124		Son	Unm	15	M	Silkwinder	Herts	St Albans
1586	MUNT	Sarah	124		Dau	Unm	14	F	Silkwinder	Herts	St Albans
1587	MUNT	Charles	124		Son		11	M	Silkwinder	Herts	St Albans
1588	MUNT	Abel	124		Son		9	M	Silkwinder	Herts	St Albans
1589	MUNT	John	124		Son		6	M	Scholar	Herts	St Albans
1590	MUNT	Emma	124		Dau		4	F	Scholar	Herts	St Albans
1591	MUNT	Thomas	124		Son		3	M	Scholar	Herts	St Albans
1592	HEDGES	Hannah	125	Snatchup Alley	Head	Widow	76	F	Pauper (Plaiter)	Herts	Sandridge
1593	FITZJOHN	Sarah	125		Sister	Unm	64	F	Pauper (Plaiter)	Herts	Sandridge

	SURNAME	FORENAME	SCHEDULE NUMBER	ADDRESS	RELATIONSHIP	STATUS	AGE	SEX	OCCUPATION	COUNTY OF BIRTH	PLACE OF BIRTH
1594	GROOM	Daniel	126	Snatchup Alley	Head	Mar	60	M	Agric Lab	Herts	Hitchin
1595	GROOM	Hannah	126		Wife	Mar	55	F		Herts	Hitchin
1596	GROOM	William	126		Son	Unm	15	M	Agric Lab	Herts	St Peter
1597	GROOM	Frederick	126		Son	Unm	21	M	Agric Lab	Herts	St Peter
1598	DELL	Henry	126	Snatch Alley	Head	Mar	28	M	Works Brickmaker	Bucks	West Wickham
1599	DELL	Eliza	126		Wife	Mar	26	F	Straw Hat Worker	Herts	St Peters
1600	DELL	Jane	126		Dau		5	F		Herts	St Peters
1601	DELL	Harriet	126		Dau		3	F		Herts	Ware
1602	DELL	William	126		Son		9m	M		Herts	Bell Bar, North Mimms
1603	BOURNE	Sophy	127	Snatch Alley	Head	Widow	73	F		Herts	St Peters
1604	BURGOINE	Joseph	128	Snatch Alley	Head	Mar	35	M	Agric Lab	Herts	Wheathampstead
1605	BURGOINE	Sarah	128		Wife	Mar	30	F		Herts	St Peters
1606	BURGOINE	Jesse	128		Son		10	M	Agric Lab	Herts	St Peters
1607	BURGOINE	John	128		Son		6	M		Herts	St Peters
1608	BURGOINE	Ann	128		Dau		4m	F		Herts	St Peters
1609	SWAIN	Stephen	129	Snatch Alley	Head	Mar	26	M	Brewers Man	Herts	Sandridge
1610	SWAIN	Elizabeth	129		Wife	Mar	28	F		Scotland	Unknown
1611	MCKINLEY	Elizabeth	129		Dau		9	F		Herts	Watford
1612	SWAIN	John	129		Son		2	M		Herts	St Albans
1613	SWAIN	Rose	129		Dau		10m	F		Herts	St Albans
1614	BIGGS	James	130	Snatch Alley	Head	Mar	45	M	Works Bricklayer	Herts	Sandridge
1615	BIGGS	Eliza Ann	130		Wife	Mar	52	F	Schoolmistress	London	
1616	LEWIS	Henry	131	Snatch Alley	Head	Mar	50	M	Agric Lab	Herts	Sandridge
1617	LEWIS	Mary	131		Dau	Unm	29	F	Straw Hat Maker	Herts	St Stephens
1618	LEWIS	Emily	131		Grandau		11	F	Straw Hat Maker	Herts	St Peters
1619	FINDELL	William	132	Snatch Alley	Head	Mar	42	M	Brickmaker	Herts	Harpenden
1620	FINDELL	Ann	132		Wife	Mar	39	F		Herts	Hitchin
1621	FINDELL	Alfred	132		Son	Unm	17	M		Herts	St Peters
1622	FINDELL	Ebenezer	132		Son		15	M		Herts	St Peters
1623	FINDELL	Edwin	132		Son		12	M		Herts	St Peters
1624	FINDELL	James	132		Son		9	M		Herts	St Peters
1625	FINDELL	Sarah	132		Dau		4	F		Herts	St Peters
1626	FINDELL	John	132		Son		1	M		Herts	St Peters
1627	FINDELL	Mary A	132		Sister		37	F		Herts	Harpenden
1628	LORANCE	William	133	Snatch Alley	Head	Mar	36	M	Labourer	Herts	St Peters
1629	LORANCE	Jane	133		Wife	Mar	29	F	Straw Hat Maker	Herts	St Peters
1630	BRACKLEY	Caroline	133		Sister	Unm	23	F	Straw Hat Maker	Herts	St Peters
1631	LARGE	Susan	134	Snatch Alley	Head	Unm	52	F	Nurse	Herts	St Albans
1632	SEARS	Reuben	134		Nephew	Unm	19	M	Outdoor Servant	Herts	St Albans
1633	SMART	William	135	Snatch Alley	Head	Mar	42	M	Labourer	Herts	St Peters
1634	SMART	Elizabeth	135		Wife	Mar	55	F	Straw Worker	Herts	St Peters
1635	LAURENCE	James	135		Grandson		6	M		Herts	St Peters
1636	FINDELL	William	136	Snatch Alley	Head	Mar	63	M	Labourer	Herts	[Unknown]
1637	FINDELL	Mary	136		Wife	Mar	53	F	Straw Worker	Herts	St Stephens

1638	CARTER	Elizabeth	137	Snatch Alley	Head	Widow	55	F	Straw Worker	[Unknown]	
1639	CARTER	Sarah	137		Dau	Unm	28	F	Straw Worker	[Unknown]	
1640	CARTER	Elizabeth	137		Dau	Unm	26	F	Straw Worker	[Unknown]	
1641	CARTER	Harriet	137		Dau	Unm	20	F	Straw Worker	[Unknown]	
1642	CARTER	Henry	137		Son	Unm	17	M	Straw Worker	[Unknown]	
1643	CARTER	George	137		Son	Unm	14	M	Straw Worker	[Unknown]	
1644	BOURNE	Samuel	138	Snatch Alley	Head	Mar	31	M	Labourer	Herts	St Peters
1645	BOURNE	Elizabeth	138		Wife	Mar	33	F	Straw Worker	Herts	St Michaels
1646	BOURNE	Sophia	138		Dau		11	F	Straw Worker	Herts	St Peters
1647	BOURNE	Eliza	138		Dau		9	F		Herts	St Peters
1648	BOURNE	George	138		Son		7	M		Herts	St Peters
1649	BOURNE	Sarah	138		Dau		5	F		Herts	St Peters
1650	BOURNE	John	138		Son		3	M		Herts	St Peters
1651	BOURNE	Jane	138		Dau		1	F		Herts	St Peters
1652	BOURNE	Joseph	138		Son		2m	M		Herts	St Peters
1653	CROUCH	John	139	Snatch Alley	Head	Mar	43	M	Labourer	Herts	St Peters
1654	CROUCH	Susan	139		Wife	Mar	42	F		Herts	St Michaels
1655	CROUCH	James	139		Son	Unm	19	M	Labourer	Herts	St Peters
1656	CROUCH	Ann	139		Dau	Unm	17	F	Straw Hat Maker	Herts	St Peters
1657	CROUCH	Emma	139		Dau		15	F	Straw Hat Maker	Herts	St Peters
1658	CROUCH	William	139		Son		11	M	Straw Hat Maker	Herts	St Peters
1659	CROUCH	Samuel	139		Son		7	M		Herts	St Peters
1660	CROUCH	Fanny	139		Dau		5	F		Herts	St Peters
1661	CROUCH	George	139		Son		3	M		Herts	St Peters
1662	CROUCH	Lydia	139		Dau		1	F		Herts	St Peters

Registrar's District: St Albans   **Enumeration District 1c**   Ref. HO 107/1713 folios 280-307

The part east of St Albans Parish and south west of the road from St Albans to Barnet including Key Field, Hare and Hounds public house, Green School and adjoining houses.

1663	HARDWICKE	Frances	1	London Road	Head	Widow	47	F		Beds	Luton
1664	HARDWICKE	Fanny	1		Dau	Unm	26	F	Bonnet Sewer	Herts	St Albans
1665	HARDWICKE	Henry	1		Son	Unm	20	M	Bonnet Trimming Weaver	Herts	St Albans
1666	DENNIS	Thomas	2	London Road	Head	Mar	61	M	Labourer	Herts	Wheathampstead
1667	DENNIS	Elizabeth	2		Wife	Mar	60	F	Shop Keeper	Herts	South Mimms
1668	RIDDLE	Emma	3	London Road	Wife	Mar	28	F	Weaver	Herts	St Peters
1669	RIDDLE	Jeanet	3		Son	Unm	8	M	Weaver	Herts	St Peters
1670	RIDDLE	James	3		Son	Unm	7	M		Herts	St Peters
1671	RIDDLE	Fergus	3		Son	Unm	9	M		Herts	St Peters
1672	AVIS	Charlotte	3		Lodger	Widow	64	F	Char Woman	Herts	Codicote
1673	NORWOOD	Mary	3		Lodger	Unm	36	F	Weaver	Herts	St Peters
1674	NORWOOD	Maria	3		Lodger	Unm	32	F	Weaver	Herts	St Peters
1675	WILSON	Isabella	3		Lodger	Unm	20	F	Weaver	Herts	St Peters

	SURNAME	FORENAME	SCHEDULE NUMBER	ADDRESS	RELATIONSHIP	STATUS	AGE	SEX	OCCUPATION	COUNTY OF BIRTH	PLACE OF BIRTH
1676	HEWITT	William	4	London Road	Head	Mar	50	M	Labourer	Berks	[Unknown]
1677	HEWITT	Elizabeth	4		Wife	Mar	51	F	Brazilian Hat Maker	Beds	Sandy
1678	HEWITT	Jemima	4		Dau	Unm	23	F	Brazilian Hat Maker	Herts	St Peters
1679	HEWITT	John	4		Son	Unm	17	M	Silk Throwster	Herts	St Stephens
1680	HEWITT	Elizabeth	4		Dau	Unm	12	F	Brazilian Hat Maker	Herts	St Peters
1681	PARROTT	Ann	4		Visitor	Unm	25	F	Canvas Weaver	Herts	Hatfield
1682	BATCHELOR	Richard	5	London Road	Head	Mar	41	M	Baker	Bucks	Hammersham [Amersham]
1683	BATCHELOR	Harriet	5		Wife	Mar	46	F		Wilts	Wroughton
1684	BATCHELOR	James	5		Son	Unm	13	M		Herts	St Peters
1685	BATCHELOR	Richard	5		Son	Unm	12	M		Herts	St Peters
1686	BATCHELOR	Susannah	5		Dau	Unm	9	F		Herts	St Peters
1687	BATCHELOR	John	5		Son	Unm	7	M		Herts	St Peters
1688	HARTWELL	John	6	London Road	Head	Mar	42	M	Carpenter & Joiner	Herts	St Albans
1689	HARTWELL	Maria	6		Wife	Mar	40	F		Herts	Shenley
1690	HARTWELL	Louisa	6		Dau	Unm	17	F	Bonnet Sewer	Herts	St Peters
1691	HARTWELL	James	6		Son	Unm	15	M		Herts	St Peters
1692	HARTWELL	George	6		Son	Unm	10	M		Herts	St Peters
1693	HARTWELL	Maria	6		Dau	Unm	8	F		Herts	St Peters
1694	HARTWELL	Ellen	6		Dau	Unm	1	F		Herts	St Peters
	[missed out]		7								
1695	HOWARD	Jane	8	London Road	Wife	Mar	30	F	Beer Shop Keeper	Middx	[Unknown]
1696	HOWARD	Joseph	8		Son	Unm	12	M		Herts	St Peters
1697	HOWARD	Charles	8		Son	Unm	9	M		Herts	St Peters
1698	HOWARD	Mary Ann	8		Dau	Unm	5	F	At Home	Herts	St Peters
1699	HOWARD	Sarah	8		Dau	Unm	4	F	At Home	Herts	St Peters
1700	HOWARD	Emily	8		Dau	Unm	3	F	At Home	Herts	St Peters
1701	HOWARD	Elizabeth	8		Dau	Unm	2	F	At Home	Herts	St Peters
1702	HOWARD	Tom	8		Son	Unm	1	M	At Home	Herts	St Peters
1703	WATSON	John	9	London Road	Head	Mar	27	M	Nurseryman	Herts	St Albans
1704	WATSON	Elizabeth	9		Wife	Mar	32	F		Herts	St Peters
1705	WATSON	John A.	9		Son		7	M	At Home	Herts	St Albans
1706	WATSON	Jane E.	9		Dau		5	F	At Home	Herts	St Albans
1707	FREEMAN	George	9		Appr	Unm	17	M	Apprentice	Herts	Harpenden
1708	HAYWARD	Thomas	10	London Road	Head	Unm	76	M	Independent	Middx	St Georges, Hanover Square
1709	HEELES	Elizabeth	10		Serv	Unm	37	F	Servant	Herts	St Albans
1710	KEIGHTLEY	Jane	11	London Road	Head	Unm	33	F	Brazilian Hat Manufacturer	Bucks	Newport Pagnell
1711	KEIGHTLEY	Charles	11		Father	Mar	75	M	Ostler	Bucks	Newport Pagnell
1712	KEIGHTLEY	Hannah	11		Mother	Mar	70	F		Beds	Leagrave
1713	KEIGHTLEY	Eliza	11		Niece	Unm	14	F	Dressmaker	Herts	St Albans
1714	DUMPLETON	Emma	11		Cousin	Unm	25	F		Beds	Woburn
1715	MEAD	Joseph	12	London Road	Head	Mar	40	M	Master Carpenter employing 3 Men	Bucks	Newport Pagnell
1716	MEAD	Hannah	12		Wife	Mar	41	F		Leics	[Unknown]
1717	MEAD	Edward	12		Son	Unm	8	M	Scholar	Herts	St Albans

1718	MEAD	Arthur	12		Son	Unm	10 m	M	At Home	Herts	St Albans
1719	HALE	William	13	London Road	Head	Mar	52	M	Farrier	Herts	Hertford
1720	HALE	Elizabeth	13		Wife	Mar	50	F		Middx	Cowley
1721	HALE	George	13		Son	Unm	18	M	Farrier	Herts	St Albans
1722	HALE	Mary	13		Dau	Unm	16	F	At Home	Herts	St Albans
1723	ASHWELL	William	14	Watsons Row	Head	Mar	23	M	Silk Throwster	Herts	St Peters
1724	ASHWELL	Elizabeth	14		Wife	Mar	24	F	Cook	Norfolk	[Unknown]
1725	KENTISH	William	15	Watsons Row	Head	Mar	66	M	Gardener	Herts	St Michaels
1726	KENTISH	Sarah	15		Wife	Mar	61	F		Herts	Cheshunt
1727	KENTISH	Edward	15		Son	Unm	24	M	Bonnet Trimming Weaver	Herts	St Albans
1728	BURNE	William	15		Lodger	Unm	21	M	Bonnet Trimming Weaver	Suffolk	[Unknown]
1729	FRANCIS	Thomas	16	Watsons Row	Head	Mar	23	M	Farrier	Middx	Chiswick
1730	FRANCIS	Ellen	16		Wife	Mar	27	F		Middx	St Marylebone
1731	UNWIN	Charles T.	16		Lodger	Unm	28	M	Farrier	Essex	Lawford
1732	GRIFFIN	Martha	17	Watsons Row	Head	Unm	37	F	Dressmaker	Herts	St Albans
1733	RAKE	William	18	Watsons Row	Head	Mar	62	M	Formerly a Farmer	Somerset	Yeovil
1734	RAKE	Ann	18		Wife	Mar	57	F		Dorset	Weymouth
1735	RAKE	Esther	18		Dau	Unm	21	F	Dressmaker	Somerset	Stapleton
1736	RAKE	Ellen	18		Dau	Unm	16	F		Somerset	Stapleton
Empty			19								
1737	JONES	William	20	Watsons Row	Head	Mar	38	M	Primitive Methodist Minister	Berks	Aston
1738	JONES	Eliza	20		Wife	Mar	28	F		Herts	Hertford
1739	JONES	Emily	20		Dau	Unm	4	F	At Home	Hants	Portsmouth
1740	JONES	William	20		Son	Unm	3	M	At Home	Kent	Canterbury
1741	JONES	Fanny	20		Dau	Unm	1	F	At Home	Herts	St Albans
1742	BURRIDGE	Edward	21	Watsons Row	Head	Mar	22	M	Bricklayer	Herts	St Albans
1743	BURRIDGE	Eliza	21		Wife	Mar	23	F	Bonnet Trimming Weaver	Herts	Gaddesden Row, Hemel Hempstead
1744	BURRIDGE	Horace W.	21		Son	Unm	1 m	M	At Home	Herts	St Albans
1745	MACKEY	Francis	22	Watsons Row	Head	Mar	39	M	Straw Plait Manufacturer	Ireland	Armagh
1746	MACKEY	Ellen	22		Wife	Mar	30	F	Straw Plait Manufacturer	Beds	Luton
1747	MACKEY	Ellen	22		Dau	Unm	9	F	Scholar	Beds	Luton
1748	MACKEY	Peter	22		Son	Unm	7	M	Scholar	Beds	Luton
1749	MACKEY	James	22		Son	Unm	5	M	Scholar	Beds	Luton
1750	MACKEY	William	22		Son	Unm	2	M	At Home	Herts	St Albans
1751	MACKEY	Frances	22		Dau	Unm	6 m	F	At Home	Herts	St Albans
1752	FRENCH	Mary	22		Appr	Unm	26	F	Straw Bonnet Maker	Leics	Foxton
1753	WHITEHOUSE	William	23	Watsons Row (Part of house)	Head	Mar	33	M	Cordwainer	Herts	Hertford
1754	WHITEHOUSE	Ann	23		Wife	Mar	30	F	Shoe Binder	Herts	St Albans
1755	WHITEHOUSE	Thomas	23		Son	Unm	3	M	At Home	Herts	St Albans
1756	AMSDEN	Alfred	24	Watsons Row	Head	Mar	26	M	Straw Hat Manufacturer	Herts	Tring
1757	AMSDEN	Martha	24		Wife	Mar	32	F	Straw Hat Manufacturer	Herts	St Albans
1758	AMSDEN	Frederick	24		Son	Unm	2	M	At Home	Herts	St Albans

	SURNAME	FORENAME	SCHEDULE NUMBER	ADDRESS	RELATIONSHIP	STATUS	AGE	SEX	OCCUPATION	COUNTY OF BIRTH	PLACE OF BIRTH
1759	RICHARDSON	Eliza	24		Serv	Unm	22	F	Servant	Middx	Holloway
1760	WARREN	John	25	London Road	Head	Mar	39	M	Miller	Herts	Wheathampstead
1761	WARREN	Elizabeth	25		Wife	Mar	39	F	Plaiter	Herts	Harpenden
1762	WARREN	Alfred	25		Son	Unm	12	M	Scholar	Herts	Wheathampstead
1763	WARREN	Mary Ann	25		Dau	Unm	9	F	Scholar	Herts	Harpenden
1764	WARREN	Emily	25		Dau	Unm	7	F	Scholar	Herts	Harpenden
1765	WARREN	Elizabeth	25		Dau	Unm	5	F	At Home	Herts	St Stephens
1766	WARREN	Jane	25		Dau	Unm	3	F	At Home	Herts	St Peters
1767	WARREN	George	25		Son	Unm	9m	M	At Home	Herts	St Peters
1768	SEABROOK	Rebecca	25		Mother-in-law	Widow	72	F	Plaiter	Herts	St Peters
1769	PUDDEPHATT	Samuel	26	London Road	Head	Mar	72	M	Labourer	Bucks	Ellesborough
1770	PUDDEPHATT	Maria	26		Wife	Mar	73	F		Herts	Redbourn
1771	PUDDEPHATT	Elizabeth	26		Dau	Unm	32	F	Plaiter	Herts	Redbourn
1772	FLETCHER	Elizabeth	26		Grandau	Unm	13	F	Plaiter	Herts	Redbourn
1773	JACKSON	Elizabeth	27	London Road	Head	Widow	76	F	Laundress	Kent	Dartford
1774	BAKER	Mary	27		Lodger	Widow	30	F	Bonnet Sewer	Herts	St Peters
1775	BAKER	George	27		Lodgers Son		8	M	Scholar	Herts	Wheathampstead
1776	RICHARDSON	Samuel J.	28	London Road	Head	Mar	59	M	Painter	Northants	Peterborough
1777	RICHARDSON	Mary	28		Wife	Mar	49	F		Beds	Luton
1778	RICHARDSON	Ann	28		Dau	Unm	25	F	Plaiter	Herts	St Albans
1779	RICHARDSON	Frederick	28		Son	Unm	21	M	Painter	Herts	St Albans
1780	RICHARDSON	Edward	28		Son	Unm	18	M	Cabinet Maker	Herts	St Albans
1781	RICHARDSON	Susan	28		Dau	Unm	15	F	Plaiter	Herts	St Albans
1782	RICHARDSON	Elizabeth	28		Dau	Unm	13	F	Scholar	Herts	St Albans
1783	RICHARDSON	Maria	28		Dau	Unm	11	F	Scholar	Herts	St Albans
1784	RICHARDSON	Emma	28		Dau	Unm	9	F	Scholar	Herts	St Albans
1785	HALE	James	29	London Road	Head	Mar	60	M	Dealer	Herts	Park Street [St Stephens]
1786	HALE	Ann	29		Wife	Mar	56	F		Herts	Hemel Hempstead
1787	PERRY	Mary Ann	29		Lodger	Unm	8	F	Scholar	Herts	Abbots Langley
1788	MILEMAN	George	29		Lodger		26	M	Labourer	Herts	Park Street [St Stephens]
1789	MEAD	Ellen	30	London Road	Head	Widow	64	F	Annuitant	Bucks	Wovingdon [Wolverton]
1790	MEAD	Sarah	30		Dau	Unm	37	F	Bonnet Sewer	Bucks	Newport Pagnell
1791	MEAD	Ann	30		Dau	Unm	27	F	Dressmaker	Bucks	Newport Pagnell
1792	MEAD	Eliza	30		Dau	Unm	22	F	Bonnet Sewer	Herts	St Albans
1793	HOLLAND	Thomas	31	London Road	Head	Mar	40	M	Bricklayer	Oxon	Thame
1794	HOLLAND	Elizabeth	31		Wife	Mar	40	F		Herts	Sandridge
1795	HOLLAND	Emma	31		Dau	Unm	16	F	Brazilian Hat Maker	Herts	St Stephens
1796	HOLLAND	Frances	31		Dau	Unm	14	F	Brazilian Hat Maker	Herts	St Stephens
1797	HOLLAND	Marcus	31		Son	Unm	13	M	Bonnet Trimming Weaver	Herts	St Stephens
1798	HOLLAND	Thomas	31		Son	Unm	11	M	Bonnet Trimming Weaver	Herts	St Peters
1799	HOLLAND	Samuel	31		Son	Unm	9	M	Bonnet Trimming Weaver	Herts	St Peters
1800	HOLLAND	Elizabeth	31		Dau	Unm	7	F	Bonnet Trimming Weaver	Herts	St Peters
1801	HOLLAND	William	31		Son	Unm	4	M	At Home	Herts	St Peters

1802	HOLLAND	Roseanne	31		Dau	Unm	1	F	At Home	Herts	St Peters
1803	WHITE	John	31		Lodger	Unm	18	M	Bonnet Trimming Weaver	Herts	St Peters
1804	EDWARDS	James	32	London Road	Head	Mar	26	M	Labourer	Herts	St Peters
1805	EDWARDS	Elizabeth	32		Wife	Mar	26	F	Beer House Keeper	Herts	Great Gaddesden
1806	EDWARDS	Sarah Ann	32		Dau	Unm	4	F	At Home	Herts	St Peters
1807	EDWARDS	Mary Anne	32		Dau	Unm	3	F	At Home	Herts	St Peters
1808	EDWARDS	James W.	32		Son	Unm	1	M	At Home	Herts	St Peters
1809	KENTISH	Josiah	33	London Road	Head	Mar	26	M	Bonnet Trimming Weaver	Herts	St Peters
1810	KENTISH	Esther	33		Wife	Mar	23	F		Herts	Redbourn
1811	KENTISH	Thomas	33		Son	Unm	5 m	M	At Home	Herts	St Peters
1812	LAWRENCE	Sarah	34	London Road	Head	Unm	60	F		Herts	North Mimms
1813	LITTLE	Charles	35	London Road	Head	Mar	27	M	Shoemaker	Herts	Hertford
1814	LITTLE	Elizabeth	35		Wife	Mar	25	F		Herts	St Albans
1815	LITTLE	George	35		Son	Unm	4	M	At Home	Herts	St Albans
1816	LITTLE	Frederick	35		Son	Unm	2	M	At Home	Herts	St Albans
1817	FITZJOHN	John	35		[Lodger]	Mar	55	M	Agric Lab	Herts	St Albans
1818	FITZJOHN	Eliza	35		[Lodgers Wife]	Mar	43	F	Agric Labs Wife	Herts	St Albans
1819	FERBORN [?]	Emma	35		[Lodger]		13	F	Scholar	Herts	St Albans
1820	FRANCIS	William	36	London Road	Head	Mar	43	M	Labourer	Herts	Hatfield
1821	FRANCIS	Maria	36		Wife	Mar	33	F	Plaiter	Herts	St Michaels
1822	FRANCIS	James	36		Son		7	M	Plaiter	Herts	St Peters
1823	FRANCIS	Ann	36		Dau		2	F	At Home	Herts	St Peters
1824	FRANCIS	Jane	36		Dau		4	F	At Home	Herts	St Peters
1825	SLOUGH	David	36		[Lodger]	Mar	40	M	Labourer	Herts	Harpenden
1826	SLOUGH	Ann	36		[Lodgers Wife]	Mar	40	F	Plaiter	Herts	St Michaels
1827	GREEN	James	37	London Road	Head	Mar	50	M	Carrier	Herts	Stevenage
1828	GREEN	Mary	37		Wife	Mar	50	F		Herts	Stevenage
1829	GREEN	George	37		Son	Unm	20	M	Groom	Herts	Stevenage
1830	GREEN	Eliza	37		Dau		13	F	Plaiter	Herts	Hatfield
1831	GREEN	Maria	37		Dau		10	F	Scholar	Herts	St Peters
1832	CROUCH	Ann	37		Lodger	Mar	34	F	Bonnet Trimming Weaver	Herts	Abbey [St Albans]
1833	CROUCH	Charles	37		Lodger		7	M		Herts	Abbey [St Albans]
1834	HOPKINS	James	38	London Road	Head	Mar	63	M	Brazilian Hat Manufacturer	Beds	Luton
1835	HOPKINS	Keziah	38		Wife	Mar	59	F	Brazilian Hat Manufacturer	Beds	Luton
1836	HOPKINS	John	38		Son	Mar	20	M	Painter	Herts	St Albans
1837	HOPKINS	Susan	38		Dau-in-law	Mar	20	F		Herts	St Albans
1838	DENNITS	Sarah	38		Niece	Unm	20	F	Brazilian Hat Maker	Beds	Luton
1839	MIST	Elizabeth	38		Lodger		10	F	Brazilian Hat Maker	Herts	St Albans
1840	RICHARDSON	Susan	38		Lodger		15	F	Brazilian Hat Maker	Herts	St Albans
1841	BULL	Samuel	39	London Road	Head	Mar	51	M	Broker	Suffolk	Bungay
1842	BULL	Elizabeth	39		Wife	Mar	64	F		Suffolk	Bungay
1843	BULL	Henry M.	39		Son	Unm	26	M	Brokers Son	Herts	St Albans
1844	WILTON	Robert	40	London Road	Head	Unm	63	M	Greenwich Pensioner	Middx	St Lukes

	SURNAME	FORENAME	SCHEDULE NUMBER	ADDRESS	RELATIONSHIP	STATUS	AGE	SEX	OCCUPATION	COUNTY OF BIRTH	PLACE OF BIRTH
1845	FRAY	Hannah	40		Visitor	Unm	26	F	Bonnet Trimming Weaver	Herts	St Albans
1846	PRYOR	James	41	London Road	Head	Mar	43	M	General Labourer	Herts	Barnet
1847	PRYOR	Elizabeth	41		Wife	Mar	33	F	Brazilian Hat Maker	Herts	Harpenden
1848	PRYOR	Emma	41		Dau	Unm	12	F	Brazilian Hat Maker	Herts	Harpenden
1849	PRYOR	Mary Ann	41		Dau	Unm	9	F	Brazilian Hat Maker	Herts	St Michaels
1850	PRYOR	John	41		Son	Unm	2	M	At Home	Herts	St Peters
1851	PRYOR	Rachael	41		Dau	Unm	5dys	F	At Home	Herts	St Peters
1852	MUNT	James	42	London Road	Head	Mar	42	M	Labourer	Herts	Wheathampstead
1853	MUNT	Mary	42		Wife	Mar	40	F	Plaiter	Herts	Sandridge
1854	MUNT	William	42		Son	Unm	18	M	Labourer	Herts	Sandridge
1855	MUNT	David	42		Son	Unm	16	M	Labourer	Herts	St Peters
1856	LEWIS	Charity	42		Mother-in-law	Widow	86	F		Dorset	Hammoon [?]
1857	ASHTON	Thomas	43	London Road	Head	Mar	53	M	Labourer	Middx	Brentford
1858	ASHTON	Ann	43		Wife	Mar	56	F		Lancs	Liverpool
1859	ASHTON	Sarah	43		Dau	Unm	16	F	Bonnet Trimming Weaver	Hants	Alton
1860	STEWART	Catherine	44		Head	Widow	74	F	Cap Seller	Ireland	Kilkenny
1861	STEWART [?]	George K.	44		Grandson	Unm	7	M	Scholar	Herts	St Peters
1862	GRIMSHAW	Caleb	45	London Road	Head	Unm	46	M	Confectioner	Beds	Hockcliffe [?]
1863	GRIMSHAW	Alfred	45		Son	Unm	14	M	Confectioner	Herts	St Albans
1864	STELL	John	46	London Road	Head	Mar	25	M	Dealer	Beds	Shefford
1865	STELL	Emma	46		Wife	Mar	23	F		Herts	St Peters
1866	STELL	Samuel	46		Son	Unm	5	M	At Home	Herts	St Peters
1867	STELL	John	46		Son	Unm	3	M	At Home	Herts	St Peters
1868	STELL	Frederick	46		Son	Unm	5m	M	At Home	Herts	St Peters
1869	BIBBY	William	47	London Road	Head	Mar	45	M		[Unknown]	
1870	BIBBY	Elizabeth	47		Wife	Mar	48	F		[Unknown]	
1871	BIBBY	William	47		Son	Unm	16	M		[Unknown]	
1872	SLADE	George	48	London Road	Head	Mar	30	M	Bonnet Trimming Manufacturer	Middx	London
1873	SLADE	Lucy	48		Wife	Mar	31	F	Bonnet Trimming Manufacturer	Bucks	Newport Pagnell
1874	SLADE	Charles G.	48		Son	Unm	7	M	Bonnet Trimming Manufacturer	Herts	St Albans
1875	SLADE	Alfred J.	48		Son	Unm	3	M	At Home	Herts	St Albans
1876	SLADE	Emma E.	48		Dau	Unm	1	F	At Home	Herts	St Albans
1877	SLADE	Horace	48		Son	Unm	1m	M		Herts	St Albans
1878	KING	Eliza	48		Visitor	Unm	33	F	Straw Bonnet Maker	Herts	St Albans
1879	BURTON	Eliza	48		Serv	Unm	19	F	House Servant	Herts	Hoddesdon
1880	BURGESS	Richard	49	Cross Street, London Road	Head	Mar	40	M	Carrier	Herts	Tewin
1881	BURGESS	Mary	49		Wife	Mar	47	F		Beds	Shillington
One empty house			50								
1882	HISKETT	Charles	51	Cross Street, London Road	Head	Mar	38	M	Shoemaker	Middx	London
1883	HISKETT	Elizabeth	51		Wife	Mar	35	F		Herts	Ware
1884	HISKETT	Henry W.	51		Son	Unm	16	M	Shoemaker	Herts	St Albans
1885	HISKETT	Elizabeth	51		Dau	Unm	12	F	Scholar	Herts	St Albans

1886	HISKETT	Frederick	51		Son	Unm	9	M	Scholar	Herts	St Albans
1887	HISKETT	Charlotte	51		Dau	Unm	7	F	Scholar	Herts	St Albans
1888	HISKETT	Hannah	51		Dau	Unm	5	F	At Home	Herts	St Albans
1889	HISKETT	Caroline	51		Dau	Unm	3	F	At Home	Herts	St Albans
1890	HISKETT	Charles	51		Son	Unm	11 m	M	At Home	Herts	St Albans
1891	BURNETT	Henry	51		Lodger	Unm	17	M	Shoemakers Apprentice	Herts	Wheathampstead
1892	DRAPER	Frederick	51		Lodger	Mar	34	M	Tailor	Somerset	Bath
1893	DRAPER	Hannah	51		Lodgers Wife	Mar	33	F		Herts	Shenley
1894	DRAPER	Emma	51		Lodgers Dau	Unm	8	F	Scholar	Herts	St Albans
1895	DRAPER	Frederick	51		Lodgers Son	Unm	5	M	Scholar	Herts	St Albans
1896	FOUNTAIN	Henry	52	Cross Street, London Road	Head	Mar	23	M	Servant	Herts	[Unknown]
1897	FOUNTAIN	Elizabeth	52		Wife	Mar	21	F	Servant	Herts	[Unknown]
1898	FOUNTAIN	Elleanor	52		Dau	Unm	8 m	F	At Home	Herts	[Unknown]
1899	NORTH	Samuel	53	Cross Street, London Road	Head	Mar	24	M	Labourer	Herts	St Stephens
1900	NORTH	Mary Ann	53		Wife	Mar	23	F	Bonnet Trimming Maker	Herts	St Peters
1901	NORTH	Sarah	53		Dau	Unm	10 m	F	At Home	Herts	St Peters
1902	WELLS	Mary	53		Visitor	Widow	57	F	Dressmaker	Herts	Kimpton
1903	WELLS	Susan	53		Visitor	Unm	26	F	Bonnet Trimming Maker	Herts	St Peters
1904	CHERRY	Patience	54	Cross Street, London Road	Wife	Widow	45	F	Brazilian Hat Maker	Herts	Park Street [St Stephens]
1905	CHERRY	Sarah	54		Dau	Unm	19	F	Bonnet Sewer	Herts	St Michaels
1906	CHERRY	Elizabeth	54		Dau	Unm	17	F	Bonnet Trimming Maker	Herts	St Michaels
1907	CHERRY	Ann	54		Dau	Unm	12	F	Brazilian Hat Maker	Herts	St Michaels
1908	CHERRY	William	54		Son	Unm	8	M	Brazilian Hat Maker	Herts	St Michaels
1909	CHERRY	Emma	54		Dau	Unm	4	F	Brazilian Hat Maker	Herts	St Michaels
1910	BROWN	Daniel	55	Cross Street, London Road (Part of house)	Head	Mar	35	M	Gardener	Herts	North Mimms
1911	BROWN	Elizabeth	55		Wife	Mar	36	F	Brazilian Hat Maker	Middx	St Pancras
1912	BROWN	Caleb	55		Son	Unm	7	M	Brazilian Hat Maker	Herts	North Mimms
1913	BROWN	Errick	55		Son	Unm	4	M	At Home	Herts	North Mimms
1914	BROWN	Ira	55		Son	Unm	3	M	At Home	Herts	St Peters
1915	BROWN	Mary	55		Dau	Unm	3 m	F	At Home	Herts	St Peters
1916	RUSHTON	William	56	Cross Street, London Road	Head	Mar	74	M	Spring Maker	Staffs	[Unknown]
1917	RUSHTON	Margaret	56		Wife	Mar	63	F		Warks	[Unknown]
1918	RUSHTON	Matilda	56		Dau	[Unm]	24	F	Bonnet Trimming Weaver	Herts	[Unknown]
1919	RUSHTON	Eliza	56		Dau	[Unm]	18	F	Bonnet Trimming Weaver	Bucks	[Unknown]
1920	EDMONDS	Mary	56		Lodger	[Unm]	24	F	Bonnet Trimming Weaver	Herts	[Unknown]
1921	EDMONDS	Walter	56		Lodger		5	M	Scholar	Herts	[Unknown]
1922	BIGNALL	Sarah	56		Lodger		3	F	At Home	Herts	[Unknown]
1923	WOOLLAMS	Edward	57	Cross Street, London Road	Head	Mar	53	M	Bricklayer	Bucks	Great Missenden
1924	WOOLLAMS	Sarah	57		Wife	Mar	43	F	Silk Throwster	Herts	St Albans
1925	WOOLLAMS	Harriet	57		Dau	Unm	16	F	Silk Throwster	Herts	Tring
1926	WOOLLAMS	Emily	57		Dau	Unm	5	F	Scholar	Herts	St Peters
1927	WOOLLAMS	John	57		Son	Unm	4	M	Scholar	Herts	St Peters

	SURNAME	FORENAME	SCHEDULE NUMBER	ADDRESS	RELATIONSHIP	STATUS	AGE	SEX	OCCUPATION	COUNTY OF BIRTH	PLACE OF BIRTH
1928	SPRIGGS	John	58	Cross Street, London Road	Head	Mar	34	M	Labourer	Herts	Bushey
1929	SPRIGGS	Ann	58		Wife	Mar	32	F	Bonnet Trimming Weaver	Herts	St Stephens
1930	SPRIGGS	Ann	58		Lodger	Mar	75	F	Washerwoman	Herts [Middx]	Uxbridge
1931	SPRIGGS	John	58		Son	Unm	7	M	At Home	Herts	St Albans
1932	SPRIGGS	Hannah	58		Dau	Unm	6	F	At Home	Herts	St Peters
1933	SPRIGGS	James	58		Son	Unm	5	M	At Home	Herts	St Peters
1934	GOODMAN	Emma	59	London Road	Head	Unm	43	F		Cambs	March
1935	LAWRENCE	Kate E.	59		Niece	Unm	18	F		Middx	Hampstead
1936	LAWRENCE	John A.	59		Nephew	Unm	11	M		Middx	Hampstead
1937	MUMFORD	Ann	59		Cook	Unm	20	F	Cook	Essex	Stanstead
1938	KNIGHTS	Elizabeth	59		Housemaid	Unm	19	F	Housemaid	Herts	Bishop Stortford
1939	SMITH	Stephen	60	London Road	Head	Mar	43	M	J.P. No Occupation	Herts	St Albans
1940	SMITH	Jane	60		Wife	Mar	38	F		Kent	Dartford
1941	SMITH	Ada	60		Dau	Unm	12	F		Herts	Bushey
1942	SMITH	William	60		Son	Unm	10	M	Scholar	Herts	Bushey
1943	SMITH	Henry	60		Son	Unm	8	M	Scholar	Herts	Bushey
1944	SMITH	Charles	60		Son	Unm	5	M		Herts	Bushey
1945	SMITH	Irene	60		Dau	Unm	3	F		Herts	Bushey
1946	SMITH	Georgianna	60		Dau	Unm	1	F		Herts	St Albans
1947	EDWARDS	Eliza	60		Serv	Unm	26	F	House Servant	Herts	St Albans
1948	SPITTLE	Ann	61	London Road	Head	Widow	78	F	Independent	Leics	Asfordby
1949	ATKINS	Harriet	61		Serv	Unm	29	F	Maid Servant	Oxon	Witney
1950	SIBLEY	William	62	London Road	Head	Mar	61	M	No Occupation	Beds	Luton
1951	SIBLEY	Elizabeth	62		Wife	Mar	45	F	No Occupation	Gloucs	Kings Stanley
1952	SIBLEY	Joseph	62		Son	Unm	14	M	Scholar	Herts	St Albans
1953	SIBLEY	Thomas	62		Son	Unm	11	M	Scholar	Herts	St Albans
1954	SIBLEY	Sophia	62		Dau	Unm	9	F		Herts	St Albans
1955	JUDD	Emma	62		Serv	Unm	17	F	House Servant	Herts	London Colney
1956	MARSTIN	William	63	London Road	Serv	Mar	55	M	Servant	Herts	St Albans
1957	MARSTIN	Hannah	63		Visitor	Mar	22	F	Bonnet Trimming Weaver	Herts	St Albans
1958	NARROWAY	Caroline	63		Visitor	Unm	19	F	Dressmaker	Herts	St Albans
1959	SHUFFORD	Ann	64	London Road	Wife	Mar	34	F		Beds	Woburn
1960	SHUFFORD	Henry T.	64		[Son]	Unm	4	M		Herts	St Peters
1961	VARNAM	Ann	64		Visitor	Unm	33	F	Bonnet Trimming Weaver	Kent	Woolwich
1962	KEER	George	65	London Road	Head	Mar	25	M	Waiter	Herts	St Albans
1963	KEER	Jennet	65		Wife	Mar	24	F	Brazilian Hat Maker	Herts	St Peters
1964	KEER	Emily	65		Dau	Unm	1	F		Herts	St Peters
1965	NORRIS	William	66	London Road	Head	Mar	55	M	Chelsea Pensioner	Herts	Hatfield
1966	NORRIS	Ann	66		Wife	Mar	33	F		Herts	Hatfield
1967	NORRIS	Elizabeth	66		Dau	Unm	16	F	Brazilian Hat Maker	E. Indies	
1968	ARNOLD	Samuel	67	London Road	Head	Mar	49	M	Labourer	[Unknown]	
1969	ARNOLD	Isabella	67		Wife	Mar	52	F		[Unknown]	
1970	WRIGHT	Jane	67		Dau-in-law	Unm	25	F		[Unknown]	
1971	HARDWICK	William	68	London Road	Head	Mar	55	M	Labourer	Beds	Dunstable

1972	HARDWICK	Matilda	68		Wife	Mar	60	F		[Unknown]	
1973	HARDWICK	Sophia	68		Dau	Unm	30	F		Herts	St Albans
1974	HARDWICK	Susan	68		Dau	Unm	25	F	Bonnet Trimming Maker	Herts	St Albans
1975	HARDWICK	Charles	68		Son	Unm	18	M	Bonnet Trimming Maker	Herts	St Albans
1976	HARDWICK	Emily	68		Grandau	Unm	7	F	Scholar	Herts	St Albans
1977	HARDWICK	John	68		Grandson	Unm	5	M	Scholar	Herts	St Albans
1978	PURSELL	Ann	68		Lodger	Unm	24	F	Bonnet Trimming Maker	Herts	St Albans
1979	GOSS	James	69	London Road	Head	Mar	62	M	Sawyer	Herts	St Michaels
1980	GOSS	Mary	69		Wife	Mar	52	F		Herts	St Albans
1981	GOSS	Henry	69		Son	Unm	17	M	Sawyer	Herts	St Peters
1982	GOSS	Caroline	69		Dau	Unm	13	F	Bonnet Trimming Weaver	Herts	St Peters
1983	GOSS	William	69		Son	Unm	15	M	Brazilian Hat Maker	Herts	St Peters
1984	LUNNON	William	70	London Road	Head	Mar	24	M	Hat Blocker	Herts	St Michaels
1985	LUNNON	Rebecca	70		Wife	Mar	22	F		Herts	North Mimms
1986	LUNNON	Sarah	70		Dau	Unm	1m	F		Herts	St Peters
1987	COMPTON	James	71	London Road	Head	Mar	38	M	Labourer	[Unknown]	
1988	COMPTON	Sarah	71		Wife	Mar	40	F	Brazilian Hat Maker	Bucks	High Wycombe
1989	COMPTON	Louisa	71		Dau	Unm	18	F	Brazilian Hat Maker	Devon	[Unknown]
1990	COMPTON	Sarah	71		Dau	Unm	13	F	Brazilian Hat Maker	Middx	London
1991	COMPTON	Rachael	71		Dau	Unm	11	F	Brazilian Hat Maker	Middx	London
1992	GULLINGHAM	William	71		Lodger	Unm	15	M	Labourer	Middx	London
1993	DAVIS	Daniel	71		Lodger	Unm	13	M	Labourer	Cumb	Carlisle
1994	NORTHWOOD	Daniel	71		Lodger	Unm	14	M	Carpenter	Beds	Luton
1995	FENSOM	George	72	London Road	Head	Mar	44	M	Groom	Beds	Combworth [Colmworth]
1996	FENSOM	Elizabeth	72		Wife	Mar	36	F		Herts	St Peters
1997	FENSOM	Alice	72		Dau	Unm	13	F	Silk Throwster	Herts	St Peters
1998	FENSOM	Elizabeth	72		Dau	Unm	10	F	Silk Throwster	Herts	St Peters
1999	FENSOM	George	72		Son	Unm	2	M		Herts	St Peters
2000	SMITH	Sophia	73	London Road	Wife	Mar	55	F		Herts	St Peters
2001	SMITH	Eliza	73		Dau	Unm	22	F	Brazilian Hat Maker	Herts	Shenley
2002	SMITH	George	73		Son	Unm	20	M	Brazilian Hat Maker	Herts	Shenley
2003	SMITH	Louisa	73		Dau	Unm	14	F	Bonnet Trimming Weaver	Herts	Ridge
2004	DAWES	William	74	London Road	Head	Mar	55	M	Sawyer	Herts	Sandridge
2005	DAWES	Elizabeth	74		Wife	Mar	66	F		Herts	Hitchin
2006	DAWES	Elizabeth	74		Dau	Unm	21	F		Herts	St Peters
2007	DAWES	Ann	74		Lodger	Unm	58	F		Herts	Sandridge
2008	SMALL	James	75	London Road	Head	Widower	60	M	Bookseller	Surrey	Lambeth
2009	SMALL	Sophia	75		Dau	Unm	23	F	Brazilian Hat Maker	Herts	St Albans
2010	NORRIE	William	76	London Road	Head	Mar	49	M	Pastry Cook	Sussex	Salehurst
2011	NORRIE	Susan	76		Wife	Mar	42	F	Bonnet Trimming Maker	Herts	St Albans
2012	CAMPBELL	Emma	76		Dau-in-law	Unm	19	F	Bonnet Trimming Maker	Herts	St Peters
2013	LEWIS	Jane	76		Dau-in-law	Unm	16	F	Bonnet Trimming Maker	Herts	St Peters
2014	GOODMAN	Henry	77	London Road	Head	Mar	55	M	Groom	Bucks	Stony Stratford

	SURNAME	FORENAME	SCHEDULE NUMBER	ADDRESS	RELATIONSHIP	STATUS	AGE	SEX	OCCUPATION	COUNTY OF BIRTH	PLACE OF BIRTH
2015	GOODMAN	Mary Ann	77		Wife	Mar	30	F		Bucks	Ringshall
2016	GOODMAN	Mary Ann	77		Dau	Unm	15	F	Silk Throwster	Herts	St Albans
2017	GOODMAN	Edward	77		Son	Unm	9	M	Silk Throwster	Herts	St Albans
2018	GOODMAN	Elizabeth	77		Dau	Unm	2	F		Herts	St Albans
	One empty house		78								
2019	NASH	Henry	79	London Road	Head	Mar	27	M	Hat Blocker	Herts	St Stephens
2020	NASH	Rebecca	79		Wife	Mar	32	F	Bonnet Trimming Weaver	Herts	Tring
2021	NASH	Thomas	79		Son	Unm	7	M		Herts	St Albans
2022	NASH	Sarah	79		Dau	Unm	5	F		Herts	St Peters
2023	NASH	Ann	79		Dau	Unm	3	F		Herts	St Peters
2024	FUSEDALE	Edwin	79		[blank]	Unm	10	M		Herts	St Peters
2025	BENTLEY	William	80	London Road	Head	Mar	71	M	Gardener	Herts	Ayot St Lawrence
2026	BENTLEY	Elizabeth	80		Wife	Mar	68	F	Housekeeper	Essex	Low Layton
2027	WISE	Winsler	81	Toll Gate, London Road	Head	Mar	50	M	Toll Gate Keeper	Herts	St Peters
2028	LEWIS	John	82	Old London Road	Head	Mar	50	M	Labourer	Herts	Sandridge
2029	LEWIS	Ann	82		Wife	Mar	40	F	Brazilian Hat Maker	Herts	St Peters
2030	LEWIS	Mary Ann	82		Dau	Unm	21	F	Brazilian Hat Maker	Herts	St Peters
2031	LEWIS	Eliza	82		Dau	Unm	19	F	Brazilian Hat Maker	Herts	St Peters
2032	LEWIS	Emma	82		Dau	Unm	11	F	Brazilian Hat Maker	Herts	St Peters
2033	LEWIS	George	82		Son	Unm	9	M	Brazilian Hat Maker	Herts	St Peters
2034	LEWIS	Selina	82		Dau	Unm	5	F		Herts	St Peters
2035	SLAUGHTER	Benjamin	83	Old London Road	Head	Mar	49	M	Labourer	Herts	St Peters
2036	SLAUGHTER	Martha	83		Wife	Mar	44	F	Bonnet Trimming Weaver	Herts	St Albans
2037	SLAUGHTER	Eliza	83		Dau	Unm	11	F	Brazilian Hat Maker	Herts	St Peters
2038	BIGNALL	Lucy	83		Lodger	Unm	9	F	Brazilian Hat Maker	Herts	St Peters
2039	JUSTICE	George	84	Old London Road	Head	Mar	36	M	Labourer	Bucks	Swing [Wing]
2040	JUSTICE	Sarah	84		Wife	Mar	52	F	Wife	Herts	Hemel Hempstead
2041	TARBOX	Fanny	84		Dau	Unm	19	F	Brazilian Hat Maker	Herts	Great Gaddesden
2042	TARBOX	Thomas	84		Son	Unm	16	M	Brazilian Hat Maker	Herts	Great Gaddesden
2043	JUSTICE	Emma	84		Dau	Unm	14	F	Brazilian Hat Maker	Herts	Great Gaddesden
2044	JUSTICE	George	84		Son	Unm	11	M	Brazilian Hat Maker	Herts	Hemel Hempstead
2045	FIELD	Mary	85	Old London Road	Head	Unm	30	F	Brazilian Hat Maker	Herts	Shenley
2046	FIELD	Lucy	85		Sister	Unm	27	F	Brazilian Hat Maker	Herts	Shenley
2047	FIELD	William	85		Brother	Unm	24	M	Bonnet Trimming Weaver	Herts	Shenley
2048	FIELD	Martha	85		Sister	Unm	18	F	Brazilian Hat Maker	Herts	Shenley
2049	FIELD	Henry	85		Nephew	Unm	6	M	Brazilian Hat Maker	Herts	St Peters
2050	FIELD	Ellen	85		Dau	Unm	3	F		Herts	St Albans
2051	FIELD	Emily	85		Niece	Unm	2	F		Herts	St Stephens
2052	BURDEN	Thomas	86	Old London Road	Head	Mar	61	M	Labourer	Herts	Flamstead
2053	BURDEN	Martha	86		Wife	Mar	63	F		Herts	St Michaels
2054	WHITE	William	86		Lodger	Unm	22	M	Bonnet Trimming Weaver	Herts	St Albans
2055	EAMES	Henry	86		Lodger	Unm	23	M	Miller	Herts	Redbourn
2056	CATLIN	George	87	Old London Road	Head	Mar	28	M	Agric Lab	Herts	St Stephens

2057	CATLIN	Ann	87		Wife	Mar	25	F	Bonnet Trimming Weaver	Herts	St Stephens
2058	CATLIN	Sarah Ann	87		Dau	Unm	5	F	Scholar	Herts	St Stephens
2059	CATLIN	William	87		Son	Unm	1	M		Herts	St Albans
2060	CATLIN	James	87		Brother	Unm	26	M	Agric Lab	Herts	St Albans
2061	MILEMAN	Mary Ann	87		Sister-in-law	Unm	14	F	Servant	Herts	St Stephens
2062	WILSON	Sarah	87		Lodger	Unm	21	F	Bonnet Trimming Weaver	Herts	St Albans
2063	LOW	William	88	Old London Road	Head	Mar	39	M	Labourer	Herts	St Peters
2064	LOW	Charlotte	88		Wife	Mar	38	F		Herts	Colney Heath
2065	LOW	Shadrac	88		Son	Unm	17	M	Bonnet Trimming Weaver	Herts	St Peters
2066	LOW	Emma	88		Dau	Unm	15	F	Brazilian Hat Maker	Herts	St Peters
2067	LOW	Sarah	88		Dau	Unm	10	F	Brazilian Hat Maker	Herts	St Peters
2068	LOW	Nathaniel	88		Son	Unm	7	M		Herts	St Peters
2069	GREY	William	89	Old London Road	Head	Mar	43	M	Labourer	Herts	Wheathampstead
2070	GREY	Elizabeth	89		Wife	Mar	37	F		Herts	St Stephens
2071	GREY	George	89		Son	Unm	21	M	Silk Throwster	Herts	St Stephens
2072	GREY	William	89		Son	Unm	10	M	Scholar	Herts	St Stephens
2073	GREY	Daniel	89		Son	Unm	8	M	Scholar	Herts	St Peters
2074	GREY	Mary Ann	89		Dau	Unm	3	F		Herts	St Peters
2075	GREY	Sarah	89		Dau	Unm	2	F		Herts	St Peters
2076	WEATHERLY	William	89		Lodger	Unm	33	M	Labourer	Herts	St Stephens
2077	HAWKINS	Sarah	90	Old London Road	Wife	Mar	32	F		Herts	St Albans
2078	HAWKINS	George	90		Son	Unm	3	M		Herts	St Albans
2079	KIFF	Barnard	91	Old London Road	Head	Mar	67	M	Labourer	Herts	St Stephens
2080	KIFF	Barbara	91		Wife	Mar	65	F		N'thumb	[Unknown]
2081	KIFF	William	91		Son	Unm	21	M	Labourer	Herts	St Stephens
2082	VERNNIER	John	92	Old London Road	Head	Mar	41	M	Shoemaker	Herts	Hertford
2083	VERNNIER	Ann	92		Wife	Mar	40	F	Shoe Binder	Ireland	[Unknown]
2084	VERNNIER	John	92		Son	Unm	9	M	Bonnet Trimming Weaver	Herts	St Albans
2085	VERNNIER	Emily	92		Dau	Unm	5	F	Scholar	Herts	St Albans
2086	NORRIS	Charles	93	Old London Road	Head	Mar	53	M	Carpenter	Herts	St Stephens
2087	NORRIS	Lillia	93		Wife	Mar	38	F		Somerset	Bruton
2088	NORRIS	Charles	93		Son	Unm	22	M	Sawyer	Herts	St Stephens
2089	NORRIS	William	93		Son	Unm	19	M	Baker	Herts	St Stephens
2090	NORRIS	George	93		Son	Unm	17	M	Baker	Herts	St Stephens
2091	ATTWOOD	Thomas	94	Old London Road	Head	Mar	75	M	Labourer	Herts	Harpenden
2092	ATTWOOD	Susanna	94		Wife	Mar	70	F		Herts	St Albans
2093	PETTIT	John	95	Old London Road	Head	Mar	23	M	Plumbers Labourer	Herts	St Albans
2094	PETTIT	Sarah	95		Wife	Mar	24	F	Bonnet Trimming Weaver	Herts	St Peters
2095	PETTIT	Harriet	95		Dau	Unm	3	F		Herts	St Michaels
2096	BATCHELOR	Maria	95		Lodger	Unm	22	F	Brazilian Hat Maker	Herts	Rickmansworth
2097	EAMES	Samuel	96	Old London Road	Head	Mar	34	M	Hurdle Maker	Herts	St Peters
2098	EAMES	Elizabeth	96		Wife	Mar	37	F		[Unknown]	
2099	EAMES	Sarah	96		Niece	Unm	5	F		Herts	St Peters

SURNAME	FORENAME	SCHEDULE NUMBER	ADDRESS	RELATIONSHIP	STATUS	AGE	SEX	OCCUPATION	COUNTY OF BIRTH	PLACE OF BIRTH
2100	OAKLEY	George	97	Old London Road	Head	Mar	23	M	Silk Throwster	Herts	St Albans
2101	OAKLEY	Caroline	97		Wife	Mar	28	F		Bucks	Shenley
2102	OAKLEY	James	97		Son	Unm	3	M		Herts	St Peters
2103	SEARS	John	97		Lodger	Unm	28	M	Silk Throwster	Herts	Watford
2104	FINCHER	Daniel	97		Lodger	Unm	24	M	Silk Throwster	Herts	Tring
2105	PRATT	Susanna	98	Old London Road	Wife	Mar	51	F	Bonnet Sewer	Unknown	
2106	PRATT	Eliza	98		Dau	Unm	23	F	Bonnet Sewer	Middx	London
2107	BROTHERS	James	99	Old London Road	Head	Mar	25	M	Labourer	Herts	St Albans
2108	BROTHERS	Ann	99		Wife	Mar	24	F		Northants	Northampton
2109	BROTHERS	Ann	99		Dau	Unm	3 m	F		Herts	St Albans
2110	SADDINGTON	Mary	99		Sister-in-law	Unm	21	F		Herts	St Albans
2111	PLUMMER	Joseph	100	Old London Road	Head	Mar	40	M	Labourer	Herts	Harpenden
2112	PLUMMER	Sarah	100		Wife	Mar	32	F	Plaiter	Beds	Toddington
2113	PLUMMER	Alfred	100		Son	Unm	3	M		Herts	St Peters
2114	JENKINS	Eliza	100		Lodger	Unm	22	F	Plaiter	Herts	Harpenden
2115	LONG	John	101	Old London Road	Head	Mar	55	M	Journeyman Baker	Herts	St Stephens
2116	LONG	Mary	101		Wife	Mar	45	F		Herts	St Peters
2117	LONG	Isaac	101		Son		11	M	Scholar	Herts	St Peters
2118	ALLIN	Joseph	102	Old London Road	Head	Mar	65	M		Herts	St Albans
2119	ALLIN	Sarah	102		Wife	Mar	72	F		Herts	St Albans
2120	KEEN	Daniel	103	Old London Road	Head	Mar	23	M	Journeyman Bricklayer	Beds	Dunstable
2121	KEEN	Sarah Ann	103		Wife	Mar	28	F		Herts	Great Gaddesden
2122	TARBOX	Margaret	103		Sister-in-law	Unm	18	F	Brazilian Hat Maker	Herts	Great Gaddesden
2123	FLETCHER	John	104	Old London Road	Head	Mar	49	M	Labourer	Herts	St Albans
2124	FLETCHER	Martha	104		Wife	Mar	54	F		Herts	St Albans
2125	FLETCHER	George	104		Son	Unm	20	M	Labourer	Herts	St Albans
2126	ELSE	William	105	Old London Road	Head	Mar	35	M	Labourer	Herts	St Albans
2127	ELSE	Martha	105		Wife	Mar	31	F	Bonnet Trimming Weaver	Herts	St Albans
2128	ELSE	Joseph	105		Son	Unm	7	M	Scholar	Herts	St Albans
2129	ELSE	Elizabeth	105		Dau	Unm	4	F	Scholar	Herts	St Albans
2130	SMITH	Joseph	106	Old London Road	Head	Mar	52	M	Labourer	Herts	Sandridge
2131	SMITH	Ann	106		Wife	Mar	56	F	Blind	Herts	Tring
2132	SMITH	William	106		Son	Unm	17	M	Errand Boy	Herts	St Albans
2133	SMITH	Eliza	106		Dau	Unm	19	F	Brazilian Hat Maker	Herts	St Albans
2134	JOHNSON	William	107	Old London Road	Head	Mar	34	M	Groom	Herts	Kensworth
2135	JOHNSON	Martha	107		Wife	Mar	37	F	Shop Keeper	Oxon	[Unknown]
2136	JOHNSON	Martha	107		Dau	Unm	13	F		Herts	St Peters
2137	JOHNSON	Jane	107		Dau	Unm	12	F		Herts	St Peters
2138	JOHNSON	William	107		Son	Unm	9	M		Herts	St Peters
2139	JOHNSON	Mark	107		Son	Unm	6	M		Herts	St Peters
2140	JOHNSON	Emma	107		Dau	Unm	3	F		Herts	St Peters
2141	ELSE	Edward	108	Old London Road	Head	Mar	59	M	Agric Lab	Beds	[Unknown]
2142	ELSE	Ann	108		Wife	Mar	50	F		Herts	St Albans
2143	ELSE	Caroline	108		Dau	Unm	21	F	Bonnet Trimming Weaver	Herts	St Albans

2144	ELSE	Mary	108		Dau	Unm	21	F	Brazilian Hat Maker	Herts	St Albans
2145	ELSE	Louisa	108		Dau	Unm	19	F	Bonnet Trimming Weaver	Herts	St Albans
2146	COLINGS	Charles	109	Old London Road	Head	Mar	28	M	Labourer	Herts	St Albans
2147	COLINGS	Jane	109		Wife	Mar	29	F		Herts	St Albans
2148	COLINGS	Henry	109		Son	Unm	2	M		Herts	St Albans
2149	JOHNSON	Charlotte	109		Mother	Widow	60	F	Washerwoman	Beds	Markyate Street
2150	MARSTON	Dinah	110	Old London Road	Wife	Mar	55	F	Brazilian Hat Maker	Herts	Shenley
2151	MARSTON	Mary	110		Dau	Unm	14	F	Bonnet Trimming Weaver	Herts	St Albans
2152	MARTINGALE	Elizabeth	111	Old London Road	Head	Widow	80	F	Proprietor of Houses	Herts	St Peters
2153	MARTINGALE	Mary Ann	111		Dau-in-Law	Widow	50	F	Dressmaker	Hunts	Stilton
2154	DEAYTON	Joseph	112	Old London Road	Head	Mar	44	M	Labourer	Herts	St Albans
2155	DEAYTON	Sarah	112		Dau	Unm	18	F	Plaiter	Herts	St Albans
2156	DEAYTON	Caroline	112		Dau	Unm	16	F	Plaiter	Herts	St Albans
2157	DEAYTON	Samuel	112		Son	Unm	13	M	Labourer	Herts	St Albans
2158	DEAYTON	Emma	112		Dau	Unm	10	F		Herts	St Albans
2159	DEAYTON	Mary Ann	112		Dau	Unm	8	F		Herts	St Albans
2160	HILL	Moses	113	Old London Road	Head	Mar	46	M	Labourer	Herts	St Stephens
2161	HILL	Ann	113		Wife	Mar	45	F		Warks	Warwick
2162	HILL	Ann	113		Dau	Unm	16	F		Herts	St Peters
2163	HILL	John	113		Son	Unm	13	M		Herts	St Peters
2164	HILL	Jane	113		Dau	Unm	10	F		Herts	St Peters
2165	HILL	Isabella	113		Dau	Unm	8	F		Herts	St Peters
2166	HILL	William	113		Son	Unm	5	M		Herts	St Peters
2167	SIMKINS	Thomas	114	Old London Road	Head	Mar	30	M	Bonnet Trimming Weaver	Herts	St Albans
2168	SIMKINS	Ann	114		Wife	Mar	33	F	Bonnet Trimming Weaver	Herts	St Albans
2169	SIMKINS	Susan	114		Dau	Unm	10	F	Bonnet Trimming Weaver	Herts	St Albans
2170	SIMKINS	Samuel	114		Son	Unm	7	M		Herts	St Albans
2171	SIMKINS	Sarah	114		Dau	Unm	3	F		Herts	St Albans
2172	SIMKINS	(Infant)	114		Son	Unm	14dys	M		Herts	St Albans
2173	SIMKINS	Susan	115	Old London Road	Head	Widow	54	F	Washerwoman	Herts	Shenley
2174	SIMKINS	Fanny	115		Dau	Unm	19	F	Bonnet Trimming Weaver	Herts	St Albans
2175	SIMKINS	Emma	115		Dau	Unm	12	F	Bonnet Trimming Weaver	Herts	St Albans
2176	SLOW	George	116	Old London Road	Head	Mar	37	M	Labourer	Herts	Wheathampstead
2177	SLOW	Saphira	116		Wife	Mar	34	F	Bonnet Trimming Weaver	Herts	Shenley
2178	SLOW	Lucy	116		Dau	Unm	10	F		Herts	St Albans
2179	SLOW	Eliza	116		Dau	Unm	8	F		Herts	St Albans
2180	SLOW	William	116		Son	Unm	6	M		Herts	St Albans
2181	SLOW	George	116		Son	Unm	3	M		Herts	St Albans
2182	SLOW	Alfred	116		Son	Unm	1	M		Herts	St Albans
2183	JUSTICES	James	117	Old London Road	Head	Mar	61	M	Labourer	Herts	Studham
2184	JUSTICES	Charlotte	117		Wife	Mar	56	F		Herts	Great Gaddesden
2185	JUSTICES	Charles	117		Son	Unm	27	M		Herts	Studham
2186	JUSTICES	Harry	117		Son	Unm	22	M		Herts	Studham

	SURNAME	FORENAME	SCHEDULE NUMBER	ADDRESS	RELATIONSHIP	STATUS	AGE	SEX	OCCUPATION	COUNTY OF BIRTH	PLACE OF BIRTH
2187	JUSTICES	Emily	117		Dau	Unm	19	F		Herts	Studham
2188	JUSTICES	Elijah	117		Son		13	M		Herts	Great Gaddesden
2189	WEATHERLEY	Esther	118	Old London Road	Head	Widow	65	F		Herts	St Peters
2190	WEATHERLEY	Zilpert [?]	118		Dau	Unm	32	F		Herts	St Peters
2191	WEATHERLEY	Susan	118		Dau	Unm	30	F		Herts	St Peters
2192	WEATHERLEY	Sarah	118		Dau	Unm	24	F		Herts	St Peters
2193	WEATHERLEY	James	118		Son	Unm	22	M		Herts	St Peters
2194	WEATHERLEY	William	118		Grandson	Unm	15	M		Herts	St Peters
2195	WEATHERLEY	Alfred	118		Grandson	Unm	12	M		Herts	St Peters
2196	WEATHERLEY	Ellen	118		Grandau	Unm	5	F		Herts	St Peters
2197	WEATHERLEY	George	118		Grandson	Unm	7	M		Herts	St Peters
2198	BLAIN	Mary	118		Dau	Unm	36	F		Herts	St Peters
2199	BLAIN	Thomas	118		Grandson	Unm	11	M		Herts	Redbourn
2200	BLAIN	Susan	118		Grandau	Unm	9	F		Herts	Redbourn
2201	BLAIN	William	118		Grandson	Unm	5	M		Herts	Harpenden
2202	LINES	William	119	Old London Road	Head	Mar	50	M	Journeyman Blacksmith	Herts	Hemel Hempstead
2203	LINES	Sarah	119		Wife	Mar	50	F		Herts	Harpenden
2204	LINES	Elizabeth	119		Dau	Unm	15	F	Brazilian Hat Maker	Herts	St Albans
2205	LINES	Abel	119		Son	Unm	12	M	Brazilian Hat Maker	Herts	St Albans
2206	LINES	Fanny	119		Dau	Unm	6	F		Herts	St Albans
2207	LINES	Mary	120	Old London Road	Head	Widow	60	F		Herts	St Albans
2208	LINES	Susan	120		Niece	Unm	19	F	Brazilian Hat Maker	Herts	St Albans
2209	COOK	Richard	121	Old London Road	Head	Mar	63	M	Labourer	[Unknown]	
2210	COOK	Sarah	121		Wife	Mar	60	F	Charwoman	[Unknown]	
2211	COOK	Hannah	121		Dau	Unm	23	F	Silk Throwster	Herts	St Peters
2212	COOK	James	121		Son	Unm	24	M	Labourer	Herts	St Peters
2213	COOK	Richard	121		Son	Unm	16	M	Labourer	Herts	St Peters
2214	COOK	George	121		Son	Unm	14	M		Herts	St Peters
2215	COOK	James	121		Grandson	Unm	6	M		Herts	St Peters
2216	COOK	Ann	121		Grandau	Unm	19	F		Herts	St Peters
2217	DIGGINS	Edward	122	Old London Road	[blank]	Widower	60	M	Journeyman Carpenter	Berks	[Unknown]
2218	HILL	William	122		Head	Mar	30	M	Labourer	Herts	St Peters
2219	HILL	Martha	122		Wife	Mar	32	F		Herts	Caddington
2220	HILL	Sarah	122		Dau	Unm	6	F		Herts	St Peters
2221	HILL	Eliza	122		Dau	Unm	3	F		Herts	St Peters
2222	HILL	George	122		Son	Unm	12	M		Herts	St Peters
2223	BRIDEN	George	123	Old London Road	Head	Mar	27	M	Silk Throwster	Herts	St Stephens
2224	BRIDEN	Elizabeth	123		Wife	Mar	30	F		Beds	Lidlington
2225	HANSCOMB	Thomas	124	Old London Road	Head	Mar	24	M	Labourer	Herts	St Peters
2226	HANSCOMB	Judith	124		Wife	Mar	30	F		Herts	Kimpton
2227	HANSCOMB	James	124		Son	Unm	3 m	M		Herts	St Peters
2228	MARDELL	James	125	Old London Road	Head	Mar	67	M	Agric Lab	Herts	St Stephens
2229	MARDELL	Sarah	125		Wife	Mar	66	F		Herts	North Mimms
2230	MARDELL	Edward	125		Son	Unm	23	M	Agric Lab	Herts	St Michaels
2231	LEE	William	126	Old London Road	Head	Mar	37	M	Agric Lab	Herts	Redbourn

2232	LEE	Elizabeth	126		Wife	Mar	40	F		Oxon	[Unknown]
2233	LEE	Emma	126		Dau	Unm	1	F		Herts	St Peters
2234	HEMMINGTON	John	127	Old London Road	Head	Mar	35	M	Agric Lab	Herts	Redbourn
2235	HEMMINGTON	Jane	127		Wife	Mar	33	F	Plaiter	Herts	Redbourn
2236	HEMMINGTON	Ann	127		Dau	Unm	12	F	Plaiter	Herts	Redbourn
2237	BARTRAM	Sarah	128	Old London Road	Head	Unm	34	F	Brazilian Hat Maker	Herts	Redbourn
2238	BARTRAM	Caroline	128		Sister	Unm	23	F	Plaiter	Herts	Redbourn
2239	BARTRAM	Sarah	128		Dau	Unm	16	F	Brazilian Hat Maker	Herts	Redbourn
2240	BARTRAM	George	128		Nephew	Unm	4	M		Herts	Redbourn
2241	ADAMS	Mary	128		Lodger	[blank]	70	F		Herts	St Albans
2242	STREET	James	129	Old London Road	Head	Mar	38	M	Tin Plate Worker	Herts	Hitchin
2243	STREET	Frances	129		Wife	Mar	38	F		Herts	Hitchin
2244	STREET	Elizabeth	129		Sister	Unm	18	F	Weaver	Herts	Hitchin
2245	STREET	Emily	129		Visitor	Unm	5	F	Scholar	Herts	St Albans
2246	STREET	Thomas	129		Visitor	Unm	18	M	Painter	Herts	Watford
2247	WALKER	James	130	Old London Road	Head	Widower	46	M	Dealer	Herts	St Albans
2248	WALKER	Thomas	130		Son	Unm	20	M	Journeyman Shoemaker	Herts	St Albans
2249	WALKER	Eliza	130		Dau	Unm	19	F		Herts	St Albans
2250	WALKER	Susan	130		Dau	Unm	17	F		Herts	St Albans
2251	WALKER	James	130		Son	Unm	15	M		Herts	St Albans
2252	WALKER	Ann	130		Dau	Unm	14	F		Herts	St Albans
2253	WALKER	Samuel	130		Son	Unm	10	M		Herts	St Albans
	One empty house		*131*								
2254	SMITH	William	132	Old London Road	Head	Mar	43	M	Journeyman Shoemaker	Norfolk	Norwich
2255	SMITH	Elizabeth	132		Wife	Mar	45	F	Shoe Binder	Norfolk	Great Yarmouth
2256	SMITH	William	132		Son	Unm	23	M	Boot Closer	Norfolk	Norwich
2257	SMITH	Elizabeth	132		Dau	Unm	19	F	Shoe Binder	Norfolk	Norwich
2258	SMITH	Emma	132		Dau	Unm	12	F		Norfolk	Norwich
2259	SILLCOCK	James	133	Old London Road	Head	Mar	65	M	Grocer	Bucks	Northall
2260	SILLCOCK	Hannah	133		Wife	Mar	45	F		Herts	St Albans
2261	SILLCOCK	Mary	133		Dau	Unm	39	F		Herts	St Albans
2262	SILLCOCK	Catherine	133		Dau	Unm	29	F		Herts	St Albans
2263	ELSTONE	Hannah	134	Old London Road	Head	Mar	45	F	Bonnet Trimming Weaver	Middx	[Unknown]
2264	ELSTONE	Hannah	134		Dau	Unm	11	F	Bonnet Trimming Weaver	Herts	St Albans
2265	ELSTONE	Caroline	134		Dau	Unm	9	F	Bonnet Trimming Weaver	Herts	St Albans
2266	ELSTONE	Elizabeth	134		Dau	Unm	7	F	Bonnet Trimming Weaver	Herts	St Albans
2267	ELSTONE	Mary	134		Dau	Unm	4	F		Herts	St Peters
2268	AUSTIN	Mary	134		Lodger	Unm	23	F	Bonnet Trimming Weaver	Kent	Queenborough
2269	AUSTIN	William	134		Lodger	Unm	6	M	Bonnet Trimming Weaver	Herts	St Peters
2270	HALSEY	George	135	Old London Road	Head	Mar	39	M	Agric Lab	Herts	Sandridge
2271	HALSEY	Sarah	135		Wife	Mar	38	F	Plaiter	Herts	Harpenden
2272	HALSEY	Sarah	135		Dau	Unm	16	F	Bonnet Sewer	Herts	St Albans
2273	HALSEY	Eliza	135		Dau	Unm	12	F	Scholar	Herts	St Peters

	SURNAME	FORENAME	SCHEDULE NUMBER	ADDRESS	RELATIONSHIP	STATUS	AGE	SEX	OCCUPATION	COUNTY OF BIRTH	PLACE OF BIRTH
2274	ANDREWS	Sarah	136	Old London Road	Head	Unm	56	F	Plaiter	Herts	St Stephens
2275	ANDREWS	Mary	136		Mother	Widow	82	F		Herts	St Michaels
2276	SAMS	Henry	137	Old London Road	Head	Mar	33	M	Journeyman Butcher	Herts	Lemsford Mills
2277	SAMS	Eliza	137		Wife	Mar	34	F		Herts	St Albans
2278	SAMS	Mary Ann	137		Dau	Unm	10	F		Herts	St Albans
2279	SAMS	James	137		Son	Unm	7	M	Scholar	Herts	St Albans
2280	SAMS	Henry	137		Son	Unm	4	M	Scholar	Herts	St Albans
2281	SAMS	Jane	137		Dau	Unm	11 m	F		Herts	St Albans
2282	HARTWELL	William	138	Old London Road	Head	Mar	40	M	Carpenter	Herts	St Albans
2283	HARTWELL	Elizabeth	138		Wife	Mar	41	F		Herts	St Albans
2284	HARTWELL	Emily	138		Dau	Unm	17	F		Herts	St Albans
2285	HARTWELL	Sarah	138		Dau	Unm	15	F		Herts	St Albans
2286	HARTWELL	Eliza	138		Dau	Unm	13	F		Herts	St Albans
2287	HARTWELL	Fanny	138		Dau	Unm	4	F		Herts	St Albans
2288	KIFF	Richard	139	Old London Road	Head	Mar	26	M	Cattle Dealer	Herts	St Stephens
2289	KIFF	Rebecca	139		Wife	Mar	18	F		Beds	Great Barford
2290	KIFF	Jane	139		Dau	Unm	4m	F		Herts	St Peters
2291	CLARK	Ambrose	139		Lodger	Unm	26	M	Labourer	Middx	Holloway
2292	OSBORN	Thomas H.	140	Old London Road	Head	Mar	44	M	Bonnet Trimming Manufacturer	Herts	St Albans
2293	OSBORN	Martha	140		Wife	Mar	26	F		Herts	St Albans
2294	OSBORN	Thomas	140		Son	Unm	8	M		Herts	St Albans
2295	OSBORN	Emma	140		Dau	Unm	3	F		Herts	St Albans
2296	OSBORN	Elizabeth	140		Dau	Unm	10 m	F		Herts	St Albans
2297	PUDDEPHAT	Mary	140		Aunt	Unm	50	F	Straw Bonnet Maker	Herts	St Albans
2298	LUDLAM	Thomas	141	Old London Road	Head	Widower	61	M	Independent Minister	Yorks	Sheffield
2299	LUDLAM	Ann E.	141		Dau	Unm	24	F	Straw Hat Manufacturer	Kent	Tunbridge Wells
2300	LUDLAM	Thomas T.	141		Son	Unm	22	M	Straw Hat Manufacturer	Essex	Walthamstow
2301	CUMBERLAND	Elizabeth	141		Serv	Unm	25	F	Straw Hat Manufacturer	Beds	Houghton Regis
2302	WRIGHT	Ellen J.	141		Serv	Unm	18	F	Straw Hat Manufacturer	Middx	London
2303	FRAZIER	Jane	141		Serv	Unm	16	F	House Servant	Kent	Hawkhurst
2304	HOWARD	William	142	Old London Road	Head	Unm	31	M	Coal Dealer	Surrey	Brixton
2305	HOWARD	Charles	142		Brother	Unm	34	M	Bricklayer - Journeyman	Herts	St Albans
2306	HOWARD	Mary Ann	142		Sister	Unm	39	F	Brazilian Hat Maker	Herts	St Albans
2307	HOWARD	Emma	142		Sister	Unm	26	F	Brazilian Hat Maker	Surrey	Brixton
2308	MITCHELL	John	143	Old London Road	Head	Mar	36	M	Master Coach Builder	Herts	Hemel Hempstead
2309	MITCHELL	Ann	143		Wife	Mar	43	F		Herts	St Albans
2310	READ	Emma	143		Niece	Unm	7	F	Scholar	Herts	Redbourn
2311	PARROTT	Mary	143		Mother-in-law	Widow	67	F		Herts	St Albans
2312	DUDLEY	Thomas	144	Old London Road	Head	Mar	53	M	Straw Dealer	Beds	Edjington [Eggington]
2313	DUDLEY	Susan	144		Wife	Mar	48	F		Herts	Bedmond [Abbots Langley]
2314	DUDLEY	Sarah	144		Mother	Widow	78	F		Beds	Eaton Bray
2315	GRAY	Sarah	144		[Lodger]	Widow	53	F		Herts	Redbourn
2316	GRAY	Henry	144		[Lodger]	Unm	18	M	Canvas Weaver	Herts	Redbourn

2317	LOWERY	Robert	145	Old London Road	Head	Mar	41	M	Lecturer	N'thumb	North Shields
2318	LOWERY	Sarah	145		Wife	Mar	42	F		N'thumb	North Shields
2319	LOWERY	Sarah	145		Dau	Unm	22	F	Straw Hat Maker	N'thumb	North Shields
2320	LOWERY	Jessie	145		Grandau	Unm	6	F	Scholar	Scotland	Aberdeen
2321	ARCHER	Thomas	146	Old London Road	Head	Mar	56	M	Labourer	Herts	Aldenham
2322	ARCHER	Sarah	146		Wife	Mar	51	F		Herts	St Albans
2323	ARCHER	Ann	146		Dau	Unm	21	F		Herts	St Albans
2324	ARCHER	Thomas	146		Son	Unm	15	M	Labourer	Herts	St Albans
2325	MAYLES	Jeremiah	147	Old London Road	Head	Mar	34	M	Foreman of Canvas Factory	Beds	Leagrave
2326	MAYLES	Emma	147		Wife	Mar	33	F	Bonnet Sewer	Middx	Whetstone
2327	SIMMONS	Archibald	148	Old London Road	Head	Mar	31	M	Cordwainer	Herts	Watford
2328	SIMMONS	Sarah	148		Wife	Mar	28	F		Bucks	Newport Pagnell
2329	SIMMONS	George	148		Son	Unm	7	M		Herts	St Albans
2330	SIMMONS	Emily	148		Dau	Unm	5	F		Herts	St Albans
2331	SMITH	Charles	149	Hare & Hounds, Old London Road	Head	Widower	64	M	Victualler	Northants	Hackleton
2332	BROWN	Manuel	149		Lodger	Unm	21	M	Labourer	Herts	St Albans
2333	LINES	William	149		Lodger	Unm	20	M	Labourer	Herts	St Albans
2334	WILSON	Edward	149		Lodger	Unm	22	M	Labourer	Herts	St Albans
2335	GOODWIN	William	149		Lodger	Mar	28	M	Hawker	Unknown	
2336	GOODWIN	Ann	149		Lodger	Mar	24	F		Unknown	
2337	PARLES	Thomas	149		Lodger	Unm	23	M	Sawyer	Herts	St Albans
2338	BLOW	William	150	Old London Road	Head	Mar	63	M	Brazilian Hat Blocker	Herts	Caddington
2339	BLOW	Sophia	150		Wife	Mar	53	F		Beds	Luton
2340	BLOW	William	150		Son	Unm	30	M	Hat Blocker	Herts	Knebworth
2341	BLOW	Emma	150		Dau	Unm	25	F	Bonnet Sewer	Herts	St Albans
2342	BLOW	Alfred	150		Son	Unm	18	M	Hat Blocker	Herts	St Albans
2343	BLOW	Ellen	150		Dau	Unm	16	F	Bonnet Sewer	Herts	St Albans
2344	BLOW	Frederick	150		Son	Unm	14	M		Herts	St Albans
2345	BLOW	Mary	150		Dau	Unm	8	F		Herts	St Albans
2346	BLOW	Jane	150		Dau	Unm	3	F		Herts	St Albans
2347	BLOW	James	151	Old London Road	Head	Mar	28	M	Hat Blocker	Herts	Caddington
2348	BLOW	Charlotte	151		Wife	Mar	27	F		Herts	St Albans
2349	BLOW	Walter	151		Son	Unm	5 m	M		Herts	St Albans
2350	JOHNSON	Francis	152	Keyfield Terrace	Head	Mar	30	M	Baker	Herts	Flamstead
2351	JOHNSON	Mary	152		Wife	Mar	30	F		Herts	St Albans
2352	JOHNSON	Sarah	152		Dau [Sister?]	Unm	25	F	Bonnet Sewer	Herts	St Albans
2353	BURGESS	Phoebe	152		Sister-in-law	Unm	32	F	Bonnet Sewer	Herts	St Albans
2354	WESTALL	Harriet	152		Lodger	Unm	12	F	Bonnet Sewer	Herts	St Albans
2355	DYTON	John	153	Keyfield Terrace	Head	Mar	50	M	Labourer	Herts	Cheshunt
2356	DYTON	Mary	153		Wife	Mar	40	F		Herts	Aldenham
2357	DYTON	Joseph	153		Son	Unm	21	M	Bonnet Trimming Weaver	Herts	St Peters
2358	DYTON	Eliza	153		Dau	Unm	16	F	Brazilian Hat Maker	Herts	St Peters
2359	DYTON	William	153		Son	Unm	14	M	Silk Throwster	Herts	St Peters
2360	DYTON	John	153		Son	Unm	12	M	Silk Throwster	Herts	St Peters

	SURNAME	FORENAME	SCHEDULE NUMBER	ADDRESS	RELATIONSHIP	STATUS	AGE	SEX	OCCUPATION	COUNTY OF BIRTH	PLACE OF BIRTH
2361	DYTON	James	153		Son	Unm	9	M	Silk Throwster	Herts	St Peters
2362	DYTON	Henry	153		Son	Unm	7	M		Herts	St Peters
2363	DYTON	Elizabeth	153		Dau	Unm	1	F		Herts	St Peters
One empty house			154								
2364	WESTALL	P.	155	Keyfield Terrace	Head	Widow	46	F	Laundress	Berks	[Unknown]
2365	WESTALL	Daniel	155		Son	Unm	22	M	Labourer	Berks	[Unknown]
2366	WESTALL	Mary	155		Dau	Unm	15	F	Bonnet Trimming Weaver	Berks	[Unknown]
2367	WESTALL	John	155		Son	Unm	13	M	Bonnet Trimming Weaver	Berks	[Unknown]
2368	WESTALL	Isaac	155		Son	Unm	8	M	Bonnet Trimming Weaver	Herts	St Peters
2369	BROWN	William	156	Keyfield Terrace	Head	Mar	47	M	Carpenter	Herts	Hatfield
2370	BROWN	Unnamed	156		Wife	Mar	46	F		Herts	St Albans
2371	BROWN	Eliza	156		Dau	Mar	24	F	Bonnet Trimming Weaver	Herts	St Albans
2372	GAIZLEY	Stephen	156		Lodger	Mar	26	M	Bonnet Trimming Weaver	Unknown	
2373	BROWN	George	156		Son	Unm	19	M	Bonnet Trimming Weaver	Herts	St Albans
2374	BROWN	Elizabeth	156		Dau	Unm	16	F	Brazilian Hat Maker	Herts	St Albans
2375	BROWN	John	156		Son	Unm	11	M	Brazilian Hat Maker	Herts	St Albans
2376	BROWN	William	156		Son	Unm	8	M	Brazilian Hat Maker	Herts	St Albans
2377	EVANS	John	157	Keyfield Terrace	Head	Mar	59	M	Labourer	Herts	St Albans
2378	EVANS	Susannah	157		Wife	Mar	49	F		Herts	St Albans
2379	EVANS	Elizabeth	157		Dau	Unm	20	F	Plaiter	Herts	St Albans
2380	EVANS	John	157		Son	Unm	15	M	Plaiter	Herts	St Albans
2381	EVANS	Susannah	157		Dau	Unm	10	F	Plaiter	Herts	St Albans
2382	EVANS	William	157		Son	Unm	7	M	Plaiter	Herts	St Albans
2383	WRIGHT	William	158	Keyfield Terrace	Head	Mar	33	M	Labourer	Herts	St Albans
2384	WRIGHT	Ann	158		Wife	Mar	33	F		Herts	St Albans
2385	WRIGHT	Charles	158		Son	Unm	11	M		Herts	St Albans
2386	WRIGHT	Samuel	158		Son	Unm	9	M		Herts	St Albans
2387	WRIGHT	Mary	158		Dau	Unm	6	F		Herts	St Albans
2388	WRIGHT	Emma	158		Dau	Unm	1	F		Herts	St Albans
2389	WELCH	Arthur	159	Keyfield Terrace	Head	Mar	25	M	Bonnet Trimming Weaver	Herts	Redbourn
2390	WELCH	Mary Ann	159		Wife	Mar	21	F	Bonnet Trimming Weaver	Middx	London
2391	WILSON	David	160	Keyfield Terrace	Head	Mar	25	M	Silk Throwster	Herts	Watford
2392	WILSON	Eleanor	160		Wife	Mar	30	F		Herts	St Albans
2393	WILSON	William H.	160		Son	Unm	3	M		Herts	St Albans
2394	WILSON	Joseph	160		Son	Unm	1	M		Herts	St Albans
2395	WILSON	John	160		Brother	Unm	13	M		Herts	Watford
2396	WRIGHT	Thomas	161	Keyfield Terrace	Head	Widower	73	M	Labourer	Herts	St Albans
2397	WRIGHT	Elizabeth	161		Dau	Unm	44	F	Laundress	Herts	St Peters
2398	WRIGHT	Ann	161		Dau	Unm	42	F	Bonnet Trimming Weaver	Herts	Redbourn
2399	WRIGHT	Mary	161		Dau	Unm	39	F	Bonnet Trimming Weaver	Herts	Redbourn
2400	WRIGHT	John	161		Son	Unm	20	M	Bonnet Trimming Weaver	Herts	St Peters
2401	GARNER	Mary Ann	162	Keyfield Terrace	Head	Widow	31	F		Middx	[Unknown]

2402	GARNER	Emily	162		Dau	Unm	11	F		Herts	St Albans
2403	GARNER	Rose	162		Dau	Unm	9	F		Herts	St Albans
2404	GARNER	Eliza	162		Dau	Unm	6	F		Herts	St Albans
2405	GARNER	John	162		Son	Unm	1	M		Herts	St Albans
2406	CORLEY	Martha	163	Keyfield Terrace	Head	Mar	58	F		Herts	St Albans
2407	CORLEY	Martha	163		Dau	Unm	24	F		Herts	St Albans
2408	HINTON	Mary	163		Lodger	Widow	69	F		Herts	Shenley
2409	COLLINGS	Robert	164	Keyfield Terrace	Head	Mar	28	M	Bricklayer	Norfolk	East Harling
2410	COLLINGS	Mary Ann	164		Wife	Mar	29	F	Bonnet Trimming Weaver	Herts	St Albans
2411	COLLINGS	George	164		Son	Unm	7	M		Herts	St Albans
2412	COLLINGS	Louisa	164		Dau	Unm	5	F		Herts	St Albans
2413	COLLINGS	Thomas	164		Son	Unm	4	M		Herts	St Albans
2414	COLLINGS	Mark	164		Son	Unm	9 m	M		Herts	St Albans
2415	HAWES	Sarah	165	Keyfield Terrace	Head	Widow	54	F	Laundress	Essex	Harwich
2416	HAWES	Robert	165		Son	Unm	16	M	Butchers Boy	Herts	St Albans
2417	HAWES	Jane	165		Dau	Unm	13	F	Brazilian Hat Maker	Herts	St Albans
2418	STONING	Elizabeth	165		[Lodger]	Widow	31	F	Bonnet Sewer	Herts	Redbourn
2419	STONING	John	165		[Lodgers Son]	Unm	6	M		Middx	Bow
2420	ROBERSON	John	166	Keyfield Terrace	Head	Mar	49	M	Labourer	Herts	St Albans
2421	ROBERSON	Ann	166		Wife	Mar	40	F	Brazilian Hat Maker	Bucks	Weedon
2422	ROBERSON	William	166		Son	Unm	15	M	Brazilian Hat Maker	Herts	St Albans
2423	ROBERSON	George	166		Son	Unm	13	M	Brazilian Hat Maker	Herts	St Albans
2424	ROBERSON	Joseph	166		Son	Unm	11	M	Brazilian Hat Maker	Herts	St Albans
2425	ROBERSON	Mary	166		Dau	Unm	8	F		Herts	St Albans
2426	ROBERSON	James	166		Son	Unm	4	M		Herts	St Albans
2427	TAYLOR	Sarah	167	Keyfield Terrace	Head	Widow	84	F	Blind	Herts	St Albans
2428	PHILLPOTT	Mary	167		Lodger	Unm	38	F		Herts	St Albans
2429	JONES	John	168	Keyfield Terrace	Head	Mar	46	M	Labourer	Herts	St Michaels
2430	JONES	Ann	168		Wife	Mar	56	F		Middx	London
2431	JONES	Susan	168		Dau	Unm	25	F		Herts	St Albans
2432	JONES	Emma	168		Dau	Unm	21	F	Plaiter	Herts	St Michaels
2433	JONES	William	168		Son	Unm	19	M		Herts	St Michaels
2434	JONES	Maria	168		Dau	Unm	14	F	Bonnet Trimming Weaver	Herts	Redbourn
2435	JONES	George	168		Son	Unm	12	M	Brazilian Hat Maker	Herts	Redbourn
2436	RAYMENT	John	169	Keyfield Terrace	Head	Mar	68	M		Beds	Luton
2437	RAYMENT	Ann	169		Wife	Mar	67	F		Beds	Luton
2438	HOLLAND	John	170	Keyfield Terrace	Head	Mar	40	M	Labourer	Herts	St Peters
2439	HOLLAND	Alice	170		Wife	Mar	30	F	Bonnet Trimming Weaver	Herts	St Peters
2440	HOLLAND	William	170		Son	Unm	8	M		Herts	St Peters
2441	HOLLAND	James	170		Son	Unm	6	M		Herts	St Peters
2442	HOLLAND	Sarah	170		Dau	Unm	4	F		Herts	St Peters
2443	HOLLAND	Hannah	170		Dau	Unm	1	F		Herts	St Peters
2444	SAUNDERS	Phillis	170		Sister-in-law	Unm	22	F	Bonnet Trimming Weaver	Herts	Redbourn

	SURNAME	FORENAME	SCHEDULE NUMBER	ADDRESS	RELATIONSHIP	STATUS	AGE	SEX	OCCUPATION	COUNTY OF BIRTH	PLACE OF BIRTH
2445	SAUNDERS	William	171	Keyfield Terrace	Head	Mar	35	M	Labourer	Herts	St Albans
2446	SAUNDERS	Harriet	171		Wife	Mar	28	F	Bonnet Trimming Weaver	Herts	St Albans
2447	SAUNDERS	Samuel	171		Son	Unm	3	M		Herts	St Albans
2448	SAUNDERS	Eliza	171		Dau	Unm	1 m	F		Herts	St Albans
2449	BIGGS	Elizabeth	172	Keyfield Terrace	Head	Mar	55	F		Herts	[Unknown]
2450	BIGGS	Ann	172		Dau	Unm	30	F		Herts	Stevenage
2451	BIGGS	Maria	172		Grandau	Unm	10	F		Herts	St Peters
2452	BIGGS	Louisa	172		Grandau	Unm	6	F		Herts	St Peters
2453	BIGGS	Eliza	172		Grandau	Unm	2	F		Herts	St Peters
2454	BIGGS	Elizabeth	172		Grandau	Unm	16	F		Herts	St Peters
2455	WILLIS	William	173	Keyfield Terrace	Head	Widower	71	M	Chelsea Pensioner	Herts	St Stephens
2456	WILLIS	Samuel	173		Son	Unm	20	M	Labourer	Herts	St Peters
2457	WELLS	Edward	174	Keyfield Terrace	Head	Mar	22	M	Labourer	Herts	Harpenden
2458	WELLS	Rebecca	174		Wife	Mar	21	F	Brazilian Hat Maker	Herts	Sandridge
2459	WELLS	Susannah	174		Dau	Unm	1	F		Herts	St Peters
2460	WELLS	Shadrach	174		Son	Unm	10 m	M		Herts	St Peters
2461	EVANS	George	175	Keyfield Terrace	Head	Mar	47	M	Labourer	Herts	St Peters
2462	EVANS	Ann	175		Wife	Mar	47	F	Brazilian Hat Maker	Beds	Tilsworth
2463	EVANS	Maria	175		Dau	Unm	17	F	Brazilian Hat Maker	Herts	St Albans
2464	CORDELL	Abraham	176	Keyfield Terrace	Head	Mar	66	M	Labourer	Herts	St Pauls Walden
2465	CORDELL	Maria	176		Wife	Mar	69	F		Herts	Kimpton
2466	CORDELL	Charles	176		Son	Mar	47	M	Agric Lab	Herts	Ayot St Lawrence
2467	CORDELL	Mary	176		Dau	Mar	45	F	Bonnet Trimming Weaver	Herts	St Albans
2468	CORDELL	Charles George	176		Grandson	Unm	18	M	Bonnet Trimming Weaver	Herts	St Albans
2469	MUNT	Eliza	177	Keyfield Terrace	Head	Unm	40	F	Bonnet Trimming Weaver	Herts	St Albans
2470	SMITH	George	178	Keyfield Terrace	Head	Mar	27	M	Labourer	Herts	St Albans
2471	SMITH	Elizabeth	178		Wife	Mar	28	F	Brazilian Hat Maker	Herts	Hatfield
2472	SMITH	George	178		Son	Unm	6	M		Herts	St Michaels
2473	SMITH	Frederick	178		Son	Unm	3	M		Herts	St Albans
2474	SMITH	Jane	178		Dau	Unm	6 m	F		Herts	St Peters
2475	ARNOLD	William	179	Keyfield Terrace	Head	Mar	49	M	Labourer	Middx	Enfield
2476	ARNOLD	Susannah	179		Wife	Mar	49	F		Beds	Eaton Bray
2477	ARNOLD	Caroline	179		Dau	Unm	24	F	Brazilian Hat Maker	Herts	Harpenden
2478	ARNOLD	Amelia	179		Dau	Unm	4	F		Herts	Harpenden
2479	BRACEY	William	179		Lodger	Unm	22	M	Labourer	Herts	Harpenden
2480	WANSBY	William	180	Keyfield Terrace	Head	Mar	40	M	Labourer	Bucks	Beaconsfield
2481	WANSBY	Rebecca	180		Wife	Mar	39	F		Herts	Wheathampstead
2482	WANSBY	David	180		Son	Unm	15	M	Agric Lab	Herts	St Peters
2483	WANSBY	Joseph	180		Son	Unm	13	M	Labourer	Herts	St Peters
2484	WEBB	Thomas	181	Keyfield Terrace	Head	Mar	37	M	Dealer	Beds	[Unknown]
2485	WEBB	Mary Ann	181		Wife	Mar	40	F		Herts	Flamstead
2486	WEBB	William	181		Son	Unm	18	M	Labourer	Herts	St Albans
2487	WEBB	Thomas	181		Son	Unm	9	M		Herts	St Albans
2488	WEBB	Sarah	181		Dau	Unm	7	F		Herts	St Albans

2489	LEWIS	Richard	182	Keyfield Terrace	Head	Mar	35	M	Agric Lab	Herts	Wheathampstead
2490	LEWIS	Hannah	182		Wife	Mar	33	F	Plaiter	Herts	Wheathampstead
2491	LEWIS	Frederick	182		Son	Unm	13	M	Silk Throwster	Herts	St Albans
2492	LEWIS	Richard	182		Son	Unm	9	M	Silk Throwster	Herts	St Albans
2493	LEWIS	Henry	182		Son	Unm	6	M		Herts	St Albans
2494	LEWIS	Emma	182		Dau	Unm	4	F		Herts	St Michaels
2495	LEWIS	William	182		Son	Unm	1	M		Herts	St Peters
2496	LOWE	Abbey	182		Sister	Unm	20	F	Brazilian Hat Maker	Herts	Wheathampstead
2497	COLLINS	Mary	183	Keyfield Terrace	Head	Widow	60	F	Plaiter	Beds	[Unknown]
2498	COLLINS	Emma	183		Dau	Unm	19	F	Bonnet Trimming Weaver	Herts	St Peters
2499	JEANS	John	184	Keyfield Terrace	Head	Mar	24	M	Labourer	Herts	St Michaels
2500	JEANS	Elleanor	184		Wife	Mar	26	F	Brazilian Hat Maker	Herts	Harpenden
2501	JEANS	George	184		Son	Unm	2	M		Herts	Harpenden
2502	SMITH	Henry	185	Keyfield Terrace	Head	Mar	38	M	Labourer	Herts	St Albans
2503	SMITH	Mary Ann	185		Wife	Mar	33	F	Bonnet Trimming Weaver	Herts	Berkhamsted
2504	SMITH	Georgiana	185		Dau	Unm	2	F		Herts	St Peters
2505	SMITH	Georgiana	186	Keyfield Terrace	Head	Unm	28	F	Brazilian Hat Maker	Herts	St Albans
2506	SMITH	Louisa	186		Sister	Unm	20	F	Brazilian Hat Maker	Herts	St Albans
2507	WILSON	Henry	187	Keyfield Terrace	Head	Mar	48	M	Agric Lab	Herts	St Michaels
2508	WILSON	Charlotte	187		Wife	Mar	45	F		Herts	St Stephens
2509	WILSON	Samuel	187		Son	Unm	16	M	Brazilian Hat Maker	Herts	St Peters
2510	WILSON	Charles	187		Son	Unm	14	M	Brazilian Hat Maker	Herts	St Peters
2511	WILSON	Thomas	187		Son	Unm	12	M	Brazilian Hat Maker	Herts	St Peters
2512	WILSON	George	187		Son	Unm	9	M	Brazilian Hat Maker	Herts	St Peters
2513	WILSON	Maria	187		Dau	Unm	6	F		Herts	St Peters
2514	WILSON	Henry	187		Son	Unm	4	M		Herts	St Peters
2515	PURSELL	William	188	Keyfield Terrace	Head	Mar	50	M	Shoemaker	Herts	St Peters
2516	PURSELL	Elizabeth	188		Wife	Mar	46	F	Dressmaker	Herts	Stevenage
2517	PURSELL	Thomas	188		Son	Mar	25	M	Shoemaker	Herts	St Peters
2518	PURSELL	Charlotte	188		Dau-in-law	Mar	25	F	Brazilian Hat Maker	Herts	St Peters
2519	PURSELL	Selina	188		Dau	Unm	15	F	Brazilian Hat Maker	Herts	St Peters
2520	PURSELL	Sabina	188		Dau	Unm	13	F	Brazilian Hat Maker	Herts	St Peters
2521	PURSELL	Alexander	188		Son	Unm	11	M	Brazilian Hat Maker	Herts	St Peters
2522	PURSELL	Mary	188		Dau	Unm	4	F	Scholar	Herts	St Peters
2523	WESTALL	Amy	188		Lodger	Unm	15	F	Brazilian Hat Maker	Berks	[Unknown]

Chapter Nine

The Out-hamlets in the liberty of St Albans

Registrar's District: St Albans   Enumeration District 2a   Ref. HO 107/1713 folios 308-24

Sleap and Smallford Hamlet, north of the St Albans and Hatfield Road, and the houses abutting on such road and the houses at Ellenbrook.

Parish of St Stephens

1	IVORY	Joseph	1	Tyttenhanger Green	Head	Mar	37	M	Farm Labourer	Herts	Great Berkhamsted
2	IVORY	Mary	1		Wife	Mar	31	F	Plaiter	Herts	Tyttenhanger Green
3	IVORY	David	1		Son	Unm	12	M		Herts	Tyttenhanger Green
4	IVORY	William	1		Son	Unm	11	M		Herts	Tyttenhanger Green
5	IVORY	Elizabeth	1		Dau	Unm	7	F		Herts	Tyttenhanger Green
6	IVORY	Charlotte	1		Dau	Unm	5	F		Herts	Tyttenhanger Green
7	IVORY	James	1		Son	Unm	4	M		Herts	Tyttenhanger Green
8	IVORY	Sarah	1		Dau	Unm	3	F		Herts	Tyttenhanger Green
9	IVORY	Richard	1		Son	Unm	1	M		Herts	Tyttenhanger Green
10	DOCKERY	William	2	Tyttenhanger Green	Head	Mar	40	M	Agric Lab	Herts	Broad Colney [Shenley]
11	DOCKERY	Maria	2		Wife	Mar	31	F	Straw Plaiter	Herts	St Albans
12	DOCKERY	Thomas	2		Son	Unm	12	M		Herts	Tyttenhanger Green
13	DOCKERY	Shadric	2		Son	Unm	9	M		Herts	Tyttenhanger Green
14	DOCKERY	James	2		Son	Unm	6	M		Herts	Tyttenhanger Green
15	DOCKERY	George	2		Son	Unm	2	M		Herts	Tyttenhanger Green
16	REEVES	John	3	Tyttenhanger Green	Head	Mar	40	M	Agric Lab	Herts	Whitwell
17	REEVES	Elizabeth	3		Wife	Mar	39	F		Essex	Parndon
18	REEVES	William	3		Son	Unm	19	M	Agric Lab	Essex	Parndon
19	REEVES	Marshal	3		Son	Unm	15	M	Straw Plaiter	Herts	St Peters
20	REEVES	Elijah	3		Son	Unm	13	M	Straw Plaiter	Herts	St Peters
21	REEVES	David	3		Son	Unm	7	M		Herts	St Peters
22	REEVES	Sophia	3		Dau	Unm	5	F		Herts	St Peters
23	REEVES	Betsey	3		Dau	Unm	4	F		Herts	St Peters

Figure 9 : THE OUT-HAMLETS OF ST ALBANS

413

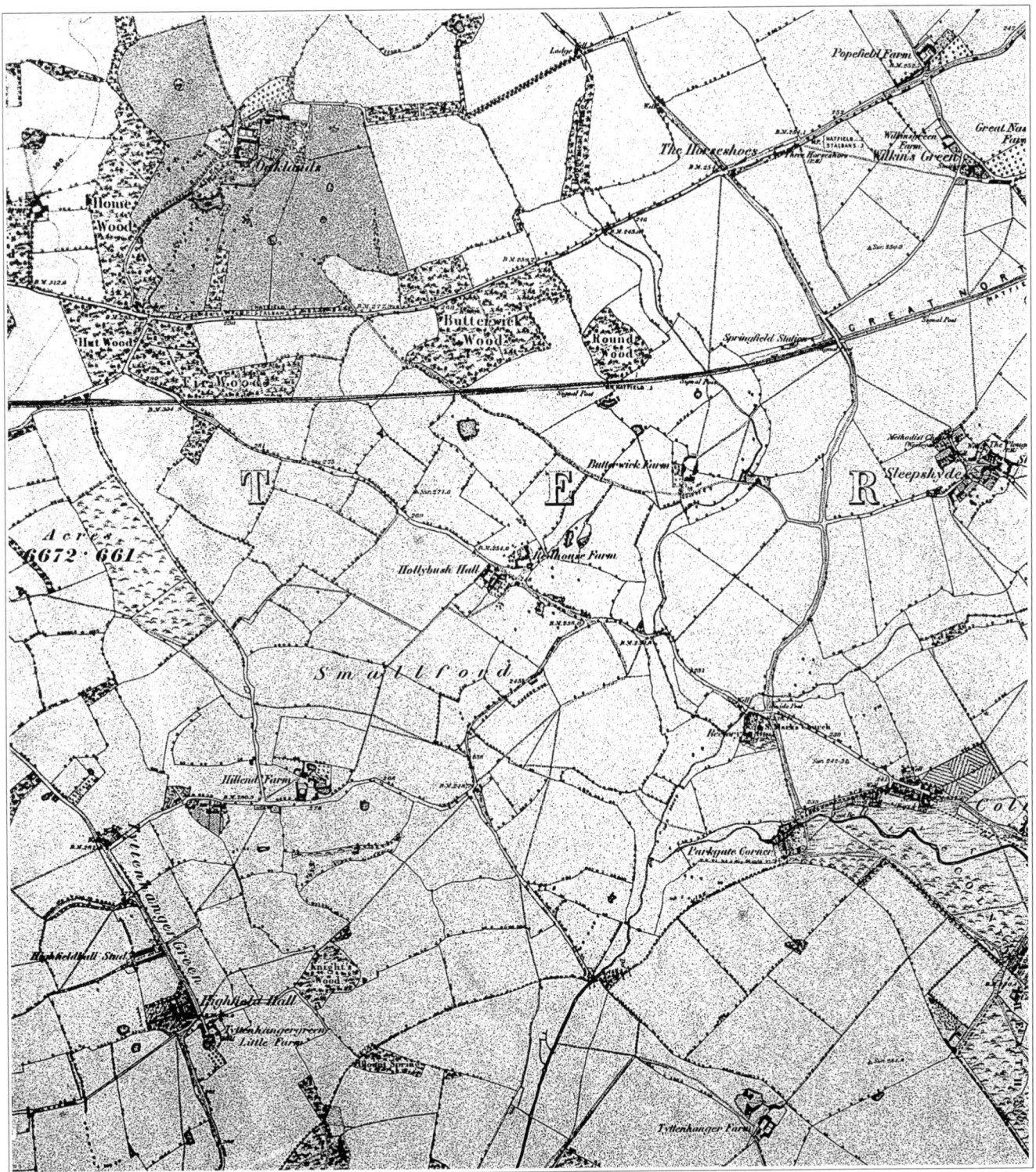

From the first edition of the 6 inch Ordinance Survey of Hertfordshire (1878), Sheet XXXV

Approximate scale of reproduction: 1cm = 106m

	SURNAME	FORENAME	SCHEDULE NUMBER	ADDRESS	RELATIONSHIP	STATUS	AGE	SEX	OCCUPATION	COUNTY OF BIRTH	PLACE OF BIRTH
24	REEVES	Mary	3		Dau	Unm	1	F		Herts	Tyttenhanger Green
25	BRINKLOW	Deborah	4	Tyttenhanger Green	Head	Widow	63	F	Farmer	Hunts	St Neots
26	BRINKLOW	William	4		Son	Mar	36	M	Bailiff	Bucks	Great Brickhill
27	BRINKLOW	Ann	4		Dau-in-law	Mar	40	F		Lincs	Burton
28	BRINKLOW	Alfred	4		Brother	Unm	27	M	Servant	Bucks	Great Brickhill
29	BRINKLOW	George	4		Son	Unm	6	M		Herts	Shenley Hill
30	BRINKLOW	William	4		Son	Unm	4	M		Herts	Tyttenhanger Green
31	BRINKLOW	Emma	4		Dau	Unm	2	F		Herts	Tyttenhanger Green
32	BRINKLOW	Amelia	4		Dau	Unm	2	F		Herts	Tyttenhanger Green
33	WATKINS	Frederick	4		Nephew	Unm	11	M		Middx	Marylebone
34	FIELD	Elizabeth	4		Serv	Unm	17	F	Servant	Herts	St Stephens
35	KIFF	James	4		Serv	Unm	20	M	Farm Lab	Herts	Tyttenhanger Green
36	KIFF	John	4		Serv	Unm	14	M	Farm Lab	Herts	Tyttenhanger Green
37	HOW	Joseph	4		Serv	Unm	12	M	Farm Lab	Herts	Tyttenhanger Green
38	REYNOLDS	George	5	Tyttenhanger Green	Head	Mar	62	M	Farmer of 60 acres employing 2 men & 2 boys	Herts	St Stephens
39	REYNOLDS	Ann E.	5		Wife	Mar	65	F	Farmers Wife	Herts	St Albans
40	REYNOLDS	William	5		Son	Unm	32	M		Herts	St Stephens
41	REYNOLDS	Ann	5		Dau	Unm	21	F		Herts	St Stephens
42	DOCKERY	Caleb	5		Serv	Unm	13	M	Agric Lab	Herts	St Peters
43	ALLEN	Henry	5		Serv	Unm	13	M	Agric Lab	Herts	St Peters
44	KIFF	William	6	Tyttenhanger Green	Head	Widower	50	M	Agric Lab	Herts	Westwick Row [St Michaels]
45	KIFF	Sarah	6		Dau	Unm	24	F	Housekeeper	Herts	Colney Heath
46	HOW	Elizabeth	6		Visitor	Unm	10	F	Scholar	Herts	Tyttenhanger Green
47	HOW	George	7	Tyttenhanger Green	Head	Mar	52	M	Agric Lab	Herts	Colney Heath
48	HOW	Sarah	7		Wife	Mar	49	F	Housekeeper	Herts	Sandridge
49	HOW	James	7		Son	Unm	25	M	Agric Lab	Herts	St Peters
50	HOW	George	7		Son	Unm	22	M	Agric Lab	Herts	Colney Heath
51	HOW	William	7		Son	Unm	17	M	Agric Lab	Herts	Tyttenhanger Green
52	HOW	Henry	7		Son	Unm	15	M	Agric Lab	Herts	Tyttenhanger Green
53	HOW	John	7		Son	Unm	8	M	Agric Lab	Herts	Tyttenhanger Green
54	ALLEN	Thomas	8	Tyttenhanger Green	Head	Mar	29	M	Agric Lab	Herts	Tyttenhanger Green
55	ALLEN	Hannah	8		Wife	Mar	29	F	Straw Hat Maker	Herts	St Peters
56	ALLEN	Mary Ann	8		Dau	Unm	7	F	Scholar	Herts	London Colney
57	ALLEN	Frederick	8		Son	Unm	1	M		Herts	Tyttenhanger Green
58	HUTSON	Thomas	9	Tyttenhanger Green	Head	Mar	81	M	Brewer	Essex	Hockley
59	HUTSON	Margaret	9		Wife	Mar	61	F	Brewers Wife	Herts	Weston
60	HUTSON	Margaret	9		Dau	Unm	29	F	Dressmaker	Herts	Harpenden
61	LAMBERT	William H	9		Grandson	Unm	4	M	Scholar	Herts	Markyate
62	KIFF	Joseph	10	Tyttenhanger Green	Head	Mar	40	M	Agric Lab	Herts	St Albans
63	KIFF	Mary	10		Wife	Mar	38	F	Straw Plaiter	Herts	London Colney

64	KIFF	Mary	10		Dau	Unm	11	F	Scholar	Herts	Tyttenhanger Green
65	KIFF	John	10		Son	Unm	6	M		Herts	Tyttenhanger Green
66	TYLER	James	11	Tyttenhanger Green	Head	Mar	80	M	Agric Lab	Herts	Sleapshyde
67	TYLER	Ann	11		Wife	Mar	78	F		Beds	South Hill
68	WHITE	John	11		Lodger	Unm	30	M	Agric Lab	Herts	St Albans
69	COOK	George	12	Tyttenhanger Green	Head	Mar	56	M	Agric Lab	Herts	Sandridge
70	COOK	Sarah	12		Wife	Mar	55	F	Agric Labs Wife	Herts	Ellenbrook [St Peters]
71	FUSEDALE	Sarah	12		Visitor	Mar	29	F	Bonnet Trimming Weaver	Herts	Beastney [St Peters]
72	COOK	Emma	12		Dau	Unm	17	F	Bonnet Trimming Weaver	Herts	Beastney [St Peters]
73	COOK	Henry	12		Son	Unm	15	M	Agric Lab	Herts	Beastney [St Peters]
74	FUSEDALE	Walter	12		Visitor	Unm	4	M	Scholar	Herts	London Colney
75	FUSEDALE	Ruth	12		Visitor	Unm	2	F	At Home	Herts	London Colney
76	HARRIS	John	13	Tyttenhanger Green	Head	Mar	40	M	Agric Lab	Herts	[Unknown]
77	HARRIS	Maria	13		Wife	Mar	40	F	Agric Labs Wife	Middx	[Unknown]
78	HARRIS	Martha	13		Dau	Unm	18	F	Brazilian Grass Hat Maker	Essex	[Unknown]
79	HARRIS	Maria	13		Dau	Unm	16	F	Brazilian Grass Hat Maker	Herts	[Unknown]
80	HARRIS	Susan	13		Dau	Unm	13	F	Brazilian Grass Hat Maker	Herts	[Unknown]
81	HARRIS	George	13		Son	Unm	11	M	Brazilian Grass Hat Maker	Herts	[Unknown]
82	HARRIS	Caroline	13		Dau	Unm	9	F	Brazilian Grass Hat Maker	Herts	[Unknown]
83	HARRIS	Joseph	13		Son	Unm	7	M	Brazilian Grass Hat Maker	Herts	[Unknown]
84	HARRIS	Rachel	13		Dau	Unm	5	F	Scholar	Herts	[Unknown]
85	HARRIS	James	13		Son	Unm	3	M	At Home	Herts	[Unknown]
86	REYNOLDS	Francis	14	Tyttenhanger Green	Head	Unm	27	M	Wheelwright	Herts	St Stephens
87	PICKET	Charlotte	14		[blank]	Unm	23	F		Herts	Shenley
88	PICKET	Edward	14		Son	Unm	4	M	At Home	Herts	Shenley
89	PICKET	Francis	14		Son	Unm	2	M	At Home	Herts	Shenley
90	PICKET	William	14		Son	Unm	2m	M	At Home	Herts	St Stephens
91	HIPGRAVE	Benjamin	15	Tyttenhanger Green	Head	Mar	35	M	Agric Lab	Suffolk	Ipswich
92	HIPGRAVE	Rose	15		Wife	Mar	30	F	Straw Plaiter	Herts	Ellenbrook [St Peters]
93	HIPGRAVE	William	15		Son	Unm	7	M		Herts	Smallford
94	HIPGRAVE	Harriet	15		Dau	Unm	4	F	At Home	Herts	Blue Houses [North Mimms]
95	HIPGRAVE	Rachael	15		Dau	Unm	7dys	F	At Home	Herts	Tyttenhanger Green
96	CHILDS	Joseph	16	Tyttenhanger Green (Part of house)	Head	Mar	31	M	Agric Lab	Middx	Mimms
97	CHILDS	Eliza	16		Wife	Mar	25	F		Herts	Tyttenhanger Green
98	CHILDS	James R	16		Son	Unm	7	M	At Home	Herts	Tyttenhanger Green
99	CHILDS	Jane	16		Dau	Unm	3	F	At Home	Herts	Tyttenhanger Green
100	CHILDS	William E	16		Son	Unm	9m	M	At Home	Herts	Tyttenhanger Green
101	LARFORD	Joseph	17	Tyttenhanger Green	Head	Mar	50	M	Agric Lab	Herts	North Mimms
102	LARFORD	Susan	17		Wife	Mar	50	F		Herts	Smallford
103	LARFORD	Mary	17		Dau	Unm	21	F	Bonnet Trimming Weaver	Herts	Smallford

	SURNAME	FORENAME	SCHEDULE NUMBER	ADDRESS	RELATIONSHIP	STATUS	AGE	SEX	OCCUPATION	COUNTY OF BIRTH	PLACE OF BIRTH
104	LARFORD	David	17		Son	Unm	16	M	Agric Lab	Herts	Smallford
105	LARFORD	Thomas	17		Son	Unm	10	M	Scholar	Herts	Tyttenhanger Green
106	CROCKET	John	17		Lodger	Unm	15	M	Agric Lab	Herts	St Stephens
107	POTTER	William	18	Tyttenhanger Green	Head	Mar	30	M	Agric Lab	Herts	London Colney
108	POTTER	Martha	18		Wife	Mar	30	F		Herts	Bengeo
109	POTTER	Martha	18		Dau	Unm	11	F	Brazilian Hat Maker	Herts	Tyttenhanger Green
110	POTTER	William	18		Son	Unm	9	M	Brazilian Hat Maker	Herts	Tyttenhanger Green
111	POTTER	Betsey	18		Dau	Unm	7	F	Brazilian Hat Maker	Herts	Tyttenhanger Green
112	FALKNALL	James	19	Tyttenhanger Green	Head	Mar	40	M	Agric Lab	Herts	St Peters
113	FALKNALL	Eliza	19		Wife	Mar	31	F		Herts	St Peters
114	FALKNALL	Sarah	19		Dau	Unm	16	F	Brazilian Hat Maker	Herts	St Peters
115	FALKNALL	Elizabeth	19		Dau	Unm	11	F	Brazilian Hat Maker	Herts	St Peters
116	FALKNALL	Emma	19		Dau	Unm	9	F	Brazilian Hat Maker	Herts	St Peters
117	FALKNALL	Eliza	19		Dau	Unm	8	F	Brazilian Hat Maker	Herts	St Peters
118	FALKNALL	Marian	19		Dau	Unm	5	F	Brazilian Hat Maker	Herts	St Peters
119	FALKNALL	Rebecca	19		Dau	Unm	3	F	At Home	Herts	St Peters
120	FALKNALL	John	20	Tyttenhanger Green (Part of house)	Head	Mar	37	M	Agric Lab	Herts	St Peters
121	FALKNALL	Hannah	20		Dau	Unm	11	F	Brazilian Hat Maker	Herts	St Peters
122	FALKNALL	James	20		Son	Unm	9	M	Brazilian Hat Maker	Herts	St Peters
123	REYNOLDS	George	21	Tyttenhanger Green	Head	Mar	33	M	Agric Lab	Herts	St Stephens
124	REYNOLDS	Anna	21		Wife	Mar	24	F		Herts	St Stephens
125	REYNOLDS	George	21		Son	Unm	2	M	At Home	Herts	St Stephens
126	REYNOLDS	William	21		Son	Unm	1	M	At Home	Herts	St Stephens
127	LEE	William	21		Lodger	Unm	23	M	Agric Lab	Beds	Millow
128	SMITH	John	22	Tyttenhanger Green	Head	Mar	32	M	Agric Lab	Herts	St Albans
129	SMITH	Jane	22		Wife	Mar	30	F	Bonnet Trimming Weaver	Herts	St Peters
130	SMITH	William	22		Son	Unm	6	M	At Home	Herts	St Peters
131	SMITH	Mary	22		Dau	Unm	3	F	At Home	Herts	St Peters
132	SMITH	William	23	Tyttenhanger Green (Part of house)	Lodger	Unm	20	M	Agric Lab	Herts	St Peters
133	FIELD	Joseph	23		Lodger	Unm	20	M	Agric Lab	Herts	St Peters
134	CROCKETT	William	23		Lodger	Unm	14	M	Agric Lab	Herts	St Peters
135	DELL	Mary	24		Wife	Widow	40	F	Public House Keeper	Herts	Sandridge
136	DELL	William	24		Son	Unm	13	M	Agric Lab	Herts	St Stephens
137	DELL	George	24		Son	Unm	10	M	At Home	Herts	St Stephens
138	DELL	Elizabeth	24		Dau	Unm	7	F	At Home	Herts	St Stephens
139	DELL	Henry	24		Son	Unm	4	M	At Home	Herts	St Stephens
140	DELL	Caroline	24		Dau	Unm	1	F	At Home	Herts	St Stephens
141	CHICKETT	William	25	Tyttenhanger Green (Part of house)	Head	Mar	30	M	Agric Lab	Suffolk	[Unknown]
142	CHICKETT	Lucy	25		Wife	Mar	38	F		Suffolk	[Unknown]
143	DAVIS	David	26	Tyttenhanger Green	Head	Mar	25	M	Agric Lab	Beds	Dunton
144	DAVIS	Hannah	26		Wife	Mar	29	F	Plaiter	Beds	Dunton
145	DAVIS	John	26		Son	Unm	2	M	At Home	Beds	Dunton
146	GOODWICH	Eliza	27	Tyttenhanger Green	Wife	[Mar]	22	F	Plaiter	Herts	Hatfield

147	GOODWICH	Emily	27		Dau	Unm	3	F	At Home	Herts	Hatfield
148	BROWN	Thomas	28	Hill End	Head	Mar	32	M	Farmer of 300 acres employing 3 labourers	Beds	Dunton
149	BROWN	Penelope	28		Wife	Mar	30	F		Herts	Baldock
150	BROWN	William	28		Son	Unm	13	M	Scholar	Beds	Dunton
151	BROWN	Alfred	28		Son	Unm	9	M	Scholar	Beds	Dunton
152	BROWN	Elizabeth	28		Dau	Unm	7	F	Scholar	Beds	Dunton
153	ROW	Mary Ann	28		Governess	Unm	19	F	Governess	Middx	Highgate
154	MORTON	Mary	28		Serv	Unm	20	F	House Servant	Herts	Colney Heath
155	HARRIS	Benjamin	28		Serv	Unm	22	M	Agric Lab	Herts	Kimpton
156	BEACH	John	28		Serv	Unm	17	M	Agric Lab	Herts	Colney Heath
157	WHITE	Thomas	29	Hill End	Head	Mar	42	M	Agric Lab	Herts	St Albans
158	WHITE	Hannah	29		Wife	Mar	38	F		Warks	[Unknown]
159	WHITE	Emma	29		Dau	Unm	8	F	Scholar	Herts	Smallford
160	WHITE	Rachael	29		Dau	Unm	4	F	At Home	Herts	Smallford
161	GURNEY	George	29		Lodger	Unm	23	M	Agric Lab	Herts	Smallford
162	BROWN	William	30	Sion Cottage	Head	Mar	37	M	Dealer In Beer	Monm'th	[Unknown]
163	BROWN	Elizabeth	30		Wife	Mar	38	F		Middx	London
164	BROWN	Ann	30		Dau	Unm	15	F		Glos	[Unknown]
165	BROWN	George	30		Son	Unm	11	M		Herts	[Unknown]
166	BROWN	Elard Jane	30		Dau	Unm	8	F		Herts	[Unknown]
167	ALLEN	Thomas	30		[blank]	Unm	22	M	Agric Lab	Herts	[Unknown]
168	HOY	James	31	Sion Cottage	Head	Mar	30	M	Agric Lab	Herts	[Unknown]
169	HOY	Jane	31		Wife	Mar	26	F	Plaiter	Herts	[Unknown]
170	HOY	William	31		Son	Unm	7	M	Plaiter	Herts	[Unknown]
171	PERRY	Thomas	32	Sion Cottage	Head	Mar	42	M	Shepherd	Herts	Smallford
172	PERRY	Charlotte	32		Wife	Mar	42	F	Brazilian Hat Maker	Shrop	[Unknown]
173	PERRY	Ellen	32		Dau	Unm	18	F	Brazilian Hat Maker	Herts	Shenley
174	PERRY	Emma	32		Dau	Unm	17	F	Brazilian Hat Maker	Herts	Shenley
175	PERRY	Louisa	32		Dau	Unm	14	F	Brazilian Hat Maker	Herts	Shenley
176	PERRY	William	32		Son	Unm	12	M	Agric Lab	Herts	Shenley
177	PERRY	Charlotte	32		Dau	Unm	10	F	Brazilian Hat Maker	Herts	St Peters
178	PERRY	Harriett	32		Dau	Unm	8	F	Brazilian Hat Maker	Herts	St Peters
179	PERRY	Shadrack	32		Son	Unm	5	M	Brazilian Hat Maker	Herts	Smallford
180	PERRY	Mary Ann	32		Dau	Unm	3	F	Brazilian Hat Maker	Herts	Smallford
181	PERRY	Alice	32		Dau	Unm	1	F	At Home	Herts	Smallford
182	HOY	John	33	Sion Cottage	Head	Mar	40	M	Agric Lab	Herts	St Stephens
183	HOY	Sarah	33		Wife	Mar	27	F		Herts	St Stephens
184	HOY	George	33		Son	Unm	8	M	Agric Lab	Herts	St Peters
185	HOY	James	33		Son	Unm	5	M	At Home	Herts	St Stephens
186	HOWARD	Ann	34	Sion Cottage (Part of house)	Wife	Mar	64	F	Charwoman	Herts	St Stephens
187	HOWARD	John	34		Son	Unm	30	M	Agric Lab	Herts	St Stephens
188	KING	Abraham	35	Sion Cottage	Head	Mar	47	M	Gardener	Herts	St Albans
189	KING	Harriet	35		Wife	Mar	57	F		Sussex	[Unknown]
190	RAWRIDGE	Jane	36	Sion Cottage	Wife	Mar	35	F	Plaiter	Herts	St Peters

	SURNAME	FORENAME	SCHEDULE NUMBER	ADDRESS	RELATIONSHIP	STATUS	AGE	SEX	OCCUPATION	COUNTY OF BIRTH	PLACE OF BIRTH
191	RAWRIDGE	John	36		Son	Unm	17	M	Agric Lab	Herts	St Peters
192	FALKNALL	Henry	36		Visitor	Unm	40	M	Agric Lab	Herts	St Peters
193	HARRIS	Joseph	37	Sion Cottages	Head	Mar	42	M	Agric Lab	Herts	Hatfield
194	HARRIS	Mary	37		Wife	Mar	42	F	Plaiter	Herts	Ippollitts
195	HARRIS	John	37		Son	Unm	16	M	Agric Lab	Herts	Kimpton
196	HARRIS	Ann	37		Dau	Unm	14	F	Brazilian Hat Maker	Herts	Kimpton
197	HARRIS	Joseph	37		Son	Unm	8	M	Agric Lab	Herts	St Stephens

End of St Stephens parish

The parish of St Peters

	SURNAME	FORENAME	SCHEDULE NUMBER	ADDRESS	RELATIONSHIP	STATUS	AGE	SEX	OCCUPATION	COUNTY OF BIRTH	PLACE OF BIRTH
198	REYNOLDS	George	38	Horse Shoes	Head	Mar	36	M	Agric Lab	Herts	St Peters
199	REYNOLDS	Susan	38		Wife	Mar	36	F	School Mistress	Herts	St Peters
200	REYNOLDS	George	38		Son	Unm	7	M		Herts	St Peters
201	REYNOLDS	Levi	38		Son	Unm	5	M		Herts	St Peters
202	REYNOLDS	Marian	38		Dau	Unm	2	F		Herts	St Peters
203	BERRY	William	39	Horse Shoes	Head	Mar	65	M	Turnpike Toll Collector	Surrey	Bookham
204	BERRY	Elizabeth	39		Wife	Mar	55	F		Herts	Hertford
205	WRIGHT	William	40	Horse Shoes	Head	Mar	74	M	Corn Salesman	Bucks	Cheddington
206	WRIGHT	Sarah	40		Wife	Mar	52	F		Beds	Toddington
207	WRIGHT	William	40		Son	Unm	9	M	Scholar	Herts	St Peters
208	RANDALL	Eliza	40		Dau-in-law	Unm	17	F		Herts	St Peters
209	HILL	Robert	41	Horse Shoes	Head	Mar	49	M	Agric Lab	Herts	St Peters
210	HILL	Hannah	41		Wife	Mar	45	F	Plaiter	Herts	St Peters
211	HILL	Sarah	41		Dau	Unm	18	F	Brazilian Hat Maker	Herts	St Peters
212	HILL	William	41		Son	Unm	14	M	Agric Lab	Herts	St Peters
213	HILL	Henry	41		Son	Unm	12	M	Agric Lab	Herts	St Peters
214	HILL	Robert	41		Son	Unm	5	M		Herts	St Peters
215	COLLINS	Thomas	41		Visitor	Unm	25	M	Agric Lab	Herts	St Peters
216	SLEET	Frederick	41		Visitor	Unm	19	M	Carpenter	Herts	St Peters
217	SIMKINS	Henry	42	Horse Shoes	Head	Mar	40	M	Agric Lab	Herts	North Mimms, Bell Bar
218	SIMKINS	Dinah	42		Wife	Mar	35	F	Plaiter	Herts	St Peters
219	SIMKINS	Mary	42		Dau	Unm	12	F	Plaiter	Herts	St Peters
220	SIMKINS	Eliza	42		Dau	Unm	7	F	Plaiter	Herts	St Peters
221	SIMKINS	James	42		Son	Unm	9	M	Plaiter	Herts	St Peters
222	SIMKINS	John	42		Son	Unm	6 m	M	At Home	Herts	St Peters
223	WEBB	Sarah	42		Cousin	Unm	17	F	Plaiter	Herts	St Peters
224	GIDDINS	Samuel	43	Horse Shoes	Head	Mar	50	M	Agric Lab	Beds	Clifton
225	GIDDINS	Ann	43		Wife	Mar	49	F		Beds	Storfold [Stotfold]
226	GIDDINS	Mary Ann	43		Dau	Unm	14	F		Beds	Artsey [Arlesey]
227	WYKER	Thomas	44	Horse Shoes	Head	Mar	28	M	Gamekeeper	Herts	Hemel Hempstead
228	WYKER	Eliza	44		Wife	Mar	27	F		Herts	St Peters
229	WYKER	Thomas John	44		Son	Unm	1	M	At Home	Herts	St Peters
230	CLIFFEN	William	45	Horse Shoes	Head	Mar	46	M	Agric Lab	Herts	Kensworth

231	CLIFFEN	Charlotte	45		Wife	Mar	41	F	Plaiter	Herts	St Peters
232	MESENGER	Mary	45		Lodger	Unm	25	F	Plaiter	Herts	St Peters
233	MESENGER	George	45		Lodger	Unm	7	M		Herts	St Peters
234	MESENGER	Mary Ann	45		Lodger	Unm	1	F	At Home	Herts	St Peters
235	GIBBS	Mary	46	Horse Shoes	Head	Widow	70	F	Washerwoman	Middx	Limehouse
236	SIMPKIN	John	47	Horse Shoes	Head	Mar	32	M	Agric Lab	Herts	St Peters
237	SIMPKIN	Emma	47		Wife	Mar	27	F	Plait Manufacturer	Herts	St Peters
238	SIMPKIN	William	47		Son	Unm	4	M	At Home	Herts	St Peters
239	SIMPKIN	Thomas	47		Son	Unm	2	M	At Home	Herts	St Peters
240	WARD	Martha	48	Horse Shoes	Head	Widow	59	F		Herts	St Peters
241	WARD	John	48		[blank]	Unm	33	M	Agric Lab	Herts	St Peters
242	WARD	Mary	48		Dau	Unm	23	F	Plaiter	Herts	St Peters
243	RAU	William	49	Horse Shoes	Head	Mar	64	M	Agric Lab	Herts	Hatfield
244	RAU	Mary	49		Wife	Mar	44	F	Washerwoman	Middx	[Unknown]
245	RAU	George	49		Son	Unm	18	M	Brazilian Hat Maker	Herts	Northaw
246	RAU	Joseph	49		Son	Unm	15	M	Agric Lab	Herts	Northaw
247	RAU	Emma	49		Dau	Unm	14	F		Herts	Northaw
248	RAU	Rosy	49		Dau	Unm	8	F		Herts	St Peters
249a	DEARMAN	Abraham	50	Horse Shoes	Head	Mar	45	M	Victualler. Chelsea Pensioner	Herts	St, Albans
249b	DEARMAN	Sarah	50		Wife	Mar	55	F	Deaf	Herts	St Albans
250	DEARMAN	Joshua	50		Son	Unm	20	M	Cattle Dealer	Herts	St Peters
251	DEARMAN	Mary	50		Dau	Unm	18	F	Dressmaker	Herts	St Peters
252	DEARMAN	Jemima	50		Dau	Unm	15	F	Dressmaker	Herts	St Peters
253	GILBERT	William	50		Serv	Unm	29	M	Agric Lab	Herts	St Peters
254	SOUTH	George	50		Serv	Unm	23	M	Agric Lab	Herts	Welwyn
255	SIMPKINS	William	51	Horse Shoes	Head	Mar	45	M	Agric Lab	Herts	North Mimms
256	SIMPKINS	Rebecca	51		Wife	Mar	39	F	Plaiter	Herts	St Peters
257	SIMPKINS	William	51		Son	Unm	23	M	Agric Lab	Herts	North Mimms
258	SIMPKINS	Richard	51		Son	Unm	21	M	Agric Lab	Herts	St Peters
259	SIMPKINS	Eliza	51		Dau	Unm	17	F	Brazilian Hat Maker	Herts	St Peters
260	SIMPKINS	Rebecca	51		Dau	Unm	15	F	Brazilian Hat Maker	Herts	St Peters
261	SIMPKINS	Emily	51		Dau	Unm	13	F	Brazilian Hat Maker	Herts	St Peters
262	WEBB	James	52	Horse Shoes	Head	Mar	40	M	Agric Lab	Herts	North Mimms
263	WEBB	Mary	52		Wife	Mar	43	F	Plaiter	Herts	St Peters
264	WEBB	Joseph	52		Son	Unm	17	M	Blacksmith	Herts	St Peters
265	WEBB	Eliza	52		Dau	Unm	10	F	Plaiter	Herts	St Peters
266	WEBB	Anne	52		Dau	Unm	7	F	Plaiter	Herts	St Peters
267	WEBB	Emma	52		Dau	Unm	4	F	At Home	Herts	St Peters
268	WEBB	James	52		Son	Unm	1	M	At Home	Herts	St Peters
269	WEBB	Edward	52		Son	Unm	1	M	At Home	Herts	St Peters
270	LINES	Edward	52	Horse Shoes (Part of house)	Head	Widower	70	M	Blacksmith	Herts	Harpenden
271	LINES	Sophia	52		Dau	Unm	37	F	Plaiter	Herts	St Peters
272	LINES	Elizabeth	52		Dau	Unm	9	F	Plaiter	Herts	St Peters
273	LINES	Harriet	52		Dau	Unm	6	F	Plaiter	Herts	St Peters

	SURNAME	FORENAME	SCHEDULE NUMBER	ADDRESS	RELATIONSHIP	STATUS	AGE	SEX	OCCUPATION	COUNTY OF BIRTH	PLACE OF BIRTH
274	FIELD	John	53	Pope Field Farm	Head	Mar	52	M	Farmer of 190 acres employing 6 labourers	Herts	Stevenage
275	FIELD	Catherine	53		Wife	Mar	49	F		Herts	Digswell
276	FIELD	Thomas E	53		Son	Unm	21	M	Farmer	Herts	St Albans
277	FIELD	Arthur	53		Son	Unm	17	M	Farmer	Herts	St Albans
278	TITMUS	Catherine	53		Visitor	Unm	9	F	Farmers Daughter	Herts	Digswell
279	WEBB	Sarah	53		Serv	Unm	21	F	House Servant	Herts	St Albans
280	McNAIR	William	54	Ellen Brook	Head	Unm	24	M	Blacksmith	Scotland	[Unknown]
281	McNAIR	John	54		Brother	Unm	22	M	Wheelwright	Scotland	[Unknown]
282	SIBLEY	John	54		Visitor	Unm	34	M	Blacksmith	Herts	Wheathampstead
283	JANES	James	55	Ellen Brook	Head	Mar	33	M	Agric Lab	Herts	St Michaels
284	JANES	Mary	55		Wife	Mar	24	F	Plaiter	Herts	St Peters
285	DAY	William	56	Ellen Brook	Head	Mar	60	M	Agric Lab	Herts	Hatfield
286	DAY	Elizabeth	56		Wife	Mar	59	F	Plaiter	Beds	Upper Gravenhurst
287	DAY	Marian	56		Dau	Unm	21	F	Brazilian Hat Maker	Herts	St Peters
288	DOGGETT	Joseph	57	Ellen Brook	Head	Mar	38	M	Agric Lab	Herts	Little Gaddesden
289	DOGGETT	Eliza	57		Wife	Mar	29	F	Plaiter	Herts	St Peters
290	DOGGETT	James	57		Son	Unm	2	M	At Home	Herts	St Peters
291	DAY	James	58	Ellen Brook	Head	Mar	38	M	Agric Lab	Herts	St Peters
292	DAY	Elizabeth	58		Wife	Mar	34	F		Herts	St Peters
293	DAY	Martha	58		Dau	Unm	12	F	Brazilian Hat Maker	Herts	St Peters
294	DAY	Eliza	58		Dau	Unm	10	F	Brazilian Hat Maker	Surrey	Wandsworth
295	DAY	John	58		Son	Unm	6	M		Herts	St Peters
296	DAY	Walter	58		Son	Unm	5	M	At Home	Herts	St Peters
297	DAY	Rachel	58		Dau	Unm	3	F	At Home	Herts	St Peters
298	DAY	Sarah	58		Dau	Unm	2	F	At Home	Herts	St Peters
299	DAY	Mary	58		Dau	Unm	6	F		Herts	St Peters
300	GRAY	Richard	59	Ellen Brook	Head	Mar	34	M	Agric Lab	Herts	Hatfield
301	GRAY	Emma	59		Wife	Mar	32	F	Brazilian Hat Maker	Herts	St Peters
302	MAYNARD	Mary	60	Ellen Brook	Wife	Mar	38	F	Plaiter	Herts	Hatfield
303	MAYNARD	Samuel	60		Son	Unm	18	M	Agric Lab	Herts	Hitchin
304	MAYNARD	Shadrack	60		Son	Unm	13	M	Agric Lab	Herts	Hitchin
305	MAYNARD	John	60		Son	Unm	8	M		Herts	St Peters
306	DAY	George	61	Ellen Brook	Head	Mar	23	M	Agric Lab	Herts	St Peters
307	DAY	Sophia	61		Wife	Mar	24	F	Brazilian Hat Maker	Herts	St Peters
308	YOUNG	William	62	Ellen Brook	Head	Mar	40	M	Agric Lab	Beds	Luton
309	YOUNG	Sarah	62		Wife	Mar	36	F		Herts	Little Wymondley
310	YOUNG	Emma	62		Dau	Unm	17	F	Brazilian Hat Maker	Herts	Sandridge
311	YOUNG	Eliza	62		Dau	Unm	13	F	Brazilian Hat Maker	Herts	St Peters
312	YOUNG	Samuel	62		Son	Unm	9	M		Herts	St Peters
313	YOUNG	Harriet	62		Dau	Unm	6	F		Herts	St Peters
314	YOUNG	John	62		Son	Unm	1	M	At Home	Herts	St Peters
315	THOMAS	William	63	Ellen Brook	Head	Mar	39	M	Master Wheelwright	Surrey	Cheam
316	THOMAS	Sarah	63		Wife	Mar	35	F		Herts	Hatfield
317	THOMAS	Sarah	63		Dau	Unm	12	F		Herts	Hatfield

318	THOMAS	James D	63		Son	Unm	11	M	Scholar	Middx	Enfield	
319	THOMAS	John	63		Son	Unm	9	M	Scholar	Middx	Enfield	
320	THOMAS	Frank	63		Son	Unm	7	M	Scholar	Middx	Enfield	
321	THOMAS	Mary A F	63		Dau	Unm	5	F	At Home	Herts	St Albans	
322	HICKS	William	63		Lodger	Unm	25	M	Agric Lab	Beds	Markyate Street	
323	PAPPER	James	63		Lodger	Unm	41	M	Railway Lab	Herts	Watton	
324	SHORBY	Henry	64	Harpsfield Hall	Head	Mar	29	M	Agric Lab	Herts	Northaw	
325	SHORBY	Elizabeth	64		Wife	Mar	24	F		Herts	Hatfield	
326	SHORBY	Emily	64		Dau	Unm	3	F	At Home	Herts	Hatfield	
327	SHORBY	Sarah Ann	64		Dau	Unm	1	F	At Home	Herts	Hatfield	
328	SHELDRAKE	Richard	64	Harpsfield Hall	Head	Mar	50	M	Agric Lab	Suffolk	Barham	
329	SHELDRAKE	Susannah	64		Wife	Mar	47	F		Suffolk	Westerfield	
330	SHELDRAKE	Joshua	64		Son	Unm	19	M	Agric Lab	Suffolk	Hemingstone	
331	SHELDRAKE	Richard	64		Son	Unm	17	M	Agric Lab	Suffolk	Hemingstone	
332	SHELDRAKE	Thomas	64		Son	Unm	10	M		Suffolk	Rattlesden	
333	SHELDRAKE	Sarah	64		Dau	Unm	15	F		Suffolk	Hemingstone	
334	SHELDRAKE	Mary Ann	64		Dau	Unm	8	F		Suffolk	Rattlesden	
335	NOWLSON	James S.	65	Harpsfield Hall Farm	Head	Mar	46	M	Farmer of 500 acres employing 30 labourers	Wilts	Baverstock	
336	NOWLSON	Elizabeth	65		Wife	Mar	45	F		Wilts	Wilton	
337	NOWLSON	Elizabeth N.	65		Dau	Unm	4	F	At Home	Herts	Harpsfield Hall [St Peters]	
338	NOWLSON	Mary	65		Dau	Unm	4	F	At Home	Herts	Harpsfield Hall [St Peters]	
339	NOWLSON	Jane S	65		Dau	Unm	2	F	At Home	Herts	Harpsfield Hall [St Peters]	
340	NOWLSON	Mary Maria	65		Visitor	Unm	35	F	Annuitant	Dorset	Corfe Mullen	
341	WEBB	Alice	65		Visitor	Unm	20	F	Farmers Daughter	Herts	Northaw	
342	FORD	Emma	65		Serv	Unm	19	F	House Servant	Herts	Hatfield	
343	SKINNER	Mary	65		Serv	Unm	16	F	House Servant	Herts	Hatfield	
344	MARDLIN	William	65		Serv	Unm	20	M	Agric Lab	Herts	St Peters	
345	MARDLIN	John	65		Serv	Unm	35	M	Agric Lab	Herts	Hatfield	
346	MADDENS	Stephen	65		Serv	Unm	20	M	Agric Lab	Herts	Hatfield	
347	HARRIS	William	66	Sleve Hall	Head	Mar	48	M	Agric Lab	Herts	Harpenden	
348	HARRIS	Mary	66		Wife	Mar	44	F		Herts	Flamstead	
349	HARRIS	Sarah	66		Dau	Unm	15	F	Brazilian Hat Maker	Herts	Sandridge	
350	HARRIS	Thomas	66		Son	Unm	12	M	Agric Lab	Herts	Harpenden	
351	HARRIS	James	66		Son	Unm	9	M	Agric Lab	Herts	Sandridge	
352	HARRIS	George	66		Son	Unm	6	M		Herts	St Peters	
353	HARRIS	Edward	66		Son	Unm	3	M		Herts	St Peters	
Empty			67	Sleve Hall								
354	ADDINGTON	William	68	Sleve Hall	Head	Mar	47	M	Agric Lab	Herts	Sandridge	
355	ADDINGTON	Hester	68		Wife	Mar	48	F		Herts	St Pauls Walden	
356	ADDINGTON	Ann	68		Dau	Unm	22	F	Brazilian Hat Maker	Herts	Sandridge	
357	ADDINGTON	Joseph	68		Son	Unm	19	M	Agric Lab	Herts	Sandridge	
358	ADDINGTON	Maryann	68		Dau	Unm	17	F	Brazilian Hat Maker	Herts	Sandridge	
359	ADDINGTON	Jane	68		Dau	Unm	14	F	Brazilian Hat Maker	Herts	Sandridge	
360	ADDINGTON	John	68		Son	Unm	12	M	Agric Lab	Herts	Sandridge	

	SURNAME	FORENAME	SCHEDULE NUMBER	ADDRESS	RELATIONSHIP	STATUS	AGE	SEX	OCCUPATION	COUNTY OF BIRTH	PLACE OF BIRTH
361	BROWN	Elizabeth	69	Shoe Hall	Head	Widow	74	F	Beer House Keeper	Herts	Wheathampstead
362	RAY	Caroline	69		Grandau	Unm	16	F	Brazilian Hat Maker	Herts	St Peters
363	HARRIS	Ann	69		Visitor	Unm	17	F	Brazilian Hat Maker	Herts	Sandridge
364	KERLEY	Henry	70	Beach Farm	Head	Widower	57	M	Farmer of 196 acres employing 5 labourers	Berks	[Unknown]
365	MORRIS	Mary Ann	70		H'keeper	Widow	55	F	Farmers Wife	Berks	[Unknown]
366	SIMONDS	John	70		Serv	Mar	56	M	Servant	Berks	[Unknown]
367	HEDGES	John	70		Serv	Unm	21	M	Servant	Berks	[Unknown]
368	PAYNE	Joseph	70		Serv	Unm	16	M	Servant	Berks	[Unknown]
369	BONE	Thomas	70		Serv	Unm	14	M	Servant	Herts	St Albans
370	BRACEY	Joshua	71	Ash Cottage	Head	Mar	31	M	Agric Lab	Herts	Harpenden
371	BRACEY	Sophia	71		Wife	Mar	34	F		Beds	Luton
372	BRACEY	George	71		Son	Unm	12	M	Agric Lab	Herts	Harpenden
373	BRACEY	William	71		Son	Unm	11	M	Agric Lab	Herts	Harpenden
374	BRACEY	Emma	71		Dau	Unm	6	F		Herts	Harpenden
375	BRACEY	Elizabeth	71		Dau	Unm	4	F	At Home	Herts	St Peters
376	ANDREWS	Elizabeth	71		Visitor	Unm	26	F	Brazilian Hat Maker	Herts	Harpenden
377	KING	Keziah	71		Visitor	Unm	24	F	Plaiter	Herts	Sandridge
378	BRACEY	Charlotte	71		Dau	Unm	1	F	At Home	Herts	St Peters
379	GEORGE	William	72	Oak Farm	Head	Mar	36	M	Farmer of 360 acres employing 14 labourers	Herts	Sandridge
380	GEORGE	Maria	72		Wife	Mar	33	F		Herts	Flamstead
381	GEORGE	William	72		Son	Unm	5	M		Herts	St Peters
382	GEORGE	Marian	72		Dau	Unm	4	F		Herts	St Peters
383	GEORGE	Henry	72		Son	Unm	2	M		Herts	St Peters
384	GEORGE	Susan	72		Dau	Unm	1	F		Herts	St Peters
385	DICKINSON	Emma	72		Serv	Unm	19	F		Herts	St Peters
386	DICKINSON	Jane	72		Serv	Unm	15	F		Herts	St Peters
387	BROWN	Samuel	72		Serv	Unm	21	M		Herts	North Mimms
388	SWAIN	William	72		Serv	Unm	16	M		Herts	St Peters
389	HOWARD	James	72		Serv	Unm	15	M		Herts	St Peters
390	GRAY	Charles	73	Newgate Farm	Head	Mar	31	M	Farmer of 20 acres	Herts	Ickleford
391	GRAY	Sarah	73		Wife	Mar	28	F		Herts	St Peters
392	GRAY	Alfred	73		Son	Unm	6	M	Scholar	Herts	Aldenham
393	GRAY	Sarah	73		Dau	Unm	4	F		Middx	South Mimms
394	GRAY	Rosa	73		Dau	Unm	1	F		Herts	Hemel Hempstead
395	ALDERSON	James S.	74	Oaklands	Head	Mar	38	M	Land Steward	Durham	Darlington
396	ALDERSON	Elizabeth	74		Wife	Mar	40	F		Middx	Staines
397	RADLEY	Jemima	74		Serv	Unm	23	F	Cook	Essex	Woodford
398	SANDERS	Rhoda	74		Serv	Unm	22	F	Housemaid	Herts	Cheshunt
399	WANALE	John	74		Serv	Unm	25	M	Groom	Herts	St Stephens
400	JELLIFF	George	74		Serv	Unm	14	M	Foot Boy	Herts	St Stephens
401	MILEN	Alexander	75	Oaklands	Head	Widower	41	M	Gardener	Scotland	[Unknown]
402	MILEN	George	75		Son	Unm	9 m	M		Herts	St Peters
403	BUSHNELL	Sarah	75		Sister-in-law	Unm	19	F		Wilts	[Unknown]
404	BUSHNELL	Ellen	75		Sister-in-law	Unm	9	F		[Unknown]	[Unknown]

405	WOOLLNOUGH	William	76	Oaklands	Head	Mar	36	M	Farming Man	Norfolk	[Unknown]
406	WOOLLNOUGH	Charlotte	76		Wife	Mar	36	F		Norfolk	[Unknown]
407	WOOLLNOUGH	Emma	76		Dau	Unm	9	F		Herts	St Peters
408	WOOLLNOUGH	Sarah	76		Dau	Unm	7	F		Herts	St Peters
409	WOOLLNOUGH	William	76		Son	Unm	3	M		Herts	St Peters
410	WOOLLNOUGH	George	76		Son	Unm	2	M		Herts	St Peters
411	WOOLLNOUGH	James	76		Son	Unm	9m	M		Herts	St Peters
412	LOW	Charles	77	Oaklands	Head	Mar	27	M	Shepherd	Herts	Wheathampstead
413	LOW	Mary	77		Wife	Mar	28	F		Ireland	Queens County
414	LOW	Edward	77		Son	Unm	2m	M		Herts	St Peters
415	PAYNE	Joseph	78	Oaklands	Head	Mar	27	M	Agric Lab	Herts	St Peters
416	PAYNE	Elizabeth	78		Wife	Mar	23	F		Herts	North Mimms
417	PAYNE	Sarah	78		Dau	Unm	3	F		Herts	St Peters
418	PAYNE	Samson	78		Son	Unm	2	M		Herts	St Peters
419	PAYNE	Infant	78		Dau	Unm	3dys	F		Herts	St Peters
420	PAYNE	Elizabeth	78		[blank]	Mar	40	F	Monthly Nurse	Herts	Hertingfordbury
Empty			79	Hut Toll Gate							
421	SAYER	William	80	Hut Toll Gate	Head	Mar	55	M	Farmer of 64 acres employing 4 labourers	Suffolk	Thwaite
422	SAYER	Mary Ann	80		Wife	Mar	46	F		Herts	St Albans
423	SAYER	Richard	80		Nephew	Unm	19	M	Saddler	Sth. Am.	New Granada
424	CALVERT	Thomas	80		Nephew	Unm	10	M	Scholar	Middx	London
425	WEBB	Sophia	80		Serv	Unm	20	F	Servant	Herts	St Peters
426	LARFORD	William	80		Serv	Unm	18	M	Agric Lab	Herts	Smallford
427	EAMES	Ephraim	80		Serv	Unm	15	M	Agric Lab	Herts	St Peters
428	PACK	Isaac	81	Hut Toll Gate	Head	Mar	47	M	Farmer of 230 acres employing 9 labourers	Northants	Geddington
429	PACK	Anne	81		Wife	Mar	55	F		Leics	Quorndon
430	PACK	Thomas	81		Son	Unm	19	M	Farmers Son	Northants	Geddington
431	PACK	Elizabeth Anne	81		Dau	Unm	16	F		Northants	Glapthorn
432	HEARN	James	81		Serv	Unm	30	M	Agric Lab	Herts	St Peters
433	HILL	Joseph	81		Serv	Unm	22	M	Agric Lab	Herts	St Peters
434	NORRIS	Stephen	81		Serv	Unm	16	M	Agric Lab	Herts	St Peters
435	PEACOCK	Samuel	81		Serv	Unm	12	M	Agric Lab	Herts	St Peters
436	SEABROOK	John	82	Hut Toll Gate	Head	Mar	26	M	Gamekeeper	Herts	Redbourn
437	SEABROOK	Martha	82		Wife	Mar	29	F		Herts	Harpenden
438	SEABROOK	Edward	82		Son	Unm	6	M	Scholar	Herts	Redbourn
439	SEABROOK	Ann	82		Dau	Unm	4	F		Beds	Whipsnade
440	SEABROOK	Henry	82		Son	Unm	2	M		Beds	Whipsnade
441	WARDEN	Thomas	83	Hall Heath	Head	Mar	34	M	Agric Lab	Herts	St Stephens
442	WARDEN	Ann	83		Wife	Mar	42	F		Herts	St Stephens
443	WARDEN	Robert	83		Son	Unm	11	M		Herts	Smug Oak [St Stephens]
444	WARDEN	Thomas	83		Son	Unm	8	M		Herts	Smug Oak [St Stephens]
445	WARDEN	Elizabeth	83		Dau	Unm	5	F		Herts	Smug Oak [St Stephens]
446	WARDEN	Hannah	83		Dau	Unm	2	F		Herts	Smug Oak [St Stephens]

	SURNAME	FORENAME	SCHEDULE NUMBER	ADDRESS	RELATIONSHIP	STATUS	AGE	SEX	OCCUPATION	COUNTY OF BIRTH	PLACE OF BIRTH
447	WARDEN	Mary Ann	83		Dau	Unm	7 m	F		Herts	Hall Heath
448	HILL	John	84	Hall Heath	Head	Mar	29	M	Agric Lab	Herts	St Michaels
449	HILL	Elizabeth Clara	84		Wife	Mar	34	F		Berks	Beenham
450	HILL	Mary Elizabeth	84		Dau	Unm	2	F		Herts	St Peters
451	SLOUGH	William	85	Sandpit Lane	Head	Mar	56	M	Agric Lab	Herts	Harpenden
452	SLOUGH	Esther	85		Wife	Mar	60	F		Herts	St Peters
453	SLOUGH	Esther	85		Dau	Unm	30	F	Plaiter	Herts	St Peters
454	SLOUGH	Eliza	85		Dau	Unm	28	F	Plaiter	Herts	St Peters
455	SLOUGH	Ann	85		Dau	Unm	16	F	Dressmaker	Herts	St Peters
456	SLOUGH	William	85		Son	Unm	4	M		Herts	St Peters
457	LONG	Henry	86	Sandpit Lane	Head	Mar	58	M	Agric Lab	Herts	St Michaels
458	LONG	Mary	86		Wife	Mar	56	F	Schoolmistress	Herts	Redbourn
459	KIFF	Barbara	86		Lodger	Unm	23	F	Needlewoman	Herts	St Stephens
460	ANDERSON	Daniel	87	Sandpit Lane	Head	Mar	56	M	Agric Lab	Herts	St Michaels
461	ANDERSON	Phebe	87		Wife	Mar	51	F	Laundress	Herts	St Peters
462	ANDERSON	William	87		Son	Unm	24	M	Agric Lab	Herts	St Peters
463	ANDERSON	Richard	87		Son	Unm	12	M	Agric Lab	Herts	St Peters
464	WRIGHT	William	88	Sandpit Lane	Head	Mar	43	M	Agric Lab	Herts	St Stephens
465	WRIGHT	Ann	88		Wife	Mar	33	F	Plaiter	Herts	Hitchin
466	WRIGHT	Sarah	88		Dau	Unm	7	F		Herts	St Peters
467	WRIGHT	Susan	88		Dau	Unm	4	F		Herts	St Peters
468	WRIGHT	Thomas	88		Son	Unm	2	M		Herts	St Peters
469	PARSONS	Charles	89	Sandpit Lane	Head	Mar	60	M	Baker Journeyman	Herts	Sandridge
470	PARSONS	Elizabeth	89		Wife	Mar	59	F		Herts	Sandridge
471	PARSONS	Elizabeth	89		Dau	Unm	32	F		Herts	Sandridge
472	PARSONS	Ellen	89		Dau	Unm	15	F		Herts	Codicote
473	PARSONS	Mary	89		Grandau	Unm	2	F		Herts	St Peters
474	SMITH	William	90	Sandpit Lane	Head	Mar	47	M	Agric Lab	Herts	Sandridge
475	SMITH	Sarah	90		Wife	Mar	44	F		Herts	Hatfield
476	SMITH	Hannah	90		Dau	Unm	19	F		Herts	Sandridge
477	SMITH	George	90		Son	Unm	15	M		Herts	Sandridge

Registrar's District: St Albans   Enumeration District 2b   Ref. HO 107/1713 folios 325-45

Sleap and Smallford Hamlet south of St Albans and Hatfield Road, except the houses abutting on such road and those at Ellenbrook.

Parish of St Stephens

	SURNAME	FORENAME	SCHEDULE NUMBER	ADDRESS	RELATIONSHIP	STATUS	AGE	SEX	OCCUPATION	COUNTY OF BIRTH	PLACE OF BIRTH
478	LONGSTAFF	George	1	Smallford	Head	Mar	30	M	Farmer of 118 acres employing 6 men	Herts	North Mimms
479	LONGSTAFF	Mary	1		Wife	Mar	36	F		Herts	North Mimms
480	LONGSTAFF	Eliza	1		Dau		7	F		Herts	North Mimms
481	LONGSTAFF	William	1		Son		2 m	M		Herts	St Stephens
482	EAMES	George	1		Serv	Unm	27	M		Herts	St Peters
483	GAZELEY	Charles	1		Serv	Unm	17	M		Herts	St Michaels
484	WISE	William	2	Smallford	Head	Mar	66	M	Farmer of 108 acres employing 4 men	Herts	St Peters

485	WISE	Elizabeth	2		Wife	Mar	60	F		Northants	Ringstead
486	WISE	Thomas	2		Son	Unm	27	M	Farm Labourer	Herts	St Stephens
487	PECK	George	2		Serv	Unm	32	M		Herts	St Peters
488	DIMOCK	Samuel	2		Serv	Unm	16	M		Herts	St Peters
489	FIELD	Emma	2		Serv	Unm	17	F	General Servant	Herts	St Stephens
490	GUTTERIDGE	James	3	Smallford	Head	Mar	43	M	Farm Labourer	Herts	St Stephens
491	GUTTERIDGE	Elizabeth	3		Wife	Mar	41	F	Straw Hat Maker	Herts	St Stephens
492	GUTTERIDGE	Eliza	3		Dau	Unm	17	F	Straw Hat Maker	Herts	St Stephens
493	GUTTERIDGE	Charlotte	3		Dau		11	F	Straw Hat Maker	Herts	St Stephens
494	GUTTERIDGE	Eliza	3		Visitor		8	F	Straw Hat Maker	Herts	St Stephens
495	GIDDENS	William	4	Smallford	Head	Mar	54	M	Farm Labourer	Herts	St Peters
496	GIDDENS	Elizabeth	4		Wife	Mar	52	F	Laundress	Oxon	Pittenmore [?]
497	GIDDENS	Eliza	4		Dau	Unm	17	F	Straw Hat Maker	Herts	St Stephens
498	GIDDENS	Emma	4		Dau		15	F	Straw Hat Maker	Herts	St Stephens
499	GIDDENS	Sarah	4		Dau		13	F	Straw Hat Maker	Herts	St Stephens
500	GIDDENS	Martha	4		Dau		12	F	Straw Hat Maker	Herts	St Stephens
501	GIDDENS	Samuel	4		Son	Unm	19	M	At Home	Herts	St Stephens
502	GIDDENS	Jesse	4		Son		6	M	At Home	Herts	St Stephens
503	FLINT	John	5	Smallford	Head	Mar	45	M	Farm Labourer	Herts	St Stephens
504	FLINT	Sarah	5		Wife	Mar	35	F		Herts	North Mimms
505	FLINT	James	5		Son		12	M	Farm Labourer	Herts	North Mimms
506	KEMP	Eliza	5		Dau		12	F	Straw Hat Maker	Herts	North Mimms
507	FLINT	John	5		Son		7	M	At Home	Herts	North Mimms
508	FLINT	Charles	5		Son		5	M	At Home	Herts	St Stephens
509	FLINT	William	5		Son		2	M	At Home	Herts	St Stephens
510	FLINT	Emma	5		Dau		7dys	F		Herts	St Stephens
511	ALLEN	James	6	Smallford	Head	Mar	46	M	Farm Labourer	Herts	St Stephens
512	ALLEN	Bethia	6		Wife	Mar	43	F		Herts	Sandridge
513	ALLEN	Samuel	6		Son	Unm	21	M	Farm Labourer	Herts	St Peters
514	ALLEN	Thomas	6		Son	Unm	18	M	Farm Labourer	Herts	St Peters
515	ALLEN	Eliza	6		Dau	Unm	16	F	Straw Hat Maker	Herts	St Peters
516	ALLEN	Sarah	6		Dau		13	F	Scholar	Herts	St Stephens
517	ALLEN	William	7	Smallford	Head	Mar	43	M	Farm Labourer	Herts	St Peters
518	ALLEN	Fanny	7		Wife	Mar	41	F		Herts	St Stephens
519	ALLEN	Joseph	7		Son		12	M	Labourer	Herts	St Stephens
520	ALLEN	Anne	7		Dau		10	F	Straw Plaiter	Herts	St Stephens
521	ALLEN	George	7		Son		7	M	Scholar	Herts	St Stephens
522	ALLEN	Elizabeth	7		Dau		5	F	Scholar	Herts	St Stephens
523	ALLEN	Susan	7		Dau		2	F		Herts	St Stephens
524	PECK	Thomas	7		Lodger	Unm	34	M	Farm Labourer	Herts	St Stephens
525	TURNEY	Barnett	8	Smallford	Head	Mar	41	M	Farm Labourer	Herts	St Stephens
526	TURNEY	Sarah	8		Wife	Mar	41	F		Herts	St Peters
527	TURNEY	Mary	8		Dau	Unm	16	F	Hat Maker	Herts	St Peters
528	TURNEY	Louisa	8		Dau		11	F	Hat Maker	Herts	St Peters
529	TURNEY	Emma	8		Dau		4	F		Herts	St Stephens

Parish of St Peters

	SURNAME	FORENAME	SCH	ADDRESS	RELATIONSHIP	STATUS	AGE	SEX	OCCUPATION	COUNTY	PLACE OF BIRTH
530	ALLEN	James	9	Smallford	Head	Mar	70	M	Farm Labourer	Herts	St Peters
531	ALLEN	Sarah	9		Wife	Mar	71	F		Herts	St Peters
532	ALLEN	George	9		Son	Unm	30	M	Farm Labourer	Herts	St Peters
533	ALLEN	Susan	9		Dau	Unm	32	F	Straw Plaiter	Herts	St Peters
534	TURNER	Joseph	10	Splash, Smallford	Head	Mar	35	M	Farm Labourer	Herts	St Peters
535	TURNER	Eliza	10		Wife	Mar	32	F	Straw Plaiter	Herts	St Peters
536	TURNER	Mary Anne	10		Dau		12	F	At Home	Herts	St Peters
537	TURNER	Henry	10		Son		10	M		Herts	St Peters
538	TURNER	Elizabeth	10		Dau		7	F		Herts	St Peters
539	TURNER	Sarah	10		Dau		4	F		Herts	North Mimms
540	TURNER	Henry	11	Smallford	Head	Mar	55	M	Farm Labourer	Herts	Park Street [St Stephens]
541	TURNER	Elizabeth	11		Wife	Mar	56	F	Straw Plaiter	Beds	Barton
542	ALLEN	James	12	Smallford	Head	Mar	38	M	Farm Labourer	Herts	St Stephens
543	ALLEN	Susan	12		Wife	Mar	35	F	Straw Plaiter	Herts	St Peters
544	ALLEN	Ann	12		Dau		12	F	Straw Plaiter	Herts	St Stephens
545	ALLEN	William	12		Son		9	M	Goes to School	Herts	St Stephens
546	ALLEN	George	12		Son		5	M	Goes to School	Herts	St Stephens
547	ALLEN	Charles	12		Son		2	M		Herts	St Peters
548	ALLEN	Hannah	12		Dau		1wk	F		Herts	St Peters
549	TURNER	Maria	12		Mother-in-law	Widow	62	F	Straw Plaiter	Herts	Sandridge
550	ROCHE	William	13	Smallford	Head	Mar	43	M	Perpetual Curate. M.A.	Middx	London
551	ROCHE	Catherine	13		Wife	Mar	36	F		Middx	Islington
552	ROCHE	Mark	13		Son		3m	M		Herts	St Peters
553	MATHEWS	Ellen	13		Serv	Unm	19	F	House Servant	Surrey	Farnham
554	TURNEY	Rebecca	13		Serv		14	F	House Servant	Herts	St Peters
555	MANSFIELD	Charles	14	Sleapshyde	Head	Mar	29	M	Shoemaker	Herts	Cheshunt
556	MANSFIELD	Rebecca	14		Wife	Mar	26	F		Herts	North Mimms
557	KINGHAM	William	14		Nephew	Unm	21	M	Shoemaker	Middx	Enfield
558	GRAY	William	15	Sleapshyde	Head	Mar	27	M	Agric Lab	Herts	Hatfield
559	GRAY	Sarah	15		Wife	Mar	38	F		Herts	Digswell
560	MANCER	William	15		Son		13	M	Agric Lab	Herts	Hatfield
561	MANCER	George	15		Son		10	M		Herts	Hatfield
562	GRAY	Henry	15		Son		3	M		Herts	Hatfield
563	GRAY	Thomas	15		Son		2m	M		Herts	Hatfield
564	HART	William	16	Sleapshyde	Head	Mar	43	M	Farmer of 145 acres employing 5 men	Herts	North Mimms
565	HART	Mary	16		Wife	Mar	42	F		Herts	Hatfield
566	HART	Eliza	16		Dau	Unm	22	F		Herts	North Mimms
567	HART	Jane	16		Dau		15	F		Herts	St Peters
568	HART	Emma	16		Dau		12	F	Scholar	Herts	St Peters
569	HART	Mary Ann	16		Dau		9	F	Scholar	Herts	St Peters
570	HART	Susan	16		Dau		8	F	Scholar	Herts	St Peters
571	HART	Elizabeth	16		Dau		5	F	Scholar	Herts	St Peters

No.	Surname	Forename		Place	Relation	Status	Age	Sex	Occupation	County	Birthplace
572	HART	Thomas William	16		Son		3	M	Scholar	Herts	St Peters
573	HART	Sarah	16		Dau		8m	F		Herts	St Peters
574	RAY	John	17	Sleapshyde	Head	Mar	47	M	Farm Labourer	Herts	St Peters
575	RAY	Ann	17		Wife	Mar	44	F		Herts	Sandridge
576	RAY	Hannah	17		Dau	Unm	17	F	Straw Plaiter	Herts	Sleapshyde
577	RAY	Jane	17		Dau		14	F	Straw Plaiter	Herts	Sleapshyde
578	RAY	Joseph	17		Son		9	M		Herts	Sleapshyde
579	RAY	John	17		Son		6	M		Herts	Sleapshyde
580	HILL	George	18	Sleapshyde	Head	Mar	30	M	Agric Lab	Herts	St Peters
581	HILL	Eliza	18		Wife	Mar	34	F	Straw Plaiter	Herts	St Peters
582	CROCKELL	James	19	Sleapshyde	Head	Mar	48	M	Agric Lab	Herts	St Peters
583	CROCKELL	Sarah	19		Wife	Mar	46	F	Straw Plaiter	Herts	Sandridge
584	CROCKELL	Ann	19		Dau	Unm	23	F	Straw Plaiter	Herts	Sleapshyde
585	CROCKELL	William	19		Son		13	M		Herts	Hatfield
586	CROCKELL	Joseph	19		Son		11	M		Herts	Hatfield
587	CROCKELL	Emma	19		Dau		7	F		Herts	St Peters
588	SWAIN	Susan	20	Sleapshyde	Head	Widow	39	F	Straw Plaiter	Herts	Hertingfordbury
589	SWAIN	Joseph	20		Son		10	M		Herts	Sleapshyde
590	SWAIN	John	20		Son		7	M		Herts	Sleapshyde
591	SWAIN	Sarah	20		Dau		5	F		Herts	Sleapshyde
592	SWAIN	Mary	20		Dau		3	F		Herts	Sleapshyde
593	TAYLOR	William	21	Sleapshyde	Head	Mar	44	M	Agric Lab	Herts	St Peters
594	TAYLOR	Ann	21		Wife	Mar	46	F		Herts	Bengeo
595	LITTLE	Harriet	21		Dau	Widow	23	F	Hat Maker	Herts	Stapleford
596	TAYLOR	William	21		Son	Unm	20	M	Agric Lab	Herts	St Peters
597	TAYLOR	Mary Ann	21		Dau		14	F		Herts	St Peters
598	TAYLOR	Phillis	21		Dau		11	F		Herts	St Peters
599	LITTLE	Sarah Ann	21		Grandau		3	F		Herts	St Peters
600	LITTLE	Maria	21		Grandau		2	F		Herts	St Peters
601	WEBB	Elizabeth	22	Sleapshyde	Head	Widow	37	F	Straw Plaiter	Herts	St Pauls Walden
602	WEBB	Caroline	22		Dau		10	F		Herts	Wheathampstead
603	WEBB	Matelda	22		Dau		8	F		Herts	Wheathampstead
604	WEBB	Charles	22		Son		6	M		Herts	Wheathampstead
605	WEBB	John	22		Son		4	M		Herts	Colney Heath
606	WEBB	James	22		Son		2	M		Herts	St Peters
607	WEBB	William	22		Son		3m	M		Herts	St Peters
608	HARVEY	William	23	Sleapshyde	Head	Mar	25	M	Agric Lab	Herts	St Peters
609	HARVEY	Elizabeth	23		Wife	Mar	26	F		Herts	St Peters
610	HARVEY	Alfred	23		Son		6	M		Herts	Sleapshyde
611	HARVEY	David	23		Son		2	M		Herts	Sleapshyde
612	HARVEY	William	23		Son		2m	M		Herts	Sleapshyde
613	RAY	James	23		Father-in-law	Mar	80	M	Agric Lab	Herts	Sleapshyde
614	RAY	Sarah	23		Mother-in-law	Mar	60	F		Herts	St Peters
615	FIELD	Thomas	24	Sleapshyde	Head	Mar	28	M	Agric Lab	Herts	Colney Heath

	SURNAME	FORENAME	SCHEDULE NUMBER	ADDRESS	RELATIONSHIP	STATUS	AGE	SEX	OCCUPATION	COUNTY OF BIRTH	PLACE OF BIRTH
616	FIELD	Elizabeth	24		Wife	Mar	27	F	Straw Plaiter	Herts	Sleapshyde
617	BECK	Joseph	24		Father	Widower	71	M	Agric Lab	Herts	Sleapshyde
618	HULL	Samuel	25	Sleapshyde	Head	Mar	64	M	Agric Lab	Herts	St Stephens
619	HULL	Hannah	25		Wife	Mar	62	F		Herts	Sleapshyde
620	HULL	Henry	25		Son	Unm	21	M	Agric Lab	Herts	Sleapshyde
621	HALL	Samuel	26	Sleapshyde	Head	Mar	42	M	Agric Lab	Herts	Sleapshyde
622	HALL	Elizabeth	26		Wife	Mar	37	F		Herts	Colney Heath
623	HALL	William	26		Son		12	M	Straw Plaiter	Herts	Sleapshyde
624	HALL	Mary	26		Dau		11	F		Herts	Sleapshyde
625	HALL	George	26		Son		9	M		Herts	Sleapshyde
626	HALL	Susan	26		Dau		5	F		Herts	Sleapshyde
627	HALL	James	26		Son		5m	M		Herts	Sleapshyde
628	DAY	James	27	Sleapshyde	Head	Mar	62	M	Farmer of 140 acres employing 6 men	Herts	Stevenage
629	DAY	Emma	27		Wife	Mar	33	F		Beds	Luton
630	DAY	James	27		Son		2	M		Herts	St Peters
631	SMITH	Ann	27		Serv	Unm	19	F	House Servant	Herts	Aldenham
632	DAY	Joseph	27		Nephew	Unm	19	M	Agric Lab	Herts	Welwyn
633	SIMKINS	James	27		Serv	Unm	20	M	Agric Lab	Herts	Sandridge
634	SKEGGS	John	27		Serv	Unm	19	M	Agric Lab	Herts	Bishops Stortford
635	PEW	William	28	Sleapshyde	Head	Mar	49	M	Agric Lab	Herts	Colney Heath
636	PEW	Mary	28		Wife	Mar	44	F		Herts	Sleapshyde
637	PEW	Rebecca	28		Dau	Unm	19	F		Herts	Sleapshyde
638	PEW	William	28		Son		14	M	Agric Lab	Herts	Sleapshyde
639	PEW	James George	28		Son		10	M	Straw Plaiter	Herts	Sleapshyde
640	PEW	Susan	28		Dau		6	F		Herts	Sleapshyde
641	PEW	Thomas	28		Son		4	M		Herts	Sleapshyde
642	WILSHIRE	James	28		Lodger	Widower	72	M	Agric Lab	Herts	Hatfield
643	BLISTOW	John	29	Sleapshyde	Head	Mar	26	M	Agric Lab	Herts	Welwyn
644	BLISTOW	Sophia	29		Wife	Mar	21	F		Herts	Sleapshyde
645	BLISTOW	Joseph	29		Son		1	M		Herts	Sleapshyde
646	KING	Charlotte	29		Mother	Widow	60	F	Straw Plaiter	Herts	Sandridge
647	RAY	Richard	30	Sleapshyde	Head	Mar	34	M	Agric Lab	Herts	St Peters
648	RAY	Ann	30		Wife	Mar	35	F		Herts	North Mimms
649	RAY	James	30		Son		13	M	Agric Lab	Herts	Hatfield
650	PEW	Thomas	31	Sleapshyde	Head	Mar	47	M	Gardener	Herts	St Peters
651	PEW	Mary Ann	31		Wife	Mar	45	F		Herts	St Stephens
652	RAY	James	32	Sleapshyde	Head	Mar	43	M	Agric Lab	Herts	St Peters
653	RAY	Sarah	32		Wife	Mar	48	F		Herts	St Peters
654	RAY	Samuel	32		Son	Unm	18	M	Agric Lab	Herts	St Peters
655	RAY	Emma	32		Dau		14	F		Herts	St Peters
656	RAY	Eliza	32		Dau		12	F		Herts	St Peters
657	RAY	Mary Anne	32		Dau		9	F		Herts	St Peters
658	RAY	Harriett	32		Dau		6	F		Herts	St Peters
659	HALL	George	33	Sleapshyde	Head	Mar	31	M	Agric Lab	Herts	Sleapshyde

	Surname	Forename		Place	Relation	Status	Age	Sex	Occupation	County	Place of birth
660	HALL	Eliza	33		Wife	Mar	32	F		Herts	North Mimms
661	KILBY	Thomas	33		Lodger	Unm	55	M	Agric Lab	Herts	St Stephens
662	ALLEN	Joseph	33		Lodger	Unm	32	M	Agric Lab	Middx	London
663	FRANKLIN	John	34	Sleapshyde	Head	Mar	66	M	Agric Lab	Herts	Sandridge
664	FRANKLIN	Charlotte	34		Wife	Mar	56	F		Herts	Smallford
665	FRANKLIN	James	34		Son	Unm	33	M	Agric Lab	Herts	Sleapshyde
666	FRANKLIN	John	34		Son	Unm	22	M	Agric Lab	Herts	Sleapshyde
667	FRANKLIN	Rebecca	34		Dau		12	F	Needlewoman	Herts	Sleapshyde
668	HART	William	34		Visitor	Unm	23	M	Agric Lab	Herts	Royston
669	ROW	William	35	Sleapshyde	Head	Mar	59	M	Farmer of 17 acres	Hants	Houghton
670	ROW	Mary Ann	35		Wife	Mar	54	F		Middx	Fulham
671	ROW	Thomas	35		Son	Unm	16	M	Agric Lab	Middx	Highgate
672	ROW	Caroline	35		Dau		14	F		Middx	Highgate

End of the village of Sleapshyde

	Surname	Forename		Place	Relation	Status	Age	Sex	Occupation	County	Place of birth
673	BRIANT	William	36	Colney Heath	Head	Unm	25	M	Servant	Herts	St Albans
674	FRANKLIN	Phillip	37	Colney Heath	Head	Mar	30	M	Agric Lab	Herts	Colney Heath
675	FRANKLIN	Margaret	37		Wife	Mar	25	F		Herts	Colney Heath
676	GODFREY	Joseph	38	Colney Heath	Head	Unm	31	M	No Trade	Herts	North Mimms
677	DIMMOCK	Sarah	39	Colney Heath	Head	Widow	37	F	Dressmaker	Herts	St Peters
678	DIMMOCK	Thomas	39		Son	Unm	17	M	Agric Lab	Herts	St Peters
679	DIMMOCK	Eliza	39		Dau		12	F	Scholar	Herts	St Peters
680	DIMMOCK	George	39		Son		7	M	Scholar	Herts	St Peters
681	DIMMOCK	Emma	39		Dau		4	F	Scholar	Herts	St Peters
682	FRANKLIN	James	40	Colney Heath	Head	Mar	39	M	Agric Lab	Herts	North Mimms
683	FRANKLIN	Mary	40		Wife	Mar	30	F		Herts	North Mimms
684	FRANKLIN	William	40		Son	Unm	16	M	Agric Lab	Herts	North Mimms
685	FRANKLIN	Elizabeth	40		Dau		14	F		Herts	North Mimms
686	FRANKLIN	George	40		Son		12	M		Herts	North Mimms
687	FRANKLIN	Louisa	40		Dau		10	F		Herts	North Mimms
688	FRANKLIN	James	40		Son		6	M		Herts	North Mimms
689	FRANKLIN	Mary	40		Dau		4	F		Herts	North Mimms
690	BIRD	George	41	Colney Heath	Head	Mar	30	M	Agric Lab	Herts	St Michaels
691	BIRD	Eliza	41		Wife	Mar	28	F		Herts	St Peters
692	BROWN	James	41		Son-in-law		9	M	At Home	Herts	St Peters
693	BROWN	Hannah	41		Dau-in-law		6	F	At Home	Herts	St Peters
694	BIRD	Betsey	41		Dau		3	F		Herts	St Peters
695	BIRD	Louisa	41		Dau		1	F		Herts	St Peters
696	CATO	Jesse	42	Colney Heath	Head	Mar	57	M	Pensioner	Bucks	Ivinghoe
697	CATO	Elizabeth	42		Wife	Mar	37	F	Dressmaker	Bucks	North End
698	CURTIS	John	42		Visitor	Unm	58	M	Pensioner	Middx	Marylebone
699	FRANKLIN	William	43	Colney Heath	Head	Mar	37	M	Agric Lab	Herts	St Peters
700	FRANKLIN	Hannah	43		Wife	Mar	40	F		Herts	North Mimms
701	FRANKLIN	Joseph	43		Son		12	M		Herts	St Peters
702	FRANKLIN	Isaac	43		Son		7	M		Herts	St Peters

	SURNAME	FORENAME	SCHEDULE NUMBER	ADDRESS	RELATIONSHIP	STATUS	AGE	SEX	OCCUPATION	COUNTY OF BIRTH	PLACE OF BIRTH
703	FRANKLIN	Rebecca	43		Dau		5	F		Herts	St Peters
704	TURNEY	Joseph	44	Colney Heath	Head	Widower	80	M	Agric Lab	Beds	Toddington
705	TURNEY	Edith	44		Dau	Mar	47	F	Housekeeper	Herts	St Stephens
706	CLARK	John	45	Colney Heath	Head	Mar	47	M	Agric Lab	Suffolk	Willingham
707	CLARK	Jane	45		Wife	Mar	41	F		Kent	Seal
708	CLARK	Edward	45		Son	Unm	17	M	Agric Lab	Kent	Seal
709	CLARK	James	45		Son		11	M	Agric Lab	Herts	St Peters
710	CLARK	David	45		Son		8	M	Scholar	Herts	St Peters
711	CLARK	Jane	45		Dau		4	F	At Home	Herts	St Peters
712	CLARK	Mathew	45		Son		2	M	At Home	Herts	St Peters
713	CLARK	Elizabeth	45		Dau		1 m	F		Herts	St Peters
714	SAKER	Mary	45		Visitor	Widow	64	F		Kent	Shipbourne
715	HENRY	James	45		Lodger	Unm	38	M	Agric Lab	Kent	Maidstone
716	GRAY	William	46	School House	Head	Mar	46	M	School Master R.W.A.	Bucks	Preston Bisset
717	GRAY	Sarah	46		Wife	Mar	40	F	School Mistress S&c	Herts	Harpenden
718	WOOD	Joseph	46		Boarder		10	M	Scholar	Middx	London
719	JACKSON	Edward	46		Boarder		9	M	Scholar	Middx	Hornsey
720	HEARLE	Joseph William	46		Boarder		4	M	Scholar	Middx	London
721	DICKINSON	Thomas	47	Colney Heath	Head	Mar	52	M	Boot & Shoemaker	Herts	Aldenham
722	DICKINSON	Charlotte	47		Wife	Mar	52	F		Herts	St Stephens
723	TAYLOR	Mary	47		Dau	Mar	25	F	Straw Plaiter	Herts	St Peters
724	DICKINSON	Sampson	47		Son	Unm	24	M	Shoemaker	Herts	St Peters
725	DICKINSON	Solomon	47		Son	Unm	22	M	Shoemaker	Herts	St Peters
726	DICKINSON	David	47		Son		13	M	Shoemaker	Herts	St Peters
727	DICKINSON	Joseph	47		Son		10	M	At Home	Herts	St Peters
728	TAYLOR	Thomas	47		Grandson		1	M		Herts	St Peters
729	HENRY	John	48	Colney Heath	Head	Mar	70	M	Agric Lab	Herts	Colney
730	HENRY	Mary	48		Wife	Mar	60	F		Oxon	Bicester
731	HENRY	William	48		Son		15	M	Agric Lab	Herts	Colney Heath
732	FIELD	Mary	49	Colney Heath	Head	Widow	71	F		Essex	Ilford
733	PECK	William	49		Visitor	Mar	21	M	Agric Lab	Herts	St Peters
734	PECK	Eliza	49		Visitor	Mar	21	F	Straw Plaiter	Herts	St Peters
735	RIFFIEN	William	50	Colney Heath	Head	Widower	48	M	Hawker in Cutlery	Herts	St Peters
736	OAKLEY	Edmund	51	Colney Heath	Head	Mar	32	M	Farmer of 60 acres	Herts	St Peters
737	OAKLEY	Hannah	51		Wife	Mar	33	F		Herts	St Michaels
738	OAKLEY	Edmund	51		Son		7	M	At Home	Herts	Abbots Langley
739	OAKLEY	Sarah	51		Dau		4	F		Herts	Abbots Langley
740	OAKLEY	Emma	51		Dau		7	F		Herts	Abbots Langley
741	COOPER	Charlotte	51		Visitor	Unm	25	F	Needlewoman	Herts	St Michaels
742	CLINSON	John	51		Visitor	Unm	29	M	Agric Lab	Herts	Kings Langley
743	BROWN	William	51		Visitor	Unm	16	M	Agric Lab	Herts	Abbots Langley
744	KENNY	Jerrymiah	52	Licenced House	Head	Mar	50	M	Victualler	Herts	Colney Heath
745	KENNY	Sarah	52		Wife	Mar	39	F		Herts	North Mimms
746	WICKS	William	52		Lodger	Unm	24	M	Carpenter	Surrey	Epsom

747	CHAPPEL	John	53	Colney Heath	Head	Mar	39	M	Dealer	Herts	North Mimms
748	CHAPPEL	Sarah	53		Wife	Mar	30	F		Essex	Harlow
749	CHAPPEL	Sarah	53		Dau		9	F		Herts	North Mimms
750	CHAPPEL	William	53		Son		7	M		Herts	Bayford
751	CHAPPEL	George	53		Son		2	M		Herts	St Peters

Three houses building

752	SIBLEY	Samuel	54	Colney Heath	Head	Mar	27	M	Agric Lab	Herts	Broad Colney [Shenley]
753	SIBLEY	Martha	54		Wife	Mar	30	F		Herts	St Peters
754	SIBLEY	Henry	54		Son		6	M		Herts	Shenley
755	SIBLEY	Emma	54		Dau		4	F		Herts	Colney Heath
756	SIBLEY	James	54		Son		6m	M		Herts	Colney Heath
757	GREENHAM	William	55	Colney Heath	Head	Mar	30	M	Agric Lab	Herts	Hatfield
758	GREENHAM	Mary Ann	55		Wife	Mar	25	F		Middx	Enfield
759	GREENHAM	Ann Maria	55		Dau		5	F		Herts	St Peters
760	GREENHAM	William Thomas	55		Son		3	M		Herts	St Peters
761	GREENHAM	George	55		Son		1	M		Herts	St Peters
762	SMITH	George	56	Colney Heath	Head	Mar	51	M	Agric Lab	Beds	Unknown
763	SMITH	Kitty	56		Wife	Mar	50	F		Herts	St Peters
764	SMITH	Mary	56		Dau	Unm	21	F	Hat Maker	Herts	St Peters
765	SMITH	Samuel	56		Son	Unm	18	M	Agric Lab	Herts	St Peters
766	SMITH	James	56		Son		14	M	Agric Lab	Herts	Colney Heath
767	SMITH	Levi	56		Son		11	M		Herts	St Stephens

Two houses uninhabited

768	MANSELL	Charles	57	Colney Heath	Head	Mar	30	M	Agric Lab	Herts	North Mimms
769	MANSELL	Eliza	57		Wife	Mar	29	F		Herts	St Peters
770	HAY	William	57		Father-in-law	Widower	79	M	Agric Lab	Herts	Stannen [Standon?]
771	TYLER	James	58	Colney Heath	Head	Mar	38	M	Agric Lab	Herts	St Peters
772	TYLER	Mary	58		Wife	Mar	38	F		Herts	Trowley Bottom
773	TYLER	James	58		Son	Unm	16	M	Agric Lab	Herts	St Peters
774	TYLER	Samuel	58		Son		15	M	Agric Lab	Herts	St Peters
775	TYLER	Mary	58		Dau		11	F		Herts	St Peters
776	TYLER	Jane	58		Dau		7	F		Herts	St Peters
777	TYLER	Sarah	58		Dau		5	F		Herts	St Peters
778	TYLER	Ann	58		Dau		5	F		Herts	St Peters
779	TYLER	Joseph	58		Son		2	M		Herts	St Peters
780	HILL	Joseph	59	Colney Heath	Head	Mar	38	M	Agric Lab	Herts	St Peters
781	HILL	Mary	59		Wife	Mar	33	F		Herts	Colney Heath
782	HILL	William	59		Son		9	M		Herts	Colney Heath
783	HILL	John	59		Son		3	M		Herts	Colney Heath
784	GEORGE	Mary	59		Mother-in-law	Widow	74	F	Needle Woman	Herts	St Peters
785	HARDIN	John	60	Colney Heath	Head	Mar	54	M	Agric Lab	Herts	Tewin
786	HARDIN	Mary	60		Wife	Mar	52	F	Straw Plaiter	Herts	Colney Heath
787	HARDIN	John	60		Son	Unm	24	M	Agric Lab	Herts	Colney Heath

	SURNAME	FORENAME	SCHEDULE NUMBER	ADDRESS	RELATIONSHIP	STATUS	AGE	SEX	OCCUPATION	COUNTY OF BIRTH	PLACE OF BIRTH
788	HARDIN	William	60		Son		5	M		Herts	Colney Heath
789	REYNOLDS	William	61	Licenced House	Head	Mar	63	M	Victualler	Herts	St Stephens
790	REYNOLDS	Sarah	61		Wife	Mar	51	F		Herts	St Michaels
791	HAYWARD	Sarah	61		Dau	Mar	34	F		Herts	Ridge
792	HAYWARD	Samuel G.	61		Grandson		11	M	Scholar	Middx	Soho
793	SMITH	Joseph	61		Lodger	Unm	20	M	Agric Lab	Herts	St Peters
794	CARVINTON?	Richard	61		Lodger	Unm	46	M	Bricklayer	Derby	[Unknown]
795	SAUNDERS	Marbet [?]	61		Lodger	Unm	21	M	Agric Lab	Herts	Bengeo
796	WEBSTER	William	62	Colney Heath	Head	Widower	59	M	Meat Dealer	Herts	Shenley
797	HILL	William	63	Colney Heath	Head	Mar	50	M	Agric Lab	Herts	St Peters
798	HILL	Sophia	63		Wife	Mar	48	F		Herts	North Mimms
799	HILL	Mary Ann	63		Dau	Unm	20	F	Straw Hat Maker	Herts	St Peters
800	HILL	William	63		Son	Unm	20	M	Agric Lab	Herts	North Mimms
801	HILL	James	63		Son	Unm	18	M	Agric Lab	Herts	North Mimms
802	HILL	Sarah	63		Dau	Unm	16	F	Straw Hat Maker	Herts	North Mimms
803	HILL	Sophia	63		Dau		14	F	Straw Hat Maker	Middx	South Mimms
804	HILL	Ann	63		Dau		10	F	Straw Hat Maker	Herts	St Peters
805	HILL	David	63		Son		7	M	Scholar	Herts	St Peters
806	HILL	Emily	63		Dau		7m	F		Herts	St Peters
807	FIELD	Joseph	63		Son-in-law [Brother-in-law]	Mar	28	M	Agric Lab	Herts	St Peters
808	FIELD	Eliza	63		Dau-in-law [Sister]	Mar	29	F	Straw Hat Maker	Herts	North Mimms
809	FIELD	Susan	63		Niece		5	F		Herts	North Mimms
810	FIELD	William	63		Nephew		2	M		Herts	North Mimms
811	HILL	Samuel	64	Colney Heath	Head	Mar	43	M	Agric Lab	Herts	Sleapshyde
812	HILL	Mary	64		Wife	Mar	39	F	Straw Plaiter	Herts	Sandridge
813	HILL	James	64		Son	Unm	18	M	Agric Lab	Herts	Sleapshyde
814	HILL	John	64		Son		12	M	Agric Lab	Herts	Colney Heath
815	HILL	George	64		Son		9	M	At Home	Herts	Colney Heath
816	HILL	Mary	64		Dau		5	F		Herts	Colney Heath
817	HILL	Emma	64		Dau		1	F		Herts	Colney Heath
818	DIMOCK	Jeremiah	65	Colney Heath	Head	Mar	50	M	Agric Lab	Herts	North Mimms
819	DIMOCK	Ann	65		Wife	Mar	40	F	Straw Plaiter	Herts	St Peters
820	DIMOCK	Sarah	65		Dau	Unm	16	F	Straw Plaiter	Herts	North Mimms
821	DIMOCK	Jeremiah	65		Son	Unm	21	M	Agric Lab	Herts	St Peters
822	DIMOCK	Mary	65		Dau		9	F		Herts	St Peters
823	DIMOCK	Isaac	65		Son		4	M		Herts	North Mimms
824	DIMOCK	Thomas	65		Son		10 [mths, wks?]	M		Herts	St Peters
825	BROWN	James	66	Colney Heath	Head	Mar	51	M	Agric Lab	Herts	Hatfield
826	BROWN	Hannah	66		Wife	Mar	52	F		Herts	Bramfield
827	BROWN	Benjamin	66		Son	Unm	26	M	Agric Lab	Herts	St Peters
828	BROWN	Ester	66		Dau	Unm	19	F	Straw Hat Maker	Herts	St Peters
829	LONG	James	67	Colney Heath	Head	Mar	54	M	Agric Lab	Herts	Potters Crouch [St Michaels]
830	LONG	Ann	67		Wife	Mar	51	F	Straw Plaiter	Herts	Colney Heath

831	LONG	Maria	67		Dau	Unm	17	F	Straw Hat Maker	Herts	Colney Heath
832	LONG	William	67		Son		12	M	Agric Lab	Herts	Colney Heath
833	EDMONDS	William	68	Colney Heath	Head	Widower	54	M	Agric Lab	Herts	Chipperfield
834	EDMONDS	Therrey	68		Dau	Unm	16	F	Straw Hat Maker	Herts	St Peters
835	JACKSON	William	69	Round House	Head	Mar	37	M	Farmer of 70 acres employing 3 men	Herts	Colney Heath
836	JACKSON	Eliza	69		Wife	Mar	30	F		Herts	Smallford
837	JACKSON	Eliza	69		Dau		1	F		Herts	Colney Heath
838	PARSONS	Mary	69		Lodger	Widow	77	F	Annuitant	Herts	Colney Heath
839	BOFFLE	Martha	69		Serv	Unm	17	F	General Servant	Beds	Northill
840	HUTCHINS	James	69		Serv	Unm	22	M	Agric Lab	Herts	Colney Heath
841	BALDWIN	Samuel	69		Serv		15	M	Agric Lab	Herts	Colney Heath
842	WILSON	John	70	Colney Heath	Head	Mar	54	M	Wheelwright	Herts	Langley
843	WILSON	Charlotte	70		Wife	Mar	55	F		Herts	St Peters
844	WILSON	Louisa	70		Dau	Unm	20	F		Herts	St Peters
845	WILSON	John	70		Son	Unm	18	M	Wheelwright	Herts	St Peters
846	RAY	John	71	Colney Heath	Head	Mar	65	M	Agric Lab	Herts	St Peters
847	RAY	Elizabeth	71		Wife	Mar	67	F		Bucks	Unknown
848	COBB	William	72	Colney Heath	Head	Mar	38	M	Agric Lab	Herts	Sandridge
849	COBB	Rebecca	72		Wife	Mar	36	F	Straw Plaiter	Herts	St Peters
850	COBB	Eliza	72		Dau		7	F	Scholar	Herts	St Peters
851	COBB	Susan	72		Dau		3	F	Scholar	Herts	St Peters
852	HOY	Elizabeth	72		Scholar		12	F	Scholar	Herts	St Peters
853	DAY	Thomas	73	Colney Heath	Head	Mar	46	M	Carpenter	Herts	Ickleford
854	DAY	Ann	73		Wife	Mar	45	F	Plaiter	Herts	St Albans
855	DAY	George	73		Son	Unm	22	M	Agric Lab	Herts	Hatfield
856	DAY	Amos	73		Son	Unm	18	M	Agric Lab	Herts	Hatfield
857	DAY	Charles	73		Son		15	M	Agric Lab	Herts	Hatfield
858	DAY	David	73		Son		12	M	Scholar	Herts	St Peters
859	DAY	John	73		Son		9	M	Scholar	Herts	St Peters
860	JORDAN	Abraham	74	Colney Heath	Head	Mar	61	M	Cordwainer	Suffolk	Wenston [Wenhaston]
861	JORDAN	Harriett	74		Wife	Mar	61	F	Shoe Binder	Suffolk	Wenston [Wenhaston]
862	JORDAN	John	74		Son	Unm	31	M	Cordwainer	Suffolk	Wenston [Wenhaston]
863	JORDAN	Lydia	74		Dau		10	F	Scholar	Herts	St Peters
864	PARISH	Joshua	75	Colney Heath	Head	Mar	29	M	Agric Lab	Herts	North Mimms
865	PARISH	Charlotte	75		Wife	Mar	35	F	Plaiter	Malta	[Unknown]
866	PARISH	Thomas	75		Son		2	M		Herts	St Peters
867	HILL	Amos	76	Colney Heath	Head	Mar	24	M	Agric Lab	Herts	St Peters
868	HILL	Sarah	76		Wife	Mar	34	F	Straw Plaiter	Herts	St Peters
869	HILL	William	76		Son		3	M		Herts	St Peters
870	PAIN	William	76		Father-in-law	Widower	70	M	Agric Lab	Herts	St Peters
871	PAIN	Eliza	76		Dau	Unm	27	F	Straw Plaiter	Herts	St Peters
872	LOFORD	John	77	Colney Heath	Head	Mar	45	M	Agric Lab	Herts	North Mimms
873	LOFORD	Sarah	77		Wife	Mar	48	F	Straw Plaiter	Herts	St Peters

	SURNAME	FORENAME	SCHEDULE NUMBER	ADDRESS	RELATIONSHIP	STATUS	AGE	SEX	OCCUPATION	COUNTY OF BIRTH	PLACE OF BIRTH
874	WEBSTER	Thomas	77		Lodger	Widower	71	M	Agric Lab	Herts	St Peters
875	HILL	John	78	Colney Heath	Head	Mar	46	M	Agric Lab	Herts	St Peters
876	HILL	Rose	78		Wife	Mar	36	F	Straw Plaiter	Suffolk	Wenston [Wenhaston]
877	HILL	Louisa	78		Dau		3	F		Herts	St Peters
878	HILL	Abraham	78		Son		6m	M		Herts	St Peters
879	HILL	William	78		Lodger	Unm	74	M	Agric Lab	Herts	St Stephens
880	FREEMAN	James	79	Roe Green	Head	Mar	38	M	Victualler & Dealer	Herts	St Peters
881	FREEMAN	Mary	79		Wife	Mar	34	F		Sussex	Hellingly
882	FREEMAN	Harriett	79		Dau		11	F	Scholar	Herts	North Mimms
883	FREEMAN	Eliza	79		Dau		8	F	Scholar	Herts	North Mimms
884	FREEMAN	James	79		Son		6	M	Scholar	Herts	North Mimms
885	FREEMAN	Rosa	79		Dau		4	F		Herts	St Peters
886	FREEMAN	Laura	79		Dau		1	F		Herts	St Peters
887	SOY	Rebecca	79		Serv	Unm	14	F	General Servant	Herts	Hatfield
888	FIELD	William	79		Lodger	Unm	40	M	Agric Lab	Herts	Hatfield
889	MANSELL	James	80	Colney Heath	Head	Mar	50	M	Agric Lab	Herts	Northall
890	MANSELL	Charlotte	80		Wife	Mar	53	F	Agric Lab	Herts	North Mimms
891	MANSELL	Mary Ann	80		Dau	Unm	17	F		Herts	North Mimms
892	HILL	George	81	Colney Heath	Head	Mar	26	M	Bricklayers Labourer	Middx	Hadley
893	HILL	Susan	81		Wife	Mar	23	F	Straw Hatter	Herts	Hatfield
894	HILL	William	81		Son		2	M		Herts	Hatfield
895	FORD	Fanny	81		[blank]		6	F		Herts	Hatfield
896	KUMIN	John	82	Colney Heath	Head	Mar	49	M	Farm Steward	Suffolk	Rattlesden
897	KUMIN	Mary Anne	82		Wife	Mar	47	F	Farm Stewards Wife	Suffolk	Rattlesden
898	KUMIN	Mary Anne	82		Dau	Unm	21	F	Farm Stewards Daughter	Suffolk	Rattlesden
899	KUMIN	John	82		Son	Unm	29	M	Agric Lab	Suffolk	Rattlesden
900	HUPPY	William	82		Visitor	Unm	23	M	Agric Lab	Suffolk	Rattlesden
901	JACKSON	Abraham	83	Colney Heath	Head	Mar	28	M	Farmer of 16 acres	Herts	Colney Heath
902	JACKSON	Emma	83		Wife	Mar	37	F	Dressmaker	Herts	Welham Green
903	JACKSON	William	83		Son		3	M		Herts	Welham Green
904	JACKSON	Flora	83		Dau		3m	F		Herts	St Peters
905	MAINFIELD	John	84	Colney Heath	Head	Mar	42	M	Beerhouse Keeper & Shoemaker	Herts	Northall
906	MAINFIELD	Hannah	84		Wife	Mar	35	F		Herts	St Peters
907	MAINFIELD	Betsey	84		Dau		13	F	Straw Hat Maker	Herts	St Peters
908	MAINFIELD	Susan	84		Dau		5	F	Scholar	Herts	St Peters
909	MAINFIELD	Jane	84		Dau		3	F		Herts	St Peters
910	MAINFIELD	Sophia	84		Dau		1	F		Herts	St Peters
911	WRIGHT	James	84		Serv	Unm	37	M	Shoemaker	Herts	Settle Green [?]
912	GREY	Martha	85	Colney Heath	Head	Widow	40	F	Straw Plaiter	Herts	Roestock
913	GREY	Harriett	85		Dau		4	F	At Home	Herts	Roestock
914	GREY	William	85		Son		3m	M		Herts	Roestock
915	BEACH	John	86	Colney Heath	Head	Mar	45	M	Agric Lab	Herts	Hatfield
916	BEACH	Sarah	86		Wife	Mar	40	F		Herts	Hatfield
917	BEACH	Mary Anne	86		Dau		15	F	Brazilian Hat Maker	Herts	St Peters

	Surname	Name			Relation		Age	Sex	Occupation	County	Birthplace
918	BEACH	Emma	86		Dau		12	F		Herts	St Peters
919	BEACH	Hannah	86		Dau		5	F		Herts	St Peters
920	BEACH	Job	86		Son		2	M		Herts	St Peters
921	FIELD	William	87	Colney Heath	Head	Mar	57	M	Agric Lab	Herts	St Peters
922	FIELD	Mary	87		Wife	Mar	55	F		Beds	Cheddington
923	FIELD	Elizabeth	87		Dau	Mar	29	F		Herts	Roe Green [St Peters]
924	FINCH	James	87		Son-in-law	Mar	34	M	Agric Lab	Herts	Hatfield
925	FINCH	William	87		Nephew		10	M		Herts	Hatfield
926	WILSON	Alfred	87		Nephew		10	M		Herts	Hatfield
927	WILSON	Martha	87		Niece		7	F		Herts	Roe Green [St Peters]
928	WILSON	Eliza	87		Niece		5	F		Herts	Roe Green [St Peters]
929	WILSON	James	87		Nephew		2	M		Herts	Roe Green [St Peters]
930	WILSON	Mary Ann	87		Niece		9wks	F		Herts	Roe Green [St Peters]
931	WICKS	William	88	Colney Heath	Head	Mar	29	M	Agric Lab	Herts	Hatfield
932	WICKS	Sarah	88		Wife	Mar	35	F		Herts	Hatfield
933	WICKS	Ann Maria	88		Dau		10	F	Scholar	Herts	Hatfield

End of the village of Colney Heath

	Surname	Name			Relation		Age	Sex	Occupation	County	Birthplace
934	WHEATLEY	Thomas	89	Hatfield Road	Head	Mar	44	M	Dyer	Herts	Childwick [St Michaels]
935	WHEATLEY	Elizabeth	89		Wife	Mar	36	F		Dorset	Emlock [Hemyock?]
936	WHEATLEY	Caroline	89		Dau		14	F		Somerset	Yeovil
937	WHEATLEY	Jane	89		Dau		10	F		Herts	St Albans
938	WHEATLEY	Martha	89		Dau		8	F		Herts	St Albans
939	WHEATLEY	Ann	89		Dau		6	F		Herts	St Albans
940	WHEATLEY	Elizabeth	89		Dau		4	F		Herts	St Albans
941	WHEATLEY	Emily	89		Dau		2	F		Herts	St Albans
942	CRAIG	Amelia	90	Hatfield Road	Head	Widow	37	F	Landed Proprietor	Warks	Chilvers Coton
943	CRAIG	Adelaide	90		Dau		10	F	Scholar at Home	Northants	Burton Latimer
944	CRAIG	Edward	90		Son		1	M		Middx	Islington
945	COLE	Ellen	90		Governess	Unm	32	F	Governess	Bucks	Aylesbury
946	HAWKINS	Hannah	90		Serv	Unm	33	F	General Servant	Herts	Stapleford
947	ELDRIDGE	Elizabeth	90		Serv	Unm	38	F	General Servant	Herts	St Albans
948	DUAM	Mary Ann	90		Serv	Unm	20	F	General Servant	Somerset	Taunton
949	CHIPPENDALE	John	91	Hatfield Road	Head	Mar	25	M	Curate of St Peters, St Albans	Lancs	Manchester
950	CHIPPENDALE	Eliza	91		Wife	Mar	25	F	Curates Wife	Kent	Bexley
951	CHIPPENDALE	John Theodore	91		Son		1	M	Curates Son	Herts	St Albans
952	WELSH	Emma Margaret	91		Visitor	Unm	22	F	Barristers Daughter	Middx	Lambeth
953	CHAPPEL	Anne	91		Serv	Unm	30	F	Cook	Essex	Upminster
954	DEAYTON	Eliza	91		Serv	Unm	27	F	Housemaid	Herts	Watford
955	BLAKE	Harriet	91		Serv	Unm	40	F	Nurse	Suffolk	Little Stonham
956	BENNETT	Joseph	92	Hatfield Road	Head	Widower	44	M	Builder & Surveyor employing 8 men & 2 boys	Middx	Hackney
957	EASONE	Ann	92		Serv	Unm	35	F	Servant	Herts	Shenley

	SURNAME	FORENAME	SCHEDULE NUMBER	ADDRESS	RELATIONSHIP	STATUS	AGE	SEX	OCCUPATION	COUNTY OF BIRTH	PLACE OF BIRTH
958	GURNEY	William	93	Hatfield Road	Head	Mar	44	M	Victualler	Herts	Gaddesden
959	GURNEY	Elizabeth	93		Wife	Mar	42	F		Herts	St Michaels
960	GURNEY	Harriett	93		Dau	Unm	16	F		Herts	St Michaels
961	GURNEY	John	93		Son		15	M		Middx	Paddington
962	CRAWLEY	Barnard	93		Lodger	Unm	20	M	Agric Lab	Herts	St Peters

Two houses building

	SURNAME	FORENAME	SCHEDULE NUMBER	ADDRESS	RELATIONSHIP	STATUS	AGE	SEX	OCCUPATION	COUNTY OF BIRTH	PLACE OF BIRTH
963	PINNOCK	James	94	Hatfield Road	Head	Mar	33	M	Brazilian Hat Maker	Herts	Baldock
964	PINNOCK	Mary Ann	94		Wife	Mar	31	F		Herts	Colney Heath
965	PINNOCK	Clara	94		Dau		7	F		Herts	St Peters
966	PINNOCK	James	94		Son		3	M		Herts	St Peters
967	PINNOCK	Mary Anne	94		Dau		2	F		Herts	St Peters
968	PINNOCK	Charles	94		Son		6wks	M		Herts	St Peters
969	OSMAN	Sarah	95	Hatfield Road	Head	Widow	62	F	Straw Bonnet Maker	Herts	St Peters
970	OSMAN	Ann	95		Dau	Unm	27	F	Straw Bonnet Maker	Herts	St Peters
971	GILBERT	Susan	96	The Lodge	Head	Widow	42	F	Straw Bonnet Maker	Herts	Sandridge
972	HARCOURT	Thomas	97	Hatfield Road	Head	Widower	49	M	Labourer	Herts	St Albans
973	HARCOURT	Georgenaie	97		Dau		12	F	Straw Plaiter	Herts	St Peters

End of the Hatfield Road St Peters

	SURNAME	FORENAME	SCHEDULE NUMBER	ADDRESS	RELATIONSHIP	STATUS	AGE	SEX	OCCUPATION	COUNTY OF BIRTH	PLACE OF BIRTH
974	GRAINGE	James	98	Butterwick	Head	Mar	45	M	Farmer of 175 acres employing 3 men	Herts	Shenley
975	GRAINGE	Sarah	98		Wife	Mar	48	F		Worcs	Unknown
976	GRAINGE	John	98		Son	Unm	21	M	Farmers Son	Herts	Little Munden
977	GRAINGE	Charles	98		Son	Unm	18	M	Farmers Son	Herts	Little Munden
978	DAVIS	Mary	98		Serv	Unm	20	F	Servant	Middx	Clerkenwell
979	DAVIS	David	98		Visitor	Widower	57	M	Carpenter	S. Wales	[Unknown]
980	HARDING	James	99	Butterwick	Head	Mar	28	M	Agric Lab	Herts	St Peters
981	HARDING	Martha	99		Wife	Mar	29	F	Grass Hat Maker	Herts	St Peters
982	HARDING	Ann	99		Dau		6	F	Grass Hat Maker	Herts	St Peters
983	HARDING	David	99		Son		3	M		Herts	St Peters
984	HARDING	Emily	99		Dau		2	F		Herts	St Peters
985	LAWFORD	George	100	Butterwick	Head	Mar	26	M	Agric Lab	Herts	St Peters
986	LAWFORD	Sarah	100		Wife	Mar	21	F	Grass Hat Maker	Middx	Enfield

End of the Hamlet of Butterwick

Registrar's District: St Albans   Enumeration District 3   Ref. HO 107/1713 folios 346-61

Tyttenghanger Hamlet

Parish of St Peters

	SURNAME	FORENAME	SCHEDULE NUMBER	ADDRESS	RELATIONSHIP	STATUS	AGE	SEX	OCCUPATION	COUNTY OF BIRTH	PLACE OF BIRTH
987	EAMES	Joseph	1	Camp	Head	Mar	53	M	Labourer	Herts	St Peters
988	EAMES	Ann	1		Wife	Mar	46	F	Straw Plaiter	Herts	St Peters
989	EAMES	Jesse	1		Son	Unm	19	M	Labourer	Herts	St Peters
990	CHARKLEY	William	2	Camp	Head	Mar	25	M	Agric Lab	Herts	St Peters
991	CHARKLEY	Sarah	2		Wife	Mar	26	F	Straw Plaiter	Herts	St Peters
992	CHARKLEY	Sarah	2		Dau		1	F		Herts	St Peters

No.	Surname	Forename		Place	Relation	Status	Age	Sex	Occupation	County	Parish
993	CHARKLEY	William	2		Son		1 m	M		Herts	St Peters
994	HOWARD	Joshua	3	Camp	Head	Mar	28	M	Agric Lab	Herts	St Peters
995	HOWARD	Sarah	3		Wife	Mar	25	F	Straw Plaiter	Herts	St Stephens
996	HOWARD	George	3		Son		5	M		Herts	St Peters
997	HOWARD	David	3		Son		1	M		Herts	St Peters
998	PEACOCK	James	4	Camp	Head	Mar	38	M	Gardener	Herts	[Unknown]
999	PEACOCK	Hannah	4		Wife	Mar	34	F	Hand Loom Weaver	Herts	[Unknown]
1000	PEACOCK	Joseph	4		Son		7	M	Scholar	Herts	St Stephens
1001	PEACOCK	William	4		Son		4	M		Herts	St Stephens
1002	WEBB	Henry	5	Camp	Head	Mar	27	M	Agric Lab	Herts	Sandridge
1003	WEBB	Ann	5		Wife	Mar	25	F	Hand Loom Worker	Herts	North Mimms
1004	WEBB	Emma	5		Dau		5	F		Herts	St Peters
1005	WEBB	Mary	5		Dau		3	F		Herts	St Peters
1006	WEBB	Sarah	5		Sister	Unm	21	F	Bonnet Sewer	Herts	St Peters
1007	OAKLEY	John	6	Camp	Head	Mar	60	M	Agric Lab	Herts	St Peters
1008	OAKLEY	Elizabeth	6		Wife	Mar	61	F	Straw Plaiter	Herts	St Peters
1009	DELL	Thomas	7	Camp	Head	Mar	50	M	Brickmaker	Bucks	Great Marlow
1010	DELL	Mary	7		Wife	Mar	50	F	Brickmakers Wife	Bucks	Great Marlow
1011	MAJOR	Sarah	7		Niece		11	F		Herts	St Albans
1012	OAKLEY	Edward	8	Camp	Head	Mar	41	M	Agric Lab	Herts	St Peters
1013	OAKLEY	Eliza	8		Wife	Mar	35	F	Straw Plaiter	Herts	St Peters
1014	OAKLEY	Isaac	8		Son		6	M	Scholar	Herts	St Peters
1015	OAKLEY	Mary A.	8		Dau		5	F		Herts	St Peters
1016	OAKLEY	Richard	8		Son		3	M		Herts	St Peters
1017	OAKLEY	John	8		Son		11 m	M		Herts	St Peters
1018	HAWKINS	George	9	Camp	Head	Mar	24	M	Agric Lab	Herts	Hatfield
1019	HAWKINS	Mary	9		Wife	Mar	23	F	Straw Plaiter	Herts	Stevenage
1020	HAWKINS	George	9		Son		2	M		Herts	St Peters
1021	HAWKINS	Henry	9		Son		6 m	M		Herts	St Peters
1022	LAWRENCE	John	10	Camp	Head	Mar	73	M	Agric Lab	Herts	Brent Pelham
1023	LAWRENCE	Mary	10		Wife	Mar	59	F		Essex	Berden
1024	JARVIS	William	11	Camp	Head	Mar	39	M	Agric Lab	Berks	[Unknown]
1025	JARVIS	Sarah	11		Wife	Mar	32	F	Hat Maker	Herts	St Albans
1026	JARVIS	Hannah	11		Dau		11	F	Hat Maker	Herts	St Peters
1027	JARVIS	Mary A.	11		Dau		9	F	Hat Maker	Herts	St Peters
1028	JARVIS	James	11		Son		7	M	Scholar	Herts	St Peters
1029	JARVIS	Emma	11		Dau		5	F		Herts	St Peters
1030	JARVIS	Jane	11		Dau		10 m	F		Herts	St Peters
1031	HOWARD	John	12	Camp	Head	Mar	59	M	Agric Lab	Herts	St Pauls Walden
1032	HOWARD	Mary	12		Wife	Mar	58	F	Laundress	Herts	St Herts [St Peters?]
1033	HOWARD	John	12		Son	Mar	27	M	Agric Lab	Herts	St Peters
1034	MUSKETT	John	13	Camp	Head	Mar	40	M	Agric Lab	Herts	St Peters
1035	MUSKETT	Eliza	13		Wife	Mar	35	F	Straw Plaiter	Herts	St Peters
1036	MUSKETT	William	13		Son	Unm	16	M	Agric Lab	Herts	St Peters

	SURNAME	FORENAME	SCHEDULE NUMBER	ADDRESS	RELATIONSHIP	STATUS	AGE	SEX	OCCUPATION	COUNTY OF BIRTH	PLACE OF BIRTH
1037	MUSKETT	Ellen	13		Dau		11	F	Hat Maker	Herts	St Peters
1038	MUSKETT	Jane	13		Dau		8	F	Hat Maker	Herts	St Peters
1039	MUSKETT	James	13		Son		4	M		Herts	St Peters
1040	MUSKETT	Eliza	13		Dau		2m	F		Herts	St Peters
1041	CANNON	William	14	Camp	Head	Mar	67	M	Agric Lab	Herts	St Peters
1042	CANNON	Elizabeth	14		Wife	Mar	60	F	Straw Plaiter	Herts	St Peters
1043	CANNON	William	14		Son	Unm	19	M	Agric Lab	Herts	St Peters
1044	OAKLEY	John	15	Camp	Head	Mar	32	M	Carpenter	Herts	St Peters
1045	OAKLEY	Sarah	15		Wife	Mar	41	F	Straw Plaiter	Herts	Sandridge
1046	OAKLEY	Mary	15		Dau		9	F	Scholar	Herts	St Peters
1047	OAKLEY	Thomas	15		Son		5	M	Scholar	Herts	St Peters
1048	OAKLEY	John	15		Son		3	M		Herts	St Peters
1049	OAKLEY	Thomas	16	Camp	Head	Mar	57	M	Farmer of 38 acres employing 2 labourers	Herts	St Peters
1050	OAKLEY	Sarah	16		Wife	Mar	65	F	Wife	Herts	Wheathampstead
1051	CONSTABLE	James	17	Camp	Head	Mar	48	M	Agric Lab	Herts	St Peters
1052	CONSTABLE	Mary	17		Wife	Mar	47	F	Straw Plaiter	Herts	St Peters
1053	CONSTABLE	John C.	17		Son	Unm	25	M	Agric Lab	Herts	St Peters
1054	CONSTABLE	William	17		Son	Unm	22	M	Agric Lab	Herts	St Peters
1055	CONSTABLE	Eliza	17		Dau		14	F	Hat Maker	Herts	St Peters
1056	CONSTABLE	Hannah	17		Dau		11	F	Hat Maker	Herts	St Peters
1057	CONSTABLE	Mary	17		Dau		6	F		Herts	St Peters
1058	CONSTABLE	Jonah	17		Son		2	M		Herts	St Peters
1059	LITTLE	Ann	18	Beastneys	Head	Unm	75	F	Receiving Relief from the Parish, formerly Plait Woman	Herts	Wheathampstead
1060	LITTLE	Mary	18		Sister	Unm	70	F	Job Woman	Herts	Wheathampstead
1061	EAMES	David	18		Lodger	Unm	23	M	Agric Lab	Herts	St Peters
1062	CRAWLEY	James	18		Lodger	Unm	17	M	Journeyman Brickmaker	Herts	Wheathampstead
1063	TURNER	Charles	19	Beastneys	Head	Mar	24	M	Agric Lab	Bucks	High Wycombe
1064	TURNER	Harriett	19		Wife	Mar	23	F	Hat Maker	Berks	[Upper] Culham
1065	TURNER	Joseph	19		Son		1	M		Herts	St Peters
1066	HARCOURT	Joseph	20	Beastneys	Head	Mar	42	M	Brickmaker	Herts	St Albans
1067	HARCOURT	Emley	20		Wife	Mar	36	F	Straw Plaiter	Herts	Wheathampstead
1068	HARCOURT	Eliza	20		Dau		11	F		Herts	St Albans
1069	HARCOURT	Emma	20		Dau		9	F		Herts	St Albans
1070	HARCOURT	Jane	20		Dau		8m	F		Herts	St Peters
1071	MUNT	Joseph	20		Lodger	Unm	47	M	Agric Lab	Herts	Wheathampstead
1072	POCOCK	Samuel	21	Beastneys	Head	Mar	59	M	Foreman for Thomas Mill Farmer, 100 acres employing 4 labourers	Herts	St Peters
1073	POCOCK	Elizabeth	21		Wife	Mar	57	F	Wife	Herts	St Peters
1074	POCOCK	Ann	21		Dau	Unm	26	F	Hat Maker	Herts	St Peters
1075	POCOCK	Charles	21		Son	Unm	22	M	Labourer	Herts	St Peters
1076	POCOCK	Emma	21		Dau	Unm	18	F	Hat Maker	Herts	St Peters
1077	FILLPOT	Henry	21		Serv	Unm	30	M	Agric Lab	Herts	Codicote
1078	IVORY	David	21		Serv		12	M		Herts	St Peters
1079	ALLEN	Thomas	22	London Colney	Head	Mar	43	M	Agric Lab	Herts	St Peters

1080	ALLEN	Sarah	22		Wife	Mar	39	F	Charwoman	Staffs	Wolverhampton
1081	ALLEN	John	22		Son		14	M	Agric Lab	Herts	St Peters
1082	ALLEN	William	22		Son		10	M		Herts	St Peters
1083	ALLEN	Elizabeth	22		Dau		7	F		Herts	St Peters
1084	ALLEN	Ann	22		Dau		5	F		Herts	St Peters
1085	ALLEN	James	23	London Colney	Head	Mar	70	M	Agric Lab	Herts	St Peters
1086	ALLEN	Elizabeth	23		Wife	Mar	66	F	Charwoman	Herts	St Peters
1087	ALLEN	James	23		Son	Unm	22	M	Agric Lab	Herts	St Peters
1088	ALLEN	Richard	23		Son	Unm	17	M		Herts	St Peters
1089	JONES	Thomas	24	London Colney	Head	Mar	63	M	Innkeeper	Herts	St Peters
1090	JONES	Elizabeth	24		Wife	Mar	56	F		Beds	Streatley
1091	JONES	Joshua	24		Son	Unm	30	M	Carpenter	Herts	Harpenden
1092	PALMER	Henry	24		Serv	Unm	48	M	Ostler (Inn)	Beds	Chalgrave
1093	SADDLER	Robert	24		Lodger	Mar	50	M	Traveller	Middx	Hammersmith
1094	SADDLER	Sarah	24		Wife	Mar	50	F	Wife	Surrey	Lambeth
1095	WESTON	James	25	London Colney	Head	Mar	42	M	Victualler	Northants	Barby
1096	WESTON	Hannah	25		Wife	Mar	42	F	Wife	Kent	Pembury
1097	TOWNER	Herbert	25		Step-son		9	M		Kent	Pembury
1098	WESTON	Joseph	25		Son		9	M		France	Sen Rolebise [?]
1099	WESTON	Hannah	25		Dau		7	F	Scholar	Northants	Whelford [Welford]
1100	WESTON	John	25		Son		5	M		Yorks	Morley
1101	HOSEFIELD	Benjamin	26	London Colney	Head	Mar	63	M	Bricklayer	Herts	St Peters
1102	HOSEFIELD	Mary	26		Wife	Mar	67	F		Surrey	Wheddone
1103	HOSEFIELD	Thomas	26		Son	Unm	27	M	Bricklayer	Herts	Shenley
1104	HOSEFIELD	William	26		Grandson		11	M	Scholar	Herts	St Michaels
1105	SMITH	Sarah	26		[blank]	Widow	88	F		Unknown	Unknown
1106	OAKLEY	Charles	27	London Colney	Head	Mar	32	M	Gardener	Herts	St Peters
1107	OAKLEY	Carriline	27		Wife	Mar	30	F	Straw Plaiter	Herts	St Michaels
1108	OAKLEY	Mary A.	27		Dau		6	F		Herts	St Peters
1109	OAKLEY	Sarah	27		Dau		3	F		Herts	St Peters
1110	OAKLEY	James	27		Son		8 m	M		Herts	St Peters
1111	SMITH	Joseph	27		Lodger	Unm	23	M	Agric Lab	Herts	St Peters
1112	LOW	William	28	London Colney	Head	Mar	67	M	Agric Lab	Herts	Redbourn
1113	LOW	Mary	28		Wife	Mar	63	F	Wife	Herts	Studham
1114	PRIDMORE	Fanney	29	London Colney	Head	Widow	46	F	Dressmaker	Herts	St Peters
1115	PRIDMORE	Fanney	29		Dau	Unm	26	F	Dressmaker	Herts	St Peters
1116	PRIDMORE	Joseph	29		Son	Unm	23	M	Seaman	Herts	St Peters
1117	LAURENCE	Hearey	29		Visitor	Unm	29	M	Seaman	Unknown	Unknown
1118	OAKLEY	Richard	30	London Colney	Head	Mar	57	M	Agric Lab	Herts	St Albans
1119	OAKLEY	Sarah	30		Wife	Mar	54	F	Straw Plaiter	Herts	St Albans
1120	OAKLEY	William	30		Son	Unm	17	M	Agric Lab	Herts	St Peters
1121	WINTER	William	31	London Colney	Head	Mar	25	M	Agric Lab	Middx	Marylebone
1122	WINTER	Sarah	31		Wife	Mar	20	F		Herts	St Peters
1123	WINTER	William	31		Son		2	M		Herts	Shenley

	SURNAME	FORENAME	SCHEDULE NUMBER	ADDRESS	RELATIONSHIP	STATUS	AGE	SEX	OCCUPATION	COUNTY OF BIRTH	PLACE OF BIRTH
1124	WINTER	John	31		Son		3m	M		Herts	St Peters
1125	HOAR	James	32	London Colney	Head	Mar	51	M	Agric Lab	Herts	Hemel Hempstead
1126	HOAR	Mary	32		Wife	Mar	50	F	Charwoman	Herts	Bovingdon
1127	HOAR	Eliza	32		Dau		14	F		Herts	St Peters
1128	HOAR	Mary Ann	32		Dau		12	F		Herts	St Peters
1129	TOMLIN	Mary A.	33	London Colney	Head	Widow	34	F	Bonnet Sewer	Herts	St Albans
1130	TOMLIN	William	33		Son		3	M		Herts	St Peters
1131	TOMLIN	Mary A.	33		Dau		2	F		Herts	St Peters
1132	TOMLIN	David	33		Son		3m	M		Herts	St Peters
1133	GOATLY	Ruth	33		Lodger	Widow	57	F		Middx	Marylebone
1134	GOATLY	Emily	33		Lodgers Dau		11	F		Herts	St Peters
1135	GORDON	Joseph C.	34	London Colney	Head	Unm	74	M	Annuitant	Middx	[Unknown]
1136	CROSS	James	35	London Colney	Head	Mar	60	M	Carpenter	Herts	Puckeridge
1137	CROSS	Sarah	35		Wife	Mar	59	F		Middx	South Mimms
1138	REYNOLDS	James	36	London Colney	Head	Mar	35	M	Agric Lab	Beds [Herts]	Lilley
1139	REYNOLDS	Sarah	36		Wife	Mar	29	F	Straw Plaiter	Herts	Hatfield
1140	REYNOLDS	Sarah	36		Dau		7	F		Herts	St Peters
1141	REYNOLDS	Sophia	36		Dau		4	F		Herts	St Peters
1142	REYNOLDS	Mary Ann	36		Dau		1	F		Herts	St Peters
1143	HORTON	Thomas	37	London Colney	Head	Mar	48	M	Agric Lab	Herts	St Peters
1144	HORTON	Elizabeth	37		Wife	Mar	45	F	Hat Maker	Herts	St Peters
1145	HORTON	Catherine	37		Dau	Unm	18	F	Agric Lab	Herts	St Peters
1146	HORTON	Alfred	37		Son		10	M	Scholar	Herts	St Peters
1147	CARNEY	Martin	37		Visitor	Unm	20	M	Agric Lab	Ireland	[Unknown]
1148	GREEN	Matthew	37	London Colney	Head	Mar	36	M	Agric Lab	Herts	St Peters
1149	GREEN	Sarah	37		Wife	Mar	23	F		Herts	St Peters
1150	GREEN	Alfred	37		Son		14	M		Herts	St Peters
1151	GREEN	Eliza	37		Dau		10	F		Herts	St Peters
1152	GREEN	George	37		Son		7	M		Herts	St Peters
1153	GREEN	Jane	37		Dau		2	F		Herts	St Peters
1154	CHILES	Thomas	38	London Colney	Head	Mar	24	M	Agric Lab	Herts	St Peters
1155	CHILES	Eliza	38		Wife	Mar	23	F		Herts	St Peters
1156	CHILES	Elizabeth	38		Dau		1	F		Herts	St Peters
1157	FAIN	George	38	London Colney	Head	Mar	30	M	Agric Lab	Herts	St Peters
1158	FAIN	Ann	38		Wife	Mar	28	F		Herts	St Peters
1159	FAIN	Emma	38		Dau		6	F		Herts	St Peters
1160	FAIN	George	38		Son		8	M		Herts	St Peters
1161	FAIN	James	38		Son		3	M		Herts	St Peters
1162	FAIN	William	38		Son		10m	M		Herts	St Peters
1163	HYDE	Henry	39	London Colney	Head	Mar	32	M	Church of England Schoolmaster	Hants	Winton St Michael
1164	HYDE	Amelia	39		Wife	Mar	35	F		Hants	Gosport, Alverstoke
1165	HYDE	Ann	39		Sister		14	F		Hants	Winton St Michael
1166	WHEELER	Thomas	39		Visitor		9	M		Middx	Pimlico, St Peters

1167	NIGHTINGALE	Edith	40	London Colney	Head	Widow	72	F	Independent	Middx	London
1168	NIGHTINGALE	Prudence	40		Dau	Unm	39	F	Independent	Herts	Stevenage
1169	NIGHTINGALE	Mary	40		Dau	Unm	37	F	Independent	Herts	Stevenage
1170	NIGHTINGALE	Thomas	40		Son	Unm	35	M	Independent	Beds	Ex Parochial
1171	NIGHTINGALE	Anne	40		Dau	Unm	30	F	Independent	Herts	Hatfield
1172	PEARMAN	David	40	London Colney	Head	Mar	55	M	Police Officer	Herts	Sandridge
1173	PEARMAN	Sarah	40		Wife	Mar	56	F		Lancs	Cherry
1174	BROWN	Sarah	40		Dau		27	F		Middx	Edmonton
1175	BROWN	Sarah	40		Grandau		5	F		Herts	Elstree
1176	COOK	Charles	41	London Colney	Head	Mar	34	M	Labourer	Herts	St Peters
1177	COOK	Elizabeth	41		Wife	Mar	36	F	Labourers Wife	Herts	St Peters
1178	COOK	James J.	41		Son		10	M		Herts	St Peters
1179	COOK	George	41		Son		8	M		Herts	St Peters
1180	COOK	Benjamin	41		Son		6	M		Herts	St Peters
1181	COOK	Hannah E.	41		Dau		3	F		Herts	St Peters
1182	COOK	Sarah	41		Dau		1	F		Herts	St Peters
1183	MUNT	John	42	London Colney	Head	Mar	52	M	Agric Lab	Herts	[Unknown]
1184	MUNT	Martha	42		Wife	Mar	37	F		Herts	St Peters
1185	MUNT	Martha	42		Dau		3	F		Herts	St Peters
1186	MUNT	Joseph	42		Son		8 m	M		Herts	St Peters
1187	WELCH	John	42		Lodger	Widower	21	M		Herts	Stevenage
1188	WELCH	Elizabeth A.	42		Lodgers Dau		1 m	F		Herts	St Peters
1189	JENKINS	John R.	43	London Colney	Head	Mar	54	M	Annuitant	Essex	Snaresbrook
1190	JENKINS	Charlotte	43		Wife	Mar	53	F	Annuitants Wife	Middx	Aldgate
1191	BRIANT	Emma B.	43		Sister	Unm	46	F	Annuitant	Middx	Wapping
1192	LONGSTAFF	Hannah	43		Serv	Unm	20	F	House Servant	Herts	North Mimms
1193	ROBERTS	Joseph	44	London Colney	Head	Mar	52	M	Labourer	Herts	North Mimms
1194	ROBERTS	Eliza	44		Wife	Mar	48	F	Bonnet Sewer	Herts	Sandridge
1195	ROBERTS	Esrom	44		Son	Unm	16	M	Labourer	Herts	St Peters
1196	SEABROOK	Joseph	45	London Colney	Head	Mar	25	M	Agric Lab	Herts	St Michaels
1197	SEABROOK	Hannah	45		Wife	Mar	21	F	Straw Bonnet Maker	Herts	St Michaels
1198	GREEN	Lucy	46	London Colney	Head	Mar	33	F	Straw Bonnet Maker	Beds	Bedford
1199	GREEN	Edward	46		Son		3	M	Scholar	Beds	Bedford
1200	TEBBOTH	Elizabeth	46		Visitor	Unm	30	F	Hand Loom Weaver	Herts	St Albans
1201	SUTTON	William	47	London Colney	Head	Mar	78	M	Butcher Out of Business (Deaf)	Herts	Barkway
1202	SUTTON	Ann	47		Wife	Mar	67	F		Herts	Great Hormead
1203	ATKINS	Edmond	48	London Colney	Head	Mar	22	M	Coal Dealer	Herts	St Peters
1204	ATKINS	Eliza	48		Wife	Mar	16	F	Hat Maker	Herts	St Peters
1205	COLLINS	William	49	London Colney	Head	Mar	25	M	Agric Lab	Herts	St Peters
1206	COLLINS	Mary	49		Wife	Mar	21	F		Herts	St Peters
1207	POTTER	Henry	50	London Colney	Head	Mar	32	M	Agric Lab	Herts	St Peters
1208	POTTER	Harriett	50		Wife	Mar	22	F		Herts	St Peters
1209	POTTER	Susannah	50		Dau		2	F		Herts	St Peters
1210	CATLIN	William	51	London Colney	Head	Mar	26	M		Herts	Wheathampstead

	SURNAME	FORENAME	SCHEDULE NUMBER	ADDRESS	RELATIONSHIP	STATUS	AGE	SEX	OCCUPATION	COUNTY OF BIRTH	PLACE OF BIRTH
1211	CATLIN	Dinah	51		Wife	Mar	28	F		Herts	Hatfield
1212	CATLIN	Emley	51		Dau		9	F		Herts	Hatfield
1213	CATLIN	Jane	51		Dau		6	F		Herts	St Peters
1214	CATLIN	James	51		Son		1	M		Herts	St Peters
1215	MARTIN	Susan	52	London Colney	Head	Widow	42	F	Charwoman	Herts	St Peters
1216	MARTIN	William	52		Son	Unm	16	M	Agric Lab	Herts	St Peters
1217	MARTIN	Joseph	52		Son		12	M	Agric Lab	Herts	St Peters
1218	MARTIN	Emma	52		Dau		9	F	Scholar	Herts	St Peters
1219	MARTIN	John	52		Son		6	M	Scholar	Herts	St Peters
1220	MARTIN	Charlotte	52		Dau		1	F		Herts	St Peters
1221	SMITH	Emma	52		Visitor	Unm	23	F		Herts	St Peters
1222	SMITH	George	52		Visitor	Unm	25	M		Herts	St Peters
			53	Mrs Wiilton absent on the night of the 31 [sic] of March.							
1223	FACSDALE	George W.	54	London Colney	Head	Mar	35	M	Tailor	Herts	Shenley
1224	FACSDALE	Susannah	54		Wife	Mar	40	F	Dressmaker	Middx	Mill Hill
1225	FACSDALE	George	54		Son		11	M	Scholar	Herts	St Peters
1226	FACSDALE	Hannah	54		Dau		10	F	Scholar	Herts	St Peters
1227	FACSDALE	Charles	54		Son		6	M	Scholar	Herts	St Peters
1228	FACSDALE	John	54		Son		3	M	Scholar	Herts	St Peters
1229	FACSDALE	Knott	54		Son		2	M	Scholar	Herts	St Peters
1230	SKEGGS	William	55	London Colney	Head	Mar	47	M	Agric Lab	Herts	Anstey
1231	SKEGGS	Sarah	55		Wife	Mar	46	F	Charwoman	Herts	St Stephens
1232	SKEGGS	Shadrach	55		Son		14	M	Agric Lab	Middx	South Mimms
1233	SKEGGS	Emma	55		Dau		12	F	Scholar	Middx	South Mimms
1234	SKEGGS	William	55		Son		4	M	Scholar	Herts	St Stephens
1235	EAMES	Daniel	56	London Colney	Head	Mar	31	M	Agric Lab	Herts	St Peters
1236	EAMES	Sarah	56		Wife	Mar	29	F	Hat Maker	Herts	St Albans
1237	EAMES	Elenior	56		Dau		4	F		Herts	St Peters
1238	EAMES	George	56		Son		1	M		Herts	St Peters
1239	WHITTEY	Elenior	56		Sister-in-law	Unm	27	F	Hat Maker	Herts	St Albans
1240	CHESHER	George	57	London Colney	Head	Mar	42	M	Baker	Middx	South Mimms
1241	CHESHER	Mary A.	57		Wife	Mar	41	F	Bakers Wife	Herts	St Stephens
1242	DICKINSON	Charlotte	57		Relative		15	F		Herts	St Stephens
1243	SMITH	Alfred	57		Serv	Unm	17	M	Journeyman	Herts	Ridge
1244	DOLAMORE	John	58	London Colney	Head	Mar	48	M	Grocer & Draper	Herts	St Peters
1245	DOLAMORE	Lydia	58		Wife	Mar	50	F		Kent	Greenwich
1246	DOLAMORE	James	59	London Colney	Head	Mar	44	M	Shoemaker	Herts	St Stephens
1247	DOLAMORE	Ann	59		Wife	Mar	40	F		Middx	Edgware
1248	DOLAMORE	John	59		Son	Unm	20	M	Shoemaker	Herts	Kings Langley
1249	DOLAMORE	James	59		Son	Unm	16	M	Servant	Herts	Hemel Hempstead
1250	DOLAMORE	Jabez	59		Son		14	M	Servant	Herts	Hemel Hempstead
1251	DOLAMORE	Harriet	59		Dau		10	F		Herts	Rickmansworth
1252	DOLAMORE	Henry	59		Son		8	M	Scholar	Herts	Hemel Hempstead
1253	DOLAMORE	Thomas	59		Son		5	M	Scholar	Herts	St Peters

1254	DOLAMORE	Emma	59		Dau		3	F		Herts	St Peters
1255	DOLAMORE	William	59		Son		6m	M		Herts	St Peters
1256	HALSEY	John	60	London Colney	Head	Mar	38	M	Butcher	Herts	St Peters
1257	HALSEY	Lusa [?]	60		Wife	Mar	46	F		Herts	St Albans
1258	HALSEY	Caleb	60		Son	Unm	17	M	Journeyman	Herts	St Peters
1259	HALSEY	Harriett	60		Dau		15	F		Herts	St Peters
1260	HALSEY	John	60		Son		7	M		Herts	St Peters
1261	HALSEY	George	60		Son		5	M		Herts	St Peters
1262	HALSEY	James T.	60		Son		18dys	M		Herts	St Peters
1263	DICKINSON	John	61	London Colney	Head	Mar	70	M	Shoemaker & Publican	Herts	Aldenham
1264	DICKINSON	Jane	61		Wife	Mar	56	F	Shoemaker & Publicans Wife	Sussex	Newhaven
1265	FEAST	Jennett	61		Dau	Unm	20	F		Herts	Wheathampstead
1266	COSTIN	William	61		Lodger	Unm	28	M	Shepherd	Herts	St Peters
1267	HOAR	Thomas	61		Lodger	Unm	53	M	Dealer	Herts	Hemel Hempstead
1268	MUNT	Joseph	61		Lodger	Unm	61	M	Agric Lab	Herts	Westwick Row [St Michaels]
1269	WEBB	William	61		Lodger	Unm	39	M	Painter	Suffolk	Bungay
1270	FACSDALE	John	61		Lodger	Mar	56	M	Tailor	Herts	St Peters
1271	BERNARD	Markland	62	London Colney	Head	Mar	48	M	Perpetual Curate of Colney	Berks	Sonning
1272	BERNARD	Emma T.	62		Wife	Mar	45	F		London	Christs Hospital
1273	BERNARD	Emma C.	62		Dau	Unm	21	F		Herts	St Peters
1274	BERNARD	Markland	62		Son	Unm	19	M	Scholar	Herts	Colney
1275	BAKER	Eleanor	62		Visitor	Unm	57	F		Surrey	Croydon
1276	DOLAMORE	Jane	62		Serv	Unm	35	F	Cook	Herts	St Stephens
1277	COSTIN	Mary Ann	62		Serv	Unm	20	F	Housemaid	Herts	St Peters
1278	HARRIS	John	62		Serv	Unm	28	M	Footman	Herts	St Stephens
1279	FIELD	Benjamin	63	London Colney	Head	Mar	56	M	Blacksmith	Herts	Hatfield
1280	FIELD	Sarah	63		Wife	Mar	59	F	Straw Plaiter	Herts	Tewin
1281	CLARK	Robert	63		Son-in-law	Mar	35	M	Labourer	Kent	Tumbridge [Tonbridge]
1282	CLARK	Sarah	63		Dau	Mar	30	F	Straw Plaiter	Herts	St Stephens
1283	FIELD	Charlotte	63		Dau	Unm	21	F	Straw Plaiter	Herts	St Stephens
1284	FIELD	Elizabeth	63		Dau	Unm	18	F	Straw Plaiter	Herts	Aldenham
1285	CLARK	Nathaniel	63		Grandson		2	M		Herts	St Peters
1286	TANSLEY	William	64	London Colney	Head	Mar	30	M	Master Wheelwright	Herts	Shenley
1287	TANSLEY	Caroline	64		Wife	Mar	26	F	Wife	Hants	East Tisted
1288	TANSLEY	Sarah	64		Dau		2	F		Herts	St Peters
1289	TANSLEY	Thomas	64		Son		2m	M		Herts	St Peters
1290	BENNETT	Mary	65	London Colney	Head	Widow	51	F	Labourer Woman	Middx	Edmonton
1291	BENNETT	James	65		Son	Unm	20	M	Labourer	Herts	St Peters
1292	BENNETT	George	65		Son	Unm	17	M	Labourer	Herts	St Peters
1293	BENNETT	Jane	65		Dau		10	F	Scholar	Herts	St Peters
1294	BENNETT	Joseph	65		Lodger	Unm	45	M	Labourer	Herts	Shenley
1295	TERENE	William	66	London Colney	Head	Mar	40	M	Labourer	Herts	Aldenham
1296	TERENE	Mary	66		Wife	Mar	32	F	Straw Hat Maker	Herts	Flamstead
1297	TERENE	Mary Ann	66		Dau		9	F	Scholar	Herts	St Peters

	SURNAME	FORENAME	SCHEDULE NUMBER	ADDRESS	RELATIONSHIP	STATUS	AGE	SEX	OCCUPATION	COUNTY OF BIRTH	PLACE OF BIRTH
1298	TERENE	Maria	66		Dau		7	F	Scholar	Herts	St Peters
1299	TERENE	Fancy	66		Dau		3	F		Herts	St Peters
1300	GEORGE	George	67	London Colney	Head	Mar	33	M	Labourer	Herts	St Peters
1301	GEORGE	Mary	67		Wife	Mar	32	F	Straw Hat Maker	Herts	Welwyn
1302	GEORGE	Mary Ann	67		Dau		11	F	Straw Hat Maker	Herts	St Peters
1303	GEORGE	Rebecca	67		Dau		8	F	Scholar	Herts	St Peters
1304	GEORGE	George	67		Son		2	M		Herts	St Peters
1305	MASLIN	John	68	London Colney	Head	Mar	37	M	Labourer	Herts	St Peters
1306	MASLIN	Elizabeth	68		Wife	Mar	26	F	Straw Plaiter	Middx	Whetstone
1307	MASLIN	John	68		Son		1 m	M		Herts	St Peters
1308	SMITH	Emily	69	London Colney	Head	Widow	40	F	Victualler	Herts	Wheathampstead
1309	BAKER	Fanny	69		Mother	Widow	77	F	Formerly Victualler	Beds	Luton
1310	ROSON	George	69		Lodger	Unm	27	M		Herts	St Peters
1311	WHITE	Henry	70	London Colney	Head	Mar	30	M	Labourer	Bucks	Little Marlow
1312	WHITE	Ann	70		Wife	Mar	26	F		Herts	Hemel Hempstead
1313	WHITE	William	70		Son		3	M		Herts	St Michaels
1314	WHITE	Emma	70		Dau		1	F		Herts	St Michaels
1315	ROSON	Samuel	71	London Colney	Head	Mar	50	M	Dog Breaker	Herts	St Peters
1316	ROSON	Rebecca	71		Wife	Mar	26	F		Herts	St Stephens
1317	ROSON	Samuel	71		Son	Unm	18	M		Herts	St Peters
1318	ROSON	Edward	71		Son		14	M		Herts	St Peters
1319	ROSON	Lewesor	71		Dau		9	F		Herts	St Peters
1320	HILLS	Eleanor	72	London Colney	Head	Widow	67	F	Annuitant	N'thumb	[Unknown]
1321	GIBSON	Elizabeth	72		Inmate	Widow	64	F	Annuitant	Middx	London
1322	PARSONS	William	73	London Colney	Head	Mar	30	M	Baker	Herts	Sandridge
1323	PARSONS	Mary	73		Wife	Mar	35	F		Berks	Warfield
1324	PARSONS	William	73		Son		2	M		Herts	St Peters
1325	PARSONS	Ann	73		Dau		10 m	F		Herts	St Peters
1326	COLLINS	William	73		Serv	Unm	17	M	Servant	Unknown	Unknown
1327	PARSONS	Ellen	73		Visitor		15	F		Herts	St Peters
1328	ATKINS	William	74	London Colney	Head	Mar	46	M	Farmer of 73 acres employing 1 labourer	Herts	St Albans
1329	ATKINS	Sarah	74		Wife	Mar	54	F	Farmers Wife	Sussex	Newhaven
1330	ATKINS	Frederick	74		Son	Unm	16	M	Farmers Son	Herts	St Albans
1331	ATKINS	George	74		Son		13	M	Farmers Son	Herts	St Albans

One house uninhabited

	SURNAME	FORENAME	SCHEDULE NUMBER	ADDRESS	RELATIONSHIP	STATUS	AGE	SEX	OCCUPATION	COUNTY OF BIRTH	PLACE OF BIRTH
1332	BUNN	Mary	75	London Colney	Head	Unm	48	F	Proprietor of House	Herts	St Peters
1333a	BISNEY	John	76	London Colney	Head (absent)	Mar	Not Known				
1333b	BISNEY	Elizabeth	76		Wife	Mar	34	F	Annuitant	Middx	London
1334	BISNEY	John J.	76		Son		10	M	Scholar	Herts	St Peters
1335	BISNEY	George G.	76		Son		8	M	Scholar	Herts	St Peters
1336	BISNEY	Edwin C.	76		Son		6	M	Scholar	Herts	St Peters
1337	BISNEY	Elizabeth C.	76		Dau		4	F	Scholar	Herts	St Peters
1338	BISNEY	Ann G.	76		Dau		1	F		Herts	St Peters

1339	PEACH	Sarah	76		Visitor	Unm		74	F	Independent	Middx	London
1340	JUDD	Harriett	76		Inmate			12	F	Servant of all Work	Herts	St Peters
1341	WING	Matthew	77	London Colney	Head	Mar		40	M	Victualler	Middx	Mimms
1342	WING	Harriett	77		Wife	Mar		32	F		Devon	Brixham
1343	WING	Harriett	77		Dau			3	F		Herts	St Peters
1344	WING	James	77		Son			1	M		Herts	St Peters
1345	BIRD	Eleneor	77		Serv	Unm		17	F	Servant	Herts	Radlett
1346	REID	William	77		Lodger	Widower		35	M		Herts	St Peters
1347	BENNETT	Charles	78	London Colney	Head	Mar		36	M	Agric Lab	Herts	Mimms
1348	BENNETT	Jane	78		Wife	Mar		33	F	Charwoman	Berks	Reading
1349	BENNETT	Ellen	78		Dau			9	F	Scholar	Herts	St Peters
1350	BENNETT	William	78		Son			5	M	Scholar	Herts	St Peters
1351	STOKES	Thomas	79	London Colney	Head	Mar		37	M	Agric Lab	Herts	St Peters
1352	STOKES	Susanna	79		Wife	Mar		36	F	Straw Hatter	Herts	Hempstead
1353	STOKES	Charlotte	79		Dau			10	F	Scholar	Herts	St Peters
1354	STOKES	John	79		Son			8	M	Scholar	Herts	St Peters
1355	STOKES	Sarah M.	79		Dau			1	F		Herts	St Peters
1356	STOKES	William	79		Son			1 m	M		Herts	St Peters
1357	FANE	Mary	80	London Colney	Head	Widow		69	F	Charwoman	Herts	Totteridge
1358	FANE	Sarah	80		Dau	Unm		39	F	Straw Plaiter	Herts	St Stephens
1359	BRAHAM	Benjamin	81	London Colney	Head	Mar		36	M		Herts	St Stephens
1360	BRAHAM	Ann	81		Wife	Mar		44	F		[Unknown]	[Unknown]
1361	COOK	John	82	London Colney	Head	Mar		62	M	Labourer on the Road	Beds	Steppingley
1362	COOK	Ann	82		Wife	Mar		51	F	Dressmaker	Herts	St Peters
1363	COOK	William	82		Son	Unm		17	M	Gardener	Herts	St Peters
1364	COSTIN	Robert	83	London Colney	Head	Mar		55	M	Shoemaker	Herts	St Stephens
1365	COSTIN	Ann	83		Dau			13	F		Herts	St Peters
1366	HALSEY	Elizabeth	83		Visitor			8	F		Herts	St Peters
1367	MUNT	Sarah	84	London Colney	Head	Widow		56	F		Herts	Aldenham
1368	MUNT	William	84		Son	Mar		26	M	Labourer	Herts	St Stephens
1369	MUNT	Sarah	84		Dau	Unm		17	F		Herts	St Peters
1370	MUNT	Jane	84		Dau			6	F		Herts	St Peters
1371	MUNT	Frederick	84		Son			4	M		Herts	St Peters
1372	EAMES	Sarah	85	London Colney	Head	Widow		63	F	Charwoman	Herts	St Albans
1373	POTTER	Joseph	85		Son	Unm		28	M	Agric Lab	Herts	St Peters
1374	POTTER	James	85		Son	Unm		24	M	Agric Lab	Herts	St Peters
1375	KIFF	George	85		Son-in-law	Mar		26	M	Agric Lab	Herts	St Stephens
1376	KIFF	Sarah	85		Wife	Mar		27	F	Straw Plaiter	Herts	St Stephens
1377	TEACHER	Joseph	86	London Colney	Head	Mar		43	M	Labourer	Herts	St Peters
1378	TEACHER	Loucia	86		Wife	Mar		35	F	Straw Plaiter	Herts	St Stephens
1379	TEACHER	Maria	86		Dau			12	F	Straw Plaiter	Herts	St Peters
1380	TEACHER	Henry	86		Son			14	M	Labourer	Herts	St Peters
1381	TEACHER	Loucia	86		Dau			5	F	Scholar	Herts	St Peters
1382	TEACHER	Enif [?]	86		Dau			4	F	Scholar	Herts	St Peters
1383	TEACHER	Caroline	86		Dau			3	F	Scholar	Herts	St Peters

	SURNAME	FORENAME	SCHEDULE NUMBER	ADDRESS	RELATIONSHIP	STATUS	AGE	SEX	OCCUPATION	COUNTY OF BIRTH	PLACE OF BIRTH
1384	TEACHER	William	86		Son		2	M		Herts	St Peters
1385	HANLEY	Frederick	87	London Colney	Head	Mar	32	M	Police Constable	London	City
1386	HANLEY	Mary Ann	87		Wife	Mar	26	F	Dressmaker	Middx	Kentish Town
1387	BAKER	Jane	88	London Colney	Wife	Mar	47	F	Dressmaker	Somerset	Widcombe Cres., Bath
1388	BAKER	Charles G.	88		Son		15	M	Pupil Teacher	Middx	Earl St., Paddington
1389	BUCKLAND	Jonathan	89	London Colney	Head	Mar	52	M	Plumber, Glazier & Painter employing 1 man	Kent	Dartford
1390	BUCKLAND	Mary	89		Wife	Mar	46	F		Surrey	Chobham
1391	BUCKLAND	Mary	89		Dau	Unm	16	F		Herts	St Peters
1392	DRAGE	Jane	90	London Colney	Head	Widow	71	F	Annuitant	Bucks	Milton Keynes
1393	DRAGE	William F.	90		Son	Unm	47	M	Druggist	Northants	Harwick
1394	SCALES	Eliza	90		Serv	Unm	18	F	House Servant	Herts	St Peters
1395	NICHOLSON	William	91	London Colney	Head	Mar	40	M	Gardener	Ireland	County Wicklow
1396	NICHOLSON	Charlotte	91		Wife	Mar	30	F	Gardeners Wife	Norfolk	Norwich
1397	NICHOLSON	Eliza	91		Dau		3	F		Herts	St Peters
1398	NICHOLSON	Ellen	91		Dau		1	F		Herts	St Peters
1399	GEORGE	James	92	London Colney	Head	Widower	66	M	Agric Lab	Herts	St Michaels
1400	SMALL	Ann	93	Napsbury Farm	Head	Widow	55	F	Farmer of 419 acres employing 6 men and 2 boys	Herts	St Albans
1401	SMALL	Alexander	93		Son	Unm	25	M	Farmers Son	Herts	St Albans
1402	SMALL	George	93		Son	Unm	24	M	Farmers Son	Herts	St Peters
1403	SMALL	Elizabeth	93		Dau	Unm	19	F	Farmers Daughter	Herts	St Peters
1404	SMALL	Ann	93		Dau	Unm	16	F	Farmers Daughter	Herts	St Peters
1405	BURTT	Joseph	93		Serv	Unm	22	M	Shepherd	Beds	Houghton Regis
1406	PARKINS	Thomas	93		Serv		15	M	Plough Boy	Herts	Shenley
1407	ADAMS	George	94	Sheephouse Farm (Mr. Jarman, Farmer)	Head	Mar	26	M	Agric Lab, 106 acres employing 3 men	Essex	Weeley
1408	ADAMS	Mary	94		Wife	Mar	26	F		Essex	Baniley [?] [Barley?]
1409	ADAMS	Emma	94		Dau		4	F		Essex	Baniley [?] [Barley?]
1410	ADAMS	George	94		Son		1	M		Essex	Weeley
1411	CLARK	William	94		Lodger	Unm	25	M	Agric Lab	Suffolk	[Unknown]
1412	EDWARDS	Charles	95	Newhouse Farm	Head	Mar	33	M	Farmer of 205 acres employing 11 men	London	[Unknown]
1413	EDWARDS	Jane E.	95		Wife	Mar	28	F		Warks	[Unknown]
1414	EDWARDS	Elizabeth J.	95		Dau		7m	F		Herts	St Peters
1415	POTTER	Rachael	95		Serv	Unm	18	F		Herts	St Peters
1416	BENNETT	James	95		Serv		12	M		Herts	St Peters
1417	BRADBURY	John	96	Golden Lion Farm	Head	Mar	62	M	Farmer of 115 acres employing 5 labourers	Bucks	Great Horwood
1418	BRADBURY	Ann	96		Wife	Mar	62	F		Northants	Wicken
1419	BRADBURY	Susanna	96		Visitor	Unm	50	F		Northants	Wicken
1420	SCALES	Thomas	96		Serv		14	M		Herts	St Peters
1421	MARTIN	Thomas	96		Serv		14	M		Herts	St Peters
1422	WILKS	James	97	Gib Cottage	Head	Mar	33	M	Agric Lab	Herts	St Peters
1423	WILKS	Mary A.	97		Wife	Mar	35	F		Essex	Bocking
1424	WILKS	Mary A.	97		Dau		7	F		Herts	St Peters

1425	WILKS	Emily	97		Dau		4	F		Herts	St Peters
1426	WILKS	George	97		Son		5 m	M		Herts	St Peters
1427	HEWEL	Richard	97		Lodger	Unm	23	M		Herts	St Peters
1428	SMITH	William C.	98	New Barns Mill	Head	Mar	43	M	Miller	Herts	St Stephens
1429	SMITH	Ann	98		Wife	Mar	38	F		Surrey	Lambeth
1430	SULLIVAN	Lucy	98		Relative	Unm	32	F		Surrey	Lambeth
1431	ELLWOOD	Joseph	98		Serv	Unm	23	M		Herts	St Stephens
1432	COOK	Elizabeth	99		Serv	Unm	40	F	Dairymaid	Middx	Twickenham
1433	CROCKETT	William	99		Serv	Unm	37	M	Ploughman	Herts	St Stephens
1434	PICKETT	Joseph	99		Serv	Unm	30	M	Ploughman	Herts	Harpenden
1435	PEW	Philip	99		Serv	Unm	17	M	Farm Boy	Herts	North Mimms
1436	HALSEY	David	99		Serv		14	M	Farm Boy	Herts	St Peters
1437	DAVIS	William	99		Serv	Unm	16	M	Farm Boy	Herts	St Peters
1438	HIDE	James	100	Mansion (repairing)	Serv	Mar	33	M	Painter	London	City
1439	CARPENTER	George	100		Serv	Mar	36	M	Bricklayer	London	London
1440	DANL	George	100		Serv	Unm	25	M	Servant	Herts	St Michaels
1441	WISE	Sarah	101	Wool Pack, Mile House London Rd	Wife	Mar	50	F	Victuallers Wife	Herts	St Peters
1442	WISE	Jemima	101		Dau	Unm	26	F	Victuallers Daughter	Herts	St Peters
1443	WISE	Cecilia	101		Dau	Unm	23	F	Victuallers Daughter	Herts	St Peters
1444	WISE	Frederick	101		Son	Unm	21	M	Victuallers Son	Herts	St Peters
1445	BROWN	David	101		Lodger	[blank]	27	M	Painter	Essex	[Unknown]
1446	WEAVING	William	101		Lodger	[blank]	35	M	Painter	Middx	[Unknown]
1447	KIRKHAM	John	101		Lodger	[blank]	40	M	Painter	Middx	[Unknown]
1448	DURHAM	William	101		Lodger	[blank]	42	M	Painter	Ireland	Cork
1449	FIELD	Thomas	101		Lodger	[blank]	55	M	Labourer	Herts	St Peters
1450	FIELD	Joseph	101		Lodger	[blank]	60	M	Labourer	Herts	St Peters
1451	POCOCK	Richard	102	Hedges Farm	Head	Unm	60	M	Farmer of 549 acres employing 22 men	Herts	St Stephens
1452	STROUD	Sarah	102		Serv	Unm	50	F	Housekeeper	Oxon	South Newington
1453	NORWOOD	Elizabeth	102		Serv	Unm	18	F		Herts	St Stephens
1454	FIGGETT	Charles	102		Serv	Unm	17	M		Herts	Sandridge
1455	FLETCHER	Mark	102		Serv	Unm	16	M		Herts	St Peters
1456	GOURING	Frederick	103	Great Cell Barns Farm	Head	Unm	24	M	Farmer of 208 acres employing 8 men	Norfolk	Norwich
1457	MARRIOTT	Ann	103		Serv	Unm	28	F		Yorks	Burstwick
1458	WARD	Robert	103		Serv	Unm	19	M		Suffolk	Mickfield
1459	ARNOLD	George	104	Little Cell Barns Farm	Head	Mar	54	M	Farmer of 140 acres employing 4 men	Herts	[Unknown]
1460	ARNOLD	Elizabeth	104		Wife	Mar	46	F		Herts	[Unknown]
1461	ARNOLD	Edward	104		Son		8	M	Farmers Son	Herts	[Unknown]
1462	DICKINSON	Sarah	104		Sister	Unm	34	F	Farmers Daughter	Herts	[Unknown]
1463	MEREDITH	Elizabeth	104		Serv	Unm	18	F	House Servant	Wales	[Unknown]
1464	COOK	Abraham	104		Serv	Unm	19	M	Farm Labourer	Wales	[Unknown]
1465	MUSKETT	George	104		Serv		14	M	Farm Boy	Wales	[Unknown]
1466	GOUGH	Frederick	105	Cunningham Hill Farm	Head	Mar	70	M	Farmer of 180 acres	Beds	Silsoe
1467	GOUGH	Sarah	105		Wife	Mar	74	F	Farmers Wife	Herts	St Peters

	SURNAME	FORENAME	SCHEDULE NUMBER	ADDRESS	RELATIONSHIP	STATUS	AGE	SEX	OCCUPATION	COUNTY OF BIRTH	PLACE OF BIRTH
1468	GOUGH	Peter	105		Son	[blank]	38	M	Farmers Son	Herts	St Peters
1469	DRINKWATER	Edward	105		Serv	Unm	20	M	Farm Servant	Herts	St Albans
1470	[blank]	Harriett	105		Serv	[blank]	21	F	Farm Servant	Herts	Barnet

Chapter Ten

The parish of St Albans in the borough

of St Albans

Registrar's District: St Albans   Enumeration District 4a   Ref. HO 107/1713 folios 362-97

Middle Ward, comprising High Street, Chequer Street, Market Place, Back Street with the adjoining yards, and Verulam Street and Dagnall Lane.

1	GARROD	John	1	High Street	Head	Mar	47	M	Cordwainer	Suffolk	Ipswich
2	GARROD	Mary	1		Wife	Mar	46	F		Essex	Ramsey
3	BOTT	Alfred	1		Apprentice	Unm	17	M	Cordwainers Apprentice (Deaf & Dumb)	Herts	Park Street [St Stephens]
4	PAUL	Thomas	2	High Street	Head	Mar	28	M	Staymaker	Herts	Hitchin
5	PAUL	Mary Ann Rebecca	2		Wife	Mar	27	F	Staymaker	Herts	Hitchin
6	PAUL	John Thomas Fensom	2		Son	Unm	1	M		Herts	St Albans
7	DUNSAY	Mary Ann	2		Serv	Unm	17	F	General Servant	Middx	Chelsea
8	ALLEN	George	3	High Street	Head	Mar	32	M	Grocer & Dealer in Glass & China	Sussex	Lancing
9	ALLEN	Elizabeth	3		Wife	Mar	28	F		Herts	Hertford
10	ALLEN	Frances Elizabeth	3		Dau	Unm	6	F	Scholar	Herts	St Albans
11	ALLEN	Catherine Lucy	3		Dau	Unm	3m	F		Herts	St Albans
12	ARNOT	Sarah	3		Serv	Unm	14	F	General Servant	Bucks	Denham
13	THEOBALD	Ann	4	High Street	Head	Widow	57	F	Annuitant	Norfolk	Thetford
14	FISK	William	5	High Street	Head	Mar	43	M	Linen Draper	Essex	St Osyth
15	FISK	Louisa	5		Wife	Mar	43	F		Essex	Tiptree
16	FISK	William	5		Son	Unm	15	M	Linen Drapers Shopman	Herts	St Albans
17	FISK	Louisa	5		Dau	Unm	11	F	Scholar	Herts	St Albans
18	FISK	Sarah	5		Dau	Unm	9	F	Scholar	Herts	St Albans
19	FISK	Frances	5		Dau	Unm	7	F	Scholar	Herts	St Albans
20	FISK	Ebenezar	5		Son	Unm	6	M	Scholar	Herts	St Albans
21	FISK	Eleanor	5		Dau	Unm	3	F		Herts	St Albans
22	FISK	Alban	5		Son	Unm	3m	M		Herts	St Albans
23	LAKE	Joseph	5		Visitor	Unm	39	M	Linen Draper	Essex	Kelvedon
24	SMART	John	5		Apprentice	Unm	17	M	Linen Drapers Apprentice	Herts	Welwyn
25	SMITH	Mary	5		Serv	Unm	29	F	General Servant	Essex	Thorpe

From the first edition of the 6 inch Ordinance Survey of Hertfordshire (1878), Sheet XXXIV

Approximate scale of reproduction: 1cm = 110m

26	BARNFEATHER	Jane	5			Nurse	Widow	47	F	Nurse	Herts	St Albans
27	EVANS	Charles	6	High Street	Head	Mar	38	M	Publican	Beds	Eversholt
28	EVANS	Sarah	6		Wife	Mar	31	F		Herts	Northaw
29	EVANS	Noble	6		Son		3	M		Herts	Hatfield
30	EVANS	Horatio	6		Son		1	M		Herts	St Albans
31	BLAKE	Jacob	7	High Street	Head	Mar	66	M	Shop Keeper & Registrar of Births, Deaths & Marriages	Middx	Old Brentford
32	BLAKE	Mary	7		Wife	Mar	46	F		Channel I	Guernsey
33	NARROWAY	Hannah	7		Serv	Unm	19	F	House Servant	Herts	St Albans
34	FURNESS	Anne	8	High Street	Head	Widow	55	F	Butcher, employing 2 men	Bucks	Stony Stratford
35	ARISS	Daniel John	8		Nephew	Unm	34	M	Annuitant	Herts	St Albans
36	MASON	John	9	High Street	Head	Unm	42	M	Town Councillor & Ironmonger	Herts	St Albans
37	MASON	Mary	9		Sister	Unm	40	F	Housekeeper	Herts	St Albans
38	OAKLEY	Eliza	9		Serv	Unm	38	F	House Servant	Herts	London Colney
39	SHEPHEARD	William	10	High Street	Head	Mar	35	M	Linen Draper	Bucks	Maids Moreton
40	SHEPHEARD	Maria	10		Wife	Mar	27	F		Herts	Lilley
41	SHEPHEARD	William Henry	10		Son	Unm	5	M		Herts	St Albans
42	SHEPHEARD	Emily Jane	10		Dau	Unm	11 m	F		Herts	St Albans
43	PRATT	George J.	10		Shopman	Unm	25	M	Shopman	Essex	Otton Belchamp
44	COLEMAN	Herbert	10		Shopman	Unm	21	M	Shopman	Gloucs	Stroud
45	MILES	Mary	10		Serv	Unm	19	F	House Servant	Northants	Towcester
46	PULLEN	Mary Ann	10		Serv	Unm	17	F	Nurse - Servant	Herts	London Colney
47	YOUNGER	Thomas	11	High Street	Head	Widower	57	M	Upholsterer	N'thumb	Berwick Upon Tweed
48	YOUNGER	Henry	11		Son	Mar	27	M	Upholsterer	Herts	St Albans
49	YOUNGER	Caroline	11		Dau-in-law	Mar	27	F		Herts	St Albans
50	YOUNGER	Elizabeth	11		Dau	Unm	30	F		Herts	St Albans
51	HOWELL	Frederick	11		Apprentice	Unm	14	M	Apprentice [Upholsterer]	Middx	London
52	LANGLEY	William	12	High Street	Head	Mar	60	M	Alderman & Stationer	Middx	Shoreditch
53	LANGLEY	Mary	12		Wife	Mar	60	F		Herts	Sandon
54	WELLS	Sarah	12		Serv	Unm	48	F	Servant	Herts	St Albans
55	GIBSON	James	13	High Street	Head	Unm	41	M	Draper & Clothier, employing 14 men	Middx	Pentonville
56	HOLT	Charles	13		Shopman	Unm	32	M	Shopman	Lancs	Hollingswood [Hollingworth?]
57	YOUNG	John	13		Apprentice	Unm	16	M	Apprentice	Herts	Watford
58	MARTINGAL	Henry John	13		Apprentice	Unm	15	M	Apprentice	Herts	Bedmond [Abbots Langley]
59	GOODMAN	William	13		Serv	Unm	19	M	Porter	Herts	St Albans
60	RICHARDS	Sophia	13		Serv	Unm	42	F	Housekeeper	Middx	Clerkenwell
61	EVANS	Barron	14		Assistant to a chemist	Unm	23	M	Assistant to a Chemist	Sussex	Brighton
62	WARD	John	15	High Street	Head	Mar	50	M	Innkeeper	Herts	St Albans
63	WARD	Sarah	15		Wife	Mar	30	F		Herts	St Albans
64	WARD	George	15		Son	Unm	22	M	Innkeepers Son	Herts	St Albans
65	WARD	Charles	15		Son	Unm	20	M	Innkeepers Son	Herts	St Albans
66	WARD	Emma	15		Dau	Unm	17	F	Innkeepers Daughter	Herts	St Albans

	SURNAME	FORENAME	SCHEDULE NUMBER	ADDRESS	RELATIONSHIP	STATUS	AGE	SEX	OCCUPATION	COUNTY OF BIRTH	PLACE OF BIRTH
67	WARD	John	15		Son	Unm	12	M	Scholar	Herts	St Albans
68	WARD	Rosana	15		Dau	Unm	9	F	Scholar	Herts	St Albans
69	WARD	Sarah	15		Dau	Unm	7	F	Scholar	Herts	St Albans
70	WARD	David	15		Son	Unm	5	M	Scholar	Herts	St Albans
71	SLATER	Jeremiah	15		Lodger	Unm	32	M	Labourer	Herts	St Albans
72	BRITTAND	George	15		Serv	Unm	28	M	Ostler	Herts	St Albans
73	I Man not known		15		Lodger	[blank]		M	[Unknown]	[Unknown]	
74	I Man not known		15		Lodger	[blank]		M	[Unknown]	[Unknown]	
75	BEAUMONT	Elizabeth	16	Chequer Street	Head	Mar	30	F		[Unknown]	
76	GEORGE	Rachael	16		Serv	Unm	26	F	House Servant	Herts	High St. [St Albans]
77	GREEN	Solomon	16		Serv	Unm	15	M	General Servant	Herts	Windridge [St Michaels]
78	SALMON	Rebecca	17	Chequer Street	Head	Unm	63	F	Annuitant	Herts	St Albans
79	NEATH	William	17		Visitor	Widower	78	M	Annuitant	Herts	Welwyn
80	BRADSHAW	Thomas	18		Lodger	Mar	71	M	Watchmaker	Kent	Dover
81	BRADSHAW	Mary	18		Lodger Wife	Mar	70	F	Watchmakers Wife	Kent	Eltham
82	LEWIS	John	19	Chequer Street	Head	Widower	35	M	Chemist & Druggist	Herts	Rickmansworth
83	LEWIS	Henry	19		Son	Unm	5	M		Herts	St Albans
84	LEWIS	Ann	19		Dau	Unm	9	F	Scholar	Herts	St Albans
85	TAYLOR	Harriett	19		Visitor	Widow	33	F	Housekeeper	Kent	Rochester
86	UPTON	Eustace James	19		Apprentice	Unm	18	M	[Apprentice] Chemist & Druggist	Herts	St Albans
87	BIRD	Louisa	19		Serv	Unm	29	F	House Servant	Herts	London Colney
88	HARRIS	Thomas	20	Chequer Street	Head	Mar	47	M	Straw Hat & Canvas Manufacturer employing 300 hands	Herts	St Albans
89	HARRIS	Sarah	20		Wife	Mar	36	F	Assisting in Manufactory	Herts	Wheathampstead
90	HARRIS	Mary Ann	20		Dau	Unm	17	F	Straw Hat Maker	Herts	St Albans
91	DAY	Emma	20		Step-dau	Unm	16	F	Straw Hat Maker	Herts	Wheathampstead
92	HARRIS	Hadorgenos [?]	20		Dau	Unm	3 m	F		Herts	St Albans
93	RUSSELL	George	20		Nephew	Unm	7	M	Scholar	Herts	Harpenden
94	KENT	Thomas Weedon	21	Chequer Street	Head	Widower	44	M	Maltster & Brewer	Herts	St Albans
95	KENT	Maria	21		Dau	Unm	15	F	Scholar	Herts	St Albans
96	KENT	Susanna	21		Dau	Unm	14	F	Scholar	Herts	St Albans
97	KENT	Thomas	21		Son	Unm	12	M	Scholar	Herts	St Albans
98	KENT	Charles	21		Son	Unm	9	M	Scholar	Herts	St Albans
99	GILBERT	Sarah	21		Serv	Widow	36	F	Housekeeper	Herts	St Albans
100	FIELD	Elizabeth	22	Chequer Street	Serv	[blank]	34	F	Servant	Herts	Kings Walden
101	KENT	John Walter	23	Chequer Street	Head	Unm	42	M	Plumber, employing 5 men	Herts	St Albans
102	KENT	Ruth Hannah	23		Sister	Unm	38	F		Herts	St Albans
103	KENT	Frederic	23		Brother	Unm	32	M	Clerk	Herts	St Albans
104	HAWKINS	Ann	23		Serv	Unm	29	F	House Servant	Herts	Harpenden
105	MASON	Richard David	24	Chequer Street	Head	Mar	32	M	Plumber & Painter	Herts	St Albans
106	MASON	Susan	24		Wife	Mar	37	F		Middx	London
107	MASON	Richard William	24		Son		5	M		Herts	St Albans

108	MASON	Lucretia Statham	24		Dau		3	F		Herts	St Albans
109	MASON	John Joseph	24		Son		3 m	M		Herts	St Albans
110	BAKER	Susanna	25	Chequer Street	Head	Widow	71	F	Charwoman	Herts	St Albans
111	BAKER	Sarah	25		Dau	Unm	28	F	Silk Throwster	Herts	St Albans
112	BAKER	Elizabeth	25		Grandau	Unm	16	F	Silk Throwster	Herts	St Albans
113	KIBBLES	Elizabeth	25		Lodger	Unm	24	F	Silk Throwster	Herts	Watford
114	HEDGES	Mary	25		Lodger	Unm	24	F	Dressmaker	Herts	Redbourn
115	BAKER	George	26	Chequer Street	Head	Mar	42	M	Labourer	Herts	St Albans
116	BAKER	George	26		Son	Unm	15	M	Silk Throwster	Herts	St Albans
117	POINTON	Charles	27	Chequer Street	Head	Mar	25	M	Shoemaker	Herts	Hatfield
118	POINTON	Elizabeth	27		Wife	Mar	24	F		Herts	St Albans
119	POINTON	George	27		Son		5	M		Herts	St Albans
120	POINTON	Charles	27		Son		2	M		Herts	St Albans
121	CURRIER	Elizabeth	27		Mother-in-law	Widow	50	F	Not Known	Northants	Northampton
122	BINGHAM	Sarah	28	Chequer Street	Head	Widow	61	F	Straw Bonnet Maker	Herts	Hitchin
123	MAWBEY	William	29	Chequer Street	Head	Mar	48	M	Hair Dresser	Beds	Wilden
124	MAWBEY	Emma	29		Dau	Unm	17	F	Dressmaker	Herts	St Albans
125	MAWBEY	William	29		Son	Unm	12	M		Herts	St Albans
126	MAWBEY	Edwin Charles	29		Son	Unm	5	M		Herts	St Albans
127	VARNEY	James	30	Chequer Street	Head	Mar	52	M	Publican	Herts	Harpenden
128	VARNEY	Amelia	30		Wife	Mar	43	F		Beds	Luton
129	VARNEY	William	30		Son	Unm	17	M	Publicans Son	Beds	Totternhoe
130	VARNEY	Matilda	30		Dau	Unm	15	F	Hat Maker	Beds	Dunstable
131	VARNEY	Elizabeth	30		Dau	Unm	13	F	Hat Maker	Beds	Dunstable
132	VARNEY	James	30		Son	Unm	6	M	Scholar	Herts	St Albans
133	VARNEY	Harriett	30		Dau	Unm	2	F		Herts	St Albans
134	CASTLE	George	30		Lodger	Widower	50	M	Tailor	London	
135	PERRY	David	30		Lodger	Unm	33	M	Not Known	Herts	Harpenden
136	Unknown man		30		Lodger	[blank]		M	Not Known	[Unknown]	
137	Unknown man		30		Lodger	[blank]		M	Not Known	[Unknown]	
138	Unknown man		30		Lodger	[blank]		M	Not Known	[Unknown]	
139	Unknown man		30		Lodger	[blank]		M	Not Known	[Unknown]	
140	Unknown man		30		Lodger	[blank]		M	Not Known	[Unknown]	
141	Unknown man		30		Lodger	[blank]		M	Not Known	[Unknown]	
142	Unknown woman		30		Lodger	[blank]		F	Not Known	[Unknown]	
143	Unknown woman		30		Lodger	[blank]		F	Not Known	[Unknown]	
144	Unknown child		30		Lodger	[blank]		M	Not Known	[Unknown]	
145	Unknown child		30		Lodger	[blank]		M	Not Known	[Unknown]	
146	KING	James	31	Chequer Street	Head	Mar	60	M	Collar Harness Maker	Herts	St Albans
147	KING	Sarah	31		Wife	Mar	56	F		Herts	St Albans
148	KING	Ann	31		Dau	Unm	16	F	Hat Maker	Herts	St Albans
149	KING	Eliza	31		Dau	Unm	35	F	Hat Maker	Herts	St Albans

	SURNAME	FORENAME	SCHEDULE NUMBER	ADDRESS	RELATIONSHIP	STATUS	AGE	SEX	OCCUPATION	COUNTY OF BIRTH	PLACE OF BIRTH
150	KING	Edward	31		Son	Unm	15	M		Herts	St Albans
151	KING	Frederick	31		Son	Unm	14	M		Herts	St Albans
152	CAUSTON	Thomas Dilworth	32	Chequer Street	Head	Mar	43	M	Grocer	Herts	St Albans
153	CAUSTON	Sarah	32		Wife	Mar	37	F		Middx	Shoreditch
154	CAUSTON	Sarah	32		Dau	Unm	12	F		Herts	St Albans
155	CAUSTON	Rosanna	32		Dau	Unm	8	F		Herts	St Albans
156	CAUSTON	Mary	32		Dau	Unm	6	F		Herts	St Albans
157	CAUSTON	Eliza	32		Dau	Unm	1	F		Herts	St Albans
158	CAUSTON	Elizabeth	32		Dau	Unm	2 m	F		Herts	St Albans
159	FORSTER	Susan	32		Serv	Unm	23	F	General Servant	Herts	Watford
160	CHERRY	Jesse	33	Chequer Street	Head	Mar	46	M	Linen Draper	Herts	St Albans
161	CHERRY	Harriett	33		Wife	Mar	34	F	Wife of Draper	Herts	North Mimms
162	CHERRY	Jesse	33		Son	Unm	9	M	Scholar	Herts	St Albans
163	BATES	Ann	33		Serv	Widow	56	F	Charwoman	Herts	St Albans
164	CHERRY	William	34	Chequer Street	Head	Mar	48	M	Tailor & Draper	Herts	St Albans
165	CHERRY	Eleanor	34		Wife	Mar	47	F		London	
166	TURNEY	John	34		Nephew	Unm	17	M	Tailor	London	
167	VALLANCE	Thomas	35	High Street	Head	Mar	33	M	Ironmonger	Herts	St Albans
168	VALLANCE	Ann	35		Wife	Mar	26	F		Middx	Westminster
169	VALLANCE	Elizabeth	35		Dau	Unm	3	F		Herts	St Albans
170	GROVENOR	William	36	High Street	Head	Mar	26	M	Hatter	London	
171	GROVENOR	Jane	36		Wife	Mar	25	F		London	
172	GILES	William	37	High Street	Head	Mar	50	M	Drapers Assistant	Herts	St Albans
173	GILES	Jane	37		Wife	Mar	40	F		Middx	London
174	GILES	Jane	37		Dau	Unm	21	F	Toy Shop Keeper	Middx	Hammersmith
175	GILES	Harriett	37		Dau	Unm	19	F	Toy Shop Keeper	Middx	Hammersmith
176	GILES	Amelia	37		Dau	Unm	12	F	Scholar	Middx	Hammersmith
177	HART	Thomas Hawkins	38	High Street	Head	Mar	41	M	Butcher, employing 2 men	Herts	North Mimms
178	HART	Charlotte	38		Wife	Mar	36	F		Herts	St Albans
179	WILBY	Mary Ann	38		Serv	Unm	18	F	General Servant	Herts	Hatfield
180	WELLS	Joseph	39	High Street	Head	Mar	37	M	Watchmaker & Jeweller	London	St Lukes
181	WELLS	Maria	39		Wife	Mar	36	F	Jewellers Wife	[Herts]	South Mimms
182	WELLS	John	39		Son	Unm	6	M	Jewellers Son	Herts	St Albans
183	WELLS	Jane	39		Dau	Unm	5	F		Herts	St Albans
184	WELLS	Emma	39		Dau	Unm	2	F		Herts	St Albans
185	ROBERTS	Margaret	39		Sister-in-law	Unm	38	F	Annuitant	Herts	Hemel Hempstead
186	DELL	Thomas	39		Apprentice	Unm	16	M	Jewellers Apprentice	Herts	Patchendon [?] [Stapleford]
187	OSBORN	Jarvis	40	High Street	Head	Mar	50	M	Baker	Northants	Nassington
188	OSBORN	Mary	40		Wife	Mar	31	F		Herts	St Stephens
189	OSBORN	Helen	40		Dau	Unm	4	F		Herts	St Albans
190	OSBORN	Hannah	40		Dau	Unm	2	F		Herts	St Albans
191	FOXALL	Richard	41	High Street	Head	Mar	42	M	Victualler	London	Bermondsey
192	FOXALL	Sophia	41		Wife	Mar	40	F		London	
193	FOXALL	Sophia S.	41		Dau	Unm	7	F		Herts	St Albans

194	FOXALL	Sarah Ann	41		Dau	Unm	5	F		Herts	St Albans
195	FOXALL	Henrietta Matilda	41		Dau	Unm	4	F		Herts	St Albans
196	FOXALL	Richard Joseph	41		Son	Unm	1	M		Herts	St Albans
197	SPAKESBY [?]	Joseph	41		Serv	Unm	55	M	Servant	Herts	St Albans
198	ABBOTT	Rowland T.	42	High Street	Head	Mar	29	M	M.N.C.S. England, practising as general practioner	Suffolk	Eye
199	ABBOTT	Sarah F.	42		Wife	Mar	33	F		London	
200	ABBOTT	Fanny M.	42		Dau	Unm	3	F		Herts	St Albans
201	ABBOTT	Bessie K.	42		Dau	Unm	1	F	Surgeons Daughter	Herts	St Albans
202	SCRIVENER	Mary	42		Serv	Unm	26	F	Cook	Herts	Ayot St Lawrence
203	LOOKER	Louisa	42		Serv	Unm	38	F	Housemaid	Cambs	Comberton
204	LOOKER	Kezia	42		Serv	Unm	21	F	Nurse	Middx	London
205	LITCHFIELD	Elizabeth	43	George Street	Head	Unm	32	F	Linen Draper	Herts	St Stephens
206	LITCHFIELD	Charlotte	43		Sister	Unm	30	F	Linen Draper	Herts	St Stephens
207	WHITEHEAD	Henry	44	George Street	Head	Widower	43	M	Butcher	Beds	Silsoe
208	BEALE	Mary	44		Sister	Widow	41	F	Housekeeper	Beds	Silsoe
209	WHITEHEAD	Sarah	44		Dau	Unm	13	F	Scholar	Herts	St Albans
210	WHITEHEAD	William	44		Son	Unm	8	M	Scholar	Herts	St Albans
211	CROFT	Mary	44		Serv	Unm	19	F	House Servant	Herts	St Stephens
212	DAVIS	George	45	George Street	Head	Mar	38	M	Boot Maker	Herts	St Albans
213	DAVIS	Mary	45		Wife	Mar	40	F	Bonnet Maker	Herts	St Albans
214	CROUCH	John	46	George Street	Head	Mar	51	M	Watchmaker	Herts	St Albans
215	CROUCH	Anna	46		Wife	Mar	30	F		Kent	Godden Green [?] [Goddington]
216	CROUCH	John Thomas	46		Son	Unm	28	M	Watchmaker	Herts	St Albans
217	CROUCH	George Henry	46		Son		6 m	M		Herts	St Albans
218	IRONMONGER	Joseph	47	George Street	Head	Mar	50	M	Grocer	Beds	Luton
219	IRONMONGER	Matilda	47		Wife	Mar	37	F		Essex	Woodford
220	IRONMONGER	Sarah	47		Dau	Unm	18	F		Herts	St Albans
221	IRONMONGER	Isaac	47		Son	Unm	15	M	Grocers Shopman	Herts	St Albans
222	IRONMONGER	Matilda	47		Dau	Unm	9	F	Scholar	Herts	St Albans
223	IRONMONGER	Jeannette	47		Dau	Unm	8	F	Scholar	Herts	St Albans
224	IRONMONGER	Mary Louisa	47		Dau	Unm	7	F	Scholar	Herts	St Albans
225	IRONMONGER	Thomas	47		Nephew	Unm	22	M	Grocers Shopman	Beds	Luton
226	FOSTER	Mary Ann	47		Serv	Unm	19	F	House Servant	Herts	Shenley
227	FIELD	Henry	48	George Street	Head	Mar	28	M	Butcher	Herts	St Albans
228	FIELD	Elizabeth	48		Wife	Mar	29	F	Butchers Wife	Herts	Stevenage
229	FIELD	George	48		Son	Unm	1	M	Butchers Son	Herts	St Albans
230	FIELD	Kate	48		Dau	Unm	2 m	F		Herts	St Albans
231	BURR	Eliza	48		Serv	Unm	13	F	House Servant	Herts	St Albans
232	RAYMENT	George	49	High Street	Head	Mar	30	M	Chemist & Druggist	Herts	Brent Pelham
233	RAYMENT	Anne	49		Wife	Mar	30	F	Chemist & Druggists Wife	Kent	Wrotham
234	FOWLER	Caroline	49		Serv	Unm	16	F	House Servant	Herts	Shenley
235	STORY	John Samuel	50	High Street	Head	Mar	69	M	Solicitor	W. Indies	

	SURNAME	FORENAME	SCHEDULE NUMBER	ADDRESS	RELATIONSHIP	STATUS	AGE	SEX	OCCUPATION	COUNTY OF BIRTH	PLACE OF BIRTH
236	WADE	Elizabeth	50		Dau	Mar	40	F		Herts	St Albans
237	STORY	Samuel (Jnr)	50		Son	Unm	38	M	Solicitor	Herts	St Albans
238	STORY	Francis	50		Son	Unm	23	M	Solicitor	Herts	St Albans
239	STORY	Evelyn	50		Grandau	Unm	11	F		Herts	St Albans
240	STORY	Venetia	50		Grandau	Unm	8	F		Herts	St Albans
241	STORY	Blanche	50		Grandau	Unm	4	F		Herts	St Albans
242	LAVONT	Madame	50		Governess	Unm	38	F	Governess	France	
243	DAY	Samuel	50		Serv	Mar	45	M	Servant	Herts	Redbourn
244	MARTIN	Mary	50		Serv	Unm	25	F	House Servant	Herts	St Stephens
245	NOTT	Susan	50		Serv	Unm	26	F	House Servant	Herts	St Michaels
246	GHOST	Mary	50		Serv	Unm	25	F	Nurse	Herts	St Albans
247	CHERRY	Samuel	51	Chequer Street	Head	Mar	42	M	Linen Draper	Herts	St Albans
248	CHERRY	Sarah	51		Wife	Mar	34	F		Herts	St Albans
249	CHERRY	Frederic Henry	51		Son	Unm	6	M	Scholar	Herts	St Albans
250	CHERRY	Elizabeth Ann	51		Dau	Unm	4	F		Herts	St Albans
251	PARSONS	Hannah	51		Serv	Unm	37	F	House Servant	Herts	Rickmansworth
252	VASS	George	52	George Street	Head	Mar	52	M	Bricklayer & Publican	Herts	Redbourn
253	VASS	Sarah	52		Wife	Mar	50	F	Bricklayer & Publicans Wife	London	
254	VASS	George	52		Son	Unm	19	M	Bricklayer & Publicans Son	Herts	St Albans
255	VASS	Mary	52		Dau	Mar	24	F	Bricklayer & Publicans Daughter	Herts	St Albans
256	VASS	Elizabeth	52		Dau	Unm	15	F	Bricklayer & Publicans Daughter	Herts	St Albans
257	VASS	Joseph	52		Son	Unm	13	M	Bricklayer & Publicans Son	Herts	St Albans
258	VASS	Fanny	52		Dau	Unm	10	F	Bricklayer & Publicans Daughter	Herts	Abbots Langley
259	VASS	Catherine	52		Dau	Unm	8	F	Bricklayer & Publicans Daughter	Herts	Abbots Langley
260	COHEN	Moses	52		Lodger	[blank]	55	M	Traveller	Germany	
261	SLING	Daniel	53	George Street	Head	Unm	53	M	Master Butcher	Herts	St Albans
262	SLING	Hannah	53		Mother	Widow	76	F	Proprietor of Houses	Herts	St Albans
263	BISNEY	Louisa	53		Niece	Unm	45	F	Fundholder	Herts	Hatfield
264	POTTER	Eliza	53		Serv	Unm	25	F	Servant	Herts	London Colney
265	WELLS	William	53		Serv	Unm	18	M	Servant	Herts	Bushey
266	HARDING	James	54	George Street	Head	Mar	42	M	Fruiterer	Herts	St Albans
267	HARDING	Mary	54		Wife	Mar	40	F	Fruiterers Wife	Middx	Clerkenwell
268	BRISTOW	Emma	54		Serv	Unm	17	F	Servant	Surrey	Newington
269	CLIMANCE	Richard	55	George Street	Head	Mar	37	M	Master Baker	London	
270	CLIMANCE	Jane	55		Wife	Mar	42	F		Herts	St Albans
271	HIGDON	Mary	55		Sister	Unm	40	F	Servant	Herts	St Albans
272	CLIMANCE	Elizabeth	55		Dau	Unm	13	F	Scholar	Herts	St Albans
273	CLIMANCE	Anne	55		Dau	Unm	10	F	Scholar	Herts	St Albans
274	CLIMANCE	William	55		Son	Unm	5	M	Scholar	Herts	St Albans

One house uninhabited

	SURNAME	FORENAME	SCHEDULE NUMBER	ADDRESS	RELATIONSHIP	STATUS	AGE	SEX	OCCUPATION	COUNTY OF BIRTH	PLACE OF BIRTH
275	CHERRY	Rose	56	George Street	Head	Widow	79	F	Formerly Laundress	Herts	Kings Walden
276	CHERRY	William	56		Son	Unm	57	M	Blacksmith	Herts	St Albans

277	CHERRY	Mary Ann	56		Dau	Unm	48	F	Laundress	Herts	St Albans
278	CHERRY	Ann	56		Dau	Unm	46	F	Laundress	Herts	St Albans
279	CHERRY	Henry	56		Grandson	Unm	19	M	Butcher	Herts	St Albans
280	CHERRY	George	56		Grandson	Unm	11	M	Scholar	Herts	St Albans
281	GOOCH	Henry	57	George Street	Head	Mar	40	M	Gunmaker	Kent	Canterbury
282	GOOCH	Catherine	57		Wife	Mar	42	F	Staymaker	Middx	Elstree
283	GOOCH	Georgiana	57		Dau	Unm	19	F	Bonnet Maker	Herts	St Albans
284	GOOCH	Harriett	57		Dau	Unm	15	F	Bonnet Maker	Herts	St Albans
285	GOOCH	Emma	57		Dau	Unm	13	F		Herts	St Albans
286	GOOCH	Sarah Ann	57		Dau	Unm	7	F	Scholar	Herts	St Albans
287	WAGGETT	Mary Anne	63	George Street	Head	Mar	43	F	Houseowner	Herts	Harpenden
288	WAGGETT	M.A.E.	63		Dau	Unm	15	F	Hat Maker	Middx	Hammersmith
289	WAGGETT	G.S.	63		Son	Unm	13	M	Scholar	Herts	St Albans
290	MAIN	Andrew	62	George Street	Head	Mar	36	M	Basket Maker	Germany	
291	MAIN	Isabella	62		Wife	Mar	45	F		Scotland	[Unknown]
292	MAIN	Margaret	62		Dau		9	F		Kent	Woolwich
293	TILLEY	William	61	George Street	Head	Mar	29	M	Cordwainer	Northants	Daventry
294	TILLEY	Mary Anne	61		Wife	Mar	34	F	Weaver	Beds	Barton
295	WALLER	Jane	61		Dau	Unm	11	F	Hat Maker	Herts	St Albans
296	EDWARDS	Daniel	61	George Street	Head	Mar	54	M	Coach Builder	Herts	St Albans
297	EDWARDS	Sarah	61		Wife	Mar	58	F		Herts	St Albans
298	PATES	William	60	George Street	Head	Unm	33	M	Tailor	[Herts]	Lilley
299	PALMER	Emma	60		[blank]	Unm	22	F	Houseowner	[Unknown]	
300	GUTTERIDGE	Ann	58	George Street	Head	Unm	53	F	Dressmaker	Herts	Redbourn
301	FRANKLIN	Thomas	64	George Street	Head	Mar	40	M	Provision Dealer	Herts	Hemel Hempstead
302	FRANKLIN	Ann	64		Wife	Mar	30	F		Wilts	Marlborough [?]
303	BURT	Sarah	64		Visitor	Unm	45	F	Cook	Wilts	Marlborough [?]
304	WICKHAM	William Faircloth	65	George Street	Head	Mar	45	M	Solicitor	Essex	Chigwell
305	WICKHAM	Margaret	65		Wife	Mar	36	F	Solicitors Wife	Suffolk	Hawick [?] [Hawkedon]
306	WICKHAM	Emily	65		Dau	Unm	10	F	Solicitors Daughter	Herts	St Albans
307	WICKHAM	Caroline	65		Dau	Unm	5	F	Solicitors Daughter	Herts	St Albans
308	WICKHAM	Jane	65		Dau	Unm	3	F	Solicitors Daughter	Herts	St Albans
309	MOORE	Thomas	66	George Street	Head	Mar	38	M	Baker & Lodging House Keeper	Herts	St Albans
310	MOORE	Eliza	66		Wife	Mar	46	F	Baker & Lodging House Keepers Wife	Herts	Redbourn
311	SADDINGTON	Eliza	66		Dau	Unm	21	F	Baker & Lodging House Keepers Dau	Herts	St Albans
312	CHURCH	Rebecca	66		Niece	Unm	13	F		Herts	Kings Langley
313	BEVAN	Philip	66		Lodger	Mar	27	M	Stone Mason	Wales	Swansea
314	TUCK [?]	Stephen	66		Lodger	Mar	34	M	Stone Mason	[Unknown]	
315	GREEN	James	66		Lodger	Mar	33	M	Shoemaker	Cheshire	Nantwich
316	SCARRATT	James	66		Lodger	Unm	30	M	Boot and Shoemaker	Lancs	Warrington
317	BEWLY	Thomas	66		Lodger	Unm	30	M	Boot and Shoemaker	Shrop	Shrewsbury
318	NOWELL	John	66		Lodger	Mar	34	M	Stone Mason	Wilts	Warminster
319	COX	John	66		Lodger	Mar	36	M	Labourer	Berks	Wallingford

	SURNAME	FORENAME	SCHEDULE NUMBER	ADDRESS	RELATIONSHIP	STATUS	AGE	SEX	OCCUPATION	COUNTY OF BIRTH	PLACE OF BIRTH
320	EDWARDS	Charles	66		Lodger	Unm	25	M	Labourer	Lancs	Manchester
321	SANDERS	William	67	Spicer Street	Head	Mar	60	M	Labourer	[Herts]	St Pauls Walden
322	SANDERS	Eliza	67		Wife	Mar	40	F	House Servant	London	St Pancras
323	BUCKLE	William	67		Lodger	Unm	20	M	Not Known	London	St Pancras
324	COE	George	67		Lodger	Unm	23	M	Labourer	[Unknown]	
325	KEYSEY	James Odell	67		Lodger	Unm	56	M	Hawker	Ireland	
326	KEYSEY	John	67		Lodgers Son	Unm	9	M		Herts	St Albans
327	STEEL	Dennis	67		Lodger	Unm	50	M	Traveller	Ireland	
328	CLARK	Ann	67		Lodger	Mar	30	F	Traveller	Warks	Coventry
329	HARDWICK	James	67		Lodger	Mar	37	M	Traveller	Yorks	Kingston Upon Hull
330	HARDWICK	Elizabeth	67		Lodgers Wife	Mar	33	F	Traveller	Notts	Sutton
331	HARDWICK	Elizabeth	67		Lodgers Dau	Unm	12	F		Warks	Birmingham
332	HARDWICK	James	67		Lodgers Son	Unm	10	M		Yorks	Kingston Upon Hull
333	HARDWICK	Mary	67		Lodgers Dau	Unm	5	F		Yorks	Kingston Upon Hull
334	HARDWICK	William	67		Lodgers Son	Unm	2	M		Wales	[Unknown]
335	TURNER	Charles	68	George Street	Head	Mar	47	M	Tailor	Yorks	Sheffield
336	TURNER	Mary	68		Wife	Mar	45	F	Dressmaker	Herts	St Albans
337	TURNER	Harriett	68		Dau	Unm	20	F	Straw Hat Maker	Herts	St Albans
338	TURNER	Maria	68		Dau	Unm	15	F	Straw Hat Maker	Herts	St Albans
339	TURNER	Frances	68		Dau	Unm	13	F	Silk Throwster	Herts	St Albans
340	TURNER	Mary Anne	68		Dau	Unm	11	F	Scholar	Herts	St Albans
341	TURNER	Lucy	68		Dau	Unm	9	F	Scholar	Herts	St Albans
342	TURNER	Thomas	68		Son		3	M	Scholar	Herts	St Albans
343	TURNER	Charlotte	68		Dau		7	F	Scholar	Herts	St Albans
344	JOSLING	Robert	69	George Street	Head	Mar	47	M	Seedsman	Hants	Portsea
345	JOSLING	Ann	69		Wife	Mar	48	F	Seedsmans Wife	Suffolk	Bungay
346	JOSLING	Jane	69		Dau	Unm	19	F	Seedsmans Daughter	Herts	St Albans
347	BILBY	Maria	69		Serv	Unm	16	F	House Servant	Herts	St Albans
348	BURROWS	James	70	George Street	Head	Mar	40	M	Machine Maker	Herts	Rickmansworth
349	BURROWS	Ellen	70		Wife	Mar	25	F		Bucks	Long Crendon
350	BURROWS	Maria	70		Dau	Unm	7	F		Bucks	Long Crendon
351	BURROWS	Fanny	70		Dau	Unm	1	F		Herts	St Albans
352	BUCKINGHAM	George	71	George Street	Head	Mar	46	M	Maltster & Corn Dealer	Herts	Little Gaddesden
353	BUCKINGHAM	Elizabeth Ann	71		Wife	Mar	32	F		Herts	St Albans
354	BUCKINGHAM	E.J.	71		Dau	Unm	19	F		Herts	Flamstead
355	BUCKINGHAM	George	71		Son	Unm	16	M		Herts	Two Waters [Hemel Hempstead]
356	BUCKINGHAM	Elizabeth	71		Dau	Unm	12	F	Scholar	Herts	Two Waters [Hemel Hempstead]
357	BUCKINGHAM	Mary Ann	71		Dau	Unm	11	F	Scholar	Herts	Two Waters [Hemel Hempstead]
358	BUCKINGHAM	Emily Ann	71		Dau	Unm	4	F	Scholar	Herts	St Albans
359	BROOKS	Robert	72	George Street	Head	Mar	58	M	Assistant Overseer	Beds	Biggleswade

No	Surname	Forename	HH	Address	Relation	Cond	Age	Sex	Occupation	County	Place
360	BROOKS	Emma	72		Wife	Mar	61	F		Herts	St Albans
361	BROOKS	John	72		Son	Unm	30	M	Teacher of Music & Singing	Herts	St Albans
362	BROOKS	Emma	72		Dau	Unm	20	F		Herts	St Albans
363	BROOKS	George	72		Son	Unm	22	M	Assistant to Mr Brooks [Teacher]	Herts	St Albans
364	BROOKS	Robert	72		Grandson	Unm	2	M		Herts	St Albans
365	POTTON	Ann	72		Serv	Unm	17	F	General Servant	Herts	Kimpton
366	PARSONS	Jonathan	73	George Street	Head	Mar	32	M	Greengrocer employing 1 labourer	Herts	Sandridge
367	PARSONS	Mary	73		Wife	Mar	27	F	Greengrocers Wife	Herts	Wheathampstead
368	PARSONS	Catharine Joel	73		Dau	Unm	2	F	Scholar	Herts	St Albans
369	PARSONS	Elizabeth Susan	73		Dau	Unm	1	F	Scholar	Herts	St Albans
370	LAWRENCE	Susanna Jane	73		Visitor	Unm	16	F	Dressmaker	Herts	Sandridge
371	BONET	Jane	73		Visitor	Unm	14	F	Scholar	Herts	Sandridge
372	BONET	Ann	73		Visitor	Unm	11	F	Scholar	Herts	Sandridge
373	BEDFORD	Charles	73		Lodger	Unm	20	M	Shoemaker	Bucks	Wing
374	BEDFORD	John	73		Lodger	Unm	15	M	Shoemaker	Bucks	Wing
375	HEALEY	George	74	George Street	Head	Mar	33	M	Innkeeper & Brewer	Kent	Deptford
376	HAYWARD	John	74		Lodger	Unm	36	M	Annuitant	Herts	St Albans
377	STANTON	Anne	74		Serv	Unm	28	F	Barmaid & Housekeeper	Warks	Warwick
378	STRATFORD	M.E.	74		Cousin	Unm	24	F	Barmaid	Herts	Redbourn
379	ANDREWS	Elizabeth	74		Serv	Unm	35	F	Cook	Herts	Abbots Langley
380	LINGE	Matilda	74		Serv	Unm	28	F	Waitress	Norfolk	Runton [?]
381	KENT	George	74		Serv	Unm	30	M	Ostler	Herts	Redbourn
382	ASHBY	Thomas	74		Serv	Unm	16	M	Potboy	Herts	Commonwood [Watford]
383	PRATT	John	75	George Street	Head	Mar	58	M	Poulterer & Carrier	Herts	Preston
384	PRATT	Harriett	75		Wife	Mar	60	F		Herts	Abbots Langley
385	PRATT	Robert	75		Son	Unm	28	M	Poulterer & Carrier	Herts	St Albans
386	BROOKS	Robert	76	George Street	Head	Widower	32	M	Tallow Chandler	Herts	St Albans
387	GREGORY	Edward	76		Serv	Unm	20	M	Shopman	Herts	St Albans

One house uninhabited

No	Surname	Forename	HH	Address	Relation	Cond	Age	Sex	Occupation	County	Place
388	GRIFFIN	William	77	Verulam Street	Head	Mar	42	M	Butcher	Herts	St Albans
389	GRIFFIN	Susan	77		Wife	Mar	28	F		Herts	St Albans
390	GRIFFIN	Saunders	77		Son	Unm	3	M		Herts	St Albans
391	GRIFFIN	Susan	77		Dau	Unm	1	F		Herts	St Albans
392	SMITH	Joseph	78	Verulam Street	Head	Mar	21	M	Beer Shop Keeper	Herts	St Albans
393	SMITH	Mary Ann	78		Wife	Mar	20	F	Beer Shop Keeper	Herts	St Albans
394	AXTELL	Maria	78		Lodger	Mar	42	F	Nurse	Herts	St Stephens
395	MACINTOSH	Charlotte	78		Lodger	Mar	34	F	Needlewoman	Herts	St Stephens
396	MACINTOSH	John	78		Lodger	Unm	6m	M		London	St Lukes
397	COLE	Edward	78		Lodger	Widower	43	M	Labourer	Herts	St Stephens
398	DEAN	William	78		Lodger	Unm	52	M	Hawker	Herts	Berkhamsted
399	EWER	William	78		Lodger	Unm	18	M	Labourer	Herts	St Albans
400	WESTALL	Joseph	78		Lodger	Unm	17	M	Labourer	Berks	[Unknown]
401	KIFF	Charles	78		Lodger	Unm	21	M	Labourer	Herts	St Albans

	SURNAME	FORENAME	SCHEDULE NUMBER	ADDRESS	RELATIONSHIP	STATUS	AGE	SEX	OCCUPATION	COUNTY OF BIRTH	PLACE OF BIRTH
402	PATON	Robert	78		Lodger	Mar	42	M	Hatter	Middx	Bow
403	PATON	Charlotte	78		Lodgers Wife	Mar	40	F		London	St Lukes
404	BAYLEY	Alfred Thomas	79	Verulam Street	Head	Mar	40	M	Newspaper Reporter	Herts	Codicote
405	BAYLEY	Harriett	79		Wife	Mar	33	F		Herts	St Albans
406	BAYLEY	Elizabeth	79		Mother	Widow	63	F		Essex	Epping
407	SMITH	George	80	Verulam Road	Head	Mar	45	M	Carpenter	Beds	Eversholt
408	SMITH	Susanna	80		Wife	Mar	43	F		Beds	Lewsey Farm [Leagrave]
409	SMITH	Ephraim	80		Son	Mar	22	M	Weaver	Beds	Houghton Regis
410	SMITH	Matilda	80		Dau-in-law	Mar	19	F	Dressmaker	Ireland	[Unknown]
411	SMITH	Hannah	80		Dau	Unm	14	F	Bonnet Maker	Herts	St Albans
412	SMITH	John	80		Son	Unm	11	M	Scholar	Herts	St Albans
413	SMITH	Ebenezer	80		Son	Unm	5	M	Scholar	Herts	St Albans
414	SMITH	Elizabeth	80		Dau	Unm	3	F		Herts	St Albans
415	SMITH	Sarah Jane	80		Dau	Unm	1	F		Herts	St Albans
416	MAWBEY	Elizabeth	80		Lodger	Unm	50	F	Dressmaker	Beds	Wilden
417	PELLEY	Luke	81	Verulam Road	Head	Mar	32	M	Painter & Glazier	Dorset	Compton
418	PELLEY	Sarah	81		Wife	Mar	28	F		Beds	Holywell [Holwellbury]
419	PELLEY	William	81		Son	Unm	3	M		Herts	St Albans
420	PELLEY	Rose	81		Dau	Unm	1	F		Herts	St Albans
421	BIGGS	Joseph	82	Verulam Street	Head	Mar	40	M	Builder	Herts	Sandridge
422	BIGGS	Amelia	82		Wife	Mar	40	F		Herts	Sandridge
423	BIGGS	C.F.	82		Son	Unm	14	M	Builder	Herts	St Albans
424	BIGGS	Eliza	82		Dau	Unm	16	F		Herts	St Albans
425	PEW	George	82		Visitor	Unm	22	M	Carpenter	Herts	Wheathampstead
426	CRAMPHORN	David	82		Visitor	Unm	20	M	Labourer	Herts	St Albans
427	MORRIS	James	82		Lodger	Unm	30	M	Labourer	Herts	Watford
428	WALTON	Thomas	83	Verulam Street	Head	Mar	62	M	Carpenter	Durham	Houghton le Spring
429	WALTON	Ann	83		Wife	Mar	59	F	Carpenters Wife	Kent	Woolwich
430	WALTON	Ann Margaret	83		Dau	Unm	36	F	Carpenters Daughter	London	St Lukes
431	WALTON	Stephen John	83		Son	Unm	20	M	Carpenters Son	London	St Lukes
432	BATES	James	83		Lodger	Unm	19	M	Assistant in Straw Bonnet Factory	Herts [Beds]	Westoning
433	AGUTTER	Benjamin	84	Verulam Street	Head	Mar	41	M	Tailor & Draper	Herts	St Albans
434	AGUTTER	Maria	84		Wife	Mar	39	F	Tailor & Drapers Wife	Oxon	Oxford
435	HOUSE	Francis Thomas	84		Son-in-law	Unm	12	M	Tailor & Drapers Stepson	Herts	St Albans
436	AGUTTER	Ben	84		Son	Unm	6	M	Tailor & Drapers Son	Herts	St Albans
437	AGUTTER	E.M.	84		Dau	Unm	2	F	Tailor & Drapers Daughter	Herts	St Albans
438	AGUTTER	Henry Odell	84		Son	Unm	2m	M		Herts	St Albans
439	MORETON	Elizabeth	84		Serv	Unm	20	F	House Servant	Herts	Colney Heath
440	AGUTTER	Benjamin	85	Verulam Street	Head	Mar	70	M	Tailor & Draper	Herts	St Albans
441	AGUTTER	Sarah	85		Wife	Mar	65	F	Tailor & Drapers Wife	Herts	St Albans
442	AGUTTER	Mary Ann	85		Dau	Unm	29	F	Tailor & Drapers Daughter	Herts	St Albans
443	AGUTTER	Rosanna	85		Dau	Unm	27	F	Tailor & Drapers Daughter	Herts	St Albans

	Surname	Forename		Street	Relation	Status	Age	Sex	Occupation	County	Place
444	NORRIS	Joseph	86	Verulam Street	Head	Unm	33	M	Baker	Herts	Great Berkhamsted
445	NORRIS	Mary	86		Sister	Unm	27	F	Housekeeper	Herts	Hemel Hempstead
446	CLAYTON	Thomas	86		Serv	Unm	17	M	Baker	Herts	St Albans
447	POWELL	Thomas	86		Serv	Unm	14	M	Baker	Herts	St Albans
448	DAVIS	Thomas	87	Verulam Street	Head	Mar	62	M	Retired Draper	Montgom	Welshpool
449	DAVIS	Elizabeth	87		Wife	Mar	65	F	Retired Drapers Wife	Montgom	Meifod
450	BUCK	Mary	87		Serv	Unm	62	F	House Servant	Suffolk	Wickham Market
451	MARTON	Mary	87		Serv	Unm	24	F	House Servant	Herts	St Albans
452	SHRUBB	Samuel	88	Verulam Street	Head	Widower	71	M	Harness & Rope Maker	Herts	St Albans
453	HAMMOND	Ann	88		Serv	Unm	21	F	Housekeeper	Northants	Ravensthorpe
454	JOSLING	Arthur	88		Nephew	Unm	12	M	Scholar	Herts	St Albans
455	HILTON	Mary	88		Sister	Widow	66	F		Herts	St Albans
456	HILTON	Mary	88		Niece	Unm	6	F	Scholar	Herts	St Albans
457	SKINNER	Hannah Baker	89		Wife	Mar	41	F	Carpenters Wife	Herts	St Albans
458	BROAD	Mary Ann	89		Niece		14	F	Brazilian Hat Maker	Herts	Watford
459	HIGDON	William Henry	89		Lodger	Unm	38	M	Cordwainer (Dumb)	Herts	St Albans
460	LAPISH	George	89		Visitor	Mar	33	M	Stone Mason	Northants	Northampton
461	LAPISH	Emma	89		Visitors Wife	Mar	24	F	Stone Masons Wife	Sussex	West Ham
462	BRADSHAW	Mary	90	Verulam Street	Head	Widow	48	F	Annuitant	Herts	Kimpton
463	DIXON	Sarah	90		Serv	Unm	13	F	Servant	Herts	Watford
464	PAGE	John	91		Lodger	Widower	72	M	Auctioneer	Herts	St Albans
465	LINES	Robert	92	Verulam Street	Head	Mar	35	M	Victualler	Herts	St Albans
466	LINES	Maria	92		Wife	Mar	30	F	Victuallers Wife	Herts	St Albans
467	LINES	Ann	92		Dau	Unm	1	F		Herts	St Albans
468	LINES	Thomas	92		Brother	Unm	19	M	Painters Apprentice	Herts	St Albans
469	GIDDINGS	Eliza	92		Serv	Unm	14	F	House Servant	Herts	Welwyn
470	GLASSCOCK	Hannah	93	Verulam Street	Head	Widow	30	F	Grocer & Tea Dealer	Herts	Kensworth
471	GLASSCOCK	John	93		Son	Unm	9	M	Scholar	Herts	St Albans
472	GLASSCOCK	James	93		Son	Unm	11	M	Scholar	Herts	St Albans
473	GLASSCOCK	Alfred	93		Son	Unm	7	M	Scholar	Herts	St Albans
474	LOVETT	Ann	93		Serv	Unm	15	F	Servant	Herts	St Albans
475	STEPHENS	John	94	Verulam Street	Head	Mar	29	M	Baker	Middx	[Unknown]
476	STEPHENS	Elizabeth	94		Wife	Mar	31	F	Bakers Wife	Herts	[Unknown]
477	GOOCH	Charlotte	94		Lodger	Unm	38	F	Gunsmiths Daughter	Kent	Canterbury
478	ALDRIDGE	Jonathan	94		Serv	Unm	17	M	Bakers Apprentice	Herts	St Albans
479	SWAIN	Henry	96	Verulam Street	Head	Mar	35	M	Saddle & Harness Maker	Herts	St Albans
480	SWAIN	Charlotte	96		Wife	Mar	36	F	Bonnet Sewer	Beds	Leighton
481	SWAIN	Charlotte	96		Dau	Unm	10	F	Scholar	Herts	St Albans
482	SWAIN	Elizabeth	96		Dau	Unm	5	F	Scholar	Herts	St Albans
483	SWAIN	Emily	96		Dau	Unm	3	F	Scholar	Herts	St Albans
484	SMITH	Elizabeth	96		Aunt	Widow	63	F	Bonnet Sewer	Herts	St Albans
485	HEATH	Thomas M.	95	Verulam Street	Head	Mar	26	M	Painter	Herts	St Albans
486	HEATH	Jane	95		Wife	Mar	27	F	Painters Wife	Herts	St Albans

	SURNAME	FORENAME	SCHEDULE NUMBER	ADDRESS	RELATIONSHIP	STATUS	AGE	SEX	OCCUPATION	COUNTY OF BIRTH	PLACE OF BIRTH
487	HEATH	Frederic	95		Son	Unm	5	M		Herts	St Albans
488	HEATH	Thomas	95		Son	Unm	2	M		Herts	St Albans
489	MAWBEY	Joseph	97	Verulam Street	Head	Mar	39	M	Hair Dresser	Herts	Bushey
490	MAWBEY	Eliza	97		Wife	Mar	37	F		Beds	Dunstable
491	MAWBEY	William	97		Son	Unm	12	M	Scholar	Herts	St Albans
492	MAWBEY	Elizabeth	97		Dau	Unm	10	F	Scholar	Herts	St Albans
493	MAWBEY	Sophia	97		Dau	Unm	9	F	Scholar	Herts	St Albans
494	MAWBEY	Eliza	97		Dau	Unm	2	F	Scholar	Herts	St Albans
495	GODDWICH	William	98	Verulam Road	Head	Mar	30	M	Coach Builder	Middx	Islington
496	GODDWICH	Maria	98		Wife	Mar	30	F		Middx	St Lukes
497	GODDWICH	William	98		Son	Unm	5	M	Scholar	Herts	St Albans
498	GODDWICH	George	98		Son	Unm	2	M		Herts	St Albans
499	SMITH	Robert	98		Lodger	Mar	24	M	Iron Founder	Middx	Hampstead
500	SMITH	Mary	98		Lodgers Wife	Mar	30	F	Straw Weaver	Middx	Hampstead
501	MORRIS	Joseph	99	Verulam Road	Head	Mar	38	M	Straw Bonnet Manufacturer	Middx	Mile End
502	MORRIS	Eliza	99		Wife	Mar	38	F	Straw Bonnet Manufacturers Wife	Warks	Coventry
503	MORRIS	Julia	99		Dau	Unm	18	F	Straw Bonnet Manufacturers Dau	Warks	Coventry
504	PEARS	Job	99		Father-in-law	Widower	67	M	Brewer	Warks	Coventry
505	HYDE	Sarah	99		Serv	Unm	23	F	House Servant	Herts	Bishops Stortford

One house building

	SURNAME	FORENAME	SCHEDULE NUMBER	ADDRESS	RELATIONSHIP	STATUS	AGE	SEX	OCCUPATION	COUNTY OF BIRTH	PLACE OF BIRTH
506	HAILES	George	100	Verulam Road	Head	Mar	50	M	Foreman of Bonnet Factory	Herts	Barley
507	HAILES	Charlotte	100		Wife	Mar	40	F		Essex	Ongar
508	HAILES	Sarah Susan	100		Dau	Unm	17	F		London	St Georges East
509	HAILES	Esther	100		Dau	Unm	11	F		London	St Georges East
510	PEARCE	Charles	100		Visitor	Mar	23	M	Labourer	Oxon	Henley
511	PEARCE	Ann	100		Visitors Wife	Mar	27	F	Labourer	Herts	St Stephens
512	FLETCHER	Francis	101	Verulam Road	Head	Mar	62	M	Groom	Herts	Caddington
513	FLETCHER	Jane	101		Wife	Mar	55	F		Herts	Hitchin
514	DOLLIMORE	Elizabeth	102	Verulam Road	Head	Widow	66	F	Straw Plaiter	Herts	Kings Walden
515	BUCKINGHAM	William	102		Visitor	Mar	34	M		Herts	St Albans
516	WABEY	Thomas	103	Verulam Road	Head	Mar	57	M	Agric Lab	Herts	St Albans
517	WABEY	Deborah	103		Wife	Mar	52	F		Herts	St Albans
518	JENKINS	Sarah	104	Verulam Road	Head	Widow	55	F	Plaiter	Herts	St Albans
519	JENKINS	Elizabeth	104		Dau	Unm	35	F	Plaiter	Herts	St Albans
520	REYNOLDS	Elizabeth	104		Visitor	Unm	20	F	Bonnet Sewer	Herts	North Mimms
521	BEARDON	Elizabeth	105		Wife	Mar	63	F	Labourers Wife	Herts	St Albans
522	GIDDINS	George	105		Lodger	Mar	40	M	Waiter	Beds	Dunstable
523	GIDDINS	Sarah	105		Lodgers Wife	Mar	38	F	Waiters Wife	Herts	Hatfield
524	GIDDINS	Eustace	105		Lodgers Son		3	M	Waiters Son	Herts	St Albans
525	EDWARDS	Amelia	105		Lodger	Unm	25	F	Silk Throwster	Herts	Rickmansworth
526	EDWARDS	Martha	105		Lodger	Unm	14	F	Silk Throwster	Herts	Rickmansworth
527	WINGRAVE	John	106	Verulam Road	Head	Widower	72	M	Straw Manufacturer	Beds	Luton

528	BLOOMFIELD	Mary	106		Dau	Widow	48	F	Housekeeper	Beds	Luton
529	PELHAM	Elizabeth	106		Serv	Unm	29	F	General Servant	London	
530	TIDD	William	107	Verulam Road	Head	Mar	48	M	Carpenter	Lincs	Grantham
531	ASTELL	Emma	107		Cousin	Unm	14	F		London	
532	COLEY	Charles	107		Lodger	Unm	30	M	Stone Mason	Unknown	
533	POCOCK	Samuel	108	Verulam Road	Head	Mar	31	M	Cordwainer	Herts	Harpenden
534	POCOCK	Ellen	108		Wife	Mar	29	F		Herts	St Albans
535	POCOCK	William	108		Son	Unm	12	M	Scholar	Herts	St Albans
536	JAYS	Mary	109	Verulam Road	Head	Unm	51	F	Laundress	Northants	North Haddon
537	JAYS	Hannah	109		Sister	Unm	37	F	Laundress	Herts	St Albans
538	BAYNES	Richard	110	Verulam Road	Head	Mar	66	M	Cabinet Maker	Durham	Sunderland
539	BAYNES	Ann	110		Wife	Mar	66	F	Cabinet Makers Wife	London	
540	EARLE	Richard	111	Verulam Road	Head	Mar	58	M	Whitesmith	Bucks	Chesham
541	EARLE	Mary	111		Wife	Mar	59	F	Whitesmiths Wife	Bucks	Hawridge [?]
542	PENN	George	112	Verulam Road	Head	Mar	30	M	Whitesmith	Middx	Stanmore
543	PENN	Emma	112		Wife	Mar	31	F	Whitesmiths Wife	Herts	Berkhamsted
544	PENN	Emma	112		Dau	Unm	9m	F		Herts	St Albans
545	GREGORY	Abraham	113	Verulam Road	Head	Mar	57	M	Statuary & Mason	Cheshire	Waverton
546	GREGORY	Elizabeth	113		Wife	Mar	59	F	Statuary & Masons Wife	Northants	Harlestone
547	GREGORY	Emma	113		Dau	Unm	37	F	Dressmaker	Cheshire	Waverton
548	GREGORY	Isaac	113		Son	Unm	22	M	Stone & Marble Mason	Herts	St Albans
549	GREGORY	Sarah Ann	113		Grandau	Unm	7	F	Scholar	Herts	St Albans
550	DUDLEY	Joseph	114	Verulam Road	Head	Mar	35	M	Straw Factor	Beds	Egginton
551	DUDLEY	Harriett	114		Wife	Mar	27	F	Straw Factors Wife	Herts	St Albans
552	DUDLEY	Jesse	114		Son		7	M		Herts	St Albans
553	DUDLEY	Emma	114		Dau		5	F		Herts	St Albans
554	DUDLEY	Sarah	114		Dau		3	F		Herts	St Albans
555	CAUSTON	George	114		Lodger	Mar	26	M	Stone Cutter	Herts	Redbourn
556	PENNY	Henry	114		Lodger	Widower	55	M	Labourer	Herts	Redbourn
557	MITCHEL	William	115	Cross Street	Head	Mar	36	M	Tailor	London	
558	MITCHEL	Elizabeth	115		Wife	Mar	37	F	Dressmaker	Herts	St Albans
559	RICHARDSON	James C.	116	Market Place	Head	Mar	37	M	Upholsterer employing 1 man	Gloucs	Tewkesbury
560	RICHARDSON	Sarah	116		Wife	Mar	37	F		Herts	Bushey
561	RICHARDSON	Sarah F.	116		Dau	Unm	3	F		Herts	St Albans
562	RICHARDSON	Jane F.	116		Dau	Unm	1	F		Herts	St Albans
563	GOLDSBY	Henry	117	Market Place	Head	Mar	37	M	Bricklayer	Herts	St Albans
564	GOLDSBY	Mary	117		Wife	Mar	39	F	Washer Woman	Herts	Redbourn
565	GOLDSBY	Charles	117		Son	Unm	15	M	Labourer	Herts	St Albans
566	GOLDSBY	William	117		Son	Unm	12	M	Silk Throwster	Herts	St Albans
567	GOLDSBY	Mary Ann	117		Dau	Unm	6	F	Scholar	Herts	St Albans
568	SMITH	Charles	118	Market Place	Head	Mar	50	M	Victualler	Herts	St Albans
569	SMITH	Maria	118		Wife	Mar	49	F	Victuallers Wife	Herts	St Albans
570	SMITH	Margaret Ann	118		Dau	Unm	26	F	Victuallers Daughter	Herts	Watford
571	SMITH	Charles	118		Son	Unm	18	M	Victuallers Son	Herts	St Albans

	SURNAME	FORENAME	SCHEDULE NUMBER	ADDRESS	RELATIONSHIP	STATUS	AGE	SEX	OCCUPATION	COUNTY OF BIRTH	PLACE OF BIRTH
572	SMITH	Emma	118		Dau	Unm	9	F	Victuallers Daughter	Herts	St Albans
573	EVANS	Edward	118		Lodger	Unm	25	M	Shoemaker	Herts	Sandridge
574	WALKER	James	119	Market Place	Head	Mar	34	M	Tailor and Hatter	Cumb	Penrith
575	WALKER	Ann	119		Wife	Mar	29	F		Beds	Ampthill
576	WALKER	Henry	119		Son	Unm	7	M	Scholar	Beds	Ampthill
577	WALKER	Sarah Ann	119		Dau	Unm	5	F	Scholar	Beds	Ampthill
578	WALKER	James	119		Son	Unm	3	M	Scholar	Beds	Ampthill
579	WALKER	Charlotte	119		Dau	Unm	1	F		Herts	St Albans
580	WARNER	Emma	119		Serv	Unm	15	F	House Servant	Herts	Childwick [St Michaels]
581	MARTIN	Henry Gillam	120	Market Place	Head	Unm	25	M	Chemist	Herts	St Albans
582	MARTIN	Alice	120		Sister	Unm	42	F	Hatters Daughter	Herts	St Albans
583	MARTIN	Ann	120		Sister	Unm	39	F	Hatters Daughter	Herts	St Albans
584	MARTIN	Emma	120		Sister	Unm	36	F	Hatters Daughter	Herts	St Albans
585	DRIVER	Frederick	120		Serv	Unm	15	M	Fishmongers Son	London	
586	HARDING	Jemima	121	Market Place	Head	Unm	67	F	Needlewoman	Herts	Hemel Hempstead
587	DAVIS	Kezia	121		Sister	Mar	64	F	Needlewoman	Herts	Abbots Langley
588	FOWLER	Ann	121		Visitor	Unm	43	F	Charwoman	Herts	St Albans
589	TURNER	Elizabeth	122	Market Place	Head	Widow	42	F	Grocer	Herts	St Albans
590	TURNER	Charles	122		Son	Unm	20	M	Grocer	Herts	St Albans
591	RICHARDSON	Thomas	123	Market Place	Head	Mar	32	M	Breeches Maker	Beds	Biggleswade
592	RICHARDSON	Sarah	123		Wife	Mar	30	F		Middx	Hillingdon
593	KENT	John	124	Market Place	Head	Mar	43	M	Grocer	Herts	Redbourn
594	KENT	Ann	124		Dau	Unm	16	F	Grocers Daughter	Beds	Dunstable
595	KENT	William	124		Son	Unm	15	M	Grocers Son	Herts	St Albans
596	KENT	Henry	124		Son	Unm	7	M	Scholar	Herts	St Albans
597	ALDRIDGE	Henry	125	Market Place	Head	Mar	29	M	Butcher	Herts	St Albans
598	ALDRIDGE	Fanny	125		Wife	Mar	31	F	Butchers Wife	Herts	St Albans
599	ALDRIDGE	Edward	125		Son	Unm	2	M		Herts	St Albans
600	BIRD	Hannah	125		Serv	Unm	14	F	House Servant	Herts	St Albans
601	STUCKEY	Elizabeth	125		Lodger	Unm	70	F	Sempstress	Herts	Cobdenhill [?] [Aldenham]
602	DAY	Emma	125		Lodger	Unm	15	F	Bonnet Sewer	Herts	St Albans
603	WOOD	Joseph	126	Market Place	Head	Unm	43	M	Master Cooper	Middx	Clerkenwell
604	MASON	Esther	127	Market Place	Head	Widow	57	F		Herts	Shenley
605	MASON	James George	127		Son	Unm	28	M	Painter	Herts	St Albans
606	MASON	Mary Elizabeth	127		Dau	Unm	25	F	Bonnet Sewer	Herts	St Albans
607	MASON	Hannah Rachael	127		Dau	Unm	20	F	Bonnet Sewer	Herts	St Albans
608	MASON	Susanna Esther	127		Dau	Unm	14	F	Bonnet Sewer	Herts	St Albans
609	TILCOCK	John	128	Market Place	Head	Mar	32	M	Greengrocer	Beds	Greenfield [?]
610	TILCOCK	Elizabeth	128		Wife	Mar	32	F	Greengrocers Wife	Beds	Greenfield [?]
611	TILCOCK	John	128		Son	Unm	12	M	Greengrocers Son	Beds	Greenfield [?]
612	TILCOCK	Eliza	128		Dau	Unm	13	F	Greengrocers Daughter	Beds	Greenfield [?]
613	SKILLETON	Eliza	128		Niece	Unm	19	F	Greengrocers Niece	Beds	Greenfield [?]

One empty house

614	SYRETT	Thomas	129	Market Place	Head	Mar	49	M	Linen Draper	Suffolk	Waldingfield
615	SYRETT	Mary Anne	129		Wife	Mar	50	F		Surrey	Southwark
616	SYRETT	Francis	129		Brother	Unm	36	M	Linen Draper	Suffolk	Bildeston
617	DOUGLAS	Thomas	129		Assistant	Unm	25	M	Linen Drapers Assistant	Oxon	
618	LONDON	Henry	129		Assistant	Unm	23	M	Linen Drapers Assistant	Kent	Maidstone
619	PAYNE	Frank Edward	129		Apprentice	Unm	15	M	Linen Drapers Apprentice	Sussex	Worthing
620	BULL	George Osman	129		Apprentice	Unm	16	M	Linen Drapers Apprentice	Middx	Islington
621	SHARP	Martha	129		Serv	Unm	24	F	General Servant	Herts	Ayot St Peter
622	ROBERTS	Albinius	130	Market Place	Head	Mar	37	M	Chemist	Sussex	Hurstpierpont
623	ROBERTS	Sarah Ann	130		Wife	Mar	33	F		Herts	St Albans
624	LAINE	Robert	130		Assistant	Unm	21	M	Chemists Assistant	Hants	Alresford
625	HUCKLE	Mary	130		Serv	Mar	30	F	General Servant	Herts	Chipperfield [Kings Langley]
626	LANGRIDGE	Edward	131	Market Place	Head	Mar	58	M	Justice & Councillor & Wine Merchant	Sussex	East Grinstead
627	LANGRIDGE	Sarah Elizabeth	131		Wife	Mar	60	F		[Herts]	Aldenham
628	LANGRIDGE	Jessie	131		Dau	Unm	22	F		Herts	St Albans
629	LANGRIDGE	Phillip	131		Son	Unm	18	M	Shop Assistant	Herts	St Albans
630	GATES	Edward William	131		Grandson	Unm	5	M	Visitor	Bucks	Aylesbury
631	GATES	Charles	131		Grandson	Unm	4	M	Visitor	Bucks	Aylesbury
632	ROBINS	Sarah	131		Serv	Unm	16	F	General Servant	Herts	Little Berkhamsted
633	MILLS	Thomas	132	Market Place	Head	Mar	52	M	Publican	Herts	St Albans
634	MILLS	Harriett	132		Wife	Mar	52	F	Publicans Wife	Herts	St Albans
635	MILLS	John	132		Son	Unm	24	M	Publicans Son	Herts	St Albans
636	MILLS	Thomas	132		Son	Unm	22	M	Publicans Son	Herts	St Albans
637	MILLS	Edward	132		Son	Unm	17	M	Publicans Son	Herts	St Albans
638	PHIPPS	Sarah	132		Serv	Unm	21	F	General Servant	Herts	Essendon
639	TYLER	Ann	133	Dagnall Lane	Head	Widow	53	F	School Mistress	Herts	Hatfield
640	TYLER	Mary Ann	133		Dau	Unm	27	F	School Mistress	Herts	Hatfield
641	TYLER	Charles	133		Son	Unm	25	M	Cordwainer	Herts	Hatfield
642	TYLER	Emily	133		Dau	Unm	22	F	Dressmaker	Herts	Hatfield
643	TYLER	Cecilia	133		Dau	Unm	20	F	Dressmaker	Herts	Hatfield
644	TYLER	Lavinia	133		Dau	Unm	18	F	Dressmaker	Herts	Hatfield
645	CONQUEST	Mary Ann	134	Verulam Street	Head	Mar	57	F	Hat Maker	Herts	Hitchin
646	CONQUEST	Emily	134		Dau	Unm	27	F	Straw Bonnet Maker	Herts	Colney
647	WILLIAMS	Henry	136	Verulam Street	Head	Mar	39	M	Accountant	Beds	Biggleswade
648	WILLIAMS	Mary	136		Wife	Mar	29	F	Milliner	Suffolk	Ipswich
649	WILLIAMS	Henry John	136		Son	Unm	15	M		Suffolk	Ipswich
650	WILLIAMS	Catharine	136		Dau	Unm	10	F	Scholar	Suffolk	Ipswich
651	BURTON	John	137	Verulam Street	Head	Mar	52	M	Confectioner employing 1 man	Beds	Biggleswade
652	BURTON	Amelia	137		Wife	Mar	53	F		Herts	St Albans
653	WARD	George	138	Verulam Street	Head	Unm	33	M	Postmaster	Herts	St Albans
654	WARD	Lydia	138		Sister	[blank]	37	F		Herts	St Albans
655	PERRY	George	139	Verulam Street	Head	Mar	53	M	Plumber	Herts	Digswell

	SURNAME	FORENAME	SCHEDULE NUMBER	ADDRESS	RELATIONSHIP	STATUS	AGE	SEX	OCCUPATION	COUNTY OF BIRTH	PLACE OF BIRTH
656	PERRY	Sarah	139		Wife	Mar	53	F		Herts	Clothall
657	PERRY	George	139		Son	Unm	24	M	Painter	Herts	St Albans
658	PERRY	Jane	139		Dau	Unm	19	F		Herts	St Albans
659	PERRY	Sarah	139		Dau	Unm	10	F	Scholar	Herts	St Albans
660	LATHWOOD	William	140	Dagnall Lane	Head	Mar	48	M	Plasterer	London	Marylebone
661	LATHWOOD	Mary Ann	140		Wife	Mar	45	F	Stay Maker	At Sea	
662	FOUNTAIN	Mary	141	Dagnall Lane	Head	Mar	48	F	Charwoman	Herts	St Albans
663	ROBINSON	William	142	Dagnall Lane	Head	Mar	63	M	Cordwainer	Herts	St Stephens
664	ROBINSON	Susanna	142		Wife	Mar	64	F		Middx	Highgate
665	COOPER	Susanna	143	Dagnall Lane	Head	Mar	46	F	Straw Bonnet Maker	Herts	St Albans
666	COOPER	Ellen	143		Dau	Unm	24	F	Straw Bonnet Maker	[Middx]	Enfield
667	CLARK	Ann	143		Visitor	Unm	23	F	Straw Bonnet Maker	Herts	St Albans
668	PUGH	Ann E.	143		Visitor	Unm	23	F	Straw Bonnet Maker	Herts	Watford
669	POWELL	Samuel	144	Dagnall Lane	Head	Mar	46	M	Pipe Maker	London	
670	POWELL	Sophia	144		Wife	Mar	28	F	Pipe Makers Wife	Herts	Whitwell
671	ARNOLD	Martha	144		Sister	Unm	17	F	Straw Plaiter	Herts	Whitwell
672	CARTER	Sarah	145	Dagnall Lane	Head	Unm	30	F	Bonnet Sewer	Beds	Luton
673	CARTER	Albert	145		Son	Unm	12	M	Scholar	Beds	Luton
674	HILLYARD	Sarah	145		Sister	Unm	12	F	Apprentice	Beds	Clophill
675	WEBB	James	146	Dagnall Lane	Head	Mar	55	M	Builder employing 8 men	Middx	Enfield
676	WEBB	Susan	146		Wife	Mar	52	F		Beds	Hockliffe
677	WEBB	Anna	146		Dau	Unm	17	F	Builders Daughter	Herts	St Albans
678	VARNEY	Anna	146		Serv	Unm	13	F	General Servant	Herts	St Albans
679	WEBB	William	147	Dagnall Lane	Head	Mar	30	M	Bricklayer	Herts	St Albans
680	WEBB	Harriett	147		Wife	Mar	25	F	Dressmaker	Herts	St Albans
681	WEBB	Harriett	147		Dau	Unm	2	F		Herts	St Albans
682	WEBB	William	147		Son	Unm	1	M		Herts	St Albans
683	WEBB	Emily	147		Dau	Unm	1 m	F		Herts	St Albans
684	BRITTON	Maurice	148	Dagnall Lane	Head	Mar	48	M	Wesleyan Minister	Gloucs	Bitton
685	BRITTON	Anne	148		Wife	Mar	44	F		Beds	Luton
686	BRITTON	Maurice W.	148		Son	Unm	14	M	Assistant in Straw Factory	Hunts	St Ives
687	BRITTON	Ann Elizabeth	148		Dau	Unm	12	F	Scholar	Wilts	Swindon
688	BRITTON	Mary Hanison [?]	148		Dau	Unm	8	F	Scholar	Gloucs	Dursley
689	BRITTON	Joseph Willis	148		Son	Unm	4	M		Wales	Pontypridd
690	BRITTON	Martha Vipond	148		Dau	Unm	1	F		Herts	St Albans
691	CHAPMAN	Rebecca	148		Serv	Unm	20	F	General Servant	Beds	Hodley [?]
692	CHALKLEY	Richard	149	Dagnall Lane	Head	Mar	62	M	Master Stone Mason employing 1 man	Hants	Petersfield
693	CHALKLEY	Elizabeth	149		Wife	Mar	55	F		Herts	St Albans
694	CHALKLEY	Samuel	149		Son	Unm	22	M	Stonemason	Herts	St Albans
695	CHALKLEY	Sarah	149		Dau	Unm	20	F	Chip Hat Maker	Herts	St Albans
696	CHALKLEY	Susan	149		Dau	Unm	16	F	Brazilian Hat Maker	Herts	St Albans
697	CHALKLEY	Jane	149		Dau	Unm	12	F	Chip Hat Maker	Herts	St Albans
698	CHALKLEY	Elizabeth	149		Grandau	Unm	10	F		Herts	St Albans

699	CHALKLEY	Martha	149		Grandau	Unm	4	F	Scholar	Herts	St Albans
700	GIBBS	Richard	150	Dagnall Lane	Head	Mar	46	M	Printer & Bookseller	Bucks	Aylesbury
701	GIBBS	Frances	150		Wife	Mar	43	F	Printer & Booksellers Wife	Oxon	Bicester
702	GIBBS	Frances Rolls	150		Dau	Unm	21	F	Printer & Booksellers Daughter	Herts	St Albans
703	GIBBS	Sarah Rolls	150		Dau	Unm	19	F	Printer & Booksellers Daughter	Herts	St Albans
704	GIBBS	Richard	150		Son	Unm	17	M	Printer	Herts	St Albans
705	GIBBS	Emma	150		Dau	Unm	13	F	Scholar	Herts	St Albans
706	GIBBS	Robert Rolls	150		Son	Unm	8	M	Scholar	Herts	St Albans
707	GIBBS	Albert	150		Son	Unm	5	M	Scholar	Herts	St Albans
708	GIBBS	Mary Rolls	150		Dau	Unm	1	F		Herts	St Albans
709	MCCLANE	Thomas	150		Visitor	Unm	25	M	British Schoolmaster	Scotland	Kirkcudbright
710	DEELEY	Mary Ann	150		Serv	Unm	22	F	General Servant	Bucks	Waddesdon
711	LACEY	John	151	Kings Head Inn, Market Street	Head	Mar	51	M	Licensed Victualler	Hants	Ropley Dean
712	LACEY	Phoebe	151		Wife	Mar	57	F	Laundress	Warks	Dunchurch
713	LACEY	Sarah	151		Dau	Unm	10	F	Bonnet Sewer	Herts	St Albans
714	GODSELL	Aquila Ann	151		Lodger	Widow	26	F	School Mistress	Somerset	Taunton Cotterel
715	GODSELL	Elizabeth	151		Lodgers Dau	Unm	7	F	Scholar	Cheshire	Congleton
716	GODSELL	William	151		Lodgers Son	Unm	4	M	Scholar	Lancs	Manchester
717	GODSELL	Thomas	151		Lodgers Son	Unm	3	M		Lancs	Manchester
718	GODSELL	Eliza	151		Lodgers Dau		1	F		Staffs	Stafford
719	PEARCE	George	151		Lodgers	Mar	23	M	Actor	Middx	St Lukes
720	PEARCE	Sarah	151		Lodgers Wife	Mar	22	F	Actress	Middx	Islington
721	HIGDON	John	151		Lodger	Widower	66	M	Millwright	Somerset	Bruton
722	COLEMAN	Vincent	152	Market Street	Head	Mar	43	M	Dissenting Minister	Somerset	Clifton
723	COLEMAN	Elizabeth	152		Wife	Mar	40	F	Fancy Toy Shop Keeper	Herts	St Albans
724	COLEMAN	George Davenport	152		Son	Unm	12	M	Scholar	Herts	St Albans
725	BLETSO	Ann	152		Niece	Unm	17	F	Assistant in Toy Shop	London	
726	WILLS	Edward Sutton	153	Market Place	Head	Mar	38	M	Grocer & Tallow Chandler	Beds	Worthill [Worthy End?]
727	WILLS	Mary	153		Wife	Mar	42	F		Beds	Houghton Regis
728	CHURCH	Eliza	153		Dau-in-law	Unm	13	F	Scholar	Herts	St Albans
729	LUMMON [?]	Sarah	153		Serv	Unm	32	F	General Servant	Herts	St Albans
730	MATTING	William	154	Market Place	Head	Mar	28	M	Pastry Cook	Northants	Northampton
731	MATTING	Maria	154		Wife	Mar	29	F		Surrey	Brixton
732	MATTING	William Henry	154		Son	Unm	1	M		Herts	St Albans
733	HOWELL	Eliza	154		Serv	Unm	24	F	General Servant	Herts	Cheshunt
734	CLIMANCE	George	155	Market Place	Head	Mar	33	M	Baker & Corn Dealer	London	
735	CLIMANCE	Sarah	155		Wife	Mar	33	F		Durham	Durham
736	BROOMFIELD	Sarah	155		Dau-in-law	Unm	11	F		Hants	Winchester
737	FENSOM	Mary	155		Serv	Unm	23	F	General Servant	Herts	St Albans
738	SADLER	William	155		Serv	Unm	28	M	Labourer	Herts	St Albans

One empty house

	SURNAME	FORENAME	SCHEDULE NUMBER	ADDRESS	RELATIONSHIP	STATUS	AGE	SEX	OCCUPATION	COUNTY OF BIRTH	PLACE OF BIRTH
739	STEABBEN	George	156	Market Place	Head	Mar	40	M	Grocer	Herts	St Albans
740	STEABBEN	Ann Elizabeth	156		Wife	Mar	31	F	Grocers Wife	Middx	Stamford Hill
741	STEABBEN	Elizabeth	156		Dau	Unm	10	F	Grocers Daughter	Herts	St Albans
742	LIMBAY	William	156		Serv	Unm	22	M	Grocers Shopman	Beds	Dunstable
743	HINSELL	Joseph	156		Serv	Unm	18	M	Grocers Shopman	Middx	Marylebone
744	HARDING	Sarah Ann	156		Serv	Unm	18	F	General Servant	Herts	Boxmoor [Hemel Hempstead]
745	TIDD	Mary Ann	156		Nurse	Mar	55	F	Carpenters Wife [Nurse]	Middx	Marylebone
746	BOND	George	157	Market Place	Head	Mar	40	M	Clothier & Shoe Warehouse	Herts	Markyate Street
747	BOND	Anne	157		Wife	Mar	41	F			[Unknown]
748	BOND	Alfred	157		Son	Unm	18	M	Shopman	Herts	Codicote
749	BOND	Susannah	157		Dau	Unm	16	F	Dressmaker	Herts	Sandridge
750	BOND	Mary	157		Dau	Unm	11	F	Dressmaker	Herts	Sandridge
751	EVANS	Charles	157		Nephew	Unm	14	M	Errand Boy	Herts	Sandridge
752	BRYAN	Martha	158	Fleur de Lis Inn	Head	Unm	40	F	Innkeeper	Middx	Edmonton
753	BRYAN	Ann	158		Mother	Widow	80	F	Late Innkeeper	Wilts	[Unknown]
754	BRYAN	William	158		Brother	Unm	48	M	House Servant	Middx	Poplar
755	BUCKINGHAM	John Henry	158		Lodger	Widower	50	M	Portrait Painter	Middx	Hendon
756	BULL	Mary	159	Back Street	Head	Widow	54	F	Butcher	Herts	Flamstead
757	BULL	William C.	159		Son	Unm	21	M	Butcher	Herts	St Albans
758	SMITH	Neptune	160	St Christopher Inn, Back Street	Head	Mar	33	M	Victualler	Herts	Barnet
759	SMITH	Susannah	160		Wife	Mar	40	F		Essex	Civil Cunningham [Sible Hedingham]
760	GRIFFIN	William	160		Visitor	Unm	6	M		Herts	St Albans
761	TURNEY	George	161	Back Street	Head	Mar	30	M	Labourer	Herts	St Albans
762	TURNEY	Susan	161		Wife	Mar	29	F	Weaver	Herts	St Albans
763	WATKINS	Edward	162	Back Street	Head	Mar	72	M	Cordwainer	Herts	St Albans
764	WATKINS	Catharine	162		Wife	Mar	71	F		Herts	St Albans
765	WATKINS	Thomas	162		Son	Unm	39	M	Cordwainer	Herts	St Albans
766	WATKINS	Edward	162		Son	Unm	40	M	Coach Painter	Herts	St Albans
767	YOUNG	William	163	The Dog, Back Street	Head	Mar	39	M	Victualler	Herts	St Albans
768	YOUNG	Maria	163		Wife	Mar	40	F		Herts	Hemel Hempstead
769	YOUNG	Louisa	163		Dau	Unm	15	F		Herts	Hemel Hempstead
770	YOUNG	Eliza	163		Dau	Unm	12	F		Herts	Hemel Hempstead
771	YOUNG	Edwin	163		Son	Unm	8	M		Herts	Hemel Hempstead
772	PRIM	Mary	163		Lodger	Unm	35	F	Labourer	Herts	Hemel Hempstead
773	BUCKINGHAM	F.W.	163		Lodger	Widower	43	M	Labourer	Ceylon	Colombo (British Subject)
774	JEFFERIES	E.	163		Lodger	Mar	22	M	Tailor	Beds	Sandy
775	JEFFERIES	Ann	163		Lodgers Wife	Mar	24	F		Hants	[Unknown]
776	ANDREWS	Thomas	163		Lodger	Unm	24	M	Labourer	Herts	Bedmond [Abbots Langley]
777	GOOCH	George	164	Back Street	Head	Mar	45	M	Gun Maker	Suffolk	Ipswich
778	GOOCH	Sarah	164		Wife	Mar	31	F		Herts	Hemel Hempstead
779	GOOCH	George	164		Son	Unm	3	M		Herts	St Albans

780	GOOCH	William	164		Son	Unm	2	M		Herts	St Albans
781	GOOCH	Ellen	164		Dau		5 m	F		Herts	St Albans
782	ANSELL	Elizabeth	164		Serv	Unm	18	F	General Servant	Herts	Digswell
783	BURFORD	Frederick	165	Back Street	Head	Mar	33	M	Brazilian Hat Manufacturer	Beds	Luton
784	BURFORD	Mary Ann	165		Wife	Mar	32	F		Beds	Luton
785	BURFORD	Thomas	165		Son	Unm	9	M		[Lancs]	Liverpool
786	BURFORD	Rowena	165		Dau	Unm	1	F		Herts	St Albans
787	BIGNELL	Eliza	165		Serv	Unm	36	F	General Servant	Herts	Royston
788	GILLIGEN	Elizabeth	165		Serv	Unm	14	F	General Servant	Ireland	Boyle

One empty house

789	NEGUS	Robert	166	Market Place	Head	Mar	65	M	Cooper	Beds	Bedford
790	NEGUS	Mary	166		Wife	Mar	65	F		Bucks	Lavendon
791	NEGUS	Mary	166		Dau	Unm	39	F	Blind	Beds	Bedford
792	NEGUS	Ann	166		Dau	Unm	37	F	Bonnet Sewer	Beds	Bedford
793	NEGUS	William	166		Son	Unm	35	M	Cooper	Beds	Bedford
794	NEGUS	Jane	166		Dau	Unm	32	F	Bonnet Sewer	Herts	St Albans
795	NEGUS	Sophia	166		Dau	Unm	29	F	Bonnet Sewer	Herts	St Albans
796	NEGUS	Robert	166		Son	Unm	27	M	Cooper	Herts	St Albans
797	PERRY	Joseph	167	Verulam Street	Head	Mar	28	M	Plumber	Herts	St Albans
798	PERRY	Matilda	167		Wife	Mar	27	F		London	
799	HUGHES	John Philip	168	Verulam Street	Head	Mar	47	M	Upholsterer	Shrop	Shrewsbury
800	HUGHES	Ann	168		Wife	Mar	46	F	Upholsterers Wife	Hereford	Ross
801	DOUGLAS	Joseph	169	St Peter Street	Head	Mar	63	M	Superintendent of Police	Herts	Shenley
802	DOUGLAS	Mary Farr	169		Wife	Mar	45	F	Superintendents Wife	Beds	Holcot
803	DOUGLAS	Elizabeth M.	169		Dau		16	F	Superintendents Daughter	Herts	St Albans
804	DAVIS	Susanna	170	Market Place	Head	Widow	49	F	Fishmonger	London	
805	PEARCE	James	170		Serv	Unm	25	M	Shopman	Herts	St Albans

Two houses uninhabited

806	LATTIMORE	Jeremiah	171	Dagnall Lane	Head	Mar	64	M	Carpenter	Herts	St Albans
807	LATTIMORE	Mary	171		Wife	Mar	53	F		Beds	Woburn
808	HIBBERT	Mary	172	Dagnall Lane	Head	Widow	70	F	Sempstress	Surrey	Amplinton [?] [Addington]
809	HANKS	Lucy	173	Dagnall Lane	Head	Widow	80	F	Laundress	Worcs	Wolverley
810	HANKS	Eliza	173		Dau	Unm	49	F	Bonnet Sewer	Middx	Marylebone
811	HANKS	Amelia	173		Grandau	Unm	13	F	Bonnet Sewer	Middx	Stoke Newington
812	WRIGHT	George	174	Dagnall Lane	Head	Mar	38	M	Stone Mason	Derby	Ashover
813	WRIGHT	Jane	174		Wife	Mar	33	F	Stone Masons Wife	Suffolk	Gusford
814	COZIER	Elizabeth	175	Albion Place	Head	Widow	72	F	Fundholder	Bucks	Brill
815	COZIER	Ann	175		Dau	Unm	36	F	Fundholder	Herts	St Albans
816	MERRINGTON	Alice	175		Sister	Widow	80	F	Fundholder	Bucks	Brill
817	HAGGAR	James	176	Dagnall Lane	Head	Mar	55	M	Servant	Herts	Welwyn
818	HAGGAR	Emma	176		Wife	Mar	48	F		Herts	Hitchin
819	HAGGAR	Caroline	176		Dau	Unm	30	F	Bonnet Sewer	Herts	Hitchin

	SURNAME	FORENAME	SCHEDULE NUMBER	ADDRESS	RELATIONSHIP	STATUS	AGE	SEX	OCCUPATION	COUNTY OF BIRTH	PLACE OF BIRTH
820	HAGGAR	Ann Elizabeth	176		Dau	Unm	18	F	Bonnet Sewer	Herts	Welwyn
821	HAGGAR	Thomas	176		Son	Unm	21	M	Painter	Herts	Ickleford
822	HAGGAR	James	176		Son	Unm	15	M	Servant	Herts	St Albans
823	HAGGAR	Emma	176		Dau	Unm	10	F	Scholar	Herts	St Albans
824	THORN	Anthony	176		Serv	Unm	13	M	Servant	Herts	Colney
825	WILDBOAR	Caroline	177	Dagnall Lane	Head	Unm	38	F	Annuitant	Herts	St Albans
826	WILDBOAR	Hannah	177		Sister	Unm	36	F	Annuitant	Herts	St Albans
827	EMILY?	Sarah	177		Serv	Widow	60	F	House Servant	Herts	St Albans
828	HITCHAM	James	178	The Hope Beer Shop, Dagnall Lane	Head	Mar	50	M	Beer & Coal Seller	Suffolk	Wrentham
829	HITCHAM	Mary	178		Wife	Mar	44	F		Suffolk	Wrentham
830	BLUNDELL	George	178		Lodger	Unm	22	M	Coach Maker	Herts	Baldock
831	STRATTON	Thomas	178		Lodger	Unm	21	M	Coach Maker	Herts	St Albans
832	LITTLE	Charles	178		Lodger	Mar	26	M	Shoemaker	Middx	Hounslow
833	LITTLE	[Unnamed]	178		Lodgers Wife	Mar	28	F	Shoemakers Wife	Middx	Hounslow
834	LITTLE	Charles	178		Lodgers Son	Unm	3	M	Shoemakers Son	Middx	Hounslow
835	GAYTES	George	178		Lodger	Widower	69	M	Butcher	Herts	Stevenage
836	VARNEY	Ann	179	Dagnall Lane	Head	Widow	80	F	Annuitant	Bucks	Wing
837	JOHNSTON	Ann	179		Dau	Mar	42	F	Annuitant	Herts	St Albans
838	HARRIS	Elizabeth	179		Visitor	Mar	48	F		Herts	Ware
839	HYLAND	Elizabeth	180	Dagnall Lane	Head	Widow	42	F	School Mistress	Herts	Colney
840	HYLAND	Elizabeth	180		Dau	Unm	11	F		Herts	St Albans
841	HYLAND	Martha	180		Dau	Unm	7	F		Herts	St Albans
842	WOODFINE	Richard	181	Dagnall Lane	Head	Mar	31	M	Wesleyan Minister	Cheshire	Tushingham
843	WOODFINE	Sophia	181		Wife	Mar	26	F	Ministers Wife	Oxon	Banbury
844	WOODFINE	Alice Ann	181		Dau	Unm	9 m	F		Herts	St Albans
845	HATTON	Amelia	181		Serv	Unm	17	F	General Servant	Hunts	Brampton
846	BROWN	William	182	Dagnall Lane	Head	Mar	60	M	Baker	Beds	Luton
847	BROWN	Eliza	182		Wife	Mar	59	F		Herts	Hemel Hempstead
848	BROWN	Maria	182		Dau	Unm	30	F	Straw Bonnet Maker	Herts	Hemel Hempstead
849	BROWN	Henry	182		Son	Unm	23	M	Plumber	Herts	Hemel Hempstead
850	BROWN	Richard	182		Son	Unm	19	M	Baker	Herts	Hemel Hempstead
851	DAY	Thomas	183	Dagnall Lane	Head	Mar	45	M	Bonnet Blocker	Herts	Wheathampstead
852	DAY	Sarah	183		Wife	Mar	40	F	Plaiter	Herts	Harpenden
853	DAY	Thomas	183		Son	Unm	13	M	Silk Throwster	Herts	Harpenden
854	DAY	Abel	183		Son	Unm	11	M	Silk Throwster	Herts	Harpenden
855	DAY	Eliza Ann	183		Dau	Unm	9	F	Silk Throwster	Herts	Harpenden
856	DAY	Frederick	183		Son	Unm	7	M	Scholar	Herts	Harpenden
857	BUTLER	Thomas	184	Dagnall Lane	Head	Widower	73	M	Tailor	Beds	Woburn
858	BUTLER	Ann	184		Dau	Unm	42	F	Bonnet Maker	Herts	Bushey
859	LATTIMORE	Elizabeth	184		Lodger	Unm	40	F	Bonnet Maker	Herts	St Albans
860	GIDDINS	William	185	Dagnall Lane	Head	Mar	38	M	Post Boy	Beds	Dunstable
861	GIDDINS	Elizabeth	185		Wife	Mar	38	F		Hants	Basingstoke
862	HAMIRE [?]	Mary Ann	186	Dagnall Lane	Head	Mar	43	F	Shoe Binder	London	

863	HAMIRE [?]	Ellen	186		Dau	Unm	20	F	Shoe Binder	Herts	St Albans
864	HAMIRE [?]	Sarah	186		Dau	Unm	14	F	Shoe Binder	Herts	St Albans
865	HAMIRE [?]	Mattey	186		Son	Unm	7	M		Herts	St Albans
866	PUGH	Harriett	187	Dagnall Lane	Head	Unm	52	F	Laundress	Herts	Smallford [St Peters]
867	STONE	George	188	Dagnall Lane	Head	Mar	52	M	Baker	Middx	Pinner
868	STONE	Elizabeth	188		Wife	Mar	52	F		Cambs	Wisbech
869	STONE	Emma	188		Dau	Unm	27	F	Brazilian Hat Maker	London	
870	STONE	Joseph	188		Son	Mar	21	M	Silk Throwster	Herts	St Albans
871	STONE	Charlotte	188		Dau-in-law	Mar	20	F	Silk Throwster	Herts	St Albans
872	STONE	Betsey	188		Dau	Unm	13	F	Hat Maker	Herts	St Albans
873	STONE	Eliash	188		Son	Unm	5	M		Herts	St Albans
874	STONE	Ellen	188		Grandau	Unm	1	F		Herts	St Albans
875	HINDLE	Agnes	189	Dagnall Lane	Head	Widow	49	F	Silk Throwster	Herts	St Albans
876	HINDLE	Henry	189		Son	Unm	22	M	Labourer	Herts	St Albans
877	HINDLE	Mary	189		Dau	Unm	13	F	Hat Maker	Herts	St Albans
878	HOLLOWAY	Jane	189		Lodger	Unm	21	F	Hat Maker	Herts	Harpenden
879	ARNOLD	Amelia	189		Lodger	Unm	19	F	Silk Throwster	Herts	Harpenden
880	ARNOLD	Eliza	189		Lodger	Unm	18	F		Herts	St Albans
881	WARNER	John	190	Dagnall Lane	Head	Mar	55	M	Chimney Sweeper	Beds	Ridgmont
882	WARNER	Sarah	190		Wife	Mar	57	F		London	St Lukes
883	WARNER	John	190		Son	Unm	30	M	Butcher	Beds	Bedford
884	WARNER	George	190		Son	Unm	16	M	Chimney Sweeper	Herts	St Albans
885	WARNER	Susan	190		Dau	Unm	25	F	Chip Hat Maker	Herts	St Albans
886	WARNER	Elizabeth	190		Dau	Unm	21	F	Chip Hat Maker	Herts	St Albans
887	WARNER	Julia	190		Grandau	Unm	4	F	Chip Hat Maker	Herts	St Albans
888	GIDDINS	George	191	Dagnall Lane	Head	Mar	73	M	Post Boy	Beds	Dunstable
889	GIDDINS	Ann	191		Wife	Mar	61	F		Beds	Dunstable
890	GIDDINS	Eliza	191		Dau	Unm	32	F	Dressmaker	Herts	St Albans
891	GIDDINS	Arthur	191		Grandson	Unm	7	M		Herts	St Albans
892	JERMYN	Hannah	192	Dagnall Lane	Head	Unm	74	F	House Owner	Suffolk	Bungay
893	ROLLS	Sarah	192		Lodger	Unm	41	F	Annuitant	Oxon	Bicester
894	GIBBS	Selina A.	192		Niece	Unm	15	F	Scholar	Herts	St Albans
895	MARRIETTE	C.J.A.	193	Dagnall Lane	Head	Unm	23	F	Professor of Languages	France	
896	WELLS	Harry	194	Dagnall Lane	Head	Unm	21	M	Bankers Clerk	Berks	Reading
897	COOPER	Samuel Bolton	195	Dagnall Lane	Head	Mar	41	M	Coach Builder	Lincs	Louth
898	COOPER	Charlotte	195		Wife	Mar	43	F		Cambs	Westwick [?]
899	BURROWS	Ann	195		Mother-in-law	Widow	79	F		Herts	Broomfield [Hatfield]
900	WILKINS	Ann	195		Lodger	Widow	81	F	Retired Coach Builder	Herts	St Albans
901	GARLAND	George	196	Dagnall Lane	Head	Mar	40	M	Mason	Kent	Folkestone
902	GARLAND	Ruth	196		Wife	Mar	28	F		Kent	Chatham
903	GARLAND	Ruth	196		Dau	Unm	8	F	Scholar	Sussex	Cuckfield
904	GARLAND	Martha	196		Dau	Unm	7	F	Scholar	Bucks	Aylesbury
905	GARLAND	Mary	196		Dau	Unm	5	F	Scholar	Sussex	Brighton
906	GARLAND	Esther	196		Dau	Unm	3	F		Norfolk	Lynn [Kings Lynn]

	SURNAME	FORENAME	SCHEDULE NUMBER	ADDRESS	RELATIONSHIP	STATUS	AGE	SEX	OCCUPATION	COUNTY OF BIRTH	PLACE OF BIRTH
907	MARLOW	Elizabeth	196		Serv	Unm	21	F	General Servant	Herts	St Albans
908	BASSIL	Mary	197	Dagnall Lane	Head	Widow	49	F	Proprietor of Houses	Northants	Northampton
909	BASSIL	Jane	197		Dau	Unm	18	F	Dressmaker	Herts	Wheathampstead
910	HUMPHREY	James	198	Abbey Passage, High St	Head	Mar	55	M	Policeman	Herts	Wheathampstead
911	HUMPHREY	Susan	198		Wife	Mar	50	F		[Unknown]	Queens Town [?]
912	HUMPHREY	Ellen	198		Dau	Unm	23	F	Milliner	Herts	Wheathampstead
913	HUMPHREY	Phoebe	198		Dau	Unm	17	F		Herts	St Albans
914	STAMMERS	Charlotte	199		Lodger	Widow	64	F	Annuitant	London	
915	JONES	Simon	200	Abbey Passage, High St	Head	Mar	33	M	Jeweller	Poland	
916	JONES	Martha	200		Wife	Mar	32	F		Bucks	Buckingham
917	JONES	Adelhade	200		Dau	Unm	4	F		Beds	Luton
918	JONES	Indor	200		Son	Unm	2m	M		Herts	St Albans
919	SILVESTER	F.R.	201	London Road	Head	Mar	37	M	Mayor of St Albans	Essex	Colchester
920	SILVESTER	Charlotte	201		Wife	Mar	37	F		[Bucks]	Ditton
921	CLARKE	Emily	201		Serv	Unm	18	F	General Servant	Herts	Lemsford Mills [Hatfield]
922	LONG	Ann	202	London Road	Head	Unm	76	F	Fundholder (Blind)	Herts	Ware
923	WRIGHT	Sarah	202		Visitor	Unm	36	F	Visitor	Bucks	Grove
924	PLUMMER	Rebecca	202		Serv	Unm	34	F	Servant	Herts	Sandridge
925	CHARTERS	John G.	203	London Road	Head	Mar	31	M	Surveyor of Taxes	N'thumb	Berwick-on-Tweed
926	CHARTERS	Sophia A.	203		Wife	Mar	31	F		London	
927	WARRINGTON	Kate	203		Dau-in-law	Unm	7	F	Scholar	Bucks	Colnbrook
928	CHARTERS	Frank H.	203		Son	Unm	6m	M		Herts	St Albans
929	HIBBERT	Sarah	203		Serv	Unm	21	F	General Servant	Herts	Kings Langley
930	WOOD	Joseph	204	4 London Road	Head	Mar	54	M	Proprietor of Houses	Herts	St Albans
931	WOOD	Elizabeth	204		Wife	Mar	51	F		Middx	Islington
932	PARSONS	Elizabeth	204		Serv	Unm	21	F	General Servant	Herts	Kimpton
933	BARRANCE	Henry	205	4 London Road	Head	Mar	37	M	Out of Business at present	Herts	Aldbury
934	BARRANCE	Emma	205		Wife	Mar	27	F		Herts	St Albans
935	BARRANCE	Harry Francis	205		Son	Unm	4	M		Herts	St Albans
936	BARRANCE	John	205		Son	Unm	2	M		Herts	St Albans
937	BARRANCE	Charlotte	205		Dau	Unm	1	F		Herts	St Albans
938	COOK	Alice	205		Serv	Unm	15	F	General Servant	Herts	St Albans
939	STRACEY	Henry	206	3 London Road	Head	Mar	62	M	Dyer	London	Not stated
940	STRACEY	Susanna	206		Wife	Mar	57	F		London	Not stated
941	STRACEY	Susanna	206		Dau	Unm	35	F	Governess	London	Not stated
942	STRACEY	Rebecca	206		Dau	Unm	28	F		London	Not stated
943	STRACEY	Sarah	206		Dau	Unm	25	F	Milliner	London	Not stated
944	STRACEY	George	206		Son	Unm	20	M	Draper	[Herts]	Buntingford
945	AMBROSE	Mary	206		Apprentice	Unm	17	F	Dressmaker	Herts	Hitchin
946	GROVER	Elizabeth	206		Boarder	Unm	11	F	Scholar	Herts	Abbots Langley
947	WILKINS	Letitia	207	London Road	Head	Widow	40	F	Independent	London	
948	WILKINS	Joseph	207		Son	Unm	10	M	Scholar	Herts	Harpenden
949	WILKINS	Letitia	207		Dau	Unm	9	F	Scholar	Herts	Harpenden

950	WILKINS	Ann	207		Dau	Unm	7	F	Scholar	Herts	Harpenden
951	WILKINS	Mary	207		Dau	Unm	5	F	Scholar	Herts	Harpenden
952	WILKINS	Sarah	207		Dau	Unm	4	F		Herts	Harpenden
953	PUDDEPHATT	Mary	207		Serv	Unm	16	F	General Servant	London	
954	HARVEY	George	207		Serv	Unm	15	M	Errand Boy	Herts	St Albans
955	UPTON	William	208	8 London Road	Head	Mar	54	M	Dissenting Minister	London	
956	UPTON	Eliza	208		Wife	Mar	47	F	Principal of Ladies School	Herts	St Albans
957	UPTON	Sarah Amelia	208		Dau	Unm	27	F	Assistant of Ladies School	Herts	St Albans
958	UPTON	Martha Matilda	208		Dau	Unm	15	F	Scholar	Herts	St Albans
959	UPTON	Mary Louisa	208		Dau	Unm	10	F	Scholar	Herts	St Albans
960	WELLS	Mary	208		Pupil	Unm	18	F	Scholar	London	
961	HARRIS	Sarah Ann	208		Pupil	Unm	15	F	Scholar	Herts	Berkhamsted
962	SMITH	Sophia	208		Pupil	Unm	8	F	Scholar	Herts	Elstree
963	BEAUMONT	Georgiana	208		Pupil	Unm	10	F	Scholar	Herts	Park Street [St Stephens]
964	SAKER	Eliza Helen	208		Pupil	Unm	10	F	Scholar	[Cornwall]	Saltash
965	WILKINS	Letitia	208		Pupil	Unm	9	F	Scholar	Herts	Harpenden
966	WOOD	Mary Ann	208		Pupil	Unm	12	F	Scholar	London	
967	WILKINS	Ann	208		Pupil	Unm	8	F	Scholar	Herts	Harpenden
968	WILKINS	Mary	208		Pupil	Unm	6	F	Scholar	Herts	Harpenden
969	WELLS	Miranda	208		Pupil	Unm	13	F	Scholar	Yorks	Leeds
970	OLNEY	Ann	208		Serv	Unm	32	F	Servant	Herts	London Colney
971	FLOYD	William	209	London Road	Head	Mar	28	M	Coach Smith	Herts	Wheathampstead
972	FLOYD	Eliza	209		Wife	Mar	30	F	Weaver	Herts	St Albans
973	ROBESBY [?]	Charles	210	London Road	Head	Mar	47	M	Labourer	Herts	St Albans
974	ROBESBY [?]	Elizabeth	210		Wife	Mar	47	F		Herts	St Albans
975	ROBESBY [?]	Eliza	210		Dau	Unm	21	F	Weaver	Herts	St Albans
976	ROBESBY [?]	Jane	210		Dau	Unm	15	F	Weaver	Herts	St Albans
977	ROBESBY [?]	Frederick	210		Son	Unm	12	M	Errand Boy	Herts	St Albans
978	ROBESBY [?]	Emma	210		Dau	Unm	11	F	Brazilian Hat Maker	Herts	St Albans
979	ROBESBY [?]	Charles	210		Son	Unm	6	M	Scholar	Herts	St Albans
980	ROBESBY [?]	Mary Ann	210		Dau	Unm	1	F		Herts	St Albans
981	HOPKINS	James	211	London Road	Head	Mar	31	M	Labourer	Herts	St Albans
982	HOPKINS	Hannah	211		Wife	Mar	32	F		Herts	St Albans
983	HOPKINS	Henry	211		Son	Unm	8	M		Herts	St Albans
984	HOPKINS	Frederick	211		Son	Unm	6	M		Herts	St Albans
985	HOPKINS	James	211		Son	Unm	10 m	M		Herts	St Albans
986	OAKLEY	William	211		Father	Mar	60	M		Herts	St Albans
987	KEARSLEY	Mark	212	London Road	Head	Mar	41	M	Ostler	Berks	Coxwell
988	KEARSLEY	Mary	212		Wife	Mar	43	F		Berks	Wallingford
989	KEARSLEY	Joseph	212		Son		13	M		Berks	Wallingford
990	KEARSLEY	John	212		Son		11	M		Berks	Wallingford
991	RADWAY	Charles	212		Visitor		2	M		London	Not stated
992	MARSHALL	Charles	213	Woolpack Tap, London Road	Head	Mar	48	M	Victualler	Essex	Takeley
993	MARSHALL	Jane	213		Wife	Mar	51	F	Victuallers Wife	Essex	Dunmow

	SURNAME	FORENAME	SCHEDULE NUMBER	ADDRESS	RELATIONSHIP	STATUS	AGE	SEX	OCCUPATION	COUNTY OF BIRTH	PLACE OF BIRTH
994	RAIMENT	Edward	213		Lodger	Unm	22	M	Mariner	Herts	St Albans
995	TEBBOTH	Richard	214	Peahen Tap, London Road	Head	Mar	55	M	Victualler	Herts	Hertford
996	TEBBOTH	Elizabeth	214		Wife	Mar	65	F		Herts	Barnet
997	LAURENCE	John	215	Cross Street	Head	Mar	37	M	Carpenter	Herts	St Albans
998	LAURENCE	Susan	215		Wife	Mar	37	F		Herts	St Albans
999	LAURENCE	Eliza	215		Dau	Unm	15	F	Scholar	Herts	St Albans
1000	LAURENCE	George	215		Son	Unm	13	M	Scholar	Herts	St Albans
1001	LAURENCE	Emma	215		Dau	Unm	12	F	Scholar	Herts	St Albans
1002	LAURENCE	Louisa	215		Dau	Unm	10	F	Scholar	Herts	St Albans
1003	LAURENCE	John	215		Son	Unm	8	M	Scholar	Herts	St Albans
1004	LAURENCE	Mary	215		Dau	Unm	6	F	Scholar	Herts	St Albans
1005	KEEN	William	216	Cross Street	Head	Mar	43	M	Labourer	Herts	Flamstead
1006	KEEN	Deborah	216		Wife	Mar	42	F	Charwoman	London	
1007	KEEN	Martha	216		Dau	Unm	13	F	Hat Maker	Herts	St Albans
1008	SMITH	John	216		Visitor	Unm	48	M	Annuitant	Herts	St Albans
1009	MARLOW	Mary	217	Cross Street	Head	Widow	58	F	Laundress	Herts	St Albans
1010	MARLOW	Eliza	217		Dau	Unm	20	F	Silk Throwster	Herts	St Albans
1011	MARLOW	Maria	217		Dau	Unm	14	F	Hat Maker	Herts	St Albans
1012	JAMES	Henry	218	Cross Street	Head	Mar	33	M	Labourer	[Bucks]	Shabbington
1013	JAMES	Elizabeth	218		Wife	Mar	31	F	Brazilian Hat Maker	Herts	St Albans
1014	JAMES	Henry	218		Son	Unm	9	M	Scholar	Herts	St Albans
1015	JAMES	Arthur	218		Son		3	M	Scholar	Herts	St Albans
1016	JAMES	Emily	218		Dau		1	F		Herts	St Albans
1017	BALLARD	Martha	218		Lodger	Mar	62	F	Plaiter	Herts	St Albans
1018	BALLARD	Ellen	218		Lodgers Dau	Mar	22	F	Chip Hat Maker	Herts	St Albans
1019	HARPER	Catherine	220	Cross Street	Head	Unm	42	F	Straw Plaiter	Herts	Codicote
1020	PARROTT	Amos	220		Nephew	Unm	18	M	Servant	Herts	Datchworth
1021	PARROTT	Caroline	220		Niece	Unm	14	F	Silk Throwster	Herts	Hertford
1022	CUSTANCE	John	221	Cross Street	Head	Mar	46	M	Ostler	Beds	Dunstable
1023	CUSTANCE	Ann	221		Wife	Mar	50	F	Straw Plaiter	Herts	Redbourn
1024	CUSTANCE	Thomas	221		Son	Unm	17	M	Servant	Herts	St Albans
1025	CUSTANCE	Henry	221		Son	Unm	14	M	Silk Throwster	Herts	St Albans
1026	CUSTANCE	William	221		Son	Unm	8	M	Scholar	Herts	St Albans
1027	CUSTANCE	Daniel	222	Cross Street	Head	Mar	30	M	Cordwainer	Herts	St Albans
1028	CUSTANCE	Eliza	222		Wife	Mar	28	F	Weaver	Herts	St Albans
1029	CUSTANCE	Mary Ann	222		Dau	Unm	7	F	Scholar	Herts	St Albans
1030	CUSTANCE	Rachael	222		Dau	Unm	6	F	Scholar	Herts	St Albans
1031	CUSTANCE	Harriett	222		Dau	Unm	4	F	Scholar	Herts	St Albans
1032	CUSTANCE	Albert	222		Son	Unm	1 m	M		Herts	St Albans
1033	COLLINS	John	223	Cross Street	Head	Mar	46	M	Cooper	Middx	Westminster
1034	BOWMAN	Thomas Dixon	224	London Road	Head	Mar	56	M	Landed Proprietor	Durham	Gateshead
1035	BOWMAN	Catherine	224		Wife	Mar	73	F		Herts	Redbourn
1036	DIXON	Mary	224		Visitor	Unm	82	F	Annuitant	Herts	Redbourn
1037	MOSS	Emma	224		Serv	Unm	21	F	House Servant	Herts	Essendon

1038	VARNEY	Matthew	225	Cross Street	Head	Mar	36	M	Bricklayer	Herts	St Albans
1039	VARNEY	Eliza	225		Wife	Mar	37	F		Herts	St Albans
1040	VARNEY	Sam C. Henry	225		Son	Unm	13	M		Herts	St Albans
1041	VARNEY	Eliza	225		Dau	Unm	10	F		Herts	St Albans
1042	VARNEY	Frederic	225		Son	Unm	8	M		Herts	St Albans
1043	VARNEY	Alfred	225		Son	Unm	6	M		Herts	St Albans
1044	VARNEY	Ann Harriett	225		Dau	Unm	3	F		Herts	St Albans
1045	VARNEY	Henry	225		Son	Unm	4 m	M		Herts	St Albans
1046	WHITE	Charlotte	226	Cross Street	Head	Mar	48	F	Charwoman	Herts	Letchmore Heath [Aldenham]
1047	WHITE	Ben	226		Son	Unm	28	M	Labourer	Herts	Watford
1048	WHITE	William	226		Son	Unm	21	M	Labourer	Herts	Watford
1049	WHITE	Sarah	226		Dau	Unm	14	F	Straw Hat Maker	Herts	Watford
1050	WHITE	John	226		Son	Unm	12	M	Straw Hat Maker	Herts	Watford
1051	WHITE	Daniel	226		Son	Unm	10	M	Straw Hat Maker	Herts	Watford
1052	WHITE	Ann	226		Dau	Unm	4	F	Straw Hat Maker	Herts	St Albans
1053	WELLS	Harriett	227	London Road	Head	Unm	27	F	Principal of Establishment	Middx	Islington
1054	UPTON	Maria	227		Partner	Unm	29	F	Partner of Establishment	Herts	St Albans
1055	ASHWELL	Edward	227		Scholar	Unm	7	M	Scholar	Herts	St Albans
1056	WALKER	Henry	227		Scholar	Unm	8	M	Scholar	Herts	Harpenden
1057	WRIGHT	John Irvine	227		Scholar	Unm	8	M	Scholar	Beds	Luton
1058	BUTTENSHAW	Samuel Edward	227		Scholar	Unm	10	M	Scholar	London	
1059	BUTTENSHAW	Richard James	227		Scholar	Unm	7	M	Scholar	London	
1060	BEAUMONT	William Henry	227		Scholar	Unm	8	M	Scholar	Herts	Park Street [St Stephens]
1061	WILES	Julia	227		Assistant	Unm	16	F	Assistant	Herts	St Albans
1062	ANTHONY	Eliza	227		Serv	Unm	18	F	General Servant	Herts	London Colney
1063	EVANS	James	228	Dog Yard	Head	Mar	33	M	Bricklayers Labourer	Herts	St Albans
1064	EVANS	Mary	228		Wife	Mar	30	F	Weavers Labourer	Herts	St Albans
1065	EVANS	Eliza	228		Dau	Unm	9	F	Silk Throwster	Herts	St Albans
1066	EVANS	Henry	228		Son	Unm	7	M		Herts	St Albans
1067	EVANS	William	228		Son	Unm	3	M		Herts	St Albans
1068	EVANS	James	228		Son	Unm	11 m	M		Herts	St Albans
1069	FORMAN	Sarah	229	Dog Yard	Head	Unm	60	F	Straw Plaiter	Herts	Kings Walden
1070	WEBSTER	Sophia	230	Dog Yard	Head	Widow	68	F	Washerwoman	Surrey	Wandsworth
1071	WEBSTER	Ann	230		Dau	Unm	40	F	Weaver	Herts	St Albans
1072	WEBSTER	Ann	230		Grandau	Unm	5	F		Herts	St Albans
1073	HARCOURT	William	231	Christopher Yard	Head	Mar	63	M	Labourer	Herts	St Albans
1074	HARCOURT	Charlotte	231		Wife	Mar	25	F		Herts	St Albans
1075	HARCOURT	Betsey	231		Dau	Unm	20	F	Hat Maker	Herts	St Albans
1076	HARCOURT	Frederic	231		Son	Unm	16	M	Labourer	Herts	St Albans
1077	HARCOURT	Charles	231		Son	Unm	9	M	Scholar	Herts	St Albans
1078	HARCOURT	Samuel	231		Son	Unm	8	M	Scholar	Herts	St Albans
1079	HARCOURT	William	231		Son	Unm	5	M	Scholar	Herts	St Albans
1080	HARCOURT	Alfred	231		Son	Unm	2	M	Scholar	Herts	St Albans

	SURNAME	FORENAME	SCHEDULE NUMBER	ADDRESS	RELATIONSHIP	STATUS	AGE	SEX	OCCUPATION	COUNTY OF BIRTH	PLACE OF BIRTH
1081	HARCOURT	Emma	231		Dau	Unm	5 m	F		Herts	St Albans
1082	ANDERSON	Sarah	232	Christopher Yard	Head	Unm	54	F	Charwoman	Beds	Hockcliffe
1083	ANDERSON	Anna	232		Sister	Unm	53	F	Charwoman	Beds	Hockcliffe
1084	PERKINS	Rebecca	232		Sister	Widow	50	F	Charwoman	Beds	Hockcliffe
1085	PERKINS	Sarah	232		Grandau		7	F		Beds	Hockcliffe
1086	WILSON	William	233	Christopher Yard	Head	Mar	40	M	Labourer	Herts	St Albans
1087	WILSON	Anna	233		Wife	Mar	38	F	Weaver	Herts	St Albans
1088	WILSON	Mary	233		Dau	Unm	15	F	Silk Throwster	Herts	St Albans
1089	WILSON	William	233		Son	Unm	13	M	Silk Throwster	Herts	St Albans
1090	WILSON	Joseph	233		Son	Unm	10	M	Silk Throwster	Herts	St Albans
1091	DEAMER	James	234	Christopher Yard	Head	Mar	39	M	Cloth Cap Maker	Herts	St Albans
1092	DEAMER	Phoebe	234		Wife	Mar	39	F		Herts	St Albans
1093	BONNICK [?]	William	234		Lodger	Mar	23	M	Tailor	Herts	Redbourn
1094	BONNICK [?]	Charlotte	234		Lodgers Wife	Mar	22	F	Hat Maker	Herts	Rickmansworth
1095	PEACOCK	Thomas	235	Christopher Yard	Head	Mar	56	M	Labourer	Herts	St Albans
1096	PEACOCK	Rebecca	235		Wife	Mar	44	F	Weaver	Herts	St Albans
1097	PEACOCK	Henry	235		Son	Unm	22	M	Labourer	Herts	St Albans
1098	PEACOCK	Eliza	235		Dau	Unm	14	F	Weaver	Herts	St Albans
1099	PEACOCK	Ann	235		Dau	Unm	8	F	Silk Throwster	Herts	St Albans
1100	PEACOCK	Mary	235		Dau	Unm	4	F		Herts	St Albans
1101	KING	John	235		Visitor	Mar	34	M	Sawyer	Herts	St Albans
1102	KING	Martha	235		Visitors Wife	Mar	24	F	Weaver	Herts	St Albans
1103	KING	John	235		Visitors Son	Unm	9	M		Herts	St Albans
1104	KING	Frederic	235		Visitors Son	Unm	5	M		Herts	St Albans
1105	KINGHAM	Emma	236	Christopher Yard	Head	Unm	30	F	Weaver	Herts	St Albans
1106	HALL	William	236		Lodger	Unm	30	M	Labourer	Herts	London Colney
1107	SKINNER	Rebecca	237	Christopher Yard	Head	Mar	62	F	Washerwoman	Herts	St Albans
1108	PEARCE	Jane	238	Christopher Yard	Head	Unm	25	F	Weaver	Herts	St Albans
1109	SKINNER	Robert	238		Lodger	Unm	27	M	Labourer	Herts	St Albans
1110	WHITE	Joseph	238		Lodger	Unm	24	M	Silk Throwster	Herts	St Albans
1111	MARTINDALE	Samuel	239	Christopher Yard	Head	Mar	48	M	Labourer	Herts	Watford
1112	MARTINDALE	Ann	239		Wife	Mar	45	F		Herts	St Albans
1113	GURNEY	Eliza	239		Dau	Unm	23	F	Weaver	Herts	St Albans
1114	MARTINDALE	Ann	239		Dau	Unm	20	F	Weaver	Herts	St Albans
1115	MARTINDALE	Sarah	239		Dau	Unm	15	F	Silk Throwster	Herts	St Albans
1116	MARTINDALE	Elizabeth	239		Dau	Unm	12	F	Silk Throwster	Herts	St Albans
1117	MARTINDALE	Emma	239		Dau	Unm	9	F	Silk Throwster	Herts	St Albans
1118	MARTINDALE	James	239		Son	Unm	6	M	Scholar	Herts	St Albans
1119	MARTINDALE	Jane	239		Dau	Unm	2	F		Herts	St Albans
1120	KINGS	Mary	240	Christopher Yard	Head	Widow	70	F	Sempstress	Herts	St Albans
1121	KINGS	Elizabeth	240		Dau	Unm	35	F	Weaver	Herts	St Albans
1122	SCRIVENER	Thomas	240		Lodger	Unm	36	M	Chair Bottomer	Herts	St Albans
1123	NORTH	Joseph	241	Christopher Yard	Head	Mar	45	M	Labourer	Herts	St Albans
1124	NORTH	Elizabeth	241		Wife	Mar	43	F	Weaver	Herts	St Albans

1125	NORTH	William	241		Son	Unm	14	M	Silk Throwster	Herts	St Albans
1126	NORTH	George	241		Son	Unm	12	M	Silk Throwster	Herts	St Albans
1127	NORTH	Betsey	241		Dau	Unm	8	F	Silk Throwster	Herts	St Albans
1128	NORTH	Thomas	241		Son	Unm	4	M	Scholar	Herts	St Albans
1129	PEARCE	Sarah	241		Mother-in-law	Widow	73	F	Weaver	Herts	St Albans
1130	PEACOCK	William	242	Christopher Yard	Head	Mar	43	M	Bricklayer	Herts	St Albans
1131	PEACOCK	Mary	242		Wife	Mar	40	F	Weaver	Herts	St Albans
1132	PEACOCK	Joseph	242		Son	Unm	21	M	Labourer	Herts	St Albans
1133	PEACOCK	Emma	242		Dau	Unm	19	F	Weaver	Herts	St Albans
1134	PEACOCK	William	242		Son	Unm	16	M	Horsekeeper	Herts	St Albans
1135	PEACOCK	Selina	242		Dau		7wks	F		Herts	St Albans
1136	DENTON	Martha	243	Christopher Yard	Head	Mar	48	F	Plaiter	Herts	Wheathampstead
1137	DENTON	Charles	243		Son	Unm	20	M	Servant at Ironmongers	Herts	Wheathampstead
1138	DENTON	George	243		Son	Unm	16	M		Herts	Sandridge
1139	DENTON	Mary Ann	243		Dau	Unm	18	F	Hat Work	Herts	Sandridge
1140	DENTON	Henry	243		Son	Unm	11	M		Herts	Hemel Hempstead
1141	STRATTON	James	244	Christopher Yard	Head	Mar	46	M	Labourer	Herts	St Albans
1142	STRATTON	Sarah	244		Wife	Mar	42	F		Herts	St Albans
1143	STRATTON	George	244		Son	Unm	22	M	Labourer	Herts	St Albans
1144	STRATTON	Joseph	244		Son	Unm	16	M	Labourer	Herts	St Albans
1145	STRATTON	James	244		Son	Unm	14	M	Silk Throwster	Herts	St Albans
1146	STRATTON	William	244		Son	Unm	11	M	Silk Throwster	Herts	St Albans
1147	STRATTON	Ann	244		Dau	Unm	7	F		Herts	St Albans
1148	STRATTON	Emma	244		Dau	Unm	5	F		Herts	St Albans
1149	STRATTON	Thomas	244		Son	Unm	3	M		Herts	St Albans
1150	MANLOVE	Charles	245	Market Place	Head	Mar	38	M	Ironmonger	Herts	St Albans
1151	MANLOVE	Dorcas	245		Wife	Mar	38	F		Herts	St Albans
1152	MANLOVE	Rosanna	245		Dau	Unm	8	F		Herts	St Albans
1153	MANLOVE	Susanna	245		Dau	Unm	6	F		Herts	St Albans
1154	MANLOVE	Anne Young	245		Dau	Unm	5	F		Herts	St Albans
1155	MANLOVE	Hannah	245		Dau	Unm	4	F		Herts	St Albans
1156	MANLOVE	Dorcas	245		Dau	Unm	3	F		Herts	St Albans
1157	MANLOVE	Emma	245		Dau	Unm	1	F		Herts	St Albans
1158	DAY	Sarah	245		Serv	Unm	20	F	General Servant	Herts	North Mimms
1159	COLES	Alfred	246	Market Place	Head	Unm	24	M	Bread & Biscuit Baker	Bucks	Buckingham
1160	COLES	Samuel	246		Brother	Unm	14	M	Bread & Biscuit Makers Brother	Bucks	Buckingham
1161	COLES	Rebecca	246		Sister	Unm	14	F	Bakers Sister	Bucks	Buckingham
1162	TAYLOR	George	247	Market Place	Head	Mar	46	M	Boot Maker	Herts	St Albans
1163	TAYLOR	Eliza	247		Wife	Mar	34	F	Boot Makers Wife	Middx	Islington
1164	SLAUGHTER	John	247		Nephew		12	M	Scholar	Herts	St Albans
1165	HARTLEY	Elizabeth	248	Christopher Yard	Head	Widow	69	F	Rag Maker	Herts	St Albans
1166	HARTLEY	Esther	248		Dau	Unm	29	F	Weaver	Herts	St Albans
1167	HARTLEY	Mary	248		Dau	Unm	27	F	Charwoman	Herts	St Albans
1168	HARTLEY	Martha	248		Dau	Unm	23	F	Weaver	Herts	St Albans

	SURNAME	FORENAME	SCHEDULE NUMBER	ADDRESS	RELATIONSHIP	STATUS	AGE	SEX	OCCUPATION	COUNTY OF BIRTH	PLACE OF BIRTH
1169	HARTLEY	William	248		Son	Unm	6	M		Herts	St Albans
1170	HARTLEY	Sarah	248		Dau	Unm	3	F		Herts	St Albans
1171	HARTLEY	Emma	248		Dau	Unm	1	F		Herts	St Albans
1172	FRAY	Charlotte	248		Lodger	Mar	33	F	Silk Throwster	Herts	St Albans
1173	FRAY	James	248		Lodgers Son	Unm	15	M	Silk Throwster	Herts	St Albans
1174	FRAY	Ann	248		Lodgers Dau	Unm	12	F	Silk Throwster	Herts	St Albans
1175	FRAY	Rose	248		Lodgers Dau	Unm	6	F		Herts	St Albans
1176	FRAY	Eliza	248		Lodgers Dau	Unm	3	F		Herts	St Albans
1177	FRAY	Emma	248		Lodgers Sister	Unm	20	F	Trimming Feathers	Herts	St Albans
1178	BROOKS	William	249	London Road	Head	Widower	64	M	Retired Architect	London	Holborn
1179	BROOKS	Sophia	249		Dau	Unm	28	F		London	Islington
1180	WALBLATE	Sarah	249		Serv	Unm	20	F	General Servant	Herts	St Albans
1181	COCKEL	Ann	250	Half Moon Yard	Head	Widow	67	F	Sempstress	Herts	St Albans
1182	MOLES	Susan	250		Niece	Unm	25	F	Bonnet Sewer	Herts	St Albans
1183	SMITH	Mary	250		Visitor	Unm	15	F	Silk Throwster	Herts	Watford
1184	CRAMPHORN	Robert	251	Half Moon Yard	Head	Mar	44	M	Gardener	Herts	Widford
1185	CRAMPHORN	Mary	251		Wife	Mar	44	F		Middx	Edgware
1186	CRAMPHORN	David	251		Son	Unm	20	M	Bricklayers Labourer	Herts	St Albans
1187	CRAMPHORN	Mary	251		Dau	Unm	18	F	Brazilian Hat Maker	Herts	St Albans
1188	CRAMPHORN	Henry	251		Son	Unm	16	M	Brazilian Hat Maker	Herts	St Albans
1189	CRAMPHORN	Caroline	251		Dau	Unm	14	F	Brazilian Hat Maker	Herts	St Albans
1190	CRAMPHORN	Sarah	251		Dau	Unm	12	F	Brazilian Hat Maker	Herts	St Albans
1191	CRAMPHORN	Frederic	251		Son	Unm	10	M	Scholar	Herts	St Albans
1192	CRAMPHORN	James	251		Son	Unm	6	M		Herts	St Albans
1193	CRAMPHORN	Anna	251		Dau	Unm	4	F		Herts	St Albans
1194	HARVEY	William	252	Half Moon Yard	Head	Mar	57	M	Tailor	Herts	St Albans
1195	HARVEY	Susan	252		Wife	Mar	55	F	Weaver	Herts	St Albans
1196	HARVEY	Frederic	252		Son	Unm	22	M	Labourer	Herts	St Albans
1197	HARVEY	Joseph	252		Son	Unm	20	M	Labourer	Herts	St Albans
1198	HARVEY	Alfred	252		Son	Unm	16	M	Silk Throwster	Herts	St Albans
1199	HARVEY	Thomas	252		Son	Unm	12	M	Silk Throwster	Herts	St Albans
1200	HARVEY	Edwin	252		Son	Unm	9	M		Herts	St Albans
1201	JONES	Samuel	253	Half Moon Yard	Head	Mar	43	M	Groom	Herts	Codicote
1202	JONES	Mary	253		Wife	Mar	43	F		Herts	Kimpton
1203	JONES	Sarah	253		Dau	Unm	13	F	Scholar	Herts	St Albans
1204	JONES	Emma	253		Dau	Unm	11	F	Scholar	Herts	St Albans
1205	OAKLEY	William	254	Half Moon Yard	Head	Mar	60	M	Brewer	Beds	Woburn
1206	OAKLEY	Elizabeth	254		Wife	Mar	65	F		Beds	Eversholt
1207	OAKLEY	William	254		Son	Unm	28	M	Silk Throwster	Herts	St Albans

Three houses uninhabited

	SURNAME	FORENAME	SCHEDULE NUMBER	ADDRESS	RELATIONSHIP	STATUS	AGE	SEX	OCCUPATION	COUNTY OF BIRTH	PLACE OF BIRTH
1208	OAKLEY	John	255	Half Moon Yard	Head	Mar	26	M	Silk Throwster	Herts	St Albans
1209	OAKLEY	Susan	255		Wife	Mar	28	F	Weaver	London	
1210	OAKLEY	William	255		Son		7	M	Scholar	Herts	St Albans

Two houses uninhabited

1211	MABLETON	Robert	256	Half Moon Yard	Head	Mar	55	M	Labourer	Herts	St Albans
1212	MABLETON	Mary	256		Wife	Mar	54	F		Herts	St Stephens
1213	ANDERSON	William Morris	256		Father	Widower	88	M	Carpenter	Herts	St Stephens
1214	ANDERSON	Emma	256		Grandau [Niece]	Unm	13	F		Herts	St Albans
1215	JONES	Henry	257	Half Moon Yard	Head	Mar	23	M	Groom	Herts	Welwyn
1216	JONES	Alice	257		Wife	Mar	31	F		Essex	Dagenham
1217	BACON	Elizabeth	258	Half Moon Yard	Head	Widow	60	F	Bonnet Sewer	Herts	St Albans
1218	BACON	Charles	258		Son	Mar	26	M	Labourer	Herts	St Albans
1219	BACON	Eliza	258		Dau	Mar	23	F	Brazilian Hat Maker	Herts	St Albans
1220	BACON	George	258		Son	Unm	20	M	Labourer	Herts	St Albans
1221	BACON	Ellen	258		Dau	Unm	17	F	Bonnet Sewer	Herts	St Albans
1222	COPLEY	Joseph (Jnr)	259	Half Moon Yard	Head	Mar	32	M	Labourer	Herts	St Albans
1223	COPLEY	Harriett	259		Wife	Mar	32	F	Trimming Weaver	Herts	Hemel Hempstead
1224	COPLEY	Charles	259		Son	Unm	12	M	Scholar	Herts	St Albans
1225	COPLEY	Sarah	259		Dau	Unm	9	F	Scholar	Herts	St Albans
1226	COPLEY	Henry	259		Son	Unm	7	M	Scholar	Herts	St Albans
1227	COPLEY	Ellen	259		Dau	Unm	4	F	Scholar	Herts	St Albans
1228	COPLEY	Joseph	260	Half Moon Yard	Head	Mar	54	M	Labourer	London	
1229	COPLEY	Diana	260		Wife	Mar	58	F		Herts	St Albans
1230	WEBSTER	George	261	Half Moon Yard	Head	Mar	36	M	Ostler	Herts	St Albans
1231	WEBSTER	Elizabeth	261		Wife	Mar	30	F	Needlewoman	Herts	Little Munden
1232	WEBSTER	Charles	261		Son	Unm	10	M	Scholar	Herts	St Albans
1233	WEBSTER	George	261		Son	Unm	6	M	Scholar	Herts	St Albans
1234	WEBSTER	William	261		Son	Unm	4	M	Scholar	Herts	St Albans
1235	WEBSTER	Emma	261		Dau	Unm	1	F		Herts	St Albans
1236	WARBEY	Charlotte	262	Half Moon Yard	Head	Widow	25	F	Hat Worker	Herts	Welwyn
1237	WARBEY	Alfred	262		Son	Unm	5	M		Herts	St Albans
1238	WARBEY	James	262		Son	Unm	2	M		Herts	St Albans
1239	WARBEY	Fanny	262		Dau	Unm	6wks	F		Herts	St Albans
1240	SMITH	Sarah	262		Sister	Unm	28	F	Weaver	Herts	Welwyn
1241	SMITH	Eliza	262		Dau [Niece]	Unm	9	F	Silk Throwster	Herts	Hatfield
1242	SMITH	Emily	262		Dau [Niece]	Unm	2m	F		Herts	St Albans
1243	FULKNER	Thomas	263	Half Moon Yard	Head	Mar	70	M	Labourer	Herts	Markyate St
1244	FULKNER	Rosanna	263		Wife	Mar	45	F		Herts	St Albans
1245	FULKNER	Ebenezer	263		Son	Unm	19	M	Labourer	Herts	St Albans
1246	HART	George	264	Half Moon Yard	Head	Mar	24	M	Labourer	Beds	Luton
1247	HART	Mary	264		Wife	Mar	28	F	Straw Plaiter	Beds	Luton
1248	PINNOCK	William	265	Half Moon Yard	Head	Mar	40	M	Blacksmith	Herts	Baldock
1249	PINNOCK	Hannah	265		Wife	Mar	41	F		Herts	Park Street [St Stephens]
1250	PINNOCK	Jane	265		Dau	Unm	18	F		Herts	Park Street [St Stephens]
1251	PINNOCK	Eliza	265		Dau	Unm	15	F	Blacksmiths Daughter	Herts	Park Street [St Stephens]

	SURNAME	FORENAME	SCHEDULE NUMBER	ADDRESS	RELATIONSHIP	STATUS	AGE	SEX	OCCUPATION	COUNTY OF BIRTH	PLACE OF BIRTH
1252	PINNOCK	Samuel	265		Son	Unm	10	M		Herts	St Albans
1253	PINNOCK	Rosanna	265		Dau	Unm	8	F		Herts	St Albans
1254	COOPER	Joseph	266	Half Moon Yard	Head	Mar	55	M	Labourer	Herts	St Albans
1255	COOPER	Sarah	266		Wife	Mar	61	F	Laundress	Herts	St Albans
1256	NEVILLE	Edward	267	Half Moon Yard	Head	Mar	32	M	Tailor	Norfolk	Norwich
1257	NEVILLE	Sarah	267		Wife	Mar	27	F	Tailors Wife	Beds	Wootton
1258	NEVILLE	Elizabeth	267		Dau	Unm	2	F		Herts	St Albans
1259	BACON	Anthony	268	Half Moon Yard	Head	Mar	25	M	Labourer	Herts	St Albans
1260	BACON	Elizabeth	268		Wife	Mar	27	F		Herts	St Albans
1261	BACON	George Bassil	268		Son	Unm	10	M	Silk Throwster	Herts	St Albans
1262	BACON	Eliza	268		Dau	Unm	8	F		Herts	St Albans
1263	BACON	Alfred	268		Son	Unm	5	M		Herts	St Albans
1264	NEWELL	John	269	Half Moon Yard	Head	Mar	67	M	Labourer	Beds	[Unknown]
1265	NEWELL	Elizabeth	269		Wife	Mar	66	F		Herts	[Unknown]
1266	MEAD	Mary	270	Half Moon Yard	Head	Widow	40	F	Plaiter	Herts	Wheathampstead
1267	KEMPSTER	Elizabeth	271	Half Moon Yard	Head	Widow	26	F	Straw Plaiter	Bucks	Stewkley
1268	KEMPSTER	Charles Oakley	271		Son	Unm	9	M		Bucks	Cublington
1269	KEMPSTER	Albert Barrows	271		Son	Unm	4	M		Bucks	Aylesbury
1270	RICHARDSON	John Pitt	272	High Street	Head	Mar	43	M	Bookseller	Gloucs	Tewkesbury
1271	RICHARDSON	Jane	272		Wife	Mar	46	F	Milliner	Beds	Luton
1272	KAY	Mary Jane	272		Serv	Unm	18	F	Booksellers Assistant	Lancs	Warrington
1273	JONES	Sarah	272		Serv	Unm	16	F	Milliners Apprentice	Beds	Luton
1274	COOPER	Eliza	272		Serv	Unm	17	F	House Servant	Essex	Swiston [?] [Stisted?]

Registrar's District: St Albans   Enumeration District 4b   Ref. HO 107/1713 folios 398-428

Holywell Ward, comprising Holywell House, Sopwell Lane, with all the yards in Holywell Hill and Sopwell Lane.

	SURNAME	FORENAME	SCHEDULE NUMBER	ADDRESS	RELATIONSHIP	STATUS	AGE	SEX	OCCUPATION	COUNTY OF BIRTH	PLACE OF BIRTH
1275	WHEELER	Frederick	1	Holywell Hill	Head	Mar	42	M	Chemist	Hants	Andover
1276	WHEELER	Emma	1		Wife	Mar	42	F	Chemists Wife	Middx	Holborn
1277	WHEELER	Elizabeth	1		Dau	Unm	12	F	Scholar	Herts	St Albans
1278	WHEELER	Selina	1		Dau		10	F	Scholar	Herts	St Albans
1279	WHEELER	Frederika	1		Dau		6	F	Scholar	Herts	St Albans
1280	HARMON	William Bridon	1		Assistant	Unm	25	M	Chemists Assistant	Middx	Hayes
1281	FIRMAN	Elizabeth	1		Serv	Unm	54	F	Domestic Servant	Herts	Hertford
1282	NASH	John Brossbridge	2	Holywell Hill	Head	Unm	54	M	Alderman and Stationer	Herts	St Albans
1283	KIMPTON	Eliza	2		Serv	Unm	29	F	Servant Housekeeper	Bucks	Stewkley
1284	PEW	Mary	2		Serv	Unm	23	F	Servant	Herts	St Peters
1285	INCE	Sarah	3	Holywell Hill	Head	Unm	54	F	Annuitant	India	Bombay
1286	HULKS	Jesse	4	Holywell Hill	Head	Mar	46	M	Boot And Shoemaker	Herts	St Albans
1287	HULKS	Isabella	4		Wife	Mar	45	F	Boot And Shoemakers Wife	Herts	St Albans
1288	HULKS	David	4		Son		8	M	Scholar	Herts	St Albans
1289	HULKS	Jesse	4		Son		6	M	Scholar	Herts	St Albans
1290	HULKS	Ebenezer	4		Son		3	M		Herts	St Albans

Address	Relation	Condition	Age	Sex	Occupation	County	Birthplace
	Serv	[Unm]	17	F	Servant	Herts	Harpenden
	Visitor	Unm	27	M	Grocer	Herts	St Albans
olywell Hill	Head	Mar	25	M	Linen Draper	Norfolk	Aylsham
	Wife	Mar	29	F	Linen Draper Wife	Herts	Hemel Hempstead
	Son	Unm	2	M	Linen Draper Son	Herts	St Albans
	Brother	Unm	17	M	Linen Draper Assistant	Norfolk	Aylsham
	Serv	Unm	17	F	House Servt Assistant	Wales	[Unknown]
olywell Hill	Head	Mar	30	M	Harness Maker	Middx	Hadley
	Wife	Mar	28	F	Harness Maker Wife	Middx	Southgate
	Son	Unm	7	M	Scholar	Herts	St Albans
	Son	Unm	6	M	Scholar	Herts	St Albans
	Dau	Unm	4	F	Scholar	Herts	St Albans
	Son	Unm	2	M	Scholar	Herts	St Albans
lywell Hill	Head	Mar	36	M	Fruiterer	Herts	St Albans
	Wife	Mar	31	F	Fruiterer Wife	Herts	Redbourn
	Dau	Unm	9	F	Scholar	Herts	St Albans
	Dau	Unm	4	F		Herts	St Albans
	Dau	Unm	1	F		Herts	St Albans
lywell Hill	Head	Mar	44	M	Grocer	Herts	St Albans
	Wife	Mar	42	F	Grocer Wife	Berks	Sulhampstead
	Dau	Unm	13	F	Scholar	Herts	St Albans
	Son	Unm	11	M	Scholar	Herts	St Albans
	Dau	Unm	9	F	Scholar	Herts	St Albans
	Dau	Unm	7	F	Scholar	Herts	St Albans
	Dau	Unm	5	F	Scholar	Herts	St Albans
	Dau	Unm	4	F		Herts	St Albans
	Son	Unm	2	M		Herts	St Albans
ywell Hill	Head	Mar	40	M	Boot & Shoemaker	Herts	Watford
	Wife	Mar	37	F	Boot & Shoemaker Wife	Herts	St Albans
	Dau	Unm	12	F	Scholar	Herts	Watford
	Dau	Unm	4	F		Herts	St Albans
	Cousin	Unm	28	F	Shoe Binder	Herts	Hemel Hempstead
well Hill	Head	Widow	70	F	Grocer	Herts	North Mimms
	Dau	Unm	35	F		Herts	St Albans
	Son	Unm	23	M	Grocers Son	Herts	St Albans
well Hill	Head	Mar	45	M	Hairdresser	Herts	St Albans
	Wife	Mar	50	F	Hairdressers Wife	Herts	St Albans
	Son	Unm	15	M	Solicitors Clerk	Herts	St Albans
	Sister-in-law	Unm	33	F	Dressmaker	Herts	St Albans
well Hill	Head	Mar	47	M	Baker	Oxon	Oxford
	Wife	Mar	49	F	Bakers Wife	Herts	Gaddesden
	Son	Unm	22	M	Artist Painting	Herts	St Albans
	Son	Unm	20	M	Baker	Herts	St Albans
	Son	Unm	16	M	Baker	Herts	St Albans

	SURNAME	FORENAME	SCHEDULE NUMBER	ADDRESS	RELATIONSHIP	STATUS	AGE	SEX	OCCUPATION	COUNTY OF BIRTH	PLACE OF BIRTH
1335	WESTALL	Slenia [?]	12		Dau	Unm	12	F		Herts	St Albans
1336	WESTELL	Mary	12		Dau	Unm	10	F		Herts	St Albans
1337	WESTELL	Thomas	12		Son	Unm	6	M		Herts	St Albans
1338	CLAY [DAY?]	William	13	Holywell Hill	Head	Mar	24	M	Tin Plate Worker	Herts	St Albans
1339	CLAY [DAY?]	Elizabeth	13		Wife	Mar	25	F	Tin Plate Workers Wife	Herts	St Albans
1340	CLAY [DAY?]	Emma	13		Dau	Unm	6	F	Scholar	Herts	St Albans
1341	CLAY [DAY?]	Celina	13		Dau	Unm	1	F		Herts	St Albans
1342	NASH	Edwd	14	Holywell Hill	Head	Mar	34	M	Labourer	Herts	St Albans
1343	NASH	Mary	14		Wife	Mar	29	F	Straw Plait Worker	Herts	St Albans
1344	NASH	Fanny	14		Dau	Unm	10	F	Scholar	Herts	St Albans
1345	BISNEY	Mary Ann	14	Holywell Hill	Head	Widow	60	F	Proprieter of Houses	Herts	St Albans
1346	HISKETH	Elizabeth	15	Holywell Hill	Head	Widow	73	F	Shoemaker	Herts	Hatfield
1347	ANGEL	Elizabeth	15		Dau	Mar	43	F	Milliner	Middx	St James
1348	ANGEL	William	15		Son-in-law	Mar	29	M	Plumber	Herts	Hatfield
1349	HISKETH	William	15		Son	Unm	33	M	Bootmaker	Middx	St James
1350	HISKETH	Emma	15		Dau	Unm	26	F	Milliner	Herts	St Albans
1351	ANGEL	Alfred	15		Grandson	Unm	5	M		Herts	St Albans
1352	ANGEL	Robert	15		Grandson	Unm	2	M		Herts	St Albans
1353	TURNER	Ann	16	Holywell Hill	Head	Unm	23	F	Hatmaker	Herts	Watford
1354	HAYWARD	Francis	17	Holywell Hill	Head	Unm	40	M	Victualler	Sussex	[Unknown]
1355	HAYWARD	Elizabeth	17		Dau	Unm	17	F	Hatmaker	Herts	St Albans
1356	MOLES	Thomas	17		Boarder	Unm	41	M	Labourer	India	
1357	HONNOR	John Walter	18	Holywell Hill	Head	Mar	56	M	Grocer	Herts	St Stephens
1358	HONNOR	Sarah	18		Wife	Mar	61	F	Grocer Wife	Herts	Hatfield
1359	HOWE	George	18		Serv	Unm	23	M	Shopman	Herts	Abbots Langley
1360	ENGLAND	Joseph	18		Serv	Unm	19	M	Porter	Herts	St Stephens
1361	JARVIS	Martha	19	Holywell Hill	Head	Widow	57	F	Lodger House Keeper	Somerset	Axbridge
1362	DODD	Robert James	20	Holywell Hill	Head	Unm	16	M	Carpenter & Joiner	Middx	Spitalfields
1363	EWER	James	21	Holywell Hill	Head	Mar	32	M	Painter	N'thumb	North Shields
1364	NUNN	Charles	22	Holywell Hill	Head	Unm	28	M	Tinplate Worker	Suffolk	Beccles
1365	DAY	Jemima	23	Holywell Hill	Head	Mar	52	F	Housekeeper	Herts	Colney Heath
1366	DAY	Charles	23		Son	Unm	32	M	Straw Trimming Weaver	Middx	Shenley
1367	GREGORY	Ann	23		Dau	Mar	27	F	Domestic	Middx	Shenley
1368	GREGORY	George	23		Son-in-law	Mar	27	M	Stone Mason	Herts	St Albans
1369	GOODYEAR	Emma	23		Dau	Mar	21	F	Straw Bonnet Sewer	Herts	St Albans
1370	GREGORY	Emma	23		Grandau	Unm	5	F	Scholar	Herts	St Albans
1371	GOODYEAR	Frederick	23		Grandson	Unm	10 m	M		Herts	St Albans
1372	JACKSON	Sarah	23		Visitor	Unm	28	F	Visitor	Herts	Redbourn
1373	NICHOLSON	Henry	24	Holywell Hill	Head	Mar	55	M	Rector Of St Albans	Middx	Marylebone
1374	NICHOLSON	Mary	24		Wife	Mar	48	F	Rector Of St Albans Wife	Surrey	Esher
1375	ANDREWS	Susan	24		Serv	Unm	25	F	Cook	Norfolk	Marhan
1376	CHERRY	Emma	24		Serv	Unm	22	F	Housemaid	Herts	St Albans
1377	LAWFORD	James	24		Serv	Unm	17	M	Footman	Herts	St Albans

on p. 568 (currently numbered 171-186)

1378	DEBENHAM	George	25	Orchard House	Head	Mar	44	M	Attorney At Law	Suffolk	Ixworth Thorpe
1379	DEBENHAM	Fanny	25		Wife	Mar	36	F	Wife	Kent	Lewisham
1380	DEBENHAM	Lucilia Margaret	25		Dau	Unm	9	F	Scholar	Kent	Lee
1381	DEBENHAM	Cecilia	25		Dau	Unm	11	F	Scholar	Kent	Lee
1382	DEBENHAM	Rosalie Fanny	25		Dau	Unm	5	F	Scholar	Kent	Lee
1383	DEBENHAM	Alfred Herbert	25		Son	Unm	2	M		Kent	Lee
1384	WILLMOTT	Catherine	25		Sister-in-law	Unm	32	F		Kent	Lewisham
1385	BULLEN	Thomas G	25		Nephew	Unm	17	M	Articled Clerk	Suffolk	Bury St Edmunds
1386	BULLEN	Susan Dora	25		Niece	Unm	14	F	Scholar	Suffolk	Bury St Edmunds
1387	BROAD	Esther Mary	25		Serv	Unm	40	F	Domestic Servant	Middx	St Georges
1388	HOLTON	Jane Phelps	25		Serv	Unm	25	F	Domestic Servant	Middx	Fulham
1389	LIVICK	James	25		Serv	Unm	26	M	Domestic Servant	Suffolk	Ixworth
1390	SITTLE	Annah	25		Serv	Widow	22	F	Domestic Servant	Suffolk	Tostock
1391	WEBSTER	Fred F	26	Holywell Hill	Head	Mar	39	M	Surgeon	Herts	St Albans
1392	WEBSTER	Sarah	26		Wife	Mar	35	F	Surgeon Wife	Herts	Markyate
1393	WEBSTER	Sarah Ridley	26		Dau	Unm	14	F	Scholar	Herts	St Albans
1394	WEBSTER	Fanny Anne	26		Dau	Unm	13	F	Scholar	Herts	St Albans
1395	HARRIS	John	27	Holywell Hill	Head	Mar	67	M	Independent Minister	Shrop	Shrewsbury
1396	HARRIS	Ann	27		Wife	Mar	70	F	Independent Ministers Wife	Notts	Nottingham
1397	HARRIS	Mary Ann	27		Dau	Unm	36	F		Shrop	Whitchurch
1398	DOTTKIN	Ann	27		Serv	Unm	21	F	Servant	Cambs	Melbourn
1399	BUNN	Robert	28	Holywell Hill	Head	Mar	29	M	Millwright	Suffolk	Ipswich
1400	BUNN	Mary Ann	28		Wife	Mar	34	F	Dressmaker	Northants	Gayton
1401	BACON	Rosana	28		Niece	Unm	3	F		Herts	St Albans
1402	UNWIN	George	29	Holywell Hill	Head	Unm	19	M	Weaver	Herts	St Albans
1403	SMITH	William	30	Holywell Hill	Head	Unm	17	M	Weaver	Herts	St Albans
1404	WELCH	John	31	Holywell Hill	Head	Unm	22	M	Baker	Herts	St Albans
1405	EDWARDS	John	32	Holywell Hill	Head	Unm	21	M	Weaver	Herts	St Albans
1406	WILLSON	Simpson	33	Holywell Hill	Head	Mar	23	M	Publican	Herts	St Albans
1407	WILLSON	Maria	33		Wife	Mar	23	F	Publican Wife	Herts	St Albans
1408	WILLSON	Sarah	33		Dau	Unm	7m	F		Herts	St Albans
1409	CHARFONT	Abel	34	Holywell Hill	Head	Mar	49	M	Carrier	Middx	Hammersmith
1410	CHARFONT	Eliza	34		Wife	Mar	32	F	Carrier Wife	Herts	St Albans
1411	CHARFONT	Maryann Jane	34		Dau	Unm	7m	F		Herts	St Albans
1412	DAVIS	George	35	Holywell Hill	Head	Unm	36	M	Bootmaker	Herts	St Albans
1413	DAVIS	Mary Ann	35		Sister	Unm	30	F	Grocer	Herts	St Albans
1414	DAVIS	Jane	35		Sister	Unm	22	F	Grocer	Herts	St Albans
1415	RADWAY	Edward	36	Holywell Hill	Head	Unm	60	M	Currier	Gloucs	Cirencester
1416	DICKIE	John	37	Holywell Hill	Head	Unm	21	M	Draper	Scotland	[Unknown]
1417	COLLINGWOOD	Thomas	38		Lodger	Mar	33	M	Cordwainer	Middx	Harefield
1418	MAUGER	John	38		Lodger	Mar	32	M	Musician	Germany	
1419	MAUGER	Elizabeth	38		Lodge'rs Wife	Mar	23	F	Musicians Wife	Bucks	West Wycombe

	SURNAME	FORENAME	SCHEDULE NUMBER	ADDRESS	RELATIONSHIP	STATUS	AGE	SEX	OCCUPATION	COUNTY OF BIRTH	PLACE OF BIRTH
1420	DOUGLAS	Robert	38		Lodger	Mar	28	M	Actor	Scotland	[Unknown]
1421	DOUGLAS	Ann	38		Lodgers Wife	Mar	23	F	Actress	Scotland	[Unknown]
1422	EVERETT	James	39	Holywell Hill	Head	Mar	44	M	Publican	Essex	South Weald
1423	EVERETT	Jane	39		Wife	Mar	47	F	Publicans Wife	Herts	Welwyn
1424	EVERETT	Jane S	39		Dau	Unm	15	F	Dress Maker	Herts	St Albans
1425	EVERETT	Charles	39		Son	Unm	14	M	Scholar	Herts	St Albans
1426	EVERETT	George	39		Son	Unm	7	M	Scholar	Herts	St Albans
1427	EVERETT	Sarah Ann	39		Dau	Unm	5	F	Scholar	Herts	St Albans
1428	NUTKINS	Charles	39		Nephew	Unm	20	M	Labourer	Herts	St Albans
1429	KING	Stephen	39		Lodger	Widower	70	M	Hairdresser	Herts	St Albans
1430	SMITH	Henry Tony	39		Lodger	Unm	61	M	Labourer	Herts	St Stephens
1431	BREECH	John	39		Lodger	Mar	50	M	Hairdresser	Herts	St Albans
1432	ROBINSON	Thomas	39		Lodger	Unm	21	M	Tailor	Chester [Cheshire]	Whitegate
1433	FARRUL	Jevoy	39		Lodger	Unm	20	M	Tailor	Ireland	
1434	BARNARD	William	40	Holywell Hill	Head	Mar	33	M	Baker	Suffolk	Honington
1435	BARNARD	Elizabeth	40		Wife	Mar	27	F	Baker Wife	Middx	London
1436	BARNARD	James	40		Son	Unm	5	M		Yorks	Bradford
1437	BARNARD	William	40		Son	Unm	1	M		Herts	St Albans
1438	BREWER	William	41	Holywell Hill	Head	Unm	41	M	Labourer	Bucks	Newport Pagnell
1439	BREWER	Eliza	41		Dau	Unm	11	F	Scholar	Herts	St Albans
1440	DEAYTON	Thomas	42	Holywell Hill	Head	Mar	44	M	Sergeant At Mace	Herts	St Albans
1441	DEAYTON	Lydia	42		Wife	Mar	35	F	Wife	Herts	Hatfield
1442	DEAYTON	Thomas	42		Son	Unm	16	M	Straw Hat Maker	Herts	St Albans
1443	DEAYTON	James	42		Son	Unm	14	M	Straw Hat Maker	Herts	St Albans
1444	DEAYTON	Lydia	42		Dau	Unm	12	F		Herts	St Albans
1445	DEAYTON	William Edward	42		Son	Unm	10	M		Herts	St Albans
1446	GREGORY	Samuel	42	Holywell Hill	Head	Mar	60	M	Mason	Cheshire	Waverton
1447	GREGORY	Elizabeth	42		Wife	Mar	55	F	Baker	Kent	Dover
1448	GREGORY	Elizabeth	42		Dau	Unm	31	F	Bonnet Sewer	Middx	Brentford
1449	GREGORY	Ann	42		Dau	Unm	18	F	Bonnet Sewer	Herts	St Albans
1450	GREGORY	Alfred	42		Son		15	M	Servant	Herts	St Albans
1451	GREGORY	Samuel	42		Son		12	M	Servant	Herts	St Albans
1452	GREGORY	Jane	42		Dau		10	F	Scholar	Herts	St Albans
1453	DAVIS	Elizabeth	42		Dau	Mar	27	F	Bonnet Sewer	Herts	St Albans
1454	DAVIS	Emma	42		Grandau		5	F	Scholar	Herts	St Albans
1455	DAVIS	Samuel	42		Grandson		4	M	Scholar	Herts	St Albans
1456	OAR	Ann	43	Holywell Hill	Head	Widow	71	F	Hat Maker	Herts	Hatfield
1457	OAR	Eliza	43		Dau	Unm	24	F	Weaver	Herts	Berkhamsted
1458	OAR	Cornelius	43		Grandson	Unm	7	M		Herts	St Albans
1459	OAR	William	43		Grandson	Unm	1	M		Herts	St Albans
1460	WILSON	William	44	Holywell Hill	Head	Mar	45	M	Tailor	Herts	St Albans
1461	WILSON	Mary Ann	44		Wife	Mar	43	F	Tailors Wife	Herts	St Albans
1462	WILSON	Charlton	44		Son	Unm	25	M	Tailor	Herts	St Albans
1463	WILSON	Henry	44		Son	Unm	23	M	Silk Throwster	Herts	St Albans

1464	WILSON	William	44		Son	Unm	21	M	Groom	Herts	St Albans
1465	WILSON	Alfred	44		Son	Unm	15	M	Weaver	Herts	St Albans
1466	WILSON	Walter	44		Son	Unm	13	M	Scholar	Herts	St Albans
1467	WILSON	John	44		Son	Unm	11	M	Scholar	Herts	St Albans
1468	MILLIGAN	Mary	44		[blank]	Widow	75	F		Bucks	Chalfont St Peter
1469	OSBORN	William Thomas	45	Holywell Hill	Head	Mar	69	M	School Master	Herts	Redbourn
1470	OSBORN	Elizabeth	45		Wife	Mar	80	F	School Masters wife	Herts	Markyate
1471	OSBORN	Charles G H	45		Son	Unm	37	M	Salem Poor Law Commissioner	Herts	St Albans
1472	OSBORN	Catherine	45		Sister	Unm	65	F	Housekeeper	Herts	Redbourn
1473	GREGORY	Mary	46	Holywell Hill	Head	Widow	56	F	Baker	Essex	Notley
1474	GREGORY	Eliza	46		Dau	Unm	35	F	School Mistress	Herts	St Albans
1475	BLIGHT	Ann	46		Niece	Unm	9	F	Scholar	Staffs	Wolverhampton
1476	BROOKS	James	46		Serv	Unm	21	M	Baker	Herts	Redbourn
1477	STEPNEY	Jersey	46		Serv	Unm	15	M	Baker	Herts	St Albans
1478	DEAR	John	47	Holywell Hill	Head	Unm	54	M	Grocer	Herts	Baldock
1479	SEWELL	James	48	Holywell Hill	Head	Unm	65	M	Veterinary Surgeon	Herts	Wheathampstead
1480	TITMUSS	Mary	48		Serv	Unm	28	F	Housekeeper	Herts	Wheathampstead
1481	OAKLEY	George	49	Holywell Hill	Head	Mar	30	M	Baker	Herts	Barnet
1482	OAKLEY	Eliza	49		Wife	Mar	30	F	Bakers Wife	Middx	London
1483	OAKLEY	Eliza	49		Dau	Unm	12	F	Hat Maker	Herts	St Albans
1484	OAKLEY	George	49		Son	Unm	10	M	Hat Maker	Herts	St Albans
1485	OAKLEY	Thomas	49		Son	Unm	8	M	Scholar	Herts	St Albans
1486	OAKLEY	Ann	49		Dau	Unm	7	F	Scholar	Herts	St Albans
1487	OAKLEY	William	49		Son	Unm	6	M	Scholar	Herts	St Albans
1488	OAKLEY	Emma	49		Dau	Unm	3	F		Herts	St Albans
1489	FITCH	James	50	Holywell Hill	Head	Unm	74	M	Propretor Of Houses	Middx	London
1490	RICHARDSON	Eliza	50		Niece	Unm	20	F	Housekeeper	Herts	Hatfield
1491	SHANE	Eliza	50		Serv	Unm	30	F	Domestic Servt	Somerset	Bruton
1492	OSBALDESTON	F.I.	51	Holywell Hill	Head	Mar	49	M	Solicitor & Coroner for Herts	Herts	Hatfield
1493	OSBALDESTON	Rose	51		Wife	Mar	39	F	Wife	Herts	Hatfield
1494	OSBALDESTON	Rose	51		Dau	Unm	17	F		Herts	St Albans
1495	OSBALDESTON	Henry	51		Son	Unm	15	M		Herts	St Albans
1496	OSBALDESTON	Lavinia	51		Dau	Unm	13	F		Herts	St Albans
1497	OSBALDESTON	Charles	51		Son	Unm	12	M		Herts	St Albans
1498	OSBALDESTON	Francis	51		Son	Unm	10	M		Herts	St Albans
1499	OSBALDESTON	Catherine	51		Dau	Unm	9	F		Herts	St Albans
1500	OSBALDESTON	Helen M	51		Dau	Unm	3	F		Herts	St Albans
1501	MARMERY	Susan	51		Serv	Unm	62	F	Domestic Servant	Northants	Daventry
1502	HIBBERT	Leonard	52	Holywell Hill	Head	Mar	53	M	Butcher	Surrey	Croydon
1503	HIBBERT	Elizabeth Chapple	52		Wife	Mar	50	F	Hatmaker	Herts	Bedmond [Abbots Langley]
1504	HIBBERT	Ann	52		Dau	Unm	24	F	Hatmaker	Herts	Kings Langley
1505	HIBBERT	Elizabeth	52		Dau	Unm	22	F	Hatmaker	Herts	Kings Langley
1506	HIBBERT	Frances	52		Dau	Unm	19	F	Hatmaker	Herts	Kings Langley
1507	HIBBERT	Henry Shay	52		Son	Unm	17	M	Butcher	Herts	Kings Langley

	SURNAME	FORENAME	SCHEDULE NUMBER	ADDRESS	RELATIONSHIP	STATUS	AGE	SEX	OCCUPATION	COUNTY OF BIRTH	PLACE OF BIRTH
1508	HIBBERT	Thomas	52		Son	Unm	16	M	Errand Boy	Herts	Kings Langley
1509	HIBBERT	William	52		Son	Unm	13	M	Hatmaker	Herts	Bedmond [Abbots Langley]
1510	HIBBERT	George	52		Son	Unm	11	M	Hatmaker	Herts	St Albans
1511	HAIR	William	53	Holywell Hill	Head	Unm	56	M	Clerk to Solicitors Office	Scotland	[Unknown]
1512	HAIR	Sarah	53		Sister	Unm	58	F	House Keeper	Herts	St Albans
1513	HAIR	Annie E.	53		Niece	Unm	24	F		London	St Andrews
1514	SANDERS	George	54	Holywell Hill	Head	Mar	33	M	Coal Merchant	Herts	St Michaels
1515	SANDERS	Amy	54		Wife	Mar	38	F	Wife	Beds	Houghton Conquest
1516	NORWOOD	Susan	54		Serv	Unm	35	F	Domestic Servant	Herts	St Stephens
1517	DRAPER	John	55	Holywell Hill	Head	Mar	35	M	Inland Revenue Officer	Wilts	Chippenham
1518	DRAPER	Elizabeth	55		Wife	Mar	37	F	Wife	London	
1519	DRAPER	James I	55		Son	Unm	7	M	Scholar	London	
1520	DRAPER	John	55		Son	Unm	5	M	Scholar	Northants	Northampton
1521	DRAPER	Sarah E	55		Dau	Unm	3	F	Scholar	Herts	St Albans
1522	DRAPER	Henry	55		Son		7m	M		Herts	St Albans
1523	FERNEL	Esther	56	Holywell Hill	Head	Widow	59	F	Landed Proprietress	London	
1524	FERNEL	Emma	56		Dau	Unm	36	F		London	
1525	SHAWBROOK	Ann	56		Serv	Unm	16	F	Domestic Servt	Herts	Wheathampstead
1526	YORSTON	Eliza	57	Holywell Hill	Head	Mar	28	F		Ne'lands	Ghent
1527	YORSTON	John	57		Son	Unm	7	M		Middx	Turnham Green
1528	YORSTON	Sheridan	57		Son	Unm	5	M		Herts	St Albans
1529	YORSTON	William	57		Son	Unm	2	M		Essex	Chelmsford
1530	YORSTON	Walker	57		Son	Unm	6m	M		Herts	St Albans
1531	EDWARDS	Caroline	57		Serv	Unm	19	F	House Servant	Herts	St Albans
1532	DISHER	Henry	58	Holywell Hill	Head	Mar	34	M	Brazier	Herts	Redbourn
1533	DISHER	Harriett	58		Wife	Mar	27	F	Brazier Wife	Herts	St Albans
1534	MARTIN	Thomas	59	Holywell Hill	Head	Mar	25	M	Blacksmith	Herts	St Stephens
1535	MARTIN	Hannah	59		Wife	Mar	25	F	Weaver	Herts	St Peters
1536	MARTIN	Elizabeth	59		Mother	Widow	56	F	Dressmaker	Herts	St Stephens
1537	MARTIN	Charles	59		Brother	Unm	23	M	Blacksmith	Herts	St Stephens
1538	MARTIN	Susan	59		Sister	Unm	13	F	Hatmaker	Herts	St Stephens
1539	LOGGAN	Charles	60	Holywell Hill	Head	Mar	31	M	Gardener	Herts	St Albans
1540	LOGGAN	Elizabeth	60		Wife	Mar	30	F	Wife	Cambs	Linton
1541	LOGGAN	Theodore	60		Son	Unm	3	M		Herts	St Albans
1542	LOGGAN	William	60		Son	Unm	1	M		Herts	St Albans
1543	JEFFS	Ann	61	Holywell Hill	Head	Widow	73	F	Laundress	Essex	Stratford
1544	WILKINS	Elizabeth	61		Niece	Unm	35	F	Hatmaker	Essex	Stratford
1545	WILKINS	William	61		Nephew	Unm	27	M	Shoemaker	Herts	St Albans
1546	WILKINS	Charles	61		Nephew	Unm	7m	M		Herts	St Albans
1547	HALE	M A	62	Holywell Hill	Head	Mar	32	F	Straw Bonnet Maker	Herts	Markyate
1548	HALE	Archibald	62		Son	Unm	7m	M		Herts	St Albans
1549	HOWARD	William	62		Visitor	Mar	23	M	Silk Throwster	Herts	St Albans
1550	HOWARD	Ellenor	62		Visitors Wife	Mar	23	F	Silk Throwsters Wife	Middx	Highgate
1551	HOWARD	George	62		Visitors Son	Unm	1m	M		Herts	St Albans

1552	CATLIN	John	63	Holywell Hill	Head	Mar	32	M	Beer Seller	Herts	St Stephens
1553	CATLIN	Elizabeth	63		Wife	Mar	35	F	Beer Sellers Wife	Herts	St Stephens
1554	CATLIN	Eliza	63		Dau	Unm	8	F	Scholar	Herts	St Stephens
1555	CATLIN	Martha	63		Dau	Unm	5	F	Scholar	Herts	St Stephens
1556	CATLIN	Emma	63		Dau	Unm	1	F		Herts	St Stephens
1557	CATLIN	George	63		Visitor	Unm	31	M	Labourer	Herts	St Peters
1558	MALES	Joseph	63		Visitor	Unm	32	M	Labourer	Herts	St Albans
1559	PENNEY	James	63		Visitor	Unm	31	M	Labourer	Herts	Redbourn
1560	CASTLE	Ann	64	Holywell Hill	Head	Unm	23	F	Dress Maker	Herts	Flamstead
1561	CASTLE	Charles MacDaniel	64		Son	Unm	3	M		Herts	St Albans
1562	CASTLE	Caroline	64		Sister	Unm	17	F	Straw Hat Maker	Herts	Flamstead
1563	SMITH	Matilda	65	Holywell Hill	Head	Unm	24	F	Trimming Weaver	Herts	Kinsbourne Green [Harpenden]
1564	SLOUGH	James	66	Holywell Hill	Head	Mar	47	M	Gardener	Herts	Wheathampstead
1565	SLOUGH	Tessa	66		Wife	Mar	46	F	Gardener Wife	Herts	St Albans
1566	SLOUGH	Joseph	66		Son	Unm	22	M	Silk Throwster	Herts	St Albans
1567	SLOUGH	Lucy	66		Dau	Unm	15	F	Straw Hat Maker	Herts	St Albans
1568	SLOUGH	Mary	66		Dau	Unm	14	F	Straw Hat Maker	Herts	St Albans
1569	SLOUGH	Mark	66		Son	Unm	4	M		Herts	St Albans
1570	DOUSE	James	67	Holywell Hill	Head	Mar	33	M	Labourer	Herts	Abbots Langley
1571	DOUSE	Eliza	67		Wife	Mar	31	F	Straw Hat Maker	Herts	Flamstead
1572	CADDINGTON	Emma	67		Niece	Unm	12	F	Straw Hat Maker	Beds	Pepperstock [?]
1573	FARNESS	Mary	67		Visitor	Unm	19	F	Straw Hat Maker	Herts	Watford
1574	RUSSELL	Joseph	68	Holywell Hill	Head	Unm	47	M	Gentleman	Herts	St Albans
1575	REECE	Mary	68		Serv	Unm	40	F	Servant	Gloucs	Bristol
1576	LIGHTFOOT	Thomas	69	Holywell Hill	Head	Mar	33	M	Maltster	Herts	Childwick [St Michaels]
1577	LIGHTFOOT	Lydia	69		Wife	Mar	35	F	Maltsters wife	Herts	Walden
1578	LIGHTFOOT	Mary Ann	69		Dau	Unm	8	F	Scholar	Herts	St Albans
1579	LIGHTFOOT	George	69		Son	Unm	7	M	Scholar	Herts	St Albans
1580	LIGHTFOOT	Ann	69		Dau	Unm	3	F		Herts	St Albans
1581	LIGHTFOOT	Hellen	69		Dau	Unm	1	F		Herts	St Albans
1582	HEALEY	George	70	Holywell Hill	Head	Unm	26	M	Commercial Traveller	Herts	St Albans
1583	LIGHTFOOT	Joseph	70		Visitor	Unm	36	M	Labourer	Herts	Childwick [St Michaels]
1584	ATTWOOD	Caroline	70		Visitor	Unm	19	F	Bonnet Sewer	Herts	Harpenden
1585	LANE	Charlotte?	70		Visitor	Unm	15	F	Silk Throwster	Somerset	[Unknown]
1586	BROWN	William	70		Head	Mar	54	M	Grocer	Middx	Hadly
1587	BROWN	Mary	70		Wife	Mar	54	F		Herts	Aldenham
1588	BROWN	Mary	70		Dau	Unm	17	F		Herts	Hemel Hempstead
1589	BROWN	Robert	70		Son	Unm	13	M		Herts	St Albans
1590	ELSTON	John	70		Visitor	Mar	55	M	Eating House Keeper	Middx	Staines
1591	HAWKINS	William	70		[blank]	Mar	65	M		Middx	Staines
1592	HARDING	Thomas	71	Sopwell Lane	Head	Mar	67	M	Fishmonger	London	
1593	HARDING	Mary	71		Wife	Mar	69	F		Herts	St Albans
1594	THORNTON	Jane	71		Dau-in-law	[blank]	38	F		Herts	St Albans

	SURNAME	FORENAME	SCHEDULE NUMBER	ADDRESS	RELATIONSHIP	STATUS	AGE	SEX	OCCUPATION	COUNTY OF BIRTH	PLACE OF BIRTH
1595	SMITH	Keziah	72	Sopwell Lane	Head	Widow	50	F	Loom Weaver	Herts	St Albans
1596	POWELL	Hannah	72		[blank]	Unm	20	F	Loom Weaver	Herts	Sandridge
1597	RUSKEN	Hannah	72		[blank]	Unm	20	F	Loom Weaver	Herts	St Stephens
1598	HIGGINS	Mary	73	Sopwell Lane	Head	Widow	70	F		Herts	Great Gaddesden
1599	HIGGINS	Mary Anne	73		Dau	Unm	40	F	Trimming Maker Hats	Herts	St Albans
1600	HIGGINS	Elizabeth	73		Dau	Unm	33	F	Trimming Maker Hats	Herts	St Albans
1601	HIGGINS	Charlotte	73		Dau	Unm	29	F	Trimming Maker Hats	Herts	St Albans
1602	HIGGINS	William	73		Son	Unm	20	M	Trimming Maker Hats	Herts	St Albans
1603	HIGGINS	Eliza	73		Dau	Unm	18	F	Trimming Maker Hats	Herts	St Albans
1604	CORLEY	Susan	74	Sopwell Lane	Head	Widow	54	F	Trimming Manufacturer	Herts	St Albans
1605	CORLEY	Harriet	74		Dau	Unm	27	F	Trimming Manufacturer	Herts	St Albans
1606	CORLEY	Ann	74		Dau	Unm	30	F	Trimming Manufacturer	Herts	St Albans
1607	GILES	Fanny	75	Sopwell Lane	Head	Widow	66	F	Nurse	Herts	Hemel Hempstead Bushey
1608	GILES	Elizabeth	75		Dau	Unm	40	F	Silk Weaver	Herts	
1609	GILES	George	75		Son	Unm	36	M	Loom Weaver	Herts	Great Stanmore
1610	GILES	Emma	75		Dau		13	F	Hat Maker	Herts	St Albans
1611	GILES	Charles	75		Son		8	M	Hat Maker	Herts	St Albans
1612	GILES	James	75		Son		3	M		Herts	St Albans
1613	HALL	James	76	Sopwell Lane	Head	Mar	32	M	Labourer	Herts	St Peters
1614	HALL	Anne	76		Wife	Mar	30	F		Herts	St Albans
1615	NEWELL	Henry	77	Sopwell Lane	Head	Mar	33	M	Labourer	Herts	St Albans
1616	NEWELL	Eliza	77		Wife	Mar	30	F		Herts	St Albans
1617	NEWELL	William	77		Son		5	M		Herts	St Albans
1618	NEWELL	John	77		Son		3	M		Herts	St Albans
1619	CORLEY	John	78	Sopwell Lane	Head	Mar	32	M	Pipe Maker	Herts	St Albans
1620	CORLEY	Martha	78		Wife	Mar	31	F		Herts	St Albans
1621	CORLEY	Elizabeth	78		Dau		8	F		Herts	St Albans
1622	CORLEY	William	78		Son		6	M		Herts	St Albans
1623	CORLEY	Clara	78		Dau		4	F		Herts	St Albans
1624	CORLEY	John	78		Son		1	M		Herts	St Albans
1625	HALL	Thomas	78		Lodger	Unm	19	M	Labourer	Herts	St Albans
1626	HARDEY	John	79	Sopwell Lane	Head	Mar	33	M	Sawyer	Herts	St Albans
1627	HARDEY	Elizabeth	79		Wife	Mar	33	F		Beds	Bedford
1628	HARDEY	Eliza	79		Dau		6	F	Scholar	Herts	St Albans
1629	HARDEY	Ann	79		Dau		1	F		Herts	St Albans
1630	KING	Rosannah	80	Sopwell Lane	Head	Unm	25	F	Trimming Maker	Herts	St Albans
1631	KING	Medora	80		Dau		6	F	Scholar	Herts	St Albans
1632	FOFIELD	Catherine	80		Lodger	Unm	22	F	Silk Worker	Bucks	Chesham
1633	WELCH	James	81	Sopwell Lane	Head	Unm	33	M	Silk Throwster	Warks	Birmingham
1634	PRATT	William	82	Sopwell Lane	Head	Mar	51	M	Timber Merchant	Surrey	Peckham
1635	PRATT	Sarah	82		Wife	Mar	55	F	Bonnet Maker	Herts	St Stephens
1636	CORLEY	Eliza	82		Grandau		8	F	Scholar	Herts	St Albans
1637	COOPER	Eliza	82		Lodger	Unm	26	F	Bonnet Sewer	Herts	St Michaels
1638	CORLEY	William	83	Sopwell Lane	Head	Mar	32	M	Straw Hat Manufacturer	Herts	St Albans

1639	CORLEY	Eliza	83		Wife	Mar	30	F	Straw Hat Manufacturer	Herts	St Albans
1640	CORLEY	Emily	83		Dau		6	F		Herts	St Albans
1641	CORLEY	Alice	83		Dau		4	F		Herts	St Albans
1642	CORLEY	Alfred	83		Son		2	M		Herts	St Albans
1643	FULLER	Eliza	83		Visitor	[blank]	26	F	Bonnet Sewer	Herts	Hatfield
1644	GURNEY	Thomas	84	Sopwell Lane	Head	Mar	48	M	Labourer	Herts	St Stephens
1645	GURNEY	Hannah	84		Wife	Mar	56	F		Herts	St Albans
1646	GURNEY	Elizabeth	84		Dau	Unm	27	F	Bonnet Sewer	Herts	St Albans
1647	BIGGS	John	85	Sopwell Lane	Head	Mar	29	M	Bricklayer	Herts	Sandridge
1648	BIGGS	Eliza	85		Wife	Mar	32	F	Bonnet Sewer	Herts	St Albans
1649	BIGGS	Ellen	85		Dau		8	F	Scholar	Herts	St Albans
1650	BIGGS	Charles	85		Son		6	M	Scholar	Herts	St Albans
1651	HUGHES	George	86	Sopwell Lane	Head	Mar	82	M	Gardener	Hants	Strathfield Saye
1652	HUGHES	Maria	86		Wife	Mar	70	F	Laundress	Ireland	[Unknown]
1653	HOWARD	Joseph	86		Head	Mar	50	M	Labourer	Herts	South Mimms
1654	HOWARD	Hannah	86		Wife	Mar	46	F		Herts	Hadley
1655	HOWARD	Emma	86		Dau		11	F	Hatmaker	Herts	St Albans
1656	HOWARD	David	86		Son		8	M		Herts	St Albans
1657	EDWARDS	Samuel	87	Sopwell Lane	Head	Mar	35	M	Maltster	Herts	St Stephens
1658	EDWARDS	Lydia	87		Wife	Mar	29	F		Herts	Gaddesden
1659	EDWARDS	John	87		Son		10	M		Herts	Bushey
1660	EDWARDS	William	87		Son		7	M		Herts	Bushey
1661	EDWARDS	Eliza	87		Dau		5	F		Herts	St Albans
1662	EDWARDS	Amelia	87		Dau		2	F		Herts	St Albans
1663	EDWARDS	Sarah	87		Dau		1 m	F		Herts	St Albans
1664	COOK	Eliza	87		Lodger	Unm	20	F	Weaver	Herts	St Albans
1665	HOWARD	Emma	87		Lodger	Unm	18	F	Straw Worker	Herts	St Albans

One house unoccupied

1666	WATKINS	Henry	88	Sopwell Lane	Head	Mar	28	M	Labourer	Herts	St Albans
1667	WATKINS	Eliza	88		Wife	Mar	29	F		Herts	Berkhamsted
1668	LOW	James	89	Sopwell Lane	Head	Mar	66	M	Labourer	Beds	[Unknown]
1669	LOW	Betsey	89		Wife	Mar	51	F		Herts	[Unknown]
1670	ANDERSON	John	90	Sopwell Lane	Head	Mar	61	M	Carpenter	Herts	Baldock
1671	ANDERSON	Kitty	90		Wife	Mar	59	F	Bonnet Sewer	Herts	Markyate
1672	ANDERSON	Harriet	90		Dau	Unm	24	F	Trimming Maker	Herts	St Albans
1673	ANDERSON	Emma	90		Dau	Unm	22	F	Trimming Maker	Herts	St Albans
1674	KING	William	91	Sopwell Lane	Head	Mar	53	M	Labourer	Warks	Long Compton
1675	KING	Ann	91		Wife	Mar	49	F		Herts	Harpenden
1676	KING	Selina	91		Dau	Unm	19	F	Hatmaker	Herts	Harpenden
1677	KING	Maria	91		Dau	Unm	17	F	Hatmaker	Herts	St Albans
1678	KING	Louisa	91		Dau	Unm	15	F	Hatmaker	Herts	St Albans
1679	KING	Eliza	91		Dau		11	F	Scholar	Herts	St Albans
1680	KING	William	91		Son		6	M	Scholar	Herts	Harpenden
1681	SKINNER	William	92	Sopwell Lane	Head	Mar	37	M	Labourer	Herts	St Michaels

	SURNAME	FORENAME	SCHEDULE NUMBER	ADDRESS	RELATIONSHIP	STATUS	AGE	SEX	OCCUPATION	COUNTY OF BIRTH	PLACE OF BIRTH
1682	SKINNER	Martha	92		Wife	Mar	40	F		Herts	Shenley
1683	SHARP	Thomas	92		Brother-in-law	Unm	23	M	Lamp Lighter	Herts	St Albans
1684	BUTCHER	Mary	93	Sopwell Lane	Head	Mar	63	F	Harness Makers wife	Herts	St Albans
1685	CATLIN	William	94	Sopwell Lane	Head	Mar	62	M		Herts	St Albans
1686	CATLIN	Susan	94		Wife	Mar	35	F		Herts	St Albans
1687	CATLIN	William	94		Son		15	M	Scholar	Herts	St Albans
1688	CATLIN	Joseph	94		Son		12	M	Scholar	Herts	St Albans
1689	CATLIN	Elizabeth	94		Dau		10	F	Scholar	Herts	St Albans
1690	CATLIN	Henry	94		Son		5	M	Scholar	Herts	St Albans
1691	CATLIN	Isaac	94		Son		2	M		Herts	St Albans
1692	EDMONDS	William	95	Sopwell Lane	Head	Mar	52	M	Publican	Herts	St Albans
1693	EDMONDS	Ann	95		Wife	Mar	52	F	Plait Dealer	Herts	Sandridge
1694	LAMBETH	Joseph	95		Nephew	Unm	21	M	Bonnet Presser	Herts	Sandridge
1695	LACY	John	95		Visitor	Unm	23	M	Unknown	London	
1696	GRIFFEN	Elizabeth	95		Visitor	Unm	19	F	Milliner & Bonnet Maker	Devon	Bradford
1697	JOHNSON	William	96	Sopwell Lane	Head	Unm	23	M	Coal Dealer	Middx	Chelsea
1698	COX	Thomas	97	Sopwell Lane	Head	Mar	50	M	Horse Keeper	Beds	Gayns [?]
1699	COX	Mary	97		Wife	Mar	51	F	Trimming Maker	Herts	Cashell [Cassio?]
1700	SEARS	Joseph	97		Lodger	Unm	22	M	Hand Weaver	Herts	St Albans
1701	NORTHWOOD	Francis	98	Sopwell Lane	Head	Mar	57	M	Pensioner	Beds	Maulden
1702	NORTHWOOD	Elizabeth	98		Wife	Mar	49	F		Herts	St Albans
1703	NORTHWOOD	Frederick	98		Son		12	M	Labourer	Herts	Colney
1704	NORTHWOOD	Charles	98		Son		10	M	Labourer	Herts	Colney
1705	NORTHWOOD	James	98		Son		5	M	Scholar	Herts	St Albans
1706	LAMBETH	Samuel	99	Sopwell Lane	Head	Mar	49	M	Porter	Herts	St Albans
1707	LAMBETH	Jane	99		Dau	Unm	19	F	Weaver	Herts	Colney
1708	LAMBETH	James	99		Son	Unm	16	M	Horse Keeper	Herts	Colney
1709	LAMBETH	Sarah	99		Dau		13	F	Hat Maker	Herts	St Albans
1710	BLENDALL	John Robert	100	Sopwell Lane	Head	Unm	19	M	Handloom Weaver	Herts	Stanstead
1711	CRAWLEY	James	101	Sopwell Lane	Head	Mar	47	M	Labourer	Middx	Stanmore
1712	CRAWLEY	Charlotte	101		Wife	Mar	38	F		Herts	St Albans
1713	CRAWLEY	Emma	101		Dau		12	F	Scholar	Herts	St Albans
1714	CRAWLEY	William	101		Son		10	M	Scholar	Herts	St Albans
1715	CRAWLEY	Sarah	101		Dau		2	F		Herts	St Albans
1716	DAWSON	Sarah	102	Sopwell Lane	Head	Widow	62	F	Laundress	Herts	St Albans
1717	OSMAN	William	103	Sopwell Lane	Head	Mar	32	M	Labourer	Herts	Great Berkhamsted
1718	OSMAN	Mary	103		Wife	Mar	32	F	Hand Loom Weaver	Herts	St Albans
1719	OSMAN	John	103		Son		4	M		Herts	St Albans
1720	OSMAN	Harriet	103		Dau		2	F		Herts	St Albans
1721	EVANS	Harriet	103		Mother	[blank]	69	F	Formerly Laundress	London	St Faith
1722	POCOCK	Margaret	104	Sopwell Lane	Head	Unm	70	F	Hawker	Herts	St Stephens
1723	RUSKIN	Charlotte	105	Sopwell Lane	Head	Mar	42	F	Trimming Weaver	Herts	Hatfield
1724	RUSKIN	Elizabeth	105		Dau	Unm	18	F	Trimming Weaver	Herts	St Peters

1725	RUSKIN	Emily	105		Dau	Unm	15	F	Trimming Weaver	Herts	St Stephens
1726	RUSKIN	Eliza	105		Dau		14	F	Trimming Weaver	Herts	St Albans
1727	RUSKIN	William	105		Son		10	M	Scholar	Herts	St Albans
1728	RUSKIN	Mary Ann	105		Dau		6	F	Scholar	Herts	St Albans
1729	RUSKIN	Louisa	105		Dau		4	F	Scholar	Herts	St Albans
1730	RUSKIN	James	105		Son		2	M		Herts	St Albans
1731	CROW	Elizabeth	106	Sopwell Lane	Head	Widow	60	F	Grocer	Lincs	Cottesgrove
1732	CRAWLEY	Caroline	106		Serv	Unm	15	F	Servant	Herts	St Albans
1733	PARKS	Joseph	107	Sopwell Lane	Head	Mar	27	M	Carpenter	Herts	St Albans
1734	PARKS	Harriet	107		Wife	Mar	24	F	Trimming Manufacturer	Herts	St Albans
1735	HIGDON	James	108	Sopwell Lane	Head	Unm	46	M	Butcher	Herts	Hatfield
1736	BUDD	Mary	108		H'keeper	Unm	33	F	Housekeeper	Surrey [Hants]	Liphook
1737	HALL	James	109	Sopwell Lane	Head	Mar	38	M	Labourer	Herts	Park Street [St Stephens]
1738	HALL	Mary	109		Wife	Mar	32	F	Straw Hat Maker	Herts	Park Street [St Stephens]
1739	HALL	Emily	109		Dau		10	F	Straw Hat Maker	Herts	Park Street [St Stephens]
1740	HALL	Mary	109		Dau		7	F		Herts	Park Street [St Stephens]
1741	HALL	Arthur	109		Son		5	M		Herts	Park Street [St Stephens]
1742	HALL	George	109		Son		3	M		Herts	Park Street [St Stephens]
1743	HALL	Sarah Jane	109		Dau		4m	F		Herts	Park Street [St Stephens]
1744	GLASSCOCK	George	110	Sopwell Lane	Head	Mar	40	M	Grocer	Herts	St Albans
1745	GLASSCOCK	Jemima	110		Wife	Mar	22	F		Herts	St Albans
1746	GLASSCOCK	William	110		Son	Unm	15	M		Herts	St Albans
1747	GLASSCOCK	Mary Ann	110		Dau		13	F		Herts	St Albans
1748	GLASSCOCK	Hannah	110		Dau		8	F		Herts	St Albans
1749	GLASSCOCK	George	110		Son		10	M	Scholar	Herts	St Albans
1750	GLASSCOCK	Edward	110		Son		5	M	Scholar	Herts	St Albans
1751	GLASSCOCK	Francis	110		Son		3m	M		Herts	St Albans
1752	DAVIS	Thomas	111	Sopwell Lane	Head	Mar	46	M	Salesman	Herts	Wheathampstead
1753	DAVIS	Ann	111		Wife	Mar	30	F	Bonnet Sewer	Herts	St Michaels
1754	DAVIS	Henry	111		Son		13	M	Hat Maker	Herts	Wheathampstead
1755	DAVIS	Nathaniel	111		Son		11	M	Hat Maker	Herts	Wheathampstead
1756	BURGOINE	Mary	112	Sopwell Lane	Head	Widow	42	F	Plaiter	Beds	Luton
1757	BURGOINE	Mary	112		Dau	Unm	18	F	Canvas Weaver	Herts	Wheathampstead
1758	BURGOINE	Martha	112		Dau	Unm	16	F	Canvas Weaver	Herts	Wheathampstead
1759	BURGOINE	James	112		Son		13	M	Straw Hat Maker	Herts	St Peters
1760	BURGOINE	Joseph	112		Son		11	M	Straw Hat Maker	Herts	St Peters
1761	BURGOINE	Thomas	112		Son		7	M	Straw Hat Maker	Herts	St Peters
1762	BURGOINE	Elizabeth	112		Dau		5	F		Herts	St Peters
1763	BURGOINE	William	112		Son		3	M		Herts	St Peters
1764	BURGOINE	Charles	112		Son		2m	M		Herts	St Albans
1765	SHUFFIELD	John	113	Sopwell Lane	Head	Mar	37	M	Labourer	Herts	North Mimms
1766	SHUFFIELD	Flowers	113		Wife	Mar	38	F	Plaiter	Herts	St Peters
1767	SHUFFIELD	William	113		Son	Unm	16	M	Farm Labourer	Herts	St Peters

	SURNAME	FORENAME	SCHEDULE NUMBER	ADDRESS	RELATIONSHIP	STATUS	AGE	SEX	OCCUPATION	COUNTY OF BIRTH	PLACE OF BIRTH
1768	SHUFFIELD	Joseph	113		Son		12	M	Farm Labourer	Herts	St Peters
1769	SHUFFIELD	James	113		Son		9	M	Farm Labourer	Herts	St Peters
1770	SHUFFIELD	John	113		Son		7	M		Herts	St Peters
1771	SHUFFIELD	Charles	113		Son		5	M		Herts	St Peters
1772	SHUFFIELD	Ann	113		Dau		2	F		Herts	St Peters
1773	BOWDON	William	114	Sopwell Lane	Head	Mar	40	M	Labourer	Herts	St Albans
1774	BOWDON	Ann	114		Wife	Mar	39	F	Labourers Wife	Herts	St Albans
1775	BOWDON	Ann	114		Dau		4	F		Herts	St Albans
1776	BOWDON	William	114		Son		2	M		Herts	St Albans
1777	LEE	Mary	115	Sopwell Lane	Head	Unm	22	F	Straw Plaiter	Beds	Dunstable
1778	SHARP	Amelia	116	Sopwell Lane	Head	Mar	45	F		Middx	Uxbridge
1779	SHEARS	Amelia	116		Dau	Mar	27	F	Trimming Maker	Herts	St Stephens
1780	SHARP	Matilda	116		Dau	Unm	20	F	Trimming Maker	Herts	St Stephens
1781	SHARP	Stephen	116		Grandson		6	M		Herts	St Stephens
1782	SHARP	Jane	116		Grandau		1	F		Herts	St Stephens
1783	FURNESS	William	116		Boarder		6	M		Herts	St Michaels
1784	GARDNER	Frederick	117	Sopwell Lane	Head	Mar	32	M	Labourer	Beds	Dunstable
1785	GARDNER	Sarah	117		Wife	Mar	28	F	Trimming Maker Hat	Herts	St Albans
1786	NEWELL	John	118	Sopwell Lane	Head	Unm	21	M	Trimming Maker Hat	Kent [Middx]	Brompton
1787	GLADMAN	Mary	119	Sopwell Lane	Head	Mar	63	F		Herts	St Stephens
1788	GLADMAN	Fanny	119		Dau	Unm	20	F	Straw Hat Maker	Herts	St Albans
1789	BAKER	Mary	119		Grandau		11	F	Straw Hat Maker	Herts	St Albans
1790	GLADMAN	Sarah	119		Grandau		10 m	F		Herts	St Albans
1791	CROFT	Hannah	119		Boarder	Widow	45	F	Silk Throwster	London	
1792	MUNT	Charlotte	119		Boarder	Mar	29	F	Silk Throwster	Herts	St Albans
1793	BRACEY	George	119		Boarder	Unm	25	M	Silk Throwster	Herts	Hatfield
1794	BATEMAN	James	119		Boarder		4	M		Herts	St Albans
1795	FISHER	George	119		Boarder	Unm	30	M	Silk Throwster	Herts	Hatfield
1796	CORLEY	Jane	120	Sopwell Lane	Head	Widow	34	F	Dressmaker	Herts	St Albans
1797	CORLEY	John	120		Son	Unm	15	M	Canvas Maker	Herts	St Albans
1798	CORLEY	William	120		Son		10	M	Silk Throwster	Herts	St Albans
1799	CORLEY	Louisa	120		Dau		8	F	Brazilian Hat Maker	Herts	St Albans
1800	CORLEY	Samuel	120		Son		6	M		Herts	St Albans
1801	CORLEY	George	120		Son		4	M		Herts	St Albans
1802	CORLEY	Joseph	120		Son		3wks	M		Herts	St Albans
1803	OAKLEY	George	121	Sopwell Lane	Head	Mar	37	M	Labourer	Herts	St Albans
1804	OAKLEY	Sarah	121		Wife	Mar	35	F	Labourers Wife	Herts	St Albans
1805	OAKLEY	George	121		Son		6	M	Labourers Son	Herts	St Albans
1806	OAKLEY	Maria	121		Dau		2	F	Labourers Daughter	Herts	St Albans
1807	DAVIS	William	122	Sopwell Lane	Head	Mar	40	M	Verger Of The Abbey	Herts	St Albans
1808	DAVIS	Eliza	122		Wife	Mar	40	F	Laundress	Herts	St Albans
1809	DAVIS	Ellen	122		Dau	Unm	17	F	Brazilian Hat Maker	Herts	St Albans
1810	DAVIS	Eliza	122		Dau		15	F	Brazilian Hat Maker	Herts	St Albans
1811	DAVIS	Jane Sarah	122		Dau		9	F	Scholar	Herts	St Albans

1812	DAVIS	Mary Ann	122		Dau		6	F	Scholar	Herts	St Albans
1813	DAVIS	Samuel	122		Son		4	M	Scholar	Herts	St Albans
1814	DAVIS	Emma	122		Dau		1	F		Herts	St Albans
1815	BROWN	Elijah	123	Sopwell Lane	Head	Mar	51	M	Labourer	Bucks	Helsborough
1816	BROWN	Elizabeth	123		Wife	Mar	49	F	Shoe Binder	[Unknown]	On The Lea
1817	BRANDEN	Samuel	123		Boarder	Unm	22	M	Labourer	Herts	St Albans
1818	JEFFS	William	124	Sopwell Lane	Head	Mar	69	M	Labourer	Herts	St Peters
1819	JEFFS	Ann	124		Wife	Mar	56	F	Plaiter	Herts	St Peters
1820	JEFFS	Joseph	124		Son	Unm	26	M	Labourer	Herts	St Albans
1821	JEFFS	John	124		Son	Unm	22	M	Hand Loom Weaver	Herts	St Albans
1822	JEFFS	Ann	124		Dau	Unm	19	F	Brazilian Hat Maker	Herts	St Albans
1823	JEFFS	Jane	124		Dau	Unm	16	F	Brazilian Hat Maker	Herts	St Albans
1824	JEFFS	William	124		Son		8	M	Brazilian Hat Maker	Herts	St Albans
1825	STRATTON	John	125	Sopwell Lane	Head	Unm	53	M	Labourer	Herts	St Peters
1826	STRATTON	William	125		Son	Unm	18	M	Labourer	Herts	St Albans
1827	STRATTON	John	125		Son		11	M	Brazilian Hatter	Herts	St Albans
1828	STAPLES	Samuel	126	Sopwell Lane	Head	Mar	53	M	Labourer	Herts	St Albans
1829	STAPLES	Sarah	126		Wife	Mar	49	F	Trimming Maker	Herts	Hatfield
1830	STAPLES	Jane	126		Dau	Unm	21	F	Silk Throwster	Herts	St Albans
1831	STAPLES	Henry	126		Son		11	M	Silk Throwster	Herts	St Albans
1832	STAPLES	Sarah	126		Dau		8	F	Brazilian Hat Maker	Herts	Harpenden
1833	ARNOLD	Charles	127	Sopwell Lane	Head	Mar	28	M	Groom	Herts	Marford
1834	ARNOLD	Harriet	127		Wife	Mar	21	F	Grooms Wife	Herts	St Albans
1835	ARNOLD	Ann	127		Dau		1	F	Grooms Daughter	Herts	St Albans
1836	ARNOLD	Edward Dolling	127		Son		4m	M	Grooms Son	Herts	St Albans
1837	BATES	Ann	127		Visitor	Unm	15	F	Plaiter	Herts	Park Street [St Stephens]
1838	GRIMSHAW	Mary	128	Sopwell Lane	Head	Unm	22	F	Bonnet Sewer	Beds	Leighton Buzzard
1839	HARDY	William	129	Sopwell Lane	Head	Mar	63	M	Carrier	Herts	St Albans
1840	HARDY	Elizabeth	129		Wife	Mar	65	F		Bucks	Brickhill
1841	HARDY	William	129		Son	Unm	18	M	Carrier	Herts	St Albans
1842	KNIGHT	George	130	Sopwell Lane	Head	Mar	44	M	Green Grocer	Herts	Hardmead [Great Amwell]
1843	KNIGHT	Maria	130		Wife	Mar	50	F	Green Grocers Wife	Beds	Leighton Buzzard
1844	KNIGHT	Sarah	130		Dau	Unm	13	F	Green Grocers Daur	Beds	Dunstable
1845	LINES	Susanah	130		Head	Widow	74	F	House Holder	Beds	Stanford
1846	VILES	Ann	130		Grandau	Unm	29	F	Disabled	Herts	St Albans
1847	VILES	Sarah	130		Grandau	Unm	25	F	Straw Worker	Herts	St Albans
1848	VILES	Eliza	130		Grandau	Unm	22	F	Silk Worker	Herts	St Albans
1849	VILES	Thomas	130		Grandson	Unm	19	M	Silk Worker	Herts	St Albans
1850	LEWIS	Thomas	131	Sopwell Lane	Head	Mar	50	M	Labourer	Herts	Wheathampstead
1851	LEWIS	Mary	131		Wife	Mar	54	F	Labourer Wife	Herts	Baldock
1852	WARWICK	Jane	131		Grandau	Mar	32	F		Herts	St Albans
1853	WARWICK	William	131		Grandson [in-law]	Mar	29	M	Masons Labourer	Herts	St Albans
1854	WARWICK	Jane	131		Gt. Grandau		7	F	Straw Worker	Herts	St Albans

	SURNAME	FORENAME	SCHEDULE NUMBER	ADDRESS	RELATIONSHIP	STATUS	AGE	SEX	OCCUPATION	COUNTY OF BIRTH	PLACE OF BIRTH
1855	WARWICK	Ann	131		Gt. Grandau		5	F		Herts	St Albans
1856	WARWICK	George	131		Gt. Grandson		2	M		Herts	St Albans
1857	WARWICK	Alfred	131		Gt. Grandau		4m	M		Herts	St Albans
1858	LEWIS	Charlotte	131		Dau	Unm	25	F	Brazilian Hat Maker	Herts	St Michaels
1859	LEWIS	Sarah	131		Dau	Unm	23	F	Brazilian Hat Maker	Herts	St Peters
1860	LEWIS	William	131		Son	Unm	17	M	Brazilian Hat Maker	Herts	St Peters
1861	LEWIS	Ruth	131		Dau		14	F	Brazilian Hat Maker	Herts	St Peters
1862	LEWIS	George	131		Grandson		2	M		Herts	St Albans
1863	LEWIS	Mary	131		Grandau		2	F		Herts	St Albans
1864	MARBY [MAILEY]	George	131		Visitor	Unm	26	M	Labourer	Herts	St Michaels
1865	STEARN	George	132	Sopwell Lane	Head	Mar	44	M	Shoemaker	Middx	London
1866	STEARN	Phillis	132		Wife	Mar	40	F		Herts	Kensworth
1867	BAREHAM	Sarah	132		[Step-]Dau	Unm	16	F	Scholar	Bucks	Aylesbury
1868	STEARN	Harriet	132		Dau		8	F	Scholar	Bucks	Aylesbury
1869	STEARN	Emma	132		Dau		3	F	Scholar	Herts	St Albans
1870	STEARN	Phillis	132		Dau		1m	F		Herts	St Albans
1871	WHITE	William	133	Sopwell Lane	Head	Mar	42	M	Labourer	Herts	Kimpton
1872	WHITE	Ruth	133		Wife	Mar	52	F	Plaiter	Herts	Digswell
1873	DRAPER	Charles	133		Nephew		14	M	Hatter	Herts	Kimpton
1874	SHARPE	William	134	Sopwell Lane	Head	Mar	32	M	Labourer	Herts	Colney Street [St Peters]
1875	SHARPE	Elizabeth	134		Wife	Mar	31	F	Weaver	Herts	Sandridge
1876	SCRIVENER	Thomas	135	Sopwell Lane	Head	Mar	60	M	Sieve Maker	Herts	St Albans
1877	SCRIVENER	Mary	135		Wife	Mar	56	F	Seive Makers Wife	Ireland	Caslow
1878	SCRIVENER	Edward	135		Son	Unm	33	M	Labourer	Herts	St Albans
1879	BLAKE	George	135		Grandson	Unm	7	M		Herts	St Albans
1880	BLAKE	Sarah	135		Boarder	Widow	30	F	Weaver	Herts	St Albans
1881	SMITH	William	136	Sopwell Lane	Head	Mar	50	M	Labourer	Herts	St Peters
1882	SMITH	Esther	136		Wife	Mar	78	F		Herts	St Albans
1883	SMITH	William	136		Son	Unm	30	M	Labourer	Herts	St Albans
1884	SMITH	Mary	136		Dau	Unm	27	F	Trimming Weaver	Herts	St Albans
1885	SMITH	Sarah	136		Dau	Unm	24	F	Trimming Weaver	Herts	St Albans
1886	SMITH	Henry	136		Grandson		5	M		Herts	St Albans
1887	SMITH	Shadrach	136		Grandson		1	M		Herts	St Albans
1888	ELTHERIDGE [?]	Elizabeth	137	Sopwell Lane	Head	Widow	42	F	Silk Worker	Herts	Flamstead
1889	ROSE	Thomas	137		Son		10	M	Scholar	Herts	St Albans
1890	HALE	Jane	138	Sopwell Lane	Head	Unm	18	F	Silk Worker	Herts	Tring
1891	DOLLING	Ann	139	Sopwell Lane	Head	Widow	63	F	Victualler	Bucks	Chesham
1892	DOLLING	Edward	139		Son	Unm	35	M	Victualler	Herts	St Albans
1893	DOLLING	Emma	139		Dau	Unm	19	F	Bonnet Sewer	Herts	St Albans
1894	NORRIS	Ann	139		Boarder	Widow	50	F	Char Woman	Herts	Kimpton
1895	NORRIS	Sarah	139		Boarders Dau	Unm	23	F	Straw Worker	Herts	Wheathampstead
1896	HOWARD	George	139	Sopwell Lane	Head	Mar	25	M	Silk Throwster	Herts	Berkhamsted
1897	HOWARD	Harriett	139		Wife	Mar	26	F	Silk Reel Picker	Herts	Hatfield
1898	TOLBATE [?]	Elizabeth	139		Aunt	Unm	60	F	Bonnet Sewer	Bucks	Chesham

1899	SMITH	William	140	Sopwell Lane	Head	Mar	35	M	Shoemaker	Herts	Redbourn
1900	SMITH	Sarah	140		Wife	Mar	35	F	Brazilian Hat Maker	Herts	St Albans
1901	SMITH	Susannah	140		Dau		13	F	Brazilian Hat Maker	Herts	St Albans
1902	SMITH	Samuel	140		Son		11	M	Brazilian Hat Maker	Herts	St Albans
1903	SMITH	Ann	140		Dau		9	F		Herts	St Albans
1904	SMITH	John	140		Son		4	M		Herts	St Albans
1905	SMITH	Martha	140		Dau		10 m	F		Herts	St Albans
1906	SEARS	Ann	141	Sopwell Lane	Head	Widow	71	F		Somerset	St Pilton
1907	NEWELL	Jane	141		Grandau	Unm	14	F	Straw Hat Maker	Herts	St Albans
1908	HOWES	William	141		Boarder		6	M		Herts	St Albans
1909	COLLINS	Joseph	142	Sopwell Lane	Head	Mar	53	M	Labourer	Herts	St Albans
1910	COLLINS	Susannah	142		Wife	Mar	62	F	Straw Plaiter	Herts	Welwyn
1911	COLLINS	William	142		Son		23	M	Labourer	Herts	St Albans
1912	COLLINS	Louisa	142		Dau		19	F	Hat Maker	Herts	St Albans
1913	CROUCH	Martha	143	Sopwell Lane	Head	Widow	45	F	Trimming Weaver	Herts	St Albans
1914	PETERS	William	143		Nephew		7	M		Herts	St Albans
1915	LINES	Henry	144	Sopwell Lane	Head	Mar	32	M	Silk Spinner	Herts	St Peters
1916	LINES	Mary	144		Wife	Mar	30	F	Trimming Weaver	Worcs	St Nicholls [?]
1917	LINES	James	144		Son		4	M	Scholar	Herts	St Albans
1918	LINES	John	144		Son		2	M		Herts	St Albans
1919	BARTLETT	Alice	145	Sopwell Lane	Head	Unm	23	F	Silk Winder	Herts	Colney Street [St Peters]
1920	COULSTON	Mary	145		Boarder	Unm	22	F	Trimming Weaver	Herts	Sandridge
1921	SHARP	John	146	Sopwell Lane	Head	Unm	25	M	Labourer	Herts	St Albans
1922	LAWRENCE	Susan	146		Boarder	Unm	21	F	Brazilian Hatter	Herts	St Albans
1923	LAWRENCE	William	146		[Boarders] Son		2	M		Herts	St Albans
1924	LAWRENCE	James	146		[Boarders] Son		1	M		Herts	St Albans
1925	STEPNEY	John	147	Sopwell Lane	Head	Mar	47	M	Shoemaker	Beds	Luton
1926	STEPNEY	Mary	147		Wife	Mar	50	F	Shoemakers Wife	Herts	St Albans
1927	STEPNEY	Sarah	147		Dau	Unm	20	F	Shoemakers Daughter	Herts	St Albans
1928	STEPNEY	David	147		Son	Unm	12	M	Shoemakers Son	Herts	St Albans
1929	CROUCH	Elvia	147		Grandau	Unm	12	F	Watchmakers Dau	Herts	St Albans
1930	CROUCH	Jane	147		Grandau	Unm	14	F	Watchmakers Dau	Herts	St Albans
1931	CROUCH	Frederick	147		Grandson	Unm	10	M	Watchmakers Son	Herts	St Albans
1932	CROUCH	Alfred	147		Grandson		6	M	Watchmakers Son	Herts	St Albans
1933	STOCKWELL	Samuel	148	Sopwell Lane	Head	Mar	54	M	Tailor	Somerset	Thorne
1934	STOCKWELL	Anna Maria	148		Wife	Mar	42	F		London	
1935	STOCKWELL	Albert Edward	148		Son		1	M		Herts	St Albans
1936	BROWN	Joseph	148		Son-in-law		9	M		Herts	St Albans
1937	CARRINGTON	David	149	Sopwell Lane	Head	Unm	33	M	Labourer	Herts	St Albans
1938	HORNER	Elizabeth	149		Boarder	Widow	29	F	Weaver	Herts	Hatfield
1939	HORNER	Martha	149		Boarders [Dau]	Unm	11	F	Hatter	Herts	Hatfield
1940	HORNER	Elizabeth	149		Boarders [Dau]		7	F	Scholar	Herts	St Albans
1941	HORNER	Mary	149		Boarders [Dau]		2	F		Herts	St Albans

	SURNAME	FORENAME	SCHEDULE NUMBER	ADDRESS	RELATIONSHIP	STATUS	AGE	SEX	OCCUPATION	COUNTY OF BIRTH	PLACE OF BIRTH
1942	CASTLE	William	149		Boarder	Unm	52	M	Pensioner (Chelsea)	Herts	Hatfield
1943	CASTLE	Hannah	149		Boarder	Unm	15	F	Hatter	Herts	Hatfield
1944	GELL	William	150	Sopwell Lane	Head	Mar	54	M	Engine Driver	Leics	Shepshed
1945	GELL	Ann	150		Wife	Mar	59	F		Derby	Coymor [?]
1946	WELCH	John	151	Sopwell Lane	Head	Mar	68	M	Labourer	Berks [Oxon]	Horley
1947	WELCH	Mary	151		Wife	Mar	58	F	Dressmaker	Worcs	Hartlebury
1948	HUGHES	Ann	151		Dau	Widow	25	F	Dressmaker	Worcs	St Nichols [?]
1949	WELCH	Amelia	151		Dau	Unm	20	F	Trimming Weaver	Warks	Birmingham
1950	WELCH	George	151		Son	Unm	16	M	Trimming Weaver	Herts	St Albans
1951	HUGHES	George	151		Grandson		3	M	Scholar	Herts	St Albans
1952	WALLER	James	152	Sopwell Lane	Head	Mar	73	M	Gardener	Herts	Weston
1953	WALLER	Sarah	152		Wife	Mar	55	F	Needlewoman	Herts	Bunkers Farm [Abbots Langley]
1954	WALLER	Emma	152		Dau	Mar	26	F	Hatter	Herts	St Albans
1955	WALLER	Charles	152		Son	Mar	25	M	Hat Presser	Herts	St Albans
1956	WALLER	Emma	152		Grandau		4	F		Herts	St Albans
1957	WALLER	Elizabeth	152		Grandau		1	F		Herts	St Albans
1958	WALLER	Frederick	152		Grandson		6	M		Herts	St Albans
1959	GILES	William	153	Sopwell Lane	Head	Mar	30	M	Silk Weaver	Herts	St Albans
1960	GILES	Eliza	153		Wife	Mar	25	F	Loom Weaver	Herts	Wheathampstead
1961	GILES	Frederick	153		Son		6	M		Herts	St Albans
1962	GILES	Henry	153		Son		3	M		Herts	St Albans
1963	DIXON	Mary	154	Sopwell Lane	Head	Widow	40	F	Straw Hat Maker	Herts	Ayot St Lawrence
1964	DIXON	Richard	154		Son	Unm	17	M	Pipe Maker	Herts	St Albans
1965	DIXON	Henry	154		Son		14	M	Labourer	Herts	St Albans
1966	DIXON	James	154		Son		13	M	Straw Hat Maker	Herts	St Albans
1967	DIXON	Ann	154		Dau		10	F		Herts	St Albans
1968	DIXON	William	154		Son		6	M		Herts	St Albans
1969	DIXON	Mary	154		Dau		3	F		Herts	St Albans
1970	PEARCE	Thomas	155	Sopwell Lane	Head	Mar	48	M	Labourer	Herts	St Albans
1971	PEARCE	Sophia	155		Wife	Mar	48	F	Labourer	Herts	St Albans
1972	PEARCE	Sarah	155		Dau	Unm	19	F	Brazilian Hat Maker	Herts	St Albans
1973	PEARCE	Joseph	155		Son		15	M	Brazilian Hat Maker	Herts	St Albans
1974	PEARCE	Jessey	155		Son		13	M	Brazilian Hat Maker	Herts	St Albans
1975	PEARCE	George	155		Son		11	M	Brazilian Hat Maker	Herts	St Albans
1976	PEARCE	Alfred	155		Grandson		7m	M		Herts	St Albans
1977	PEARCE	William	155		Brother	Widower	38	M	Labourer	Herts	St Albans
1978	PEARCE	Emma	155		Niece	[Unm]	17	F	Brazilian Hat Maker	Herts	St Albans
1979	HARVEY	Elizabeth	156	Sopwell Lane	Head	Unm	60	F	Charwoman	Herts	St Albans
1980	HAWTREE	James	157	Sopwell Lane	Head	Mar	43	M	Publican	Herts	St Stephens
1981	HAWTREE	Caroline	157		Wife	Mar	42	F	Publican	Herts	Abbots Langley
1982	HAWTREE	James	157		Son	Unm	18	M	Labourer	Herts	St Stephens
1983	HAWTREE	Richard	157		Son		13	M		Herts	St Stephens
1984	HAWTREE	Elizabeth	157		Dau		11	F	Scholar	Herts	St Stephens
1985	HAWTREE	Thomas	157		Son		8	M	Scholar	Herts	St Albans

1986	HAWTREE	Harriet Jane	157		Dau		5	F	Scholar	Herts	St Albans
1987	HAWTREE	Edward	157		Son		2	M		Herts	St Albans
1988	HAWTREE	Eliza	157		Dau		3wks	F		Herts	St Albans
1989	FLY	Meshech	157		Visitor	Unm	47	M		Herts	St Michaels
1990	KIPP	James	158	Sopwell Lane	Head	Mar	40	M	Pipe Maker	Herts	St Albans
1991	KIPP	Elizabeth	158		Wife	Mar	46	F		Herts	St Albans
1992	HOLLOWAY	James	158		Son-in-law	Unm	15	M	Pipe Maker	Herts	St Albans
1993	KIPP	George	158		Son		11	M	Scholar	Herts	St Albans
1994	KIPP	Ann	158		Dau		7	F		Herts	St Albans
1995	JEFFS	Thomas	159	Sopwell Lane	Head	Mar	31	M	Carrier	Herts	St Albans
1996	JEFFS	Elizabeth	159		Wife	Mar	38	F	Work At Silk Mill	Somerset	Shepton Mallet
1997	JEFFS	Eliza	159		Dau		5	F	Scholar	Herts	St Albans
1998	CHISED	Charles	160	Sopwell Lane	Head	Unm	21	M	Trimming Weaver	Herts	St Albans
1999	CHISED	William	160		Brother	Unm	19	M	Trimming Weaver	Herts	St Albans
2000	CHISED	Theresa	160		Sister	Unm	14	F	Straw Hat Maker	Herts	St Albans
2001	CHISED	Mary	160		Sister		6	F	Straw Hat Maker	Herts	St Albans
2002	GRAVESTOCK	Ann	161	Sopwell Lane	Head	Mar	55	F	Straw Hat Maker	Beds	Dunstable
2003	GRAVESTOCK	Ann	161		Dau	Unm	20	F	Trimming Weaver	Herts	Shenley
2004	GRAVESTOCK	Fanny	161		Dau	Unm	17	F	Straw Hat Maker	Herts	Shenley
2005	GRAVESTOCK	Sarah	161		Dau	Unm	13	F	Straw Hat Maker	Herts	Shenley
2006	GRAVESTOCK	Sarah	161		Grandau		5	F		Herts	St Albans
2007	GRAVESTOCK	John	161		Grandson		4	M		Herts	St Albans
2008	WESTAL	Elizabeth	161		Boarder		6	F		Herts	St Peters
2009	DEAMER	Samuel	162	Sopwell Lane	Head	Mar	57	M	Labourer	Herts	Sandridge
2010	DEAMER	Sarah	162		Wife	Mar	52	F	Plaiter	Beds [Herts]	Markyate
2011	DEAMER	Samuel	162		Son	Unm	17	M	Labourer	Herts	St Michaels
2012	DEAMER	Mary	162		Dau		14	F	Straw Hat Maker	Herts	St Michaels
2013	DEAMER	William	162		Son		10	M		Herts	St Michaels
2014	COOPER	Thomas	163	Crown Yard	Head	Mar	56	M	Labourer	Herts	St Michaels
2015	COOPER	Ann	163		Wife	Mar	54	F	Labourers Wife	Northants	Northampton
2016	BUTLER	John	164	Sopwell Lane	Head	Mar	38	M	Cordwainer	Herts	Redbourn
2017	BUTLER	Elizabeth	164		Wife	Mar	43	F	Shoe Binder	London	
2018	BUTLER	Argent	164		Son		12	M	Brazilian Hatter	Herts	Redbourn
2019	BUTLER	John	164		Son		10	M	Brazilian Hatter	Herts	Redbourn
2020	BUTLER	Sarah	164		Dau		8	F	Brazilian Hatter	Herts	Redbourn
2021	BUTLER	Henry	164		Son		6	M		Herts	Redbourn
2022	BUTLER	David	164		Son		4	M		Herts	Redbourn
2023	BUTLER	Anne	164		Dau		2	F		Herts	St Albans
2024	RUSSELL	Lydia	165	Crown Yard	Head	Widow	63	F	Formerly Dressmaker	Bucks	Aylesbury
2025	BURNBY	Richard	165		Nephew	Mar	26	M	Butcher	Surrey	Croydon
2026	BURNBY	Georgianna	165		Niece	Mar	25	F	Butchers Wife	Herts	St Albans
2027	BURNBY	Richard	165		[Nephews] Son		4	M	Butchers Son	Herts	St Albans
2028	BURNBY	James	165		[Nephews] Son		2	M	Butchers Son	Herts	St Albans
2029	BURNBY	Edward	165		[Nephews] Son		8 m	M	Butchers Son	Herts	St Albans

	SURNAME	FORENAME	SCHEDULE NUMBER	ADDRESS	RELATIONSHIP	STATUS	AGE	SEX	OCCUPATION	COUNTY OF BIRTH	PLACE OF BIRTH
2030	BURNBY	Henry	165		Nephew		9	M	Scholar	Surrey	Croydon
2031	GREGORY	Henry	165		Boarder	Widower	53	M	Baker	Herts	St Albans
2032	NORRIS	Frederick	166	Holywell Hill	Head	Mar	27	M	Butcher	Herts	St Albans
2033	NORRIS	Harriet	166		Wife	Mar	22	F		Herts	St Albans
2034	NORRIS	Kate	166		Dau		2	F		Herts	St Albans
2035	GREEN	Ellen	166		Serv	[Unm]	16	F	Servant	Herts	St Stephens
2036	GROVER	George	167	Holywell Hill	Head	Mar	57	M	Brazier	Herts	Hemel Hempstead
2037	GROVER	Elizabeth	167		Wife	Mar	49	F		Herts	Markyate Street
2038	GROVER	Harriet	167		Dau	Unm	19	F	Bonnet Sewer	Herts	St Albans
2039	GROVER	Emily	167		Grandau		6	F		Herts	St Albans
2040	GRIMSHAW	Amilia	167		[blank]		11	F	Scholar	Herts	St Albans
2041	WALKER	Thomas	168	Holywell Hill	Head	Mar	35	M	Dealer	Herts	St Albans
2042	WALKER	Lucy	168		Wife	Mar	33	F		Herts	St Peters
2043	WALKER	John	168		Son	Unm	14	M	Brazilian Hat Maker	Herts	St Peters
2044	WALKER	Elizabeth	168		Dau	Unm	12	F	Brazilian Hat Maker	Herts	St Peters
2045	WALKER	Joseph	168		Son		9	M	Scholar	Herts	St Peters
2046	WALKER	Eliza	168		Dau		7	F	Scholar	Herts	St Peters
2047	WALKER	Emma	168		Dau		5	F		Herts	St Peters
2048	KNIGHT	Thomas	169	Holywell Hill	Head	Mar	41	M	Coach Trimmer	Yorks	Hull
2049	KNIGHT	Susan	169		Wife	Mar	33	F	Coach Trimmers Wife	Herts	St Albans
2050	CROUCH	Henry	169		Nephew		2	M		Herts	St Albans
2051	EDWARDS	Joseph	170	Holywell Hill	Head	Mar	46	M	Labourer	Beds	Bedford
2052	EDWARDS	Mary	170		Wife	Mar	47	F	Labourers Wife	Suffolk	Ipswich
2053	EDWARDS	Caroline	170		Dau		11	F		Herts	St Albans
2054	WALKER	Thomas	170	Holywell Hill	Head	Mar	70	M	Baker	Yorks	Leeds
2055	WALKER	Eliza	170		Wife	Mar	60	F	Bakers Wife	Herts	Hatfield
2056	WALKER	Selina	170		Dau	Unm	17	F	At Home	Herts	St Albans

One unoccupied house

	SURNAME	FORENAME	SCHEDULE NUMBER	ADDRESS	RELATIONSHIP	STATUS	AGE	SEX	OCCUPATION	COUNTY OF BIRTH	PLACE OF BIRTH
2057	COLEMAN	Thomas	171	Holywell Hill	Head	Mar	55	M	Trainer Of Horses	Herts	Hertingfordbury
2058	COLEMAN	Sarah	171		Wife	Mar	50	F	Wife Of Trainer	[Gloucs]	Bristol
2059	COLEMAN	George Thomas	171		Son	Unm	29	M	Son Of Trainer	Herts	Tewin
2060	COLEMAN	Thomas	171		Son	Unm	21	M	Son Of Trainer	Herts	St Albans
2061	COLEMAN	Edward	171		Son	Unm	18	M	Son Of Trainer	Herts	St Albans
2062	COLEMAN	James	171		Son	Unm	14	M	Son Of Trainer	Herts	St Albans
2063	HURST	John	171		Serv	Unm	20	M	Servant To Horse Trainer	Yorks	Bradford
2064	DRAWWATER	Augustus Charles	172	Holywell Hill	Head	Mar	64	M	Retired Half Pay Army	Notts	Eastwood
2065	DRAWWATER	Catherine	172		Wife	Mar	60	F		N. Scotia	Windsor
2066	MORLEY	Thomas	172		Serv	Unm	25	M	Domestic Servant	Notts	Ratcliffe [Upon Soar]
2067	LESTER	Henrietta	172		Serv	[blank]	37	F	Domestic Servant	Rutland	Uppingham
2068	SHARPE	Jane	172		Serv	[blank]	32	F	Cook	Lincs [Norfolk]	Burston
2069	BLANKS	John Thomas	173	Holywell Hill	Head	Mar	36	M	Licensed Victualler	Essex	Springfield
2070	BLANKS	Eliza	173		Wife	Mar	34	F		Essex	Rochford

2071	BLANDS	Thomas White	173		Son		11	M		Essex	Rochford
2072	BLANKS	Frederick	173		Son		8	M		Essex	Southminster
2073	BLANKS	Charles	173		Son		6	M		Essex	Southminster
2074	BLANKS	Walter	173		Son		3	M		Herts	Southminster
2075	BLANKS	Eliza	173		Dau		1	F		Herts	St Albans
2076	HAWES	John	173		Lodger for night	Unm	24	M	Valet	Herts	Bushey
2077	DAWING [?]	Sarah	173		Serv	Unm	39	F	Servant	Herts	St Albans
2078	WALL	Octavius Charles	173		Head	Mar	48	M	Engineer	Middx	Limehouse
2079	WALL	Charlotte	173		Wife	Mar	30	F		Middx	Clerkenwell
2080	ARGENT	James	173		Brother-in-law	Unm	25	M	Engineer	Middx	Clerkenwell
2081	ARGENT	Susan Charlotte	173		Niece		2	F		Middx	Clerkenwell
2082	PARKES	William	174	White Hart Yard	Head	Mar	55	M	Carpenter	Herts	Harpenden
2083	PARKES	Martha	174		Wife	Mar	55	F	Carpenters Wife	Herts	Harpenden
2084	PARKES	George	174		Son	Unm	18	M	Labourer	Herts	St Albans
2085	PARKES	Henry	174		Son	Unm	16	M	Labourer	Herts	St Albans
2086	MARSTON	George Edward	175	White Hart Yard	Head	Mar	41	M	Baker	Herts	St Albans
2087	MARSTON	Mary	175		Wife	Mar	46	F	Bakers Wife	Herts	St Albans
2088	HILL	Joseph	176	White Hart Yard	Head	Mar	55	M	Drayman	Herts	St Albans
2089	HILL	Eliza	176		Wife	Mar	45	F	Laundress	Middx	Barnet
2090	HILL	Eliza	176		Dau	Unm	24	F	Bonnet Sewer	Herts	St Albans
2091	HILL	Sarah	176		Dau	Unm	22	F	Laundress	Herts	St Albans
2092	HILL	William	176		Son	Unm	20	M	Groom	Herts	St Albans
2093	HILL	James	176		Son	Unm	18	M	Groom	Herts	St Albans
2094	HILL	Anne	176		Dau		12	F	Scholar	Herts	St Albans
2095	HILL	Frederick	176		Son		8	M	Scholar	Herts	St Albans
2096	BENT	David	176		Visitor	Unm	21	M	Formerly Gents Servant	Beds	Luton
2097	JOHNSON	William	177	Holywell Hill	Head	Mar	50	M	Hat Manufacturer	Herts	Wheathampstead
2098	JOHNSON	Mary	177		Wife	Mar	49	F		Herts	Wheathampstead
2099	JOHNSON	George	177		Son	Unm	24	M	Hat Manufacturer	Herts	Wheathampstead
2100	JOHNSON	Charles	177		Son	Unm	19	M	Hat Manufacturer	Herts	Wheathampstead
2101	JOHNSON	Susan	177		Dau	Unm	18	F	Bonnet Sewer	Herts	Wheathampstead
2102	JOHNSON	Lucy	177		Dau	Unm	16	F	Bonnet Sewer	Herts	Wheathampstead
2103	JOHNSON	James	177		Son		13	M	Scholar	Herts	St Albans
2104	JOHNSON	Jane	177		Dau		7	F		Herts	St Albans
2105	SEYMOUR	William	178	Saracens Holywell Hill	Head	Mar	35	M	Coach Proprietor	Herts	Hatfield
2106	SMITH	Sarah	178		H'keeper	Unm	28	F	Housekeeper	Herts	Hitchin
2107	SEYMOUR	Eliza	178		Niece		7	F		Herts	Moorgreen [Ardeley]
2108	LACY	Emma	179	Saracens Head Yard	Head	Unm	21	F	Hat & Bonnet Maker	Herts	St Albans
2109	LACY	Rosanna	179		Sister	Unm	16	F	Straw Bonnet Sewer	Herts	St Albans
2110	KEIGHTLEY	Joseph	180	Saracens Head Yard	Head	Mar	37	M	Tailor	Bucks	Newport Pagnell
2111	KEIGHTLEY	Jane	180		Wife	Mar	32	F	Tailors Wife	Herts	St Albans
2112	KEIGHTLEY	Charles	180		Son		8	M	Scholar	Herts	St Albans
2113	KEIGHTLEY	Sarah	180		Dau		6	F	Scholar	Herts	St Albans

	SURNAME	FORENAME	SCHEDULE NUMBER	ADDRESS	RELATIONSHIP	STATUS	AGE	SEX	OCCUPATION	COUNTY OF BIRTH	PLACE OF BIRTH
2114	KEIGHTLEY	Joseph	180		Son		4	M		Herts	St Albans
2115	KEIGHTLEY	William	180		Son		3m	M		Herts	St Albans
2116	BOURNE	John	181	Saracens Head Yard	Head	Mar	39	M	Straw Bonnet Presser	Kent	Faversham
2117	BOURNE	Sarah	181		Wife	Mar	36	F	Straw Bonnet Sewer	Herts	St Albans
2118	BOURNE	Emily	181		Dau		15	F	Straw Bonnet Sewer	Herts	St Albans
2119	BOURNE	John	181		Son		13	M		Herts	St Albans
2120	BOURNE	Frederick	181		Son		11	M		Herts	St Albans
2121	BOURNE	Sarah	181		Dau		9	F		Herts	St Albans
2122	BOURNE	Charles	181		Son		6	M		Herts	St Albans

Two uninhabited houses

	SURNAME	FORENAME	SCHEDULE NUMBER	ADDRESS	RELATIONSHIP	STATUS	AGE	SEX	OCCUPATION	COUNTY OF BIRTH	PLACE OF BIRTH
2123	WILLOUGHBY	Sarah	182	Saracens Head Yard	Head	Mar	45	F	Laundress	Herts	St Albans
2124	WILLOUGHBY	Emma	182		Dau	Unm	12	F	Brazilian Hat Maker	Herts	St Albans
2125	WILLOUGHBY	John	182		Son	Unm	7	M	Scholar	Herts	St Albans
2126	WILLOUGHBY	Elizabeth	182		Dau		5	F		Herts	St Albans
2127	HUMBLES	John	183	Saracens Head Yard	Head	Mar	33	M	Accountant	Herts	St Albans
2128	HUMBLES	Elizabeth	183		Wife	Mar	32	F	Straw Hat Maker	Middx	Bartholemew Close [London]
2129	HUMBLES	William	183		Son		7	M	At Home	Herts	St Albans
2130	POCOCK	William	184	Saracens Head Yard	Head	Mar	32	M	Coach Trimmer	Herts	Harpenden
2131	POCOCK	Susannah	184		Wife	Mar	30	F	Brazilian Hat Maker	Herts	St Albans
2132	POCOCK	William	184		Son		9	M	Scholar	Herts	St Albans
2133	POCOCK	Thomas	184		Son		7	M	Scholar	Herts	St Albans
2134	POCOCK	George	184		Son		5	M	Scholar	Herts	St Albans
2135	POCOCK	Edward	184		Son		3	M		Herts	St Albans
2136	POCOCK	Charles	184		Son		1	M		Herts	St Albans
2137	SADDINGTON	Pheobe	185	Saracens Head Yard	Head	Widow	40	F	Lace Maker	Oxon	Merton
2138	SADDINGTON	Emma	185		Dau		8	F	Brazilian Hat Maker	Herts	St Albans
2139	SADDINGTON	James	185		Son		7	M	Scholar	Herts	St Albans
2140	SADDINGTON	Sarah	185		Dau		6	F		Herts	St Albans
2141	BROWN	Alice	186	Saracens Head Yard	Head	Mar	60	F	Charwoman	Northants	Brompton [?]
2142	CAPPEL	William	186		Dau	Mar	23	F	Weaver	Herts	St Peters
2143	CAPPEL	William	186		Grandson		4	M		Herts	St Peters
2144	CARTER	William	187	Saracens Head Yard	Head	Mar	55	M	Porter	Herts	[Hertford] All Saints
2145	CARTER	Charlotte	187		Wife	Mar	46	F	Domestic Household	Herts	Wheathampstead
2146	CARTER	Sarah	187		Dau	Unm	21	F	Brazilian Hat Maker	Middx	Kensington
2147	CARTER	Charles	187		Son		12	M	Scholar	Herts	St Albans
2148	CARTER	James	187		Son		9	M	Scholar	Herts	St Albans
2149	CARTER	Emma	187		Dau		6	F	Scholar	Herts	St Albans
2150	WOOTTON	John	188	Saracens Head Yard	Head	Mar	30	M	Coach Painter	Herts	Little Berkhamsted
2151	WOOTTON	Mary	188		Wife	Mar	31	F	Silk Weaver	Herts	St Albans
2152	PHORLEY	Edward	188		Nephew		4	M	Scholar	Bucks	Beaconsfield
2153	WOOD	Edmund	189	Holywell Hill	Head	Mar	48	M	Saddler	Herts	St Albans
2154	WOOD	Sarah	189		Wife	Mar	46	F	Saddlers Wife	Herts	Harpenden
2155	WOOD	Sarah Jane	189		Dau	Unm	16	F	Saddlers Daughter	Herts	St Albans

2156	MAGER	William	190	Holywell Hill	Head	Mar	40	M	Painter employing 1 man	Herts	Hertford
2157	MAGER	Sarah	190		Wife	Mar	30	F	Painters Wife	Beds	Eversholt
2158	MAGER	John Thomas	190		Son		4	M	Painters Son	Herts	St Albans
2159	BRADSHAW	John	191	Holywell Hill	Head	Mar	37	M	Carpenter	Herts	Hatfield
2160	BRADSHAW	Phillis	191		Wife	Mar	40	F		Herts	Welwyn
2161	BRADSHAW	Martha	191		Dau		5	F	Scholar	Herts	Hatfield
2162	DAY	John	192	Holywell Hill	Head	Mar	50	M	Butcher	Herts	St Albans
2163	DAY	Mary	192		Wife	Mar	53	F	Butchers Wife	Hereford	Glasbury
2164	DAY	John A	192		Son	Unm	22	M	Butcher	Herts	St Albans
2165	DAY	Henrietta J	192		Dau	Unm	20	F	Butchers Daughter	Herts	St Albans
2166	DAY	Mary Ann	192		Dau	Unm	18	F	Butchers Daughter	Herts	St Albans
2167	DAY	Mary Ann	192		Sister	Unm	51	F	Fund Holder	Herts	St Albans
2168	WEADON	Edward	192		Serv	Unm	50	M	House Servant	Beds	Luton
2169	CANNON	Joseph	192		Serv	Unm	16	M	House Servant	Herts	Hatfield
2170	KING	Sarah	192		Serv	Unm	18	F	House Servant	Bucks	Aylesbury
2171	GALES	George	192		Serv	Widower	60	M	Brewer	Unknown	
2172	TEBBOTH	Thomas	193	Holywell Hill	Head	Mar	28	M	Baker	Herts	St Albans
2173	TEBBOTH	Elizabeth	193		Wife	Mar	22	F	Weaver	Northants	Sibbertoft
2174	TEBBOTH	Oliver	193		Brother	[blank]	59	M	Baker	Herts	Hertford
2175	BROWN	Cornelius	194	Marstons Yard	Head	Widower	65	M	Gardener	Herts	St Albans
2176	BROWN	Emma	194		Dau	Unm	32	F	Dressmaker	Herts	St Albans
2177	BROWN	Thomas	194		Son	Unm	26	M	Canvas Weaver	Herts	St Albans
2178	BROWN	Robert	194		Son	Unm	22	M	Gardener	Herts	St Albans
2179	BROWN	William	194		Son	Unm	20	M	Trimming Weaver	Herts	St Albans
2180	MITCHELL	David	195	Marstons Yard	Head	Mar	38	M	Painter	Scotland	[Unknown]
2181	MITCHELL	Eliza	195		Wife	Mar	36	F		Herts	St Albans
2182	MITCHELL	Joseph	195		Son		15	M	Silk Minder	Herts	St Albans
2183	MITCHELL	Elizabeth	195		Dau		11	F		Herts	St Albans
2184	MITCHELL	Emily	195		Dau		8	F		Herts	St Albans
2185	WARD	Rebecca	196	Marstons Yard	Head	Widow	69	F		Cambs	Cambridge
2186	WARD	Mary	196		Dau	Unm	34	F	Hand Loom Weaver	Herts	St Albans
2187	WARD	Charles	196		Grandson	Unm	15	M	Silk Throwster	Herts	St Albans
2188	MARSTON	Thomas	197	Marstons Yard	Head	Mar	31	M	Baker	Herts	St Albans
2189	MARSTON	Eliza Ann	197		Wife	Mar	26	F		London	
2190	POWELL	Thomas	198	Marstons Yard	Head	Mar	24	M	Labourer	Herts	St Peters
2191	POWELL	Elizabeth	198		Wife	Mar	24	F		Herts	St Albans
2192	WHITE	Susan	198		Boarder		4	F		Herts	St Peters
2193	POWELL	Charles	198		Son		9m	M		Herts	St Michaels
2194	HOWARD	James	199	Marstons Yard	Head	Mar	44	M	Labourer	Herts	St Albans
2195	HOWARD	Hannah	199		Wife	Mar	50	F		Herts	Hatfield
2196	HOWARD	Mary	199		Dau	Unm	29	F	Trimming Maker	Herts	Hatfield
2197	HOWARD	Susan	199		Dau	Unm	24	F	Trimming Maker	Herts	Hatfield
2198	HOWARD	George	199		Son	Unm	21	M	Labourer	Herts	Hatfield
2199	HOWARD	William	199		Son	Unm	19	M	Labourer	Herts	St Michaels

	SURNAME	FORENAME	SCHEDULE NUMBER	ADDRESS	RELATIONSHIP	STATUS	AGE	SEX	OCCUPATION	COUNTY OF BIRTH	PLACE OF BIRTH
2200	HOWARD	Joseph	199		Son	Unm	16	M	Labourer	Herts	St Albans
2201	HOWARD	Emily	199		Dau		4	F		Herts	St Albans
2202	TOMBS	George	200	Marstons Yard	Head	Mar	45	M	Farm Labourer	Herts	St Stephens
2203	TOMBS	Caroline	200		Wife	Mar	38	F	Trimming Weaver	Herts	St Stephens
2204	TOMBS	William	200		Son	Unm	20	M	Labourer	Herts	St Stephens
2205	TOMBS	James	200		Son	Unm	18	M	Labourer	Herts	St Stephens
2206	TOMBS	Sarah	200		Dau	Unm	16	F	Trimming Weaver	Herts	St Stephens
2207	TOMBS	Frederick	200		Son		11	M	Brazilian Hat Maker	Herts	St Stephens
2208	TOMBS	John	200		Son		9	M	Brazilian Hat Maker	Herts	St Stephens
2209	TOMBS	Robert	200		Son		6	M	Brazilian Hat Maker	Herts	St Albans
2210	REEVES	Harvey	201	Holywell Hill	Head	Mar	31	M	Draper	Herts	St Albans
2211	REEVES	Creseat	201		Wife	Mar	25	F		Herts	St Albans
2212	REEVES	Creseat	201		Dau		7	F		Herts	St Albans
2213	REEVES	William	201		Son		6	M		Herts	St Albans
2214	VORMER	Frederick	201		Apprentice	Unm	25	M	Drapers Apprentice	Beds	Bedford
2215	BRAY	Ann	201		Serv	Unm	36	F	Servant	Beds	Bedford
2216	LIPSCOMB	John Thomas	202	Holywell Hill	Head	Mar	58	M	Magistrate, Alderman M.R.C.S. Eng. Gen Practioner	Hants	Hunton
2217	LIPSCOMB	Elizabeth Sarah	202		Wife	Mar	52	F		Herts	St Albans
2218	LIPSCOMB	John Thomas Nicholson	202		Son	Unm	31	M	General Practioner M.D. St Andrews, M.R.C.S. Eng.	Herts	St Albans
2219	LIPSCOMB	Frederick	202		Son	Unm	26	M	MA Oxon, Curate of Abbots Langley	Herts	St Albans
2220	LIPSCOMB	Mary	202		Dau	Unm	24	F		Herts	St Albans
2221	LIPSCOMB	Richard Nicholson	202		Son	Unm	21	M	Scholar At Home	Herts	St Albans
2222	LIPSCOMB	Ellen	202		Dau	Unm	14	F	Scholar At Home	Herts	St Albans
2223	LIPSCOMB	Henry Alchorn	202		Son	Unm	12	M	Scholar	Herts	St Albans
2224	COOPER	Caroline	202		Serv	Unm	36	F	Cook	Herts	South Mimms
2225	BASIL	Caroline Sarah	202		Serv	Unm	27	F	Housemaid	Herts	Ayot St Peter
2226	SAUNDERS	Joseph	203	Holywell Hill	Head	Mar	59	M	Coach Maker	Herts	St Albans
2227	SAUNDERS	Catherine	203		Wife	Mar	61	F	Coach Makers Wife	Herts	St Albans
2228	BLUCHER	Anne	203		Serv	Unm	18	F	Servant	Herts	St Albans
2229	RAYMENT	Betsey Ann	204	Holywell Hill	Head	Widow	61	F	Annuitant	Essex	[Unknown]
2230	LAWRENCE	Jemima	204		Serv	Unm	34	F	Servant	Herts	[Unknown]
2231	COCKING	Joseph	205	Holywell Hill	Head	Mar	53	M	Innkeeper	Lincs	Ludford
2232	COCKING	Emma	205		Wife	Mar	55	F	Innkeepers Wife	Herts	St Albans
2233	SMITH	William	205		Brother	Unm	57	M	Dumb	Herts	St Albans
2234	LAWES	Robert	205		Coachman	Unm	24	M	Driver Of Omnibus	Surrey	Clapham
2235	KELLY	James	205		Serv	Unm	15	M	Boots	Berks	Wallingford
2236	WOOD	Thomas	205		Serv	Unm	17	M	Under Ostler	Herts	Berkhamsted
2237	DRAPER	Emma	205		Serv	Unm	23	F	Chamber Maid	Cambs [Herts]	Royston
2238	BENNETT	Maria	205		Serv	Unm	46	F	Cook	Derby	Derby
2239	MARKS	Mary	206	Holywell Hill	Head	Widow	56	F	Innkeeper	Herts	Sandridge
2240	MARKS	William	206		Son	Unm	22	M	Farmer	Herts	St Albans
2241	MARKS	Ellen	206		Dau	Unm	19	F		Herts	St Albans

2242	BROOKS	Richard	206		Visitor	Unm	24	M	Assistant Surgeon	Staffs [Cheshire]	Macclesfield
2243	PARSONS	Ellen H	206		Niece	Unm	8	F	Scholar	Middx	Islington
2244	BADGER	Samuel	206		Visitor	Mar	43	M	House & Law Agent	Shrop	Shrewsbury
2245	EVANS	Susan	206		Serv	Unm	32	F	Servant	Herts	St Peters
2246	BELL	Jane	206		Serv	Unm	25	F	Servant	Herts	Hitchin
2247	HAZZARD	Thomas	206		Serv	Unm	64	M	Porter	Beds	Tottenhoe
2248	SIMONS	William	206		Serv	Widower	52	M	Housekeeper	Herts	Welwyn
2249	SAMMONS	John	206		Serv	Unm	17	M	Porter	Herts	Bell Bar [North Mimms]
2250	TETCH	Linford	206		Serv	Widower	52	M	Postboy	Beds	Dunstable

Registrar's District: St Albans   **Enumeration District 4c**   **Ref. HO 107/1713 folios 429-61**

Fishpool Ward comprising part of Fishpool Street, Lower Dagnall Lane, College Street, Spicer Street, College Place, New England Place and Abbey Mill Lane.

2251	FORSHAM	Edward A.	1	College Street	Head	Unm	80	M	Landed Proprietor & Fundholder	Herts	Kelshall
2252	BOURNE	Mary	1		Serv	Unm	72	F	Housekeeper	Hants	Milton
2253	MASON	Catherine	1		Serv	Unm	42	F	General Serv	Herts	Sandridge

Two houses uninhabited

2254	WOOD	Thomas	2	College Street	Head	Mar	52	M	Retired, Harness Maker	Herts	St Albans
2255	WOOD	Mary	2		Wife	Mar	54	F		Beds	Luton
2256	WOOD	Martha	2		Dau	Unm	17	F		Herts	St Albans
2257	WOOD	Mary Anne	2		Dau	Unm	24	F		Herts	St Albans
2258	YOUNG	Elizabeth	3	College Street	Head	Widow	67	F	Annuitant	Middx	London
2259	YOUNG	Susanna Goodfellow	3		Dau	Unm	37	F	Fundholder	Middx	Islington
2260	STENING	Fanny	3		Serv	Unm	15	F	General Servant	Middx	Bethnal Green
2261	SIMCOCK	Susanna	4	College Street	Head	Unm	74	F	Retired Schoolmistress	Herts	St Albans
2262	READING	Mary	4		Serv	Unm	57	F	General Servant	Herts	St Albans
2263	OSBORN	Ann	5	College Street	Head	Widow	74	F	Retired Pastry Cook	Bucks	Quainton
2264	YOUNG	Elizabeth	5		Serv	Unm	40	F	General Servant	Beds	Luton
2265	LANGTON	Edward J.	6	College Street	Head	Mar	29	M	Inland Revenue Officer	Devon	High Rickington [?]
2266	LANGTON	Jane	6		Wife	Mar	33	F		Middx	St Georges, Westminster
2267	LANGTON	Edward J.	6		Son		2	M		Bucks	Aylesbury
2268	LANGTON	Jane	6		Dau		2m	F		Herts	St Albans
2269	WILES	Hannah	7	College Street	Head	Widow	79	F	Baker	Beds	North Hill [Northill]
2270	WILES	Hannah	7		Dau	Unm	43	F		Beds	Roxton
2271	WILES	Elizabeth	7		Dau	Unm	32	F		Beds	Blunham
2272	HORTON	Ann	8	College Street	Head	Unm	70	F	Annuitant	Beds	Chellington
2273	PAYNE	Sarah	8		Niece	Unm	39	F	Annuitant	Herts	St Albans
2274	FIELD	Ann	8		Serv	Mar	64	F	Nurse	Herts	Redbourn
2275	HENMAN	Frances	9	College Street	Head	Widow	53	F	Straw Bonnet Sewer	Herts	St Albans
2276	HENMAN	Emma	9		Dau	Unm	27	F	Straw Bonnet Sewer	Herts	St Albans
2277	HENMAN	Elizabeth	9		Dau	Unm	24	F	Straw Bonnet Sewer	Herts	Hatfield
2278	SCARBOROUGH	George	9		Visitor	Unm	24	M	Inland Revenue Officer	Herts	Hatfield

SURNAME	FORENAME	SCHEDULE NUMBER	ADDRESS	RELATIONSHIP	STATUS	AGE	SEX	OCCUPATION	COUNTY OF BIRTH	PLACE OF BIRTH

Three houses uninhabited

	SURNAME	FORENAME	SCHEDULE NUMBER	ADDRESS	RELATIONSHIP	STATUS	AGE	SEX	OCCUPATION	COUNTY OF BIRTH	PLACE OF BIRTH
2279	HARKNESS	James	10	College Street	Head	Mar	38	M	Tea Dealer	Scotland	[Unknown]
2280	HARKNESS	Harriet	10		Wife	Mar	38	F		Herts	St Michaels
2281	HARKNESS	James T.	10		Son		3	M		Herts	St Albans
2282	HARKNÉSS	Harriet	10		Dau		1	F		Herts	St Albans
2283	BUTLER	Susanna	10		Mother-in-law	Widow	72	F	Proprietor of Houses	Herts	Hemel Hempstead
2284	MCADAM	James	10		Visitor	Unm	28	M	Travelling Draper	Scotland	[Unknown]
2285	MCADAM	Roger	10		Visitor	Unm	24	M	Travelling Draper	Scotland	[Unknown]
2286	MCADAM	Robert	10		Visitor	Unm	19	M	Travelling Draper	Scotland	[Unknown]
2287	LATTIMORE	Osborn	11	College Street	Head	Mar	32	M	Journeyman Tallow Chandler	Herts	St Albans
2288	LATTIMORE	Rachael	11		Wife	Mar	27	F	Dressmaker	Herts	St Albans
2289	MASON	Emine	12	College Street	Head	Unm	30	F	Straw Bonnet Sewer	Herts	St Peters
2290	MASON	Esther C.	12		Sister	Unm	26	F	Straw Bonnet Sewer	Herts	St Peters
2291	MORGAN	Ellen	13	College Street	Head	Widow	36	F	Housekeeper	Ireland	[Unknown]
2292	WARLEY	Joseph	14	Dagnall Lane	Head	Mar	67	M	Agric Lab	Herts	St Albans
2293	WARLEY	Mary	14		Wife	Mar	66	F		Herts	St Albans
2294	WARLEY	Mary	14		Grandau		16	F	Brazilian Hatmaker	Herts	St Albans
2295	HOWARD	Joseph	15	Dagnall Lane	Head	Mar	23	M	Silk Throwster	Herts	St Albans
2296	HOWARD	Emma	15		Wife	Mar	20	F	Silk Throwster	Herts	St Albans
2297	LETTS	Richard	16	Dagnall Lane	Head	Widower	47	M	Plumber & Glazier	Northants	Guilsborough
2298	LETTS	Richard	16		Son	Unm	13	M	Scholar	Herts	St Albans
2299	LETTS	Edward	16		Son	Unm	11	M	Scholar	Herts	St Albans
2300	LETTS	Thomas	16		Son	Unm	7	M	Scholar	Herts	St Albans
2301	DAWSON	Mary	16		Serv	Widow	47	F	Housekeeper	Herts	St Albans
2302	WELSH	Henry	17	Dagnall Lane	Head	Mar	39	M	Carpenter	Herts	Welwyn
2303	WELSH	Charlotte	17		Wife	Mar	38	F		Herts	Bedmond [Abbots Langley]
2304	FRAIL	John [?]	18	Dagnall Lane	Head	Mar	64	M	Engineer	Herts	St Peters
2305	TITMASS	Elizabeth	19	Dagnall Lane	Head	Unm	35	F	Brazilian Hat Maker	Herts	Wheathampstead
2306	WELCH	Jane	19		Aunt	Widow	79	F	Annuitant	Herts	Wheathampstead
2307	WARNE	Daniel	20	Dagnall Lane	Head	Unm	31	M	Malster	Herts	Wheathampstead
2308	DRAPER	George	20		Brother-in-law	Mar	26	M	Agric Lab	Herts	Wheathampstead
2309	DRAPER	Sarah	20		Sister	Mar	28	F		Herts	Wheathampstead
2310	DRAPER	Hannah	20		Niece		2	F		Herts	St Albans
2311	WARNER	William	20		Nephew		1	M		Herts	St Albans
2312	REEVES	Thomas	21	Dagnall Lane	Head	Mar	33	M	Grocer	Herts	St Albans
2313	REEVES	Sarah	21		Wife	Mar	37	F		Herts	Harpenden
2314	SUTTON	Matthew	22	College Place	Head	Mar	34	M	Engineer	Herts	Kings Langley
2315	SUTTON	Susannah	22		Wife	Mar	35	F		Herts	St Albans
2316	SUTTON	Charlotte	22		Dau		4	F		Herts	St Albans
2317	SUTTON	Sarah J.	22		Dau		2	F		Herts	St Albans
2318	SUTTON	Bessy [?]	22		Dau		4m	F		Herts	St Albans
2319	BLIGH	Martin	23	College Place	Head	Mar	24	M	Silk Throwster	Herts	Tring
2320	BLIGH	Emma	23		Wife	Mar	23	F	Silk Throwster	Herts	Watford

2321	BLIGH	William	23		Son			3	M		Herts	Watford
2322	BLIGH	Mary Ann	23		Dau			1	F		Herts	Watford
2323	SMITH	Thomas	24	College Place	Head	Mar	50	M	Carpenter	Herts	Redbourn
2324	SMITH	Jane	24		Wife	Mar	51	F		Herts	St Albans
2325	SMITH	George	24		Son	Unm	18	M	Appr [Carpenter]	Herts	St Albans
2326	SMITH	Alfred	24		Son		14	M	Silk Throwster	Herts	St Albans
2327	SMITH	Joseph	24		Son		10	M	Silk Throwster	Herts	St Albans
2328	MATES	William	25	College Place	Head	Widower	67	M	Chelsea Pensioner (Blind)	Herts	St Albans
2329	MATES	Sarah	25		Dau	Unm	35	F		Sth. Am.	
2330	TAYLOR	James	26	College Place	Head	Widower	50	M	Brewers Labourer	Herts	St Albans
2331	SEARS	Betsy	27	College Place	Head	Unm	23	F	Brazilian Hat Maker	Herts	St Albans
2332	WELDALE	James	28	College Place	Head	Mar	25	M	Brazilian Hat Blocker	Herts	Harpenden
2333	WELDALE	Mary Ann	28		Wife	Mar	23	F		Herts	Harpenden
2334	WELDALE	Ann	28		Dau		1	F		Herts	St Albans
2335	GARLAND	John [?]	29	College Place	Head	Mar	29	M	Stone Mason	Devon	Plymouth
2336	GARLAND	Ann	29		Wife	Mar	28	F		Devon	Ilfracombe
2337	GARLAND	Mary Ann	29		Dau	Unm	5	F	Scholar	Middx	London
2338	GARLAND	John [?]	29		Son		4	M		Middx	London
2339	GARLAND	Susan	29		Dau		1	F		Devon	Plymouth
2340	GARLAND	Phoebe	29		Cousin		8	F	Scholar	Middx	London
2341	VARNEY	John	30	College Place	Head	Mar	39	M	Carpenter	Herts	St Albans
2342	VARNEY	Jane	30		Wife	Mar	35	F		Herts	St Albans
2343	VARNEY	Fanny	30		Dau		4	F		Middx	London
2344	CRAWLEY	Thomas	31	College Place	Head	Widower	46	M	Brewers Labourer	Herts	Aldenham
2345	CRAWLEY	Eliza	31		Dau	Unm	19	F	Dressmaker	Herts	St Albans
2346	CRAWLEY	Mary	31		Dau		12	F	Scholar	Herts	St Albans
2347	CRAWLEY	Sarah	31		Dau		8	F	Scholar	Herts	St Albans
2348	HIGGINS	Mary	32	College Place	Head	Widow	59	F	Shoe Binder	Middx	Highgate
2349	HIGGINS	Eliza	32		Dau	Unm	24	F	Dressmaker	Herts	Hatfield
2350	HIGGINS	Emma	32		Dau	Unm	23	F	Bonnet Sewer	Herts	London Colney
2351	HOLLOWAY	Joseph	33	College Place	Head	Unm	22	M	Brazilian Hat Blocker	Beds	Barton
2352	FLOOD	Ann	34	College Place	Head	Mar	27	F	Bonnet Sewer	Northants	Northampton
2353	LUCK	Edmund	35	College Place	Head	Mar	58	M	Straw Factor	Herts	Harpenden
2354	LUCK	Charlotte	35		Wife	Mar	51	F		Herts	Codicote
2355	LUCK	Alfred	35		Grandson		8	M		Herts	St Albans
2356	PARREY	Joseph	36	College Place	Head	Unm	18	M	Straw Factor	Herts	Hemel Hempstead
2357	WALKER	William	37	College Place	Head	Mar	42	M	Boot Maker	Herts	St Albans
2358	WALKER	Maria	37		Wife	Mar	45	F		Herts	Bengeo
2359	WALKER	Thomas	37		Son	Unm	18	M	Silk Throwster	Herts	St Albans
2360	WALKER	William	37		Son		15	M	Silk Throwster	Herts	St Albans
2361	WALKER	Charles	37		Son		12	M	Silk Throwster	Herts	St Albans
2362	WALKER	James	37		Son		11	M	Silk Throwster	Herts	St Albans
2363	WALKER	Emma	37		Dau		8	F	Scholar	Herts	St Albans
2364	GARLAND	John	38	College Place	Head	Mar	43	M	Stonemason	Gloucs	Bristol

	SURNAME	FORENAME	SCHEDULE NUMBER	ADDRESS	RELATIONSHIP	STATUS	AGE	SEX	OCCUPATION	COUNTY OF BIRTH	PLACE OF BIRTH
2365	GARLAND	Elizabeth	38		Wife	Mar	44	F	Appr [Stonemason]	Kent	Chatham
2366	TAYLOR	Mary	38		Mother-in-law	Widow	84	F	Laundress	Essex	East Ham
2367	SPORTAN	John	38		Nephew		15	M	Agric Lab	Notts	Unknown
2368	SILSY	Lydia	39	College Place	Head	Widow	63	F	Laundress	Herts	Newnham
2369	SEARS	William	39		Son-in-law	Mar	26	M		Herts	St Albans
2370	SEARS	Caroline	39		Dau	Mar	30	F		Herts	St Albans
2371	SEARS	John Thomas	39		Grandson		4	M		Herts	St Albans
2372	FISHER	George	40	College Place	Head	Mar	55	M	Coach Painter	Herts	St Albans
2373	FISHER	Elizabeth	40		Wife	Mar	50	F		Middx	London
2374	FISHER	Robert	40		Son	Unm	29	M	Agric Lab	Herts	St Albans
2375	FISHER	Elizabeth	40		Dau	Unm	25	F	Bonnet Sewer	Herts	St Albans
2376	FISHER	Selina	40		Dau	Unm	23	F	Bonnet Sewer	Herts	St Albans
2377	FISHER	John	40		Son		13	M	Errand Boy	Herts	St Albans
2378	BOWERS	Mary	41	College Place	Head	Widow	59	F	Brazilian Hat Maker	Herts	Sandridge
2379	DUNHAM	Emma	41		Dau	Unm	33	F		Herts	Wheathampstead
2380	BOWERS	Elizabeth	41		Dau	Unm	24	F	Straw Bonnet Sewer	Herts	St Albans
2381	BOWERS	Susanna	41		Dau	Unm	22	F	Brazilian Hat Maker	Herts	St Albans
2382	BOWERS	Joseph	41		Son	Unm	20	M	Carpenter	Herts	St Albans
2383	LAWRENCE	Harriet	42	College Place	Head	Unm	18	F	Brazilian Hat Maker	Herts	Harpenden
2384	BENNETT	Amelia	43	College Place	Head	Widow	47	F	Seamstress	Herts	Kimpton
2385	BENNETT	Maria	43		Dau	Unm	19	F		Herts	Redbourn
2386	BENNETT	Joseph	43		Son		11	M	Scholar	Herts	St Albans
2387	WELLS	Edward	44	College Place	Head	Mar	64	M	Bricklayer	Herts	Codicote
2388	WELLS	Sarah	44		Wife	Mar	57	F		Herts	St Albans
2389	WELLS	Eliza	44		Dau	Unm	35	F	Silk Throwster	Herts	St Albans
2390	WELLS	Ann	44		Dau	Unm	28	F	Silk Throwster	Herts	St Albans
2391	WELLS	Mary	44		Dau	Unm	19	F	Brazilian Hat Maker	Herts	St Albans
2392	BROWN	Caroline	45	College Place	Head	Unm	17	F	Brazilian Hat Maker	Herts	Harpenden
2393	BROWN	Emily	45		Sister	Unm	15	F	Brazilian Hat Maker	Herts	Harpenden
2394	BROWN	Ann	45		Sister	Unm	11	F	Brazilian Hat Maker	Herts	Harpenden
2395	BROWN	Cicely	45		Sister	Unm	7	F	Scholar	Herts	Harpenden
2396	KEEP	William	45		Nephew		6	M	Scholar	Middx	Whitechapel
2397	KEEP	Charles	45		Nephew		4	M	Scholar	Middx	Whitechapel
2398	KEEP	Alfred	45		Nephew		1	M		Middx	Whitechapel
2399	CLOWES	Henry	46	College Place	Head	Mar	30	M	Tailor	Cheshire	Macclesfield
2400	CLOWES	Mary Ann	46		Wife	Mar	29	F	Straw Bonnet Sewer	Warks	Coventry
2401	CLOWES	Francis R.	46		Son		6	M	Scholar	Herts	St Albans
2402	CLOWES	Thomas H.	46		Son		4	M	Scholar	Herts	St Albans
2403	CLOWES	Emma	46		Dau		2	F		Herts	St Albans
2404	CLOWES	Jane	46		Dau		under 1 m	F		Herts	St Albans
2405	CLOWES	Ellen	46		Dau		under 1 m	F		Herts	St Albans
2406	COLEMAN	Ann	47	College Place	Head	Mar	40	F	Charwoman	Herts	Hertford
2407	COLEMAN	Mary	47		Dau	Unm	18	F	Brazilian Hat Maker	Herts	St Albans
2408	COLEMAN	Emma	47		Dau		15	F	Brazilian Hat Maker	Herts	St Albans

2409	COLEMAN	Eliza	47		Dau		13	F	Silk Throwster	Herts	St Albans
2410	COLEMAN	Ellen	47		Dau		11	F	Brazilian Hat Maker	Herts	St Albans
2411	COLEMAN	Amelia	47		Dau		9	F	Brazilian Hat Maker	Herts	St Albans
2412	COLEMAN	William	47		Son		4	M	Scholar	Herts	St Albans
2413	TRUSALL	Joseph	48	College Place	Head	Mar	50	M	Agric Lab	Herts	St Albans
2414	TRUSALL	Ann	48		Wife	Mar	45	F	Brazilian Hat Maker	Herts	St Albans
2415	TRUSALL	Mary Ann	48		Dau	Unm	22	F	Brazilian Hat Maker	Herts	St Albans
2416	TRUSALL	Sarah	48		Dau	Unm	20	F	Brazilian Hat Maker	Herts	St Albans
2417	TRUSALL	David	48		Son	Unm	14	M	Brazilian Hat Maker	Herts	St Albans
2418	TRUSALL	John	48		Son	Unm	12	M	Brazilian Hat Maker	Herts	St Albans
2419	TRUSALL	Joshua	48		Son		6	M	Brazilian Hat Maker	Herts	St Albans
2420	TRUSALL	Eliza	48		Dau		4	F		Herts	St Albans
2421	CLOWES	William	49	College Place	Head	Mar	58	M	Millwright	Cheshire	Buglawton
2422	CLOWES	Elizabeth	49		Wife	Mar	50	F		Cheshire	Macclesfield
2423	CLOWES	Levi	49		Son	Unm	18	M	Engineer	Cheshire	Macclesfield
2424	CLOWES	James	49		Son	[Unm]	16	M	Silk Throwster	Cheshire	Macclesfield
2425	CLOWES	Edward	49		Son		12	M	Silk Throwster	Herts	Watford
2426	CLOWES	Caroline	49		Dau		10	F	Scholar	Herts	Watford
2427	MITCHELL	Peter	50	College Place	Head	Widower	33	M	Tailor	Dorset	Dalwood
2428	MITCHELL	Mary	50		Mother	Widow	58	F		Dorset	Dalwood
2429	MITCHELL	Daniel	50		Son		10	M	Scholar	Herts	St Albans
2430	MITCHELL	John	50		Son		8	M	Scholar	Herts	St Albans
2431	MITCHELL	Walter	50		Son		3	M	Scholar	Herts	St Albans
2432	MITCHELL	Henry	50		Son		1	M		Herts	St Albans
2433	ENGLAND	Caroline	50		Serv		11	F	General Servant	Herts	St Albans
2434	NORMAN	Mary	51	College Place	Head	Widow	50	F	Annuitant	Bucks	Winslow
2435	NORMAN	Adelaide	51		Dau	Unm	19	F	Dressmaker	Bucks	Newport Pagnall
2436	NORMAN	Sarah C.	51		Dau		10	F	Scholar	Bucks	Fenny Stratford
2437	FISHER	Thomas	52	College Place	Head	Mar	58	M	Painter	Beds	Bedford
2438	FISHER	Elizabeth	52		Wife	Mar	60	F		Beds	Eversholt
2439	BETTLES	Ann	53	College Place	Head	Widow	79	F	Receiving Alms Late Shoebinder	Herts	St Albans
2440	HARVEY	Henry	54	College Place	Head	Mar	28	M	Tailor	Herts	St Albans
2441	HARVEY	Ann	54		Wife	Mar	23	F	Dressmaker	Herts	Great Gaddesden
2442	WHITFORD	John	55	College Place	Head	Mar	56	M	Inland Revenue Officer	Ireland	[Unknown]
2443	WHITFORD	Rachael	55		Wife	Mar	56	F		Cumb	Workington
2444	HATTON	Thomas	56	Dagnall Lane	Head	Mar	52	M	Cordwainer	Herts	St Albans
2445	HATTON	Jane	56		Wife	Mar	45	F		Beds	Unknown
2446	HATTON	Jane	56		Dau		15	F	Silk Throwster	Herts	St Albans
2447	HATTON	Hannah	56		Dau		12	F	Silk Throwster	Herts	St Albans
2448	LEWIS	Charles	57	Dagnall Lane	Head	Mar	25	M	Tailor	Herts	St Albans
2449	LEWIS	Winifred	57		Wife	Mar	23	F	Silk Throwster	Herts	St Albans
2450	LEWIS	Walter	57		Son		2	M		Herts	St Albans
2451	LEWIS	Emma	57		Dau		1	F		Herts	St Albans
2452	LUCK	Phillis	58	Dagnall Lane	Head	Widow	32	F	Straw Bonnet Sewer	Herts	St Albans

	SURNAME	FORENAME	SCHEDULE NUMBER	ADDRESS	RELATIONSHIP	STATUS	AGE	SEX	OCCUPATION	COUNTY OF BIRTH	PLACE OF BIRTH
2453	LUCK	Edmund	58		Son		8	M	Scholar	Herts	St Albans
2454	LUCK	Frederick	58		Son		6	M	Scholar	Herts	St Albans
2455	LUCK	Harriet	58		Dau		3	F	Scholar	Herts	St Albans
2456	HATCHETT	Thomas	58		Visitor	Mar	34	M	Gardener	Surrey	North Brixton
2457	HATCHETT	Ann	58		Visitors Wife	Mar	36	F	Laundress	Surrey	North Brixton
2458	HALE	Joseph	59	Dagnall Lane	Head	Mar	23	M	Ostler	Herts	St Albans
2459	HALE	Mary	59		Wife	Mar	22	F		Herts	St Albans
2460	HALE	Elizabeth	59		Dau		1	F		Herts	St Albans
2461	RUDD	William	60	Dagnall Lane	Head	Mar	34	M	Agric Lab	Herts	Park Street [St Stephens]
2462	RUDD	Jane	60		Wife	Mar	29	F		Herts	Park Street [St Stephens]
2463	RUDD	William	60		Son		7	M	Scholar	Herts	Park Street [St Stephens]
2464	RUDD	Mary Ann	60		Dau		4	F	Scholar	Herts	Park Street [St Stephens]
2465	RUDD	Betsy	60		Sister	Unm	28	F	Dressmaker	Herts	Park Street [St Stephens]
2466	JORDAN	William	61	Dagnall Lane	Head	Mar	35	M	Grocers Assistant	Herts	St Albans
2467	JORDAN	Eliza	61		Wife	Mar	33	F	Brazilian Hat Maker	Herts	St Albans
2468	DUNHAM	Benjamin	62	Dagnall Lane	Head	Mar	26	M	Carpenter	Herts	St Albans
2469	DUNHAM	Mary Ann	62		Wife	Mar	28	F	Straw Bonnet Sewer	Herts	St Albans
2470	DUNHAM	Maria	62		Dau		2m	F		Herts	St Albans
2471	WOOLFIELD	Sophia	63	Dagnall Lane	Head	Mar	59	F	Bonnet Sewer	Warks	Birmingham
2472	WOOLFIELD	Eliza	63		Dau	Unm	30	F	Bonnet Sewer	Warks	Birmingham
2473	WOOLFIELD	Maria	63		Dau	Unm	14	F	Bonnet Sewer	Herts	St Albans
2474	BAKER	Alfred D.	63		Visitor		10	M		Middx	London
2475	POLKE	Ellen	63		Visitor		11	F		Middx	London
2476	POLKE	Henry	63		Visitor		2	M		Middx	London
2477	CLARKE	Joseph	64	Dagnall Lane	Head	Mar	50	M	Butcher	Herts	St Albans
2478	CLARKE	Ann	64		Wife	Mar	27	F		Herts	Park Street [St Stephens]
2479	CLARKE	Mary	64		Dau		12	F		Herts	St Albans
2480	CLARKE	James	64		Son		3	M	Scholar	Herts	St Albans
2481	DOWDEL	James	64		Head	Unm	31	M	Straw Cutter	Surrey	Croydon

One house uninhabited

	SURNAME	FORENAME	SCHEDULE NUMBER	ADDRESS	RELATIONSHIP	STATUS	AGE	SEX	OCCUPATION	COUNTY OF BIRTH	PLACE OF BIRTH
2482	HEALY	William Alfred	65	New England Place	Head	Mar	32	M	Tea Dealer	Lancs	Bardsley [?]
2483	HEALY	Caroline	65		Wife	Mar	28	F		Middx	London
2484	HEALY	Catherine	65		Dau		4	F		Middx	London
2485	HEALY	William	65		Son		2	M		Middx	London
2486	PARLES	Eliza	66	New England Place	Head	Widow	29	F	Brazilian Hat Maker	Herts	St Albans
2487	PARLES	Charlotte	66		Dau		9	F	Brazilian Hat Maker	Herts	St Albans
2488	PARLES	Charles	66		Son		4	M	Scholar	Herts	Watford
2489	PARLES	Harry	66		Son		1	M		Herts	St Albans
2490	STROWEN	Mary	67	New England Place	Head	Unm	19	F	Silk Throwster	Herts	Rickmansworth
2491	MADON	Richard	68	New England Place	Head	Mar	41	M	Painter and Glazier	Lancs	Preston
2492	MADON	Richard	68		Son		12	M	Silk Throwster	Middx	London
2493	MADON	Alice	68		Dau		10	F	Scholar	Middx	London

2494	MADON	Thomas	68		Son		8	M	Scholar	Middx	London
2495	MADON	William	68		Son		3	M		Middx	London
2496	ANDERSON	Sarah	69	New England Place	Head	Widow	50	F	Straw Bonnet Wirer	Herts	Harpenden
2497	ANDERSON	Emma	69		Dau	Unm	19	F	Brazilian Hat Maker	Herts	St Albans
2498	ANDERSON	Josiah	69		Son		12	M		Herts	Park Street [St Stephens]
2499	ANDERSON	William	69		Son		8	M	Brazilian Grass Opener	Herts	Park Street [St Stephens]
2500	SKINNER	John	70	New England Place	Head	Mar	40	M	Agric Lab	Unknown	
2501	HATTON	George	71	New England Place	Head	Mar	23	M	Silk Throwster	Herts	St Albans
2502	HATTON	Eliza	71		Wife	Mar	24	F	Silk Throwster	Herts	St Albans
2503	HATTON	Alice	71		Mother	Mar	64	F	Charwoman	Herts	St Albans
2504	LOGGAN	William	72	New England Place	Head	Mar	40	M	Gardener	Herts	St Albans
2505	LOGGAN	Jane	72		Wife	Mar	30	F		Bucks	Princes Risborough
2506	LOGGAN	Arthur	72		Nephew	Unm	17	M	Gardener	Herts	St Albans
2507	LOGGAN	Eliza	72		Sister	Unm	30	F		Herts	St Albans
2508	ANDERSON	James	73	New England Place	Head	Mar	40	M	Carpenter	Herts	St Stephens
2509	ANDERSON	James	73		Son	Unm	20	M	Carpenter	Herts	St Albans
2510	THOMPSON	Robert	74	New England Place	Head	Mar	75	M	Receiving Alms Late Gardener	Herts	Watford
2511	THOMPSON	Ann	74		Wife	Mar	79	F		Suffolk	Preston
2512	STONE	William	75	New England Place	Head	Widower	64	M	Agric Lab	Middx	Pinner
2513	WHITE	Charles	75		Son-in-law	Widower	25	M	Agric Lab	Herts	St Albans
2514	SMITH	James	76	New England Place	Head	Mar	28	M	Carpenter	Herts	St Albans
2515	SMITH	Louisa	76		Wife	Mar	25	F	Hand Loom Weaver Trimming	Herts	St Albans
2516	SMITH	Jane	76		Dau		6	F	Scholar	Herts	St Albans
2517	SMITH	Emilia	76		Dau		4	F	Scholar	Herts	St Albans
2518	SMITH	Lydia	76		Dau		11 m	F		Herts	St Albans
2519	BUTLER	Thomas	77	New England Place	Head	Mar	33	M	Agric Lab	Herts	Redbourn
2520	BUTLER	Esther	77		Wife	Mar	30	F	Straw Plaiter	Herts	Harpenden
2521	BUTLER	Anne	77		Dau		7	F	Straw Plaiter	Herts	Redbourn
2522	BUTLER	John	77		Son		4	M		Herts	Harpenden
2523	ARCHER	George O.	77		Visitor	Mar	35	M	Grocers Clerk	Middx	London
2524	COOPER	John	78	New England Place	Head	Mar	38	M	Silk Throwster	Middx	London
2525	COOPER	Eliza	78		Wife	Mar	42	F		Herts	St Albans
2526	COOPER	Mary Ann	78		Dau		11	F	Brazilian Hat Maker	Essex	Sewardstone
2527	COOPER	Charles	78		Son		9	M	Scholar at Home	Essex	Sewardstone
2528	COOPER	Thomas	78		Son		7	M	Scholar at Home	Essex	Sewardstone
2529	COOPER	Louisa	78		Dau		3	F		Herts	St Albans
2530	NICHOLLS	Helen	79	New England Place	Head	Widow	43	F	Straw Bonnet Sewer	Suffolk	Ipswich
2531	NICHOLLS	Joseph	79		Son	Unm	20	M	Brazilian Grass Splitter	Herts	St Albans
2532	NICHOLLS	Elizabeth	79		Dau	Unm	18	F	Hand Loom Weaver Trimmer	Herts	St Albans
2533	NICHOLLS	Eliza	79		Dau	Unm	16	F	Hand Loom Weaver Trimmer	Herts	St Albans
2534	NICHOLLS	Frances	79		Dau		12	F	Silk Throwster	Herts	St Albans
2535	NICHOLLS	Louisa	79		Dau		10	F	Silk Throwster	Herts	St Albans
2536	NICHOLLS	Isaac	79		Son		7	M	Scholar	Herts	St Albans

	SURNAME	FORENAME	SCHEDULE NUMBER	ADDRESS	RELATIONSHIP	STATUS	AGE	SEX	OCCUPATION	COUNTY OF BIRTH	PLACE OF BIRTH
2537	FISHER	Samuel	80	New England Place	Head	Mar	52	M	Agric Lab	Herts	St Albans
2538	FISHER	Sarah	80		Wife	Mar	53	F		Middx [Herts]	Ridge
2539	FISHER	Henry	80		Son	Unm	23	M	Silk Throwster	Herts	St Albans
2540	FISHER	John	80		Son	Unm	19	M	Silk Throwster	Herts	St Albans
2541	FISHER	George	80		Son		12	M	Scholar	Herts	St Albans
2542	GOSSEY	Robert	81	New England Place	Head	Mar	43	M	Agric Lab	Beds	Shambrook
2543	GOSSEY	Hannah	81		Wife	Mar	40	F	Seamstress	Herts	Sandridge
2544	GOSSEY	Richard	81		Son		11	M	Brazilian Hat Maker	Beds	Dunstable
2545	GOSSEY	Elizabeth	81		Dau		12	F	Brazilian Hat Maker	Beds	Dunstable
2546	GOSSEY	Hannah	81		Dau		11	F	Brazilian Hat Maker	Beds	Dunstable
2547	GOSSEY	Alfred	81		Son		8	M	Scholar	Herts	St Albans
2548	GOSSEY	Jane	81		Dau		6	F		Herts	St Peters
2549	GOSSEY	John H.	81		Son		1	M		Herts	St Albans
2550	CROUCH	Edward	82	New England Place	Head	Mar	35	M	Police Officer	Beds	Hockliffe
2551	CROUCH	Sophia	82		Wife	Mar	31	F		Herts	Redbourn
2552	CROUCH	John	82		Son		9	M	Scholar	Northants	Northampton
2553	CROUCH	Charlotte	82		Dau		8	F	Scholar	Beds	Caddington
2554	CROUCH	Maria	82		Dau		7	F		Herts	St Albans

One house uninhabited

	SURNAME	FORENAME	SCHEDULE NUMBER	ADDRESS	RELATIONSHIP	STATUS	AGE	SEX	OCCUPATION	COUNTY OF BIRTH	PLACE OF BIRTH
2555	GAINER	John	83	New England Place	Head	Mar	40	M	Stone Mason	Wales	Talgarth
2556	GAINER	Mary	83		Wife	Mar	50	F		Wales	Talgarth
2557	GAINER	Ann	83		Dau	Unm	19	F		Wales	Talgarth
2558	GAINER	Mary	83		Dau	[Unm]	16	F		Wales	Crickhowell
2559	GAINER	Harry	83		Son		5	M	Scholar	Sussex	Brighton
2560	GAINER	Jim	83		Son		3	M	Scholar	Surrey	Reigate
2561	WHITE	John	84	New England Place	Head	Mar	62	M	Cordwainer	Bucks	Wing
2562	WHITE	Caroline	84		Wife	Mar	58	F		Herts	Colney
2563	WEBB	Thomas	85	New England Place	Head	Mar	42	M	Builder employing 3 men	Bucks	Hanslope
2564	WEBB	Eliza	85		Wife	Mar	42	F		Herts	St Albans
2565	WEBB	Sarah	85		Dau		12	F	Scholar	Herts	St Albans
2566	WEBB	Maria	85		Dau		11	F	Scholar	Herts	St Albans
2567	WEBB	Thomas	85		Son		8	M	Scholar	Herts	St Albans
2568	WEBB	Martha	85		Dau		7	F	Scholar	Herts	St Albans
2569	TOWERSEY	Joseph	86	New England Place	Head	Mar	24	M	Waterproof Hat Manufacturer	Bucks	Aylesbury
2570	TOWERSEY	Maria	86		Wife	Mar	28	F		Africa	
2571	TWITCHELL [?]	Mary	87	New England Place	Head	Widow	59	F	Brazilian Hat Maker	Lincs	Boston
2572	TWITCHELL [?]	Louisa	87		Dau	Unm	25	F	Brazilian Hat Maker	Herts	Watford
2573	TWITCHELL [?]	Elizabeth	87		Dau	Unm	23	F	Brazilian Hat Maker	Herts	Watford
2574	TWITCHELL [?]	Rebecca	87		Dau	Unm	16	F	Brazilian Hat Maker	Herts	Shenley
2575	TWITCHELL [?]	Emily	87		Grandau		4	F		Herts	St Albans
2576	ELBORN	James	88	Dagnall Lane	Head	Mar	36	M	Coal Dealer	Herts	Hemel Hempstead
2577	ELBORN	Esther	88		Wife	Mar	48	F		Herts	St Stephens
2578	TEARLE	Esther	88		Step-dau	Unm	16	F	Bonnet Maker	Herts	St Michaels

2579	ELBORN	Thomas	88		Son		8	M	Scholar	Herts	St Albans
2580	ELBORN	Sophia	88		Dau		7	F	Scholar	Herts	St Albans
2581	ELBORN	John	88		Son		5	M	Scholar	Herts	St Albans
2582	JAYS	Susan	89	Wellclose Place	Head	Widow	61	F	Annuitant	Yorks	Selby
2583	REEVE	Ann	89		Dau	Unm	40	F	Annuitant	Yorks	Kingston
2584	LANE	John	90	Wellclose Place	Head	Mar	61	M	Proprietor of Houses	Cheshire	Prestbury [?]
2585	LANE	Ann	90		Wife	Mar	61	F		Herts	Kensworth
2586	ATKINS	Edward	91	Dagnall Lane	Head	Mar	44	M	Shoemaker Master	Herts	St Albans
2587	ATKINS	Jane	91		Wife	Mar	43	F	Shoe Binder	Herts	St Albans
2588	CONQUEST	Charles	92	Dagnall Lane	Head	Mar	34	M	Watchman	Beds	Luton
2589	CONQUEST	Sarah	92		Wife	Mar	40	F	Straw Plaiter	Herts	St Albans
2590	CONQUEST	William	92		Son		8	M	Scholar	Herts	St Albans
2591	LEATHER	John H.	93	Dagnall Lane	Head	Mar	36	M	Sub-Bailiff of St Albans County Court	Cambs	Sutton, Ely
2592	LEATHER	Mary Ann	93		Wife	Mar	30	F		Norfolk	Reepham
2593	POTTS	Robert	94	Dagnall Lane	Head	Mar	48	M	Tailor and News Agent	Yorks	Sheffield
2594	POTTS	Hannah	94		Wife	Mar	41	F		Herts	St Albans
2595	POTTS	George	94		Son	Unm	19	M	Silk Throwster	Herts	St Albans
2596	POTTS	Robert	94		Son	Unm	17	M	Silk Throwster	Herts	St Albans
2597	POTTS	Harriet	94		Dau		8	F	Scholar	Herts	St Albans
2598	POTTS	James	94		Son		4	M	Scholar	Herts	St Albans
2599	POTTS	Hannah	94		Dau		1	F		Herts	St Albans
2600	CROUCH	Charles	95	Dagnall Lane	Head	Mar	31	M	Shoemaker	Herts	St Albans
2601	CROUCH	Julliet	95		Wife	Mar	31	F	Shoe Binder	Herts	Hunton Bridge [Abbots Langley]
2602	CROUCH	Sarah	95		Dau		11	F	Scholar	Herts	St Albans
2603	CROUCH	Mary Ann	95		Dau		7	F	Scholar	Herts	St Albans
2604	CROUCH	Jemima	95		Dau		5	F	Scholar	Herts	St Albans
2605	CROUCH	Jane	95		Sister	Unm	22	F	Hand Loom Weaver (Trimmer)	Herts	St Albans
2606	HANSCOMBE	James	96	Dagnall Lane	Head	Mar	75	M	Agric Lab	Beds [Bucks]	Shipton [?]
2607	HANSCOMBE	Charlotte	96		Wife	Mar	63	F	Charwoman	Herts	St Albans
2608	HANSCOMBE	Ann	96		Dau	Unm	33	F	Hand Loom Weaver (Trimming)	Herts	Markyate Street
2609	HANSCOMBE	Emma	96		Dau	Unm	19	F	Hand Loom Weaver (Trimming)	Herts	Markyate Street
2610	HANSCOMBE	William	96		Grandson		10	M	Scholar	Herts	St Albans
2611	HANSCOMBE	Thomas	96		Grandson		7	M	Scholar	Herts	St Albans
2612	HANSCOMBE	Rosannah	96		Grandau		3	F	Scholar	Herts	St Albans
2613	HANSCOMBE	Edith	96		Grandau		5m	F		Herts	St Albans
2614	KERR	John	97	Dagnall Lane	Head	Mar	60	M	Road Labourer	Sussex	Unknown
2615	KERR	Sarah	97		Wife	Mar	57	F	Charwoman	Middx	London
2616	HEDGES	Ann	97		Dau-in-law	Unm	32	F	Trimming Weaver	Herts	St Albans
2617	KERR	Margaret	97		Dau	Unm	20	F	Trimming Weaver	Herts	St Albans
2618	KERR	Isaac	97		Son	Unm	18	M	Silk Throwster	Herts	St Albans
2619	HEDGES	Albert	97		Grandson		9	M	Scholar	Herts	St Albans
2620	HEDGES	Arthur	97		Grandson		6	M	Scholar	Herts	St Albans
2621	HEDGES	Henry	97		Grandson		4	M	Scholar	Herts	St Albans

	SURNAME	FORENAME	SCHEDULE NUMBER	ADDRESS	RELATIONSHIP	STATUS	AGE	SEX	OCCUPATION	COUNTY OF BIRTH	PLACE OF BIRTH
2622	REED	Caroline	98	Dagnall Lane	Head	Unm	69	F	Laundress	Herts	St Albans
2623	DEAYTON	Jeremiah	99	Dagnall Lane	Head	Mar	62	M	Bailiff	Herts	St Albans
2624	DEAYTON	Sarah	99		Wife	Mar	62	F	Brazilian Hat Maker	Herts	Markyate Street
2625	DEAYTON	Henry	99		Son	Unm	27	M	Brazilian Hat Blocker	Herts	St Albans
2626	DEAYTON	Charles	99		Son	Unm	25	M	Brazilian Hat Blocker	Herts	St Albans
2627	DEAYTON	Maria	99		Dau	Unm	20	F	Brazilian Hat Maker	Herts	St Albans
2628	DEAYTON	James	99		Son	Mar	32	M	Brazilian Hat Blocker	Herts	St Albans
2629	DEAYTON	Dinah	99		Dau-in-law	Mar	37	F	Brazilian Hat Maker	Kent	Queenborough
2630	DEAYTON	Maria	99		Grandau		7	F		Herts	St Albans
2631	DEAYTON	James	99		Grandson		6	M		Herts	St Albans
2632	DEAYTON	Mary	99		Grandau		4	F		Herts	St Albans
2633	DEAYTON	Sarah	99		Grandau		1	F		Herts	St Albans
2634	FISHER	William	100	Dagnall Lane	Head	Mar	49	M	Grocer	Herts	St Albans
2635	FISHER	Sarah	100		Wife	Mar	55	F		Herts	St Albans
2636	FISHER	George	100		Son	Unm	26	M	Agric Lab	Herts	St Albans
2637	FISHER	Emma	100		Dau	Unm	19	F	Dressmaker	Herts	St Albans
2638	FISHER	David	100		Son		16	M	Agric Lab	Herts	St Albans
2639	NEWMAN	George	101	Dagnall Lane	Head	Mar	30	M	Iron Founder employing 1 man	Essex	Colchester
2640	NEWMAN	Emily	101		Wife	Mar	31	F		Herts	Ware
2641	NEWMAN	Emily	101		Dau		4	F		Herts	St Albans
2642	NEWMAN	George	101		Son		7m	M		Herts	St Albans
2643	ATKINS	Jane	101		Serv		12	F	General Servant	Herts	Abbots Langley
2644	LINES	Joseph	102	Dagnall Lane	Head	Mar	31	M	Carpenter	Herts	St Albans
2645	LINES	Deborah	102		Wife	Mar	32	F		Herts	St Albans
2646	LINES	Joseph	102		Son		8	M	Scholar	Herts	St Albans
2647	LINES	Henry	102		Son		7	M	Scholar	Middx	Holloway
2648	LINES	Deborah	102		Dau		4	F		Herts	St Albans
2649	LINES	Alfred	102		Son		2	M		Herts	St Albans
2650	LINES	Frederick	102		Son		2m	M		Herts	St Albans
2651	ALLISON	Thomas	103	Dagnall Lane	Head	Widower	62	M	Agric Lab	Beds	Toddington
2652	ALLISON	Levi	103		Son	Unm	17	M	Trimming Weaver	Herts	St Albans
2653	ALLISON	Jilpha	103		Dau		14	F		Herts	St Albans
2654	BRANDON	Ann	104	Ranshaws Alms Houses	Head	Widow	62	F	Receiving Alms (Seamstress)	Herts	St Albans
2655	MUNT	Elizabeth	105	Ranshaws Alms Houses	Head	Widow	60	F	Receiving Alms (Straw Plaiter)	Herts	St Albans
2656	WOODWARDS	Ann	106	Ranshaws Alms Houses	Head	Widow	74	F	Receiving Alms (Charwoman)	Herts	London Colney
2657	WOODWARDS	John	106		Grandson		9	M	Silk Throwster	Herts	St Albans
2658	SWAIN	Mary	107	Ranshaws Alms Houses	Head	Widow	62	F	Receiving Alms (Seamstress)	Herts	St Albans
2659	SWAIN	Ann H.	107		Grandau		10	F	Brazilian Hat Maker	Herts	St Albans
2660	NICHOLLS	Mary	108	Ranshaws Alms Houses	Head	Widow	91	F	Receiving Alms (Housekeeper)	Herts	St Albans
2661	QUINTON	Ann	108		Visitor	Unm	40	F	Dressmaker	Herts	St Albans
2662	GOSBELL	Mary	109	Ranshaws Alms Houses	Head	Unm	71	F	Receiving Alms (Housekeeper)	Herts	Elstree
2663	RICHARDSON	Mary	110	Ranshaws Alms Houses	Head	Widow	82	F	Receiving Alms (Innkeeper)	Beds	Shillingston

2664	GRUBB	Ann	111	Ranshaws Alms Houses	Head	Widow	72	F	Receiving Alms (Charwoman)	Norfolk	Brandon
2665	SCRIVENER	Susan	112	Ranshaws Alms Houses	Head	Widow	62	F	Receiving Alms	Essex	Saffron Walden
2666	LARGE	Ellen	113	Ranshaws Alms Houses	Head	Widow	79	F	Receiving Alms (Agric Labs Wife)	Wales	[Unknown]
2667	OAKLEY	James	114	Spicer Street	Head	Mar	40	M	Furniture Broker	Herts	St Albans
2668	OAKLEY	Elizabeth	114		Wife	Mar	36	F		Herts	St Albans
2669	OAKLEY	Mary Ann	114		Dau		12	F		Herts	St Albans
2670	OAKLEY	Martha	114		Dau		10	F	Scholar	Herts	St Albans
2671	OAKLEY	Emma	114		Dau		5	F	Scholar	Herts	St Albans
2672	OAKLEY	William	114		Son		3	M		Herts	St Albans
2673	PERRIN	Sarah	115	Spicer Street	Head	Widow	40	F	Lodging House Keeper & Chimney Sweep employing 8 Chimney Sweeps	Herts	Hitchin
2674	PERRIN	James	115		Son	Unm	16	M	Chimney Sweeper	Herts	Hitchin
2675	HYDE	Charles	115		Nephew		7	M	Chimney Sweeper	Herts	Hitchin
2676	WATTS	Henry	115		Serv	Unm	23	M	Chimney Sweeper	Warks	Birmingham
2677	BROWN	William	115		Serv	Unm	23	M	Chimney Sweeper	Kent	Deptford
2678	WHEELER	William	115		Serv	Unm	21	M	Chimney Sweeper	Middx	Balls Pond
2679	COOK	Matthew	115		Serv	Unm	21	M	Chimney Sweeper	Beds	Dunstable
2680	HAWKINS	Samuel	115		Serv	Unm	18	M	Chimney Sweeper	Herts	Hitchin
2681	CASSEY	Charles	115		Serv	Unm	15	M	Chimney Sweeper	Herts	Hitchin
2682	BANATAKER	Tunny [?]	115		Serv	Unm	24	M	Chimney Sweeper	Italy	
2683	EAMES	John	115		Lodger	Mar	27	M	Tramp Agric Lab	Herts	St Albans
2684	EAMES	Louisa	115		Lodger	[Mar]	36	F	Tramp Laundress	Middx	Stoke Newington
2685	TIDDEMAN	Elizabeth	115		Lodger		14	F	Tramp Silk Weaver	Middx	West Hackney
2686	EAMES	Mary	115		Lodger		4	F	Tramp	Herts	St Albans
2687	EAMES	John	115		Lodger		1	M	Tramp	Herts	St Albans
2688	GIBBS	Charles	116	Spicer Street	Lodger	Mar	58	M	Tramp Baker	Essex	Hadleigh
2689	GIBBS	Eliza	116		Lodger	Mar	58	F	Tramp Needlewoman	Leics	Leicester
2690	COLLINS	Timothy	116		Lodger	Mar	41	M	Tramp Labourer	Ireland	[Unknown]
2691	COLLINS	Johannah	116		Lodgers Wife	Mar	40	F	Tramp Laundress	Ireland	[Unknown]
2692	COLLINS	Margaret	116		Lodgers Dau		13	F	Tramp	Middx	Hendon
2693	COLLINS	John	116		Lodgers Son		6	M	Tramp	Herts	Hemel Hempstead
2694	COLLINS	Timothy	116		Lodgers Son		7m	M	Tramp	Surrey	Croydon
2695	POCOCK	Robert	116		Lodger	Unm	54	M	Tramp Labourer	Herts	Redbourn
2696	MACDONALD	John	116		Lodger	Unm	28	M	Tramp N. K.	Ireland	[Unknown]
2697	COLLINS	Mary	116		Lodgers Wife	Mar	30	F	Tramp N. K.	Ireland	[Unknown]
2698	COLLINS	James	116		Lodger	Mar	30	M	Tramp N. K.	Ireland	[Unknown]
2699	COLLINS	James	116		Lodgers Son		1	M	Tramp	Somerset [Gloucs]	Bristol
2700	COLLINS	Daniel	116		Lodgers Son		8	M	Tramp	Somerset [Gloucs]	Bristol
2701	COLLINS	Timothy	116		Lodgers Son		6	M	Tramp	Somerset [Gloucs]	Bristol
2702	SOUTH	Elizabeth	116		Lodger	Widow	91	F	Tramp	Herts	Wheathampstead
2703	DOCRAM	George	117		Lodger	Mar	34	M	Tramp	Middx	London
2704	SOUTH	George	118	Spicer Street	Head	Unm	30	M	Beggar	Herts	Wheathampstead

	SURNAME	FORENAME	SCHEDULE NUMBER	ADDRESS	RELATIONSHIP	STATUS	AGE	SEX	OCCUPATION	COUNTY OF BIRTH	PLACE OF BIRTH
2705	TEARLE	Richard	119	Spicer Street	Head	Mar	50	M	Gardener	Herts	St Albans
2706	TEARLE	Frances	119		Wife	Mar	50	F	Laundress	Beds	Hockliffe
2707	TEARLE	Sarah	119		Dau	Unm	21	F	Brazilian Hat Maker	Herts	St Albans
2708	TEARLE	Hannah	119		Dau		12	F	Trimming Weaver	Herts	St Albans
2709	CHURCHOUSE	John S.	120	Spicer Street	Head	Mar	38	M	Blacksmith	Beds	Luton
2710	CHURCHOUSE	Louisa	120		Wife	Mar	38	F	Blacksmiths wife	Herts	St Albans
2711	CHURCHOUSE	Enoch	120		Son		14	M	Agric Lab	Middx	Hampstead
2712	CHURCHOUSE	Louisa J.	120		Dau		8	F	Scholar	Middx	Hampstead
2713	CHURCHOUSE	Hannah	120		Dau		7	F	Scholar	Herts	St Albans
2714	CHURCHOUSE	David T.	120		Son		6	M	Scholar	Herts	St Albans
2715	CHURCHOUSE	Abel	120		Son		4	M	Scholar	Herts	St Albans
2716	CHURCHOUSE	Joshua	120		Son		3	M		Herts	St Albans
2717	CHURCHOUSE	Mary	120		Dau		5m	F		Herts	St Albans
2718	TEARLE	Charles	121	Spicer Street	Head	Mar	25	M	Queens Messenger (Postman)	[Unknown]	
2719	TEARLE	Caroline	121		Wife	Mar	22	F	Straw Bonnet Sewer	[Unknown]	
2720	LADDINGTON	James	122	Spicer Street	Head	Mar	25	M	General Dealer	Herts	St Albans
2721	LADDINGTON	Sarah	122		Wife	Mar	25	F		Herts	St Albans
2722	LADDINGTON	James	122		Son		5	M		Herts	St Albans
2723	LADDINGTON	Emma	122		Dau		3	F		Herts	St Albans
2724	LADDINGTON	Sarah	122		Dau		2	F		Herts	St Albans
2725	PUTMAN	Robert	123	Spicer Street	Head	Unm	18	M	Trimming Weaver	Herts	St Albans
2726	PUTMAN	Ann	123		Sister	Unm	20	F	Brazilian Hat Maker	Herts	St Albans
2727	BARKER	George	124	Spicer Street	Head	Unm	29	M	Tailor	Herts	St Albans
2728	WALKLATE	Joseph	125	Spicer Street	Head	Mar	56	M	Harness Maker	Herts	St Albans
2729	WALKLATE	Ann	125		Wife	Mar	56	F		Herts	St Albans
2730	WALKLATE	James	125		Son	Unm	17	M	Harness Maker	Herts	St Albans
2731	WALKLATE	Edward	125		Son		14	M	Scholar	Herts	St Albans
2732	WALKLATE	Richard	125		Son		10	M	Scholar	Herts	St Albans
2733	BAYFORD	Mary Kate	125		Grandau		8	F	Scholar	Herts	Welwyn
2734	BAYFORD	Joseph	125		Grandson		6	M	Scholar	Herts	Welwyn
2735	LOWERY	William	126	Spicer Street	Head	Unm	37	M	Agric Lab	Ireland	[Unknown]
2736	MARSTIN	Thomas	127	Spicer Street	Head	Mar	27	M	Confectioner	Herts	St Albans
2737	MARSTIN	Susan	127		Wife	Mar	22	F		Herts	St Stephens
2738	MARSTIN	Joseph	127		Son		1m	M		Herts	St Albans
2739	MILEMAN	Ann	127		Mother-in-law	Widow	50	F	Charwoman	Beds	Leighton
2740	MILEMAN	Sarah	127		Sister-in-law	Unm	26	F	Dressmaker	Herts	St Stephens
2741	MILEMAN	James	127		Brother-in-law	Unm	18	M	Farm Labourer	Herts	St Stephens
2742	MILEMAN	Abraham	127		Brother-in-law	Unm	17	M	Servant	Herts	St Stephens
2743	MANNING	Martha	128	Spicer Street	Head	Unm	65	F	Dressmaker	Herts	Hunton Bridge [Abbots Langley]
2744	MANNING	Edward	128		Son		9	M	Scholar	Herts	St Albans
2745	FLOWER	Joseph	129	Spicer Street	Head	Mar	73	M	Beadle	Wilts	Warminster
2746	FLOWER	Ann	129		Wife	Mar	71	F		Herts	St Albans
2747	FLOWER	Ann	129		Dau	Unm	26	F	Sempstress	Herts	St Albans

2748	MARRINER	Richard	129		Visitor	Mar	45	M	Printer	Kent	Chatham
2749	WATTS	John	129		Visitor	Mar	40	M	Stonemason	Somerset	Bath
2750	HALE	William	130	Spicer Street	Head	Mar	47	M	Post Boy	Middx	Barnet
2751	HALE	Sarah	130		Wife	Mar	42	F		Herts	Bells Bar [North Mimms]
2752	HALE	Eliza	130		Dau	Unm	20	F	Trimming Weaver	Herts	St Albans
2753	HALE	Mary Ann	130		Dau	Unm	18	F	Brazilian Hat Maker	Herts	St Albans
2754	HALE	William	130		Son		15	M	Scholar	Herts	St Albans
2755	HALE	Jane	130		Dau		12	F	Scholar	Herts	St Albans
2756	HALE	John	130		Son		10	M	Scholar	Herts	St Albans
2757	HALE	Benjamin	130		Son		7	M	Scholar	Herts	St Albans
2758	HALE	Hannah	130		Dau		2	F		Herts	St Albans
2759	THOMPSON	James	131	Shrubbs Yard	Head	Mar	28	M	Bricklayers Labourer	Herts	St Albans
2760	THOMPSON	Elizabeth	131		Wife	Mar	28	F	Brazilian Hat Maker	Herts	St Albans
2761	WHITE	Ann	131		Niece		4	F	Scholar	Herts	St Albans
2762	NORTH	Henry	132	Shrubbs Yard	Head	Mar	60	M	Receiving Alms (Soldier)	Herts	Hertford
2763	NORTH	Sarah	132		Wife	Mar	59	F	Laundress	Herts	St Albans
2764	NORTH	Emma	132		Dau	Unm	20	F	Straw Hat Maker	Herts	St Albans
2765	PEACOCK	John	133	Shrubbs Yard	Head	Mar	20	M	Bricklayers Lab	Herts	St Albans
2766	PEACOCK	Sarah	133		Wife	Mar	26	F	Trimming Weaver	Herts	St Albans
2767	PEACOCK	Frederick	133		Son		10	M	Scholar	Herts	St Albans
2768	PEACOCK	Ann	133		Dau		5	F	Scholar	Herts	St Albans
2769	PEACOCK	Jane	133		Dau		2	F		Herts	St Albans
2770	STRATTON	William	134	Shrubbs Yard	Head	Mar	36	M	Rope Maker	Herts	St Albans
2771	STRATTON	Elizabeth	134		Wife	Mar	35	F	Trimming Weaver	Herts	St Albans
2772	STRATTON	Eliza	134		Dau		11	F	Silk Throwster	Herts	St Albans
2773	STRATTON	Joseph	134		Son		5	M	Scholar	Herts	St Albans
2774	STRATTON	Mary	134		Dau		2	F	Scholar	Herts	St Albans
2775	STRATTON	Sarah	134		Mother	Widow	74	F		Herts	St Albans
2776	TAYLOR	David	135	Shrubbs Yard	Head	Mar	34	M	Painter	Herts	St Albans
2777	TAYLOR	Charlotte	135		Wife	Mar	33	F	Trimming Weaver	Herts	Wheathampstead
2778	TAYLOR	Jane	135		Dau		9	F	Silk Throwster	Herts	St Albans
2779	TAYLOR	Eliza	135		Dau		7	F	Silk Throwster	Herts	St Albans
2780	TAYLOR	Mary	135		Dau		2	F		Herts	St Albans
2781	TAYLOR	William	135		Son		4m	M		Herts	St Albans
2782	CRAMPTON	David	136	Spicer Street	Head	Mar	36	M	Bricklayers Labourer	Herts	St Albans
2783	CRAMPTON	Matilda	136		Wife	Mar	29	F	Trimming Weaver	Herts	Bells Bar
2784	CRAMPTON	Rebecca	136		Dau		10	F	Silk Throwster	Herts	St Albans
2785	CRAMPTON	Mary	136		Dau		5	F	Scholar	Herts	St Albans
2786	CRAMPTON	Ann	136		Dau		2	F		Herts	St Albans
2787	CLARKE	George	137	Spicer Street	Head	Mar	37	M	Carrier	Herts	St Albans
2788	CLARKE	Eliza	137		Wife	Mar	36	F		Herts	St Albans
2789	CLARKE	George	137		Son		14	M	Scholar	Herts	St Albans
2790	CLARKE	Eliza	137		Dau		12	F	Scholar	Herts	St Albans
2791	CLARKE	Walter	137		Son		10	M	Scholar	Herts	St Albans

	SURNAME	FORENAME	SCHEDULE NUMBER	ADDRESS	RELATIONSHIP	STATUS	AGE	SEX	OCCUPATION	COUNTY OF BIRTH	PLACE OF BIRTH
2792	CLARKE	Alfred	137		Son		8	M	Scholar	Herts	St Albans
2793	CLARKE	Charles	137		Son		6	M	Scholar	Herts	St Albans
2794	CLARKE	Emma	137		Dau		4	F	Scholar	Herts	St Albans
2795	CLARKE	William	137		Son		2	M		Herts	St Albans
2796	POLLANT	Mary	138	Spicer Street	Head	Widow	55	F	Laundress	Herts	St Albans
2797	COMPTON	Charles	139	Spicer Street	Head	Mar	36	M	Greengrocer	Herts	St Albans
2798	COMPTON	Isabella	139		Wife	Mar	29	F		Sussex	Hartfield
2799	COMPTON	George	139		Son		4	M	Scholar	Herts	St Albans
2800	COMPTON	Jane	139		Dau		8	F	Scholar	Herts	St Albans
2801	GARMENT	John	140	Spicer Street	Head	Mar	37	M	Greengrocer	Herts	Tring
2802	GARMENT	Mary	140		Wife	Mar	37	F		Herts	Redbourn
2803	GARMENT	George	140		Son		14	M	Errand Boy	Herts	Tring
2804	GARMENT	Josiah	140		Son		8	M	Scholar	Herts	Tring
2805	GARMENT	Ann	140		Dau		6	F	Scholar	Herts	St Albans
2806	GARMENT	Enoch	140		Son		2	M		Herts	St Albans
2807	GARMENT	Jonathan	140		Son		7m	M		Herts	St Albans
2808	DARWELL	Elizabeth	140		Sister-in-law	Unm	27	F	Straw Bonnet Sewer	Herts	Redbourn
2809	DARWELL	Emma	140		Sister-in-law	Unm	19	F	Straw Bonnet Sewer	Bucks	Chesham
2810	WILLIS	Ann	141	Spicer Street	Head	Mar	55	F	Straw Plaiter	Oxon	Odenton [Oddington]
2811	WILLIS	Joseph	141		Son	Unm	22	M	Journeyman Tailor	Middx	London
2812	WILLIS	Frances	141		Dau	Unm	21	F	Bonnet Sewer	Middx	London
2813	WILLIS	Caroline	141		Dau		11	F	Bonnet Sewer	Herts	Tring
2814	MANSELL	David	142	Spicer Street	Head	Mar	23	M	Wheelwright	Herts	St Albans
2815	MANSELL	Elizabeth	142		Wife	Mar	24	F		Herts	St Albans
2816	MANSELL	David	142		Son		2	M		Herts	St Albans
2817	MANSELL	Ann	142		Dau		1	F		Herts	St Albans
2818	BACON	John	143	Spicer Street	Head	Mar	30	M	Bricklayer	Herts	St Albans
2819	BACON	Hannah	143		Wife	Mar	26	F		Herts	Hatfield
2820	BACON	Rosanna	143		Dau		3	F	Scholar	Herts	St Albans
2821	BACON	Robert	143		Son		3m	M		Herts	St Albans
2822	AMBROSE	John	144	Spicer Street	Head	Mar	27	M	Ironfounder	Essex	Chelmsford
2823	AMBROSE	Mary Ann	144		Wife	Mar	22	F		Middx	London
2824	EASTHALL	Robert	145	Spicer Street	Head	Mar	38	M	Plumber and Glazier	Norfolk	Old Buckenham
2825	EASTHALL	Sophia	145		Wife	Mar	30	F		Beds	Clophill
2826	EASTHALL	Francis	145		Son		9	M	Scholar	Beds	Biggleswade
2827	EASTHALL	Ellen	145		Dau		6	F	Scholar	Beds	Biggleswade
2828	EASTHALL	Adriana	145		Dau		2	F		Bucks	Fenny Stratford
2829	FARRIS	William	146	Fishpool Street	Head	Mar	30	M	Paper Stainer employing 1 man & 1 boy	Middx	St Pancras
2830	FARRIS	Elizabeth	146		Wife	Mar	35	F		Herts	St Albans
2831	FARRIS	Eliza	146		Dau		10	F	Scholar	Middx	St Pancras
2832	FARRIS	Sarah	146		Dau		8	F	Scholar	Middx	St Pancras
2833	FARRIS	Alice	146		Dau		6	F	Scholar	Middx	St Pancras
2834	FARRIS	Elizabeth	146		Dau		4	F	Scholar	Middx	St Pancras
2835	BRADSHAW	Edward	146		Visitor	[Mar]	34	M	House Servant	Kent	Canterbury

2836	BRADSHAW	Eliza	146		Visitors [Wife]	[Mar]	29	F		Herts	St Albans
2837	FARRIS	Emily	146		Dau		2	F		Middx	St Pancras
2838	ALDRIDGE	Charlotte	147	Fishpool Street	Head	Mar	57	F	Publicans Wife	Herts	Hoddesden
2839	ALDRIDGE	Charlotte	147		Dau	Unm	23	F		Herts	St Albans
2840	ALDRIDGE	Richard	147		Son	Unm	21	M	Butcher	Herts	St Albans
2841	ALDRIDGE	Joseph	147		Son	Unm	21	M	Butcher	Herts	St Albans
2842	BEDFORD	Ann	147		Serv		15	F	General Servant	Herts	St Albans

One house uninhabited

2843	OWEN	Charles	148	Fishpool Street	Head	Mar	47	M	Builder	Wales	[Unknown]
2844	OWEN	Mary Ann	148		Wife	Mar	46	F		Herts	St Albans
2845	OWEN	Annie	148		Dau		15	F		Herts	St Albans
2846	OWEN	Emma	148		Dau		12	F	Scholar	Herts	St Albans
2847	OWEN	Evan E.	148		Son		9	M	Scholar	Herts	St Albans
2848	OWEN	Owen C.	148		Son		7	M	Scholar	Herts	St Albans
2849	OWEN	James H.	148		Son		6	M		Herts	St Albans
2850	MCGEORGE	Thomas	149	Fishpool Street	Head	Mar	40	M	Publican	Kent	Gravesend
2851	MCGEORGE	Susanna	149		Wife	Mar	23	F		Herts	St Stephens
2852	MCGEORGE	Alfred	149		Son		15	M	Scholar	Middx	London
2853	MCGEORGE	Horatio	149		Dau		9	M	Scholar	Middx	London
2854	MCGEORGE	Ellen	149		Dau		8	F	Scholar	Herts	St Albans
2855	MCGEORGE	Isabella	149		Dau		2	F	Scholar	Herts	St Albans
2856	MCGEORGE	Sarah Ann	149		Dau		1	F		Herts	St Albans
2857	MCGEORGE	Mary Ann	149		Dau		13	F	Scholar	Herts	St Albans
2858	FAWELL	John	150	Fishpool Street	Head	Mar	44	M	Carpenter and Builder employing 6 men	Herts	St Albans
2859	FAWELL	Ann	150		Wife	Mar	30	F	Dressmaker	Herts	Sandridge
2860	FAWELL	Susan A.	150		Dau		6	F	Scholar	Herts	St Albans
2861	FAWELL	Elizabeth M.	150		Dau		4	F	Scholar	Herts	St Albans
2862	FAWELL	Rosa	150		Dau		3	F		Herts	St Albans
2863	FAWELL	Maria	150		Dau		1	F		Herts	St Albans
2864	HARRIS	Mary	151	Fishpool Street	Head	Unm	31	F	Milliner and Dressmaker	Middx	Bloomsbury
2865	HARRIS	Sarah Ann	151		Sister	Unm	21	F	Milliner and Dressmaker	Herts	Cheshunt
2866	BAYTON	Ann	152	Fishpool Street	Head	Unm	64	F	Annuitant	Essex	Braintree
2867	FLOWER	John	153	Fishpool Street	Head	Mar	33	M	Tin Worker	Herts	St Albans
2868	FLOWER	Mercy	153		Wife	Mar	33	F		Herts	St Albans
2869	FLOWER	John	153		Son		4	M	Scholar	Herts	St Albans
2870	FLOWER	Joseph	153		Son		2	M		Herts	St Albans
2871	CHERRY	Mark	154	Fishpool Street	Head	Mar	32	M	Draper	Herts	St Albans
2872	CHERRY	Alice	154		Wife	Mar	29	F		Herts	Hemel Hempstead
2873	CHERRY	Ann	154		Dau		7	F	Scholar	Beds	Bedford
2874	CHERRY	George	154		Son		6	M	Scholar	Beds	Bedford
2875	CHERRY	Sarah	154		Dau		4	F	Scholar	Beds	Bedford
2876	POTTER	Emma	154		Serv	Unm	22	F	General Servant	Herts	London Colney
2877	PEPPERCORN	Samuel	155	Fishpool Street	Head	Unm	31	M	Solicitors General Clerk	Herts	St Albans

	SURNAME	FORENAME	SCHEDULE NUMBER	ADDRESS	RELATIONSHIP	STATUS	AGE	SEX	OCCUPATION	COUNTY OF BIRTH	PLACE OF BIRTH
2878	WILES	Joseph	156	Fishpool Street	Head	Mar	24	M	Baker	Beds	Blunham
2879	WILES	Jane W.	156		Wife	Mar	29	F		Middx	Islington
2880	WILES	Jane	156		Dau		1	F		Herts	St Albans
2881	SIMS	William George	156		Serv	Unm	23	M	Journeyman Baker	Middx	St Pancras
2882	CLAYTON	William John	156		Serv	Unm	20	M	Journeyman Baker	Herts	St Albans
2883	ELWOOD	Charlotte	156		Serv	Unm	17	F	General Servant	Herts	St Stephens
2884	HALL	Henry	157	Fishpool Street	Head	Mar	31	M	Clergyman without cure	Cambs	Wisbech
2885	HALL	Elizabeth	157		Wife	Mar	25	F	Clergymans wife	Cambs	Wisbech
2886	WILKINSON	Joseph	157		Pupil	Unm	18	M	Pupil	Lincs	Spalding
2887	FAIRPELL	Frederick	157		Pupil	Unm	15	M	Pupil	Cambs	Wisbech
2888	GIBSON	Finlay	157		Pupil	Unm	12	M	Pupil	Essex	Ongar
2889	LAYDALE	Walter	157		Pupil	Unm	17	M	Pupil	Notts	Nottingham
2890	LEACH	Henry	157		Pupil	Unm	14	M	Pupil	Cambs	Wisbech
2891	BAKER	Henry	157		Pupil	Unm	13	M	Pupil	Cambs	Whittlesey
2892	WELLING	Charles	157		Pupil	Unm	14	M	Pupil	Norfolk	Lynn
2893	SEDGEWICK	Arthur	157		Pupil	Unm	13	M	Pupil	Herts	Rickmansworth
2894	BAXTER	Charles	157		Pupil	Unm	14	M	Pupil	Cambs	Whittlesey
2895	ROBERTS	Albinus	157		Pupil	Unm	14	M	Pupil	Middx	London
2896	WOTTON	Charles	157		Pupil	Unm	14	M	Pupil	Herts	Kings Langley
2897	JOHNSON	Robert	157		Pupil	Unm	13	M	Pupil	Cambs	Whittlesey
2898	WARD	Henry	157		Pupil	Unm	15	M	Pupil	Cambs	Wisbech
2899	WHITTAKER	William	158		Pupil	Unm	14	M	Pupil	Middx	London
2900	BOWER	Thomas	158		Pupil	Unm	15	M	Pupil	Cambs	Whittlesey
2901	WATSON	John	158		Pupil	Unm	16	M	Pupil	Cambs	Wisbech
2902	BOYCE	Gibson	158		Pupil	Unm	12	M	Pupil	Cambs	Whittlesey
2903	LIP	William	158		Pupil	Unm	14	M	Pupil	Northants	Peterborough
2904	GROOME	Richard	158		Pupil	Unm	11	M	Pupil	Herts	Kings Langley
2905	HAZLEHURST	Alfred	158		Pupil	Unm	11	M	Pupil	Essex	Ilford
2906	WRIGHT	Walter	158		Pupil	Unm	10	M	Pupil	Herts	Hitchin
2907	SABERTON	John	158		Pupil	Unm	13	M	Pupil	Cambs	Witcham
2908	SABERTON	Thomas	158		Pupil	Unm	9	M	Pupil	Cambs	Witcham
2909	BENNETT	William	158		Pupil	Unm	11	M	Pupil	Herts	St Albans
2910	GIBSON	Philip	158		Pupil	Unm	11	M	Pupil	Essex	Ongar
2911	DONALDSON	A	158		Pupil	Unm	12	M	Pupil	Middx	London
2912	BLUNT	John	158		Pupil	Unm	12	M	Pupil	Cambs	Whittlesey
2913	SEDGWICK	Gordon	158		Pupil	Unm	10	M	Pupil	Herts	Rickmansworth
2914	BOWKER	Fred	159		Pupil	Unm	11	M	Pupil	Cambs	Whittlesey
2915	HEDGES	Hannah	159		Serv	Unm	27	F	Cook	Herts	Redbourn
2916	WARNER	Rebecca	159		Serv	Unm	20	F	Domestic Servant	Cambs	Thorney
2917	LEES	Celia S.	159		Serv	Unm	21	F	Domestic Servant	Middx	London
2918	HUNT	Mary Ann	159		Serv	Unm	19	F	Domestic Servant	Norfolk	Emneth
2919	DUNHAM	William	160	Fishpool Street	Head	Mar	34	M	Bricklayer	Herts	St Albans
2920	DUNHAM	Charlotte	160		Wife	Mar	34	F	Hat Maker	Beds	Ashley [?] [Apsley]
2921	JAMES	Joshua	161	Fishpool Street	Head	Unm	38	M	Labourer	Herts	St Stephens

2922	TURNER	Martha	162	Fishpool Street	Head	Widow	48	F	Straw Bonnet Maker	Beds	Luton
2923	TURNER	Nathaniel B.	162		Son	Unm	22	M	Sexton of the Abbey	Herts	St Albans
2924	TURNER	Sarah	162		Dau	Unm	25	F	Straw Bonnet Maker	Herts	St Albans
2925	TURNER	Elizabeth	162		Dau		13	F	Straw Bonnet Maker	Herts	St Albans
2926	TURNER	Emma	162		Dau		10	F	Scholar	Herts	St Albans
2927	TURNER	Samuel M.	162		Son		7	M	Scholar	Herts	St Albans
2928	MEAD	John	162		Nephew		12	M	Silk Throwster	Herts	Wallington
2929	RADWAY	John	163	Fishpool Street	Head	Mar	62	M	Currier	Gloucs	Cirencester
2930	RADWAY	Elizabeth	163		Wife	Mar	54	F	Curriers Wife	Notts	Granby
2931	RADWAY	Thomas	163		Son	Unm	31	M	Animal Painter	Notts	Granby
2932	RADWAY	William	163		Son	Unm	23	M	Curriers Son	Herts	St Albans
2933	RADWAY	Clara	163		Dau	Unm	15	F	Scholar	Herts	St Albans
2934	BLAGG	Thomas Ward	164	Fishpool Street	Head	Mar	49	M	Solicitor	Staffs	Cheadle
2935	BLAGG	Elizabeth	164		Wife	Mar	45	F	Solicitors Wife	Wilts	Marlborough
2936	EDMONDS	Jane A.	164		Visitor	Unm	22	F		Devon	Woodleigh
2937	BECKINGHAM	Elizabeth	164		Serv	Unm	24	F	Domestic Servant	Wilts	Marlborough
2938	COLE	Jane	164		Serv	Unm	34	F	Domestic Servant	Middx	Shadwell
2939	PRYAM	Mainet [?]	164		Serv	Unm	17	F	Domestic Servant	Ireland	[Unknown]
2940	JOHNSON	John	165	Fishpool Street	Head	Mar	70	M	Millwright	Dorset	Sherborne
2941	JOHNSON	Hannah	165		Wife	Mar	70	F	Millwrights Wife	Herts	Ridge
2942	JOHNSON	Thomas	165		Son	Mar	36	M	Bootmaker	Herts	St Albans
2943	JOHNSON	Jane C.	165		Dau-in-law	Mar	40	F	Bootmakers wife	London	
2944	JOHNSON	William	165		Son	Unm	24	M	Bootmaker	Herts	St Albans
2945	JOHNSON	Sarah	165		Dau	Unm	22	F	Shoe Binder	Herts	St Albans
2946	HAWKINS	Elizabeth M.	165		Visitor	Unm	10	F	Scholar	Kent	Greenwich
2947	BAILEY	John	165		Serv	Unm	20	M	Apprentice	Herts	Wheathampstead
2948	PALMER	William	165		Serv	Unm	17	M	Apprentice	Herts	Wheathampstead
2949	HARRAWAY	William	166	Fishpool Street	Head	Mar	53	M	Bricklayer	Herts	St Albans
2950	HARRAWAY	Ann	166		Wife	Mar	53	F	Hat Maker	Herts	Shenley
2951	HARRAWAY	Fanny	166		Dau	Unm	21	F	Loom Weaver	Herts	St Albans
2952	HARRAWAY	Eliza	166		Dau	Unm	10	F	Scholar	Herts	St Albans
2953	TALLETT	Thomas Kings	167	Fishpool Street	Head	Mar	47	M	Painter and Grocer	Oxon	Oxford
2954	TALLETT	Catherine	167		Wife	Mar	44	F	Painters wife	Herts	St Albans
2955	TALLETT	Samuel K.	167		Son	Unm	14	M	Apprentice	Herts	St Albans
2956	TALLETT	Henry	167		Son	Unm	13	M	Servant	Herts	St Albans
2957	TALLETT	Mary	167		Dau	Unm	11	F	Silk Throwster	Herts	St Albans
2958	TALLETT	Catherine	167		Dau	Unm	10	F	Silk Throwster	Herts	St Albans
2959	TALLETT	Elizabeth	167		Dau	Unm	8	F	Scholar	Herts	St Albans
2960	TALLETT	Charlotte	167		Dau	Unm	6	F	Scholar	Herts	St Albans
2961	TALLETT	Martha	167		Dau	Unm	3	F	Scholar	Herts	St Albans
2962	COLEMAN	Sarah	168	Fishpool Street	Head	Unm	36	F	Silk Throwster	Herts	St Albans
2963	COLEMAN	John	168		Son	Unm	18	M	Silk Throwster	Herts	St Albans
2964	COLEMAN	Samuel	168		Son	Unm	16	M	Silk Throwster	Herts	St Albans
2965	HILLIARD	Henry	169	Fishpool Street	Head	Mar	37	M	Schoolmaster	Herts	St Albans

	SURNAME	FORENAME	SCHEDULE NUMBER	ADDRESS	RELATIONSHIP	STATUS	AGE	SEX	OCCUPATION	COUNTY OF BIRTH	PLACE OF BIRTH
2966	HILLIARD	Charlotte	169		Wife	Mar	34	F	Schoolmaster	Bucks	Amersham
2967	HILLIARD	Henry	169		Son	Unm	9	M	Scholar	Herts	St Albans
2968	HILLIARD	James	169		Son	Unm	7	M	Scholar	Herts	St Albans
2969	HILLIARD	William	169		Son	Unm	5	M	Scholar	Herts	St Albans
2970	RANCE	Fanny	169		Sister-in-law	Unm	29	F	Bonnet Sewer	Bucks	Amersham
2971	BLYTH	Thomas	170	Fishpool Street	Head	Mar	41	M	Iron Worker	Norfolk	Norwich
2972	BLYTH	Mary Ann	170		Wife	Mar	41	F	Shoe Binder	Norfolk	Norwich
2973	JUNIPER	Elizabeth	172	Fishpool Street	Head	Mar	29	F	Dressmaker	Unknown	
2974	JUNIPER	William	172		Son		2	M		London	
2975	COMPTON	Mary A.	173	Fishpool Street	Head	Unm	46	F	Brazilian Hat Maker	Herts	St Albans
2976	COMPTON	Eliza	173		Sister	Unm	40	F	Brazilian Hat Maker	Herts	St Albans
2977	BATES	Thomas H.	174	Fishpool Street	Head	Mar	52	M	Groom	Herts	St Albans
2978	BATES	Margaret	174		Wife	Mar	43	F	Laundress	Herts	St Albans
2979	BATES	Emilia	174		Dau		7	F	Scholar	Herts	St Albans
2980	GHOST	William	174		Father-in-law	Widower	67	M	Cooper	Herts	Great Berkhamsted
2981	SELSBY	Jane	174		Visitor	Unm	34	F	Dressmaker	Herts	St Albans
2982	PERKINS	Rebecca	174		Visitor	Unm	34	F	Plait Maker	London	

One house uninhabited

	SURNAME	FORENAME	SCHEDULE NUMBER	ADDRESS	RELATIONSHIP	STATUS	AGE	SEX	OCCUPATION	COUNTY OF BIRTH	PLACE OF BIRTH
2983	GLADMAN	William	176	Fishpool Street	Head	Unm	72	M	Rope Maker	Unknown	
2984	DUNHAM	John	177	Fishpool Street	Head	Widower	61	M	Builder	Herts	Wheathampstead
2985	DUNHAM	Ann	177		Dau	Unm	38	F	Housekeeper	Herts	St Albans
2986	DUNHAM	Francis	177		Son	Unm	19	M	Bricklayer	Herts	St Albans
2987	SEARLE	Emma	177		Serv	Unm	19	F	Domestic Servant	Herts	Bishops Stortford
2988	WHITE	Charles	178	Fishpool Street	Head	Mar	28	M	Carpenter	Herts	Watford
2989	WHITE	Mary Ann	178		Wife	Mar	25	F	Carpenters Wife	Herts	St Albans
2990	WHITE	Mary Ann	178		Dau		6	F		Herts	St Albans
2991	WHITE	Charles	178		Son		4	M		Herts	St Albans
2992	WHITE	Rose Hannah	178		Dau		3	F		Herts	St Albans
2993	WHITE	Emily	178		Dau		1	F		Herts	St Albans
2994	SADLER	Mary	178		Gd Mother	Widow	58	F	Nurse	Herts	St Albans
2995	ATKINS	Joseph	179	Fishpool Street	Head	Mar	33	M	Dealer	Herts	Bedmond [Abbots Langley]
2996	ATKINS	Tamer	179		Wife	Mar	33	F	Hatmaker	Herts	Buxhill [Buckshill, Watford?]
2997	ATKINS	Reuben	179		Son		12	M	Silk Throwster	Herts	Bedmond [Abbots Langley]
2998	ATKINS	Cavilione [?]	179		Dau		10	F	Silk Throwster	Herts	Bedmond [Abbots Langley]
2999	ATKINS	Edemond	179		Son		9	M	Silk Throwster	Herts	Chipperfield [Kings Langley]
3000	ATKINS	Eli	179		Son		6	M	Scholar	Herts	Bedmond [Abbots Langley]
3001	ATKINS	Amos	179		Son		5	M	Scholar	Herts	Nashwell [Nash Mills?]
3002	ATKINS	Amelia	179		Dau		1	F		Herts	Bedmond [Abbots Langley]
3003	TINSON	Susannah	179		Visitor	Unm	23	F	Hatmaker	Herts	Woodhall
3004	DEAYTON	Thomas	180	Fishpool Street	Head	Mar	64	M	Carpenter	Herts	St Albans
3005	DEAYTON	Mary	180		Wife	Mar	57	F	Carpenters Wife	Herts	St Albans
3006	DEAYTON	Jane	180		Dau	Unm	21	F	Dressmaker	Herts	St Albans

3007	SINFIELD	Joseph	181	Fishpool Street	Head	Mar	25	M	Victualler	Beds	Maulden
3008	SINFIELD	Susannah	181		Wife	Mar	25	F	Victuallers Wife	Herts	St Michaels
3009	DEACON	David	182	Fishpool Street	Head	Mar	29	M	Hat Blocker	Beds	Dunstable
3010	DEACON	Isabelle	182		Wife	Mar	35	F		Bucks	Aylesbury
3011	MILLARD	Henry	183	Fishpool Street	Head	Mar	43	M	General Dealer	Somerset	Bath
3012	MILLARD	Jane	183		Wife	Mar	28	F	General Dealers wife	N'thumb	[Unknown]
3013	FOUNTAIN	William	184	Fishpool Street	Head	Mar	32	M	Labourer	Beds	Eaton Bray
3014	FOUNTAIN	Harriett	184		Wife	Mar	29	F	Labourers Wife	Herts	Aldenham
3015	PARROTT	Mary	185	Fishpool Street	Head	Widow	58	F	Laundress	Herts	Kings Walden
3016	PARROTT	Joseph	185		Son	Unm	25	M	Son	Herts	St Albans
3017	WATTS	Hannah	185		Niece	Unm	24	F	Hatmaker	Herts	Redbourn
3018	DAWSON	John	186	Fishpool Street	Head	Mar	34	M	Rope Maker	Herts	Welwyn
3019	DAWSON	Caroline	186		Wife	Mar	28	F	Weaver	Middx	Battle Bridge [?]
3020	GOLDING	Sarah	186		Serv		8	F	Domestic Servant	Herts	St Albans
3021	GOLDING	Mary Ann	187		Lodger	Unm	24	F	Weaver	Bucks	Chesham
3022	CHARLES	Hannah	188	Fishpool Street	Head	Widow	74	F	Laundry Proprietress	Durham	Durham
3023	BIDNESS	Mary	188		Serv	Unm	54	F	Domestic Servant	Bucks	Buckingham
3024	CARRICK	Benjamin	189	Fishpool Street	Head	Mar	34	M	Tailor	Kent	Tunbridge Wells
3025	CARRICK	Mary	189		Wife	Mar	34	F	Tailors Wife	Beds	New Mill End [?]
3026	CARRICK	Henry	189		Son		11	M	Scholar	Beds	Dunstable
3027	CARRICK	Caroline	189		Dau		9	F	Scholar	Herts	St Albans
3028	CARRICK	Thomas	189		Son		7	M	Scholar	Herts	St Albans
3029	CARRICK	William	189		Son		5	M	Scholar	Herts	St Albans
3030	CARRICK	Isabella	189		Dau		2	F	Scholar	Herts	St Albans
3031	CARRICK	Fanny	189		Dau		1 m	F		Herts	St Albans
3032	REDRUP	Caroline	190	Fishpool Street	Head	Unm	23	F	Hatmaker	Herts	St Albans
3033	REDRUP	Maria	190		Sister	Unm	16	F	Hatmaker	Herts	St Albans
3034	CHERRY	Luke	191	Fishpool Street	Head	Widower	76	M	Retired Tailor	Beds	Luton
3035	CHERRY	Ann	191		Dau	Unm	37	F		Herts	St Albans
3036	GREEN	Sarah	191		Serv	Unm	36	F	Domestic Servant	Herts	Redbourn
3037	LUNDY	Eliza	192	Fishpool Street	Head	Widow	41	F	Hatmaker	Herts	Hemel Hempstead
3038	LUNDY	Jane	192		Dau	Unm	22	F	Hatmaker	Herts	St Albans
3039	LUNDY	John	192		Son	Unm	18	M	Iron Founder	Herts	St Albans
3040	LUNDY	Alfred	192		Son	Unm	13	M	Scholar	Herts	St Albans
3041	LUNDY	Frederick	192		Son	Unm	11	M	Silk Throwster	Herts	St Albans
3042	LUNDY	Emily	192		Dau	Unm	7	F	Brazilian Hatmaker	Herts	St Albans
3043	BARR	Sarah	193	Fishpool Street	Head	Widow	56	F	Plaiter	Herts	St Albans
3044	BARR	Sarah Ann	193		Dau	Unm	18	F	Hatmaker	Herts	St Albans
3045	CRICKETT [?]	George W.A.C.	194	Fishpool Street	Head	Mar	46	M	Painter	Kent	Colchester
3046	CRICKETT [?]	Martha	194		Wife	Mar	41	F	Painters Wife	Lancs	Liverpool
3047	CRICKETT [?]	Harriett	194		Dau	Unm	17	F	Trimming Weaver	Herts	St Albans
3048	CRICKETT [?]	Charles Alexander	194		Son		15	M	Apprentice	Herts	St Albans
3049	CRICKETT [?]	Amelia	194		Dau		13	F		Herts	St Albans

	SURNAME	FORENAME	SCHEDULE NUMBER	ADDRESS	RELATIONSHIP	STATUS	AGE	SEX	OCCUPATION	COUNTY OF BIRTH	PLACE OF BIRTH
3050	EWER	Francis	195	Fishpool Street	Head	Mar	29	M	Brazilian Hat Presser	Herts	St Albans
3051	EWER	Eliza	195		Wife	Mar	33	F	Hat Pressers Wife	Herts	Markyate
3052	EWER	Sarah	195		Dau		6	F	Scholar	Herts	St Albans
3053	EWER	Charles	195		Son		3	M		Herts	St Albans
3054	WELLS	William	196	Fishpool Street	Head	Mar	30	M	Labourer	Herts	Flamstead
3055	WELLS	Hannah	196		Wife	Mar	38	F	Labourers Wife	Herts	Tring
3056	PEARCE	Thomas	197	Fishpool Street	Head	Mar	36	M	Carpenter	Herts	Sandridge
3057	PEARCE	Eliza	197		Wife	Mar	31	F	Carpenters Wife	Herts	St Albans
3058	PEARCE	Joseph	197		Son		12	M	Scholar	Herts	St Albans
3059	PEARCE	Eliza	197		Dau		9	F	Scholar	Middx	Paddington
3060	PEARCE	Thomas Albert	197		Son		5	M	Scholar	Herts	Essendon
3061	PEARCE	Elizabeth	197		Dau		3	F		Herts	St Albans
3062	BURRIDGE	William	198	Fishpool Street	Head	Mar	27	M	Shoemaker	London	
3063	BURRIDGE	Elizabeth	198		Wife	Mar	28	F	Shoemakers Wife	Herts	Great Gaddesden
3064	BURRIDGE	Sarah	198		Dau		6	F		Herts	Hemel Hempstead
3065	BURRIDGE	Mary	198		Dau		5	F		Herts	Great Gaddesden
3066	BURRIDGE	Joseph	198		Son		2	M		Herts	Great Gaddesden
3067	BURRIDGE	Ann	198		Dau		7m	F		Herts	St Albans
3068	HAINES	Thomas	199	Fishpool Street	Head	Mar	49	M	Blacksmith	Ireland	Roscommon
3069	HAINES	Alice	199		Wife	Mar	47	F	Plaiter	Herts	Sandridge
3070	HAINES	Sophia	199		Dau	Unm	18	F	Hatmaker	Herts	Wheathampstead
3071	HAINES	Maria	199		Dau		15	F	Hatmaker	Herts	Wheathampstead
3072	HAINES	Thomas	199		Son		13	M	Grass Opener	Herts	Redbourn
3073	HAINES	James	199		Son		10	M	Hat Worker	Herts	St Albans
3074	HAINES	Edwin	199		Son		8	M	Hat Worker	Herts	Cubit Green [?]
3075	HAINES	Joseph	199		Son		6	M	Scholar	Herts	St Albans
3076	HAINES	Elizabeth	199		Dau		3	F		Herts	St Albans
3077	FRANKLIN	James	200	Fishpool Street	Head	Mar	30	M	Brazilian Hat Presser	Herts	Sandridge
3078	FRANKLIN	Elizabeth	200		Wife	Mar	30	F	Hat Pressers Wife	Herts	St Albans
3079	FRANKLIN	Elizabeth	200		Dau		8	F	Scholar	Herts	St Albans
3080	FRANKLIN	James	200		Son		6	M	Scholar	Herts	St Albans
3081	FRANKLIN	Joseph	200		Son		3	M	Scholar	Herts	St Albans
3082	FRANKLIN	Samuel	200		Son		2	M	Scholar	Herts	St Albans
3083	SMITH	William	201	Fishpool Street	Head	Mar	32	M	Hat and Bonnet Presser	Herts	St Albans
3084	SMITH	Elizabeth	201		Wife	Mar	36	F	Hat Worker	Herts	St Albans
3085	LAWRANCE	David	201		Father-in-law	Widower	56	M	Farm Labourer	Herts	St Albans
3086	CARRINGTON	Mary	202	Fishpool Street	Head	Widow	50	F	Nurse	Herts	[Unknown]
3087	FENSOM	Samuel	203	Fishpool Street	Head	Mar	79	M	Labourer	Herts	St Albans
3088	FENSOM	Ann	203		Wife	Mar	75	F	Labourers Wife	Cambs	Chesterton
3089	TURNER	John	204	Fishpool Street	Head	Mar	31	M	Common Brewer	Herts	Watford
3090	TURNER	M Ann	204		Wife	Mar	34	F	Common Brewers Wife	Herts	Flamstead
3091	TURNER	John	204		Son	Unm	12	M	Scholar	Herts	St Albans
3092	TURNER	William	204		Son	Unm	10	M	Scholar	Herts	St Albans

3093	TURNER	Charles	204		Son	Unm	7	M	Scholar	Herts	St Albans
3094	TURNER	Henry	204		Son	Unm	5	M	Scholar	Herts	St Albans
3095	TURNER	Frank	204		Son	Unm	3	M	Scholar	Herts	St Albans
3096	TURNER	Mary	204		Dau	Unm	1	F		Herts	St Albans
3097	FISHER	William	205	Fishpool Street	Head	Unm	30	M	Labourer	Herts	Redbourn
3098	LAMBDEN	William	206	Fishpool Street	Head	Unm	22	M	Labourer	Surrey	[Unknown]
3099	WILSON	William	207	Fishpool Street	Head	Unm	27	M	Labourer	Herts	St Michaels
3100	JOHNSON	Ruth	208	Fishpool Street	Head	Widow	52	F	Hat Manufacturer	Herts	Redbourn
3101	JOHNSON	Sarah	208		Dau	Unm	25	F	Assistant [Hat Manufacturer]	Herts	Redbourn
3102	JOHNSON	Emma	208		Dau	Unm	24	F	Assistant [Hat Manufacturer]	Herts	Redbourn
3103	JOHNSON	Rosa	208		Dau	Unm	20	F	Assistant [Hat Manufacturer]	Herts	Redbourn
3104	JOHNSON	Ruth	208		Dau	Unm	17	F	Assistant [Hat Manufacturer]	Herts	Redbourn
3105	JOHNSON	Thomas	208		Son		15	M	Assistant [Hat Manufacturer]	Herts	Redbourn
3106	JOHNSON	Ellen	208		Dau		13	F	Assistant [Hat Manufacturer]	Herts	Redbourn
3107	JOHNSON	Elizabeth	208		Dau		10	F	Assistant [Hat Manufacturer]	Herts	St Albans
3108	ROGERS	J	208		Visitor	Mar	24	M	Draper	Beds	Ampthill
3109	ROGERS	Mary	208		Visitors Wife	Mar	23	F	Drapers Wife	Herts	St Albans
3110	ROGERS	Kate	208		Visitors Dau		9 m	F		Kent	Bexley
3111	WEST	Samuel	209	Fishpool Street	Head	Mar	32	M	Hat Manufacturer	Surrey	Epsom
3112	WEST	Eliza	209		Wife	Mar	26	F	Hat Manufacturers Wife	Herts	St Albans
3113	WEST	William	209		Son	Unm	7	M	Scholar	Herts	St Albans
3114	WEST	Eliza	209		Dau	Unm	5	F	Scholar	Herts	St Albans
3115	WEST	Ann	209		Dau	Unm	4	F	Scholar	Herts	St Albans
3116	WEST	Mary	209		Dau	Unm	1	F		Herts	St Albans
3117	RUDDOCK	R. H.	209		Serv	Unm	14	M	Clerk	Herts	Hertford
3118	BARFATHER	Jane	209		Serv	Unm	19	F	Domestic Servant	London	
3119	PLAYSOME	Frances	209		Serv	Unm	14	F	Domestic Servant	Herts	St Albans
3120	HUTCHINS	John	210	Fishpool Street	Head	Mar	21	M	Brewer	Herts	Bedmond [Abbots Langley]
3121	HUTCHINS	Mary Ann	210		Wife	Mar	23	F	Hat Worker	Surrey	Lambeth
3122	WESTALL	Hannah	211	Fishpool Street	Head	Unm	17	F	Hat Worker	Unknown	
3123	SMITH	James	212	Fishpool Street	Head	Mar	61	M	Hat Maker	Herts	St Albans
3124	SMITH	Ann	212		Wife	Mar	60	F		Herts	St Albans
3125	SMITH	Martha	212		Dau	Unm	17	F	Fancy Hat Trimmer	Herts	St Albans
3126	WELLS	Caroline	213	Fishpool Street	Head	Widow	26	F	Dress Maker	Herts	Ware
3127	WELLS	Caroline	213		Dau		3	F		Herts	Ware
3128	CASS	Ann	213		Sister	Unm	19	F	Dress Maker	Herts	Ware
3129	PAYNE	Ellen	214	Fishpool Street	Head	Widow	30	F	Bonnet Sewer	Herts	St Albans
3130	PAYNE	Hannah	214		Dau		7	F	Scholar	Herts	Watford
3131	PAYNE	Ellen	214		Dau		3	F		Herts	Watford
3132	PAYNE	Eliza	214		Dau		2	F		Herts	Watford
3133	CROW	George	215	Fishpool Street	Head	Mar	42	M	Victualler	Herts	Hatfield
3134	CROW	Sarah	215		Wife	Mar	41	F		Essex	Colchester

	SURNAME	FORENAME	SCHEDULE NUMBER	ADDRESS	RELATIONSHIP	STATUS	AGE	SEX	OCCUPATION	COUNTY OF BIRTH	PLACE OF BIRTH
3135	CROW	William G.	215		Son	Unm	19	M		Surrey	Lambeth
3136	GLASS	Mary	215		Mother-in-law	Widow	60	F		Essex	Colchester
3137	GLADMAN	William	216	Fishpool Street	Head	Mar	65	M	Dyer	Herts	St Albans
3138	GLADMAN	Martha	216		Wife	Mar	60	F	Dyers Wife	Kent	[Unknown]
3139	STOCKWELL	David	217	Fishpool Street	Head	Unm	19	M	Tailor	Herts	St Albans
3140	PAYNE	Thomas	218	Fishpool Street	Head	Mar	26	M	Sawyer	Herts	St Peters
3141	PAYNE	Milson	218		Wife	Mar	29	F	Weaver	Herts	St Albans
3142	PAYNE	William	218		Son		4	M		Herts	St Peters
3143	PAYNE	Thomas	218		Son		1	M		Herts	St Peters
3144	SMITH	Joseph	219	Fishpool Street	Head	Mar	22	M	Hat Blocker	Herts	St Albans
3145	SMITH	Jane	219		Wife	Mar	30	F	Hatcaner	Herts	St Albans
3146	SMITH	Henry	219		Son		7	M	Grass Opener	Herts	St Albans
3147	SMITH	William	219		Son		5	M		Herts	St Albans
3148	SMITH	Joseph	219		Son		2	M		Herts	St Albans
3149	BELLHAM	John	220	Fishpool Street	Head	Mar	40	M	Gardener	Norfolk	Necton
3150	BELLHAM	Ann	220		Wife	Mar	46	F	Gardeners Wife	Herts	Whitwell
3151	BELLHAM	James	220		Son		9	M	Scholar	Herts	Whitwell
3152	BELLHAM	Jane	220		Dau		7	F	Weaver	Herts	Whitwell
3153	BREWER	William	221	Fishpool Street	Head	Mar	39	M	Labourer	Herts	St Albans
3154	BREWER	Hannah	221		Wife	Mar	32	F	Trimming Weaver	Herts	St Albans
3155	BREWER	Mary Ann	221		Dau		9	F	Scholar	Herts	St Albans
3156	MOON	James	222	Fishpool Street	Head	Mar	46	M	Marine Store Dealer	Herts	St Albans
3157	MOON	Eliza	222		Wife	Mar	25	F	Trimming Weaver	Herts	St Albans
3158	MOON	Louisa I.	222		Dau		4	F		Herts	St Albans
3159	MOON	Thomas	222		Son		1	M		Herts	St Albans
3160	COMPTON	William	223	Fishpool Street	Head	Mar	42	M	Shoemaker	Herts	St Albans
3161	COMPTON	Mary	223		Wife	Mar	41	F	Hatmaker	Herts	St Albans
3162	COMPTON	Hannah	223		Dau	Unm	18	F	Hatmaker	Herts	St Albans
3163	COMPTON	William	223		Son		12	M	Hatmaker	Middx	Westminster
3164	COMPTON	Mary	223		Dau		8	F	Hatmaker	Herts	St Albans
3165	COMPTON	Charles	223		Son		3	M	Hatmaker	Herts	St Albans
3166	BRIDEN	Edward	224	Fishpool Street	Head	Mar	58	M	Baker	Herts	Markyate
3167	BRIDEN	Sarah	224		Wife	Mar	44	F	Bakers Wife	Beds	Leighton [Buzzard]
3168	PEACOCK	William	225	Fishpool Street	Head	Mar	55	M	Grocers Shopman	Middx	Isleworth
3169	PEACOCK	Elizabeth	225		Wife	Mar	47	F	Governess	Middx	London
3170	BAKER	William	226	Fishpool Street	Head	Mar	59	M	Whitesmith	Middx	London
3171	BAKER	Elizabeth	226		Wife	Mar	62	F	Whitesmiths Wife	[Unknown]	
3172	BAKER	Thomas	226		Son	Unm	35	M	Whitesmith	Herts	Sandridge
3173	BAKER	Emanuel	226		Son	Unm	27	M	Whitesmith	Herts	Sandridge
3174	TRIPP	Eliza	226		Serv	Unm	21	F	Domestic Servant	Herts	Watford
3175	SMITH	George	227	Fishpool Street	Head	Unm	31	M	Shoemaker	Suffolk	Nayland
3176	PORTER	George	228	Fishpool Street	Head	Unm	19	M	Shoemaker	Northants	Northampton
3177	WARRILOW	Thomas	229	Fishpool Street	Head	Unm	26	M	Shoemaker	Staffs	Stone
3178	FENSOM	James	230	Fishpool Street	Head	Unm	26	M	Shoemaker	Herts	Wheathampstead

3179	EMMERTON	John	231	Fishpool Street	Head	Mar	38	M	Labourer	Beds	Biddle Hill [Biddenham?]
3180	EMMERTON	Sarah	231		Wife	Mar	33	F	Labourers Wife	Herts	St Albans
3181	EMMERTON	Mary	231		Dau		11	F	Silk Throwster	Herts	St Albans
3182	EMMERTON	Elizabeth	231		Dau		9	F	Silk Throwster	Herts	St Albans
3183	EMMERTON	William	231		Son		7	M	Scholar	Herts	St Albans
3184	EMMERTON	Susan	231		Dau		5	F	Scholar	Herts	St Albans
3185	EMMERTON	Sarah	231		Dau		2	F	Scholar	Herts	St Albans
3186	WINGRAVE	Josiah	232	Fishpool Street	Head	Mar	38	M	Straw Plait Merchant	Beds	Luton
3187	WINGRAVE	Caroline	232		Wife	Mar	30	F	Straw Plait Merchants Wife	Herts	St Albans
3188	WINGRAVE	Josiah	232		Son		10	M		Herts	St Albans
3189	WINGRAVE	Thomas H	232		Son		8	M		Herts	St Albans
3190	WINGRAVE	John Wood	232		Son		6	M		Essex	Wethersfield
3191	WINGRAVE	Robert	232		Son		4	M		Herts	St Albans
3192	WINGRAVE	Frederick	232		Son		3	M		Herts	St Albans
3193	WINGRAVE	William	232		Son		3	M		Herts	St Albans
3194	WINGRAVE	Catherine	232		Dau		8m	F		Herts	St Albans
3195	WOOD	Thomas William	232		Brother	Unm	26	M	Straw Plait Merchant	Herts	St Albans
3196	NASH	Ann	232		Serv	Unm	24	F	Domestic Servant	Essex	Wethersfield
3197	ANDERSON	Emma	232		Serv	Unm	16	F	Domestic Servant	Herts	Park Street [St Stephens]
3198	FELLS	Robert King	233	Fishpool Street	Head	Mar	26	M	Manager of Iron Foundry	Herts	Barkway
3199	FELLS	Susannah	233		Wife	Mar	21	F	Managers Wife	Herts	Ware
3200	FELLS	Rosa Wells	233		Dau		1	F		Herts	St Albans
3201	WELLS	Sara Ann	233		Sister	Unm	19	F	Visitor	Herts	Ware
3202	BATES	Eliza	233		Serv	Unm	18	F	Domestic Servant	Herts	Nash Mills [Kings Langley]
3203	BELL	Eliza	234	Fishpool Street	Head	Widow	45	F	Landed Proprietress	Hunts	St Ives
3204	BELL	Ellen	234		Dau	Unm	20	F	Landed Proprietress	Norfolk	Norwich
3205	GHOST	Harriot	234		Serv	Unm	21	F	Domestic Servant	Herts	St Albans
3206	CASEY	Thomas	235	Fishpool Street	Head	Mar	55	M	Physician MD Edinburgh	Ireland	[Unknown]
3207	CASEY	Ann	235		Wife	Mar	50	F	Physicians Wife	Herts	Kimpton
3208	CASEY	Anne	235		Dau		14	F	Scholar at home	Ireland	[Unknown]
3209	CASEY	Mary Anne	235		Dau		12	F	Scholar at home	Ireland	[Unknown]
3210	CASEY	Henry Ernest	235		Son		10	M	Scholar	Ireland	[Unknown]
3211	CASEY	Edward	235		Son		8	M	Scholar	Herts	St Albans
3212	BEAN	Eliza	235		Serv	Unm	22	F	Domestic Servant	Herts	St Albans
3213	BURGOYNE	William	236	Fishpool Street	Head	Mar	48	M	Carpenter	Beds	Eversholt
3214	BURGOYNE	Mary	236		Wife	Mar	49	F	Carpenters Wife	Beds	Stopsley
3215	WRIGHT	Harriot	236		Dau-in-law	Unm	24	F	Hatmaker	Herts	Hitchin
3216	BURGOYNE	William	236		Son		15	M	Carpenters Son	Herts	St Albans
3217	BURGOYNE	Emma	236		Dau		10	F	Hatmaker	Herts	St Albans
3218	BURGOYNE	Susannah	236		Dau		14	F	Scholar	Herts	St Albans
3219	BURGOYNE	Rachael	236		Dau		8	F	Scholar	Herts	St Albans
3220	BURGOYNE	Fanny	236		Dau		5	F	Scholar	Herts	St Albans
3221	BURGOYNE	Claire	236		Dau		1	F		Herts	St Albans

SURNAME	FORENAME	SCHEDULE NUMBER	ADDRESS	RELATIONSHIP	STATUS	AGE	SEX	OCCUPATION	COUNTY OF BIRTH	PLACE OF BIRTH
3222	DEAYTON	John	237	Prison	Head	Mar	36	M	Governor of Prison	Herts	St Albans
3223	DEAYTON	Susannah Marton	237		Wife	Mar	34	F	Governors Wife	Surrey	Southwark
3224	DEAYTON	Susannah Sarah	237		Dau		8	F	Scholar	Herts	St Albans
3225	DEAYTON	Amelia Jane	237		Dau		6	F	Scholar	Herts	St Albans
3226	DEAYTON	John Thomas	237		Son		5	M	Scholar	Herts	St Albans
3227	DEAYTON	Ann Ford	237		Dau		2	F		Herts	St Albans
3228	ALLEN	John Scott	237		Head	Mar	36	M	Head Turnkey of Prison	Middx	St Marylebone
3229	ALLEN	Eliza	237		Wife	Mar	36	F	Matron of Prison	Hants	Stockbridge
3230	ALLEN	Catherine Louise	237		Dau		12	F	Scholar at home	Hants	Stockbridge
3231	ALLEN	Eliza Ann	237		Dau		10	F	Scholar at home	Middx	St Marylebone
3232	ALLEN	Thomas	237		Son		9	M	Scholar at home	Middx	St Lukes
3233	ALLEN	John Scott	237		Son		5	M	Scholar at home	Herts	St Albans
3234	ALLEN	Frances Charlotte	237		Dau		3	F		Herts	St Albans
3235	ALLEN	Rosetta	237		Dau		1	F		Herts	St Albans
3236	TOMS	Eliza	237		Serv	Unm	19	F	General Servant	Herts	Park Street [St Stephens]
3237	HUNT	Charles	238		Prisoner	Unm	19	M	Labourer	Herts	Rickmansworth
3238	COREY	Henry	238		Prisoner	Mar	48	M	Mariner	Middx	Hackney
3239	KINGSBURY	William	238		Prisoner	Unm	21	M	Labourer	London	St Georges
3240	MUNT	Richard	238		Prisoner	Unm	27	M	Labourer	Beds	St Michaels
3241	TURNER	John	238		Prisoner	Unm	19	M	Labourer	Herts	Rickmansworth
3242	WILSON	Joseph	238		Prisoner	Mar	24	M	Bricklayer	Herts	Watford
3243	SHARPE	Thomas	238		Prisoner	Unm	19	M	Labourer	Herts	Flamstead
3244	PERRY	George	238		Prisoner	Unm	16	M	Labourer	Herts	Redbourn
3245	BURGESS	John	238		Prisoner	Unm	24	M	Labourer	Warks	Coventry
3246	FORD	Isaac	238		Prisoner	Unm	36	M	Labourer	Herts	Barnet
3247	GODFREY	John	238		Prisoner	Unm	36	M	Labourer	Middx	Friern Barnet
3248	HARPER	James	238		Prisoner	Unm	30	M	Labourer	Herts	Northaw
3249	GREEN	Eliza	238		Prisoner	Widow	29	F	Labourer	Devon	Plymouth
3250	SMITH	James	239		Prisoner	Mar	60	M	Labourer	Herts	Abbots Langley
3251	WELSH	Martin	239		Prisoner	Unm	18	M	Labourer	Ireland	Galway
3252	BAUGH	George	239		Prisoner	Unm	47	M	Labourer	Shrop	[?]
3253	BURNHILL	John	239		Prisoner	Unm	57	M	Schoolmaster	Herts	St Michaels
3254	STRATTON	James	239		Prisoner	Mar	45	M	Labourer	Herts	St Albans
3255	HOWARD	William	239		Prisoner	Mar	17	M	Carpenter	Herts	Watford
3256	FREEMAN	William	239		Prisoner	Unm	32	M	Bookkeeper	Lancs	Manchester
3257	KEEGAN	John	239		Prisoner	Unm	25	M	Labourer	Herts	Bedmond [Abbots Langley]
3258	WILSON	Robert	239		Prisoner	Unm	60	M	Labourer	Ireland	West Meath [?]
3259	HUMPHREY	George	239		Prisoner	Mar	18	M	Labourer	Herts	Hemel Hempstead
3260	SEWDELL	Henry	239		Prisoner	Unm	30	M	Chair Maker	Herts	St Stephens
3261	FOUNTAIN	Joseph	239		Prisoner	Unm	17	M	Labourer	Herts	Hatfield
3262	DOUGLAS	John	239		Prisoner	Unm	26	M	Labourer	Herts	Rickmansworth
3263	NORTON	William	239		Prisoner	Mar	27	M	Labourer	Ireland	Langford
3264	MALLARD	James	239		Prisoner	Unm	21	M	Labourer	Kent	Dartford

3265	GULSTON	Thomas	240		Prisoner	Unm	19	M	Labourer	Herts	Watford
3266	FISHER	Emma	240		Prisoner	Unm	11	F	Labourer	Herts	Codicote
3267	STEVENS	John	240		Prisoner	Mar	43	M	Labourer	Herts	Great Gaddesden
3268	HUNT	Charles	240		Prisoner	Mar	48	M	Shoemaker	Herts	Rickmansworth
3269	HAWKINS	Joseph	240		Prisoner	Unm	21	M	Labourer	Herts	Rickmansworth
3270	PHILLIPS	John	240		Prisoner	Unm	18	M	Labourer	Somerset	Bath
3271	HOUSE	George	240		Prisoner	Unm	22	M	Labourer	Herts	Abbots Langley
3272	MARTINDALE	Mark	240		Prisoner	Unm	31	M	Labourer	Herts	Abbots Langley
3273	NETHERCOTE	John	240		Prisoner	Unm	19	M	Labourer	Berks	Wallingford
3274	BENNETT	George	240		Prisoner	Unm	18	M	Labourer	Herts	Abbots Langley
3275	CLAY	George	240		Prisoner	Unm	45	M	Labourer	Herts	St Michaels
3276	NOAH	Daniel	240		Prisoner	Mar	41	M	Labourer	Bucks	Chesham
3277	MCGREGOR	John	240		Prisoner	Unm	28	M	Labourer	Herts	Barnet
3278	GRAY	James	240		Prisoner	Unm	19	M	Labourer	Herts	Datchworth
3279	COWLEY	William	240		Prisoner	Unm	31	M	Labourer	Ireland	County Meath
3280	LAING	George	241	Abbey Mill Lane	Head	Mar	66	M	Gentleman	Middx	London
3281	LAING	Mary Ann	241		Wife	Mar	63	F	Gentlemans Wife	Middx	London
3282	MCKEENE	John	241		Serv	Unm	23	M	Servant	Scotland	Inverness
3283	MCKEENE	Mary	241		Serv	Unm	31	F	Servant	Scotland	Inverness
3284	TERRY	Matilda	241		Serv	Unm	20	F	Servant	Scotland	Inverness
3285	SURTEES	Benjamin	242	Abbey Mill Lane	Head	Mar	22	M	Boot Maker	Surrey	Walworth
3286	SURTEES	Eliza	242		Wife	Mar	21	F	Hat Maker	Herts	Redbourn
3287	SURTEES	Alfred	242		Son		3m	M		Herts	St Albans
3288	WELCH	Samuel	242		Brother-in-law	Unm	16	M	Silk Weaver	Herts	St Albans
3289	BISHOP	Joseph	243	Abbey Mill Lane	Head	Mar	36	M	Carpenter	Herts	St Albans
3290	BISHOP	Mary Ann	243		Wife	Mar	32	F	Carpenters Wife	Middx	London
3291	BISHOP	Joseph J.	243		Son		12	M	Silk Winder	Herts	St Albans
3292	BISHOP	Robert	243		Son		6	M	Scholar	Herts	St Albans
3293	BISHOP	Littlesher [?Letitia]	243		Dau		4	F	Scholar	Herts	St Albans
3294	BISHOP	Elizabeth	243		Dau		2	F		Herts	St Albans
3295	BISHOP	Martha	243		Dau		4m	F		Herts	St Albans
3296	RUFFETT	George	244	Abbey Mill Lane	Head	Mar	21	M	Licensed Victualler	Surrey	Ditton
3297	RUFFETT	Jane	244		Wife	Mar	22	F	Licensed Victuallers wife	Wilts	Ramsbury
3298	MINALL	Eliza	244		Sister-in-law		9	F	Visitor	Wilts	Ramsbury
3299	WOOLLAM	John	245	Abbey Mill Lane	Head	Mar	61	M	Silk Throwster	Wales	Wrexham
3300	WOOLLAM	Mary	245		Wife	Mar	47	F		[Gloucs]	Bristol
3301	WOOLLAM	Penelope	245		Dau	Unm	25	F		Middx	Hampstead
3302	WOOLLAM	Catharine	245		Dau	Unm	20	F		Middx	Hamsptead
3303	WOOLLAM	Charles	245		Son	Unm	19	M	Scholar	Middx	Hampstead
3304	WARD	Frances J.	245		Visitor	Unm	34	F		[Gloucs]	Bristol
3305	CAPEL	Mary	245		Serv	Unm	47	F	Domestic Servant	Kent	Crocombe
3306	PAYNE	Elizabeth	245		Serv	Unm	28	F	Domestic Servant	Herts	Flaunden
3307	MAILON	Sarah	245		Serv	Unm	17	F	Domestic Servant	Herts	St Albans
3308	ATKINS	George	245		Labourer	Widower	42	M	Labourer	Herts	St Albans

	SURNAME	FORENAME	SCHEDULE NUMBER	ADDRESS	RELATIONSHIP	STATUS	AGE	SEX	OCCUPATION	COUNTY OF BIRTH	PLACE OF BIRTH
3309	BARKER	George	246	Abbey Mill Lane	Head	Mar	36	M	Silk Throwster	Herts	Hatfield
3310	BARKER	Ann	246		Wife	Mar	39	F	Silk Winder	Herts	St Albans
3311	JOHNSON	John	247	Abbey Mill Lane	Head	Mar	44	M	Millwright	Herts	St Albans
3312	JOHNSON	Hannah	247		Wife	Mar	42	F	Millwrights wife	Herts	St Albans
3313	JOHNSON	Hannah	247		Dau	Unm	20	F	Bonnet Sewer	Herts	St Albans
3314	JOHNSON	Clara	247		Dau		9	F	Scholar	Herts	St Albans
3315	BREWER	Henry	248	Abbey Mill Lane	Head	Mar	36	M	Silk Throwster	Herts	St Albans
3316	BREWER	Ann	248		Wife	Mar	41	F	Silk Throwsters wife	Herts	St Albans
3317	WELCH	Emma	248		Dau-in-law	Unm	17	F	Silk Winder	Herts	St Albans
3318	BREWER	Henry	248		Son	Unm	12	M	Scholar	Herts	St Albans
3319	BREWER	Jesse William	248		Son	Unm	11	M	Scholar	Herts	St Albans
3320	BREWER	Charles	248		Son	Unm	7	M	Scholar	Herts	St Albans
3321	BREWER	Catherine	248		Dau	Unm	4	F	Scholar	Herts	St Albans
3322	HALSEY	Daniel	249	Abbey Mill Lane	Head	Mar	31	M	Labourer	Herts	St Albans
3323	HALSEY	Maria	249		Wife	Mar	31	F	Weaver	Herts	St Albans
3324	TEBBUTT	Samuel	250	Abbey Mill Lane	Head	Mar	30	M	Cordwainer	Beds	Shambrook
3325	TEBBUTT	Ann	250		Wife	Mar	25	F	Weaver	Beds	Leighton [Buzzard]
3326	TEBBUTT	Frederick	250		Son		6	M	Scholar	Herts	St Albans
3327	TEBBUTT	Rebecca	250		Dau		3	F	Scholar	Herts	St Albans
3328	CASTLE	John	251	Abbey Mill Lane	Head	Mar	26	M	Labourer	Herts	Hatfield
3329	CASTLE	Ann	251		Wife	Mar	21	F	Weaver	Somerset	Barton
3330	CASTLE	Sarah	251		Dau		3	F		Herts	St Albans
3331	CASTLE	Jane	251		Dau		1	F		Herts	St Albans
3332	POWELL	Maria	252	Abbey Mill Lane	Head	Unm	22	F	Hat Maker	Herts	St Albans
3333	HAYNES	Edward	253	Abbey Mill Lane	Head	Mar	42	M	Cabinet Maker	Cambs	Wisbech
3334	HAYNES	Hannah	253		Wife	Mar	37	F	Cabinet Makers wife	Herts	St Albans
3335	HAYNES	Joseph Edward	253		Son		15	M	Hat Worker	Herts	St Albans
3336	WARBEY	Charles	254	Abbey Mill Lane	Head	Mar	24	M	Straw Weaver	Herts	St Albans
3337	WARBEY	Mary	254		Wife	Mar	28	F	Straw Weavers wife	Herts	St Albans
3338	WARBEY	Arthur	254		Son		4	M	Scholar	Herts	St Albans
3339	WARBEY	Frederick	254		Son		11 m	M		Herts	St Albans
3340	RICHARDSON	John	255	Abbey Mill Lane	Head	Mar	43	M	Gardener	Herts	St Albans
3341	RICHARDSON	Fanny	255		Wife	Mar	48	F	Gardeners wife	Herts	St Albans
3342	RICHARDSON	Charles	255		Son	Unm	16	M	Scholar	Herts	St Albans
3343	RICHARDSON	George	255		Son	Unm	13	M	Scholar	Herts	St Albans
3344	RICHARDSON	William	255		Son	Unm	9	M	Scholar	Herts	St Albans
3345	RICHARDSON	James	255		Son	Unm	9	M	Scholar	Herts	St Albans
3346	SHORT	Mary Harriet	256	Abbey Mill Lane	Head	Widow	46	F	Seamstress	Herts	St Albans
3347	SHORT	Joseph James	256		Son	Unm	22	M	Clerk in Solicitors Office	Herts	St Albans
3348	SHORT	Christiana	256		Dau	Unm	19	F	Servant	Herts	St Albans
3349	SHORT	Walter Charles	256		Son	Unm	15	M	Scholar	Herts	St Albans
3350	SHORT	Emma Main	256		Dau	Unm	10	F	Scholar	Herts	St Albans
3351	SHORT	Jane Sarah	256		Dau	Unm	9	F	Scholar	Herts	St Albans

3352	DORANT	James Annerly	257	Abbey Mill Lane	Head	Mar	53	M	Solicitor	Middx	St James
3353	DORANT	Harriett	257		Wife	Mar	31	F		Middx	Kentish Town
3354	DORANT	Pauline	257		Dau		8 m	F		Herts	St Albans
3355	MANSELL	Eliza	257		Serv	Unm	20	F	General Servant	Herts	St Albans
3356	COOTE	Jeannette	258	Rome Land	Head	Widow	65	F	Annuitant	Essex	Woodford
3357	COOTE	Eliza	258		Dau	Unm	32	F	Governess	Essex	Woodford
3358	TURNER	Henry	259	Rome Land	Head	Unm	36	M	Assistant Master in Grammar School	Kent	Deptford
3359	BEAN	Joseph	260	Rome Land	Head	Mar	54	M	Sawyer	Herts	Harpenden
3360	BEAN	Elizabeth	260		Wife	Mar	48	F	Sawyers wife	Herts	St Michaels
3361	BEAN	Charlotte	260		Dau	Unm	13	F	Scholar	Herts	St Albans
3362	BEAN	Jane	260		Dau	Unm	10	F	Scholar	Herts	St Albans
3363	BEAN	Thomas	260		Son	Unm	8	M	Scholar	Herts	St Albans
3364	BEAN	William	260		Son	Unm	6	M	Scholar	Herts	St Albans
3365	BEAN	George	260		Son	Unm	6	M	Scholar	Herts	St Albans
3366	CAWDREY	John	261	Rome Land	Head	Mar	33	M	Labourer	Herts	Abbots Langley
3367	CAWDREY	Mary	261		Wife	Mar	26	F		Herts	St Albans
3368	CAWDREY	Mary Ann	261		Dau		9 m	F		Herts	Abbey [St Albans]
3369	KINE	James	262	Rome Land	Head	Mar	52	M	Boot Maker	Herts	St Albans
3370	KINE	Esther	262		Wife	Mar	59	F	Boot Makers Wife	Herts	St Albans
3371	WILLIS	William	262		Serv	Unm	14	M	Apprentice	Herts	Tring

Chapter Eleven

The parish of St Michaels in the borough of St Albans

Registrar's District: St Albans   Enumeration District 5a   Ref. HO 107/1713 folios 462-93

All the houses in the Parish and Borough, including part of Fishpool Street, St Michaels and Pound Field.

1	BRANDON	William	1	Fishpool Street	Head	Mar	50	M	Greenwich Out Pensioner Shoe Binder	Bucks	Chesham
2	BRANDON	Susan	1		Wife	Mar	44	F	Shoe Binder	Herts	St Albans
3	HOLLAND	Sarah	1		Mother-in-law	Widow	86	F	Pauper	Herts	St Albans
4	GAZELEY	Charles	1		Nephew	Unm	17	M	Trimming Weaver	Herts	St Albans
5	SALMON	Jane	2	Fishpool Street	Head	Widow	72	F		[Surrey]	Shere [?]
6	SALMON	Eliza	2		Dau	Unm	28	F	Trimming Weaver	Herts	St Michaels
7	SALMON	Sarah	2		Dau	Unm	24	F	Hat Maker	Herts	St Michaels
8	TAYLOR	Edward	3	Fishpool Street	Head	Mar	37	M	Bricklayers Labourer	Herts	St Albans
9	TAYLOR	Dianah	3		Wife	Mar	36	F		Herts	St Michaels
10	TAYLOR	Jane	3		Dau		13	F	Hat Maker	Herts	St Michaels
11	TAYLOR	Emma	3		Dau		11	F	Hat Maker	Herts	St Michaels
12	TAYLOR	Elizabeth	3		Dau		8	F	Hat Maker	Herts	St Michaels
13	TAYLOR	Frederick	3		Son		6	M	Scholar	Herts	St Michaels
14	KIFF	George	4	Fishpool Street	Head	Mar	30	M	Agric Lab	Herts	St Michaels
15	KIFF	Elizabeth	4		Wife	Mar	28	F	Trimming Weaver	Herts	Harpenden
16	KIFF	Betsy	4		Dau		7	F	Hat Maker	Herts	St Michaels
17	KIFF	Emma	4		Dau		5	F	Scholar	Herts	St Michaels
18	KIFF	Susan	4		Dau		1	F		Herts	St Michaels
19	STEPNEY	William	5	Fishpool Street	Head	Mar	45	M	Labourer	Beds	Luton
20	STEPNEY	Ann Maria	5		Wife	Mar	43	F		Herts	St Michaels
21	STEPNEY	Mary Ann	5		Dau		13	F	Hat Maker	Beds	Luton
22	STEPNEY	John	5		Son		8	M	Hat Maker (Deaf & Dumb)	Beds	Luton
23	STEPNEY	Sarah Maria	5		Dau		5	F		Herts	St Albans
24	STEPNEY	Eliza	5		Dau		1	F		Herts	St Albans
25	SEABROOKE	David	6	Fishpool Street	Head	Mar	39	M	Bricklayers Lab	Herts	Hempstead [Hemel]
26	SEABROOKE	Ann	6		Wife	Mar	38	F		Herts	Sandridge
27	SEABROOKE	Charles	6		Son		12	M	Hat Maker	Herts	St Michaels

28	SEABROOKE	Sarah	6		Dau		10	F	Hat Maker	Herts	St Michaels
29	SEABROOKE	Eliza	6		Dau		5	F		Herts	St Michaels
30	SEABROOKE	Maria	6		Dau		2	F		Herts	St Michaels
31	SKEGG	Ann	7	Fishpool Street	Head	Mar	60	F		Essex	[Unknown]
32	SKEGG	James	7		Son	Unm	33	M	Lab in a coal yard	Herts	St Michaels
33	SKEGG	Eliza	7		Dau	Unm	24	F		Herts	St Michaels
34	FREEMAN	Thomas	8	Fishpool Street	Head	Mar	47	M	Gardener	Herts	Kimpton
35	FREEMAN	Ann	8		Wife	Mar	46	F		Herts	Redbourn
36	FREEMAN	Sophia	8		Dau	Unm	18	F	Trimming Weaver	Herts	St Michaels
37	FREEMAN	Joseph	8		Son		14	M	Hat Maker	Herts	St Michaels
38	FREEMAN	Sarah	8		Dau		10	F	Hat Maker	Herts	St Michaels
39	FREEMAN	Mary Ann	8		Dau		10	F	Hat Maker	Herts	St Michaels
40	GAZELEY	William	9	Fishpool Street	Head	Mar	49	M	Agric Lab	Herts	St Michaels
41	GAZELEY	Sarah	9		Wife	Mar	52	F		Herts	Hatfield
42	GAZELEY	Joseph	9		Son	Unm	23	M	Trimming Weaver	Herts	St Michaels
43	GAZELEY	Elizabeth	9		Dau	Unm	19	F	Hat Maker	Herts	St Michaels
44	GAZELEY	William	9		Son	Unm	18	M	Grass Splitter	Herts	St Michaels
45	GAZELEY	Henry	9		Son		15	M		Herts	St Michaels
46	GAZELEY	Isaac	9		Son		13	M		Herts	St Michaels
47	BLAKE	Joseph	10	Fishpool Street	Head	Mar	32	M	Agric Lab	Herts	St Michaels
48	BLAKE	Mary	10		Wife	Mar	29	F	Hat Maker	Herts	Hatfield
49	BLAKE	Louisa	10		Dau		7	F	Scholar	Herts	St Michaels
50	BLAKE	Philip	10		Son		5	M		Herts	St Michaels
51	GAZELEY	Eliza	10		Sister	Unm	25	F	Trimming Weaver	Herts	St Michaels

One house uninhabited

52	BRAMPTON	Charlotte	11	Fishpool Street	Head	Widow	50	F	Sorter of Rags	Beds	Willington
53	BRAMPTON	Emma	11		Dau	Unm	19	F	Sorter of Rags	Beds	Cotten End
54	SHRIMPTON	John	12	Fishpool Street	Head	Mar	40	M	Rag Merchant	Herts	Watford
55	SHRIMPTON	Hannah	12		Wife	Mar	44	F		Herts	Market Street [St Albans]
56	SHRIMPTON	Charlotte	12		Dau		13	F	Scholar	Herts	Stevenage
57	SHRIMPTON	John	12		Son		10	M	Scholar	Herts	Stevenage
58	SHRIMPTON	Joseph	12		Son		6	M	Scholar	Herts	Stevenage
59	SHRIMPTON	Samuel	12		Son		4	M	Scholar	Herts	Stevenage
60	ATKINS	Sarah	13	Fishpool Street	Head	Mar	67	F		Herts	Ickleford
61	FINCH	Eliza	13		Grandau		16	F	Straw Hat Maker	Herts	St Michaels
62	FINCH	Ann	13		Grandau		13	F	Straw Hat Maker	Herts	St Michaels
63	CURNICK	Richard	14	Fishpool Street	Head	Mar	59	M	Post Boy	Beds	Brick Hill
64	CURNICK	Emma	14		Wife	Mar	34	F		Bucks	Chesham
65	CURNICK	Emma	14		Dau		1	F		Herts	St Michaels
66	BROWN	Edward	15	Fishpool Street	Head	Mar	29	M	Shoemaker employing 2 men	Herts	St Michaels
67	BROWN	Rhoda	15		Wife	Mar	29	F		Herts	Redbourn
68	BROWN	Edward	15		Son		5	M	Scholar	Herts	St Michaels
69	BROWN	William	15		Son		1	M		Herts	St Michaels
70	BROWN	Henry	15		Brother	Unm	25	M	Shoemaker	Herts	St Michaels

	SURNAME	FORENAME	SCHEDULE NUMBER	ADDRESS	RELATIONSHIP	STATUS	AGE	SEX	OCCUPATION	COUNTY OF BIRTH	PLACE OF BIRTH
71	GREENWOOD	James	16	Fishpool Street	Head	Mar	58	M	Relieving Officer	Yorks	[Unknown]
72	GREENWOOD	Harriet	16		Wife	Mar	51	F		Worcs	[Unknown]
73	GREENWOOD	Mary	16		Dau	Unm	25	F	Schoolmistress	Ireland	Dublin
74	GREENWOOD	James	16		Son	Unm	21	M	Assistant Relieving Officer	Middx	St Georges
75	GREENWOOD	Jane L	16		Dau		14	F	Scholar	Herts	St Stephens
76	GREENWOOD	Charles J	16		Son		7	M	Scholar	Herts	St Michaels
77	HALSEY	Thomas	17	Fishpool Street	Head	Mar	63	M	Gardener	Beds	[Unknown]
78	HALSEY	Eliza	17		Wife	Mar	60	F	Laundress	Herts	St Albans
79	GAPE	Thomas F	18	Fishpool Street	Head	Unm	62	M	Landed Proprietor	Herts	St Michaels
80	GAPE	Jane E	18		Sister	Unm	60	F	Fundholder	Herts	St Michaels
81	GAPE	Martha	18		Sister	Unm	50	F	Fundholder	Herts	St Michaels
82	GAPE	Elizabeth	18		Sister	Unm	46	F	Fundholder	Herts	St Michaels
83	PLAYLE	John H	18		Serv	Unm	39	M	Butler	Essex	Stamford River
84	AMBROSE	William	18		Serv	Unm	25	M	Footman	Herts	Abbots Langley
85	LANE	George	18		Serv	Unm	26	M	Groom	Rutland	Burley
86	OLIFF	Harriet	18		Serv	Unm	45	F	Ladys Maid	Unknown	
87	PARKINS	Amelia	18		Serv	Unm	33	F	Cook	Northants	Duncote [?]
88	WRIGHT	Elizabeth	18		Serv	Unm	28	F	Housemaid	Herts	Wadesmill [Thundridge]
89	CLARK	Lydia	18		Serv	Unm	22	F	Kitchen Maid	Rutland	Uffington
90	AUSTIN	David	19	Fishpool Street	Head	Mar	28	M	Wheelwright	Herts	St Albans
91	AUSTIN	Esther	19		Wife	Mar	27	F	Bonnet Sewer	Herts	St Albans
92	AUSTIN	William	19		Son		6	M	Scholar	Herts	St Albans
93	AUSTIN	Emily	19		Dau		2	F		Herts	St Albans
94	AUSTIN	Sarah	19		Dau		8m	F		Herts	St Albans
95	COLGRAVE	Samuel	20	Fishpool Street	Head	Mar	21	M	Shoemaker	Beds	Thurleigh
96	COLGRAVE	Eliza	20		Wife	Mar	20	F	Shoe Binder	Beds	Cople
97	WHEELER	Davey	20		Lodger	Widower	67	M	Shoemaker	Sussex	Lindfield
98	PAIN	Joseph	21	Fishpool Street	Head	Mar	67	M	Gardener	Beds	Luton
99	PAIN	Ann	21		Wife	Mar	66	F		Herts	St Albans
100	PAIN	George	21		Son	Widower	25	M	Letter Carrier	Herts	St Albans
101	PAIN	William	21		Grandson		5	M	Scholar	Herts	St Albans
102	PAIN	Eliza Ann	21		Grandau		3	F	Scholar	Herts	St Albans
103	DUNHAM	John B	22	Fishpool Street	Head	Mar	29	M	Carpenter	Herts	St Albans
104	DUNHAM	Mary	22		Wife	Mar	27	F		Herts	St Albans
105	DUNHAM	John S	22		Son		7m	M		Herts	St Albans
106	VARNEY	Matilda	22		Serv		15	F	House Servant	Herts	St Albans
107	MORRIS	Joseph	23	Fishpool Street	Head	Mar	48	M	Hat Manufacturer	Notts	Radcliff
108	MORRIS	Sarah	23		Wife	Mar	41	F		Beds	Salford
109	MORRIS	Susannah	23		Dau		9	F	Scholar	Herts	St Michaels
110	MORRIS	Joseph C	23		Son		7	M	Scholar	Herts	St Michaels
111	MORRIS	John E	23		Son		3	M		Herts	St Michaels
112	MORRIS	Mary E	23		Dau		5m	F		Herts	St Michaels
113	GREENWOOD	Sophia	23		Serv	Unm	42	F	House Servant	Bucks	Newport

One house uninhabited

114	SHEPHERD	John	24	Fishpool Street	Head	Mar	42	M	Blacksmith	Herts	St Peters
115	SHEPHERD	Ann	24		Wife	Mar	40	F		Herts	St Stephens
116	SHEPHERD	John	24		Son	Unm	16	M	Groom	Herts	St Peters
117	SHEPHERD	Henry	24		Son		13	M		Herts	St Peters
118	SHEPHERD	William	24		Son		11	M	Silk Spinner	Herts	St Albans
119	SHEPHERD	George	24		Son		7	M	Scholar	Herts	St Albans
120	SHEPHERD	Jane	24		Dau		5	F	Scholar	Herts	St Peters
121	PHILIPS	Mary A	25	Fishpool Street	Head	Mar	28	F	Trimming Weaver	Ireland	[Unknown]
122	CADWELL	Amelia	25		Sister	Unm	28	F	Trimming Weaver	Ireland	[Unknown]
123	EWINGTON	Ethaelda	25		Dau		14	F	Silk Spinner	Herts	Welwyn
124	EWINGTON	Edward	25		Son		12	M	Silk Spinner	Herts	Welwyn
125	EWINGTON	Frederick	25		Son		10	M	Silk Spinner	Herts	Welwyn
126	CADWELL	Sidney	25		Nephew		1	M		Herts	St Michaels
127	BLAKEMORE	John	26	Fishpool Street	Head	Mar	37	M	Servant	Somerset	Clifton
128	BLAKEMORE	Elizabeth	26		Wife	Mar	44	F		Herts	St Albans
129	BLAKEMORE	John Wm	26		Son	Unm	17	M	Groom	Herts	St Albans
130	BLAKEMORE	Charles	26		Son	Unm	16	M	Footman	Herts	St Albans
131	BLAKEMORE	Mary Ann	26		Dau		14	F	Servant	Herts	St Albans
132	BLAKEMORE	Amelia E	26		Dau		14	F	Hat Maker	Herts	St Albans
133	BLAKEMORE	James M	26		Son		12	M	Hat Maker	Herts	St Albans
134	BLAKEMORE	Harriet	26		Dau		10	F	Hat Maker	Herts	St Albans
135	BLAKEMORE	Sarah	26		Dau		1	F		Herts	St Albans
136	WALKER	Ann	27	Fishpool Street	Head	Widow	75	F	Seamstress	Herts	London Colney
137	WALKER	James	27		Son	Unm	36	M	Bricklayers Lab	Herts	St Albans
138	WALKER	George	27		Son	Unm	26	M	Groom	Herts	St Albans
139	WALKER	William	27		Son	Unm	24	M	Ag Lab	Herts	St Albans
140	BIBBY	Mary	27		Dau	Widow	43	F	Straw Plaiter	Herts	St Albans
141	CAUDLE	Bridget	28	Fishpool Street	Head	Widow	50	F	Laundress	Ireland	
142	CURRANT	James	29	Fishpool Street	Head	Widower	50	M	Ag Lab	Beds	Dunstable
143	CURRANT	Ann	29		Dau	Unm	20	F	Hat Maker	Herts	St Michaels
144	CURRANT	David	29		Son	Unm	18	M	Agric Lab	Herts	St Michaels
145	CURRANT	George	29		Son		15	M	Hat Maker	Herts	St Michaels
146	CURRANT	Eliza	29		Dau		11	F	Silk Spinner	Herts	St Michaels
147	GAZELEY	Sarah	29		Lodger	Unm	19	F	Hat Maker	Herts	St Albans
148	AUSTIN	Samuel	30	Fishpool Street	Head	Mar	30	M	Wheelwright	Herts	St Albans
149	AUSTIN	Martha	30		Wife	Mar	34	F	Bonnet Sewer	Herts	St Albans
150	AUSTIN	Samuel	30		Son		6	M	Scholar	Herts	St Albans
151	AUSTIN	Martha	30		Dau		4	F	Scholar	Herts	St Albans
152	AUSTIN	John	30		Son		6m	M		Herts	St Albans
153	PARKINS	Ann	31	Fishpool Street	Head	Unm	43	F	Dressmaker	Herts	St Michaels
154	KNOTT	Sarah	31		Assistant	Unm	17	F	Dressmaker	Herts	St Michaels
155	SAWYER	Ann	32	Fishpool Street	Head	Widow	30	F	Bonnet Sewer	Herts	Redbourn
156	SAWYER	William H	32		Son		2	M		Herts	Redbourn
157	MAJOR	William	33	Fishpool Street	Head	Mar	29	M	Bonnet Presser	Herts	St Albans
158	MAJOR	Mary	33		Wife	Mar	26	F	Bonnet Maker	Unknown	

	SURNAME	FORENAME	SCHEDULE NUMBER	ADDRESS	RELATIONSHIP	STATUS	AGE	SEX	OCCUPATION	COUNTY OF BIRTH	PLACE OF BIRTH
159	MAJOR	Emma J	33		Dau		9	F	Scholar	Herts	St Michaels
160	MAJOR	Harriet L	33		Dau		3	F		Herts	St Michaels
161	MAJOR	William E	33		Son		1	M		Herts	St Michaels
162	MAJOR	Elizabeth	33		Mother	Widow	72	F	Formerly Laundress	Herts	St Albans
163	MAJOR	Sarah	33		Sister	Unm	39	F	Bonnet Manufacturer	Herts	St Albans
164	TOMLIN	James	34	Fishpool Street	Head	Mar	55	M	Carpenter	Beds	Luton
165	TOMLIN	Eleanor	34		Wife	Mar	52	F	Bonnet Sewer	Herts	St Albans
166	TOMLIN	James	34		Son	Unm	22	M	Hat Presser	Herts	St Albans
167	TOMLIN	Eliza	34		Dau	Unm	20	F	Hat Maker	Herts	St Albans
168	TOMLIN	Matilda	34		Dau		15	F	Hat Maker	Herts	St Albans
169	TOMLIN	Emily	34		Dau		10	F	Hat Maker	Herts	St Albans
170	GEORGE	William	35	Fishpool Street	Head	Mar	44	M	Sawyer	Herts	St Albans
171	GEORGE	Rebecca	35		Wife	Mar	44	F		Herts	St Albans
172	GEORGE	Jane	35		Dau		15	F	Trimming Weaver	Herts	St Albans
173	GEORGE	Thomas	35		Son		11	M	Scholar	Herts	St Albans
174	GEORGE	Elizabeth	35		Dau		8	F	Scholar	Herts	St Albans
175	GEORGE	George	35		Son		6	M	Scholar	Herts	St Albans
176	GEORGE	Ann	35		Dau		4	F	Scholar	Herts	St Albans
177	HULL	James	36	Fishpool Street	Head	Mar	55	M	Gardener	Herts	St Albans
178	HULL	Louisa	36		Wife	Mar	52	F		Kent	Greenwich
179	HULL	Sarah	36		Dau	Unm	18	F	Hat Maker	Herts	St Albans
180	HULL	John	36		Son		16	M		Herts	St Albans
181	HULL	Maria	36		Dau		14	F	Hat Maker	Herts	St Albans
182	HULL	James	36		Son		8	M	Hat Maker	Herts	St Albans
183	GENTLE	Philip	37	Fishpool Street	Head	Mar	45	M	Shoemaker	Herts	Abbots Langley
184	GENTLE	Jane	37		Wife	Mar	44	F	Shoe Binder	Herts	Abbots Langley
185	GENTLE	James	37		Son	Unm	20	M	Hat Presser	Herts	Abbots Langley
186	GENTLE	Hannah	37		Dau	Unm	17	F	Hat Maker	Herts	Abbots Langley
187	GENTLE	Samuel	37		Son		15	M	Errand Boy	Herts	Abbots Langley
188	GENTLE	Thomas	37		Son		13	M	Silk Spinner	Herts	Abbots Langley
189	GENTLE	Philip	37		Son		11	M	Silk Spinner	Herts	Abbots Langley
190	GENTLE	Reuben	37		Son		8	M	Scholar	Herts	Abbots Langley
191	GENTLE	George	37		Son		6	M	Scholar	Herts	Abbots Langley
192	GENTLE	Amos	37		Son		4	M		Herts	Abbots Langley
193	GENTLE	Alice	37		Dau		1	F		Herts	Abbots Langley
194	KENTISH	Joseph	38	Fishpool Street	Head	Unm	75	M	Annuitant	Herts	St Michaels
195	CLAYTON	Dinah	38		Niece	Widow	44	F	Stay Maker	Herts	St Michaels
196	CLAYTON	James	38		Nephew		15	M	Labourer	Herts	St Michaels
197	CLAYTON	Jesse	38		Nephew		12	M	Scholar	Herts	St Michaels
198	CLAYTON	Richard	38		Nephew		9	M	Scholar	Herts	St Michaels
199	BIRCHMORE	Eliza	38		Niece	Unm	27	F	Bonnet Sewer	Herts	St Michaels
200	LAURENCE	Richard	39	Fishpool St. Cock & Flower Pot	Head	Mar	58	M	Publican	Herts	North Mimms
201	LAURENCE	Elizabeth	39		Wife	Mar	52	F		Herts	St Michaels
202	HOLLAND	John	40	Fishpool Street	Head	Mar	49	M	Agric Lab	Herts	St Michaels
203	HOLLAND	Rebecca	40		Wife	Mar	56	F	Lace Maker	Bucks	

204	ELLTRAYS	Mary	41	Fishpool Street	Head	Mar	54	F	Charwoman	Herts	St Stephens
205	ROBINSON	Edward	42	Fishpool Street	Head	Mar	52	M	Annuitant	Middx	London
206	ROBINSON	Sarah	42		Wife	Mar	43	F		Shrop	Bridgnorth
207	ROBINSON	Arthur D	42		Son	Unm	17	M	Scholar	Middx	Chelsea
208	ROBINSON	Sarah C	42		Dau		15	F	Scholar	Middx	Chelsea
209	ROBINSON	Edward	42		Son		13	M	Scholar	Middx	Chelsea
210	ROBINSON	Hester A	42		Dau		10	F	Scholar	Middx	Chelsea
211	ROBINSON	Alfred	42		Son		7	M	Scholar	Middx	Chelsea
212	CHALK	Jane	42		Serv	Unm	23	F	House Servant	Bucks	Penn
213	EASTLAND	John	43	Fishpool Street	Head	Unm	67	M	Annuitant	Bucks	Newport Pagnell
214	PRATT	Frances	43		Serv	Unm	30	F	House Servant	Herts	Hitchin
215	BROTHERS	Henry	44	Fishpool Street	Head	Mar	52	M	Agric Lab	Herts	Hitchin
216	BROTHERS	Charlotte	44		Wife	Mar	52	F	Cotton Spinner	Herts	St Albans
217	BROTHERS	George	44		Son	Unm	27	M	Agric Lab	Herts	St Albans
218	BROTHERS	Sarah	44		Dau	Unm	24	F	Weaver	Herts	St Albans
219	BROTHERS	Eliza	44		Dau		12	F	Scholar	Herts	St Albans
220	BROTHERS	William	44		Son		9	M	Servant	Herts	St Albans
221	HANDSCOMB	Mary A	45	Fishpool Street	Head	Unm	27	F	Hat Maker	Herts	St Peters
222	HANDSCOMB	Mary A	45		Dau		7m	F		Herts	St Michaels
223	GILBERT	William	46	Fishpool Street	Head	Mar	22	M	Brazilian Grass Splitter	Herts	St Albans
224	GILBERT	Eliza	46		Wife	Mar	23	F	Brazilian Hat Maker	Herts	St Albans
225	GILBERT	Sarah	46		Dau		1m	F		Herts	St Albans
226	CRAWLEY	William	46		Lodger	Unm	19	M	Silk Weaver	Herts	St Albans
227	HANDSCOMB	Joseph	47	Fishpool Street	Head	Mar	32	M	Agric Lab	Herts	Market Street [St Albans]
228	HANDSCOMB	Charlotte	47		Wife	Mar	32	F	Trimming Weaver	Herts	St Michaels
229	HANDSCOMB	Louisa Ann	47		Dau		10	F	Hat Maker	Herts	St Albans
230	BIRD	Amelia	47		Sister	Unm	23	F	Hat Maker	Herts	St Peters
231	STEABBEN	John	48	Fishpool Street	Head	Mar	46	M	Grocer	Herts	St Albans
232	STEABBEN	Elizabeth	48		Wife	Mar	32	F		Herts	St Albans
233	REYNOLDS	John	48		[blank]	Unm	33	M	Shopman	London	Marylebone
234	STEABBEN	Isaac	48		Nephew		13	M	Grocers Apprentice	Lancs	Manchester
235	KINE	Joseph	49	Fishpool Street	Head	Mar	51	M	Shoemaker	Herts	St Albans
236	KINE	Susan	49		Wife	Mar	52	F		Herts	St Michaels
237	KINE	Emma	49		Dau	Unm	24	F	Silk Spinner	Herts	St Albans
238	KINE	James	49		Son	Unm	19	M	Silk Spinner	Herts	St Albans
239	KINE	John	49		Son		17	M	Shoemaker	Herts	St Albans
240	KINE	Josiah	49		Son		9	M	Scholar	Herts	St Albans
241	REAY	Caroline	49		Lodger	Unm	19	F	Hat Maker	Middx	Marylebone
242	EWER	Thomas	50	Fishpool Street	Head	Mar	54	M	Agric Lab	Herts	St Michaels
243	EWER	Ann	50		Wife	Mar	55	F		Herts	St Michaels
244	EWER	Hannah	50		Dau	Unm	23	F	Hat Maker	Herts	St Michaels
245	EWER	Elizabeth	50		Dau	Unm	20	F	Hat Maker	Herts	St Michaels
246	EWER	John	50		Son		15	M	Agric Lab	Herts	St Michaels
247	EWER	Eliza	50		Dau		12	F	Hat Maker	Herts	St Michaels

	SURNAME	FORENAME	SCHEDULE NUMBER	ADDRESS	RELATIONSHIP	STATUS	AGE	SEX	OCCUPATION	COUNTY OF BIRTH	PLACE OF BIRTH
248	EWER	Robert	50		Son		6	M	Scholar	Herts	St Michaels
249	GROOM	Daniel	51	Fishpool Street	Head	Mar	30	M	Agric Lab	Beds	Winfield
250	GROOM	Charlotte	51		Wife	Mar	31	F	Trimming Weaver	Herts	St Michaels
251	GROOM	William	51		Son		5	M	Scholar	Herts	St Michaels
252	GROOM	Henry	51		Son		3	M		Herts	St Michaels
253	ASTIN	Susan	52	Fishpool Street	Head	Widow	80	F	Pauper	Herts	St Michaels
254	ASTIN	Mary	52		Dau	Unm	54	F	Plait Maker	Herts	St Michaels
255	ASTIN	Elizabeth	52		Dau	Unm	52	F		Herts	St Michaels
256	ASTIN	Thomas	52		Son	Unm	40	M	Agric Lab	Herts	St Michaels
257	BROTHERS	John	52		Nephew		15	M	Brazilian Grass Splitter	Herts	St Michaels
258	HOLLAND	William	53	Fishpool Street	Head	Mar	57	M	Agric Lab	Herts	St Michaels
259	HOLLAND	Hannah	53		Wife	Mar	57	F		Bucks	[Unknown]
260	BAILEY	Robert	54	Fishpool Street	Head	Mar	55	M	Agric Lab	Beds	Sewell
261	BAILEY	Hannah	54		Wife	Mar	64	F	Straw Plaiter	Herts	Wigginton
262	EWER	William	54		Grandson		10	M	Hat Maker	Herts	St Albans
263	LUNNON	Thomas	55	Fishpool Street	Head	Widower	60	M	Agric Lab	Herts	Flamstead
264	LUNNON	Pamela	55		Dau	Unm	19	F	Brazilian Hat Maker	Herts	St Albans
265	PLASOM	James	56	Fishpool Street	Head	Mar	52	M	Agric Lab	Herts	Harpenden
266	PLASOM	Frances	56		Wife	Mar	50	F	Laundress	Herts	St Albans
267	PLASOM	Sarah	56		Dau	Unm	25	F	Invalid	Herts	St Albans
268	PLASOM	George	56		Son	Unm	19	M	Gardener	Herts	St Albans
269	PLASOM	Harriet	56		Dau	Unm	17	F	Bonnet Sewer	Herts	St Albans
270	PLASOM	Maria	56		Dau	Unm	16	F	Brazilian Hat Maker	Herts	St Albans
271	SAWYER	Elizabeth	56		Sister	Widow	65	F	Laundress	Herts	St Albans
272	WELCH	Charles	57	Fishpool Street	Head	Mar	32	M	Baker	Herts	Redbourn
273	WELCH	Jane	57		Wife	Mar	28	F		Herts	St Albans
274	WELCH	Henry C	57		Son		8	M	Scholar	Herts	St Albans
275	WELCH	Charles G	57		Son		6	M	Scholar	Herts	St Albans
276	WELCH	Emma	57		Dau		4	F		Herts	St Albans
277	WELCH	Edward J	57		Son		3	M		Herts	St Albans
278	WELCH	James	57		Son		1	M		Herts	St Albans
279	WHEELER	Eliza	57		Niece		8	F		Unknown	
280	EADES	William	58	Fishpool Street	Head	Mar	26	M	Baker	London	Marylebone
281	EADES	Caroline	58		Wife	Mar	28	F		Herts	St Stephens
282	EADES	William	58		Son		2	M		Herts	Kings Langley
283	EADES	Kate	58		Dau		6m	F		Herts	St Michaels
284	WRIGHT	Harriet	58		Sister	Unm	42	F	Visitor	Herts	St Stephens
285	SARGENT	Caroline	58		Niece		9	F	Scholar	Hants	Isle of Wight
286	GROVER	Joseph	59	Fishpool Street	Head	Mar	33	M	Agric Lab	Herts	Flaunden
287	GROVER	Elizabeth	59		Wife	Mar	31	F	Trimming Weaver	Herts	St Michaels
288	GROVER	William	59		Son		10	M	Hat Maker	Herts	St Michaels
289	GROVER	John	59		Son		8	M	Hat Maker	Herts	St Michaels
290	GROVER	Ann	59		Dau		6	F		Herts	St Michaels
291	GROVER	Dorcas	59		Dau		4	F		Herts	St Michaels
292	GROVER	Edward	59		Son		2	M		Herts	St Michaels

293	GROVER	Joseph	59		Son		4m	M		Herts	St Michaels

One house uninhabited

294	SIMMONDS	Elizabeth	60	Fishpool Street	Head	Widow	45	F	Needlewoman	Gloucs	[Unknown]
295	SIMMONDS	Ellen	60		Dau	Unm	16	F	Hat Maker	Herts	Little Gaddesden
296	SIMMONDS	Eliza	60		Dau		14	F	Hat Maker	Herts	Little Gaddesden
297	SIMMONDS	Jane	60		Dau		11	F	Hat Maker	Herts	Little Gaddesden
298	WALKLATE	William	61	Fishpool Street	Head	Mar	33	M	Gardener	Herts	Watford
299	WALKLATE	Mary	61		Wife	Mar	39	F		Essex	Illingham
300	WALKLATE	Eliza	61		Dau		11	F	Scholar	London	
301	WALKLATE	John	61		Son		6	M		Herts	St Michaels
302	WALKLATE	Henry	61		Son		3	M		Herts	St Michaels
303	WALKLATE	Elizabeth	61		Dau		7m	F		Herts	St Michaels
304	LINES	Maria	62	Fishpool Street	Head	Mar	42	F	Laundress	Herts	Harpenden
305	WILSON	Joseph	63	Fishpool Street	Head	Widower	46	M	Agric Lab	Herts	St Albans
306	WILSON	Edmond	63		Son		15	M	Hat Maker	Herts	St Michaels
307	WILSON	Joseph	63		Son		11	M	Hat Maker	Herts	St Michaels
308	WILSON	Frederick	63		Son		9	M	Hat Maker	Herts	St Michaels
309	KIFF	James	64	Fishpool Street	Head	Mar	34	M	Agric Lab	Herts	St Albans
310	KIFF	Susan	64		Wife	Mar	35	F	Hat Maker	Herts	Redbourn
311	KIFF	Alfred	64		Son		2	M		Herts	St Michaels
312	KIFF	Kate	64		Mother	Widow	77	F	Plaiter	Herts	Kimpton
313	THISTLE	Ann	65	Fishpool Street	Head	Unm	25	F	Hat Maker	Herts	St Michaels
314	THISTLE	Isabella	65		Dau		4	F		Herts	St Michaels
315	THISTLE	Robert	65		Son		2	M		Herts	St Michaels
316	THISTLE	George	65		Brother	Unm	30	M	Agric Lab	Herts	St Michaels
317	THISTLE	Thomas	65		Brother	Unm	28	M	Groom	Herts	St Michaels
318	THISTLE	John	65		Brother	Unm	19	M	Agric Lab	Herts	St Michaels
319	PERRY	William	66	Fishpool Street	Head	Mar	49	M	Marine Store Gatherer	Herts	Redbourn
320	PERRY	Elizabeth	66		Wife	Mar	30	F	Trimming Weaver	Herts	Hatfield
321	MITCHELL	David	66		Son		8	M	Scholar	Herts	North Mimms
322	KIFF	Susan	67	Fishpool Street	Head	Mar	39	F	Straw Plaiter	Herts	St Michaels
323	KIFF	James	67		Son	Unm	16	M	Trimming Weaver	Herts	St Michaels
324	KIFF	Mary A	67		Dau		11	F	Hat Maker	Herts	St Michaels
325	KIFF	Eliza	67		Dau		3	F		Herts	St Michaels
326	TURNEY	James	68	Fishpool Street	Head	Mar	71	M	Pauper	Herts	[Unknown]
327	TURNEY	Charlotte	68		Wife	Mar	71	F		Herts	[Unknown]
328	CREW	Martha	69	Fishpool Street	Head	Unm	53	F	Straw Plaiter	Herts	St Michaels
329	CREW	Elizabeth	69		Dau	Unm	35	F	Trimming Weaver	Herts	St Michaels
330	GAZELEY	Emma	70	Fishpool Street	Head	Unm	20	F	Hat Maker	Herts	St Michaels
331	GAZELEY	Sophia	70		Dau		4m	F		Herts	St Albans
332	NEWELL	William	71	Fishpool Street	Head	Mar	41	M	Painter	Herts	Hexton
333	NEWELL	Rachael	71		Wife	Mar	43	F	Schoolmistress	Herts	St Michaels
334	BROCKLEY	William	71		Nephew	Unm	23	M	Barometer Maker	Herts	St Michaels
335	BRANDON	James	72	Fishpool Street	Head	Mar	48	M	Cowman	Bucks	Chesham

	SURNAME	FORENAME	SCHEDULE NUMBER	ADDRESS	RELATIONSHIP	STATUS	AGE	SEX	OCCUPATION	COUNTY OF BIRTH	PLACE OF BIRTH
336	BRANDON	Ann F	72		Wife	Mar	45	F	Laundress	Herts	St Albans
337	BRANDON	Elizabeth	72		Dau	Unm	24	F	Hat Maker	Herts	St Albans
338	BRANDON	George	72		Son	Unm	23	M	Hat Blocker	Herts	St Albans
339	BRANDON	Sarah	72		Dau	Unm	14	F	Hat Maker	Herts	St Albans
340	UNWIN	Mary	72		Lodger	Unm	25	F	Trimming Weaver	London	
341	FOSTER	Martha	73	Fishpool Street	Head	Mar	68	F		Herts	Hempstead [Hemel]
342	FOSTER	Charlotte	73		Dau	Unm	30	F	Weaver	Herts	St Albans
343	GILBERT	Thomas	74	Fishpool Street	Head	Mar	57	M	Agric Lab	Herts	St Albans
344	GILBERT	Sarah	74		Wife	Mar	52	F	Hat Maker	Beds	Whipsnade
345	GILBERT	Emma	74		Dau	Unm	19	F	Hat Maker	Herts	St Albans
346	GILBERT	Jane	74		Dau		14	F	Hat Maker	Herts	St Albans
347	ELLINGHAM	Joseph	74		Son	Unm	19	M	Weaver	Herts	St Albans
348	GREEN	Rhoda	75	Fishpool Street	Head	Widow	44	F	Pauper	Herts	St Michaels
349	GREEN	Sarah	75		Dau	Unm	20	F	Hat Maker	Herts	St Michaels
350	GREEN	Mary A	75		Dau	Unm	18	F	Hat Maker	Herts	St Michaels
351	GREEN	John	75		Son		15	M	Hat Maker	Herts	St Michaels
352	GREEN	David	75		Son		12	M	Hat Maker	Herts	St Michaels
353	GREEN	Ann	75		Dau		9	F	Scholar	Herts	St Michaels
354	GREEN	Elizabeth	75		Dau		7	F	Scholar	Herts	St Michaels
355	GREEN	Harriet	75		Dau		5	F	Scholar	Herts	St Michaels
356	HESTER	Fanny	76	Fishpool Street	[blank]	Widow	80	F	Pauper	Oxon	[Unknown]
357	PEW	James	77	Fishpool Street	Head	Mar	48	M	Brewers Lab	Herts	St Peters
358	PEW	Sabina	77		Wife	Mar	52	F		Herts	Abbots Langley
359	PEW	Ann	77		Dau	Unm	21	F	Bonnet Sewer	Herts	St Albans
360	PEW	Sarah	77		Dau	Unm	19	F	Straw Hat Maker	Herts	St Michaels
361	PEW	Rose H	77		Dau		13	F	Scholar	Herts	St Michaels
362	COOPER	James	78	Fishpool Street	Head	Mar	57	M	Agric Lab	Herts	St Michaels
363	COOPER	Ann	78		Wife	Mar	58	F		Herts	St Michaels
364	BIRD	Esther A	78		Dau	Unm	20	F	Hat Maker	Herts	St Peters
365	BIRD	Alfred	78		Son	Unm	18	M	Agric Lab	Herts	Shenley
366	CONSTABLE	Benjamin	79	Fishpool Street	Head	Mar	39	M	Agric Lab	Herts	St Michaels
367	CONSTABLE	Susannah	79		Wife	Mar	40	F	Dressmaker	Herts	Redbourn
368	CONSTABLE	Mary A	79		Dau		9	F	Scholar	Herts	St Peters
369	CONSTABLE	George	79		Son		4	M		Herts	St Michaels
370	BIRCHMORE	Joseph	80	Fishpool Street	Head	Mar	36	M	Agric Lab	Herts	St Michaels
371	BIRCHMORE	Ann	80		Wife	Mar	32	F		Herts	St Michaels
372	BIRCHMORE	Susan	80		Dau		15	F	Hat Maker	Herts	St Michaels
373	BIRCHMORE	Ann M	80		Dau		5	F	Scholar	Herts	St Michaels
374	BIRCHMORE	Georgiana	80		Dau		3	F		Herts	St Michaels
375	BIRCHMORE	Sarah	80		Dau		2	F		Herts	St Michaels
376	ALDRIDGE	Elizabeth	81	Fishpool Street, Unicorn	Head	Widow	45	F	Licensed Victualler	Essex	Nazeing
377	ALDRIDGE	Henry	81		Son	Unm	20	M	Carrier	Herts	St Albans
378	ALDRIDGE	John	81		Son		16	M	Bakers Apprentice	Herts	St Albans
379	ALDRIDGE	William	81		Son		14	M		Herts	St Albans

380	KITCHENER	William	81		Lodger	Unm	55	M	Blind	Beds	Ampthill
381	MUNT	Jesse	81		Lodger	Unm	23	M	Agric Lab	Herts	St Albans
382	BRANDON	John	81		Lodger	Unm	22	M	Agric Lab	Kent	Unknown
383	WILES	George	81		Lodger	Unm	25	M	Gardener	Herts	St Albans
384	LUNNON	Joseph	81		Lodger	Unm	18	M	Agric Lab	Herts	St Albans
385	MUNT	Elizabeth	81		Lodger	Unm	21	F	Hat Maker	Herts	St Albans
386	BIRCHMORE	Elizabeth	82	Fishpool Street	Head	Mar	74	F		Herts	St Michaels
387	BLAKE	John	82		Son	Unm	40	M	Agric Lab	Herts	St Michaels
388	MUNT	William	82		Nephew	Unm	37	M	Agric Lab	Herts	Abbots Langley
389	HOWARD	William	83	Fishpool Street	Head	Widower	66	M	Agric Lab	Herts	St Michaels
390	HOWARD	Emma	83		Dau		15	F	Brazilian Hat Maker	Herts	St Michaels
391	HOWARD	Francis	83		Son		13	M	Brazilian Hat Maker	Herts	St Michaels
392	GOODSPEED	Henry	84	Fishpool Street Black Lion	Head	Mar	62	M	Victualler	Beds	Woburn
393	GOODSPEED	Sarah	84		Wife	Mar	64	F		Herts	St Albans
394	GOODSPEED	William	84		Son	Unm	34	M	Butcher	Herts	St Albans
395	GOODSPEED	Elizabeth	84		Dau	Unm	24	F	Dressmaker	Herts	St Albans
396	GOODSPEED	Frederick	84		Grandson		10	M	Scholar	Herts	St Albans

End of the Old Parliamentary Borough of St Albans

397	WILLSHIN	Thomas	1	Kingsbury House	Head	Mar	38	M	Farmer of 600 acres employing 26 men	Middx	Northolt
398	WILLSHIN	Hannah	1		Wife	Mar	32	F		Herts	St Stephens
399	WILLSHIN	George	1		Son		9	M		Herts	St Stephens
400	WILLSHIN	Hannah	1		Dau		6	F		Herts	St Stephens
401	WILLSHIN	Kate	1		Dau		5	F		Herts	St Stephens
402	WILLSHIN	Sophia	1		Dau		2	F		Herts	St Michaels
403	GARDENER	Christopher	1		Pupil	Unm	25	M	Pupil	Cambs	Unknown
404	CALLOW	Rebecca	1		Governess	Unm	21	F	Governess	Middx	St Pancras
405	BUNCE	Ann	1		Serv	Unm	22	F	Servant	Herts	Ware
406	COE	Maria	1		Serv	Unm	20	F	Servant	Herts	St Albans
407	CUTLER	James	1		Serv	Unm	22	M	Ploughman	Bucks	Dagnall
408	MUNT	Samuel	1		Serv	Unm	18	M	Groom	Herts	St Albans
409	HUNT	George	1		Serv		15	M	Agric Lab	Herts	Harpenden
410	GROOM	James	1		Serv	Unm	17	M	Agric Lab	Herts	St Albans
411	EDWARDS	George	2	Kingsbury Mill	Head	Mar	30	M	Miller employing 1 man	Beds	Burton [Barton?]
412	EDWARDS	Georgiana A	2		Wife	Mar	25	F		Herts	Aston
413	EDWARDS	George F.	2		Son		4	M		Beds	Burton [Barton?]
414	EDWARDS	Georgiana K.	2		Dau		6 m	F		Herts	St Michaels
415	EDWARDS	Frederick	2		Brother	Unm	25	M	Miller	Beds	Burton [Barton?]
416	WING	Emma	2		Serv		15	F	House Servant	Herts	Cottered
417	BURRIDGE	Joseph	3	St Michaels	Head	Mar	57	M	Auctioneers Clerk	Herts	St Albans
418	BURRIDGE	Elizabeth	3		Wife	Mar	58	F		Derby	Bretby
419	BURRIDGE	Elizabeth	3		Dau	Unm	28	F	Needlewoman	Herts	St Albans
420	BURRIDGE	George	3		Son	Unm	23	M	Labourer	Herts	St Albans
421	BURRIDGE	John	3		Son	Unm	23	M	Servant	Herts	St Albans

	SURNAME	FORENAME	SCHEDULE NUMBER	ADDRESS	RELATIONSHIP	STATUS	AGE	SEX	OCCUPATION	COUNTY OF BIRTH	PLACE OF BIRTH
422	BURRIDGE	Mary	3		Dau		15	F	Dressmakers Apprentice	Herts	St Albans
423	HORSLEY	William	3		Visitor		8	M	Scholar	Essex	Henny
424	SKINNER	Thomas	4	St Michaels	Head	Mar	28	M	Hawker	Surrey	Wandsworth
425	SKINNER	Jane	4		Wife	Mar	33	F		Herts	St Michaels
426	SKINNER	Thomas	4		Son		7	M	Scholar	Herts	St Michaels
427	SKINNER	Jane	4		Dau		5	F	Scholar	Herts	St Michaels
428	SKINNER	James	4		Son		3	M		Herts	St Michaels
429	SKINNER	William	4		Son		2m	M		Herts	St Michaels
430	SKINNER	George	5	St Michaels	Head	Mar	60	M	Oil Miller	Surrey	Wandsworth
431	SKINNER	Eliza	5		Wife	Mar	55	F		Middx	Uxbridge
432	SKINNER	Charlotte	5		Dau		13	F	Scholar	Kent	Frindsbury
433	WEATHERLEY	Francis	6	St Michaels	Head	Mar	63	M	Brewers Labourer	Herts	Sandridge
434	WEATHERLEY	Hettey	6		Wife	Mar	58	F		Herts	Sandridge
435	WEATHERLEY	Thomas	6		Son	Unm	19	M	Agric Lab	Herts	Sandridge
436	WEATHERLEY	Joshua	6		Son	Unm	16	M	Coal Yard Labourer	Herts	Sandridge
437	PLUMMER	Elizabeth	6		Niece	Unm	16	F	Hat Maker	Herts	Sandridge
438	PICKET	William	6		Lodger	Unm	28	M	Brewers Labourer	Herts	Sandridge
439	CARRINGTON	Thomas	7	St Michaels	Head	Mar	28	M	Drayman	Herts	Harpenden
440	CARRINGTON	Mary Ann	7		Wife	Mar	28	F		Herts	Redbourn
441	CARRINGTON	Mary Ann	7		Dau		3	F		Herts	St Michaels
442	PEARCE	Richard	8	St Michaels	Head	Mar	52	M	Chelsea Out Pensioner	Somerset	[Unknown]
443	PEARCE	Emma	8		Wife	Mar	38	F	Chelsea Out Pensioners Wife	Gloucs	[Unknown]
444	PEARCE	Mary J.	8		Dau		12	F		Middx	Westminster
445	PEARCE	Richard	8		Son		10	M	Hat Maker	Herts	St Michaels
446	PEARCE	George	8		Son		8	M	Scholar	Herts	St Michaels
447	PEARCE	Charles J.	8		Son		7	M	Scholar	Herts	St Michaels
448	PEARCE	William	8		Son		4	M	Scholar	Herts	St Michaels
449	PEARCE	Joseph	8		Son		1	M		Herts	St Michaels
450	RUSSELL	John	9	St Michaels (Rose & Crown)	Head	Mar	43	M	Publican	Somerset	Shepton Mallet
451	RUSSELL	Ann	9		Wife	Mar	49	F		Durham	Hurworth
452	BUDDEN	Mary A.	9		Dau	Unm	16	F	Dressmaker	Herts	St Michaels
453	BUDDEN	Jane H.	9		Dau		11	F	Scholar	Herts	St Michaels
454	READ	Samuel	9		Lodger	Mar	59	M	Formerly Butler	Herts	St Michaels
455	BARNES	William	9		Serv	Unm	48	M	Ostler (Inn)	Herts	Redbourn
456	MONK	Joseph	9		Lodger	Unm	19	M	Coal Yard Labourer	Herts	Harpenden
457	CANDY	Robert	9		Lodger	Mar	30	M	Servant	Dorset	Wilton
458	HALSEY	Charlotte	10	St Michaels	Head	Widow	37	F	Charwoman	Herts	St Albans
459	HALSEY	Sarah	10		Dau		12	F		Herts	St Stephens
460	HALSEY	Thomas	10		Son		9	M	Hat Maker	Herts	St Stephens
461	HALSEY	William	10		Son		7	M	Hat Maker	Herts	St Stephens
462	HALSEY	Edward	10		Son		4	M	Scholar	Herts	St Michaels
463	HALSEY	Mary Ann	10		Dau		3	F		Herts	St Michaels
464	NORTH	Mary	11	St Michaels	Head	Unm	23	F	Hat Maker	Herts	St Michaels
465	NORTH	Emily	11		Sister		15	F	Hat Maker	Herts	St Michaels

466	NORTH	Martha	11		Sister		7	F	Hat Maker	Herts	St Michaels
467	NORTH	James	11		Brother		9	M	Scholar	Herts	St Michaels
468	NORTH	Jane	11		Sister		5	F	Scholar	Herts	St Michaels
469	ELMORE	Harriet	11		Lodger	Mar	40	F	Charwoman	Middx	[Unknown]
470	GEORGE	William	12	St Michaels	Head	Mar	78	M	Pauper	Herts	Redbourn
471	GEORGE	Maria	12		Wife	Mar	74	F	Laundress	Herts	Berkhamsted
472	TYERS	Rosanna	12		Lodger	Unm	23	F	Silk Spinner	Herts	Watford
473	SKINNER	George	13	St Michaels	Head	Mar	26	M	Hat Presser	Surrey	Ockbridge
474	SKINNER	Caroline	13		Wife	Mar	27	F		Herts	St Albans
475	SKINNER	Eliza	13		Dau		5	F	Scholar	Herts	St Michaels
476	SKINNER	George	13		Son		2	M		Herts	St Michaels
477	SKINNER	Emma	13		Dau		3m	F		Herts	St Michaels
478	STREADER	Maria	14	St Michaels	Head	Widow	30	F	Laundress	Northants	Northampton
479	STREADER	Joseph	14		Son		12	M	Horse Keepers Boy	Herts	St Michaels
480	STREADER	John	14		Son		9	M	Scholar	Herts	St Michaels
481	STREADER	Mary Ann	14		Dau		3m	F		Herts	St Michaels
482	RIDGEWAY	John	15	St Michaels	Head	Mar	28	M	Agric Lab	Herts	Gaddesden
483	RIDGEWAY	Mary Ann	15		Wife	Mar	26	F		Herts	Redbourn
484	RIDGEWAY	Eliza	15		Dau		4	F		Herts	Redbourn
485	RIDGEWAY	William	15		Son		1	M		Herts	Redbourn
486	ALLEN	Charlotte	15		Mother	Mar	66	F	Nurse	Herts	Unknown
487	BROWN	George	15		Nursechild		9m	M		Beds	Luton
488	WILSON	Edward	16	St Michaels	Head	Mar	59	M	Agric Lab	Herts	Kensworth
489	WILSON	Mary	16		Wife	Mar	54	F	Charwoman	Herts	Kensworth
490	WILSON	Caroline	16		Dau	Unm	24	F	Hat Maker	Herts	St Michaels
491	WILSON	Emma	16		Dau	Unm	19	F	Hat Maker	Herts	St Michaels
492	ROBINSON	George	17	St Michaels	Head	Mar	26	M	Silk Mill Labourer	[London]	Farringdon
493	ROBINSON	Maria	17		Wife	Mar	28	F	Silk Mill Labourer	Herts	Sarrat
494	ROBINSON	Levi	17		Son		4	M	Scholar	Herts	Watford
495	ROBINSON	Sarah	17		Dau		2	F		Herts	Watford
496	GEORGE	Joseph	18	St Michaels	Head	Mar	41	M	Carman	Herts	St Michaels
497	GEORGE	Ann	18		Wife	Mar	42	F		Herts	St Michaels
498	GEORGE	Edward	18		Son		14	M	Assistant to his Father	Herts	St Michaels
499	GEORGE	Harriet	18		Dau		11	F	Scholar	Herts	St Michaels
500	GEORGE	Martha	18		Dau		9	F	Scholar	Herts	St Michaels
501	GEORGE	Henry	18		Son		7	M	Scholar	Herts	St Michaels
502	KIFF	Stephen	19	St Michaels	Head	Mar	29	M	Corn Mill Labourer	Herts	St Michaels
503	KIFF	Ann	19		Wife	Mar	28	F		Herts	Redbourn
504	KIFF	Frederick	19		Son		6	M	Scholar	Herts	St Michaels
505	KIFF	Henry	19		Son		3	M	Scholar at Home	Herts	St Michaels
506	KIFF	Sarah	19		Dau		2	F		Herts	St Michaels
507	TITMAS	Charles	20	St Michaels	Head	Mar	28	M	Silk Mill Labourer	Herts	Watford
508	TITMAS	Ann	20		Wife	Mar	32	F		Herts	Bushey
509	TITMAS	Eliza	20		Dau		7	F	Scholar	Herts	Watford
510	TITMAS	Charles	20		Son		3	M	Scholar at Home	Herts	Bushey

	SURNAME	FORENAME	SCHEDULE NUMBER	ADDRESS	RELATIONSHIP	STATUS	AGE	SEX	OCCUPATION	COUNTY OF BIRTH	PLACE OF BIRTH
511	TITMAS	William	20		Son		1	M		Herts	St Michaels
512	EVANS	Elizabeth	20		Lodger	Mar	25	F	Employed at a Silk Mill	Herts	Bushey
513	STRATTON	Fanny	20		Lodger	Unm	22	F	Employed at a Silk Mill	Herts	Rickmansworth
514	SEABROOKE	Daniel	21	St Michaels	Head	Mar	25	M	Silk Mill Labourer	Herts	Watford
515	SEABROOKE	Sarah	21		Wife	Mar	23	F		Herts	Rickmansworth
516	SEABROOKE	Henry	21		Son		2	M		Herts	Rickmansworth
517	SEABROOKE	Hannah	21		Dau		5m	F		Herts	St Michaels
518	SEARS	Samuel	21		Lodger	Widower	27	M	Silk Mill Labourer	Herts	Watford
519	PEACOCK	Ann	22	St Michaels	Head	Unm	78	F	Pauper (Bedridden)	Herts	St Michaels
520	ABBOTT	Elizabeth	22		Sister	Widow	55	F		Herts	St Michaels
521	PAYNE	Charles	23	St Michaels	Head	Mar	51	M	Blacksmith	Herts	St Albans
522	PAYNE	Charlotte	23		Wife	Mar	49	F		Herts	St Albans
523	PAYNE	Jemima	23		Dau	Unm	23	F	Bonnet Sewer	Herts	St Albans
524	PAYNE	Joseph	23		Son	Unm	16	M	Blacksmith	Herts	St Albans
525	PAYNE	Emma	23		Dau		13	F	Bonnet Sewer	Herts	St Albans
526	PAYNE	Eliza	23		Dau		9	F	Scholar	Herts	St Albans
527	BROWN	Daniel	24	St Michaels	Head	Mar	34	M	Blacksmith	Beds	Luton
528	BROWN	Harriet	24		Wife	Mar	35	F		Herts	St Peters
529	BROWN	Mary	24		Dau		12	F	Hat Maker	Herts	St Michaels
530	BROWN	Harriet	24		Dau		9	F	Scholar	Herts	St Michaels
531	BROWN	Emma	24		Dau		6	F	Scholar	Herts	St Michaels
532	BROWN	William	24		Son		2	M		Herts	St Michaels
533	SEBEY	Esther	24		Lodger	Unm	60	F	Silk Spinner	Herts	St Michaels
534	DOVER	Susannah	25	St Michaels	Head	Widow	66	F		Bucks	[Unknown]
535	SOPER	William	25		Son	Unm	34	M	Gardener	Middx	St Andrews
536	DEACON	Thomas	26	St Michaels (Six Bells)	Head	Mar	60	M	Maltster	Herts	Aldenham
537	DEACON	Ann	26		Wife	Mar	59	F		Herts	Aubury
538	DEACON	Mary A.	26		Dau	Unm	31	F	Straw Worker	Herts	Gaddesden
539	DEACON	Sarah	26		Dau	Unm	24	F	Straw Worker	Herts	Hemel Hempstead
540	HOSIER	Amelia	26		Dau	Mar	27	F	Straw Worker	Herts	Gaddesden
541	HOSIER	Sarah	26		Grandau		10 m	F		Herts	St Michaels
542	DEACON	Naomi	26		Grandau		7	F	Scholar	Herts	St Michaels
543	WILSON	John	26		Brother	Widower	50	M	Agric Lab	Herts	Aubury
544	FREEMAN	George	26		Serv	Unm	20	M	Agric Lab	Herts	St Michaels
545	HARROWELL	John	26		Serv	Unm	18	M	Agric Lab	Herts	Hemel Hempstead
546	BUTLER	William	26		Lodger	Unm	38	M	Tailor	Herts	Hemel Hempstead
547	SMITH	Penelope	27	St Michaels	Head	Widow	52	F	Straw Plaiter	Herts	St Michaels
548	SMITH	Edward	27		Son	Unm	19	M	Brazilian Grass Splitter	Herts	Hemel Hempstead
549	BIDDLE	Joseph	28	St Michaels	Head	Unm	45	M	Annuitant	Herts	St Albans
550	BIDDLE	Frederick	28		Brother	Unm	39	M	Annuitant	Herts	St Albans
551	BIDDLE	Edward	28		Brother	Unm	29	M	Annuitant	Herts	St Albans
552	BIDDLE	Harriet	28		Sister	Unm	40	F	Annuitant	Herts	St Albans
553	BIDDLE	Georgiana	28		Sister	Unm	30	F	Annuitant	Herts	St Albans
554	SMITH	Eliza	28		Aunt	Widow	70	F	Annuitant	Herts	St Albans

555	HOWARD	Anna	28		Cousin	Unm	40	F	Annuitant	Herts	St Albans
556	STAMFORD	Ann	28		Serv	Unm	42	F	Cook	Cambs	[Unknown]
557	STAMFORD	Lydia	28		Serv	Unm	38	F	Housemaid	Cambs	[Unknown]
558	FENSOM	Charles	28		Serv	Unm	19	M	Footman	Herts	St Albans

Two houses uninhabited

559	PAIN	Edward	29	St Michaels	Head	Mar	26	M	Agric Lab	Beds	Caddington
560	PAIN	Judith	29		Wife	Mar	27	F	Weaver	Herts	St Michaels
561	JANES	Elizabeth	29		Mother	Widow	67	F	Pauper	Herts	St Michaels
562	HUTCHINSON	Benjamin	30	St Michaels Vicarage	Head	Mar	41	M	Vicar of St Michaels	Northants	Cranford
563	HUTCHINSON	Mary Ann	30		Wife	Mar	39	F		Yorks	Halifax
564	HUTCHINSON	Emily C.	30		Dau		11	F		Shrop	Whitchurch
565	HUTCHINSON	Anna S.	30		Dau		9	F		Shrop	Whitchurch
566	HUTCHINSON	Henry E.	30		Son		8	M		Shrop	Whitchurch
567	HUTCHINSON	Emma	30		Dau		5	F		Staffs	Hilderstone
568	HUTCHINSON	Ernest B.	30		Son		3	M		Herts	St Michaels
569	HUTCHINSON	Benjamin	30		Son		1	M		Herts	St Michaels
570	MAROIN	Elizabeth A.	30		Serv	Unm	33	F	Nurse	Kent	Farnborough
571	PAIN	Sarah	30		Serv	Unm	25	F	Cook	Sussex	Pagham
572	MORRIS	Mary	30		Serv	Unm	20	F	Housemaid	Sussex	Bognor
573	PERRY	Hannah	30		Serv		15	F	Under Nurse	Herts	Hoddesdon
574	CHAPMAN	William	31	St Michaels	Head	Mar	41	M	Agric Lab	Beds	[Unknown]
575	CHAPMAN	Hannah	31		Wife	Mar	40	F		Oxon	[Unknown]
576	CHAPMAN	Mary	31		Dau	Unm	18	F	Hat Maker	Herts	St Stephens
577	CHAPMAN	James	31		Son		12	M	Scholar	Herts	St Stephens
578	CHAPMAN	Susan	31		Dau		9	F	Scholar	Herts	St Stephens
579	CHAPMAN	Sarah	31		Dau		7	F	Scholar	Herts	St Stephens
580	CHAPMAN	Emma	31		Dau		4	F	Scholar	Herts	Abbey [St Albans]
581	CHAPMAN	William	31		Son		2	M		Herts	St Michaels
582	NORWOOD	William	32	St Michaels	Head	Mar	42	M	Agric Lab	Herts	St Michaels
583	NORWOOD	Hannah	32		Wife	Mar	50	F	Straw Plaiter	Herts	St Michaels
584	NORWOOD	Emma	32		Dau		13	F	Hat Maker	Herts	St Michaels
585	NORWOOD	Elizabeth	32		Dau		9	F	Scholar	Herts	St Michaels
586	WREN	George	33	St Michaels	Head	Mar	38	M	Coal Yard Labourer	Herts	Codicote
587	WREN	Ann	33		Wife	Mar	33	F		Herts	Sandridge
588	WREN	Elizabeth	33		Dau		12	F	Hat Maker	Herts	Sandridge
589	WREN	Sarah	33		Dau		9	F	Scholar	Herts	Sandridge
590	WREN	William	33		Son		6	M	Scholar	Herts	St Michaels
591	WREN	Emma	33		Dau		3	F		Herts	St Michaels
592	WREN	Henry	33		Son		1	M		Herts	St Michaels
593	ATKINS	William	34	St Michaels	Head	Mar	45	M	Chelsea Out Pensioner	Herts	St Michaels
594	ATKINS	Jane	34		Wife	Mar	40	F		Ireland	Dublin
595	ATKINS	John	34		Son		12	M	Silk Spinner	Middx	Westminster
596	ATKINS	William	34		Son		9	M	Silk Spinner	London	Tower
597	ATKINS	Thomas	34		Son		2	M		Middx	Westminster

	SURNAME	FORENAME	SCHEDULE NUMBER	ADDRESS	RELATIONSHIP	STATUS	AGE	SEX	OCCUPATION	COUNTY OF BIRTH	PLACE OF BIRTH
598	CREED	Henry	35	New House	Head	Mar	39	M	Captain Half-Pay Artillery East India Company Service	Middx	London
599	CREED	Amelia	35		Wife	Mar	21	F	Lady	France	
600	CREED	Mary	35		Dau		4	F		E. Indies	Poona
601	CREED	Emily A.	35		Sister	Unm	33	F	Lady	France	Paris
602	BULKELEY	Constance	35		Visitor	Unm	24	F	Lady	Middx	London
603	HANMORE	Harriett	35		Serv	Unm	23	F	Cook	Middx	London
604	BIRCH	Mary A.	35		Serv	Unm	30	F	Ladys Maid	Middx	Uxbridge
605	ALLEN	Jane	35		Serv	Unm	23	F	Housemaid	Berks	Cookham Dean
606	STEVENS	Henry	35		Serv	Unm	16	M	Man Servant	Devon [Somerset]	Pawlett
607	WALLEN	Thomas	36	St Michaels	Head	Mar	49	M	Coachman & Gardener	Essex	Upminster
608	WALLEN	Elizabeth	36		Wife	Mar	41	F	Laundress	Devon	Kennford
609	WALLEN	Elizabeth	36		Dau		2	F		Essex	Dagenham
610	HALSEY	Daniel	37	St Michaels	Head	Mar	65	M	Agric Lab	Unknown	
611	HALSEY	Lucy	37		Wife	Mar	64	F		Herts	St Albans
612	NORWOOD	William	38	St Michaels	Head	Mar	33	M	Agric Lab	Herts	St Michaels
613	NORWOOD	Ellen	38		Wife	Mar	34	F		Herts	Gaddesden
614	NORWOOD	Mary A.	38		Dau		12	F	Hat Maker	Herts	St Michaels
615	NORWOOD	Sarah	38		Dau		10	F	Scholar	Herts	St Michaels
616	NORWOOD	Uriah	38		Son		7	M	Scholar	Herts	St Michaels
617	NORWOOD	Amelia	38		Dau		4	F		Herts	St Michaels
618	NORWOOD	Emily	38		Dau		1	F		Herts	St Michaels
619	LEGG	Thomas	39	St Michaels	Head	Widower	50	M	Agric Lab	Herts	Redbourn
620	LEGG	Ellen	39		Dau	Unm	20	F	Hat Maker	Herts	St Michaels
621	LEGG	Louisa	39		Dau		12	F	Hat Maker	Herts	St Michaels
622	COMPTON	Joseph	40	St Michaels	Head	Mar	47	M	Baker	Herts	St Albans
623	COMPTON	Maria	40		Wife	Mar	40	F		Herts	Langley
624	COMPTON	Emma	40		Dau	Unm	22	F	Hat Maker	Herts	St Albans
625	COMPTON	Joseph	40		Son	Unm	20	M	Groom	Herts	St Albans
626	COMPTON	Ann	40		Dau		12	F	Hat Maker	Herts	St Albans
627	COMPTON	Eliza	40		Dau		9	F	Hat Maker	Herts	St Albans
628	COMPTON	Elizabeth	40		Dau		3	F		Herts	St Albans
629	SMITH	Elizabeth	41	St Michaels	Head	Widow	76	F	Pauper	Herts	Watford
630	SMITH	William	41		Son	Unm	46	M	Gardener	Herts	St Michaels
631	JANES	Benjamin	42	St Michaels	Head	Mar	42	M	Coal Yard Labourer	Herts	St Michaels
632	JANES	Eliza	42		Wife	Mar	36	F		Herts	St Michaels
633	JANES	Mary	42		Dau	Unm	16	F	Dressmakers Apprentice	Herts	St Michaels
634	JANES	Elizabeth	42		Dau		13	F	Hat Maker	Middx	South Mimms
635	JANES	Eliza	42		Dau		11	F	Hat Maker	Middx	Hadley
636	JANES	Martha	42		Dau		9	F	Scholar	Herts	St Michaels
637	JANES	William	42		Son		6	M	Scholar	Herts	St Michaels
638	JANES	Sophia	42		Dau		4	F	Scholar	Herts	St Michaels
639	JANES	Frances	42		Dau		1	F		Herts	St Michaels
640	GARNER	Frances	42		Mother-in-law	Widow	68	F	Nurse	Herts	Hatfield

641	LAWFORD	Mary	43	St Michaels	Head	Mar	45	F	Laundress	Herts	St Albans
642	LAWFORD	Henry	43		Son		13	M	Carpenters Apprentice	Herts	St Albans
643	JAVAHLAW	Charles	43		Lodger	Unm	23	M	Servant	Suffolk	Hixworth [Ixworth]
644	MONK	John	44	St Michaels	Head	Mar	48	M	Parish Clerk & Boot Maker (2 men)	Herts	St Michaels
645	MONK	Mary	44		Wife	Mar	53	F		Essex	Farnham
646	MONK	Elizabeth C.	44		Dau	Unm	20	F	Dressmaker	Herts	St Michaels
647	BALLARD	Eliza	44		Serv		14	F	House Servant	Herts	St Michaels
648	SMITH	William	45	St Michaels	Head	Unm	38	M	Annuitant	Herts	St Albans
649	SANDERS	William R.	46	St Michaels	Head	Mar	37	M	Baker	Herts	St Michaels
650	SANDERS	Elizabeth	46		Wife	Mar	32	F		Herts	Ridge
651	SANDERS	William	46		Son		9	M	Scholar	Herts	St Michaels
652	SANDERS	George	46		Son		7	M	Scholar	Herts	St Michaels
653	THOROGOOD	James	46		Serv	Unm	26	M	Servant	Herts	Hemel Hempstead
654	WILSON	Sarah	46		Serv	Unm	22	F	Servant	Herts	Hatfield
655	WARWICK	Joseph	47	St Michaels	Head	Mar	25	M	Silk Spinner	Herts	St Peters
656	WARWICK	Eliza	47		Wife	Mar	28	F	Trimming Weaver	Herts	St Michaels
657	WARWICK	Charles	47		Son		3	M		Herts	St Michaels
658	WARWICK	William	47		Son		1	M		Herts	St Michaels
659	GARNER	William	48	St Michaels	Head	Mar	45	M	Pauper	Beds	Dunstable
660	GARNER	Mary	48		Wife	Mar	45	F	Dressmaker	Herts	St Albans
661	GARNER	George	48		Son		14	M	Errand Boy	Herts	St Albans
662	GARNER	Charles	48		Son		11	M	Hat Maker	Herts	St Albans
663	GARNER	Emma	48		Dau		8	F	Scholar	Herts	St Albans
664	GARNER	Jane	48		Dau		6	F	Scholar	Herts	St Albans
665	GARNER	John	48		Son		3	M		Herts	St Albans
666	FOSTER	Mary	48		Lodger	Unm	64	F	Annuitant	Middx	Unknown
667	MONK	Frederick C.	49	St Michaels	Head	Mar	22	M	School Master	Herts	St Michaels
668	MONK	Sarah	49		Wife	Mar	22	F	Trimming Weaver	Herts	Wheathampstead
669	KENT	Walter J.	50	St Michaels	Head	Mar	36	M	Carpenter	Herts	Redbourn
670	KENT	Lucy	50		Wife	Mar	30	F		Herts	St Michaels
671	KENT	Eleanor J.	50		Dau		12	F		Middx	Spittalfields
672	BALLARD	Eliza	51	St Michaels	Head	Mar	44	F		Herts	Wheathampstead
673	BALLARD	Joseph	51		Son	Unm	18	M	Odd Man	Herts	St Michaels
674	BALLARD	Susan	51		Dau	Unm	16	F	Hat Maker	Herts	St Michaels
675	BALLARD	Maria	51		Dau		9	F	Scholar	Herts	St Michaels
676	BALLARD	William	51		Son		6	M	Scholar	Herts	St Michaels
677	BALLARD	Hannah	51		Dau		4	F		Herts	St Michaels
678	BALLARD	Unnamed Infant	51		Dau		2wks	F		Herts	St Michaels
679	NORTH	Sarah	51		Nurse	Widow	44	F	Nurse	Herts	St Michaels
680	PIKE	Samuel	52	St Michaels	Head	Mar	63	M	Agric Lab	Herts	St Michaels
681	PIKE	Susannah	52		Wife	Mar	63	F		Herts	St Michaels
682	PIKE	Charlotte	52		Dau	Unm	39	F		Herts	St Michaels
683	PIKE	Alfred	52		Son	Unm	21	M	Shoemaker	Herts	St Michaels

SURNAME	FORENAME	SCHEDULE NUMBER	ADDRESS	RELATIONSHIP	STATUS	AGE	SEX	OCCUPATION	COUNTY OF BIRTH	PLACE OF BIRTH
684	ATKINS	Shadrach	53	Branch Road	Head	Mar	32	M	Brewers Labourer	Herts	Pimlico
685	ATKINS	Ann	53		Wife	Mar	24	F		Herts	Watford
686	ATKINS	Sarah A.	53		Dau		4	F		Herts	St Albans
687	ATKINS	Henry W.	53		Son		2	M		Herts	St Albans
688	ATKINS	Frederick	53		Son		3 m	M		Herts	St Albans
689	TAYLOR	Emma	53		Sister-in-law		11	F	Scholar	Herts	Watford
690	WILLIAMS	Herbert	54	Kingsbury Lodge	Head	Unm	26	M	B.A. 2nd Master St Albans Grammar School	Somerset	Bath
691	WILLIAMS	Margaret M.J.	54		Sister	Unm	28	F	Lady	Somerset	Bath
692	GRESHAM	William	54		Pupil		12	M	Pupil	Beds	Dunstable
693	FELTHAM	Louisa	54		Serv	Unm	19	F	Servant	Wilts	Clourton [Coulston]
694	TREOBAR	Mary Ann	54		Serv	Unm	19	F	Servant	Bucks	Chesham
695	CARTER	William	55	Kingsbury Toll Gate	Head	Mar	64	M	Toll Gate Keeper	Herts	St Peters
696	ORCHARD	Samuel	56	Verulam Road, Angel Inn	Head	Mar	58	M	Inn Keeper	Somerset	Bath
697	ORCHARD	Sarah	56		Wife	Mar	57	F		Surrey	Epsom
698	DYER	James	56		Visitor	Mar	32	M	Carpenter	Herts	Kings Langley
699	DYER	Ann	56		Visitors Wife	Mar	28	F		Wilts	Melksham
700	DYER	Emma	56		Visitors Dau		6 m	F		Herts	St Peters
701	SILVERTHORN	Rhoda	56		Serv	Unm	18	F	House Servant	Wilts	Westbury
702	SCARANCKE	Francis J.	57	Verulam Road	Head	Mar	41	M	Brewer & Maltster employing 10 men	Herts	St Albans
703	SCARANCKE	Maria	57		Wife	Mar	24	F		Italy	Florence
704	SCARANCKE	Francis N.	57		Son		2	M		Herts	St Michaels
705	PHILIPS	Sarah	57		Serv	Widow	50	F	House Servant (Cook)	Hants	Ringwood
706	BRODERICK	Emma	57		Serv	Unm	29	F	House Servant (Nurse)	Middx	London
707	BEXHALL	Hannah	57		Serv	Unm	22	F	House Servant (Housemaid)	Surrey	Shelford [Shalford]
708	HARRISON	Catherine	58	Verulam Road	Head	Widow	46	F	Fundholder	Beds	Luton
709	HARRISON	D.W.	58		Dau	Unm	29	F		Herts	St Albans
710	HARRISON	Martha G.	58		Dau	Unm	18	F		Herts	St Albans
711	GARDNER	Mary	58		Serv	Unm	24	F	House Servant	Oxon	Drayton

One house uninhabited

712	ASHWELL	George	59	Verulam Road	Head	Mar	41	M	Solicitor	Notts	Newark
713	ASHWELL	Ann	59		Wife	Mar	38	F		Notts	Hawton
714	ASHWELL	Helen	59		Dau		5	F		Herts	St Albans
715	ASHWELL	Stephen	59		Son		3	M		Herts	St Albans
716	ASHWELL	Henry	59		Son		1	M		Herts	St Albans
717	STARKINS	Fanny	59		Serv	Unm	38	F	House Servant	Herts	Redbourn
718	JONES	Mary	59		Serv	Unm	19	F	House Servant	Herts	Welwyn
719	CLARK	Sarah	59		Serv	Unm	17	F	House Servant	Herts	St Michaels
720	PAREZ	Charles	60	Verulam Road	Head	Mar	48	M	Landscape Painter	Northants	Northampton
721	PAREZ	Elizabeth	60		Wife	Mar	49	F		London	
722	ADAMS	Susan	60		Serv	Unm	19	F	House Servant	Herts	Wheathampstead
723	GROOM	Ann	61		Serv	Unm	27	F	House Servant	Herts	Harpenden
724	WEBSTER	Louisa	62	Verulam Road	Head	Unm	33	F	Daily Governess	Herts	St Albans

725	WEBSTER	Eliza	62		Sister	Unm	31	F	Daily Governess	Herts	St Albans
726	BELSON	William E.	63	Verulam Road	Head	Unm	24	M	Curate of St Michaels	Kent	Rochester
727	HARRIS	Harriet	63		Serv	Unm	46	F		Kent	Yalding
728	GOSLING	Mary	64	Verulam Road	Head	Widow	60	F	Annuitant	Surrey	Wondish [Wonersh]
729	EDMONDS	Hannah	64		Sister	Widow	62	F	Annuitant	Surrey	Wondish [Wonersh]
730	MANLOVE	Richard	65	Kentish Villas	Head	Mar	63	M	Fundholder	[Unknown]	
731	MANLOVE	Hannah	65		Wife	Mar	60	F		Herts	St Albans
732	MANLOVE	Robert	65		Son	Unm	28	M	Ironmonger	Herts	St Albans
733	SURRIDGE	Emma	65		Serv	Unm	21	F	House Servant	Herts	Watton
734	EVANS	Joseph	66	Verulam Road	Head	Unm	70	M	Annuitant	Worcs	St Clement, Worcester
735	EVANS	Rebecca	66		Niece	Unm	56	F	Annuitant	Worcs	St Clement, Worcester
736	COMPTON	Kitty	66		Serv		15	F	House Servant	Middx	London

One house uninhabited

737	KENTISH	Ann	67	Verulam Road	Head	Widow	58	F	House Proprietor	Beds	Dunstable
738	KENTISH	Emma	67		Dau	Unm	21	F		Herts	St Peters
739	KENTISH	Ann	67		Dau	Unm	18	F		Herts	St Peters
740	MARTIN	Sarah	67		Serv	Unm	29	F	House Servant	Herts	St Michaels
741	LOVETT	Eliza	67		Serv	Unm	19	F	House Servant	Herts	St Michaels

Five houses building

742	SPRIGINGS	George	68	Verulam Road	Head	Mar	65	M	Gardener	Herts	St Michaels
743	SPRIGINGS	Elizabeth	68		Wife	Mar	46	F		Herts	St Michaels
744	SPRIGINGS	William	68		Son	Unm	18	M	Helper in Garden	Herts	St Michaels
745	SPRIGINGS	Eliza	68		Dau	Unm	16	F	Hat Maker	Herts	St Michaels
746	SPRIGINGS	Charlotte	68		Dau		13	F	Scholar	Herts	St Michaels
747	SPRIGINGS	Edward	68		Son		9	M	Scholar	Herts	St Michaels
748	GREGORY	Charles	69	Verulam Road	Head	Mar	25	M	Stone & Marble Mason	Herts	St Albans
749	GREGORY	Keziah	69		Wife	Mar	26	F	Straw Hat & Bonnet Sewer	Herts	St Albans

One house uninhabited

750	WINTERBORN	James	70	Verulam Road	Head	Mar	45	M	Builder employing 8 men	Middx	Hackney
751	WINTERBORN	Maria	70		Wife	Mar	43	F		Surrey	Bermondsey
752	WINTERBORN	Maria	70		Dau	Unm	22	F	Bonnet Sewer	Middx	Hackney
753	WINTERBORN	Lucy	70		Dau	Unm	20	F	Milliner & Dressmaker	Middx	Hackney
754	WINTERBORN	Elizabeth	70		Dau		15	F	Bonnet Sewer	Middx	Bethnal Green
755	WINTERBORN	James	70		Son		13	M	Scholar	Middx	Bethnal Green
756	WINTERBORN	Emma	70		Dau		11	F	Scholar	Herts	Bishops Stortford
757	WINTERBORN	Josiah	70		Son		8	M	Scholar	Herts	Bishops Stortford
758	INNS	Jane	70		Sister-in-law	Widow	35	F	Dressmaker	Surrey	Bermondsey
759	YOUNG	Frederick	71	Pound Field	Head	Mar	34	M	Tailor	Beds	Dunstable
760	YOUNG	Eliza	71		Wife	Mar	29	F		Herts	Bovingdon
761	YOUNG	Robert	71		Son		4	M	Scholar	Herts	St Michaels
762	YOUNG	Frederick	71		Son		1	M		Herts	St Michaels
763	HAIGH	George	71		Lodger	Unm	31	M	House Painter	Herts	Kitts End, Abbots Langley

SURNAME	FORENAME	SCHEDULE NUMBER	ADDRESS	RELATIONSHIP	STATUS	AGE	SEX	OCCUPATION	COUNTY OF BIRTH	PLACE OF BIRTH
764	AUSTIN	Sarah	72	Pound Field	Head	Widow	63	F	Annuitant	Herts	Cuck Street [Cock Lane, St Albans?]
765	STEVENS	James	73	Pound Field	Head	Mar	40	M	General Dealer	Beds	Henlow
766	STEVENS	Eliza	73		Wife	Mar	38	F		Herts	[Unknown]
767	STEVENS	James	73		Son		15	M	Hat Maker	Beds	Bedford
768	STEVENS	George	73		Son		13	M	Grass Opener	Herts	St Michaels
769	STEVENS	William	73		Son		10	M	Grass Opener	Herts	St Michaels
770	STEVENS	Jane	73		Dau		7	F	Scholar	Herts	St Michaels
771	CLARK	Henry	74	Pound Field	Head	Mar	30	M	Tailor	Herts	St Albans
772	CLARK	Mary	74		Wife	Mar	32	F		Essex	Great Waltham
773	CLARK	Mary	74		Dau		5	F		Herts	St Albans
774	CLARK	Ebenezer	74		Son		3	M		Herts	St Albans
775	CLARK	Sarah	74		Dau		2	F		Herts	St Albans
776	CLARK	Henry	74		Son		11 m	M		Herts	St Albans
777	DELVES	Elizabeth	75	Pound Field	Head	Unm	22	F	Dressmaker	Staffs	Wolstanton
778	MADDOX	Eliza	76	Pound Field	Head	Widow	43	F	Laundress	Essex	Great Waltham
779	MADDOX	James	76		Son	Unm	16	M	Out Door Servant	Herts	St Albans
780	MADDOX	Eliza	76		Dau		14	F	Hat Maker	Herts	St Albans
781	MADDOX	Jonathan	76		Son		12	M	Silk Spinner	Herts	St Albans
782	MADDOX	Richard	76		Son		10	M	Scholar	Herts	St Albans
783	MADDOX	George	76		Son		7	M	Scholar	Herts	St Albans
784	MADDOX	Ann	76		Dau		3	F		Herts	St Albans
785	MEDLOCK	James	77	Pound Field	Head	Widower	61	M	Master Baker	Beds	Tempsford
786	MEDLOCK	Elizabeth	77		Dau	Unm	29	F	House Keeper	Northants	Cottingham
787	MEDLOCK	Harriet	77		Dau	Unm	27	F	Fancy Hat Maker	Northants	Cottingham
788	MEDLOCK	Ann	77		Dau	Unm	24	F	Straw Bonnet Maker	Beds	Riseley
789	MEDLOCK	Mary	77		Dau	Unm	18	F	Fancy Hat Maker	Herts	St Albans
790	CHILDS	William	78	Pound Field	Head	Mar	56	M	Carpenter	Cambs	West Wickham
791	CHILDS	Mary	78		Wife	Mar	55	F		Herts	Kensworth
792	WEBB	Thomas	79	Pound Field	Head	Mar	24	M	Milkman	Herts	Sandridge
793	WEBB	Elizabeth	79		Wife	Mar	22	F	Trimming Weaver	Herts	Park Street
794	WEBB	George	79		Son		2	M		Herts	St Michaels
795	WEBB	William	79		Son		3 m	M		Herts	St Michaels
796	ENGLAND	Mary	79		Sister-in-law	Unm	17	F	Trimming Weaver	Herts	Sandridge
797	MARDEL	Richard	80	Pound Field	Head	Mar	30	M	Agric Lab	Herts	[Unknown]
798	MARDEL	Leah	80		Wife	Mar	30	F		Bucks	[Unknown]
799	MARDEL	George	80		Son		2	M		Herts	St Michaels
800	COLLINS	Caroline	80		Lodger	Widow	60	F	Pauper	Beds	[Unknown]
801	GOODGAME	Mary	81	Pound Field	Wife	Mar	41	F	Millers Wife	Herts	Flamstead
802	GOODGAME	Isabella	81		Dau		14	F	Hat Maker	Middx	Islington
803	GOODGAME	William	81		Son		12	M	Hat Maker	Middx	Islington
804	GOODGAME	Charlotte	81		Dau		10	F	Hat Maker	Middx	Islington
805	GOODGAME	Fanny	81		Dau		8	F	Scholar	Herts	St Albans
806	GOODGAME	Charles	81		Son		6	M	Scholar	Herts	St Albans
807	GOODGAME	Rose	81		Dau		4	F	Scholar	Herts	St Albans

808	GOODGAME	Matilda	81		Dau			3	F	Scholar	Herts	St Albans
809	GOODGAME	Selina	81		Dau			5 m	F		Herts	Hemel Hempstead
810	SEARS	Thomas	82	Pound Field	Head	Mar		50	M	Agric Lab	Herts	St Albans
811	SEARS	Fanny	82		Wife	Mar		42	F		Herts	Redbourn
812	SEARS	Jane	82		Dau	Unm		20	F	Hat Maker	Herts	St Albans
813	SEARS	Thomas	82		Son	Unm		18	M	Hat Maker	Herts	St Albans
814	SEARS	William	82		Son			14	M	Hat Maker	Herts	St Albans
815	SEARS	Maria	82		Dau			12	F	Scholar	Herts	St Albans
816	SEARS	Susan	82		Dau			9	F	Scholar	Herts	St Albans
817	SEARS	Rhoda	82		Dau			6	F	Scholar	Herts	St Albans
818	SEARS	Fanny	82		Dau			4	F		Herts	St Albans
819	BROWN	Mary	83	Pound Field	Head	Unm		59	F	Straw Plaiter	Herts	St Michaels
820	BROWN	Emma	83		Sister	Unm		51	F	Schoolmistress	Herts	St Michaels
821	HIGGINS	George T.	83		Lodger	Unm		26	M	Carpenter	Herts	Radlett
822	PIKE	David	84	Pound Field	Head	Mar		34	M	Agric Lab	Herts	St Michaels
823	PIKE	Eliza	84		Wife	Mar		39	F		Herts	Wheathampstead
824	PIKE	Thomas	84		Son			13	M	Errand Boy	Herts	St Michaels
825	PIKE	Daniel	84		Son			10	M	Scholar	Herts	St Michaels
826	PIKE	Edward	84		Son			9	M	Scholar	Herts	St Michaels
827	PIKE	James	84		Son			7	M	Scholar	Herts	St Michaels
828	PIKE	Charlotte	84		Dau			5	F	Scholar	Herts	St Michaels
829	PIKE	Susan	84		Dau			2	F	Scholar	Herts	St Michaels
830	PIKE	David	84		Son			1 m	M		Herts	St Michaels
831	WARE	Mary	85	Pound Field	Head	Widow		44	F	Charwoman	Herts	Ware
832	WARE	Sarah	85		Dau	Unm		19	F	Bonnet Sewer	Herts	Redbourn
833	WARE	Ann	85		Dau	Unm		18	F	Brazilian Hat Maker	Herts	Redbourn
834	WARE	James	85		Son			15	M	Grass Splitter	Herts	Redbourn
835	WARE	George	85		Son			13	M	Errand Boy	Herts	Redbourn
836	WARE	Charles	85		Son			9	M	Hat Maker	Herts	Redbourn
837	WARE	Elizabeth	85		Dau			6	F	Scholar	Herts	St Albans
838	WARE	Emma	85		Grandau			1	F		Herts	St Albans
839	COCKLE	Rose A.	86	Pound Field	Head	Widow		59	F	Laundress	Herts	Wheathampstead
840	COCKLE	William	86		Son	Unm		27	M	Bricklayers Labourer	Herts	St Michaels
841	COCKLE	Frederick	86		Grandson			10	M	Scholar	Herts	St Michaels
842	ROBINSON	Elizabeth	87	Pound Field	Head	Widow		72	F		Herts	Hitchin
843	MANN	Abel	88	Pound Field	Head	Mar		58	M	Agric Lab	Beds	Shillington
844	MANN	Mary	88		Wife	Mar		68	F		Herts	Lilley
845	MANN	Joshua	88		Son	Unm		26	M	Bricklayer	Herts	St Michaels
846	COLLINS	John	89	Pound Field	Head	Mar		36	M	Shoemaker	Herts	St Albans
847	COLLINS	Sarah	89		Wife	Mar		35	F		Herts	Harpenden
848	COLLINS	Samuel	89		Son			2	M		Herts	St Albans
849	COLLINS	Ephraim	89		Son			1	M		Herts	St Albans
850	MANN	Henry	89		Son-in-law			11	M	Errand Boy	Herts	St Albans
851	OAKLEY	Ann	90	Pound Field	Head	Mar		70	F	Pauper	Herts	St Albans

SURNAME	FORENAME	SCHEDULE NUMBER	ADDRESS	RELATIONSHIP	STATUS	AGE	SEX	OCCUPATION	COUNTY OF BIRTH	PLACE OF BIRTH
852	OAKLEY	Esther	90		Dau	Unm	33	F	Trimming Weaver	Herts	St Albans
853	OAKLEY	Eliza	90		Dau	Unm	23	F	Trimming Weaver	Herts	St Albans
854	BARR	James	91	Pound Field	Head	Mar	42	M	Greenwich Pensioner	Herts	Redbourn
855	BARR	Alice	91		Wife	Mar	35	F	Shoe Binder	Bucks	[Unknown]
856	BARR	Julia A.	91		Dau		5	F	Scholar	Herts	Hemel Hempstead
857	BASSETT	William	92	Pound Field	Head	Mar	73	M	Pauper	London	
858	BASSETT	Mary	92		Wife	Mar	64	F	Nurse	Beds	Podington
859	HUCKLE	John	93	Pound Field	Head	Mar	36	M	Agric Lab	Herts	Sandridge
860	HUCKLE	Mary	93		Wife	Mar	30	F		Herts	Kings Langley
861	HUCKLE	Mary A.	93		Dau		1	F		Herts	St Albans
862	BAKERSTAFF	Mary	93		Lodger	Widow	60	F	Charwoman	Herts	Kings Langley
863	GRACE	Thomas	94	Pound Field	Head	Mar	45	M	Water Cress Grower	Herts	Redbourn
864	GRACE	Harriet	94		Wife	Mar	43	F		Herts	St Michaels
865	GRACE	Eliza	94		Dau	Unm	22	F	Brazilian Hat Maker	Herts	St Michaels
866	GRACE	David	94		Son		11	M	Brazilian Hat Maker	Herts	St Michaels
867	GRACE	Frederick	94		Son		6	M	Scholar	Herts	St Michaels
868	HANNELL	William	94		Lodger	Unm	23	M	Pipe Maker	Herts	St Michaels
869	WINMILL	George	95	Pound Field	Head	Mar	36	M	Coachman	Herts	St Michaels
870	WINMILL	Eliza	95		Wife	Mar	36	F		Herts	St Albans
871	PIKE	George	96	Pound Field	Head	Mar	32	M	Bricklayer	Herts	St Michaels
872	PIKE	Hannah E.	96		Wife	Mar	33	F		Herts	North Mimms
873	PIKE	Edwin	96		Son		8	M	Scholar	Herts	St Peters
874	PIKE	Arthur	96		Son		5	M	Scholar	Herts	St Michaels
875	PIKE	Eliza	96		Dau		2	F	Scholar	Herts	St Michaels
876	PIKE	Charlotte M.	96		Dau		3m	F		Herts	St Michaels
877	POTTON	William	97	Pound Field	Head	Mar	38	M	Coal Dealer	Herts	Great Berkhamsted
878	POTTON	Elizabeth	97		Wife	Mar	38	F		Bucks	Ringsall
879	POTTON	James	97		Son		12	M	Assistant to his Father	Herts	Northchurch
880	POTTON	Frederick	97		Son		7	M	Scholar	Herts	St Albans
881	POTTON	Jonathan	97		Son		6	M	Scholar	Herts	St Albans
882	POTTON	Elizabeth	97		Dau		3	F		Herts	St Albans
883	ROWLAND	Eliza	97		Lodger	Unm	16	F	Hat Maker	Herts	St Albans
884	CADDINGTON	Joseph	98	Pound Field	Head	Mar	26	M	Brewers Labourer	Herts	St Albans
885	CADDINGTON	Elizabeth	98		Wife	Mar	22	F		Herts	St Albans
886	CADDINGTON	Charles	98		Son		1	M		Herts	St Albans
887	PIKE	Joseph	99	Pound Field	Head	Mar	24	M	Agric Lab	Herts	St Albans
888	PIKE	Ann	99		Wife	Mar	30	F		Herts	Abbots Langley
889	PIKE	Alfred	99		Son		3	M		Herts	Abbots Langley
890	PIKE	Ann	99		Dau		1	F		Herts	St Albans
891	LITCHFIELD	William	100	Pound Field (Portland Cottage)	Head	Mar	66	M	Annuitant	Herts	St Stephens
892	LITCHFIELD	Fanny	100		Wife	Mar	65	F		Herts	St Stephens
893	HAWKINS	Robert	101	Pound Field	Head	Mar	50	M	Agric Lab	Herts	[Unknown]
894	HAWKINS	Hannah	101		Wife	Mar	47	F		Beds [Herts]	Pirton

895	HAWKINS	Betsy	101		Dau	Unm	20	F	Hat Maker	Herts	[Unknown]
896	HAWKINS	Emma	101		Dau		11	F	Scholar	Herts	Sandridge
897	HAWKINS	Eliza	101		Dau		7	F	Scholar	Herts	Sandridge
898	HAWKINS	Frederick	101		Son		6	M	Scholar	Herts	St Michaels
899	ARBORN	William	102	Pound Field	Head	Mar	35	M	Agric Lab	Herts	[Unknown]
900	ARBORN	Rebecca	102		Wife	Mar	40	F	Trimming Weaver	Herts	[Unknown]
901	ARBORN	Tresa	102		Dau	Unm	21	F	Hat Maker	Herts	North Mimms
902	ARBORN	Reuben	102		Son		13	M	Agric Lab	Herts	Redbourn
903	WACKETT	Tresa	102		Niece		3	F		Herts	St Michaels
904	HARRIS	Thomas	103	Pound Field	Head	Mar	26	M	Carpenter	Beds	Harrold
905	HARRIS	Eliza	103		Wife	Mar	24	F		Beds	Compton [Campton]
906	HARRIS	William	103		Son		3	M		Herts	[Unknown]
907	HARRIS	Arthur J.	103		Son		1	M		Herts	[Unknown]
908	BUNN	Joseph	104	Pound Field	Head	Mar	56	M	Agric Lab	Bucks	Marsworth
909	BUNN	Charlotte	104		Wife	Mar	59	F		Herts	St Peters
910	BUNN	Fanny	104		Dau	Unm	28	F	Hat Maker	Herts	Sandridge
911	BUNN	Edith	104		Dau	Unm	23	F	Hat Maker	Herts	Sandridge
912	SMITH	Maria	105	Pound Field	Head	Widow	50	F	Proprietor of Houses	Oxon	Weston-on-the-Green
913	SMITH	Ann	105		Dau		14	F	Dressmaker	Herts	St Stephens
914	SMITH	Rhoda M.	105		Dau		12	F	Scholar	Herts	St Stephens
915	SMITH	Caroline	105		Dau		11	F	Scholar	Herts	St Stephens
916	LOVETT	Alice	106	Pound Field	Wife	Mar	56	F		Leics	Goadby
917	LOVETT	William	106		Son	Unm	23	M	Agric Lab	Herts	St Michaels
918	LOVETT	James	106		Son	Mar	22	M	Rag Merchant	Herts	St Michaels
919	LOVETT	Harriet	106		Dau	Mar	28	F		Middx	St Giles
920	BAIL	William	107	Pound Field	Head	Mar	36	M	Bricklayers Labourer	Herts	St Albans
921	BAIL	Eliza	107		Wife	Mar	37	F		Herts	St Albans
922	BAIL	William	107		Son		11	M	Hat Maker	Herts	St Albans
923	BAIL	George	107		Son		10	M	Scholar	Herts	St Albans
924	BAIL	Charles	107		Son		7	M	Hat Maker	Herts	St Albans
925	BAIL	Mary J.	107		Dau		2	F		Herts	St Albans
926	LOWE	Ann	107		Mother-in-law	Widow	75	F	Pauper	Herts	St Albans
927	WINMILL	John	108	Pound Field	Head	Mar	33	M	Bricklayer	Herts	St Albans
928	WINMILL	Mary A.	108		Wife	Mar	30	F	Hat Maker	Bucks	Unknown
929	WINMILL	William	108		Son		10	M	Scholar	Herts	St Michaels
930	WINMILL	Hannah	108		Dau		8	F	Scholar	Herts	St Michaels
931	WINMILL	George	108		Son		5	M		Herts	St Michaels
932	HILL	Sarah	109	Pound Field	Head	Widow	42	F	Hat Maker	Herts	Ridge
933	HILL	Eliza	109		Dau		13	F	Hat Maker	Herts	Watford
934	HILL	George	109		Son		11	M	Hat Maker	Herts	Watford
935	HILL	Sarah	109		Dau		7	F	Scholar	Herts	St Michaels
936	HILL	William	109		Son		5	M	Scholar	Herts	St Michaels
937	HILL	John	109		Son		2	M		Herts	St Michaels
938	WITHERINGTON	Oliver	109		Nephew	Unm	23	M	Silk Worker	Herts	St Albans

	SURNAME	FORENAME	SCHEDULE NUMBER	ADDRESS	RELATIONSHIP	STATUS	AGE	SEX	OCCUPATION	COUNTY OF BIRTH	PLACE OF BIRTH
939	WINMILL	William	110	Pound Field	Head	Mar	64	M	Agric Lab	Beds	Luton
940	WINMILL	Mary	110		Wife	Mar	67	F		Beds	Luton
941	WINMILL	Hannah	110		Dau	Unm	26	F	Hat Maker	Herts	St Michaels
942	WINMILL	Charles	110		Son	Unm	21	M	Bricklayers Labourer	Herts	St Michaels
943	DELL	Kitty	110		Dau	Mar	41	F	Plaiter	Beds	Luton
944	DELL	Harriet	110		Grandau	Unm	17	F	Hat Maker	Herts	St Michaels

One house uninhabited

	SURNAME	FORENAME	SCHEDULE NUMBER	ADDRESS	RELATIONSHIP	STATUS	AGE	SEX	OCCUPATION	COUNTY OF BIRTH	PLACE OF BIRTH
945	WESTLEY	William	111	Pound Field	Head	Mar	49	M	Agric Lab	Herts	St Albans
946	WESTLEY	Sarah	111		Wife	Mar	49	F		Herts	St Albans
947	WESTLEY	Selina	111		Dau	Unm	22	F	Bonnet Maker	Herts	St Albans
948	WESTLEY	Eliza A.	111		Dau	Unm	17	F	Hat Maker	Herts	St Albans
949	WESTLEY	George	111		Son		14	M	Hat Maker	Herts	St Albans
950	WESTLEY	Martha	111		Dau		12	F	Hat Maker	Herts	St Albans
951	WESTLEY	Mary	111		Dau		12	F	Hat Maker	Herts	St Albans
952	WESTLEY	Henry	111		Son		7	M	Scholar	Herts	St Albans
953	WESTLEY	Emma	111		Grandau		1	F		Herts	St Albans
954	HANNELL	John	112	Pound Field	Head	Mar	42	M	Hat Maker	Herts	St Michaels
955	HANNELL	Ann	112		Wife	Mar	42	F	Hat Maker	Beds	Barton
956	HANNELL	Ann	112		Dau	Unm	20	F	Hat Maker	Herts	St Michaels
957	HANNELL	Newman	112		Son	Unm	18	M	Hat Maker	Herts	St Michaels
958	HANNELL	John	112		Son	Unm	16	M	Hat Maker	Herts	St Michaels
959	HANNELL	David	112		Son		14	M	Hat Maker	Herts	St Michaels
960	HANNELL	Francis	112		Son		12	M	Hat Maker	Herts	St Michaels
961	HANNELL	Mary	112		Dau		10	F	Hat Maker	Herts	St Michaels
962	HANNELL	Eliza	112		Dau		8	F	Hat Maker	Herts	St Michaels
963	HANNELL	Elizabeth	112		Dau		4	F	Hat Maker	Herts	St Michaels
964	GEORGE	Charles	113	Pound Field, Portland Arms	Head	Mar	30	M	Publican	Herts	St Albans
965	GEORGE	Sarah	113		Wife	Mar	28	F		Herts	St Albans
966	GEORGE	Emily	113		Dau		7	F	Scholar	Herts	St Albans
967	GEORGE	Louisa	113		Dau		4	F	Scholar	Herts	St Albans
968	GEORGE	Harry	113		Son		2	M		Herts	St Albans
969	GEORGE	Eliza	113		Dau		6 m	F		Herts	St Albans
970	WOODMAN	Josh	113		Lodger	Unm	60	M	Agric Lab	Herts	St Albans
971	WOODMAN	John	113		Lodger	Unm	25	M	Agric Lab	Herts	St Albans
972	WHITE	William	114	Pound Field	Head	Mar	53	M	Chelsea Out Pensioner (Blind)	Herts	Watford
973	WHITE	Sarah	114		Wife	Mar	38	F	Straw Plaiter	Herts	St Peters
974	ROWLAND	Hannah	114		Lodger	Unm	20	F	Trimming Weaver	Herts	St Michaels
975	COOPER	Henry	114		Visitor		5	M	Scholar	Herts	St Albans
976	BITCHENCE [?]	William	115	Pound Field	Head	Unm	39	M	Agric Lab	Herts	St Michaels
977	BITCHENCE [?]	George	115		Brother	Unm	27	M	Agric Lab	Herts	St Michaels
978	SCRIVENER	James	116	Pound Field	Head	Mar	30	M	Journeyman Cordwainer	Herts	Kimpton
979	SCRIVENER	Ellen H.	116		Wife	Mar	26	F		Herts	St Albans
980	SCRIVENER	Ellen C.	116		Dau		3	F		Herts	St Albans
981	SCRIVENER	James E.	116		Son		7 m	M		Herts	St Albans

982	LOGGAN	Martha	117	Pound Field	Head	Widow	76	F	Formerly Laundress	Herts	St Albans
983	LOGGAN	Georgiana	117		Grandau	Unm	16	F	Bonnet Sewer	Herts	St Albans
984	PEW	Howell	118	Pound Field	Head	Mar	62	M	Agric Lab	Herts	Flamstead
985	PEW	Martha	118		Wife	Mar	56	F	Plaiter	Herts	St Albans
986	WINDMILL	Joseph	119	Pound Field	Head	Mar	27	M	Bricklayer	Herts	St Michaels
987	WINDMILL	Ann	119		Wife	Mar	26	F	Hat Maker	Herts	St Peters
988	WINDMILL	Maria	119		Dau		5	F	Scholar	Herts	St Michaels
989	WINDMILL	Edward	119		Son		3	M		Herts	St Michaels
990	CAWDREY	George P.	120	Pound Field	Head	Mar	34	M	Hat Presser	Herts	Abbots Langley
991	CAWDREY	Hannah	120		Wife	Mar	32	F		Herts	St Michaels
992	CAWDREY	Emily	120		Dau		10	F	Hat Maker	Herts	St Michaels
993	CAWDREY	Sarah	120		Dau		7	F	Scholar	Herts	St Michaels
994	CAWDREY	Hannah	120		Dau		4	F		Herts	St Michaels
995	CAWDREY	Lucy	120		Dau		2	F		Herts	St Michaels
996	CAWDREY	George	120		Son		1 m	M		Herts	St Michaels
997	PITTS	Sarah	121	Pound Field	Head	Widow	40	F	Trimming Weaver	Herts	Redbourn
998	PITTS	Selina	121		Dau	Unm	20	F	Trimming Weaver	Herts	St Albans
999	PITTS	Thomas	121		Son		15	M	Silk Spinner	Herts	St Albans
1000	FENSOM	William	122	Pound Field	Head	Mar	23	M	Boot Maker	Herts	St Albans
1001	FENSOM	Sarah	122		Wife	Mar	26	F	Hat Maker	Herts	Rickmansworth
1002	SLAUGHTER	Harriet	122		Dau		7	F	Scholar	Herts	Watford
1003	JANES	James	123	Pound Field	Head	Mar	39	M	Baker	Herts	St Michaels
1004	JANES	Catherine	123		Wife	Mar	44	F		Herts	St Michaels
1005	LONG	William	124	Pound Field	Head	Mar	40	M	Bricklayer	Bucks	Amersham
1006	LONG	Susan	124		Wife	Mar	40	F		Herts	St Albans
1007	LONG	William	124		Son		10	M	Scholar	Herts	St Albans
1008	LONG	Frederick	124		Son		3	M		Herts	St Albans
1009	LEWIS	Eliza	124		Visitor		9	F	Scholar	Middx	London
1010	LEWIS	Frederick	124		Visitor		7	M	Scholar	Herts	St Albans
1011	THOMPSON	Matthew	124		Visitor	Unm	42	M	Sawyer	Herts	Harpenden
1012	COLES	Susan	124		Visitor	Unm	26	F	Hat Maker	Essex	Ridgewell
1013	CARRINGTON	Letitia	124		Visitor	Widow	70	F	Annuitant (Blind)	Herts	Hitchin
1014	EWER	George	125	Pound Field	Head	Mar	33	M	Agric Lab	Herts	St Peters
1015	EWER	Eliza	125		Wife	Mar	28	F	Trimming Weaver	Herts	St Michaels
1016	EWER	Emma	125		Dau		8	F	Trimming Weaver	Herts	St Michaels
1017	EWER	Charles	125		Son		3	M		Herts	St Michaels
1018	EWER	Eliza A.	125		Dau		1	F		Herts	St Michaels
1019	EWER	Harriet	125		Sister	Unm	29	F	Trimming Weaver	Herts	St Peters
1020	LAWRENCE	William	126	Pound Field	Head	Mar	29	M	Bricklayers Labourer	Herts	St Peters
1021	LAWRENCE	Louisa	126		Wife	Mar	26	F	Trimming Weaver	Herts	St Michaels
1022	LAWRENCE	Georgiana	126		Dau		6	F	Scholar	Herts	St Michaels
1023	LAWRENCE	Mary Ann	126		Dau		2	F		Herts	St Michaels
1024	LAWRENCE	Emily S.	126		Dau		5m	F		Herts	St Michaels
1025	LAWRENCE	Emma	126		Sister	Unm	19	F	Trimming Weaver	Herts	St Peters

	SURNAME	FORENAME	SCHEDULE NUMBER	ADDRESS	RELATIONSHIP	STATUS	AGE	SEX	OCCUPATION	COUNTY OF BIRTH	PLACE OF BIRTH
1026	HEWITT	Aaron	127	Pound Field	Head	Mar	25	M	Cordwainer	Northants	Wellingborough
1027	HEWITT	Mary Ann	127		Wife	Mar	29	F		Beds	Bedford
1028	HEWITT	George R.	127		[Son]		3	M		Beds	Bedford
1029	HEWITT	Maria E.	127		[Dau]		1	F		Herts	St Albans
1030	LEESON	Elizabeth	128	Pound Field	Head	Unm	45	F	Annuitant	Northants	Braunston
1031	LEESON	Alfred	128		Son		14	M	Grocers Apprentice	Herts	Whitwell
1032	OAKLEY	William	129	Pound Field	Head	Mar	38	M	Agric Lab	Herts	St Michaels
1033	OAKLEY	Mary	129		Wife	Mar	42	F		Bucks	Dinton
1034	OAKLEY	Anne	129		Dau		8	F	Scholar	Herts	St Michaels
1035	OAKLEY	James	129		Son		5	M	Scholar	Herts	St Michaels
1036	TOMPKINS	John	130	Pound Field	Head	Mar	26	M	Grocer	Beds	Salford
1037	TOMPKINS	Mary	130		Wife	Mar	25	F		Beds	Salford
1038	TOMPKINS	Thomas	130		Son		2	M		Herts	St Albans
1039	TOMPKINS	Edward	130		Son		2m	M		Herts	St Albans
1040	DURLEY	James	131	Pound Field	Head	Widower	48	M	Straw Bonnet Manufacturer	Bucks	Unknown
1041	DURLEY	Betsy	131		Dau	Unm	20	F	Straw Bonnet Maker	Herts	Unknown
1042	DURLEY	Mary Ann	131		Dau	Unm	17	F	Straw Bonnet Maker	Herts	Unknown
1043	DURLEY	William	131		Son		11	M	Scholar	Beds	Luton

One house uninhabited

	SURNAME	FORENAME	SCHEDULE NUMBER	ADDRESS	RELATIONSHIP	STATUS	AGE	SEX	OCCUPATION	COUNTY OF BIRTH	PLACE OF BIRTH
1044	LAWRENCE	Joseph	132	Pound Field	Head	Mar	41	M	Labourer	Herts	Sandridge
1045	LAWRENCE	Esther	132		Wife	Mar	49	F		Herts	St Albans
1046	LAWRENCE	Sarah	132		Dau		14	F	Hat Maker	Herts	St Albans
1047	BAIL	Henry	133	Pound Field	Head	Mar	23	M	House Servant	Herts	Redbourn
1048	BAIL	Harriet	133		Wife	Mar	25	F	Trimming Weaver	Herts	St Albans
1049	BAIL	Henry	133		Son		2	M		Herts	St Michaels
1050	TILCOCK	John	134	Pound Field	Head	Mar	62	M	Agric Lab	Bucks	Northill
1051	TILCOCK	Elizabeth	134		Wife	Mar	63	F		Bucks	Ivinghoe
1052	TILCOCK	Mary Ann	134		Dau	Unm	24	F	Trimming Weaver	Herts	St Albans
1053	KEYS	Benjamin	135	Pound Field	Head	Mar	37	M	Bricklayers Labourer	Essex	Ridgewell
1054	KEYS	Lidia	135		Wife	Mar	34	F	Hat Maker	Essex	Ridgewell
1055	KEYS	Sarah A.	135		Dau		14	F	Hat Maker	Essex	Ridgewell
1056	KEYS	Martha	135		Dau		11	F	Hat Maker	Herts	St Michaels
1057	KEYS	Frederick	135		Son		9	M	Errand Boy	Herts	St Michaels
1058	KEYS	Emily	135		Dau		6	F	Scholar	Herts	St Michaels
1059	KEYS	Mary Ann	135		Dau		4	F		Herts	St Michaels
1060	KEYS	John	135		Son		1	M		Herts	St Michaels
1061	BROWN	John	136	Pound Field	Head	Mar	61	M	Agric Lab	Herts	Codicote
1062	BROWN	Susannah	136		Wife	Mar	60	F		Herts	Sandridge
1063	BROWN	Mary A.	136		Dau	Unm	34	F	Bonnet Sewer	Herts	St Albans
1064	BROWN	Harriet	136		Dau	Unm	27	F	Bonnet Sewer	Herts	St Albans
1065	BROWN	Susannah	136		Dau	Unm	22	F	Bonnet Sewer	Herts	St Albans
1066	BROWN	Maria	136		Dau	Unm	17	F	Bonnet Sewer	Herts	St Albans
1067	WINGROVE	John	137	Pound Field	Head	Mar	45	M	Brewers Labourer	Herts	St Michaels
1068	WINGROVE	Hannah	137		Wife	Mar	46	F		Herts	Wheathampstead

1069	WINGROVE	George	137		Son			13	M	Errand Boy	Herts	St Michaels
1070	WINGROVE	Ann	137		Dau		10	F	Scholar	Herts	St Michaels
1071	WINGROVE	Mary A.	137		Dau		8	F	Scholar	Herts	St Michaels
1072	WINGROVE	Eliza	137		Dau		6	F	Scholar	Herts	St Michaels
1073	WINGROVE	Emma	137		Dau		4	F	Scholar	Herts	St Michaels
1074	BAIL	John	138	Pound Field	Head	Mar	28	M	Bricklayers Labourer	Herts	St Albans
1075	BAIL	Elizabeth	138		Wife	Mar	32	F		Beds	Dunstable
1076	BAIL	Ann E.	138		Dau		3m	F		Herts	St Albans
1077	DAY	William	139	Pound Field	Head	Mar	41	M	Agric Lab	Herts	Harpenden
1078	DAY	Sophia	139		Wife	Mar	40	F		Herts	Harpenden
1079	DAY	Charles	139		Son		15	M	Hat Maker	Herts	St Michaels
1080	DAY	Emma	139		Dau		13	F	Hat Maker	Herts	Harpenden
1081	DAY	William	139		Son		11	M	Hat Maker	Herts	Harpenden
1082	DAY	Hannah	139		Dau		7	F	Hat Maker	Herts	Harpenden
1083	DAY	George	139		Son		3	M		Herts	St Michaels
1084	DAY	Martha	139		Dau		9m	F		Herts	St Michaels
1085	MAUNDER	Vincent	140	Pound Field	Head	Mar	37	M	Gardener	Oxon	Thame
1086	MAUNDER	Maria	140		Wife	Mar	38	F		Herts	St Albans
1087	MAUNDER	Elizabeth	140		Dau	Unm	18	F	Hat Maker	Oxon	Thame
1088	MAUNDER	James	140		Son		7	M	Scholar	Herts	St Peters
1089	MAUNDER	Joseph	140		Son		5	M	Scholar	Herts	St Peters
1090	MAUNDER	Eliza	140		Dau		2	F		Herts	St Michaels
1091	MAUNDER	Sarah	140		Dau		2m	F		Herts	St Michaels

The end of the Municipal Borough of St Albans

Chapter Twelve

The parish of St Michaels in the liberty of St Albans

Registrar's District: St Albans   Enumeration District 5b   Ref. HO 107/1713 folios 494-504

Childwick side of St Michaels Parish.

	Surname	Forename		Place	Relation	Status	Age	Sex	Occupation	County	Birthplace
I	FENSOM	William	I	Back Lane	Head	Mar	42	M	Gardener	Herts	St Albans
I	FENSOM	Sarah	I		Wife	Mar	40	F	Gardeners Wife	Herts	St Albans
I	FENSOM	Emma	I		Dau	Unm	18	F	Gardeners Daughter	Herts	St Albans
I	FENSOM	Samuel	I		Son	Unm	15	M	Errand Boy	Herts	St Albans
I	PARROTT	Abraham	2	Back Lane	Head	Mar	42	M	Shepherd	Herts	Wheathampstead
I	PARROTT	Elizabeth	2		Wife	Mar	49	F		Herts	Great Gaddesden
I	PARROTT	Charles H.	2		Son	Unm	12	M	Scholar at Home	Herts	Hemel Hempstead
I	GEORGE	James	3	Back Lane	Head	Mar	62	M	Carpenter	Herts	St Michaels
I	GEORGE	Susannah	3		Wife	Mar	62	F		Herts	St Peters
I	HOWARD	Charlotte	3		Lodger	Unm	42	F	Plaiter	Herts	Abbots Langley
I	BAILLIE	Henry	4	Prae House	Head	Mar	48	M	Member of Parliament	Gloucs	Bristol
I	BAILLIE	Phillippa	4		Wife	Mar	31	F	M.P.s Wife	Sweden	
I	BAILLIE	Hugh	4		Son		8	M	Scholar at Home	London	
I	BAILLIE	Francis	4		Son		7	M	Scholar at Home	London	
I	BAILLIE	George	4		Son		5	M	Scholar at Home	London	
I	BAILLIE	Ellen	4		Dau		3	F		London	
I	KINGSMILL	William M.	4		Tutor	Unm	26	M	Clergyman Church of England B.A. Cambs (Coll. Jesus)	Hants	Southampton
I	SLIGO (Marquis of)	George John	4		Visitor	Mar	31	M	Peer	Ireland	Westport
I	SLIGO (Marchioness of)	Ellen	4		Visitor	Mar	27	F	Wife of Peer	Oxon	Charlbury
I	BROWNE	Catherine Ellen	4		Niece	Unm	11 m	F	Peer's Daughter	Ireland	Westport
I	WELFARD	Ellen	4		Serv	Unm	29	F	Nurse	Oxon	Charlbury
I	CAZE	Clotilde	4		Serv	Unm	31	F	Second Nurse	France	
I	PIPET	Eliz.	4		Serv	Unm	28	F	Nurse	Scotland	Stonehaven
I	WIGLIE	Anne	4		Serv	Unm	30	F	Ladys Maid	London	
I	RUNEY	Clara	4		Serv	Mar	35	F	Ladys Maid	France	

Figure 11 : ST MICHAELS (RURAL)

557

From the first edition of the 6 inch Ordinance Survey of Hertfordshire (1878), Sheet XXXIV

Approximate scale of reproduction: 1cm = 165m

	SURNAME	FORENAME	SCHEDULE NUMBER	ADDRESS	RELATIONSHIP	STATUS	AGE	SEX	OCCUPATION	COUNTY OF BIRTH	PLACE OF BIRTH
26	LINFIELD	Mary	4		Serv	Unm	50	F	Cook	Sussex	Rudgwick
27	WILDING	Alice	4		Serv	Unm	29	F	Housemaid	Wales	Radnor
28	WHITE	Mary	4		Serv	Unm	24	F	Kitchen Maid	Notts	Collingham
29	COLES	William	4		Serv	Unm	21	M	Footman	Wilts	Maningford
30	BOWERS	John	4		Serv	Unm	30	M	Footman	Kent	Hythe
31	CLIMANCE	William	5	Prae Mill House	Head	Mar	60	M	Master Miller employing 2 men	Herts	Braughing
32	CLIMANCE	Mary	5		Wife	Mar	50	F		Middx	London
33	CLIMANCE	Eliza	5		Dau	Unm	30	F		Herts	St Albans
34	CLIMANCE	Alfred	5		Son	Unm	21	M	Miller	Herts	St Albans
35	CHANDLER	William	5		Nephew	Unm	19	M	Baker	Middx	London
36	GOODGAME	William	6	Prae Mill	Head	Mar	37	M	Miller	Middx	Cowley
37	CLIMANCE	Benjamin	7	Prae Mill	Head	Mar	27	M	Labourer	Herts	Braughing
38	CLIMANCE	Harriet	7		Wife	Mar	29	F	Labourers Wife	Herts	Cuffley [Northaw]
39	PRATT	Harriet	7		Dau-in-law		5	F	Scholar	Herts	Northaw
40	CLIMANCE	Benjamin	7		Son		1	M		Herts	St Albans
41	CLIMANCE	Eliza	7		Dau		2m	F		Herts	St Albans
42	CLIMANCE	Jane	7		Dau		2m	F		Herts	St Albans
43	STARKINS	Thomas	8	Redbourn Road	Head	Mar	69	M	Labourer	Herts	St Albans
44	STARKINS	Hannah	8		Wife	Mar	52	F	Labourers Wife	Bucks	Great Kimble
45	STARKINS	Sarah	8		Dau	Unm	23	F	Bonnet Sewer	Herts	St Albans
46	STARKINS	John	8		Son	Unm	18	M	Labourer	Herts	St Albans
47	STARKINS	Thomas	8		Son		11	M	Scholar	Herts	St Albans
48	DUNHAM	William	9	Redbourn Road	Head	Mar	73	M	Labourer	Herts	St Albans
49	DUNHAM	Hounour	9		Wife	Mar	48	F	Bonnet Sewer	Middx	London
50	DUNHAM	Elizabeth	9		Dau	Unm	18	F	Bonnet Sewer	Herts	St Albans
51	DUNHAM	Ann	9		Dau		13	F	Hatter	Herts	St Albans
52	DUNHAM	Selina	9		Dau		9	F	Scholar	Herts	St Albans
53	DUNHAM	Henry	9		Son		7	M	Scholar at Home	Herts	St Albans
54	PARSONS	Jonathan	10	Shafford Mill	Head	Widower	57	M	Farmer & Miller, 200 acres employing 9 labourers	Herts	Sandridge
55	PARSONS	William	10		Son	Mar	29	M	Farmers Son	Herts	Sandridge
56	PARSONS	Eliza	10		Dau-in-law	Mar	25	F	Housekeeper	Middx	Somers Town, St Pancras
57	PARSONS	Jesse	10		Son	Unm	28	M	Miller	Herts	Sandridge
58	PARSONS	Henry	10		Son	Unm	26	M	Miller	Herts	Sandridge
59	PARSONS	George	10		Son	Unm	22	M	Draper	Herts	Sandridge
60	GILBERT	Harriet	10		Serv	Unm	19	F	House Servant	Herts	St Albans
61	DEARMAN	William	10		Serv	Unm	16	M	Farm Servant	Herts	St Peters
62	CURRALL	John	10		Serv	Unm	16	M	Farm Servant	Herts	Redbourn
63	SMITH	Robert	11	Childwick, Hedges Farm	Head	Mar	35	M	Farmer of 292 acres employing 15 labourers	Beds	Luton
64	SMITH	Ruth	11		Wife	Mar	30	F		Beds	Luton
65	SMITH	Robert	11		Son		7	M	Scholar at Home	Herts	St Michaels
66	SMITH	Levi	11		Son		4	M		Herts	St Michaels
67	FOSKET	Car(oline)	11		Serv	Unm	19	F	House Servant	Bucks	Grandborough
68	BENNETT	William	11		Serv	Unm	17	M	Farm Servant	Herts	Harpenden

69	BYGRAVE	Thomas	11		Serv	Unm	16	M	Farm Servant	Beds	Sundon
70	ALLEN	Frederick	11		Serv		15	M	Farm Servant	Herts	St Pauls Walden
71	KING	George	12	Childwick	Head	Mar	31	M	Labourer (Shepherd)	Bucks	Great Horwood
72	KING	Mary	12		Wife	Mar	28	F	Plaiter	Herts	Wheathampstead
73	WHEATLEY	Richard	13	Childwick	Head	Mar	70	M	Labourer	Herts	St Michaels
74	WHEATLEY	Mary Ann	13		Wife	Mar	63	F		Herts	St Michaels
75	WHEATLEY	Elizabeth	13		Dau	Unm	32	F		Herts	St Michaels
76	WHEATLEY	George	13		Son	Widower	26	M	Labourer	Herts	St Michaels
77	WHEATLEY	Ann	13		Dau		2	F		Herts	St Michaels
78	GREENHILL	Edward J.	13		[blank]		12	M	Scholar	Herts	St Michaels
79	JENNINGS	Joshua	13		Visitor	Unm	34	M	Game Keeper	Middx	[Unknown]
80	TIMPERON	Arthur	14	Childwick Hall	Head	Unm	37	M	Esquire	Herts	St Albans
81	TIMPERON	Anne	14		Mother	Widow	61	F		Middx	Hammersmith
82	WORLEY	Isabella	14		Sister	Mar	33	F		Herts	St Albans
83	TOWERS	Elizabeth	14		Nurse	Widow	78	F	Nurse	Berks	Wokingham
84	TIMPERON	Mary Anne	14		Sister	Unm	34	F		Herts	St Albans
85	BASTIN	Sarah	14		Serv	Unm	38	F	Nursemaid	Hants	Winchester
86	CLARKE	Mary A.	14		Serv	Unm	33	F	Ladies Maid	Berks	Kingston
87	ROBERTS	Ann	14		Serv	Unm	40	F	Ladies Maid	Lincs	Fillingham
88	GRAY	Sarah	14		Serv	Unm	29	F	Housemaid	Herts	Welwyn
89	COOK	Elizabeth	14		Serv	Unm	40	F	Dairy Woman	Middx	Twickenham
90	PARR	Sarah	14		Serv	Unm	40	F	Cook	Sussex	Chichester
91	KENNY	Martha	14		Serv	Unm	24	F	Kitchen Maid	Herts	St Albans
92	SHAW	Thomas	14		Serv	Mar	65	M	Coachman	Beds	Leighton Buzzard
93	TAYLOR	Thomas	14		Serv	Unm	24	M	Footman	Beds	Luton
94	HAWKINS	George	14		Serv	Mar	38	M	Groom	Herts	Harpenden
95	BENNETT	William	15	Near Childwick Hall	Head	Mar	43	M	Labourer	Herts	Harpenden
96	BENNETT	Hannah	15		Wife	Mar	30	F	Labourers Wife	Herts	Harpenden
97	BENNETT	Henry	15		Son		10	M	Scholar	Herts	Redbourn
98	BENNETT	Sarah	15		Dau		7	F	Scholar	Herts	St Michaels
99	BENNETT	Charles	15		Son		4	M	Scholar	Herts	St Michaels
100	BENNETT	John	15		Son		2	M	Scholar	Herts	St Michaels
101	BENNETT	Henry	16	Near Childwick Hall	Head	Widower	73	M	Labourer	Herts	[Unknown]

One house uninhabited

102	BLAGG	William	17	Near Childwick Bury	Head	Mar	35	M	Coachman	Notts	Gateford
103	BLAGG	Elizabeth	17		Wife	Mar	28	F		Norfolk	Taverham
104	BLAGG	William	17		Son		6	M	Scholar	Norfolk	Ringland
105	BLAGG	Frederic	17		Son		2	M		Middx	St James
106	BLAGG	Charles	17		Son		2m	M		Herts	Childwick [St Michaels]
107	SPINKES	Elizabeth	17		Visitor	Unm	18	F		Norfolk	Taverham
108	JODDREL	Richard Paul	18	Childwick Bury	Head	Mar	32	M	Landed Proprietor	London	St Marylebone
109	JODDREL	Isabella Anna Maria	18		Wife	Mar	22	F	Peers Daughter	Ireland	County Cork
110	DOUGLAS	William	18		Serv	Unm	22	M	House Servant	Surrey	Wandsworth
111	HAGGAR	Henry	18		Serv	Unm	27	M	House Servant	Herts	Hitchin

	SURNAME	FORENAME	SCHEDULE NUMBER	ADDRESS	RELATIONSHIP	STATUS	AGE	SEX	OCCUPATION	COUNTY OF BIRTH	PLACE OF BIRTH
112	COX	James	18		Serv	Unm	17	M	House Servant	Beds	Kensworth
113	SAWYER	Mary	18		Serv	Unm	36	F	House Servant	Herts	Hertford
114	JACKSON	Alice	18		Serv	Unm	29	F	House Servant	Herts	Royston
115	FRISBY	Caroline	18		Serv	Unm	21	F	House Servant	Cambs	Cambridge
116	KENTISH	Mary	18		Serv	Unm	17	F	House Servant	Herts	Bricket Wood [St Stephens]
117	ANNESLY	Sophia	18		Visitor	Unm	40	F	Spinster	Trinidad	
118	WHITEHEAD	Samuel	19	Childwick Green	Head	Widower	57	M	Labourer (Farm)	Herts	St Michaels
119	WHITEHEAD	George	19		Son	Unm	22	M	Labourer (Shepherd)	Herts	St Michaels
120	WHITEHEAD	Eliza	19		Dau	Unm	16	F	Plaiter	Herts	St Michaels
121	DAY	John	20	Childwick Green	Head	Mar	38	M	Labourer (Farm)	Herts	Kimpton
122	DAY	Jane	20		Wife	Mar	39	F	Plaiter	Herts	St Michaels
123	DAY	Joseph	20		Son	Unm	9	M	Scholar at Home	Herts	St Michaels
124	DAY	James	20		Son	Unm	11	M	Errand Boy	Herts	St Michaels
125	DAY	Judith	20		Dau	Unm	8	F	Plaiter	Herts	St Michaels
126	DAY	Elizabeth	20		Dau	Unm	6	F		Herts	St Michaels
127	DAY	Henry	20		Son	Unm	3	M		Herts	St Michaels
128	DAY	Ellen	20		Dau	Unm	2m	F		Herts	St Michaels
129	DAY	William	21	Childwick Green	Head	Mar	33	M	Cordwainer	Herts	Kimpton
130	DAY	Mary	21		Wife	Mar	30	F	Plaiter	Herts	[Unknown]
131	DAY	Eliza	21		Dau		5	F	Scholar	Herts	St Michaels
132	DAY	Louisa	21		Dau		4	F		Herts	St Michaels
133	DAY	Daniel	21		Son		2	M		Herts	St Michaels
134	WHITBREAD	Henry	21		Lodger	Mar	55	M	Gardener	Unknown	
135	DAY	Sarah	22	Childwick Green	Head	Widow	69	F	Beer Seller	Herts	Codicote
136	DAY	Susan	22		Grandau	Unm	13	F	Plaiter	Herts	St Michaels
137	BROWN	Bradley	22		Lodger	Unm	23	M	Agric Lab	Herts	Harpenden
138	SWAINE	Joseph	23	Childwick Green	Head	Mar	41	M	Agric Lab	Herts	Kimpton
139	SWAINE	Elizabeth	23		Wife	Mar	45	F	Plaiter	Herts	Kimpton
140	SWAINE	Eliza	23		Dau	Unm	15	F	Trimming Weaver	Herts	St Michaels
141	SWAINE	Frederic	23		Son	Unm	12	M	Shepherd	Herts	St Michaels
142	SWAINE	Emma	23		Dau	Unm	7	F		Herts	St Michaels
143	SWAINE	Fanny	23		Dau		5	F		Herts	St Michaels
144	CHALK	George	24	Childwick Green	Head	Mar	37	M	Agric Lab	Herts	Abbots Langley
145	CHALK	Jane	24		Wife	Mar	38	F	Plaiter	Herts	Hitchin
146	CHALK	Rosanna	24		Dau		9	F	Plaiter	Herts	St Michaels
147	CHALK	Charles	24		Son		2	M		Herts	St Michaels
148	STONE	James	25	Childwick Green	Head	Mar	47	M	Sawyer	Bucks	Risborough [Princes Risborough]
149	STONE	Ann	25		Wife	Mar	40	F	Sawyers Wife	Bucks	Risborough [Princes Risborough]
150	STONE	John	25		Son	Unm	25	M	Sawyer	Bucks	Risborough [Princes Risborough]
151	STONE	Thomas	25		Son	Unm	19	M	Sawyer	Bucks	Risborough [Princes Risborough]
152	STONE	Benjamin	25		Son	Unm	16	M	Agric Lab	Bucks	Risborough [Princes

											Risborough]
153	STONE	Ann	25		Dau	Unm	13	F	Plaiter	Bucks	Risborough [Princes Risborough]
154	STONE	Oliver	25		Son		8	M	Scholar	Bucks	Risborough [Princes Risborough]
155	STONE	William	25		Son		3	M		Bucks	Risborough [Princes Risborough]
156	EALING	Thomas	26	Childwick Green	Head	Mar	21	M	Agric Lab	Herts	Harpenden
157	EALING	Hannah	26		Wife	Mar	23	F	Plaiter	Herts	Abbots Langley
158	GRAY	William	27	Childwick Green	Head	Mar	29	M	Agric Lab	Herts	Codicote
159	GRAY	Mary	27		Wife	Mar	28	F	Plaiter	Herts	St Pauls Walden
160	GRAY	William	27		Son		9	M		Herts	St Pauls Walden
161	GRAY	Charles	27		Son		4	M		Herts	Kimpton
162	GRAY	Mary A.	27		Dau		1	F		Herts	Kimpton
163	WELCH	John	28	Childwick Green	Head	Mar	65	M	Straw Plait Dealer	Herts	Flamstead
164	WELCH	Hannah	28		Wife	Mar	55	F	Straw Plait Dealer	Herts	St Michaels
165	EALEY	Eliza	28		Lodger	Unm	27	F	Hatter	Herts	St Albans
166	MASON	William	29	Childwick Green	Head	Mar	40	M	Farm Labourer	Herts	Sandridge
167	MASON	Elizabeth	29		Wife	Mar	38	F	Plaiter	Middx	Hackney
168	MASON	Samuel	29		Son	Unm	15	M	Farm Labourer	Herts	St Michaels
169	MASON	Edward	29		Son		11	M	Errand Boy	Herts	St Michaels
170	MASON	James	29		Son		9	M	Plaiter	Herts	St Michaels
171	MASON	Stephen	29		Son		5	M		Herts	St Michaels
172	MASON	Nathan	29		Son		3	M		Herts	St Michaels
173	MASON	David	29		Son		2	M		Herts	St Michaels
174	HUNT	James	30	Childwick Green	Head	Mar	54	M	Farm Labourer	Beds	Dunstable
175	HUNT	Mary	30		Wife	Mar	55	F	Hatter	Beds	Tebworth
176	HUNT	Mary A.	30		Dau	Unm	26	F	Hatter	Herts	Harpenden
177	HUNT	Louisa	30		Dau	Unm	22	F	Hatter	Herts	Harpenden
178	WARNER	Elizabeth	31	Childwick Green	Head	Widow	57	F	Straw Plaiter	Herts	St Michaels
179	WARNER	Mary	31		Dau	Unm	25	F	Weaver (Trimming)	Herts	St Michaels
180	WARNER	Betsey	31		Dau	Unm	20	F	Weaver (Trimming)	Herts	St Michaels
181	KING	[?]	31		Lodger	Unm	23	M	Farm Labourer	Herts	Sandridge
182	BOLTER	William	32	Childwick Green	Head	Unm	56	M	Farmer of 300 acres employing 11 labourers	Oxon	Sarsden
183	BOLTER	Charles	32		Nephew	Unm	30	M	Visitor	Oxon	Lyneham
184	SLOW	Daniel	32		Serv	Unm	20	M	House Servant	Herts	Wheathampstead
185	SHARP	William	32		Serv	Unm	21	M	House Servant	Herts	Sandridge
186	GOOLING	William	32		Serv	Unm	13	M	Farm Labourer	Herts	St Albans
187	JEFFRIES	Ann	32		Serv	Unm	24	F	House Servant	Bucks	Aylesbury
188	KNOWLES	James	33	Childwick Green	Head	Mar	48	M	Farm Labourer	Herts	Redbourn
189	KNOWLES	Esther	33		Wife	Mar	46	F	Hatter	Herts	Wheathampstead
190	KNOWLES	Julia	33		Dau		14	F	Hatter	Herts	St Michaels
191	KNOWLES	Emma	33		Dau		12	F	Hatter	Herts	St Michaels
192	KNOWLES	Mary A.	33		Dau		9	F	Scholar at Home	Herts	St Michaels
193	KNOWLES	Lettice S.	33		Dau		6	F	Scholar at Home	Herts	St Michaels

	SURNAME	FORENAME	SCHEDULE NUMBER	ADDRESS	RELATIONSHIP	STATUS	AGE	SEX	OCCUPATION	COUNTY OF BIRTH	PLACE OF BIRTH
194	DUNHAM	George	34	Childwick Green	Head	Mar	25	M	Formerly Baker	Herts	Wheathampstead
195	DUNHAM	Hannah	34		Wife	Mar	26	F	Bakers Wife	Herts	Wheathampstead
196	DUNHAM	Emma	34		Dau		5	F		Herts	Harpenden
197	DUNHAM	Anne	34		Dau		4	F		Herts	Harpenden
198	BEAN	Joseph	35	Childwick Green	Head	Mar	31	M	Wood Sawyer	Herts	Harpenden
199	BEAN	Susan	35		Wife	Mar	28	F	Straw Bonnet Maker	Herts	St Michaels
200	LIGHTFOOT	William	36	Childwick Green	Head	Mar	61	M	Farm Labourer	Herts	Hertford
201	LIGHTFOOT	Mary	36		Wife	Mar	56	F	Charwoman	Herts	St Michaels
202	LIGHTFOOT	Emma	36		Dau	Unm	17	F	Straw Bonnet Maker	Herts	Wheathampstead
203	WELCH	Isaac	37	Old Roson, Luton Road	Head	Mar	54	M	Farm Labourer	Herts	Wheathampstead
204	WELCH	Hannah	37		Wife	Mar	45	F	Plaiter	Herts	Wheathampstead
205	WELCH	John	37		Son	Unm	24	M	Farm Labourer	Herts	Kimpton
206	WELCH	Susan	37		Dau	Unm	21	F	Plaiter	Herts	Harpenden
207	WELCH	Isaac	37		Son	Unm	15	M	Farm Labourer	Herts	Harpenden
208	WELCH	William	37		Grandson	Unm	3m	M		Herts	St Michaels
209	CARTER	James	38	Old Roson, Luton Road	Head	Mar	27	M	Farm Labourer	Herts	Wheathampstead
210	CARTER	Eliza	38		Wife	Mar	25	F	Plaiter	Herts	Kimpton
211	DAY	Joseph	39	Old Roson, Luton Road	Head	Mar	45	M	Victualler	Herts	Codicote
212	DAY	Mary	39		Wife	Mar	44	F	Victuallers Wife	Herts	Hatfield
213	DAY	Emma	39		Dau	Unm	19	F		Herts	St Michaels
214	DAY	Elizabeth	39		Dau	Unm	14	F		Herts	St Michaels
215	DAY	Sarah	39		Dau	Unm	12	F	Scholar	Herts	St Michaels
216	DAY	Joseph	39		Son		9	M	Scholar	Herts	St Michaels
217	DAY	Susan	39		Dau		5	F		Herts	St Michaels
218	DAY	Jane	39		Dau		4m	F		Herts	St Michaels
219	MOSS	Thomas	39		Visitor	Widower	64	M	Carpenter	Herts	Kimpton
220	LINTON	J.H.	39		Visitor	Widower	47	M	Gentleman	London	
221	STALLARD	Samuel	39		Visitor	[blank]	60	M	Gentleman	London	St Brides
222	DICKINSON	Charles	40	Greens Farm	Head	Mar	30	M	Farmer of 110 acres	Herts	Sandridge
223	DICKINSON	Emily	40		Wife	Mar	27	F	Farmers Wife	Beds	Toddington
224	DICKINSON	George	40		Son		5m	M		Herts	St Michaels
225	DICKINSON	William	40		Brother	Unm	44	M	Farmer of 11 acres	Herts	Sandridge
226	COOK	William	41	Bernards Heath	Head	Mar	55	M	Dealer in Ashes & Manure	Middx	Shoreditch
227	COOK	Maria	41		Wife	Mar	48	F		Herts	Shenley
228	COOK	Elizabeth	41		Dau	Unm	19	F	Hatter	Herts	St Peters
229	COOK	George	41		Son	Unm	18	M	Dealer	Herts	St Peters
230	COOK	Caroline	41		Dau	Unm	17	F	Hatter	Herts	St Peters
231	COOK	Jane	41		Dau	Unm	15	F	Hatter	Herts	St Peters
232	GODFREY	John	41		Serv	Unm	27	M	Labourer	Herts	Sandridge
233	FRISTER	John	42	Bernards Heath	Head	Mar	46	M	Farm Labourer	Herts	Hemel Hempstead
234	FRISTER	Louisa	42		Wife	Mar	34	F	Hatter	Herts	St Michaels
235	FRISTER	Charles	42		Son		10	M	Hatter	Herts	St Peters
236	FRISTER	William	42		Son		8	M	Hatter	Herts	St Peters
237	FRISTER	Eliza	42		Dau		6	F		Herts	St Peters

No.	Surname	Name	#	Address	Relation	Cond.	Age	Sex	Occupation	County	Birthplace
238	FRISTER	Charlotte	42		Dau		4	F		Herts	St Peters
239	FRISTER	Henry	42		Son		2	M		Herts	St Michaels
240	HORTON	Mary	43	Bernards Heath	Head	Mar	55	F	Sempstress	Beds	Luton
241	HORTON	Thomas	43		Son	Mar	31	M	Farm Labourer	Beds	Luton
242	HORTON	William	43		Son	[Unm]	20	M	Farm Labourer	Herts	Sandridge
243	HORTON	James	43		Son	[Unm]	16	M	Farm Labourer	Herts	Sandridge
244	BARBER	James	43		Grandson		3	M		Herts	St Michaels
245	GOLDING	James	44	Bernards Heath	Head	Mar	64	M	Farm Labourer	Herts	Chipperfield
246	GOLDING	Louisa	44		Wife	Mar	48	F	Hatter	Bucks	Chenies
247	GOLDING	Sophia	44		Dau	Unm	20	F	Trimming Weaver	Herts	Sarratt
248	GOLDING	George	44		Son	Unm	26	M	Grass Splitter (Palm Leaf)	Herts	Sarratt
249	GOLDING	Emma	44		Dau	Unm	5	F		Herts	St Michaels

Five houses uninhabited

No.	Surname	Name	#	Address	Relation	Cond.	Age	Sex	Occupation	County	Birthplace
250	CULLUM	Samuel Henry	45	Townsend Farm	Head	Unm	38	M	Farmer	London	City
251	ROBERTS	Ann	45		Serv	Unm	40	F	Housekeeper	Beds	[Unknown]
252	HAYF'	Nievens	45		Serv	Unm	16	M	Housekeeper	Herts	St Albans
253	SCOTT	Elizabeth	46	Oster House	Head	Widow	53	F	Landed Proprietor	Oxon	Oxford
254	SCOTT	Elizabeth A.	46		Dau	Unm	30	F		London	
255	SCOTT	Emma	46		Dau	Unm	21	F		London	
256	SCOTT	Frances M.	46		Dau	Unm	18	F		London	
257	SCOTT	Laura	46		Dau	Unm	17	F		London	
258	SCOTT	Alice	46		Dau		15	F		London	
259	WHALEY	Catherine	46		Visitor	Widow	58	F	Annuitant	Oxon	Oxford
260	SCOTT	Walter	46		Visitor		2	M		Middx	Islington
261	SCOTT	Arthur	46		Visitor		11 m	M		Middx	Islington
262	GILES	Ellen	46		Serv	Mar	29	F	Servant (Wet Nurse)	London	
263	ELLIS	Elizabeth	46		Serv	Unm	32	F	Servant (Cook)	Herts	Weston
264	BAKER	Maria	46		Serv	Unm	26	F	House Servant	Suffolk	Sudbury
265	HUMPHRYS	Charles	46		Serv	Unm	24	M	Groom	Herts	Wheathampstead
266	HAMMOND	Richard	47	Oster Hill	Head	Mar	33	M	Gardener	Devon	Bishopsteignton
267	HAMMOND	Elizabeth	47		Wife	Mar	35	F	Gardeners Wife	Devon	Newton Abbot
268	HAMMOND	William	47		Son		11	M	Scholar at Home	Devon	Bishopsteignton
269	HAMMOND	George	47		Son		9	M	Scholar at Home	Devon	Bishopsteignton
270	HAMMOND	Mary	47		Dau		6	F	Scholar at Home	Devon	Bishopsteignton
271	HAMMOND	John	47		Son		1	M		Herts	St Michaels

Registrar's District: St Albans   Enumeration District 5c   Ref. HO 107/1713 folios 505-25

Gorhambury Side and Chapelry of Leverstock Green, with Westwick Row, in the Parish of St Michaels.

Gorhambury Side

No.	Surname	Name	#	Address	Relation	Cond.	Age	Sex	Occupation	County	Birthplace
1	KING	Joseph	1	Silk Mill Cottage	Head	Mar	52	M	Silk Throwster	Herts	St Albans
1	KING	Ann	1		Wife	Mar	54	F		Herts	St Albans
1	KING	Sarah	1		Dau		14	F	Silk Winder	Herts	St Michaels
1	WELLS	George	2	Silk Mill Cottage	Head	Mar	32	M	Silk Throwster	Herts	St Albans

	SURNAME	FORENAME	SCHEDULE NUMBER	ADDRESS	RELATIONSHIP	STATUS	AGE	SEX	OCCUPATION	COUNTY OF BIRTH	PLACE OF BIRTH
1	WELLS	Emma	2		Wife	Mar	34	F		Herts	St Albans
2	WELLS	Sarah	2		Dau		6	F	Scholar	Herts	St Albans
3	WELLS	Emma	2		Dau		4	F	Scholar	Herts	St Albans
4	CHANCE	Maria	2		Lodger	Unm	55	F	Silk Winder	Herts	St Michaels
5	LOMAS	Samuel	3	Silk Mill Cottage	Head	Mar	52	M	Silk Throwster	Cheshire	Congleton
6	LOMAS	Mary	3		Wife	Mar	50	F		Cheshire	Congleton
7	LOMAS	Samuel	3		Son		14	M	Scholar	Lancs	Manchester
8	LOMAS	Ann	3		Dau		12	F		Lancs	Manchester
9	LOMAS	Edward	3		Son		9	M	Scholar	Lancs	Manchester
10	LOMAS	Sarah Ellen	3		Dau		5	F		Lancs	Manchester
11	CARTER	William	4	Verulam Hills	Head	Mar	25	M	Agric Lab	Herts	St Albans
12	CARTER	Sarah	4		Wife	Mar	26	F		Herts	St Stephens
13	CARTER	Elizabeth M.	4		Dau		10 m	F		Herts	St Stephens
14	GLASSCOCK	James	5	St Stephens Farm	Head	Mar	52	M	Farm Bailiff	Essex	Clavering
15	GLASSCOCK	Rebecca	5		Wife	Mar	54	F		Essex	Baden [Berden]
16	SELLS	Arthur	5		Grandson		4	M		Essex	Clavering
17	BRADLEY	James	5		Serv	Unm	26	M	Waggoner	Bucks	[Unknown]
18	FRANKLIN	Henry	5		Serv	Unm	22	M	Shepherd	Herts	Sandridge
19	ENGLAND	James	5		Serv	Unm	20	M	Farm Labourer	Herts	Sandridge
20	ATKINS	Daniel	5		Serv	Unm	17	M	Farm Labourer	Beds	Caddington
21	SEYMOUR	William	6	King Harry	Head	Mar	56	M	Victualler	Hunts	Huntingdon
22	SEYMOUR	Elizabeth	6		Wife	Mar	52	F		Herts	Barnet
23	SEYMOUR	Charles	6		Son	Unm	17	M	Ostler	Herts	Hatfield
24	SEYMOUR	James	6		Grandson		8	M		Herts	Buntingford
25	LEWIS	Thomas	6		Lodger	Unm	29	M	Agric Lab	Herts	St Stephens
26	PENNINGTON	James	7	St Stephens Green	Head	Mar	71	M	One of Her Majesty's Yeomen	Notts	Oldicots [Oldcoates]
27	PENNINGTON	Elizabeth	7		Wife	Mar	69	F		Notts	Kingsthorpe
28	ORCHARD	James	8	St Stephens Green	Head	Unm	46	M	Farmer of 10 acres employing 1 labourer	Herts	St Michaels
29	SADDINGTON	Ann	8		Serv	Widow	60	F	House Servant	Northants	Aldwinkle
30	FEARY	Elizabeth	9	St Stephens Green	Head	Widow	69	F	Annuitant	Middx	London
31	SPRIGGINS	David	10	St Stephens Green	Head	Mar	32	M	Nurseryman (3 men/3 apprentices)	Herts	St Michaels
32	SPRIGGINS	Emma	10		Wife	Mar	27	F		Middx	St Martins
33	SPRIGGINS	Mary Ann	10		Dau		7	F	Scholar at Home	Herts	Hertford
34	SPRIGGINS	Ann	10		Dau		3	F		Herts	St Michaels
35	SPRIGGINS	George C.	10		Son		3 m	M		Herts	St Michaels
36	BRACEY	John	10		Appr	Unm	19	M	Nurseryman (Appr)	Herts	Wheathampstead
37	ALLEN	Charles	10		Appr	Unm	15	M	Nurseryman (Appr)	Herts	Harpenden
38	WALLER	James	11	West Fields	Head	Mar	29	M	Farm Labourer	Beds	Barton
39	WALLER	Hannah	11		Wife	Mar	26	F	Straw Plaiter	Herts	St Albans
40	WALLER	Thomas	11		Son		4	M		Herts	St Albans
41	WALLER	William	11		Son		2	M		Herts	St Albans
42	HALLEY	Newman	12	West Farm	Head	Mar	66	M	Farmer of 115 acres employing 6 labourers	Herts	Kings Langley
43	HALLEY	Elizabeth	12		Wife	Mar	56	F		Middx	St Lukes
44	GEE	Mary	12		Serv	Unm	24	F	House Servant	Lincs	Bourne

45	MOOR	Rebecca	12		Serv	Unm	23	F	House Servant	Oxon	Milton
46	TINNEY	William	12		Widower	Unm	62	M	Farm Labourer	Bucks	Waddesdon
47	GREEN	William	13	Windridge Cottage	Head	Mar	45	M	Agric Lab	Herts	St Stephens
48	GREEN	Mary	13		Wife	Mar	42	F		Herts	St Albans
49	GREEN	Thomas	13		Son		10	M	Agric Lab	Herts	St Michaels
50	GREEN	Mary	13		Dau		7	F		Herts	St Michaels
51	GREEN	George	13		Son		6	M		Herts	St Michaels
52	GREEN	Elizabeth	13		Dau		1	F		Herts	St Michaels
53	NORWOOD	William	14	Windridge Cottage	Head	Mar	49	M	Agric Lab	Herts	St Michaels
54	NORWOOD	Ann	14		Wife	Mar	51	F	Brazilian Grass Plaiter	Herts	St Michaels
55	NORWOOD	Ann	14		Dau		13	F	Brazilian Grass Plaiter	Herts	St Stephens
56	DELL	Elizabeth	14		Mother-in-law	Widow	73	F	Straw Plaiter	Herts	St Michaels
57	HOWARD	James	15	Windridge Farm	Head	Mar	76	M	Farmer of 350 acres employing 8 labourers	Herts	[Unknown]
58	HOWARD	Ann Maria	15		Wife	Mar	53	F		Middx	Tottenham
59	HOWARD	James Sparks	15		Son	Mar	31	M	Farmers Son employed on Farm	Herts	St Michaels
60	HOWARD	Fanny	15		Dau-in-Law	Mar	23	F		Herts	Cheshunt
61	HOWARD	Thomas G.	15		Son	Unm	29	M	Farmers Son employed on Farm	Herts	St Michaels
62	HOWARD	Robert S.	15		Son		14	M	Farmers Son employed on Farm	Herts	St Michaels
63	HOWARD	Ruth E.	15		Dau		10	F		Herts	St Michaels
64	SKEGGS	Jane	15		Serv	Unm	23	F	House Serv	Herts	Hunsdon
65	STARKINS	William	15		Serv	Unm	16	M	Farm Lab	Herts	St Michaels
66	LEA	George	15		Serv	Unm	16	M	Errand Boy	Herts	St Stephens
67	CLEAVER	John	15		Serv	Unm	30	M	Shepherd	Berks	Wargrave
68	CATLIN	Isaac	16	Potters Crouch	Head	Mar	35	M	Farm Bailiff	Herts	St Michaels
69	CATLIN	Sarah	16		Wife	Mar	33	F		Herts	Hemel Hempstead
70	CROUCH	William	16		Lodger	Widower	77	M	Pauper (Agric Lab)	Herts	Hatfield
71	WHITE	George	16		Serv	Unm	16	M	Farm Servant	Herts	Watford
72	HOSIER	Benjamin	16		Lodger	Unm	18	M	Farm Lab	Herts	Hemel Hempstead
73	NORWOOD	Thomas	17	Potters Crouch	Head	Mar	29	M	Coal Carter (Blind)	Herts	St Stephens
74	NORWOOD	Susannah	17		Wife	Mar	30	F		Herts	St Michaels
75	NORWOOD	William	17		Son		2	M		Herts	St Stephens
76	TWITCHELL	James	18	Potters Crouch	Head	Mar	59	M	Agric Lab	Herts	Berkhamsted
77	TWITCHELL	Sarah	18		Wife	Mar	55	F		Herts	St Michaels
78	TWITCHELL	Sarah	18		Dau	Unm	31	F	General Serv	Herts	Hemel Hempstead
79	TWITCHELL	Jane	18		Dau	Unm	28	F	General Serv	Herts	Hemel Hempstead
80	TWITCHELL	Emma	18		Dau	Unm	26	F	General Serv	Herts	Hemel Hempstead
81	TWITCHELL	Ann	18		Dau	Unm	18	F	General Serv	Herts	Abbots Langley
82	TWITCHELL	William	18		Son	Unm	21	M	Agric Lab	Herts	Abbots Langley
83	HANNELL	Levina	19	Holly Bush	Head	Widow	32	F	Victualler	Herts	St Michaels
84	HANNELL	William	19		Son-in-law	Unm	23	M	Agric Lab	Herts	St Michaels
85	HANNELL	Alfred	19		Son-in-law	Unm	17	M	Agric Lab	Herts	St Michaels
86	HANNELL	Emma	19		Dau		14	F	Bonnet Sewer	Herts	St Michaels

	SURNAME	FORENAME	SCHEDULE NUMBER	ADDRESS	RELATIONSHIP	STATUS	AGE	SEX	OCCUPATION	COUNTY OF BIRTH	PLACE OF BIRTH
87	WILSON	James	19		Lodger	Unm	20	M	Agric Lab	Unknown	Unknown
88	ROBINS	George	20	Potters Crouch	Head	Mar	34	M	Farmer of 270 acres employing 12 labourers	Herts	Hertingfordbury
89	ROBINS	Sarah A.	20		Wife	Mar	33	F		Herts	St Michaels
90	ROBINS	George	20		Son		4	M		Herts	St Michaels
91	ROBINS	Benjamin	20		Son		2	M		Herts	St Michaels
92	GREEN	Henry	20		Serv	Unm	18	M	Farm Servant	Herts	Hemel Hempstead
93	ARNOLL	Benjamin	20		Serv	Unm	16	M	Farm Servant	Herts	Abbots Langley
94	ROBINS	Ann	20		Visitor	Mar	39	F	Nurse	Herts	Little Berkhamsted
95	PARROTT	Edward	21	Potters Crouch	Head	Mar	65	M	Carpenter	Herts	St Michaels
96	PARROTT	Mary	21		Wife	Mar	58	F		Herts	Langley
97	PARROTT	William	21		Son	Unm	26	M	Carpenter	Herts	St Michaels
98	PARROTT	Eliza	21		Dau	Unm	19	F		Herts	St Michaels
99	COOPER	Daniel	22	Potters Crouch	Head	Mar	26	M	Hay Dealer	Herts	St Michaels
100	COOPER	Betsey	22		Wife	Mar	27	F		Herts	Hemel Hempstead
101	ROBINS	William	23	Potters Crouch	Head	Mar	47	M	Agric Lab	Herts	Hertingfordbury
102	ROBINS	Elizabeth	23		Dau	Unm	19	F	Bonnet Sewer	Herts	Berkhamsted
103	ROBINS	William	23		Son		12	M	Agric Lab	Herts	Berkhamsted
104	ROBINS	Eliza	23		Dau		10	F	Scholar	Herts	Berkhamsted
105	SEABROOKE	Joseph	24	Apps Pond	Head	Mar	34	M	Game Keeper	Herts	Redbourn
106	SEABROOKE	Charlotte	24		Wife	Mar	32	F		Herts	Redbourn
107	SEABROOKE	Charlotte	24		Dau		11	F	Scholar	Herts	St Michaels
108	SEABROOKE	Joseph	24		Son		8	M	Scholar	Herts	Redbourn
109	SEABROOKE	William	24		Son		3	M		Herts	St Michaels
110	SEABROOKE	Frances	24		Dau		1	F		Herts	St Michaels
111	GADBERY	Ann	25	Apps Pond	Head	Widow	85	F	Pauper	Beds	Alington [Harlington]
112	GADBERY	Frances	25		Dau	Unm	55	F	Straw Plaiter	Herts	St Stephens
113	GADBERY	Sarah	25		Grandau	Unm	23	F	Straw Plaiter	Herts	Hadley
114	GADBERY	Mary Ann	25		Grandau	Unm	19	F	Pauper	Middx	St Pauls
115	ORSBORN	William	26	Apps Pond	Head	Mar	30	M	Agric Lab	Bucks	Chesham
116	ORSBORN	Kezia	26		Wife	Mar	30	F		Herts	Watford
117	ORSBORN	Maria	26		Dau		7	F	Scholar	Herts	Bedmond [Abbots Langley]
118	ORSBORN	Ellen	26		Dau		5	F	Scholar	Herts	Bedmond [Abbots Langley]
119	ORSBORN	Joseph	26		Son		6m	M		Herts	St Michaels
120	BURRIDGE	Hannah	27	Apps Pond	Head	Widow	53	F		Berks	Fawley
121	BURRIDGE	Isaac	27		Son	Unm	24	M	Agric Lab	Herts	Abbots Langley
122	BURRIDGE	Kitty	27		Dau	Unm	19	F	Hat Maker	Herts	Abbots Langley
123	BURRIDGE	Ann	27		Dau		15	F	Hat Maker	Herts	Abbots Langley
124	BURRIDGE	Jane	27		Dau		13	F	Hat Maker	Herts	St Michaels
125	BURRIDGE	George	27		Grandson		1	M		Herts	St Michaels
126	ROBERTS	Elizabeth	28	Maidens Crouch	Head	Widow	60	F	Farmer of 100 acres employing 2 labourers	Herts	Brickendon
127	ROBERTS	Richard	28		Son	Unm	29	M	Farmers Son employed at Home	Herts	St Michaels
128	VINE	Richard	28		Serv		14	M	Farm Servant	Herts	Bedmond [Abbots Langley]

129	SAUNDERS	Thomas	29	Hills End Farm	Head	Widower	60	M	Farmer of 220 acres employing 7 labourers		Herts	Redbourn
130	SAUNDERS	James	29		Son	Unm	39	M	Farmers Son at Home		Herts	Redbourn
131	ROGERS	John	29		Grandson		6	M			Herts	Watford
132	WEBB	Ellen	29		Serv		15	F	House Serv		Herts	St Michaels
133	SMITH	James	29		Serv	[Unm]	20	M	Ploughman		Unknown	Unknown
134	JAMES	Henry	29		Serv	[Unm]	17	M	Horsekeeper		Unknown	Unknown
135	SIMPSON	Frederick	30	Stud Cottage, Gorhambury Park	Head	Unm	23	M	Carpenter		Lincs	Grantham
136	SIMPSON	Mary	30		Sister	Unm	19	F	Housekeeper		Derby	Eckington
137	SIMPSON	Elizabeth	30		Sister	Unm	16	F			Derby	Eckington
138	OAKLEY	John	31	The Old Temple, Gorhambury Park	Head	Mar	55	M	Gardeners Labourer		Herts	St Peters
139	OAKLEY	Mary	31		Wife	Mar	55	F			Herts	St Michaels
140	OAKLEY	David	31		Son		10	M			Herts	St Michaels
141	OAKLEY	John [?]	31		Grandson		2	M			Herts	St Michaels
142	CARD	Martha	32	The Old Temple, Gorhambury Park	Head	Widow	67	F	Late Park Keepers Wife		Sussex	Breed [Brede]
143	SPARKS	Richard	32		Son-in-law	Mar	38	M	General Serv		Herts	Hertingfordbury
144	SPARKS	Elizabeth	32		Dau	Mar	38	F			Herts	St Michaels
145	SPARKS	Elizabeth	32		Grandau		8	F			Herts	St Michaels
146	HOLINSHEAD	Thomas	33	Kettlewells Farm	Head	Unm	44	M	Farmer of 287 acres employing 6 labourers		Herts	Freisden [Frithsden]
147	SAUNDERS	Ann	33		Serv	Widow	66	F	Housekeeper		Herts	Redbourn
148	HIGGINS	Mary Ann	33		Serv	Unm	20	F	House Serv		Oxon	Piddington [?]
149	BARTON	William	33		Serv	Unm	22	M	Farm Lab		Herts	Great Gaddesden
150	WELLS	John	33		Serv	Unm	22	M	Farm Lab		Herts	Redbourn
151	SQUIRES	George	33		Serv	Unm	21	M	Farm Lab		Herts	Redbourn
152	PUNTER	Charles	33		Serv	Unm	19	M	Farm Lab		Beds	Caddington
153	WILSON	William	33		Serv	Unm	16	M	Farm Lab		Herts	St Michaels
154	BENNETT	William	33		Serv	Unm	15	M	Farm Lab		Herts	St Michaels
155	BOGUE	George	34	Garden House, Gorhambury Park	Head	Mar	43	M	Gardener		Scotland	[Unknown]
156	BOGUE	Martha	34		Wife	Mar	45	F			Dorset	Abbotsbury
157	DELL	Isaac	34		Appr	Unm	24	M	Gardeners Apprentice		Herts	Abbots Langley
158	SAUNDERS	Lucas	34		Appr	Unm	23	M	Gardeners Apprentice		Herts	Hemel Hempstead
159	TRIPP	Jesse	35	Garden House, Gorhambury Park	Head	Mar	32	M	Gardeners Lab		Herts	Albury
160	TRIPP	Sarah	35		Wife	Mar	28	F			Herts	Abbots Langley
161	TRIPP	Edward	35		Son		4	M			Herts	Hemel Hempstead
162	TRIPP	George	35		Son		8m	M			Herts	Hemel Hempstead
163	NASH	Henry	36	Park Gate Lodge	Head	Mar	36	M	Groom		Suffolk	Newmarket
164	NASH	Harriet	36		Wife	Mar	32	F	Laundress		Devon	Credick [Craddock?]
165	NASH	Samuel	36		Son		3	M			Herts	St Michaels
166	NASH	Charlotte	36		Dau		3	F			Herts	St Michaels
167	NASH	Elizabeth	36		Dau		11m	F			Herts	St Michaels
168	JARRAT	Martha	36		Serv		12	F	House Servant		Herts	St Michaels
169	CURL	William	37	Old Park Gate Lodge	Head	Mar	42	M	Shepherd		Herts	Fields End
170	CURL	Charlotte	37		Wife	Mar	40	F			Herts	Rickmansworth

	SURNAME	FORENAME	SCHEDULE NUMBER	ADDRESS	RELATIONSHIP	STATUS	AGE	SEX	OCCUPATION	COUNTY OF BIRTH	PLACE OF BIRTH
171	WATERTON	Sophia	37		Visitor	Unm	15	F	Straw Plaiter	Herts	Berkhamsted
172	MILLS	Caroline	37		Visitor	Unm	26	F	Straw Plaiter	Herts	Berkhamsted
173	VERULAM	Dowager Countess of	38	Gorhambury	Mother	Widow	66	F	Peeress	London	London
174	VERULAM	Earl of	38		Head	Mar	42	M	Peer. Lord Lieutenant of Herts	London	London
175	VERULAM	Countess of	38		Wife	Mar	25	F	Peeress	London	London
176	GRIMSTON	Harriett E.	38		Dau		5	F		London	London
177	GRIMSTON	Jane	38		Dau		2	F		Herts	St Albans
178	GRIMSTON	Robert	38		Brother	Unm	34	M	Barrister at Law	London	London
179	ADDINGTON	Henry Unwin	38		Visitor	Mar	61	M	Under Secretary of State for Foreign Affairs	Oxon	Blount Court
180	ADDINGTON	Eleanor Anne	38		Visitors wife	Mar	46	F	Wife of the above	London	London
181	GREEN	Elizabeth	38		Serv	Unm	42	F	Housekeeper	Notts	St Peters, Nottingham
182	ALLEN	Eliza	38		Serv	Unm	27	F	Ladys Maid	Middx	Kensington
183	THOMPSON	Flora	38		Serv	Unm	30	F	Cook	Scotland	[Unknown]
184	SAUNDERS	Caroline	38		Visitors Serv	Unm	27	F	Maid to Dowager Countess of Verulam	Herts	Watford
185	BRAGLEY	Mary	38		Visitors Serv	Unm	30	F	Maid to Mrs. Addington	Devon	Fuleigh [Filleigh]
186	FRY	Bridget	38		Serv	Unm	29	F	Laundry Maid	Devon	Broad Clyst
529	WADKIN	Elizabeth	38		Serv	Unm	37	F	Housemaid	Yorks	Brandsby [?]
530	COLLYER	Caroline	39	Gorhambury	Serv	Unm	26	F	Housemaid	Hants	Steep
531	HITCHCOCK	Jane	39		Serv	Unm	23	F	Housemaid	Kent	Sevenoaks
532	POOL	Sarah	39		Serv	Unm	32	F	Still Room Maid	Essex	Tackley [Takeley]
533	MCDONALD	Isabella	39		Serv	Unm	28	F	Kitchen Maid	Scotland	Inverness
534	GREATOREX	Louisa	39		Serv	Unm	20	F	Scullery Maid	Essex	Thirsk
535	ATLINCH [?]	Mary	39		Serv	Unm	26	F	Dairy Maid	Bucks	Allscott [?]
536	COTTON	Fanny	39		Serv	Unm	22	F	Nursemaid	Shrop	Shipnal
537	BARTON	Emma	39		Serv	Unm	19	F	Laundry Maid	Middx	London
538	SHEPHERD	Mary	39		Serv	Unm	44	F	Nurse	Ireland	Dublin
539	MOUNTJOY	Martin	39		Serv	Mar	45	M	House Steward	Hants	Winchester
540	JUNIPER	Samuel	39		Serv	Mar	30	M	Under Butler	Essex	Springfield
541	MAULT	Thomas	39		Serv	Unm	27	M	Footman	Northants	Lowick
542	STEED	Francis	39		Serv	Unm	26	M	Footman	Lancs	Liverpool
543	HOGG	Thomas	39		Serv	Unm	25	M	Coachman	Durham	Darlington
544	GURTON	Edward	39		Serv	Unm	17	M	Stewards Room Boy	Essex	Goldhanger
478	STILES	Henry	40	Gorhambury	Serv	Unm	25	M	Helper in Stables	Gloucs	Letchley [Lechlade?]
479	COVERTON	Edward	40		Visitors Serv	Unm	29	M	Servant to Dowg. Countess of Verulam	Born at Sea	
480	ARCHER	John	40		Visitors Serv	Unm	24	M	Servant to Mr. Addington	Middx	Hackney
481	PICKETT	John	40		Serv	Unm	35	M	Cowman	Beds	Luton
482	BOUCH	William	40		Serv	Unm	21	M	Helper	Cumb	[Unknown]
483	CLARK	Robert	40		Serv	Unm	16	M	Post Boy	Herts	Wheathampstead
484	CLIMANCE	Elizabeth	40		Serv	Widow	58	F	Charwoman	Herts	Ware
485	PURROTT	John	41	Maynes Farm	Head	Mar	59	M	Farmer	Bucks	Amersham
486	PURROTT	Harriet	41		Wife	Mar	57	F		Surrey	Ditton [Thames Ditton]
487	PURROTT	John	41		Son	Unm	28	M	Farmers Son	Herts	St Michaels

No.	Surname	Forename	Sch.	Address	Relation	Cond.	Age	Sex	Occupation	County	Place
488	PURROTT	Charlotte	41		Dau	Unm	19	F	Farmers Daughter	Herts	St Michaels
489	DAY	Mary	41		Serv	Unm	29	F	House Servant	Bucks	Chearsley
490	BALLARD	William	41		Serv	Mar	45	M	Farm Labourer	Herts	St Michaels
491	LOVETT	Jonathan	41		Serv	Mar	64	M	Farm Labourer	Bucks	Chesham
492	MARSHALL	Charles	41		Serv	Unm	19	M	Ploughman	Herts	Redbourn
493	CLARK	William	41		Serv	Unm	18	M	Ploughman	Herts	St Michaels
494	LOW	William	41		Serv	Unm	30	M	Shepherd	Northants	Rudton [Rudham?]
495	PAYNE	Edward	41		Serv	Mar	25	M	Ploughman	Beds	Caddington
496	CONSTABLE	Thomas	42	Pondyards	Head	Mar	47	M	Under Keeper & Watchman	Herts	St Michaels
497	CONSTABLE	Susannah	42		Wife	Mar	47	F		Herts	St Michaels
498	CLARK	Matthew	43	The Grove	Head	Mar	43	M	Ploughman	Beds	Luton
499	CLARK	Hannah	43		Wife	Mar	44	F		Beds	Caddington
500	CLARK	Mary Ann	43		Dau	Unm	20	F	Bonnet Sewer	Herts	St Michaels
501	CLARK	Eliza	43		Dau		13	F	Scholar	Herts	St Michaels
502	CLARK	Noah	43		Son		10	M	Farm Servant	Herts	St Michaels
503	CLARK	Matilda	43		Dau		8	F	Scholar	Herts	St Michaels
504	CLARK	Betsey	43		Dau		6	F	Scholar	Herts	St Michaels
505	CLARK	Edward	43		Son		4	M		Herts	St Michaels
506	CLARK	Charles	43		Son		4m	M		Herts	St Michaels
507	PAYNE	Joseph	44	The Grove	Head	Mar	39	M	Agric Lab	Herts	Colney Heath
508	PAYNE	Maria	44		Wife	Mar	39	F		Beds	Bedford
509	PAYNE	William	44		Son		14	M	Agric Lab	Herts	Colney Heath
510	PAYNE	Elizabeth A.	44		Dau		12	F	Hat Maker	Herts	Colney Heath
511	PAYNE	Harriett	44		Dau		10	F	Scholar	Herts	St Michaels
512	PAYNE	Sarah	44		Dau		8	F	Scholar	Herts	St Michaels
513	PAYNE	Mary	44		Dau		6	F	Scholar	Herts	St Michaels
514	PAYNE	John	44		Son		4	M		Herts	St Michaels
515	PAYNE	Charlotte	44		Dau		2	F		Herts	St Michaels
516	DUNN	John	45	Prae Wood	Head	Mar	58	M	Game Keeper	Sussex	Mountfield
517	DUNN	Judith	45		Wife	Mar	60	F		Kent	Wittersham
518	DUNN	Mary	45		Dau	Unm	25	F		Herts	St Michaels
519	DUNN	Ann	45		Dau	Unm	19	F	Bonnet Sewer	Herts	St Michaels
520	CANDY	Harriett	45		Dau	Mar	28	F	Bonnet Sewer	Herts	St Michaels
521	CANDY	Mary A.	45		Grandau		2	F		Herts	St Michaels
522	CANDY	[?]	45		Grandson		1dy	M		Herts	St Michaels
523	BITCHENOE	John	46	Prae Wood Farm	Head	Mar	65	M	Agric Lab	Herts	North Mimms
524	BITCHENOE	Elizabeth	46		Wife	Mar	65	F		Herts	St Michaels
525	BITCHENOE	Samuel	46		Son	Unm	34	M	Agric Lab	Herts	St Michaels
526	WARNER	Harriett	46		Dau	Mar	37	F		Herts	St Michaels
527	WARNER	Thomas	46		Son-in-Law	Mar	30	M	Agric Lab	Beds	Sundon
528	WARNER	Hannah	46		Grandau		1	F		Herts	St Michaels

One house building

No.	Surname	Forename	Sch.	Address	Relation	Cond.	Age	Sex	Occupation	County	Place
529	TIMSON	William	47	Blue House Hill	Head	Mar	55	M	Agric Lab	Herts	St Stephens
530	TIMSON	Sarah	47		Wife	Mar	50	F	Hat Maker	Herts	Albury

	SURNAME	FORENAME	SCHEDULE NUMBER	ADDRESS	RELATIONSHIP	STATUS	AGE	SEX	OCCUPATION	COUNTY OF BIRTH	PLACE OF BIRTH
531	TIMSON	William	47		Son		13	M	Shepherd	Herts	St Peters
532	TIMSON	Sarah	47		Dau		10	F	Hat Maker	Herts	St Peters
533	LOWE	Thomas	48	Blue House Hill	Head	Mar	41	M	Gardeners Lab	Herts	St Michaels
534	LOWE	Ann	48		Wife	Mar	38	F		Herts	St Albans
535	LOWE	Sarah	48		Dau	Unm	16	F	Silk Winder	Herts	St Michaels
536	LOWE	Jane	48		Dau		13	F	Hat Maker	Herts	St Michaels
537	LOWE	William	48		Son		11	M	Scholar	Herts	St Michaels
538	LOWE	Alfred	48		Son		8	M	Scholar	Herts	St Michaels
539	LOWE	Hannah	48		Dau		4	F	Scholar	Herts	St Michaels
540	LOWE	Elizabeth	48		Dau		1	F		Herts	St Michaels
541	BIRCHMORE	William	49	Blue House Hill	Head	Mar	40	M	Agric Lab	Herts	St Michaels
542	BIRCHMORE	Ann	49		Wife	Mar	39	F	Hat Maker	Herts	St Michaels
543	BLAKE	Ann	49		Niece		9	F	Hat Maker	Herts	St Albans
544	GRAY	Thomas	50	Blue House Hill	Head	Mar	25	M	Agric Lab	Herts	Wheathampstead
545	GRAY	Mary Ann	50		Wife	Mar	23	F	Weaver	Herts	St Peters
546	MANSELL	William	51	Blue House Hill	Head	Mar	46	M	Wheelwright	Herts	North Mimms
547	MANSELL	Hannah	51		Wife	Mar	45	F		Herts	St Michaels
548	MANSELL	Mary	51		Dau	Unm	18	F	Hat Maker	Herts	St Albans
549	MANSELL	James	51		Son		12	M	Scholar	Herts	St Albans
550	MANSELL	William	51		Son		8	M	Scholar	Herts	St Peters
551	ALDRIDGE	Joseph	52	St Germans Farm	Head	Mar	53	M	Farmer of 90 acres employing 10 labourers	Herts	Amwell
552	ALDRIDGE	George C.	52		Son	Unm	22	M	Farmers Son emp. on Farm	Herts	St Albans
553	ALDRIDGE	Charles C.	52		Son	Unm	20	M	Farmers Son emp. on Farm	Herts	St Albans
554	FLITTON	Edward	52		Serv	Unm	47	M	Farm Servant	Herts	St Michaels
555	ADAMS	Aaron	52		Serv	Unm	20	M	Farm Servant	Herts	Sandridge
556	NEWELL	James	52		Serv	Unm	18	M	Farm Servant	Herts	Frithsden

The end of Gorhambury Side

Chapelry of Leverstock Green

	SURNAME	FORENAME	SCHEDULE NUMBER	ADDRESS	RELATIONSHIP	STATUS	AGE	SEX	OCCUPATION	COUNTY OF BIRTH	PLACE OF BIRTH
557	DANES	George	1	Westwick Hall Farm	Head	Mar	50	M	Farmer of 319 acres employing 12 labourers	Unknown	Unknown
558	DANES	Susan	1		Wife	Mar	55	F		Unknown	Unknown
559	JOINER	Ann	1		Serv	Unm	25	F	House Serv	Unknown	Unknown
560	LOVETT	Raz	1		Serv	Unm	21	M	Farm Servant	Unknown	Unknown
561	SMART	Henry	1		Serv	Unm	21	M	Farm Servant	Unknown	Unknown
562	SIMMONS	James	1		Serv	Unm	18	M	Farm Servant	Unknown	Unknown

Two houses uninhabited

	SURNAME	FORENAME	SCHEDULE NUMBER	ADDRESS	RELATIONSHIP	STATUS	AGE	SEX	OCCUPATION	COUNTY OF BIRTH	PLACE OF BIRTH
563	COOPER	Thomas	2	Westwick Row	Head	Mar	58	M	Agric Lab	Herts	Redbourn
564	COOPER	Mary	2		Wife	Mar	54	F		Herts	Hemel Hempstead
565	COOPER	Rose Anna	2		Dau	Unm	27	F	Straw Plaiter	Herts	St Michaels
566	COOPER	Hannah	2		Dau	Unm	20	F	Straw Plaiter	Herts	St Michaels
567	COOPER	Sarah M.	2		Dau	Unm	18	F	Straw Plaiter	Herts	St Michaels
568	COOPER	George	2		Son	Unm	16	M	Agric Lab	Herts	St Michaels
569	COOPER	Samuel	2		Son		12	M	Agric Lab	Herts	St Michaels

570	COOPER	Maria	2		Grandau		4	F		Herts	St Michaels
571	WHITEHEAD	Richard	3	Westwick Row	Head	Mar	34	M	Agric Lab	Herts	St Michaels
572	WHITEHEAD	Elizabeth	3		Wife	Mar	32	F		Herts	St Michaels
573	WHITEHEAD	Ann	3		Dau		12	F	Scholar	Herts	St Michaels
574	WHITEHEAD	Mary E.	3		Dau		9	F	Scholar	Herts	St Michaels
575	WILKINS	Edward	4	Westwick Row	Head	Mar	52	M	Agric Lab	Herts	Hemel Hempstead
576	WILKINS	Mary A.	4		Wife	Mar	58	F		Herts	St Michaels
577	MUCKLE	Thomas	4		Son-in-law	Unm	28	M	Shepherd	Herts	St Michaels
578	WILKINS	William	4		Son	Unm	24	M	Shepherd	Herts	St Michaels
579	WILKINS	George	4		Son	Unm	22	M	Agric Lab	Herts	St Michaels
580	WILKINS	Mary A.	4		Dau	Unm	20	F		Herts	St Michaels
581	WILKINS	Jane	4		Dau	Unm	18	F		Herts	St Michaels
582	WILKINS	Alfred T.H.	4		Grandson		2	M		Herts	St Michaels
583	MUCKLE	Hannah	5	Westwick Row	Head	Mar	28	F	Straw Plaiter	Herts	St Michaels
584	DELL	Frances	6	Westwick Row	Wife	Mar	29	F	Carrier & Dealers Wife	Herts	Dagnall
585	KARL	Thomas	6		Serv	Unm	20	M	Carriers Servant	Unknown	Unknown
586	PARKINS	Elizabeth	6		Visitor	Unm	19	F	Plaiter	Herts	St Michaels
587	FOSTER	John	7	Westwick Row	Head	Mar	49	M	Agric Lab	Herts	Hemel Hempstead
588	FOSTER	Hannah	7		Wife	Mar	40	F	School Mistress	Herts	St Michaels
589	HEADECH	Daniel	8	Westwick Row	Head	Unm	38	M	Farmer of 145 acres employing 2 labourers	Herts	St Michaels
590	WOOD	James	8		Serv	Unm	18	M	Farm Servant	Herts	St Pauls Walden
591	COOK	George	8		Serv	Unm	18	M	Farm Servant	Herts	St Stephens
592	BARNES	Joseph	9	Westwick Row	Head	Mar	42	M	Carpenter	Herts	Hemel Hempstead
593	BARNES	Mary	9		Wife	Mar	34	F	Straw Plaiter	Herts	Abbots Langley
594	MILLARD	Charlotte	9		Dau-in-law	Unm	15	F	Straw Plaiter	Herts	Hemel Hempstead
595	MILLARD	Mary	9		Dau-in-law	Unm	14	F	Straw Plaiter	Herts	Hemel Hempstead
596	BARNES	Sophia	9		Dau		13	F	Straw Plaiter	Herts	Hemel Hempstead
597	BARNES	Maria	9		Dau		12	F	Straw Plaiter	Herts	St Michaels
598	BARNES	Reuben	9		Son		7	M		Herts	St Michaels
599	BARNES	Frances	9		Dau		5	F		Herts	St Michaels
600	BARNES	Joseph	9		Son		4	M	Scholar	Herts	St Michaels
601	BARNES	Sarah A.	9		Dau		2	F		Herts	St Michaels
602	BARNES	Elizabeth	9		Dau		4m	F		Herts	St Michaels
603	RACKLEY	Henry	10	Westwick Row	Head	Mar	35	M	Paper Makers Lab	Herts	Rickmansworth
604	RACKLEY	Sarah	10		Wife	Mar	28	F		Herts	Hemel Hempstead
605	RACKLEY	William	10		Son		9	M		Herts	Hemel Hempstead
606	RACKLEY	Jane	10		Dau		3	F		Herts	St Michaels
607	RACKLEY	George	10		Son		1	M		Herts	St Michaels
608	BROWN	James	11	Westwick Row	Head	Mar	37	M	Paper Makers Lab	Herts	Hitchin
609	BROWN	Mary	11		Wife	Mar	30	F		Herts	St Michaels
610	BROWN	Mary A.	11		Dau		12	F	Scholar	Herts	St Michaels
611	BROWN	Margarett	11		Dau		9	F	Scholar	Herts	St Michaels
612	BROWN	Charlotte	11		Dau		6	F		Herts	St Michaels

	SURNAME	FORENAME	SCHEDULE NUMBER	ADDRESS	RELATIONSHIP	STATUS	AGE	SEX	OCCUPATION	COUNTY OF BIRTH	PLACE OF BIRTH
613	BROWN	Emma	11		Dau		4	F		Herts	St Michaels
614	BROWN	Eliza	11		Dau		2	F		Herts	St Michaels
615	EAST	Edward	12	Westwick Row	Head	Mar	27	M	Agric Lab	Herts	St Michaels
616	EAST	Ann	12		Wife	Mar	26	F		Herts	Aldenham
617	EAST	Eliza	12		Dau		3	F		Herts	St Michaels
618	EAST	Mary A.	12		Dau		1	F		Herts	St Michaels
619	GIFKINS	James	13	Westwick Row	Head	Mar	44	M	Agric Lab	Herts	St Michaels
620	GIFKINS	Amey	13		Wife	Mar	46	F		Herts	Shenley
621	GIFKINS	Louisa	13		Dau	Unm	18	F		Herts	St Michaels
622	GIFKINS	Eliza	13		Dau		13	F	Scholar	Herts	St Michaels
623	PARKINS	William	14	Westwick Row	Head	Mar	55	M	Agric Lab	Herts	Flamstead
624	PARKINS	Priscilla	14		Wife	Mar	53	F		Herts	Redbourn
625	PARKINS	Priscilla	14		Dau	Unm	16	F		Herts	St Michaels
626	PARKINS	William	14		Son	Unm	12	M	Agric Lab	Herts	St Michaels
627	PARKINS	Sylba	14		Dau		9	F	Scholar	Herts	St Michaels
628	MARTIN	George	15	Westwick Row	Head	Mar	25	M	Agric Lab	Herts	St Michaels
629	MARTIN	Catherine	15		Wife	Mar	21	F		Herts	St Michaels
630	MARTIN	Sarah	15		Dau		2m	F		Herts	St Michaels

One house uninhabited

	SURNAME	FORENAME	SCHEDULE NUMBER	ADDRESS	RELATIONSHIP	STATUS	AGE	SEX	OCCUPATION	COUNTY OF BIRTH	PLACE OF BIRTH
631	CHARGE	William	16	Westwick Row	Head	Mar	33	M	Agric Lab	Herts	Flaunden
632	CHARGE	Mary A.	16		Wife	Mar	30	F		Herts	Studham
633	CHARGE	Eliza	16		Dau		9	F	Scholar	Herts	Hemel Hempstead
634	CHARGE	Mary A.	16		Dau		5	F	Scholar	Herts	Hemel Hempstead
635	CHARGE	Lydia	16		Dau		3	F		Herts	St Michaels
636	CHARGE	David	16		Son		9wks	M		Herts	St Michaels
637	TRAVELL	Isaac	17	Westwick Row	Head	Mar	28	M	Agric Lab	Herts	Redbourn
638	TRAVELL	Sarah	17		Wife	Mar	25	F		Herts	Hemel Hempstead
639	TRAVELL	Henry	17		Son		6	M	Scholar	Herts	St Michaels
640	DOLLING	James	18	Westwick Row	Head	Mar	30	M	Agric Lab	Herts	Shenley
641	DOLLING	Sarah	18		Wife	Mar	28	F		Herts	Aldenham
642	DOLLING	Ann	18		Dau		9	F		Herts	Aldenham
643	DOLLING	John	18		Son		6	M		Herts	Abbots Langley
644	DOLLING	James	18		Son		10m	M		Herts	Watford

One house uninhabited

	SURNAME	FORENAME	SCHEDULE NUMBER	ADDRESS	RELATIONSHIP	STATUS	AGE	SEX	OCCUPATION	COUNTY OF BIRTH	PLACE OF BIRTH
645	ATTWOOD	William	19	Westwick Row	Head	Mar	36	M	Agric Lab	Herts	Hemel Hempstead
646	ATTWOOD	Mary A.	19		Wife	Mar	32	F		Herts	Berkhamsted
647	ATTWOOD	George	19		Son		9	M	Scholar	Herts	Hemel Hempstead
648	ATTWOOD	Mary A.	19		Dau		5	F		Herts	Hemel Hempstead
649	ATTWOOD	Emma	19		Dau		2	F		Herts	Hemel Hempstead
650	ATTWOOD	Joseph	19		Son		1m	M		Herts	St Michaels
651	BARNS	Charles	20	Westwick Row	Head	Mar	70	M	Agric Lab	Herts	Flaunden
652	BARNS	Frances	20		Wife	Mar	64	F		Herts	Hemel Hempstead

653	BENNETT	Mary	21	Westwick Row	Head	Widow	79	F	Pauper (Farmers Widow)	Herts	St Michaels
654	LINFIELD	Jane	21		Grandau		7	F	Scholar	Herts	St Michaels
655	LINFIELD	James	22	Westwick Row	Head	Mar	43	M	Agric Lab	Herts	Kings Walden
656	LINFIELD	Elizabeth	22		Wife	Mar	40	F		Herts	Hemel Hempstead
657	LINFIELD	John	22		Son		15	M	Agric Lab	Herts	Hemel Hempstead
658	LINFIELD	James	22		Son		10	M		Herts	Hemel Hempstead
659	LINFIELD	George	22		Son		5	M	Scholar	Herts	St Michaels

One house uninhabited

660	SAUNDERS	John	23	Westwick Row	Head	Mar	63	M	Farmer of 162 acres employing 3 men & 2 boys	Herts	St Michaels
661	SAUNDERS	Charlotte	23		Wife	Mar	55	F		Herts	St Michaels
662	SAUNDERS	John	23		Son	Unm	21	M	Bankers Clerk	Herts	St Michaels
663	SAUNDERS	Daniel	23		Son	Unm	20	M	Farmers Son employed at Home	Herts	St Michaels
664	SAUNDERS	George H.	23		Son	Unm	18	M	Solicitors General Clerk	Herts	St Michaels
665	SAUNDERS	Charlotte E.	23		Dau	Unm	15	F	Farmers Dau employed at Home	Herts	St Michaels
666	SAUNDERS	William L.	23		Son		12	M	Scholar	Herts	St Michaels
667	SMITH	Henry	23		Serv	Unm	19	M	Farm Lab	Herts	St Michaels
668	PUNTER	Alfred	23		Serv	Unm	16	M	Farm Lab	Herts	Harpenden
669	WINGROVE	Henry	24	Beech Tree	Head	Widower	76	M	Pauper (Agric Lab)	Herts	Redbourn
670	WILSON	Joseph	24		Son-in-Law	Mar	49	M	Agric Lab	Herts	St Albans
671	WILSON	Hannah	24		Dau	Mar	50	F		Herts	Redbourn
672	WILSON	Joseph	24		Grandson		8	M	Scholar	Herts	St Michaels
673	WEBB	Richard	25	Beech Tree	Head	Mar	48	M	Carpenter	Oxon	Deddington
674	WEBB	Hannah	25		Wife	Mar	50	F		Bucks	Tingewick
675	WEBB	Hannah	25		Dau	Unm	19	F	Dressmaker	Bucks	Haversham
676	WEBB	Thomas	25		Son	Unm	17	M	Carpenter	Bucks	Haversham
677	WEBB	Emiley	25		Dau		9	F		Herts	St Michaels
678	WEBB	John	25		Son		7	M	Scholar	Herts	St Michaels
679	BOWRA	William	26	Beech Tree	Head	Mar	34	M	Game Keeper	Kent	Sevenoaks
680	BOWRA	Harriett	26		Wife	Mar	32	F		Surrey	Lambeth
681	BOWRA	Harriett	26		Dau		8	F		Herts	St Michaels
682	BOWRA	Elizabeth	26		Dau		6	F		Herts	St Michaels
683	CATLIN	Mary	27	Beech Tree	Head	Unm	55	F	Straw Plaiter	Herts	Rickmansworth
684	MARTIN	James	28	Beech Tree	Head	Mar	71	M	Agric Lab	Herts	Kensworth
685	MARTIN	Sarah	28		Wife	Mar	67	F		Herts	Harpenden
686	MARTIN	William	28		Son	Unm	20	M	Agric Lab	Herts	St Michaels

One house uninhabited

687	PANGBORN	Mary	29	Hempstead Road	Head	Widow	65	F	Charwoman	Herts	Cromer Hyde
688	HAWKINS	Jonathan	45	30	Hempstead Road	Head	Mar	45	M	Agric Lab	Herts	St Michaels
689	HAWKINS	Mary	30		Wife	Mar	48	F		Herts	St Michaels
690	HAWKINS	Sarah	30		Dau	Unm	14	F		Herts	St Michaels
691	DEAR	John	30		Brother-in-law	Unm	55	M	Agric Lab	Herts	St Michaels

	SURNAME	FORENAME	SCHEDULE NUMBER	ADDRESS	RELATIONSHIP	STATUS	AGE	SEX	OCCUPATION	COUNTY OF BIRTH	PLACE OF BIRTH
692	FINCH	Joseph	31	Corner Farm	Head	Mar	54	M	Farmer of 260 acres employing 9 labourers	Herts	St Michaels
693	FINCH	Jane	31		Wife	Mar	43	F		Herts	Flamstead
694	FINCH	Joseph	31		Son	Unm	22	M	Farmers Son employed on Farm	Herts	St Michaels
695	FINCH	Jane	31		Dau	Unm	18	F		Herts	St Michaels
696	FINCH	Maria	31		Dau		11	F	Scholar	Herts	St Michaels
697	FINCH	George	31		Son		9	M	Scholar	Herts	St Michaels
698	FINCH	Susan	31		Dau		7	F	Scholar	Herts	St Michaels
699	FINCH	Sarah	31		Dau		5	F		Herts	St Michaels
700	FINCH	William	31		Son		2	M		Herts	St Michaels
701	DIXON	Hannah	31		Serv	Unm	17	F	House Serv	Bucks	Stoke Mandeville
702	WRIGHT	William	31		Serv	Unm	17	M	Farm Servant	Herts	Kings Langley
703	COOPER	Thomas	32	Hempstead Road	Head	Mar	31	M	Agric Lab	Herts	St Michaels
704	COOPER	Matilda	32		Wife	Mar	23	F		Bucks	Thornborough
705	COOPER	Ann	32		Dau		3	F		Herts	St Michaels
706	COOPER	George	32		Son		1	M		Herts	St Michaels
707	EAST	George	32		Lodger	Unm	22	M	Agric Lab	Herts	Hemel Hempstead
708	WARD	William	33	The Red Lion	Head	Mar	51	M	Victualler	Herts	St Michaels
709	WARD	Charlotte	33		Wife	Mar	48	F		Herts	St Michaels
710	WARD	William	33		Son	Unm	27	M	Agric Lab	Herts	St Michaels
711	WARD	Hannah	33		Dau		13	F		Herts	St Michaels
712	WARD	Jeremiah	33		Son		11	M		Herts	St Michaels
713	SMITH	William	33		Lodger	Unm	18	M	Agric Lab	Unknown	Unknown
714	BUCKOAK	Benjamin	33		Lodger	Unm	24	M	Agric Lab	Unknown	Unknown
715	WARD	Harriett	33		Dau	Unm	17	F		Herts	St Michaels
716	RICHARDSON	Richard	34	Parsonage House	Head	Mar	39	M	M.A. Incumbent of Leverstock Green	Cheshire	Capenhurst
717	RICHARDSON	Fanny	34		Wife	Mar	27	F	Clergymans Wife	Kent	Canterbury
718	RICHARDSON	Fanny G.	34		Dau		4m	F		London	London
719	BAILEY	Benjamin	34		Serv	Mar	41	M	Gardener & Coachman	Middx	Hadley
720	BOYS	Eliza	34		Serv	Unm	24	F	Nurse	Kent	Godmersham
721	PAGE	Ellen	34		Serv	Unm	21	F	Housemaid	Kent	Faversham
722	EAST	Samuel	35	Leverstock Green	Head	Mar	54	M	Agric Lab	Herts	Wheathampstead
723	EAST	Charlotte	35		Wife	Mar	50	F		Herts	St Michaels
724	EAST	Mary	35		Dau	Unm	20	F		Herts	Hemel Hempstead
725	EAST	Ann	35		Dau	Unm	17	F		Herts	Hemel Hempstead
726	EAST	Emma	35		Dau		12	F	Scholar	Herts	Hemel Hempstead
727	EAST	John	35		Son		9	M	Scholar	Herts	Hemel Hempstead
728	EAST	Susannah	35		Dau		7	F	Scholar	Herts	Hemel Hempstead
729	ALLEN	Richard	36	Leverstock Green	Head	Mar	39	M	Agric Lab	Herts	Little Gaddesden
730	ALLEN	Elizabeth	36		Wife	Mar	42	F		Herts	St Michaels
731	ALLEN	Joseph	36		Son	Unm	17	M	Agric Lab	Herts	St Michaels
732	ALLEN	John	36		Son		12	M	Agric Lab	Herts	St Michaels
733	ALLEN	William	36		Son		11	M	Scholar	Herts	St Michaels
734	ROLFE	John	37	Leverstock Green	Head	Mar	42	M	Agric Lab	Herts	Sandridge

735	ROLFE	Charlotte	37		Wife	Mar	40	F		Herts	St Michaels
736	ROLFE	Mary	37		Dau	Unm	20	F		Herts	Wheathampstead
737	ROLFE	Eliza	37		Dau	Unm	18	F		Herts	Wheathampstead
738	ROLFE	Elizabeth	37		Dau	Unm	16	F		Herts	Wheathampstead
739	ROLFE	Emma	37		Dau		11	F	Scholar	Herts	Wheathampstead
740	ROLFE	John	37		Son		8	M		Herts	St Michaels
741	ROLFE	George	37		Son		3	M		Herts	St Michaels
742	LUCK	William	38	Leverstock Green	Head	Mar	57	M	Agric Lab	Herts	Kings Walden
743	LUCK	Mary	38		Wife	Mar	57	F		Herts	Hemel Hempstead
744	LUCK	Elizabeth	38		Dau		15	F		Herts	St Michaels
745	BENNETT	John	39	Leverstock Green	Head	Mar	47	M	Agric Lab	Herts	Hemel Hempstead
746	BENNETT	Hannah	39		Wife	Mar	37	F		Herts	Hemel Hempstead
747	BENNETT	John	39		Son		13	M	Agric Lab	Herts	St Michaels
748	BENNETT	David	39		Son		10	M	Scholar	Herts	St Michaels
749	BENNETT	Eve	39		Dau		9	F	Scholar	Herts	St Michaels
750	BENNETT	Hannah	39		Dau		6	F		Herts	St Michaels
751	BENNETT	Elijah	39		Son		4	M	Scholar	Herts	St Michaels
752	BENNETT	Elisha	39		Son		3	M		Herts	St Michaels
753	BENNETT	Eliza	39		Dau		11 m	F		Herts	St Michaels
754	WILSON	Benjamin	40	Leverstock Green	Head	Mar	41	M	Agric Lab	Herts	Great Gaddesden
755	WILSON	Sarah	40		Wife	Mar	41	F		Herts	Hemel Hempstead
756	WILSON	George	40		Son	Unm	21	M	Agric Lab	Herts	St Michaels
757	WILSON	Sophia	40		Dau	Unm	19	F		Herts	Hemel Hempstead
758	WILSON	Benjamin	40		Son		13	M	Agric Lab	Herts	Hemel Hempstead
759	WILSON	Godfrey	40		Son		11	M	Agric Lab	Herts	Hemel Hempstead
760	WILSON	James	40		Son		9	M	Scholar	Herts	St Michaels
761	WILSON	Mary A.	40		Dau		7	F	Scholar	Herts	St Michaels
762	WILSON	Sarah	40		Dau		4	F		Herts	St Michaels
763	WILSON	Daniel	40		Son		2	M		Herts	St Michaels
764	BREWER	Joseph	41	Leverstock Green	Head	Widower	56	M	School Master	Herts	St Albans
765	STEVENS	Elizabeth	42	Leverstock Green	Wife	Mar	35	F	Straw Factors Wife	Herts	Abbots Langley
766	STEVENS	Mary A.	42		Dau	Unm	17	F		Herts	Abbots Langley
767	STEVENS	Lucy A.	42		Dau		13	F	Scholar	Herts	Kings Langley
768	STEVENS	Amos	42		Son		10	M	Scholar	Herts	Kings Langley
769	STEVENS	Sarah A.	42		Dau		6	F	Scholar	Herts	Kings Langley
770	STEVENS	Nathan	42		Son		4	M	Scholar	Herts	Kings Langley
771	BOULTON	Sarah	43	Leverstock Green	Head	Widow	50	F	Tinman & Braziers (Widow)	Herts	Hemel Hempstead
772	BOULTON	Alfred	43		Son	Unm	18	M	Tinman & Brazier	Herts	St Michaels
773	BOULTON	Jesse	43		Son		10	M	Scholar	Herts	St Michaels
774	WINGRAVE	William	44	Leather Bottle	Head	Mar	37	M	Victualler	Herts	Hemel Hempstead
775	WINGRAVE	Sophia	44		Wife	Mar	33	F		Middx	Harrow-on-the-Hill
776	WINGRAVE	Amelia S.	44		Dau		3	F		Herts	St Michaels

	SURNAME	FORENAME	SCHEDULE NUMBER	ADDRESS	RELATIONSHIP	STATUS	AGE	SEX	OCCUPATION	COUNTY OF BIRTH	PLACE OF BIRTH
777	WINGRAVE	Mary A.	44		Dau		1	F		Herts	St Michaels
778	BUCKINGHAM	Ellen	44		Sister-in-law		14	F	Nurse	Middx	Harrow
779	HOW	Daniel	44		Lodger	[blank]	47	M	Labourer	Herts	Hemel Hempstead
780	SEABROOK	Joseph	45	Leverstock Green	Head	Mar	32	M	Agric Lab	Herts	Hemel Hempstead
781	SEABROOK	Ann	45		Wife	Mar	27	F		Beds	Caddington
782	WARNER	Jane	45		Sister-in-law		7	F		Bucks	Lower Winchendon
783	WELLS	Thomas	46	Leverstock Green	Head	Mar	51	M	Agric Lab	Herts	Flamstead
784	WELLS	Hannah	46		Wife	Mar	43	F		Herts	Flamstead
785	WELLS	Elizabeth	46		Dau	Unm	20	F		Herts	Flamstead
786	WELLS	Job	46		Son	Unm	16	M	Agric Lab	Herts	St Michaels
787	WELLS	Hannah	46		Dau		14	F	Scholar	Herts	St Michaels
788	WELLS	William	46		Son		7	M	Scholar	Herts	St Michaels
789	WELLS	Thomas	46		Son		3	M		Herts	St Michaels
790	WELLS	George	46		Son		3m	M		Herts	St Michaels
791	SEARS	Sarah	47	Leverstock Green	Sister-in-law, H'keeper	Unm	25	F	Straw Plaiter	Herts	St Michaels
792	HANNELL	William	47		Son		7	M	Scholar	Herts	St Michaels
793	HANNELL	Joseph	47		Son		3	M	Scholar	Herts	St Michaels
794	SMART	William	48	Leverstock Green	Head	Mar	46	M	Agric Lab	Beds	Dunstable
795	SMART	Rebecca	48		Wife	Mar	62	F		Bucks	Mussford [?]
796	SMART	Hannah	48		Dau	Unm	18	F	Straw Plaiter	Herts	Redbourn
797	CHILD	John	49	Leverstock Green	Head	Unm	23	M	Wheelwright	Herts	St Michaels
798	CHILD	Anna	49		Mother	Widow	54	F		Herts	St Albans
799	CHILD	James	49		Brother	Unm	19	M	Wheelwright (Journeyman)	Herts	St Michaels
800	CHILD	George	49		Brother	Unm	17	M	Wheelwright (Appr)	Herts	St Michaels
801	CHILD	Simeon	49		Brother		14	M		Herts	St Michaels
802	CHILD	Thomas	49		Brother		11	M	Scholar	Herts	St Michaels
803	GINGER	James	50	Leverstock Green	Head	Mar	45	M	Shoemaker	Herts	Hemel Hempstead
804	GINGER	Ellen	50		Wife	Mar	45	F		Beds	Sundon
805	GINGER	Ann	50		Dau		9	F	Scholar	Herts	Hemel Hempstead
806	GINGER	Thomas	50		Son		7	M	Scholar	Herts	St Michaels
807	GINGER	Eliza	50		Dau		5	F		Herts	St Michaels
808	GINGER	James	50		Son		2	M		Herts	St Michaels
809	ASHWELL	Daniel	50		Son-in-Law	Unm	22	M	Agric Lab	Herts	Hemel Hempstead
810	ASHWELL	David	50		Son-in-Law	Unm	19	M	Agric Lab	Herts	Hemel Hempstead
811	ASHWELL	Sarah	50		Dau-in-Law	Unm	16	F	Straw Plaiter	Herts	Hemel Hempstead
812	ASHWELL	Jane	50		Dau-in-Law		13	F	Scholar	Herts	Hemel Hempstead
813	ABBISS	Enoch	51	Leverstock Green	Head	Mar	41	M	Agric Lab	Herts	Hilington [?]
814	ABBISS	Eliza	51		Wife	Mar	40	F		Herts	North Mimms
815	ABBISS	Emma	51		Dau		14	F		Herts	Gaddesden
816	ABBISS	Sarah	51		Dau		12	F		Herts	Hemel Hempstead
817	ABBISS	George	51		Son		9	M	Scholar	Herts	Hemel Hempstead

818	ABBISS	David	51		Son		7	M	Scholar	Herts	Hemel Hempstead
819	ABBISS	James	51		Son		3	M		Herts	St Michaels
820	ABBISS	Eliza	51		Dau		1	F		Herts	St Michaels
821	ROSE	George	52	Leverstock Green	Head	Mar	33	M	Agric Lab	Herts	Bovingdon
822	ROSE	Mary A.	52		Wife	Mar	39	F		Herts	Kings Langley
823	ROSE	Alfred	52		Son		11	M	Shepherd Boy	Herts	St Michaels
824	ROSE	Lucy	52		Dau		10	F	Scholar	Herts	St Michaels
825	ROSE	George	52		Son		5	M	Scholar	Herts	St Michaels
826	LEA	Joseph	53	Leverstock Green	Head	Mar	60	M	Grocer & Gardener	Oxon	Benson
827	LEA	Elizabeth	53		Wife	Mar	56	F		Beds	Caddington
828	TRAVELL	James	54	The White Horse Beer Shop	Head	Mar	31	M	Dealer in Pigs etc.	Herts	Hemel Hempstead
829	TRAVELL	Ann	54		Wife	Mar	29	F		Herts	Hemel Hempstead
830	TRAVELL	Mary A.	54		Dau		3m	F		Herts	St Michaels
831	BUTLER	Joseph	54		Lodger	Unm	36	M	General Dealer	Middx	St Marylebone
832	SOUSTER	Newman	54		Lodger	Widower	68	M	Agric Lab	Herts	Hemel Hempstead

One house uninhabited

833	WILSON	George	55	Leverstock Green	Head	Mar	39	M	Agric Lab	Herts	Gaddesden
834	WILSON	Sarah	55		Wife	Mar	24	F	Straw Plaiter	Herts	St Michaels
835	WILSON	William	55		Son		9	M		Herts	St Michaels
836	HALL	Thomas	56	Leverstock Green	Head	Mar	39	M	Agric Lab	Herts	Flamstead
837	HALL	Fanny	56		Wife	Mar	31	F		Herts	Redbourn
838	HALL	Mary A.	56		Dau		12	F		Herts	Redbourn
839	HALL	Emma	56		Dau		6	F		Herts	St Michaels
840	HALL	Amos	56		Son		4	M		Herts	Abbots Langley
841	HALL	Henry	56		Son		2	M		Herts	Abbots Langley
842	GURNEY	Mary	57	Leverstock Green	Head	Widow	63	F	Straw Plaiter	Herts	Flaunden
843	GURNEY	Joseph	57		Son	Unm	33	M	Agric Lab	Herts	Abbots Langley
844	GURNEY	William	57		Son	Unm	30	M	Agric Lab	Herts	Abbots Langley
845	PARKINS	Mary	57		Lodger	Unm	19	F	Straw Plaiter	Herts	Abbots Langley
846	GURNEY	James	58	Leverstock Green	Head	Mar	27	M	Agric Lab	Herts	Abbots Langley
847	GURNEY	Hannah	58		Wife	Mar	23	F	Hat Maker	Herts	Abbots Langley
848	GURNEY	Mary A.	58		Dau		2	F		Herts	St Michaels
849	COOPER	Thomas	59	Three Horseshoes Beer Shop	Head	Mar	40	M	Corn Salesman	Herts	Hemel Hempstead
850	COOPER	Maria	59		Wife	Mar	38	F		Herts	St Michaels
851	COOPER	Mary A.	59		Dau	Unm	14	F		Herts	St Michaels
852	COOPER	William	59		Son		11	M	Scholar	Herts	St Michaels
853	COOPER	Charlotte	59		Dau		9	F	Scholar	Herts	St Michaels
854	COOPER	Joseph	59		Son		7	M	Scholar	Herts	St Michaels
855	COOPER	Emily	59		Dau		5	F	Scholar	Herts	St Michaels
856	COOPER	Elizabeth	59		Dau		2	F	Scholar	Herts	St Michaels
857	WILSON	David	59		Nephew	Unm	16	M	Servant	Herts	St Michaels
858	EASY	William	60	Leverstock Green	Head	Mar	56	M	Tailor & Schoolmaster	Herts	Abbots Langley
859	EASY	Martha	60		Wife	Mar	57	F		Herts	Northchurch

	SURNAME	FORENAME	SCHEDULE NUMBER	ADDRESS	RELATIONSHIP	STATUS	AGE	SEX	OCCUPATION	COUNTY OF BIRTH	PLACE OF BIRTH
860	EASY	Henry	60		Son	Unm	21	M	Agric Lab	Herts	Hemel Hempstead
861	EASY	Alfred	60		Son		12	M	Scholar	Herts	Hemel Hempstead
862	MARTIN	James	61	Leverstock Green	Head	Mar	28	M	Agric Lab	Herts	St Michaels
863	MARTIN	Elizabeth	61		Wife	Mar	21	F		Bucks	Haversham
864	MARTIN	Lucy	61		Dau		2	F		Herts	St Michaels
865	DELL	George	62	Leverstock Green	Head	Mar	31	M	Agric Lab	Herts	St Michaels
866	DELL	Sarah	62		Wife	Mar	31	F		Herts	St Michaels
867	DELL	Mary A.	62		Dau		4	F		Herts	St Michaels
868	DELL	John	62		Son		1	M		Herts	St Michaels
869	MARTIN	Mary	62		Visitor		10	F	Scholar	Herts	St Michaels
870	HALE	Sarah	63	Leverstock Green	Head	Widow	79	F	School Mistress	Herts	Watford
871	ORCHARD	Thomas	64	Bottom House	Head	Mar	58	M	Farmer, 90 acres emp 4 Lab	Herts	Abbots Langley
872	ORCHARD	Levina	64		Wife	Mar	38	F		Herts	Hemel Hempstead
873	MOSS	Mary	64		Serv	Widow	65	F	House Serv	Unknown	Unknown
874	FOUNTAIN	William	64		Serv	Unm	18	M	Farm Servant	Herts	Hemel Hempstead
875	SMITH	George	64		Serv	Unm	15	M	Farm Servant	Herts	St Stephens
876	SEARS	Richard	65	Breakspeare	Head	Mar	51	M	Agric Lab	Herts	Hemel Hempstead
877	SEARS	Maria	65		Wife	Mar	45	F		Herts	Hemel Hempstead
878	SEARS	Richard	65		Son	Unm	24	M	Agric Lab	Herts	Hemel Hempstead
879	SEARS	Jesse	65		Son		13	M		Herts	Hemel Hempstead
880	SEARS	David	65		Son		10	M		Herts	Hemel Hempstead
881	SEARS	Mary A.	65		Dau		6	F		Herts	St Michaels
882	PARTRIDGE	John	66	Breakspeare	Head	Mar	45	M	Agric Lab	Herts	Hemel Hempstead
883	PARTRIDGE	Hannah	66		Wife	Mar	44	F		Herts	Hemel Hempstead
884	PARTRIDGE	Charlotte	66		Dau	Unm	21	F		Herts	Hemel Hempstead
885	PARTRIDGE	Eliza	66		Dau	Unm	17	F		Herts	Hemel Hempstead
886	PARTRIDGE	James	66		Son		13	M	Agric Lab	Herts	Hemel Hempstead
887	PARTRIDGE	Ann	66		Dau		9	F	Scholar	Herts	Hemel Hempstead
888	PARTRIDGE	John	66		Son		7	M	Scholar	Herts	St Michaels
889	PARTRIDGE	Emma	66		Dau		5	F	Scholar	Herts	St Michaels
890	PARTRIDGE	David	66		Son		3	M		Herts	St Michaels
891	PARTRIDGE	Sarah A.	66		Grandau		2	F		Herts	St Michaels
892	HALSEY	Thomas	67	Megdell	Head	Mar	45	M	Agric Lab	Herts	St Stephens
893	HALSEY	Ann	67		Wife	Mar	44	F		Herts	North Mimms
894	HALSEY	Thomas	67		Son		1	M		Herts	St Michaels
895	HALSEY	Thomas	67		Father	Widower	81	M	Pauper (Agric Lab)	Herts	St Stephens
896	SHUFFIELD	Nanny	67		Mother-in-law	Widow	79	F	Pauper	Herts	St Stephens
897	WHITE	William	68	Megdell	Head	Mar	34	M	Agric Lab	Herts	Hatfield
898	WHITE	Hannah	68		Wife	Mar	32	F		Herts	Sandridge
899	WHITE	William	68		Son		13	M		Herts	Sandridge
900	WHITE	Joseph	68		Son		11	M		Herts	St Michaels

901	WHITE	Zackery	68		Son			9	M		Herts	St Michaels
902	WHITE	Charlotte	68		Dau			7	F	Scholar	Herts	St Michaels
903	WHITE	Charles	68		Son			5	M	Scholar	Herts	St Michaels
904	WHITE	Edith	68		Dau			2	F		Herts	St Michaels
905	WHITE	Clara J.	68		Dau			5 m	F		Herts	St Michaels
906	MATHEWS	William	69	Megdell	Head	Mar		43	M	Agric Lab	Beds	Luton
907	MATHEWS	Anne	69		Wife	Mar		37	F		Herts	St Michaels
908	MATHEWS	William	69		Son			6	M	Scholar	Herts	Redbourn
909	MATHEWS	George	69		Son			5 m	M		Herts	St Michaels

End of Chapelry of Leverstock Green with Westwick Row

Chapter Thirteen

St Albans Workhouse

Registrar's District: St Albans   Enumeration District n/a   Ref. HO107/1713 folios 526-33

Parish of St Michaels, Township of St Albans

1	WEIR	William	St Albans Union Workhouse	Master	Mar	58	M	Workhouse Master	Scotland	Paisley
2	WEIR	Helen	St Albans Union Workhouse	Matron	Mar	58	F	Workhouse Matron	Scotland	Paisley
3	WEIR	Marion	St Albans Union Workhouse	Dau	Unm	20	F		Ireland	Dublin
4	WEIR	James	St Albans Union Workhouse	Son	Unm	16	M		Herts	Sandridge
5	WEIR	Helen Ann	St Albans Union Workhouse	Dau		14	F		Herts	Sandridge
6	MUNDAY	Elizabeth	St Albans Union Workhouse	Nurse	Unm	40	F	Nurse	Middx	London
7	HARRIS	Robert	St Albans Union Workhouse	School Master	Mar	33	M	School Master	Herts	St Stephens
8	HARRIS	Mary Ann	St Albans Union Workhouse	School Mistress	Mar	32	F	School Mistress	Herts	St Stephens
9	HARRIS	Henry	St Albans Union Workhouse	Son		10	M		Herts	St Stephens
10	HARRIS	Mary Ann	St Albans Union Workhouse	Dau		9	F		Herts	St Michaels
11	COOK	Sophia	St Albans Union Workhouse	Pauper	Unm	58	F	Plaiter	Herts	St Albans
12	MEAD	Joseph	St Albans Union Workhouse	Pauper	Widower	80	M	Farm Steward	Herts	Redbourn
13	SLY	Mary	St Albans Union Workhouse	Pauper	Unm	56	F	Idiot	Herts	St Michaels
14	GLADMAN	William	St Albans Union Workhouse	Pauper	Unm	61	M	Labourer	Herts	St Albans
15	HOLLOWAY	Henry	St Albans Union Workhouse	Pauper		14	M	Scholar	Herts	St Albans
16	DEAYTON	James	St Albans Union Workhouse	Pauper	Mar	71	M	Victualler	Herts	St Albans
17	DEAYTON	Edith	St Albans Union Workhouse	Pauper	Mar	72	F	Victualler	Oxford	Easingdon
18	LONG	Eliza	St Albans Union Workhouse	Pauper		13	F	Scholar	Herts	St Albans
19	LONG	Thomas	St Albans Union Workhouse	Pauper		11	M	Scholar	Herts	St Albans
20	HALL	Mary	St Albans Union Workhouse	Pauper	Unm	37	F	Straw Plaiter	Herts	St Albans
21	HALL	Mary	St Albans Union Workhouse	Pauper		11	F	Scholar	Herts	St Albans
22	GARDENER	Alice	St Albans Union Workhouse	Pauper		9	F	Scholar	Herts	St Albans
23	COLLINS	Sarah	St Albans Union Workhouse	Pauper	Widow	72	F	Charwoman	Middx	London
24	RUSH	George	St Albans Union Workhouse	Pauper		15	M	Scholar	Herts	St Albans
25	RUSH	Harry	St Albans Union Workhouse	Pauper		11	M	Scholar	Herts	St Albans
26	NORMAN	James	St Albans Union Workhouse	Pauper	Widower	73	M	Toll Gate Keeper	Herts	Hatfield
27	SHEPHERD	Israel	St Albans Union Workhouse	Pauper	Widower	59	M	Labourer	Herts	St Albans
28	WOODBINE	Matthew	St Albans Union Workhouse	Pauper	Mar	75	M	Labourer	Herts	St Stephens
29	MOORE	Thomas	St Albans Union Workhouse	Pauper	Widower	74	M	Gardener	Herts	Hatfield
30	HULL	Thomas	St Albans Union Workhouse	Pauper	Mar	60	M	Bricklayers Labourer	Herts	St Albans

31	HIGDON	Thomas	St Albans Union Workhouse	Pauper	Mar	72	M	Turner		Somerset	Bruton
32	HIGDON	Elizabeth	St Albans Union Workhouse	Pauper	Mar	71	F	Knitter		Somerset	Bruton
33	NEAL	Matthew	St Albans Union Workhouse	Pauper		7	M	Scholar		Middx	London
34	HENMAN	Elizabeth	St Albans Union Workhouse	Pauper	Unm	57	F	Needlework		Herts	Sandridge
35	HIGDON	Richard	St Albans Union Workhouse	Pauper	Unm	45	M	Labourer		Herts	St Albans
36	ABLETT	Frederick	St Albans Union Workhouse	Pauper	Unm	20	M	Idiot		Herts	St Albans
37	SHEPHERD	Fanny	St Albans Union Workhouse	Pauper	Unm	51	F	Blind		Herts	St Albans
38	COMPTON	George	St Albans Union Workhouse	Pauper		12	M	Scholar		Gloucs	Cheltenham
39	COMPTON	Jane	St Albans Union Workhouse	Pauper		10	F	Scholar		Gloucs	Cheltenham
40	COMPTON	Thomas	St Albans Union Workhouse	Pauper		8	M	Scholar		Gloucs	Cheltenham
41	COMPTON	Eliza	St Albans Union Workhouse	Pauper		6	F	Scholar		Gloucs	Cheltenham
42	CONQUEST	Joseph	St Albans Union Workhouse	Pauper	Mar	65	M	Maltster		Beds	Luton
43	EAMES	Ann	St Albans Union Workhouse	Pauper	Unm	24	F	Servant		Herts	St Albans
44	GLADMAN	Jeremiah	St Albans Union Workhouse	Pauper	Mar	67	M	Bricklayer (journeyman)		Herts	St Albans
45	HIGDON	Charles	St Albans Union Workhouse	Pauper	Unm	17	M	Labourer		Herts	St Albans
46	STONE	George	St Albans Union Workhouse	Pauper	Mar	54	M	Baker		Middx	Pinner
47	DUNTON	Mary	St Albans Union Workhouse	Pauper	Widow	58	F	Cook		Worcs	Bisshampton
48	PONEY	Mary	St Albans Union Workhouse	Pauper	Unm	35	F	Servant		Herts	St Albans
49	FRANCIS	William	St Albans Union Workhouse	Pauper	Widower	73	M	Brewers Servant		Herts	Hatfield
50	BREWER	Jacob	St Albans Union Workhouse	Pauper	Widower	77	M	Butler		Yorks	Hull
51	EDWARDS	Henrietta	St Albans Union Workhouse	Pauper		11	F	Scholar		Herts	St Albans
52	BRACEY	Mary	St Albans Union Workhouse	Pauper	Unm	41	F	Plaiter		Herts	St Albans
53	BRACEY	George	St Albans Union Workhouse	Pauper		11	M	Scholar		Herts	St Albans
54	BRACEY	William	St Albans Union Workhouse	Pauper		7	M	Scholar		Herts	St Albans
55	EDMONDS	Thomas	St Albans Union Workhouse	Pauper	Widower	63	M	Labourer		Herts	Colney
56	PEACOCK	Ann	St Albans Union Workhouse	Pauper	Unm	34	F	Servant		Middx	London
57	PEACOCK	Frederick	St Albans Union Workhouse	Pauper		5	M	Scholar		Herts	St Albans
58	PEACOCK	George	St Albans Union Workhouse	Pauper		1	M			Herts	St Albans
59	THOMAS	Elizabeth	St Albans Union Workhouse	Pauper	Unm	41	F	Servant		Herts	Hatfield Road
60	SAUNDERS	William	St Albans Union Workhouse	Pauper	Mar	69	M	Stonemason		Herts	Abbots Langley
61	SAUNDERS	Hannah	St Albans Union Workhouse	Pauper	Mar	57	F	Charwoman		Middx	London
62	ALWAY	James	St Albans Union Workhouse	Pauper	Unm	62	M	Painter		Herts	St Albans
63	HERBERT	Ann	St Albans Union Workhouse	Pauper	Unm	79	F	Servant		Beds	Dunstable
64	FIELD	John	St Albans Union Workhouse	Pauper	Widower	86	M	Labourer		Herts	Studham
65	ROWSON	Mary	St Albans Union Workhouse	Pauper	Widow	87	F	Charwoman		Gloucs	Lydney
66	BRACEY	Underwood	St Albans Union Workhouse	Pauper	Widower	77	M	Labourer		Herts	Knebworth
67	HEARN	William	St Albans Union Workhouse	Pauper	Widower	74	M	Game Keeper		Herts	St Stephens
68	WYKES	Joseph	St Albans Union Workhouse	Pauper	Unm	62	M	Tallow Chandler		Herts	St Stephens
69	HARMAN	James	St Albans Union Workhouse	Pauper	Unm	62	M	Labourer		Herts	Colney
70	HENRY	Honnor	St Albans Union Workhouse	Pauper	Mar	71	M	Labourer		Herts	St Stephens
71	MATTHEWS	Rilly	St Albans Union Workhouse	Pauper	Unm	50	F	Needlework		Middx	London
72	BROWN	William	St Albans Union Workhouse	Pauper	Widower	81	M	Labourer		Herts	Shenley
73	KINES	Sarah	St Albans Union Workhouse	Pauper	Widow	78	F	Washerwoman		Herts	St Albans
74	LONG	Sarah	St Albans Union Workhouse	Pauper	Widow	75	F	Charwoman		Kent	Dartford
75	ANDREW	John	St Albans Union Workhouse	Pauper	Mar	68	M	Labourer		Herts	Hatfield

	SURNAME	FORENAME	SCHEDULE NUMBER	ADDRESS	RELATIONSHIP	STATUS	AGE	SEX	OCCUPATION	COUNTY OF BIRTH	PLACE OF BIRTH
76	ANDREW	Elizabeth		St Albans Union Workhouse	Pauper	Mar	67	F	Charwoman	Herts	Hatfield
77	POWELL	Elizabeth		St Albans Union Workhouse	Pauper	Unm	36	F	Plaiter	Herts	St Albans
78	KINGHAM	Rachael		St Albans Union Workhouse	Pauper		7	F	Scholar	Middx	London
79	KINGHAM	Richard		St Albans Union Workhouse	Pauper		3	M	Scholar	Middx	London
80	PEW	George		St Albans Union Workhouse	Pauper	Widower	82	M	Labourer	Herts	St Peters
81	IRONS	Susan		St Albans Union Workhouse	Pauper	Unm	31	F	Blind	Herts	St Albans
82	ALLEN	George		St Albans Union Workhouse	Pauper	Unm	41	M	Wheelwright	Herts	St Peters
83	OSMAN	Thomas		St Albans Union Workhouse	Pauper	Widower	69	M	Labourer	Herts	Redbourn
84	BURGESS	Thomas		St Albans Union Workhouse	Pauper		3	M	Scholar	Herts	St Albans
85	TURNER	James		St Albans Union Workhouse	Pauper	Widower	67	M	Labourer	Herts	St Michaels
86	TATT	Henry		St Albans Union Workhouse	Pauper	Unm	17	M	Labourer	Herts	St Albans
87	CAMPBELL	George		St Albans Union Workhouse	Pauper	Unm	22	M	Labourer	Middx	Enfield
88	HARBOURN	Sarah		St Albans Union Workhouse	Pauper	Unm	35	F	Charwoman	Middx	London
89	MAWBEY	Mary		St Albans Union Workhouse	Pauper	Unm	41	F	Servant	Herts	St Albans
90	WALLER	James		St Albans Union Workhouse	Pauper	Widower	76	M	Labourer	Beds	Shillington
91	MONK	George		St Albans Union Workhouse	Pauper	Unm	24	M	Tailor	Middx	London
92	WICKES	Ann		St Albans Union Workhouse	Pauper	Mar	37	F	Servant	Herts	St Peters
93	JONES	Charles		St Albans Union Workhouse	Pauper	Unm	54	M	Labourer	Cheshire	Chester
94	ADAMS	Susan		St Albans Union Workhouse	Pauper	Widow	62	F	Washerwoman	Herts	Flamstead
95	GRAY	Elizabeth		St Albans Union Workhouse	Pauper	Unm	64	F		Herts	St Albans
96	HOLLAND	James		St Albans Union Workhouse	Pauper	Widower	78	M	Labourer	Bucks	Ivinghoe
97	MORRIS	Sarah		St Albans Union Workhouse	Pauper	Widow	70	F	Needlework	Herts	St Albans
98	FOUNTAIN	John		St Albans Union Workhouse	Pauper	Widower	75	M	Labourer	Herts	St Michaels
99	GRACE	Charles		St Albans Union Workhouse	Pauper	Unm	24	M	Idiot	Herts	St Albans
100	HUMPHRIES	Michael		St Albans Union Workhouse	Pauper	Mar	74	M	Labourer	Herts	St Albans
101	GEEVES	Elizabeth		St Albans Union Workhouse	Pauper	Widow	70	F	Charwoman	Herts	St Albans
102	WOOLER	Jane		St Albans Union Workhouse	Pauper	Unm	45	F	Silk Spinner	Middx	London
103	GOLDING	Phoebe		St Albans Union Workhouse	Pauper	Unm	68	F	Idiot	Herts	St Albans
104	JOHNSON	William		St Albans Union Workhouse	Pauper	Widower	70	M	Labourer	Herts	Wheathampstead
105	HORROD	John		St Albans Union Workhouse	Pauper		2	M		Herts	Leverstock Green
106	HAWS	James		St Albans Union Workhouse	Pauper		14	M	Scholar	Herts	St Albans
107	DEAYTON	Elizabeth		St Albans Union Workhouse	Pauper	Unm	57	F	Servant	Herts	Bedmond [Abbots Langley]
108	CROUCH	William		St Albans Union Workhouse	Pauper	Unm	47	M	Labourer	Herts	Hempstead [Hemel]
109	ANDERSON	Benjamin		St Albans Union Workhouse	Pauper	Unm	69	M	Labourer	Herts	St Albans
110	DOWNING	Thomas		St Albans Union Workhouse	Pauper	Unm	53	M	Blacksmith	Herts	St Albans
111	SIMMONDS	William		St Albans Union Workhouse	Pauper	Unm	35	M	Idiot	Herts	St Stephens
112	HAWS	Mary		St Albans Union Workhouse	Pauper	Unm	30	F	Servant	Herts	St Stephens
113	LEWIS	John		St Albans Union Workhouse	Pauper	Widower	74	M	Labourer	Herts	Wheathampstead
114	WINDELL	James		St Albans Union Workhouse	Pauper	Widower	81	M	Labourer	Herts	Little Hormead
115	HAMMETT	William		St Albans Union Workhouse	Pauper		8	M	Scholar	Herts	Bedmond [Abbots Langley]
116	CLARK	Robert		St Albans Union Workhouse	Pauper	Unm	42	M	Labourer	Herts	St Stephens
117	SMITH	James		St Albans Union Workhouse	Pauper	Mar	73	M	Labourer	Herts	St Peters
118	SMITH	Elizabeth		St Albans Union Workhouse	Pauper	Mar	67	F	Charwoman	Herts	St Albans
119	HALSEY	James		St Albans Union Workhouse	Pauper	Widower	71	M	Labourer	Herts	St Michaels
120	HUMPHREY	William		St Albans Union Workhouse	Pauper	Mar	71	M	Labourer	Herts	Bushey

121	HUMPHREY	Jane	St Albans Union Workhouse	Pauper	Mar	79	F	Plaiter	Leics	Boosley
122	GREEN	Charlotte	St Albans Union Workhouse	Pauper	Unm	42	F	Servant	Norfolk	Beason [Beeston?]
123	HILL	James	St Albans Union Workhouse	Pauper	Mar	90	M	Farmer	Herts	Hatfield
124	ENGLAND	Mary	St Albans Union Workhouse	Pauper	Unm	37	F	Servant	Herts	St Stephens
125	ENGLAND	Harriet	St Albans Union Workhouse	Pauper		10	F	Scholar	Herts	St Stephens
126	ENGLAND	Mary	St Albans Union Workhouse	Pauper		7	F	Scholar	Herts	St Stephens
127	ENGLAND	Joseph	St Albans Union Workhouse	Pauper		5	M	Scholar	Herts	St Stephens
128	BIDMEAD	Harvey	St Albans Union Workhouse	Pauper	Widow	39	F	Servant	Middx	London
129	BIDMEAD	Charles	St Albans Union Workhouse	Pauper		11	M	Scholar	Middx	London
130	BIDMEAD	William	St Albans Union Workhouse	Pauper		9	M	Scholar	Middx	London
131	DIMMOCK	Thomas	St Albans Union Workhouse	Pauper	Widower	78	M	Labourer	Herts	Great Berkhamsted
132	MUNT	Elizabeth	St Albans Union Workhouse	Pauper	Widow	72	F	Charwoman	Herts	St Stephens
133	WHITE	Benjamin	St Albans Union Workhouse	Pauper		11	M	Scholar	Herts	St Albans
134	OAKLEY	Thomas	St Albans Union Workhouse	Pauper	Unm	41	M	Labourer	Herts	St Stephens
135	BILBEY	John	St Albans Union Workhouse	Pauper	Widower	70	M	Shepherd	Bucks	Ivinghoe
136	DRAPER	Esther	St Albans Union Workhouse	Pauper	Unm	86	F	Plaiter	Herts	Sandridge
137	CROFT	Harriet	St Albans Union Workhouse	Pauper	Unm	38	F	Plaiter	Herts	Sandridge
138	POWELL	John	St Albans Union Workhouse	Pauper		11	M	Scholar	Herts	St Albans
139	GOLSBY	Edwin	St Albans Union Workhouse	Pauper		7	M	Scholar	Herts	St Albans
140	LUDGATE	William	St Albans Union Workhouse	Pauper	Widower	73	M	Labourer	Herts	St Albans
141	HARBOURN	Eliza	St Albans Union Workhouse	Pauper	Unm	15	F	Servant	Herts	St Albans
142	HARBOURN	Louisa	St Albans Union Workhouse	Pauper		13	F	Scholar	Herts	St Albans
143	FLOYD	George	St Albans Union Workhouse	Pauper	Widower	77	M	Labourer	Herts	Wheathampstead
144	GODFREY	Henry	St Albans Union Workhouse	Pauper		11	M	Scholar	Herts	St Albans
145	HALSEY	Elizabeth	St Albans Union Workhouse	Pauper	Unm	32	F	Straw Plaiter	Herts	Sandridge
146	ARCHER	Charles	St Albans Union Workhouse	Pauper	Widower	71	M	Labourer	Herts	St Albans
147	PARKINS	William	St Albans Union Workhouse	Pauper	Unm	55	M	Labourer	Herts	Sandridge
148	RUDD	Philip	St Albans Union Workhouse	Pauper	Widower	71	M	Labourer	Herts	Preston
149	LILLEY	John	St Albans Union Workhouse	Pauper	Mar	71	M	Labourer	Herts	Tewin
150	LILLEY	Margaret	St Albans Union Workhouse	Pauper	Mar	58	F	Plaiter	Herts	Wheathampstead
151	EAMES	William	St Albans Union Workhouse	Pauper	Widower	51	M	Labourer	Herts	St Peters
152	SQUIRES	Eliza	St Albans Union Workhouse	Pauper	Unm	27	F	Servant	Herts	Hitchin
153	SQUIRES	William	St Albans Union Workhouse	Pauper		3	M		Herts	St Albans
154	HARRIS	John	St Albans Union Workhouse	Pauper	Mar	73	M	Labourer	Kent	Cocks Heath
155	SIMPSON	Sarah	St Albans Union Workhouse	Pauper	Unm	54	F	Plaiter	Herts	Redbourn
156	FELLS	Ann	St Albans Union Workhouse	Pauper	Unm	71	F	Idiot	Herts	Redbourn
157	READING	Daniel	St Albans Union Workhouse	Pauper		12	M	Scholar	Herts	Redbourn
158	MORGAN	William	St Albans Union Workhouse	Pauper		10	M	Scholar	Unknown	
159	FOWLER	Ann	St Albans Union Workhouse	Pauper	Widow	75	F	Servant	Beds	Sundon
160	COX	Mary	St Albans Union Workhouse	Pauper	Widow	51	F	Plaiter	Herts	Redbourn
161	COCKLE	James	St Albans Union Workhouse	Pauper		9	M	Scholar	Herts	Redbourn
162	COCKLE	Mary	St Albans Union Workhouse	Pauper		7	F	Scholar	Herts	Redbourn
163	HADNUTT	Joseph	St Albans Union Workhouse	Pauper	Widower	76	M	Sack Carrier	Herts	Bovingdon
164	ALLEN	Richard	St Albans Union Workhouse	Pauper	Mar	71	M	Labourer	Herts	Redbourn
165	AUSTIN	Fanny	St Albans Union Workhouse	Pauper	Unm	45	F	Plaiter	Herts	Redbourn

	SURNAME	FORENAME	SCHEDULE NUMBER	ADDRESS	RELATIONSHIP	STATUS	AGE	SEX	OCCUPATION	COUNTY OF BIRTH	PLACE OF BIRTH
166	CAM	Mary		St Albans Union Workhouse	Pauper	Widow	75	F	Washerwoman	Herts	Hatfield
167	FISHER	Joseph		St Albans Union Workhouse	Pauper	Widower	80	M	Labourer	Herts	Redbourn
168	WHITE	John		St Albans Union Workhouse	Pauper	Unm	66	M	Labourer	Herts	Redbourn
169	ARNOLD	Aaron		St Albans Union Workhouse	Pauper	Mar	81	M	Basket Maker	Herts	Watford
170	ARNOLD	Mary		St Albans Union Workhouse	Pauper	Mar	81	F		Beds	Luton
171	FREEMAN	John		St Albans Union Workhouse	Pauper	Unm	56	M	Labourer	Herts	Flamstead
172	HOMAN [?]	George		St Albans Union Workhouse	Pauper	Mar	71	M	Master Bricklayer	Herts	Flamstead
173	HOMAN [?]	Hannah		St Albans Union Workhouse	Pauper	Mar	60	F		Herts	Redbourn
174	BURGESS	John		St Albans Union Workhouse	Pauper	Unm	54	M	Shepherd	Beds	Luton
175	BONFIELD	William		St Albans Union Workhouse	Pauper	Unm	47	M	Labourer	Herts	St Albans
176	BOWSTREET	John		St Albans Union Workhouse	Pauper	Unm	60	M	Labourer	Herts	Redbourn
177	FOWLER	Mary		St Albans Union Workhouse	Pauper	Unm	39	F	Plaiter	Herts	Redbourn
178	FOWLER	Sarah		St Albans Union Workhouse	Pauper		2	F		Herts	Redbourn
179	BONNICK	Samuel		St Albans Union Workhouse	Pauper	Widower	86	M	Labourer	Beds	Chargrove
180	REID	Joseph		St Albans Union Workhouse	Pauper	Unm	55	M	Labourer	Herts	Harpenden
181	BARNES	George		St Albans Union Workhouse	Pauper		12	M	Scholar	Herts	Harpenden
182	PITKIN	Henry		St Albans Union Workhouse	Pauper		13	M	Scholar	Herts	Harpenden
183	BARKER	Solomon		St Albans Union Workhouse	Pauper	Widower	88	M	Labourer	Bucks	Ivinghoe
184	HARDEY	Robert James		St Albans Union Workhouse	Pauper		12	M	Scholar	Middx	London
185	WARREN	Amos		St Albans Union Workhouse	Pauper		12	M	Scholar	Herts	Harpenden
186	SWALLOW	Charles		St Albans Union Workhouse	Pauper		12	M	Scholar	Herts	Harpenden
187	DOWNES	Elizabeth		St Albans Union Workhouse	Pauper	Widow	72	F	Charwoman	Herts	Harpenden
188	KEEP	Mary		St Albans Union Workhouse	Pauper	Widow	83	F	Charwoman	Unknown	
189	FARR	Fanny		St Albans Union Workhouse	Pauper		8	F	Scholar	Beds	Luton
190	FELLS	William		St Albans Union Workhouse	Pauper	Widower	73	M	Sawyer	Herts	Harpenden
191	MITCHELL	James		St Albans Union Workhouse	Pauper	Widower	75	M	Labourer	Herts	Flidwick [Flitwick, Beds?]
192	ROWE	Joseph		St Albans Union Workhouse	Pauper	Mar	71	M	Labourer	Herts	Caddington
193	BAXTER	Thomas		St Albans Union Workhouse	Pauper	Widower	81	M	Labourer	Herts	Harpenden
194	RIVERS	Jane		St Albans Union Workhouse	Pauper	Unm	60	F	Servant	Berks	West Hendred
195	BARBER	Elizabeth		St Albans Union Workhouse	Pauper	Mar	29	F	Charwoman	Beds	Luton
196	BARBER	George		St Albans Union Workhouse	Pauper		7	M	Scholar	Herts	St Albans
197	BARBER	Thomas		St Albans Union Workhouse	Pauper		2	M		Herts	St Albans
198	MANNING	Thomas		St Albans Union Workhouse	Pauper	Unm	29	M	Labourer	Herts	Harpenden
199	WINCH	Sarah		St Albans Union Workhouse	Pauper	Widow	47	F	Plaiter	Herts	Luton
200	SYGROVE	James		St Albans Union Workhouse	Pauper		14	M	Scholar	Herts	Harpenden
201	SYGROVE	George		St Albans Union Workhouse	Pauper		11	M	Scholar	Herts	Harpenden
202	PESTELL	Thomas		St Albans Union Workhouse	Pauper	Widower	72	M	Labourer	Herts	Harpenden
203	PLUMB	William		St Albans Union Workhouse	Pauper	Unm	65	M	Labourer	Herts	Welwyn
204	HUMPHREY	Sarah		St Albans Union Workhouse	Pauper	Unm	77	F	Plaiter	Herts	Wheathampstead
205	JOHNSON	Elizabeth		St Albans Union Workhouse	Pauper	Widow	82	F	Charwoman	[Unknown]	
206	FOSTER	Sarah		St Albans Union Workhouse	Pauper	Widow	80	F	Plaiter	Middx	London
207	WHEELER	Sarah		St Albans Union Workhouse	Pauper	Unm	33	F	Plaiter	Herts	Wheathampstead
208	WHEELER	Emma		St Albans Union Workhouse	Pauper		13	F	Scholar	Herts	Wheathampstead
209	WHEELER	Sarah		St Albans Union Workhouse	Pauper		7	F	Scholar	Herts	St Albans
210	PEACOCK	Sarah		St Albans Union Workhouse	Pauper	Unm	49	F	Plaiter	Beds	Woburn

211	WHEELER	George	St Albans Union Workhouse	Pauper	Unm	24	M	Idiot	Herts	Wheathampstead
212	WALKER	Mary	St Albans Union Workhouse	Pauper		12	F	Scholar	Herts	Baldock
213	WALKER	Emma	St Albans Union Workhouse	Pauper		10	F	Scholar	Herts	Baldock
214	WALKER	James	St Albans Union Workhouse	Pauper		8	M	Scholar	Herts	Baldock
215	ABBESS	Sarah	St Albans Union Workhouse	Pauper	Unm	61	F	Plaiter	Herts	Wheathampstead
216	WILES	Sarah	St Albans Union Workhouse	Pauper	Widow	61	F	Plaiter	Herts	Wheathampstead
217	WHEELER	John	St Albans Union Workhouse	Pauper	Mar	75	M	Labourer	Hereford	Hentland
218	WHEELER	Elizabeth	St Albans Union Workhouse	Pauper	Mar	64	F	Plaiter	Herts	Wheathampstead
219	DAY	Joseph	St Albans Union Workhouse	Pauper	Unm	17	M	Labourer	Herts	Harpenden
220	SCRIVENER	Sarah	St Albans Union Workhouse	Pauper	Widow	41	F	Needlework	Herts	Ware
221	SCRIVENER	Elizabeth	St Albans Union Workhouse	Pauper		10	F	Scholar	Herts	Ware
222	SCRIVENER	Sarah	St Albans Union Workhouse	Pauper		8	F	Scholar	Herts	St Albans
223	SCRIVENER	William	St Albans Union Workhouse	Pauper		4	M	Scholar	Herts	St Albans
224	TOBEY	Thomas	St Albans Union Workhouse	Pauper	Widower	69	M	Labourer	Herts	Kimpton
225	STEAD	Elisha	St Albans Union Workhouse	Pauper	Widower	72	M	Labourer	Beds	Luton
226	HARCOURT	Ann	St Albans Union Workhouse	Pauper		9	F	Scholar	Herts	St Albans
227	HARCOURT	Jonathan	St Albans Union Workhouse	Pauper		7	M	Scholar	Herts	St Albans
228	STEALE	Ellen	St Albans Union Workhouse	Pauper	Widow	62	F	Washerwoman	Ireland	[Unknown]
229	GAZELEY	Mary	St Albans Union Workhouse	Pauper	Unm	28	F	Plaiter	Herts	St Albans
230	GAZELEY	Kezia	St Albans Union Workhouse	Pauper		6	F	Scholar	Herts	St Albans
231	BARBER	Charlotte	St Albans Union Workhouse	Pauper	Widow	81	F	Charwoman	Herts	Abbots Langley
232	EVANS	Isabella	St Albans Union Workhouse	Pauper		10	F	Scholar	Middx	London
233	COLLINS	John	St Albans Union Workhouse	Pauper	Widower	80	M	Labourer	Herts	St Michaels
234	HILL	Elizabeth	St Albans Union Workhouse	Pauper	Widow	65	F	Servant	Herts	Hatfield
235	BURRIDGE	Martha	St Albans Union Workhouse	Pauper	Widow	72	F	Charwoman	Suffolk	Glandford
236	EVANS	William	St Albans Union Workhouse	Pauper	Mar	71	M	Labourer	Herts	Studham
237	DUGGIN	Caroline	St Albans Union Workhouse	Pauper	Unm	26	F	Servant	Derby	Litchfield
238	BULL	Martha	St Albans Union Workhouse	Pauper	Widow	72	F	Charwoman	Beds	Luton
239	STANLEY	William	St Albans Union Workhouse	Pauper	Mar	62	M	Labourer	Herts	Clothall
240	CROSS	Eleanor	St Albans Union Workhouse	Pauper	Unm	72	F	Charwoman	Staffs	Litchfield
241	BRADBURY	Mary	St Albans Union Workhouse	Pauper	Widow	62	F	Washerwoman	Staffs	Litchfield
242	SKINNER	John	St Albans Union Workhouse	Pauper	Mar	65	M	Labourer	Beds	Dunstable Houghton
243	LAWRENCE	John	St Albans Union Workhouse	Pauper	Unm	23	M	Labourer (Blind)	Herts	St Albans

Chapter 14

The parish of St Stephens in the liberty

of St Albans

Registrar's District: St Albans   Enumeration District 6a   Ref. HO 107/1713 folios 534-48

Park Ward west of the Edgeware Road, except the houses abutting on such road.

Park Ward West

1	SHARP	Job	1	Spooners	Head	Mar	49	M	Agric Lab	Herts	Tring
2	SHARP	Harriett	1		Wife	Mar	50	F		Herts	St Michaels
3	SHARP	Emma	1		Dau	Unm	20	F	Brazilian Hat Maker	Herts	St Stephens
4	SHARP	Eliza	1		Dau	Unm	11	F	Scholar	Herts	St Stephens
5	SHARP	Thomas	1		Son	Unm	9	M	Scholar	Herts	St Stephens
6	SHARP	John	1		Son	Unm	6	M	Scholar	Herts	St Stephens
7	COSTIN	Thomas	2	Spooners	Head	Mar	28	M	Higgler	Herts	St Stephens
8	COSTIN	Mary Ann	2		Wife	Mar	29	F		Herts	St Stephens
9	COSTIN	Thomas	2		Son	Unm	6	M	Scholar	Herts	St Stephens
10	COSTIN	Henry	2		Son	Unm	4	M	Scholar	Herts	St Stephens
11	COSTIN	Elizabeth	2		Dau	Unm	1	F		Herts	St Stephens
12	GREEN	Augustus William	3	Park Lane Cottage	Head	Unm	28	M	Curate Holy Trinity St Stephens	Middx	St Marylebone
13	PICTON	Susan	3		Serv	Widow	52	F	House Servant	Essex	Hatfield
14	ROGERS	Francis	3		Serv	Unm	19	M	House Servant	Herts	Abbots Langley
15	DAYTON	John	4	Park Street Lane	Head	Mar	63	M	Agric Lab	Herts	St Stephens
16	DAYTON	Charlotte	4		Wife	Mar	57	F		Middx	Edmonton
17	DAYTON	Sophia	4		Dau	Unm	30	F	Straw Plaiter	Herts	St Stephens
18	DAYTON	Catherine	4		Dau	Unm	25	F	Brazilian Hat Maker	Herts	St Stephens
19	DAYTON	Kitty	4		Grandau		9	F	Scholar	Herts	St Stephens
20	CATLIN	Daniel	5	Park Street Lane	Head	Mar	74	M	Agric Lab	Herts	St Stephens
21	CATLIN	Esther	5		Wife	Mar	64	F		Herts	St Stephens
22	CATLIN	Adelaide	5		Cousin	Unm	21	F	Brazilian Hat Maker	Herts	St Stephens
23	CHARGE	John	6	Park Street Lane	Head	Mar	31	M	Agric Lab	Herts	St Stephens
24	CHARGE	Mary Ann	6		Wife	Mar	32	F	Brazilian Hat Maker	Herts	St Stephens
25	CHARGE	Mary Ann	6		Dau		5	F		Herts	St Stephens
26	CHARGE	Jane	6		Dau		3	F		Herts	St Stephens

Figure 12 : ST STEPHENS

587

From the first edition of the 6 inch Ordinance Survey of Hertfordshire (1878), Sheets XXXIV and XXXIX

Approximate scale of reproduction: 1cm = 220m

	SURNAME	FORENAME	SCHEDULE NUMBER	ADDRESS	RELATIONSHIP	STATUS	AGE	SEX	OCCUPATION	COUNTY OF BIRTH	PLACE OF BIRTH
27	HOSTLER	James	7	Park Street Lane	Head	Widower	47	M	Agric Lab	Herts	Abbots Langley
28	HOSTLER	George	7		Son		10	M	Scholar	Herts	St Stephens
29	HOSTLER	Sarah	7		Dau		5	F		Herts	St Stephens
30	HOSTLER	Daniel	7		Son		3	M		Herts	St Stephens
31	GURNEY	James	8	Park Street Lane	Head	Widower	52	M	Agric Lab	Herts	St Stephens
32	PETERS	Sarah	8		Dau	Widow	27	F	Straw Plaiter	Herts	St Stephens
33	GURNEY	Susan	8		Dau	Unm	27	F	Brazilian Hat Maker	Herts	St Stephens
34	GURNEY	Philip	8		Son	Unm	22	M	Agric Lab	Herts	St Stephens
35	PETERS	Joseph	8		Grandson		3	M		Herts	St Stephens
36	BONNICK	Thomas	9	Park Street Lane	Head	Mar	52	M	Agric Lab	Beds	Caddington
37	BONNICK	Martha	9		Wife	Mar	44	F	Straw Plaiter	Herts	St Stephens
38	BONNICK	George	9		Son	Unm	20	M	Groom	Herts	St Stephens
39	BONNICK	Eliza	9		Dau	Unm	18	F	Straw Plaiter	Herts	St Stephens
40	BONNICK	Jane	9		Dau		11	F	Scholar	Herts	St Stephens
41	BONNICK	Charles	9		Son		8	M	Scholar	Herts	St Stephens
42	BONNICK	Caroline	9		Dau		5	F		Herts	St Stephens
43	LINNEY	Susan	10	Park Street Lane	Head	Mar	37	F	Straw Plaiter	Herts	St Stephens
44	LINNEY	Emma	10		Dau		12	F	Scholar	Herts	St Stephens
45	LINNEY	George	10		Son		10	M	Scholar	Herts	St Stephens
46	LINNEY	Thomas	10		Son		8	M	Scholar	Herts	St Stephens
47	LINNEY	Sarah	10		Dau		6	F	Scholar	Herts	St Stephens
48	LINNEY	Frederick	10		Son		4	M		Herts	St Stephens
49	NORTH	Henry	11	How Wood	Head	Mar	25	M	Farm Bailiff	Bucks	Towersey
50	NORTH	Sarah	11		Wife	Mar	21	F		Oxon	Chinnor
51	SMITH	John	12	Slowmans	Head	Widower	69	M	Farmer of 150 acres employing 6 labourers	Herts	St Stephens
52	HUGHES	Anna Maria	12		Serv	Widow	48	F	Housekeeper	Worcs	Tenbury
53	SMITH	James	12		Serv	Unm	15	M	Agric Lab	Herts	St Stephens
54	ELLWOOD	Thomas	13	Darley Hall	Head	Mar	34	M	Agric Lab	Herts	St Stephens
55	ELLWOOD	Susan	13		Wife	Mar	33	F		Herts	St Stephens
56	ELLWOOD	George	13		Son	Unm	10	M	Agric Lab	Herts	St Stephens
57	ELLWOOD	Mary Ann	13		Dau		8	F	Scholar	Herts	St Stephens
58	ELLWOOD	Thomas	13		Son		6	M	Scholar	Herts	St Stephens
59	ELLWOOD	Joseph	13		Son		2	M		Herts	St Stephens
60	WARDEN	Caroline	13		Niece		9	F	Scholar	Herts	St Stephens
61	HILL	Sarah	14	Darley Hall	Head	Widow	70	F		Herts	St Stephens
62	HILL	Sarah	14		Dau	Unm	34	F	Brazilian Hat Maker	Herts	St Stephens
63	HILL	Sarah	14		Grandau	Unm	14	F	Brazilian Hat Maker	Herts	St Stephens
64	WARDEN	Sarah	14		Visitor	Unm	20	F	Brazilian Hat Maker	Herts	St Stephens
65	HOBBS	William	15	Smug Oak	Head	Widower	60	M	Agric Lab	Beds	Caddington
66	HOBBS	Caroline	15		Dau	Unm	27	F	Straw Plaiter	Herts	St Stephens
67	HOBBS	James	15		Son	Unm	19	M	Agric Lab	Herts	St Stephens
68	WEEDON	Henry	16	Smug Oak	Head	Widower	43	M	Agric Lab	Herts	St Stephens
69	WEEDON	Eliza	16		Dau	Unm	24	F	Straw Plaiter	Herts	St Stephens
70	WEEDON	Ellis	16		Son		10	M	Brazilian Hat Maker	Herts	St Stephens
71	WEEDON	Louisa	16		Dau		8	F	Brazilian Hat Maker	Herts	St Stephens

72	WEEDON	Caroline	16		Dau		4	F		Herts	St Stephens
73	WEEDON	Maria	16		Dau		1	F		Herts	St Stephens
74	SLAUGHTER	Job	17	Smug Oak	Head	Mar	40	M	Beer Shop Keeper	Herts	St Stephens
75	SLAUGHTER	Eliza	17		Wife	Mar	46	F		Herts	Watford
76	SLAUGHTER	George	17		Son	Unm	20	M	Agric Lab	Herts	St Stephens
77	SLAUGHTER	Mary Ann	17		Dau		14	F	Brazilian Hat Maker	Herts	St Stephens
78	SLAUGHTER	William	17		Son		12	M	Scholar	Herts	St Stephens
79	SLAUGHTER	Robert	17		Son		8	M	Scholar	Herts	St Stephens
80	DEACON	David	17		Lodger	Unm	22	M	Agric Lab	Herts	Abbots Langley
81	HAWTREE	Alexander	17		Lodger	Unm	19	M	Agric Lab	Herts	St Stephens
82	HARRISON	Thomas	18	Smug Oak	Head	Mar	45	M	Agric Lab	Herts	Watford
83	HARRISON	Phillis	18		Wife	Mar	48	F		Herts	St Stephens
84	HARRISON	William	18		Son	Unm	18	M	Agric Lab	Herts	St Stephens
85	HARRISON	Mary Ann	18		Dau	Unm	15	F	Brazilian Hat Maker	Herts	St Stephens
86	HARRISON	Thomas	18		Son	Unm	12	M		Herts	St Stephens
87	HARRISON	David	18		Son	Unm	9	M		Herts	St Stephens
88	WEEDON	William	19	Smug Oak	Head	Mar	40	M	Agric Lab	Herts	St Stephens
89	WEEDON	Rebecca	19		Wife	Mar	38	F	Brazilian Hat Maker	Herts	St Stephens
90	WEEDON	Betsey	19		Dau	Unm	15	F	Brazilian Hat Maker	Herts	St Stephens
91	WEEDON	Caroline	19		Dau	Unm	12	F	Brazilian Hat Maker	Herts	St Stephens
92	WEEDON	Thomas	19		Son	Unm	9	M		Herts	St Stephens
93	WEEDON	Susannah	19		Dau	Unm	6	F		Herts	St Stephens
94	WEEDON	John	19		Son	Unm	3	M		Herts	St Stephens
95	WEEDON	William	19		Son	Unm	4 m	M		Herts	St Stephens
96	JOINER	Thomas	20	Smug Oak	Head	Mar	27	M	Dealer in Wood etc.	Herts	St Stephens
97	JOINER	Sarah Ellen	20		Wife	Mar	22	F		Herts	Bushey
98	JOINER	Ellen	20		Dau		1	F		Herts	St Stephens
99	BROWN	James	21	Smug Oak	Head	Mar	48	M	Agric Lab	Herts	Little Munden
100	BROWN	Sarah	21		Wife	Mar	50	F	Straw Plaiter	Herts	St Stephens
101	ATKINS	John	22	Smug Oak	Head	Mar	49	M	Agric Lab	Herts	St Stephens
102	ATKINS	Mary	22		Wife	Mar	49	F	Straw Plaiter	Herts	St Stephens
103	ATKINS	William	22		Son	Unm	25	M	Agric Lab	Herts	St Stephens
104	ATKINS	John	22		Son	Unm	23	M	Agric Lab	Herts	St Stephens
105	ATKINS	Thomas	22		Son	Unm	21	M	Agric Lab	Herts	St Stephens
106	ATKINS	Emma	22		Dau	Unm	17	F	Brazilian Hat Maker	Herts	St Stephens
107	ATKINS	Edward	22		Son		15	M	Agric Lab	Herts	St Stephens
108	ATKINS	James	22		Son		12	M	Agric Lab	Herts	St Stephens
109	CHARGE	Thomas	23	Smug Oak	Head	Mar	42	M	Agric Lab	Herts	St Stephens
110	CHARGE	Rachael	23		Wife	Mar	42	F	Straw Plaiter	Herts	Wheathampstead
111	CHARGE	Eliza	23		Dau	Unm	20	F	Brazilian Hat Maker	Herts	St Stephens
112	CHARGE	William	23		Son	Unm	12	M	Brazilian Hat Maker	Herts	St Stephens
113	CHARGE	Alfred	23		Son	Unm	10	M		Herts	St Stephens
114	CHARGE	Mary Ann	23		Dau	Unm	6	F		Herts	St Stephens
115	CHARGE	James	23		Son	Unm	4	M		Herts	St Stephens
116	CHARGE	Susannah	23		Dau	Unm	2	F		Herts	St Stephens

	SURNAME	FORENAME	SCHEDULE NUMBER	ADDRESS	RELATIONSHIP	STATUS	AGE	SEX	OCCUPATION	COUNTY OF BIRTH	PLACE OF BIRTH
117	CHARGE	Hannah	23		Dau	Unm	11 m	F		Herts	St Stephens
118	BECKLEY	William	24	Smug Oak	Head	Widower	93	M	Agric Lab	Bucks	Chesham
119	HAWTREE	William	25	Smug Oak	Head	Mar	46	M	Agric Lab	Herts	St Stephens
120	HAWTREE	Mary	26		Wife	Mar	52	F	Straw Plaiter	London	London
121	DEACON	James	26	Smug Oak	Head	Mar	45	M	Shoemaker	Herts	Watford
122	DEACON	Caroline	26		Wife	Mar	43	F		Herts	Watford
123	DEACON	James	26		Son	Unm	17	M	Agric Lab	Herts	Watford
124	DEACON	Elizabeth	26		Dau	Unm	15	F	Brazilian Hat Maker	Herts	Abbots Langley
125	DEACON	Mary Ann	26		Dau	Unm	13	F	Brazilian Hat Maker	Herts	Abbots Langley
126	DEACON	William	26		Son	Unm	11	M	Brazilian Hat Maker	Herts	Watford
127	DEACON	George	26		Son	Unm	8	M	Brazilian Hat Maker	Herts	St Stephens
128	DEACON	Henry	26		Son	Unm	6	M	Brazilian Hat Maker	Herts	St Stephens
129	DEACON	Darcus	26		Dau	Unm	2	F		Herts	St Stephens
130	WIGGS	Thomas	27	Smug Oak	Head	Mar	72	M	Agric Lab	Herts	St Stephens
131	WIGGS	Mary	27		Wife	Mar	70	F		Bucks	Soulbury
132	WIGGS	Thomas	28	Smug Oak	Head	Mar	34	M	Dealer	Herts	St Stephens
133	WIGGS	Mary	28		Wife	Mar	34	F	Brazilian Hat Maker	Herts	St Stephens
134	WIGGS	Susan	28		Dau	Unm	12	F	Brazilian Hat Maker	Herts	St Stephens
135	WIGGS	Jane	28		Dau	Unm	10	F	Brazilian Hat Maker	Herts	St Stephens
136	WIGGS	William	28		Son	Unm	8	M	Scholar	Herts	St Stephens
137	WIGGS	Charlotte	28		Dau	Unm	7	F		Herts	St Stephens
138	WIGGS	Thomas	28		Son	Unm	5	M		Herts	St Stephens
139	WIGGS	George	28		Son	Unm	3	M		Herts	St Stephens
140	WIGGS	Robert	28		Son	Unm	1	M		Herts	St Stephens
141	STOW	Samuel	29	Smug Oak	Head	Mar	34	M	Farmer of 180 acres employing 8 labourers	Herts	St Stephens
142	STOW	Esther	29		Wife	Mar	24	F		Herts	St Stephens
143	STOW	William	29		Son	Unm	3	M		Herts	St Stephens
144	STOW	Ann Maria	29		Dau		1	F		Herts	St Stephens
145	STOW	Thomas	29		Son		2 m	M		Herts	St Stephens
146	KING	Susan	29		Serv	Unm	24	F	House Servant	Herts	St Stephens
147	TEBBOTH	Thomas	29		Serv	Unm	19	M	Agric Lab	Herts	St Stephens
148	SMITH	Henry	29		Serv	Unm	16	M	Agric Lab	Herts	Aldenham
149	JOLLIFF	William	30	Smug Oak	Head	Mar	36	M	Game Keeper	Hants	Hursley
150	JOLLIFF	Sarah	30		Wife	Mar	35	F		Middx	Bloomsbury
151	JOLLIFF	William	30		Son	Unm	12	M	Game Keepers Helper	Hants	Compton
152	JOLLIFF	Mary Ann	30		Dau	Unm	10	F	Scholar	Devon	Stoke Gabriel
153	JOLLIFF	Ellen	30		Dau	Unm	8	F	Scholar	Devon	Stoke Gabriel
154	JOLLIFF	Emma	30		Dau	Unm	6	F		Herts	St Stephens
155	JOLLIFF	Edwin	30		Son	Unm	4	M		Herts	St Stephens
156	JOLLIFF	Jane	30		Dau	Unm	2	F		Herts	St Stephens
157	EDMONDS	William	31	Smug Oak	Head	Mar	53	M	Brazilian Hat Maker	Herts	Abbots Langley
158	EDMONDS	Harriett	31		Wife	Mar	48	F	Brazilian Hat Maker	Herts	Abbots Langley
159	EDMONDS	Harriett	31		Dau	Unm	18	F	Brazilian Hat Maker	Herts	Abbots Langley
160	EDMONDS	Robert	31		Son	Unm	15	M	Brazilian Hat Maker	Herts	Abbots Langley
161	EDMONDS	Elizabeth	31		Dau	Unm	13	F	Brazilian Hat Maker	Herts	Abbots Langley

162	EDMONDS	Maria	31		Dau	Unm	11	F	Brazilian Hat Maker	Herts	Abbots Langley
163	EDMONDS	Sarah	31		Dau	Unm	10	F	Brazilian Hat Maker	Herts	Abbots Langley
164	EDMONDS	John	31		Grandson	Unm	5	M		Herts	St Stephens
165	ENGLAND	Charles	32	Smug Oak	Head	Mar	52	M	Agric Lab	Herts	Shenley
166	ENGLAND	Mary	32		Wife	Mar	49	F	Brazilian Hat Maker	Herts	St Stephens
167	ENGLAND	Mary	32		Dau	Unm	19	F	Brazilian Hat Maker	Herts	St Stephens
168	ENGLAND	Allice	32		Dau	Unm	17	F	Brazilian Hat Maker	Herts	St Stephens
169	ENGLAND	Betsey	32		Dau	Unm	13	F	Brazilian Hat Maker	Herts	St Stephens
170	KING	James	33	Smug Oak	Head	Mar	71	M	Agric Lab	Herts	St Stephens
171	KING	Frances	33		Wife	Mar	71	F		Herts	St Stephens
172	KING	Mary	33		Dau	Unm	25	F	Straw Plaiter	Herts	St Stephens
173	KING	Benjamin	33		Son	Unm	19	M	Agric Lab	Herts	St Stephens
174	KING	William	33		Son	Unm	11	M	Scholar	Herts	St Stephens
175	HEWITT	William	34	Smug Oak	Head	Mar	50	M	Agric Lab	Herts	Barnet
176	HEWITT	Sarah	34		Wife	Mar	43	F	Straw Plaiter	Herts	Aldenham
177	HEWITT	Mary Ann	34		Dau	Unm	11	F	Scholar	Herts	St Stephens
178	HEWITT	Edward	34		Son	Unm	8	M		Herts	St Stephens
179	HEWITT	John	34		Son	Unm	6	M		Herts	St Stephens
180	CHAPEL	Edward	35	Smug Oak	Head	Mar	52	M	Agric Lab	Herts	Abbots Langley
181	CHAPEL	Ann	35		Wife	Mar	47	F	Straw Plaiter	Herts	St Stephens
182	CHAPEL	Edward	35		Son	Unm	26	M	Agric Lab	Herts	St Stephens
183	CHAPEL	Emma	35		Dau	Unm	19	F	Brazilian Hat Maker	Herts	St Stephens
184	CHAPEL	Mary	35		Dau	Unm	15	F	Brazilian Hat Maker	Herts	St Stephens
185	CHAPEL	Thomas	35		Son	Unm	12	M	Agric Lab	Herts	St Stephens
186	CHAPEL	Sarah Ann	35		Dau	Unm	10	F	Scholar	Herts	St Stephens
187	CHARGE	John	36	Smug Oak	Head	Mar	51	M	Agric Lab	Herts	Aldenham
188	CHARGE	Ann	36		Wife	Mar	58	F	Brazilian Hat Maker	Herts	Abbots Langley
189	CHARGE	Sarah	36		Dau	Unm	22	F	Brazilian Hat Maker	Herts	St Stephens
190	CHARGE	Eliza	36		Dau	Unm	19	F	Brazilian Hat Maker	Herts	St Stephens
191	CHARGE	Kitty	36		Dau	Unm	17	F	Brazilian Hat Maker	Herts	St Stephens
192	CHARGE	Isabelle	36		Grandau	Unm	3	F		Herts	St Stephens
193	HAWKINS	Betsey	36		Lodger	Unm	27	F	Brazilian Hat Maker	Herts	St Stephens
194	HAWKINS	William	36		Lodgers Son	Unm	3	M		Herts	St Albans
195	MILEMAN	William	37	Smug Oak	Head	Mar	72	M	Agric Lab	Herts	St Stephens
196	MILEMAN	Sarah	37		Wife	Mar	60	F		Herts	Watford
197	MILEMAN	Matthew	37		Son	Mar	33	M	Agric Lab	Herts	Watford
198	MILEMAN	Eliza	37		Dau-in-law	Mar	35	F		Herts	St Stephens
199	MILEMAN	Hannah	37		Grandau		3	F		Herts	St Stephens
200	MILEMAN	Jane	37		Grandau		8 m	F		Herts	St Stephens
201	MILEMAN	Sarah	37		Grandau		8 m	F		Herts	St Stephens
202	LINE	George	38	Little Hanstead	Head	Mar	60	M	Farmer of 75 acres employing 2 men	Warks	Church Law[ford]
203	LINE	Ann	38		Wife	Mar	57	F		Northants	Asby
204	HANDLEY	George	38		Nephew	Mar	27	M	Farmers Nephew	Leics	Lorten [?]
205	HANDLEY	Margaret	38		Niece	Mar	27	F		Middx	Christchurch
206	SHARP	George	38		Serv	Unm	14	M	Agric Lab	Herts	St Stephens

	SURNAME	FORENAME	SCHEDULE NUMBER	ADDRESS	RELATIONSHIP	STATUS	AGE	SEX	OCCUPATION	COUNTY OF BIRTH	PLACE OF BIRTH
207	EDWARDS	Henry	39	Great Hanstead	Head	Mar	48	M	Farmer of 150 acres employing 9 labourers	Herts	St Albans
208	EDWARDS	Harriett	39		Wife	Mar	49	F	Farmers Wife	Herts	St Albans
209	EDWARDS	Hayward	39		Son	Unm	22	M	Farmers Son	Herts	St Albans
210	EDWARDS	Frank	39		Son	Unm	18	M	Farmers Son	Herts	St Albans
211	EDWARDS	Henry	39		Son	Unm	21	M	Farmers Son	Herts	St Albans
212	EDWARDS	John	39		Son		8	M	Farmers Son	Herts	St Albans
213	EDWARDS	Harriett	39		Dau		7	F	Farmers Daughter	Herts	St Albans
214	BUTLER	Sarah	39		Serv	Unm	20	F	House Servant	Oxon	Oxford
215	EPHGRAVE	George	40	Great Hanstead	Head	Mar	37	M	Blacksmith & Publican employing 1 man	Herts	Sandridge
216	EPHGRAVE	Rhoda	40		Wife	Mar	34	F		Sussex	Cuckfield
217	EPHGRAVE	George Alfred	40		Son	Unm	1	M		Herts	St Stephens
218	EPHGRAVE	Mary	40		Mother-in-law	Widow	57	F	Annuitant	Essex	Dunmow
219	EPHGRAVE	William	40		Brother	Unm	27	M	Blacksmith	Herts	Sandridge
220	HAWKINS	William	40		Lodger	Widower	60	M	Agric Lab	Herts	Abbots Langley
221	HOLINSHEAD	John	41	Little Munden	Head	Mar	39	M	Farmer of 140 acres employing 5 labourers	Beds	Hudnall
222	HOLINSHEAD	Catherine	41		Wife	Mar	34	F	Farmers Wife	Herts	Chipping Barnet
223	HOLINSHEAD	John Edward	41		Son	Unm	4	M	Farmers Son	Herts	North Mimms
224	HOLINSHEAD	Joseph Thomas	41		Son	Unm	2	M	Farmers Son	Herts	North Mimms
225	ROBERTS	Mary	41		Serv	Unm	18	F	House Servant	Bucks	Waddesdon
226	HEWITT	William	41		Serv	Unm	19	M	Agric Lab	Herts	St Stephens
227	KEEN	Thomas	41		Serv	Unm	18	M	Agric Lab	Herts	Rickmansworth
228	LYON	John	42	Bricket Wood	Head	Mar	63	M	Farmer of 5 acres	Herts	Wilstone
229	LYON	Sarah	42		Wife	Mar	63	F		Herts	Stevenage
230	EDMONDS	John	43	Bricket Wood	Head	Mar	26	M	Agric Lab	Herts	Abbots Langley
231	EDMONDS	Hannah	43		Wife	Mar	24	F		Herts	St Stephens
232	EDMONDS	John	43		Son	Unm	5	M	Scholar	Herts	St Stephens
233	EDMONDS	William	43		Son	Unm	2	M		Herts	St Stephens
234	EDMONDS	Hannah	43		Dau	Unm	1 m	F		Herts	St Stephens
235	HANDLEY	William	44	Bricket Wood	Head	Mar	37	M	Agric Lab	Herts	Kings Walden
236	HANDLEY	Maria	44		Wife	Mar	32	F	Straw Plaiter	Herts	St Peters
237	HANDLEY	Mary Ann	44		Dau	Unm	8	F	Scholar	Herts	Wheathampstead
238	HANDLEY	Susannah	44		Dau	Unm	6	F	Scholar	Herts	St Stephens
239	HANDLEY	Sarah	44		Dau	Unm	4	F		Herts	St Stephens
240	HANDLEY	Emily	44		Dau	Unm	2	F		Herts	St Stephens
241	HANDLEY	Elizabeth	44		Dau	Unm	9 wks	F		Herts	St Stephens
242	HYOM	Henry	45	Bricket Wood	Head	Mar	22	M	Agric Lab	Herts	Hatfield
243	HYOM	Mary Ann	45		Wife	Mar	21	F		Herts	St Stephens
244	HYOM	William	45		Son	Unm	1	M		Herts	Watford
245	COLLEY	Jesse	46	Bricket Wood	Head	Mar	36	M	Agric Lab	Herts	Watford
246	COLLEY	Sarah	46		Wife	Mar	42	F		Herts	St Stephens
247	COLLEY	George	46		Son	Unm	7	M	Scholar	Herts	St Stephens
248	COLLEY	Samuel	46		Son	Unm	5	M	Scholar	Herts	St Stephens
249	ROFFE	James	47	Bricket Wood	Head	Mar	62	M	Carpenter	Herts	St Stephens
250	ROFFE	Phillis	47		Wife	Mar	50	F		Herts	St Stephens

251	ROFFE	Charles	47		Son	Unm	17	M	Agric Lab	Herts	St Stephens
252	ROFFE	Ann	47		Grandau	Unm	7	F	Scholar	Herts	St Stephens
253	KILBY	James	48	Bricket Wood	Head	Mar	52	M	Agric Lab	Herts	St Stephens
254	KILBY	Susannah	48		Wife	Mar	51	F		Herts	St Stephens
255	KILBY	William	48		Son	Unm	17	M	Agric Lab	Herts	Aldenham
256	KILBY	Hannah	48		Dau	Unm	14	F	Brazilian Hat Maker	Herts	Aldenham
257	KILBY	Peter	48		Son	Unm	10	M	Agric Lab	Herts	Aldenham
258	DYKE	Matilda	49	Bricket Wood	Head	Unm	29	F	Schoolmistress	Middx	St Georges, Stepney
259	BURMINGHAM	Mary Ann	49		Visitor	Unm	24	F	Schoolmistress	Surrey	Wandsworth
260	GATHERN	John	50	Bricket Wood	Head	Mar	69	M	Agric Lab	Herts	St Stephens
261	GATHERN	Sarah	50		Wife	Mar	55	F		Herts	St Stephens
262	GATHERN	George	50		Son	Unm	15	M	Agric Lab	Herts	St Stephens
263	HUMPHRYES	John	51	Bricket Wood	Head	Mar	36	M	Agric Lab	Herts	St Stephens
264	HUMPHRYES	Jane	51		Wife	Mar	34	F		Herts	St Stephens
265	HUMPHRYES	George	51		Son	Unm	13	M	Agric Lab	Herts	St Stephens
266	HUMPHRYES	James	51		Son	Unm	11	M	Scholar	Herts	St Stephens
267	HUMPHRYES	Alfred	51		Son	Unm	6	M	Scholar	Herts	St Stephens
268	HUMPHRYES	Emma	51		Dau	Unm	3	F		Herts	St Stephens
269	HUMPHRYES	Eliza	51		Dau	Unm	11 m	F		Herts	St Stephens
270	HAYLOCK	Giles	52	Bricket Wood	Head	Mar	35	M	Game Keeper	Suffolk	Cowlinge
271	HAYLOCK	Jane	52		Wife	Mar	35	F		Herts	Anstey
272	HAYLOCK	Sidney	52		Son	Unm	14	M		Herts	Anstey
273	HAYLOCK	Henry	52		Son	Unm	7	M	Scholar	Herts	Anstey
274	HAYLOCK	George	52		Son	Unm	4	M	Scholar	Herts	St Stephens
275	HAYLOCK	Emma	52		Dau	Unm	2	F		Herts	St Stephens
276	BARTLAM	Samuel	53	Bricket Wood	Head	Mar	44	M	Agric Lab	Herts	Great Gaddesden
277	BARTLAM	Hannah	53		Wife	Mar	30	F	Straw Plaiter	Herts	St Stephens
278	BARTLAM	Mary	53		Dau	Unm	8	F	Scholar	Herts	St Stephens
279	BARTLAM	Sarah	53		Dau	Unm	5	F	Scholar	Herts	St Stephens
280	BARTLAM	William	53		Son	Unm	2	M		Herts	St Stephens
281	FLITT	Henry	54	Bricket Wood	Head	Mar	27	M	Horse Breaker	Middx	Pinner
282	FLITT	Hannah	54		Wife	Mar	31	F	Dressmaker	Herts	St Stephens
283	FLITT	Fanncy	54		Dau	Unm	3	F		Herts	Abbots Langley
284	FLITT	Mary Ann	54		Dau	Unm	1	F		Herts	St Stephens
285	FLITT	Sarah	54		Dau	Unm	2 m	F		Herts	St Stephens
286	DEACON	Edward	55	Bricket Wood	Head	Mar	26	M	Agric Lab	Herts	St Stephens
287	DEACON	Ann	55		Wife	Mar	27	F		Herts	St Stephens
288	DEACON	Mary Ann	55		Dau	Unm	3	F		Herts	St Stephens
289	DEACON	John	55		Son	Unm	1	M		Herts	St Stephens
290	DEACON	Joseph	55		Father	Widower	70	M	Agric Lab	Herts	St Stephens
291	ASHBY	William	56	Bricket Wood	Head	Mar	77	M	Agric Lab	Herts	Abbots Langley
292	ASHBY	Sarah	56		Wife	Mar	66	F	Straw Plaiter	Herts	St Stephens
293	ASHBY	Joseph	56		Son	Unm	39	M	Agric Lab	Herts	St Stephens
294	QUICKS	William	57	Bricket Wood	Head	Mar	50	M	Agric Lab	Herts	St Stephens
295	QUICKS	Barbary	57		Wife	Mar	42	F		Herts	St Stephens

	SURNAME	FORENAME	SCHEDULE NUMBER	ADDRESS	RELATIONSHIP	STATUS	AGE	SEX	OCCUPATION	COUNTY OF BIRTH	PLACE OF BIRTH
296	QUICKS	William	57		Son	Unm	19	M	Agric Lab	Herts	St Stephens
297	QUICKS	Mary	57		Dau	Unm	11	F	Scholar	Herts	St Stephens
298	QUICKS	Alfred	57		Son	Unm	6	M	Scholar	Herts	St Stephens
299	QUICKS	James	57		Son	Unm	4	M		Herts	St Stephens
300	KENTISH	Daniel	58	Bricket Wood	Head	Mar	57	M	Beershop & Agric Lab	Herts	St Stephens
301	KENTISH	Charlotte	58		Wife	Mar	48	F		Herts	St Stephens
302	KENTISH	Ann	58		Dau	Unm	22	F	Brazilian Hat Maker	Herts	St Stephens
303	KENTISH	Charlotte	58		Dau	Unm	12	F	Scholar	Herts	St Stephens
304	SMITH	Samuel	59	Bricket Wood	Head	Mar	48	M	Agric Lab	Herts	Aldenham
305	SMITH	Elizabeth	59		Wife	Mar	52	F	Straw Plaiter	Herts	Wheathampstead
306	SMITH	Sarah	59		Dau	Unm	22	F	Brazilian Hat Maker	Herts	St Stephens
307	SMITH	Joseph	59		Son	Unm	14	M	Agric Lab	Herts	St Stephens
308	SMITH	Samuel	59		Son	Unm	11	M	Agric Lab	Herts	St Stephens
309	SMITH	George	59		Son	Unm	9	M	Scholar	Herts	St Stephens
310	SMITH	William	59		Son	Unm	1	M		Herts	St Stephens
311	WOODWARD	William	60	Bricket Wood	Head	Mar	60	M	Agric Lab	Herts	Abbots Langley
312	WOODWARD	Ann	60		Wife	Mar	56	F		Herts	St Stephens
313	WOODWARD	Eliza	60		Dau	Unm	23	F	Brazilian Hat Maker	Herts	St Stephens
314	WOODWARD	Joseph	60		Son	Unm	14	M	Agric Lab	Herts	St Stephens
315	WOODWARD	Emma	60		Dau	Unm	11	F	Scholar	Herts	St Stephens
316	KENTISH	Thomas	61	Bricket Wood	Head	Mar	25	M	Gardener	Herts	St Stephens
317	KENTISH	Susan	61		Wife	Mar	29	F		Cornwall	[Unknown]
318	KENTISH	Mary Ann	61		Dau	Unm	2	F		Herts	St Stephens
319	KENTISH	Jane	61		Dau	Unm	1 m	F		Herts	St Stephens
320	GATHERN	William	62	Bricket Wood	Head	Mar	23	M	Agric Lab	Herts	St Stephens
321	GATHERN	Susan	62		Wife	Mar	22	F		Herts	St Stephens
322	SMITH	Philip	63	Bricket Wood	Head	Mar	33	M	Agric Lab	Beds	Luton
323	SMITH	Elizabeth	63		Wife	Mar	29	F		Herts	St Stephens
324	SMITH	Caroline	63		Dau	Unm	6	F	Scholar	Herts	St Stephens
325	SMITH	George	63		Son	Unm	1	M		Herts	St Stephens
326	NORWOOD	Thomas	64	Bricket Wood	Head	Mar	42	M	Agric Lab	Herts	Watford
327	NORWOOD	Mary	64		Wife	Mar	38	F		Herts	Abbots Langley
328	NORWOOD	Fanny	64		Dau	Unm	19	F	Brazilian Hat Maker	Herts	Abbots Langley
329	NORWOOD	Edward	64		Son	Unm	13	M	Agric Lab	Herts	Watford
330	NORWOOD	Maria	64		Dau	Unm	9	F	Scholar	Herts	Watford
331	NORWOOD	Ann	64		Dau	Unm	9	F	Scholar	Herts	Watford
332	NORWOOD	James	64		Son	Unm	7	M	Scholar	Herts	St Stephens
333	NORWOOD	Louisa	64		Dau	Unm	1	F		Herts	St Stephens
334	NORWOOD	William	64		Son	Unm	2 wks	M		Herts	St Stephens
335	NORWOOD	Samuel	64		Grandson	Unm	1 m	M		Herts	St Stephens
336	DOUSE	John	65	Bricket Wood	Head	Widower	66	M	Agric Lab	Herts	Abbots Langley
337	NORWOOD	John	65		Grandson	Unm	15	M	Agric Lab	Herts	St Stephens
338	HOOPER	John	66	Bricket Wood	Head	Mar	27	M	Carpenter & Beershop	Herts	Aldenham
339	HOOPER	Mary	66		Wife	Mar	33	F		Herts	St Stephens
340	HOOPER	Mary	66		Dau	Unm	10 m	F		Herts	St Stephens

341	NEALE	Maria	67	Bricket Wood	Head	Widow	48	F		Herts	St Stephens
342	NEALE	Thomas	67		Son	Unm	15	M	Agric Lab	Herts	St Stephens
343	NEALE	William	67		Son	Unm	14	M	Agric Lab	Herts	St Stephens
344	NEALE	George	67		Son	Unm	12	M	Agric Lab	Herts	St Stephens
345	NEALE	Richard	67		Son	Unm	10	M	Agric Lab	Herts	St Stephens
346	NEALE	Jane	67		Dau	Unm	9	F	School	Herts	St Stephens
347	BIGNALL	Samuel	67		Lodger	Unm	25	M	Agric Lab	Herts	Abbots Langley
348	LOUGH	Mary	68	Aldenham Abbey	Head	Widow	51	F	Housekeeper	N'thumb	Berwick-upon-Tweed
349	KELLY	Susan	68		Serv	Unm	40	F	Housemaid	Kent	Woolwich
350	JONES	Elizabeth	68		Serv	Unm	27	F	Laundry Maid	Kent	Greenwich
351	EAMES	Esther	68		Serv	Unm	17	F	Laundry Maid	Herts	Aldenham
352	CUTHBERK	James	68		Serv	Unm	26	M	Gardener	Scotland	[Unknown]
353	TOOKEY	Stephen	69	Blackbirds	Head	Mar	48	M	Farmer of 140 acres employing 7 labourers	Herts	Watford
354	TOOKEY	Sarah	69		Wife	Mar	50	F	Farmers Wife	Bucks	Wycombe
355	TOOKEY	Stephen	69		Son	Unm	24	M	Farmers Son	Herts	Watford
356	TOOKEY	Sarah	69		Dau	Unm	23	F	Farmers Daur	Herts	Watford
357	TOOKEY	Emma	69		Dau	Unm	19	F	Farmers Daur	Herts	Watford
358	CLARKE	William	69		Serv	Unm	60	M	Agric Lab	Bucks	Bledlow Ridge
359	WHITE	William	69		Serv	Unm	21	M	Agric Lab	Bucks	Bledlow Ridge
360	YOUNG	John	70	Newlands	Head	Mar	49	M	Farmer of 70 acres employing 2 labourers	Oxon	Over Norton
361	YOUNG	Sarah	70		Wife	Mar	42	F	Farmers Wife	London	London
362	YOUNG	Sarah Ann	70		Dau	Unm	8	F	Farmers Daughter	London	London
363	YOUNG	Amelia	70		Dau	Unm	4	F	Farmers Daughter & Scholar	Herts	St Stephens
364	ANDREWS	William	70		Serv	Unm	14	M	Agric Lab	Herts	Aldenham
365	LOVELL	Joseph	71	The Hill Farm	Head	Mar	58	M	Farmer of 350 acres employing 14 labourers	Herts	St Stephens
366	LOVELL	Elizabeth	71		Wife	Mar	63	F		Herts	Sandridge
367	LOVELL	Henry	71		Son	Unm	28	M	Farmers Son	Herts	St Stephens
368	CLARK	Eliza	71		Serv	Unm	17	F	House Servant	Herts	St Stephens
369	SLAUGHTER	William	71		Serv	Unm	40	M	Agric Lab	Herts	St Stephens
370	FIGEON/FITZJOHN	John	71		Serv	Unm	24	M	Agric Lab	Herts	St Pauls Walden
371	CONSTABLE	William	71		Serv	Unm	19	M	Agric Lab	Herts	Aldenham
372	TIMSON	George	71		Serv	Unm	15	M	Agric Lab	Herts	Aldenham
373	PICTON	John	71		Serv	Unm	14	M	Agric Lab	Herts	St Stephens
374	SMITH	Ralph	72	The Wild Farm	Head	Unm	60	M	Farmer of 300 acres employing 10 men & 5 boys	Herts	St Stephens
375	WAGHORN	Ann	72		Sister	Widow	72	F	Housekeeper	Herts	St Stephens
376	WAGHORN	Sarah	72		Visitor	Unm	63	F	Fund Holder	Essex	Romford
377	WEEDON	Sarah	72		Serv	Unm	18	F	Cook	Herts	St Stephens
378	HOW	Ann	72		Serv	Unm	15	F	Housemaid	Herts	Aldenham
379	PEARCE	George	72		Serv	Unm	24	M	Agric Lab	Herts	Wheathampstead
380	KING	Philip	72		Serv	Unm	18	M	Agric Lab	Herts	St Peters
381	TURNER	William	73	Wild Farm Cottages	Head	Mar	29	M	Agric Lab	Herts	St Albans
382	TURNER	Elizabeth	73		Wife	Mar	35	F		Herts	St Stephens
383	TURNER	William	73		Son	Unm	7	M	Scholar	Herts	St Stephens
384	TURNER	Sarah	73		Dau	Unm	5	F	Scholar	Herts	St Stephens

	SURNAME	FORENAME	SCHEDULE NUMBER	ADDRESS	RELATIONSHIP	STATUS	AGE	SEX	OCCUPATION	COUNTY OF BIRTH	PLACE OF BIRTH
385	TURNER	Eliza	73		Dau	Unm	8 m	F		Herts	St Stephens
386	BEVERSTOCK	Jasper	73		Lodger	Unm	29	M		Wilts	Corton
387	PLACEHAM	William	74	Wild Farm Cottages	Head	Mar	26	M	Agric Lab	Herts	Harpenden
388	PLACEHAM	Ann	74		Wife	Mar	27	F	Straw Plaiter	Herts	Hatfield
389	PLACEHAM	William	74		Son	Unm	2	M		Herts	St Stephens
390	SHARP	Matthew	75	Wild Farm Cottages	Head	Mar	25	M	Agric Lab	Herts	St Stephens
391	SHARP	Martha	75		Wife	Mar	22	F	Brazilian Hat Maker	Herts	St Stephens
392	SHARP	James	75		Son	Unm	1	M		Herts	St Stephens
393	WALLER	John	76	Wild Farm Cottages	Head	Mar	63	M	Agric Lab	Beds	Streatley
394	WALLER	Elenor	76		Wife	Mar	58	F		Herts	St Stephens
395	WALLER	John	76		Son	Mar	28	M	Agric Lab	Herts	St Stephens
396	WALLER	Harriett	76		Dau-in-law	Mar	25	F	Brazilian Hat Maker	Oxon	Piddington
397	WALLER	Mary Ann	76		Grandau	Unm	1	F		Herts	St Stephens
398	WEEDON	James	77	Bottom House	Head	Mar	33	M	Farmer of 80 acres employing 2 labourers	Herts	St Stephens
399	WEEDON	Eliza	77		Wife	Mar	37	F		Herts	Abbots Langley
400	WEEDON	Mary Ann	77		Dau	Unm	12	F	Scholar	Herts	St Stephens
401	WEEDON	James	77		Son	Unm	10	M	Scholar	Herts	St Stephens
402	WEEDON	Emma	77		Dau	Unm	7	F	Scholar	Herts	St Stephens
403	WEEDON	Hannah	77		Dau	Unm	5	F		Herts	St Stephens
404	WEEDON	Ann	77		Dau	Unm	4	F		Herts	St Stephens
405	WEEDON	Letitia	77		Dau	Unm	1	F		Herts	St Stephens
406	MUNT	Letitia	77		Mother	Widow	71	F		Herts	Bovingdon
407	WHITE	Ephraim	78	Lodge Cottage	Head	Mar	28	M	Gardener	Herts	St Stephens
408	WHITE	Mary Ann	78		Wife	Mar	28	F	Laundress	Herts	Shenley
409	WHITE	James	78		Son	Unm	3	M		Herts	Aldenham
410	WHITE	John	78		Son	Unm	5 m	M		Herts	Aldenham
411	ASHBURNHAM	Theodona	79	Lodge Cottage	Head	Unm	38	F	Earl's Daughter	Suffolk	Barking Heath
412	MARSHALL	Mary	79		Serv	Unm	24	F	House Servant	Kent	Lee
413	RUMENS	Sarah	79		Serv	Unm	17	F	House Servant	Kent	Lee
414	YOUNGER	William	79		Serv	Unm	27	M	House Servant	London	London
415	COOK	Alfred	80	Moor Mill	Head	Mar	30	M	Miller employing 2 Millers & 1 Agric Lab	Herts	Hemel Hempstead
416	COOK	Amy	80		Wife	Mar	31	F		Bucks	Stony Stratford
417	COOK	Louisa	80		Dau	Unm	4	F		Herts	Hemel Hempstead
418	COOK	Ebenezer	80		Son	Unm	3	M		Herts	Hemel Hempstead
419	COOK	Ruth	80		Dau	Unm	1	F		Herts	St Stephens
420	COOK	Amy	80		Dau	Unm	3 wks	F		Herts	St Stephens
421	BARNES	Dinah	80		Serv	Unm	28	F	House Servant	Herts	Abbots Langley
422	BAILEY	Mary	80		Nurse	Widow	45	F	Nurse	Herts	St Albans
423	FENN	Thomas	81	Pest House	Head	Mar	67	M	Farmer of 6 acres	Herts	Aubury [Albury?]
424	FENN	Sarah	81		Wife	Mar	61	F		Herts	St Stephens
425	FENN	Ann	81		Dau	Unm	30	F	Brazilian Hat Maker	Herts	St Stephens
426	FENN	George	81		Son	Unm	22	M	Agric Lab	Herts	St Stephens
427	FENN	John	81		Son	Unm	20	M	Agric Lab	Herts	St Stephens
428	ELLWOOD	Edward	82	Pest House	Head	Mar	56	M	Agric Lab	Herts	Rickmansworth
429	ELLWOOD	Abigail	82		Wife	Mar	55	F	Straw Plaiter	Herts	St Stephens

430	RICE	Ann	82		Dau & Visitor	Mar	31	F	Straw Plaiter	Herts	St Stephens
431	ELLWOOD	Hannah	82		Dau	Unm	27	F	Brazilian Hat Maker	Herts	St Stephens
432	ELLWOOD	John	82		Son	Unm	13	M	Agric Lab	Herts	St Stephens
433	ELLWOOD	Abraham	82		Son	Unm	11	M	Scholar	Herts	St Stephens
434	FENN	Thomas	83	Pest House	Head	Mar	25	M	Agric Lab	Herts	St Stephens
435	FENN	Ann	83		Wife	Mar	20	F	Brazilian Hat Maker	Herts	St Michaels

One house uninhabited

End of the District of Park Ward West

Registrar's District: St Albans   Enumeration District 6b   Ref. HO 107/1713 folios 549-72

Park Ward east of the Edgeware Road and also the houses in such ward, abutting on such road.

Park Ward, Borough of St Albans

436	STAMMERS	John B.	1	Holywell House	Head	Mar	44	M	Gas Manufacturer	Middx	London
437	STAMMERS	Samuel J.	1		Son		13	M	Scholar	Surrey	Clapham
438	STAMMERS	Charlotte	1		Dau		11	F	Scholar	Surrey	Clapham
439	STAMMERS	Arthur N.	1		Son		8	M	Scholar	Surrey	Clapham
440	STAMMERS	Charles H.	1		Son		6	M		Herts	St Albans
441	STAMMERS	Alice	1		Dau		3	F		Herts	St Albans
442	QUILCH	Emma	1		Serv	Unm	18	F	House servant	Herts	Chenies
443	HARDY	William	2	Gas works	Head	Mar	25	M	Gas Man	Ireland	Belfast
444	HARDY	Maria	2		Wife	Mar	27	F		Herts	Rickmansworth
445	HARDY	Susan E.	2		Dau		3	F		Surrey	Lambeth
446	HARDY	Andrew	2		Son		0	M		Herts	St Albans
447	GIBBS	William	2		Son-in-law		9	M	Scholar	Herts	Rickmansworth
448	GIBBS	James	3	Gas works	Head	Mar	26	M	Lab at gas works	Herts	Chorley Wood
449	GIBBS	Rebecca	3		Wife	Mar	23	F		Herts	Chorley Wood
450	GIBBS	Eliza	3		Dau		2	F		Herts	Chorley Wood

End of the Borough of St Albans within the Parish of St Stephens.

Park Ward

451	HOLT	Edward	4	Sportsmans Hall	Head	Mar	55	M	Agric Lab	Herts	Great Gaddesden
452	HOLT	Hannah	4		Wife	Mar	48	F	Weaver	Herts	St Michaels
453	HOLT	Emma	4		Dau	Unm	23	F	Weaver of canvas	Herts	St Peters
454	HOLT	George	4		Son	Unm	19	M	Weaver	Herts	St Stephens
455	HOLT	Eliza	4		Dau	Unm	16	F	Weaver. Shoot filler	Herts	St Stephens
456	HOLT	Edmond	4		Son		8	M	Scholar	Herts	St Stephens
457	HOLT	Ann	4		Dau		6	F	Scholar	Herts	St Stephens
458	HOLT	Harriott	4		Dau		4	F		Herts	St Stephens
459	HOLT	Frederick	4		Grandson		3	M		Herts	St Stephens
460	LAWRENCE	George	5	Sportsmans Hall	Head	Mar	38	M	Miller (Journeyman)	Herts	Harpenden
461	LAWRENCE	Mary	5		Wife	Mar	32	F		Herts	Harpenden
462	LAWRENCE	David	5		Son		9	M	Scholar	Herts	Harpenden
463	LAWRENCE	George	5		Son		6	M	Scholar	Herts	St Albans
464	LAWRENCE	Hannah	5		Dau		2	F		Herts	St Albans

	SURNAME	FORENAME	SCHEDULE NUMBER	ADDRESS	RELATIONSHIP	STATUS	AGE	SEX	OCCUPATION	COUNTY OF BIRTH	PLACE OF BIRTH
465	CHAD	Sarah	5		Mother-in-law	Widow	69	F	Formerly Agric Labs wife	Herts	Wheathampstead
466	LONG	Abraham	6	Sopwell Mill	Head	Unm	25	M	Agric Lab	Herts	Hexton
467	SNOXALL	David	7	New Barns	Head	Mar	45	M	Agric Lab	Beds	Dunstable
468	SNOXALL	Jane	7		Wife	Mar	36	F	Laundress	Herts	St Peters
469	SNOXALL	Eliza	7		Dau	Unm	17	F	Laundress	Herts	St Peters
470	SNOXALL	Sarah	7		Dau		11	F	Laundress	Herts	St Peters
471	SNOXALL	David	7		Son		8	M	Scholar	Herts	St Peters
472	SNOXALL	Jane	7		Dau		3	F		Herts	St Stephens
473	SNOXALL	George	7		Son		8 m	M		Herts	St Stephens
474	WEATHERLEY	George	8	Sopwell Barns	Head	Mar	34	M	Agric Lab	Herts	St Stephens
475	WEATHERLEY	Jane	8		Wife	Mar	35	F		Herts	St Michaels
476	WEATHERLEY	Joseph	8		Father	Widower	70	M	Agric Lab	Herts	Sandridge
477	HANSHAW	Thomas	9	Sopwell Barns	Head	Widower	76	M	Agric Lab (shepherd)	Bucks	Weston Favel

Village of Park Street

	SURNAME	FORENAME	SCHEDULE NUMBER	ADDRESS	RELATIONSHIP	STATUS	AGE	SEX	OCCUPATION	COUNTY OF BIRTH	PLACE OF BIRTH
478	WRIGHT	William	10	Bury Dell	Head	Widower	68	M	Wheelwright	Herts	St Stephens
479	SARGENT	Sarah	10		Dau	Mar	36	F		Herts	St Stephens
480	SARGENT	Robert	10		Son-in-law	Mar	39	M	Painter	Middx	Shoreditch
481	SARGENT	Emily	10		Grandau		7	F	Scholar	Middx	Grays Inn
482	SARGENT	Alice	10		Grandau		5	F		Middx	Grays Inn
483	SARGENT	Frederick	10		Grandson		3	M		Middx	Edgware
484	SARGENT	Eliza	10		Grandau		9 m	F		Middx	Edgware
485	WILLSON	Henry	11	Bury Dell	Head	Mar	30	M	Police Constable (rural)	Herts	Hatfield
486	WILLSON	Hannah	11		Wife	Mar	30	F		Beds	Dunstable
487	STARKINS	James	12	Bury Dell	Head	Mar	41	M	Agric Lab	Herts	Redbourn
488	STARKINS	Sarah	12		Wife	Mar	43	F		Beds	Shefford
489	STARKINS	George	12		Son		10	M	Scholar	Herts	St Stephens
490	STARKINS	Joseph	12		Son		8	M		Herts	St Stephens
491	STARKINS	Thomas	12		Son		5	M	Scholar	Herts	St Stephens
492	STARKINS	John	12		Son		3	M		Herts	St Stephens
493	STARKINS	Fanny	12		Dau		1	F		Herts	St Stephens
494	BOFF	James	13	Bury Dell	Head	Mar	35	M	Sawyer	Herts	St Stephens
495	BOFF	Charlotte	13		Wife	Mar	31	F		Herts	St Stephens
496	BOFF	Samuel	13		Son		2	M		Herts	St Stephens
497	BOFF	Eliza Jane	13		Dau		1	F		Herts	St Stephens
498	ANDERSON	Benjamin	14	Bury Dell	Head	Mar	25	M	Agric Lab	Herts	St Stephens
499	ANDERSON	Eliza	14		Wife	Mar	24	F		Herts	St Stephens
500	ANDERSON	Susan	14		Dau		4	F		Herts	St Stephens
501	ANDERSON	Lydia	14		Dau		11 m	F		Herts	St Stephens
502	ENGLAND	George	14		Lodger	Unm	36	M	Agric Lab	Herts	St Stephens
503	BOFF	James	15	Bury Dell	Head	Mar	60	M	Sawyer	Herts	St Stephens
504	BOFF	Anne	15		Wife	Mar	55	F		Herts	St Stephens
505	BOFF	Samuel	15		Son	Unm	30	M	Sawyer (Deaf and Dumb)	Herts	St Stephens
506	BOFF	Joseph	15		Son	Unm	30	M	Shoemaker (Deaf and Dumb)	Herts	St Stephens
507	BOFF	Mary	15		Dau	Unm	27	F	Straw bonnet maker	Herts	St Stephens

508	BOFF	Arthur	15		Son	Unm	16	M	Sawyer	Herts	St Stephens
509	BOFF	George	16	Park Street	Head	Mar	33	M	Timber merchant employing 2 men	Herts	St Stephens
510	BOFF	Mary Ann	16		Wife	Mar	33	F		Herts	St Stephens
511	BOFF	Frederick	16		Son		10	M	Scholar (Blind)	Herts	St Stephens
512	BOFF	Sarah	16		Dau		8	F	Scholar	Herts	St Stephens
513	BOFF	Mary Ann	16		Dau		5	F	Scholar	Herts	St Stephens
514	BOFF	Henry	16		Son		1	M		Herts	St Stephens
515	BARR	Thomas	17	Park Street	Head	Mar	44	M	Agric Lab	Herts	St Stephens
516	BARR	Elizabeth	17		Wife	Mar	49	F		Bucks	Cheddington
517	BARR	Catherine	17		Dau	Unm	17	F	Brazilian Hat Maker	Herts	St Stephens
518	BARR	Philip	17		Son		10	M	Scholar	Herts	Boxmoor
519	BARR	Louisa	17		Niece		9	F	Scholar	Herts	St Stephens
520	ENGLAND	Joseph	17		Lodger	Unm	34	M	Agric Lab	Herts	St Stephens
521	DICKINSON	William	18	Park Street	Head	Mar	34	M	Higgler	Herts	St Stephens
522	DICKINSON	Mary	18		Wife	Mar	37	F		Herts	Berkhamsted
523	DICKINSON	Herbert	18		Son		11	M	Scholar	Herts	St Stephens
524	COOK	John	19	Park Street	Head	Mar	55	M	Agric Lab	Herts	Redbourn
525	COOK	Dorcas	19		Wife	Mar	56	F		Herts	St Stephens
526	COOK	Emma	19		Dau		12	F	Scholar	Herts	St Stephens
527	EAST	George	20	Park Street	Head	Mar	37	M	Agric Lab	Herts	Abbots Langley
528	EAST	Ruth	20		Wife	Mar	39	F		Herts	Abbots Langley
529	EAST	William	20		Son		14	M	Agric Lab	Herts	Aldenham
530	EAST	George	20		Son		12	M	Agric Lab	Herts	Aldenham
531	EAST	Sarah	20		Dau		10	F	Scholar	Herts	Aldenham
532	EAST	Joseph	20		Son		8	M	Agric Lab	Herts	St Stephens
533	EAST	Martha	20		Dau		5	F		Herts	St Stephens
534	EAST	Samuel	20		Son		2	M		Herts	St Stephens
535	BEAMENT	George	21	Park Street	Head	Mar	43	M	Miller employing 3 men	Middx	South Mimms
536	BEAMENT	Ann	21		Wife	Mar	36	F		Herts	St Stephens
537	BEAMENT	Edwin	21		Son	Unm	20	M	Miller	Herts	St Stephens
538	BEAMENT	Ann	21		Dau	Unm	14	F		Herts	St Stephens
539	BEAMENT	Charles	21		Son		15	M	Scholar	Herts	St Stephens
540	BEAMENT	James	21		Son		2	M		Herts	St Stephens
541	HILL	Sarah	21		Serv	Mar	24	F	Cook	Herts	Hatfield
542	HANSCOMBE	Hepzibah	21		Serv	Unm	17	F	Nursemaid	Herts	St Albans
543	FENSOM	Edward	22	Park Street	Head	Mar	53	M	Baker	Herts	St Stephens
544	FENSOM	Pricilla	22		Wife	Mar	53	F		Herts	St Stephens
545	FENSOM	Thomas	22		Son	Unm	29	M	Baker	Herts	St Stephens
546	FENSOM	Martha	22		Mother	Widow	47	F	Formerly grocer	Herts	Kinsworth
547	TOMS	Hannah	23	Park Street	Head	Widow	44	F	Straw Plaiter	Herts	St Stephens
548	HALL	Elizabeth	23		Sister	Unm	27	M	Pauper	Herts	St Stephens
549	TOMS	William	23		Son	Mar	26	M	Agric Lab	Herts	St Stephens
550	TOMS	Mary Anne	23		Dau	Unm	24	F	Straw Plaiter	Herts	St Stephens
551	TOMS	Ruth	23		Dau-in-law	Mar	26	F		Cambs	Caxton
552	HALL	Emma	23		Grandau		3	F		Herts	St Stephens

	SURNAME	FORENAME	SCHEDULE NUMBER	ADDRESS	RELATIONSHIP	STATUS	AGE	SEX	OCCUPATION	COUNTY OF BIRTH	PLACE OF BIRTH
553	TOMS	Julia	23		Grandau		1	F		Herts	St Stephens
554	MARTIN	George	24	Park Street	Head	Mar	28	M	Master Blacksmith	Herts	St Stephens
555	MARTIN	Susannah	24		Wife	Mar	24	F		Northants	Blakesley
556	MARTIN	George Henry	24		Son		4	M	Scholar	Herts	St Stephens
557	MARTIN	Ann Maria	24		Dau		3	F		Herts	St Stephens
558	MARTIN	Albert	24		Son		3 m	M		Herts	St Stephens
559	MARTIN	Alfred	24		Brother	Unm	19	M	Journeyman Blacksmith	Herts	St Stephens
560	CLARK	Mary	25	Park Street	Head	Widow	52	F	Charwoman	Herts	Sandridge
561	CLARK	Charlotte	25		Dau	Unm	24	F	Brazilian Hat Maker	Herts	St Stephens
562	CLARK	Hannah	25		Dau	Unm	19	F	Housemaid	Herts	St Stephens
563	CLARK	William	25		Son		15	M	Agric Lab	Herts	St Stephens
564	FLETCHER	Samuel	26	Park Street	Head	Mar	39	M	Hat manufacturer	Herts	Sandridge
565	FLETCHER	Eliza	26		Wife	Mar	37	F	Hat manufacturer	Herts	Harpenden
566	FLETCHER	Eliza	26		Dau		13	F	Hat manufacturer	Herts	St Stephens
567	FLETCHER	Elizabeth	26		Dau		11	F	Hat manufacturer	Herts	St Stephens
568	FLETCHER	Samuel	26		Son		8	M	Scholar	Herts	St Stephens
569	MARTIN	Ann	27	Park Street	Head	Widow	52	F	Annuitant	Herts	St Albans
570	SMITH	Joseph	27		Brother	Unm	60	M	Annuitant	Herts	St Albans
571	SMITH	Elizabeth	27		Sister	Unm	45	F	Annuitant	Herts	St Albans
572	MORTON	William	27		Nephew		5	M	Scholar	Middx	London
573	INWOOD	Ann	28	Park Street	Head	Widow	65	F	Dressmaker	Herts	Welwyn
574	ANDERSON	Joseph	29	Park Street	Head	Mar	76	M	Master Carpenter	Herts	St Stephens
575	ANDERSON	Elizabeth	29		Wife	Mar	76	F		Herts	St Stephens
576	ANDERSON	William	30	Park Street	Head	Mar	56	M	Carpenter (Journeyman)	Herts	St Stephens
577	ANDERSON	Maryann	30		Wife	Mar	50	F	Laundress	Herts	St Stephens
578	ANDERSON	Susan	30		Dau	Unm	20	F	Brazilian Hat Maker	Herts	St Stephens
579	ANDERSON	Sarah	30		Dau	Unm	18	F	Brazilian Hat Maker	Herts	St Stephens
580	SMITH	John	31	Park Street	Head	Mar	55	M	Agric Lab	Essex	Bambury
581	SMITH	Sarah	31		Wife	Mar	63	F	Formerly laundress	Beds	Luton
582	SMITH	James	31		Son-in-Law	Mar	33	M	Agric Lab	Kent	Chatham
583	SMITH	Mary	31		Dau	Mar	31	F		Beds	Luton
584	SMITH	Sarah	31		Grandau		4	F		Herts	St Stephens
585	SMITH	John	31		Grandson		2	M		Herts	St Stephens
586	HILL	Ann	32	Park Street	Head	Mar	75	F	Seamstress	Middx	Sheperton
587	ENTICKNAP	Margaret	32		Sister	Unm	65	F	Seamstress	Middx	Sheperton
588	BOTTOM	William	33	Park Street	Head	Mar	46	M	Bricklayer employing 7 men	Herts	St Stephens
589	BOTTOM	Charlotte	33		Wife	Mar	40	F		Herts	Abbots Langley
590	BOTTOM	William	33		Son	Unm	16	M	Bricklayers son	Herts	St Stephens
591	BOTTOM	Francis	33		Son		14	M	Bricklayers son	Herts	St Stephens
592	BOTTOM	Ann	33		Dau		11	F	Scholar	Herts	St Stephens
593	BOTTOM	Mark	33		Son		9	M	Scholar	Herts	St Stephens
594	BOTTOM	John	33		Son		6	M	Scholar	Herts	St Stephens
595	BOTTOM	George	33		Son		6	M	Scholar	Herts	St Stephens
596	BOTTOM	Charlotte	33		Dau		1	F		Herts	St Stephens
597	FENSOM	Elizabeth	33		Cousin	[Unm]	24	F	Servant	Herts	St Stephens

598	HARRIS	Joseph	34	Park Street	Head	Mar	27	M	General dealer	Herts	St Stephens
599	HARRIS	Mary Ann	34		Wife	Mar	27	F		Herts	St Stephens
600	HARRIS	Ann	34		Dau		5	F	Scholar	Herts	St Stephens
601	ANDERSON	Martha	34		Sister-in-law		11	F	Scholar	Herts	St Stephens
602	LEE	William	35	Park Street	Head	Mar	46	M	Agric Lab	Herts	St Stephens
603	LEE	Sarah	35		Wife	Mar	52	F		Herts	St Stephens
604	LEE	Sam	35		Son	Unm	18	M	Agric Lab	Herts	St Stephens
605	LEE	Sarah	35		Dau		13	F	Scholar	Herts	St Stephens
606	LEE	Mary	35		Dau		11	F	Scholar	Herts	St Stephens
607	MITCHELL	Samuel	36	Park Street	Head	Mar	49	M	Agric Lab	Herts	Great Gaddesden
608	MITCHELL	Mahala	36		Wife	Mar	46	F		Sussex	East Dean
609	MITCHELL	Joseph Wm.	36		Son		11	M	Scholar	Herts	St Stephens
610	FOSTER	Joseph	37	Park Street	Head	Mar	59	M	Shoemaker	Beds	Luton
611	FOSTER	Mary	37		Wife	Mar	52	F		Herts	St Stephens
612	SEABROOK	Mary	38	Park Street	Head	Widow	50	F	Charwoman	Herts	St Albans
613	HOW	Isaac	39	Park Street	Head	Mar	55	M	Agric Lab	Herts	Bovingdon
614	HOW	Sarah	39		Wife	Mar	58	F		Herts	Bovingdon
615	HOW	Isaac	39		Son	Unm	20	M	Agric Lab	Herts	Park Street [St Stephens]
616	WRIGHT	Frederick	40	Park Street	Head	Mar	37	M	Tailor	Herts	St Stephens
617	WRIGHT	Ann	40		Wife	Mar	40	F	Tailors wife	Herts	St Stephens
618	WRIGHT	William	40		Son		8	M	Scholar	Herts	St Stephens
619	WRIGHT	Frederick	40		Son		6	M	Scholar	Herts	St Stephens
620	DAWE	Mark	40		Nursechild		2	M		Middx	London
621	WRIGHT	Caroline	40		Sister	Widow	48	F	Midwife	Herts	St Stephens
622	WRIGHT	Thomas	40		Nephew		14	M	Scholar	Herts	St Stephens
623	GARFORTH	George	41	Park Street	Head	Mar	31	M	Agric Lab	Herts	St Stephens
624	GARFORTH	Ann	41		Wife	Mar	26	F	Straw Plaiter	Herts	St Stephens
625	GARFORTH	Esther Ann	41		Dau		2	F		Herts	Aldenham
626	GARFORTH	Sarah	41		Dau		11 m	F		Herts	St Stephens
627	SHARP	Henry	42	Park Street	Head	Mar	39	M	Publican	Herts	Batchworth Heath
628	SHARP	Maria Elizabeth	42		Wife	Mar	38	F		Middx	Harefield
629	SHARP	Betsey	42		Dau		4	F		Herts	Aldenham
630	HOLLMAN	William	42		Lodger	Widower	64	M	Tailor	Herts	Berkhamsted
631	PAIN	William	43	Park Street	Head	Mar	50	M	Baker employing 1 man	Herts	St Stephens
632	PAIN	Sarah	43		Wife	Mar	38	F		Hants	Southampton
633	PAIN	Charles	43		Son	Unm	20	M	Baker	Herts	St Stephens
634	PAIN	Susan	43		Dau	Unm	17	F	Bonnet Sewer	Herts	St Stephens
635	PAIN	Elizabeth	43		Dau		14	F		Herts	St Stephens
636	PAIN	Francis	43		Son		11	M	Scholar	Herts	St Stephens
637	PAIN	Mary	43		Dau		9	F	Scholar	Herts	St Stephens
638	PAIN	Sarah	43		Dau		7	F	Scholar	Herts	St Stephens
639	PAIN	Charlotte	43		Dau		8 m	F		Herts	St Stephens
640	WARREN	Thomas	44	Park Street	Head	Mar	29	M	Miller (Journeyman)	Herts	Wheathampstead
641	WARREN	Sarah	44		Wife	Mar	28	F	Bonnet Sewer	Herts	St Stephens
642	WARREN	William	44		Son		7	M	Scholar	Herts	St Stephens

	SURNAME	FORENAME	SCHEDULE NUMBER	ADDRESS	RELATIONSHIP	STATUS	AGE	SEX	OCCUPATION	COUNTY OF BIRTH	PLACE OF BIRTH
643	WARREN	Sarah Ann	44		Dau		5	F	Scholar	Herts	St Stephens
644	WARREN	Hannah Maria	44		Dau		3	F		Herts	St Stephens
645	WARREN	Eliza Jane	44		Dau		8 m	F		Herts	St Stephens
646	EAMES	William	45	Park Street	Head	Mar	36	M	Agric Lab	Herts	St Stephens
647	EAMES	Eliza	45		Wife	Mar	36	F		Herts	North Mimms
648	EAMES	Emma	45		Dau		10	F	Scholar	Herts	St Stephens
649	EAMES	Amelia	45		Dau		9	F	Scholar	Herts	St Stephens
650	EAMES	Eliza	45		Dau		6	F	Scholar	Herts	St Stephens
651	EAMES	Ellen	45		Dau		5	F		Herts	St Stephens
652	EAMES	Anne Maria	45		Dau		1	F		Herts	St Stephens
653	WEEDON	Joseph	46	Park Street	Head	Mar	39	M	Agric Lab	Herts	St Stephens
654	WEEDON	Sarah	46		Wife	Mar	47	F		Cambs	Caxton
655	WEEDON	Joseph	46		Son		14	M	Agric Lab	Cambs	Caxton
656	WEEDON	Eliza	46		Dau		7	F	Scholar	Herts	St Stephens
657	BIGNALL	Thomas	47	Park Street	Head	Mar	46	M	Agric Lab	Herts	Great Gaddesden
658	BIGNALL	Sarah	47		Wife	Mar	45	F		Herts	Abbots Langley
659	BIGNALL	Mary	47		Dau		13	F	Brazilian Hat Maker	Herts	St Stephens
660	BIGNALL	Thomas	47		Son		11	M	Scholar	Herts	Abbots Langley
661	BIGNALL	Job	47		Son		9	M		Herts	Abbots Langley
662	BIGNALL	Jane	47		Dau		4	F		Herts	St Stephens
663	BIGNALL	Rhoda	47		Dau		2	F		Herts	St Stephens
664	CRAFT	George	48	Park Street	Head	Mar	56	M	Agric Lab	Bucks	Horn Hill
665	CRAFT	Sarah	48		Wife	Mar	54	F	Seamstress	Middx	Great Chelsea
666	HILL	James	49	Park Street	Head	Mar	24	M	Carpenter (Journeyman)	Herts	St Stephens
667	HILL	Elizabeth	49		Wife	Mar	25	F	Bonnet Sewer	Herts	St Albans
668	HILL	James	49		Son		1	M		Herts	St Albans
669	SHAW	John	50	Park Street	Head	Mar	25	M	Groom	Middx	London
670	SHAW	Maria	50		Wife	Mar	25	F		Herts	North Mimms
671	SHAW	Thomas	50		Son		1 m	M		Herts	St Stephens
672	ANDREW	Joseph	51	Park Street	Head	Mar	25	M	Bricklayers lab	Herts	St Stephens
673	ANDREW	Sarah Ann	51		Wife	Mar	23	F		Herts	St Stephens
674	HARDING	Walter	52	Park Street	Head	Mar	32	M	Agric Lab	Herts	Redbourn
675	HARDING	Hannah	52		Wife	Mar	28	F		Herts	St Stephens
676	HARDING	Sarah Ann	52		Dau		7	F	Scholar	Herts	St Stephens
677	HARDING	Emma	52		Dau		5	F		Herts	St Stephens
678	HARDING	Frederick	52		Son		3	M		Herts	St Stephens
679	HARDING	John	52		Son		2	M		Herts	St Stephens
680	HARDING	Eliza	52		Dau		3 m	F		Herts	St Stephens
681	ANDERSON	Benjamin	53	Park Street	Head	Mar	77	M	Carpenter	Herts	St Stephens
682	ANDERSON	Ann	53		Wife	Mar	65	F		Herts	Offley
683	HOW	Henry	54	Park Street	Head	Mar	34	M	Agric Lab	Herts	Bovingdon
684	HOW	Lydia	54		Wife	Mar	27	F		Herts	Leverstock Green
685	HOW	Mary Ann	54		Dau		8	F	Scholar	Herts	St Stephens
686	HOW	George	54		Son		3	M		Herts	St Stephens
687	HOW	Daniel	54		Son		1 m	M		Herts	St Stephens

688	BECKINGTON	William	55	Park Street	Head	Mar	51	M	Shoemaker	Herts	St Stephens
689	BECKINGTON	Elizabeth	55		Wife	Mar	45	F		Herts	St Stephens
690	BECKINGTON	William	55		Son	Unm	18	M	Agric Lab	Herts	St Stephens
691	BECKINGTON	Frederic	55		Son		8	M	Scholar	Herts	St Stephens
692	EAMES	Joseph	56	Park Street	Head	Mar	63	M	Agric Lab	Herts	St Stephens
693	EAMES	Elizabeth	56		Wife	Mar	63	F		Herts	St Stephens
694	EAMES	Mary Ann	56		Dau	Unm	28	F	Brazilian Hat Maker	Herts	St Stephens
695	EAMES	Louisa	56		Grandau		9	F	Scholar	Herts	St Stephens
696	EAMES	George	56		Grandson		5	M		Herts	St Stephens
697	WEEDON	Elizabeth	57	Park Street	Head	Widow	66	F	Straw Plaiter	Herts	St Stephens
698	WEEDON	James	57		Son	Unm	29	M	Agric Lab	Herts	St Stephens
699	WEEDON	Eliza	57		Dau	Unm	24	F	Brazilian Hat Maker	Cambs	Caxton
700	WEEDON	Edwin	57		Grandson		5	M		Herts	St Stephens
701	WEEDON	George	57		Grandson		2	M		Herts	St Stephens
702	WEEDON	George	58	Park Street	Head	Mar	36	M	Agric Lab	Herts	St Stephens
703	WEEDON	Charlotte	58		Wife	Mar	31	F		Herts	St Stephens
704	WEEDON	Sarah Ann	58		Dau		8	F	Scholar	Herts	St Stephens
705	WEEDON	Lydia	58		Dau		6	F	Scholar	Herts	St Stephens
706	WEEDON	Charlotte	58		Dau		3	F		Herts	St Stephens
707	GODMAN	George	59	Park Street	Head	Mar	74	M	Agric Lab	Herts	Chipperfield
708	GODMAN	Hannah	59		Wife	Mar	59	F	Washerwoman	Herts	St Stephens
709	DAYTON	William	59		Son-in-law	Mar	32	M	Agric Lab	Herts	St Stephens
710	DAYTON	Ann	59		Dau	Mar	32	F	Straw Plaiter	Herts	St Stephens
711	WEATHERLEY	Thomas	60	Park Street	Head	Unm	41	M	Agric Lab	Herts	St Stephens
712	GODMAN	Hannah	61	Park Street	Head	Widow	60	F	Schoolmistress	Herts	Abbots Langley
713	GODMAN	George	61		Son	Widower	26	M	School Master	Herts	Abbots Langley
714	STOCKSLEY	Francis	62	Park Street	Head	Mar	63	M	Victualler	Beds	Carrington
715	STOCKSLEY	Sarah	62		Wife	Mar	49	F		Herts	St Stephens
716	STOCKSLEY	Susan	62		Dau	Unm	22	F	Bonnet Sewer	Herts	St Michaels
717	STOCKSLEY	James	62		Son	Unm	20	M	Agric Lab	Herts	St Michaels
718	STOCKSLEY	George	62		Son		14	M	Agric Lab	Herts	St Michaels
719	STOCKSLEY	Emily	62		Grandau		3	F		Herts	St Albans
720	WEEDON	George	62		Lodger	Unm	27	M	Agric Lab	Herts	St Stephens
721	HORNETT	George	62		Lodger	Unm	44	M	Agric Lab	Herts	St Stephens
722	DEWY	Amelia	63	Park Street	Head	Unm	22	F	Parish Schoolmistress	Surrey	Camberwell
723	GREEN	Betsey	63		Serv		14	F	House servant	Herts	St Stephens
724	WOODSTOCK	John Wm	64	Park Street	Head	Mar	67	M	Proprietor of houses	Cambs	Newmarket
725	WOODSTOCK	Sophia	64		Wife	Mar	59	F	Fundholder Annuitant	Essex	Colchester
726	GRAVESTOCK	Daniel	65	Park Street	Head	Mar	46	M	Gardener	Herts	St Stephens
727	GRAVESTOCK	Susannah	65		Wife	Mar	47	F		Herts	St Stephens
728	GRAVESTOCK	Jane	65		Dau	Unm	17	F	Brazilian Hat Maker	Herts	St Stephens
729	GRAVESTOCK	William	65		Son		14	M	Servant	Herts	St Stephens
730	GRAVESTOCK	Elizabeth	65		Dau		11	F	Scholar	Herts	St Stephens
731	GRAVESTOCK	Susan	65		Dau		8	F	Scholar	Herts	St Stephens
732	TERRY	James	65		Head	Mar	35	M	Carpenter	Oxon	Thame

	SURNAME	FORENAME	SCHEDULE NUMBER	ADDRESS	RELATIONSHIP	STATUS	AGE	SEX	OCCUPATION	COUNTY OF BIRTH	PLACE OF BIRTH
733	TERRY	Jane	65		Wife	Mar	27	F	Dressmaker	Bucks	Wendover
734	KIRBY	Charles	66	Park Street	Head	Mar	42	M	Agric Lab	Oxon	Tackly
735	KIRBY	Elizabeth	66		Wife	Mar	44	F		Berks	Beden
736	KIRBY	Charles	66		Son	Unm	17	M	Agric Lab	Oxon	Tackly
737	KIRBY	Thomas	66		Son		15	M	Agric Lab·	Oxon	Tackly
738	KIRBY	William	66		Son		10	M	Scholar	Berks	Hampstead
739	KIRBY	John	66		Son		8	M	Scholar	Berks	Hampstead
740	KIRBY	George	66		Son		4	M		Herts	St Stephens
741	KIRBY	Albert	66		Son		10 m	M		Herts	St Stephens
742	SHARP	James	66		Lodger	Unm	24	M	Agric Lab	Herts	St Stephens
743	DICKINSON	Abel	66	Park Street	Head	Mar	54	M	Farmer of 165 acres employing 10 labourers	Herts	Abbots Langley
744	DICKINSON	Mary	66		Wife	Mar	51	F	Farmers wife	Herts	Kings Langley
745	DICKINSON	Mary	66		Dau	Unm	23	F	Farmers daur	Herts	St Stephens
746	DICKINSON	Susan	66		Dau	Unm	21	F	Farmers daur	Herts	St Stephens
747	DICKINSON	Sarah Ann	66		Dau	Unm	15	F	Farmers daur	Herts	St Stephens
748	HAYES	Richard	66		Serv	Unm	25	M	Agric Lab	Herts	St Stephens
749	KNOWLES	James	66		Serv	Unm	20	M	Agric Lab	Herts	St Stephens
750	HOWARD	Thomas	66		Serv	Unm	17	M	Agric Lab	Herts	St Stephens
751	ANDREW	George	66		Serv		13	M	Agric Lab	Herts	St Stephens
752	SHAW	James	67	Park Street	Head	Mar	29	M	Journeyman Miller	Middx	St Marylebone
753	SHAW	Keziah	67		Wife	Mar	34	F		Herts	St Stephens
754	ANDERSON	Charles	68	Park Street	Head	Mar	28	M	Carpenter	Herts	St Stephens
755	ANDERSON	Betsey	68		Wife	Mar	28	F		Beds	Luton
756	ANDERSON	Betsey	68		Dau		6	F	Scholar	Herts	St Stephens
757	SHAW	Jane	69		Wife	Mar	67	F	Coachmans wife	Bucks	Whaddon
758	EGGLETON	Selina	69		Grandau		14	F	Scholar	Middx	Pentonville
759	WARRELL	George	70	Park Street	Head	Mar	32	M	Straw hat and bonnet manufacturer	Herts	St Stephens
760	WARRELL	Catherine	70		Wife	Mar	27	F	Straw hat and bonnet manufacturer	Herts	St Albans
761	WARRELL	Emma	70		Dau		6	F	Scholar	Herts	St Stephens
762	WARRELL	Edmond	70		Son		3	M	Scholar	Herts	St Stephens
763	OAKLEY	Eliza	70		Sister-in-law	Unm	17	F	Bonnet Sewer	Herts	St Albans
764	WARRELL	George	70		Son		2 m	M		Herts	St Stephens
765	SHEARS	Thomas	71	Park Street	Head	Mar	60	M	Agric Lab	Kent	Dartford
766	SHEARS	Sarah	71		Wife	Mar	51	F		Herts	Abbots Langley
767	SHEARS	Ann	71		Dau	Unm	34	F	Brazilian Hat Maker	Herts	St Stephens
768	SHEARS	William	71		Son	Unm	22	M	Agric Lab	Herts	St Stephens
769	SHEARS	John	71		Son	Unm	20	M	Agric Lab	Herts	St Stephens
770	SHEARS	Henry	71		Son		15	M	Brazilian Hat Maker	Herts	St Stephens
771	SHEARS	Susan	71		Dau		14	F	Brazilian Hat Maker	Herts	St Stephens
772	SHEARS	Emma	71		Dau		11	F	Brazilian Hat Maker	Herts	St Stephens
773	SHEARS	Betsy	71		Dau		10	F	Brazilian Hat Maker	Herts	St Stephens
774	SHEARS	James	71		Grandson		6	M	Brazilian Hat Maker	Herts	St Stephens
775	ANDREW	Joseph	72	Park Street	Head	Mar	50	M	Agric Lab	Herts	Hemel Hempstead
776	ANDREW	Hannah	72		Wife	Mar	49	F		Herts	St Stephens
777	ANDREW	Sarah	72		Dau	Unm	17	F	Brazilian Hat Maker	Herts	St Stephens

778	ANDREW	Thomas	72		Son		10	M	Agric Lab	Herts	St Stephens
779	ANDREW	William	72		Son		7	M	Scholar	Herts	St Stephens
780	ANDREW	Frances	72		Dau		3	F		Herts	St Stephens
781	HOLLMAN	William	72		Lodger	Unm	25	M	Shoemaker	Herts	Berkhamsted
782	BECKINGTON	Thomas	73	Park Street	Head	Mar	72	M	Shoemaker	Herts	St Stephens
783	BECKINGTON	Ann	73		Wife	Mar	68	F		Herts	St Stephens
784	BECKINGTON	Hannah	73		Dau	Unm	27	F	Brazilian Hat Maker	Herts	St Stephens
785	STUART	Jane B.	73		Grandau		7	F	Scholar	Herts	St Stephens
786	BECKINGTON	William	73		Grandson		4	M	Scholar	Herts	St Stephens
787	HARRIS	Mary	74	Park Street	Head	Widow	49	F	Washerwoman	Herts	North Mimms
788	HARRIS	Frederick	74		Son	Unm	21	M	Tailor (Apprentice)	Herts	St Stephens
789	HARRIS	Francis	74		Son	Unm	18	M	Servant	Herts	St Stephens
790	HARRIS	Mary Ann	74		Dau		15	F	Bonnet Sewer	Herts	St Stephens

Two houses uninhabited

791	SMITH	Hannah	75	Park Street	Head	Widow	51	F	Grocer	Herts	Redbourn
792	HARDING	James	75		Son	Unm	24	M	Agric Lab	Herts	St Albans
793	HARDING	Sarah	75		Dau		14	F	Scholar	Herts	St Stephens
794	SMITH	Ann	75		Dau		11	F	Scholar	Herts	St Stephens
795	PURT	William	76	Park Street	Head	Mar	52	M	Waggoner	Berks	Wantage
796	PURT	Hannah	76		Wife	Mar	46	F	Charwoman	Herts	St Stephens
797	PURT	Aubrey	76		Son	Unm	16	M	Agric Lab	Herts	St Stephens
798	PURT	Charlotte	76		Dau		10	F	Scholar	Herts	St Stephens
799	RIXSON	Catherine	76		Visitor	Unm	26	F	Bonnet Sewer	Middx	Hendon
800	RIXSON	Sarah	76		Visitor	Unm	19	F	House Servant	Middx	Hendon
801	KNOWLES	John	77	Park Street	Head	Mar	45	M	Agric Lab	Herts	Abbots Langley
802	KNOWLES	Mary	77		Wife	Mar	48	F		Herts	St Stephens
803	KNOWLES	Eliza	77		[Dau]		12	F	Scholar	Herts	St Stephens
804	GARFORTH	John	78	Park Street	Head	Mar	42	M	Grocer and carrier	Herts	St Stephens
805	GARFORTH	Caroline	78		Wife	Mar	43	F	Grocers wife	Herts	Shenley
806	GARFORTH	Caroline	78		Dau	Unm	17	F	Bonnet Sewer	Herts	St Albans
807	GARFORTH	Jane	78		Dau	Unm	15	F	Grocer (assistant)	Herts	St Stephens
808	GARFORTH	Edwin	78		Son		12	M	Grocers son employed at home	Herts	St Stephens
809	GARFORTH	Elizabeth	78		Dau		8	F	Scholar	Herts	St Stephens
810	GARFORTH	Ellen	78		Dau		6	F	Scholar	Herts	St Stephens
811	GARFORTH	Ann	78		Dau		3	F	Scholar	Herts	St Stephens
812	HORNETT	William	79	Park Street	Head	Mar	37	M	Agric Lab	Herts	St Stephens
813	HORNETT	Eliza	79		Wife	Mar	28	F		Herts	St Stephens
814	HORNETT	Mary	79		Dau		7	F	Scholar	Herts	St Stephens
815	HORNETT	George	79		Son		6	M	Scholar	Herts	St Stephens
816	HORNETT	Eliza	79		Dau		4	F		Herts	St Stephens
817	HORNETT	Emily	79		Dau		1	F		Herts	St Stephens
818	FLETCHER	Charles	80	Park Street	Head	Mar	75	M	Agric Lab	Herts	Harpenden
819	FLETCHER	Elizabeth	80		Wife	Mar	79	F		Herts	Wheathampstead
820	EASON	Robert	81	Park Street	Head	Mar	35	M	Agric Lab	Herts	St Stephens
821	EASON	Sarah	81		Wife	Mar	35	F		Herts	St Stephens

	SURNAME	FORENAME	SCHEDULE NUMBER	ADDRESS	RELATIONSHIP	STATUS	AGE	SEX	OCCUPATION	COUNTY OF BIRTH	PLACE OF BIRTH
822	EASON	Sarah Ann	81		[Dau]		8	F	Scholar	Herts	St Stephens
823	EASON	Thomas	81		[Son]		6	M	Scholar	Herts	St Stephens
824	EASON	James E.	81		[Son]		3	M		Herts	St Stephens
825	EASON	Caroline	81		[Dau]		9 m	F		Herts	St Stephens
826	GIDDINS	Henry	82	Park Street	Head	Mar	31	M	Journeyman Miller	Herts	Welwyn
827	GIDDINS	Amelia	82		Wife	Mar	29	F		Herts	Kimpton
828	GIDDINS	Sarah	82		Dau		6	F	Scholar	Herts	Whitwell
829	GIDDINS	Eliza	82		Dau		4	F		Middx	Hadley
830	GIDDINS	Henry	82		Son		2 m	M		Herts	St Albans
831	RENTOWL	Lydia	83	Red Lion	Head	Widow	39	F	Victualler	Hunts	Hemmingford
832	RENTOWL	Jane	83		Dau		7	F	Scholar	Herts	St Stephens
833	RENTOWL	George	83		Son		5	M	Scholar	Herts	St Stephens
834	READER	Sarah	83		Sister	Mar	49	F	Sailors wife	Hunts	Hemmingford
835	READER	Elizabeth	83		Niece		6	F	Scholar	Pemb	Pater
836	WRIGHT	John	84	Frogmoor	Head	Unm	39	M	Master Tailor employing 2 men	Herts	St Stephens
837	WRIGHT	Mary	84		Mother	Widow	73	F		Herts	Kings Langley
838	WRIGHT	Sarah	84		Sister	Unm	35	F	Dressmaker	Herts	St Stephens
839	WRIGHT	John	84		Nephew	Unm	19	M	Tailor	Herts	St Stephens
840	GEORGE	James	85	Frogmoor	Head	Mar	38	M	Gardener	Herts	St Peters
841	GEORGE	Elizabeth	85		Wife	Mar	39	F	Straw Plaiter	Herts	St Stephens
842	GEORGE	Sarah	85		Dau	Unm	18	F	Straw Plaiter	Herts	St Stephens
843	GEORGE	Eliza	85		Dau		14	F	Scholar	Herts	St Stephens
844	GEORGE	Henry	85		Son		11	M	Scholar	Herts	St Stephens
845	GEORGE	Mary	85		Dau		7	F	Scholar	Herts	St Stephens
846	ENGLAND	William	86	Frogmoor	Head	Mar	50	M	Agric Lab	Herts	St Stephens
847	ENGLAND	Sarah	86		Wife	Mar	28	F		Herts	Hatfield
848	PEARCE	Ann	87		Serv	Unm	27	F	Laundress	Middx	Fulham
849	BRADSHAW	Thomas	88	Frogmoor	Head	Mar	61	M	Agric Lab	Herts	Hemel Hempstead
850	BRADSHAW	Ann	88		Wife	Mar	60	F		Herts	St Stephens
851	COSTEN	Mary	89	Frogmoor	Head	Widow	96	F	Almswoman	Herts	Colney
852	MILEMAN	Kezia	90	Frogmoor	Nurse	Widow	72	F	Nurse	Herts	St Stephens
853	ROWE	Elizabeth	91	Frogmoor	Head	Widow	83	F	Almswoman	Herts	Abbots Langley
854	LINNEY	Eliza	91		Serv		14	F	Servant	Herts	St Stephens
855	DICKINSON	William	92	Frogmoor	Head	Mar	60	M	Boot and Shoemaker	Herts	Aldenham
856	DICKINSON	Martha	92		Wife	Mar	58	F		Herts	St Stephens
857	DICKINSON	Frederick	92		Son	Unm	19	M	Gardener	Herts	St Stephens
858	DICKINSON	Jane	92		Dau	Unm	18	F	Brazilian Hat Maker	Herts	St Stephens
859	DICKINSON	Emma	92		Dau		11	F	Scholar	Herts	St Stephens
860	WILLIAMS	Henry	92		Grandson		5	M	Scholar	Middx	St Marylebone
861	WILLIAMS	Charles	92		Grandson		4	M		Herts	St Stephens
862	EASON	Robert	93	Frogmoor	Head	Mar	61	M	Agric Lab	Middx	St Marylebone
863	EASON	Caroline	93		Dau	Unm	30	F	Brazilian Hat Maker	Herts	St Stephens
864	EASON	James	93		Son	Unm	26	M	Agric Lab	Herts	St Stephens

Two houses building

	SURNAME	FORENAME	SCHEDULE NUMBER	ADDRESS	RELATIONSHIP	STATUS	AGE	SEX	OCCUPATION	COUNTY OF BIRTH	PLACE OF BIRTH
865	SMITH	Maria	94	Frogmoor	Head	Widow	68	F	Pauper	Essex	Romford

866	NORWOOD	James	95	Frogmoor	Head	Mar	66	M	Agric Lab	Herts	St Stephens
867	NORWOOD	Elinor	95		Wife	Mar	57	F	Straw Plaiter	Herts	Hemel Hempstead
868	ROWE	Daniel	95		Lodger	Unm	45	M	Agric Lab	Herts	St Stephens
869	TEBBOTH	Ann	96	Frogmoor	Head	Widow	60	F	Charwoman	Herts	St Stephens
870	PEDDAR	Mary	96		Sister	Unm	45	F	Straw Plaiter	Herts	St Stephens
871	TEBBOTH	Eliza	96		Dau	Unm	32	F	Brazilian Hat Maker	Herts	St Stephens
872	PEDDAR	William	96		Nephew	Unm	22	M	Sawyers Lab	Herts	St Stephens
873	DICKINSON	Benjamin	97	Frogmoor	Head	Mar	58	M	Shoemaker	Herts	Aldenham
874	DICKINSON	Martha	97		Wife	Mar	57	F		Herts	St Stephens
875	DICKINSON	John	97		Son	Unm	18	M	Shoemaker	Herts	St Stephens
876	TURNER	Susan	97		Dau	Widow	29	F		Herts	St Stephens
877	TURNER	Sarah	97		Grandau		5	F	Scholar	Herts	St Stephens

One uninhabited house

878	READ	John	98	The Lamb	Head	Mar	38	M	Dealer and beershop keeper	Bucks	Sulhamstead
879	READ	Mary	98		Wife	Mar	38	F		Herts	St Stephens
880	READ	John	98		Son		6	M	Scholar	Herts	St Stephens
881	READ	William	98		Son		3	M	Scholar	Herts	St Stephens
882	READ	Joseph	98		Son		1	M		Herts	St Stephens
883	COSTEN	Ann	99	Frogmoor	Head	Widow	54	F	Carrier employing 2 men	Herts	St Stephens
884	COSTEN	Henry	99		Son	Unm	18	M	Carrier employed at home	Herts	St Stephens
885	COSTEN	Elizabeth	99		Dau	Unm	20	F	Brazilian Hat Maker	Herts	St Stephens
886	INWOOD	Robert	100	Frogmoor	Head	Mar	38	M	Master Wheelwright	Herts	Little Berkhamsted
887	INWOOD	Ann	100		Wife	Mar	32	F		Herts	St Stephens
888	INWOOD	Sarah	100		Dau		9	F	Scholar	Herts	St Stephens
889	INWOOD	Thomas	100		Son		10	M	Scholar	Herts	St Stephens
890	INWOOD	Ann	100		Dau		6	F	Scholar	Herts	St Stephens
891	INWOOD	Elizabeth	100		Dau		4	F	Scholar	Herts	St Stephens
892	INWOOD	Sam	100		Brother	Unm	24	M	Wheelwright	Herts	Hatfield
893	WRIGHT	Frances	100		Mother-in-law	Widow	67	F	Annuitant	Herts	Kings Walden
894	SHARP	James	101	Frogmoor	Head	Mar	48	M	Carrier	Herts	St Stephens
895	SHARP	Elizabeth	101		Wife	Mar	46	F		Herts	St Stephens
896	SHARP	Ann	101		Dau	Unm	25	F	Bonnet Sewer	Herts	St Stephens
897	BURGESS	John	101		Nephew		10	M	Scholar	Herts	St Stephens
898	HOSTLER	George	102	Frogmoor	Head	Unm	44	M	Agric Lab	Herts	Hemel Hempstead
899	HOSTLER	George	102		Lodger	Unm	22	M	Agric Lab	Herts	St Stephens
900	SHARP	William	103	Frogmoor	Head	Mar	52	M	Agric Lab	Herts	St Stephens
901	SHARP	Mary	103		Wife	Mar	50	F		Herts	St Stephens
902	SHARP	William	103		Son	Unm	30	M	Agric Lab	Herts	St Stephens
903	SHARP	James	103		Son	Unm	26	M	Pauper (Agric. Lab)	Herts	St Stephens
904	SHARP	Sarah	103		Dau	Unm	16	F	Brazilian Hat Maker	Herts	St Stephens
905	SHARP	Eliza	103		Dau		12	F	Scholar	Herts	St Stephens
906	SHARP	Alfred	103		Son		10	M	Scholar	Herts	St Stephens
907	SHARP	Emma	103		Dau		4	F		Herts	St Stephens
908	STILWELL	Henry	104	Frogmoor	Head	Mar	32	M	Gardener	Surrey	Ash

	SURNAME	FORENAME	SCHEDULE NUMBER	ADDRESS	RELATIONSHIP	STATUS	AGE	SEX	OCCUPATION	COUNTY OF BIRTH	PLACE OF BIRTH
909	STILWELL	Frances	104		Wife	Mar	34	F		Surrey	Wandsworth

One uninhabited house

End of the Village of Park Street

Village of Colney Street

	SURNAME	FORENAME	SCHEDULE NUMBER	ADDRESS	RELATIONSHIP	STATUS	AGE	SEX	OCCUPATION	COUNTY OF BIRTH	PLACE OF BIRTH
910	DAVIS	Daniel	105	Red Cow	Head	Mar	37	M	Publican	Middx	Ealing
911	DAVIS	Elizabeth	105		Wife	Mar	34	F		Middx	Heston
912	DAVIS	William	105		Son		5	M	Scholar	Herts	St Stephens
913	DAVIS	Elizabeth	105		Dau		3	F		Herts	St Stephens
914	TOMBS	George	106	Red Cow	Head	Mar	22	M	Agric Lab	Herts	St Stephens
915	TOMBS	Esther	106		Wife	Mar	22	F	Brazilian Hat Maker	Herts	St Stephens
916	GODMAN	John	107	Red Cow	Head	Mar	31	M	Dealer	Herts	St Stephens
917	GODMAN	Susannah	107		Wife	Mar	26	F		Herts	St Stephens
918	FIELD	James	107		Serv	Unm	16	M	Drover	Herts	St Stephens
919	KIFF	George	108	Red Cow	Head	Widower	70	M	Agric Lab	Herts	St Stephens
920	OAKLEY	James	109	Red Cow	Head	Mar	56	M	Agric Lab	Herts	St Stephens
921	OAKLEY	Esther	109		Wife	Mar	56	F		Herts	St Stephens
922	OAKLEY	Mary	109		Dau	Unm	33	F	Brazilian Hat Maker	Herts	St Stephens
923	OAKLEY	Emanuel	109		Son	Unm	28	M	Chelsea Pensioner	Herts	St Stephens
924	OAKLEY	James	109		Son	Unm	20	M	Agric Lab	Herts	St Stephens
925	OAKLEY	Ann	109		Dau	Unm	19	F	Brazilian Hat Maker	Herts	St Stephens
926	OAKLEY	Alice	109		Grandau		9	F	Scholar	Herts	St Stephens
927	OAKLEY	Eliza	109		Grandau		5	F	Scholar	Herts	St Stephens
928	BARR	William	110	Red Cow	Head	Mar	23	M	Agric Lab	Herts	Shenley
929	BARR	Hannah	110		Wife	Mar	22	F	Brazilian Hat Maker	Herts	St Stephens
930	BARR	John Wm.	110		Son		1	M		Herts	St Stephens

Two uninhabited houses

	SURNAME	FORENAME	SCHEDULE NUMBER	ADDRESS	RELATIONSHIP	STATUS	AGE	SEX	OCCUPATION	COUNTY OF BIRTH	PLACE OF BIRTH
931	TOMS	James	111	Red Cow	Head	Mar	38	M	Agric Lab	Herts	St Stephens
932	TOMS	Keziah	111		Wife	Mar	37	F		Herts	Sandridge
933	TOMS	Alice	111		Dau		15	F	Scholar	Herts	St Stephens
934	TOMS	Ellen	111		Dau		11	F	Scholar	Herts	St Stephens
935	SHEARS	Thomas	111		Lodger		27	M	Agric Lab	Herts	St Stephens
936	GARRATT	William	112	Red Cow	Head	Mar	33	M	Journeyman Miller	Herts	Hemel Hempstead
937	GARRATT	Ann	112		Wife	Mar	28	F		Herts	St Stephens
938	GARRATT	William	112		Son		7	M	Scholar	Herts	St Stephens
939	GARRATT	James	112		Son		5	M	Scholar	Herts	St Stephens
940	GARRATT	Elizabeth	112		Dau		3	F		Herts	St Stephens
941	GARRATT	Ann	112		Dau		1	F		Herts	St Stephens
942	WYATT	Robert	113	New Park Bury	Head	Mar	68	M	Farmer of 234 acres employing 9 labourers	Northants	Kings Sutton
943	WYATT	Sarah	113		Wife	Mar	68	F	Farmers wife	Oxon	Bletchington
944	WYATT	Mary E.	113		Dau	Unm	35	F	Farmers daur	Northants	Kings Sutton
945	WYATT	Henry	113		Son	Unm	30	M	Farmers son	Northants	Kings Sutton
946	WOODWARD	Caroline	113		Serv	Unm	18	F	House Servant	Herts	Aldenham
947	BOULTER	Daniel	114	Old Park Bury	Head	Mar	40	M	Farmer of 357 acres.	Oxon	Sarsden
948	BOULTER	Sarah	114		Wife	Mar	36	F		Oxon	Salford

949	BOULTER	Joseph	114		Son	Unm	15	M	Farmers son	Bucks	Little Brickill
950	BOULTER	Sydney	114		Son		4 m	M		Herts	St Stephens
951	WARN	Eliza	114		Serv	Unm	17	F	House servant	Herts	Watford
952	REYNOLDS	George	114		Serv	Unm	35	M	Agric Lab	Herts	London Colney
953	FISHER	Samuel	114		Serv	Unm	20	M	Agric Lab	Herts	Ippollitts
954	KIFF	William	114		Serv	Unm	15	M	Agric Lab	Herts	St Stephens
955	GREEN	Matthew	115	Upper Wild Farm	Serv	Unm	34	M	Agric Lab (shepherd)	Herts	St Stephens
956	WOODWARDS	William	115		Serv	Unm	17	M	Agric Lab	Herts	Aldenham
957	HAWTREE	William	116	Colney Street Bridge	Head	Mar	82	M	Agric Lab	Herts	St Stephens
958	HAWTREE	Sarah	116		Wife	Mar	73	F	Pauper	Herts	St Stephens
959	HAWTREE	George	116		Son	Unm	36	M	Agric Lab (pauper)	Herts	St Stephens
960	BETTS	Sarah	117	Colney Street Bridge	Head	Widow	48	F	Straw Plaiter (Pauper)	Herts	St Stephens
961	BETTS	Jane	117		Dau		12	F	Straw Plaiter	Herts	Shenley
962	BETTS	Mary Ann	117		Dau		10	F	Scholar	Herts	Colney
963	PICTON	William	118	Colney Street Bridge	Head	Mar	61	M	Pauper (Agric. Lab)	Herts	Northchurch
964	PICTON	Elizabeth	118		Wife	Mar	59	F	Straw Plaiter	Herts	St Stephens
965	PICTON	Elizabeth	118		Dau		12	F	Scholar	Herts	St Stephens
966	HILL	Joseph	119	Colney Street Bridge	Head	Mar	49	M	Pauper (Ag.ric Lab)	Herts	St Stephens
967	HILL	Charlotte	119		Wife	Mar	57	F		Herts	St Stephens
968	HILL	William	119		Son	Mar	29	M	Agric Lab	Herts	St Stephens
969	HILL	Mathew	119		Son	Unm	26	M	Agric Lab	Herts	St Stephens
970	HILL	James	119		Son	Unm	21	M	Agric Lab	Herts	St Stephens
971	HILL	George	119		Son		14	M	Agric Lab	Herts	St Stephens
972	GREEN	Ann	120	Colney Street Bridge	Head	Widow	80	F	Pauper	Herts	Hemel Hempstead
973	GREEN	Thomas	120		Son	Unm	46	M	Agric Lab	Herts	St Stephens
974	GREEN	Mary	120		Dau	Unm	49	F	Straw Plaiter	Herts	St Stephens
975	HILL	John	120		Gt. Grandson		11	M		Herts	St Stephens
976	ROYDS	George	121	Park Bury Lodge	Head	Mar	33	M	Landed Proprietor and Fundholder	Middx	London
977	ROYDS	Jane	121		Wife	Mar	33	F		Middx	London
978	ROYDS	Henry John	121		Son		6	M	Scholar at Home	Middx	London
979	ROYDS	Jane Louisa	121		Dau		5	F	Scholar at Home	Middx	London
980	ROYDS	Fanny	121		Dau		2	F		Middx	London
981	RAULEY	Frances	121		Serv	Unm	30	F	Nurse	Surrey	Cobham
982	ANTHONY	Elizabeth	121		Serv	Unm	16	F	Nursemaid	Herts	London Colney
983	COOK	Mary	121		Serv	Unm	25	F	Cook	Herts	London Colney
984	LAMMAS	Sarah	121		Serv	Unm	25	F	Housemaid	Middx	Hendon
985	FOWLER	Amos	122	Colney Street	Head	Mar	28	M	Gardener	Herts	Shenley
986	FOWLER	Emma	122		Wife	Mar	32	F	Laundress	Middx	South Mimms
987	FOWLER	Emma	122		Dau		5	F	Scholar	Herts	Shenley
988	FOWLER	Maria Jane	122		Dau		3	F		Herts	Shenley
989	FOWLER	Frederick G.	122		Son		1	M		Middx	South Mimms
990	THORNTON	James	123	Colney Street	Head	Mar	36	M	Agric Lab	Herts	St Stephens
991	THORNTON	Elizabeth	123		Wife	Mar	36	F		Herts	St Stephens
992	THORNTON	Ann	123		Dau		9	F	Scholar	Herts	St Stephens
993	THORNTON	William	123		Son		7	M	Scholar	Herts	St Stephens

	SURNAME	FORENAME	SCHEDULE NUMBER	ADDRESS	RELATIONSHIP	STATUS	AGE	SEX	OCCUPATION	COUNTY OF BIRTH	PLACE OF BIRTH
994	THORNTON	Thomas	123		Son		4	M	Scholar	Herts	St Stephens
995	THORNTON	David Elias	123		Son		11 m	M		Herts	St Stephens
996	CRAIK	Samuel	123		Lodger	Unm	19	M	Gardener	Herts	Borehamwood
997	THOMPSON	Henry	123		Lodger	Unm	21	M	Agric Lab	Herts	Aldenham
998	THORNTON	Ann	124	Colney Street	Head	Mar	68	F	Brazilian Hat Maker	Herts	St Stephens
999	GURNEY	Thomas	124		Grandson-in-law	Mar	25	M	Agric Lab	Herts	St Stephens
1000	GURNEY	Phillis	124		Grandau	Mar	24	F	Brazilian Hat Maker	Herts	St Stephens
1001	TIMSON	Mary	124		Grandau	Unm	21	F	Brazilian Hat Maker	Herts	St Stephens
1002	ENGLAND	Hannah	124		Lodger	Unm	20	F	Brazilian Hat Maker	Herts	St Stephens
1003	SMITH	Thomas	125	Colney Street	Head	Mar	30	M	Agric Lab	Herts	Colney
1004	SMITH	Sarah	125		Wife	Mar	28	F		Herts	Aldenham
1005	SMITH	Eliza	125		Dau		1	F		Herts	St Stephens
1006	CHARGE	Martha	125		Mother-in-law	Widow	61	F	Straw Plaiter	Bucks	Missenden
1007	CHARGE	John	125		Brother-in-law	Unm	21	M	Agric Lab	Herts	St Stephens
1008	WRIGHT	James	126	Colney Street	Head	Mar	43	M	Blacksmith	Herts	St Stephens
1009	WRIGHT	Eliza	126		Wife	Mar	38	F	Linen Draper	Herts	St Stephens
1010	WRIGHT	Sarah	126		Dau	Unm	16	F	Brazilian Hat Maker	Herts	St Stephens
1011	WRIGHT	James	126		Son	Unm	15	M	Blacksmith at home	Herts	St Stephens
1012	WRIGHT	Eliza	126		Dau		13	F	Brazilian Hat Maker	Herts	St Stephens
1013	WRIGHT	Martha	126		Dau		10	F	Scholar	Herts	St Stephens
1014	WRIGHT	George	126		Son		8	M	Scholar	Herts	St Stephens
1015	WRIGHT	Mary	126		Dau		5	F	Scholar	Herts	St Stephens
1016	WRIGHT	Matilda	126		Dau		3	F		Herts	St Stephens
1017	LYALLS	Ann	127	Colney Street	Head	Widow	62	F	Schoolmistress	Yorks	Sheffield
1018	PURT	Esther	127		Visitor	Unm	22	F	Bonnet Sewer	Herts	St Stephens
1019	WILKINSON	William	128	Colney Street	Head	Mar	35	M	Agric Lab	Herts	Radlett
1020	WILKINSON	Ann	128		Wife	Mar	35	F		Herts	St Stephens
1021	WILKINSON	Mary	128		Dau		10	F	Scholar	Herts	Radlett
1022	WILKINSON	Elizabeth	128		Dau		6	F	Scholar	Herts	Radlett
1023	WILKINSON	Jane	128		Dau		3	F		Herts	Radlett
1024	SLAUGHTER	Sarah	129	Colney Street	Head	Widow	72	F	pauper	Herts	Radlett
1025	WALLER	George	129		Grandson-in-law	Mar	30	M	Agric Lab	Herts	Radlett
1026	WALLER	Phillis	129		Grandau	Mar	28	F		Herts	Radlett
1027	WALLER	Eliza	129		Gt. Grandau		9	F	Scholar	Herts	Watford
1028	WALLER	John	129		Gt. Grandson		7	M	Scholar	Herts	Watford
1029	WALLER	Phillis E.	129		Gt. Grandau		5	F	Scholar	Herts	Watford
1030	WALLER	George	129		Gt. Grandson		8 m	M		Herts	St Stephens
1031	MUNT	Elizabeth	130	Colney Street	Head	[Mar]	47	F	Straw Plaiter	Herts	St Stephens
1032	TOMS	James	130		Son-in-law	[Mar]	29	M	Agric Lab	Herts	St Stephens
1033	MUNT	Hannah	130		Dau	[Mar]	20	F	Brazilian Hat Maker	Herts	St Stephens
1034	MUNT	Benjamin	130		Son	Unm	18	M	Agric Lab	Herts	St Stephens
1035	MUNT	Charles	130		Son	Unm	16	M	Agric Lab	Herts	Shenley
1036	MUNT	Reuben	130		Son		7	M	Scholar	Herts	St Stephens
1037	TOMS	Mary	131	Colney Street	Head	Widow	79	F	Pauper	Herts	Aldenham

1038	TOMS	Richard	131		Son	Unm	39	M	Agric Lab	Herts	St Stephens
1039	ELLIOTT	William	132	Colney Street	Head	Mar	46	M	Agric Lab	Herts	Great Hormead
1040	ELLIOTT	Dinah	132		Wife	Mar	36	F		Herts	St Stephens
1041	ELLIOTT	Nathaniel	132		Son	Unm	15	M	Agric Lab	Herts	St Stephens
1042	ELLIOTT	Jane	132		Dau		11	F	Scholar	Herts	St Stephens
1043	ELLIOTT	Emma	132		Dau		9	F	Scholar	Herts	St Stephens
1044	TOMS	Bridget	132		Dau-in-Law		10	F	Scholar	Somerset	Bristol
1045	ELLIOTT	Elizabeth	132		Dau		2	F		Herts	St Stephens
1046	ELLIOTT	Daniel	132		Son		6 m	M		Herts	St Stephens
1047	WOODWARD	Thomas	133	Black Horse	Head	Mar	45	M	Licensed Victualler	Herts	Kings Langley
1048	WOODWARD	Catherine	133		Wife	Mar	45	F		Herts	Kings Langley
1049	WOODWARD	Jane	133		Dau		7	F	Scholar	Herts	Hatfield
1050	SWAIN	George	133		Lodger	Unm	21	M	Agric Lab	Herts	Harpenden
1051	TOMKINS	Henry	133		Lodger	Unm	19	M	Agric Lab (shepherd)	Bucks	Aylesbury
1052	WIGGS	William	134	Colney Street	Head	Mar	31	M	Agric Lab	Herts	St Stephens
1053	WIGGS	Sarah Jane	134		Wife	Mar	28	F		Herts	St Albans
1054	WIGGS	William	134		Son		5	M	Scholar	Herts	St Stephens
1055	WIGGS	Robert	134		Son		3	M		Surrey	Peckham
1056	WIGGS	Thomas	134		Son		2	M		Herts	St Albans
1057	ELLIOTT	William	134		Lodger	Unm	21	M	Agric Lab	Herts	St Albans
1058	THORNTON	John	135	Colney Street	Head	Mar	40	M	Higgler	Herts	St Stephens
1059	THORNTON	Elizabeth	135		Wife	Mar	39	F		Herts	St Stephens
1060	THORNTON	Caroline A.	135		Dau		15	F	Brazilian Hat Maker	Herts	St Stephens
1061	WELSH	Thomas	136	The George	Head	Widower	39	M	Publican	Herts	Flamstead
1062	WELSH	Mary	136		Dau		13	F		Herts	St Stephens
1063	WELSH	William	136		Son		6	M	Scholar	Herts	St Stephens
1064	PRAT	George	136		Lodger	Unm	20	M	Agric Lab	Herts	St Stephens
1065	GARFORTH	William	137	Colney Street	Head	Mar	32	M	Grocer and carrier	Herts	St Stephens
1066	GARFORTH	Charlotte	137		Wife	Mar	33	F		Herts	Aldenham
1067	GARFORTH	Alice Jane	137		Dau		12	F		Herts	Aldenham
1068	GARFORTH	Jane	137		Dau		10	F		Herts	Aldenham
1069	GARFORTH	Henry	137		Son		9	M	Scholar	Herts	Aldenham
1070	GARFORTH	William	137		Son		7	M	Scholar	Herts	Aldenham
1071	GARFORTH	Maria	137		Dau		4	F	Scholar	Herts	Aldenham
1072	GARFORTH	Charlotte	137		Dau		1	F		Herts	Aldenham
1073	TIMSON	Thomas	138	Colney Street	Head	Mar	52	M	Agric Lab	Herts	St Stephens
1074	TIMSON	Sarah	138		Wife	Mar	42	F		Durham	Sunderland
1075	TIMSON	Sarah	138		Dau	Unm	18	F	Brazilian Hat Maker	Herts	St Stephens
1076	TIMSON	William	138		Son		7	M	Scholar	Herts	St Albans
1077	TIMSON	George	138		Son		5	M	Scholar	Herts	St Stephens
1078	TIMSON	Frederick	138		Son		1	M		Herts	St Stephens
1079	LOVETT	William	139	Colney Street Farm	Head	Mar	29	M	Farmer of 154 acres employing 6 labourers	Herts	St Stephens
1080	LOVETT	Jane	139		Wife	Mar	36	F		Herts	Aldenham
1081	LOVETT	Joseph	139		Son		4	M		Herts	St Stephens
1082	LOVETT	Henry Isaac	139		Son		2	M		Herts	St Stephens

	SURNAME	FORENAME	SCHEDULE NUMBER	ADDRESS	RELATIONSHIP	STATUS	AGE	SEX	OCCUPATION	COUNTY OF BIRTH	PLACE OF BIRTH
1083	LOVETT	Alfred	139		Son		3 m	M		Herts	St Stephens
1084	FREEMAN	Sarah	139		Mother-in-law	Widow	76	F	Formerly Farmers wife	Berks	Childrey
1085	FREEMAN	James	139		Serv	Widower	67	M	Agric Lab	Herts	Hemel Hempstead
1086	WHITE	Rebecca	140	Colney Street	Head	Widow	43	F	Grocer	Bucks	Chenies
1087	WHITE	Rebecca	140		Dau	Unm	15	F	Bonnet Sewer	Bucks	Chenies
1088	WHITE	Maria	140		Dau		14	F	Brazilian Hat Maker	Herts	St Stephens
1089	WHITE	Harriett	140		Dau		10	F	Scholar	Herts	St Stephens
1090	WHITE	Caroline	140		Dau		9	F	Scholar	Herts	St Stephens
1091	WHITE	Elizabeth S.	140		Dau		5	F	Scholar	Herts	St Stephens
1092	SWAIN	Caroline	140		Serv	Unm	20	F	Grocer (assistant)	Bucks	Chenies
1093	HAWES	Sarah	141	Colney Street	Head	Widow	65	F	Domestic	Herts	St Stephens
1094	EAMES	James	141		Son-in-law	Widower	45	M	Agric Lab	Herts	St Stephens
1095	EAMES	Thomas	141		Grandson	Unm	18	M	Agric Lab	Herts	St Stephens
1096	EAMES	John	141		Grandson	Unm	15	M	Agric Lab	Herts	St Stephens
1097	GREEN	William	142	Colney Street	Head	Mar	52	M	Agric Lab	Herts	St Stephens
1098	GREEN	Ann	142		Wife	Mar	45	F		Herts	Hemel Hempstead
1099	SHARP	William	142		Father-in-law	Widower	80	M	Pauper (Agric Lab)	Herts	St Pauls Walden
1100	GREEN	George	142		Son	Unm	17	M	Agric Lab	Herts	St Stephens
1101	GREEN	William	142		Son		9	M	Scholar	Herts	St Stephens
1102	GREEN	Shadrack	142		Son		3	M		Herts	St Stephens
1103	HUMBLES	Sarah	143	Colney Street	Head	Widow	35	F	Washerwoman	Herts	St Stephens
1104	HUMBLES	George	143		Son		14	M	Agric Lab	Herts	St Stephens
1105	HUMBLES	William	143		Son		11	M	Agric Lab	Herts	St Stephens
1106	HUMBLES	Robert	143		Son		6	M	Scholar	Herts	St Stephens
1107	HUMBLES	Henry	143		Son		4	M		Herts	St Stephens
1108	HUMBLES	Thomas	143		Son		11 m	M		Herts	St Stephens
1109	ENGLAND	William	144	Colney Street	Head	Widower	60	M	Agric Lab	Herts	Watford
1110	ENGLAND	Mary	144		Dau	Unm	18	F	Brazilian Hat Maker	Herts	St Stephens
1111	ENGLAND	James	144		Son		14	M	Agric Lab	Herts	St Stephens
1112	ENGLAND	Thomas	144		Son		12	M	Agric Lab	Herts	St Stephens
1113	ENGLAND	John	144		Son		10	M	Agric Lab	Herts	St Stephens
1114	CLARK	Jeremiah	145	Colney Street	Head	Mar	74	M	Agric Lab	Herts	Aldenham
1115	CLARK	Charlotte	145		Wife	Mar	65	F		Oxon	Sanford Mills
1116	WHITE	George	146	Colney Street	Head	Mar	38	M	Agric Lab	Herts	Abbots Langley
1117	WHITE	Mary	146		Wife	Mar	32	F		Herts	Watford
1118	WHITE	David	146		Son		9	M	Scholar	Herts	St Stephens
1119	WHITE	Emma	146		Dau		7	F	Scholar	Herts	St Stephens
1120	WHITE	Hannah	146		Dau		5	F	Scholar	Herts	St Stephens
1121	WHITE	Elizabeth	146		Dau		2	F		Herts	St Stephens
1122	WHITE	Sarah	146		Dau		5 m	F		Herts	St Stephens
1123	BELCHER	William	147	Colney Street	Head	Mar	32	M	Agric Lab	Herts	Harpenden
1124	BELCHER	Mary	147		Wife	Mar	32	F		Herts	St Stephens
1125	BELCHER	Eliza	147		Dau		7	F	Scholar	Herts	St Stephens
1126	BELCHER	Mary	147		Dau		6	F	Scholar	Herts	St Stephens
1127	BELCHER	Emma	147		Dau		4	F		Herts	St Stephens

1128	BELCHER	Jane	147		Dau		2	F		Herts	St Stephens
1129	ENGLAND	David	148	Colney Street	Head	Mar	55	M	Agric Lab	Herts	St Stephens
1130	ENGLAND	Mary	148		Wife	Mar	35	F		Herts	St Stephens
1131	ENGLAND	David	148		Son	Unm	16	M	Agric Lab	Herts	St Stephens
1132	ENGLAND	Joseph	148		Son		14	M	Agric Lab	Herts	St Stephens
1133	ENGLAND	James	148		Son		12	M	Agric Lab	Herts	St Stephens
1134	ENGLAND	Benjamin	148		Son		10	M	Brazilian Hat Maker	Herts	Watford
1135	ENGLAND	Hannah	148		Dau		7	F	Scholar	Herts	Abbots Langley
1136	ENGLAND	Betsey	148		Dau		5	F	Scholar	Herts	St Stephens
1137	ENGLAND	Alfred	148		Son		3	M		Herts	St Stephens
1138	ENGLAND	Susan	148		Dau		6 m	F		Herts	St Stephens
1139	THOMPSON	Henry	149	Colney Street	Head	Mar	57	M	Agric Lab	Herts	Knebworth
1140	THOMPSON	Mary	149		Wife	Mar	47	F		Herts	Hitchin
1141	THOMPSON	Charles	149		Son		11	M	Agric Lab	Herts	Aldenham
1142	THOMPSON	George	149		Son		7	M	Scholar	Herts	St Stephens
1143	THOMPSON	Joseph	149		Son		5	M	Scholar	Herts	St Stephens
1144	WARREN	William	150	Colney Street	Head	Mar	33	M	Agric Lab	Herts	Harpenden
1145	WARREN	Mary	150		Wife	Mar	31	F		Herts	Abbots Langley
1146	WARREN	Mary Ann	150		Dau		11	F	Scholar	Herts	Abbots Langley
1147	WARREN	Hannah	150		Dau		5	F	Scholar	Herts	St Peters
1148	WARREN	George Albert	150		Son		1 m	M		Herts	St Stephens
1149	DIMMOCK	Joseph	150		Father-in-law	Widower	60	M	Agric Lab	Herts	Abbots Langley
1150	GREEN	Joseph	151	Colney Street	Head	Mar	45	M	Agric Lab	Herts	St Stephens
1151	GREEN	Elizabeth	151		Wife	Mar	44	F		Herts	St Peters
1152	GREEN	Rose	151		Dau	Unm	21	F	Brazilian Hat Maker	Herts	St Stephens
1153	GREEN	Mary Ann	151		Dau	Unm	19	F	Brazilian Hat Maker	Herts	St Stephens
1154	GREEN	George	151		Son		8	M	Scholar	Herts	St Stephens
1155	GREEN	Catherine	151		Dau		6	F	Scholar	Herts	St Stephens
1156	GREEN	Elizabeth	151		Dau		3	F		Herts	St Stephens
1157	FIELD	William	152	Colney Street	Head	Mar	51	M	Agric Lab	Herts	St Stephens
1158	FIELD	Charlotte	152		Wife	Mar	51	F		Herts	Shenley
1159	FIELD	Sarah	152		Dau	Unm	21	F		Herts	St Stephens
1160	FIELD	Charlotte	152		Dau		12	F	Scholar	Herts	St Stephens
1161	FIELD	William	152		Son		10	M	Scholar	Herts	St Stephens
1162	FIELD	Rebecca	152		Dau		8	F	Scholar	Herts	St Stephens
1163	COOK	Thomas	152		Brother-in-law	Unm	30	M	Agric Lab	Herts	Shenley
1164	FITZJOHN	George	152		Lodger	Unm	26	M	Agric Lab	Herts	Aldenham
1165	WITHERS	Louisa	153	Colney Street	Head	Unm	32	F	Landed Proprietor and Fundholder	Leics	Leicester
1166	WITHERS	Mary Ann	153		Mother	Mar	58	F	Gentlewoman	Leics	Leicester
1167	MUNNS	Sarah	153		Serv	Unm	29	F	General servant	Cambs	Fordham

End of the Village of Colney Street

1168	GOMME	John	154	St Julians Farm	Head	Widower	58	M	Farmer 362 acres employing 18 labourers	Bucks	Chesham
1169	GOMME	John Talbot	154		Son	Unm	28	M	Farmers son	Herts	Rickmansworth
1170	GOMME	Frederick T.	154		Son	Unm	26	M	Farmers son	Herts	St Stephens

	SURNAME	FORENAME	SCHEDULE NUMBER	ADDRESS	RELATIONSHIP	STATUS	AGE	SEX	OCCUPATION	COUNTY OF BIRTH	PLACE OF BIRTH
1171	GOMME	Sarah T.	154		Dau	Unm	24	F	Farmers daur	Herts	St Stephens
1172	GOMME	Emma T.	154		Dau	Unm	19	F	Farmers daur	Herts	St Stephens
1173	GOMME	James T.	154		Son	Unm	17	M	Farmers son	Herts	St Stephens
1174	DAVIS	Lucy`	154		Serv	Unm	15	F	Housemaid	Herts	Shenley
1175	STIERS	William	154		Serv	Unm	20	M	Agric Lab (ploughman)	Beds	Sundon
1176	WEST	Edward	154		Serv	Unm	19	M	Agric Lab	Beds	Toddington
1177	STARKINS	James	154		Serv	Unm	16	M	Agric Lab	Herts	St Stephens
1178	PUNTER	William	154		Serv	Unm	58	M	Agric Lab	Beds	Caddington
1179	DEACON	Mary	155	St Stephens	Head	Widow	62	F	Washerwoman	Herts	Hemel Hempstead
1180	DEACON	Thomas	155		Son	Unm	35	M	Agric Lab	Herts	Watford
1181	DEACON	Mary	155		Dau	Unm	19	F	Straw Plaiter	Herts	St Stephens
1182	BLY	James	156	St Stephens	Head	Mar	36	M	Agric Lab (shepherd)	Herts	St Peters
1183	BLY	Lydia	156		Wife	Mar	36	F		Herts	Hunsdon
1184	BLY	Hannah	156		Dau		14	F	Scholar	Herts	Shenley
1185	BLY	Mary Ann	156		Dau		13	F	Scholar	Herts	Shenley
1186	BLY	Lydia	156		Dau		11	F	Scholar	Herts	Shenley
1187	BLY	Eliza	156		Dau		9	F	Scholar	Herts	Shenley
1188	BLY	Thomas	156		Son		7	M	Scholar	Herts	St Stephens
1189	BLY	Amy	156		Dau		4	F		Herts	St Stephens
1190	BLY	John	156		Son		2	M		Herts	St Stephens
1191	BLY	James	156		Son		1 m	M		Herts	St Stephens
1192	GRAY	George	157	St Stephens	Head	Mar	24	M	Agric Lab	Beds	Luton
1193	GRAY	Elizabeth	157		Wife	Mar	22	F		Bucks	Ellesborough

End of District

Registrar's District: St Albans   Enumeration District 6c   Ref. HO 107/1713 folios 573-85

Windridge Ward

	SURNAME	FORENAME	SCHEDULE NUMBER	ADDRESS	RELATIONSHIP	STATUS	AGE	SEX	OCCUPATION	COUNTY OF BIRTH	PLACE OF BIRTH
1194	COTLIN	Isaac	1	Ragged Hall	Head	Mar	67	M	Agric Lab	Herts	St Stephens
1195	COTLIN	Elizabeth	1		Wife	Mar	66	F		Herts	St Peters
1196	BURTON	Sarah	2	Ragged Hall	Head	Widow	65	F	Straw Plaiter (Pauper)	Herts	St Stephens
1197	BURTON	George	2		Son	Unm	29	M	Agric Lab	Herts	St Stephens
1198	BURTON	Sarah	2		Dau	Unm	25	F	Straw Plaiter	Herts	St Stephens
1199	ANDERSON	Samuel	3	Ragged Hall	Head	Widower	73	M	Carpenter	Herts	St Stephens
1200	MOORE	Richard	3		Lodger	Widower	46	M	Agric Lab	Oxon	Milton

One uninhabited house

	SURNAME	FORENAME	SCHEDULE NUMBER	ADDRESS	RELATIONSHIP	STATUS	AGE	SEX	OCCUPATION	COUNTY OF BIRTH	PLACE OF BIRTH
1201	BURTON	Thomas	4	Ragged Hall	Head	Mar	28	M	Agric Lab	Herts	St Stephens
1202	BURTON	Mary	4		Wife	Mar	24	F	Brazilian Hat Maker	Herts	St Stephens
1203	ANDERSON	Samuel	5	Ragged Hall	Head	Mar	48	M	Carpenter	Herts	St Stephens
1204	ANDERSON	Sarah	5		Wife	Mar	50	F		Herts	St Stephens
1205	ANDERSON	Sarah	5		Dau	Unm	25	F	Dressmaker	Middx	Edmonton
1206	ANDERSON	Joseph	5		Son	Unm	16	M	Carpenters son	Herts	St Albans
1207	HOWARD	Arnott	6	Cuckmans	Head	Unm	43	M	Farmer of 212 acres employing 8 labourers	Herts	St Stephens
1208	HOWARD	Mary	6		Sister	Unm	47	F	Annuitant	Herts	St Stephens
1209	HOWARD	Eliza	6		Sister	Unm	44	F	Annuitant	Herts	St Stephens

1210	WILLMOTT	Lucretia	6		Sister	Widow	49	F	Annuitant	Herts	St Stephens
1211	GREEN	Mary	6		Serv	Widow	69	F	House Servant	Herts	St Peters
1212	MARTINDALE	William	6		Serv	Unm	17	M	Agric Lab	Herts	Abbots Langley
1213	GRAVESTOCK	Thomas	6		Serv		14	M	Agric Lab	Herts	St Stephens
1214	HOWARD	John	6		Serv	Unm	17	M	Agric Lab	Herts	St Stephens
1215	HOLT	William	7	Plaistows	Head	Mar	44	M	Farmer of 170 acres employing 11 labourers	Middx	Tottenham
1216	HOLT	Sophia	7		Wife	Mar	44	F		Bucks	Burcott
1217	ADAMS	Elizabeth Maria	7		Sister-in-law	Unm	35	F	Visitor	Bucks	Burcott
1218	ADAMS	Catherine Medora	7		Sister-in-law	Unm	27	F	Visitor	Bucks	Burcott
1219	ADAMS	Ann Jennet	7		Sister-in-law	Unm	23	F	Visitor	Bucks	Burcott
1220	SWEETING	Caroline	7		Serv	Unm	18	F	House Servant	Herts	Watford
1221	HILL	Robert	7		Serv	Unm	23	M	Agric Lab	Herts	St Peters
1222	BURRIDGE	James	7		Serv	Unm	22	M	Agric Lab	Herts	Abbots Langley
1223	FENN	Jesse	7		Serv	Unm	17	M	Agric Lab	Herts	St Stephens
1224	SHARP	William	7		Serv		13	M	Agric Lab	Herts	St Stephens
1225	ELLINGHAM	Charlotte	8	Bourne Hill	Head	Widow	42	F	Farmer of 186 acres employing 6 labourers	Middx	St Sepulchre
1226	ELLINGHAM	John	8		Son	Unm	20	M		Herts	St Stephens
1227	ELLINGHAM	Louisa	8		Dau	Unm	16	F		Herts	St Stephens
1228	ELLINGHAM	Alfred	8		Son		13	M	Scholar	Herts	St Stephens
1229	ELLINGHAM	Gabriel	8		Son		11	M	Scholar	Herts	St Stephens
1230	ELLINGHAM	Charlotte	8		Dau		8	F	Scholar	Herts	St Stephens
1231	ELLINGHAM	Anne	8		Dau		6	F	Scholar	Herts	St Stephens
1232	KIFF	Jonathan	8		Serv	Unm	18	M	Agric Lab	Herts	St Stephens
1233	CHARGE	Thomas	8		Serv	Unm	17	M	Agric Lab	Herts	St Stephens
1234	MILLIARD	James	9	Deanswick	Head	Mar	32	M	Agric Lab	Herts	Sandridge
1235	MILLIARD	Caroline	9		Wife	Mar	31	F	Straw Plaiter	Herts	St Albans
1236	MILLIARD	William	9		Son		6	M	Labs son	Herts	St Stephens
1237	MILLIARD	Mary Ann	9		Dau	Unm	1 m	F		Herts	St Stephens
1238	PEDDER	James	10	The Noke	Head	Mar	32	M	Agric Lab	Herts	Great Gaddesden
1239	PEDDER	Susan	10		Wife	Mar	33	F	Brazilian Hat Maker	Herts	Kings Langley
1240	PEDDER	George	10		Son		10	M	Scholar	Herts	St Stephens
1241	PEDDER	William	10		Son		8	M	Scholar	Herts	St Stephens
1242	PEDDER	Emma	10		Dau		4	F		Herts	St Stephens
1243	PEDDER	Reuben	10		Son		1	M		Herts	St Stephens
1244	MAILS	William	11	The Noke	Head	Mar	67	M	Agric Lab	Herts	Great Gaddesden
1245	MAILS	Elizabeth	11		Wife	Mar	54	F	Straw Plaiter	Herts	Datchworth
1246	TRIPP	John	11		Lodger	Widower	50	M	Agric Lab	Herts	Tring
1247	MAILS	John	11		Son	Unm	29	M	Agric Lab	Herts	St Michaels
1248	FIELD	Joseph	12	The Noke	Head	Mar	69	M	Agric Lab	Herts	Kings Walden
1249	DANCER	Rhoda	12		Dau	Mar	23	F	Brazilian Hat Maker	Herts	St Stephens
1250	DANCER	Thomas	12		Son-in-law	Mar	24	M	Agric Lab	Herts	Abbots Langley
1251	PHILLPOTT	William	13	The Noke	Head	Widower	65	M	Agric Lab	Herts	St Peters
1252	HILL	James	14	The Noke	Head	Unm	56	M	Agric Lab	Herts	St Stephens
1253	HILL	Samuel	14		Brother	Unm	47	M	Agric Lab	Herts	St Stephens

	SURNAME	FORENAME	SCHEDULE NUMBER	ADDRESS	RELATIONSHIP	STATUS	AGE	SEX	OCCUPATION	COUNTY OF BIRTH	PLACE OF BIRTH
1254	BROWN	George	15	The Holt	Head	Unm	22	M	Farmers son	Hunts	Eynesbury
1255	HOLAH	Ellen	15		Visitor	Unm	30	F		Middx	Kingsland
1256	HOLAH	Emma	15		Visitor	Unm	25	F		Middx	Kingsland
1257	CLAYDON	Elizabeth	15		Serv	Unm	22	F	House Servant	Bucks	
1258	SEABROOK	William	15		Serv	Unm	20	M	Agric Lab	Herts	St Stephens
1259	CAPEL	John	15		Serv		14	M	Agric Lab	Herts	Watford
1260	KINDER	John	16	Searches	Head	Unm	25	M	Farmer of 156 acres employing 7 men	Herts	St Stephens
1261	BARNS	William	16		Lodger	Mar	29	M	Farm Labourer	Bucks	Chesham
1262	BARNS	Mary	16		Lodgers Wife	Mar	27	F	Straw Plaiter	Bucks	Chesham
1263	BARNS	Robert	16		Lodgers Son		3	M		Herts	Rickmansworth
1264	TUFNALL	John	16		Serv	Unm	25	M	Agric Lab	Beds	Luton
1265	BOTSWORTH	Thomas	16		Serv	Unm	21	M	Agric Lab	Beds	Luton
1266	HEWITT	Walter	16		Serv		14	M	Agric Lab	Herts	St Stephens
1267	STOW	Samuel	17	White House	Head	Widower	78	M	Farmer of 155 acres employing 9 men	Herts	St Stephens
1268	KINDER	Thomas	17		Nephew	Unm	32	M	Farm bailiff	Herts	Hemel Hempstead
1269	WHITE	Ann	17		Serv	Unm	40	F	House Servant	Bucks	Aylesbury
1270	ABBEY	George	17		Serv	Unm	18	M	Agric Lab	Herts	Rickmansworth
1271	KIMPTON	Samuel	17		Serv		12	M	Agric Lab	Herts	Abbots Langley
1272	SIBLEY	Esther E	17		Visitor	Unm	21	F	Farmers daur	Herts	Wheathampstead
1273	MUNT	Joseph	18	Serge Hill	Head	Mar	39	M	Agric Lab	Herts	St Stephens
1274	MUNT	Ann	18		Wife	Mar	33	F	Brazilian Hat Maker	Herts	Abbots Langley
1275	MUNT	George	18		Son		9	M	Scholar	Herts	St Stephens
1276	MUNT	Joseph	18		Son		6	M	Scholar	Herts	St Stephens
1277	MUNT	John	18		Son		3	M		Herts	St Stephens
1278	MUNT	Reuben	18		Son		11 m	M		Herts	St Stephens
1279	MUNT	Ann	18		Mother	Widow	70	F	Charwoman	Herts	St Stephens
1280	DOUSE	Isaac	18		Lodger	Widower	60	M	Agric Lab	Herts	Abbots Langley
1281	LETCHFORD	George	18		Lodger		15	M	Agric Lab	Herts	St Michaels
1282	KIFF	Jonathan	19	Serge Hill	Head	Mar	54	M	Agric Lab	Herts	St Stephens
1283	KIFF	Ann	19		Wife	Mar	50	F	Agric Labs Wife	Herts	Abbots Langley
1284	KIFF	Frederick	19		Son	Unm	20	M	Agric Lab	Herts	Abbots Langley
1285	KIFF	Prudence	19		Dau	Unm	23	F	Brazilian Hat Maker	Herts	Abbots Langley
1286	KIFF	Silvey	19		Dau		13	F	Brazilian Hat Maker	Herts	St Stephens
1287	KIFF	Thomas	19		Son		10	M	Scholar	Herts	St Stephens
1288	KIFF	Sarah Ann	19		Visitor		2	F		Herts	St Stephens
1289	SOLLY	Samuel R	20	Serge Hill	Head	Widower	70	M	Magistrate	London	
1290	SOLLY	W. H.	20		Son	Unm	36	M	Barrister	London	
1291	MAWE	Thomas	20		Serv	Mar	47	M	Gardener	Middx	South Mimms
1292	MAWE	Mercy	20		Servs Wife	Mar	54	F		Rutland	Whissendine
1293	MAWE	Sarah Ann	20		Servs Niece	Unm	17	F		Rutland	Pilton [?]
1294	TWITCHELL	James	21	Bedmond House	Head	Widower	78	M	Farmer of 80 acres employing 2 men	Bucks	Chesham
1295	JIFFKINS	Sarah	21		Sister	Widow	67	F	Housekeeper	Bucks	Chesham
1296	DEAN	Thomas	21		Serv	Unm	20	M	Agric Lab	Herts	Abbots Langley
1297	KING	Isaac	22	Ninings Farm	Head	Mar	62	M	Servant	Wilts	Gt. Bedding

1298	KING	Elizabeth	22		Wife	Mar	67	F	Laundress	Hants	Kings Clare [Kingsclere]
1299	KING	James	22		Son	Mar	30	M	Wheelwright	Middx	Chelsea
1300	KING	Emelia	22		Dau-in-law	Mar	26	F	Laundress	Middx	South Mimms
1301	KING	Elizabeth	22		Grandau	Unm	10 m	F		Herts	Abbots Langley
1302	HALSEY	John	23	Ninings Farm	Head	Mar	57	M	Agric Lab	Herts	St Michaels
1303	HALSEY	Ann	23		Wife	Mar	53	F		Herts	St Albans
1304	HALSEY	William	23		Son	Unm	24	M	Agric Lab	Herts	Abbots Langley
1305	BAILEY	John Edmond	24	Mill House	Head	Mar	48	M	Farmer of 180 acres employing 11 men	Herts	St Stephens
1306	BAILEY	Elizabeth	24		Wife	Mar	43	F	Farmers wife	Herts	St Michaels
1307	BAILEY	John	24		Son	Unm	16	M	Farmers son	Herts	St Stephens
1308	BAILEY	Elizabeth	24		Dau		14	F	Scholar at home	Herts	St Stephens
1309	BAILEY	Jane	24		Dau		10	F	Scholar at home	Herts	St Stephens
1310	BAILEY	Thomas	24		Son		8	M	Scholar at home	Herts	St Stephens
1311	BAILEY	Emma	24		Dau		5	F	Scholar at home	Herts	St Stephens
1312	BAILEY	Frederick	24		Son		2	M		Herts	St Stephens
1313	BAILEY	Mary	24		Mother	Widow	80	F	Annuitant	Herts	Kinsworth
1314	DICKINSON	Elizabeth	24		Niece	Unm	20	F	Governess	Herts	St Stephens
1315	DELL	Caroline	24		Serv	Unm	17	F	House Servant	Herts	St Stephens
1316	SEABROOK	John	24		Serv	Unm	42	M	Agric Lab	Herts	St Stephens
1317	PERRY	William	24		Serv	Unm	19	M	Agric Lab	Herts	St Michaels
1318	DICKINSON	Charlotte	24		Niece	Unm	17	F	Farmers daur	Herts	St Stephens
1319	PEDDER	Thomas	25	Knowlsons	Head	Mar	27	M	Agric Lab	Herts	Abbots Langley
1320	PEDDER	Mary	25		Wife	Mar	29	F	Brazilian Hat Maker	Herts	St Stephens
1321	PEDDER	George	25		Son		8	M	Scholar	Herts	St Stephens
1322	PEDDER	John	25		Son		3	M		Herts	St Stephens
1323	HUTCHINS	James	26	Knowlsons	Head	Mar	28	M	Agric Lab	Herts	Abbots Langley
1324	HUTCHINS	Ann	26		Wife	Mar	34	F	Brazilian Hat Maker	Herts	St Stephens
1325	HUTCHINS	Sophia	26		Dau		10	F	Scholar	Herts	St Stephens
1326	HUTCHINS	William	26		Son		5	M	Scholar	Herts	St Stephens
1327	HUTCHINS	Sarah	26		Dau		3	F		Herts	St Stephens
1328	STOW	John	27	Tenements	Head	Mar	30	M	Farmer of 180 acres employing 7 men	Herts	St Stephens
1329	STOW	Sarah Ann	27		Wife	Mar	23	F	Farmers wife	Herts	St Stephens
1330	STOW	Emily Ann	27		Dau		4	F		Herts	St Stephens
1331	STOW	Ann Elizabeth	27		Dau		2	F		Herts	St Stephens
1332	STOW	John William	27		Son	Unm	10 m	M		Herts	St Stephens
1333	WHITE	John	27		Serv	Unm	25	M	Agric Lab	Herts	Abbots Langley
1334	BATES	David	27		Serv	Unm	19	M	Agric Lab	Herts	Abbots Langley
1335	PRICE	Emma	27		Serv	Unm	23	F	House Servant	Oxon	Thame
1336	CROFT	Joseph	28	Coles Bottom	Head	Mar	59	M	Agric Lab	Herts	Abbots Langley
1337	CROFT	Charlotte	28		Wife	Mar	56	F	Straw Plaiter	Herts	St Stephens
1338	CROFT	William	28		Son	Unm	22	M	Agric Lab	Herts	St Stephens
1339	CROFT	Maria	28		Dau		15	F	Straw Plaiter	Herts	St Stephens
1340	TIBBLES	James	29	Coles Bottom	Head	Mar	60	M	Agric Lab	Herts	St Stephens
1341	TIBBLES	Martha	29		Wife	Mar	59	F	Charwoman	Herts	Hitchin

	SURNAME	FORENAME	SCHEDULE NUMBER	ADDRESS	RELATIONSHIP	STATUS	AGE	SEX	OCCUPATION	COUNTY OF BIRTH	PLACE OF BIRTH
1342	TIBBLES	William	29		Son	Unm	40	M	Agric Lab	Herts	St Stephens
1343	TIBBLES	John	29		Son	Unm	20	M	Agric Lab	Herts	St Stephens
1344	BROWN	Robert	30	Waterdell	Head	Unm	27	M	Farm bailiff	Unknown	
1345	GODMAN	Richard	31	Black Boy	Head	Mar	54	M	Surveyor of land and timber	Herts	St Stephens
1346	GODMAN	Sarah	31		Wife	Mar	44	F		London	Rotherhithe
1347	GODMAN	Mary Ann	31		Dau		12	F	Brazilian Hat Maker	Herts	St Stephens
1348	GODMAN	Jane Hilson	31		Dau		10	F	Brazilian Hat Maker	Herts	St Peters
1349	GODMAN	Henry White	31		Son		7	M		Herts	St Peters
1350	GODMAN	William Bailey	31		Son		4	M		Herts	St Stephens
1351	GODMAN	Emily Lucy	31		Dau		1	F		Herts	St Stephens
1352	DANCER	James	32	Black Boy	Head	Mar	48	M	Agric Lab	Herts	St Stephens
1353	DANCER	Martha	32		Wife	Mar	47	F		Bucks	Winchendon
1354	DANCER	William	32		Son	Unm	23	M	Agric Lab	Herts	St Stephens
1355	DANCER	Hannah	32		Dau		11	F	Scholar	Herts	St Stephens
1356	DANCER	Lydia	32		Dau		6	F	Scholar	Herts	St Stephens
1357	SIMONS	Thomas	32		Lodger	Unm	24	M	Agric Lab	Herts	Abbots Langley
1358	PAYNE	Charlotte	33	Black Boy	Head	Unm	41	F	Brazilian Hat Maker	Herts	St Stephens
1359	PAYNE	Mary	33		Sister	Unm	38	F	Brazilian Hat Maker	Herts	St Stephens
1360	BROOKS	James	34	Black Boy	Head	Mar	50	M	Agric Lab	Herts	Hemel Hempstead
1361	BROOKS	Eliza	34		Wife	Mar	39	F		Herts	Watford
1362	WATKINS	Elizabeth	34		Dau		10	F	Scholar	Herts	Abbots Langley
1363	JOINER	Eliza	35	Black Boy	Head	Unm	34	F	Straw Plaiter	Herts	St Stephens
1364	JOINER	Emma	35		Sister	Unm	18	F	Brazilian Hat Maker	Herts	St Stephens
1365	JOINER	Benjamin	35		Brother		14	M	Agric Lab	Herts	St Stephens
1366	JOINER	Ann	35		Sister		10	F	School	Herts	St Stephens
1367	JORDAN	James	36	Black Boy	Head	Mar	50	M	Publican	Herts	Elstree
1368	JORDAN	Elizabeth	36		Wife	Mar	50	F		Herts	Watford
1369	BONCE	William	36		Son-in-law	Mar	27	M	Agric Lab	Herts	Watford
1370	BONCE	Charlotte	36		Son-in-laws wife	Mar	24	F	Brazilian Hat Maker	Herts	St Stephens
1371	JORDAN	George	36		Son	Unm	23	M	Agric Lab	Herts	St Stephens
1372	JORDAN	Mary	36		Dau	Unm	17	F	Brazilian Hat Maker	Herts	St Stephens
1373	JORDAN	James	36		Son		15	M	Farm Labourer	Herts	St Stephens
1374	JORDAN	Thomas	36		Son		13	M	Farm Labourer	Herts	St Stephens
1375	JORDAN	Hannah	36		Dau		11	F	Scholar	Herts	St Stephens
1376	JORDAN	Benjamin	36		Son		8	M	Scholar	Herts	St Stephens
1377	JOINER	George	37	Black Boy	Head	Mar	30	M	Agric Lab	Herts	St Stephens
1378	JOINER	Sarah	37		Wife	Mar	19	F		Herts	St Stephens
1379	WILLIAM	Adam	38	Black Boy	Head	Mar	36	M	Toll Collector	Sussex	Barcombe
1380	WILLIAM	Elizabeth	38		Wife	Mar	30	F	Toll Collectors wife	Sussex	Waldron
1381	WILLIAM	William	38		Son		6	M		Sussex	Barcombe
1382	WILLIAM	John	38		Son		2	M		Oxon	Chipping Norton
1383	WEEDON	Elijah	39	Mount Pleasant	Head	Mar	23	M	Agric Lab	Unknown	
1384	WEEDON	Hannah	39		Wife	Mar	24	F	Straw Plaiter	Herts	St Stephens
1385	WEEDON	Mary	39		Dau		2	F		Herts	St Stephens

1386	WEEDON	Caroline	39		Dau		1	F		Herts	St Stephens
1387	EWER	John	39		Brother-in-law	Widower	36	M	Agric Lab	Herts	St Stephens
1388	EWER	William	39		Nephew		9	M	Scholar	Herts	St Stephens
1389	FENN	Daniel	40	Mount Pleasant	Head	Mar	34	M	Agric Lab	Herts	St Stephens
1390	FENN	Sarah	40		Wife	Mar	26	F	Straw Plaiter	Herts	Watford
1391	EWER	John	41	Mount Pleasant	Head	Mar	60	M	Agric Lab	Herts	St Michaels
1392	EWER	Ann	41		Wife	Mar	61	F		Herts	St Stephens
1393	EWER	Elizabeth	41		Dau	Unm	30	F	Straw Plaiter	Herts	St Stephens
1394	EWER	James	41		Son	Unm	27	M	Agric Lab	Herts	St Stephens
1395	EWER	George	41		Son	Unm	18	M	Agric Lab	Herts	St Stephens
1396	ENGLAND	William	42	Mount Pleasant	Head	Mar	32	M	Agric Lab	Herts	St Stephens
1397	ENGLAND	Susannah	42		Wife	Mar	51	F	Straw Plaiter	Herts	St Stephens
1398	ENGLAND	David	42		Son	Unm	18	M	Agric Lab	Herts	St Stephens
1399	ENGLAND	William	42		Son		15	M	Agric Lab	Herts	St Stephens
1400	ENGLAND	George	43	Mount Pleasant	Head	Mar	23	M	Agric Lab	Herts	St Stephens
1401	ENGLAND	Hannah	43		Wife	Mar	21	F	Brazilian Hat Maker	Herts	St Stephens
1402	ENGLAND	John	43		Son		2	M		Herts	St Stephens
1403	ENGLAND	Mary	43		Dau		3 m	F		Herts	St Stephens
1404	NORWOOD	Francis	43		Lodger	Widower	53	M	Agric Lab	Herts	Watford
1405	BOTWRIGHT	Benjamin	44	Mount Pleasant	Head	Mar	32	M	Agric Lab	Herts	North Mimms
1406	BOTWRIGHT	Caroline	44		Wife	Mar	26	F	Brazilian Hat Maker	Herts	Abbots Langley
1407	BOTWRIGHT	John	44		Son		5	M		Herts	St Stephens
1408	BOTWRIGHT	Mary	44		Dau		3	F		Herts	St Stephens
1409	BOTWRIGHT	Ann	44		Dau		1	F		Herts	St Stephens
1410	BOTWRIGHT	Susan	44		Visitor	Widow	66	F	Annuitant	Suffolk	Warpole [Walpole]
1411	BOTWRIGHT	Sarah	44		Visitor	Unm	28	F	Brazilian Hat Maker	Herts	St Stephens
1412	BATES	Henry	45	Bricket Wood	Head	Mar	33	M	Game Keeper	Herts	Aldenham
1413	BATES	Elizabeth	45		Wife	Mar	35	F		Herts	Aldenham
1414	BATES	Henry	45		Son		10	M	Scholar	Herts	Aldenham
1415	BATES	Richard	45		Son		5	M		Herts	Aldenham
1416	BATES	John	45		Son		3	M		Herts	St Stephens
1417	BATES	Mary Ann	45		Dau		8	F		Herts	St Stephens
1418	HOWARD	James	46	Black Green	Head	Mar	28	M	Agric Lab	Herts	St Stephens
1419	HOWARD	Mary	46		Wife	Mar	22	F	Brazilian Hat Maker	Herts	St Stephens
1420	TIMSON	James	47	Black Green	Head	Mar	48	M	Agric Lab	Herts	St Stephens
1421	TIMSON	Susan	47		Wife	Mar	47	F	Brazilian Hat Maker	Herts	St Stephens
1422	TIMSON	Eliza	47		Dau	Unm	18	F	Brazilian Hat Maker	Herts	St Stephens
1423	TIMSON	Ann	47		Dau	Unm	16	F	Brazilian Hat Maker	Herts	St Stephens
1424	TIMSON	Emma	47		Dau		13	F	Brazilian Hat Maker	Herts	St Stephens
1425	TIMSON	David	47		Son		11	M	Agric Lab	Herts	St Stephens
1426	TIMSON	George	47		Son		6	M		Herts	St Stephens
1427	WARRELL	James	48	Black Green	Head	Mar	71	M	Agric Lab	Herts	St Stephens
1428	WARRELL	Ann	48		Wife	Mar	63	F		Herts	St Stephens
1429	WARRELL	Henry	48		Son	Unm	29	M	Brazilian Hat Maker	Herts	St Stephens
1430	BROWN	Richard	49	Lye Lane	Head	Mar	52	M	Farmer of 270 acres employing 4 men	Beds	Wilden

	SURNAME	FORENAME	SCHEDULE NUMBER	ADDRESS	RELATIONSHIP	STATUS	AGE	SEX	OCCUPATION	COUNTY OF BIRTH	PLACE OF BIRTH
1431	BROWN	Eliza	49		Wife	Mar	50	F	Farmers wife	Middx	Bishopsgate
1432	BROWN	John	49		Son	Unm	21	M	Farmers son	Hunts	Eynesbury
1433	WARRELL	Sarah	49		Serv	Unm	24	F	House Servant	Herts	St Stephens
1434	HORNCASTLE	John	50	Burston Farm	Head	Mar	52	M	Farmer of 225 acres employing 10 men	Surrey	Battersea
1435	HORNCASTLE	Elizabeth	50		Dau	Mar	24	F	Farmers daughter	Herts	Hatfield
1436	HORNCASTLE	Jane Augusta	50		Dau	Unm	19	F	Farmers daughter	Herts	Hatfield
1437	HORNCASTLE	Ann	50		Dau	Unm	17	F	Farmers daughter	Herts	Watford
1438	WEEDON	Charles	50		Serv	Unm	16	M	Agric Lab	Herts	St Stephens
1439	BONNICK	Thomas	50		Serv		13	M	Agric Lab	Herts	St Stephens
1440	HOWARD	James	51	Burston Gate	Head	Mar	60	M	Agric Lab	Herts	Abbots Langley
1441	HOWARD	Elizabeth	51		Wife	Mar	57	F	Straw Plaiter	Herts	Aldenham
1442	HOWARD	William	51		Son	Unm	30	M	Agric Lab	Herts	St Stephens
1443	STOW	John	52	Burston Gate	Head	Mar	47	M	Agric Lab	Herts	Abbots Langley
1444	STOW	Elizabeth	52		Wife	Mar	48	F	Brazilian Hat Maker	Herts	St Michaels
1445	STOW	M.E.	52		Dau	Unm	19	F	Brazilian Hat Maker	Herts	Abbots Langley
1446	STOW	Sarah	52		Dau	Unm	16	F	Brazilian Hat Maker	Herts	St Stephens
1447	STOW	William	52		Visitor	Widower	88	M	Agric Lab	Herts	St Stephens
1448	FIELD	John	53	Brick Field	Head	Mar	48	M	Agric Lab	Herts	St Michaels
1449	FIELD	Eliza	53		Wife	Mar	30	F	Brazilian Hat Maker	Herts	St Stephens
1450	FIELD	Frederick	53		Son		2	M		Herts	St Stephens
1451	SHARP	James	53		Lodger	Mar	70	M	Agric Lab	Herts	St Stephens
1452	SHARP	Sarah	53		Lodgers Dau	Unm	16	F	Brazilian Hat Maker	Herts	St Stephens
1453	PANGBORN	John	54	Brick Field	Head	Mar	70	M	Agric Lab	Herts	St Michaels
1454	PANGBORN	Elizabeth	54		Wife	Mar	65	F	Straw Plaiter	Herts	St Michaels
1455	PANGBORN	William	54		Son	Unm	27	M	Agric Lab	Herts	St Michaels
1456	PANGBORN	John	54		Son	Unm	24	M	Agric Lab	Herts	St Michaels
1457	PANGBORN	George	54		Son	Unm	17	M	Agric Lab	Herts	St Michaels
1458	HILL	Elizabeth	55	Brick Field	Head	Unm	41	F	Brazilian Hat Maker	Herts	St Stephens
1459	HILL	Hannah	55		Dau		14	F	Brazilian Hat Maker	Herts	St Stephens
1460	ROFFE	Thomas	56	Brick Field	Head	Mar	50	M	Agric Lab	Herts	Harpenden
1461	ROFFE	Elizabeth	56		Wife	Mar	52	F	Straw Plaiter	Herts	St Stephens
1462	ROFFE	Hannah	56		Dau		12	F	Straw Plaiter	Herts	St Stephens
1463	SIMMONDS	David	57	Brick Field	Head	Mar	29	M	Agric Lab	Herts	St Michaels
1464	SIMMONDS	Sarah	57		Wife	Mar	24	F	Straw Plaiter	Herts	St Stephens
1465	SIMMONDS	Frederick	57		Son		1 m	M		Herts	St Stephens
1466	KING	Thomas	58	Brick Field	Head	Mar	36	M	Agric Lab	Herts	St Stephens
1467	KING	Eliza	58		Wife	Mar	34	F	Brazilian Hat Maker	Herts	Abbots Langley
1468	KING	William	58		Son		12	M	Agric Lab	Herts	St Stephens
1469	KING	George	58		Son		10	M	Agric Lab	Herts	St Stephens
1470	KING	Emma	58		Dau		1	F		Herts	St Stephens
1471	HARRISON	Henry	59	Brick Field	Head	Mar	42	M	Agric Lab	Herts	St Stephens
1472	HARRISON	Charlotte	59		Wife	Mar	41	F	Brazilian Hat Maker	Herts	St Stephens
1473	HARRISON	Joseph	59		Son		12	M	Agric Lab	Herts	St Stephens
1474	HARRISON	Susan	59		Dau		9	F	Brazilian Hat Maker	Herts	St Stephens
1475	HARRISON	Maria	59		Dau		7	F	Brazilian Hat Maker	Herts	St Stephens

1476	HARRISON	Hannah	59		Dau		5	F	Brazilian Hat Maker	Herts	St Stephens
1477	HARRISON	Ruth	59		Dau		3	F		Herts	St Stephens
1478	JANES	Thomas	60	Chiswell Green	Head	Mar	56	M	Farm Labourer	Bucks	Edlesborough
1479	JANES	Elizabeth	60		Wife	Mar	55	F		Herts	Hatfield
1480	JANES	Ruth	60		Mother	Widow	81	F	Straw Plaiter	Bucks	Dagnall
1481	LITCHFIELD	James	61	Chiswell Green	Head	Mar	55	M	Agric Lab	Herts	St Stephens
1482	LITCHFIELD	Susan	61		Wife	Mar	55	F	Charwoman	Herts	St Stephens
1483	LITCHFIELD	Charlotte	61		Dau	Unm	16	F	Brazilian Hat Maker	Herts	St Stephens
1484	LITCHFIELD	Frederick	61		Son		4	M		Herts	St Stephens
1485	LITCHFIELD	William	61		Brother	Unm	59	M	Agric Lab	Herts	St Stephens
1486	NORWOOD	William	62	Chiswell Green	Head	Mar	68	M	Agric Lab	Herts	St Stephens
1487	NORWOOD	Elizabeth	62		Wife	Mar	68	F	Blind	Herts	St Stephens
1488	NORWOOD	Charlotte	62		Dau	Unm	30	F		Herts	St Stephens
1489	KIFF	William	63	Chiswell Green	Head	Unm	47	M	Agric Lab	Herts	St Stephens
1490	HOWARD	Thomas	64	Chiswell Green	Head	Mar	54	M	Agric Lab	Herts	St Stephens
1491	HOWARD	Susannah	64		Wife	Mar	44	F	Brazilian Hat Maker	Herts	St Stephens
1492	HOWARD	James	64		Son	Unm	22	M	Agric Lab	Herts	St Stephens
1493	HOWARD	Sarah	64		Dau		14	F	Brazilian Hat Maker	Herts	St Stephens
1494	HOWARD	Jane	64		Dau		11	F	Brazilian Hat Maker	Herts	St Stephens
1495	HOWARD	Hannah	64		Dau		9	F	Brazilian Hat Maker	Herts	St Stephens
1496	HOWARD	William	64		Son		5	M		Herts	St Stephens
1497	HOWARD	Emily	64		Dau		3	F		Herts	St Stephens
1498	HOWARD	Ann	64		Dau		2 m	F		Herts	St Stephens
1499	LIVINGS	Stephen	65	Chiswell Green	Head	Mar	30	M	Agric Lab	Herts	St Stephens
1500	LIVINGS	Elizabeth	65		Wife	Mar	32	F	Straw Plaiter	Herts	St Stephens
1501	LIVINGS	Frederick	65		Son		5	M		Herts	St Stephens
1502	LIVINGS	Louisa	65		Dau		3	F		Herts	St Stephens
1503	LIVINGS	Stephen	65		Son		1	M		Herts	St Stephens
1504	MARTIN	William	66	Bunker Hill	Head	Mar	54	M	Blacksmith and licensed brewer	Herts	St Stephens
1505	MARTIN	Hannah	66		Wife	Mar	53	F		Herts	Sandridge
1506	MARTIN	William	66		Son	Unm	23	M	Blacksmith	Herts	St Stephens
1507	MARTIN	George	66		Son	Unm	21	M	Baker	Herts	St Stephens
1508	MARTIN	Isaac	66		Son	Unm	18	M	Blacksmith	Herts	St Stephens
1509	MARTIN	John	66		Son	Unm	16	M	Blacksmith	Herts	St Stephens
1510	MARTIN	Eliza	66		Dau		13	F	Brazilian Hat Maker	Herts	St Stephens
1511	MARTIN	Ann	66		Dau		10	F		Herts	St Stephens
1512	GOODWIN	John	67	St Stephens	Head	Mar	38	M	Coachman	Herts	St Stephens
1513	GOODWIN	Jane	67		Wife	Mar	42	F	Laundress	Hants	Basingstoke
1514	GOODWIN	George	67		Son		11	M	Scholar	Herts	St Stephens
1515	GOODWIN	Emma	67		Dau		3	F		Herts	St Stephens
1516	HINLEY	Elizabeth	68	St Stephens	Head	Widow	77	F	Annuitant	Middx	Tottenham
1517	SIMONDS	Hannah	68		Companion	Unm	36	F		Suffolk [Hunts]	Molesworth
1518	ROWLERSON	Selina	68		Serv	Unm	30	F	House Servant	Kent	Strood
1519	DAY	John	68		Serv	Mar	24	M	House Servant	Beds	Luton
1520	HUTCHINS	William	69	St Stephens	Head	Mar	36	M	Higgler	Herts	Abbots Langley

	SURNAME	FORENAME	SCHEDULE NUMBER	ADDRESS	RELATIONSHIP	STATUS	AGE	SEX	OCCUPATION	COUNTY OF BIRTH	PLACE OF BIRTH
1521	HUTCHINS	Allice	69		Wife	Mar	36	F		Oxon	Thame
1522	KIRTLAND	Esther	69		Niece	Unm	17	F	Bonnet Sewer	Oxon	Thame
1523	ENGLAND	Ephraim	69		Lodger	Unm	46	M	Agric Lab	Herts	St Stephens
1524	SEYMOUR	E	69		Lodger		4	F		Surrey	Twickenham
1525	READ	Charles	70	St Stephens	Head	Mar	38	M	Agric Lab	Herts	Harpenden
1526	READ	Matilda	70		Wife	Mar	35	F	Straw Plaiter	Herts	Redbourn
1527	READ	Hannah	70		Dau		13	F	Brazilian Hat Maker	Herts	St Michaels
1528	READ	William	70		Son		7	M	Brazilian Hat Maker	Herts	St Michaels
1529	WARD	Ann	71	St Stephens	Head	Widow	68	F	Annuitant	Middx	St Marylebone
1530	BOSHER	Frances	71		Serv	Unm	24	F	House servant	Herts	St Stephens
1531	HALL	Mary	72	St Stephens	Head	Unm	65	F	Fund holder	Middx	St James
1532	BULL	Mary	72		Niece	Widow	50	F	Annuitant	Middx	Kensington
1533	BULL	Mary	72		Gt. Niece		13	F	Scholar at home	Middx	Islington
1534	BRANDOM	Jane	72		Serv		15	F	House Servant	Herts	St Michaels
1535	GODMAN	John	73	St Stephens	Head	Mar	49	M	Land and Timber Surveyor	Herts	St Stephens
1536	GODMAN	Louisa	73		Wife	Mar	50	F		Herts	Hitchin
1537	GODMAN	John	73		Son	Unm	22	M	Land and Timber Surveyor	Herts	St Stephens
1538	GODMAN	Frederick J.	73		Son	Unm	18	M	Land and Timber Surveyor	Herts	St Stephens
1539	GODMAN	Catherine J.	73		Dau		13	F		Herts	St Stephens
1540	GODMAN	Emma L.	73		Dau		10	F	Scholar	Herts	St Stephens
1541	GODMAN	Arthur	73		Son		8	M	Scholar	Herts	St Stephens
1542	GODMAN	Elenor J.	73		Dau		6	F	Scholar	Herts	St Stephens
1543	COX	Henry	74	St Stephens	Head	Unm	60	M	Farmer of 100 acres employing 10 men	Herts	Hatfield
1544	COMPLIN	Sarah	74		Friend	Unm	53	F	House Keeper	Hants	Wick [Wickham?]
1545	SPRIGGS	Marianne	74		Serv	Unm	23	F	Cook	Herts	Lemsford Mill [Hatfield]
1546	ASHBY	Maria	74		Serv	Unm	20	F	House Servant	Herts	Abbots Langley
1547	BOOTHBY	Cunningham	75	Vicarage	Head	Mar	31	M	Officiating Minister St Stephens	Lancs	Liverpool
1548	BOOTHBY	Jane	75		Wife	Mar	22	F		Scotland	Moffatt
1549	BOOTHBY	James W A	75		Son		1	M		Essex	Haydens
1550	TODD	William	75		Visitor	Unm	21	M	Student	Scotland	Moffatt
1551	HARVEY	Nancy P.	75		Serv	Unm	27	F	House Servant	Devon	[Unknown]
1552	WEBB	Fanny	75		Serv	Unm	35	F	House Servant	Herts	Datchworth
1553	WALLER	Jane	75		Serv	Unm	23	F	House Servant	Herts	St Stephens

One uninhabited house

End of Windridge Ward, St Stephens.

Name index

The various districts into which the enumerators' returns have been divided are described in Part One, Chapter Three, above pp. 31–3. They are identified in the index by an appropriate abbreviation, and each district is treated in a separate chapter in Part Two. These abbreviations, the chapters to which they pertain and the relevant page references, are as follows:

				Pages
A	St Albans parish	Chapter	10	449
H	Harpenden parish	Chapter	5	231
MR	St Michaels parish (rural)	Chapter	12	556
MU	St Michaels parish (urban)	Chapter	11	530
OH	Out-hamlets, Liberty of St Albans	Chapter	9	412
P	St Peters parish, Borough of St Albans	Chapter	8	352
R	Redbourn parish	Chapter	6	279
S	St Stephens parish	Chapter	14	586
SA	Sandridge parish	Chapter	7	330
W	Wheathampstead parish	Chapter	4	185
WK	St Albans Union Workhouse	Chapter	13	580

A

ABBESS
Sarah — WK215

ABBEY
George — S1270

ABBISS
David — MR818
Eliza — MR814
Eliza — MR820
Emma — MR815
Enoch — MR813
George — MR817
James — MR819
Mary Ann — H722
Sarah — MR816

ABBOTT
Amos — H964
Ann — H991
Ann — R118
Ann — R743
Ann — R745
Ann — R985
Ann — R1025
Ann — R1142
Bessie K. — A201
Bryomer — H960
Charles — R277
Charles — R1139
Charles — R1712
Charlotte — R280
Daniel — R283
Daniel — R742
Daniel — R744
Eliza — R278
Elizabeth — MU520
Elizabeth A — W243
Emma — R279
Fanny M. — A200
George — H458
George — R282
Georgiana — R1530
Hannah — R1140
Hannah — R1143
Henry — R281
Henry — W237
James — R1529
Jane — H963
Jane — H1608
Jane — W242
John — R275
John — R1024
John — R1711
Lydia — H992
Mary Ann — R1141
Mary Ann — W238
Meheler R. — H961
Rosa — H990
Rowland T. — A198
Sarah — R276
Sarah — R1039
Sarah — R1467
Sarah F. — A199
Thomas — R117
Thomas — R1468
William — H959
William — H962
William — R119
William — R984

ABLETT
Frederick — WK36

ABRAHAMS
Caroline — R780

ABRAHAMS
George — H1826

William — R779

ABRAMS
Ann — R1112
Eliza — R1113
Joseph — R1108
Mary — R1109
Mary — R1110
Sarah — R1111
William — R2068

ADAMS
Aaron — MR555
Abel — W356
Albert — W1760
Alfred — R494
Ann — SA776
Ann Jennet — S1219
Anne — W1759
Arthur — R493
Catherine Medora — S1218
Daniel — R166
Daniel — R490
Daniel — W352
Elizabeth — SA777
Elizabeth — W2
Elizabeth — W354
Elizabeth Maria — S1217
Emma — H134
Emma — OH1409
Emma — P261
Frederick — R495
George — OH1407
George — OH1410
George — P338
Harriet — W355
James — P341
John — H132
John — P339
Joseph — H1914
Mary — H1913
Mary — OH1408
Mary — P2241
Ruth — W353
Sarah — H133
Sarah — H1912
Sarah — R491
Sarah — P337
Sarah — P340
Susan — SA774
Susan — WK94
Susan — MU722
Susana — SA728
Thomas — R492
Thomas — SA775
Walter — R496
William — H1911
William — R396
William — SA773
William — W1
William — W1758

ADDINGTON
Ann — H46
Ann — OH356
Charles — SA283
Eleanor Anne — MR455
Eliza — P698
Emma — W221
Hannah — SA538
Henry Unwin — MR454
Hester — OH355
James — W1223
Jane — OH359
John — OH360
Joseph — OH357
Lizzey — SA539

Maryann — OH358
Sarah — SA540
Sarah — W1211
William — SA537
William — OH354

ADEY
Goodson — H806
Priscilla — H807

AGGELTON
Mary — P1505

AGUTTER
Ben — A436
Benjamin — A433
Benjamin — A440
E.M. — A437
Emma — P213
Henry Odell — A438
Maria — A434
Mary Ann — A442
Rosanna — A443
Sarah — A441
Sarah — P214

ALDERSON
Elizabeth — OH396
James S. — OH395

ALDRIDGE
Ann — SA559
Charles — SA558
Charles C. — MR553
Charlotte — A2838
Charlotte — A2839
Edward — SA562
Edward — A599
Elizabeth — MU376
Fanny — A598
George C. — MR552
Henry — SA418
Henry — A597
Henry — MU377
Isabel — SA44
James — SA556
John — MU378
Jonathan — A478
Joseph — A2841
Joseph — MR551
Mary — SA557
Richard — A2840
Susan — SA560
William — SA561
William — MU379

ALLCOCK
Charlotte — R1206
Daniel — R1205

ALLEN
Allice — SA841
Ann — H68
Ann — R224
Ann — OH544
Ann — W727
Ann — OH1084
Anne — OH520
Bethia — OH512
Catherine Louise — A3230
Catherine Lucy — A11
Charles — OH547
Charles — MR312
Charlotte — H1256
Charlotte — SA838
Charlotte — MU486
Eliza — R222
Eliza — R987
Eliza — OH515
Eliza — A3229
Eliza — MR457

Eliza Ann — A3231
Elizabeth — OH522
Elizabeth — OH1083
Elizabeth — OH1086
Elizabeth — A9
Elizabeth — MR730
Elvia Maria — H1214
Fanny — OH518
Frances Charlotte — A3234
Frances Elizabeth — A10
Frederick — OH57
Frederick — MR70
George — SA654
George — OH521
George — OH532
George — OH546
George — A8
George — WK82
Hannah — OH55
Hannah — OH548
Henry — OH43
Henry — W729
Isabella — SA840
James — OH511
James — OH530
James — OH542
James — OH1085
James — OH1087
James — W1478
Jane — MU605
John — H66
John — H70
John — R986
John — SA837
John — OH1081
John — MR732
John — W725
John C. — R221
John Scott — A3228
John Scott — A3233
Joseph — OH519
Joseph — OH662
Joseph — MR731
Lewis — H1210
Louisa — H69
Louisa — SA839
Lousia S. — H1213
Lydia — R223
Mahalla — SA639
Maria — H114
Mary — H116
Mary — H1211
Mary — R1420
Mary — SA640
Mary Ann — OH56
Matilda — H115
Richard — OH1088
Richard — WK164
Richard — MR729
Rosetta — A3235
Samuel — OH513
Sarah — H67
Sarah — OH516
Sarah — OH531
Sarah — OH1080
Sarah — W728
Sophia — W726
Susan — OH523
Susan — OH533
Susan — OH543
Thomas — H117
Thomas — OH54
Thomas — OH167
Thomas — OH514

Thomas	OH1079	Samuel	S1199	Mary	W1273	Maria	W604
Thomas	A3232	Samuel	S1203	**ANTHONY**		Mary	W574
William	H71	Sarah	A1082	Eliza	A1062	Mary Ann	W603
William	H118	Sarah	A2496	Elizabeth	S982	Rebecca	SA534
William	H1212	Sarah	S579	**APPLEBY**		Rose	H1736
William	R225	Sarah	S1204	Elizabeth	P284	Sarah	H1476
William	SA638	Sarah	S1205	**APTED [?]**		Sarah	H1650
William	OH517	Susan	S500	Emma	P1127	Sarah	H1654
William	OH545	Susan	S578	**ARBER**		Sarah	H1742
William	OH1082	William	OH462	Mary Ann	H837	Sarah	SA162
William	MR733	William	A2499	**ARBORN**		Sarah	SA165
ALLIN		William	S576	Eliza	R1084	Sarah	P2322
Joseph	P2118	William Morris	A1213	Emma	R1086	Sarah	W576
Sarah	P2119	**ANDERSSON**		Hannah	R1085	Sarah	W606
ALLISON		Laura M	SA480	Joseph	R1082	Sarah	W1218
Jilpha	A2653	**ANDREW**		Rebecca	MU900	Susan	H16
Levi	A2652	Ann	H1011	Reuben	MU902	Susannah	W797
Thomas	A2651	Eliza	H1012	Sarah	R1083	Thomas	H1477
ALLWAY		Elizabeth	H1010	Theresa	R1087	Thomas	H1651
Elizabeth	P520	Elizabeth	WK76	Tresa	MU901	Thomas	SA531
James	WK62	Emma	H380	William	MU899	Thomas	SA674
AMBROSE		Frances	S780	**ARBOROUGH**		Thomas	P2321
John	A2822	George	S751	Emma	R905	Thomas	P2324
Mary	A945	Hannah	S776	Jane	R906	Thomas	W794
Mary Ann	A2823	Jabez	H381	John	R903	Thomas	W796
William	MU84	John	WK75	Mary	R904	Thomas	W1217
AMERY		Joseph	S672	**ARCHER**		William	H1302
Elizabeth	R1633	Joseph	S775	Alfred	SA535	William	H1649
Robert	R1632	Priscilla	H379	Ann	H1150	William	H1652
AMES		Sarah	S777	Ann	H1746	William	SA161
Mary	SA630	Sarah Ann	S673	Ann	SA532	William	SA533
AMSDEN		Thomas	S778	Ann	SA536	William	W573
Alfred	P1756	William	H378	Ann	P2323	William	W856
Benjamin	P76	William	S779	Ann	W602	Willm	SA419
Frances	P77	**ANDREWS**		Ann	W860	**[ARCHER ?]**	
Frederick	P1758	Elizabeth	SA759	Charles	WK146	Infant	SA168
Harriet F.	P78	Elizabeth	OH376	Charles	P1458	**ARGENT**	
Martha	P1757	Elizabeth	A379	Edward	H1734	James	A2080
Mary A.	P79	George	SA758	Edward	SA166	Susan Charlotte	A2081
ANDERSON		James	SA753	Elizabeth	H1743	**ARISS**	
Ann	S682	Laura	R1604	Elizabeth	SA160	Daniel John	A35
Ann	W1861	Maria	SA754	Elizabeth	W577	**ARMSTRONG**	
Anna	A1083	Mary	SA755	Elizabeth	W608	Agnes	P121
Arthur	W1862	Mary	P2275	Elizabeth	W795	Andrew	P125
Benjamin	WK109	Sarah	SA757	Ellen	H1739	Ann	P120
Benjamin	S498	Sarah	P2274	Emely	SA484	Mary	P119
Benjamin	S681	Susan	A1375	Emily	H1744	**ARNOLD**	
Betsey	S755	Thomas	A776	Emily	W1221	Aaron	WK169
Betsey	S756	William	SA756	Emma	H1738	Albert	W100
Charles	S754	William	S364	Emma	SA164	Amelia	A879
Charles	W1863	**ANGEL**		Esther	W605	Amelia	P2478
Daniel	OH460	Alfred	A1351	Frederick	H1747	Ann	R1424
Eliza	S499	Elizabeth	A1347	George	H1475	Ann	A1835
Elizabeth	S575	Robert	A1352	George	H1653	Ann	W117
Emma	A1214	William	A1348	George	SA167	Ann	W536
Emma	A1673	**ANGLE**		George	W575	Ann	W1554
Emma	A2497	Charles	H488	George	W601	Ann	W1556
Emma	A3197	Charlotte	H493	George O.	A2523	Caroline	P2477
Harriet	A1672	Eliza	H491	Hannah	H1735	Charles	A1833
James	A2508	George	H494	Hannah	W859	Charlotte	P768
James	A2509	Hannah	H490	Hannah	W1220	David	P765
John	A1670	Henry	H492	James	SA163	David	P770
John	P1531	Mary	H489	James	W858	Edward	OH1461
John	W1860	**ANNESLY**		James	W1219	Edward Dolling	A1836
Joseph	S574	Sophia	MR117	Jane	H1745	Eliza	A880
Joseph	S1206	**ANSELL**		Jane	SA542	Elizabeth	R648
Josiah	A2498	Amelia	P470	Jane	W607	Elizabeth	OH1460
Kitty	A1671	Ann	R341	Jane	W857	Elizabeth	W1734
Lydia	S501	Ann	W1274	Jessie	H1748	Emily	W120
Martha	S601	Charles	W1272	John	H1737	Esther	P771
Maryann	S577	Charlotte	W1171	John	H1741	Francis Joseph	P772
Phebe	OH461	Elizabeth	A782	John	SA397	George	H901
Richard	OH463	George	P469	John	MR480	George	H904
Richard	W1864	John J.	R340	Joseph	W861	George	OH1459

George	W211
George	W1559
George Farr	P238
Harriet	A1834
Harriet	W214
Isabella	P1969
James	R647
James	P769
James	W116
James	W244
James	W535
James	W1557
James	W1733
Jane	W121
John	R1423
John	SA510
John	W1751
Joseph	W109
Julia	W1752
Julia M	W213
Martha	H905
Martha	A671
Mary	R1426
Mary	WK170
Mary	W212
Mary A	W1749
Mary Ann	H903
Mary Ann	P766
Mary Ann	P767
Matthew	W1553
Matthew	W1555
Oliver	W1748
Patty	R1422
Robert	P42
Ruth	W108
Samuel	P1968
Sarah	H902
Sarah	W118
Sarah	W245
Sarah	W1747
Susan	H45
Susan E	W1750
Susannah	P239
Susannah	P2476
Thomas	H906
William	R1421
William	R1425
William	P2475
William	W119
William	W1558
ARNOLL	
Benjamin	MR368
ARNOT	
Sarah	A12
ASHBURNHAM	
Theodona	S411
ASHBY	
Ann	R335
Catherine	R337
Catherine	R593
Charles	H185
Daniel	R296
Daniel	R334
Elizabeth	R338
Frances	R592
Georgiana	R336
Harriott	H1451
John	R330
John S.	R71
John T.	R333
Joseph	R75
Joseph	S293
Maria	S1546
Maria A.	R70

Maria E.	R73
Mary	R76
Mary Ann	R297
Mary D.	R591
Samuel	R74
Sarah	R294
Sarah	R295
Sarah	R331
Sarah	R332
Sarah	R590
Sarah	S292
Sarah A.	R72
Thomas	R69
Thomas	A382
Thomas (Snr)	R589
William	R293
William	R1583
William	S291
ASHTON	
Ann	P1858
Sarah	P1859
Thomas	P1857
ASHWELL	
Ann	MU713
Daniel	MR809
David	MR810
Edward	A1055
Elizabeth	P1724
George	MU712
Georgianna	P536
Helen	MU714
Henry	MU716
Jane	MR812
Sarah	MR811
Stephen	MU715
Thomas	P537
William	P535
William	P538
William	P1723
ASLIN	
Ann	R1912
Avery	R1126
Avery	R1829
Benjamin	R701
Charles	R1907
Charlotte E.	R703
Edmund	R1908
Eliza	R702
Emily	R1911
Frederick	R97
George	R1913
John	R704
Maria	R1910
Mary	R1127
Mary	R1827
Mary	R1906
Robert	R1822
Rose	R1828
Samuel	R705
Susan	R1820
Susan	R1830
Thomas	R1819
Thomas	R1904
Thomas	R1905
Walter	R706
William	R1821
William	R1826
William	R1909
ASTELL	
Emma	A531
ASTIN	
Elizabeth	MU255
Mary	MU254
Susan	MU253

Thomas	MU256
ATKINS	
Amelia	A3002
Amos	A3001
Ann	MU685
Cavilione [?]	A2998
Daniel	MR295
Edemond	A2999
Edmond	OH1203
Edward	A2586
Edward	S107
Eli	A3000
Eliza	OH1204
Emma	S106
Frederick	OH1330
Frederick	MU688
George	OH1331
George	A3308
Harriet	P1949
Henry W.	MU687
James	S108
Jane	A2587
Jane	A2643
Jane	MU594
John	MU595
John	S101
John	S104
Joseph	A2995
Mary	S102
Phoebe	W1468
Reuben	A2997
Sarah	OH1329
Sarah	MU60
Sarah	P1233
Sarah A.	MU686
Shadrach	MU684
Tamer	A2996
Thomas	MU597
Thomas	S105
William	OH1328
William	MU593
William	MU596
William	S103
ATLINCH [?]	
Mary	MR468
ATTWOOD	
Alfred	A1312
Alfred	W1028
Amos	H913
Amos	W413
Ann	H1655
Ann	H1663
Ann	A1311
Ann	W1029
Caroline	A1584
Charles	A1317
Charles	W1026
Charlotte	W965
Creser	A1316
Eliza	H1662
Eliza	H1664
Eliza	W966
Elizabeth	H912
Emily	H1979
Emma	MR649
Eyden [?]	A1314
Frank	H1291
Frank	H1661
George	H914
George	MR647
George	W968
Harriet	W967
James	H1218
Joseph	R1075

Joseph	MR650
Joseph	W964
Lydia	H881
M Ann	A1310
Mary	H1469
Mary	W1030
Mary A.	MR646
Mary A.	MR648
Razer	A1315
Rose	H1665
Sarah	H882
Sarah	A1313
Sarah	W1027
Sarah	W1094
Susanna	P2092
Thomas	H1666
Thomas	P2091
William	H880
William	H911
William	R1074
William	A1309
William	MR645
AUBERN	
Ann	R1882
Eliza	R1885
Emma	R1883
George	R1884
John	R1881
Sarah	R823
AUNSCOMBE	
Allen	R231
AUSTEN	
William	P798
Alice	R140
Ann	R463
Ann	W1408
Charles	R1835
David	MU90
Eliza	R1832
Eliza	P1468
Elizabeth	R1769
Emily	MU93
Esther	MU91
Fanny	WK165
George	R1678
Hannah	R1677
Henry	R1338
John	R1676
John	MU152
Joseph	R1767
Joseph	P1467
Martha	MU149
Martha	MU151
Mary	R1768
Mary	P2268
Rose	R1834
Samuel	R1679
Samuel	MU148
Samuel	MU150
Sarah	R1339
Sarah	MU94
Sarah	MU764
Thomas	R1831
William	MU92
William	P2269
William	W1407
AVIS	
Charlotte	P1672
Mary	P810
AXTELL	
Daniel	R1462
Francis	R1501
James	R1460
Joseph	R1503

John	R736
Mary	R737

BLAKE

Ann	MR543
George	A1879
Harriet	OH955
Jacob	A31
John	MU387
Joseph	MU47
Louisa	MU49
Mary	A32
Mary	MU48
Philip	MU50
Sarah	A1880

BLAKEMORE

Amelia E	MU132
Charles	MU130
Elizabeth	MU128
Elizabeth	P719
Harriet	MU134
James M	MU133
John	MU127
John Wm	MU129
Mary Ann	MU131
Sarah	MU135

BLAND

James	W155
Sarah	W156

BLANDS

Thomas White	A2071

BLANKS

Charles	A2073
Eliza	A2070
Eliza	A2075
Frederick	A2072
John Thomas	A2069
Walter	A2074

BLENDALL

John Robert	A1710

BLETSO

Ann	A725

BLEWITT

Charles	P1230

BLIGH

Emma	A2320
Martin	A2319
Mary Ann	A2322
William	A2321

BLIGHT

Ann	A1475

BLISTOW

John	OH643
Joseph	OH645
Sophia	OH644

BLOOMFIELD

Mary	A528

BLOW

Alfred	P2342
Ann	W71
Ann	W75
Charlotte	P2348
Ellen	P2343
Emma	P2341
Emma	W73
Frederick	P2344
Harriet	W74
James	P2347
Jane	P2346
Mary	P2345
Robert	W72
Robert	W1591
Sophia	P2339
Walter	P2349
William	P2338

William	P2340
William	W70

BLOWS

Louisa	H336

BLUCHER

Anne	A2228

BLUNDELL

George	A830

BLUNT

Charlotte	P206
John	A2912

BLY

Amy	S1189
Eliza	S1187
Hannah	S1184
James	S1182
James	S1191
John	S1190
Lydia	S1183
Lydia	S1186
Mary Ann	S1185
Thomas	S1188

BLYTH

Mary Ann	A2972
Thomas	A2971

BOFF

Anne	S504
Arthur	S508
Charlotte	S495
Eliza Jane	S497
Frederick	S511
George	S509
Henry	S514
James	S494
James	S503
Joseph	S506
Mary	H1515
Mary	S507
Mary Ann	S510
Mary Ann	S513
Samuel	S496
Samuel	S505
Sarah	S512

BOFFLE

Martha	OH839

BOGGIS

George	R953
George	R956
Mary	R954
Mary Ann	R955

BOGUE

George	MR430
Martha	MR431

BOLTER

Charles	MR183
William	MR182

BOLTON

Joseph	P1377

BONCE

Charlotte	S1370
William	S1369

BOND

Alfred	A748
Anne	A747
George	A746
Mary	A750
Susannah	A749

BONE

Thomas	OH369

BONET

Ann	A372
Jane	A371

BONFIELD

John	H1882

Sarah	H1883
William	WK175

BONNIC

Ann	R723
Charles	R722
George	R721
James	R718
Martha	R716
Mary	R720
Samuel	R715
Samuel	R717
Thomas	R719

BONNICK

Caroline	S42
Charles	S41
Eliza	S39
George	S38
Jane	S40
Martha	S37
Samuel	WK179
Thomas	S36
Thomas	S1439

BONNICK [?]

Charlotte	A1094
William	A1093

BOOBYER

Adam Edwin	P313
Emily Carpenter	P311
Emma Diana Jane	P314
Henry Richard	P317
James Clarke	P315
Mary Ann Ruth	P312
Sarah Priscilla	P316
William	P310

BOOKER

Mary Ann	H1197

BOOME

Henry	P1223

BOON

Elizabeth	W824
Ellen	W736
Emma	W828
George	W872
Hannah	W427
Harriet	W830
Henry	W823
Henry	W825
John	W735
Susan	W829
William	W426

BOOTH

Elizabeth	SA406

BOOTHBY

Cunningham	S1547
James W A	S1549
Jane	S1548

BORDERS

Amos	H1430
Isaac	H639
John	H388
William	H637

BOSHER

Emma	W752
Frances	S1530
James	W751
Julia	W753

BOSWORTH

Eliza	H752
Henry	H751
Sarah	H753

BOTSWORTH

Thomas	S1265

BOTT

Alfred	A3

BOTTOM

Ann	S592
Charlotte	S589
Charlotte	S596
Francis	S591
George	S595
John	S594
Mark	S593
William	S588
William	S590

BOTWRIGHT

Ann	S1409
Benjamin	S1405
Caroline	S1406
John	S1407
Mary	S1408
Sarah	S1411
Susan	S1410

BOUCH

William	MR482

BOULTER

Daniel	S947
Joseph	S949
Sarah	S948
Sydney	S950

BOULTON

Alfred	MR772
Charles	H1314
Jesse	MR773
Louisa	H1315
Sarah	MR771

BOURNE

Charles	A2122
Eliza	P1647
Elizabeth	P1645
Emily	A2118
Frederick	A2120
George	P1648
Jane	P1651
John	A2116
John	A2119
John	P1650
Joseph	P1652
Mary	A2252
Samuel	P1644
Sarah	A2117
Sarah	A2121
Sarah	P1649
Sophia	P1646
Sophy	P1603

BOUTELL

Mary E L	SA478

BOWATER

Susannah	P1416

BOWDLER

Elizabeth	R172
Fanny	R171
Joseph	R167
Mary Ann	R169
Sarah	R168
Thomas	R170

BOWDON

Ann	A1774
Ann	A1775
William	A1773
William	A1776

BOWEN

Aubrey William Percy	
	P205
Aubrey William Spencer	
	P201
Elizabeth Ann	P202
Henry Francis	P204

Eliza	H1525	Mary	W1085	Jane	MR399	John	A2016
James	H1523	Mary	W1102	John	MU421	John	A2019
James	H1579	Peter	W1086	Joseph	A3066	John	A2522
Maria	H1533	Sarah	P1605	Joseph	MU417	Joseph	MR831
Martha	H1580	Stephen	W1087	Kitty	MR397	Mary Ann	P50
Mary	H1534	Thomas	A1761	Martha	WK235	Sarah	A2020
Mary	H1582	William	A1763	Mary	A3065	Sarah	S214
Thomas	H1532	William	W1097	Mary	MU422	Susanna	A2283
BURCHMORE		**BURGOYNE**		Mary	P936	Thomas	A857
Ann	R132	Claire	A3221	Mary Anne Elizabeth	P940	Thomas	A2519
Charlotte	R131	Edith	W1662	Sarah	A3064	William	MU546
Elizabeth Hannah	H474	Emma	A3217	Susan	R1998	**BUTTENSHAW**	
George	H472	Fanny	A3220	Sydney Edward Perkins		Richard James	A1059
Hannah	H473	George	R425		P939	Samuel Edward	A1058
Mary Ann	R133	Henry	W1664	William	A3062	**BUTTERWORTH**	
Sarah	R1996	Infant	W1665	**BURROWS**		Robert	H1137
William	R1995	Jane	R233	Ann	A899	**BYGRAVE**	
BURDEN		John	W1658	Ellen	A349	John	W329
Martha	P2053	Joyce	W1660	Fanny	A351	Martha	W331
Thomas	P2052	Lucy	W1661	James	A348	Sarah	W330
BURFORD		Mary	A3214	Maria	A350	Thomas	MR69
Frederick	A783	Mary	W1659	**BURT**		**BYLES**	
Mary Ann	A784	Rachael	A3219	Sarah	A303	George	SA329
Rowena	A786	Sarah	R424	**BURTON**		James E	W281
Thomas	A785	Susannah	A3218	Amelia	A652		
BURGESS		Thomas	W1314	Charles	W836	**C**	
Alfred	H669	William	R475	Edward	W1753	**COCKLE**	
Ann	H668	William	A3213	Edward	W1757	David	R1283
Ann	R373	William	A3216	Eliza	P1879	**CADDINGTON**	
Charles	W1671	**BURMINGHAM**		Eliza	W1754	Charles	MU886
Edward	H670	Mary Ann	S259	Emily	P14	Elizabeth	MU885
Elizabeth	H367	**BURN**		Emma	W833	Emma	A1572
Elizabeth	R1499	Benjamin	R1587	George	S1197	Joseph	MU884
Frederick	W1676	Joseph	R1584	Hannah	W832	**CADWELL**	
Hannah	H221	Joseph	R1586	Harriet	W1755	Amelia	MU122
Hannah	R1500	Kitty	R1588	Jeremiah	R368	Sidney	MU126
John	A3245	[?]	R1585	John	A651	**CALLOW**	
John	WK174	**BURNBY**		Joseph	W834	Rebecca	MU404
John	S897	Edward	A2029	Maria	W839	**CALVERT**	
Joseph	H222	Georgianna	A2026	Mary	S1202	Thomas	OH424
Maria	W1672	Henry	A2030	Mary A.	R766	**CAM**	
Mary	R1498	James	A2028	Sarah	S1196	Mary	WK166
Mary	P1881	Richard	A2025	Sarah	S1198	**CAMBERS**	
Phoebe	P2353	Richard	A2027	Sarah	W838	Jane	R1680
Richard	P1880	**BURNE**		Sarah A	W1756	**CAMPBELL**	
Thomas	H220	William	P1728	Sophia	W835	Emma	P2012
Thomas	H366	**BURNETT**		Thomas	S1201	George	WK87
Thomas	WK84	Henry	P1891	William	W831	**CANDLE**	
William	R372	**BURNHILL**		William	W837	Ann	P778
BURGIN		John	A3253	**BURTT**		Elizabeth	P774
Eliza	SA632	**BURR**		Joseph	OH1405	Elizabeth	P776
Joseph	W1571	Eliza	A231	**BUSH**		Frederick	P777
William	SA631	**BURRETT**		William	SA434	Joseph	P775
BURGOINE		Daniel	R1620	**BUSHNELL**		Thomas	P773
Alfred	W1100	Elizabeth	R1618	Ellen	OH404	**CANDY**	
Ann	P1608	Keziah	R1619	Sarah	OH403	Harriett	MR520
Ann	W1098	Maria	R1681	**BUTCHER**		Mary A.	MR521
Charles	A1764	William	R1617	Amey	P662	Robert	MU457
Eliza	W1101	**BURRIDGE**		Charles	P661	[?]	MR522
Elizabeth	A1762	Ann	A3067	George	P663	**CANNON**	
Emily	W1099	Ann	MR398	James	P664	Elizabeth	OH1042
Esther	W1083	Edward	P1742	Mary	A1684	Emily	P267
George	W1082	Eliza	P1743	Mary	W378	Harriet	P1237
James	A1759	Elizabeth	A3063	Rebecca	W379	Joseph	A2169
Jesse	P1606	Elizabeth	MU418	Thomas	H1312	Maria	P1238
John	P1607	Elizabeth	MU419	**BUTLER**		William	OH1041
John	W1084	Esther	P938	Ann	A858	William	OH1043
Joseph	A1760	George	MR400	Anne	A2023	William	P1236
Joseph	P1604	George	MU420	Anne	A2521	**CAPEL**	
Joyce	R12	Hannah	MR395	Argent	A2018	John	S1259
Lucy	P1477	Harriet	P937	David	A2022	Mary	A3305
Martha	A1758	Horace W.	P1744	Elizabeth	A2017	**CAPPEL**	
Mary	A1756	Isaac	MR396	Esther	A2520	William	A2142
Mary	A1757	James	S1222	Henry	A2021	William	A2143

CARD		William	W388	Rosanna	A155	Emma	S183
Martha	MR417	William	W389	Sarah	A153	Mary	S184
CARNEY		William	W767	Sarah	A154	Sarah Ann	S186
Martin	OH1147	**CARVINTON [?]**		Thomas Dilworth	A152	Thomas	S185
CARPENTER		Richard	OH794	**CAWDLE**		**CHAPMAN**	
Eliza	R1616	**CASEY**		Ann	P1552	Alice E	W1507
George	OH1439	Ann	A3207	Mary A	P1553	Ann	P1517
CARR		Anne	A3208	William	P1551	Ann	W1279
Amelia	P1085	Edward	A3211	William	P1554	Ann	W1283
Edwin	P1091	Henry Ernest	A3210	**CAWDREY**		Charles	W104
Elizabeth	P1084	Mary Anne	A3209	Emily	MU992	Emma	MU580
Frederick	P1090	Thomas	A3206	George	MU996	Emma	W1281
John	P1088	**CASS**		George P.	MU990	Hannah	MU575
Joseph	P1089	Ann	A3128	Hannah	MU991	Hannah	W1506
Margaret	H857	**CASSEY**		Hannah	MU994	Henry	P550
Mary Ann	P1092	Charles	A2681	John	A3366	James	MU577
Sophia	P1087	**CASTLE**		Lucy	MU995	James	W1500
William	P1083	Ann	A1560	Mary	A3367	John	SA435
William	P1086	Ann	A3329	Mary Ann	A3368	John	W1505
CARRICK Benjamin		Caroline	A1562	Sarah	MU993	Louisa	W102
A3024		Charles MacDaniel		**CAZE**		Lucy	W1284
Caroline	A3027		A1561	Clotilde	MR22	Maria	W105
Fanny	A3031	Frances	R1782	**CHAD**		Mary	MU576
Henry	A3026	George	A134	Sarah	S465	Rebecca	A691
Isabella	A3030	Hannah	A1943	**CHALK**		Richard	W1278
Mary	A3025	Jane	A3331	Ann	P655	Samuel	W1282
Thomas	A3028	John	A3328	Charles	MR147	Sarah	MU579
William	A3029	Sarah	A3330	George	MR144	Susan	MU578
CARRIDGE		William	A1942	Jane	MR145	William	MU574
Elizabeth	P1260	**CATLEY**		Jane	MU212	William	MU581
Samuel	P1259	Emma	W56	Rosanna	MR146	William	W106
CARRINGTON		Naomi	W55	**CHALKLEY**		William	W1280
Amos	R153	**CATLIN**		Charles	H1107	**CHAPPEL**	
David	A1937	Adelaide	S22	Eleanor	P460	Anne	OH953
Letitia	MU1013	Ann	P1291	Eliza	R674	George	OH751
Mary	A3086	Ann	P2057	Elizabeth	H1105	John	OH747
Mary Ann	MU440	Daniel	S20	Elizabeth	A693	Sarah	OH748
Mary Ann	MU441	Dinah	OH1211	Elizabeth	A698	Sarah	OH749
Thomas	MU439	Eliza	A1554	Emma	R675	William	OH750
Thomas	W1159	Elizabeth	A1553	George	R673	**CHAPPLE YOUNG**	
CARTER		Elizabeth	A1689	James	H1106	Frances	P369
Albert	A673	Emley	OH1212	Jane	A697	Samuel	P368
Amelia	W391	Emma	A1556	Joseph	R1999	**CHARFONT**	
Ann M	W392	Esther	S21	Louisa	W361	Abel	A1409
Caroline	W390	George	A1557	Martha	A699	Eliza	A1410
Caroline	W764	George	P2056	Richard	A692	Maryann Jane	A1411
Charles	A2147	George	W748	Samuel	A694	**CHARGE**	
Charlotte	A2145	Henry	A1690	Sarah	A695	Alfred	S113
Eliza	MR210	Isaac	A1691	Susan	A696	Ann	S188
Elizabeth	P1328	Isaac	MR343	Thomas	H1104	David	MR636
Elizabeth	P1638	James	OH1214	William	P459	Eliza	MR633
Elizabeth	P1640	James	P2060	**CHALKLY**		Eliza	S111
Elizabeth M.	MR288	Jane	OH1213	Ann	R1407	Eliza	S190
Emma	A2149	John	A1552	David	R1408	Hannah	S117
George	P1643	Joseph	A1688	James	R1406	Isabelle	S192
George	W762	Martha	A1555	Mary	R1405	James	S115
Harriet	P1641	Mary	MR683	Mary	R1409	Jane	S26
Henry	P1642	Sarah	MR344	William	R1404	John	S23
James	A2148	Sarah Ann	P2058	**CHAMBERS**		John	S187
James	MR209	Susan	A1686	Ann	R1652	John	S1007
James	P1574	William	OH1210	Emma	H1949	Kitty	S191
Jane	P276	William	A1685	George	H1950	Lydia	MR635
Mary	W763	William	A1687	Hannah	R1651	Martha	S1006
Mercy	W766	William	P2059	John	H1947	Mary A.	MR632
Moses	W393	**CATO**		Sarah	H1948	Mary A.	MR364
Richard	P1327	Elizabeth	OH697	William	R1650	Mary Ann	S24
Sarah	A672	Jesse	OH696	**CHANCE**		Mary Ann	S25
Sarah	A2146	**CAUDLE**		Maria	MR279	Mary Ann	S114
Sarah	MR287	Bridget	MU141	**CHANDLER**		Rachael	S110
Sarah	P1639	**CAUSTON**		William	MR35	Sarah	S189
Sarah	W765	Eliza	A157	**CHAPEL**		Susannah	S116
William	A2144	Elizabeth	A158	Ann	S181	Thomas	S109
William	MR286	George	A555	Edward	S180	Thomas	S1233
William	MU695	Mary	A156	Edward	S182	William	MR631

William	S112	Sarah	R230	Rebecca	A312	Mary	W344
CHARKLEY		Sarah	A248	**CHURCHILL**		Mary	W1796
Sarah	OH991	Sarah	A2875	George C.	H1681	Mary A	W1800
Sarah	OH992	Sarah	P1905	**CHURCHOUSE**		Mary Ann	H1838
William	OH990	William	A164	Abel	A2715	Mary Ann	H1840
William	OH993	William	A276	David T.	A2714	Mary Ann	MR500
CHARLES		William	P1908	Enoch	A2711	Mathew	OH712
Albert	SA795	**CHESHER**		Hannah	A2713	Matilda	MR503
Alfred	SA793	George	OH1240	John S.	A2709	Matthew	MR498
Alfred	SA857	Mary A.	OH1241	Joshua	A2716	Nathaniel	OH1285
Elizabeth	SA852	**CHICKETT**		Louisa	A2710	Noah	MR502
Fanny	SA853	Lucy	OH142	Louisa J.	A2712	Robert	OH1281
George	SA851	William	OH141	Mary	A2717	Robert	WK116
Hanna	SA792	**CHILD**		**CLARIDGE**		Robert	MR483
Hannah	A3022	Anna	MR798	George	H1685	Sarah	OH1282
Jane	SA794	Elizabeth	H1167	James	W1425	Sarah	MU719
Jesse	SA854	George	MR1891	Joseph	W1489	Sarah	MU775
Sarah	SA855	Harry	H1116	Joshua	W1484	Sarah	W336
Walter	SA856	James	MR799	Lydia	W1485	Sarah	W338
William	SA791	John	MR797	Sophia	W1487	Susan	R18
CHARTERS		Mary	H1115	Thomas	W1488	Thomas	W1799
Frank H.	A928	Simeon	MR801	William	W1486	William	R219
John G.	A925	Thomas	MR802	**CLARK**		William	R666
Sophia A.	A926	William	H1114	Alfred	H1841	William	OH1411
CHASE		**CHILDS**		Ambrose	P2291	William	MR493
Amelia	H1173	David	P146	Ann	R1705	William	S563
Caroline	H1175	Eliza	OH97	Ann	A328	William	W337
Emily	H1174	Eliza	P143	Ann	A667	William	W1795
Frederick	H1170	Emma	P150	Betsey	MR504	William	W1801
Frederick J.	H1172	Frances	P27	Catherine	W1797	**CLARKE**	
Horace	P1226	Francoise	P26	Charles	MR506	Alfred	A2792
Sarah	H1171	Henry	P25	Charles	W340	Ann	A2478
Sydney	P1227	James R	OH98	Charlotte	R268	Charles	A2793
CHATER		Jane	OH99	Charlotte	S561	Edmund	P531
Esther	H1111	Jesse	P142	Charlotte	S1115	Eira [?]	P166
CHEESEMAN		Jesse	P144	David	OH710	Eliza	A2788
Elizabeth	R306	Joseph	OH96	Ebenezer	MU774	Eliza	A2790
Joseph	R305	Mary	MU791	Edward	H1839	Elizabeth	P532
CHENNELLS		Mary Ann	P145	Edward	R17	Emily	A921
Ann	W1699	Susan	P148	Edward	OH708	Emma	A2794
Esther	W1700	Walter	P149	Edward	MR505	George	A2787
Mary	W1872	William	MU790	Eliza	R665	George	A2789
William	W1871	William	P147	Eliza	R667	Harriet	P299
Amelia	W283	William E	OH100	Eliza	MR501	Hester	P405
George	W284	**CHILES**		Eliza	S368	James	A2480
John	W285	Eliza	OH1155	Elizabeth	R220	James	P160
CHERRY		Elizabeth	OH1156	Elizabeth	OH713	Jenny	P301
Alice	A2872	Thomas	OH1154	Esther	W343	Joseph	A2477
Ann	A278	**CHIPPENDALE**		George	R664	Lydia	P159
Ann	A2873	Eliza	OH950	George	W335	Lydia	P162
Ann	A3035	John	OH949	George	W342	Margaret	P164
Ann	P1907	John Theodore	OH951	George	W502	Maria	P165
Eleanor	A165	**CHIPPERFIELD**		George	W1798	Mary	A2479
Elizabeth	P1906	Charles	R768	Hannah	MR499	Mary A.	MR86
Elizabeth Ann	A250	Mary	R157	Hannah	S562	Mary Ann	P161
Emma	A1376	Mary	R767	Henry	MU771	Robert	P158
Emma	P1909	**CHISED**		Henry	MU776	Samuel	P324
Frederic Henry	A249	Charles	A1998	Isaac	R1886	Susan	P1172
George	A280	Mary	A2001	James	R1703	Sydney	P533
George	A2874	Theresa	A2000	James	R1704	Walter	A2791
Harriett	A161	William	A1999	James	OH709	William	A2795
Henry	A279	**CHRISTMAS**		Jane	R594	William	P163
Jabez	R226	Elizabeth	R681	Jane	OH707	William	S358
Jesse	A160	Emma	R682	Jane	OH711	**CLAY**	
Jesse	A162	John	R676	Jane	W339	George	A3275
Luke	R229	Mary	R679	Jeremiah	S1114	Joseph	P707
Luke	A3034	Mary Ann	R677	John	H1837	Josiah	H1208
Mark	A2871	Owen W.	R680	John	R267	Martha	P706
Mary Ann	A277	Sarah	R678	John	OH706	Sarah	P705
Patience	P1904	**CHURCH**		Lydia	MU89	**CLAY [DAY]**	
Rose	A275	Anne	R413	Maria	W345	Celina	A1341
Samuel	R228	Eliza	A728	Mary	MU772	Elizabeth	A1339
Samuel	A247	Hannah	R412	Mary	MU773	Emma	A1340
Sarah	R227	John	R411	Mary	S560	William	A1338

CLAYDON
Elizabeth — S1257

CLAYTON
Dinah — MU195
James — MU196
Jesse — MU197
Richard — MU198
Thomas — A446
William — R532
William John — A2882

CLEAVER
John — MR342

CLIFFEN
Charlotte — OH231
William — OH230

CLIMANCE
Alfred — MR34
Anne — A273
Benjamin — MR37
Benjamin — MR40
Eliza — MR33
Eliza — MR41
Elizabeth — A272
Elizabeth — MR1575
George — A734
Harriet — MR38
Jane — A270
Jane — MR42
Mary — MR32
Richard — A269
Sarah — A735
William — A274
William — MR31

CLINSON
John — OH742

CLOWES
Caroline — A2426
Edward — A2425
Elizabeth — A2422
Ellen — A2405
Emma — A2403
Francis R. — A2401
Henry — A2399
James — A2424
Jane — A2404
Levi — A2423
Mary Ann — A2400
Thomas H. — A2402
William — A2421

COALMAN
Charlotte — W849
Elizabeth — W855
Henry — W854
Louisa — W852
Sarah A — W851
Thomas — W853
William — W848
William — W850

COBB
Eliza — OH850
Rebecca — OH849
Susan — OH851
William — OH848

COCKEL
Ann — A1181

COCKING
Emma — A2232
Joseph — A2231

COCKINGTON
John — P1332
Susan — P1333

COCKLE
Abel — R1281
Emily — P572
Emma — R1284
Frederick — MU841
George — R2027
Hannah — R1935
James — WK161
James — P570
Maria — R1833
Mary — R1282
Mary — WK162
Rose A. — MU839
Sarah — P571
William — R1934
William — MU840

COCKS
Mary — H1140

COE
Ann — H1420
George — A324
Louisa — P1504
Maria — MU406
Philip — P1502
Sarah — P1503

COHEN
Moses — A260

COLE
Celia — R88
Edward — A397
Elizabeth — R631
Ellen — OH945
Jane — R632
Jane — A2938
Mary Ann — R1631
Robert W. — R90
Sarah A. — R89
William — R87
William (Snr) — R630
William G. — R91

COLEMAN
Amelia — A2411
Amelia — P717
Ann — A2406
Arthur — W115
Charles — R8
Dinah — W113
Edward — A2061
Eliza — A2409
Elizabeth — A723
Ellen — A2410
Emma — A2408
George Davenport — A724
George Thomas — A2059
Herbert — A44
James — A2062
John — A2963
Mary — R1855
Mary — A2407
Samuel — A2964
Sarah — R1856
Sarah — SA324
Sarah — A2058
Sarah — A2962
Susannah — R1854
Thomas — A2057
Thomas — A2060
Thomas — W112
Vincent — A722
William — A2412
William — W114

COLES
Alfred — A1159
Ann — R651
Joseph — R649
Rebecca — A1161
Rose — R650
Samuel — A1160
Sarah — R652
Susan — MU1012
William — MR29

COLEY
Charles — A532

COLGRAVE
Eliza — MU96
Samuel — MU95

COLINGS
Charles — P2146
Henry — P2148
Jane — P2147

COLLEY
George — S247
Jesse — S245
Samuel — S248
Sarah — S246

COLLIER
Thomas — R895

COLLINGS
George — P2411
Henry — H1866
Louisa — P2412
Mark — P2414
Mary Ann — P2410
Robert — P2409
Thomas — P2413

COLLINGWOOD
Thomas — A1417

COLLINS
Ann — W1166
Caroline — R2066
Caroline — MU800
Charles — H297
Daniel — A2700
Edward — R2065
Elizabeth — H296
Elizabeth — H298
Emma — P2498
Ephraim — MU849
Francis — W1165
Frederic — H300
George — W1168
James — A2698
James — A2699
Johannah — A2691
John — H299
John — A1033
John — A2693
John — WK233
John — MU846
Joseph — A1909
Louisa — A1912
Margaret — A2692
Mary — R2064
Mary — OH1206
Mary — A2697
Mary — P2497
Samuel — MU848
Sarah — WK23
Sarah — MU847
Susannah — A1910
Thomas — OH215
Timothy — A2690
Timothy — A2694
Timothy — A2701
William — H295
William — OH1205
William — OH1326
William — A1911
William — W1167

COLLYER
Caroline — MR463

COMPLIN
Sarah — S1544

COMPTON
Ann — MU626
Charles — A2797
Charles — A3165
Eliza — A2976
Eliza — WK41
Eliza — MU627
Elizabeth — MU628
Emma — MU624
George — A2799
George — WK38
Hannah — A3162
Isabella — A2798
James — P1987
Jane — A2800
Jane — WK39
Joseph — MU622
Joseph — MU625
Kitty — MU736
Louisa — P1989
Maria — MU623
Mary — A3161
Mary — A3164
Mary A. — A2975
Rachael — P1991
Sarah — P1988
Sarah — P1990
Thomas — WK40
William — A3160
William — A3163

CONNELLY
Thomas — P685

CONQUEST
Charles — A2588
Emily — A646
Joseph — WK42
Mary Ann — A645
Sarah — A2589
William — A2590

CONSTABLE
Ann — H1460
Ann — P981
Benjamin — MU366
Charles — H1692
Charles — H1695
Eliza — OH1055
George — MU369
Hannah — OH1056
James — OH1051
James — P980
Jane — P658
John C. — OH1053
Jonah — OH1058
Joseph — H1459
Mary — H1693
Mary — OH1052
Mary — OH1057
Mary A — MU368
Susannah — MR497
Susannah — MU367
Thomas — MR496
William — H1694
William — OH1054
William — P657
William — S371

COOK
Abraham — OH1464
Alfred — S415
Alice — A938
Amy — S416
Amy — S420

Charlotte	A1712	**CRISP**		Jane	A2605	William	A1026
Daniel	P541	Clara L	W263	Jemima	A2604	**CUTHBERK**	
Eliza	A2345	Fanny	W261	John	A214	James	S352
Eliza	P81	George C A	W264	John	A2552	**CUTLER**	
Elizabeth	P964	Harriet	W260	John	P1653	James	MU407
Elizabeth	P1316	Marianne	W262	John Thomas	A216	**CUTTS**	
Emily	W403	**CROCKELL**		Julliet	A2601	Ann	P1263
Emma	A1713	Ann	OH584	Lydia	P1662		
George	P1547	Emma	OH587	Maria	A2554	**D**	
George	P1549	James	OH582	Martha	A1913	**DALTON**	
James	H1855	Joseph	OH586	Mary Ann	A2603	Jane	P1099
James	OH1062	Sarah	OH583	Samuel	P1659	Mary	P1100
James	A1711	William	OH585	Sarah	A2602	**DANCER**	
John	H1528	**CROCKET**		Sophia	A2551	Hannah	S1355
Joseph	P963	John	OH106	Susan	P1654	James	S1352
Joseph	P966	**CROCKETT**		William	WK108	Lydia	S1356
Marian	P967	William	OH134	William	MR345	Martha	S1353
Martha	P968	William	OH1433	William	P1658	Rhoda	S1249
Mary	H1178	**CROFT**		**CROULON**		Thomas	S1250
Mary	H1854	Ann	W140	Thomas	H422	William	S1354
Mary	A2346	Charlotte	S1337	**CROW**		**DANES**	
Mary	P965	Elizabeth	SA695	Elizabeth	A1731	George	MR557
Mary	W402	Emily	P502	George	A3133	Susan	MR558
Mary Ann	H1529	George	R2037	Sarah	A3134	**DANESON**	
Mary Ann	P545	Hannah	A1791	William G.	A3135	George	P357
Richard	H1526	Harriet	WK137	**CULLUM**		George	P358
Richard	P543	Harriet	W141	Samuel Henry	MR250	**DANIELS**	
Rosetta	P1319	Harriotte	SA696	**CUMBERLAND**		Amelia	P1068
Sarah	A1715	Henry	R1929	Elizabeth	P2301	**DANL**	
Sarah	A2347	Henry	R2035	**CURBY**		George	OH1440
Sarah	P544	James	P499	Jane	P140	**DARBON**	
Susanah	H1527	Joseph	S1336	**CURD**		John	H1141
Thomas	H1853	Louisa	R2039	Ann	R754	Sarah	H1142
Thomas	A2344	Lucy	P503	Clara	R753	William	W450
William	A1714	Maria	S1339	**CURELL**		**DARLOW**	
William	MU226	Martha	H342	George	SA382	James	SA374
William	P1315	Mary	R1930	**CURL**		**DARWELL**	
William	P1550	Mary	R2034	Charlotte	MR445	Elizabeth	A2808
William	W1579	Mary	A211	William	MR444	Emma	A2809
CREED		Mary Ann	R2041	**CURNICK**		**DAUBIN**	
Amelia	MU599	Maryanne	P501	Emma	MU64	Jane	W673
Emily A.	MU601	Matilda	R2036	Emma	MU65	Mary	W674
Henry	MU598	Rosa	SA82	Richard	MU63	Susan	W672
Mary	MU600	Sarah	R2040	**CURRALL**		Thomas	W675
CREW		Susan	R1931	John	MR62	William	W671
Benjamin	W1530	Susan	R2038	**CURRANT**		**DAVAY**	
Caleb	P360	Susan	P500	Ann	MU143	John	H1160
Charles	P634	William	R2033	David	MU144	**DAVIES**	
Elizabeth	MU329	William	SA694	Eliza	MU146	Charles Thomas	H179
Emily	H1248	William	S1338	George	MU145	Elisabeth	H158
Frederick	P365	William	W139	James	MU142	George	H161
Gary [?]	H1249	**CROSS**		**CURRELL**		Mary	H176
Henry	H1070	Eleanor	WK240	Eliza	R165	Mary	H177
Louisa	P366	James	OH1136	Elizabeth	R695	Sarah	H155
Martha	MU328	John	R1818	Thomas	P1466	Sarah	H156
Mary	P361	Sarah	OH1137	**CURRIER**		Sarah	H178
Mary	P363	**CROUCH**		Elizabeth	A121	William	H154
Mary	W1301	Alfred	A1932	**CURTIS**		William	H157
Mary Ann	W1302	Ann	P1656	Catherine	H1109	William	H175
Sarah	H1245	Ann	P1832	James	H1108	**DAVIS**	
Sophia	P633	Anna	A215	John	OH698	Ann	H1865
Susannah	P364	Charles	A2600	Leah	R175	Ann	A1753
Thomas	P632	Charles	P1833	**CUSTANCE**		Caroline	R581
Vincent	H1244	Charlotte	A2553	Albert	A1032	Daniel	P1993
Vincent	H1246	Edward	A2550	Ann	A1023	Daniel	S910
William	H1247	Elvia	A1929	Daniel	A1027	David	OH143
William	P362	Emma	P1657	Eliza	A1028	David	OH979
William	W1303	Fanny	P1660	Harriett	A1031	Eliza	R582
CRICKETT [?]		Frederick	A1931	Henry	A1025	Eliza	A1808
Amelia	A3049	George	P1661	Jenny	P359	Eliza	A1810
Charles Alexander	A3048	George Henry	A217	John	A1022	Elizabeth	A449
George W.A.C.	A3045	Henry	A2050	Mary Ann	A1029	Elizabeth	A1453
Harriett	A3047	James	P1655	Rachael	A1030	Elizabeth	S911
Martha	A3046	Jane	A1930	Thomas	A1024	Elizabeth	S913

Name	Ref
Mary	P2356
William	P2359

E

EACOTT
Mary A	P1179

EADES
Caroline	MU281
Kate	MU283
William	MU280
William	MU282

EAGLE
Ann	P347
Eliza	P346

EAGLESFIELD
Abigail	P1366

EALEY
Eliza	MR165
Hannah	MR157
Thomas	MR156

EAMES
Alfred	P667
Amelia	S649
Ann	R840
Ann	OH988
Ann	WK43
Ann	P673
Ann	P742
Anne Maria	S652
Daniel	OH1235
David	OH1061
Elenior	OH1237
Eliza	R838
Eliza	P669
Eliza	S647
Eliza	S650
Elizabeth	R839
Elizabeth	P16
Elizabeth	P666
Elizabeth	P2098
Elizabeth	S693
Ellen	S651
Ellen J.	R499
Emma	S648
Ephraim	OH427
Ephraim	P743
Esther	S351
George	OH482
George	OH1238
George	P15
George	P17
George	S696
Henry	P2055
James	P670
James	S1094
Jeffrey	P1530
Jesse	OH989
John	R203
John	A2683
John	A2687
John	S1096
Joseph	OH987
Joseph	P672
Joseph	S692
Louisa	A2684
Louisa	S695
Mary	R498
Mary	R837
Mary	A2686
Mary A.	R205
Mary Ann	S694
Mathew	P741
Robert	P665
Samuel	R497
Samuel	P2097
Sarah	R204
Sarah	OH1236
Sarah	OH1372
Sarah	P671
Sarah	P2099
Thomas	P668
Thomas	S1095
William	WK151
William	S646

EAMEY [?]
James	H1340
Rebecca	H1341

EARLE
Mary	A541
Richard	A540

EASON
Caroline	S825
Caroline	S863
James	S864
James E.	S824
Robert	S820
Robert	S862
Sarah	S821
Sarah Ann	S822
Thomas	S823

EASONE
Ann	OH957

EAST
Ann	MR616
Ann	MR725
Ann	W137
Charles	W136
Charlotte	MR723
Edward	MR615
Eliza	MR617
Eliza	W135
Eliza	W1188
Emma	MR726
George	MR707
George	S527
George	S530
George	W132
Jane	SA378
John	MR727
Joseph	S532
Martha	S533
Mary	MR724
Mary	W133
Mary A.	MR618
Matthew	SA381
Ruth	S528
Samuel	MR722
Samuel	S534
Sarah	SA380
Sarah	S531
Susan	W131
Susannah	MR728
Thomas	W138
William	SA377
William	SA379
William	S529
William	W134

EASTHALL
Adriana	A2828
Ellen	A2827
Francis	A2826
Robert	A2824
Sophia	A2825

EASTLAND
John	MU213

EASY
Alfred	MR861
Henry	MR860
Martha	MR859
William	MR858

EBBORN
Alfred	P978
Charles	P976
Fanny	P974
George	P975
Joseph	P979
William	P973
William	P977

EDMONDS
Alfred	W1767
Amelia	P1131
Ann	A1693
Anne	P1133
Eliza	W803
Elizabeth	S161
Elizabeth	W362
Elizabeth	W802
George	W615
Hannah	MU729
Hannah	S231
Hannah	S234
Hannah	W800
Harriett	S158
Harriett	S159
James	W798
Jane	W363
Jane A.	A2936
John	P167
John	S164
John	S230
John	S232
Maria	S162
Mary	P168
Mary	P1920
Mary	W799
Mary	W1728
Mary A	W1766
Robert	S160
Sarah	P304
Sarah	S163
Sarah	W801
Therrey	OH834
Thomas	WK55
Walter	P1921
William	SA589
William	OH833
William	A1692
William	S157
William	S233
William	W1765

EDMONS
Arther	W691
Elizabeth	W687
Elizabeth	W689
Harriet	W692
John	W686
Sarah	W688
Walter	W690

EDMUNDS
Charlotte	W223
Eliza	W224
Elizabeth	W222
George	W225
John	W13
William	W1845

EDWARDS
Amelia	A525
Amelia	A1662
Caroline	A1531
Caroline	A2053
Charles	OH1412
Charles	A320
Daniel	A296
Eliza	A1661
Eliza	P1947
Elizabeth	P110
Elizabeth	P1805
Elizabeth J.	OH1414
Ellen	SA609
Frank	S210
Frederick	SA606
Frederick	MU415
George	H850
George	MU411
George F.	MU413
Georgiana A.	MU412
Georgiana K.	MU414
Harriett	S208
Harriett	S213
Hayward	S209
Henrietta	WK51
Henry	S207
Henry	S211
James	H1152
James	SA608
James	P1292
James	P1804
James W.	P1808
Jane E.	OH1413
Jocelene	SA607
John	A1405
John	A1659
John	S212
Joseph	A2051
Lydia	A1658
Maria	SA438
Martha	A526
Mary	A2052
Mary	P1293
Mary A	P1294
Mary Anne	P1807
Robert	P1295
Samuel	A1657
Sarah	A297
Sarah	A1663
Sarah Ann	P1806
Thomas	P111
William	A1660

EGAN
Hannah Maria	P428
William	P19

EGGLETON
Selina	S758

ELBORN
Esther	A2577
James	A2576
John	A2581
Sophia	A2580
Thomas	A2579

ELDRIDGE
Elizabeth	OH947

ELLINGHAM
Alfred	S1228
Anne	S1231
Charlotte	S1225
Charlotte	S1230
Edmond	H942
Gabriel	S1229
John	S1226
John	W1793
Joseph	MU347
Louisa	S1227
Maria	H941
Mary	W1794
Sarah	P1425
Thomas	H940

F

FACSDALE
Charles	OH1227
George	OH1225
George W.	OH1223
Hannah	OH1226
John	OH1228
John	OH1270
Knott	OH1229
Susannah	OH1224

FAIN
Ann	OH1158
Emma	OH1159
George	OH1157
George	OH1160
James	OH1161
William	OH1162

FAIRCLOTH
Eliza	R974
Emma	R976
Frederick	R971
Mary Ann	R975
Sophia	R657
Susan	R972
Susan	R973

FAIRPELL
Frederick	A2887

FAIRTHORNE
Sarah W	P1159
Thomas	P1158

FALKNALL
Ann	P157
Eliza	OH113
Eliza	OH117
Elizabeth	OH115
Emma	OH116
Hannah	OH121
Henry	OH192
James	OH112
James	OH122
John	OH120
Marian	OH118
Rebecca	OH119
Sarah	OH114

FALLDER
Ann	R1341
Charles	R1070
David	R1340
Elizabeth	R1067
Emma	R940
George	R1069
George	R1342
Hannah	R939
Hannah	R941
John	R1065
Mary Ann	R1072
Rose	R1073
Rose	R1479
Sophia	R1066
Thomas	R1071
Thomas	R1478
William	R938
William	R1068
William	R1480

FANE
Mary	OH1357
Sarah	OH1358

FAREY
Ann	R113
Fanny	R94
George	R93
James	R92
Samuel	R112

FARNELL

Charles	W537
Frederick	H1126
Jane	W538
John	H1125

FARNESS
Mary	A1573

FARR
Alfred	H1940
Ann	H1929
Ann	H1939
Charles	W1338
Edward	H532
Elisha	P211
Elizabeth	SA76
Emma	H1549
Emma	H1928
Emma	P212
Fanny	WK189
Francis	H1925
Frederick E.	W1337
George	H823
George	H1550
George	H1927
George	H1938
George	W1334
Hannah	H1926
Harriett	H1551
Jane	H533
Jane	H534
John	H1548
John	SA75
Joseph	H1791
Maria	H826
Mary	H535
Mary	H1789
Mary	H1792
Robert	H821
Robert	H1788
Sarah	H536
Sarah	H820
Sarah	H822
Sophia	W1335
Sophia	W1336
Thomas	H819
Thomas	H824
Thomas	H1930
William	H825
William	H1790

FARRIS
Alice	A2833
Eliza	A2831
Elizabeth	A2830
Elizabeth	A2834
Emily	A2837
Sarah	A2832
William	A2829

FARRUL
Jevoy	A1433

FAULDER
Elizabeth	W976
Henry	SA804
Jane	SA806
Maria	SA803
Rhoda	SA802
Sarah	SA805
Thomas	W975

FAULKNER
Eliza	H1427
Maria	H1426

FAWELL
Ann	A2859
Elizabeth M.	A2861
John	A2858
Maria	A2863

Rosa	A2862
Susan A.	A2860

FEARY
Elizabeth	MR305

FEAST
Jennett	OH1265

FELLOWS
Caroline	R1641
Elizabeth	R1637
Emma	R1640
James	R1636
James	R1639
Jane	R1638
William	R1642

FELLS
Ann	WK156
Catherine	H755
Eliza	H1638
Emma	H776
George	H756
George	H1635
George	H1637
John	H757
John	H775
Maria	H758
Mary	H801
Matilda	H759
Robert King	A3198
Rosa Wells	A3200
Susan	H1636
Susannah	A3199
William	H754
William	WK190

FELTHAM
Louisa	MU693

FENDELL
Ann	H768
James	H767
James	H769

FENN
Alfred J.	R960
Ann	S425
Ann	S435
Catherine	R962
Daniel	S1389
Elizabeth	R958
Emma S.	R959
George	S426
Jane	R961
Jesse	S1223
John	R946
John	S427
Louisa	R963
Mary Ann	R957
Sarah	S424
Sarah	S1390
Thomas	S423
Thomas	S434

FENSOM
Alice	P1997
Ann	H1772
Ann	H1907
Ann	R708
Ann	A3088
Ann M	W1118
Charles	MU558
David	H1774
Edward	H1784
Edward	S543
Eliza	W1145
Elizabeth	R707
Elizabeth	P1996
Elizabeth	P1998
Elizabeth	S597

Emma	MR3
George	H1910
George	P1995
George	P1999
James	A3178
James	W871
James	W1138
Jim	H1908
John	W1116
Joseph	H1969
Maria	H1773
Maria	W1139
Mark	SA568
Martha	S546
Mary	A737
Mary A.	R155
Pricilla	S544
Samuel	H1775
Samuel	A3087
Samuel	MR4
Sarah	MR2
Sarah	MU1001
Thomas	S545
William	H1771
William	H1906
William	H1909
William	MR1
William	MU1000

FENSOME
Elizabeth	W1587

FENSON
Emily	P1428
Emily	W1117
Harriet	P1427
William	P1426

FERBORN [?]
Emma	P1819

FERNEL
Emma	A1524
Esther	A1523

FIELD
Ann	A2274
Ann	W658
Ann	W929
Arthur	OH277
Benjamin	OH1279
Catherine	OH275
Charlotte	OH1283
Charlotte	S1158
Charlotte	S1160
Charlotte	W654
Eliza	H1158
Eliza	OH808
Eliza	S1449
Eliza	W657
Eliza	W930
Elizabeth	H151
Elizabeth	OH34
Elizabeth	OH616
Elizabeth	OH923
Elizabeth	OH1284
Elizabeth	A100
Elizabeth	A228
Elizabeth	W959
Ellen	P2050
Emily	P2051
Emma	OH489
Emma	W1232
Frederick	S1450
George	A229
Harriett	W961
Harriett	W1231
Henry	A227
Henry	P2049

James	MU74
Jane L	MU75
John	P1221
Mary	MU73
Sophia	MU113
Thomas	P1222

GREGG

Edmond	R741

GREGORY

Abraham	A545
Alfred	A1450
Ann	A1367
Ann	A1449
Charles	MU748
Charlotte	H1237
Charlotte	H1241
Edward	A387
Eliza	A1474
Elizabeth	A546
Elizabeth	A1447
Elizabeth	A1448
Elizabeth	W1773
Emma	R1272
Emma	A547
Emma	A1370
George	H1238
George	R1273
George	A1368
Henry	A2031
Isaac	A548
James	H1240
Jane	A1452
Keziah	MU749
Mary	A1473
Samuel	A1445
Samuel	A1451
Sarah Ann	A549
William	H1239
William	R1271

GRESHAM

William	MU692

GREY

Ann	H707
Ann	W1876
Daniel	P2073
Edward	H218
Eliza	H323
Elizabeth	P2070
Frederic	H324
George	H708
George	P2071
Harriett	OH913
James	W1848
John	H320
Martha	OH912
Mary	H162
Mary	H709
Mary Ann	H219
Mary Ann	P2074
Phillis	H322
Samuel	H321
Sarah	H319
Sarah	P2075
Sophia	P522
Thomas	H318
Thomas	H706
William	OH914
William	P2069
William	P2072

GRIFFEN

Elizabeth	A1696
Martha	P1732
Saunders	A390
Susan	A389
Susan	A391
William	A388
William	A760

GRIFFITHS

Ernest H	SA441
Frederick W	SA440

GRIGG

Ellen	W1569
William A	W1568

GRIMSDALE

Ann	W1837
Arthur	W1839
Elizabeth	W1838
George	W1836

GRIMSHAW

Alfred	P1863
Amilia	A2040
Caleb	P1862
Mary	A1838

GRIMSHEAD

Frances	R655

GRIMSHEAD (ESQ.)

Thomas	R654

GRIMSTON

Harriett E.	MR451
Jane	MR452
Robert	MR453

GRISSEL

Eliza	W172
Emma	W171
Rebecca	W173
William	W174

GROOM

Ann	MU723
Ann	W319
Ann	W321
Anne	W1575
Arthur	W324
Arthur	W1804
Charles	W1574
Charles	W322
Charlotte	MU250
Daniel	MU249
Daniel	P1594
Elizabeth	R1244
Elizabeth	P787
Elizabeth	W1578
Frederick	P1597
George	H7
George	W325
Hannah	P1595
Henry	MU252
James	R1246
James	MU410
James	W295
James	W298
James	W1608
John	W1577
Mary	H8
Mary Ann	R1245
Reuben	W1610
Sarah	P1349
Susan	W1576
Susan	W1609
Susanna	W296
Thomas	W318
Thomas	W320
William	R1243
William	MU251
William	P1596
William	W297
William	W323
William	W1802

GROOME

Richard	A2904

GROVENOR

Jane	A171
William	A170

GROVER

Ann	R709
Ann	MU290
Caroline	H1545
Dorcas	MU291
Edward	MU292
Eliza	H1544
Elizabeth	A946
Elizabeth	A2037
Elizabeth	MU287
Emily	A2039
George	H1546
George	A2036
Harriet	A2038
John	MU289
Joseph	MU286
Joseph	MU293
Maria	H1543
William	H1542
William	MU288

GRUBB

Ann	A2664
George	P764

GRUNDON

Ann E	W78

GULLINGHAM

William	P1992

GULSTON

Sarah	H1087
Thomas	A3265

GURNEY

Eliza	SA800
Eliza	A1113
Elizabeth	OH959
Elizabeth	A1646
George	R2031
George	OH161
Hannah	SA801
Hannah	A1645
Hannah	MR847
Harriett	OH960
James	MR846
James	S31
John	OH961
Joseph	MR843
Mary	MR842
Mary A.	MR848
Philip	S34
Phillis	S1000
Susan	S33
Thomas	A1644
Thomas	S999
William	SA799
William	OH958
William	MR844

GURTON

Edward	MR477

GUTTERIDGE

Ann	A300
Charlotte	OH493
Eliza	OH492
Eliza	OH494
Elizabeth	OH491
George	R232
James	OH490

H

HADAWAY

Ann	SA715
Edward	SA718
Eliza	SA692
Henry	SA691
James	SA719
Jane	SA714
Lakey	SA712
Lizzy	SA717
Patience	SA713
William	SA716

HADNUTT

Jemima	P1
Joseph	WK163

HAGGAR

Ann Elizabeth	A820
Caroline	A819
Emma	A818
Emma	A823
Henry	MR111
James	A817
James	A822
Thomas	A821
Alfred	P39
Henry	P40
Louisa	P38

HAIGH

George	MU763

HAILES

Charlotte	A507
Esther	A509
George	A506
Sarah Susan	A508

HAINES

Alice	A3069
Edwin	A3074
Elizabeth	A3076
James	A3073
Joseph	A3075
Maria	A3071
Sophia	A3070
Thomas	A3068
Thomas	A3072

HAIR

Annie E.	A1513
Sarah	A1512
William	A1511

HALE

Ann	P9
Ann	P1786
Archibald	A1548
Benjamin	A2757
Daniel	SA628
Eliza	H95
Eliza	H1863
Eliza	R1720
Eliza	A2752
Eliza	W1321
Eliza	W1323
Elizabeth	A2460
Elizabeth	P1720
Emma	H974
Frederick	W1322
George	P1721
Hannah	R1719
Hannah	R1722
Hannah	A2758
Harriet	W1324
Helen	H1861
James	P1785
Jane	A1890
Jane	A2755
John	H1860
John	A2756
Joseph	A2458
M A	A1547

Name	Ref
Maria	P1339
Martha	H973
Mary	R1721
Mary	SA629
Mary	A2459
Mary	P1722
Mary A	P1472
Mary Ann	A2753
Sarah	A2751
Sarah	MR870
Sarah	W1325
Thomas	H975
Thomas	W1320
William	H94
William	H1862
William	R1718
William	A2750
William	A2754
William	P1471
William	P1719
William	W1326

HALES

Ann	H1642
Eliza	P1101

HALL

Abraham	R1043
Amos	MR840
Anne	A1614
Arthur	A1741
Betsey	R100
Charlotte	R1041
Eliza	OH660
Elizabeth	R504
Elizabeth	OH622
Elizabeth	A2885
Elizabeth	S548
Emily	A1739
Emma	MR839
Emma	S552
Fanny	MR837
George	R98
George	OH625
George	OH659
George	A1742
Henry	R1775
Henry	A2884
Henry	MR841
James	OH627
James	A1613
James	A1737
John	R1040
Mary	R502
Mary	R1042
Mary	OH624
Mary	A1738
Mary	A1740
Mary	WK20
Mary	WK21
Mary	S1531
Mary A.	MR838
Matilda	R505
Ruth	R99
Samuel	OH621
Sarah Jane	A1743
Susan	OH626
Thomas	R501
Thomas	A1625
Thomas	MR836
William	R503
William	OH623
William	A1106

HALLEY

Elizabeth	MR318
Newman	MR317

HALSEY

Amy	R1788
Ann	R627
Ann	MR893
Ann	S1303
Caleb	OH1258
Charles B	W570
Charlotte	R1200
Charlotte	MU458
Daniel	A3322
Daniel	MU610
David	R1204
David	OH1436
Edmund	R1201
Edward	R1787
Edward	MU462
Eliza	R629
Eliza	R752
Eliza	R1055
Eliza	MU78
Eliza	P2273
Elizabeth	R1784
Elizabeth	OH1366
Elizabeth	WK145
Elizabeth	W1780
Elizabeth B	W572
Emanuel	R1317
Emily	R1054
Emma	R628
Fanny	SA751
George	H840
George	R489
George	R1049
George	OH1261
George	P2270
George B	W571
Harriett	OH1259
Henry	R1051
James	R1199
James	R1316
James	WK119
James	W1193
James T.	OH1262
Jane	R1772
Jane	R1838
John	R1786
John	R1836
John	OH1256
John	OH1260
John	S1302
John	W567
Joseph	W563
Joseph	W564
Josiah	R1052
Louisa	R1839
Lucy	MU611
Lusa [?]	OH1257
Maria	R1048
Maria	A3323
Mary	R1053
Mary	R1197
Mary Ann	MU463
Matilda	R750
Mercy	W569
Nancy	R1198
Phebe	R1202
Richard	R749
Richard Snr	R894
Rose	R1837
Samuel	SA752
Sarah	R751
Sarah	R1050
Sarah	MU459
Sarah	P2271

Sarah	P2272
Sarah	W565
Sarah	W1781
Susan	W568
Thomas	R1196
Thomas	R1318
Thomas	R1785
Thomas	MR892
Thomas	MR894
Thomas	MR895
Thomas	MU77
Thomas	MU460
Walter	R1203
William	SA748
William	MU461
William	S1304
William	W566

HAMIRE [?]

Ellen	A863
Mary Ann	A862
Mattey	A865
Sarah	A864

HAMMETT

Henry	SA548
William	WK115

HAMMOND

Ann	A453
Elizabeth	MR267
George	MR269
John	MR271
Mary	MR270
Richard	MR266
William	MR268

HAMMONDS

Martha	P651

HAMPSON

Jane	R459
William S.	R460

HANDLEY

Charles	SA122
Charles	SA252
Elizabeth	S241
Emily	S240
George	SA123
George	S204
Jesse	SA124
John	R1974
John	SA117
John	W1618
Margaret	S205
Maria	S236
Mary Ann	S237
Richard	SA120
Sarah	SA119
Sarah	S239
Sarah	W1619
Susan	SA118
Susan	SA121
Susannah	S238
William	S235

HANDSCOMB

Charlotte	MU228
Joseph	MU227
Louisa Ann	MU229
Mary A	MU221
Mary A	MU222

HANKS

Amelia	A811
Eliza	A810
Lucy	A809

HANLEY

Frederick	OH1385
Mary Ann	OH1386

HANMORE

Harriett	MU603

HANNAL

Mary A	SA331

HANNELL

Alfred	MR360
Ann	MU955
Ann	MU956
David	MU959
Eliza	MU962
Elizabeth	MU963
Emma	MR361
Francis	MU960
John	MU954
John	MU958
Joseph	MR7934
Levina	MR358
Mary	MU961
Newman	MU957
William	MR359
William	MR792
William	MU868

HANSCOMB

James	P2227
Judith	P2226
Thomas	P2225

HANSCOMBE

Ann	R824
Ann	A2608
Ann Caroline	H58
Charles	H1151
Charlotte	A2607
Edith	A2613
Elizabeth	H1014
Emma	H608
Emma	A2609
Fanny	SA395
Hepzibah	S542
James	A2606
Jane	R825
John	H57
Mary	H1013
Rosannah	A2612
Thomas	A2611
William	H697
William	A2610
William M.	H59

HANSELL

Charles	P1060
Edward	P1058
Elizabeth	P1059
Frederick	P1061
Thomas	P1062

HANSHAW

Caroline	A1321
Thomas	S477
Thomas Ambrose	A1318
Tilney	A1319
Tilney Ann	A1320

HAPPY

Emma	W1537
Mary	W1536
William	W1535

HARBOROUGH

Caroline	R827
Charlotte	R828
Elizabeth	R830
Emma	R831
Henry	R829
Micael	R826

HARBOURN

Eliza	WK141
Louisa	WK142
Sarah	WK88

HARBURN

Benjamin	P1257

HARCOURT

Alfred	A1080
Ann	WK226
Betsey	A1075
Charles	A1077
Charlotte	A1074
Eliza	OH1068
Emley	OH1067
Emma	OH1069
Emma	A1081
Frederic	A1076
Georgenaie	OH973
Jane	OH1070
Jonathan	WK227
Joseph	OH1066
Mary	P1581
Samuel	A1078
Thomas	OH972
Thomas	P1469
William	A1073
William	A1079
William	P1580

HARDEY

Ann	A1629
Eliza	A1628
Elizabeth	A1627
John	A1626
Robert James	WK184

HARDIN

John	OH785
John	OH787
Mary	OH786
William	OH788

HARDING

Ann	OH982
David	OH983
Eliza	S680
Emily	OH984
Emma	S677
Frederick	S678
Hannah	S675
James	OH980
James	A266
James	P329
James	S792
Jemima	A586
John	S679
Martha	OH981
Mary	A267
Mary	A1593
Mary Ann	P330
Sarah	S793
Sarah Ann	A744
Sarah Ann	S676
Susan	P660
Thomas	A1592
Walter	S674
William	P659

HARDWICK

Charles	P1975
Elizabeth	A330
Elizabeth	A331
Emily	P1976
George	P1180
James	R1009
James	A329
James	A332
John	P1977
Joseph	R1012
Mary	A333
Mary Ann	R1010
Mary Ann	R1015
Matilda	P1972

Sarah	R1013
Sophia	P1973
Susan	R1014
Susan	P1974
William	R1011
William	A334
William	P1971

HARDWICKE

Fanny	P1664
Frances	P1663
Henry	P1665

HARDY

Andrew	S446
Ann	H11
Eliza	H1369
Elizabeth	H1364
Elizabeth	A1840
George	H1363
George	SA432
Henry	H1371
James	H10
James	H1366
James	SA83
Jane	H1370
John	H9
Maria	H1367
Maria	S444
Mary	H1365
Rebecca	SA77
Susan E.	S445
William	H1368
William	A1839
William	A1841
William	S443

HARKNESS

Harriet	A2280
Harriet	A2282
James	A2279
James T.	A2281

HARMAN

James	WK69

HARMON

William Bridon	A1280

HARPER

Catherine	A1019
Charlotte	H550
George William	H546
James	A3248
Jane Elizabeth	H551
Mary	H547
Mary Ann	H549
Sarah	H548

HARRADINE

Charlotte	R95
Katherine	R96

HARRAWAY

Ann	A2950
Eliza	A2952
Fanny	A2951
William	A2949

HARRIS

Ann	OH196
Ann	OH363
Ann	A1396
Ann	S600
Arthur J.	MU907
Benjamin	OH155
C	W83
Caroline	OH82
Charlotte	R363
Charlotte	W1127
Edward	OH353
Eliza	MU905
Elizabeth	H104

Elizabeth	R202
Elizabeth	A838
Elizabeth	P1125
Elizabeth	W1544
Francis	S789
Frederick	S788
George	OH81
George	OH352
George	W1546
Hadorgenos [?]	A92
Harriet	MU727
Henry	WK9
James	R641
James	OH85
James	OH351
Jemima	W81
John	OH76
John	OH195
John	OH1278
John	A1395
John	WK154
John	W1125
Joseph	OH83
Joseph	OH193
Joseph	OH197
Joseph	S598
Joseph	W1547
Maria	OH77
Maria	OH79
Martha	OH78
Mary	OH194
Mary	OH348
Mary	A2864
Mary	S787
Mary	W84
Mary A	W1545
Mary Ann	A90
Mary Ann	A1397
Mary Ann	WK8
Mary Ann	WK10
Mary Ann	S599
Mary Ann	S790
Rachel	OH84
Robert	WK7
Sarah	OH349
Sarah	A89
Sarah	P1126
Sarah	W1124
Sarah Ann	A961
Sarah Ann	A2865
Susan	OH80
Thomas	R1549
Thomas	OH350
Thomas	A88
Thomas	MU904
Thomas	W1126
Thomas	W1543
William	OH347
William	MU906
William	W80
William	W82
William	W1123
William	W1548

HARRIS?

Elizabeth	H1505

HARRISON

Catherine	MU708
Charlotte	S1472
D.W.	MU709
David	S87
Hannah	S1476
Henry	S1471
James	R442
Joseph	S1473

Maria	S1475
Martha G.	MU710
Mary Ann	S85
Phillis	S83
Ruth	S1477
Susan	S1474
Thomas	S82
Thomas	S86
William	S84

HARROWELL

John	MU545

HART

Charlotte	A178
Eliza	SA452
Eliza	OH566
Elizabeth	OH571
Ellen	SA455
Emma	OH568
Emma	P412
George	A1246
James	SA453
Jane	OH567
John	SA454
Mary	OH565
Mary	A1247
Mary Ann	OH569
Mathew	SA451
Sarah	OH573
Susan	OH570
Thomas Hawkins	A177
Thomas William	OH572
William	SA456
William	OH564
William	OH668

HARTLEY

Anna	SA144
Elizabeth	A1165
Emma	A1171
Esther	A1166
Frederick	SA142
Martha	A1168
Mary	A1167
Sarah	SA143
Sarah	SA146
Sarah	A1170
Thomas	SA145
William	A1169

HARTWELL

Eliza	P2286
Elizabeth	P2283
Ellen	P1694
Emily	P2284
Fanny	P2287
George	P1692
James	P1691
John	P864
John	P1688
Louisa	P1690
Maria	P1689
Maria	P1693
Sarah	P865
Sarah	P2285
William	P2282

HARVEY

Alfred	OH610
Alfred	A1198
Ann	A2441
David	OH611
Edwin	A1200
Elizabeth	OH609
Elizabeth	A1979
Frederic	A1196
George	A954
Harriet	P1080

HELBORN	
Eliza	R1104
Elizabeth	R1101
George	R1098
George	R1100
James	R1105
Joseph	R1107
Mary	R1103
Sarah	R1099
Sarah	R1102
William	R1106
HEMMINGTON	
Ann	P2236
Jane	P2235
John	P2234
HENLY	
Emma	W815
George	W814
Louisa	W812
Martha	W1055
Mary	W1050
Sarah	W811
Sarah	W1056
Sophia	W1054
Thomas	W810
William	W813
HENMAN	
Elizabeth	A2277
Elizabeth	WK34
Emma	A2276
Frances	A2275
Mary Ann	P275
HENRY	
Honnor	WK70
James	OH715
John	OH729
Mary	OH730
William	OH731
HENSLOW	
Ann F	P1512
Charlotte	P1513
Eleanor	P1514
Frances	P1511
John Prentis	P1510
Louisa	P1515
HERBERT	
Ann	WK63
HERRON	
George	R114
George	R116
William	R115
HESTER	
Ann	R1613
Ann	P912
Fanny	MU356
George	R1615
James	R1612
James	R1614
Thomas	P913
HEWEL	
Richard	OH1427
HEWITT	
Aaron	MU1026
Charles	P28
Edward	S178
Elizabeth	P1677
Elizabeth	P1680
Emma	P458
George R.	MU1028
Jemima	P1678
John	P1679
John	S179
Maria E.	MU1029
Mary	P29
Mary Ann	MU1027
Mary Ann	S177
Sarah	S176
Thomas	R2032
Walter	S1266
William	P1676
William	S175
William	S226
HEWSON	
Alfred W	W1673
Edward	W1675
Laura	W1674
HIBBERT	
Ann	A1504
Elizabeth	A1505
Elizabeth Chapple	A1503
Frances	A1506
George	A1510
Henry Shay	A1507
Leonard	H1632
Leonard	A1502
Mary	A808
Sarah	A929
Thomas	A1508
William	A1509
HICKMAN	
William	P141
HICKS	
Ellen	R1977
William	OH322
HIDE	
James	OH1438
HIGDEN	
Elizabeth	P378
Emma	P380
Joseph	P377
Thomas	P379
HIGDON	
Charles	WK45
Elizabeth	WK32
James	A1735
John	A721
Mary	A271
Richard	WK35
Thomas	WK31
William Henry	A459
HIGGARD	
Joseph	SA547
HIGGINS	
Charlotte	A1601
Eliza	A1603
Eliza	A2349
Elizabeth	A1600
Elizabeth	P1373
Emma	A2350
George T.	MU821
John	SA603
Joseph	W233
Mary	A1598
Mary	A2348
Mary Ann	MR423
Mary Anne	A1599
Phoebe	W234
Sarah	SA602
William	A1602
HILL	
Abraham	OH878
Albert A	P1194
Amos	OH867
Angenina	P1193
Ann	OH804
Ann	P2161
Ann	P2162
Ann	S586
Anne	A2094
Arthur James	P59
Charlotte	S967
Clara A.	P1195
Daniel	P1189
David	OH805
Dinah	R36
Eliza	OH581
Eliza	A2089
Eliza	A2090
Eliza	MU933
Eliza	P1190
Eliza	P2221
Elizabeth	R38
Elizabeth	R141
Elizabeth	WK234
Elizabeth	S667
Elizabeth	S1458
Elizabeth Clara	OH449
Emily	OH806
Emma	SA679
Emma	OH817
Emmelina	P1192
Frederick	A2095
Frederick	P61
George	OH580
George	OH815
George	OH892
George	MU934
George	P62
George	P2222
George	S971
Hannah	OH210
Hannah	P983
Hannah	S1459
Harriotte	SA678
Henry	OH213
Horace Hade	P63
Isaac	R1410
Isabella	P2165
James	OH801
James	OH813
James	A2093
James	WK123
James	S666
James	S668
James	S970
James	S1252
Jane	P2164
John	OH448
John	OH783
John	OH814
John	OH875
John	MU937
John	P2163
John	S975
Joseph	R35
Joseph	SA549
Joseph	OH433
Joseph	OH780
Joseph	A2088
Joseph	S966
Josiah	R759
Lizzy	SA680
Louisa	R1412
Louisa	OH877
Margaret	H838
Martha	P2219
Mary	R1411
Mary	SA677
Mary	OH781
Mary	OH812
Mary	OH816
Mary	P57
Mary	P982
Mary Ann	R1414
Mary Ann	OH799
Mary Ann	P417
Mary Elizabeth	OH450
Mathew	S969
Matthew	R21
Moses	P2160
Robert	OH209
Robert	OH214
Robert	S1221
Rose	OH876
Samuel	R1413
Samuel	R1887
Samuel	OH811
Samuel	S1253
Sarah	SA681
Sarah	OH211
Sarah	OH802
Sarah	OH868
Sarah	A2091
Sarah	MU932
Sarah	MU935
Sarah	P984
Sarah	P2220
Sarah	S61
Sarah	S62
Sarah	S63
Sarah	S541
Sophia	OH798
Sophia	OH803
Sophia	W433
Susan	OH893
Thomas	P58
William	R37
William	R1415
William	SA676
William	OH212
William	OH782
William	OH797
William	OH800
William	OH869
William	OH879
William	OH894
William	A2092
William	MU936
William	P56
William	P60
William	P2166
William	P2218
William	S968
HILLIARD	
Alfred	P827
Charlotte	A2966
Fanny	H138
George	P829
Henry	A2965
Henry	A2967
Henry	P830
James	H137
James	A2968
John	P828
Sarah	P826
William	A2969
William	P825
HILLS	
Albert	W1604
Ann	W1603
Eleanor	OH1320
Fanny	W1606
Harriet	W1607
Jane	W1602
John	W1601
Louisa	W1605

John	H1122	Hannah	S1495	Rosetta	P1105	Jesse	A1289
Sarah	W1473	Harriet	W822	Sarah E.	R447	John Francis	P270
Thomas	W1472	Harriett	A1897	**HOY**		John Joseph	P272
HOW		James	OH389	Elizabeth	OH852	Joseph	W124
Ann	S378	James	A2194	George	OH184	Joseph	W127
Charlotte	R1292	James	MR332	James	OH168	Joshua	R301
Daniel	MR779	James	P1072	James	OH185	Lydia	W130
Daniel	S687	James	S1418	Jane	OH169	Mary	R299
Elizabeth	OH46	James	S1440	John	OH182	Mary	P271
George	OH47	James	S1492	Sarah	OH183	Ruth	P1449
George	OH50	James Sparks	MR334	William	OH170	Sarah	W128
George	S686	Jane	R33	**HUCKBODY**		Susan	W129
Henry	R1291	Jane	P1695	Elizabeth	H1825	Thomas	W126
Henry	OH52	Jane	S1494	**HUCKELL**		**HULL**	
Henry	S683	Jane	W821	Thomas	R1825	Adelaide	R1375
Isaac	S613	Jane Ann	W819	**HUCKLE**		Ann	R1373
Isaac	S615	Jesse	P1076	John	MU859	Ann	P990
James	OH49	John	OH187	Mary	A625	Betsy	R1374
Jane	R2016	John	OH1031	Mary	MU860	Caroline	H1518
John	H1827	John	OH1033	Mary A.	MU861	Catherine	H1520
John	H1970	John	P1074	Thomas	SA202	Daniel	H501
John	R2015	John	S1214	**HUCKLESBY**		David	H499
John	OH53	Joseph	A1653	Dinah	R1430	Eliza	R1376
Joseph	R68	Joseph	A2200	Eliza	R1393	Eliza	P568
Joseph	R530	Joseph	A2295	George	R1392	Eliza	P1019
Joseph	OH37	Joseph	P1147	James	R1429	Elizabeth	H1522
Lydia	S684	Joseph	P1696	James	W1061	Elizabeth	P309
Margaret	R2013	Joshua	OH994	John	R1431	Emma	P989
Mary	R2012	Lydia	P1075	William	R1394	George	H498
Mary	R2014	Mary	OH1032	William	R1432	George	H878
Mary Ann	S685	Mary	A2196	**HUDSON**		George	P22
Sarah	OH48	Mary	S1208	Elizabeth	R1621	George	P1286
Sarah	S614	Mary	S1419	Frederick	R206	Hannah	OH619
Susannah	R531	Mary Ann	P1145	**HUGGETT**		Helen	P992
William	H813	Mary Ann	P1698	Henry	P1141	Henry	OH620
William	OH51	Mary Ann	P2306	**HUGHES**		Henry	P1284
HOWARD		Robert S.	MR337	Alfred	SA742	Infant	P1022
Ann	OH186	Ruth E.	MR338	Ann	A800	Isabella	P991
Ann	S1498	Sarah	OH995	Ann	A1948	James	H496
Ann Maria	MR333	Sarah	P1146	Anna Maria	S52	James	H500
Anna	MU555	Sarah	P1149	Charles	H1349	James	H1588
Arnott	S1207	Sarah	P1699	Charles	H1353	James	MU177
Charles	P1697	Sarah	S1493	Eliza	H1355	James	MU182
Charles	P2305	Susan	A2197	Eliza	SA743	Jane	H497
Charles E	W818	Susannah	S1491	Elizabeth	H844	John	H1517
Charlotte	MR10	Thomas	P1144	Elizabeth	H1352	John	H1680
David	OH997	Thomas	S750	Elizabeth	SA744	John	R1372
David	A1656	Thomas	S1490	Fanny	SA740	John	MU180
Elisabeth	P1148	Thomas G.	MR336	Frederick	H1351	Joseph	H1521
Eliza	S1209	Tom	P1702	George	A1651	Louisa	MU178
Elizabeth	P1073	William	H476	George	A1951	Maria	MU181
Elizabeth	P1701	William	A1549	Henry	SA741	Mary	H876
Elizabeth	S1441	William	A2199	James	SA738	Mary	P569
Ellen	R1114	William	A3255	James	SA746	Samuel	OH618
Ellenor	A1550	William	MU389	John	H1354	Sarah	H1519
Emily	A2201	William	P2304	John Philip	A799	Sarah	MU179
Emily	P1700	William	S1442	Maria	A1652	Sarah	P566
Emily	S1497	William	S1496	Phoebe	H1350	Sarah	P1285
Emma	R1115	William	W820	Sophia	SA739	Susan	P988
Emma	A1655	**HOWE**		Susan	SA745	Susan	P1018
Emma	A1665	George	A1359	**HULKS**		Susan	P1020
Emma	A2296	**HOWELL**		Alfred	R298	Thomas	H879
Emma	MU390	Charles	H1832	Alfred	R300	Thomas	WK30
Emma	P2307	Eliza	A733	Charles	R303	Thomas	P567
Esther	P1077	Frederick	A51	Charlotte	P1450	Thomas	P987
Fanny	MR335	Henry	W1462	David	A1288	Thomas	P1017
Francis	MU391	James	W1459	Ebenezer	A1290	Thomas	P1288
George	OH996	Sarah	W1460	Eliza	P1448	Thomas James	P1021
George	A1551	William	W1461	Eliza	W125	William	H875
George	A1896	**HOWES**		Frederick	R304	William	H877
George	A2198	William	A1908	Hannah	R367	William	H1002
Hannah	R34	**HOWIE**		Henry	R302	William	P565
Hannah	A1654	Robert	R445	Isabella	A1287	William	P993
Hannah	A2195	Rose F.	R446	Jesse	A1286	William	P1287

William	W424

J

JACKSON

Abraham	OH901
Alice	MR114
Edward	OH719
Eliza	OH836
Eliza	OH837
Eliza	W103
Elizabeth	P1773
Emma	OH902
Flora	OH904
Hannah	R574
Hannah	R1293
Mary	R2025
Sarah	A1372
William	R120
William	R2010
William	OH835
William	OH903

JAMES

Arthur	A1015
Elizabeth	A1013
Emily	A1016
Fanny	SA504
George	R1893
Henry	A1012
Henry	A1014
Henry	MR409
John E	W1732
Joshua	A2921

JANES

Benjamin	MU631
Catherine	MU1004
Eliza	MU632
Eliza	MU635
Elizabeth	MU561
Elizabeth	MU634
Elizabeth	S1479
Frances	MU639
James	OH283
James	MU1003
Martha	MU636
Mary	OH284
Mary	MU633
Ruth	S1480
Sophia	MU638
Thomas	S1478
William	MU637

JAQUES

Charles	P334
Peter	P333
Rosetta Jane	P336
Susannah	P335

JARMIN

Ann	R1565
Ann	R1567
Benjamin	R1564
Catherine	R1570
Charles	R1566
David	R1575
Edward	R1569
Elizabeth	R1573
George	R1571
Joseph	R1568
Sarah	R1574
Thomas	R1572

JARRAT

Martha	MR443

JARVIS

Ann	W1378
David	W1377
Elizabeth	P612

Emma	OH1029
Hannah	OH1026
James	OH1028
Jane	OH1030
Martha	A1361
Mary A.	OH1027
Sarah	OH1025
Steven	SA373
William	OH1024

JAURER [?]

Charles	P656
Deborah	P654
John	P653

JAVAHLAW

Charles	MU643

JAYS

Hannah	A537
Mary	A536
Susan	A2582

JEANS

Elleanor	P2500
George	P2501
John	P2499

JEEVES

Ann	SA131
Ann	W720
Eliza	W722
Emma	W721
Jesse	SA130
Louis	W723
Sophia	W719
Susannah	W724
William	W718

JEFFERIES

Ann	A775
E.	A774

JEFFERY

Samuel	R2026

JEFFREYS

Henry	P745

JEFFRIES

Ann	MR187

JEFFS

Ann	A1543
Ann	A1819
Ann	A1822
Eliza	A1997
Elizabeth	A1996
James	P809
Jane	A1823
John	A1821
Joseph	A1820
Thomas	A1995
William	A1818
William	A1824

JELLIFF

George	OH400

JENKINS

Charlotte	OH1190
Eliza	P2114
Elizabeth	A519
Hector	R290
John R.	OH1189
Sarah	A518

JENKINSON

Mary	P1394

JENNINGS

Ann	W32
Benjamin	W31
Emma	P411
Frederick	W34
Joshua	R469
Joshua	MR79
Julia	R470

Martha	W35
Sarah A	W33

JERMYN

Hannah	A892

JIFFKINS

Sarah	S1295

JODDREL

Isabella Anna Maria	MR109
Richard Paul	MR108

JOHNSON

Ann	P1142
Caroline	P274
Charles	A2100
Charlotte	P2149
Clara	A3314
Elizabeth	R884
Elizabeth	A3107
Elizabeth	WK205
Ellen	A3106
Emma	A3102
Emma	P2140
Francis	P2350
George	A2099
Hannah	A2941
Hannah	A3312
Hannah	A3313
James	A2103
James	W1722
Jane	A2104
Jane	P2137
Jane C.	A2943
John	R886
John	R1309
John	R1314
John	A2940
John	A3311
John	P132
Lucy	A2102
Mark	P2139
Martha	P2135
Martha	P2136
Mary	R883
Mary	A2098
Mary	P2351
Mary A.	R1312
Mary Ann	P273
Robert	SA610
Robert	A2897
Rosa	A3103
Ruth	A3100
Ruth	A3104
Sarah	R1310
Sarah	A2945
Sarah	A3101
Sarah	P2352
Susan	A2101
Thomas	R1313
Thomas	A2942
Thomas	A3105
William	R882
William	R885
William	R1311
William	A1697
William	A2097
William	A2944
William	WK104
William	P2134
William	P2138

JOHNSTON

Ann	A837

JOINER

Ann	MR559
Ann	S1366
Benjamin	S1365

Edmund	W1616
Eliza	S1363
Ellen	S98
Emma	S1364
Emma	W1642
Frederick	W1614
George	S1377
Henry	W1617
Jane	W1613
John	W1611
Joseph	W1315
Joyce	W1316
Matilda	W1615
Sarah	S1378
Sarah	W1612
Sarah Ellen	S97
Thomas	S96

JOLLIFF

Edwin	S155
Ellen	S153
Emma	S154
Jane	S156
Mary Ann	S152
Sarah	S150
William	S149
William	S151

JONES

Adelhade	A917
Alice	A1216
Ann	R244
Ann	P2430
Charles	WK93
Eliza	P1738
Elizabeth	OH1090
Elizabeth	S350
Ellen	R245
Emily	P1739
Emma	A1204
Emma	P2432
Fanny	P1741
George	P2435
Henry	A1215
Indor	A918
John	P931
John	P2429
Joshua	OH1091
Maria	P2434
Martha	A916
Mary	A1202
Mary	MU718
Mary Ann	P343
Samuel	A1201
Samuel	P898
Sarah	A1203
Sarah	A1273
Simon	A915
Susan	P2431
Thomas	SA366
Thomas	OH1089
William	SA858
William	P1737
William	P1740
William	P2433
William C.	R246

JORDAN

Abraham	OH860
Benjamin	S1376
Eliza	A2467
Elizabeth	P1155
Elizabeth	S1368
George	S1371
Hannah	S1375
Harriett	OH861
James	S1367

Name	Code
Eliza	P237
Eliza	P1878
Eliza	S1467
Elizabeth	S1298
Elizabeth	S1301
Emelia	S1300
Emma	S1470
Ephraim	SA646
Frances	S171
Frederic	A1104
Frederick	A151
George	SA642
George	SA647
George	MR71
George	S1469
Hannah	R758
Hannah	SA645
Harriet	OH189
Isaac	S1297
James	A146
James	S170
James	S1299
James	W1288
John	R755
John	A1101
John	A1103
Joseph	R757
Joseph	MR272
Keziah	OH377
Louisa	A1678
Maria	A1677
Maria	P916
Martha	A1102
Mary	MR72
Mary	S172
Mary	W1286
Medora	A1631
Philip	S380
Rosannah	A1630
Sarah	A147
Sarah	A2170
Sarah	MR274
Selina	A1676
Sophia	SA643
Stephen	A1429
Susan	S146
Thomas	R835
Thomas	P917
Thomas	S1466
William	A1674
William	A1680
William	P915
William	S174
William	S1468
William	W1285
William	W1287
[?]	MR181

KINGHAM

Caroline	R1146
Edward	R1147
Emma	A1105
George	R1144
George	W1477
Hannah	R1148
James	W313
Mary Ann	W314
Rachael	R1145
Rachael	WK78
Richard	WK79
Susan	R1149
William	SA376
William	OH557

KINGHORN

Frederick	P231

KINGS

Elizabeth	A1121
Mary	A1120

KINGSBURY

William	A3239

KINGSMILL

William M.	MR17

KINGSTON

Elizabeth	R1997

KIPP

Ann	A1994
Elizabeth	A1991
George	A1993
James	A1990

KIRBY

Albert	S741
Charles	S734
Charles	S736
Elizabeth	S735
George	S740
John	S739
Thomas	S737
William	S738

KIRKHAM

John	OH1447

KIRTLAND

Esther	S1522

KITCHENER

Frederick	R575
James	R579
Kezia A.	R578
Pamelia	R576
William	R577
William	MU380

KNIGHT

George	A1842
Maria	A1843
Sarah	A1844
Susan	A2049
Thomas	A2048

KNIGHTS

Elizabeth	P1938

KNOTT

Sarah	MU154

KNOWLES

Eliza	S803
Emma	MR191
Esther	MR189
James	MR188
James	S749
John	S801
Julia	MR190
Lettice S.	MR193
Mary	S802
Mary A.	MR192
Sarah	P191

KUMIN

John	OH896
John	OH899
Mary Anne	OH897
Mary Anne	OH898

L

LACEY

Caroline	R517
Jabez	R516
James	R519
John	A711
Phoebe	A712
Ruth	R518
Sarah	A713

LACY

Emma	A2108
John	A1695

Name	Code
Rosanna	A2109

LADDINGTON

Emma	A2723
James	A2720
James	A2722
Sarah	A2721
Sarah	A2724

LAINE

Robert	A624

LAING

George	A3280
Mary Ann	A3281

LAKE

Joseph	A23

LAMBDEN

William	A3098

LAMBERT

William H	OH61

LAMBETH

James	A1708
Jane	A1707
Joseph	A1694
Samuel	A1706
Sarah	A1709

LAMMAS

Sarah	S984

LANE

Ann	A2585
Charlotte?	A1585
George	MU85
George	P23
Henry Thomas	P392
James William	P20
John	A2584
John	P390
John	P394
Maria	P391
Mary Ann	P393
Mary Elizabeth	P21

LANGLEY

Mary	A53
William	A52

LANGRIDGE

Edward	A626
Jessie	A628
Phillip	A629
Sarah Elizabeth	A627

LANGTON

Edward J.	A2265
Edward J.	A2267
Jane	A2266
Jane	A2268

LAPISH

Emma	A461
George	A460

LARFORD

David	OH104
Joseph	OH101
Mary	OH103
Susan	OH102
Thomas	OH105
William	OH426

LARGE

Amos	R431
Ann	R434
Ellen	R430
Ellen	A2666
Emma	R435
Hannah	W1458
James (Jnr)	R429
James (Snr)	R432
John	R436
Matthew	R437
Sarah	R433

Name	Code
Susan	P1631
William	W1457

LARMAN

Matthew	SA175

LASCELLES

Eliza Angelina	P575
Precious	P574
Ralph	P573

LATCHFORD

Ann	W1262
Ann	W1498
James	W1178
James	W1846
John	W1495
Joseph	SA762
Lizzie	W1499
Mary	SA763
Mary	SA765
Sarah	SA764
Sarah	W1179
Sarah	W1496
Susan	SA767
Thomas	W410
Thomas	W1261
Thomas	W1497
William	SA766
William	W1501
William	W1847

LATHWOOD

Mary Ann	A661
William	A660

LATTIMORE

Ann	W20
Anne	W257
Charles F	W22
Charles Higby	W256
Elizabeth	A859
Hannah	W1834
Jeremiah	A806
John	SA768
Joseph	SA769
Joshua	SA51
Mary	SA52
Mary	A807
Mary	W258
Osborn	A2287
Rachael	A2288
Sophia	W23
Thomas	W1833
William	W18
William H	W21
William Higby	W19

LAURENCE

Eliza	A999
Elizabeth	MU201
Elizabeth	W1173
Emma	A1001
George	A1000
Hearey	OH1117
James	P1635
John	A997
John	A1003
Louisa	A1002
Mary	A1004
Mary	W1144
Richard	MU200
Susan	A998
Thomas	W1172

LAVONT

Madame	A242

LAWES

Robert	A2234

LAWFORD

George	OH985

Fanny	P2206
Frederick	A2650
George	W597
George	W1205
George	W1827
Georgiana	R156
Harriet	OH273
Harriet	W595
Henry	A1915
Henry	A2647
Henry	W935
James	A1917
James	W1832
Jessey	W1203
John	SA592
John	SA595
John	A1918
John	P1053
John	W936
John	W1199
John	W1204
John	W1830
Joseph	A2644
Joseph	A2646
Joseph	W1201
Ketturah	W1895
Kitty	W1829
Maria	A466
Maria	MU304
Mary	A1916
Mary	P2207
Mary	W943
Mary	W1826
Mary A	W1730
Mary A	W1897
Mary Ann	W1202
Robert	A465
Sarah	P2203
Sarah	W1200
Sophia	SA596
Sophia	OH271
Susan	P2208
Susanah	A1845
Thomas	A468
William	P2202
William	P2333
William	W593
William	W933
William	W938

LINFIELD

Elizabeth	MR656
George	MR659
James	MR655
James	MR658
Jane	MR654
John	MR657
Mary	MR26

LINFORD

Alfred	W1538
Maria	W431
Mary A	W1539

LINGE

Matilda	A380

LINNELL

Richard	P18

LINNEY

Eliza	S854
Emma	S44
Frederick	S48
George	S45
Rosannah	P303
Sarah	S47
Susan	S43
Thomas	S46

LINTON

J.H.	MR220

LIP

William	A2903
Lipscomb Elizabeth	
Sarah	A2217
Ellen	A2222
Frederick	A2219
Henry Alchom	A2223
John Thomas	A2216
John Thomas Nicholson	
	A2218
Mary	A2220
Richard Nicholson	A2221

LITCHFIELD

Charlotte	A206
Charlotte	S1483
Elizabeth	A205
Fanny	MU892
Frederick	S1484
Harriot	P234
James	S1481
Susan	S1482
William	MU891
William	P235
William	S1485

LITTEL

George	P972

LITTLE

Ann	OH1059
Caroline	P850
Charles	A832
Charles	A834
Charles	P1310
Charles	P1813
Eliza	P851
Elizabeth	P1308
Elizabeth	P1814
Frederick	P1816
George	P1815
Harriet	OH595
Henry	P849
Henry	P928
James	R1298
Jane	R1299
Maria	OH600
Martha	P1309
Mary	OH1060
Rosanna	P852
Sarah	P929
Sarah	P1306
Sarah Ann	OH599
Sarah Anne	P930
Sophy	SA566
Thomas	P1307
William	SA221
William	P1305
[Unnamed]	A833

LIVICK

James	A1389

LIVINGS

Elizabeth	S1500
Frederick	S1501
Louisa	S1502
Stephen	S1499
Stephen	S1503

LOFORD

John	OH872

LOFORD

Sarah	OH873

LOGGAN

Arthur	A2506
Charles	A1539
Eliza	A2507

Elizabeth	A1540
Georgiana	MU983
Jane	A2505
Joseph	P253
Martha	MU982
Mary	P254
Theodore	A1541
William	A1542
William	A2504

LOMAS

Ann	MR283
Edward	MR284
Mary	MR281
Samuel	MR280
Samuel	MR282
Sarah Ellen	MR285

LONDON

Daniel	R1706
Edward	R1723
George	R1708
Henry	A618
Sarah	R1707
Susan	R1724

LONG

Abraham	S466
Ann	OH830
Ann	A922
Eliza	WK18
Frederick	MU1008
Henry	OH457
Isaac	P2117
James	OH829
John	P2115
Maria	OH831
Mary	OH458
Mary	P2116
Sarah	WK74
Susan	MU1006
Thomas	WK19
William	OH832
William	MU1005
William	MU1007

LONGHURST

George	R500

LONGSTAFF

Eliza	OH480
George	OH478
Hannah	OH1192
Mary	OH479
William	OH481

LOOKER

Kezia	A204
Louisa	A203
Louisa	P635

LORANCE

Jane	P1629
William	P1628

LORD

Ann	R193
Ann	P302
Frederick	R195
Thomas	R196
William	R192
William	R194

LOUGH

Mary	S348

LOUGHTON

James	P800
Sarah	P799
Sarah	P801

LOVELL

Ann	R620
Ann E.	R622
Elizabeth	S366

Henry	S367
Joseph	S365
William	R621

LOVETT

Alfred	S1083
Alice	MU916
Ann	A474
Betsey	SA109
Eliza	MU741
Esther	R567
Hannah	P1235
Harriet	MU919
Henry Isaac	S1082
James	MU918
Jane	S1080
John	P24
Jonathan	MR491
Joseph	S1081
Raz	MR560
William	MU917
William	S1079

LOW

Betsey	A1669
Charles	OH412
Charlotte	P2064
Edward	OH414
Emma	P2066
James	A1668
Mary	OH413
Mary	OH1113
Nathaniel	P2068
Sarah	P2067
Shadrac	P2065
William	OH1112
William	MR494
William	P2063

LOWE

Abbey	P2496
Alfred	MR538
Amos	P1027
Ann	MR534
Ann	MU926
Ann	P1124
Caroline	P1029
David	SA250
Eliza	P1025
Elizabeth	A1329
Elizabeth	MR540
Ellen	R568
George	P1023
Hannah	MR539
Jane	MR536
Richard G	P1122
Robert	P1028
Sarah	MR535
Susan	P1024
Thomas	MR533
William	MR537
William	P1026

LOWERY

Jessie	P2320
Robert	P2317
Sarah	P2318
Sarah	P2319
William	A2735

LUCK

Alfred	A2355
Charlotte	A2354
Edmund	A2353
Edmund	A2453
Elizabeth	MR744
Frederick	A2454
Harriet	A2455
Joseph	R540

John	R514	Maria	W1269	Emma	W160	Henry	SA796
Rebecca	R515	Mary	MR595	George	W161	Philip	W1887
MESSENGER		Rhoda	W369	Henry	W157	Sarah	SA797
Emma	R237	William	W241	Rebecca	W159	Sarah	W1889
Hannah	R236	William	W1268	**MONK**		**MORRIS**	
Henry	R234	**MILLER**		Elizabeth C.	MU646	Eliza	A502
Henry	SA821	Adolphus	R862	Frederick C.	MU667	Emma	W181
James	SA817	Ann	R925	George	WK91	James	A427
James	SA820	Augusta	R864	John	MU644	John	W182
John	SA819	Harry	R861	Joseph	MU456	John E	MU111
Mary	R235	Herbert	R860	Mary	MU645	Joseph	A501
Mary	SA818	Jesse	R863	Sarah	MU668	Joseph	MU107
Sarah	R238	Martha	R859	**MONTAGUE**		Joseph C	MU110
Thomas	R239	Thomas	R858	Daniel	R1542	Julia	A503
Thomas	SA822	Thomas	R866	Emily	R1541	Mary	MU572
MESSER		Walter	R865	John	R1538	Mary Ann	OH365
Alfred	W1688	**MILLIARD**		John	R1540	Mary E	MU112
Ebenezer	W1686	Caroline	S1235	Kezia	R1539	Sarah	WK97
James	W1684	James	S1234	**MOODY**		Sarah	MU108
John	W1682	Mary Ann	S1237	Amy	R1188	Sarah	W180
John	W1690	William	S1236	Edward	R1961	Sarah	W183
Mary	W1683	**MILLIGAN**		Elizabeth	R1194	Susannah	MU109
Mary	W1689	Mary	A1468	George	R1186	William	W179
Thomas	W1685	**MILLS**		George	R1958	**MORTON**	
William	W1687	Ann	P1093	Harriett	R1959	Mary	OH154
MEXEY [?]		Caroline	MR447	Henry	R1185	William	S572
Ann	P425	Edward	A637	Henry	R1189	**MOSS**	
MIAS		Harriett	A634	Henry	R1960	Anna M.	R138
Elizabeth	W1450	John	A635	John	R1962	Emma	A1037
Esther	W1448	Susan	P1094	Moses	R1193	Mary	MR873
James	W1452	Thomas	A633	Sarah	R1187	Thomas	MR219
John	W1451	Thomas	A636	Sarah	R1195	**MOUNTJOY**	
William	W1449	**MINALL**		William	R1963	Martin	MR472
MICHELL		Ann	SA505	**MOON**		**MOWBRAY**	
Frederick	P410	Eliza	A3298	Eliza	A3157	Elizabeth	W1727
MILEMAN		**MINNARD**		James	A3156	**MUCKLE**	
Abraham	A2742	Martha	SA356	Louisa I.	A3158	Eliza	P1529
Ann	A2739	Mary A	SA355	Thomas	A3159	Hannah	MR583
Eliza	S198	Sarah	SA353	**MOOR**		Thomas	MR577
George	P1788	William	SA352	Mary	P842	**MULLER**	
Hannah	S199	William	SA354	Rebecca	MR320	Julia	P298
James	A2741	**MIST**		**MOORCROFT**		**MUMFORD**	
Jane	S200	Elizabeth	P1839	Caroline [?]	R846	Ann	P1937
Kezia	S852	**MITCHEL**		Charles	R847	John	W286
Mary Ann	P2061	Elizabeth	A558	Ebenezer	R848	**MUNDAY**	
Matthew	S197	William	A557	Elizabeth	R851	Elizabeth	WK6
Sarah	A2740	**MITCHELL**		Emily	R849	**MUNNINGS**	
Sarah	S196	Ann	P2309	John	R845	Hannah	P1493
Sarah	S201	Daniel	A2429	Maria	R852	**MUNNS**	
William	S195	David	A2180	William	R850	Elizabeth	P517
MILEN		David	MU321	**MOORE**		James	P516
Alexander	OH401	Eliza	A2181	Eliza	A310	Maria	P518
George	OH402	Elizabeth	R392	Henry	P927	Sarah	S1167
MILES		Elizabeth	A2183	Richard	S1200	**MUNT**	
Ann	SA288	Elizabeth	P1370	Thomas	A309	Aaron	SA292
Anna	SA287	Emily	A2184	Thomas	WK29	Abel	P1588
James	SA289	George	P1369	**MORETON**		Alfred	W1109
Lizzy	SA286	Henry	A2432	Anne	P319	Alfred	W1344
Mary	A45	James	WK191	Elizabeth	A439	Alfred	W1655
Ruth	SA285	John	A2430	Emma	P943	Amos	W1654
William	SA284	John	P2308	**MORFITT**		Ann	S1274
MILLARD		Joseph	A2182	Elizabeth	P1392	Ann	S1279
Charlotte	MR594	Joseph Wm.	S609	**MORGAN**		Anne	W1657
Daniel	W364	Mahala	S608	Elizabeth	P114	Benjamin	S1034
Daniel	W1271	Mary	A2428	Ellen	A2291	Charles	SA398
David	W1270	Peter	A2427	Henry	SA605	Charles	P1587
Elizabeth	W367	Samuel	S607	Margaret	W1712	Charles	S1035
Emma	W365	Walter	A2431	William	WK158	Charles	W1651
Frances	W365	William	P1371	William	W1711	Charlotte	A1792
Frances S	W366	**MOLES**		**MORLEY**		David	P1855
Henry	A3011	Susan	A1182	Thomas	A2066	Eliza	P2469
Jane	A3012	Thomas	A1356	**MORRICE**		ELiza	W1107
Jane	W371	**MONDIN**		Eliza	W1888	Eliza	W1341
John D	W368	Eliza	W158	Elizabeth	SA798	Eliza	W1343

Ann	W1906
Charlotte	MR735
Charlotte	W1147
Eliza	MR737
Elizabeth	MR1829
Elizabeth	W1150
Emma	MR739
George	MR741
George	W1149
George	W1907
James	W1905
John	MR734
John	MR740
Mary	MR736
Mathew	W1146
Mathew	W1148
Thomas	W1160
ROLLS	
Sarah	A893
ROLPH	
John	W448
ROLT	
Elizabeth	H1358
George	H1189
Sarah	H1187
Sarah	H1361
Thomas	H1186
Thomas	H1362
William	H1188
ROSE	
Alfred	MR823
George	MR821
George	MR825
Lucy	MR824
Mary A.	MR822
Thomas	A1889
ROSON	
Edward	OH1318
George	OH1310
Lewesor	OH1319
Rebecca	OH1316
Samuel	OH1315
Samuel	OH1317
ROSS	
Elizabeth	P1393
ROW	
Caroline	OH672
Charles	W1192
Edward	W1189
Edward	W1191
Elisabeth	H712
Eliza	H713
Emma	H663
Hannah	W1190
James	H714
John	H661
Lucy	H662
Mary	H711
Mary Ann	OH153
Mary Ann	OH670
Thomas	H710
Thomas	OH671
William	OH669
ROWE	
Daniel	S868
Elizabeth	H436
Elizabeth	S853
James	H435
Joseph	WK192
Mary	R1428
Thomas	R1427
ROWED	
Elizabeth	H1123
ROWEN	
Albert H	P1354
John B	P1353
Sarah	P1351
William E	P1352
ROWLAND	
Eliza	MU883
Hannah	MU974
ROWLERSON	
Selina	S1518
ROWSON	
Mary	WK65
ROYDS	
Fanny	S980
George	S976
Henry John	S978
Jane	S977
Jane Louisa	S979
ROYER	
Sarah	H37
RUDD	
Ann	W1736
Betsy	A2465
Daniel	W1737
Elizabeth	SA579
Jane	A2462
Joseph	W1738
Mary	SA580
Mary Ann	A2464
Philip	WK148
Philip	W1739
Samuel	H1337
William	A2461
William	A2463
William	W1735
RUDDOCK	
R. H.	A3117
RUFFETT	
George	A3296
Jane	A3297
RUFFETT [RUSSELL]	
George	P1509
John	P1508
Margaret	P1507
Thomas	P1506
RUMBALL	
Arthur G.	H1617
Aubrey	P282
Charles	P281
Eliza Ann	P278
Frederick	H36
George	H33
George Horace	P279
Henry John	P285
James	H35
James R.	H31
John Horner	P277
Martha	R507
Rebecca	H32
Rosa Mary	P283
Sampson John	P280
Selina	H34
Stanley	P1231
Stewart	P1232
William	R506
RUMENS	
Sarah	S413
RUMNEY	
Jane	SA365
RUMSLEY	
Thomas	W470
RUNEY	
Clara	MR25
RUSH	
Frederick	P870
George	WK24
Hannah	P869
Harry	WK25
William	R822
RUSHTON	
Eliza	P1919
Margaret	P1917
Mary	P1247
Matilda	P1918
William	P1916
RUSKEN	
Hannah	A1597
RUSKIN	
Charlotte	A1723
Eliza	A1726
Elizabeth	A1724
Emily	A1725
James	A1730
Louisa	A1729
Mary Ann	A1728
William	A1727
RUSSEL	
Ann M	W581
Emily	W1379
Francis	W578
James	SA463
Louisa	W1380
Lucy	W579
Sarah J	W580
RUSSELL	
Alexander Thomas	P5
Ann	MU451
Ellen	H1360
George	A93
George	H1359
Harry Goodman B.	P6
Jane	P4
John	MU450
Joseph	A1574
Joseph	H1390
Lydia	A2024
Sarah	P843
William Alexander	P3
RUTHERFORD	
Peter	H439
Sarah	H440
RUTTY	
Sarah	H1294
Stephen H.	H1293
S	
SABERTON	
John	A2907
Thomas	A2908
SADDINGTON	
Ann	MR304
Eliza	A311
Emma	A2138
James	A2139
Mary	P2110
Pheobe	A2137
Sarah	A2140
SADDLER	
Robert	OH1093
Sarah	OH1094
Mary	A2994
William	A738
SAGE	
Ann	R1090
Charlotte	R1091
Eliza	P758
Elizabeth	R1089
George	R1092
Thomas	R1088
William	R1093
SAKER	
Eliza Helen	A964
Mary	OH714
SALES	
Sarah	W1131
SALMON	
Eliza	MU6
Elizabeth	SA97
Jane	MU5
Rebecca	A78
Sarah	MU7
SAMMONS	
John	A2249
SAMS	
Ann	P760
Eliza	P2277
Henry	P2276
Henry	P2280
James	P2279
Jane	P2281
Joseph	P759
Joseph	P761
Joseph H	W282
Margaret	P762
Mary Ann	P2278
Sarah	P763
William	W468
SANDERS	
Amy	A1515
Charlotte	P1418
Eliza	A322
Elizabeth	MU650
Elizabeth	P1419
George	A1514
George	MU652
Henry	R877
James	P1417
James	R853
Julia	R856
Mary	R854
Rhoda	OH398
Sarah	P1420
Susan	R2028
Thomas	P1421
Walter	R855
William	A321
William	MU651
William	P1422
William R.	MU649
SANDISON	
Sarah	P1365
SAPWELL	
Ann	H1835
Ellen	H1834
James	H1836
William	H1833
SARGENT	
Alice	S482
Caroline	MU285
Eliza	S484
Emily	S481
Frederick	S483
Robert	S480
Sarah	S479
SAUNDERS	
Abraham	W623
Alfred	W622
Alfred W.	R896
Amy M.	R923
Ann	MR422
Anne	R897
Caroline	MR459
Catherine	A2227

Charlotte	MR661	Mary Ann	OH422	Ann	R993	Mary	S612
Charlotte E.	MR665	Richard	OH423	Caroline	H1699	Mary	W24
Daniel	MR663	Robert	SA582	Charles	H1701	Mary	W882
Edward	R259	Samuel	SA586	Charles	H446	Mary A	W885
Eliza	P2448	Sarah	SA583	Charles	R952	Mary Ann	H746
Emily	R924	William	OH421	Charlotte	P796	Mary Ann	R1487
Emily	W627	**SCALES**		Charlotte	R49	Mary Ann	R1625
Fanny	R921	Eliza	OH1394	Charlotte	R951	Mary Ann	R3
Frederick	H1408	Thomas	OH1420	David	SA499	Mary Anne	W198
George	W1386	**SCARBOROUGH**		Edward	OH438	Matthew	W1879
George	W624	George	A2278	Eliza	H197	Michael	W195
George H.	MR664	**SCARRATT**		Eliza	H437	Micheal	H442
George T.	R920	James	A316	Eliza	H447	Mille	W886
Hannah	WK61	**SCHOOLING**		Eliza	R1488	Rebecca	P1768
Harriet	P2446	Martha	P1518	Eliza	R2011	Robert	H449
Henrietta	H1471	**SCOREY**		Eliza	R916	Sarah	R1486
Henry	W628	Joseph	W464	Elizabeth	H127	Sarah	R2078
James	MR405	**SCOTT**		Elizabeth	H744	Sarah	R5
Jane F.	R922	Alice	MR258	Elizabeth	R43	Sarah	W1880
Jane M.	R473	Arthur	MR261	Elizabeth	W884	Sarah	W197
John	H1470	Elizabeth	MR253	Elizabeth	W891	Selina Alice	H438
John	MR660	Elizabeth A.	MR254	Ellen	R970	Susannah	R912
John	MR662	Emma	MR255	Emma	H1698	Thomas	H1696
John	W620	Frances M.	MR256	Emma	H444	Thomas	R217
John Frederick	H1458	Laura	MR257	Emma	W887	Thomas	R968
Joseph	A2226	Walter	MR260	Emma M.	R7	Thomas	W1723
Louisa	H1473	**SCRIVENER**		Emma M.	R918	Walter	R47
Lucas	MR433	Ann		Frances	H193	William	H192
Marbet [?]	OH795	Elizabeth	H568	Frances	R2009	William	H198
Mark	W626	Charles	W1371	Francis	H199	William	H742
Mary	H1472	Edward	A1878	Frederic	H195	William	R1497
Mary	W625	Eliza	W1373	George	H126	William	R42
Matilda	H1407	Elizabeth	WK221	George	H1700	William	R45
Phillis	P2444	Ellen C.	MU980	George	R1	William	R950
Rose	R1949	Ellen H.	MU979	George	R913	William	R978
Samuel	P2447	Emma	W1369	George	R966	William	S1258
Sarah	H1405	George	W1365	George	R994	William	W888
Sarah	H1406	Infant	W1374	George	W196	**SEABROOKE**	
Sarah	W1387	James	MU978	George	W881	Ann	MU26
Sarah	W621	James E.	MU981	George	W883	Charles	MU27
Sophia	SA859	John	R1622	Hannah	H1697	Charlotte	MR381
Thomas	MR404	Jonathan	R1290	Hannah	H443	Charlotte	MR382
Thomas D.	R898	Maria	W1372	Hannah	OH1197	Daniel	MU514
William	H1404	Mary	A1877	Hannah	R2	David	MU25
William	P2445	Mary	A202	Harriet	W889	Eliza	MU29
William	R2043	Rose	W1367	Harriett	R6	Frances	MR1476
William	SA860	Sarah	W1366	Henry	OH440	Hannah	MU517
William	W1681	Sarah	WK220	Infant	W1881	Henry	MU516
William	WK60	Sarah	WK222	James	H196	Joseph	MR380
William L.	MR666	Sophia	R1289	James	R992	Joseph	MR383
SAVAGE		Susan	A2665	Jane	H128	Maria	MU30
Ann	P878	Susan	W1368	Jane	H448	Sarah	MU28
Daniel	P877	Thomas	A1122	John	H200	Sarah	MU515
George	P866	Thomas	A1876	John	H745	William	MR384
Harriet	P882	William	R1288	John	OH436	**SEALE**	
James	P868	William	W1370	John	R2008	Archibald A	P1213
John	P880	William	WK223	John	R4	**SEALES**	
Mary	P867	**SCRIVENOR**		John	R423	Elizabeth	SA297
Mary	P879	Catherine	H1878	John	R46	Sarah	SA298
William	P881	Henry B.	H1879	John	R914	**SEAR**	
SAVILL		John	H1880	John	S1316	Ann	R1643
Enoch	W473	Reuben	H1876	John	W890	**SEARANCKE**	
SAWBRIDGE		Sarah	H1877	Joseph	MR780	Francis J.	MU702
Jane	H1442	Sarah	H1881	Joseph	OH1196	Francis N.	MU704
SAWYER		**SEABROOK**		Joseph	R218	Maria	MU703
Ann	MU155	Alice	H861	Joseph	R48	Mary E	P1123
Elizabeth	MU271	Alice	R216	Lousia	H129	**SEARLE**	
Mary	MR113	Alice	R917	Margaret	H747	Emma	A2987
William H	MU156	Ann	H194	Maria	H445	James	R261
SAYER		Ann	MR781	Maria	R1489	**SEARS**	
Ann	P1525	Ann	OH439	Martha	OH437	Ann	A1906
Charles	SA585	Ann	R44	Mary	H743	Ann	H701
Charlotte	SA587	Ann	R915	Mary	R215	Ann	H705
Mary	SA584	Ann	R969	Mary	R967	Ann	P1055

Ann	P1186
Anne	W1411
Anne	W1413
Betsy	A2331
Caroline	A2370
Charles	H111
Charles	W1415
David	MR880
Dinah	W827
Eliza	H541
Elizabeth	R1297
Fanny	MU811
Fanny	MU818
Frederic	H109
Frederick	H704
George	R1295
Harriet	W1418
Jane	MU812
Jane	W1410
Jane	W1417
Jesse	MR879
John	H107
John	P1185
John	P1455
John	P2103
John	W1416
John Thomas	A2371
Joseph	A1700
Joseph	R1294
Maria	MR877
Maria	MU815
Mary	H108
Mary A.	MR881
Mary Ann	H110
Mary Ann	H703
Priscilla	P1184
Rebecca	R1158
Reuben	P1632
Rhoda	MU817
Richard	MR876
Richard	MR878
Samuel	MU518
Sarah	MR791
Susan	MU816
Thomas	H700
Thomas	MU810
Thomas	MU813
Thomas	P1183
Thomas	P1187
Thomas	W1409
Thomas	W1414
William	A2369
William	H540
William	H702
William	MU814
William	P1188
William	R1296
William	W1412
SEBEY	
Esther	MU533
SEDGEWICK	
Arthur	A2893
Gordon	A2913
SELLS	
Arthur	MR291
Charles	R901
Eliza	R900
William	R899
SELSBY	
Jane	A2981
SEWDELL	
Henry	A3260
SEWEERL	
A	SA424
SEWELL	
James	A1479
SEYMORE	
Emily	H750
Hannah	H749
Thomas	H748
SEYMOUR	
Charles	MR298
E	S1524
Eliza	A2107
Elizabeth	MR297
Emma	P863
James	MR299
John	P862
William	A2105
William	MR296
SHADBOLT	
Ann	W1032
George	R260
George	W1033
Richard	W1031
Sarah	W1034
SHAMBROOK	
Caroline	W397
Daniel	W394
Eliza	W398
Elizabeth	W396
Hester	W400
Joshua	W399
Martha	W401
Mary	H475
Mary	W395
SHANE	
Eliza	A1491
SHANNON	
James	H1722
SHARMAN	
James	H1048
Jane	H1047
Maria	H1050
William	H1049
SHARP	
Alfred	A1303
Alfred	S906
Alfred	SA673
Alfred	SA733
Amelia	A1778
Ann	A1299
Ann	R770
Ann	S896
Betsy	S629
Charles	SA672
Daniel	SA731
Eliza	S4
Eliza	S905
Elizabeth	R771
Elizabeth	S895
Elizabeth	SA518
Elizabeth	SA732
Emma	S3
Emma	S907
George	S206
Hannah	SA667
Hannah	SA669
Harriett	S2
Henry	S627
James	S1451
James	S392
James	S742
James	S894
James	S903
James	SA521
Jane	A1782
Job	S1
John	A1921
John	S6
John	SA666
Joseph	SA735
Lowen	A1300
Maria Elizabeth	S628
Martha	A621
Martha	S391
Mary	S901
Mary	SA523
Matilda	A1780
Matthew	S390
Rebecca	A1302
Sarah	S1452
Sarah	S904
Sarah	SA519
Sarah	SA522
Sarah	SA671
Sarah	SA734
Stephen	A1781
Susan	SA668
Thomas	A1683
Thomas	S5
Thomas	SA517
Thomas	SA520
Thomas	SA670
William	A1298
William	A1301
William	MR185
William	R769
William	S1099
William	S1224
William	S900
William	S902
SHARPE	
Ann	H856
Betsy	SA348
Elizabeth	A1875
Jane	A2068
Louisa	SA349
Lucy	H1758
Thomas	A3243
William	A1874
William	SA347
SHAW	
James	S752
Jane	S757
John	S669
Keziah	S753
Maria	S670
Thomas	MR92
Thomas	S671
SHAWBROOK	
Ann	A1525
SHEARS	
Amelia	A1779
Ann	S767
Betsy	S773
Emma	S772
Henry	S770
James	S774
John	S769
Sarah	S766
Susan	S771
Thomas	S765
Thomas	S935
William	S768
SHEFFIELD	
Eliza	H1288
Ellen	H1290
Emma	H1285
Harriet	H1284
Maria	H1286
Mary	H1289
William	H1287
SHELDRAKE	
Joshua	OH330
Mary Ann	OH334
Richard	OH328
Richard	OH331
Sarah	OH333
Susannah	OH329
Thomas	OH332
SHELLEY	
Mary	P1111
SHENSTONE	
Mary	P419
SHEPHARD	
James	H818
SHEPHEARD	
Emily Jane	A42
Maria	A40
William	A39
William Henry	A41
SHEPHERD	
Ann	MU115
Fanny	WK37
George	MU119
Henry	MU117
Israel	WK27
Jane	MU120
John	MU114
John	MU116
Mary	MR471
William	MU118
SHEPPARD	
George	R522
Sarah	H666
Sophia	R523
William	H665
SHERWOOD	
Ann	R942
John	R943
SHIRLEY	
Edwin	R637
Elizabeth	R633
Henry	R636
Josephus	R635
Mary	R634
SHIRLY	
John	R468
SHORBY	
Elizabeth	OH325
Emily	OH326
Henry	OH324
Sarah Ann	OH327
SHORT	
Christiana	A3348
Emma Main	A3350
Jane Sarah	A3351
Joseph James	A3347
Mary Harriet	A3346
Walter Charles	A3349
SHRIMPTON	
Charlotte	MU56
Hannah	MU55
John	MU54
John	MU57
Joseph	MU58
Samuel	MU59
SHRUBB	
Martha	P650
Samuel	A452
Samuel J.	P649
SHUFFIELD	
Ann	A1772
Charles	A1771
Flowers	A1766

James	A1769	Charles	R388	George	W555	Jane	MR339
John	A1765	Charles	R390	Harriett	W560	John	OH634
John	A1770	James T	P1196	Jane	R1951	Sarah	OH1231
Joseph	A1768	Mary	R389	Maria	H1456	Shadrach	OH1232
Nanny	MR896	William	R391	Maria E.	H1457	William	OH1230
William	A1767	**SILSY**		Mary	H1263	William	OH1234
SHUFFORD		Lydia	A2368	Mary	W557	**SKILLETON**	
Ann	P1959	**SILVERTHORN**		Rebecca	H1154	Eliza	A613
Henry T.	P1960	Rhoda	MU701	Robert	W559	**SKILLMAN**	
SIBLEY		**SILVESTER**		Thomas	H1749	Daniel	R273
Aaron	W897	Charlotte	A920	Thomas	S1357	Eliza	R272
Agnes	H900	F.R.	A919	William	A2248	Henry C.	R274
Ann	H895	**SIMCOCK**		William	H1153	John	R269
Charles	H899	Susanna	A2261	**SIMPKIN**		Mary	R270
Charles	W405	**SIMION[?]**		Emma	OH237	Mary Ann	R271
Charles	W439	William	H699	John	OH236	Susanna	R129
Edward	W731	**SIMKINS**		Thomas	OH239	Thomas	R128
Edwin S	W784	(Infant)	P2172	William	OH238	Thomas H.	R130
Eleanor	R310	Ann	P2168	**SIMPKINS**		**SKINNER**	
Eliza	R309	Dinah	OH218	Eliza	OH259	Alice	R1250
Eliza	W806	Eliza	OH220	Eliza	SA193	Ann	R1879
Elizabeth	H1802	Emma	P2175	Emily	OH261	Ann M.	R1880
Elizabeth	P1951	Fanny	P2174	Harriet	SA207	Caroline	MU474
Emma	H1804	Henry	OH217	James	H1867	Charlotte	MU432
Emma	OH755	James	OH221	James	SA206	Eliza	MU431
Emma	P876	James	OH633	Joseph	SA208	Eliza	MU475
Esther	W404	John	OH222	Lucy	SA256	Emma	MU477
Esther E	S1272	Mary	OH219	Mary	H1868	Emma	R1210
George	H894	Samuel	P2170	Mary	H1869	George	MU430
George	H898	Sarah	P2171	Rebecca	OH256	George	MU473
George	W900	Susan	P2169	Rebecca	OH260	George	MU476
George F	W785	Susan	P2173	Richard	OH258	Hannah Baker	A457
Henry	OH754	Thomas	P2167	Samuel	SA210	James	MU428
Henry	P875	**SIMMONDS**		Sarah	H1870	Jane	MU425
Henry	W733	David	S1463	Thomas	SA209	Jane	MU427
James	H893	Eliza	MU296	William	OH255	John	A2500
James	H896	Elizabeth	MU294	William	OH257	John	R1857
James	OH756	Ellen	MU295	William	SA251	John	WK242
James	P872	Fanny	H1052	**SIMPSON**		Joseph	R1208
James	W899	Frederick	H1053	Albert Leppard	P13	Kezia	R1858
John	OH282	Frederick	S1465	Alfred W	P1251	Martha	A1682
John	W407	Jane	MU297	Charlotte	H1296	Mary	OH343
John	W734	Mary Ann	P260	Elizabeth	MR412	Mary	R1209
Joseph	P1952	Sarah	S1464	Elizabeth	P12	Mary	R1251
Joseph	R311	William	WK111	Frederick	MR410	Rebecca	A1107
Julia	H897	**SIMMONS**		George	SA635	Robert	A1109
Maria	H1803	Ann	SA835	Henry	H1453	Thomas	MU424
Maria	W732	Archibald	P2327	James	SA633	Thomas	MU426
Martha	OH753	Charles	H1400	John A	P1252	William	A1681
Mary	P873	Charles	R124	Mary	MR411	William	MU429
Mary	W408	David	H87	Nancy W	P1250	William	R1878
Mary	W898	Emily	P2330	Sarah	H1454	**SLADE**	
Matilda	W783	Emma	H89	Sarah	WK155	Alfred J.	P1875
Robert	H1800	George	P2329	Susan	SA634	Charles G.	P1874
Samuel	OH752	George	R122	Thomas	R1371	Emma E.	P1876
Samuel	W440	George	R125	William Balcombe	P11	George	P1872
Sarah	P874	James	MR562	**SIMS**		Horace	P1877
Sarah	R307	John	SA834	William George	A2881	Lucy	P1873
Sarah	W26	John	SA836	**SIMSON**		**SLATER**	
Sophia	P1954	Mary	H90	Charlotte	SA272	Ann	SA787
Susan	H1805	Mary	R123	**SINFAIL**		Charles	H1273
Susanna	H1801	Mary Ann	R364	Elizabeth	H1265	Elizabeth	H1271
Thomas	P1953	Sarah	H88	Robert	H1264	Elizabeth	SA786
Thomas	W782	Sarah	P2328	**SINFIELD**		Emma	H1270
William	P1950	Sarah	R127	Joseph	A3007	Jeremiah	A71
William	R308	William	R126	Susannah	A3008	Joseph	SA736
William	W901	**SIMONDS**		**SITTLE**		Louisa	H1274
William	W906	Hannah	S1517	Annah	A1390	Mary	H1269
SILLCOCK		John	OH366	**SKEGG**		Sarah	SA729
Catherine	P2262	**SIMONS**		Ann	MU31	Sarah	W1399
Hannah	P2260	Ann	H1155	Eliza	MU33	Sophia	SA730
James	P2259	Ann	H1750	James	MU32	Sophia	SA788
Mary	P2261	Eliza	W556	**SKEGGS**		Susan	SA737
SILSBY		Emma	W558	Emma	OH1233	Susana	SA789

Thomas	H1268
William	H1272
SLAUGHTER	
Benjamin	P2035
Eliza	P2037
Eliza	S75
George	R61
George	S76
Harriet	MU1002
Henry	R479
Job	S74
John	A1164
John	R58
Lucy	R478
Martha	P2036
Mary Ann	S77
Robert	S79
Sarah	R59
Sarah	S1024
Thomas	R477
Walter	R481
William	R480
William	S369
William	S78
SLEET	
Frederick	OH216
SLIGO	
(Marchioness of)	
Ellen	MR19
(Marquis of)	
George John	MR18
SLING	
Daniel	A261
Hannah	A262
SLOUGH	
Alfred	W1524
Amelia	P949
Ann	OH455
Ann	P1430
Ann	P1826
Ann	W670
Arthur	W747
Charles	P1409
Charles	P848
David	P1825
Edmund	W745
Eliza	OH454
Eliza	P948
Eliza	W1356
Ellen	W1354
Emma	H717
Emma	P1410
Emma	P952
Esther	OH452
Esther	OH453
Frederick	P1406
Frederick	W669
George	H217
George	P1435
Henry	P1407
Henry	P953
Isaac	P1429
James	A1564
James	P951
Jane	H216
Jesse	P1436
John	H715
John	W746
Joseph	A1566
Joseph	P1432
Julia	P1433
Louisa	P945
Lucy	A1567
Maria	P871

Marianne	P947
Mark	A1569
Mary	A1568
Mary	P1431
Mary	W1352
Mary	W1355
Mary	W744
Mary Ann	H420
Matilda	W743
Rebecca	P1405
Rebecca	P1434
Sarah	H716
Sarah	P946
Susan	P1408
Susan	P950
Susan	W1353
Tessa	A1565
Timothy	H419
William	H215
William	OH451
William	OH456
William	P944
William	W1351
William	W742
SLOW	
Abi	H1434
Alfred	P2182
Daniel	MR184
Edmund	H1436
Edward	H1433
Eliza	P2179
Emma	H1435
George	P2176
George	P2181
James	SA282
Lucy	P2178
Mary	R556
Saphira	P2177
William	P2180
SLY	
Mary	WK13
SLYTHE	
Sarah	R653
SMALL	
Alexander	OH1401
Ann	OH1400
Ann	OH1404
Elizabeth	OH1403
George	OH1402
James	P2008
Sophia	P2009
SMALLBROOK	
Charlotte	H1339
John	H1338
SMART	
Ann	H871
Charles	R1326
Elizabeth	P1634
Emma	H873
Emma	H943
Esther	R1320
Esther	R1324
Francis	H868
Frederick	H874
George	R1322
Hannah	MR796
Hannah	SA254
Henry	MR561
John	A24
Jonas	R1319
Joseph	SA227
Josiah	H872
Maria	R1325
Matilda	H870

Rebecca	MR795
Samuel	SA253
Sarah	H869
Sophia	SA255
Susan	R1323
William	MR794
William	P1633
William	R1321
SMITH	
Abraham	R2058
Ada	P1941
Agnes	SA361
Alexander	R1471
Alfred	A2326
Alfred	OH1243
Alice	R1553
Alice	R1624
Ann	A1903
Ann	A3124
Ann	A570
Ann	MU913
Ann	OH1429
Ann	OH631
Ann	P2131
Ann	R1464
Ann	R1546
Ann	R1691
Ann	R2060
Ann	S794
Ann	SA526
Anne	W922
Betsey	R1387
Caroline	MU915
Caroline	R1891
Caroline	S324
Charles	A568
Charles	A571
Charles	H26
Charles	P1944
Charles	P2331
Charles	SA240
Charlotte	R247
Charlotte	W1721
Charlotte	W661
Dan	W1216
Daniel	R1740
Daniel	R875
Daniel (Snr)	R569
David	R1543
Dinah	SA525
Dolphin	SA357
Dorcas	R1890
Ebenezer	A413
Edmund	SA429
Edward	MU548
Edward	P598
Edward	P753
Edward	R1253
Edward	R2051
Eliza	A1241
Eliza	H638
Eliza	H799
Eliza	MU554
Eliza	P2001
Eliza	P2133
Eliza	P733
Eliza	P752
Eliza	R1438
Eliza	R1737
Eliza	R1739
Eliza	R844
Eliza	S1005
Eliza	W1259
Eliza	W25

Elizabeth	A3084
Elizabeth	A414
Elizabeth	A484
Elizabeth	H20
Elizabeth	MU629
Elizabeth	P2255
Elizabeth	P2257
Elizabeth	P2471
Elizabeth	P374
Elizabeth	P837
Elizabeth	R1693
Elizabeth	R1889
Elizabeth	S305
Elizabeth	S323
Elizabeth	S571
Elizabeth	SA363
Elizabeth	SA427
Elizabeth	SA544
Elizabeth	W1213
Elizabeth	W1254
Elizabeth	W1258
Elizabeth	WK118
Elizabeth R	P1120
Ellen	H640
Ellen	SA359
Ellen	SA430
Ellen	SA530
Emilia	A2517
Emily	A1242
Emily	OH1308
Emily	P754
Emma	A572
Emma	H1659
Emma	OH1221
Emma	P1119
Emma	P2258
Emma	R1592
Emma	SA528
Ephraim	A409
Esther	A1882
Esther	R1254
Esther	R1610
Esther	R2050
Frederick	H163
Frederick	P2473
Frederick	P734
Frederick	R1888
George	A2325
George	A3175
George	A407
George	H22
George	H25
George	H797
George	MR875
George	OH1222
George	OH477
George	OH762
George	P2002
George	P2470
George	P2472
George	R2047
George	S309
George	S325
George	SA527
George	W1720
George	W1771
George	W239
Georgiana	P2504
Georgiana	P2505
Georgianna	P1946
Hannah	A411
Hannah	H1658
Hannah	OH476
Hannah	P732

Rebecca	OH887		Edward	P932		Susannah	R355		Joseph	W240
SPACKMAN			Lydia	MU557		Walter	R361		Lucy A.	MR767
Caroline H.	H1438		STAMMERS			William	R357		Mary	P208
Frederic H.	H1440		Alice	S441		Zephah	R359		Mary	P209
Frederic R.	H1437		Arthur N.	S439		STEAD			Mary	SA404
Harriet M.	H1439		Charles H.	S440		Elisha	WK225		Mary A.	MR766
Johnson W.	H1441		Charlotte	A914		STEALE			Nathan	MR770
SPAKESBY [?]			Charlotte	S438		Ellen	WK228		Sarah A.	MR769
Joseph	A197		John B.	S436		STEARN			Susan	SA405
SPARKS			Samuel J.	S437		Emma	A1869		William	MU769
Elizabeth	MR419		STANBRIDGE			George	A1865		STEVENSTON	
Elizabeth	MR420		William	P1262		Harriet	A1868		Mary	H1220
Richard	MR418		STANLEY			Phillis	A1866		STEWART	
SPARY			Emma	P1412		Phillis	A1870		Catherine	P1860
Arthar	SA423		Emma	SA199		STEBBINGS			STEWART [?]	
David	SA420		George	SA201		Emma	W1520		George K.	P1861
Mary	SA421		Hannah	P1413		Jane	W1519		STIERS	
Rosana	SA422		John	SA198		Thomas	W1518		William	S1175
SPEEDY			Mary	P1411		STEED			STILES	
Harriet	P1134		Sarah	SA197		Elizabeth	H263		Henry	MR478
SPENCER			Sarah	SA200		Francis	MR475		STILWELL	
Leigh	H1219		William	SA196		George	H261		Frances	S909
SPICER			William	WK239		Mary	H262		Henry	S908
Anne	P1337		STANTON			STEEL			STOCKSLEY	
Frederick	P1338		Anne	A377		Dennis	A327		Emily	S719
SPINKES			STAPLES			STEER			Francis	S714
Elizabeth	MR107		Henry	A1831		Charles B	SA93		George	S718
SPITTLE			Jane	A1830		Edmund D	SA95		James	S717
Ann	P1948		Samuel	A1828		STEGGALL			Sarah	S715
SPORTAN			Sarah	A1829		Ann Elizabeth	H6		Susan	S716
John	A2367		Sarah	A1832		STELL			STOCKWELL	
SPRIGGINS			STARKEY			Emma	P1865		Albert Edward	A1935
Ann	MR309		George	H1798		Frederick	P1868		Anna Maria	A1934
David	MR306		STARKINGS			John	P1864		David	A3139
Emma	MR307		Joseph	H1417		John	P1867		Samuel	A1933
George C.	MR310		Mary	H1418		Samuel	P1866		STOKES	
Mary Ann	MR308		STARKINS			STENING			Charlotte	OH1353
SPRIGGS			Eliza	R1653		Fanny	A2260		John	OH1354
Ann	P1929		Eliza	R1666		STEPHENS			Sarah M.	OH1355
Ann	P1930		Emma	R1669		Abraham	R610		Susanna	OH1352
Ann	R1457		Esther	R1512		Ann	R611		Thomas	OH1351
Hannah	P1932		Fanny	MU717		Elizabeth	A476		William	OH1356
James	P1933		Fanny	R1668		Jesse	SA335		STONE	
John	P1928		Fanny	S493		John	A475		Ann	MR149
John	P1931		George	S489		Mary	R1496		Ann	MR153
John	R1456		Hannah	MR44		William	R2075		Benjamin	MR152
Marianne	S1545		James	R1511		STEPNEY			Betsey	A872
SPRIGINGS			James	S1177		Ann Maria	MU20		Catherine	R833
Charlotte	MU746		James	S487		David	A1928		Charlotte	A871
Edward	MU747		John	MR46		Eliza	MU24		Eliash	A873
Eliza	MU745		John	S492		Jersey	A1477		Eliza	R832
Elizabeth	MU743		Joseph	R1665		John	A1925		Elizabeth	A868
George	MU742		Joseph	S490		John	MU22		Ellen	A874
William	MU744		Mary	R1667		Mary	A1926		Emily	R486
SPRIGS			Sarah	MR45		Mary Ann	MU21		Emma	A869
John	W247		Sarah	S488		Sarah	A1927		Emma	R857
Mary	W246		Thomas	MR43		Sarah Maria	MU23		George	A867
SPRING			Thomas	MR47		William	MU19		George	WK46
Caroline	W1313		Thomas	R1513		STEVENS			Harriett	R487
Isaac	W1312		Thomas	S491		Amos	MR768		James	MR148
SQUIRES			William	MR340		Charles J	W471		John	MR150
Daniel	R1364		STEABBEN			Eliza	MU766		John	R482
Daniel	R1367		Ann Elizabeth	A740		Elizabeth	MR765		Joseph	A870
Eliza	WK152		Elizabeth	A741		George	MU768		Louisa	R834
George	MR426		Elizabeth	MU232		Hannah	SA402		Mary Ann	R483
Hannah	R1368		George	A739		Hannah	SA403		Oliver	MR154
John	R2069		Isaac	MU234		Henry	MU606		Sarah	P677
Sophia	R1365		John	MU231		Henry	W472		Sarah	R485
William	R1366		STEABBENS			James	MU765		Sophia	P678
William	WK153		Arthur	R358		James	MU767		Thomas	MR151
STALLARD			Emma	R291		James Davis	P210		Thomas	R484
Samuel	MR221		George	R360		Jane	MU770		William	A2512
STAMFORD			Joseph	R354		John	A3267		William	MR155
Ann	MU556		Joseph	R356		Joseph	SA401		William	P676

Margaret	P2122		
Thomas	P2042		
TATT			
Henry	WK86		
TAYLOR			
Amelia	P1383		
Ann	OH594		
Ann	R1160		
Ann	R1979		
Ann	R1982		
Ann	R2030		
Ann	R981		
Anna	SA72		
Benjamin	R1159		
Charles	W110		
Charlotte	A2777		
David	A2776		
David	R1152		
Dianah	MU9		
Edward	MU8		
Eliza	A1163		
Eliza	A2779		
Eliza	P955		
Eliza	P960		
Eliza	R1151		
Eliza	R1983		
Elizabeth	MU12		
Emma	H1403		
Emma	MU11		
Emma	MU689		
Emma	R982		
Frederick	MU13		
George	A1162		
George	H1401		
Harriett	A85		
Henry	P957		
James	A2330		
Jane	A2778		
Jane	MU10		
Jane	R980		
Jane	R983		
John	R1978		
Joseph	P954		
Martha	P961		
Mary	A2366		
Mary	A2780		
Mary	OH723		
Mary	P956		
Mary	R1816		
Mary Ann	OH597		
Phillis	OH598		
Sarah	H1402		
Sarah	P2427		
Sarah	P958		
Sarah	R1807		
Sarah	SA73		
Susan	P959		
Susanna	R462		
Thomas	MR93		
Thomas	OH728		
Thomas	R1806		
Thomas	R1815		
Thomas	R2029		
Thomas	SA71		
Walter J.	R1153		
William	A2781		
William	OH593		
William	OH596		
William	P962		
William	R1150		
William	R1981		
William	R979		
William	SA74		
TEACHER			
Caroline	OH1383		
Enif [?]	OH1382		
Henry	OH1380		
Joseph	OH1377		
Loucia	OH1378		
Loucia	OH1381		
Maria	OH1379		
William	OH1384		
TEARLE			
Caroline	A2719		
Charles	A2718		
Esther	A2578		
Frances	A2706		
Hannah	A2708		
Richard	A2705		
Sarah	A2707		
TEBBOTH			
Ann	S869		
Eliza	S871		
Elizabeth	A2173		
Elizabeth	A996		
Elizabeth	OH1200		
Oliver	A2174		
Richard	A995		
Thomas	A2172		
Thomas	S147		
TEBBUTT			
Ann	A3325		
Frederick	A3326		
Rebecca	A3327		
Samuel	A3324		
TEMPEL			
David	W705		
Joseph	W703		
Mary	W707		
Susan	W704		
William	W706		
TENNANT			
Ann	R1222		
Betsey	R1220		
Charity	R1218		
Eliza	R1219		
Fanny	R1224		
Joseph	R1217		
Sarah	R1223		
William	R1221		
TERENE			
Fancy	OH1299		
Maria	OH1298		
Mary	OH1296		
Mary Ann	OH1297		
William	OH1295		
TERRY			
James	S732		
Jane	S733		
Matilda	A3284		
TETCH			
Linford	A2250		
TEWIN			
Elizabeth	H1507		
Francis	H1503		
Joseph	H1501		
Sarah	H1502		
William	H1506		
TEWKESBURY			
William	P174		
THEOBALD			
Ann	A13		
THICK			
Caroline	P109		
THISTLE			
Ann	MU313		
George	MU316		
Isabella	MU314		
John	MU318		
Robert	MU315		
Thomas	MU317		
THOMAS			
Elizabeth	WK59		
Frank	OH320		
James D	OH318		
John	OH319		
Mary A F	OH321		
Sarah	OH316		
Sarah	OH317		
William	OH315		
THOMPSON			
Alice	H1587		
Ann	A2511		
Catherin Beaumont	P94		
Charles	S1141		
Charles	W713		
Elizabeth	A2760		
Elizabeth	P89		
Ellen Woollatt	P90		
Flora	MR458		
George	S1142		
George	W715		
Hannah	W711		
Henry	S1139		
Henry	S997		
James	A2759		
James	H1085		
John	W710		
John	W712		
Joseph	S1143		
Joseph Sturgo	P91		
Mary	S1140		
Mary	W714		
Matthew	MU1011		
Robert	A2510		
Samuel	P92		
Sarah	H1086		
William	H1586		
William	P88		
William	P93		
THOMSON			
Charles	W1598		
Eliza	W1594		
Hannah	W1593		
Henry	W1600		
James	W1596		
Mary	W1597		
Sophia	W1599		
Susan	W1595		
William	W1592		
THORN			
Anthony	A824		
Eliza	R1419		
Sarah	R1417		
Thomas	R1416		
Thomas	R1418		
William	H577		
THORNE			
Elizabeth	P1356		
James	P1355		
THORNTON			
Ann	S992		
Ann	S998		
Anna	A1306		
Caroline A.	S1060		
Charlotte	A1305		
Charlotte	A1307		
David Elias	S995		
Elizabeth	S1059		
Elizabeth	S991		
James	S990		
Jane	A1594		
John	A1304		
John	S1058		
Lydia	A1308		
Thomas	S994		
William	S993		
THOROGOOD			
Adeliza	R788		
Alfred	R1716		
Ann	R1713		
Ann	R511		
Betsey	R381		
Charles	R1715		
Charles	R712		
Eliza	R1629		
Eliza	R880		
Elizabeth	R879		
Emily	R791		
Emma	R243		
Emma	R697		
George	R1157		
George	R1611		
George	R784		
Henry	R696		
James	MU653		
James	R1626		
James	R512		
James	R787		
Jane	R1156		
John	R240		
John	R509		
John	R786		
Joseph	R878		
Maria	R1628		
Martha	R242		
Martha	R510		
Mary	R1627		
Mary	R513		
Mary	R785		
Mary A.	R1714		
Mary Ann	R380		
Mary Ann	R383		
Rebecca	R139		
Rosa	R385		
Sarah	R241		
Sarah	R384		
Sarah	R713		
Thomas	R1155		
Thomas	R378		
Thomas	R379		
Tryphena	R382		
Tryphena	R790		
Walter	R881		
William	R714		
William	R789		
THRALE			
Eliza	W39		
Norman	W411		
Ralph	SA391		
Ralph Norman	SA392		
Sarah	W37		
Thomas	W36		
Thomas R	W38		
William	SA393		
William	W17		
THREADER			
Emma	W455		
Hannah	W454		
Harriet	W452		
Joseph	W451		
William	W453		
William	W456		
THRUSELL			
Charles	H1306		
THRUSSELL			

Elizabeth	S382	James	S1294	Elizabeth	A131	**WADE**	
Ellen Elizabeth	P861	Jane	MR354	Fanny	A2343	Arthur G.S.	R152
Emma	A2926	Sarah	MR352	Frederic	A1042	Elizabeth	A236
Esther	R27	Sarah	MR353	Harriett	A133	Ellen E.	R151
Esther	R40	William	MR357	Henry	A1045	Mary A.M.	R150
Frances	A339	**TWITCHELL [?]**		James	A127	William	H866
Frank	A3095	Elizabeth	A2573	James	A132	William S.	R149
Harriett	A337	Emily	A2575	Jane	A2342	**WADKIN**	
Harriett	OH1064	Louisa	A2572	John	A2341	Elizabeth	MR462
Henry	A3094	Mary	A2571	Matilda	A130	**WAGGETT**	
Henry	A3358	Rebecca	A2574	Matilda	MU106	G.S.	A289
Henry	OH537	**TYERS**		Matthew	A1038	M.A.E.	A288
Henry	OH540	Rosanna	MU472	Sam C. Henry	A1040	Mary Anne	A287
Henry	R26	**TYLER**		William	A129	**WAGHORN**	
James	WK85	Ann	A639	**VASS**		Ann	S375
Jane	R2018	Ann	OH67	Catherine	A259	Sarah	S376
John	A3089	Ann	OH778	Elizabeth	A256	**WAGSTAFF**	
John	A3091	Cecilia	A643	Fanny	A258	Mary	P1330
John	A3241	Charles	A641	George	A252	**WALBLATE**	
Joseph	OH1065	Emily	A642	George	A254	Sarah	A1180
Joseph	OH534	James	OH66	James	P1151	**WALDOCK**	
Lucy	A341	James	OH771	Joseph	A257	Benjamin	R1814
M Ann	A3090	James	OH773	Maria	P1152	Eliza	R1811
Maria	A338	Jane	OH776	Mary	A255	Emily	R1790
Maria	OH549	Joseph	OH779	Sarah	A253	George	R1808
Martha	A2922	Lavinia	A644	**VAUGHAN**		Henry	R1791
Mary	A3096	Mary	OH772	Ann	W664	James	R1809
Mary	A336	Mary	OH775	Arthur	W666	James	R1812
Mary	H1112	Mary Ann	A640	Daniel	W665	Judith	R1810
Mary	R41	Michael	R258	Eliza	H1429	Maria	R1792
Mary Anne	A340	Samuel	OH774	Emma	W667	Thomas	R1789
Mary Anne	OH536	Sarah	OH777	Harriett	W668	William	R1813
Nathaniel B.	A2923			James	W662	**WALFORD**	
Samuel M.	A2927	**U**		Mary Ann	H1428	Hannah	P49
Sarah	A2924	**UCKLESBY**		Sarah	W663	John Francis	P295
Sarah	OH539	George	H816	**VERNNIER**		**WALKER**	
Sarah	P793	**UNDERWOOD**		Ann	P2083	Alfred	H398
Sarah	S384	Emily	P833	Emily	P2085	Ann	A575
Sarah	S877	Emma	P832	John	P2082	Ann	MU136
Susan	S876	James	P831	John	P2084	Ann	P1454
Thomas	A342	James	P835	**VERULAM**		Ann	P2252
Thomas	P860	Regia	P834	Countess of	MR450	Charles	A2361
Thomas	R39	Sarah	P836	Dowager Countess of		Charlotte	A579
Thomas	W409	**UNWIN**			MR448	Eliza	A2046
William	A3092	Charles T.	P1731	Earl of	MR449	Eliza	A2055
William	S381	George	A1402	**VICKERS**		Eliza	H395
William	S383	Mary	MU340	Mary Ann	R508	Eliza	P2249
TURNEY		**UPTON**		**VILES**		Elizabeth	A2044
Barnett	OH525	Eliza	A956	Ann	A1846	Ellen	H1536
TURNEY		Eustace James	A86	Eliza	A1848	Ellen	H397
Charlotte	MU327	Maria	A1054	Sarah	A1847	Emily	H394
TURNEY		Martha Matilda	A958	Thomas	A1849	Emma	A2047
Edith	OH705	Mary Louisa	A959	**VINCENT**		Emma	A2363
Emma	OH529	Sarah Amelia	A957	William	R2001	Emma	W1390
George	A761	William	A955	**VINE**		Emma	WK213
James	MU326			Richard	MR403	Fanny	H399
John	A166	**V**		**VORMER**		George	MU138
Joseph	OH704	**VALLANCE**		Frederick	A2214	Henry	A1056
Louisa	OH528	Ann	A168	**VYSE**		Henry	A576
Mary	OH527	Elizabeth	A169	George	W1275	James	A2362
Rebecca	OH554	Elizabeth	H1184	George W.	W1277	James	A574
Sarah	OH526	Martha	H1185	Sarah	W1276	James	A578
Susan	A762	Thomas	A167			James	H373
TWIDLE		William	H1183	**W**		James	MU137
Sophia	H698	**VARNAM**		**WABEY**		James	P2247
William	W15	Ann	P1961	Deborah	A517	James	P2251
TWINDELLS		**VARNEY**		Thomas	A516	James	WK214
Charles	R566	Alfred	A1043	**WACKETT**		John	A2043
Jessie	R564	Amelia	A128	Tresa	MU903	Joseph	A2045
Maria	R565	Ann	A836	**WADDINGTON**		Lucy	A2042
TWITCHELL		Ann Harriett	A1044	Henry Lee	P416	Lucy	H396
Ann	MR356	Anna	A678	Joseph	P413	Maria	A2358
Emma	MR355	Eliza	A1039	Louisa	P415	Mary	WK212
James	MR351	Eliza	A1041	Sarah	P414	Mary Ann	W1391

P568

Edward	A766	Elizabeth	MU793	Susan	A676	James	H981
Eliza	A1667	Elizabeth	OH601	Susannah	R1698	James	S398
Elizabeth	S1362	Elizabeth	SA811	Thomas	A2563	James	S401
Frederick	OH33	Elizabeth	W163	Thomas	A2567	James	S698
Henry	A1666	Ellen	MR407	Thomas	MR676	John	S94
Thomas	A765	Emiley	MR677	Thomas	MU792	Joseph	S653
WATSON		Emily	A683	Thomas	P2484	Joseph	S655
Elizabeth	P1704	Emma	OH1004	Thomas	P2487	Joseph	W1533
Frances	SA180	Emma	OH267	Thomas	W162	Joshua	S984
Jane E.	P1706	Emma	SA813	William	A679	Letitia	S405
John	A2901	Emma Clayton	P434	William	A682	Louisa	S71
John	P1703	Fanny	S1552	William	MU795	Lydia	S705
John A.	P1705	George	MU794	William	OH1269	Maria	S73
Susan	SA181	George	R1686	William	OH607	Mary	R2007
Susannah	P1388	George	R1968	William	P2486	Mary	S1385
William	SA179	George	R1971	William	P441	Mary Ann	H982
WATTS		George	W1400	William	R1696	Mary Ann	H983
Hannah	A3017	Hannah	MR674	William	SA626	Mary Ann	S400
Henry	A2676	Hannah	MR675	William	W1508	Philip	W1531
John	A2749	Hannah	P442	William	W166	Rebecca	S89
WEADON		Hannah	SA808	WEBSTER		Sarah	S377
Edward	A2168	Hannah	W1049	Ann	A1071	Sarah	S654
WEATHERHEAD		Hannah	W1404	Ann	A1072	Sarah Ann	S704
Betsy	R776	Hannah	W165	Charles	A1232	Susannah	S93
Eliza	R775	Harriett	A680	Charlotte E	W1504	Thomas	S92
Harriett	R773	Harriett	A681	Eliza	MU725	William	H986
John	R772	Henry	OH1002	Elizabeth	A1231	William	S88
John	R777	Henry	SA807	Elizabeth	W1503	William	S95
Mary Ann	R774	James	A675	Emma	A1235	WEIR	
Sophia	R778	James	OH262	Fanny	P1360	Helen	WK2
WEATHERLEY		James	OH268	Fanny Anne	A1394	Helen Ann	WK5
Alfred	P2195	James	OH606	Fred F	A1391	James	WK4
Eliza	SA816	James	SA623	George	A1230	Marion	WK3
Elizabeth	SA815	James	W1174	George	A1233	William	WK1
Ellen	P2196	Jane Cole	P443	James	W1073	WELCH	
Ellen	W868	John	H1230	Joseph	W1502	Amelia	A1949
Esther	P2189	John	MR678	Louisa	MU724	Arthur	P2389
Francis	MU433	John	OH605	Sarah	A1392	Benjamin	W1509
George	P2197	John	R1685	Sarah	P1359	Benjamin	W1512
George	S474	John	SA624	Sarah Ridley	A1393	Catherine	P8
Hettey	MU434	John	W1236	Sophia	A1070	Charles	MU272
James	P2193	John	W1239	Sophia	P1379	Charles G	MU275
Jane	S475	Joseph	OH264	Thomas	OH874	Edward	W1169
Jeremiah	SA814	Joseph	R1697	William	A1234	Edward J	MU277
Joseph	S476	Joseph	SA627	William	OH796	Elizabeth A.	OH1188
Joshua	MU436	Joseph	W1814	WEEDON		Emma	A3317
Sarah	P2192	Maria	A2566	Ann	S404	Emma	MU276
Susan	P2191	Maria	SA809	Benjaman	H987	Emma	W1511
Thomas	MU435	Maria	W1175	Betsey	S90	George	A1950
Thomas	S711	Maria	W826	Caroline	H985	George	SA508
William	P2194	Martha	A2568	Caroline	S1386	Hannah	MR164
Zilpert [?]	P2190	Mary	OH1005	Caroline	S72	Hannah	MR204
WEATHERLY		Mary	OH263	Caroline	S91	Helen	W1515
William	P2076	Mary	SA812	Charles	S1438	Henry C	MU274
WEAVER		Mary	W1237	Charlotte	S703	Isaac	MR203
Louisa Ann	P553	Mary	W1402	Charlotte	S706	Isaac	MR207
WEAVING		Mary Ann	P2485	Edwin	S700	James	A1633
William	OH1446	Maryanne Elizabeth	P435	Edwin	W1534	James	MU278
WEBB		Matelda	OH603	Elijah	S1383	Jane	A2306
Alice	OH341	Phoebe	W1405	Eliza	S399	Jane	MU273
Alice	R1699	Richard	MR673	Eliza	S656	John	A1404
Alice	W164	Ruth	R1969	Eliza	S69	John	A1946
Ann	OH1003	Sarah	A2565	Eliza	S699	John	MR163
Anna	A677	Sarah	OH1006	Elizabeth	H1486	John	MR205
Anne	OH266	Sarah	OH223	Elizabeth	S697	John	OH1187
Caroline	OH602	Sarah	OH279	Elizabeth	W1532	Mary	A1947
Caroline	R1970	Sarah	P1261	Ellis	S70	Mary	W1164
Charles	OH604	Sarah	P2488	Emma	S402	Mary	W1510
Charles	P433	Sarah	SA622	George	S701	Mary	W1514
Edith	W1406	Sarah	SA625	George	S702	Mary Ann	P2390
Edward	OH269	Sarah	W1238	George	S720	Samuel	A3288
Eliza	A2564	Sarah	W1401	Hannah	S1384	Susan	MR206
Eliza	OH265	Sarah	W1403	Hannah	S403	William	MR208
Eliza	SA810	Sophia	OH425	Henry	S68	William	W1513

Martha	R1264
Mary	H615
Mary	H623
Mary	R1259
Mary	W428
Mary A	W1129
Samuel	H616
Sarah	P1001
Sarah	R1261
Sarah	R1525
Sarah	W702
Sarah	WK207
Sarah	WK209
Selina	A1278
Thomas	H477
Thomas	OH1166
Thomas	P1000
Thomas	W739
William	A2678
William	H613
Whist	
	Mary
S	A340
Whitbread	
	Elizabeth
P	615
Henry	MR134
Henry	P614
WHITE	
Alfred	P1279
Alfred	P582
Ann	A1052
Ann	A2761
Ann	OH1312
Ann	P585
Ann	S1269
Ann Eliza	P98
Arthur	P1282
Ben	A1047
Benjamin	WK133
Caroline	A2562
Caroline	S1090
Charles	A2513
Charles	A2988
Charles	A2991
Charles	MR903
Charles	P1283
Charlotte	A1046
Charlotte	MR902
Clara J.	MR905
Daniel	A1051
David	S1118
Edith	MR904
Eliza	P1495
Eliza	P581
Elizabeth	P1276
Elizabeth	P1347
Elizabeth	P580
Elizabeth	P97
Elizabeth	S1121
Elizabeth S.	S1091
Ellen	P1280
Emily	A2993
Emily	P584
Emma	OH1314
Emma	OH159
Emma	S1119
Ephraim	S407
George	MR346
George	P1277
George	S1116
Hannah	MR898
Hannah	OH158
Hannah	S1120
Harriet	P586
Harriett	S1089
Henry	OH1311
Henry	P96
James	P587
James	S409
John	A1050
John	A2561
John	OH68
John	P1803
John	S1333
John	S410
John	WK168
Joseph	A1110
Joseph	MR900
Julia	P1281
Maria	S1088
Maria	W1874
Mary	MR28
Mary	P1346
Mary	S1117
Mary Ann	A2989
Mary Ann	A2990
Mary Ann	S408
Rachael	OH160
Rebecca	S1086
Rebecca	S1087
Rose Hannah	A2992
Ruth	A1872
Samuel	P757
Sarah	A1049
Sarah	MU973
Sarah	P1278
Sarah	P583
Sarah	S1122
Susan	A2192
Thomas	OH157
Thomas	P1494
William	A1048
William	A1871
William	MR897
William	MR899
William	MU972
William	OH1313
William	P2054
William	S359
Zackery	MR901
WHITEHEAD	
Ann	MR573
Ann	R1346
Ann	R1400
Betsy	R1345
Eliza	MR120
Elizabeth	MR572
George	MR119
Hannah	R1344
Joseph	R1348
Joseph	R1399
Mary	R996
Mary E.	MR574
Richard	MR571
Samuel	MR118
Selina	R1347
William	R1343
William	R1349
William	R995
WHITEHOUSE	
Ann	H86
Ann	P1754
Elizabeth	H1385
Jane	R316
Job	H83
Josiah	H1376
Levi	H85
Martha	H84
Mary Ann	H1377
Sophia	R317
Thomas	H1384
Thomas	P1755
William	P1753
William	R315
WHITELOCK	
Daniel	R1028
Joseph	R1026
Sarah	R1027
Sarah	R1029
WHITFORD	
John	A2442
Rachael	A2443
WHITHEAD	
Henry	A207
Sarah	A209
William	A210
WHITTAKER	
William	A2899
WHITTEY	
Elenior	OH1239
WHOOTON	
Charlotte	R733
Joshua	R735
Sarah	R732
Sarah	R734
WICKES	
Ann	WK92
WICKHAM	
Caroline	A307
Emily	A306
Jane	A308
Margaret	A305
William Faircloth	A304
WICKS	
Ann Maria	OH933
Eliza	W417
Ellen	W418
Sarah	OH932
William	OH746
William	OH931
William	W416
WIGGS	
Charlotte	S137
George	S139
Jane	S135
Mary	S131
Mary	S133
Robert	S1055
Robert	S140
Sarah Jane	S1053
Susan	S134
Thomas	S1056
Thomas	S130
Thomas	S132
Thomas	S138
William	S1052
William	S1054
William	S136
WIGLIE	
Anne	MR24
WILBY	
Mary Ann	A179
WILDBOAR	
Caroline	A825
Hannah	A826
WILDBORE	
George	P498
James	P494
Sarah	P495
Thomas	P497
William	P496
WILDING	
Alice	MR27
WILES	
Elizabeth	A2271
George	MU383
Hannah	A2269
Hannah	A2270
Jane	A2880
Jane W.	A2879
Joseph	A2878
Julia	A1061
Sarah	WK216
WILKINS	
Alfred T.H.	MR582
Ann	A900
Ann	A950
Ann	A967
Catherine Clarissa	P485
Charles	A1546
Edward	MR575
Elizabeth	A1544
Frederick	P479
Frederick John	P482
George	MR579
Harriet I.	P483
Jane	MR581
Joseph	A948
Letitia	A947
Letitia	A949
Letitia	A965
Louisa A.	P481
Mary	A951
Mary	A968
Mary	P480
Mary A.	MR576
Mary A.	MR580
Mary Martha	P484
Sarah	A952
William	A1545
William	MR578
WILKINSON	
Ann	S1020
Elizabeth	S1022
Jane	S1023
Joseph	A2886
Mary	S1021
William	S1019
WILKS	
Emily	OH1425
George	OH1426
James	OH1422
Mary A.	OH1423
Mary A.	OH1424
WILLIAM	
Adam	S1379
Elizabeth	S1380
John	S1382
William	S1381
WILLIAMS	
Ann	H1756
Anne S	SA330
Catharine	A650
Catherine	P1336
Charles	S861
Henry	A647
Henry	S860
Henry John	A649
Herbert	MU690
James	W441
Margaret M.J.	MU691
Mary	A648
WILLIS	
Ann	A2810
Caroline	A2813
Eliza	SA770
Frances	A2812

John	P236	**WILSHIRE**		Sarah	MR834	John	A527
John	SA771	Frances	W630	Sarah	MU654	John Wood	A3190
Joseph	A2811	James	OH642	Sarah	P2062	Josiah	A3186
Joseph	P257	Phoebe	H136	Sophia	MR757	Josiah	A3188
Samuel	P2456	Sarah	P721	Susannah	P367	Mary A.	MR777
Thomas	SA772	Sarah Emily	P722	Thomas	P2511	Robert	A3191
William	A3371	Susan	W1170	Thomas	R1932	Sophia	MR775
William	P2455	Thomas	H135	Walter	A1466	Thomas H	A3189
WILLMOTT		William	P720	William	A1086	William	A3193
Anne	W1157	William	W629	William	A1089	William	MR774
Catherine	A1384	**WILSON**		William	A1460	**WINGROVE**	
Charles	W1162	Alfred	A1465	William	A1464	Ann	MU1070
Charlotte	W1154	Alfred	OH926	William	A3099	Eliza	MU1072
Edward	W1156	Anna	A1087	William	MR428	Emma	MU1073
Elizabeth	H1063	Benjamin	MR754	William	MR835	George	MU1069
Elizabeth	W1151	Benjamin	MR758	William H.	P2393	Hannah	MU1068
Elizabeth	W1152	Caroline	MU490	**WILTON**		Henry	MR669
Emma	W1163	Charles	P2510	Robert	P1844	John	MU1067
Frederick	H1067	Charlotte	OH843	**WILTSHIRE**		Mary A.	MU1071
Henry	H1059	Charlotte	P2508	Joseph	W1573	**WINMILL**	
Henry	H1062	Charlton	A1462	**WIMBUSH**		Charles	MU942
Jane	H1069	Daniel	H1873	Elizabeth	P1516	Eliza	MU870
John	H1829	Daniel	MR763	**WINBOLT**		George	MU869
Joseph	H1061	David	MR857	Ann E	SA88	George	MU931
Joseph	H1299	David	P2391	Henry H	SA89	Hannah	MU930
Lousia	H1060	Dorcas	R1701	John S	SA90	Hannah	MU941
Lousia	H1065	Edmond	MU306	Mary S	SA87	John	MU927
Lucretia	S1210	Edward	MU488	Sophia S	SA91	Mary	MU940
Mary	H1300	Edward	P2334	Thomas Hy	SA86	Mary A.	MU928
Mary	W1153	Edward	W582	**WINCH**		William	MU929
Samuel	H1066	Eleanor	P2392	Caroline	W1196	William	MU939
Samuel	W1155	Eli	R1702	Charlott	W1195	**WINTER**	
Sarah	H1068	Eliza	OH928	Daniel	W1194	Catherine	P740
Sarah	H1301	Emma	MU491	Elizabeth	H1564	John	OH1124
William B.	H1064	Frederick	MU308	Elizabeth	W1423	Sarah	OH1122
WILLOUGHBY		George	MR756	Fanny	W1198	William	OH1121
Elizabeth	A2126	George	MR833	Mary Ann	H1565	William	OH1123
Emma	A2124	George	P2512	Mary Ann	W1197	**WINTERBONE**	
John	A2125	Godfrey	MR759	Matthew	W1422	Jonas	H1504
Sarah	A2123	Godfrey	R1700	Samuel	W412	**WINTERBORN**	
WILLS		Hannah	MR671	Sarah	P215	Elizabeth	MU754
Charles	SA555	Henry	A1463	Sarah	WK199	Emma	MU756
Edward Sutton	A726	Henry	P2507	**WINCHESTER**		James	MU750
Elizabeth	SA553	Henry	P2514	Bob	R1859	James	MU755
John	SA550	Isabella	P1675	Charles	R1125	Josiah	MU757
Mary	A727	James	MR362	Joseph	R1120	Lucy	MU753
Rose	SA554	James	MR760	Joseph	R1123	Maria	MU751
Sarah	SA552	James	OH929	Letitia	R134	Maria	MU752
Susan	SA551	John	A1467	Lydia	H814	**WISE**	
WILLSHIN		John	MU543	Lydia	R1121	Cecilia	OH1443
George	MU399	John	OH842	Mary	R1122	Elizabeth	OH485
Hannah	MU398	John	OH845	Susan	R1860	Frederick	OH1444
Hannah	MU400	John	P2395	William	R1124	Jemima	OH1442
Kate	MU401	Joseph	A1090	**WINDELL**		Sarah	OH1441
Sophia	MU402	Joseph	A3242	James	WK114	Thomas	OH486
Thomas	MU397	Joseph	MR670	**WINDMILL**		William	OH484
WILLSON		Joseph	MR672	Ann	MU987	Winsler	P2027
Elizabeth	W1019	Joseph	MU305	Edward	MU989	**WITHERINGTON**	
Hannah	S486	Joseph	MU307	Joseph	MU986	Oliver	MU938
Henry	S485	Joseph	P2394	Maria	MU988	**WITHERS**	
James	W1016	Louisa	OH844	**WING**		Louisa	S1165
James	W1018	Maria	P2513	Emma	MU416	Mary Ann	S1166
Maria	A1407	Martha	OH927	Harriett	OH1342	**WITHMORE**	
Mary	W1020	Mary	A1088	Harriett	OH1343	William	SA280
Sarah	A1408	Mary	MU489	James	OH1344	**WOOD**	
Simpson	A1406	Mary	R1933	Matthew	OH1341	Abraham	W788
Susan	W1017	Mary A.	MR761	**WINGRAVE**		Anna M	P1209
WILSHER		Mary Ann	A1461	Alfred	H286	Arthur	W648
John	W1691	Mary Ann	H1455	Amelia S.	MR776	Caroline	W647
John	W1696	Mary Ann	OH930	Ann	H285	Charles	P1208
Sarah	W1692	Robert	A3258	Caroline	A3187	Charles	P1210
Sarah	W1694	Samuel	P2509	Catherine	A3194	David	W1120
Thomas	W1695	Sarah	MR755	Frederick	A3192	Edmund	A2153
William	W1693	Sarah	MR762	George	H284	Edward	P1211

Elizabeth	A931	Susan	A1294	Maria	A2473	Edwin G	SA345
Ellen	W643	Thomas	R173	Sophia	A2471	Eliza	S1009
Emma	W1803	William	A1293	**WOOLLAM**		Eliza	S1012
Emma	W789	William	A1295	Catharine	A3302	Elizabeth	MU88
Frederick	H1830	**WOODSTOCK**		Charles	A3303	Elizabeth	P170
Frederick	W1528	Abenego	R1755	John	A3299	Elizabeth	P2397
Frederick	W645	Charles	R698	Mary	A3300	Elizabeth	SA343
James	MR590	Emma	R1758	Penelope	A3301	Ellen J.	P2302
James	W1122	George	R1753	**WOOLLAMS**		Emily	H1822
Jessey	W642	Hannah	R1752	Edward	P1923	Emily	R1988
John	H1943	John Wm	S724	Emily	P1926	Emily	W988
Joseph	A603	Joreal (?)	R1756	Harriet	P1925	Emma	P2388
Joseph	A930	Rose	R1757	John	P1927	Emma	SA342
Joseph	OH718	Sarah	R699	Sarah	P1924	Frances	S893
Joseph	SA509	Sherach	R1751	**WOOLLATT**		Frederick	S616
Joseph	W380	Sophia	S725	George	SA276	Frederick	S619
Louisa	W646	William	R1754	George Sidn	SA273	Frederick	W770
Maria	H1942	**WOODWARD**		Harriet	SA274	George	A812
Martha	A2256	Ann	R1649	Harriet	SA275	George	S1014
Martha	W1121	Ann	S312	Joseph	SA279	George	SA341
Mary	A2255	Caroline	S946	Katherine	SA277	George	W1115
Mary	W381	Catherine	S1048	**WOOLLNOUGH**		George	W768
Mary Ann	A966	Charles	R1646	Charlotte	OH406	Harriet	MU284
Mary Anne	A2257	Charles	SA211	Emma	OH407	Harriot	A3215
Matilda	P1212	Charles	W1572	George	OH410	James	OH911
Prentice	W644	Charlotte	W841	James	OH411	James	R1987
Sarah	A2154	Eliza	S313	Sarah	OH408	James	S1008
Sarah Jane	A2155	Elizabeth	P1007	William	OH405	James	S1011
Susan	W641	Elizabeth	P1011	William	OH409	James	SA675
Susannah	H1941	Elizabeth	SA212	**WOOLMER**		James	W772
Thomas	A2236	Elizabeth	W844	Elizabeth	SA216	Jane	A813
Thomas	A2254	Emma	P1009	James	SA219	Jane	H827
Thomas	H1944	Emma	S315	Sophia	SA217	Jane	P1970
Thomas	W640	George	P1006	Thomas	SA218	John	P2400
Thomas William	A3195	George	P1008	Walter	SA220	John	S836
William	W1529	George	SA383	William	SA215	John	S839
WOODARDS		George	W842	**WOOTTON**		John Irvine	A1057
Emma	W269	Henry	SA369	John	A2150	Martha	S1013
George	W268	James	SA213	Mary	A2151	Mary	H482
WOODBINE		James	W840	**WORBY [HORBY]**		Mary	P2387
Matthew	WK28	Jane	S1049	George	P1265	Mary	P2399
Sarah	R467	John	R1644	**WORLEY**		Mary	S1015
WOODBRIDGE		Joseph	S314	Isabella	MR82	Mary	S837
Ann	P54	Louisa	R1647	**WORRALL**		Mary	W987
Ruth	P55	Mary A	W843	Georgiana	H1479	Matilda	S1016
William	P53	Mary Ann	SA214	Joseph	H1478	Robert	W308
WOODFINE		Sarah	P1010	**WOTTON**		Rosa	SA344
Alice Ann	A844	Susan	R1645	Charles	A2896	Samuel	P2386
Richard	A842	Thomas	S1047	**WRANGLE**		Samuel	W984
Sophia	A843	William	R1648	Mary A.	R164	Sarah	A923
WOODGATE		William	S311	**WRAY**		Sarah	OH206
Caroline	SA443	**WOODWARDS**		Elizabeth	P1110	Sarah	OH466
WOODHAM		Alfred	W482	**WREN**		Sarah	S1010
William	W469	Ann	A2656	Ann	MU587	Sarah	S838
WOODHOUSE		Ann	W481	Elizabeth	MU588	Sarah	W587
Frances	P258	Anna	SA364	Emma	MU591	Sarah	W769
WOODLAND		Caroline	W477	George	MU586	Sophia	W1112
James	P902	Charlotte	W480	Henry	MU592	Susan	OH467
James	P905	Ellen	W484	Sarah	MU589	Susan	W985
John	P907	Emma	W486	William	MU590	Thomas	OH468
Joseph	P908	George	W476	**WRIGHT**		Thomas	P2396
Mary	P904	George	W485	Ann	OH465	Thomas	S622
Robert	P906	Harriet	W154	Ann	P2384	Walter	A2906
Sarah	P903	James	W479	Ann	P2398	William	H483
Sarah	P909	John	A2657	Ann	S617	William	MR702
Thomas	P910	John	W483	Ann	SA98	William	OH205
William	P230	Mary	W152	Ann	W309	William	OH207
WOODMAN		Sarah	W153	Caroline	S621	William	OH464
John	MU971	William	S956	Charles	P2385	William	P2383
Josh	MU970	William	W478	Charles	W1113	William	S478
WOODS		**WOOLER**		Charles	W986	William	S618
Charles	A1296	Jane	WK102	Daniel	R1986	William	W1111
Elizabeth	R174	**WOOLFIELD**		Daniel	W771	**WYATT**	
Maria A	P1102	Eliza	A2472	David	W1114	Abbina S.N.	H1631

Henry	S945
John	H1629
Mary E.	S944
Philis	P426
Robert	S942
Sarah	S943
Susan N.	H1630

WYKER
Eliza	OH228
Thomas	OH227
Thomas John	OH229

WYKES
Joseph	WK68

WYNTER
George Jacob	W277
Hephzibah	W278
Jane	W279

Y

YORSTON
Eliza	A1526
John	A1527
Sheridan	A1528
Walker	A1530
William	A1529

YOUNG
Amelia	S363
Ann	P718
Charles	W1330
Charlotte	P243
Daniel	P256
Edwin	A771
Eliza	A770
Eliza	MU760
Eliza	OH311
Elizabeth	A2258
Elizabeth	A2264
Emma	OH310
Frances	P245
Frederick	MU759
Frederick	MU762
George	P248
George	SA191
Harriet	OH313
Henry	P244
John	A57
John	OH314
John	S360
Louisa	A769
Maria	A768
Maria	P246
Mary	P241
Mary	SA192
Mary	W27
Mary Ann	H1462
Rebecca	W255
Robert	MU761
Samuel	OH312
Sarah	OH309
Sarah	S361
Sarah	W1331
Sarah Ann	S362
Susanna Goodfellow	A2259
Susannah	P242
Thomas	H1461
Thomas	P240
Thomas	P247
Thomas	P255
William	A767
William	OH308

YOUNGER
Caroline	A49
Elizabeth	A50
Henry	A48
Thomas	A47
William	S414

[BLANK]
Harriett	OH1470

Appendix I

Scheme for classification by social status

A   All gentry, land and property owners, higher professions (e.g. magistrates, justices of the peace, clergy, solicitors, accountants), farmers employing 20 or more labourers or owning/farming over 350 acres, people of independent means, and employer with over 25 employees.

B   Lower professions (e.g. teachers, local government officials, sureveyors, police inspectors), annuitants, farmers employing less than 20 labourers and owning/farming under 350 acres, merchants with over 5 but less than 25 employees.

C   Dealers, skilled craftsmen, clerks.

D   Semi-skilled workers, agricultural labourers, straw plaiters, servants.

E   Unskilled workers, road/general labourers, hawkers, errand boys and other menial occupations.

F   Unemployed, prisoners, paupers, vagrants.

Z   Unknown.

Protocol

In general, individuals were given the highest possible status: e.g. a "Brewer and farmer employing 25 labourers" would be classed as category A. Paupers, prison inmates and occupants of the workhouse, however, were all included in category F, regardless of any other occupational designation.

Dependents with no occupational designation were accorded the status of the head of household, husband or parents as appropriate, with parents taking priority over head of household if the staus of the two differed. The offspring of servants, lodgers and visitors were also coded as for their parents.

Any lodgers (adults and children) where no occupation or rank is indicated were coded as Z. Most of those who fall into this category were listed as visitors or lodgers in both the Relation and the Rank, Status or Occupation columns of the enumerators' schedules.

People who were retired were given the status of their former occupation.

Apprentices, assistants and the like were coded at one status group below that of their employer.

Children at boarding schools were all included in category B.

The full occupational coding scheme employed in the analysis of this data runs to over twenty pages and could not be included here. Copies are, however, available from the Centre for Regional and Local History at the University of Hertfordshire.

Appendix 2

St Albans Inns

Surname	Forename	Sex	Inn or Pub Name	Address	Additional Occupation or Other information
ALDRIDGE	George	M	Beer retailer	Fishpool Street	Pork butcher
BAKER	Elizabeth	F	Beer retailer	Fishpool Street	
BARRANCE	Henry	M	George	George Street	
BLANKS	Thomas	M	White Hart	Holywell Hill	Trimming manfacturer
BROWN	William	M	King's Head	Market Place	
CANNON	James	M	Windmill	St Peters Street	
CARRIDGE	Samuel	M	Cock	St Peters Street	
CATLIN	Elizabeth	F	Marlborough	Holywell Hill	
CLIFFEN	William	M	Ship	Hatfield Road	
COCKERELL	Thomas	M	Beer retailer	Spicer Street	
COX	Thomas	M	Beer retailer	Sopwell Lane	
DAVIS	Daniel	M	Red Cow	Colney	
DAWSON	George	M	Stag	Spencer Street	
DAY	Joseph	M	Old Roson	St Michael	
DEACON	Thomas	M	Six Bells	St Michael	
DELL	Mary	F	Beer retailer	Hill end	
DOLLING	Edward	M	Goat	Sopwell Lane	
EAMES	George	M	King William IV	St Peters Street	
EDMUNDS	Ann	F	Beer retailer	Keyfield Terrace	
EPHGRAVE	George	M	Green Man	Hanstead	
EVANS	Charles	M	Little Red Lion	High Street	
EVERETT	James	M	Post Boy	Holywell Hill	
FOREMAN	William Ellis	M	Fleur de Lis	Market Place	Commercial inn and posting house
GEORGE	Charles	M	Beer retailer	Verulam Road	
GLASCOSK	James	M	Beer retailer	Park lane cottage	
GODFREY	Edward	M	Beer retailer	Fishpool Street	
GOODSPEED	Henry	M	Black Lion	Fishpool Street	
GURNEY	William	M	Peacock	Hatfield Road	
HADDON	William	M	Angel	Verulam Road	
HALL	James	M	Beer retailer	London Road	
HALSEY	Daniel	M	Beer retailer	Abbey mill lane	
HANSELL	Edward	M	Bell	Chequer Street	
HAWTREE	James	M	Crown	Holywell Hill	
HITCHAM	James	M	Beer retailer	Dagnall lane	
HOOPER	John	M	Beer retailer	Brickett wood	
HORSFIELD	George	M	Beer retailer	London Road	Chandler's shop
HULKS	John	M	Beer retailer	St Peters	
JOHNSON	William	M	Beer retailer	London Road	Flour dealer
JORDAN	James	M	Black Boy	Waterdell	
JORDAN	John	M	Black Boy	St Stephens	
KENTISH	Daniel	M	Beer retailer	Brickett wood	

Surname	Forename	Sex	Inn or Pub Name	Address	Additional Occupation or Other information
KILBY	John	M	Sailor Boy	St Peters	
KNIGHT	George	M	Two Brewers	Holywell Hill	
LAMBDEN	Charlotte	F	Beer retailer	Fishpool Street	
LAWRENCE	Richard	M	Cock Flower Pot	Fishpool Street	
LEETE	Simeon	M	Great Red Lion	High Street	
LINES	Robert	M	Plough	Verulam Street	Tailor
LOGGAN	Joseph	M	Beer retailer	St Peters Street	
LONG	William	M	Beer retailer	Pound Field	
MACNAIR	William	M	Beer retailer	Sion cottage	
MANSELL	David	M	Beer retailer	Spicer Street	
MARKS	Mary	F	Peahen	High Street	Coach office
MARSHALL	George	M	Woolpack	London Road	
MARTIN	John Sons	M	Queen's Hotel	Chequer Street	Commercial inn, importer of foreign wines & spirits
MOORE	Thomas	M	Antelope	George Street	Marine store dealer
NICHOLLS	Isaac	M	Beer retailer	St Peters	
NORRIS	Stephen	M	Beer retailer	St Peters Street	Baker, Beer retailer
NORRIS	William	M	Queen Adelaide	St Peters Street	Butcher
OAKLEY	James	M	Beer retailer	Spicer Street	
PIDDUCK	Richard	M	Trumpet	Holywell Hill	
RATCLIFFE	William	M	Beer retailer	Hatfield Road	
RENTOWL	Lydia	F	Red Lion	Park Street	
RUSSELL	John	M	Rose Crown	St Michaels	Carpenter
SADDINGTON	James	M	Beer retailer	George Street	
SAMS	Joseph	M	Lamb	Chequer Street	
SEYMOUR	William	M	King Henry VIII	St Stephens	
SHAW	Charles	M	Beer retailer	Verulam Road	
SMITH	Charles	M	Boot	Market Place	
SMITH	Hannah	F	Falcon	Park Street	
SMITH	Neptune	M	St Christopher	Back Street	
STELLE	John	M	Beer retailer	London Road	Furniture broker
STOCKSLEY	Francis	M	White Horse	Park Street	
TALBOTT	Elizabeth	F	Beer retailer	London Road	
TRAVELL	James	M	Beer retailer	Fishpool Street	
TURNER	John	M	Beer retailer	Fishpool Street	Brewer, Beer retailer
TURNER	Thomas	M	Beer retailer	Dagnall Lane	
VARNEY	James	M	Beer retailer	Chequer Street	
VASS	Thomas	M	King's Arms	George Street	
WALKER	William	M	Crabtree	St Peters Street	
WARD	John	M	Cross Keys	Chequer Street	
WEBDALE	James	M	Beer retailer	Fishpool Street	
WELSH	Thomas	M	George	Colney Street	
WOODBRIDGE	William	M	White Horse	St Peters Street	China warehouse
WOODCOCK	William	M	Verulam Arms	Dagnall Lane	
WOODWARD	Thomas	M	Black Horse	Colney Street	
YOUNG	William	M	Greyhound	Back Street